The Handbook
of Emergent
Technologies in
Social Research

The Handbook of Emergent Technologies in Social Research

Edited by Sharlene Nagy Hesse-Biber

OXFORD
UNIVERSITY PRESS

OXFORD
UNIVERSITY PRESS

Oxford University Press, Inc., publishes works that further
Oxford University's objective of excellence
in research, scholarship, and education.

Oxford   New York
Auckland   Cape Town   Dar es Salaam   Hong Kong   Karachi
Kuala Lumpur   Madrid   Melbourne   Mexico City   Nairobi
New Delhi   Shanghai   Taipei   Toronto

With offices in
Argentina   Austria   Brazil   Chile   Czech Republic   France   Greece
Guatemala   Hungary   Italy   Japan   Poland   Portugal   Singapore
South Korea   Switzerland   Thailand   Turkey   Ukraine   Vietnam

Published by Oxford University Press, Inc.
198 Madison Avenue, New York, New York 10016

www.oup.com

Oxford is a registered trademark of Oxford University Press.

Library of Congress Cataloging-in-Publication Data
The Handbook of Emergent Technologies in Social Research / Edited by Sharlene Nagy Hesse-Biber.
  p.   cm.
Includes bibliographical references and index.
ISBN 978-0-19-537359-2
1. Social sciences—Research—Methodology.   2. Social sciences—Research—Technological
innovations.   I. Hesse-Biber, Sharlene Nagy.
H62.O94 2010   300.72—dc22   2009049402

1 3 5 7 9 8 6 4 2

Printed in the United States of America
on acid-free paper

Contents

Acknowledgments

I would like to thank all those who have supported *The Handbook of Emergent Technologies in Social Research* project. First and foremost, I thank my family: My husband, Dr. Michael Peter Biber, M.D., whose love, sense of humor, and understanding is invaluable to me; and My daughters, Sarah Alexandra Biber and Julia Ariel Biber, who supported and cheered me on but also reminded me of the importance of other things that sustain and renew us.

My gratitude to my sister, Georgia Geraghty, brother, Charles Nagy, and, of course, my mother, Helene Stockert, whose work ethic, guidance, and sound advice have inspired and sustained me throughout my academic and personal life. A heartfelt remembrance of my sister Janet Mildred Nagy Green Fisher and my father Zoltan Nagy.

Lastly, I want to thank the newest member of our family, our Portuguese water dog, Zoli, who arrived at our house at 7 weeks of age and is now a very special year old adolescent with an infectious energy. He reminds me of how important it is to also play!

A very special thanks and praise go to Boston College undergraduate research assistant Alicia Johnson '11 for providing me with invaluable insightful feedback and outstanding editorial advice and organizational support. She has worked with me throughout the *Handbook* process, allowing me the time and support to extend a range of different levels of feedback and editorial advice to each *Handbook* author as their chapters progressed to completion. My sincere appreciation is also extended to Boston College undergraduate research assistant Natalie Horbachevsky '09 for her excellent research support, and organizational and editorial skills at critical junctures in the early and later stages of the *Handbook* project. Many thanks as well to Boston College undergraduate Hilary Flowers '10 for her editorial advice at the copy-editing stage of the *Handbook*. I also want to thank Boston College's undergraduate research grants office for their partial funding of research assistance for this book project. My special thanks to Dr. William Petri, Associate Dean, Arts and Sciences, Boston College and the Boston College Undergraduate Research Fellowship Program. I would also like to thank the reviewers of the earlier drafts of the Handbook proposal whose feedback was so helpful in shaping this project.

In addition, I offer my sincere thanks to my editor, James Cook, at Oxford University Press. He is a gifted senior editor whose support, enthusiasm, knowledge of the field of research methods, and excellent editorial feedback on this book project is greatly appreciated.

I am grateful to our *Handbook* editorial board members, Dr. Norman K. Denzin, Dr. Michael Dal, Dr. Aline Gubrium, Dr. Steven Steinberg and Dr. Sheila Lakshmi Steinberg for providing outstanding advice and editorial support as the Handbook project proceeded.

This Handbook is dedicated to the authors of the *Handbook of Emergent Technologies in Social Research*. I extend my sincere gratitude to each contributors, whose commitment to this project has been unwavering and enthusiastic, for sharing their expertise in the field of emergent technologies and their applications to social research.

Handbook Editor

Sharlene Nagy Hesse-Biber, Ph. D. University of Michigan, is Professor of Sociology, and director of the Women's and Gender Studies Program at Boston College. Her monograph, *Am I Thin Enough Yet* ? (Oxford,1996), was selected as one of *Choice Magazine's* best academic books for 1996. She is author of *The Cult of Thinness* (Oxford, 2007) and *Mixed Methods Research: Merging Theory with Practice* (Guilford Publications, 2010). She is the co-author of *Working Women in America* (Oxford, 2005) and *The Practice of Qualitative Research* (Sage, 2006; 2011). She is the co-editor of *Approaches to Qualitative Research* (*Oxford, 2004*), *Feminist Perspectives on Social Research* (Oxford, 2004), *Emergent Methods in Social Research* (*Sage, 2006*) and *The Handbook of Emergent Methods* (Guilford, 2008; 2010). She is editor of *The Handbook of Feminist Research* (Sage, 2007), an AESA Critics' Choice Award winner and selected one of *Choice Magazine's* Outstanding Academic titles for 2007, and co-author of *Feminist Research Practice: A Primer* (Sage, 2007; Second Edition forthcoming, 2012). She is co-developer of Hyper RESEARCH, a software tool for analyzing qualitative data, and a transcription software tool, Hyper TRANSCRIBE (www. researchware.com).

Contributors

Anne Beaulieu is a senior research fellow at the Virtual Knowledge Studio (VKS) of the Royal Academy of Arts and Sciences in Amsterdam, and deputy programme leader of the VKS.

David P. Brown is an administrator for the Research Institute for Health and Social Change, Manchester Metropolitan University, Manchester, United Kingdom.

Patrick Brundell is a research fellow at the School of Computer Science, University of Nottingham, United Kingdom.

Victor Callaghan is a professor of computer science, leader of the Inhabited Intelligent Environments Group, and director of the Digital Lifestyles Centre at Essex University.

John M. Carroll is Edward Frymoyer Professor of information sciences and technology at Pennsylvania State University.

Jeannette Chin is a senior researcher with the Inhabited Intelligent Environments Group at Essex University.

Sunil Choenni is the head of department of the Statistical Information Management and Policy Analysis of the Research and Documentation Centre (WODC) of the Dutch Ministry of Justice and a research professor of human centered ICT at the School for Communication, Media and Information Technology, Rotterdam University of Applied Sciences in Rotterdam, the Netherlands.

Göran Collste is a professor of applied ethics at the Centre for Applied Ethics, Linköping University in Linköping, Sweden.

Gregorio Convertino is a research scientist in the augmented social computing area at the Palo Alto Research Center, California.

John W. Creswell is a professor of educational psychology in the College of Education and Human Sciences at the University of Nebraska-Lincoln in Lincoln, Nebraska.

Michael Dal is a Contributor as well as member of the Handbook editorial board. He is a professor and head of Centre for Research in Foreign and Second Language Learning at The School of Education at Iceland University.

Geert de Haan is a lecturer of media technology and a researcher in the human centered ICT group at the School for Communication, Media and Information Technology, Rotterdam University of Applied Sciences in Rotterdam, the Netherlands.

Norman K. Denzin is a member of the Handbook Editorial Board. He is a distinguished professor of communications, College of Communications Scholar, and research professor of communications, sociology, and humanities, at the University of Illinois, Urbana-Champaign.

Bella Dicks, PhD, is a reader in sociology at Cardiff University, South Wales, United Kingdom.

Karen Duggan is a project manager at Manchester Metropolitan University, Manchester, United Kingdom.

Nathan Eagle is a research scientist at the Massachusetts Institute of Technology and an Omidyar Fellow at the Santa Fe Institute.

John Findlay is CEO of Zing Technologies, a technology company from Sydney, Australia, which makes team meeting and learning systems.

Robert Fitzgerald is an associate dean research in the Faculty of Education at the University of Canberra, Australia, and senior research fellow in the Australian Institute for Sustainable Communities.

Chris Fowler is a professor in the Institute of Distance Education (IDE) at the University of Swaziland.

Karim Gherab-Martín in theoretical physics and PhD in philosophy of science and technology, is currently a visiting scholar and teaching fellow in philosophy at Harvard University.

John Griffiths is a lecturer in psychology at Manchester Metropolitan University, Manchester, United Kingdom.

Aline Gubrium is a Contributor as well as member of the Handbook editorial board. She is an assistant professor of Community Health Education in the School of Public Health and Health Sciences at the University of Massachusetts-Amherst.

David J. Gunkel is a presidential teaching professor in the Department of Communication at Northern Illinois University.

Edward J. Hackett is a professor in the School of Human Evolution and Social Change at Arizona State University, with appointments in the School of Sustainability and the Consortium for Science Policy and Outcomes.

Dr. Mariann Hardey is a social media analyst, consultant, and academic at the University of York, United Kingdom.

Barbara Herr Harthorn is an associate professor of feminist studies, anthropology, and sociology, and director of the NSF Center for Nanotechnology in Society at the University of California at Santa Barbara.

Jennifer Hawkins is an associate lecturer in education on inclusion and disability studies courses at Liverpool Hope University, Liverpool, United Kingdom.

John T. Haworth is currently a visiting research fellow in the Research Institute for Health and Social Change, at Manchester Metropolitan University, Manchester, United Kingdom.

Anne Holohan is a lecturer in sociology and a research associate of the Institute for International Integration at Trinity College Dublin.

Mette Terp Høybye is a postdoc researcher in the Department of Psychosocial Cancer Research of the Institute of Cancer Epidemiology, and an external lecturer at the Institute of Anthropology at the University of Copenhagen.

Carolyn Kagan is a professor of community social psychology and the director of the Research Institute for Health and Social Change at Manchester Metropolitan University, United Kingdom.

Sandra Kalidien is a researcher at the Department of Statistical Information Management and Policy Analysis of the Research and Documentation Center (WODC) of the Ministry of Justice, the Hague.

Anne Kellock is a senior lecturer at Sheffield Hallam University, Sheffield, United Kingdom.

Nittaya Kerdprasop is an associate professor and deputy director of Data Engineering and Knowledge Discovery (DEKD) research unit at the School of Computer Engineering, Suranaree University of Technology in Thailand.

Dawn Knight is a research associate on the ESRC-funded DReSS Project (Understanding New Forms of Digital Record project) at the University of Nottingham, United Kingdom.

Rebecca Lawthom is a reader in community practice in the Psychology and Social Change Division at Manchester Metropolitan University, Manchester, United Kingdom.

Yu-Wei Lin is a research associate at the Coordinating Hub of the ESRC-funded National Centre for e-Social Science (NCeSS) at the University of Manchester, United Kingdom.

"Bert" (Bertis Britt) Little is an associate vice president for academic research, professor of computer science and mathematics in the Department of Physics and Engineering, director of Texas Engineering Experiment Station (TEES), director of Texas Data Mining Research Institute (TDMRI), executive director of the Center for Agribusiness Excellence (CAE) at Tarleton State University—Texas A&M University System in Stephenville, Texas.

Bojana Lobe completed her PhD in social sciences methodology at the University of Ljubljana in 2006.

Bruce Mason is a research fellow in qualitative research at the University of Edinburgh, United Kingdom.

Bernard Rogers McCoy is an associate professor of journalism in the College of Journalism and Mass Communications at the University of Nebraska-Lincoln.

David L. Morgan is a university professor at Portland State University in Portland, Oregon, where he is also affiliated with the Department of Sociology.

Ilana Mountian is an honorary research fellow at Manchester Metropolitan University, Manchester, United Kingdom.

Dr Kathryn Moyle is a Professor of Educational Leadership and the Executive Director of the Centre for School Leadership, Learning and Development at Charles Darwin

University in Australia. Prior to taking up this position she held several academic and national government positions including the Director of the Secretariat for the Australian Information and Communications Technology (ICT) in Education Committee (AICTEC) which was the peak national policy committee in Australia for ICT issues that straddle the schools, vocational education and training and higher education sectors. Kathryn is internationally recognised for her research at local and whole system levels concerning school leadership, education policy and learning with technologies. Kathryn's most recent research involves listening to Australian students' views and expectations of learning with technologies. Kathryn is a member of a number of advisory committees to government and non-government agencies at national and international levels, and she is regularly invited to provide policy and strategic advice about teaching and learning with technologies.

Peter Mühlau is a lecturer in sociology and a research associate of the Institute for International Integration at Trinity College Dublin.

Ingrid Mulder is an associate professor of design techniques at ID-StudioLab, Faculty of Industrial Design Engineering of Delft University of Technology in Delft, and a research professor of human centered ICT at the School for Communication, Media and Information Technology, Rotterdam University of Applied Sciences in Rotterdam, the Netherlands.

Dhiraj Murthy is an assistant professor of sociology at Bowdoin College.

Lindsay O'Neill is a PhD candidate in the Department of Sociology at the University of Essex.

Christina Purcell is a doctoral researcher at the Research Institute for Business and Management, Manchester Metropolitan Business School, Manchester, United Kingdom.

Ross Purves is a lecturer in geography at the GIScience Centre of the Department of Geography at the University of Zurich, Switzerland.

Laura Robinson is an assistant professor of sociology at Santa Clara University.

Jeremy M Schulz is a PhD candidate in the Department of Sociology at the University of California, Berkeley.

Asiya Siddiquee is a lecturer in psychology at Manchester Metropolitan University, Manchester, United Kingdom.

Judith Sixsmith is a professor at the Research Institute for Health and Social Change, Manchester Metropolitan University, Manchester, United Kingdom.

Tom W. Smith is the director of the Center for the Study of Politics and Society at the National Opinion Research Center, University of Chicago.

John Sokolowski is a survey director at NORC at the University of Chicago in the Public Health Research Department.

Sheila Lakshmi Steinberg is a professor of sociology and director of community research for the California Center for Rural Policy at Humboldt State University in Arcata, California.

Steven J. Steinberg is a professor of geospatial analysis and director of the Institute for Spatial Analysis at Humboldt State University in Arcata, California.

K.C. Nat Turner is an assistant professor of language, literacy, and culture in teacher education and curriculum studies at the University of Massachusetts School of Education in Amherst, Massachusetts.

Joy van Helvert is a principal researcher (interdisciplinary) at the University of Essex.

Peter van Waart is a lecturer of experience branding and a researcher in the human centered ICT group at the School for Communication, Media and Information Technology, Rotterdam University of Applied Sciences in Rotterdam, the Netherlands.

Albertine Visser is an interaction designer and usability expert at the Belastingdienst CKC (Dutch Tax and Customs Administration—Center of Knowledge and Communication) in Utrecht, the Netherlands.

Claire Worley is a senior lecturer in social policy at Manchester Metropolitan University, Manchester, United Kingdom.

The Handbook
of Emergent
Technologies in
Social Research

Emergent Technologies in Social Research: Pushing Against the Boundaries of Research Praxis[1]

Sharlene Nagy Hesse-Biber

"New technologies can be used positively or negatively and in fact are at once potentially empowering and productive and disempowering and destructive, and are thus fraught with contradictions."

(Kellner, 2007, p. 19)

"Our technological powers increase, but the side effects and potential hazards also escalate."

(Toffler, 1971, p. 430)

"Computing power, neuroscience and nanotechnologies are advancing so rapidly that they will combine to produce the most significant evolutionary developments since the origin of life itself.... Imagine yourself a virtual living being... free of physical pain, able to repair any damage and with a downloaded mind that never dies."

(Paul & Cox, 1996, as cited in Dinello, 2005, p. 1)

Emergent technologies push against the boundaries of qualitative and quantitative research practices, and change the way we view all aspects of our research world. The *Handbook of Emergent Technologies* provides a wealth of information and exemplary research on how to effectively apply these technologies—including multimedia, Web 2.0, mobile, and geospatial technologies—to social research projects.

The *Handbook* provides a unique and comprehensive look at a range of emergent technologies practiced in both disciplinary and interdisciplinary environments. It explores the practice of emergent technologies outside the academic world in multimedia laboratories and research institutes. In this text, we examine the costs and benefits of utilizing new technologies in the research process, as well as the potential misuse of these techniques for methods practices.

The *Handbook* also discusses the philosophical implications of new technologies for the knowledge-building process. Emergent technologies often challenge what constitutes legitimate knowledge building within a discipline and whether these disciplines are asking the right questions. Philosopher Thomas Kuhn, in his classic work, *The Structure of Scientific*

Revolutions (1970), noted how the power of political, economic, and social factors within and outside a discipline serve to shape the knowledge-building process. Kuhn argued that science at any given historical moment is characterized by a particular paradigm. Disciplinary knowledge is then filtered through these disciplinary paradigms. Paradigms are theoretically generated views of the world that provide the core categories and concepts through and by which disciplines construct and make sense of the social world. Kuhn argued that no scientific facts lie outside a point of view or paradigm. What one discipline regards as "fact" may differ from the "facts" of another discipline's worldview. Kuhn noted that a disciplinary paradigm's dominance might arise from irrational and subjective phenomena that affect the development of science. The paradigm that emerges victorious is that which is most popular, but not necessarily the one that provides greater explanatory power. Emerging technologies have the power to transform knowledge production through the asking of new questions and upending of traditional paradigmatic "truths" that in turn may serve to challenge and/or disrupt traditional and dominant disciplinary paradigms.

The *Handbook* discusses emergent technologies as they directly impact the research process. We discuss the pros and cons of applying emergent technologies to social inquiry. The *Handbook* also looks at ethical issues arising out of the use of these technologies in the research process. Some emergent technologies, such as the social networking websites Twitter and MySpace, are user driven, allowing users to share information online in a wide variety of formats. As these social spaces open up and grow, social networking between virtual and non-virtual worlds provides opportunities for users to create new identities. Emergent technologies have also complicated the divide between public and private information. Sometimes the information gathered by researchers consists of not only textual data, but also multimedia data collected from websites that might reveal a user's identity, such as YouTube videos, Facebook photos, and so forth. Increasingly, individuals' identities both online and off-line are available for public scrutiny as new forms of digital social networking can cross-over into "real" world, face-to-face interactions.

Handbook contributors also look at possible future directions for using emergent technologies in their own disciplines and beyond. They provide a candid assessment of the new technological needs of their disciplines and the future impact of developments in technology for research practice.

What Are Emergent Technologies?

While this term encompasses a broad range of technologies, we might think of emergent technologies as those that introduce a significant break in the way individuals, groups, and society as a whole conduct their everyday activities, as well as add new dimensions to our understanding of the social world. New technologies can open up new areas of inquiry, provide researchers with the tools to answer new questions, and change the landscape of knowledge building within and across the disciplines.

However, there are downsides to the introduction of new technologies in that they can be seen as a threat to a general way of life, as in the 19th century case of the Luddites. The 1800s saw a backlash against technological change, led by the Luddites, a social movement of British textile workers in the early 1800s who protested the industrial revolution by destroying mechanized machinery, which they saw as displacing their jobs and a general way of life. Sociologist William Ogburn (1922) noted early on that emerging technologies have the potential to impact whole societies by creating a "cultural lag" (p. 1028). As technology spreads across many parts of a culture, usually the material aspects, other cultural elements that reside in non-material culture—such as values, attitudes, and long-held customs and habits—are slower to change. However, Alvin Toffler saw a more threatening factor of technologies' impact that went beyond Ogburn's ideas on "culture lag." Toffler coined the term "Future Shock" to denote the negative impacts of technological change and how it differed from what he termed "Culture Shock" (1971). He noted:

> Culture shock is the effect that immersion in a strange culture has on the unprepared visitor. . . . It is what happens when the familiar psychological cues that help an individual to function in a society are suddenly withdrawn and replaced by new ones that are strange or incomprehensible. . . . Future shock is a time phenomenon, a product of the greatly accelerated rate of change in society. It arises from the superimposition of a new culture on an old one. It is culture shock in one's own society. But its impact is far worse. . . . Take an individual out of his own culture and set him down suddenly in an environment sharply different from his own, with a different set of cues to react to—different conception of time, space, work, love, religion, sex, and everything else—then cut him off from any hope of retreat to a more familiar social landscape, and the dislocation he suffers is double severe. Moreover, if this new culture is itself in constant turmoil, and if—worse yet—its values are incessantly changing, the sense of disorientation will be still further intensified . . . most people are grotesquely unprepared to cope with it. (Toffler, 1971, p. 10–12)

Social philosophers Baudrillaud (1993), Ellul (1964), and Virilio (1995) see technology's impact as dominating and overshadowing cultures, threatening individuals' sense of their own humanity. Baudrillaud talks of "posthuman" bodies, in which individuals have lost their human bearings and identities, as they become increasingly connected to virtual worlds through mass-mediated information technologies. Virilio (1995) focuses on the social consequences that stem from the growing speed at which individuals access information: almost instantaneously. He suggests that our ability to transcend space by electronically connecting to others almost instantaneously introduces a new calculus into our thinking about what constitutes a social relationship, and may have the effect of dehumanizing our social worlds as a whole. Virilo notes:

> How can we really live if there is no more *here* and if everything is *now*? How can we survive the instantaneous telescoping of a reality that has become ubiquitous, breaking up into two orders of time, each as real as the other: that of presence here and now, and that of a telepresence at a distance, beyond the horizon of tangible appearances? How can we rationally manage the split, not only between virtual and actual realities but, more to the point, between the *apparent* horizon and the *transapparent* horizon of a screen that suddenly opens up a kind of temporal window for us to interact elsewhere, often a long way away? (1997, p. 37, emphasis in original)

Contemporary concerns about new technologies have brought about discussions of a learning and opportunity gap, or what some have termed a "digital divide" in new technologies, between those who have access to the latest technologies and those who do not (Compaine, 2001). It is estimated that "about 40% of U.S. households do not have an internet connection from home and about 30% of adults do not go online even occasionally" (Zhang, Callegaro, & Thomas, 2009, p. 6). There are also concerns about the growing "second order" digital divide, whereby those users who in fact have access to information and communication technologies do not use these technological tools (see: DiMaggio, Hargittai, Neuman, & Robinson, 2001; Donat, 2008).

Some research suggests that nonuse of new technologies may be related to levels of competency or the result of negative attitudes and values regarding technology (Donat, Brandtweiner, & Kerschbaum, 2009, p. 51). It may also be the case that the structures of these new technologies may themselves create barriers to users' willingness to access these tools if, for example, they feel that doing so may compromise their privacy (Donat et al., 2009, p. 53).

The *Handbook* provides an important social justice and social policy context within which many of these access and user issues are addressed. The wealth of knowledge on emergent technologies and their applications to social research inquiry is a critical issue in terms of the future training of social researchers and access to these emergent tools. Both sides of the digital divide will benefit from the knowledge contained within the *Handbook* chapters.

Within the context of social research practice, emergent technologies have the ability to create new multimedia data sources for the researcher, as well as make it possible for a researcher to ask and pursue new research questions. Emergent technologies bump up against the ways scientists conduct their research, often challenging them to develop new research skills and contend with thorny philosophical issues that may challenge their view of social reality. These technologies have the ability to upend disciplinary concepts and ideas. For example, the concept of what constitutes a "sampling unit" in survey research becomes challenged as one begins to think of gathering a sample from an on-line community, where users' identities may morph and also be multiple.

We can think of emergent technologies as arising from a confluence of factors. New developments in materials and methods, demand for a particular service, entrepreneurial spirit and quest for innovation, necessity, and curiosity can drive the development of emergent technologies. Serendipity also plays a role in how these factors interact, providing unique and unforeseen innovations. It is often the asking of new questions and the quest to find, solve, or explore these questions that gives rise to thinking outside one's comfort zone. Sometimes, a new technology can arise from incremental changes to an existing technology, such as moving from the use of compact discs (CDs) to digital video discs (DVDs). Both of these technologies use a similar principle, except that a DVD stores much more information on a single disc than a CD.

Popular emergent technologies tend to be characterized by innovations that have a significant impact on our everyday lives; for example, in how we listen to music (vinyl records to iPods); how we connect with others (telephone to email to Facebook and Twitter); how we travel (horse-drawn carriages to automobiles to planes); and so on. Emergent technologies disrupt traditional ways of knowing in order to create rich new knowledge by allowing researchers to access new types of data and analyze and interpret these data in a variety of innovative ways. Emergent technologies have also challenged our conceptions of space by providing nonphysical spaces, or "virtual realities," where individuals can interact with one another.

Scientists have also developed microtechnologies that can be worn or implanted in the body either to replace a body part (e.g., cochlear implants) or to enhance the workings of the body through specific "artificial intelligence" (AI), which has some capability to think.

These emergent technological tools begin to change our conception of what it means to be human when technological devices can in fact meld with the physical body to perhaps turn humans into "cybernetic organisms," or what philosopher Paul Virilio (2005, p. 136) terms, "industrialization of living matter" (see also: Clynes & Kline, 1960; Haraway, 1991; Hogle, 2005; Virilio, 1995). In his book, *The Information Bomb*, Virilo (2005) discussed how society has moved from the practice of science to a form of science he terms "techno-science." Virilio was concerned about what he sees as the increasing speed-up of technological innovation and its impact on the ethical context within which techno-science operates. He noted:

> Science, which is not so attached to "truth" as it once was, but more to immediate "effectiveness," is now drifting towards a decline, its civic fall from grace. As a panic phenomenon—a fact concealed by the success of its devices and tools—contemporary science is losing itself in the very excessiveness of its alleged progress. Much as a strategic offensive can wear itself out by the scale of its tactical conquests, so techno-science is gradually wrecking the scholarly resources of all knowledge. (Virilio, 2005, p. 2)

Handbook contributors to this volume are mindful of the negative impacts of technological change and specifically discuss the range of ethical dimensions involved in the application of the specific technological innovations they take up in their chapters. We also have a range of chapters that specifically address these concerns. Recognizing these challenges, they also focus on the enormous possibilities that new technologies hold, with optimism and faith in the possibilities of these innovations.

Part I. Emergent Technologies in a Broad Social Research Context

This first part of the *Handbook* explores some of the possibilities and challenges of employing emergent technologies in social research. We begin with Edward Hackett's chapter, "Possible Dreams: Research Technologies and Transformation of the Human Sciences." He first notes the lack of investment in research technologies in the social and behavioral sciences, unlike the heavy investment that has taken place in the physical and life sciences: "Research technologies are a transformative force that will challenge received knowledge, generate original empirical insights, and catalyze new theories" (Hackett, this volume). He specifically looks at eight areas of innovation, including: increasing the spatial, temporal, and social resolution of large data sets; addressing the increasing ethical challenges of emergent technologies; and establishing secure facilities for access to administrative (public) records and commercial transaction data.

David Gunkel's chapter, "To Tell the Truth: The Internet and Emergent Epistemological Challenges in Social Research," explores some of the philosophical dimensions of emergent technologies with regard to their impact on such foundational questions as "What is truth?" and "Who can know?" Gunkel notes that new technologies, including the internet, can alter researchers' conceptions of what reality is. For example: To what extent is the internet an extension of social reality, or a new social entity, with its own set of rules for social behavior? How do social researchers study virtual worlds?

Barbara Herr Harthorn's chapter, "Methodological Challenges Posed by Emergent Nanotechnologies and Cultural Values," looks closely at what makes technologies emergent, using the example of nanotechnologies to explore this broader question. She specifically addresses the types of research questions that lend themselves to emergent technology inquiry and examines how the emergent properties of nanotechnologies affect both the application of research methods and the kinds of questions asked. She is most concerned about the need to include the social sciences' and humanities' perspectives in informing the development and course of nanotechnologies.

The next two chapters examine some critical issues regarding the ethics of emergent technologies. While a discussion of ethical issues runs through most of the *Handbook* chapters, these contributors center ethics as a critical element in thinking about the role of technology within the research enterprise as a whole.

Göran Collste's chapter, "Under my Skin: The Ethics of Ambient Computing for Personal Health Monitoring," addresses ethical issues of using emergent technologies in social research in general, and specifically in the field of personal heath monitoring. He first discusses the problem of the ethical assessment of any emergent technology (as opposed to existing technologies) and argues for a social constructivist view of technology as "the result of social interests, forces, and choices" (Collste, this volume). He next describes ambient computing (i.e., ubiquitous computing) in general and in personal health monitoring (at home). Collste addresses many ethical questions that arise from this emergent technology, such as questions of privacy, dependence on technology, safety of personal data, technological paternalism, and identity. Finally, he looks at ethical technology assessment and advocates for the thorough ethical assessment of technologies during their emergent and developing stages.

Mariann Hardey, in "Ubiquitous Connectivity: User-Generated Data and the Role of the Researcher," tackles the ethical dilemmas associated with research using user-generated data, including confidentiality, privacy, and mixing the role of participant/observer. She provides an in-depth look at her own research experience with social networking websites such as Facebook and explores the specific ethical dilemmas associated with this type of online research. While she sees much promise in participatory research—and Web 2.0 seems to encourage ever-increasing levels of participation—she also warns that researchers must balance participation with ethical awareness.

Part II. The Rise of Internet Technologies and Social Research Practice

The second part of this Handbook covers emergent technologies that have arisen from Web 2.0 innovations and have directly impacted traditional qualitative and quantitative methods of inquiry. Early on, Sudweeks and Simoff (1999) noted, "The internet has given birth to new research fields, or has diversified existing research fields connected with human activities, including computer-mediated communication (CMC), computer-supported cooperative work (CSCW), electronic commerce, virtual communities, virtual architecture, various virtual environments and information design" (p. 29).

Since its beginning in the early 1960s, the internet has become a source for a variety of information and tools. According to Internet World Stats, the internet had almost 1.6 billion users worldwide in March 2009 (www.internetworldstats.com, accessed August 2009). Steven Jones (1999) called it an "engine of social change" in that it has "modified work habits, education, social relations generally, and…our hopes and dreams." (p. 2). The internet calls into question some traditional philosophical assumptions about the nature of social reality—is the internet merely a part of our current social reality, or a new and different environment with its own social conventions? Are positivist assumptions about the nature of social reality and interpretative models of subjective experience valid in an internet environment? (Sudweeks & Simoff, 1999, p. 31). Sudweeks and Simoff saw that researchers must adapt to an environment where "communication technologies and socio-cultural norms challenge existing research assumptions and premises" (p. 30).

An additional issue is the ever-changing nature of the internet, which has a plethora of modes for accessing multimedia information. The use of iPods, cell phones, and other devices and technology that work in a virtual environment provide even more ways to view and access data. The ability to hyperlink online data even allows for nonlinear information access (Dicks and Mason, this volume).

As you read the chapters in this part, you can observe how much Web 2.0 technologies have already permeated the practice of social research. In fact, there appears to be a dynamic interplay between emergent technologies and methods practices, such that as new technologies arise, they provide the impetus for methods innovations. A methods innovation may come about by the combining of traditional tools across different disciplines, the mixing of tools within a discipline, or the creation of new tools (see: Hesse-Biber & Leavy, 2006, 2008). This part examines some of the key methods innovations taking place within and across disciplines as a result of the development of Web 2.0 technologies. We address specific types of Web 2.0 technologies that are being utilized in the social sciences and the process by which these technologies in turn transform methods practices, often promoting the emergence of new methods practices (see Figure I.1). We examine the types of research questions one can tackle with these new technologies, as well as examine some drawbacks in their deployment for social research ends.

Bella Dicks and Bruce Mason's chapter, "Clickable Data: Hypermedia and Social Research," discusses how "clickable multimedia" or "hypermedia" can be used in all stages of the social research process. They first take a brief look at Web 2.0 as a forum for social research and the emergence of hyperlinking. They recommend hypermedia as especially useful for discovering relationships in qualitative and ethnographic research, providing

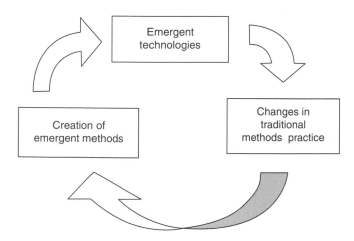

Figure I.1 Interplay between emergent technologies and methods practice.

a case study of qualitative research at Cardiff University. Next, the authors recommend software to handle multimedia data and discuss data management and archiving. For the main focus of their chapter, they talk about the use of hypermedia in analysis, as well as in authoring and dissemination. Analysis of data through the hyperlinking of records is an emergent method for "lettered," video, audio, and other multimedia data. The chapter is augmented throughout by examples from the authors' own experimentation with hypermedia. Hypermedia shows much promise for expanding the authoring of research beyond print-derived writing conventions. This method is not without its challenges, but hypermedia can provide a way for scholarly research to expand and develop across the research process

The next two chapters of this part address digital and cyber ethnography, which involve the use of both established and emergent technologies in ethnographic research. Digital and cyber ethnography can entail the examination of behavior within a technological context (e.g., an ethnography of a cyber-community) or the use of emergent technologies (e.g., digital pens or blogs) to enhance traditional methods such as fieldnotes.

Dhiraj Murthy's chapter, "Emergent Digital Ethnographic Methods for Social Research," aims "to equip social researchers in academia and industry with the knowledge to understand [five emergent] technologies and their methodological applications to digital ethnographies" (Murthy, this volume). He first defines digital ethnography, discusses some benefits and weaknesses of this method, and provides examples of digital ethnographies. Murthy next presents the core of the chapter, a thorough examination of five digital ethnographic technologies: fieldnotes with blogs/wikis, embedded ethnographic technologies, digital pens, CMS groupware, and Twitter. Despite the vast possibilities presented by emergent technologies, he argues for multiple ethnographic methods (i.e., digital methods combined with traditional, face-to-face ethnography). He rounds out the chapter with a discussion of the costs, benefits, ethical implications, and future directions of digital ethnographies. Murthy sees digital ethnographic methods for social inquiry continuing to expand with developments in ubiquitous computing.

Laura Robinson and Jeremy Schulz's chapter, "New Fieldsites, New Methods: New Ethnographic Opportunities," focuses on "three central tensions [that] have shaped the adoption of ethnographic methods in new media environments since the advent of cyberethnography in the mid 1990s: the character of mediated interaction (email, IM, blogging, texting, etc.) as a social process, text as interaction, and the relationship between the observer and observed" (this volume). Robinson and Schulz intersperse ethical dilemmas and a historical perspective on cyberethnography (including tensions arising in its development) throughout their chapter. While technologies are rapidly changing, the authors affirm that the traditional strengths of ethnography make it suitable to study behavior in technologically mediated communication, an ever-growing and vital basis for social research.

The next chapter addresses the use of the internet technology in focus group research. David Morgan and Bojana Lobe's chapter, "Online Focus Groups," provides the reader with an excellent analytical window into the praxis of online focus group research from data collection to analysis and interpretation. They present a critical assessment of the strengths and weaknesses of online technologies for social scientists looking to incorporate emergent internet technologies into the traditional focus group praxis.

Morgan and Lobe start with a discussion of the critical issues involved in the application of online technologies, specifically with regard to the benefits and challenges of synchronous and asynchronous focus groups. They proceed to discuss the nuts and bolts involved in conducting focus groups in online environments, including the challenges involved in the recruitment process, research design issues (e.g., group composition and ethical considerations), and the role of the moderator. They ground their chapter with a hands-on case study application, and end their chapter with a lively discussion of the future directions of online focus group research.

Karim Gherab-Martin's chapter, "Digital Repositories, Folksonomies, and Interdisciplinary Research: New Social Epistemology Tools," focuses on the online, interdisciplinary exchange of research and ideas, what he defines as a "trading zone." He addresses this concept and how it applies to the digital repository, "an online open access archive for collecting, preserving, and disseminating intellectual outputs, usually scientific research articles and documents" (this volume). He next looks at social tagging and the related concept "folksonomies," including advantages and drawbacks of this technique. Gherab-Martin places folksonomies in relation to other concepts and uses examples from cognitive psychology to represent their benefit to interdisciplinary relations. He closes the chapter with a number of suggestions for further development, including the introduction of social tagging to digital repositories and a deeper analysis of the "long tail" of folksonomies, or those tags that are used less (as opposed to the current focus on the most popular tags). He sees a need for current journal models to adapt to emergent technologies and to deconstruct boundaries between disciplines and existing hierarchies.

Part III. Emergent Data Collection Methods: New Forms of Data Production

This part of the *Handbook* discusses the impact of emergent data collection technologies on the practice of social research. As a result of technological development, researchers now have access to rich new sources of user-generated data. Emergent technologies provide new ways for researchers to capture user information in real time—moment to moment—and analyze these bits of information in order to arrive at an understanding of both micro and macro patterns and social processes. One might, for example, capture the day to day spending patterns of individuals, groups, and societies—what you purchased online, in the grocery store, and so on. These purchasing data are sent to a central processing technology that can make sense out of them by recontextualizing these strands of data in order to discern patterns of consumer demand for goods and services.

The contributors to this part stress the importance of looking at the ethical and privacy issues that go along with the use of these technologies, as they have the potential to invade and perhaps compromise the privacy of individual users for economic gain, social control, and even political manipulation.

Anne Beaulieu and Mette Terp Høybye's chapter, "Studying Mailing Lists: Text, Temporality, Interaction, and Materiality at the Intersection of E-Mail and the Web," discusses the mailing list, a long-used technology that the authors felt needed to be addressed, in part because it is so well known and widely used. Using two illustrative case studies throughout the chapter, they present ways of utilizing mailing lists as social data, and the many aspects that make it unique and continually emerging, especially as the mailing list can incorporate other online technologies and reflect wider social dynamics. Various topics they address include the temporality of mailing lists and the dynamics and boundaries between public and private conversations. While mailing lists were created in another stage of technological development, they continue to be a source of social knowledge and data and compliment a broad range of studies, even if not the main source of data in a particular project.

Michael Dal's chapter, "Online Data Collection and Data Analysis Using Emergent Technologies," begins by defining online data collection, an established but constantly developing method, as quantitative. Dal next looks at different types of online data collection: from websites, by sending out e-mails, from online data surveys, or from polls. He then looks at the reasons for using online data collection, including time-efficiency and cost benefits, as well as difficulties, such as participants' feelings of (in)security and informed consent. He also examines four common sources of error in data collection and how to overcome these, and provides a guide to writing and analyzing web surveys. In addition to providing exemplary research examples throughout the chapter, Dal uses a case study project to examine in-depth the use of an online survey, in this case to develop a research-based method of teaching foreign languages to dyslexic students in a European context. He ends the chapter with the emerging possibilities for presenting a survey in varied forms, including SMS surveys and visual components (see: Smith and Sokolowski, this volume). He concludes that the challenge for researchers using online data collection is to keep up with quickly advancing technology while providing simple questionnaires for respondents.

Robert Fitzgerald and John Findlay's chapter, "Collaborative Research Tools: Using Wikis and Team Learning Systems to Collectively Create New Knowledge," discusses the potential of using democratized research to solve controversial problems with no clear solution. By proposing that good research "engages participants in mutual inquiry and a dialectical or knowledge building discourse" (this volume), they frame the rest of their chapter to discuss two emerging technologies: Wikis and the Zing team learning system. They provide backgrounds for each technology and describe their applications to social research projects, specifically in focus groups and action research. Fitzgerald and Findlay conclude their chapter with an extensive discussion of the technologies' strengths and weaknesses, and emphasize the importance of "synthesis between people rather than objective analysis and truth alone" (this volume), which can be achieved with such tools as wikis and team learning systems.

Kathryn Moyle, in "Using Emerging Technologies in Focus Group Interviews," expands the discussion of team learning systems for data collection in face-to-face interviews. She begins with a description of two case studies of national education research in Australia, which are then incorporated throughout the chapter. She provides a background on the "focus group interview" and walks through traditional methods of collecting data in focus group interviews. Next, Moyle introduces the emergent technology Zing, which incorporates several keyboards and cursors that work on one screen, allowing participants to record their views and read and respond to others'. She discusses the use of Zing to collect data in focus group interviews, providing comprehensive information about such topics as how Zing can break down power relationships, what questions are suitable for using Zing, and the preparation of data for analysis. While Zing has seen limited use in educational research thus far, Moyle is confident in this technology's meaningful application to future research studies.

Gregorio Convertino and John Carroll's chapter, "Toward Experimental Methods in Collaborative Computing Research," describes methods in collaborative computing (CC) research, a term that encompasses the "research in Computer-Supported Cooperative Work (CSCW) and Groupware, which is software typically aimed at groups of knowledge workers in organizations" (this volume). They begin with a brief history of CC research and the innovative technologies used in the field, and then provide an in-depth discussion of current research methods and their deficiencies, specifically the problem of a lack of native experimental methods. In order to combat those deficiencies, Convertino and Carroll provide their own methodological approach with three distinct properties: model-based (theory-driven), centered on group process, and comprehensive in methods. They use case studies to show the use of their approach in two research projects. The chapter concludes with a valuable analysis of CC research methods' implications for social research.

Albertine Visser and Ingrid Mulder's chapter, "Emergent Technologies for Assessing Social Feelings and Experiences," provides a specific example of a recently developed technology, the "WiShare" tool, used to access experience in real time. In their chapter, Visser and Mulder introduce the concept of "sharing experiences," in which people use technology to share feelings and/or thoughts. They begin with a discussion of this concept (especially as it exists "in the moment"), as well as social feelings. Next, they provide an analysis of currently existing methods for assessing experiences, including questionnaires, the ESM, and some emergent methods. From the shortcomings of these methods, they build a set of twelve requirements that a tool must have in order to adequately assess sharing experiences. The remainder of the chapter focuses on their new tool, the WiShare, used "to let people indicate their feeling of social presence and connectedness through answering questions about sharing of context, thoughts, feelings, and wishes" (this volume). After describing the technology and two in-depth evaluation studies conducted to assess and improve the tool, they conclude with hopes for the potential of further development and use of the WiShare tool.

Quantitative methods practices have been impacted by a range of emergent technologies, as examined in the next two chapters. Bert Little's chapter, "Data Mining and Research: Applied Mathematics Reborn," analyzes and explains the workings of a variety of data mining techniques. He discusses the use of algorithms in large-scale data analysis productions, and also explains the difference between different data mining analyses, such as classification, cluster, and discriminant analysis. Little ends his chapter with a case study application of data mining, illustrating how "data mining techniques are used to extract patterns of marriage and population demographic structure that are related to the occurrence of birth defects" (this volume).

In "Knowledge Mining and Managing: Emergent Tools and Technologies in Web-Based Intelligent Learning Environments," Nittaya Kerdprasop notes that "knowledge discovery in databases or data mining has also emerged as a new field" (this volume), and it provides a valuable resource of data and knowledge. She introduces knowledge mining by looking at the current technologies for mining in web-based learning systems. She then proceeds to describe a new design based on integrated web-based intelligent learning environments (WILE) and knowledge mining in this environment using educational data on the dropout rates (number of students discontinuing enrollment) in secondary schools in the United States. She finally provides specific applications of data mining technologies to the field of educational research.

Part IV. Audiovisual, Mobile, and Geospatial Technologies' Impact on the Social Research Process

In the first three chapters of this part, we discuss audiovisual technologies, which allow the researcher to capture the movements of individuals in real time and space. Some of these technologies also have the ability to capture the existence of others in an individual's space by monitoring cell phone usage in their immediate area. Visualization technologies such as Flickr allow for the geo-tagging of photographs we capture in any given space and allow us to upload these images to a photo stream of images others have taken of that very space across time. This part specifically examines the range of ways audio and visual data can be applied in a social research context.

Tom Smith and John Sokolowski's chapter, "The Use of Audiovisuals in Surveys," looks at the emergence of audiovisual technologies in surveys. The chapter begins with a background on the use of audio, visual, and audiovisual as stimuli (within survey questions) and for data capture (within responses). The core of the chapter focuses on Computer Audio Recorded Interviewing (CARI), first explaining what CARI is and how it was developed, and then reviewing past and current technological challenges. The authors look at current uses of CARI—detecting falsification and monitoring interviewer performance—as well as future developments. They then return to audiovisual in general, discussing the advances that have allowed surveys to become more extensive and complete, as well as cautions for the researcher, such as privacy and the complications of coding and analysis. While the development and use of audiovisual technologies requires much work, they "have become a valuable tool in survey research" and will continue to do so with the advancement of other technologies (Smith and Sokolowski, this volume).

John Creswell and Bernard McCoy's chapter, "The Use of Mixed Methods Thinking in Documentary Development," analyzes a documentary film from a new, methods-based perspective. They analyze the film *Breaking Down Barriers* in the context of a mixed methods design approach, including the use of qualitative and quantitative data in the development of the documentary. They begin the chapter with an overview of mixed methods and mixed methods designs. Next, they provide information about the object of their case study, *Breaking Down Barriers*, followed by an analysis of the implementation of mixed methods in this documentary, specifically the use of concurrent and transformative mixed methods designs. Creswell and McCoy conclude their chapter with a set of recommendations for incorporating mixed methods thinking into documentaries.

Aline Gubrium and K-C Nat Turner's chapter, "Digital Storytelling as an Emergent Method for Social Research and Practice," introduces the concept of digital storytelling, both as an emergent technology and an emergent method for social research. Digital stories are short "visual narratives that synthesize images, video, audio recordings of voice and music, and text to create compelling stories" (this volume). This method allows people to create their own stories in a collaborative process with instructors and fellow storytellers. Gubrium and Turner begin their chapter with a description of the digital storytelling process. They next show digital storytelling's emergence as a research tool—both the products (digital stories) themselves, as well as the process of telling those stories. Then they provide a case study in which digital storytelling is used in the classroom to incorporate community organizing and civic engagement. In this case study, they address some of the problems and benefits of digital storytelling, including the allowance for people to "construct and represent their own experiences" (this volume). This emergent method can be incorporated with interviews, focus groups, and other existent research methods to enhance social research.

Mobile-enhanced technologies provide users access to communication "on the go." Smartphones and other mobile devices seem to carry every technology a person could need or want, from global positioning systems (GPS) and communication tools to games, computers, and cameras. The following chapters delve into several different mobile technologies that hold promise of gathering large volumes of quantitative and qualitative data in "real time" in order to enhance understanding of individuals' everyday lives in a wider social context. From mobile phones to the experience sampling method (ESM), in the next three chapters you will read about social researchers at the forefront of using and developing emergent mobile technology for studying subjective experience.

Nathan Eagle's chapter, "Mobile Phones as Sensors for Social Research," provides a wide-angle view of the impact of mobile technologies on users and researchers. With approximately 4 billion mobile phone users in the world, Eagle sees ample reason for social researchers to begin tapping into this useful tool. He explains the phone as a sensor, able to gather such information as location, communication, application use, and people nearby; he notes that data collection using phones fits neatly within the framework of existing social research methods. In addition, Eagle explains how mobile phones can answer many new questions and inform such diverse topics as mobility patterns, relationship and social networks, economic indicators, and disease monitoring. He then describes the challenges and ethical issues involved with using this pervasive technology in social and other research. Ultimately, he concludes that the mobile phone's ability to provide massive data sets will greatly complement traditional data-gathering methods.

Geert de Haan, Sunil Choenni, Ingrid Mulder, Sandra Kalidien, and Peter van Waart's chapter, "Bringing the Research Lab into Everyday Life: Exploiting Sensitive Environments to Acquire Data for Social Research," looks at the wider application of mobile technologics combined with other technologies (e.g., Web 2.0) in sensitive environments, "an intelligent infrastructure that collects sensory information of users while they move and interact" (this volume). Because such an environment can be equipped with a vast array of tools, de Haan et al. discuss the three types of data that can arise—structured, semi-structured, and unstructured—as well as how to analyze these types of data. They also discuss uncertain data, which frequently arises from those technologies that aim to serve the real-life needs of the user. Next, they provide a case study of electronic tour guides in a museum, while throughout the chapter they build upon an example of collecting data from customers in a store. The chapter closes with the benefits and future opportunities for data collected from sensitive environments.

Anne Kellock et al.'s chapter, "Using Technology and the Experience Sampling Method to Understand Real Life," highlights the experience sampling method (ESM), in which participants perform a certain task (e.g., writing in a journal or taking a photo) in response to an alert from a mobile device, in order to collect participants' status, experience, feelings, etc., in situ. Kellock et al. begin the chapter with a case study, which is tied in throughout the chapter. In the study, participants used mobile phones with integrated cameras in order to capture pictures of their experiences throughout each day for one week. Based on the results of their study, they next discuss the strengths and weaknesses of using the ESM with mobile phones/cameras and subsequent group discussions. Strengths include shared learning and participants recognizing their place in space and time; weaknesses include intrusiveness and the nontypicality of those events that happen to be captured. They also discuss the quantitative analysis conducted with the data, as well as other examples of ESM studies. The ESM method provides a new way of seeing things, while still combining different forms of data collection to contextualize the visual.

The final two chapters of this part take up emergent mobility and geospatial technologies and their application to social research practice—such systems include global positioning systems and remote sensing platforms, as well as electronic monitoring systems.

Over the past three decades, developments in geospatial technologies in the field of geography have been partly driven by critical and feminist theoretical perspectives on the concept of location in time and space, which ask new questions regarding issues of representation (see: Kwan, 2007; Nightingale, 2003). For example: Who has the power and authority to represent spatial activities and their interpretation? Who decides what to look at—for example, who decides what activities are observed in time and space at different locations? Researchers in the social sciences, humanities, and the arts have been increasingly drawn to the use of these technologies as they become more widely available, cheaper, and easier to use, and have begun to ask a range of new questions regarding the social structure of physical space.

Steven Steinberg and Sheila Steinberg's chapter, "Geospatial Analysis Technology and Social Science Research," discusses the use of geospatial technologies in social research, specifically remote sensing, global positioning systems (GPS), and geographic information systems (GIS). They present these emerging technologies as tools to expand researchers' approach to looking at space and place, and employ a computer-based socio-spatial approach. They also discuss socio-spatial grounded theory and the benefits and current status of these technologies. They look at how geospatial technologies can be incorporated into social research, enhancing the current use of geospatial data with new techniques and tools; two comprehensive case studies provide in-depth examples of their applications to social research. While there is much room to expand the use of geospatial technology across the spectrum of research fields, Steinberg and Steinberg are confident in the potential of these technologies for such tasks as participatory GIS mapping and the use of GPS in the field, and conclude succinctly, "location matters."

Ross Purves' chapter, "Methods, Examples, and Pitfalls in the Exploitation of the Geospatial Web," looks at the possibilities for research in the Geospatial Web: "the collection of data and services that allow us to collect, portray, manipulate, and analyze data with some form of geographic content from the broader Web" (this volume). After first exploring some background information, Purves provides two short case studies that explore the Geospatial Web. He then looks at how location is represented and the different forms of data available: structured and unstructured, authoritative and volunteered, and static and dynamic. After providing the methods and resources available for exploring the Geospatial Web (including application programming interfaces), he provides two extensive example analyses that are particularly relevant to social researchers. The first looks at images and labels in relation to the 2008 presidential election in the United States; the second examines the language used in association with certain concepts of natural landscapes. Ross Purves closes his chapter with the problems and promise of the Geospatial Web, which he sees as a unique, emergent method for gathering data from a geographic perspective.

Part V. The Impact of New Technologies for Studying Social Life in Naturalistic Settings

The final part of the *Handbook* addresses a point of intersection of technologies across the variety of technological areas (Web 2.0, mobile, etc.): the ubiquitous computing environment. As technology expands into every aspect of our life, encompassing most of our communication, work, school, and other activities, the logical next step is the "digital home," where the private sphere consists of appliances and other devices that are (almost) all networked, collect data, and are personalized and remote controlled. Precursors to this home environment are Living Labs, constructed but home-like, with the most advanced and emergent technologies.

Chris Fowler, Lindsay O'Neill, and Joy van Helvert's chapter, "Living Laboratories: Social Research Applications and Evaluation," offers a close look at living labs, where researchers can observe participants in a home-like environment that can monitor everything from location and appliance use to emotional response. While these spaces have largely been used for commercial research, they have much to offer social researchers. Fowler et al. begin their chapter by settling on a definition of a living lab and examining the influence of one's investigative approach and theoretical perspective on one's choice of methods. They then explore evaluation questions and data collection methods, finally providing case studies from the University of Essex's Living Lab, the "i-space." The authors conclude their chapter with a discussion of challenges faced by researchers in living labs, including sampling and ethics, and possible future directions.

Anne Holohan, Jeanette Chin, Vic Callaghan, and Peter Muhlau's chapter, "The Digital Home: A New Locus of Social Science Research," moves to the next step beyond the living lab, the "digital home," where people's own personal spaces are inundated with technology and become the site of commercial research and knowledge, and potentially social research. A digital home is a home in which most or all of the electronic appliances and systems are networked. Holohan et al. see opportunities for social research to answer such questions as, "Who will be excluded from using this new technology?" and "How will digital homes impact institutions and decision making?" They look at the emergent technologies giving way to digital homes and how new forms of information flow and decision making (in which consumers directly negotiate and exchange data with companies, government, and other organizations) provide an object of study for social research, not without ethical and other issues. The way that digital homes can empower household decision making, they conclude, ". . . has the power to allow innovative reconstitution of, existing decision making practice, and relationships between providers of resources and consumers, and governments and citizens. . . . this innovation can transform institutions and impact the existing power structure in society." (this volume).

Remaining Challenges and Future Directions of Emergent Technologies for Social Science Research

There remain important challenges in the years ahead as the pace of technological change quickens. The speed of technological change is especially characteristic of information and communications technologies (Jordan, 2008, p. 388). Government funding of science and technology corporations and research centers devoted to the production of new technologies is increasing, as well as governmental funding of new technological developments, especially in the field of military defense. The application of these new technologies in a military context adds another layer of secrecy regarding the issue of ethical research practices in the use of these technologies in the service of a military research agenda (see: Rappert, Balmer, & Stone, 2008; Wright & Wallace, 2002). The Center for Policy on Emerging Technologies notes the following with regard to findings of nanotechnologies that have specific military applications:

> Many of emerging technologies' novel capabilities are of significant interest to the military, where the potential for making materials stronger, machines smaller and faster, and bodies more resilient is directly relevant to the goals of enforcement, surveillance, and security. This interest is perhaps best illustrated by the fact that the National Nanotechnology Initiative's (NNI) budget includes more than $400 million in 2007 for research directed to nanotechnology's military applications under the auspices of the Department of Defense (DOD). The Defense Advanced Research Projects Agency (DARPA), however, is possibly the federal agency with the greatest stake in emerging technologies—proclaiming on its website to be the site of "research and technology where risk and payoff are both very high and where success may provide dramatic advances for traditional military roles and missions." Its project list ranges from the "Quantum Sensors Program" to "BioFuels" to "Self Regenerative Systems"; in all, its programs cover nearly the full gamut of the sciences, with emphasis on nanotechnology, neuroscience, and biotechnology. (Center for Policy on Emerging Technologies, 2009)

Let us now turn to the impact and future directions of emergent technologies for the social research community.

As we will observe in Part I of this *Handbook*, emergent technologies challenge basic research practices and also upend traditional disciplinary points of view regarding such foundational questions as: What is the nature of the social world? Who can know? What can be known? What seems clear is that basic structures of the social scientific enterprise as a whole are also changing and moving from a disciplinary-based practice to a more interdisciplinary and multidisciplinary environment, where social science researchers will be part of a team-based research project that may span across a variety of disciplines. Social science research will also increasingly be conducted by freestanding research institutes and corporate research environments, with some connection to universities.

As we will note in Part II of this *Handbook*, a variety of traditional research practices, such as the deployment of ethnographic and survey research methods, become transformed as they incorporate internet-based technological practices. Engaging with emergent technologies will require researchers to have a good understanding of the range of research methods—from quantitative to qualitative to mixed and multi-methods. Emergent technologies continue to blur the line between qualitative and quantitative methods with a strong leaning toward the use of multi-methods (several qualitative and quantitative methods), as well as the use of emergent methods that come out of a "trial and error" methods practice, usually promoted by the asking of new research questions.

The types of data social scientists will have access to will also grow in volume and variety, as will the ways of analyzing and interpreting these data. Issues will also arise regarding the sampling of these data, especially those data that are recorded in real time from such devices as mobile phones. These data are "streaming and ongoing." Traditional sampling techniques may need to be revised, rethought, or discarded. The concept of a "random sample," for example, may take on a new set of definitions. Issues of validity and reliability of these data will also evolve as researchers ask themselves what these data are actually measuring. Just because we have the technology to measure "a something" does not make these data useful.

Much more attention will need to be focused on how these new data sets will be utilized in the pursuit of knowledge building within the natural, behavioral, and social sciences. Who gets to decide which data sets will be utilized? To what extent do these data drive research inquiry? Issues of power and control over new data sources may also arise as researchers housed in corporations and other economic entities find that they can now market a range of new data sources for profit. The organizational structure and environment of research universities is already taking on a semicorporate structure as they link up and partner with a range of private corporations, that deal with a host of new technologies and research funding initiatives, raising a host "conflict of interest" issues with regard to, for example, what research gets funded and published.

Underlying the acquisition of these new data sources via emergent technologies will also be the possibility for the abuse of user information. As we note throughout the *Handbook*, there are numerous ethical and privacy issues surrounding the acquisition of internet data (see: Joinson, McKenna, Postmes, & Reips, 2007), where the lines between private and public information become blurred. The private lives of individuals, groups, and organizations, as seen in such data as medical records, consumer purchases, and users' locations in time and space, may be compromised, especially as emergent technologies move into naturalistic settings, as seen in the last part of this *Handbook*. What is apparent as well is that the nature of ethical research practices will also be challenged and transformed.

The current practices of university internal review boards (IRBs) that oversee the ethical dimensions of research projects and provide the approval regarding whether or not a given project meets a set of ethical standards may also need to be reassessed. For example, do IRBs possess the resources and expertise to evaluate the ethical issues surrounding the use of a specific emergent technology in a given research project? Are IRB decision makers aware of the ever-changing range of ethical consequences of emergent technologies, especially specific surveillance technologies? As research projects take on a hybrid structure that links with freestanding research institutes and corporate research environments, how will university-based IRB's ethical standards be impacted?

There may arise an "ethics gap" between an IRB's ability to understand the workings and implications of a given emergent technology and its ability to make an ethics assessment regarding a given project that uses emergent technologies. An ethics gap may place respondents at risk if certain implications of a given technology slip under the radar of traditional IRB practices. New technologies will challenge the meaning of basic terms such as "informed consent" and "privacy." For example, when a respondent agrees to be part of a research project by signing an informed consent document, to what extent do they have the technological savvy to evaluate the workings and social impact of the emergent technologies used in the project they have agreed to participate in? This is particularly problematic with regard to the use of mobile technologies that have the capability to track and record a given individual's movements in time and space. There will be an increasing need to close a growing ethics gap and this will mean a rethinking of some basic ethical concepts like informed consent. Some of this work is already taking place (see: Henry et al., 2009). How will IRBs assess these emergent technologies—their risks and benefits— if research is conducted at multisites, some of which may cross international borders? How will these multisite IRBs communicate their concerns and issues across different cultures, as well as national and research interests? While some of these concerns already exist without the rise of new technologies, adding a layer of technological innovation will make these already complex ethical issues more difficult to assess.

On the other hand, ethics boards may tend to render more conservative decisions with regard to the use of new technological innovations and might decide to outright dismiss certain projects because of a lack of understanding of the inherent ethical implications of a given research project that employs an emergent technology.

An additional issue for social research practice lies is the training of social researchers. How much training is necessary for the proper use of emergent technologies? From where will the resources come to do specific training in a given technology and who will decide who gets this type of training? Will there be a "research divide" where some researchers have access to training in these newly emergent technologies and others do not? Many researchers are trained in one primary method and set of technologies, so there already is potential for an enormous "research training gap." Implementing emergent technologies sometimes requires researchers to part from their current methods practices; even if offered such training, they may refuse to do so, perhaps creating a "secondary research divide" that may be more difficult to address. As we mentioned in Part I, emergent technologies and their practice will take a researcher out of their "methods and technology comfort zones," requiring them to confront their philosophical and methodological standpoints (see: Hesse-Biber & Leavy, 2006).

What also needs to be addressed in this process is the training of the next generation of social researchers. Training programs require resources for emergent technologies and their application to social research issues. We view this *Handbook* as moving the discipline in this direction. The incorporation of emergent technologies will require resources to implement their integration into research practice. Currently, the incorporation of new technologies in social research, especially within the social sciences, lags behind that of the natural sciences (see: Hackett, this volume). Addressing the growing number of new questions and societal problems will take a leap of learning and adjustment on the part of the social science research community. Harkening back to the work of philosopher Thomas Kuhn (1970), discussed at the beginning of this chapter, such a leap may involve a series of paradigm shifts within and between the disciplines as they begin to transform their knowledge building structures to become more interdisciplinary. There will be some inherent issues dealing with the power and control over who decides what research questions get studied and what new technologies and methods are supported and funded. Early on, there were concerns expressed of an underlying historical tension with regard to the development of new technologies that have many stakeholders: those market-driven entrepreneurial forces that push toward technological innovation of new products; a scientific community that is interested in pushing on the boundaries of intra- and inter-disciplinary knowledge building; and interest groups who demand more socially responsible development of new technologies for the common good (see: Jamison, 1989). These are by no means mutually exclusive groups, but the economic pressures to come up with new innovations and the sheer pace of innovative technological change will often require an increasing degree of economic and venture capital input, which in turn may override competing stakeholders who may not possess the economic or political capital to affect the direction that technological development ultimately takes.

In the range of emergent technologies addressed in this *Handbook* lie seeds of opportunity for social researchers to address the critical issues that our society faces now and will face in the future. Let us begin the work of addressing these issues, being mindful and respectful of the role that emergent technologies can play in this process.

Note

1. The author wishes to thank the following Boston College undergraduate research assistants: Alicia Johnson '11, for her invaluable editorial advice and assistance throughout all phases of work on this chapter, and Natalie Horbachevsky '09 and Hilary Flowers '10, for their work on editing the final drafts of this chapter.

References

Baudrillaud, J. (1993). *Symbolic exchange and death*. Thousand Oaks, CA: Sage.

Center for Policy on Emerging Technologies. (2009). Accessed September 14, 2009 at: http://www.Tc-pet.org/issues/military_applications.php.

Clynes, M. E., & Kline, N. S. (1960, September). Cyborgs and space. *Astronautics*, 26–27 and 74–75. Reprinted in Gray, Mentor, & Figueroa-Sarriera (1995). (Eds.), *The cyborg handbook* (pp. 29–34). New York: Routledge.

Compaine, B. M. (Ed.). (2001). *The digital divide: Facing a crisis or creating a myth?* Cambridge, Massachusetts: MIT Press.

DiMaggio, P., Hargittai, E., Neuman, W. R., & Robinson, J. (2001). Social implications of the internet. *Annual Review of Sociology*, *27*, 307–336.

Dinello, D. (2005). *Technophobia! Science fiction visions of posthuman technology*. Austin: University of Texas Press.

Donat, E. (2008). *Determinants of Internet usage—An in-depth analysis of the digital divide*. Hamburg: Verlag.

Donat, E., Brandtweiner, R., & Kerschbaum, J. (2009). Attitudes and the digital divide: Attitude measurement as instrument to predict Internet usage. *Informing Science*, *12*, 37–56.

Ellul, K. (1964). *The technological society*. New York: Knopf.

Haraway, D. (1991). A cyborg manifesto: Science, technology, and socialist-feminism in the late twentieth century. In *Simians, cyborgs and women: The reinvention of nature* (pp. 149–181). New York; Routledge.

Hargittai, E. (2008). The digital reproduction of inequality. In D. B. Grusky (Ed.), *Social stratification: Class, race, and gender in sociological perspective* (3rd ed., pp. 936–944).

Henry, J., Palmer, B. W., Palinkas, L., Glorioso, D. K., Caligiuri, M. P, & Jeste, D. V. (2009). Reformed consent: Adapting to new media and research participant preferences. *Ethics and Human Research*, *31*(2).

Hesse-Biber, S. N., & Leavy, P. (2006). *The practice of qualitative research*. New York: The Guilford Press.

Hesse-Biber, S. N., & Leavy, P. (2008). *Handbook of emergent methods*. Thousand Oaks, CA: Sage.

Hogle, L. F. (2005). Enhancement technologies and the body. *Annual Review of Anthropology*, *34*, 695–716.

Jamison, A. (1989). Technology's theorists: Conceptions of innovation in relation to science and technology policy. *Technology and Culture*, *30*(3), 505–533.

Joinson, A., McKenna, K., Postmes, T., & Reips, U. (2007). (Eds.). *The Oxford handbook of Internet psychology*. Great Britain: Oxford University Press.

Jones, S. (1999). Studying the net: Intricacies and issues. In S. Jones (Ed.), *Doing Internet research: Critical issues and methods for examining the net* (pp. 1–28). Thousand Oaks, CA: Sage.

Jordan, A. G. (2008). Frontiers of research and future directions in information and communication technology. *Technology and Society*, *30*(3–4), 388–396.

Kellner, D. (2007). Globalization, terrorism, and democracy: 9/11 and its aftermath. In I. Rossi (Ed.), *Frontiers of globalization research*. New York: Springer.

Kuhn, T. (1970). *The structure of scientific revolutions*. (2nd ed.) Chicago: University of Chicago Press.

Kwan, M. P. (2007). Affecting geospatial technologies: Toward a feminist politics of emotion. *Professional Geographer, 59*(1), 22–34.

Nightingale, A. (2003). A feminist in the forest: Situated knowledges and mixing methods in natural resource management. *ACME: An International E-Journal for Critical Geographies, 2*(1), 77–90.

Ogburn, W. F. (1922). *Social change with respect to culture and original nature.* New York: B. W. Huebsch.

Paul, G., & Cox, E. (1996). *Beyond humanity: Cyberevolution and future minds.* Delmar Thomson Learning.

Prieger, J. E., & Hu, W. M. (2008). The broadband digital divide and the nexus of race, competition, and quality. *Information Economics and Policy, 20,* 150–167.

Rappert, B, Blamer, B., & Stone, J. (2008). Science, technology and the military: Priorities, preoccupations and possibilities. In *The handbook of science and technology studies.* London: MIT Press.

Sudweeks, F., & Simoff, S. J. (1999). Complementary explorative data analysis: The reconciliation of quantitative and qualitative principles. In S. Jones (Ed.) *Doing Internet research: Critical issues and methods for examining the net* (pp. 29–56). Thousand Oaks, CA: Sage.

Toffler, A. (1971). *Future shock.* New York: Bantam Doubleday Dell.

Virilio, P. (1995). *The art of the motor.* Minneapolis: University of Minnesota Press.

Virilio, P. (1997). *Open sky.* New York: Verso.

Virilio, P. (2005). *The information bomb.* New York: Verso.

Wright, S., & Wallace, D. (2002). Secrecy in the biotechnology industry: Implications for the biological weapons convention. In Wright, S. (Ed.), *Biological warfare and disarmament: New problem/new perspectives.* Lanham: Rowan & Littlefield.

Zhang, C., Callegaro, M., & Thomas, M. (2009). *More than digital divide? Investigating the differences between internet and non-internet users on attitudes and behaviors.* Prepared for the Midwest Association for Public Opinion Research (MAPOR) 2008 Conference.March 2009 version (http://www.knowledgenetworks.com/ganp/docs/Digital%20Divide%20-%20full%20MAPOR%20paper%20-%20Zhang-Callegaro-Thomas%20-%2012–08.pdf) accessed.

Part I

Emergent Technologies in a Broad Social Research Context

Chapter 1

Possible Dreams: Research Technologies and the Transformation of the Human Sciences

Edward J. Hackett

The Hubble Deep Field, an iconic image in astronomy and popular culture, was made over a period of 10 days in December 1995 by focusing the telescope on an apparently empty patch of sky about the size of a dime seen from a distance of 75 feet (http://hubblesite.org/newscenter/archive/releases/1996/01). The apparent emptiness of the region means the area is devoid of nearby stars and galaxies, allowing the telescope to gaze deep into space and time. In this tiny patch of "empty" sky were found more than 1,500 galaxies, some in formation, and others from the very earliest moments of time. In astronomy, as in all sciences, technologies reveal phenomena that are otherwise unseen, permitting them to be measured, explored, explained, and understood. Investments in new research technologies are essential for the life of a science, and this is as true for the social and behavioral sciences as it is for the physical and life sciences.

Social surveys have been likened to telescopes for the social and behavioral sciences because of their power to gather, magnify, and focus (House, Juster, Kahn, Schuman, & Singer, 2004). In this chapter, the idea of the telescope will serve as a strategic example for considering the myriad intellectual, organizational, and political aspects of technological innovation in research systems. Doing so is not meant to slight research technologies that are central to other sciences: our story might be somewhat different if we were to use microscopes or particle accelerators, functional Magnetic Resonance Imaging, or linguistic archives, but its contours and implications would remain much the same (and an attempt to discuss a fair spectrum of technologies would stretch this chapter into a book). At times, the term "human sciences" will serve as another name for the social and behavioral sciences, recognizing that much excellent research on the behavior and sociality of nonhuman species compromises the goodness of fit. Finally, my apologies for the National Science Foundation (NSF)-centric perspective represented in this chapter; the National Institutes of Health (NIH) also supports large and costly surveys (such as Adolescent Health, Health and Retirement) that serve its mission while advancing fundamental research in the human sciences. Having worked at NSF, I know its research investments, sciences, and perspectives better than I know those of NIH; that said, I am convinced that partnership between the agencies holds the best prospects for transforming the research technologies of the human sciences.

The chapter begins by discussing the aspirations and rationales for selected research technologies that are under construction in the physical and life sciences, and then briefly reviews aspects of the history of large-scale social surveys. Taken together, these discussions establish a comparative framework and historical foundation for the balance of the chapter. The third section outlines emerging challenges and opportunities for the behavioral and social sciences, concluding with a series of investments that would advance the human sciences.

Ensembles of Research Technologies and the Transformation of Sciences

Technologies transform sciences. A microscope reveals life teeming in a teaspoon of pond water; a telescope gathers and focuses electromagnetic energy (and soon gravity?) to reveal unseen stars and planets; accelerators dismantle atoms, exposing their constituent particles. In astronomy, biology, engineering, geosciences, and physics, new research technologies open spheres of inquiry, stimulate theorizing, and catalyze transformative research. Planning, designing, and justifying investments in new research technologies are, in those fields, essential elements of science and science policy. For emphasis, let me repeat that such work is science by other means, and is as central to the institution of science as researching, writing, reviewing, or publishing. The social and behavioral sciences are coming to recognize this and can benefit from the experience of others. Investments of great magnitude and duration require substantial funding from the federal government, generally requiring not only the endorsement of science agency management but also approval from the White House and Congress. To meet this standard, fields must speak strongly and in unison of the scientific merits and ambitions that motivate the request. Consider the following current investments in major scientific facilities and instrumentation, paying particular attention to their aims and ambitions.

The Atacama Large Millimeter (submillimeter) Array (ALMA), being built in the Chilean Andes by an international consortium, will be "the most capable imaging radio telescope ever built…a critical complement to the leading-edge optical, infrared, ultraviolet, and x-ray astronomical instruments of the twenty-first century" (NSF, 2007, MREFC, p. 10). LIGO, the Laser Interferometer Gravitational Wave Observatory, with sites in Hanford, Washington, and Livingston, Louisiana, will detect gravity waves, or "ripples in the fabric of space-time," which are predicted by the General Theory of Relativity but have never been observed. To observe their passage through the Earth, LIGO is designed to detect distortions of about one hundred-millionth (1×10^{-16}) centimeter in a length of 4 km. LIGO is designed "to detect gravitational waves on Earth for the first time and to develop this capability into gravitational wave astronomy—a new window on the universe" (NSF, 2007, MREFC, p. 43).

From fields more similar intellectually and methodologically to the human sciences, consider the National Ecological Observatory Network (NEON), "a proposed continental-scale research platform for discovering and understanding the impacts of climate change, land-use change, and invasive species on ecology" comprising 20 research sites with comparable instrumentation that will operate in concert over a period of 30 years or more (http://www.neoninc.org/). NEON will be "a telescope that points everywhere…20 distinct climate zones and landscapes that represent the ecology of the continental United

States, plus Alaska, Hawaii, and Puerto Rico…deliver[ing] ecological information about climate and atmosphere, soils and streams, and a variety of organisms…[that] will open a frontier for ecological research" (http://www.neoninc.org/science/overview). NEON (and similar proposed project, the WATERS Network, which would focus on a sample of major watersheds in the continental U.S.) is a particularly relevant point of reference for the social and behavioral sciences for three reasons: it will be a single instrument or technology that is distributed across the continent, roughly paralleling the coordinated yet distributed character of social surveys; its mission is long-term research (30 or more years) and analysis of change at various scales (local to continental); and to attain its goal will require complementary research in the social and behavioral sciences. Much of what matters for climate and atmosphere, ecosystem and watershed, and for the organisms that inhabit such places, depends upon the patterns of human organization, behavior, and decision making. No matter how sophisticated a metrology is installed across a pristine landscape, it will not reveal what developers and planners, elected officials and home owners, consumers and producers, conservationists and educators are doing and deciding—often far from the place that will be affected–and their individual and collective actions and decisions will profoundly shape the landscape, now and for decades to come. The success of new ensembles of research technologies in the environmental sciences depends upon the development of coordinate technologies in the human sciences, the integration of the diverse streams of data that will ensue, and the invention of analytic models and synthetic theories that will explain the structure and workings of coupled natural and human systems. Thus, there is urgency for the social and behavioral sciences to develop research plans that complement those of the environmental observatories while simultaneously serving the distinct and evolving research agendas of our sciences.

The philosopher Otto Neurath compared the work of scientists to that of sailors who are challenged to continually rebuild their ships amid the turbulence and privation of the high seas (Cartwright, Cat, Fleck, & Eubel, 1996). For scientists, the turbulence arises from the ever-changing intellectual challenges, technological possibilities, and empirical phenomena that present themselves in a climate of fluid funding priorities, unpredictable patrons, and unstable contingencies of career and organization. Despite all, scientists persevere, and each of the technologies described above embodies a transformative ambition for its community, an opportunity, similar to that provided by the Hubble Deep Field, to see deeper into space and time, to observe and explain phenomena that are otherwise invisible or unknown, to test theory, and to extend the realm of the known.

New ensembles (or systems) of research technologies open spheres of inquiry, replete with new concepts, questions, relationships, and patterns of explanation. But this process does not occur without its attendant cautions and perils. Decades of scholarship and reflection have produced some firm understandings about the origins, development, and implications of ensembles of research technologies (Hackett, Conz, Parker, Bashford, & DeLay, 2004; Jacob, 1988; Mukerji, 1989; Price, 1984; Rheinberger, 1997). For example, at the same time that research systems make certain studies possible, in some instances by creating a phenomenon itself (as may happen in the construction of model systems or genetically-altered organisms; Creager, 2002), this freedom of inquiry is accompanied by constraint: "any study begins with the choice of a 'system.' On this choice depend the experimenter's freedom to manoeuvre, the nature of the questions he is free to ask, and even often the type of answer he can obtain (Jacob, 1988, p. 234). We may call such things "affordances," following Cook and Brown (1999, p. 389), a term that captures "how a material, design, or situation 'affords' doing something" and, by implication, restricts the ability to do something else. Technologies are not merely tools or techniques, but entail a constellation of methods, materials, interpretations, understandings, conventions, skills, theories, and social relationships that collectively constitute a socio-technical system or ensemble. So encompassing are such ensembles that the fates of research teams and the careers of their members may depend upon the affordances provided by the ensembles of research technologies adopted or devised by the group (Hackett et al.). For this reason many fields of science, and research groups within a field, devote concerted, systematic effort to imagining, developing, constructing, calibrating, and justifying their preferred or proposed investments in research technologies (Hackett, 2005). In those fields, science policy responds with planning grants, budget requests to the executive branch and congress, and a sophisticated development and management apparatus that aim to balance necessary accountability and controls with an appropriate degree of adaptability and responsiveness. NSF currently has a process for managing the conception, design, gestation funding, construction, testing, and commissioning of major research equipment and facilities, complete with an office director and staff, manual of policies and procedures, and penumbra of accepted practices and processes (NSF, 2007, MREFC-1-MREFC-3). Science sometimes leads to new technologies, but new technologies more often create new sciences.

Recasting "infrastructure investments" as a form of technological innovation raises awareness that the process of innovation in research, as in any realm, is shaped by historical and contextual forces. For research technologies, the most powerful forces are the epistemic standards and aims of the sciences involved. These include enduring grand challenges and "legacy" commitments (also called path dependence or technological momentum), often grounded in financial, intellectual, or reputational investments, opposed by the countervailing forces of emerging anomalies, new opportunities, and generational challenges. Science, in Thomas Kuhn's terms, is characterized by an "essential tension" between tradition and originality, between sustaining continuity with the corpus of received knowledge and theory, on the one hand, and proposing new explanations, gathering evidence of unprecedented quality, or opening new spheres of inquiry (Kuhn, 1957 [1977]). For the social and behavioral sciences, these dynamics of change are augmented by the further possibility that changes in the social world itself create novel research opportunities. European voyages of discovery, for example, and the ensuing European colonial empires created conditions that made possible the fields of anthropology and archeology, just as economics and sociology find their genesis in industrialization, urbanization, and accompanying social changes. To understand the present and near future of research technologies for the social and behavioral sciences, and to see more clearly the role social scientists and their professional societies may play in the process, it is helpful to look at episodes from the recent past. This is not the occasion (and I am not the person) to write a history of the human sciences, but two vignettes from the history of social survey research will illustrate the dynamics and establish a framework for discussing possible futures.

Episodes in the History of the Social Survey

Victorian London was a place of sewage and soot, characterized by economic upheaval, residential dislocation, poverty, and misery caused by social forces unseen and unknown.

The active, sensitive intellects of the day responded each in his own way: Charles Dickens wrote novels, Karl Marx wrote social theory, and Charles Booth conducted large-scale, systematic, empirical social research. His magnum opus, *Life and Labour of the People in London* (1902–1904 [1970]), is a 17-volume account of a meticulous, multi-method inquiry into the economic and social lives of Londoners, centered on a series of social surveys that were administered from 1886 to 1903 (archived in the London School of Economics, available online at http://booth.lse.ac.uk/static/a/3.html). In the course of his research, Booth lived with the working class and poor of London for periods of time, and his survey teams included such notables-to-be as Jesse Argyle, George Arkell, Clara Collet, George Duckworth, Beatrice Potter (later Beatrice Webb, wife of Sydney Webb), David Schloss, and Hubert Llewellyn Smith (http://booth.lse.ac.uk/static/a/3.html). Booth's surveys leveraged the data collection efforts of public officials, chiefly the door-to-door canvasses conducted by School Board visitors. His assistants also interviewed police offi-cers, factory officials, and others to acquire a deeper understanding of the economic, resi-dential, and social contexts of London's populace. The project advanced survey research methods in several respects: a numerically large population was surveyed thoroughly and systematically, using clear definitions and formal operationalizations of key concepts (e.g., categories of poverty), summarized in extensive tabulations and maps (that encoded, e.g., the poverty status of families, household-by-household, along the streets of East London), and judicious balancing of commitments to effect reform and to increase knowledge (Bulmer, Bales, & Sklar, 2001). The research was acclaimed as a transformative *scientific* (note the absence of the adverb "social") accomplishment for which Booth was awarded the highest honor of the Royal Statistical Society (he also was to become its president in 1892–94) and was elected a fellow of the Royal Society (1899). The approach pioneered by Booth and his colleagues soon crossed the Atlantic and was applied in a suite of landmark studies in Chicago, Philadelphia, and elsewhere (Bulmer et al.).

To summarize: the innovative social survey methods of the late nineteenth and early twentieth century constitute an ensemble of research technologies that included a distinc-tive approach to data collection (partnership with public officials, using data gathered in the course of their duties), diverse methods (interviews with expert informants, partici-pant observation in the form of Booth's repeated weeks-long tenancies in homes of the poor (Booth, 1902–1904 [1970], pp. 156–171)), explicit concern for spatial patterns and social contexts (including detailed mapping of social classes street-by-street), and a bal-anced commitment to academic scholarship and social reform. ("In intensity of feeling such as this, and not in statistics, lies the power to move the world. But by statistics must this power be guided if it would move the world aright" (Booth, 1902–1904 [1970], p. 178).) Concepts such as social class and poverty motivated the research, and the forces that created the teeming welter that was Victorian London provided the distinctive social circumstances that provoked Booth and others to undertake their research. An epistemic commitment to presenting social facts that exist independently of their purposes and inter-pretation pervades the work ("…the attempt has in the main been confined to show how things are. Little is said as to how they come to be as they are, or whither they are tending" (Booth, 1902–1904 [1970], p. 172)), with the author reciprocally careful to use School Board visitor data without consciously altering how they obtain their information.[1]

The nearly 50 years from Booth's research to the mid-twentieth century brought two world wars and a depression that scarred the landscape and its people. Population growth, economic and social differentiation, mass production (and marketing and consumption), and accelerating urbanization, industrialization, and migration made societies larger and more varied. Transportation and communication technologies, including the nascent broadcast media, began to knit the parts of societies together, increasing the density of interaction, homogenizing aspects of culture, and accelerating the control revolution (Beniger, 1986, pp. 291–389). Social-science theories of the day were concerned with organic solidarity and functional integration, assimilation and the rise of mass society. Scientific sampling, measurement theory, and statistical analysis transformed the scientific foundations of many fields, opening new possibilities for analytic rigor and precision in the human sciences, which responded with rising aspirations to become sciences that leave their reformist agendas in a decidedly secondary position (House et al., 2004, chapter 1). (During roughly the same period, the field of ecology maneuvered its way through a similar transition, changing from a field with a largely descriptive purpose and reformist orientation (natural history and preservation of wild lands) toward a science that would employ ecosystem models to analyze flows of energy and matter (Golley, 1993; Kingsland, 2005).

In this climate of theory, method, and social change were born the three principal research surveys that are currently supported by the National Science Foundation: the American National Election Studies (begun in 1948), the Panel Study of Income Dynamics (1968), and the General Social Survey (1972).[2] These surveys aspire to measure and explain social behavior on a national scale, applying scientific sampling and statistical inference to well-chosen samples of a few thousand people to explain the circumstances and dynamics of millions. Unlike Booth's surveys of London, characteristics of place matter chiefly in the sampling design, not as potential explanatory variables (while this is currently changing, sample sizes remain too small for extensive analyses of local contexts). Also unlike Booth's research, expert informants are not consulted, and professional interviewers are trained to apply social measurement techniques, not to work as substantive investigators in their own right. Survey researchers do not live among those they survey, supplementing their statistical analyses with qualitative observations of people, place, and social life. Nonetheless, surveys born in the mid-twentieth-century United States have succeeded admirably, becoming foundational data resources upon which are built thousands of scientific publications (and scientific careers), major advances in knowledge, extensive graduate and undergraduate education, and a heightened degree of societal self-awareness (Blow, 2007).

Survey research has become, in the words of one book title, "a telescope on society" (House et al., 2004), albeit one that more closely resembles an optical instrument on a mountaintop, not ALMA or the Hubble. NSF, NIH, and other federal agencies have provided decades of continuous funding for the surveys (a few years at a time, and with some significant conditions and limitations), as well they should, as these have become the "gold standard" of survey research, serving as models for comparable studies in other nations (e.g., Luxembourg Income Studies, British National Election Study, World Values Survey, International Social Survey Program, and various European national surveys).[3] Much has been gained in the translation and translocation of survey research from the United States back to Europe and onward to other nations. The European Social Survey (ESS), for example, is a broadly international and collaborative venture (involving more than 30 countries over the four rounds that have been completed) that received the Descartes Prize for Research and Science Communication in 2005 for "radical innovations in cross-national surveys" (http://www.europeansocialsurvey.org/). According to its planning documents, "the principal long-term aim of the project is to chart and explain the interaction between Europe's changing institutions, its political and economic structures, and the attitudes, beliefs, and behaviour patterns of its diverse populations. But an equally important shorter-term aim is to develop and demonstrate an approach to the conduct of rigorous quantitative multinational social surveys that matches that of the best national surveys in Europe and the USA" (European Social Survey, 2009, p. 6). In effect, the ESS will treat Europe as a living laboratory for the comparative study of cultural, economic, political, and social change, applying methods that were developed in national surveys, in the United States and other nations, and refined to suit the demands of large-scale, cross-national research.

In similar fashion, but with important differences in national scope, organizational form, and breadth of content, the International Social Survey Program (http://www.issp.org/) and the World Values Survey (http://www.worldvaluessurvey.org/) aspire to coordinate social inquiry and survey research across nations. The World Values Survey, for example, endeavors to "understand worldviews and changes that are taking place in the beliefs, values and motivations of people throughout the world" and claims (in its latest surveys) more than 50 national participants representing some 90% of the world's populations (World Values Survey, 2009, p. 3). In their international comparative structure and comparably collaborative forms of organization, these three surveys are ambitious and innovative, but in their sampling, survey administration, and question design they closely resemble surveys of mid-twentieth century. In this, they are superb instruments that will advance social sciences on a broad front, and for that reason alone they deserve continuing and growing support. But for those very reasons, they are also instruments of conventional design, offering partial and incomplete solutions to the opportunities and challenges confronting the behavioral and social sciences. Innovations of this sort will advance science but are unlikely to transform it, which becomes clear when we consider what lies ahead.

The Challenges Ahead

Designers of research technologies for the human sciences of the century ahead might borrow from astronomers and physicists, asking what our ALMA or LIGO or Hubble Space Telescope would look like and how it might catalyze a transition from the social-science analog of terrestrial optical astronomy toward the equivalents of radio or gravitational astronomy. They might, in fact, aspire to an integrative understanding of human behavior fashioned of the consilience of sciences that are today segregated and competing. What are the transformative opportunities, challenges, and circumstances confronting the social and behavioral sciences? What are the contemporary counterparts to the social forces of Victorian London that gave birth to Booth's path-breaking research, or to those in the mid-twentieth-century United States that shaped the major national surveys? I do not have a complete answer, but will sketch some ways that changes in society, technology, and science have combined to enlarge the ambit of the human sciences, revising the cardinal questions that guide our sciences, posing novel questions about emerging phenomena (such as social life that extends into virtual worlds), raising the standard of acceptable analysis and evidence, and restructuring the web of relationships among researchers, those we study, and those who use our findings. The essential idea I wish to convey is that the research domain of the human sciences is enlarging in the four dimensions of place, scale, time, and engagement, and that this enlargement poses new challenges for those sciences. By "place" I mean the overlapping and intersecting contexts in which people and social organizations live. Some are actual places on the ground (such as neighborhoods and communities), while others are places in cyberspace or in networks of relationships of various sorts. However virtual and fleeting such places and relationships may be, they will be real in their consequences.

"Scale" refers to the size of phenomena that are measured and explained, and for the human sciences their range now extends from the smallest scale of genes and neurons (and soon, in all likelihood, even smaller) to the largest scale of the world, including the virtual world (again, soon, in all likelihood even larger).[4] "Time," the third dimension, extends from ever-briefer measurements of activity in ever more localized areas of the brain, to the long sweep of history and prehistory, using the archaeological record to take a deep time perspective on contemporary structures and processes. In computer-mediated stock-trading markets, for example, trading time advantages on the scale of hundredths of a second may make the difference between handsome profits and mediocre returns. Finally, the dimension of "engagement" is blurring the roles of researcher, research participant (or subject), and research user (or client) and reducing the social distances between them. Sharply delineated roles and responsibilities are being supplanted by hybrid identities that have researchers reflecting on their own activities, participants taking a hand in the conduct and interpretation of research, and clients active in design, analysis, and inference.

Scientists who enter this expanded domain to conduct research will find novel intellectual possibilities that will require new ensembles of research technologies, new suites of research abilities, and new forms of research organization. After discussing the four expanded dimensions in greater detail, I will describe eight emergent areas of innovation in research technology. Change is disruptive and difficult, so this discussion of optimistic possibilities will include few words of caution. The concluding section of the chapter will offer some reflections on the difference between infrastructure and research technologies, and some tempered encouragement for organized, interdisciplinary innovation in the social and behavioral sciences.

The Enlarged Ambit of the Human Sciences

Human societies are spatially heterogeneous, and characteristics of the situation or context of a person, group, or organization shape its structure and behavior. Booth's survey of the people of London, and the studies of neighborhoods and communities in the United States that soon followed in Philadelphia and Chicago, were predicated on this principle, though during the mid-twentieth century the lesson was thrown into shadow by the bright possibilities of statistical inference, scientific sampling, and nationally representative data. In recent years, the salience of place has returned to the limelight, accompanied by the new insight that context includes not only the natural, physical, and social characteristics of a family, neighborhood, or nation, but also the distal and sometime virtual contexts of contracts, markets, networks, places, and relationships created by computers and other communication and information technologies. Texters, Twitterers, and people perpetually chatting on cell phones are simultaneously present here and elsewhere; residents of Second Life live also among us, as their avatars are tethered to people; electronic relationships and the virtual places and spaces that host them are increasingly perceived as real, and are increasingly real in their consequences (Bainbridge, 2007). Groups, organizations, and firms also function in this expanding, hybrid environment, and also find that it has real implications for their performance and survival. In this way, the research realm of the human sciences has grown to include both a richer and more consequential local context and a more extensive and influential distal context that transcends locality.

Second, disciplinarily proprietary and piecemeal explanations in the behavioral and social sciences are being supplemented by more extensive and integrated explanations that connect, for example, the neural processes of valuation and judgment, through decisions and behaviors, to the structure of markets, networks, or cities. A host of social-science specialties that are prefixed with "neuro-" are engaged in this quest, and initial results are intriguing (Glimcher, Camerer, Poldrack, & Fehr, 2008). Neuro-economics is the most developed and best known of these interdisciplinary fields, but there also is active research concerned with the neural dimensions of legal, moral, and political judgments (Tingley, 2006). In a similar fashion, genetic information and other biological data form the empirical foundation for explanations that connect biological characteristics to behavioral and social phenomena (Bearman, 2008; Freese, 2008). For example, a recent study using the Adolescent Health Survey, which combines longitudinal measures of physical health with questions about social behavior, relationships, and work experience, showed that a gene linked to a dopamine receptor that is associated with impulse control interacted with social capital and parental involvement to influence the likelihood that a boy would attend college (the gene did not affect girls' chances; see Shanahan, Vaisey, Erickson, & Smolen, 2008; for details on the Adolescent Health Survey see http://www.cpc.unc.edu/projects/addhealth/design). Other papers in this special supplement of the *American Journal of Sociology* (November 2008) examine genetic influences on alcoholism, happiness, weight, and other outcomes. Also using the Adolescent Health Survey, Fowler and his colleagues found that a person's position in his or her social network is influenced by genetic characteristics (Fowler, Dawes, & Christakis, 2009). It is heartening to see that biological data, ranging from a cheek swab or a small blood sample to a panel of medical tests, are gathered alongside social and behavioral data in other surveys, but the use of these measures to address fundamental questions of concern to the social and behavioral sciences, rather than questions of health and disease, remains in its early stages (e.g., the National Health and Nutrition Examination Survey (http://www.cdc.gov/nchs/nhis.htm)).

At the same time that research in the human sciences is extending from societies "inward" toward their constituent elements, research is also extending "outward" to compare conditions and explain patterns of change on a global scale, with research instruments increasingly coordinated to produce comparable data across nations. The European Social Survey, which was described above, takes advantage of "Europe's cultural diversity... [to] analyse differences in institutions, structures, behaviours, and beliefs across European states and relate these to explanations of human interaction" (European Science Foundation, n.d., p. 5; see for details http://www.europeansocialsurvey.org/). The World Values Survey and International Social Survey Program have similar ambitions—though the former focuses on values and beliefs, while the latter has addressed a changing assortment of topics—that are pursued in a larger number and variety of nations across the globe (http://www.worldvaluessurvey.org/; http://www.issp.org/data.shtml). Currently, these surveys provide cross-national comparisons and indicators of change over time, which are relatively straightforward (once one gets beyond the major challenges of organizing the effort, coordinating research themes, standardizing items, and translating questions across languages and cultures). These surveys also include measures that extend the human sciences to explore phenomena that are both ever-smaller and ever-larger. What they do not yet do is address the emergent challenges of explaining (1) how the smallest elements and processes operate within and across levels of organization to produce stable patterns of organization; (2) correlatively, how surprisingly large and abrupt changes arise from incremental changes in elemental behaviors (phase changes, forcings, tipping points, emergence); and (3) whether and why similar dynamics work in similar ways across national and cultural divides (more about this challenge to theory in the section that follows).

Third, patterns and processes of change are at the heart of the human sciences, and the study of change demands observations gathered over time. Yet, many important processes of human behavior and social change occur beyond the temporal limits that humans can sense, and so through instruments and other means the temporal range of the human sciences is expanding beyond those limits. At one extreme, there are consequential perceptions, preferences, judgments, and decisions that occur in a "blink," yet cumulate to form stable attitudes and preferences (Gladwell, 2005). Language acquisition, for example, depends in significant measure on the ability to identify changes in tones that occur on the scale of about 50 ms—about half a blink—and the impairment acquired from a deficit in processing sound at that time scale will endure and cumulate into a reading disability (broadly termed "dyslexia") that, in turn, will interact, over the life course, with family and friendship networks, schooling and the workplace, influencing interpersonal perceptions, social and cultural capital, and life chances. Since the likelihood of having the underlying processing disorder is strongly heritable, it may well persist across generations (Gabriell, 2009).

At the far end of the time scale there is long-term change—decadal, centennial, and millennial scale—the "late lessons" about contemporary patterns of human settlement, landscape transitions, or environmental interactions that may be learned from study of early history and prehistory (Diamond, 2004; van der Leeuw, S., Lane, & Read, 2009). Seeking theoretical bedrock, some research evokes evolutionary theory or principles of organization that span species in pursuit of explanations that are durable, parsimonious, and fundamental. Sociobiology, brought to prominence through the writings of E. O. Wilson, among others, anchors higher-order human behaviors (such as altruism or the nurturing of the young) in evolutionary theory (Wilson, 1975, 1979), and remains lively and persuasive to this day (e.g., Hrdy, 2009). Similarly, the rise and development of network science, computational social science (Lazer et al., 2009), and the science of complexity (which takes various shapes) reflect a shared urge to identify orderly patterns and underlying principles from the uncoordinated actions of constituent elements that apply across a wide spectrum of behaviors, circumstances, and species (Barabási, 2009).

Finally, the social and behavioral sciences are negotiating new terms of engagement with those who participate in and use our research. This is not the tired and tendentious tension between applied and basic research, but is instead a more collaborative mode of inquiry that is currently taking form, accompanied by expanded professional responsibilities and impacts. Research "subjects," as social and behavioral scientists have come to know them, are an endangered species that is evolving into active collaborators in our investigations. Participants will increasingly assist in the design, conduct, direction, and interpretation of inquiry—participative sensing studies do this now (Goldman et al., 2009)—and their role and attendant rights will be supported by new principles of research ethics and data ownership that will endow participants with enduring and inalienable rights to their information (Lazer et al., 2009; Pentland, 2009; Shilton, Burke, Estrin, Hansen, & Srivastava, 2008).

Similarly, those who use the results of social and behavioral research will be less inclined to do so principally through our published findings and potted policy recommendations, instead insisting upon substantive, flexible, and ongoing collaborative examination and exploration of the design, assumptions, results, reasoning, and implications of research. Such collaborations will benefit from facilities specially designed for data visualization, modeling, interpretation, and critical and speculative inquiry, such as decision theaters or similar immersive environments (http://decisiontheater.org/). The behavioral and social sciences surely will continue to observe, measure, and explain, empirically and systematically, the increasing variety of human social behaviors and organizations, but equally surely that work will be done under new terms of engagement with those who participate in our studies and make use of our findings.

In sum, ongoing changes in the importance and nature of place (from local to virtual), the scale of phenomena (from genetic or neural to global), the scope of time (from briefer than a blink to evolutionary), and the terms of engagement with research subjects and users are combining to form the ensembles of research technologies that will be developed by the social and behavioral sciences. The human sciences have left Victorian London, where smoke and soot blanketed a populace already immiserated by an emerging factory system, and where mapping poverty of various degrees, street-by-street, laid the foundation for deeper exploration. They have also left the mid-twentieth-century United States, where it sufficed that statistical analysis applied to carefully measured variables gathered from well-chosen samples yielded accurate indicators of a nation's social life. The human sciences are entering a research domain that has expanded (in cultural, spatial, and virtual dimensions) and fractionated (into segments that are smaller yet salient), which presents a spectrum of novel possibilities and requirements for research. To meet the challenges and opportunities imposed by such changes, behavioral and social scientists must initiate a process of collaborative innovation. I would suggest eight categories of innovation for consideration, inviting others to freely add, combine, or delete items from this list. Some are incremental steps that take advantage of opportunities that are at hand, while others are deeper and more extensive.

First, to meet the most pressing challenges of their expanded research realm, the social and behavioral sciences must increase the spatial, temporal, and social resolution (or granularity) of their data without sacrificing the ability to aggregate into larger units, durations, and groups. Consider spatial resolution: geographic, economic, and social contexts are powerful influences on behavior, and so geographic codes (latitude and longitude) have been added to many major national surveys. While this is a promising step, it is inadequate because countries are large and heterogeneous, so current sample sizes of a few thousand people are too small to provide statistical power sufficient to examine the influences of context. In the United States, for example, the contextual influences of neighborhood and community on households and individuals will be nested within larger patterns determined by local economic zones, states, and regions.

The rising intellectual and policy challenges of socio-environmental research have multiplied the possibilities for and the urgency of increasing the spatial resolution (or granularity) of data. At a global scale, research employing more refined spatial measurements of economic activity and climatic conditions (basically, a grid $1° \times 1°$) uncovered relationships among geographic characteristics and outcomes that are much more intricate than were obtained from comparisons of national-level data (Nordhaus, 2006). Global climate change has varied local effects, and the nature of those effects will be conditioned by a suite of local circumstances that include culture and ethnic composition, economic order and demography, and politics and institutional arrangements (Harlan, Brazel, Prashad, Stefanov, & Larsen, 2006; Ostrom, 2009). But in the absence of better data, analysts will be blind to such differences. Rising federal research investments in the environmental observatories (NEON, WATERS network) must be complemented by similar investments in coordinate social data with comparable spatial resolution in order to measure the human causes and consequences of environmental dynamics.

Consider temporal resolution: The mission of the social and behavioral sciences is to recognize, describe, and explain the patterns and processes of human behavior and social organization. But our ability to detect change depends upon the temporal resolution and duration of the data we collect; changes that occur within observational intervals may pass unnoticed; and trends that occur over durations longer than our observational periods—that outwait our impatience—will also escape notice. Annual or biennial surveys are limited by design in the dynamics they can reveal, and survey series that last only a few decades are similarly limited by their life spans. The human sciences need data gathered in shorter time-steps—some as brief as milliseconds—and over longer durations—summing, over waves of observations, to a century and more, which will require augmenting survey data with complementary data gleaned from administrative, historical, and transactional records ("reality mining"; Pentland, 2009). To acquire such data, behavioral and social scientists will need to partner with agencies of the local, state, and federal government and with proprietary firms that are in the business of gathering and linking personal data (such as Experian and Acxiom). Yes, the ethical, legal, commercial, and technical challenges are almost too much to contemplate. But to me it is more worrisome to know that such data exist but are not used for fundamental social and behavioral research.

Finally, consider social resolution: The United States is a socially, ethnically, and culturally diverse country, as are many countries today, and the differences this diversity entails are consequential for scientific understanding and social policy. Yet, the largest and best surveys funded by NSF are scarcely powerful enough to provide samples adequate for analysis of major ethnic groups, such as African Americans, Latinos, and Asians, and they achieve adequacy only by over-sampling subpopulations of interest, which is effective only for representing those particular ethnic groups that are chosen in advance for enhanced study (House et al., 2004; Isaacs, 2007). As migration and mixing continue over time, there will be growth in the number of subgroups, their intergroup perceptions and dynamics, and the complexity of their cultural and social composition. Only in retrospect will we learn, to our regret, that a group once judged to be below the threshold of study should have been surveyed in order to provide a benchmark for longitudinal analysis. With rising concern, in the United States and around the globe, for the dynamics of migration, intergroup relations, and the implications of changing ethnic geography, more highly resolved social data are essential for sound science and informed policy.

A second pressing need in the short term is to develop data that support the exploration and testing of explanations that span levels of analysis. Integrated data, analyses, and theories that connect neural and cognitive processes through behaviors to larger social patterns, for example, or that embed genetic and cognitive characteristics within the contexts of biography and family, place and social structure, are among the frontier concerns of the social and behavioral sciences (for promising examples see Conley, 2004; Lareau & Conley, 2008; Shanahan et al. 2008). Social surveys now include biological measures of various sorts (ranging from height and weight, through cheek swabs and blood tests to substantial physicals) and para-data (such as characteristics of the home or neighborhood, response lag-time and answer-changes recorded by questionnaires completed on computers)—but these collection efforts remain limited in subject matter and sample size, insufficient for large-scale, comparative analysis.

Third, increasingly powerful, portable, and pervasive computing, cyberinfrastructure, communications technologies, global positioning systems, and the tools for analyzing the data they produce have combined to create strikingly novel opportunities for research. Virtual worlds, such as Second Life, extend the social world and form a dramatic setting for original social research, including experiments that may be unworkable in "first life" (Bainbridge, 2007). Ubiquitous computing and related technologies (including cell phones, PDAs, e-mail, and the Internet) generate new forms of data in large volumes, some gathered passively as residues of their use, some requiring action on the part of the researcher, and some at the initiative of the research participant. Reality mining, which uses electronic communication and transaction records to create new measures of social interaction, geographic mobility, economic behavior, and large-scale patterns of social interaction (Greene, 2008), has the potential to advance fundamental knowledge in many disciplines. In one such application, mobile phone call records for an 18-week period were analyzed to produce a national-scale communications network (Onella et al., 2007); another found empirical regularities in the mobility patterns of 100,000 people who were traced (also using anonymized cell phone records) over a six-month period (Gonzalez, Hidalgo, & Barabási, 2008). Such analyses not only tell us something about national communication or mobility patterns, they also reveal fundamental principles of social organization and behavior, and network structure and dynamics, that will have implications across a spectrum of disciplines.[5] One network theorist, assessing the rapid advances in network science that occurred over the past decade, opined that "bottlenecks" to continued progress "are mainly data driven....If I dare to make a prediction for the next decade, it is this: Thanks to the proliferation of the many electronic devices that we use on a daily basis, from cell phones to Global Positioning Systems and the Internet, that capture everything from our communications to our whereabouts, the complex system that we are most likely to tackle first in a truly quantitative fashion may not be the cell or the Internet but rather society itself" (Barabási, 2009, p. 413).

Another class of application for these new technologies is broadly termed "participatory sensing," a research strategy that uses cell phones or PDAs (either as they are originally manufactured or augmented with additional sensors) as instruments for collaborative research among citizens and scientists. The Center for Embedded Network Sensing at the University of California in Los Angeles, for example, employed cell phones equipped with additional software to track (with consent) a person's position throughout the day. Such data are combined with measures of air quality and weather conditions (obtained from other sources) to produce a "Personalized Environmental Impact Report" (Goldman

et al., 2009, pp. 8–9) that shows how a person's daily travels influenced his or her exposure to toxic substances and responsibility for carbon emissions (the accelerometer in
the phone can distinguish walking, running, biking, driving, and riding a bus). Another
sensor-based technology used wearable sociometric badges to measure aspects of social
interaction, speech, and mobility within an organization, sharply increasing the social,
spatial, and temporal resolution of interpersonal behavior, and affording new insights
into the interaction patterns and their consequences for job performance and satisfaction
(Olguín et al., 2009). It is easy to imagine scaling up from such applications to even more
ambitious studies that include larger areas and samples of people, more extensive and
capable sensors, and a mixture of passive and active data gathering (e.g., questionnaires
or interviews). While such data collection strategies have the potential to produce large
volumes of high quality data, they present major challenges for data analysis and intricate
problems of research ethics.

Fourth, sensors and other such technologies produce volumes of data of a type
generally unfamiliar to behavioral and social scientists. A day-long time trace of speech or
interaction episodes for a group of about 20 persons, sampled in intervals of just a few sec-
onds, yields a daunting heap of data that bear little resemblance to the concepts of affinity,
emotional energy, or leadership that the research set out to measure. The first task is to
shape this mass of unfamiliar data into variables that derive from social theories, a consequential task that involves devising and validating measurement theories that connect
indicators to ideas. Having done that, there remains the further challenge of analyzing the
data in ways that take full advantage of their quality and sensitivity—higher-resolution
data expose nuances of interaction that traditional measures cannot detect—without losing sight of the research questions that motivated the study and will establish its contribution to the literature. Stated most simply, findings that leap discontinuously from the body
of settled research—grand saltations—may initially thrill their authors but are at risk of
prematurity and disbelief (Hook, 2002).

Fields as varied as cultural anthropology, linguistics, political science, psychology, sociology, and information science already confront volumes of textual, archival, and image
(still and moving) data that are cumbersome to store and access, and that require substantial amounts of expert analysts' time to examine and analyze. New research technologies
will amplify such difficulties and introduce the associated problems of devising theories,
concepts, and methods distinctly suited to such data, as well as equipping analysts with
the mathematical and computational skills and tools necessary to do the job (Lazer et al.,
2009). Initial publications have used these new forms of data to measure familiar concepts
and properties of social organization. While there is nothing wrong with doing so, greater
advantage lies with using new technologies to perceive new phenomena—remember gravitational astronomy—so the way forward begins with familiar measures, passes through a
stage of comparison and validation, then enters a realm of new ideas and indicators.

Fifth, reality mining, participative (and other) sensors, enhanced survey data (e.g.,
bio-data), and the cyber-tools to store, manage, link, share, and analyze them pose
unprecedented ethical challenges of privacy, confidentiality, research participants' rights,
researchers' obligations to one another, and the appropriate relationship between science
and the state. The responsible and ethical conduct of research is a matter of sufficiently
high national concern that it found a place in the "America COMPETES Act," leading NSF
and other research-funding agencies to initiate discussions and develop materials about
the responsible conduct of research.[6] This increased attention is timely, because researchers

deploying new technologies have been admirably sensitive to the unprecedented demands these methods impose on research ethics, proposing a "new deal on data" (Pentland, 2009) and a new dynamic of "participatory privacy" (Shilton et al., 2009). Their framing of issues constitutes an excellent starting point for discussion, but there is much more to do in drafting, codifying, and institutionalizing precepts of responsible research conduct in this new research environment. There is general agreement about the underlying principles that research participants' rights are enduring, dynamic, and negotiable—"ongoing accomplishments" of social interaction among researchers and those who provide our data, rather than a binding contract concluded at the outset of fieldwork and valid for ever after. For Pentland, for example, the foundational principles include a person's right to possess his or her data, control its use, and dispose or deploy it as he or she sees fit, whenever he or she wishes (Pentland, 2009, p. 79). But this will be a far more fluid ethical environment than the present, so implementing such principles will be a greater challenge than enunciating them. Less openly addressed are the new ethical obligations that will enjoin researchers to share data for replication and secondary analyses (and to insure that data are preserved and documented well enough to withstand such scrutiny; see Long, 2009 for a sound model of workflow design in data analysis), to shelter research participants from a curious government, and to devote enduring attention to a data set and those who participated in its production.

Sixth, secure facilities for accessing administrative (public) records and commercial transaction data would allow spatially referenced data on individuals to be used, alone or in combination with other sensitive material (from surveys, the Census, biomarkers, public records, and electronic records), thus greatly expanding analysts' ability to observe and explain human behavior, cultural and social organization and change, decision making, interaction patterns, and more. The Census Research Data Centers (http://lehd.did.census. gov/led/research/rdc.html), the NORC Data Enclave (http://www.norc.org/DataEnclave/), and other such facilities may offer the level of security necessary to persuade government agencies to share their administrative data and for the private sector to provide its extensive transactional data. In addition, these centers would also serve as repositories of expertise in the management and analysis of massive data sets and central nodes in a web of guarantors of responsible and ethical conduct. But such restrictive environments can be difficult places to do research—one analyst called them "black holes": you can bring data in but cannot take data out—and their security policies may limit or exclude the use of cyberinfrastructure for distal analysis and collaboration (so they march in the opposite direction of collaboratories and other virtual organizations). Furthermore, their wider use would invite deeper concerns about privacy and security. Beyond such concerns, which may generally be addressed with laws, contracts, and technologies, there are additional ethical matters that merit consideration. For example, government and private-sector organizations may well expect something of intellectual value in exchange for their data, and the ethical precepts guiding what that might be remain to be formulated. AOL's recent rough experience with the release of "anonymous" Web search records and a cautionary report from the U.S. National Research Council have flagged the problem for further study (Butler, 2007; Guttman & Stern, 2007).

Seventh, large-scale social surveys such as the Panel Study of Income Dynamics, the American National Election Studies, and the General Social Survey are rightly likened to telescopes, for they gather and focus data on high priority research questions and social concerns (House et al., 2004). Yet, they also offer possibilities that cannot be provided by telescopes. For example, researchers can use computers and cyberinfrastructure to communicate survey results to respondents, conduct follow-up surveys, and otherwise engage people more fully in the research (cf., participatory sensing; Goldman, 2009). New technologies allow major surveys to become instruments for enhancing public understanding of science, while also increasing their speed, flexibility, and agility. Computerized data collection, conducted face-to-face or over the Internet, also offers new ways to embed experimental designs within the survey framework, and new possibilities for asking sensitive questions in secure ways (a pioneer in such approaches is TESS, the Time-sharing Experiments for the Social Sciences, an open-access, computer-mediated questionnaire platform dedicated to experimental design embedded in or conducted through population surveys; see http://tess.experimentcentral.org/).

Finally, new forms of research organization are needed to accomplish interdisciplinary analysis and synthesis; to provide local and distal access to data and tools, skills and training; and to offer collaborative opportunities. Much has been made of cyberinfrastructure, virtual organizations, and the technological possibilities of distributed, distal, asynchronous collaboration (Olson, Zimmerman, & Bos, 2008). All that is possible, and much of it is underway. But countervailing forces are at work. Synthesis among the human sciences, across all sciences, and into the worlds of policy, practice, and decision making is essential: the grand intellectual challenges of our time demand synthetic thinking and integrative analysis, the fitting together of concepts, explanations, analyses, and data across intellectual disparate disciplines (Carpenter et al., 2009). The National Center for Ecological Analysis and Synthesis, funded by NSF since 1995, offers a successful model for this sort of organization, and it has been emulated a dozen or so times in other fields of science and in other nations (Hackett, Parker, Conz, Rhoten, & Parker, 2008). At the time of this writing (July 2010) NSF has supported several additional synthesis centers and has solicited proposals for a $30M center for environmental synthesis. Other federal science agencies (i.e., the Department of Energy and the United States Geological Survey) and other nations (e.g., Australia, the Netherlands, and Sweden) have invested in or are sponsoring competitions for similar centers. Whatever the distributed possibilities new technologies offer, the challenges ahead will demand similar investment in deeply collaborative work. Some of these collaborations will be aided by new visualization technologies to facilitate communication and understanding among the sciences and with decision makers.

Let me close this section with some words of caution: change is hard, and changing the epistemic culture of sciences is extremely hard because some change is premature (Hook, 2002), some is misguided or ill-considered, and all will meet with resistance (Barber, 1995, chapter 5; Kuhn, 1957 [1977]).

Apart from the challenges of prematurity and resistance, we must not underestimate the difficult and contentious effort that will be necessary to build theories that exploit and explain the wealth of data generated by new research technologies. Some of these theories will be imported in the minds of scientists entering the social sciences from other fields, such as physics. Writing of the challenges that multiscale phenomena (i.e., processes working at quite different social, spatial, and temporal scales) pose for the social sciences, one theorist considers that

> the toughest challenge…[for] the fundamental predictability of techno-social systems is their sensitivity and dependence on social adaptive behavior.…An interesting and ethically challenging aspect of predicting and managing the unfolding of catastrophic events

in techno-social networks is the system's adaptation to predictions when they are made publicly available. Social behaviors react and adapt to knowledge of predictions. Contrary to what happens in physical systems, the predictions themselves are part of the system dynamic. (Vespignani, 2009, p. 428)

He goes on to sketch a general strategy for meeting the predictive requirements of research on large-scale techno-social systems within the parameters of ethical behavior, but for our purposes the matter of interest is more general. In the variety of social theory implied above, human awareness and reactivity, traits which result from our sentience and free will, interfere with sound analysis and accurate forecasting. But for other social scientists,

> the goal of their discipline is not simply to understand how people behave in large groups, but to understand what motivates individuals to behave the way they do. The field cannot lose focus on that—even as it moves to exploit the power of these new technological tools, and the mathematical regularities they reveal. Comprehending capricious and uncertain human events at every scale remains one of the most challenging questions in science. (Nature, 2008, p. 698)

Building synthetic theory that explains the aggregate forces shaping human social structure and interaction, yet that accommodates individual perceptions, decisions, and values, stands as a grand intellectual challenge to accompany the technological transformation ahead. In this quest for synthesis, we are not alone: in recent decades biology has been working toward a synthesis of evolutionary theory, ecology, and development that has properties of deep time, extensive and multi-scalar contemporary space, and individual dynamic that resemble the intellective challenges confronting the social and behavioral sciences. We should learn much from their efforts.

Conclusion

In policy circles, it is common to talk about the need to invest in "research infrastructure" for the sciences. While such conversations are well intentioned, infrastructure is a misleading term for what is needed. Understood literally, infrastructure is the stuff below and within the structure—the foundation, the groundwork—upon which a structure is built. The term implies something solid, serviceable, enduring, and inert; something fabricated to the specifications necessary for what will be built upon it, then simply maintained for the life of the structure. In fact, when a foundation shifts or settles—when infrastructure changes or needs replacement—it is usually a sign of age, failure, or poor design.

Unlike much infrastructure, the ensembles of technologies used to conduct scientific research have agency, reactivity, and potential energy: they are a transformative force that challenges orthodoxy, generates empirical insights, and catalyzes new theories. Change in one part of a technological system will cause change elsewhere. New research technologies will generate data that demand explanation with synthetic theories that span disciplines and levels of organization; require analytic models and tools, and people versed in their use; set in motion new patterns of research organization, collaboration, and publication (including collaboration with those we study and those who use our results); and require values and ethics attuned to the emergent challenges of data formed across personal repositories or gathered through electronic means. In other words, the new research technologies will place demands upon what is built upon them and, in turn, the process of using those technologies will cause them to be reshaped and repurposed.

This vital quality—technologies that shape and are shaped by their use—implies the need for a process of design and construction that is iterative and reflexive. Innovative arrangements for collaboration—centers, networks, and partnerships—will be needed to organize the technologies and their application, accompanied by explicit programs of appraisal and remodeling. Openness and broad participation across disciplines and generations are essential to elicit innovative ideas and build the foundation of legitimacy and support that will be necessary for the innovations to follow. The experiences of other sciences are reasonably well documented, and we would be well advised to consult our colleagues, study their experience, and shape our path accordingly.

To educate a new generation of scholars equipped with the ideas and abilities to use these new resources in new ways is a daunting task, particularly in these constrained times, yet that process should begin soon, perhaps using NSF's Integrative Graduate Education and Research Training program or other existing training programs, because it will take a decade to achieve. This would also be an opportunity for the social and behavioral sciences to reach into K-12 education: there is no reason students in middle school and high school cannot learn science, math, and statistics using real data from experiments and surveys, and their doing so may increase the volume and quality of capable scientists who enter college interested in our fields. Finally, the new research technologies and collaborative arrangements discussed in this chapter will be possible only with new ethical principles, tailored to the challenges, securely in place.

Acknowledgments

The initial idea for this chapter arose over coffee one cold morning in Arlington, VA. I thank David Lightfoot for initiating the discussion, Mark Weiss and Frank Scioli for carrying it along during the following months. (Mark also bought the coffee.) Variants of these ideas, arguments, and examples were presented at the National Science Foundation, Indiana University, the University of Michigan, Columbia University, and Arizona State University. Thanks to Scott Long, Bob Groves, John Mutter, and Mike Barton for arranging my visits and for their ideas and advice. Insightful conversations and comments on versions of the chapter were offered by Bill Bainbridge, Jim Collins, Sharon Harlan, Sharlene Hesse-Biber, and Laurel Smith-Doerr. Bob O'Connor thought it all a bad idea and said so, which only helped. Some of the ideas reported in this chapter arose in the course of my appointment as director of the Division of Social and Economic Sciences at the National Science Foundation. The views reported in this chapter are, however, my own and do not reflect the official positions and policies of NSF.

Notes

1. Booth's intense commitment to objectivity and disinterestedness is well stated in this passage from volume 1: "With the insides of the houses and their inmates there was no attempt to meddle.

To have done so would have been an unwarrantable impertinence; and, besides, a contravention of our understanding with the School Board, who object, very rightly, to any abuse of the delicate machinery with which they work. Nor, for the same reason, did we ask the visitors to obtain information specially for us. We dealt solely with that which comes to them in a natural way in the discharge of their duties" (Booth, 1902 [1970], p. 25).

2. Soon after, large-scale surveys became a significant part of the U.S. investment in behavioral and social-science research related to health. Two recent such surveys—Health and Retirement and Adolescent Health—are discussed below.

3. From 1972 to 2008, the General Social Survey was administered 27 times—originally almost annually (with the exceptions of 1979, 1981, and 1992), then biennially since 1994—to samples ranging from 1,500 to 2,500 persons. Since 2006, the survey has included a panel component that interviews a subset of the sample in three consecutive biennial surveys. Budget limitations and national research priorities for the social sciences account for the variability in sample size and survey administration.

4. The readiest analogy to changes in store for the behavioral and social sciences is drawn from the experience of the life sciences over the past century or so: those fields of science now extend from neurons and synapses and ion channels; from genes and their constituent base pairs, the amino acids they represent and the proteins they become, to biomes, continents, and the dynamics of climate change.

5. Notably, the paper was preceded by an editorial raising questions about the fundamental epistemic purposes of the social sciences (Nature (2008), p. 698) and followed several months later by an addendum explicitly stating the various human subjects' protection committees that had reviewed and approved the project (Nature 458, p. 238).

6. Formally, the law is PL 110-69, The America Creating Opportunities to Meaningfully Promote Excellence in Technology, Education, and Science; section 7009 contains the language pertinent to ethics and responsible research.

References

Aronovici, C. (1916). *The social survey*. Philadelphia: The Harper Press.

Bainbridge, W. S. (2007). The scientific research potential of virtual worlds. *Science, 317*, 472–476.

Barabási, A. -L. (2009). Scale-free networks: A decade and beyond. *Science, 325*, 412–413.

Barber, B. (1995). Social studies of science. New Brunswick, NJ: Transaction.

Bearman, P. (2008). Introduction: Exploring genetics and social structure. *American Journal of Sociology, 114*(supplement), v–x.

Beddoe, R., Costanza, R., Farley, J., Garza, E., Kent, J., Kubiszewski, I., et al. (2009). Overcoming systemic roadblocks to sustainability: The evolutionary redesign of worldviews, institutions, and technologies. *PNAS, 106*(8), 2483–2489.

Beniger, J. (1986). *The control revolution*. Cambridge, MA: Harvard University Press.

Blow, C. (2007). Who do you think we are? *New York Times*, February 26: A27.

Booth, C. (1902–1904 [1970]). *Life and labour of the people in London*. London: Macmillan (reprinted New York: AMS Press).

Bulmer, M., Bales, K., & Sklar, K. K. (Eds.). (1991). *The social survey in historical perspective, 1880–1940*. New York: Cambridge University Press.

Butler, D. (2007). Data sharing threatens privacy. *Nature, 449*, 644–645.

Carpenter, S. R., Armbrust, E. V., Arzberger, P. W., Chapin, F. S., III, Elser, J. J., Hackett, E. J., et al. (2009). Accelerate synthesis in ecology and environmental sciences. *BioScience* 59(8): 699–701.

Cartwright, N. J., Cat, J., Fleck, L., & Uebel, T. E. (1996). *Otto Neurath: Philosophy between science and politics*. Cambridge, MA: Cambridge University Press.

Conley, D. (2004). *The pecking order: Which siblings succeed and why*. New York: Pantheon.

Cook, S. D. N. & Brown, J. S. (1999). Bridging epistemologies: The generative dance between organizational knowledge and organizational knowing. *Organization Science*, *10*(4), 381–400.

Creager, A. N. T. (2002). *The life of a virus: Tobacco mosaic virus as an experimental model system.* Chicago: University of Chicago Press.

Diamond, J. (2004). *Collapse: How societies choose to fail or succeed.* New York: Viking.

Elmer, M. C. (1914). *Social surveys of urban communities.* Ph.D. dissertation, University of Chicago, Department of Sociology, Menasha, WI: George Banta Publishing Co.

European Science Foundation, Standing Committee for the Social Sciences, Steering Committee and Methodology Committee for a European Social Survey. (n.d.). *The European Social Survey: A research instrument for the social sciences in Europe: Summary.* Strasbourg, France.

European Social Survey. (2009). Round 5 specifications for participating countries. London: Centre for Comparative Social Surveys: City University London.

Fowler, J. H. & Christakis, N. A. (2008). Dynamic spread of happiness in a large social network: Longitudinal analysis of over 20 years in the Framingham Heart Study. *BMJ*, (208)a2338 (doi: 10.1136/bmj.a2338).

Fowler, J. H., Dawes, C. T., & Christakis, N. A. (2009). Model of genetic variation in human social networks. *PNAS*, *106*(6), 1720–1724.

Freese, J. (2008). Genetics and the social science explanation of individual outcomes. *American Journal of Sociology 114*: S1–S35.

Gabriell, J. D. F. (2009). Dyslexia: A new synergy between education and cognitive science. *Science 325*, 280–283.

Gladwell, M. (2005). *Blink: The power of thinking without thinking.* New York: Little, Brown and Company.

Glimcher, P. W., Camerer, C., Poldrack, R. A., & Fehr, E. (Eds.). (2008). *Neuroeconomics: Decision making and the brain.* New York: Academic Press.

Goldman, J., Shilton, K., Burke, J., Estrin, D., Hansen, M., Ramanathan, N., et al. (2009). Participatory Sensing: A citizen-powered approach to illuminating the patterns that shape our world. Washington, DC: Woodrow Wilson International Center for Scholars.

Golley, F. B. (1993). *A history of the ecosystem concept in ecology: More than the sum of the parts.* New Haven, CT: Yale University Press.

González, M. C., Hidalgo, C. A., and Barabási, A-L. (2008). Understanding individual human mobility patterns. Nature 453: 779–782.

Greene, K. (2008). TR10: Reality mining. *Technology Review*, March–April.

Gutmann, M. P. & Stern P. C. (Eds.). (2007). Putting people on the map: Protecting confidentiality with linked social-spatial data. Washington, DC: National Academy Press.

Hackett, E. J. (2005). Essential tensions: Identity, control, and risk in research. *Social Studies of Science*, *35*(5), 787–826.

Hackett, E. J., Conz, D., Parker, J., Bashford, J., & DeLay, S. (2004). Tokamaks and turbulence: Research ensembles, policy, and technoscientific work. *Research Policy*, *33*, 747–767.

Hackett, E. J., Parker, J. N., Conz, D., Rhoten, D., & Parker, A. (2008). Ecology transformed: The National Center for Ecological Analysis and Synthesis and the changing patterns of ecological research. In *Scientific collaboration on the Internet*, Olson, G. M., Zimmerman, A., & Bos, N. (Eds.). 277–296. Cambridge, MA: MIT Press.

Harlan, S. L., Brazel, A. J., Prashad, L., Stefanov, W. L., & Larsen, L. (2006). Neighborhood microclimates and vulnerability to heat stress. *Social Science and Medicine*, *63*, 2847–2863.

Hook, E. B. (Ed.). (2002). Prematurity in scientific discovery. Berkeley: University of California Press.

House, J. S., Juster, F. T., Kahn, R. L., Schuman, H., & Singer, E. (Eds.). (2004). *A telescope on society: Survey research and social science at the University of Michigan and beyond.* Ann Arbor: University of Michigan.

Hrdy, S. B. (2009). *Mothers and others: The evolutionary origins of mutual understanding.* Cambridge, MA: Harvard University Press.

Isaacs, J. B. (2007). *Economic mobility of black and white families.* Philadelphia: Pew Charitable Trusts.

Jacob, F. (1988). *The statue within.* New York: Basic Books.

Kingsland, S. (2005). *The evolution of American ecology, 1890–2000.* Baltimore: The Johns Hopkins University Press.

Kuhn, T. S. (1957 [1977]). *The essential tension.* Chicago: University of Chicago Press.

Lareau, A., & Conley, D. C. (Eds.). (2008). *Social class: How does it work?* New York: Russell Sage Foundation.

Lazer, D., Pentland, A., Adamic, L., Aral, S., Barabási, A.-L., Brewer, D., et al. (2009). Computational social science. *Science, 323,* 721–723.

Lewis, Kevin, Kaufman, J., Gonzalez, M., Wimmer, A., & Christakis, N. A. (2008). Taste, ties, and time: A new social network dataset using Facebook.com. *Social Networks, 30,* 330–342.

Long, J. S. (2009). *The workflow of data analysis using Stata.* College Station, TX: Stata Press.

Mukerji, C. (1989). *A fragile power: Scientists and the state.* Princeton, NJ: Princeton University Press.

National Science and Technology Council, Subcommittee on Social, Behavioral, and Economic Sciences. (2009). Social, behavioral, and economic research in the federal context. Washington, DC: Office of Science and Technology Policy.

National Science Foundation. (February 2007). NSF FY2008 Budget Request to Congress. Arlington, VA: National Science Foundation (http://www.nsf.gov/about/budget/fy2008/pdf/EntirePDF.pdf).

Nature. (2008). A flood of hard data. *Nature 453,* 698.

Nordhaus, W. D. (2006). Geography and macroeconomics: New data and new findings. *PNAS, 103*(10), 3510–3517.

Olguín, D., Waber, B. N., Kim, T., Mohan, A., Ara, K., & Pentland, A. (2009). Sensible organizations: Technology and methodology for automatically measuring organizational behavior. *IEEE Transactions on Systems, Man, and Cybernetics—Part B: Cybernetics, 39*(1): 1–12.

Olson, G. M., Zimmerman, A., & Bos, N. (Eds.). (2008). *Scientific collaboration on the Internet.* Cambridge, MA: MIT Press.

Onnela, J.-P., Saramäki, J., Hyvönen, J., Szabó, G., Lazer, D., Kaski, K., et al. (2007). Structure and tie strength in mobile communication networks. *PNAS, 104*(18): 7332–7336.

Ostrom, E. (2009). A general framework for analyzing sustainability of social-ecological systems. *Science 325,* 419–422.

Pentland, A. (2009). Reality mining of mobile communications: Toward a new deal on data. Chapter 1.6 in Dutta, S. & Mia, I., (Eds.). *The global information technology report.* New York: World Economic Forum.

Price, D. J. de S. (1984). The science/technology relationship, the craft of experimental science, and policy for the improvement of high technology innovation. *Research Policy, 13,* 3–20.

Rheinberger, H.-J. (1997). *Toward a history of epistemic things: Synthesizing proteins in the test tube.* Stanford, CA: Stanford University Press.

Schrödinger, E. (1943–1944). *What is life?* Cambridge, UK: Cambridge University Press.

Shanahan, M. J., Vaisey, S., Erickson, L. D., & Smolen, A. (2008). Environmental Contingencies and Genetic Propensities: Social Capital, Educational Continuation, and Dopamine Receptor Gene DRD2. *American Journal of Sociology, 114*(S1), S260–86.

Shilton, K., Burke, J., Estrin, D., Hansen, M., & Srivastava M. B. (2008). Participatory privacy in urban sensing. Los Angeles: Center for Embedded Network Sensing. Permalink: http://escholarship.org/uc/item/90j149pp.

Tingley, D. (2006). Neurological imaging as evidence in political science: A review, critique, and guiding assessment. *Social Science Information*, *45*(5), 5–33.

van der Leeuw, S., Lane, D. A., Reed, D. W. (2009). The long-term evolution of social organization. In Lane, D. A., van der Leeuw, S., Pumain, D., & West, G. (Eds.). *Complexity: Perspectives in innovation and social change* (pp. 85–116). New york: Springer.

Vespignani, A. (2009). Predicting the behavior of techno-social systems. *Science*, *325*, 425–428.

Wilson, E. O. (1975). *Sociobiology: The new synthesis*. Cambridge, MA: Harvard University Press.

Wilson, E. O. (1979). *On human nature*. Cambridge, MA: Harvard University Press.

World Values Survey (2009). *Values change the world*. Stockholm: World Values Survey.

Chapter 2

To Tell the Truth: The Internet and Emergent Epistemological Challenges in Social Research

David J. Gunkel

During the premier episode of *The Colbert Report*, Stephen Colbert introduced what was to become one of the series' signature segments. Simply called "The Word," this first installment introduced the term "truthiness." This curious neologism, which was named word of the year by the American Dialect Society in 2005 and subsequently incorporated into the *Merriam-Webster Dictionary*, designates "the quality of preferring concepts or facts one wishes to be true, rather than concepts or facts known to be true" (Merriam-Webster, 2006). Colbert followed this up in July of 2006 with a related concept "wikiality." This neologism was, as Colbert explained, derived from the experience and features of the online encyclopedia *Wikipedia*, where "any user can change any entry, and if enough users agree with them, it becomes true" (Comedy Central, 2006). Wikiality, then, is a reality that, although not necessarily real and true, becomes real and true through user decision and agreement—in a word, truthiness. As proof of this concept, Colbert urged his viewers to go to *Wikipedia* and deliberately manipulate population statistics for the African elephant, significantly increasing the reported number so as to make it appear that the largest terrestrial mammal was not on the verge of becoming an endangered species. This collective action, although staged as a comedic prank, illustrates a very real problem that has been identified by critics like Neil Postman: "Has anyone been discussing the matter of how we can distinguish between what is true and what is false?...Those who speak enthusiastically of the great volume of statements about the world available on the Internet do not usually address how we may distinguish the true from the false" (Postman, p. 2000, 92).

No matter what kind of innovation in information and communication technology (ICT) is considered, the fundamental question inevitably has to do with "truth." This is the case whether the "t" word is used or is implied through one of its delegates: accuracy, fidelity, validity, authenticity, credibility, etc. How, for example, does one know whether the information presented on a Web page, contained in a *Wikipedia* article, or posted on a blog is in fact truthful, trustworthy, or credible? (Dreyfus, 2001; Flanagin & Metzger, 2000; Greer, 2003). How can one be certain that a digital photograph is an accurate representation of the actual state of affairs and not the result of some clever, and perhaps even malicious, manipulation facilitated by image-processing software like PhotoShop or

GIMP? (Brand, Kelly, & Kinny, 1985; Gross, Katz, & Ruby, 2003; Kittross & Gordon, 2003; Mitchell, 1994). How can one trust that the other with whom one interacts through online chat, e-mail, or a social network like Facebook or MySpace is in fact telling the truth about his/her identity? (Berman & Bruckman, 2001; Papacharissi, 2009; Stone, 1993; Tompkins, 2003). In all of these situations and inquiries there remains at least one unaddressed question: What is meant by "truth?" What do we have in mind when we deploy words like "true," "valid," "accurate," "credible," "trustworthy," and "authentic?" What is true and what is truth? More specifically, what assumptions regarding truth already inform and structure social science research practices, investigative methodologies, and accepted standards of evidence? And how do recent innovations in ICT either confirm or challenge these standard procedures and protocols?

This chapter takes up and investigates these fundamental questions, which cut to the core of social research insofar as we, both the subject and object of the social sciences, seek to uncover and tell the truth. Such an investigation will not examine any particular truth or the truth that is conveyed by any particular Internet application. Instead it will seek to disclose and investigate the general concept of truth that has been deployed and operationalized by these various instances. What will be discovered in the course of this examination is that the customary concept of truth is not (and perhaps never actually was) true. That is, the understanding of truth that has been developed in and has been constitutive of the Western intellectual tradition is not necessarily accurate or valid according to its own definition and stipulations. The investigation of this matter will be divided into four parts. The first considers the response that has typically been provided for the question "what is truth?" The second identifies and explicates a technicality that necessarily afflicts and complicates this characterization. The third part responds to this complication by advancing an alternative theory of truth that is rooted in the epistemological innovations of pragmatism and phenomenology. The fourth and final part considers the consequences of this development, demonstrating how it entails a restructuring of the concept of truth, a reevaluation of the role of technology, and a significant reconfiguration of research practices and methodologies.

The Correspondence Theory

Let us begin with what might appear to be an unlikely source—the television game show from which this essay derives its title. The program, *To Tell the Truth*, was created by Bob Stewart, produced by Mark Goodson and Bill Todman, and ran intermittently on several U.S. television networks since its premier in the mid-1950s. *To Tell the Truth* was a panel show, which like its precursor *What's My Line* (1950–1967), featured a panel of four celebrities. The panelists, who sat side-by-side behind a long rectangular desk, were confronted with a group of three individuals, or what the program's host and referee called a "team of challengers." Each member of this trio claimed to be a particular individual who had some unusual background, notable life experience, or unique occupation. The celebrity panel was charged with interrogating the three challengers and, based on the responses to their questions, decided which one of the three was actually the person he or she purported to be. In essence, they had to determine which individual was telling the truth. In this exchange, two of the challengers engaged in deliberate deception, answering the questions of the celebrity panel by pretending to be someone they were not, while the remaining challenger told the truth. The "moment of truth" came at the game's conclusion, when the program's host asked the pivotal question "Will the real so-and-so please stand up?" at which time one of the three challengers stood. In doing so, this one individual demonstrated that he or she had been telling the truth, while the other two had engaged in deliberate and calculated deception.

Although ostensibly a simple form of television entertainment, *To Tell the Truth* is based on and illustrates what is often called the "correspondence theory of truth." According to this characterization, *truth* is not something that is "out there" in things but it is essentially a relative concept. It comprises the agreement or correspondence between a statement about something, commonly called a "judgment," and the object about which the statement is made. The German philosopher Martin Heidegger illustrated this with a rather simple example: "Let us suppose that someone with his back turned to the wall makes the true statement that 'the picture on the wall is hanging askew.' This statement demonstrates itself when the man who makes it turns around and perceives the picture hanging askew on the wall" (Heidegger, 1962, p. 260). The truth of the statement, "the picture is hanging askew," is evaluated by "turning around" and comparing the content of the statement to the actual thing. If the statement agrees with or corresponds to the actual situation of the object, it is true; if not, it is false. According to Heidegger, this particular understanding of truth—truth as agreement or correspondence—dominates Western thought and can therefore be found in the seminal works of the tradition. It is, for example, evident in the scholastic definition of truth as *adaequatio intellectus et rei*, the adequation of thought to things (Heidegger, 1962, p. 257); René Descartes claimed that "the word 'truth,' in the strict sense, denotes the conformity of thought with its object" (Descartes, 1991, 139); while Immanuel Kant's *Critique of Pure Reason* grants without any critical hesitation whatsoever that truth is "the agreement of knowledge with its object" (Kant, 1965, p. 97). In the text of *Being and Time*, Heidegger traces this concept to an assertion that has been attributed to Aristotle's *De Interpretatione*: "the soul's 'experiences,' its *noemata* ('representations'), are likenings of things" (Heidegger, 1962, p. 257). Elsewhere, namely in the essay "Plato's Doctrine of Truth," he demonstrates how this concept originates with Plato's "Allegory of the Cave."

The "Allegory of the Cave," which is recounted at the beginning of book VII of the *Republic*, describes a kind of Platonic version of the game show, *Avant la lettre*. The *mise en scene*, as it is described by Socrates, consists of a subterranean cavern inhabited by men who are confined to sit before a large wall upon which are projected shadow images. The cave dwellers are chained in place from childhood and are unable to see anything other than these artificial projections, which constitute the only reality that is possible for them to know. Consequently, they operate as if everything that appears on the wall (arguably the prototype of the motion picture screen and television monitor) is in fact real. They bestow names on the different shadows, devise clever methods to predict their sequence and behavior, and hand out awards to each other for demonstrated proficiency in knowing such things (Plato, 1987, 515a–b). At the crucial turning point in the story, one of the captives is released. He is unbound by some ambiguous, external action and compelled to look at the source of the shadows—small puppets paraded in front of a large fire. Although he is initially disoriented and disappointed by discovering the light source of the shadow images, the prisoner eventually comes to understand "that what he had seen before was all a cheat and an illusion" (Plato, 1987, 515d). In this way, the former prisoner comes to see that what he and his colleagues had previously asserted about their world does not agree with what he now perceives. Like the conclusion to the game show, this prisoner now has immediate access to the real situation and is able to compare the shadowy images to the real thing itself. Understood in this way, Heidegger argues that the allegory narrates a sequence of events whereby the prisoner's gaze "becomes more correct" and truth is characterized as *orthotes*, the "correctness" of representation to the thing represented (Heidegger, 1978, pp. 230–231).

One might, on this point, dispute Heidegger's characterization on the grounds that it appears to be limited to the field of philosophy and, therefore, does not account for the way that the definition of truth seems to vary across disciplines. What "truth" is in mathematics, one could argue, does not have the same meaning as it does in religious studies, literature, physics, or philosophy. This argument, despite what might appear to be an attractive call for diversity in matters of truth, has at least one fundamental problem. It assumes that the characterization of truth provided by Heidegger (and the philosophical tradition he mobilizes) is limited to a particular discipline. Heidegger, however, is not interested in merely describing the criterion of "truth in philosophy" but instead provides an articulation of the "philosophy of truth" as it has been understood and deployed within the Western intellectual tradition irrespective of disciplinary differences. Clearly, the criterion of evidence and acceptable argumentation does in fact vary across disciplines. But what does not change is the fundamental concept of truth that underlies and informs these variations. In virtually every case, truth is commonly understood as the adequacy of a representation, such as a statement, model, or equation, to some actual state of affairs. In the field of Christian theology, for example, it is "true" that Jesus Christ was the son of God, "who was," as stated in the Apostle's Creed, "conceived of the Holy Spirit, born of the Virgin Mary, suffered under Pontius Pilate, was crucified, died, and was buried. He descended into hell. And on the third day He arose again from the dead." Within Christian theology, these statements are true and are judged to be true insofar as the person Jesus really did exist and live and die in the way that is described in the text of the Creed. Furthermore, one may consider work in the sciences. Meteorologists, for example, track and forecast weather by building computer models that simulate the Earth's atmosphere. The truthfulness of a forecast, ostensibly an assertion concerning the actual weather in a particular location for a particular period of time, is dependent upon the ability of the model to represent accurately the real system that it simulates. Even though the criterion of evidence in Christian theology and meteorology is significantly different, the basic concept of truth as the accuracy of an assertion to the thing about which the assertion is made remains invariable and remarkably consistent.

The Real Problem

The correspondence theory of truth has a long and venerable history. Like all influential theories, it has staunch advocates (e.g., David, 1994; Newman, 2002; O'Connor, 1975; Schmitt, 1995), insightful critics (e.g., Davidson, 2005; Künne, 2003; Rorty, 1990), and attentive expositors (e.g., Blackburn, 2005; Kirkham, 1992). Despite these debates, all sides acknowledge that the correspondence theory requires and relies on one crucial and fundamental assumption: in order to measure or evaluate the extent to which a particular statement or representation corresponds to the actual state of affairs, one must, at some point, have unmitigated and direct access to the real thing itself. To put it in the terms of both Heidegger's example and Plato's allegory, when one turns around, he or she must have direct and immediate access to the real thing. It is only on this basis that it becomes possible to evaluate the extent to which a statement about something corresponds to the actual thing about which the statement has been made.

Access to this "real thing" can, as the game shows of Goodson and Todman demonstrate, be furnished in one of two ways. On the one hand, the revelation of the real may be situated at the beginning. This is evident with the Platonic "doctrine of the forms," where direct access to the real is situated prior to and outside of the space and time of terrestrial experience. "For a human being," as Socrates states in the *Phaedrus*, "must understand a general idea formed by collecting into a unity by means of reason the many perceptions of the senses; and this is a recollection of those real things which our soul once beheld, when it journeyed with a god and, lifting its vision above the things which we now say exist, rose up to real being" (Plato, 1982, 249b–c). Platonic metaphysics, therefore, provides for *a priori* access to the real. This is also the procedure that is instituted and utilized by *What's My Line*, Goodson and Todman's initial panel show and the immediate precursor to *To Tell the Truth*. In *What's My Line*, four celebrity panelists interrogated one challenger in an attempt to ascertain this particular individual's occupation or line of work. Although the true identity of the challenger was concealed from the celebrity panel, it was revealed to both the studio and television audience at the beginning of the game. In this way, the studio audience and television viewer were given privileged access to the real, while the panel was restricted from knowing such information. This epistemological dissonance created a kind of dramatic tension that was undeniably entertaining. Like an omniscient being, the audience knew the truth of all things and watched the mere mortal panel try to figure out the truth from their messy involvement in and limitation to particular apparitions. Although Goodson and Todman were most likely unaware of this influence, their game show was thoroughly informed by and functioned according to the protocols of Platonism.

On the other hand, access may be situated at the end, as it is in *To Tell the Truth*. In this case, the real is not revealed until the end of the program, when the real person is asked to stand up and finally show him/herself as such. This transaction is perhaps best illustrated in contemporary science, especially physics. For the theoretical physicist, what we perceive and call "real" does not, strictly speaking, have anything to do with what actually comprises physical reality. As Brian Greene explains "physicists such as myself are acutely aware that the reality we observe—matter evolving on the stage of space and time—may have little to do with the reality, if any, that is out there" (Greene, 2004, p. ix). Greene, who is an advocate of a brand of physics called "string theory," argues that physical reality is actually composed of vibrating filaments of energy called "strings." The strings, which are estimated to be "some hundred billion billion times smaller than a single atomic nucleus" (Greene, 2004, p. 345) cannot be observed with any conceivable instrument or tested through any currently available form of experiment. Instead, their existence is calculated as the hypothetical resolution of a fundamental incompatibility between the equations of general relativity and quantum mechanics. Consequently, the real of string theory is situated outside the scope of direct experience, and what appears to us through the mediation of our senses is little more than an apparitional phenomenon that is, strictly speaking, illusory. "If superstring theory is proven correct," Greene concludes, "we will be forced to accept that the reality we have known is but a delicate chiffon draped over a thick and richly textured cosmic fabric" (Greene, 2004, p. 19).

This point is emphasized by published critiques, which specifically target and question the theory's provability. Although string theory is mathematically elegant and undeniably popular in the academy, critics such as Lee Smolen (2006) and Peter Woit (2006) assert that it lacks one of the basic requirements of science—an empirically verifiable experiment. String theory, on this account, appears to be situated just outside the threshold of what is traditionally considered to be scientific truth. This does not mean, however, that string theorists advocate a new form of "groundless idealism" that one might be tempted to call "Platonism 2.0" or are involved in perpetrating another Sokal hoax. "Nothing would," Greene declares, "please string theorists more than to proudly present the world with a list of detailed, experimentally testable predictions. Certainly, there is no way to establish that any theory describes our world without subjecting its predictions to experimental verification" (Greene, 2003, p. 210). String theorists do not reject experimental validation; they simply postpone its achievement. That is, the empirically verifiable demonstration necessary to prove string theory's predictions may be currently inaccessible but it will be made available at some point in the not-too-distant future. In support of this claim, advocates often point out that new insights in physics have often preceded experimental validation by a good number of years. "The history of physics is," Greene argues, "filled with ideas that when first presented seemed completely untestable but, through various unforeseen developments, were ultimately brought within the realm of experimental verifiability" (Greene, 2003, p. 226). Whereas mainstream Platonism, like the game show *What's my Line*, situates direct access to the real in a prior revelation that takes place outside the space and time of terrestrial experience, theoretical physics, like the game show *To Tell the Truth*, situates its revelation of the real thing within the material of empirical reality at a point in the not-too-distant future.

The problem then is not whether access is situated up front or at the end, the real problem has to do with the real itself. Although uncertainty about the real is considered to be the defining crisis of the final decades of the twentieth century, according to Slovenian philosopher Slavoj Žižek (2002, 2008a), these complications are already evident and at work in Plato. In fact, as Heidegger demonstrates, one finds that the Platonic allegory not only institutes the correspondence theory but at the same time introduces significant complications that threaten to erode it. According to the Socratic account, the shadows on the wall are succeeded by small puppets held in front of firelight. These representations, in turn, are followed by the reflection of things in water, which are again succeeded by the various objects illuminated under the light of the sun. The end point of this sequence, according to the letter of the text, rests in the sun itself. "And so, finally, I suppose, he would be able to look upon the sun itself and see its true nature, not by reflections in water or phantasms in an alien setting, but in and by itself in its own place" (Plato, 1987, 516b). Consequently, what is described in the Platonic allegory is not a simple conceptual opposition in which the real thing is distinguished from and compared to the artifice of representation, but a sequence of different modes of representation. "Thus, we may speak," John Sallis writes in his commentary on the Platonic text, "not just of two modes, but of a *continuum of modes of showing…*" (Sallis, 1986, p. 420). It is, therefore, not a matter of simply turning around and comparing shadowy images to the real things they represent. Instead, it is a complex series in which one set of representations is compared to what appears to be another, perhaps better, set of representations. Instead of gaining direct access to an immediate real thing that would be merely opposed to and released from mediated representations, Plato's emancipated prisoner encounters what appears to be an ongoing and recursive mediation.

Understood in this fashion, one never actually has immediate access to the real; everything is always and already mediated in one way or another. Evidence of this is apparent in the composition of the dialogue that describes it. Plato, for reasons that are not explicated in the dialogue itself, employs an image, the "Allegory of the Cave," to illustrate and critique the deceptive nature of images. According to Jacques Derrida, "Plato imitates the imitators in order to restore the truth of what they imitate" (Derrida, 1981, 112). A similar complication is evident with Heidegger's consideration in *Being and Time*. In order to illustrate the traditional concept of truth, Heidegger provides the example of someone who makes a statement about a picture. Is this statement about truth true? Does it, according to the standard that it articulates, agree with its object? If readers of Heidegger's text turn around, can they demonstrate the adequacy of the statement by actually perceiving someone with his/her back to the wall making statements about pictures hanging askew? Perhaps this reading is too literal. It may be the case that Heidegger's statement is not necessarily about a "real event" but is the representation of a common experience that we can easily imagine. In that case, however, the statement in the text would be demonstrated by comparing it to another kind of statement made by the reader. Asking these questions leads one in circles, in which every statement about something is compared to other statements and representations and not to the immediate perception of the real thing. Consequently, we find ourselves, like Plato's former inmate, confronted with and confined to what appears to be an endless sequence of mediations.

This complication, although already apparent in the Platonic text, comes into its own with emergent forms of ICT. Take, for example, one of the first recorded accounts of online deception in computer mediated communication (CMC) in Sandy Stone's 1991 essay "Will the Real Body Please Stand Up?" This essay, which was initially presented at the First International Conference on Cyberspace (May 4–5, 1990, University of Texas at Austin) under a different title, investigated the new opportunities and challenges introduced by the nascent virtual communities that had developed in bulletin board systems (BBS) and pre-Internet computer services like America Online, Protégé, and Compuserv. In the course of her analysis, Stone introduces readers to Julie, "a person on a computer conference in New York in 1985" (Stone, 1991 p. 82). Julie, as Stone describes her, was a severely disabled woman who compensated for her physical limitations by engaging in rather intimate conversations with other people online. She was a gregarious woman who, despite feeling trapped by her physical disabilities, was able to carry on a full and very active social life in cyberspace. The only problem, as Stone eventually points out, was that Julie did not really exist. She was, in fact, the online persona (what is now called an *avatar*) of a rather shy and introverted middle-aged male psychiatrist who decided to experiment with an alternative identity, an act that Stone provocatively called "computer cross-dressing" (Stone, 1991, p. 84). Understood in this way, Stone's narrative is organized according to and appears to play by the rules of the correspondence theory. That is, she demonstrated how the avatar Julie deviates from the actual real person, and the outrage that this deception caused in the virtual community. This procedure, according to which one compares avatar characteristics to the "real person" behind the screen, continues to be an influential and operative methodology in online social research. There is, as Thomas Boellstorff describes a "gap between virtual and actual self" and "a broadly shared cultural assumption that virtual selfhood is not identical to actual selfhood" (Boellstorff, 2008, 119–120). This "broadly shared cultural assumption" is visually exhibited in Robbie Cooper's *Alter Ego* (2007), a book of 70 composite portraits that picture computer gamers from the United States, Europe, China, and Japan alongside images of their online avatars "graphically dramatizing the gap between fantasy and reality."

Still there is more to it. If one considers the structure of Stone's article and her subsequent and expanded treatment in the essay, "In Novel Conditions: The Cross Dressing Psychiatrist" (1995), it becomes evident that Julie's true identity was not ascertained by gaining access to the real person behind the avatar. Neither Stone nor the other users of the Compuserv system had ever met the real male psychiatrist who created and controlled this virtual person. Instead, Julie's identity began to unravel due to the rather slow accumulation within the virtual environment of obvious inconsistencies and seemingly irreconcilable contradictions. The appearance of Julie, therefore, eventually betrayed itself as nothing more than a mere appearance by getting tripped up in the material of its own apparition. At some point, the real person behind Julie, whom Stone identifies as "Sanford Lewin" (Stone, 1995, p. 69), decided to end the charade and reveal himself as such. In providing this revelation, which it should be noted occurred within the space and time of the computer conference, Lewin finally unmasked Julie as a construct and came out to her online friends as a cross-dressing psychiatrist. But here is where things get exceedingly complicated, because this seemingly fantastic tale is itself something of a fabrication. As Stone (1995) later noted, her account of the Julie incident was based on an earlier publication, Lindsy Van Gelder's "The Strange Case of the Electronic Woman," which was first published in *Ms.* magazine in 1985. In retelling the story, Stone had not only taken some liberties with the narrative but even altered the names of the participants. "When I first wrote up my version of the incident," Stone explained, "I used a pseudonym for the psychiatrist, and although Van Gelder used his 'real' (legal) name, I have retained the pseudonym in this version because my treatment of him is quasifictional" (Stone, 1995, p. 191). So even in Stone's text, at that point when the real person behind Julie (which it turns out was also a pseudonym—the name reported in the original Van Gelder article was "Joan Sue Green") would be identified, we do not get the real thing; we get another fabrication and apparition. The actual thing, therefore, appears to be both logically necessary but fundamentally inaccessible and endlessly deferred, caught up in an inescapable network of apparitions and representations.

A similar difficulty is encountered in the evaluation of online information, like that provided by *Wikipedia* and other forms of user-generated content, or what is now called "Web 2.0". When one inquires about the truthfulness of the information contained in a *Wikipedia* article, such as population statistics of the African elephant, he or she questions whether the statements provided in the article agree with and correspond to the actual state of affairs. One seeks, in the idiom used by both Plato and Heidegger, to "turn around" in order to evaluate the accuracy of the reported information to the actual thing. In the case of Colbert's joke, proof of the manipulation of this data would require that one has the ability to make a credible enumeration of African elephants, which is something that is, in most cases, clearly unattainable. Consequently, the statements made in *Wikipedia* are not necessarily evaluated against the real state of affairs, which is often inaccessible as such, but by comparing the information in the *Wikipedia* article against information that is provided elsewhere, usually in some other venue or form of media. For this reason, in all but the most trivial of circumstances, when one "turns around" to test the accuracy of a statement, what is perceived is not a thing in its immediacy but another set of statements made elsewhere. It is important to emphasize that this does not mean the actual number of African elephants is somehow fictional or that the African elephant is not currently exposed to environmental pressures that adversely affect its population. What it does mean, however, is that any statement, model, or representation that comes to be made about this particular object, or any other object for that matter, is always indirect and inextricably tangled up in the sediment of mediation that cannot, it seems, ever be entirely stripped away, gotten around, or done without. Apparently human knowledge is always *in medias res* (in the middle of things).

Alternative Theories

If all this is true (to use a colloquialism that has, in the course of this analysis, become increasingly complicated), it follows that truth, as it has been customarily understood as the adequacy of a statement to the thing about which the statement is made, is itself a rather inadequate and limited description. No matter how many times one "turns around," statements are it seems only compared to other statements, images are judged against other images, and media are related to and evaluated against other forms of media. The real thing, which would have anchored the entire system, appears to be endlessly deferred and ultimately inaccessible, remaining as either an unattainable ideal or a structurally necessary fabrication. What these experiences demonstrate, therefore, is the extent to which the correspondence theory of truth is not necessarily true, but is itself a product of truthiness. For this reason, there is a need to articulate an alternative and more general definition, one that does not simply reproduce the traditional characterization and that can account for these particular complexities. Although there are a number of possible candidates advanced in the field of epistemology (i.e., coherentism, deflationism, disquotationism, etc.), there are two in particular that hold considerable promise for social research.

The first is *pragmatism*. Although attributed to the work of American philosophers Charles Sanders Peirce, William James, and John Dewey, advocates and critics alike identify precursors of pragmatist thought in the writings of Baruch Spinoza, David Hume, and Aristotle and recognize its contemporary influence in the writings of Donald Davidson, Richard Rorty, Hilary Putnam, Bruno Latour, and others. Pragmatism's conception of truth, which is by no means monolithic or homogeneous, is first formalized and defended by William James in the sixth of his 1906–1907 lectures on *Pragmatism*. Unfortunately James, like Peirce and Dewey, is often criticized by contemporary scholars for a lack of clarity, precision, and rigor (Kirkham, 1992, pp. 87–88 and Schmitt, 1995, p. 78). As a result, his rather complex account is often reduced to a simple form of utilitarian instrumentalism (i.e., "*p* is true, if it is useful to belief that *p* is true") that can only be advanced by strategically "ignoring passages" and "pruning away inconsistent remarks" (Kirkham, 1992, p. 79). This caricature, although clearly expedient for advocates of the correspondence theory, like Frederick Schmitt (1995) who uses it to argue against and to discount pragmatism, does not actually correspond to or agree with James's exposition.

James begins his "Pragmatism's Conception of Truth" with a simple and seemingly indisputable definition: "Truth, as any dictionary will tell you, is a property of certain of our ideas. It means their 'agreement,' as falsity means their disagreement, with 'reality.'

Pragmatists and intellectualists both accept this definition as a matter of course" (James, 2003, p. 99). According to James, truth can be minimally characterized as the agreement of thought to reality. The pragmatist, therefore, accepts the basic "correspondence definition" as readily as either the "tender-hearted" idealists, represented by thinkers like René Descartes and Immanuel Kant, or the "hard-headed" empiricists, represented by Bishop Berkeley and David Hume. The point of contention, James argues, does not have to do with the definition of truth, but with the way we understand the words "agreement" and "reality." Reality, James maintains, does not solely consist of the things of sense experience. It, instead, comprises three different and related elements: concrete facts, mental abstractions, and other ideas (James, 2003, 106). James's point is well taken: many of our so-called "truths" involve statements or propositions that cannot be validated by comparison to direct experience of some external and currently accessible object. The majority, in fact, "admit of no direct face-to-face verification" (James, 2003, p. 107), like those concerning ancient history or theoretical physics. James, therefore, accounts for the fact that in matters of truth we often find ourselves *in medias res*, where a representation does not necessarily correspond to an object per se but agrees with and refers to a network of other modes of representation.

In addition to this multifaceted characterization of "reality," James also argues for a more nuance understanding of "agreement." Agreement, according to James's account, does not consist in an "inert static relation" between an idea and its sensible object. "The truth of an idea," he writes, "is not a stagnant property inherent in it. Truth *happens* to an idea. It *becomes* true, is *made* true by events. Its verity *is* in fact an event, a process; the process namely of its verifying itself, its veri-*fication*" (James, 2003, p. 100). In this way, James replaces the static agreement of correspondence, whereby thought is determined either to agree with its object or not, with a dynamic process whereby truth is continually made and remade, existing in a constant state of becoming. Although this formulation has led to charges of relativism, it provides for a more accurate articulation of the way "truth" actually functions. To illustrate this, James offers an example that is surprisingly prescient of the epistemological innovations that were introduced by Thomas Kuhn: "We have to live to-day by what truth we can get to-day, and be ready to-morrow to call it falsehood. Ptolemaic astronomy, euclidean space, aristotelian logic, scholastic metaphysics, were expedient for centuries, but human experience has boiled over those limits, and now we call these things only relatively true, or true within those borders of experience" (James, 2003, p. 112). Like Kuhn (1996), James advocates an understanding of truth that is dynamic, adaptive, and relative. It is not a matter of an idea corresponding to something or not; it is about the relative expediency of thought for framing an understanding of a particular set of experiences within a particular context. Unlike static correspondence which does not, for the most part, problematize its own mode of representation, pragmatism's conception of truth understands representation as part of the truth-making process and accounts for its contributions and effects.

Pragmatism provides an alternative conceptualization of truth that does not so much contest the basic tenets of the correspondence theory as it introduces important elaborations and qualifications. A more radical and fundamental challenge is developed in the writings of Heidegger, who is not only critical of the correspondence theory, but discovers an alternative to it in a forgotten corner of the basement of Platonism. This alternative and "more original" understanding defines truth, *aletheia* in ancient Greek, in the literal sense of "unconcealing," "uncovering," or "unhiddenness." Unhiddenness, Heidegger argues, is "the fundamental trait of being itself" and, unlike the adequacy of a statement about something or the correctness of a representation to the thing represented, is not "a characteristic of the knowing of beings" (Heidegger, 1978, p. 234). If *truth* is not, as Heidegger argues, a matter of the adequacy of representation, then the status and function of any form of representation, whether spoken discourse, writing, printing, painting, photography, television, Web sites, virtual reality, etc., will also need to be situated otherwise. "To say that a statement '*is true*,'" Heidegger writes, "signifies that it uncovers the entity in itself. Such a statement, points out, 'lets' the entity 'be seen' in its uncoveredness. The *Being-true* (*truth*) of the statement must be understood as *Being-uncovered*. Thus truth has by no means the structure of an agreement between knowing and the object in the sense of a likening of one entity (the subject) to another (the object)" (Heidegger, 1962, p. 261). According to this explanation, the truth of a statement is not, as it is customarily assumed to be, a matter of the agreement of an assertion (i.e., "the picture on the wall is hanging askew") to the actual object or state of affairs about which the assertion is made. Instead, assertion constitutes a "communicatively determinative exhibition" (Heidegger, 1988, p. 210), whereby something comes to be differentiated from its undifferentiated entanglement in its environment and exhibited as such. It is the process "of taking entities out of their hiddenness and letting them be seen in their unhiddenness (their uncoveredness)" (Heidegger, 1962, p. 262).

Heidegger, for example, argues that prior to the assertions made by Sir Isaac Newton, what we now know as Newton's laws were neither true nor false. This is not because the entities (i.e., bodies and forces) that are described by these assertions did not exist in the world. It is because they did not show themselves in this particular way, that is, as bodies and forces, until Newton's theorizing differentiated and exhibited them as such (Heidegger, 1962, p. 269). This particular operation, Heidegger concludes, belongs entirely to *logos*, a word that literally means "word" and comes to be defined as discourse, language, logic, and even rationality. It is in and by *logos* that entities come to be differentiated and revealed (Heidegger, 1962, p. 262). This is, it should be noted, not merely a Heideggerian innovation but the reiteration of another fundamental turning point in the Platonic corpus, which is often called Socrates' "second voyage" (Sallis, 1986). It is in the *Phaedo*, a dialogue that narrates among other things the last moments of Socrates' life, that the aged philosopher provides an account of where it all began. In reflecting on the initiation of his endeavors, Socrates recounts how he began by trying to follow the example established by his predecessors and sought wisdom in "the investigation of nature" (Plato, 1990, 96a). He describes how this undertaking, despite its initial attraction and his best efforts, continually led him adrift, how he eventually gave it up, and how he finally decided on an alternative route by investigating the truth of things in *logos*. "So I thought," Socrates explains, "I must have recourse to *logos* and examine in them the truth of things" (Plato, 1990, 99e). In connecting truth to *logos*, therefore, Heidegger is not introducing a new concept into the Western intellectual tradition but is returning it to its origins.

Although not usually identified with Heideggerian thought per se, this alternative perspective has also been developed and deployed in the social sciences. It is evident, for example, in "the social construction of reality" or what is often simply called "social constructivism." As introduced and initially characterized by Peter L. Berger and Thomas Luckman (1966), "the social construction of reality" means that the "real world" inhabited, understood, and shared by human beings is not something that is merely given in nature but is generally shaped and structured by social interactions and language in particular.

"It is our contention," Berger and Luckman write, "that the sociology of knowledge must concern itself with whatever passes for 'knowledge' in a society, regardless of the ultimate validity or invalidity (by whatever criteria) of such 'knowledge.' And insofar as all human 'knowledge' is developed, transmitted and maintained in social situations, the sociology of knowledge must seek to understand the processes by which this is done in such a way that a taken-for-granted 'reality' congeals for the man in the street" (Berger & Luckman, 1966, 3). Although initially positioned as a contribution to what Max Scheler (1960) termed "the sociology of knowledge" or *Wissenssoziologie*, social constructivism, although not always identified by this particular moniker, has understandably found its way into the field of communication studies. Scholars of rhetoric, like Robert Scott (1967), Barry Brummett (1976), and C. Jack Orr (1978), have employed this sociological innovation to argue for an understanding of language as generative of knowledge and not just a mode of its dissemination and distribution. "I want to suggest," communication theorist James Carey writes in a passage that is indebted to Heidegger, "to play on the Gospel of St. John, that in the beginning was the word [*logos*]; words are not the names for things but, to steal a line from Kenneth Burke, things are the signs of words. Reality is not given, not humanly existent, independent of language and toward which language stands as a pale refraction. Rather, reality is brought into existence, is produced by communication—by, in short, the construction, apprehension, and utilization of symbolic forms" (Carey, 1989, p. 25). Understood in this way, communication, whether in the form of spoken discourse or newly introduced forms of ICT, does not simply transmit information about a preexisting real world but reveals what is real. For this reason, "one must," Carey continues, "examine communication, even scientific communication, even mathematical expression, as the primary phenomena of experience and not as something 'softer' and derivative from a 'realer' existent nature" (Carey, 1989, p. 26). This does not mean, it should be emphasized, that things like rocks, trees, and elephants do not exist outside the various means and mechanisms of communication. It means that these "things" are not simply given or immediately available to us. What they are and how we understand what they are is something that is, at least for our purposes, always mediated through some kind of interpretive process by which they come to show themselves as such.

Truth and Consequences

This alternative theory of truth, although holding considerable promise, is still somewhat theoretical and abstract. Let me conclude, therefore, by providing a more concrete formulation and tracing its consequences. In January of 1996, *Wired* magazine published a rather surprising interview with their self-proclaimed "patron saint," Marshall McLuhan. The interview was surprising, because at the time it was conducted, McLuhan had been deceased for over a decade. As explained in the article's introduction, "About a year ago, someone calling himself Marshall McLuhan began posting anonymously on a popular mailing list called Zone (zone@wired.com). Gary Wolf began a correspondence with the poster via a chain of anonymous remailers" (Wolf, 1996, p. 1). This situation understandably raises a number of questions concerning the identity of Wolf's online interlocutor. Who was this virtual McLuhan? Could it be the ghost of the real Marshall McLuhan? Although this sounds rather preposterous, information technology, as demonstrated by

Fredrick Kittler (1999) and Avital Ronell (1989), has always been understood as the proper realm of ghosts. Or was this an imposter engaging in a little role play? Was it someone like Stone's Sanford Lewin, who experimented with another identity and tried to pass himself off as someone else? Or was it an automated chatter bot, like Joseph Weizenbaum's ELIZA, which had been programmed with, as Wolf described it, "an eerie command of McLuhan's life and inimitable perspective" (Wolf, 1996, p. 1)? Technically there was no way to answer these questions in any definitive way. The interviewer was limited to what had appeared online and, because the exchange took place through the instrumentality of anonymous remailers (an e-mail application that strips off all identifying information), was unable to get behind the scenes or screen to ascertain the actual situation of the real thing. In the face of this irreducible indeterminacy, *Wired* did something that was, from the perspective of accepted journalistic practices, either completely wrong-headed or incredibly innovative. Instead of dismissing the whole affair as ultimately unverifiable, they decided to publish the interview as is, leaving the question about the actual situation open-ended and ultimately unresolved.

This remarkable event collects and exhibits what is at stake in this analysis. First, everything depends on how we define and operationalize the concept of truth. Even though social networks, wikis, blogs, and other forms of ICT are often considered to be merely a matter of instrumental convenience or entertainment, they are involved, whether we ever recognized it as such or not, in serious debates about and meditations on fundamental aspects of epistemology. In confronting these situations, there appears to be a default setting, as there are in many aspects of computing. This default is programmed and controlled by the correspondence theory of truth, which concerns the agreement between a statement and the real thing about which the statement is made. As long as research endeavors proceed according to this formulation, which as a default setting is often operative without having to specify it, we already know what questions matter, what evidence will count as appropriate, and what outcomes will be considered acceptable. If one examines and evaluates *Wired's* interview in light of the correspondence theory, the main question is whether what are presented as the words of McLuhan are in fact McLuhan's statements. Is this actually what McLuhan thought and said? Is the information that is presented in the interview truthful, credible, and valid, or is this all a clever deception and ultimately false? Such questions are entirely reasonable and justified. The real problem, however, is they cannot be answered by remaining within and adhering to the stipulations of the correspondence theory. Since the actual identity of the real person behind the screen (assuming, of course, that it is a person) is not able to be ascertained, there is strictly speaking no way to decide one way or the other. One can, of course, make an educated guess, but this will be nothing more than a conjecture based on, in most cases, corroborating evidence and information accessed by other means and through other forms of media. This complication is not an anomaly; it is, in fact, a rather common occurrence. Users of Internet applications, from basic e-mail and chat to more elaborate forms of social networking and online role-playing games, often find themselves in the situation of conversing and interacting with others where there is little or no possibility of ever verifying, in any satisfactory and definitive way, who or even what is on the other end of the computer-mediated conversation. As one participant in a survey of users of online role-playing games aptly described, "you never really know who is on the other side of the mask" (Boellstorff, 2008, p. 130). Without access to this information, one is, according to the stipulations of the correspondence theory, simply in no position to decide either truth or falsity. Consequently, an uncritical adherence to the correspondence theory, instead of providing researchers with a recognized standard for evaluating what is true, may in fact significantly restrict or even foreclose inquiry altogether.

Second, because of this, the correspondence theory should be understood as more the exception than the rule. This exceptional status can be demonstrated by considering another remarkable appearance of Marshall McLuhan, specifically his brief cameo in a sequence from Woody Allen's *Annie Hall* (1977). In this scene, Alvy Singer (Woody Allen) and Annie Hall (Dianne Keaton) are waiting in line to buy tickets to a film. Directly behind them is an academic who is pontificating *ad nauseam* to his companion about the films of Federico Fellini, the work of Samuel Beckett, and the views of Marshall McLuhan. Alvy, who takes particular exception to this, steps out of the line and registers his disapproval in a direct address to the camera: "What do you do, when you get stuck in a movie line with a guy like this behind you?" The man, who notices the complaint, steps forward to confront his accuser. "You don't," Alvy charges in reply to this objection, "know anything about Marshall McLuhan." The man then justifies his statements by proudly proclaiming that he happens to teach a course at Columbia called "TV, Media, and Culture" and that his "insights into Mr. McLuhan have a great deal of validity." "Oh do you?" Alvy replies, "well that's funny because I happen to have Mr. McLuhan right here." And he pulls Marshall McLuhan out from behind a large, freestanding sign. McLuhan then says to the academic, "I've heard what you're saying; you know nothing of my work.... How you got to teach a course in anything is totally amazing." Satisfied with this result, Alvy once again addresses the camera and states, "Boy, if life were only like this." The problem of course, and the point of Allen's joke, is that life is not anything like this. Correspondence, although the accepted and often unquestioned standard of truth, is the exception and not the rule. Rather than describing the actual situation of truth, the correspondence theory projects a fantastic ideal that is rarely, if ever, able to be achieved as such.

Third, due to the fact that the correspondence theory is exceptional and not, strictly speaking, true according to its own standards and requirements, researchers have advanced alternate theories. For a pragmatist, like James, truth is characterized as a dynamic and interminable process. Unlike the essentially static agreement attributed to the correspondence theory, pragmatism's conception of truth understands representation as part of the truth-making process and endeavors to account for its contributions and effects. Because the *Wired* magazine interview with McLuhan admits of no direct face-to-face verification, the truth of what was printed can only be measured by evaluating its coherence with other statements and representations. Wolf, therefore, was being entirely pragmatic when he noted that the subject of the interview possessed "an eerie command of McLuhan's life and inimitable perspective" (Wolf, 1996, p. 1). Heideggger takes things one step further, arguing for a more radical and fundamental conceptualization. For Heidegger, truth (*aletheia*) is a revealing or uncovering situated in *logos*. Understood in this way, statements do not merely represent things more or less adequately. Instead, they exhibit what Carey calls a dual capacity: "as 'symbols of' they present reality; as 'symbols for' they create the very reality they present" (Carey, 1989, p. 29). What is called "McLuhan," for example, is not some real thing existing in a kind of raw and naked state outside of and beyond the various representations that refer to this object. For us, "McLuhan" is continually made and remade according to all kinds of discursive activities, such as competing interpretations of his texts, analyses and criticisms of his various media appearances, and recollections by friends, colleagues, and relatives. For this reason, what is called "McLuhan" is, as Žižek (2008a) characterizes it, "retroactively (presup)posited" (209); it is a something that is derived from but also situated as the cause of our engagement with its various mediated representations. "Communications," Heidegger concludes, "are not a store of heaped up propositions but should be seen as possibilities by which one individual enters with the other into the same fundamental comportment toward the entity asserted about, which is unveiled in the same way" (Heidegger, 1988, p. 210). This fundamental change in perspective will, as Carey points out, necessarily mobilize an entirely different set of research questions and approaches: "How do we do this? What are the differences between these forms? What are the historical and comparative variations in them? How do changes in communication technology influence what we can concretely create and apprehend? How do groups in society struggle over the definition of what is real?" (Carey, 1989, pp. 30–31). Although this change in perspective may be cited "as insufficiently empirical" (Carey, 1989, p. 30), it is in fact attentive to the necessary restrictions and requirements of what would be a strict and serious form of empiricism—one that recognizes that human knowledge is always and only *in medias res*.

Finally, what this means for social research, especially research that engages recent innovations in ICT, is not that investigators have proceeded incorrectly. What it means is the end to a certain brand of theoretical naivety in the pursuit of these investigations. The choice of theory, especially a theory of truth, is never certain and is always open to considerable variation and debate. But the choice is always a choice, and it needs to be explicitly understood and articulated as such. The English word "theory," as we are often reminded, is derived from an ancient Greek verb, which denotes the act of seeing or vision. A theory, therefore, like the frame of a camera, always enables something to be seen by including it within the field of vision, but it also and necessarily excludes other things outside the edge of its frame. Researchers can, for instance, justifiably employ the correspondence theory of truth, and it will, in many circumstances, prove to be entirely serviceable insofar as the theory frames certain research questions and methods of investigation. This is, for example, the standard operating procedure of many forms of online social research, where researchers affirm the fact that "users can," as T. L. Taylor describes it, "construct identities that may or may not correlate to their offline persona" (Taylor, 2006, p. 95). This ability to manipulate and reconfigure identity has been either celebrated for its liberating role-playing potential or criticized for the way it facilitates potentially dangerous forms of deception. Indicative of the former is Mark Dery's claim that "online, users can float free of biological and sociocultural determinants" (Dery, 1994, p. 3). Still, this notion has grave implications, as illustrated by news reports involving identity theft, online predators, Internet scams, and other forms of deceit. Despite their many differences, the two sides of this debate share an underlying belief in and dedication to the correspondence theory. This does not mean that the correspondence theory is simply wrong. In fact, there are circumstances where correspondence is entirely appropriate and useful. Newtonian physics, although superceded by Einstein's work in relativity, is still entirely serviceable for calculating load and stress in structural engineering. Similarly, there are areas of ICT research in which the correspondence theory is perfectly suitable, such as exposing scams, measuring user demographics, or investigating online deception. Its employment, however, must be understood as limited to a highly constrained context and not something that can be, on the basis of this particular success, generalized to cover each and every circumstance. Consequently, we must explicitly recognize that this particular application of theory, like the choice of any tool or instrument, cannot be unconsciously accepted as natural and beyond critical self-reflection.

What the alternative theory of truth provides is not the one true understanding of truth but a conceptualization of truth that recognizes that truth itself is open to considerable variability, ideological pressures, and some messy theoretical negotiations. The real problem, then, is not that investigators have used one theory of truth or another. The problem is that researchers have more often than not utilized theory without explicitly recognizing which one, considering why one comes to be employed as opposed to another, or the price that must be paid for such adherence. Social research on ICT, therefore, must become a "reflexive" practice (Carey, 1989, p. 32) or what G. W. F. Hegel calls a "speculative science." For Hegel (1969), "speculative" is not, as is often the case in colloquial discourse, a pejorative term meaning groundless consideration or idle review of something that is inconclusive and indeterminate. It is not, therefore, to be construed as a kind of pointless exercise in navel gazing. Instead, Hegel understands and utilizes the word "speculative" in its strict etymological sense, which is derived from the Latin noun *speculum*. "Speculative," therefore, designates a form of self-reflective knowing. It is a method of research that makes its own protocols and procedures an object of its consideration. The strategic advantage of this particular approach, then, is not that it provides one with privileged and immediate access to the truth but that it continually conceptualizes the place from which one professes to know anything and submits to investigation the particular position that is occupied by any epistemological claim whatsoever. Understood in this way, truth is not merely a matter of measuring the correspondence of an assertion to the actual state of affairs, but is involved with evaluating how, as Žižek (2008b, 3) describes it, the position of enunciation already influences and informs what can (and cannot) be enunciated.

References

Allen, W. (1977). *Annie hall*. United Arists: Hollywood, CA.
Aristotle. (1941). *De interpretatione*. In *The basic works of Aristotle*, edited and translated by Richard McKeon. New York: Random House.
Berger, P. L. & Luckmann T. (1966). *The social construction of reality*. New York: Anchor Books.
Berman, J. & Bruckman A. S. (2001). The turing game: Exploring identity in an online environment. *Convergence 7*(3), 83–102.
Blackburn, S. (2005). *Truth: A guide*. Oxford: Oxford University Press.
Boellstorff, T. (2008). *Coming of age in second life*. Princeton, NJ: Princeton University Press.
Brand, S., Kelly K., & Kinney J. (1994). Digital retouching: The end of photography as evidence of anything. *Whole Earth Review*: 42–49.
Brummett, B. (1976). Some implications of "process" or "intersubjectivity": postmodern rhetoric. *Philosophy and Rhetoric 9*, 21–51.
Carey, J. (1989). *Communication as culture*. New York: Routledge.
Comedy Central. (2006). *The colbert report*. http://www.comedycentral.com/videos/index. jhtml?videoId=72347
Cooper, R. (2007). *Alter ego: Avatars and their creators*. London: Chris Boot Ltd.
David, M. (1994). *Correspondence and disquotation: An essay on the nature of truth*. Oxford: Oxford University Press.
Davidson, D. (2005). *Truth and prediction*. Cambridge, MA: Harvard University Press.
Derrida, J. (1981). *Disseminations*. Translated by Barbara Johnson. Chicago: University of Chicago Press.

Dery, M. (1994). *Flame wars: The discourse of cyberculture.* Durham, NC: Duke University Press.

Descartes, R. (1991). *The philosophical writings of Descartes*, vol. 3. Translated by J. Cottingham, R. Stoothoff, D. Murdock, & A. Kenny. Cambridge: Cambridge University Press.

Dreyfus, H. L. (2001). *On the internet.* New York: Routledge.

Flanagin, A. J. & Metzger M. J. (2000). Perceptions of internet information credibility. *Journalism and mass communication quarterly 77*(3), 515–540.

Greene, B. (2003). *The elegant universe.* New York: Vintage Books.

Greene, B. (2004). *The fabric of the cosmos.* New York: Vintage Books.

Greer, J. D. (2003). Evaluating the credibility of online information: A test of source and advertising influence. *Mass communication and society 6*(1), 11–28.

Gross, L., Katz J. S., & Ruby J. (2003). *Image ethics in the digital age.* Minneapolis: University of Minnesota Press.

Hegel, G. W. F. (1969). *Enzyklopädie der philosophischen wissenschaften im grundrisse.* Hamburg: Verlag von Felix Meiner.

Heidegger, M. (1962). *Being and time.* Translated by J. Macquarrie and E. Robinson. New York: Harpers & Row Publishers.

Heidegger, M. (1978). *Wegmarken.* Vittorio Klostermann: Frankfurt am Main.

Heidegger, M. (1988). *The basic problems of phenomenology.* Translated by A. Hofstadter. Bloomington, IN: University of Indiana Press.

James, W. (2003). *Pragmatism: A new name for some old ways of thinking.* New York: Barnes & Noble.

Kant, I. (1965). *Critique of pure reason.* Translated by Norman Kemp Smith. New York: St. Martin's Press.

Kirkham, R. L. (1992). *Theories of truth: A critical introduction.* Cambridge, MA: MIT Press.

Kittler, F. A. (1999). *Film, gramophone, typewriter.* Translated by G. Winthrop-Young and M. Wutz Stanford University Press: Wutz. Stanford, CA.

Kittross, J. M. & Gordon A. D. (2003). The academy and cyberspace ethics. *Journal of mass media ethics 18*(3/4), 286–307.

Kuhn, T. (1996). *The structure of scientific revolutions.* Chicago: University of Chicago Press.

Künne, W. (2003). *Conceptions of truth.* Oxford: Oxford University Press.

McLuhan, M. (1995). *Understanding media.* Cambridge, MA: MIT Press.

Merriam-Webster. (2006). *Merriam-webster's words of the year 2006.* http://www.merriam-webster.com/info/06words.htm

Mitchell, W. J. (1994). *The reconfigured eye: Visual truth in the post-photographic era.* Cambridge, MA: MIT Press.

Nesher, D. (2002). *On truth and the representation of reality.* New York: University Press of America.

Newman, A. (2002). *The correspondence theory of truth.* Cambridge: Cambridge University Press.

O'Connor, D. J. (1975). *The correspondence theory of truth.* London: Hutchingson University Library.

Orr, C. J. (1978). How shall we say: "reality is socially constructed through communication?" *Central states speech journal 29*, 263–274.

Papacharissi, Z. (2009). The virtual geographies of social networks: A comparative analysis of Facebook, LinkedIn and ASmallWorld. *New media & society 11*(1 & 2) 199–220.

Peirce, C. S. (1932). *The collected papers of Charles Sanders Peirce, vol. II, edited by C.* Hartshorne and P. Weiss. Cambridge, MA: Harvard University Press.

Plato. (1982). *Phaedrus.* Translated by H. N. Fowler. Cambridge, MA: Harvard University Press.

Plato. (1987). *Republic.* Translated by P. Shorey. Cambridge, MA: Harvard University Press.

Plato. (1990). *Phaedo.* Translated by H. N. Fowler. Cambridge, MA: Harvard University Press.

Postman, N. (2000). *Building a bridge to the 18th century.* New York: Vintage Books.

Putnam, H. (1995). *Pragmatism: An open question.* Oxford: Blackwell.

Ronell, A. (1989). *The telephone book: Technology, schizophrenia, electric speech.* Lincoln, NB: University of Nebraska Press.

Rorty, R. (1990). *Objectivity, relativism, and truth: Philosophical papers, vol. 1.* Cambridge: Cambridge University Press.

Sallis, J. (1986). *Being and logos: The way of the platonic dialogue.* Atlantic Highlands, NJ: Humanities Press International.

Scheler, M. (1960). *Die wissenformen und die gesellschaft.* Francke: Bern.

Schmitt, F. F. (1995). *Truth: A primer.* Boulder, CO: Westview Press.

Scott, R. L. (1967). On viewing rhetoric as epistemic. *Central states speech journal 18,* 9–17.

Smolen, L. (2006). *The trouble with physics: The rise of string theory, the fall of a science, and what comes next.* New York: Houghton Mifflin.

Stone, A. R. (1993). Will the real body please stand up? In *Cyberspace: First steps,* edited by Michael Benedikt. Cambridge, MA: MIT Press.

Stone, A. R. (1995). *The war of desire and technology at the close of the mechanical age.* Cambridge, MA: MIT Press.

Taylor, T. L. (2006). *Play between worlds: Exploring online game culture.* Cambridge, MA: MIT Press.

Tompkins, P. (2003). Truth, trust, and telepresence. *Journal of mass media ethics 18*(3/4), 194–212.

Van Gelder, L. (1985). The strange case of the electronic woman. *Ms.,* October, 94–95.

Wolf, G. (1996). Channeling McLuhan. *Wired 4*(1), http://www.wired.com/wired/archive/4.01/channeling_pr.html

Woit, P. (2006). *Not even wrong: The failure of string theory and the search for unity in physical law.* New York: Basic Books.

Žižek, S. (2002). *Welcome to the desert of the real.* London: Verso.

Žižek, S. (2003). *The puppet and the dwarf: The perverse core of Christianity.* Cambridge, MA: The MIT Press

Žižek, S. (2006). *The parallax view.* Cambridge, MA: The MIT Press.

Žižek, S. (2008a). *For they know not what they do.* London: Verso.

Žižek, S. (2008b). *In defense of lost causes.* London: Verson.

 Chapter 3

Methodological Challenges Posed by Emergent Nanotechnologies and Cultural Values

Barbara Herr Harthorn

Social research finds itself in an unprecedented position in the sphere of emerging nanotechnologies. Through funding of societal implications research by the National Nanotechnology Initiative (NNI) in the United States and, in particular, the Network for Nanotechnology in Society in the National Science Foundation, social researchers are able to conduct social, cultural, legal, and ethical research at a very early stage in the technological development process. These funds have also been allocated toward social research investigating the most effective methods to enhance public participation in the NNI. Researchers thus have an opportunity to provide the scientific and engineering communities with detailed research-based understandings of the societal context for their products-to-be, including public views of opportunities and threats, and for participatory involvement in the development process. However, societal awareness and familiarity with nanotechnologies is very low, so providing such contextual understanding in systematic and reliable ways poses a number of research challenges. This chapter will explore the methodological and participatory opportunities and challenges posed by this novel research context, drawing particularly on the author's own research experiences leading a research group within the National Science Foundation Center for Nanotechnology in Society at the University of California at Santa Barbara (CNS-UCSB), while also referencing other work at CNS-UCSB and in the developing nanotechnology-in-society research community. This research itself is emergent, so this analysis mirrors aspects of its unformed subject and is necessarily a work in progress.

Unlike other technologies discussed in this volume, nanotechnologies themselves are not directly altering social research practices the way geospatial, IT, and other technologies have done. These technologies are still too far upstream in many cases; they have not yet emerged from the lab into industrial and consumer realms, though they have the potential to do so. For example, nanoscale sensors will create possibilities for covert invasion of privacy far beyond those posed by current RFID (Radio-Frequency Identification) technology; human enhancement nanotechnologies are likely to provoke social disruption and conflict over distributive justice and access issues; and nanoscale biomedical devices will change the way clinical data are collected and disseminated, which will lead to confidentiality and many other patient care ethical issues. To date, however, the main challenges for social research on nanotechnologies arise from the upstream research endeavor itself, such as tasks of tracking and gauging the social response to social phenomena that are themselves invisible or emergent. Social researchers are studying a "technological revolution" (e.g., Anton, Silberglitt, & Schneider, 2001) that 70–90% of surveyed publics continue to have little or no awareness of and engaging diverse publics (which ones, where, in what social locations, etc.) in futeristic scenario-based, rather than experience-based, dialogue.

Mixed methods approaches become particularly important in such indeterminate technological development contexts where triangulation can provide better validation of findings and research is simply more exploratory of necessity. Mixed qualitative and quantitative research in particular allows movement between inductive, grounded theory approaches and deductive, hypothesis-driven work, and the nano research scape almost demands the combination of these approaches. This chapter traces how social science and humanities inquiry is being crafted to inform the development and course of these emergent nanotechnologies. This opportunity to influence the ongoing research and development of nanotechnologies requires a new kind of participatory research. It also provides the community of nanotechnological developers with a "social context of awareness" that takes into account the broader needs and goals of the wider society in its development and implementation process. In organizing research efforts to tackle these new challenges, social researchers are challenged to develop new modes of interdisciplinary collaboration in conducting research and in creating new societal dialogue around nanotechnology in the short and long term. In this chapter, I will address these issues primarily through the context of the research I lead within the CNS-UCSB while drawing secondarily on the more general experience of researchers in the CNS-UCSB, our sister CNS at Arizona State University, and the wider nanotechnology-in-society network of researchers in the United States and internationally.

Nanotechnologies as "Emergent" Technologies (Hesse-Biber & Leavy, 2008)

Before analyzing the intricacies of nanotechnology, we must first ask ourselves, "What are nanotechnologies and why are we charged with studying them? What is emergent about the technologies we are studying?" According to the U.S. National Nanotechnology Initiative, "Nanotechnology is the understanding and control of matter at dimensions between approximately 1 and 100 nanometers, where unique phenomena enable novel applications. Encompassing nanoscale science, engineering, and technology, nanotechnology involves imaging, measuring, modeling, and manipulating matter at this length scale." In quantitative terms, "a nanometer is one-billionth of a meter. A sheet of paper is about 100,000 nanometers thick; a single gold atom is about a third [of] a nanometer in diameter. Dimensions between approximately 1 and 100 nanometers are known as the nanoscale. Unusual physical, chemical, and biological properties can emerge in materials at the nanoscale level. These properties may differ in important ways from the properties of bulk materials and single atoms or molecules" (National Nanotechnology Initiative [NNI], a).

This definition of nanotechnology addresses the following elements: (1) the creation, synthesis, and fabrication of new materials rather than just the manipulation of molecules or atoms; (2) the materials in question fall within the 1–100 nanometer scale (a nanometer is 1 billionth of a meter) in at least one dimension, which means they are roughly the same size as molecules (i.e., smaller than cells; small enough to pass through the walls of cells); and (3) the materials synthesized at this scale display scale-dependent properties (physical, chemical, or optical) that can be exploited technologically and are distinct from the properties of the same materials in larger (bulk) forms.

According to the NNI's Applications and Products definition (NNI, b), "Nanotechnology is going to change the world and the way we live, creating new scientific applications that are smaller, faster, stronger, safer and more reliable." These new nanomaterials have the potential to become the building blocks for many new technologies across almost all industries. Once nanomaterials are incorporated into such new technologies, they are often discussed as "nano-enabled" devices and technologies. They have or will have the characteristics of being very strong and light, increasing their usefulness in construction materials, airplanes, protective body armor, sporting goods such as bicycles and tennis rackets, and biomaterials such as prosthetic limbs, joints, and tissue. They can also be formed into very thin films that have environmental sensing, cleaning, and protective capabilities, and they will enable the continued advancement of semiconductor capabilities to store more and more information, more cheaply, in smaller devices. Furthermore, nanoscale materials have the potential to increase exponentially the energy efficiencies of electronic devices and advance alternative energy technologies such as solar energy. Their medical applications are expected to allow far more sensitive targeted diagnosis and treatment at the cellular/molecular level, as well as remote patient care.

The fiscal year 2009 NNI budget in the United States was $1.67 billion, and total U.S. government investment since 2001 is just under $10 billion (President's Council of Advisors on Science and Technology [PCAST], 2008, p. 1; NNI n.d.[c]). Because of the breadth of potential applications, industry analysts have predicted that nanotechnologies will become a $10 trillion global industry (Lux Research, 2008). However, these estimates are contested by a number of researchers because they are simply projections based on extrapolations from the present with multiple debatable assumptions and unknown externalities. Nevertheless, it is clear that thus far nanotechnologies have ramped up quite quickly around the globe with likely significant future growth and expansion.

Dubbed by some to constitute "the next technological revolution," the form and direction taken by funding for nanotechnology research and development in the United States reflect the accumulated wisdom (and anxieties) of the U.S. Congress, which mandated public participation in the 2003 National Nanotechnology Research and Development Act that accompanied the authorization of the NNI. The original vision in Congress was for a $5 million per year "American Nanotechnology Preparedness Center" (Malakoff, 2003). In response to this mandate, the NSF took the lead on funding societal implications research and in 2004 requested proposals for a new Nanoscale Science and Engineering Center (NSEC) to be called the Center for Nanotechnology in Society. This single center would study the social, psychological, cultural, legal, and ethical implications of the new technologies, with the goal of enhancing public participation as an important theme. However, the NSF instead decided to split the award into two scaled down societal implications research centers (CNS-UCSB and CNS-ASU) in addition to funding projects at the University of South Carolina and Harvard. In addition, the NSF has funded more than 30 individual and collaborative research projects focused on societal dimensions of nanotechnology from 2003–8 (Zehr, 2008). Federal expenditures in the United States for social science research on SEIN (Social and Ethical Implications of Nanotechnology) are limited to about 2% of the NNI budget (Roco, 2008). At this writing, NSF stands alone among the 25 federal agencies that comprise the NNI in its commitment to social science societal implications research. Funding elsewhere in the world for SEIN research has been less cohesive and more modest in scope than in the United States.

Though the definition of nanotechnology above may sound precise and clear to the non-engineer, there is in fact a great deal of discussion among scientific, engineering, regulatory, and standards organizations about the exact definition of nanotechnology, its proper nomenclature, and the degree to which its many constituent elements constitute a unique class (Renn & Roco, 2006a, 2006b; Harthorn, Bryant, Satterfield, & Kandlikar, 2007). Initial discussions about nanotechnology in the societal realm in the years 2001–5 focused extensively on the degree of 'hype' in the promotion of these new technologies (Berube, 2006; Rip, 2006) and the dangers or scenarios of doom that some argued would attend their promulgation (Joy, 2000; Malakoff, 2003; ETC Group, 2006). The UK Royal Society issued an early cautionary report (2004) that focused on the potential health and safety hazards of "unbound" nanoparticles in products already on the market such as sunscreens and cosmetics. Much of the social issues research in the United States and Europe has been launched in the past 5 years and is just beginning to reach fruition.

The question of emergence has garnered particular interest as an aspect of nanoscale science and engineering (NSE) innovations and the constellation of societal issues accompanying their development and dissemination. In general, historians of science, including those associated with the CNS-UCSB, take issue with many of the claims to novelty and emergence for nanotechnology (McCray, 2005; Johnson, 2008; Mody, in press), finding nanotechnological developments far more continuous than discontinuous with past scientific discovery practice and policies; they contest the classification of nanotechnology as a revolution. Collectively, they strongly favor a profile for nanotechnological scientific innovation as one of gradual, incremental change and innovation. On the societal side as well, they trace pre-NNI patterns of special interest group activity in support of nanotechnological innovation in the United States to the 1980s (Ingram-Waters & McCray, 2007) rather than just emerging in the past years since the 2000 NNI initiation. However, in the wider social research arena in the United States and the United Kingdom, where my work has been centered, emergence itself is indeed a significant issue directly connected to challenging methods issues on both theoretical and epistemological grounds.

Nanotechnologies are, in many cases, still on the drawing board or scientifically hypothetical. For example, the nanotechnology field of spintronics exploits the spin of electrons and may one day lead to significant advances in electronics speed and storage, but it remains for now primarily in the realm of theory (McCray, 2009). Though the scientific principles for the exploration and possible development of nanotechnologies are becoming increasingly well-established, years or even decades of laboratory research lie ahead before the full potential of these technologies will be realized. Even for those applications much further along in development, commercialization constitutes a future challenge. The NNI aims to produce these applications and products, such as new medical treatments, cheap forms of energy, water filtration membranes, sensors for pollution reduction and environmental mitigation, and improved materials and new products (NNI, b). However, as noted by many researchers, the products actually on the global market fail to reflect these ambitious aims. There are hundreds of finished products on the market that may incorporate nanomaterials in some way, though the exact number is very difficult to ascertain because of the lack of regulation and tracking. A Pew Charitable Trusts-funded project at the Woodrow Wilson Center for International Scholars in Washington DC identified over 1000 consumer products as of July 2010 that purported to use or be based on nanotechnologies. The products were found in many industries, such as health and fitness (including cosmetics), home and garden, electronics and computer, food and beverage, automotive, appliance, and childcare goods, as well as "cross cutting" categories for products that are multifunctional, such as coatings (PEN, 2010). There are undoubtedly hundreds (or thousands) of additional products that incorporate nanomaterials in them without identifying or marketing them as such (e.g., sunscreens and cosmetics, electronics devices, foods, building materials, etc). In spite of this, it is reasonable to claim that the technologies themselves are "emergent" in the sense that they are just beginning to emerge from laboratory and industry settings into the commercial marketplace, although this is a very uneven process and will continue to have a highly-staggered course across industries. The scale of *projected* market involvement of nanomaterials and nano-enabled commercial products dwarfs this modest leading edge.

Since the NNI's inception in the United States in 2000, the media have paid relatively modest attention to nanotechnology. Although CNS-UCSB researchers Weaver and Bimber (2008) document an overall increase in elite print media coverage from 2000 to 2007, their analysis of the media-framing of nanotechnology (Weaver, Lively, & Bimber, 2009) indicates a lack of coalescence of views or frames among the four frames they have identified and tracked. Researchers at Lehigh (Friedman and Egolf) and University of Wisconsin (Scheufele, Dunwoody, and Brossard) have also reported similar processes for the United States. Fundamentally, nanotechnology has yet to be seen by media outlets as highly newsworthy, and there is some evidence of recent falloff in coverage rather than continued escalation (Friedman & Egolf, 2005; Weaver & Bimber, 2008; Friedman & Egolf, 2007). Friedman and Egolf (2007) have provided comparative data about the coverage in the United Kingdom that shows a more dramatic drop in media coverage of nanotechnology in 2006–7, and they, like Bimber et al., have shown that a mere handful of U.S. journalists is covering nanotechnology in elite journals. Thus, nanotechnologies are limited as far as newsworthy appeal, with issues about whether and how to regulate them as one of the main forms of coverage (Weaver & Bimber, 2008). Uncertainty about issues of Environmental Health and Safety (EHS), risk and safety also figures into the diffuseness of coverage.

Directly connected to the low-level media coverage of nanotechnologies is public awareness of nanotechnologies in the United States and abroad (with the exception of Japan), which continues at a very low level. This is supported by an array of public surveys in the United States (Sims-Bainbridge, 2002; Lee, Scheufele, & Lewenstein, 2005; Cobb, 2005; Hart, 2006; Currall, King, Lane, Madera, & Turner, 2006; Macoubrie 2006; Priest, 2006; Hart, 2007; Scheufele et al., 2007; Kahan, Slovic, Braman, Gastil, & Cohen, 2007; Kahan et al., 2008; Kahan, Braman, Gastil, Slovik, & Cohen, 2009; Satterfield, Conti, Harthorn, & Pidgeon, 2009); Scheufele et al., 2009; in Canada (Einsiedel, 2005; Priest), in the United Kingdom (Royal Society, 2004), in Switzerland (Siegrist, Keller, Kastenholz, Frey, & Wiek, 2007; Siegrist, Straemfli, & Kastenholz, 2008), in the European Union (Gaskill, Eyke, Jackson & Veltri, 2005), and in Japan (Fujita, 2006), as well as by public participation research in the United States (Kleinman & Powell, 2005; Toumey, 2006; Hamlett, Cobb, & Guston, 2008; Pidgeon, Harthorn, Bryant, & Rogers-Hayden, 2009), the United Kingdom (Royal Society, 2004; Wilsdon & Willis, 2004; Kearnes et al. 2006; Pidgeon & Rogers-Hayden, 2007; Pidgeon et al.), and throughout the European Union (Burri & Belucci, 2008; Burri, 2009; Laurent, 2007).

There is some evidence that this condition of low awareness may be beginning to change (Priest, 2008; Satterfield, Kandlikar, Beaudrie, Conti, & Harthorn, 2009), but nanotechnology is arguably still barely emergent in the views of many publics around the world. A meta-analysis of public survey data with adequate data points found that across 22 surveys in the United States, Canada, Europe, and Japan from 2002 to 2009, 65% of respondents knew "just a little" (13.8%) or "nothing at all" (51.4%) about nanotechnology, showing that familiarity with nanotechnology remains low and may not be changing much over time (Satterfield et al. 2009). The same study found that people (in a ratio of 3:1) continue to think benefits will outweigh risks but, significantly, many (44.1%) remain unsure. Reported familiarity with nanotechnology positively correlated with higher perception of benefit outweighing risks, and other variables (gender, trust, science optimism, and worldviews) also were important in some studies. Thus, there is strong evidence that public knowledge is only beginning to be formed and that because both the form and shape of future views views are largely unknown, there is a high degree of uncertainty. In such conditions of low awareness, public opinion and benefit/risk perception are likely to be particularly labile or malleable, subject to framing effects and contextual features (Slovic, 2000; Pidgeon, Kasperson, & Slovic, 2003). This emergent context thus provides an unprecedented opportunity for both naturalistic and experimental research to study public (and expert) opinion, risk perception, and cultural meaning in-the-making.

Both the United States and the European Union have articulated the need for "responsible development" (NNI [d]; European Commision [EC], 2008) of nanotechnologies. In the United States, this is mandated in the 21st Century Nanotechnology Research and Development Act (2003; 2008 – pending), the authorization for the NNI, by means of societal implications research and public participation in it. Meanwhile, the European Union more particularly states an aim of "safe, sustainable, responsible and socially acceptable development and use of nanotechnologies" (EC, 2008). While the reporting on nanotechnology thus far has strongly emphasized likely benefits (for economic development), there has been an increase in the past several years of stated concerns by governments and special interest groups about the potential environmental, health, and safety (EHS) risks that may result from workplace, community, health, and environmental exposures to these new materials. The literature to date on the toxicological, ecological, and bioaccumulation risks of nanomaterials is in its infancy (see Ostrowski, Martin, Conti, Hurt, & Harthorn, 2009; Godwin et al., 2009).

For these reasons, my discussion of the research challenges posed by early stage or emergence as a phenomenon will focus on the public reception of nanotechnological development, although I certainly acknowledge the validity of the critique of nanotechnology novelty and "emergence" offered by some researchers, particularly on the scientific discovery side (Johnson, 2008).

What Types of Research Questions Lend Themselves to This Emergent Technology Inquiry?

Because the social phenomena of nanotechnology perception, reception, and behavior are still unformed or in-the-making, and because social science researchers have never before been involved in technology social assessment activities so early in the R and D process, many exciting questions about emergent social process and the social shaping of technologies have arisen.

From a public point of view, nanotechnologies are emerging almost exclusively through a process of social construction rather than via direct contact and experience as workers, industry neighbors, or other mechanisms. Experts are familiar with the term but display ambivalence about its meaning and validity (Harthorn et al., 2007). Indeed, our expert interviews and informal interactions at many Nanoscale Science and Engineering (NSE) meetings provide evidence that the more cynical among the NSE community regard nanotechnology as an entirely socially and politically constructed category, a rubric under which a number of disparate materials and technologies are aggregated for the strategic political purpose of generating new funding for materials research. The scale-based category of nanotechnology does not reflect the conceptual or disciplinary organization of knowledge by many scientists and engineers because many of them work across several scales simultaneously, because scale is just one of the dimensions of interest in the properties they study (e.g., surface area and reactivity may be more important than size per se, although they are a function of size), or because, for example, as chemists, their discipline has been working with molecules for a very long time, and the "newness" of nanoscale science and engineering (S&E) is hard for them to embrace. In our interviews with NSE experts, it has not been uncommon for respondents to indicate they would only answer the question, "Do you consider yourself to be a nanoscientist" affirmatively if they were applying for NSE grant funds, that is, to meet the funder's requirement. Social scientists and humanists recruited to study NSE processes for technological development are thus at some risk of creating the very object we are studying, of reifying a category that may have little inherent meaning outside the funding world. Two different kinds of problem result from this situation. On the one hand, science and engineering experts are likely to be susceptible to optimistic bias about potential hazards or negative outcomes of their work, so their self reports that minimize the "newness" of the materials support denial. On the other hand, to the extent that the NNI is an elaborate mechanism for reinvigorating U.S. science and technology development, and the primary funding motivation for Social and Ethical Implications of Nanotechnology (SEIN) research is to pave the way to public acceptance, SEIN researchers' positions call for a strong stance of reflexivity (cf., Hesse-Biber & Leckenby, 2004).

The attractions of gauging response to a category that has no inherent properties, only constructed ones, are considerable for social science researchers. In the risk perception research world, it is largely unprecedented to participate in a large social experiment that studies the way meanings and courses of action emerge in response to entirely new technological phenomena. Many research questions arise about the formation of opinion and perception, and the deployment of cultural knowledge and experience in these early encounters with new technologies. In many respects, these new nanotechnologies can be seen as projective devices, onto which different publics will map a constellation of personal and collective histories (of benefit or harm, security or vulnerability, health or illness). For example, in public deliberation research in the United States and the United Kingdom, we found that people used analogies to other technologies (e.g., biotech, nuclear, automobiles) and science fiction films and texts, and drew on nuanced cultural understandings about the value of science and technology to better citizens' lives, as they began to figure out what nanotechnologies for health and energy might mean to them. Furthermore, views about new nanotechnologies interact in complex ways with attitudes toward industries and governments, culturally nuanced issues of acceptability, and ideological and political beliefs. In another example from our deliberation workshops, participants in the United Kingdom voiced reservations not about the benefits of the technologies per se but rather about their government's trustworthiness to manage new technologies safely and wisely. Given the history of risk controversies in the United

Kingdom, this is not surprising. In subtle contrast, U.S. participants expressed more concern about corporations' ability and intent to act in the public's best interests. While these processes *may* be similar to those of all technologies, we (social scientists and humanists) have never before been invited to prospectively track these ideas and beliefs, as they are in the process of formation. The upstream participation of social researchers and, in the case of the two national centers, our capacity to disseminate research widely to different stakeholder groups may enable us to impact the views and behavior of both experts/elites (scientists, regulators, industry) and the media/NGO/publics. For example, our survey research provides evidence of specific scenarios likely to increase the public's distrust in industry and government, was presented to a U.S. congressional caucus in early 2009, and could create greater commitment on the part of government to pursue more precautionary regulatory approaches.

Regulatory issues also take shape in the context of emergent nanotechnologies. Lack of standardization and nomenclature, as well as uncertainty over whether these new materials pose distinct risks necessitate discussion about new regulatory apparatuses and processes (Kuzma, 2007; Kuzma, Romanchek, & Kokotovich, 2008; Bosso, 2010). Globalization of nanotech innovation and production along global value chains varies by industry (Gereffi & Kaplinsky, 2001; Appelbaum, Parker, Cao, & Gereffi, 2010). Transnational processes for innovation, commercialization, and (eventually) consumption have raised unprecedented issues for international regulatory decision making and action (Renn & Roco, 2006b). So far, cooperation between the U.S., European Commission (EC), International Organization for Standardization (ISO), and Organization for Economic Co-operation and Development (OECD) has been good, but as competition for market share increases, this may erode if strong agreements are not in place. The EU's more precautionary approach includes the implementation of REACH (Registration, Evaluation, Authorisation and restriction of Chemicals act) in 2007 (in force June 1) and 2008 (in operation June 1), which shifts responsibility for safe nanotech (and other chemical) developments to companies and away from government, but has drawn concern from science and industry (Bowman & Calster, 2007). One study from our group has projected various scenarios for the costs of testing nanomaterials that clearly demonstrate the fiscal impossibility of universal testing for this broad class of materials (Choi, Ramachandran, & Kandlikar, 2009). Promises for the benefits of nanotechnological development are based on unquestioned assumptions about equitable development that themselves provide novel contexts for research and analysis. For example, our deliberative workshops demonstrated that new technologies, particularly those that would be consumed and delivered at the individual level such as medical treatments or devices, arouse considerable concern about distributive justice in both the United States and the United Kingdom (Pidgeon et al., 2009).

More social and economic research is studying the nanotechnology innovation system. Tracking Research and Development (R&D) investment by public and private sectors is one standard method for assessing both activity and return on investment. This can be done in a relatively straightforward way for public sector investment in most countries. For example, in the United States, NNI per annum investment in nanotech R&D is in the public record and reported annually. On the other hand, private investment in new technologies in such a highly competitive market is very difficult, if not impossible, to trace. Well-traveled bibliometric and patent database methods are being applied worldwide to studying patents for nanomaterials, nano-intermediates, and nano-enabled devices, publications by NSE researchers, and citations of those publications as measures in turn of nanoscale innovation, productivity, and quality (Appelbaum & Parker, 2008; Porter, Youtie, Shapira, & Schoeneck, 2008; Shapira & Youtie, 2008; Youtie & Shapira, 2008; Youtie, Shapira & Porter, 2008). Methodological problems here center on boundaries and definitional issues as well as data access, data reliability, and cross-cultural/cross-national differences in practices such as patenting. The diversity of classes of material and nano-enabled products, combined with lack of standard nomenclature and expert disagreement about the boundaries of the domain(s) of nanomaterials and products, provide significant challenges to defining the universe and internal classes or subclasses for nanotechnology research and development. In the publication domain, there are at least a couple of hundred thousand English language publications that can be identified as related to nanotechnology, across a wide range of disciplines and fields. For example, researchers at the Georgia Institute of Technology connected to the CNS-ASU spent 2–3 years creating and validating a set of bibliometric search terms that could reliably generate a database that included all the main classes of nanotechnology (by expert consensus) and did not include reference to technologies that included the string "nano" but did not reference actual nanoscale science and engineering research (e.g., "iPod Nano") (see Porter et al., 2008). The emerging nanotoxicology literature is far smaller in comparison, with only 1,500–2,000 articles as of early 2008, and therefore far easier to search, but even here, the interdisciplinarity of the subject is demonstrated by the fact that those articles are distributed across several hundred different journals (Ostrowski et al., 2009). Somewhat similarly, CNS-UCSB researchers Appelbaum, Gereffi, Cao, Cannady, Parker, and Ridge have had to overcome significant difficulties in obtaining, decoding, and analyzing Chinese patent data on nanotech inventions, including taking into account a cultural ethos of patenting many things that will never be developed in order to demonstrate activity to state-run laboratories and not patenting the most important discoveries to avoid piracy (R. Appelbaum, personal communication, 2009). This team will use these patent data analyses primarily to form a basis for essential field research and interviews in China, demonstrating the importance of multiple methods approaches in this emerging technology field. Nanotechnologies have proven far more challenging for the application of even tried and true quantitative methods such as bibliometric and patent data analysis. These disruptive research effects are intensified by the ongoing uncertainty about nomenclature and standards, the broad class of materials and processes encompassed by the term "nanotech," the changing economic climate for cooperation, and the global and international context for nanotech research and development.

How Do the Emergent Properties of Nanotechnologies Affect the Application of Research Methods, and Kinds of Questions Asked, Qualitative Versus Quantitative?

The emergent properties of nanotechnologies are both driving and constraining research methods in a number of respects. First, we must consider the extent to which we accept the claims of novelty of technologies. There is a strong push to study their related upstream social phenomena *prospectively* rather than *retrospectively*, and this in turn drives choice of methods powerfully. For example, CNS-UCSB political scientist Bruce Bimber and his team began collecting baseline quantitative and qualitative media coverage data from the inception of the CNS-UCSB, in January 2006, onward, expecting that they would be able to capture emergent coverage as new developments took place, thereby tracking any rising concerns or societal implications (legal, social, political, economic) as possible sources of risk amplification messages that could increase public risk perception (Pidgeon et al., 2003). They set up an electronic system to track all English language print media coverage in elite (top ten) journals using both Google News and Lexis Nexis, counting the number of stories each day (even when it was the same story, picked up over a wire service, since we were interested in the extent of public exposure to nano-related news). They also conducted content analysis to understand what issues were driving peaks of increased coverage. This study found no net increase in news coverage over time, and coverage rising and falling episodically, primarily driven by regulatory or government action (Weaver & Bimber, 2008). To look more closely at what messages the media were transmitting to the public, they also conducted a rigorous analysis of frames in nanotech media coverage from 1998–2007, identifying four main frames: progress, regulation, conflict, and generic risk/benefit. Here too, they found no one frame dominating, although regulation and conflict frames emerged in 2004–6, reducing the progress frame that accompanied the announcement of the NNI in 2000 (Weaver et al., 2009). Journalists clearly do not (yet) find nanotechnology particularly newsworthy, so emergent nanotech media studies are in baseline tracking mode until some kind of risk event generates the kind of escalating interest and coverage common in amplification events or until changing media practices cause significant shifts in media-public interactions.

Similarly CNS-UCSB sociologists Rich Appelbaum and Gary Gereffi intended to analyze China's nanotechnology R&D using a global value chain analysis (Gereffi & Kaplinsky, 2001). However, they had to shift tactics because private sector nanotech industrial development, a more downstream site in product development, is not yet fully in place in China, and the main Chinese nanotech R&D effort is taking place instead upstream in government laboratories and government-owned industrial parks. They have pursued answers to their questions about commodity chains and flows in personnel, ideas, and goods using qualitative methods, making intensive field research visits in the main sites of science and technology research and development in China, Taiwan, and Hong Kong, conducting dozens of face-to-face interviews with scientists in state-funded laboratories, technology and business specialists, and governmental officials. They are interpolating these data with the quantitative innovation data cited above, and with network analysis of collaborations from the publications data (Lenoir & Gianella, 2009). Thus, emergent nanotech phenomena are pushing researchers into new approaches, new methods, multiple methods, and greater triangulation to validate findings. As technology pushes on the boundaries of traditional disciplines and their methods practices, researchers are pressed to apply old methods in new ways, seek new ways, in this case to track a distributed technology production system, through different governmental policy and development regimes. Standards of evidence change, judgments of expertise required to tackle specific problems are shifting, and interdisciplinary collaboration greatly increases the effectiveness of the group in contexts like the nano-enterprise.

Furthermore, although survey research is essential for capturing representative groups of the public, in the nanotech case this method is burdened with the difficult challenge of studying and assessing (and forecasting) public views that do not yet exist. This has driven the decision to apply mixed methods that feed into one another in highly productive ways, blending qualitative and quantitative approaches. We have approached this problem by combining initial inductive, qualitative work with subsequent quantitative study. In 2007, we conducted deliberative forums in the United States and the

United Kingdom about nanotechnologies for energy and for health, in which in-depth, semi-structured discussions about issues of trust, responsibility, and community versus individual benefits raised a number of key issues to the surface, for both the American and British participants. This study found that benefit perceptions were strong in both U.S. and UK participants, that cross-cultural/cross-national differences were relatively subtle, and that participants in both countries were far more positive about energy applications of nanotechnologies than health and enhancement technologies. Regarding the latter, a leading concern that emerged consistently in both countries was inequality or equity surrounding the distributional justice aspects of new health technologies, as well as issues of privacy and control of sensitive medical information (Pidgeon et al., 2009). These qualitative findings served to ground and directly shape the instrument we developed for a quantitative risk perception survey in 2008 and also have guided us through the interpretive aspects of survey data analysis as well (Satterfield, Conti, Harthorn, & Pidgeon, 2009; Satterfield, Kandlikar, Beaudrie, Conti, & Harthorn, 2009). Highly suggestive findings on gender and race interactions in the deliberative context from the 2007 workshops also helped us to define and secure new funding for more deliberative workshops in 2009 that use a between groups design to look more closely at issues of inequality by gender in shaping response to emerging nanotechnologies (Harthorn & Bryant, 2008; Satterfield, 2008; Harthorn, 2008; Harthorn, Bryant & Rogers 2009. Women and participants of color clearly feel inhibited in participation in, discourse about, and ownership of new technologies, in both the United States and the United Kingdom, and this has significant implications for achieving equitable public participation in new technologies. Gender in particular is a strong factor in producing greater perceptions of risk, and is implicated with other measures of vulnerability, lower trust, for nanotechnologies in our 2008 survey, and for other technologies (Flynn, Slovic, & Mertz, 1994; Gustafson, 1998; Satterfield, Mertz, & Slovic, 2004). In particular, the first qualitative study suggested gender- and ethnicity-based differences in the number of utterances made, who initiated speech, the length of time for given responses, and the kinds of examples drawn on for analogic reasoning about new technologies. The new study will help us to examine these more closely for gender, and we plan to pursue the race/ethnicity effects in a subsequent study. These findings also provide interpretive grasp of quantitative survey data.

In conjunction with the public perception survey findings, the 2009 deliberative workshops will direct us as we head toward the next phase of quantitative survey work. The opportunity to move dialectically back and forth between qualitative and quantitative methods, but still focus on a single substantive area of research is unusual but not unprecedented in social science research. This has occurred in some long-term projects that have successfully incorporated mixed methods (e.g., Rapp, 1999; Taylor, 1998). However, the larger team enabled by national center funding and the mixed methods interdisciplinary training of the three main principals of the research group (Harthorn, Pidgeon, and Satterfield) are far from usual. In addition to the methods mentioned here, the group also uses and plans to use a number of other methods, including experimental deliberation, longitudinal methods that capture attitude change (in progress in an industry survey), experimental Web survey, and others under discussion. Both the deliberative and survey methods cited above, however, are more difficult to implement and interpret in this emergent knowledge state, since people are particularly vulnerable to researcher framing effects in such low awareness states. For example, our experimental survey data indicate that benefit and risk frames can both have powerful effects, and Kahan et al. (2009) have shown how these can interact with cultural difference to produce unexpected effects. This raises important questions about what one is actually measuring and assessing. The standard approach to tracking public opinion through surveys would be to conduct annual surveys with comparable samples (or longitudinal surveys with a standing panel or longitudinal sample) and conduct a time series. Though both CNS centers proposed more surveys, the available funding has dictated a more intermittent approach, and the continued low awareness of the public is creating an excellent opportunity to move into more experimental methods. Our 2008 survey was experimental (a complex design, looking at framing effects, primacy effects, paired comparisons, and highly controlled vignettes with numerous subsamples), and future work in planning will further the study of emergent properties of attitude and perception, trying to clarify the relative effects of perceiver attributes, nano risk object characteristics, and other contextual variables. Both our CNS-UCSB research team and that led by Dan Kahan at Yale (Kahan et al., 2007, 2008, 2009) are exploring emergence itself in response to particular, controlled nanotechnological stimuli in surveys. In this instance, emergence is driving the direction and course the research is taking and offers the prospect of theoretical advancement of understanding risk perception.

This emphasis on prospective methods has particularly challenged historians involved in the nanotechnology research process. They have resolved this epistemological dilemma in a number of ways, tracing "hidden histories" of NSE discovery (McCray, 2007), tracing recent policy history of the NNI (McCray, 2005), and providing valuable contextual background for the more contemporary studies of such social phenomena as collective action. For example, McCray and Ingram-Waters have explored the movement from pro-space to pro-nano of a small group of technology activists in the 1980s (Ingram-Waters & McCray, 2007) that provides useful background for new work, in which we plan looking at social movements in response to nanotechnology (most of which are definitely not pro-nano). The earlier work shows how collective action can form to promote not just to protest new technological development, and how relatively small groups of activists can both reflect social and cultural values and exert influence on discovery science.

How Can Social Science and Humanities Inquiry Inform the Development and Course of Nanotechnology?

Social scientists and humanities scholars involved in nanotechnological societal implications research in the United States have a perhaps unprecedented opportunity to make a difference in the unfolding societal context for nanotechnologies. This is primarily because of the upstream funding of societal implications research, by the NSF in particular. Critical analysis is vital in this context, as social researchers find themselves poised, sometimes uncomfortably, between government and industry forces that seek public acceptance for their R&D enterprises and researcher desires to promote critical reflexivity in the technology assessment process and broaden the focus to the social justice issues accompanying technological development. Feminist perspectives on situated knowledge and feminist technology studies provide excellent resources here. This funding is the direct result of congressional mandate in authorizing legislation for the NNI through the 21st Century National Nanotechnology Research and Development Act (2003; 2008-pending). This act established the mandate for societal implications research and for integration of such research in Nanoscale Science and Engineering Centers (NSECs) in order to ensure "that advances in nanotechnology bring about improvements in quality of life for all Americans," and for "public input and outreach" to be integrated in the NNI. The still pending 2008 reauthorization bill further emphasizes public participation components. The funding of the two national centers, the societal implications NSECs at UCSB and ASU, created a basis for dialogue between social science and humanities researchers and the federal government. That process is currently taking place in regular ways through annual Principal Investigator meetings for all the researchers, funded and hosted by the NSF and attended by agency personnel from other lead NNI agencies. The CNS leaders are incorporated at major NSE meetings and events as well, and our education staff works directly with other NSEC and NSE education and outreach staff. More importantly, as the research matures, CNS researchers are increasingly making invited presentations or giving testimony to national policy makers at scientific research and industry meetings. In the case of my center, we have now partnered with another new NSF/EPA center concerned with the toxicological and ecological risks of nanomaterials (UC Center for Environmental Implications of Nanotechnology), and through that have additional avenues of direct interaction with and research dissemination to regulators and other elites. Having a place at the table is a great first step. Working effectively to make use of it for promotion of social justice is a challenge, and not all (or even most) members of the nanotechnology in society research community share principles of feminist reflexivity, situated knowledge, or the politics of difference that would create a more consistent approach to these. Thus, working across difference—disciplinary, epistemological, and methodological, in addition to social location such as race/class/gender/sexuality—is a core challenge to my work as a center director and research team leader.

NSF national centers have structured obligations for education and "outreach" that also create opportunities for public participation, engagement, and dialogue. Other dialogue takes place through educational and public outreach events and activities, and through the clearinghouse functions of the centers and the nanotechnology-in-society projects. There is some tension within the nano-enterprise about the purpose of such activities (science education versus societal implications education versus other kinds of pedagogies; public participation to what end?), and we are speaking across significantly different understandings of power, knowledge, social construction, as well as values of technoscientific progress. I depend on my anthropological training to navigate these different contexts on a daily basis. Diversity is a mandated component of NSF centers and research, yet many social and economic researchers are unaccustomed to intersectional approaches that are central in a feminist methodology.

This opportunity for reflexive and participatory involvement in the course of nanotechnology R&D puts social scientists in a new position vis-à-vis science and technology. This has, in some ways, paved the way to a new, three-way dialogue among scientists and engineers, social scientists, and the public. For example, both NSF centers engage in "science café" type public outreach events that bring together nanoscientists, their social science interlocutors, and the public to have conversations about nanotechnology in a societal context that are both scientifically informed and socially grounded.[1] Longer-term efforts to engage the American citizenry about technological development have been undertaken at the University of South Carolina (Toumey, 2006), and the University of Wisconsin (Kleinman & Powell, 2005). CNS-UCSB and CNS-ASU have pursued separate research on deliberative (UCSB) and consensus (ASU) forums that examine methods for engaging diverse groups of the public (Hamlett, Cobb, & Guston, 2008; Pidgeon et al., 2009). The national centers provide new opportunities for widespread dissemination of research findings to scientific, policymaking, industrial, and other types of communities, as well as to academic social science audiences.

Other opportunities to provide feedback for research to the NSE developers of technology include CNS-UCSB's program of co-training nanoscale Science and Engineering graduate students with social science along with humanities graduate students, undergraduates, and community college interns. Social scientists are also directly involved in the new NSF/EPA UC Center for Environmental Implications of Nanotechnology at UCLA/UCSB. Harthorn leads an Interdisciplinary Research Group and works with collaborators who include Satterfield, Pidgeon, and Kandlikar from the CNS working group and environmental sociologist Bill Freudenburg, UCSB. Their work here will be to provide translational analysis of research on public concerns and priorities to toxicologists and ecologists working to characterize the risks of nanomaterials. Social scientists are welcome contributors to this multidisciplinary effort and are positioned to take an active role in helping the UC CEIN shape emergent risk communication that may be called for when particular environmental and health risks are identified.

Of course, these new positions for social scientists as researchers and agents of change are not without tensions. Scientists and engineers are understandably not seeking to be "shaped" by social scientists, although many recognize that our expertise in this field is needed and may provide valuable assistance. The mandate for our participation in the unfolding NSE enterprise does not necessarily create a large space for us at the table, but gets us in the door. Though mechanisms for our participation are being invented on the ground rather than structured into the process, this presents opportunities from which a growing number of social science and humanities researchers are benefiting. To name some of the opportunities, a veritable new industry has arisen for "ethics" scholars as science and engineering (S&E) researchers in which biomedical researchers before them deal with bioethics and grapple with new mandates for "responsible" technological development far outside their own expertise or institutional cultural experiences. This has generated a cluster of activity, including the founding of a new journal, *NanoEthics*, other publications (e.g., Allhoff & Lin, 2008), a private sector organization seeking to meet these new demands (nanoethics.org), and an expanding role for philosophers at interdisciplinary research conferences and engineering centers.

Mechanisms for all of these social science and humanities scholars to inform the research and development process for nanotechnologies are not yet in place. What is emerging, however, particularly through NSF cross-directorate activities is the acknowledgement that although these contributions account for less than 2 percent of the NNI budget (Roco, 2008), they are nonetheless essential components of the process. However, to make those connections to the larger R&D and federal project, the burden rests largely on the nanotechnology in society research community. In the CNS-UCSB, the "integration" of social science with NSE happens through a variety of mechanisms: the coeducation and training of NSE and social science graduate students in societal dimensions research and scholarship, their joint mentoring of undergraduate and community college interns who are part of a nanoscience research experience program, and the inclusion of NSE scholars at all levels of CNS-UCSB organization, which includes the executive committee, the National Advisory Board, the individual research groups, seminars, lectures, gatherings, and public outreach events. Our sister center at CNS-ASU also works concertedly at such integration by conducting annual interviews with NSE collaborators, "embedding" graduate students in labs and assessing changes in practice, as well as holding many meetings and forums in which NSE are presented public values in a way that challenges their current thinking (Guston, 2008). "Integration" should be understood here to be a goal; sociologically it is clear these steps take place across strong boundaries, but the students in particular are seeing a way forward that creates interdisciplinary spaces for science students to think about the world in which the products of their work will take on life, and for social science students to understand the scientific enterprise in its ambivalence and complexity. Integration of these technologies for research into the teaching of research methods is emergent as well—that is, we are experimenting with different modes, assessing with care, and hope to be able to contribute to a multi-stakeholder discussion about these issues over time.

In the context of the CNS-UCSB (and CNS-ASU) such training of a new generation of students takes place in an explicitly multidisciplinary environment, because of the structural requirements established by the funder, as well as the desires of the participant researchers. The centers and the research groups within them constitute just such interdisciplinary spaces. However, these are significant investments, and they may work more effectively in institutions like UCSB that have notable institutional culture that encourages and promotes interdisciplinarity. This requires attitudinal openness to new approaches, a structural context that demands them for success, an institutional setting that enables interactions in such interdisciplinary spaces, and a funder that rewards and stimulates such moves. How they become institutionalized more broadly in the long run is not clear, however.

The Toolkit for Emerging Technology Studies: Mixed Methods for "Indeterminate" Technological Development

What has worked thus far for studying the unknown (i.e., emerging nanotechnologies)? Although ethnography has much to offer as a method for studying new, unknown cultural systems of nuanced meaning or signification, it is also incredibly labor intensive and, in this context, very difficult to practice, since naturally occurring interactions with emergent technologies are not yet happening in places and spaces that we can predict other than research laboratories. Industry laboratories are highly inaccessible to such outside participant-observers, but ethnography has been used effectively to study university-based NSE lab practices (e.g., Fisher, 2007; Johansson, 2008). Closely related work in cultural studies on "cultures of knowledge" in the nanotechnology in society context is also evident among some French researchers connected with Latour (e.g., Laurent, 2007). Laurent, for example, has studied the Grenoble science research center, the largest in France, and public deployment of organized resistance as they map over onto nanotechnology a well-formed response to biotechnology. So far, this work has yet to identify anything unique to nanotechnology or its knowledge systems.

Political economy approaches to the transnational study of the global flows of goods, workers, services, and ideas demand different methods, usually highly quantitative (e.g., Gereffi & Kaplinsky, 2001). However, as our CNS-UCSB research has shown, the upstream nature of nanotechnology R&D in China, a main site of our studies, has instead necessitated a mixed methods approach. In China, nanotechnology R&D is primarily undertaken in government research labs rather than private industry, requiring an entirely new approach (Appelbaum & Parker, 2008). This research combines quantitative studies of patents, publications, and citations with qualitative interviews with laboratory scientists and government officials. The emerging, upstream technology context is necessitating retooling of methods and mixed methods approaches.

Historical research is also finding an important niche in the emerging context of nano-technology, providing contextual information on the NNI and its policy history (McCray, 2005), along with detailed histories of the entwined course of instrumentation development with technological innovation (McCray, 2007; Choi & Mody, 2008) and studies of inter-institutional connections and communities (Mody, in press).

U.S. Nanotechnology R&D is accompanied by explicit rhetoric that it should benefit the American people (and taxpayers that are paying for it) and that public participation should be integrated into the NNI. There is thus a significant emphasis, perhaps greater than ever before, on the exploration and assessment of modes of democratic participation, citing a need for: "public input and outreach to be integrated into the Program by the convening of regular and ongoing public discussions, through mechanisms such as citizens' panels, consensus conferences, and educational events, as appropriate" (21st Century National Nanotechnology Research and Development Act). There are several research efforts directed at convening and assessing public consensus and/or deliberative forums in the United States (Kleinman & Powell, 2005; Toumey, 2006; Pidgeon et al., 2009) and abroad (Wilsdon & Willis, 2004; Pidgeon & Rogers-Hayden, 2007; Burri & Bellucci, 2008; Burri, 2009). These forums would be primarily qualitative, using focus group-like methods. There is a robust and growing body of research using phone and Web-survey methods to capture the views of a representative (or quasi-representative) population of Americans (e.g., Gaskell, Eyck, Jackson, & Veltri, 2005; Currall, 2007; Scheufele, 2008), EU citizens (Gaskell et al.), and Japanese (Fujita, 2006). Current risk perception research on nanotechnological risks and benefits is moving beyond cognitive decision risk toward experimental research on construction of preference (Lichtenstein & Slovic, 2006), decision pathway analysis (Gregory et al., 1997), and cultural knowledge and beliefs (Kahan et al., 2007, 2008, 2009). This work allows dynamic interaction between researcher and respondent in the survey context, following all the pathways to decision nodes closely, for example, in decision pathway analysis, and examining the choices people make and why they make them in experimentally controlled ways. This takes experimental research out of the lab into a more naturalistic but nonetheless controlled setting, and hence allows better examination of cultural values, personal preferences, different kinds of affect rather than just negative and positive valence, and a host of other issues.

What Is Driving Our Innovative Methods and Practices?

As discussed earlier, funding agency and government mandates are playing a very significant role in creating the conditions under which the biggest pieces of nanotechnology in society research are taking place. Innovation in practice derives primarily from the emergent technology context that accounts for continued low levels of public awareness and continued upstream (and midstream) production on the laboratory science side. The global context within which nanotech development is taking place also has significant effects on the research, methods, and cultural analysis. Critical analysis/feminist work particularly examines questions about who benefits from technological development, the fracture lines along which risk flows, whether the risk takers in the development process (e.g., industry workers, consumers, neighborhoods in which industry operates, society more generally in the case of downstream waste issues) are the same as the risk makers (e.g., government? industry?), and whether those who benefit do so at the cost of harm to others, as has been the case in so many past technological development scenarios.

Collaboration—Developing Effective Collaborations

National center funding creates both a mandate and an opportunity for collaborative research, education, and outreach. Effective collaboration is always a work in progress, in its simplest form measured by funder metrics of research productivity such as publications, presentations, reports, policy briefs, and others. At CNS-UCSB, this has taken the form of multidisciplinary, mixed methods intragroup diversity of personnel and methods. CNS-ASU researchers have tended to specialize in these teams, with integration taking place at the center-wide level. We have found that the diversity of social science disciplines is necessary to meet the demands of an ever-changing nanotechnology industry. Many disciplines are represented in this societal dimensions research industry, which include anthropology, communication, English, history, political science, and sociology. Many more disciplines are reflected in the overall diversity of our collaborators, grad students, and postdoctoral researchers. The mixing of methods within my group, for example, requires knowledge about qualitative (ethnography, deliberation, focus group, interviews, elite interviews) and quantitative (survey in many forms, bibliometric research) data analysis by the group leaders, the ability to move fairly smoothly between these for validation, and appropriate mining of material from one to use in the other. For example, the identification of themes such as issues of inequality or privacy concerns in deliberative forum is then introduced into the survey and then back into subsequent qualitative contexts for further exploration.

The social project of engagement, of course, requires a different measure of collaboration effectiveness, for example, as in participatory action research (PAR). In the nanotech case, the upstream context makes stakeholder identification problematic for participatory engagement—in some respects we risk constructing the stakeholders ourselves in order to engage them. Like other citizen activist movements, education and recruitment tactics are different sides to the same coin, yet it is not yet clear even what the issues are or should be, or who will be most affected, who will benefit, or how those processes should be engaged. In the upstream context, stakeholders tend to be in expert and regulatory contexts, and public groups have thus far shown relatively little interest in nanotech, even the labor groups which have been engaged in dialogue about workplace safety issues.

As indicated above, integration of our societal dimensions work with NSE is expected by the funding agency. However, the way to go about implementing this is far from explicit or straightforward. We have arrived at a fairly new model of developing a scientifically informed social science, which involves coeducation with a two-way dialogue, and the possibilities for coeducation via a three-way dialogue with the public. We do use formal evaluation measures to capture the effectiveness of these methods, but so far the best validation for me comes from the quality of face-to-face interaction in the multidisciplinary research groups and the CNS as a whole. The cumulative effect of that interaction is impressive and unusual.

Future Directions

CNS-UCSB is currently under review for renewal funding. The new work heads in exciting new directions, exploring histories of the nano-bio interface (an area likely to provoke strong public response in the emergent synthetic biology world), impediments to responsible, citizen-driven, scientist-engaged, nano solar technology development, culture, gender, and race in experimental risk perception work, and global technological development for social equity, to name a few of the main research areas. Methods seem to become more flexible over time rather than settling into fixed patterns, and documenting and examining that emergent process is part of our task ahead. It is too soon to call this a hybrid field of study or a new kind of social science, but it is drawing from a range of disciplines and methods, in new ways that offer the possibility of new kinds of understanding of systems of meaning and power.

The critical issues of ethics in nanotechnology R&D, I would argue, are better addressed within a framework of cultural values. The nano-enterprise is constructed within a set of assumptions that embrace modernity, technological optimism, and progress narratives; reinforce masculinist assumptions about technology and society and who will benefit; and contradict scientists' own goals of contributing to the social betterment of society. Social scientists' critical engagement of both nanoscientists and the public provides a context for feminist advocacy, for examining fundamental issues of who benefits and who is harmed from technological developments that are often systematically obscured or veiled in the development process.

Conclusions

In sum, the social study of the nanotechnology "revolution" is providing a novel research context for studying emergent social phenomena and societal dimensions of upstream science, and for considering new possibilities for public participation in science and technology development. Whether and how nanotechnology is "new" is one of the constant threads of work funded through the NSF's Societal Dimensions of Nanotechnology program. Emergent phenomena and the upstream context do seem to be pressing us into new modes of research—new combinations of old methods, new approaches to old problems, and experimental work that can lead in unexpected and exciting directions. Not all of these will be successful, and failed research experiments may tell us more than the successes.

What is incontestably new in the nanotechnology social research enterprise is that social scientists and humanists are invited in by science and engineering (and funded) early in the development process to try to work together, however clumsily, in forging a new set of relationships and creating the imagined possibility of a new model of progress. This idea of progress should reflect both engineers' visions of technologies that can make a real difference in the world and social scientists' ideas of the proper indices of sustainable progress, such as equitable development, and the dedication of R&D effort toward solving the fixable problems of the world's poor. This cannot be a naïve model that ignores issues of power, risks of cooptation, and the embodiment of suffering, but it is a wonderful opportunity to attempt to put participatory research, social justice aims, and the power of experiential knowledge to work for the greater good. If small incremental change can make a difference, then the everyday work we are doing, with students from both sides of the science/society divide, in conducting rigorous substantive research, can work to convey what we learn to those in positions to make change, whether they are policymakers or citizens.

Acknowledgements

This paper is based on work supported by the National Science Foundation through cooperative agreement # SES 0531184 and grant # SES 0824042 at the Center for Nanotechnology in Society at the University of California at Santa Barbara (CNS-UCSB). This material is also based upon work supported by the National Science Foundation and the Environmental Protection Agency under Cooperative Agreement # EF 0830117. Any opinions, findings, and conclusions or recommendations expressed in this material are those of the author and do not necessarily reflect the views of the National Science Foundation or the Environmental Protection Agency. This work has not been subjected to EPA review and no official endorsement should be inferred.

The author acknowledges the many contributions of CNS-UCSB working group coleaders Nick Pidgeon (Cardiff University, Wales, UK) and Terre Satterfield (University of British Columbia), as well as collaborators Karl Bryant (SUNY New Paltz), Joseph Conti (American Bar Foundation), Adam Corner (Cardiff University, Wales, UK), Hillary Haldane (Quinnipiac University), Milind Kandlikar (UBC), Jennifer Rogers (UCSB), Tee Rogers-Hayden (University of East Anglia, UK), CNS-UCSB graduate research fellows Indy Hurt, Tyronne Martin, Alexis Ostrowski, and Joseph Summers, and UBC doctoral student Christian Beaudrie. The author also gratefully acknowledges the many helpful comments on this manuscript by editor Sharlene N. Hesse-Biber.

Note

1. Other venues where such informal engagement activities are taking place include the University of Wisconsin (Kleinman and Powell, 2005), Cornell University, and many sites of the Nanoscale Informal Science Education program (NISEnet.org).

References

Allhoff, F., & Lin, P. (Eds.). (2008). *Nanotechnology and society: Current and emerging ethical issues.* New York: Springer.

Appelbaum, R., & Parker, R. R. (2008). China's bid to be a global nanotech leader: Advancing nanotechnology through state-led programs and international collaborations. *Science and Public Policy*, 35(5), June: 319–334.

Appelbaum, R., Parker, R., Cao, C., & Gereffi, G. (2010). China's (not so hidden) developmental state: Becoming a leading nanotechnology industry in the 21st Century. In Block, F., & Keller, M., (Eds.). *State of innovation: U.S. federal technology policies, 1969–2008*. Kent, WA: Paradigm Press.

Anton, P., Silberglitt, R., & Schneider, J. (2001). *The global technology revolution: Bio/nano/ materials trends and their synergies with information technology by 2015*. Monograph/Report 1307-NIC. Santa Monica: Rand Corporation. Downloadable from: http://www.rand.org/pubs/ monograph_reports/MR1307/index.html

Berube, D. (2006). *Nano-hype*. Amherst, NY: Prometheus Books.

Bosso, C., (Ed.). (2010). *Regulatory challenges of nanotechnology*. Washington DC: Resources for the Future (RFF) Press. (Forthcoming, September.)

Bowman, D. & van Calster, G. (2007). Does REACH go too far? *Nature Nanotechnology, 2*, 525–526.

Burri, R. V. (2009). Coping with uncertainty: Assessing nanotechnologies in a citizen panel in Switzerland. Public Understanding of Science 18, 4, 498–511.

Burri, R. V. & Bellucci, S. (2008). Public perception of nanotechnology. *Journal of Nanoparticle Research, 10*, 387–391.

Choi, H. & Mody, C. (2008). The long history of molecular electronics: Microelectronics origins of nanotechnology. *Social Studies of Science, 39*(1), 11–50.

Choi, J-Y., Ramachandran,G. & Kandlikar, M. (2009). The impact of toxicity testing costs on nanomaterial regulation. *Environmental Science and Technology, 43*(9), 3030–3034.

Cobb, M. D. (2005). Framing effects on public opinion about nanotechnology. *Science Communication, 27*(2), 221–239.

Currall, S. C. (2009). Nanotechnology and society: New insights into public perceptions. *Nature Nanotechnology, 4*, 79–90.

Currall, S. C., King, E. B., Lane, N., Madera, J., & Turner, S. (2006). What drives public acceptance of nanotechnology? *Nature Nanotechnology, 1*, 153–155.

Einsiedel, E. (2005). In the public eye: The early landscape of nanotechnology among Canadian and U.S. publics. *AZojono*, online publication December 30. http://www.azonano.com/Details. asp?ArticleID=1468

ETC Group. (2006). Nanotech product recall underscores need for nanotech moratorium: Is the magic gone? April, 7. Downloadable from: http://www.etcgroup.org/en/issues/nanotechnology.html

European Commission (Hullmann, A.). (2008). European activities in the field of ethical, legal and social aspects (ELSA) and governance of nanotechnology. European Commission, DG Research Unit *Nano and Converging Sciences and Technology*, Version October 1, downloaded on January 28 from: http://ims.ukro.ac.uk/NR/rdonlyres/1EC78913–9314–4CC1-A264- DE13D4F9BA02/6354/081014_nano_societal_dimension_report.pdf

Fisher, E. (2007). Ethnographic invention: Probing the capacity of laboratory decisions. *NanoEthics, 1*(2), 155–165.

Flynn, J., Slovic, P., & Mertz, C. K. (1994). Gender, race, and perception of environmental health risks. *Risk Analysis, 14*(6), 1101–1108.

Friedman, S., & Egolf, B. P. (2005). Nanotechnology: Risks and the media. *IEEE Technology and Society Magazine, Winter*, 5–11.

Friedman, S. & Egolf, B. (2007). Changing patterns of mass media coverage of nanotechnology risks. Presentation by Friedman, S. M. Woodrow Wilson International Center for Scholars, Project on Emerging Nanotechnologies, December 18. Washington, DC. Accessible from: http://www.lehigh.edu/smf6/nanotechnology_research.html

Fujita, Y. (2006). Perception of nanotechnology among general public in Japan. *Asia Pacific Nanotech Weekly, 4*, article #6:1–2. Available at: www.nanoworld.jp/apnw/articles/library4/ pdf/4–6.pdf

Gaskell, G., Eyck, T. T., Jackson, J., & Veltri, G. (2005). Imagining nanotechnology: Cultural support for technological innovation in Europe and the United States. *Public Understanding of Science, 14*, 81–90.

Gereffi, G. & Kaplinsky, R. (Eds.). (2001). *The value of value chains: Spreading the gains from globalisation.* Special issue of the *IDS Bulletin, 32*(3), July. Brighton, UK: Institute of Development Studies at the University of Sussex.

Godwin, H., Chopra, K., Bradley, K., Cohen, Y., Harthorn, B., Hoek, E., et al. (2009). The University of California Center for the Environmental Implications of Nanotechnology. *Environmental Science and Technology, 43*(17): 6453–6457.

Gregory, R., Flynn, J., Johnson, S. M., Satterfield, T.A., Slovic,. P., & Wagner, R. (1997). Decision-pathway surveys: A tool for resource managers. *Land Economics, 73*(2), 240–254.

Gustafson, P. E. (1998). Gender differences in risk perception: Theoretical and methodological perspectives. *Risk Analysis, 18*(6), 805–811.

Guston, D. (2008). Capacity for upstream shaping of nanoscience and nanotechology to reach societal goals. Presentation in panel, *Societal dimensions of nanotechnology PI meeting.* Arlington, VA: NSF. July 28–29.

Hamlett, P., Cobb, M., & Guston, D. (2008). *National citizens' technology forum report: Nanotechnologies and human enhancement.* CNS-ASU Report #R08–0002. Tempe, AZ: Center for Nanotechnology in Society at ASU. http://cns.asu.edu/files/ NCTFSummaryReportFinalFormat08.pdf

Hart, P. D. Research Associates, Inc. (2006). *Report findings.* (September 19) Available at http:// www.nanotechproject.org/file_download/files/HartReport.pdf.

Hart, P. D. Research Associates, Inc. (2007). http://www.nanotechproject.org/news/archive/ poll_reveals_public_awareness_nanotech/

Harthorn, B. H., Bryant, K., Satterfield, T., & Kandlikar, M. (2007). Nano expert attenuation in the age of upstreaming. Paper presented at the Society for the Social Study of Science (4S), October 11. Montreal.

Harthorn, B. H. (with Bryant, K., & Rogers, J.) (2008). Deliberating nanotechnologies in the US: Gendered beliefs about benefits and risks as factors in emerging public perception and participation. NSF SES-0824042, Harthorn: Principal Investigator, 2008–2010.

Harthorn, B. H., & Bryant, K. (2008). The "white male effect" and gendered risk beliefs about emerging nanotechnologies in the US. Paper presented in the session on New Technologies, Gendered Meanings, and Social Inequalities, October 20. San Francisco: American Anthropological Association annual meetings.

Harthorn, B. H. Bryant K., & Rogers J. (2009). Gendered risk beliefs about emerging nanotechnologies in the US. *Univ of Washington Center for WorkforceDevelopment;* on-line publication posted at http://depts.washington.edu/ntethics/symposium/index.shtml.

Hesse-Biber, S. N., & Leckenby, D. (2004). How feminists practice social research. In Hesse-Biber, S. N., & Yaiser, M. L. (Eds.), *Feminist perspectives on social research,* (pp. 209–226). New York: Oxford University Press.

Hesse-Biber, S. N., & Leavy, P. (Eds.). (2008). *Handbook of emergent methods.* New York: Guilford Press.

Ingram-Waters, M., & McCray, W. P. (2007). From spaceflight to foresight: Exploring the social movement spillover between space and nano. Paper presented at the Society for the Social Study of Science (4S), October 11. Montreal.

Johansson, M. (2008). *Next to nothing: A study of nanoscientists and their cosmology at a Swedish research laboratory.* Gothenburg, Sweden: University of Gothenburg.

Johnson, A. (2008). History and the future of emerging technologies. Paper presented in panel on Anticipation: Futures of Emerging Technologies, Gordon Research Conference on Science and Technology Policy, August 20. Montana: Big Sky.

Joy, W. (2000). Why the future doesn't need us. Wired 8.04 (April). Downloadable from: http://www.wired.com/wired/archive/8.04/joy_pr.html

Kahan, D. M., Slovic, P., Braman, D., Gastil, J., & Cohen, G. (2007). Affect, values, and nanotechnology risk perceptions: An experimental investigation. (March 7). *GWU Legal Studies Research Paper* No. 261 Available at SSRN: http://ssrn.com/abstract=968652.

Kahan, D. M., Slovic, P., Braman, D., Gastil, J., Cohen, G., & Kysar, D. (2008). Biased assimiliation, polarization, and cultural credibility: An experimental study of nanotechnology risk perceptions. PEN Research Brief No. 3, February. Available at: http://www.pewtrusts.org/our_work_report_detail.aspx?id=34882

Kahan, D., Braman, D., Gastil, J., Slovic, P., & Cohen, G. (2009). Cultural cognition of the risks and benefits of nanotechnology. *Nature Nanotechnology*, *4*, 87–90.

Kearnes, M., Macnaughten, P. P., & Wilsdon, J. (2006). *Governing at the nanoscale: People, policies and emerging technologies.* London: Demos.

Kleinman, D., & Powell, M. (2005). *Report of the Madison area citizen consensus conference on nanotechnology.* http://www.nanocafes.org/files/consensus_conference_report.pdf

Kuzma, J. (2007). Moving forward responsibly: Oversight for the nanotechnology-biology interface. *Journal of Nanoparticle Research*, *9*, 165–182.

Kuzma, J., Romanchek, J., & Kokotovich, A. (2008). Upstream oversight assessment for agrifood nanotechnology. *Risk Analysis*, *28*(4), 1081–1098.

Laurent, Brice. 2007. Diverging convergences: Competing meaning of nanotechnology and converging technologies in a local context. *Innovation: The European Journal of Social Science Research*, *20*, 343–357.

Lee, C-J., Scheufele, D., & Lewenstein, B. (2005). Public attitudes toward emerging technologies. *Science Communication*, *27*(2), 240–267.

Lenoir, T., & Gianella, E. (2009). Technological platforms and the layers of patent data. In Giannella, E., Biagioli, M., Jaszi, P., & Woodmansee, M. (Eds.), *Con/texts of invention: Creative production in legal and cultural perspective*, Chicago: University of Chicago Press.

Lichtenstein, S. & Slovic, P. (Eds.). (2006). *The construction of preference.* New York: Cambridge University Press.

Lux Research. (2008). *The nanotech report* (5th ed). New York: Lux Research.

Macoubrie, J. (2006). Nanotechnology: public concerns, reasoning and trust in government. *Public Understanding of Science*, *15*, 221–241.

Malakoff, D. (2003). Congress wants studies of nanotech's "dark side." *Science*, *301*(July 4), 27.

McCray, W. P. (2005). Will small be beautiful? Making policies for our nanotech future. *History and Technology*, *21*(2), 177–203.

McCray, W. P. (2007). MBE deserves a place in the history books. *Nature Nanotechnology*, *2*(5), 2–4.

McCray, W. P. (2009). From lab to iPod: A story of discovery and commercialization in the post-cold war era. *Technology and Culture*, *50*(1), 58–81.

Mody, C. (In press). Why history matters in understanding the social issues of nanotechnology and other converging technologies. *NanoEthics*.

NanoEthics. http://www.springer.com/philosophy/ethics/journal/11569

National Nanotechnology Initiative (NNI), (n.d.[a]) What is nanotechnology? Downloaded January 29, from: http://www.nano.gov/html/facts/whatIsNano.html

National Nanotechnology Initiative (NNI), (n.d.[b]) Applications and products. Downloaded January 29, from: http://www.nano.gov/html/facts/nanoapplicationsandproducts.html

National Nanotechnology Initiative (NNI). (n.d.[c]). NNI Investments by Agency & PCA FY 2001–2010. Downloaded Aug 5, 2010 from http://nano.gov/.

National Nanotechnology Initiative (NNI), n.d. [d]. Goals of the NNI, About the NNI-Home. Downloaded Aug. 5 2010 from http://nano.gov/.

Nature Nanotechnology, Editorial. (2009). Getting to know the public. *4*, 71.

Ostrowski, A., Martin, T., Conti, J., Hurt, I., & Harthorn, B. H. (2009). Nanotoxicology: Characterizing the scientific literature, 2000–2007. *Journal of Nanoparticle Research*, *11*, 251–257.

Pidgeon, N. F., Kasperson, R. E., & Slovic, P. (Eds.). (2003). *The social amplification of risk*. Cambridge, MA: Cambridge University Press.

Pidgeon, N. F., & Rogers-Hayden, T. (2007). Opening up nanotechnology dialogue with the publics: Risk communication or "upstream engagement"? *Health, Risk and Society*, *9*, 191–210.

Pidgeon, N. F., Harthorn, B. H., Bryant, K., & Rogers-Hayden, T. (2009). Deliberating the risks of nanotechnologies for energy and health applications in the United States and United Kingdom. *Nature Nanotechnology*, *4*(2), 95–98.

Porter, A. L., Youtie, J., Shapira, P., & Schoeneck, D. (2008). Refining search terms for nanotechnology. *Journal of Nanoparticle Research*, *10*(5), 715–728.

President's Council of Advisors on Science and Technology (PCAST). (2008). The national nanotechnology initiative: Second assessment and recommendations of the national nanotechnology advisory panel. April 7. Available for download at: http://www.ostp.gov/galleries/PCAST/PCAST_NNAP_NNI_Assessment_2008.pdf

Priest, S. (2006). The North American opinion climate for nanotechnology and its products: Opportunities and challenges. *Journal of Nanoparticle Research*, *8*, 563–568.

Priest, S. (2008). Media representations of nanotechnology. Presentation in Societal Dimensions of Nanotechnology PI meeting. Arlington VA: NSF. July 28–29.

Project on Emerging Nanotechnologies (PEN). (2010). Consumer product inventory, http://www.nanotechproject.org/inventories/consumer/analysis_draft/. Download July 28.

Rapp, R. (1999). How methodology bleeds into daily life. In *Testing women, testing the fetus: The social impact of amniocentesis in America* (pp. 1–22). New York: Routledge.

Renn, O., & Roco, M. (2006a). *IRGC (International Risk Governance Council): Nanotechnology— Risk Governance*. White Paper No. 2, annexes by Roco, M., & Litten, E. Geneva, IRGC.

Renn, O., & Roco, M. (2006b). Nanotechnology and the need for risk governance. *Journal of Nanoparticle Research*, *8*(2–3), 23–45.

Rip, A. (2006). Folk theories of nanotechnologists. *Science as Culture*, *15*(4), 349–365.

Roco, M. (2008). Historical context for nanotechnology. Presentation in panel at Societal Dimensions of Nanotechnology PI meeting, July 28. Arlington, VA: NSF.

Satterfield, T. A. (2008). Reflections across a few studies of race, gender, and risk. Paper presented in session on New Technologies, Gendered Meanings, and Social Inequalities, November 20. San Francisco: American Anthropological Association meetings.

Satterfield, T. A., Mertz, C. K., & Slovic, P. (2004). Discrimination, vulnerability, and justice in the face of risk. *Risk Analysis*, *24*(1), 115–129.

Satterfield, T. A., Kandlikar, M., Beaudrie, C., Conti, J., & Harthorn, B. H. (2009). Anticipating the perceived risk of nanotechnologies. *Nature Nanotechnology* 4, 752–758.

Satterfield, T. A., Conti, J., Harthorn, B. H., & Pidgeon, N. (2009). Malleability, vulnerability and stigma in judgments about nanotechnology. Poster presented at CNS-UCSB Research Summit, January 19–20.

Scheufele, D. A., Corley, E. A., Shih, T., Dalrymple, K. E., & Ho, S. S. (2009). Religious beliefs and public attitudes toward nanotechnology in Europe and the United States. *Nature Nanotechnology*, *4*, 91–94.

Scheufele, D., Corley, E., Dunwoody, S., Shih, T., Hillback, E., & Guston, D. (2007). Scientists worry about some risks more than the public. *Nature Nanotechnology*, *2*(12), 732–734.

Shapira, P., & Youtie, J. (2008). Emergence of nanodistricts in the United States: Path dependence or new opportunities? *Economic Development Quarterly*, *22*(3).

Siegrist, M., Keller, C., Kastenholz, H., Frey, S., & Wiek, A. (2007). Laypeople's and experts' perception of nanotechnology hazards. *Risk Analysis*, *27*, 59–69.

Siegrist, M., Staempfli, N., & Kastenholz, H. (2008). Perceived risks and perceived benefits of different nanotechnology foods and nanotechnology food packaging. *Appetite*, *51*(2), 283–290.

Sims-Bainbridge, W. (2002). Public attitudes towards nanotechnology. *Journal of Nanoparticle Research*, *4*, 561–570.

Slovic, P. (2000). *The perception of risk*. London: Earthscan.

Taylor, V. (1998). Feminist methodology in social movements research. *Qualitative Sociology*, *21*(4), 357–379.

Toumey, C. (2006). Science and democracy. *Nature Nanotechnology*, *1*, 6–7.

Weaver, D., & Bimber, B. (2008). Finding news stories: A comparison of searches using LexisNexis and Google News. *Journalism and Mass Communication Quarterly*, *83*(3), 515–530.

Weaver, D., Lively, E., & Bimber, B. (2009). Searching for a frame: Media tell the story of technological progress, risk, and regulation in the case of nanotechnology. *Science Communication*. 31(2), 139–166.

Wilsdon, J., & Willis, R. (2004). *See through science: Why public engagement needs to move upstream*, September 1. London: Demos.

Youtie, J., and Shapira, P. (2008). Mapping the nanotechnology enterprise: A multi-indicator analysis of emerging nanodistricts in the US South. *Journal of Technology Transfer*, *33*(2), 209–223.

Youtie, J., Shapira, P., & Porter, A. (2008). National nanotechnology publications and citations. *Journal of Nanoparticle Research*, *10*(6), 981–986.

Zehr, S. (2008). Overview of the NSF grantees meeting on social dimensions of nanotechnology. NSF NSE Grantees Conference, NSEC Principal Investigators meeting, December 5. Arlington, VA: National Science Foundation.

Chapter 4

"Under my Skin": The Ethics of Ambient Computing for Personal Health Monitoring

Göran Collste

Introduction

If anything can be said to characterize the present age, it is constant change. One of the main impetuses for change is technology. We continuously find ourselves in new worlds that offer us new possibilities but also place new demands on us. However, are we just puppets on the technologically driven strings? Are there any ways for us to ethically assess, control, and perhaps even shape the emerging technologies? In this chapter, these questions are discussed in the context of a specific, emerging, and revolutionary technology: ambient computing for personal health monitoring. A synthesis of information and communication technologies and monitoring devices will create a new networked home environment. According to the arbiters of the new technology, this advance will transform health care and move medicine from the hospital to the home.

The chapter starts with the general problem of assessing emergent technologies from an ethical point of view. Then an overview of ambient computing and personal health monitoring is provided. In the case of personal health-care monitoring and ambient computing, there are a number of possible benefits, such as providing rapid response in case of emergency so that patients are not tied to hospitals and may stay longer in their homes. This method of monitoring potentially also allows underprivileged regions to have access to medical expertise. Still, the new medical landscape also raises a number of ethical questions. Will the emerging technologies pose a threat to patient privacy, personal autonomy, the relation between doctor and patient, and perhaps even to personal identity? In the third part of the chapter the possibility that these important values will be threatened by ambient computing for personal health monitoring is explored.

The ethical questions also draw attention to the conditions for ethical assessment of technology. Though technology might be possible to assess and influence at an early stage of development, the consequences are still uncertain at that time. At a later stage of development, the consequences are better known, including the non-intended and unpredictable consequences. However, the technology is set and more difficult to influence.

In the final part, the question of ethical technology assessment is discussed, as well as the possibilities of interactive technology assessment and value-integrated technology design.

Social Constructivism and Assessment of Emergent Technologies

Different methods for ethical assessment of technology have been developed in recent years (Reuzel, van der Wilt, ten Have, & de Vries Robb, 2001; Schot, 2001). Normally the objects for assessment are existing technologies, and the assessment focuses on, for example, their social or environmental impacts. Is it really possible to ethically assess emergent technologies when the consequences still are uncertain and there are different possible outcomes. The problem of predicting technological development is formulated by O'Hear in the following way:

> If we could predict tomorrow's technology to any degree of accuracy, we would be able to predict how it would work. But if we knew today how it would work, we would be able to develop it now. It would be today's technology.... So if technological developments are, in their nature, unpredictable, then there is a very clear sense in which the future will be radically unlike what anyone can foresee now with any degree of certainty of justification. (O'Hear, 1999, p. 104).

As emphasized by social constructivism, technology is emerging in interrelation with the social environment. New technology shapes but is also shaped by the social system. Horner argues: "We always have before us the reality of choice in the sense that we could do or have done otherwise" (Horner, 2005, p. 226).

There are different lessons learned by the theory of social constructivism. The theory is a reaction against deterministic views of technology. According to technological determinism, the development of technology is autonomous and set. We can take the production of a computer and a refrigerator as examples. At first, there is a demand to do something, that is, processing information, or cooling food down. The new technologies or technical artifacts, in this case a computer and a refrigerator, are produced in order to meet the demands. At the end of the construction process, the final artifacts, that is, the computer and the refrigerator, appear as the only possible technical solutions. They give the impression that there was only one way to technically construct them. As Andrew Feenberg expresses this: "Looking back from the later standpoint, the artifact appears purely technical, even inevitable. This is the source of the deterministic illusion" (Feenberg, 1999, p. 11).

In contrast to technological determinism, social constructivists insist that new technology is the result of social interests, forces, and choices. The theory has both descriptive and constructive implications. It informs us that technologies are not neutral, but instead serve the interests of some institutions and social groups. However, the insights may also have constructive and normative implications. If we are aware of the fact that a technology is not set but may be shaped according to our needs and values, technological development becomes an ethical challenge. The process of technological construction is intimately connected to questions of what constitutes a good life and which values we want to realize.

Let me illustrate the difference with two examples of recently emerged technologies. The first example relates to the introduction of expert systems in health care. New computer assisted expert systems have been introduced while decision making in health care is becoming more complicated. An example of this reality is expert systems for internal medicine. One of the most famous was INTERNIST-1. This program was developed in the 1980s and assisted doctors in making diagnoses. A doctor facing a diagnostic problem could transfer the relevant patient information to the system. However, after some years of using the system, the designers believed that it functioned as a "Greek Oracle." The consultant system seemed to possess "superhuman reasoning capabilities," reducing the doctor to a passive user instead of an effective decision maker. As an alternative, they developed a system called Qualitative Medical Reference (QMR). This system is designed to support the doctor's *own* diagnostic reasoning while helping him or her overcome particular difficult steps (Miller & Masarie, 1990).

From the perspective of social constructivism, the differences between the two systems may be described in the following way: The overriding values behind INTERNIST-1 were efficiency and expertise. The purpose of the system was to function as a comprehensive "expert" for diagnosis. In contrast, in the design of QMR, the values of autonomy and responsibility were already included in the design process of the new system. This should facilitate the ethical behavior of doctors by making room for both the autonomy and the responsibility of doctors in the whole diagnostic process.

Surveillance by cameras in public places is another example of how values are integrated into technological design. Nowadays, camera surveillance of squares, warehouses, taxis, and other places are commonplace. With the introduction and subsequent growth of camera surveillance, the critique against the threat to privacy has also grown. Now, the cameras can be constructed in different ways. The ordinary way is for the camera to continuously record the public space. But, it is also possible to arrange the recording so that under normal conditions the human faces are not recognizable. However, if something occurs, such as an assault, technology makes it possible to catch the perpetrators because a visual image of their faces was recorded. In line with social constructivism, one may say that the value of privacy is built into the cameras. As long as the faces are not recognizable, the privacy violations are limited.

A further problem with assessing emergent technologies is that new technological systems have both unintended results and side effects that are often important from an ethical point of view. For example, in the 1980s and 1990s, the computerization of health care made it possible to store huge amounts of patient information. In the computerized patient records, diagnoses and therapies were recorded more easily than in the paper form used earlier. The intended and partly achieved effect was to store and handle patient information more efficiently. However, sensitive personal information was also easily accessible for people who had no right to access the information. Besides the intended effects of facilitating the handling of huge amount of information, the increased vulnerability of privacy protection was an unintended effect of the new system.

The following graph illustrates different ways to assess technology (Figure 4.1). Technology is the result of (1) intentions, (2) designs, and (3) forms of production. The intentions, designs, and forms of production can be valued from different aspects. Furthermore, the technology has effects that can be direct or indirect. The technology may cause something that in its turn has an effect, etc. The (direct and indirect) effects may be

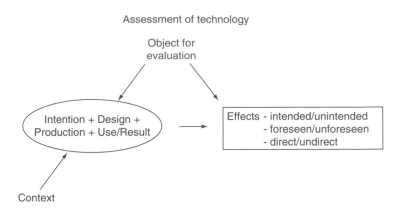

Figure 4.1

intended or unintended. Furthermore, the effects may also be unforeseen. The intended, unintended, and unforeseen effects can be valued from different perspectives, for example, from an ethical point of view. The graph illustrates how technology is assessed as both a process from intention to use (left oval) and as a causative factor producing different kind of effects.

The graph can be used to illustrate the example of computerized patient records. The context is, of course, health care. Objects for evaluation in the left oval are the *intention* to create the new systems. We can assume that this intention is valued positively; the idea is to facilitate the management of patient records. The system can be *designed* in different ways. For example, if participatory design is practiced, the end users are involved in the design process. This, then, can be valued positively as a way to engage and activate those who will use the system. For example, the *production* process can be valued according to its environmental impact. Finally, the *result* will be a system that works according to the intentions, such as facilitating the handling of sensitive information like patient records. We now turn to the right rectangle. What are the effects of the new systems? We assume that the *intended*, *foreseen*, and *direct* effects are more efficient ways to aid and treat patients. This, then, are positive values of the new system. However an *unintended*, *indirect*, and perhaps also *unforeseen* effect is the decreased protection of patient privacy. If we see privacy as a value, this effect is then something negative.

So, what are the implications for our efforts to ethically assess emergent technologies? What is the point of discussing ethical issues related to emergent technologies? Can we, at the end of the day, say anything reasonable about emerging technologies? Firstly, we have noticed the unpredictable nature of technological developments and hence the sheer difficulty in predicting tomorrow's technology. However, in contrast to forecasting the future, we are discussing *emerging* technologies. Secondly, despite this difference, one should be cautious of being too definite when discussing the ethical implications of emerging technologies. As Paul Sollie underlines, uncertainty is intimately connected with the discussion about technology assessment (Sollie, 2007).

In our assessment of emerging technologies, we know something about the intention, design, and its possible uses. We can eventually foresee some effects, for example, by making analogies to earlier technologies. Furthermore, we can sketch possible outcomes and alternatives and discuss their ethical implications. Obviously, there are some real advantages to assessing emerging technologies. At this early stage of technological development, it is still possible to influence the technology. When a technology is already implemented and in use, the ethical assessment is less meaningful. This is so because the given technology contains strong forces against change and is so much more difficult to influence in direction. Scientists and engineers have invested their brainpower, companies have invested capital, and politicians have invested their prestige and political capital.

An illustrative example of the difficulties in changing direction is the struggle over nuclear energy during the last decades. Programs to develop nuclear energy were implemented in many Western nations during the 1960s and 1970s. At this time, there were hardly any debates about the problems connected to nuclear energy. However, when the negative consequences of nuclear energy were exposed and nuclear energy was questioned, the paths in the direction of alternative "soft energy paths" were blocked (Lovins, 1977). Too many scientists and engineers were dependent on nuclear energy for their livelihood, and too much capital was invested in this energy source. A conclusion that may be drawn from the conflict over nuclear energy is that technology assessments must begin at an early stage, preferably already at the design stage.

So far, I have argued for a social constructivist view of technology that bolsters that technology is the result of human decisions and choice. Hence, when technology is designed, there are possible alternatives that will more or less fulfill human needs and interests. I have also pointed to the significance of time. The earlier the discussion and assessment of new technologies starts, the more fruitful and progressive the assessment will turn out. Thus, my preliminary conclusion is that it is possible, but not without risk, to ethically assess emerging technologies. At the end of the chapter, I will discuss in depth the theories and methodologies for the ethical assessment of technology.

Let me now turn from the more general reflections on ethical assessment of technology to a particular example of emergent technologies. As a case in point, I will discuss ambient computing for personal health monitoring. This is a bundle of technologies used for medical home care that likely will transform both the health care and home environment. Health care will move out of the hospitals and into private homes that will then be "invaded" by sensors and cameras. The technologies necessary for this transformation are more or less developed. It requires long-established technologies such as cameras and computers but also newly emergent technologies such as micro-sensors and chips that are currently under development. Ambient computing for personal health care is thus a good example of an emerging and transforming technology that is still possible to influence.

Ambient Computing for Personal Health Monitoring

In the Home

This chapter focuses on one kind of emerging technology, which is ambient computing for personal health monitoring. According to the visions of the technicians, sensors and computer devices will be, in the future, practically omnipresent. Small application-specific, network-connected information appliances will be embedded in virtually everything around us (Greenfield, 2006; Kunze, Grossmann, Stork, & Muller-Glaser, 2001). This new stage of information and communication technologies (ICT) is given different names: ambient technology, ubiquitous technology, and pervasive technology.

According to the forecast, we may predict that our homes in the future will be littered with monitoring devices. There will be microphones, cameras, microprocessors, and sensors attached to the toilet, to kitchen devices, lockers, etc., with the aim of aiding and facilitating life in different ways. Ambient ICT will also be used for health-care purposes. Sensors may be wearable and even implanted into a person's body. The sensors can monitor and register body temperature, heart rate, blood pressure, or any other bodily health-related function. Furthermore, the monitoring possibility also includes a person's movements, fall detection, location tracking, and gastrointestinal telemetry. Thus, the new electronic sensors/devices can monitor a person's activities and many of his/her bodily functions.

The devices are embedded in the environment and should ideally be unnoticed by the users. How is this possible? Firstly, they are extremely small. Nanotechnology is expected to provide material that will be miniature-sized and may be discreetly applied to the environment to be used for ambient computing in personal health monitoring; "It is a world of smart dust," writes Wright et al. (2008, p. 1). Secondly, some devices can also be directly attached to the person, connected to a person's watch, ring, and clothes, and even implanted in his or her body, for example under the skin.

Although ambient computing is a resource for different purposes, it is not least a resource for providing health care in the home. Medical treatments and drug deliveries can be distributed in the home through "intelligent" devices, such as automated functions that are programmed by health-care personnel and monitoring devices that make it possible to treat patients from a distance.

The medical use of ambient computing in combination with communication technologies is called "m-Health." It is defined as "mobile computing, medical sensors, and communication technologies for health care" (Istepanian, et al., 2004). Telematics, the combination of information technology and telecommunication, is one of the requirements for this development. It is further strengthened through wireless communication. Body-area network (BAN) is used for communication between sensors and the patient's body, personal area network (PAN) is used for communication in the personal environment of the patient, and wide area network (WAN) is used in the connection to a central data pool and information services (Kunze et al., 2001).

In sum, according to Nehmer, Becker, Karshmer, & Lamm (2006), ambient computing for health-care purposes has the following characteristics:

1. "*invisible*, i.e. embedded in clothes, watches, glasses, etc.,
2. *mobile*, i.e. being carried around,
3. *context aware*, i.e. equipped with sensors and wireless communication interfaces, making it possible to scan the local environment for useful information and spontaneously exchange information with similar nodes in their neighbourhood,
4. *anticipatory*, i.e. acting on their own behalf without explicit request from a user,
5. *communicating* naturally with potential users by voice and gestures instead by key board, mouse and text on a screen, and

6. *adaptive*, i.e. capable of reacting to all kinds of abnormal exceptional situations in a flexible way without disruption of their service." (Nehmer et al., 2006, p. 46)

So, ambient computing for personal health monitoring implies that sensors and monitoring devices will be placed in the patients' homes. These sensors and monitors are connected to clinics and hospitals on the other end.

In the Clinic—Medical Connectivity

So far, I have described how sensors and monitoring devices combined with wireless connections make it possible to send many different data about a patient to the health clinic. On the receiving end, there are personnel at a clinic watching monitors, collecting information on computer screens, and noticing signals. With the help of microphones, cameras, and other communications devices, health-care personnel are able to react to the incoming information and communicate with the patient.

On the basis of all the information received, health-care personnel will perform their work. Physicians will make their diagnosis and suggest therapies, nurses will plan for patient care, occupational therapists will prepare necessary aid, and social workers will analyze the patient's future social needs. And, due to the fact that the patient is monitored, in the case of emergency such as an accidental fall, an ambulance will in a short time be on its way.

Thus, it may seem as if ambient technologies for personal health care offer an ideal health care: the latest technology is used; there are human experts and expert systems that can diagnose any kind of incoming data and suggest treatments; through telemonitoring, health care professionals and patients can communicate with each other; and the patient does not have to travel but may be observed and cared for as if he or she were in a hospital. Although the new systems of health care have great potential, there are still some possible ethical problems that will be discussed later. However, we will first give some examples of particular projects in the pipe line.

Projects

To get an understanding of how ambient technology may be used for health-care purposes I will present some new research and development projects.

The mission of the *Healthyaim project* is to develop "devices that communicate with the outside world providing ambient intelligence to the human health level." The project is developing microsystem technologies and communication methods and connecting these to medical implants and measurements and alert systems. Information from these devices will be transmitted to health-care clinics and other relevant institutions. The data will form the basis for interpretation and diagnosis.

The products developed within the Healthyaims project are based on new, key technologies such as body area networks that enable communication from implants or from body devices to a base unit. Within the project, micro assembly techniques, implantable power sources, and biomaterials, suitable for interfacing devices in and on the body, are developed. This implies, for example, techniques for cochlear implants, retina implants, and glaucoma sensors (www.healthyaims.org).

IntelliDrugs is a project that focuses on pharmaceutical technologies. One example is an oral drug delivery device intended for patients who suffer from drug addiction or long-term diseases. The device looks like a natural tooth that is on a removable dental appliance that is placed in the mouth. It contains medicine that is administered via a microsystem, which controls the process. The medicine is released in a controlled manner according to the patient's needs and for as long as it is necessary. When emptied, the container may simply be reloaded with fresh medication. The system also includes a remote control that informs the patient and doctor when it is time to refill the device. As is stressed on the company's homepage, IntelliDrugs allows for the accuracy of every dose of medicine, the precise start and stop of the drug delivery, and the adjustment of dosage due to changing needs (www.intellidrug.org/).

MINAMI is the acronym for Micro-Nano integrated platform for transverse Ambient Intelligence applications. The project develops a mobile-centric approach to ambient intelligence. The mobile phone is a key device and the project is, in addition to the European Union, funded by Nokia. With a mobile device, the user can communicate with the surrounding environment by wirelessly reading close tags and sensors embedded in everyday objects.

The aim of MINAMI is to develop systems for home health care. One application of the technology is the so-called "Smart pillbox" that monitors medicine dosage through recognizing when the pillbox is opened. Any divergence is reported to health-care personnel via mobile phone. A second application of the technology is an ambient camera that monitors moving objects at home and alarms any suspected phenomenon such as an accidental slip by a monitored patient. The "Sleep plaster" is a third application of this technology that monitors electroencephalogram (EEG, heart rhythms) overnight. In the morning, the user can transfer the data to his or her mobile phone and transfer it to health-care personnel (www.fp6-minami.org/).

Healthyaims, IntelliDrugs, and MINAMI are just three examples of projects for ambient intelligence in home care. The overall aim is to combine the most advanced materials and computer devices in order to improve medical care and drug delivery in the home. How, then, can these emergent technologies contribute to health care?

What Is the Point?

Ambient computing is an instrument for prevalent personal health monitoring and distributed health support. It is viewed as the future of health care and will, according to the "vision" of the European Commission, "...take healthcare out of the hospital, bring it to the home and embed it into people's lives" (EurActiv, June 16, 2008).

It is not difficult to see a number of benefits with the emergent technologies. There are at least five reasons for introducing ambient computing for personal health monitoring. Firstly, the system has a potential for monitoring patients suffering from chronic illnesses and elderly people. This is a category of patients that requires long-term attention but does not necessarily need continuous treatment. In the present health-care system, when patients are too ill to live at home, but not ill enough to go to hospital, they normally move to institutions for chronically ill patients or nursing homes. With the new possibilities of personal health monitoring, staying at hospitals or nursing homes may be postponed or no longer necessary; patients will be able to stay longer in their homes while still being provided with the care they need.

The benefits for chronically ill patients and the elderly who are able to reside in their homes are both personal and economic. Typically, both chronically ill patients and elderly want to stay in their homes as long as possible, surrounded by friends and family in a familiar environment. Furthermore, the cost of institutional care is much greater than home health care. In these respects, ambient computing for personal health monitoring may benefit both the patients and the society.

Secondly, in cases of emergency and alarm personal health monitoring will facilitate necessary relief actions. For example, if an elderly person falls in his or her home, it is registered by monitoring devices such as cameras, sensors, and other monitoring devices and the information is transferred to the emergency units that can provide appropriate care.

Thirdly, the possibility of transferring expert medical advice to patients far away will have various beneficial consequences. There might be a need for immediate medical consultation when an accident happens far from a hospital, as well as for a scientific expedition in distant regions or in space. Distant medical expertise for diagnostics and therapy might also be helpful for medical service in underprivileged regions and countries. The distribution of health-care resources is usually uneven within a country and even more pronounced between developed and developing nations around the globe. The possibility of telemonitoring and distant care has the potential for limiting the gap in access to medical care.

Fourthly, personal health monitoring is not only a potential resource for the ill and elderly, but also for healthy people. It might function as an early warning system for a variety of medical conditions. The monitoring system can indicate possible health-related problems even before they are noticed by the person him/herself. Continuous health monitoring might also promote healthy life styles. It can indicate when the person behaves in a way that is detrimental to his or her health.

Finally, in a time when there is a lack of resources for employing health-care personnel, different kinds of technical support may compensate for this deficit. Nehmer et al. write: "Autonomy enhancement services ... make it possible to abandon previous manual care given by medical and social care personnel or relatives, and replace it by appropriate system support" (Nehmer et al., 2006, p. 44). Hence, ambient computing for personal health monitoring may replace health-care workers and relatives in the future.

Ethical Questions

Technology is often perceived as something given and set that is the result of invisible forces outside of anyone's control. The point of social constructivism is to "unveil" technology. It stresses that technology is the result of human decision making, social forces, and interests, and hence, that technology is changeable. We can ask questions about technology: whose interests are served by technology, what is good technology, and how would we like to change technology? These questions invite us to engage in ethical assessment of technology. We can assess the design, result, and consequences of already existent technologies in order to improve them. We can also assess emergent technologies, although the assessment is more difficult to do. We do not yet know the consequences of emergent technologies. On the other hand emergent technologies are in a process of development which makes the assessment even more pertinent. The ethical assessment might have a real, and presumably constructive, effect.

We have noticed that personal health monitoring has a number of advantages. However, in spite of the potential benefits of ambient computing for personal health monitoring, we can also envisage some threats and vulnerabilities connected to the emergent technology. Commissions in the area have pointed out that there is also a dark side to a "world of ambient intelligence." Increased surveillance of the workplace and homes poses a threat to privacy. Furthermore, vital societal practices, infrastructure, and management of personal data are dependent on the new technology. Therefore, security of the systems is of utmost importance. If or when the systems break down, damages to both society and individuals may ultimately result. For example, personal data run the risk of getting into the wrong hands, thereby posing as a risk of identity theft. Hence, it is imperative to ask about the risks associated with future health-care dependent on ambient computing. Are there any ethical problems related to the new medical landscape? In the next sections, possible ethical problems related to the advent of ambient computing for personal health monitoring will be discussed.

Hypothetically, let us assume that a nano-scaled device is implanted in a patient's body. The purpose of this device is to monitor heartbeat and other bodily functions. We can envisage a number of ethical problems related to this new medical device. Firstly, it may pose a threat to privacy. A right to privacy presupposes both a right to non-intrusion and a right to control information about oneself. How will privacy be affected by the fact that sensitive information is circulated in decentralized IT-systems? How can privacy be protected with the monitoring of patients in their homes? Secondly, ambient computing can be invisible and programmed to anticipate human action. For example, the implanted device might restrict the functioning of the patient in a way that was unanticipated and by which the patient was unaware. Does ambient computing imply a risk for technological paternalism? Thirdly, a motive behind both home-based medical care and telemonitoring is to replace health-care personnel with technical devices. For example, the implanted device will automatically transfer information to the health clinic, which will decrease the need for personal interaction between health-care personnel and the patient. However, how will this change the relational aspects of health care? Is it a moral issue if computerized health care replaces human relations? Lastly, how will wearable or implanted monitoring devices affect the identity and integrity of the patient? Will it imply a "medicalization" of the personal identity so that the *person's* self will be transformed into a *patient's* self? Thus, it seems as if existential problems of personal identity and integrity are raised by the emerging health-care technologies. Now, let me discuss these possible ethical problems in more detail.

Are Ambient Computing and Personal Health Monitoring a Threat to Privacy?

The risk of privacy violations in the wake of ambient computing is stressed by the writers of the aforementioned book *Safeguards in a World of Ambient Intelligence* (Wright et al., 2008). They warn about the threats of different facets of privacy invasions, such as disclosure of personal data, surveillance, and risks from personalized profiling. They also cite a report from the American National Academy of Science stating that due to a future scenario in which monitoring devices might be embedded everywhere, privacy "…may be at greater risk than at any previous time in history" (Wright et al., p. 19).

How will ambient computing influence home environment? What are the consequences for patients' privacy if monitoring devices are installed in the homes? "My home is my castle" is a well-known saying. Our homes are the place where we relax, are left alone, and feel secure. We meet with whomever we like, say what we want and behave without anyone watching us. Will this still be possible with personal health monitoring? One can fear that the new technology will have a negative impact on privacy. However, what does privacy really entail? Why is privacy something that we should care about?

Though privacy is an important concept in both law and ethics, its exact definition is a disputed topic. Philosopher Deborah Johnson argues that "...privacy is a complex and, in many respects, elusive concept" (Johnson, 2001, p. 120). In ethics privacy generally means one of the following: (1) to be left alone, or (2) to control information about oneself. (Tavani, 2007; Warren & Brandeis, 1890; Westin, 1967). Ambient computing for personal health monitoring seems to have implications for both these aspects of privacy. It will imply that persons/patients have monitoring devices right in their homes and even in their own bodies that will transfer a lot of sensitive information about them to the clinic.

Is ambient computing for personal health monitoring a potential threat to privacy? First it poses a threat to a patient's control of his or her private sphere. Obviously, ambient computing implies that a person's private sphere is affected. Different kinds of monitoring devices are installed in the patient's home and the private space continually shrinks. Personal health monitoring makes use of sensors that perceive aspects of the environment. They may, for example, sense emotions like stress and excitement. Furthermore, ambient computing is omnipresent and invisible. This means that the user is not always aware of the monitoring that is going on. In this way, ambient computing seems to be a real threat to privacy in the sense of control of one's private sphere.

Even informational privacy is affected by personal health monitoring. There is always a risk of leakage when sensitive information is transferred, as in the case of personal health monitoring when health-related information is transferred to health clinics (Brey, 2005).

But does that mean that personal health monitoring is a threat to the patient's *right* to privacy? If a right to privacy means a right to decide who and under what conditions other persons can enter a patient's private sphere, the right to privacy is violated if the monitoring is done without the consent of the patient. However, the presupposition behind personal health monitoring is that the patient has given his or her informed consent to the placement of computational and monitoring devices in the home and it is assumed that it is in the best interest of the patient. Furthermore, it is also assumed that the monitoring devices could be switched off when it suits the patient. Hence, if these requirements of informed consent are fulfilled, the patient's right to privacy is not violated while he or she is in control of his or her private sphere.

However, the patient is in control of his or her private sphere only if the patient has a real choice to say no to personal health monitoring. Let us imagine two scenarios: in the first scenario, the patient can choose between personal health monitoring and traditional health care based in the clinic. In the second scenario, the patient has a choice between accepting personal health monitoring and, if not accepting personal health monitoring, receiving limited health care. In the first scenario, the patient has a choice and is still in control. The patient may be aware of the benefits of personal health monitoring, but he or she still chooses traditional health care in order to avoid possible privacy intrusions. But in the second scenario, the patient's freedom is limited. In this case, if personal health monitoring is the only option to get decent health care, the cost of saying no is so great that the patient has lost control and the new system implies a violation of patients' right to privacy.

Does ambient computing and personal health monitoring then pose a threat to the control of information about oneself? There will be a constant flow of medical information from the home to the clinic. The information is of a kind that is sensitive from a privacy point of view. Of course, the transfer of patient information in health care is nothing new. However, the amount of information and the potential amount of receivers are aggravated through the use of information and communication technologies. It is safe to assume that the more sensitive the information that is transferred, the greater the risk for privacy violations. There are those who have an interest in getting access to medical information. First, we have the so-called "trusted insiders," such as personnel who have legitimate access to medical information but who may use it in an inappropriate way. There are also employers and insurance companies who might want access to patients' medical information (deCew, 1999).

One way to avoid privacy violations because of personal health monitoring is to develop privacy-enhancing technology (PET), which is an instance of so-called "value-laden design" (Nissenbaum, 2000). When it is recognized that values are embedded in the technology that are in the design stage, it is also possible to design technology so that, for example, the protection of privacy is taken into consideration. The aim of PETs is to minimize exposure of private data, through privacy protection (anonymizer and encryption tools) and technology for privacy management ensuring confidentiality (Wright et al., 2008, pp. 158, 181).

Even if patients are aware of the installation of personal health monitoring, it might go unnoticed in everyday life. This may even increase the threat to privacy while the users may forget about the monitoring and live their private life as usual. However, the invisibility of ambient computing is not only a threat to privacy, but also to control technology.

A Risk of Technological Paternalism?

We saw earlier that ambient computing in the homes will be embedded and invisible. It is unnoticed but facilitates daily life in different ways. How can we choose and stay in control of a technology that is embedded and invisible?

In a seminal article from 1991, Martin Weiser forecasted the advent of ambient or, as he calls it, "ubiquitous" computing. In his futuristic scenario he wrote: "We are therefore trying to conceive of a new way of thinking about computers, one that takes into account the human world and allows the computers themselves to vanish into the background" (Weiser, 1991, p. 3). How will this be possible? According to Weiser, two aspects are crucial: location and scale. The computer devices must be placed so that they go unnoticed and so small that they practically disappear and come to be part of common awareness. Hence, location and small scale will make the new wave of computing disguised. Weiser envisages a future where computers are invisible and when people unconsciously use them to fulfill their everyday tasks (Weiser, 1991).

Weiser's forecast seems to be realized today and ambient computing for personal health monitoring is one kind of application. Medical sampling, testing, and monitoring, as well as diagnostics and therapy are delegated to the computerized systems. Does this imply a limitation of patients' freedom? Are they targets of a new authoritarian regime, victims of paternalism?

Spiekerman and Pallas (2006) discuss the paternalistic threat of ambient computing. Paternalism implies that an agent, such as a doctor or some other authority, performs actions that control someone else, such as a patient. However, these actions are done in the best interest of the controlled subject. When this action is performed against the will of the patient, we have a case of *strong* paternalism. When it is performed in line with the will of the patient, we talk of *weak* paternalism.

Spiekerman and Pallas transfer the concept of paternalism to technological practice and coin the concept "technological paternalism." What is unique about ambient technological paternalism is that it is invisible and pervasive. The paternalistic technology is acting in a way that the users seldom have reason to question.

As a possible example of technological paternalism, let us analyze one application of ambient technology mentioned above. The aim of a smart drug system, in the form of a sensor on a pillbox connected to mobile sensors that monitor the correct drug intakes, was to enhance the control of drug addiction. Is this an example of technological paternalism? Yes, it may seem so. When the system is in practice, it might very well be perceived as a limitation to the users' freedom. Furthermore, it cannot be overruled without sacrificing functionality, it is in the users' best interest and it is performed autonomously.

Is this case of technological paternalism acceptable from a moral point of view? This question is analogous to the question of whether paternalism in health is justifiable. Arguments in favor of health-care paternalism say that it is the duty of doctors to act in a way that is beneficial to the patient, even when the patient is unable to agree, or when the patient is unable to take a stand due to incapacitation. On the other hand, arguments against paternalism emphasize the importance of autonomous decision making. According to this view, health-care paternalism is a violation of the principle of respect for autonomy. It seems that the same arguments are relevant for and against technological paternalism. As Spiekerman and Pallas rightly concede, there is a potential conflict between anti-paternalism and ambient computing. They write, "There is a clear disaccord between the concept of disappearing technologies and the attempt to remain in control" (Spiekerman and Pallas, 2006, p. 12).

One can envisage a future development of ambient computing in which the pervasiveness and invisibility of the technology may make the problem of technological paternalism more acute. Users are becoming less and less aware of the applications. For example, monitoring or smart devices for health information are installed in their best interests and automatically function despite patients being unaware of their existence. These patients lack the freedom to accept or deny them.

Ambient computing for personal health monitoring has a potential for paternalism. However, it also has a potential to affect the way we perceive ourselves. This question will be discussed in the next section.

Implications for Identity

Ambient computing for personal health monitoring implies that sensors and other monitoring devices are wearable, such as in rings or clothes, or implanted in a person's body.

Hence, the devices will be situated very close to, or even be a part of, a person's body. How will this closeness influence a person's life and well-being?

Personal health monitoring has possible implications for a person's sense of identity. Let me start with an example of another device. Many of us wear a wristwatch. A wristwatch not only poses as a convenience factor by being able to check the time, but it is also necessary in pacing oneself to be on time to an appointment, for example. The watch is intimately integrated into our work and everyday life. In order to sense the contrast, some people put their watch in a drawer when they are on holiday because there is less of a need to keep track of time. The example illustrates that the watch is more than just a practical device. It has implications for our sense of time and for our sense of freedom and dependency. It makes us more conscious of time and even structures and controls our day. Thus, the watch has not only a practical but also a symbolic function.

The wristwatch is an example of a known device that we carry close to our bodies. This example should also tell us something about the more far-reaching implications of ambient computing. How, then, will ambient computing and personal health monitoring influence our sense of ourselves and of reality? Will it have implications for our identity?

"Who am I?" This is the basic question of identity. What, then, will it mean for our sense of identity to have sensors and monitoring devices attached to our clothes or in our bodies? Even if the devices are disguised and hardly noticeable, the bearer is aware of their presence. Their presence is a constant reminder of the fact that the person suffers from some kind of chronic disease. Consequently, the person wearing the devices is constantly in the role of a patient. We can conjecture that this will affect his or her sense of identity. Who am I? A natural answer may be, "I am foremost a patient."

To be a patient (from Latin *patientia*, meaning "to suffer hardship") is to be monitored and dependent on caring and treatment. It is to be in a state of worry and hardship, causing one to wonder, "Will I recover or will I get worse?" A possible effect of ambient computing for personal health monitoring is that the personal identity is being "medicalized." A *person's* self will be transformed into a *patient's* self. If this happens, the emergent technologies affect our identity as well as our integrity. An integrated self is a self in which multiple identities are balanced. In contrast, in a disintegrated self, a specific role or identity is constantly dominant. According to my analysis of the implications of ambient computing for our identities, this might happen as a consequence of the new technology. A person is becoming a patient. The identity of being a patient takes precedence over other identities.

The new technologies may be used for monitoring not only sick patients, but also healthy patients. This has been suggested as a means for promoting healthy lifestyles (Istepanian et al., 2004). In this case, the monitoring devices are not there to detect possible malfunctions in chronically ill patients, but to report the implications of these actions on a person's lifestyle. If a person smokes or drinks too much, this will be noticed by the sensors, as well as if a person fails to take part in some health-promoting activity. A similar kind of identity transformation as the one from person to patient might then also occur as a consequence of continuous personal health monitoring of healthy people. One might even ask whether this would imply a "medicalization" of a person who is healthy. A constant reminder of our health conditions would probably not improve our health.

We noticed in the beginning of this chapter that new technologies will have both intended and unintended consequences. In this section, some possible unanticipated consequences of personal health monitoring have been pointed out, which may lead to the transformation of a monitored person's self. It might imply a change in self-perception when the patient's identity prevails over other identities. If this happens, the emergent technology has far-reaching psychological and existential implications.

The vision of ambient computing for health monitoring is to move health care into the patient's home. One argument for this transformation is to save money by substituting health-care personnel with technical devices. How will this transformation affect the social aspects of health care?

What Are the Implications for the Patient–Doctor Relationship?

Ethical aspects of the clinical encounter or consultation have long been an issue for discussion in medical ethics (Beauchamp & Childress, 2001; Pellegrino & Thomasma, 1981; Ramsey, 1970; Svenaeus, 1999). The patient is in a vulnerable situation when his or her health or life is threatened, and the clinical encounter is a means to recovery and/or of caring, with the doctor acting as a mediator (Pellegrino & Thomasma, 1981). Medicine is an "interpretive meeting" between the patient and the care giver with the aim of understanding and healing the patient who seeks help (Svenaeus, 1999, p. 28). This seemingly simple meeting may be seen as a complicated encounter, with scientific, emotional, and normative content. In this section, I will discuss the meaning of clinical encounter and how it will be affected by the emergence of ambient computing for personal health monitoring.

The patient needs the care and recognition in order to feel secure and open to the doctor. Thus, the relation between the doctor and patient is embedded in values of commitment, trust, privacy, confidentiality, and responsibility. A principle of patient–doctor relationships stresses the moral duty of health-care personnel to live up to these values and to establish a healing relationship. As a consequence, the organization of health care, as well as the technology used in health care, should facilitate the realization of this principle.

How, then, do emergent technologies used for personal health monitoring influence the patient–doctor relationship? An argument for personal health monitoring is that technology will substitute health-care personnel. For example, nurses and assistants will be redundant with the presence of monitoring and "smart" devices. This, in its turn, will save money for health care. In a time of prioritization of resources, such a gain is an important impetus for developing the new technology.

Considering the importance of the doctor–patient relationship, how will drainage of personnel affect the quality of care? If, in accordance with the arguments of Pellegrino and Thomasma, for example, we can assume that the caring relation is crucial for medicine, the answer seems to be obvious: less caring personnel will have detrimental effects on the quality of health care. Hence, those introducing information and communication technologies for personal health monitoring should consider the words of Marsden S. Blois regarding an earlier stage of medical informatics. When reflecting on the apparent distrust and disinterest of doctors toward information technology in health care, he comments:

> The most important question appears not to be "Where can we use computers?" but "Where must we use human beings?" Until this matter is thoroughly explored, tension between physicians and computer advocates will persist (Blois, 1980).

Secondly, a technology-driven implementation of personal health monitoring runs the risk of promoting a one-sided engineering perspective on the clinical encounter. In such a scenario, the relationship between patient and doctor will be of less importance. Why should one expect such a development and why is it an ethical issue? In his historical survey of the "reign of technology" over medicine, historian Stanley Reiser (1978) investigates the consequences of an increasingly technological health care. Before the advent of modern medicine in the nineteenth century, the doctor had to rely on two sources of information: listening to the patient's narratives and making the direct connection to the patients' bodies through physical examinations. Needless to say, this practice presupposed a dialogue with the patient. The introduction of medical technology places the patient in the background. And, as Reiser argues, something important was lost. He writes:

> ...the machines are denied complete access to a whole range of non-measurable facts about human being that a physician can only obtain through his own senses—questioning, observing and making judgements. (Reiser, 1978, p. 229).

Reiser's conclusion from a historical survey of how new technologies were introduced in medicine is that despite the advantages of new medical technology, an increasing dependence on technology has, in some respects, been detrimental to health care quality and the values of health care.

Reiser points at two problems with a reign of technology over medicine. Firstly, it might be detrimental to the principle of patient–doctor relationship. This will not only harm the personal and psychological aspects of the clinical encounter, but it also limits the access to the personal information the doctor needs in order to make an adequate diagnosis. Secondly, it might also have detrimental effects on the doctor's own diagnostic capacity. Diagnostic expertise, like all kinds of expertise, is developed and maintained through practice. Without continuous contact with real patients, i.e. unique persons with unique symptoms, the tacit knowledge of how to correctly diagnose a patient's disease might get lost (Reiser, 1978).

Obviously, a beneficial relationship between doctor and patient is not *necessarily* lost in a high-tech medical environment. There is no predetermined path to distance and alienation. Instead, if developed and used in a way that takes the basic values of health care into account, new technology can be both helpful and contribute to good health care (Sävenstedt, 2004). However, such an alternative way of implementing emergent technologies needs a conscious effort to assess it from a moral point of view. How is this possible? Are there methods for an ethically based technology assessment? This question is the point of departure for the next section.

Ethical Assessment of Emerging Technologies

We have noticed that emerging technologies for personal health monitoring raise important ethical questions. How should these systems be introduced and how can they achieve justification? Answers to these questions are provided by proponents of what is called constructive technology assessment (CTA) or interactive technology assessment (iTA).

Technology assessment, as a systematic activity, goes back to the 1960s. It was introduced as a response to the emerging critiques of technology that were, for example, motivated by environmental problems after industrialism and the worries about the implications of nuclear power. The aim of technology assessment is to identify, analyze, and evaluate the social consequences of the introduction and use of new technology. Technology assessment can be limited or wider in scope. It may be limited to solidity and reliability of the technology itself or involve assessment of external effects on society and environment. Obviously, the external effects that are objects for assessment might be more or less far-reaching.

Later, methods and theories for technology assessment have been enriched by ethics. There are two kinds of critiques against technology assessment from an ethical point of view. Firstly, the criteria for assessment were seen as inadequate without including ethical values. Secondly, technological assessment was carried out after the introduction of a new technology. A more constructive and effective way would be to assess new technology at the stage of design and construction. As a consequence, methods for constructive and interactive technology assessment were developed.

An example of constructive technology assessment is taken from the development of a decision-support system for diabetes care in a Swedish hospital (Collste, Shahsavar, & Gill, 1999). An information system consisting of a computer-based patient record for the collection, storage, and presentation of appropriate information, and a decision-support module to aid both patient and clinicians in diabetes care was designed and implemented. The users, such as the doctors and nurses in diabetes care, were involved in all the processes of design and implementation; thus, the principles of participatory design were in practice. Further, during the design and implementation of the system situations that rose questions of an ethical nature were detected. The system gives access to different kinds of information about patients, their yearly checkups, eye tests, laboratory results, drugs taken, and hemoglobin level. It can provide graphical presentations of the time courses of these factors and allows also sending information about the latest hemoglobin levels home to the patients.

The constructive technology assessment resulted in some obvious benefits. First, the nurses' working conditions were improved. The information both about the disease and the patients was structured in a better way and the nurses could get much easier access to the information they needed. Furthermore, the new decision-support system made it possible to decentralize the decision making. Decisions formerly made by doctors were now made by nurses. Through their greater involvement and responsibility, the nurses' satisfaction in work improved considerably. The same was true for the patients. They now were much better informed about their disease in general and their own health-care status in particular (Collste et al., 1999).

Let me now turn to a theoretical approach on ethical assessment of technology. An ethical methodology for technology assessment is based on some ethical criteria: values, and when assessing health-care technologies in particular health-care values, moral norms, and principles. An ethical methodology for assessing new technology is then to include ethical principles, for example, principles of respect for autonomy and privacy in the assessment work. This should be supplemented by an inductive approach; a *constructive* or *interactive* ethical assessment of new technology. According to this methodology, social and ethical problems surrounding technology must be addressed through a broadening of the design process. Those who are affected by the new technology, that is, the stakeholders, should then be involved in the design process as well as in the process of implementation of a new technology as a regular activity. The case of the decision-support system for diabetes care, is an example of such an interactive technology assessment.

Technological development is unpredictable. Hence, anticipation must be organized as a regular activity. According to this methodology for ethical assessment, the stakeholders will be involved in the assessment in a regular way. That this is an *ethical* assessment means that the questions raised concern values, moral principles, and norms like autonomy and privacy. That it is *constructive* means that it is integrated in the design and development of a new technology and that it is *interactive* means that it involves different stakeholders (Schot, 2001).

Constructive and interactive technology assessment is challenging technological essentialism as well as the idea of autonomous technology. Accordingly, as was argued in the opening of this chapter, technology should not be understood as autonomous and separated from its social context. Instead, it should be understood as the result of social intentions, design decisions, etc., and these intentions and decisions are not given beforehand but are instead possible to influence.

What then are the moral reasons for constructive and interactive technology assessment? Basically, it is justified by principles of autonomy, equal respect, and utility. According to a principle of autonomy, persons have a right to influence the decisions that affect their interests. According to a principal of equal respect, every person has the same right to influence decisions that affect him or her. According to a principle of utility, constructive and interactive technology assessment can be justified if it enhances the quality and beneficence of the emerging technology. A possible line of argumentation is that if those who are affected by a technology can influence its design and application, the result will be a better and more appropriate technology than otherwise. It is assumed, then, that there are better chances that the designers of technology through such a reflective and broad process will be able to anticipate possible problems with a new technology.

How is it possible to achieve a "justified" technology, such as a technology that incorporates all stakeholders' justified beliefs? Interactive technology assessment is, according to Reuzel et al. (2001), a process of valuing the consequences of technology. There are no relevant values independent of the "stakeholders," such as those who are affected by the technology. The stakeholders have different values and the goal is to come to an agreement about the conditions of a technology concerning how a specific technology should be designed and implemented to be acceptable to all affected parties.

So, what are the implications of these ideas about constructive and interactive technology assessment for the development and introduction of ambient computing and other technologies for personal health monitoring? It is difficult to anticipate what this would imply in practice. However, a basic requirement is that health-care authorities and companies involved in developing the new systems should have open minds and be willing to include the users, for example, both patients and health-care professionals in the process of design and development. The focus group methodology might be valuable in this respect.

New artifacts and systems must be tested, the views of the users must be recorded, and challenging practices must be discussed. Furthermore, during the process of design and development the ways in which new technology possibly can affect values like privacy, autonomy, and responsibility must be continuously analyzed. Thus, the introduction of new systems for information and communication in health care should involve all the affected parties, including the patients.

Ethical Issues in Research on Personal Health Monitoring

So, what are the ethical implications of these ideas about constructive and interactive technology assessment for research, development, and introduction of ambient computing and other technologies for personal health monitoring?

In their book on engineering ethics Martin and Schinzinger visualizes engineering as social experimentation (Martin & Schinzinger, 2004). Engineering, which includes both research, i.e. the invention of something new, and technology, which is to transform new ideas into artifacts, is similar to medical experimentation in the respect that it affects human beings and that it is supposed to have beneficial results. How, then can a principle of informed consent, so important for medical research, be applied to social experimentation?

In the modern world, research and technology development is intertwined. This is obvious in the area of ambient computing for personal health monitoring. As we have noticed, research in health care and ambient computing is related to the development of new technologies. For example, state agencies and European Union programs for research funding collaborate intimately with business. The huge R&D projects are supposed to result in both new knowledge and new products. There is an ethical problem connected to this merger of research and technology. Obviously the ICT-industry sees health care in private homes as a new market for its products. It might imply that the questions of what is needed and what is offered are reversed; first—with the financial support of generous grants—some new products are on the market, then the patient's needs are inquired. Instead, the primary question should be: what are the patients' needs, and the secondary: what means may satisfy the needs?

New artifacts and systems must be tested, the views of the users must be recorded, and challenging practices must be discussed. Furthermore, during the process of research, design, and development, questions on how the new technology possibly can affect values like privacy, autonomy, and responsibility must continuously be raised. Thus, the design, production and introduction of new systems for information and communication in health care should involve all the affected parties, including the patients. A complementary strategy to include ethical issues in the research process is practiced by the above mentioned MINAMI-project. The aim of MINAMI is to develop mobile systems for home health care. An ethics committee is connected to the project. It reviews continuously the ethical aspects of the research and development. They have also developed "Ethical guidelines for mobile-centred Ambient Intelligence."

I have stressed the importance of ethical assessment of emerging technologies. But, how will the assessment proceed when technologies are set and in place? This question is discussed in the next section.

A Paradox: From Visibility to Disappearance

The vision of an ethically informed technology development presupposes visibility. In line with the theory of social constructivism, I have argued that technology is the result of a chain of decisions taken by product designers and producers. In order to assess technology, questions should be raised such as, What choices are made? At what moment? By whom?

However, the visibility of a new technology and the public and moral discussion of its consequences tend to slowly vanish. This will happen when the technology is integrated in our everyday life and becomes commonplace. We no longer reflect on the pros and cons of the technology, we just take it for granted. As Mark Weiser (1991) argues, the disappearance of technology "... is a fundamental consequence not of technology but of human psychology" (p. 3). When we learn something well enough, we cease to be aware of it.

Philosopher Deborah Johnson (2000) sees technology as "instrumentation of human action" (p. 27). Ethics is about human action and, hence, when technology is set, it is the human action instrumented by technology and not the technology as such that is ethically assessed. As a consequence, Johnson argues that a focus on the ethics of a particular technology, such as computer ethics, will also slowly disappear. Johnson writes: "... once the new instrumentation is incorporated into ethical thinking, it becomes the presumed background condition" (Johnson 2000, p. 30).

Therefore, we can conclude that it is of utmost importance to focus on the process of design and development of new technology from an ethical perspective. The reason is, of course, that technology is influencing our world and our lives. However, when a technology is set and becomes integrated as instrumentation of human action, it will disappear and the ethical discussion will move to another new technology.

Conclusions

This chapter deals with ethical problems and ethical assessment of ambient computing for personal health monitoring. We have noticed that one can foresee that the emerging technologies will benefit health care in different ways. It will facilitate elderly and chronically ill patients to stay in their homes instead of being forced to go to hospitals or nursing homes. It will speed up relief in case of an emergency, it will facilitate the possibility to get expert medical opinion at a distance, and it has a potential to lower the costs of health care.

However, the transformation of health care due to ambient computing for personal health monitoring can also be expected to have some challenging ethical consequences. It might affect privacy in two ways. Firstly, ambient computing invades the patient's private sphere and even, ultimately, his or her body, which means that almost everything, except perhaps his or her thoughts and hopes, might be monitored. Secondly, even informational privacy might be threatened due to the transfer of sensitive information about the patient.

The introduction of ambient technology for personal health monitoring is of course done with the best of intentions. However, the combination of invisibility and pervasiveness might create difficulties for the patient to control the environment. Hence, the emerging technology has potential paternalistic implications; the patient loses control and autonomy is in this way confined.

We have also noticed that personal health monitoring might influence a person's sense of identity. He or she might apprehend himself or herself more and more as a patient. In the footsteps of the emerging technology, one might find an insidious medicalization of identity.

As a consequence of ambient technology for personal health monitoring, the distance between doctor and patient might increase. There will be fewer reasons for personal encounters and more distant monitoring. Health care, therefore, runs the risk of being ruled by technology.

These four possible consequences are examples of unintended but ethically relevant implications of emerging technologies in health care. Can they be avoided? Are there any options for alternative strategies? Can health care benefit from the emerging technologies without threatening important health-care values? The answer to these questions depends on many factors. The problematic effects of ambient computing for personal health monitoring are not predetermined. Through a continuous, constructive, imaginative, interactive, and ethically informed technology assessment, they might be avoided. This could be an alternative for designing emerging technologies so that their beneficial potentialities will be realized, but their negative impacts will be avoided. If this happens, ambient computing for personal health monitoring will become a helpful instrumentation of health care and embedded in our everyday lives.

References

Axisa, F., Dittmar, A., & Delhomme, G. (2003). Smart clothes for the monitoring in real time and conditions of physiological, emotional and sensorial reactions of human. *Engineering in Medicine and Biology Society. Proceedings of the 25th Annual International Conference of the IEEE* 3744–3747.

Beauchamp, T. L., & Childress, J. F. (2001). *Principles of biomedical ethics* (5th ed.). New York: Oxford University Press.

Beaudin, J. S., Intille, S. S., & Morris, M. E. (2006). To track or not to track: User reactions to concepts in longitudinal health monitoring. *Journal of Medical Internet Research, 8*(4).

Blois, M. S., (1980). Clinical judgment and computers. *North England Journal of Medicine, 303*, 192–197

Brey, P., (2005), Freedom and Privacy in Ambient Intelligence, *Ethics and Information Technology, 7*, 157–166.

Collingridge, D. (1980). *The social control of technology*. London: Frances Pinter.

Collste, G., Shahsavar, N., & Gill, H. (1999).A decision support system for diabetes care: Ethical aspects. *Methods of Information in Medicine, 38*(4–5), 313–316.

DeCew, J. W. (1999).Alternatives for protecting privacy while respecting patient care and public health needs. *Ethics and Information Technology, 1*(4), 249–255.

Feenberg, A. (1999), *Questioning Technology,*New York, Routledge.

Greenfield, A. (2006). *Everywhere. The dawning age of ubiquitous computing*. Berkely: New Riders.

Hoogenhuis, C. T., & Koelega, D. G. A. (2001). Engineers' tools for inclusive technological development. In Goujon P., & Dubreuil B. H. (Eds.), *Technology and ethics: A European quest for responsible engineering* (pp. 207–230). Leuven: Peeters.

Horner D. S. (2005). Anticipating ethical challenges: Is there a coming era of nanotechnology? In Brey, P., Grodzinsky, F., Introna, L. (Eds.), *Ethics of new information technology* (pp. 217–228) CEPE2005: University of Enschede.

Inness, J. C. (1992). *Privacy, intimacy and isolation*. New York: Oxford University Press.

Istepanian, R. S. H., Jovanov, E., & Zhang, Y. T. (2004). M-health: Beyond seamless mobility for global wireless healthcare connectivity-editorial. *IEEE transactions of information technology in biomedicine, 8*(4), 405–412.

Johnson, D. (2000). The future of computer ethics. In Collste, G. (Ed.), *Ethics in the age of information technology*, Studies in Applied Ethics, 7, Centre for Applied Ethics, Linköping: Linköping University.

Johnson, D. G. (2001). *Computer ethics*. (3rd ed.). Upper Saddle River, N.J.: Prentice Hall.

Kant, I. (1983). *Ethical philosophy*. Cambridge, MA: Hacket.

Korhonen, I., Parkka, J., & van Gils, M. (2003). Health monitoring in the home of the future. *Engineering in Medicine and Biology Magazine, IEEE, 22*(3), 66–73.

Kunze, C., Grossmann, U., Stork, W., & Muller-Glaser, K. (2001). Application of ubiquitous computing in personal health monitoring systems. *Biomedizinische Technik, 47*, 360–362.

Lovins, A. B. (1977). *Soft energy paths: Toward a durable peace.* San Francisco: Friends of the earth international.

Martin, M., & Schinzinger, R. (2004). *Ethics in Engineering,* (3rd ed.).

Milenkovic, A., Otto, C., & Jovanov, E. (2006). Wireless sensor networks for personal health monitoring: Issues and an implementation. *Computer Communications, 29*(13–14), 2521–2533.

Miller, R. A., & Masarie, F. E., Jr. (1990). The demise of the "Greek Oracle" model for medical diagnostic systems. *Methods of Information in Medicine, 29*(1), 1–2.

Nehmer, J., Becker, M., Karshmer, A., & Lamm, R. (2006). Living assistance systems: An ambient intelligence approach. *Proceedings of the 28th International Conference on Software Engineering* (p. 43). New York: ACM.

Nissenbaum, H. (2000). Values in computer system design: Bias and autonomy. In Collste, G. (Ed.), *Ethics in the age of information technology* (pp. 59–69).

O'Hear, A. (1999). *After progress: finding the old way forward,* Bloomsbury, London.

Pellegrino, E. D., & Thomasma, D. C. (1981). *A philosophical basis of medical practice: Toward a philosophy and ethic of the healing professions.* New York: Oxford University Press.

Ramsey, P. (1970). *The patient as person: Explorations in medical ethics.* New Haven: Yale University Press.

Reiser, S. J. (1978). *Medicine and the reign of technology.* Cambridge, MA: Cambridge University Press.

Reuzel, R., van der Wilt, G., ten Have, H., & de Vries Robbe, P. (2001). Interactive technology assessment and wide reflective equilibrium. *Journal of Medicine & Philosophy, 26*(3), 245.

Schot, J. (2001). Constructive technology assessment as reflexive technology politics. In *Technology and ethics: A European quest for responsible engineering.* Leuven: Peeters.

Sollie, P. (2007). Ethics, technology development and uncertainty: An outline for any future ethics of technology. *Journal of Information, Communication and Ethics in Society, 5*(4), 293.

Spiekermann, S., & Pallas, F. (2006). Technology paternalism–wider implications of ubiquitous computing. *Poiesis & Praxis: International Journal of Technology Assessment and Ethics of Science, 4*(1), 6–18.

Svenaeus, F. (1999). *The hermeneutics of medicine and the phenomenology of health: Steps towards a philosophy of medical practice,* (1st ed.). Linköping: Tema, University of Linköping.

Sävenstedt, S (2004). *Telecare of Frail Elderly: Reflections and Experiences Among Health Personnel and Family Members,* Diss. Umeå University.

Tavani, H. T. (2007). Philosophical theories of privacy: Implications for an adequate online privacy policy. *Metaphilosophy, 38*(1), 1–22.

Warren, S. D., & Brandeis, L. D. (1890). Right to privacy. *Harvard Law Review, 4*, 193.

Weiser, M., The Computer for the 21st Century, *Scientific American, 265*(3), 94–104.

Westin, A. F. (1967), *Privacy and Freedom,* Atheneum Press, New York, NY.

Westin, A. F. (2003). Social and political dimensions of privacy. *Journal of Social Issues, 59*(2), 431–453.

Wright, D., Gutwirth, S., Friedewald, M.,Vildjiounaite, E., Punie, Y. (Eds.) (2008). *Safeguards in a world of ambient intelligence.* Springer.

Internet sources

www.healthyaims.org (accessed February, 20, 2009)

http://www.intellidrug.org/ (accessed February, 20, 2009)

http://www.fp6-minami.org (accessed February, 20, 2009)

http://www.euractiv.com/en (accessed February, 20, 2009)

Chapter 5

Ubiquitous Connectivity: User-Generated Data and the Role of the Researcher

Mariann Hardey

Social science has always attempted to understand forms of sociability that arise in the spaces where people meet and interact. Since the increase in popularity of the Internet, a new set of "virtual" spaces locked within a "cyberspace" have provided unique challenges and opportunities for social researchers. Much of the initial excitement within the social science community about the Internet was based on the possibilities afforded by "playing" with identity (e.g., Turkle, 1995) and the "end of geography" (e.g., Graham, 1999). Together, these provide a range of technologies and software that can be utilized by social researchers and offer possibilities for new levels of access to research subjects (e.g., Mann & Stewart, 2000; Slater & Miller, 2000). This has been accompanied by an increased speed in the development of technologies and associated social change (Tomlinson, 2007). A consequent challenge for researchers is how to keep up with such innovations (Gane, 2006). These bring with them important methodological issues that must be addressed. Indeed, as I shall go on to explore in this chapter, what constitutes the "field" of social research is called into question as social life "goes digital" (Abbott, 1990) and takes advantage of Web-based technologies. This chapter is about the next wave of challenges and opportunities that are faced by the researcher and associated with the emergence of various new resources under the umbrella of Web 2.0 (O'Reilly, 2004). The label Web 2.0 has partly to do with the commercial identification of the next version of the Web, distinct from the Web 1.0 and the cyberspace of the 1990s. Another important element is the increasingly ubiquitous and taken-for-granted integration of Web resources into individuals' everyday lives (Hardey, 2007, 2008, 2009a; Webster, 2002).

This chapter sets out to understand the role of the researcher. The way that information is focused on the personalized preferences of the individual and their associated others as "friends" provides a challenge to the traditional role of the researcher, who has appeared as an "unengaged" and "objective" observer. For example, in the face of research that examines sociability across Social Networking Sites (SNSs) such as MySpace, Bebo, and Facebook, and blogs, the notion of the "anonymous researcher" loses ground (e.g., boyd,[1] 2006; Hardey, 2009a; Hookway, 2008). The researcher(s), while identifiable, are commonly "anonymous" in many research strategies that are built around ethical formulations that ensure that the rationale and authors of a research project are disclosed to subjects. The traditional researcher occupies a position of distance in an attempt to make objective observations and remains anonymous in the sense that he or she discloses as little as possible about his or her life and role. In the early days of mediated research, the use of pseudonyms in research based on, for example, Internet forums encouraged self-disclosure (Rheingold, 1993). Whatever the ethical issues around such a strategy, Web 2.0 social spaces have become interconnected with the real lives and identities of individuals. With such developments, my argument is that the stand-apart researcher should be recast as a subject and co-participant. The researcher should be a part of the nuances of the flows of communication, personal information, and relationships. Here, the technology makes visible collective behaviors and interactions; therefore, it is important that the researcher is placed to recognize these. What are significant here are the contributory aspects of the emerging technology. These are based on the public and open sharing of information where the accumulation of personal networks is with known and identifiable others. In essence, the researcher takes on the role of a "co-organizer" as a participant of networks of information as a part of data collection.

New Forms of Methodology

By writing and identifying oneself as a "social researcher," there is awareness of the possibilities accompanied by the development of Web information, portals, archives, and resources. Part of the challenge is *how* to translate the equivalent methods such as observation, interviews, and focus groups, which have previously proved successful for social scientists, into the Web 2.0 setting(s). Indeed, while there are numerous guides to understanding the reach, use, and role of the Internet (e.g., Jones, 1999; Hewson, Yule, & Laurent, 2003; Hine, 2005; Mann & Steward, 2000), there is little content about how to conduct research across the parameters of technologies. It is, at this juncture, relatively "easy" to identify the rapid and ever-evolving dimensions of social research, as increasing numbers of individuals take up resources such as SNSs and blogs as the sites of investigation (e.g., boyd, 2006, 2007, 2008a; Hookway, 2008; Livingstone, 2008a, 2008b). It is the "pioneers" of technological change who are the first to take steps into the *new research field* and to begin to search for appropriate research practices. One such investigator is danah boyd, a graduate student based in the United States. Her investigations, which have formed a part of her graduate research, represent explorations into a new territory of social research. She is primarily known and identified with her studies about the SNS MySpace (e.g., boyd, 2006, 2007, 2008a, 2008b). For boyd, this has meant that she occupies MySpace as an individual with personalized links and "friends," and she is identifiable as a "social scientist." Previous quantitative and survey-style research methods have made extensive use of the Internet and related Web applications for data collection (e.g., Coomber, 1997; Solomon, 2001). There is already considerable discussion about how to proceed with data collection, both in terms of data capture and how to protect participants. For example, the peer-reviewed journal *Sociological Research Online*[2] has emphasis on what it terms the "use of new media" for sociological research. Despite discussions about the utilization of the Internet for data collection, there remain limited debates about how Web-based resources should be used. boyd's work (2006, 2007) that examines social media and youth practices is of interest here and represents one of the first instances that research about a particular SNS (in this case MySpace) was created on an SNS and carried out for an extensive period. New for the Web 2.0 setting, boyd shared not only a personal profile with her potential participants, but also used this as a way to reach potential subjects.

The most recent discussions about Web-based methods have been within health and medical research (e.g., Eysenbach, 2008; Hughes, Joshi, & Wareham, 2008; Seeman, 2008) or related to innovation in teaching and learning (e.g., Bojārs, Breslina, Finna, & Deckera, 2008; Brown & Adler, 2008; MacDonald & Martinez-Uribe, 2008; McCann, Warren, & AnHai, 2008). One of the most challenging aspects is the treatment of social information that is seen as being in a very "public" domain, but is likely to contain personal and therefore "private" information (e.g., date of birth, gender, or home address). Correspondingly, it is also the open, connected, and always-available nature of the technology that invites new questions in terms of ethics and privacy. This issue is important for both the researcher and the participants. Some projects have addressed how existing tools and techniques may be adapted into "online" spaces (Mann & Stewart, 2000). For example, interview techniques and focus groups have been modified to take place within Internet forums and/or chat rooms (e.g., Davis, Bolding, Hart, Sherr, & Elford, 2004; Gaiser, 1997). However, to gain real insight into the characteristics, attitudes, and behavioral practices as they emerge, it is a *necessary* component of the research process to share, not only the same Web resources, but also the same social networks and "situations" as potential research participants. In this way, the social scientist can at once be identified as the "researcher" and "analyzer" of their data, as well as a "co-participant" both during *and* after data has been collected. Traditional and "ethnographic" studies have been developed to provide widely recognized sources of rich data or "thick description." Hine's book (2000) *Virtual Ethnography* is indicative of the attempt to transfer established research practices into new mediated spaces. Indeed, the rhetoric of what Brown (1977) and others describe as "'poetic' strategies" serve as "cognitive aesthetics" for defining the "reality" of social situations. Thus, such ethnographic research approaches, I argue, represent a particularly compelling strategy for adaptive or online research methods. Hearn, Tacchi, Foth, and Lennie (2009) reinforce this point when they emphasize the importance of "new media" applications for the research of content, technology, and social layers that are emergent across online spaces. Indeed, they go on to propose a "democratic and participatory approach" that are "particularly appropriate" for "new media projects" (Hearn et al., 2009, p. 1). From this perspective, the relationship between technology and the increasingly social and visual aspects of Web 2.0 point toward what I suggest as an increasingly reciprocal relationship between the researcher and research subjects, as well as the data and analyzed results. This approach shares much with Hearn et al.'s identification (2009, p. 1) of "new action research" that is led by an "alternative co-evolutionary perspective." An important consideration is the theoretical and conceptual assumptions about the role of technology in line with that of the researcher, especially when there is considerable emphasis on the social visibility of both. Therefore, the technological tools that are used to observe, collect data, and communicate foster collaboration between the researcher and participants. In this way, such tools are not only useful to gather and store research, but provide a context for the process of analysis, responses with participants, and the archive of research material.

My own research focuses on social media and the utilization of new Web technologies in everyday life, in particular SNSs like Facebook. Facebook is a free-access social networking Web site that launched on February 4, 2004. Users "sign up" and join networks that are organized by region, schools, and workplace. Its main purpose is to allow its users to connect with "friends" who work, study, and live around them.[3] People have a personal profile and can send messages and other notifications to inform friends about themselves. Through my own work and investigations I recognized there was a need for new methodological techniques in order to address the unique space that SNSs provide. This includes, at times, a necessary social distancing from both the research and research participants. For example, I have already argued that it is a *necessary* element of some varieties of Web research that the researcher shares the same social setting(s) as the participants. This approach quickly leads to the mass accumulation of potentially very different data sets (e.g., images, text, social network "actions" (such as the Facebook poke), comments, tagging, and so forth) that need to be sorted, classified, and analyzed. During my own research, it was an imperative that I share the same resources and social networks. As a result I have had (and continue to have) a personal profile on Facebook, which I choose to share with my research participants. One particular project that commenced in 2005 was based on interactions as they emerged across the SNS Facebook. The beginning of the investigations was *before* Facebook had reached its most recent ascent as "the world's most popular social networking site" with more than 175 million users (see Johnson & Hirsch, 2009). When the study began, there was only very limited (not any) guidance about how to conduct the research of interactions on an SNS, or the consequences of having a personal profile on the same site. Most methodological suggestions had to be "borrowed" from sociability that was related to "online" or the "virtual" communities of Web 1.0 (e.g., Wellman, 1999; Preece, 2000). During the course of the data collection, which was completed in 2008, I developed an approach that should be viewed as a *collaborative* and *collective* strategy for the conduct of research across Web 2.0. "Collaborative," in this context, denotes the formation of personal social networks as they emerged through the interactions *with* others. "Collective" is used to describe the accumulation of data that is "shared by all," reflected in the necessary social elements of the technology. This lends itself to exploring relationships and interaction, as well as the form and content of information that is exchanged by people. For example, if we were interested in how university students used SNSs to stay in contact with their parents, we could map their social network, quantify the number and frequency of direct interactions, and examine the text, images, and other content that was shared between students and parents. Reflecting previous research that focused on Internet forums, we could, for example, explore SNS groups organized around "fatness" to help understand how issues like obesity were being discussed. In other words, traditional research questions and issues that involve people's lives and relationships are open to investigation within the new mediated spaces that are becoming part of everyday life.

Recognizing Ethical Dilemmas

Part of the appeal of Web applications and related software is that they are seen to offer considerable benefits for social research. For example, due to the presentation of information, such technology provides low-cost and time effective methods to capture data within more "naturalistic" settings (Liamputtong, 2006; Liamputtong & Ezzy, 2005). One area that has recently been developed as a rich source of primarily qualitative data is blogs. A blog is a type of Web log (hence blog) that is usually maintained by an individual and formed of regular entries of commentary. The rise in popularity of blogs is that they represent "easy, inexpensive, flexible and interactive means of expression" (Herring et al., 2005). Since their development from the online diaries of the 1990s, blogs are often viewed as a "favoured medium of online self-representation" and personal expression of the author (Hookway, 2008, p. 92). Typically published in the public domain, they can offer extensive insights into the life and/or thoughts of the blog author and/or that of their readers. Research based on data from blogs has gathered momentum (e.g., Herring et al., 2005; Hookway, 2008; Thelwall, 2007). However, despite the growing research about blogs and use of published material taken from the blogosphere, the research opportunities and related discussions about academic conduct and ethics remain relatively unexplored. In addition, it is worth stating that Web applications also offer new ways of organizing research (e.g., uploading whole documents to Google Office) for data gathering and capture. Such dimensions expose new types of "research labour," as well as the strategic elements relating to research design, completion, and publication.

In a number of research projects, I have gathered data from SNSs and other Web applications such as the user review site TrustedPlaces and the Microblog site Twitter. The micro-blog has been identified as a form of free flow blogging that allows users to send brief updates and to insert micromedia such as photos or audio clips. Posts are limited by the number of characters that can be included in a blog, in the same way as a mobile phone text message or a single entry could consist of a single sentence. Updates can be posted by a variety of means that include Instant Messaging (IM), text message, and e-mail, as well as digital, audio, or video content posted from other sites such YouTube and Flickr. In addition to these observations, I found it useful to write and update regularly my own blog properfacebooketiquette[4] that explores the various dilemmas users of SNSs face in everyday life and social situations. The writing of the properfacebooketiquette blog began as a "personal quest for knowledge" and was not initially intended to be included as a part of a research project. However, over the course of a 3-year study the blog gathered a momentum with acknowledgment and discussion from blog readers about the issues that I published. As a result, properfacebooketiquette has become a research tool in its own right. Before going into the field, a researcher is aware of the role that they intend to "perform"—whether as "interviewer," "observer," etc. This is because the direction of the research effort is planned and then appropriately carried out in this way. The integration of the blog as part of my research represents a personally scaled coordination of data. By this term, I mean to highlight how the methodological procedure can be categorized as both reflexive and emergent. During the data collection, this has allowed for the organization of themes and issues that hold social significance with the participants. As a result, such data can be seen to represent a form of "group-led activity," directed by the sharing of information and cooperation with others. An interesting outcome is how the use of the blog is seen as a complement to other more traditional forms of data that I have recorded, such as face-to-face interviews and focus groups. One consequence has been the "friending" of research participants on Facebook motivated by discussions from the blog and/or in person. The recasting of the researcher into a participant, while a necessary research strategy, raises issues of confidentiality and risk. Any research must ensure that participants are not exposed to risks through the conduct of the study and so researchers should ensure that they understand the possibilities afforded by "privacy settings" on SNSs and elsewhere. For example, it may be desirable for a researcher to limit access to some of the information and networks that they maintain on an SNS, particularly as this is likely to represent their personal profile page to friends who may not be involved in the research. Confidentiality in relation to published material has become more difficult as data mining techniques (process of extracting hidden patterns from data) and search engines have become more sophisticated. While the identities of, for example, participants can be anonymized it may be possible that a direct quotation from content that they have written on the Web can be traced back to them through the simple expedient of entering some of the text into a Web search engine like Google. Depending on the nature of the research, it is important that such possibilities are recognized and that when necessary researchers put in place safeguards. For example, if appropriate, the order, word usage, and other content can be changed in a way that does not loose the meaning of the text but makes is more difficult to trace the author of a blog, SNS Wall post, private message, etc. More particularly for this kind of research that emphasizes the real communications and sources of context by participants, an important consideration is the rationale for using such methods and a close and continual tracking of the way the research may impact individual privacy.

In effect, the different forms of data—interview and focus group transcripts, blog postings, commentary, and SNS messages—provide a snapshot of the tightly structured forms of social behavior that individuals are reliant upon. The varying degrees of mediated expression that are accumulated through "Web exposure" increase the overlap between the "private" and "public" aspects of *both* participants, and the infiltration into the researcher's own social life(style). Theoretically, I have drawn on the work of Mead (1913) and Goffman (1963) to suggest that the basis of personal representation is always *social* and negotiated in relation to known others (Hardey, 2009a). Thus, there is a tension between the personal aspects of the self as these are broadcast and made available to others (such as a wall comment on an SNS or a blog post) and how these are mediated through a "privacy management" in terms of the information displayed to "friends" (Hardey, 2009a). Such approaches are reliant upon the researcher's and user's own awareness and knowledge about privacy and personal information, such as the "privacy settings" on SNSs. A particular aspect of mediated interactions is how user preferences are continually updated and modified. As a result, it is important to take into account the updates to personal user settings that emerge with the development and modification of the software. For example, the privacy settings that can be employed on Facebook today offer far more sophisticated and personalized protective measures than at the launch of the site in February 2004. The apparent "closure," or rather convergence, of the public/private divide across SNSs and elsewhere challenges the expectation of anonymity. Moreover, the metrics that work behind-the-scenes of Web search engines and social software can also conspire against the traditional practice of making sources "anonymous." Thus, research strategies must respond to the ever-emerging possibilities of limiting public disclosure, and the publication of identifiable and individual information. Researchers, therefore, need to maintain an awareness of the changing nature of the resources as they engage with others and choose to make use of technologies to work across new fields of inquiry.

On the one hand, the researcher must be aware of the transition from the "old" to the current and preferred modes of social communication. At the same time, developing technology offers new possibilities for data that can be experienced as a period of intense experimentation. These research spaces look quite different from known sources of data collection. Indeed, as researchers and users "get used" to such new technologies, there continues to be constant attention to developments that cause a proliferation of effects that can be too fast or direct to acknowledge. In response to such changes, Beer and Burrows (2007) proposed a "sociology of Web 2.0" to reflect the changing dynamics in the relations of production, consumption, and perusal of academic content. There is a touch of irony here as the authors themselves note that by the time of publication, the paper describes what has already had time to become accepted as part of the "cultural mainstream" and there are new developments with which to contend. Such time lags represent a significant issue within academic settings. The Web 2.0 technologies and resources available encourage *near instant* updates and notification of a range of social issues. However, by comparison academic publication continues to be relatively "slow" to report or to make available research findings. There are additional barriers; for example, some authors have deliberately sought to boycott journals from what they term the "archaic academic publishers" (boyd, 2008a). However, such open source publishing, which may lack a clear reviewing system, has yet to establish the scientific credibility of print-based journals and read-only formats. Open source publication can be difficult to cite correctly and/or to search for content. In traditional reviews of the literature, such work is categorized as "grey" and is accorded less academic status than the well-established print-based journal.

Compared to the "speed" of new technology innovations, the traditional academic research process is slow. Putting to one side the ability (or lack thereof) of research-funding bodies to recognize the new possibilities of new technology, the publication cycle remains slow. Typical peer-reviewed journals demand a three- to six-month reviewing process, which may be made longer if changes to the reviewed manuscript are made. Once accepted, the pressure to "publish or die" in terms of academic careers means that journals often have a backlog of issues that amount to a year or more. Under such conditions a year or more can pass before a research paper reaches an academic audience. In response to this, some journals have adopted the policy of "preprints," drafts of papers that have not yet been formally reviewed or published. Such a strategy is controversial as it may make poor research available and threatens the quality control of the peer-review system (see debate on the British Medical Journal (BMJ) Web site). Researchers can also bypass the traditional system and publish their findings on blogs or Web pages. Such "grey literature" is difficult to assess in terms of the viability of the research and publishers are generally opposed to accepting work that has previously been published on the Web. The pent up demand for publication and an increased interest in "open source" publication has led to two related developments. Firstly, a number of journals that follow peer-review conventions but are published only on the Web is growing. The advantage is not only one of lower costs but also flexibility in that length (i.e., number of paper per issue) can be varied. Moreover, images, links and other forms of dynamic content become possible. Then, secondly, the development involves a challenge to the academic journal publishing houses. Open Access Publication provides free publications (i.e., no subscription or library membership is required). Publications range from the academically prestigious and peer-reviewed to those that challenge such conventions. Researchers have more choice in where and how they publish their work than ever before. Their choice may be shaped by the desire for the academic validation of their work, speed of publication, or anticipated audience.

Embedding the *Real* in Research

Thus far, I have characterized the approach to research within Web 2.0 as "collaborative," "open," and "participatory." The openness of research design with the inclusion of "real" identities and social actions are important elements of data. Indeed, one of the main qualities of Web 2.0 resources is that individuals are taken to be, and are seen as, "real." Hence, people are not, nor do they always wish to be, anonymous in such social settings. This can pose particular problems in terms of identifying the right or most appropriate methodology. For example, to follow traditional and ethically informed ethnography practice, the names of research sites are not revealed and pseudonyms are used where necessary. The intention is to preserve anonymity and the expectation that online interactions are private and reserved for other site and forum users (cf. Hine, 2000). The lack of anonymity of participants within, for example, SNSs can make it difficult to protect individual users' identity and privacy. For example, using anonymous names may initially "hide" an individual's identity, but the publication of quoted text and/or descriptions of user preferences and behavior make it relatively easy to identify an individual. This is more likely if such material includes longer commentaries from publicly published blogs. One could argue that such data is intended for and available within the public domain, and hence concerns to protect the source and context of the material can be overplayed. However, individuals are "vulnerable" in a research context, especially if they are unaware that material has been subject to analysis that is specifically related to them and what they may consider private behavior. This issue is not new. For example, in the 1990s King's research (1996), based on material from a public Internet forum, had one respondent withdraw from the mailing list when s/he realized the group was under study. Thus, in this kind of ever-evolving field it is difficult to gauge where to draw the line between public or private material, to gain a measure of the potential level(s) of intrusiveness, or how a particular research agenda may impact participants. To follow the established conventions about protecting those involved in research provides only limited guidance about how to safeguard what participants may consider as aspects of their private lives. There is tension between the identifiability, or rather the visibility, of the individual in both the mediated spaces that are researched and the consequent publication of material. Where people communicate through a range of technologies, social implications impact differently on individuals and can result in different sets of data. For example, in the case of a blogger's identity one could question whether it matters if material is directly attributed to him/her in other contexts. However, the blog may be attached to a social network, which includes identified others. While the author may be content to be identified, the "friends" to whom they are connected may desire greater privacy and anonymity. The increasing "connectiveness" across social spaces such as SNSs, blogs, and so forth challenge traditional practices and expectations about research. As a result, issues of privacy and social surveillance are questions that are worth raising and considering before carrying out any research. Moreover, it is easy to overlook how the constitutive elements of social networks work to produce particular social effects, which range from a sharing of "friends" with other "friends," to the notification of social actions as they occur in real time.

To render anonymous any user identity can conveniently side-step many of the issues that are raised if research participants retain a clearly identifiable identity. However, to disguise just the username is to fail to acknowledge the ease with which source material and individuals can be traced. Indeed, the expression "to Google" is emblematic of such techniques where supposedly "hidden" or "protected" individuals can be found and revealed. The very premise of Tim O'Reilly's Web 2.0 vision for the future was founded on the mutual sharing of data and information that occurred on a transparent level of interaction. Web 2.0 resources in particular are affected by the use of certain cultural markers. For example, age, gender, and sexuality continue to provide key identifiers for interaction and user identity. Moreover, it is necessary that such classifications correspond to the real individual if they wish to participate with others, for example, across SNSs.

The *Social* Researcher

Increasingly, we are part of a society that seeks to make use of and have access to mediated Web resources and associated new technology. The consequent activities that we share, therefore, bring with them new responsibilities and lay new demands on researchers. In particular, Web-based applications function to enable the sharing of information and participation with others that can occur seamlessly, and at the same as, or at a similar rate to "off-line" social interactions. Data collection across this range of social situations is a constantly active and a self-reflexive process. On Web 2.0, in what traditionally would have been thought of as "entering the field," the researcher now has to begin to build social network(s) and create a User Profile. This acts as a personal page containing "snapshot" information, such as gender, age, and sexuality, and displays a visible record of some social actions, including Wall Posts and streamed social data. It is important to note that social information is not contained within the "confines" of one site and can be broadcast across an array of social networks and Web applications. For example, a Twitter update may post directly to a Facebook Status Update and images uploaded to Flickr can post simultaneously to a Facebook profile. In order to access other user profiles, the researcher must have and share his or her own personal user information. This may be a false or created identification for the research. However, in the context of Web 2.0 such "hidden" and deliberately misleading agendas are often viewed negatively and can, at best, be off-putting to participants or, at worse, harmful. These considerations share much with the analysis of chat rooms, newsgroups, and Internet forums under Web 1.0, where social scientists could take the role of a "voyeur" or "lurker" to accumulate research material. Across Web 2.0 and the future territory of Web 3.0, or the semantic Web, user-generated content is made visible through the interactions and the anticipated sharing of information *with* others. While there is still opportunity for the researcher to "lurk" online, for example, to observe streams of images on Flickr and updates on Twitter, and to create a false identity, such actions represent uncertain territory in terms of ethical precedence and point to the possibility of mistrustful results. Indeed it is my contention that, in order to understand the organizational structure of social networks and technology, the researcher *must* establish a "true" user profile. This not only allows for full access to site content in order to aggregate and identify participants, but also allows for open cooperation of research content with others. To emphasize this point, as the social scientist Seb Paquet observes, the social tools make for "ridiculously easy group-forming" (Shirky, 2008, p. 54) and these are regarded as unconstrained and seemingly straightforward research opportunities. The awareness of the personal use of technology has destabilized the previously more clear-cut boundaries between researcher and research subject(s). As the "private" individuals share more of their lives and personal information through such technology, the dichotomy between what was once described as "private" and "public" life is disrupted. To take as example the context of my own research, it is paramount that participants are as fully informed as possible about the study, and as the researcher I am seen to follow "best practice" to safeguard the participants, myself, and the data. To this end, I recommend that a certain level of familiarity with the technology before the researcher enters the field is required. Indeed, as Liamputtong (2006) notes, it is the responsibility of the researcher to ensure that individuals have "awareness" of their role and contribution to the research. This responsibility has increased significance as technology makes it relatively easy to identify the "real" and personal identity of the individual involved.

Previous social research that has explored Web interactions has highlighted the opportunity for a divergence between the online and off-line. For example, in her study of Web resources relating to breast cancer, Pitts (2004, p. 40) describes how she "can make no claims about the off-line identities of the authors (…) and I do not assume that cyber-subjects' on-line identities are necessarily identical to their off-line identities." This type of "fake" or false Web persona is increasingly removed by the visibility of *real* aspects of the self, from the use of real names rather than user names, to the identification of "friends" through a mutual network of links. We can see this shift to embodied identities through the policy of "real name attributions" on sites such as the popular shopping portal Amazon.com. On the Amazon site, it is stated that, "we believe that a community in which people use their Real Name (…) will ultimately have higher quality content, since an author willing to sign his or her real-world name on a piece of content is essentially saying 'With my real-world identity, I stand by what I have written here'."[5] King's analysis (1996) of Internet communities recommends that *all* references to any individual should be removed, including the location and form of content studied. However, such an approach is less applicable to contemporary research that may wish to blog content and SNS broadcasts that may be "findable" and identifiable on the Web. Such technology represents a convergence of the Web 1.0 newsgroups, forums, and "cyberculture" that the authors King (1996) and Pitts (2004) reference, such as SNSs that contain elements of all these media. The ways in which technologies are increasingly personal and personalized raise potential conflicts about the protection of users who may not know that they are under observation. At this point, the debate slides from a focus on anonymity to gaining a hold on the additional issues and considerations of the appropriateness of the role of the researcher in such settings. Significantly, such crossover can occur not only at the point an individual chooses to participate in a study, but remains as they are a continued part of the data. In addition, to establish and maintain the connection the researcher is mutually involved in the same network(s) as the participant. The Web 2.0 concepts of the "wisdom of crowds," "collective intelligence," and "participatory culture" help capture this synchronization of shared information (O'Reilly, 2004; Shirky, 2008; Surowiecki, 2005). These concepts are characterized by the channeling of personal information alongside mass communication for social purposes. Indeed, an important starting point for research in this context is the long-standing distinction between objective and typically "at distance" approaches and the subjective "up close" explanation of social processes. Consequently what commentators like O'Reilly (2004), Shirky (2008), and Surowiecki (2005) suggest is how "private" and "public" information is reconfigured under Web 2.0.

As a result, one stance is that data and information across Web 2.0 that is "open to all" and publicly retrievable (e.g., a Facebook listing via Google) should be treated the same as other publicly accessed content (e.g., a press publication). However, it is still important to acknowledge that such data is not necessarily clear-cut in terms of the where and how it falls in relation to privacy or methodological ethics. For example, some users are unaware of the privacy settings on SNSs, or may choose to ignore such settings, and consequently overlook the options that would make their profile listing and associated information less open to others. In addition, a public listing contains information about others, such as a friend list, which may give access to people who have not wanted to be part of a research study. Writing about data retrieved from blogs and bloggers, Hookway (2008, p. 105) suggests how there is a "strong case . . . to adopt the 'fair game-public domain' position." For blogs, the "fair-game" perspective is easier to identify and put into practice. For example, for a published blog that is "subscription only," the content, author, related links, and commentary are treated as exclusive and private material. Here, there is a wider recognition of the various privacy settings related to written and published content. Indeed, blogging is identified as "a public act of writing for an implicit audience" (Hookway, 2008, p. 105). Across SNSs, another type of audience is implicit, which includes that of identified "friends." As a result, the content management of personal information can be as basic as choosing which top line details to include on a Profile page (e.g., age, gender, etc.), to as sophisticated as specifying a particular individual to include/exclude in a friend network and the type of personal information to which they have access. However, popular media stories about "being sacked" for using Facebook (e.g., BBC News, 2008) reveal how this level awareness is on an individual basis and continues to have a very limited consensus. Thus, it is hard to see where the use of Hookway's "fair-game" (2008) in the "public domain" could be applied, as content that is publicly accessible on an SNS may be viewed as "private" by the individual and should be protected. Given the closeness of the researcher to the research subjects in such settings, it is essential that the use of ethical principles and practices be used throughout the process. For Hearn et al. (2009, p. 67) such dialogic encounters are based on relations of "mutual trust and open communication." Such approaches require careful planning before, during, and after the project. In addition, it is paramount that the researcher establishes effective communication skills for the engagement and safeguard of participants. Hence, the research should be built upon a critical reflection of the techniques for data collection as well as the continued evaluation, analysis, and archiving of the data. As a result, the use of such strategies reinforces the responsibility of the researcher and points to what Greenwood (2002, p. 117) has called for in order to "hold ourselves accountable to higher standards."

Research Principles in Practice: Watching What Happens

Hammersley and Atkinson (1989, p. 2) have argued that "the ethnographer participates, overtly or covertly, in people's daily lives for an extended period of time, *watching what happens*, listening to what is said, asking questions; in fact collecting whatever data are available to throw light on the issues with which he or she is concerned" (emphasis added). Like other approaches that seek to reveal the everyday, the scope of participation by the researcher through technology is achieved by an increased level of involvement, varying degrees of contact, and visibility with participants. This, as I have argued, creates new opportunities for the negotiation of data collection, privacy, and possible attention(s) from others. The involvement of users on SNSs reflects an increasingly prevalent social "condition" (Hardey, 2009a). Where Hammersley and Atkinson (1989, p. 2) advocate "watching what happens," there is evident tension between the motivation and visibility of the "watcher." To adopt a hidden or disguised position in relation to individuals that are open with real identities could be seen, at best, as inappropriate, and at worst deliberately deceptive. In any case, most SNSs require that a degree of personal information be provided before any individual can make use of the site. To examine the various pitfalls, I proceed with two case studies about conducting research on an SNS.

Case Study One: Closed Involvement

A Covert Observation of Students on an SNS

The researcher uses a personal user account on an SNS to trawl for data. This involves the examination and *covert* analysis of "friends" and friends-of-friends in networks. After social trends are identified (e.g., typical number of friends in a given network and the visibility of information on a Profile page), the data is captured from personal Profile pages *without* the students' knowledge or permission. At the same time, data from the students' friends' pages is used to gain access to other personal Profile pages. Where the research study is limited is that the researcher only has restricted access to information that is kept within the university-specific network. This is because it is not permissible to change a named network more than once in 3 months. Consequently, this research strategy can only capture what might be thought of as "surface" interactions and the top line information of the students on the SNS. Without open collaboration with participants, the rigor of the research material and trustworthiness of data is called into question. Most significantly, this approach intrudes on the potentially private and confidential data of others. As a result, the researcher needs to be sensitive to the lives and information of their participants, and to consider how research may impact upon them.

Case Study Two: Open Involvement

An Overt Observation of Students on an SNS

This researcher takes care to proceed in ways that protect both potential participants and the research individual. An official Web site and blog is created and all potential participants are given a link to the sites. Here individuals can follow tracts of data (e.g., user comments and e-mail response forms). The blog and Web site also act as a gateway for information and the identification of sources of the research. Permission has also been obtained from the university to allow for the researcher's personal Profile page to be present on the university network for the purposes of the research. After the identification of the types of network(s) involved in the study, the researcher makes contact with individuals through the SNS and/or by e-mail. At this time, participants share a "contact only" access to personal information and user profiles. On the SNS Facebook, this means that users can only view a whole user profile when both contacts have been added as "friends."

This allows a level of protection for those users who may not want to be involved in the research or to be identified by others. The researcher is able to respond by direct message, e-mail, or in the comments section of the blog. In the exchange of the communication, it is important that the participants be thanked for their response, made aware of the level of involvement, and visibly involved with their future contribution to the research. In addition, a dialogue is opened to discuss questions regarding the study. This marks a key turning point where individual involvement develops from being a "potential respondent" to "participant."

The first case study represents the now dated and "colonial" approach to the status of research respondents and the researcher. As this chapter has shown, such dualities are open to question in the light of Web 2.0 and related social practices. The second case study is close to my own approach. Here "participant" best describes the intensity of the involvement of the researched individual who is at once a direct contributor to the data in the same way as a "respondent" to an interview may be viewed, but whose observed social actions also represent data (cf. Holland, 2004; Reinharz, 1992). There is also an opportunity to promote the study via a blog or a Group or Fan Page on an SNS in order to recruit potential participants. Allowing individuals to approach the researcher establishes a more open agenda and has the advantage of freeing up the researcher from possible time constraints searching networks for data. Another benefit is the ability to offer a transparent approach to informing participants about the nature and conduct of the research. For example, when an individual joins a Group Page, this is published in a NewsFeed that can be read by others. This can promote the advancement of research material into the networks of others without actively infiltrating private or protected networks. What is important at all stages of the research is the clear identity of the researcher and the research project. At the centre of the still emerging guidelines about ethical online conduct are questions about conventional notions of public and private venues. It can be useful for potential researchers to look at the Association of Internet Researchers (AoIR) and published Ethics Guide.[6] Before the reproduction and inclusion of any research material, it is important that permission and agreement for involvement is obtained. Ideally, this is through the signature of a participant on an ethics form, which gives consent to participation in the study and the approval for the future publication of material. A different course of action is to make all participant identity anonymous. Here, it is vital to make explicit the use of pseudonyms and the extent to which communicated and observed material is to be used in the study. In particular, participants must be informed that while every measure is made to protect identifying information, Web-based content may still be retrieved and searched outside of the context in which the material is intended (e.g., the reproduction of an image from an SNS that is copied and republished/traced by other users). The manner in which there is a need or call for anonymity by participants must be achieved to as practical a level as possible. This is determined by the scope and sophistication of the technology. In a similar way, there are also "risks" associated with the visibility of the researcher, who must protect not only research material and participants, but also their own personal information.

In both of the above case studies, the level of involvement and role of the researcher is key to the direction of the study and nature of the data collected. Some researchers may argue that it is justifiable to "lie with intent" in order to observe interactions across social network resources. While such actions may not be intended as malicious, they set a controversial precedence for how we as researchers may explain and justify the observation and recording of research material. However, it should also be remembered that the extent and depth of data that can be collected using such strategies would be limited. One could argue that never before have individuals been so open and easy to identify for observation and analysis. From another standpoint, the techniques that can be implemented highlight a renegotiation of research parameters and appropriate distancing from data collection. Thus, the direction of social research means we must all be prepared to be included in the position of researcher, while at the same time open to the potential that we are also being *researched*.

A New Culture of *Participatory* Research

This chapter has identified shifts in the technology that make new demands on researchers and potential participants. Such shifts are pushed forward by the use of ever-more sophisticated technologies and open access, which are paralleled by the rapidly changing landscape of Web 2.0. Across these "scenes" of social information, the impulse is to be as visible and active as possible, emblematic of a particular social condition of our times (Hardey, 2009a). As a result, technologies have emerged through the information age to make increasingly visible (and observable) social information that is defined by the membership of networks. This new social exploration can take numerous forms (e.g., as a user profile, blogger identity, or Web site author). However, all appearances are identifiable and retrievable through relatively simple searches and investigation of SNSs and Web-based information. For example, typing a name into Google can retrieve user identity on more than one SNS and content from those sites. The significance and influence of such sources of social information cannot be underestimated, especially in an age when it is assumed that network information is protected and kept private between individuals. To illustrate this point, I offer the following anecdote:

> In 2007 at the beginning of the new academic year during my teaching of university undergraduates in the United Kingdom it was during our first session that I introduced the students to each other—without a prior knowledge of specific names to faces or personal description the introductions were accompanied by "snapshot" personal information such as what each individual had been doing over the weekend. My method was to use the information sheets that contained the names of my students from the university, which I had then **simply** entered into Google and retrieved the relevant Facebook Profiles. Without exception all the student Profile's were "open" and accessed by a "public" listing. Needless to say, following the seminar session **all** students introduced new privacy settings to their Facebook pages. As one student observed "no-one wanted their tutor as a 'friend' where they were able to see what they were up to.

The above demonstrates an emerging awareness driven by concern to be visible and findable to potential friends, as well as expectations shaped by a profound personal resolve to at once be a part of networks *and* retain a level of privacy—or rather a *personalized proximity* to networks. Here, the potential scope for observation and analysis shade into a cultural conventionalism that contains the subjective elements for acceptable and ethical research practices. The relative "openness" of the Web 2.0 sensibility encourages transparency, social participation, and interoperability of potential data. This might be passed over as an idealistic (unrealistic) and rose-tinted emergence of the use of the technology. Generalizations can be made about the experience of technology that takes interactions with others across a variety of social spaces. Here, it has been observed that individuals are increasingly part of a social world that is "swifter paced" and "more pressured" (Tomlinson, 2007, p. 1). These are expressed as a complex series of social networks that hinge on the *appearance* of *shared* social information. In particular, the latest Web 2.0 applications are presented as "enablers" for social networking, collaboration, filtering, social searching, file-sharing, tagging, and numerous other "actions," which are actively sought and experienced with others used to produce the ultimate architecture of participation (O'Reilly, 2004). While such tools appear promising and "fit for purpose" research opportunities, there needs to be a careful and critical assessment to establish the best code for research practice. Knowledge obtained from the substantial volumes of social information about an individual is increasingly *the* key factor for social research—one that is underpinned by a socially productive pace of life(style). The need for an ethical awareness has been noted at various points in the chapter. At one level, the sort of research that has been discussed does not require new ethical standards in terms of respect for research participants, informed choice, and so forth. At another level, it demands a knowledge and acknowledgment of the nuances and ever-changing possibilities of mediated research. The danger is that ethical committees that tend to be made up of long established researchers and academics, while rigorous in the application of ethical standards, fail to gasp, for example, the potential of data mining.

This chapter has explored some of the possibilities afforded by the emergence of what might be thought of as a *new culture of participatory social research*. The use of new Web applications such as SNSs are just one example of any number of "modern" and "in vogue" technology developments shaping everyday social situations. Consistently, it has been shown how "old" media are replaced by new forms of technology that inevitably come to constitute a cultural mainstay for interaction and communication, for example, the landline telephones, pagers, mobile phones, and e-mail. The advantages of technology to give an "anytime" and "anyplace" multi-tasking of information prompt calls for deeper engagement with research resources and outcomes. SNSs in particular represent new layers and levels of involvement in the construction of social knowledge. The immersed culture of such socially rich environments of shared information highlight engagements where researchers, and potential subjects, overlap in the same space(s) and have opportunity to survey one other's activities. Positive outcomes of these kinds of resources may be the notification of near instant social information that enables community style connections and collaboration. More negative prospects involve the potential for social surveillance and the retrieval of potentially personal content that can be taken out of context and/or used in an unintended manner. For example, Facebook unveiled in 2007 "Facebook Ads" as an "ad system" for business and third-party services to target advertising to "exact audiences" (Zuckerberg, 2007). Thus, there is potential for "unfair" intrusion into others' lives as channeled through dynamic social content. As a result, it will be necessary to revisit discussions about research ethics and professional codes of practice. One approach is to lead with what can be termed as a "closed information" scenario. In this instance, the content on an SNS, blog, wiki, and so forth is defined by the "privileges" of access put in place by the site owner (e.g., the type of access granted to one aspect of an SNS, such as a particular Group Page or identified network). As I have shown in case study one, after contact has been established with a research participant and permission is granted, the researcher gains not only communication privileges, but also access to social knowledge and other spaces that contain significant social content. In addition, (without changes to privacy) the participant(s) gain from access to the same streams of data that are about the researcher. As a result, all efforts should be made continually to preserve individuals' privacy, which may be "worked out" in collaboration with participants (e.g., by identifying points at which privacy may be an issue, such as the use and reproduction of certain images, blog content, podcasts, and vodcasts).

Conclusion: The Reconfigured Researcher

The social researcher has to take the opportunities for useful collaboration with potential research participants. However, to achieve this, a level of research vigilance is necessary to guard against what could be challenged as exploitation in relation to content, presentation, and individual involvement. When considering the use of data, it is necessary to understand and recognize the possibility for open and *fair* treatment of social information. As I have shown, the distinctions between "public and private" and "online and offline" often conflate and can coexist across a multitude of social spaces. For the purposes of designing a research strategy, it is paramount that the researcher be aware of obtaining potentially sensitive information that is intended for what may be classified by the individual as "private" use only. As we continue to move from Web 2.0 into a Web 3.0 and beyond, it is possible to foresee a reemphasis of the co-constitutive elements of the relationship between what is "offered up" through social technologies by the researcher and the meaning of the personal for the participants. Web 3.0, or "the semantic Web," relates to the view held by some that if Web 2.0 was about harnessing the collective intelligence of crowds, the further version of the Web will witness the intelligent Internet. The suggestion is that the software behind the Web will become aware of individuals' information needs and habits so that content will be tailored to their needs. Thus, such actions reveal how this follows a particular "attitude of mind," one that is less about the technology or technical aspects of the applications and more to do with the connections that the individual chooses to share and/or the types of information made explicit with others.

It is important to recognize that the research into the use and evaluation of Web 2.0-based tools is still in its infancy, despite our speeding toward a Web 3.0, a Web 4.0, and so on. Therefore, this seems an opportune moment to invite more discussion about the uses of social technologies—an invitation that leads with a call for researchers to "experiment" and test such tools in the context of the social sciences and in some formal way to report back results to the research community. The openness of a Web anchored in the acknowledged social identity of others is new to research (Hardey, 2009a). Thus, what might be claimed as a "Web pedagogy" is quite literally "in the (collaborative) making." Web-based technologies by their defining principles claim to avoid the traditional control of authoritarian influence. At once taken to be "democratizing," the potential impact and issues that such tools invoke are complex and demand a critical focus. Technologies and the researcher engage with information by collaborating *with* others. The implications for the academic community are of particular significance where researchers are not simply occupied in developing their own studies, but are actively involved in the creation and experience of social knowledge with others. In this version of events, participants have (to a greater or lesser extent) their own influence in the direction and content of research. Muirhead's description (2004) of individuals cast as "Collaborative Collectors" is useful here, where social knowledge is provided by the accumulation of new sources of social activities and information resources. This can lead to the increased participation and involvement with specified others during social monitoring. Information is seen to "flow freely" around networks and in this way such sources do not have to pass through a central authoritative body. Such sharing has relevance not only for potential data collection "sites," but is relevant to the publication of research results. Potential concerns about the distribution, editing, and authorship of studies also need to be addressed. Here, another issue is how we have moved from the potential danger of the "unreality" of interactions in virtual spaces, to concerns about a "too real" reality and intrusiveness into people's lives. Such dynamics are complex. By writing, researching, and publishing, together the intensification of different social platforms and diversification of knowledge may improve the quality of investigations. However, we must also seek to raise the levels of awareness about information that is produced through collaboration.

Future Directions

As I have suggested, more and more people are using technologies that have a strong social element. It is likely that such interactions will become the main mediated activity on the Web. The trend toward the use of visual media, such as photographs and digital content, is already evident. As the capacity to use such resources becomes both "simpler" and "faster," we may well increasingly look at interactions that have moved away from text. Such a move will make considerable demands on new modes of data collection and analysis. Indeed, methods will become increasingly participatory and reciprocal, from the initial identification and communication with participants, to the amenable feedback and update of the research (see Hardey, 2009b). The context of "open access" to research content is an important element to such methodological approaches. Indeed, a challenge for future works is the navigation of the social representations of participants in the documentation and publication of analyzed material. This suggests an inclusive and freely accessible reproduction of research material; however, there may be added complications with the need to protect individual identity and publication of material that could be subject to private restrictions (e.g., copyright material replicated on a blog). To conduct research and observe others through technology offers an innovative and creative point of entry to participants. What is important to take on board is the development of such research practices that respond to the new production of knowledge and social activities that are always in association with and increasingly formed through networks with others. My argument is that such approaches can support good analytical work and provide valuable insights into the lives and experiences of participants.

Notes

1. The sociologist danah boyd has legally changed the spelling of her name for a lower-case specification.

2. http://www.socresonline.org.uk/

3. www.facebook.com/
4. www.properfacebooketiquette.com
5. Refer to http://www.amazon.com/gp/help/customer/display.html?ie=UTF8&nodeId=14279641
6. Download content from: http://aoir.org/?page_id=54

References

Abbott, A. (1990) *The system of profession: An essay on the division of expert labor.* Chicago: University of Chicago Press.

BBC News (2008). Crew sacked over Facebook posts. (Online) (retrieved February, 2009) http://news.bbc.co.uk/1/hi/uk/7703129.stm

Beer, D., & Burrows, R. (2007). Sociology and, of and in Web 2.0: Some initial considerations. *Sociological Research online, 12*(5). (Online) (retrieved June 2008) http://www.socresonline.org.uk/12/5/17.html

Berners-Lee, T. (2000). Weaving the Web: The original design and ultimate destiny of the World Wide Web. London: Collins.

Bojārs, U., Breslina, J. G., Finna, A., & Deckera, S. (2008). Using the Semantic Web for linking and reusing data across Web 2.0 communities. *Web Semantics: Science, Services and Agents on the World Wide Web, 6*(1), 21–28.

boyd, d. m (2006a). Identity production in a networked culture: Why youth heart MySpace. *American Association for the Advancement of Science* (St. Louis, 19 February). (Online) (retrieved August 2008) http://www.danah.org/papers/AAAS2006.html

boyd, d. m. (2007). Why youth (heart) social network sites: The role of networked publics in teenage social life. In Buckingham, D. (Ed.), *MacArthur Foundation Series on Digital Learning Youth, Identity, and Digital Media Volume.* Cambridge, MA: MIT Press.

boyd, d. m. (2008a). Open-access is the future: Boycott locked-down academic journals. *Zephoria.* (Online) (retrieved August 2008) http://www.zephoria.org/thoughts/archives/2008/02/06/openaccess_is_t.html

boyd, d. m. (2008b). Facebook's privacy trainwreck: Exposure, invasion, and social convergence. *Convergence, 14*(1).

Brown, R. H. (1977). *A poetic for sociology.* New York: Cambridge University Press. (2nd ed.) Chicago, University of Chicago Press.

Brown, J. S., & Adler, R. B. (2008). Minds on fire: Open education, the long tail, and Learning 2.0. *Educause Review, 43*(1). (Online) (retrieved March, 2009) http://connect.educause.edu/Library/EDUCAUSE+Review/MindsonFireOpenEducationt/45823?time=1236939120

Carrithers, M. (1988). The anthropologist as author: Geertz's works and lives, *Anthropology Today, 5*(4), 19–22.

Coomber, R. (1997). Using the Internet for survey research, *Sociological Research Online, 2*(2). (Online) (retrieved March, 2009) http://www.socresonline.org.uk/socresonline/2/2/2.html

Davis, M., Bolding, G., Hart, G., Sherr, L., & Elford, J. (2004). Reflecting on the experience of interviewing online: Perspectives from the Internet and HIV study in London. *AIDS Care, 16*(8), 944–952.

Eysenbach, G. (2008). Medicine 2.0: Social networking, collaboration, participation, apomediation, and openness. *Journal of Medical Internet Research, 10*(3) Online) (retrieved March, 2009) http://www.pubmedcentral.nih.gov/articlerender.fcgi?artid=2626430

Gaiser, T. J. (1997). Conducting on-line focus groups: A methodological discussion, *Social Science Computer Review, 15*(2), 135–144.

Gane, N. (2006). Speed-up or slow down?: Social theory in the information age. *Information, Communication and Society, 9*(1), 20–38.

Goffman, E. (1963). *Behavior in public places: Notes on the social organization of gatherings*. The Free Press.

Graham, S. (1999). The end of geography or the explosion of place? Conceptualizing space, place and information. *Progress in Human Geography, 22*(2), 165–185.

Greenwood, D. (2002). Action research: Unfulfilled promises and unmet challenges. *Concepts and Transformation, 7*(2), 117–139.

Hammersley, M., & Atkinson, P. (1989). *Ethnography: Principles in practice*. London: Tavistock.

Hardey, M. (2007). Converging mobile technology and the sociability of the igeneration. *M/C Journal*, March 10.

Hardey, M. (2008). The formation of rules for digital interaction. *Information, Communication and Society*.

Hardey, M., & Burrows, R. (2008). New cartographies of knowing capitalism and the changing jurisdictions of empirical sociology. In Fielding, N., Lee, R.M., & Blank, G. (Eds.), *Handbook of Internet and online research methods*. London: Sage.

Hardey, M. (2009a). *Seriously social: Making connection in the information age*. PhD dissertation, York: The University of York.

Hardey, M. (2009b). The social context of online market research: An introduction to the sociability of social media. *IJMR, 51*(4).

Hardey, M. Properfacebooketiquette blog. (Online) (retrieved in June 2009) www.properfacebooketiquette.com/

Hearn, G., Tacchi, J., Foth, M., & Lennie, J. (2009). *Action research and new media*. USA: Hampton Press.

Herring, S. C., Inna K., Paolillo, J. C., Scheidt, L. A., Tyworth, M., Welsch, P., et al. (2005). Conversations in the blogosphere: An analysis "From the Bottom Up." Proceedings of the 38th Hawaii *International Conference on System Sciences* (HICSS'05), Hawaii, Los Alamitos: IEEE Press.

Hewson, C., Yule, P., & Laurent, D. (2003). *Internet research methods: A practical guide for the social and behavioural sciences*. Thousand Oaks: Sage.

Hine, C. (*2000*). *Virtual ethnography*. Thousand Oaks, CA: SAGE Publications.

Hine, C. (2005). *Virtual methods: Issues in social research on the Internet*. New York: Berg Publishers.

Holland, S. (2004). *Alternative femininities*. London: Berg.

Hookway, N. (2008). "Entering the blogosphere": Some strategies for using blogs in social research. *Qualitative Research*, February 8(1), 91–113.

Hughes, B., Joshi, I., & Wareham, J. (2008). Health 2.0 and Medicine 2.0: Tensions and controversies in the field. *Journal of Medical Internet Research, 10*(3).

Johnson, B., & Hirsch, A. (2009). Facebook backtracks after online privacy protest, *The Guardian*, Thursday February 19. (Online) (accessed February 2009) http://www.guardian.co.uk/technology/2009/feb/19/facebook-personal-data

Jones, S. (1999). *Doing Internet research: Critical issues and methods for examining the net*. London: Sage.

King, S. A. (1996). Researching Internet communities: Proposed ethical guidelines for the reporting of results. *The Information Society*, June 1, *12*(2), 119–128.

Liamputtong, P. (Eds.) (2006). *Health research in cyberspace*. New York: Nova Science Publishers.

Liamputtong, P., & Ezzy, D. (2005). *Qualitative research methods*. (2nd ed.) Melbourne: Oxford University Press.

Livingstone, S. M. (2008a). Engaging with the media-a matter of literacy? *Communication, Culture and Critique, 1*(1), 51–62.

Livingstone, S. M. (2008b). Internet literacy: Young people's negotiation of new online opportunities. In McPherson, T. (Ed.) *Digital youth, innovation, and the unexpected* (pp. 101–121) MIT Press.

Lyon, D. (2007). Surveillance, power and everyday life. In Quah, D., Silverstone, R., Mansell, R., & Avgerou, C. (Eds.), *The Oxford handbook of information and communication technologies*. Oxford: Oxford University Press.

MacDonald, S., & Martinez-Uribe, L. (2008). Libraries in the converging worlds of open data, e-research, and Web 2.0. *JISC, 32*(2), 36–40. (Online) (retrieved March, 2009) http://ie-repository.jisc.ac.uk/227/

Mann, C., & Stewart, F. (2000). *Internet communication and qualitative research: A handbook for researching online*. London: Sage.

McCann, R., Warren S., & AnHai, D. (2008). Matching schemas in online communities: A Web 2.0 approach. *Data Engineering. ICDE 2008. IEEE 24th International Conference*, 110–119.

Mead, G. H. (1913). The social self. *Journal of Philosophy, Psychology and Scientific Methods, 10*, 374–380.

Muirhead, B. (2004). Research insights into interactivity. (Online) (retrieved March 2009) http://www.itdl.org/Journal/mar_04/

O'Reilly, T. (2004). The architecture of participation. (Online) (retrieved March, 2009) http://www.oreillynet.com/pub/a/oreilly/tim/articles/

Pitts, V. (2004). Illness and Internet empowerment: Writing and reading breast cancer in cyberspace. *Health, 8*(1), 33–59.

Preece, J. (2000). *Online communities: Designing usability, supporting sociability*, Chichester, UK: John Wiley & Sons.

Reinharz, S. (1992). *Feminist methods in social researchi*. Oxford: Oxford University Press.

Rheingold, H. (*1993*). *The Virtual Community. Reading*: Addison-Wesley Publishing Company.

Savage, M., & Burrows, R. (2007). The coming crisis of empirical sociology. Sociology, Under Submission.

Seeman, N. (2008). Inside the health blogosphere: Governance, quality and the new opinion leaders. *Medicine 2.0*. (Online) (retrieved March, 2009) http://www.medicine20congress.com/ocs/viewabstract.php?id=14

Shirky, C. (2008). *Here comes everybody*. USA: Penguin Group.

Slater, D., & Miller, D. (2000). The Internet: An Ethnographic Approach. Internet Communication and Qualitative Research: A Handbook for Education, Communication and Information. *Journal of Education for Library and Information Sciences, 44*(1), 39–57.

Solomon, D. J. (2001). Conducting Web-based surveys: Practical assessment. *Research & Evaluation, 7*(19).

Surowiecki, J. (2005). *The wisdom of crowds*. USA: Anchor.

Thelwall M. (2007). Blog searching: The first general-purpose source of retrospective public. *Online Information Review, 31*(3).

Thrift, N. (2005). *Knowing capitalism*. London: Sage.

Tomlinson, J. (2007). *The culture of speed: The coming of immediacy*. London: sage.

Turkle, S. (1995). *Life on the screen: Identity in the age of the Internet*. Simon & Schuster.

Urry, J. (2003). *Global complexity*. Cambridge: Polity.

Webster, F. (2002). *Theories of the information society*. Routledge: United States.

Wellman, B. (Ed.) (1999). *Networks in the global village: Life in contemporary communities*. Boulder, CO: Westview Press.

Zuckerberg, M. (2007). Facebook unveils Facebook ads. *Facebook Press Room*. (Online) (retrieved March, 2009) http://www.facebook.com/press/releases.php?p=9176.

Part II

The Rise of Internet Technologies and Social Research Practice

➤ Chapter 6

Clickable Data: Hypermedia and Social Research

Bella Dicks and Bruce Mason

Introduction

In this chapter, we discuss how hypermedia—conventionally understood as "clickable multimedia"—can be used to inform all stages of the social research process—from data generation to dissemination of findings. Its relevance throughout the research process may seem unlikely, since the conventional idea of "clickable multimedia" would seem to limit its applicability to the computer screen. This in turn suggests that hypermedia would only be useful at the authoring and dissemination stage, where researchers might be beginning to think of Web-outlets as a means of disseminating their work. In fact, hypermedia is valuable as an aid to analysis, where it can be used to make multiple links and trails among different elements of the dataset. Beyond this, its use has implications, too, for the generation of data and for fieldwork itself. Once we start thinking about analyzing and authoring our research via hypermedia, we are sensitized to the multiple meaning-affordances of the media that shape data and characterize field settings. We become, in other words, more attuned to what can be called "multimodal" or "multisensory" research. This is because using hypermedia requires careful thinking through how data represented in different media forms relate to each other. Accordingly, we consider the dual aspects of the term "hypermedia": the idea of hyperlinking, and the idea of multimedia. Both of these have important implications for social researchers.

Before we start discussing these points, a caveat or two. First, it is important to note that the conventional conflation of hypermedia and computer-based clickable media actually blind us to the fact that hypermedia is not really a technology at all. It is enabled and enacted by computer technology but not coterminous with it. Hypermedia, rather, is an approach to ordering information that depends on multi-linear connections being put in place between different informational elements. This could hypothetically be done in any medium, including paper (although it has only become feasible with the diffusion of high-powered desk computers). It is a principle, then, rather than a technology or a method, and is actually more precise than the loose idea of "clickable media." Hyper*text* is the term originally coined by Ted Nelson, a computer "guru" who drew on original ideas from an American informatics engineer called Vannevar Bush (1945, 1986). The term refers to the linking together of diverse documents through a system that labels each link, allowing readers to follow a trail of similarly named links. Behind Bush's novel approach to indexing documents had been the concept that our minds do not work in a hierarchical manner, as do library catalogues, but through the association of ideas. Nelson was convinced that hypertext as a referencing tool would provide a degree of flexibility not possible with the type of hierarchical indexing system generally used in libraries. These visionaries saw hypertext as a more creative and "natural" form of referencing that could cope with the ever-increasing amount of available information in the postwar world. Indeed, Nelson (2009) sought to put into practice some of Bush's vision through the development of an ambitious document management system named Xanadu that he never managed to complete.

It is this ability to *name links* among data that really characterizes hypertext—and this functionality is something that the Web as currently constituted still does not provide. As Nelson claims:

> Today's popular software simulates paper. The World-Wide–Web (another imitation of paper) trivialises our original hypertext model with one-way ever-breaking links and no management of version or content. (2009)

In the process of widespread Web-diffusion, hypertext has come to mean simply "clickable text"—the now-ubiquitous highlighted or underlined words or media elements that you click on with your mouse in order to find out more. Being instantaneous and unmarked, these seem merely shortcuts to the more important information available at the "destination"; hence, the nature of the relationship between the two highlighted elements (or "nodes") is left for the reader to infer. However, as Barbules (1998) points out, links are more important than this. They specify the meaningful relationship between two elements and hence help determine how they will be read. In what follows, we try to draw out the value of being able to use both on-screen hyperlinks *per se*, and the value of being able to name them, together with the more theoretical implications of hyperlinking that allow us to think about the relationships among data in potentially more creative ways. We concentrate particularly on qualitative research projects, and especially ethnographic ones that involve periods of fieldwork. However, the discussion will also be useful to quantitative researchers who wish to supplement their numerical data with multimedia data or use screen-based design to help contextualize content.

There are two main parts to this chapter: the use of hypermedia first in analysis and second in authoring and dissemination. However, we also point out toward the end of the chapter that hypermedia involves a way of thinking about data that has implications for how we go about generating data in the field. Before turning to a discussion of the kinds of research projects to which hypermedia analysis might be applied, we briefly consider the emergence of the World Wide Web as a major electronic forum for social research that has made the world of hyperlinking and clicking so familiar. We then discuss the applications of hypermedia in data analysis, pointing out the technological requirements and illustrating the discussion with examples from our own work. Next, we look at the medium of the computer screen for authoring hypermedia scholarly work, and discuss some examples from our own experimentation with using unconventional hypermedia for dissemination purposes.

Web-Based Platforms and Social Research

It is clearly the diffusion and rapid assimilation of the Web into everyday writing and authoring practices that has helped bring hypermedia onto the social research agenda. The computer screen has become ever more firmly embedded in research practice and now stands at the heart of the social research toolkit: for representing, organizing, and analyzing data, and also for "writing it up"—especially for electronic journals and now, increasingly, e-books. Yet, it is also true that the intrinsic multi-linear qualities of hypertext that so intrigued Bush and Nelson, plus their multimedia capabilities, have so far proven unable to penetrate far into the field of academic research published online. In order to understand the barriers to hypermedia, as well as appreciate its potential, we will first address the emergence of the Web as an obvious potential channel for the dissemination of social research, but one that is considerably underused by academic researchers.

In the age of ubiquitous Web design and multimedia technologies, writing up and publishing social research today may well feel a bit like sitting on a shoreline warily eyeing the sea. Behind stretch the old and familiar landscapes of traditional print conventions, with structured, linear, written book-chapters and journal articles providing their well-trodden footpaths. In front are oceans of free-floating electronic bytes all ready to be coded into colorful images, sounds, words, and pictures and presenting endless possibilities for navigation. These are the uncharted waters now beckoning scholars to follow where bloggers, Facebookers, tweeters, and Web-designers, and all kinds of electronically minded authors have been happily bobbing about for several years now. Surely this is where academics, too, will soon be launching their research findings, potentially using all kinds of clickable media at their disposal. Yet academic publishing has so far made only cautious forays into this territory, keeping its toes, instead, on the drier ground of print-derived traditions. Though multiplying at a rate of knots, online academic journal articles and books still largely follow the familiar conventions of the scholarly "outline": a hierarchically organized structure of chapter and section titles, sub-headings, and step-by-step paragraphing, all kept together with a table of contents, and—if you are lucky—the added benefits of a search tool and hyperlinked bibliographic entries. The novel potential of the computer screen as a "writing space" as opposed to a page (Bolter, 2001)—with its mobile resources of multimedia, text, animation, and multi-linear navigation—is kept at bay.

This adherence to print-derived norms is shored up, it is clear, by the demands of the "scholarly apparatus": that whole edifice of authoring conventions that allow us to meet the demands of scholarly criteria in our published work for rigor, replicability, validity, and so forth (Biella, 1993). However, there are signs of cracks appearing in it. For a start, as the price of digital cameras and audio-recorders continues to drop, researchers are increasingly using multimedia technologies in their data-generation activities. In the pre-computer age, when the physical paper page provided the only medium for analysis and dissemination, researchers recording fieldwork data with cameras, audio, and video had to translate them into the written word for dissemination purposes—via transcription, description, quotation, and a limited amount of photographic illustration. The exception to this was film-medium outputs, of course—but these developed for social research purposes in the relatively separate domain of ethnographic and pedagogic film, where their audiences remained quite small and specialist. In the age of YouTube and easily uploaded digital video, film does not need its own specific distribution networks. In research, as a result, image-word translations seem increasingly needless. Transcription is a key test-case here; still considered essential for analysis purposes, we are nevertheless now able to access uploaded audio-files directly on-screen and attempt more in the way of analysis of speech and noise itself. The appeal of "clickability," the elasticity of the computer writing space, and the instantaneous accessibility of on-screen multimedia present a number of challenges, discussed further below, for the preservation of the scholarly apparatus.

Secondly, computer-assisted analysis software of various kinds (numerical, textual, graphical, visual, and auditory) means data-records such as fieldnotes, photographs, and interview recordings can be both generated and analyzed in the same loss-free digital formats. Further, these programs allow them to be graphically represented on-screen in multi-linear and interlinked ways, such that the multiple connections and relationships among different aspects of the analysis come to the fore. In such a context, the conventional idea of *writing up* (i.e., squeezing the resultant network of insights into mono-medium, unilinear, print-derived outline formats) appears increasingly discordant. In fact, the risk of disconnection between the activities of data generation and analysis on the one hand, and "writing up" on the other, now seems more apparent, if anything, than when most social researchers had only pens and paper or word-processors at hand. As things are, many researchers emerge from perusal of graphical, networked, and even animated representations of analysis in a qualitative coding program such as Atlas-ti or NVivo to face a very different kind of task—that of producing for the online journal a structure of sequentially ordered paragraphs of print with hierarchical headings. This may resemble trying to unravel a knitted jumper and pull out a single, straight line of wool.

It seems inevitable that, given the availability of screen-based dissemination, authors will increasingly turn to the Web for representing their research findings. Here, alternative formats can be represented. For example, Ainslie Yardley has created a Web site called Creativity Country that uses a map—similar to the London Underground map—to direct the reader to different "lines" of enquiry in her thesis on creativity (Yardley, 2004). This multi-linear map, using hyperlinks to take the reader from a "station" on a line to a text, allows her to "tell[s] a visual story, mapping the conceptual links visually and allowing the researcher to show how a specific research agenda is contained within a larger cross-disciplinary domain" (Yardley, 2008, p. 7). Hypermedia's key affordances—of clickability on the one hand and multimedia on the other—allow relatively straightforward and potentially fruitful means of showing interwoven strands of analysis. As we shall discuss below, all kinds of linkages between written exposition and data-records can be activated on-screen in digital media form. This potentially grants readers a more multidimensional and, of course, interactive engagement with both dataset and findings. Nevertheless, there are problems and losses to be recognized in relation to the use of hypermedia for social research, such as the danger of corroding scholarly standards, losing the logical coherence of analysis, and neglecting the need for synthesis and argumentation. There are also considerable issues of ethics involved in electronic forms of representation, especially using images, the topic to which we now turn.

Ethical Issues

The use of digital data is fraught with problems concerning the ownership and control of participants' personal details—especially where images and video are concerned.[1] The issues here relate both to the *storage* and *dissemination* of these potentially identifying kinds of information. The contemporary social science research landscape is replete with ethical debates, codes of conduct, and regulations. Gaining ethical approval from committees before fieldwork begins has become an increasingly standard aspect of social research. Contrary to these well-established mechanisms, there has been little debate or development of ethical best practice in relation to the storage and dissemination of qualitative multimedia data. Most researchers nowadays have had to develop quite careful procedures for dealing with participant protection: maintaining confidentiality via anonymization or pseudonymization and stringent data access management; thinking about the physical, social, and psychological well-being of respondents; and maintaining their rights. These are difficult enough to ensure during the original fieldwork period, but constructing an electronic environment for dissemination poses further problems. There is an argument that, even where informed consent has been negotiated in the original research, participants are unable to acquiesce to the reproduction of their data where it is disseminated via the Web since the potential future users—and uses—of these data become impossible to identify or predict. While this is also the case to an extent in published printed works, the amount and quality of identifying data are obviously limited in the case of the printed page. On the Web, and in hypermedia research of the kind discussed in this chapter, data-records can be reproduced in their entirety.[2] In debating the issue of consent and data reuse, both *ethics* and *law* play key roles and directly influence the practice of social science researchers.

In the case of law, it is often rather unsettling to recognize that the words spoken by a respondent in an interview remain the intellectual property of that respondent. If a researcher records the interview, the recording remains the property of the institution in which they are employed. Words transcribed from a recording also remain the copyright of the interviewee. In order for the content of recordings to be reproduced in any analysis or subsequent publication, the interviewer must ensure that the respondent assigns copyright over to the institution responsible for the recording. These issues need to be properly discussed with the participants involved. Normally, this can be done via gaining informed consent. The legal position with regard to still photographs and video recordings is quite distinct from copyright issues with sound recordings. With regards to photographs, copyright remains with the person taking the image (although not if the photograph was taken for "private" purposes). A research participant who agrees to have their photograph taken has no rights over the subsequent use of their image. Hence, research participants have no *legal* rights over their video image or any subsequent use (unless the use contravenes defamation or contract laws). However, privacy laws have been emerging that may afford the researched with more rights across a range of media. Article 8 of the European Convention on Human Rights has had some clear impacts upon the rights of individuals within the United Kingdom. In part, the article states, "Everyone has the right to respect for his private and family life, his home and his correspondence." Over the next decade or so, it is probable that laws in many countries will take privacy more seriously, potentially affecting the rights of research participants and research practice.

In terms of ethics, as distinct from law, social researchers should always seek to avoid causing, directly or indirectly, any harm or anxiety to research participants. Pink (2001) espouses the "collaborative method" in generating data, arguing that such a method assumes researcher and respondent are consciously working together to produce interviews, photographs, and video footage. Moral ownership of the data is shared in this method and respondents are empowered to change interview transcripts and edit still photographs and video footage, producing a coauthored final data product. While this method is at odds with the legal position in the United Kingdom where joint ownership of photographs and video footage is not easily established (or desirable for the researcher's employing institution), efforts can be made to ensure respondents are fully consulted as to the use and representation of the data (Corti & Backhouse, 2005). However, the temporality of consent, as something always in process, always in negotiation, and always in a state of renewal (Thorne, 1980), is something that is recognized by the main funding bodies in the United Kingdom: "Highly formalised or bureaucratic ways of securing consent should be avoided in favour of fostering relationships in which ongoing ethical regard for participants is to be sustained, even after the study itself has been completed" (Economic and Social Research Council [ESRC], 2003, p. 24, para. 3.2.2).

Much like in law, photographic and video data have a distinct set of ethical dilemmas that set them apart from the more common audio interview and subsequent written transcript. Pink (2001) acknowledges the power of the visual across cultures and is cognizant of the potential anxieties and pains associated with the medium. In research situations, where participants are often in a subordinate position to the researcher (which is certainly the case in law relating to multimedia), it is important that participants' sensitivities toward the visual are factored into the design of the study. In particular, participants should be fully consulted before any photographic or filming work begins and any objections need to be taken with great seriousness. The subsequent use of photographic and video materials also needs to be established with informants prior to data collection. This is particularly important where the participants are considered vulnerable—children, victims of crimes, criminals, disabled, and so on. Similarly, researchers working with photographic and video materials need to be acutely aware not only of the sensitivities of respondents to the visual, but also the potential legal ramifications that may result from ill-judged multimedia representations. Many of these potential pitfalls can be negated by maintaining close and trusting relationships with participants and adopting where possible Pink's notion (2001) of the collaborative method in generating visual data.

Qualitative Data Analysis and "Thick Description"

We now turn to a consideration of the kinds of research that might benefit from adopting a hypermedia approach. If we think of hypermedia in its most basic definition—as a system of multiple linkages between different media elements—it is clear that it focuses attention on the *relationships* among elements—whether numerical, textual, or graphical. Discovering these linkages and interpreting them necessarily lie at the heart of the analytic project in all social research. However, it is in qualitative and in particular ethnographic research that such relationships are particularly salient, because human beings' motivations and meanings are never straightforwardly manifest in what is said or enacted. How can one understand the culture of an office, for example? This complex task requires understanding the relationships amongst multiple orders of evidence: for example, between an interviewee's descriptions of his or her boss' behavior, the boss' own accounts of interactions with his or her employees, the researcher's observations of how work is allocated, the physical organization of the office itself, and the researcher's knowledge of organizational theory. How does one bring these together and make sense of them as a whole? Such conundrums require careful interpretation by sifting through and cross-referencing the relevant data, theory, and literature.

In using linking strategies for analysis, as we shall see below, one fieldnote, memo, or utterance is always interpreted in the light of its relationship to another, which focuses attention on the nature of the relationships at stake. It was Clifford Geertz (1973) who introduced the term "thick description" to refer to the activity of making sense of multiple layers of accounts by participants, such that the ethnographer is faced with "a multiplicity of complex conceptual structures, many of them superimposed or knotted into one another, which are at once strange, irregular, and inexplicit" (p. 49). In this sense, the interpretation of inter-relationships is key to qualitative research.

For Geertz, the need to consider such inter-relationships can be met by way of ethnographic description, that is, using the powers of observation and interpretation exercised by the anthropologist. However, other writers on qualitative methods argue for adopting *multiple methods*, which are necessarily about bringing different data together and understanding their interlinkages (or fractures). Hyperlinking can help make sense of these. Bringing a range of research instruments into the qualitative toolkit allows the object of analysis—necessarily complex and multidimensional—to be examined from a number of angles, a process that Richardson (2000) likens to grasping the many different kinds of light that a crystal refracts. Lincoln and Denzin (2003) introduce the concept of bricolage (originally from Levi Strauss) to designate the multiple webs of relationships that need attention in qualitative analysis. This has helped to fuel calls for adopting multiple techniques for data generation. For example, narrative interviewing can be combined with structured questionnaires and with naturalistic observation; video recording can be brought into focus with photographs and fieldnotes, and features of discourse can be scrutinized alongside records of observed interactions. Such are the multistranded networks of relationships that make up qualitative bricolage. For these reasons, triangulation has gained considerable followings in both quantitative and qualitative research traditions.

However, understanding relationships among different data is the key here, not the multiple kinds of data in themselves. Indeed, there is a danger in mixed-method research of ending up with data-records of different kinds that are then not properly brought into dialogue with each other. Instead, they may simply be accumulated in an additive way and used to address research questions that are implicitly different. The challenge of bricolage is to synthesize the insights they provide (Kincheloe, 2005). Hypermedia focuses attention all the time on interconnections and relationships. By instituting links among data and naming them, and allowing research data to be grasped as a network of interlinked associations, it enables researchers to bring different kinds of insight together.

This is also the case in the representation and dissemination of research findings, as we discuss below. Hypermedia authoring goes some way to meeting the demands of reflexivity and multi-linear forms of exposition that have often been called for in the so-called "reflexive turn" in qualitative research. This has emerged after a long period of self-critique amongst qualitative researchers who have recognized the subjective dimensions of writing and drawn attention to its narrative conventions. Ethnographic writing, in particular, has been shown to be highly reliant on recurrent rhetorical forms and tropes (Atkinson, 1990). It is true that, since the first appearance of critical work interrogating these authoring conventions (initiated by Clifford & Marcus, 1986), there has recently been greater tolerance of alternative and experimental forms of journal articles, yet there is still, undoubtedly, a recognizable and standard academic article structure that ethnographers and other qualitative researchers are inculcated into through their academic training; this is especially the case in social science writing. Film dissemination (the preserve mainly of anthropologists) is also characterized by long-established conventions, although here there has been more freedom to introduce innovations and a wider range of experimental practices (see Loizos, 1993; Banks, 1992; Barbash & Taylor, 1997). Hypermedia allows film and writing to be combined in creative ways. The cinematic idea of zooming in and zooming out, of representing alternative perspectives simultaneously, and of tracing multiple linkages between intertwined stories can be seen as characteristic of the contemporary ethnographic imagination (see Marcus, 1994). There are many ways in which hypermedia, in this sense, facilitates a more multifaceted and interactive engagement between authors, texts, and readers. In order to illustrate what can be done, we turn to a few illustrations from a research project in which we have been involved: an ethnographic exploration of how "science" is enacted in an interactive discovery center.

An Illustration: Hypermedia Experimentation at Cardiff University

A team of qualitative researchers based at Cardiff School of Social Sciences has long been working on hypermedia's applications for qualitative social research. A series of projects (funded by the UK Economic and Social Research Council) has explored how hypermedia might support the production and analysis of empirical datasets and findings in ways that are faithful to interpretative methodology, the capacities of contemporary technology, and the emerging possibilities for digital ethnography (for our early work in this area, see Weaver & Atkinson, 1994; Coffey, Atkinson, & Holbrook, 1996; Dicks & Mason, 1998, 1999; Mason & Dicks, 2002; Dicks & Mason, 2003; Dicks, Mason, Coffey, & Atkinson, 2005; Dicks & Mason, 2008). This experimentation has allowed us to explore a number of issues that confront the digital-age researcher: the generation of multimedia data; the capturing to computer and editing of recordings in image and sound; the complexities and challenges of multimedia data management, storage, and reuse; the facilitation of hypertextual analytical strategies; the creation and development of hyperlinks; and forms of authoring and dissemination that take advantage of hypermedia principles. From this experimentation, we have constructed a gradually evolving electronic Web-resource (password-protected) that we have termed an "ethnographic hypermedia environment" (or EHE). The EHE hosts all the multimedia datasets generated for our projects, plus three major "trails" that introduce readers to our interpretative findings, analysis, and methodology.

The original ethnographic fieldwork from which the datasets were generated was conducted at an interactive Science Discovery Centre in 2002–2003. Defining and marketing itself in opposition to the image of a traditional museum, this visitor attraction tries to make science accessible (to school-children and the general public) by blending educational and entertainment principles (hence "edutainment"). For example, in the exhibition hall children interact with machines, gadgets, and computer screens that perform actions designed to illustrate certain scientific principles. They also enter a science "theater" to participate in live shows with performers using pantomime techniques, music, and stories to illustrate scientific topics. In studying these two principal settings, our research questions focused on the production and consumption of "science"—the means by which the Centre produced interactive exhibits and displays of science and the strategies of learning and sense-making invoked by "consumers" (children, teachers, and families).

Our fieldwork comprised three objectives: (1) understanding how the various exhibits and performances provided were designed, constructed, and managed by the Centre's staff; (2) observing and analyzing how these exhibits and "performances" worked in practice; and (3) selecting two samples indicative of the two main classes of visitor (primary school classes and family groups) and investigating how they interacted with and made sense of them. These questions were addressed using a variety of techniques for observing and recording the creative decision-making processes, techniques of construction and design, staff meetings and interactions, visitor interactions, performances, and publicity activities that make up the daily life of the Centre. Data were generated in a number of different forms: fieldnotes, transcripts, live video footage, photographic images, and scanned visual materials. The analysis stage involved the construction of a complex network of named hyperlinks, establishing links between data-records, analytical memos, and interpretative texts. It was built in *Storyspace* (see below) and then exported to Web-ready HTML using custom designed templates. This brings us to the topic of software.

Software

When handling large amounts of multimedia data, there are various software aids currently available. To manage and facilitate analysis of the different data-records we used a number of different software programs:

1. *Transana*, an audiovisual transcription tool, enabled us to link segments of texts to audiovisual material through the use of time-codes (time-data recorded onto digital video tape that allow tagged excerpts of the video-record to be searched and retrieved). Hence, we could compile and annotate libraries of video data clips. Unfortunately, *Transana* does not allow hyperlinking of these video segments. In the absence of software that does, it remains to our knowledge largely impracticable to implement a hypertextual analysis strategy for video data. Such a strategy would, in our view, be invaluable as it would allow qualitative researchers working with video footage to specify and depict all kinds of complex inter-linkages between salient "scenes," moments, events, actions, or other aspects of the video recording made.
2. *Storyspace* will be unfamiliar to most social researchers as it does not routinely figure in the qualitative analysis toolkit. Although used primarily by writers engaged in Web-based literary projects, it has the potential to be used as a valuable qualitative analysis tool. It allows the researcher to set up complex networks of hypertextual links among elements of the dataset (or "data nodes") identified as significant. Crucially, it allows these links to be named. Further, since these hyperlinks are dynamic, the researcher can click on a link and be taken immediately to the pairs of data nodes concerned (the two nodes he or she has linked together). The resulting network of labeled hyperlinks can be visually

depicted *and* manipulated across entire collections of interview transcriptions and fieldnotes (see Figure 6.1). These analytic networks, for example, allowed us to depict the multiple connections and dissonances between how various Centre staff communicated with each other in meetings, what they did in work processes we observed, and what they said in interviews with us. *Storyspace* is, however, less useful in working across diverse media, since memory capacity limits the amount of audiovisual data that can be handled at any one time. A final caveat at the time of writing is that the most recent version of the program (2.5) only works on Apple computers while the Windows version (2.04) has not been updated in several years.

3.   *Adobe Premiere*, a well-known video editing package, allowed us to create both edited sequences of video as well as split-screen collages that could be used to interrogate relationships between different video data-records. Split-screen collages enabled us to inspect footage taken from two different views at the same time—allowing us to compare, for example, audience reactions to the science theater show with simultaneous footage of the performers on stage. We used edited sequences, by contrast, in an attempt at creating visual representations analogous to "video analytical fieldnotes." Editing footage together into "scenes" reflected our emergent interpretations of the video data. This allowed particular kinds of insight to be represented and analyzed; for example, edited footage of children's movements from the exhibition hall to the science theater illuminated how their bodily comportment changed from running freely around to being marshaled into a calmer and more disciplined kind of comportment suitable for the seated auditorium.

4.   *Adobe Photo Album* was used to catalogue the library of digital photographs and scanned documents. This software also has a basic indexing system, which is useful for generating hierarchies of keywords.

5.   There is also of course a whole corpus of dedicated software packages for computer-assisted qualitative data analysis (CAQDAS), such as Atlas.ti and NVivo, the former offering hypertextual functionality in its "network" views. Atlas.ti can be utilized in Web-dissemination because it is capable of exporting its coding in the generic XML data format that is widely used on the Web. In addition, both programs can handle different media relatively efficiently. However, we have not undertaken dedicated experimentation with these programs, partly because considerable work has already been undertaken by others in this area and partly because of their limited hypertextual functionality at the time of undertaking our projects.

6.   Analysis that exploits hyperlinking still requires working across several software programs simultaneously, as there is not yet, to our knowledge, a dedicated CAQDAS package that allows dynamic, labeled hyperlinking to be put in place across complex multimedia datasets, although Atlas-ti does come close to this.

Data Management and Archiving

Preparing a good digital data archive is an essential prerequisite to the analytic activities we now go on to describe. Our experience shows that hypermedia analysis/

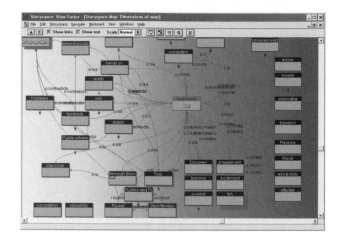

Figure 6.1 Screen shot from *StorySpace* showing map of all the nodes relating to the theme' wow factor'. Each node is itself clickable and can contain other networks of nodes within and across it.

representation can only proceed on the basis of a data archive containing the original records in such a way that allows any record to be easily found and retrieved. This data management function is something at which CAQDAS programs such as Atlas-ti and NVivo excel. But where CAQDAS programs are not being used, some other database program (such as Microsoft's Access) should be considered. It is essential, for instance, that all data-records (whether photographs, transcripts, fieldnotes, or video footage) are correctly identified and ideally given unique accession numbers (as in conventional archiving techniques). The reasons are that it is easy to lose sight of which piece of data one is dealing with while involved in the analytic activity of making a large number of links in the dataset.

In software programs such as StorySpace, which lacks the data management tools provided in CAQDAS programs, it is easy to make a copy of a piece of data and forget to label it correctly. If each record is correctly accessioned from the outset and stored in a database, and if all copies created are consistently labeled with their original record-number, the danger of losing bits of data or failing to identify which piece of data belongs to which record is minimized. The time-consuming preparatory jwork involved in assembling this database will be rewarded when it comes to constructing the networks of links (which may eventually be presented to the reader, as discussed below), for it will ensure that it is possible to navigate around the dataset without losing sight of which element of the data-record is being encountered.

Hyperlinking and Data Analysis

We now discuss in more detail how analysis of a multimedia dataset might proceed through a process of hyperlinking data-records together (albeit linking can only be done in a limited form for video). What does hyperlinking allow us to do that ordinary qualitative coding does not?

Analysis of "Lettered" Data

We turn first to analysis of interview transcripts and fieldnotes. There has been some disagreement in the published literature as to whether a meaningful distinction can be drawn between coding and hyperlinking (see Coffey et al., 1996; Kelle, 1997, Lee & Fielding, 1991). Our work suggests that these are related but distinct approaches to qualitative data analysis. Our experimentation with *StorySpace* does suggest a distinction between the largely associative activity of hyperlinking and the indexing work of coding. Hyperlinking focuses attention on the nature of the diverse relationships among segments of data, while coding focuses attention on categories of data segment—through assigning them to common categories. When a piece of data is hyperlinked to another, the nature of the relationship between them is specified (through naming it—such as "this contradicts that" or "this follows from that" or "this is an aspect of that"). When a code is assigned to a piece of data, by contrast, the relationship is usually "this is an instance of that." The advantage of hyperlinking, therefore, lies in its ability to help the researcher specify the nature of the links within the dataset and to see it as a network of semantic and thematic relationships. This is distinct from coding, since the whole point of an index is to create links between data and index, not data and data.[3] Coding, as an indexical system, tends to focus attention on groups of data-segments and their content, rather than the relationships among them.

However, it is not the case that coding is inferior to, or should be replaced by hyperlinking. On the contrary, a period of initial coding ("rough" coding) of the dataset is arguably essential before hyperlinking can proceed. Without this, hyperlinking will be a blind process at best, with the researcher making links through the dataset without a thorough knowledge of its thematic patterns and main contours. Coding allows the dataset to be thoroughly perused and its main themes noted. Once this initial coding is complete, hyperlinking can produce valuable results. Hyperlinking can consist of both data-to-data links and data-to-analytical memo links. It is data-to-data linking that offers the innovative potential of hypertext analysis, since it focuses attention on the relationships among elements of the dataset. Data-to-memo linking is more akin to traditional coding. Both complement each other. Unfortunately, there is no available off-the-shelf software that allows labeled and dynamic hyperlinking of the complex kind that *StorySpace* excels in and that can also handle large amounts of video and other multimedia data (although Atlas-ti's hyperlinking functions, though more limited, are of real value). CAQDAS development has been dominated by indexical "code and retrieve" approaches (though this is changing, and see Kelle, 2000).[4] These, as Coffey et al., (1996) argue, are not necessarily the most appropriate technique for every project. Conversely, the hypertext approach to data analysis works on a cross-referencing system where text segments are linked together due to there being a specified relationship between them. Our solution has been to use *StorySpace* for hyperlinking, and then to export the resultant networks of links to HTML.[5] However, in terms of video analysis, to which we turn now, there is no software to our knowledge that allows footage to be broken into segments and dynamically hyperlinked into networks.

Analysis of Video Data

Here, due to space restrictions, we do not deal with analysis of photographic images, but with video footage only. We can identify four stages in the analysis of video data:

1. Logging the time code (verbally describing the content of each segment of footage and making initial decisions as to what is significant and what can be discarded)
2. Storing and capturing those parts of the footage deemed significant (using digital cameras connected to computer video cards)
3. Transcribing captured video footage (in more or less detail, depending on the demands of analysis)
4. Analyzing video footage

This last is the big question that confronts hypermedia ethnographers: to what extent should video fieldwork footage be intensively analyzed in the same way as written (transcribed) material? While published work on analysis of lettered data (e.g., coding of interview transcripts; fieldnotes) is full and detailed, principles of analysis for researcher-generated visual data remain relatively unsystematized—although several textbooks have recently been produced on the topic of visual methods (Rose, 2001; Banks, 2001; Pink, 2001). Some studies propose coding video footage in a similar way to written transcripts (e.g., Nastasi, 1999). But there has been concern that coding reduces footage to a flattened plane of analysis through disaggregating it into segments and recoding it into verbal descriptions (Pink, 2001). Video footage inevitably contains multiple levels of information that are not necessarily manifest through coding. Such debates are similar to those over the merits of content analysis in media studies, and reflect long-established disagreements between realist or "factist" approaches to image analysis (e.g., Collier & Collier, 1986) and more reflexive approaches (e.g., Pink, 2001; Banks, 2001). The latter styles of analysis focus on interrogating the relationships between viewer and image and the contexts in which the image was made, rather than seeing them as neutral records of natural action. However, since these approaches are highly reflexive, they rarely provide guidelines specifying precise procedures for analysis of content *per se*.

In our own work, we found it necessary to treat our video footage both as realist *records* of the general patterns of visitor–exhibit interaction at the science center we studied (which we coded qualitatively according to broad content themes using *Transana*, as above) and as *narratives* shaped by participants' and researchers' interactions in specific fieldwork situations (which we sought to represent by producing a number of *edited sequences* of selected field activities and events, using *Adobe Premiere*, as above). The edited sequences were not treated as showing unambiguous patterns or sequences of action, but as representations that needed careful interpretation and contextualization in order to understand what was going on during a particular sequence of filming—a more holistic kind of interpretation not suited to the fragmentary activity of coding. We found this dual approach produced useful insights into the different kinds of information yielded by the same video data.

Our experience suggests that attempts to devise intricate content coding schemas for video will be suited to certain fields of inquiry (such as in close behavioral observations of psychological work or the study of kinesics) but not others. In relation to qualitative analysis of social research data in fieldwork settings, the objects of analysis comprise inevitably complex and multidimensional social worlds. In addition, the *multimodality* of video-records presents considerable barriers to coding—a term that refers to the many different kinds of semiotic resources involved in an audiovisual record (e.g., from visual modes of the face such as gesture, eye-movements, and facial expressions, to aural modes of the voice such as tone, accent, and phrasing, not to mention the many meaningful aspects captured on videotape of background soundscapes and the environments in which participants are located—see Dicks, Soyinka, & Coffey, 2006). Multimodal data in video afford meaning in specific ways—the moving image communicates differently to the soundtrack, for instance—and when a still is captured, the specific modalities of the photograph come more to the fore. The complexity of the video-record as opposed to written or spoken records alone means that its meaning is produced on a number of levels. We found that coding of video was most useful on the level of categorizing footage very broadly into general themes and patterns. For more ethnographically attuned analysis, editing the video material into narrative-governed relationships and scenes produced deeper insights into the multiple interactions at stake, namely, among filmed participants, the physical setting, the researchers, microphone, and camera.

Analysis of Sound-Data

Sound-data grants the researcher access to a whole dimension of meanings that is too often ignored. Paying attention to the soundscapes in a field setting yields, in our experience, considerable insights into its "feel" and general qualities, as well as granting more precise insights into what is going on in the setting. For example, listening carefully to the exhibition hall at Techniquest reveals everyday soundscapes of many feet running and shuffling and a background hum of multiple children's voices together with the electronic beeping sounds emitted by gadgets, creating a "feel" of science blending into fun and the randomness of visitors' interactions. As Les Back (2007) points out, recording soundscapes as objects of analysis shows up unexpected and often neglected dimensions of meaning: movement (of transport or plastic cups), distant voices (such as foreign language), as well as silences (see also his research with John Drever on The London Ear at http://www.goldsmiths.ac.uk/csisp/papers/back_london_ear.pdf). These can point to aspects of the setting that otherwise would have been missed. Similarly, Hall, Lashua, & Coffey, (2008) point to the levels of meaning that are lost when as researchers we take research participants out of the flux of everyday settings and place them in silent rooms for an interview. They have experimented with walking-tours and other mobile methods in order to capture how sound works as a key dimension of everyday social worlds. All of these considerations make audio recording—not just of interviews but soundscapes, too—an increasingly valued aspect of qualitative research.

What then can be done with the audio recording made? The analysis of sound-data is something that is still in its infancy in qualitative methodology, as most sound recordings made are then transcribed for the purposes of analysis (Lee, 2004). Indeed, the transcription of audio recordings has become a largely unquestioned and taken-for-granted aspect of qualitative research; as Lee (2004, p. 14) observes, "within the qualitative tradition there is a sense in which the tape recorder has come to be seen less as a device for recording sound, and more as a means of producing text." However, some researchers are experimenting with capturing to computer their interview and other sound-data—recorded in a digital format—and analyzing the resulting digital audio file directly on the computer screen without transcription (for an overview, see Maloney & Paolisso, 2001). This direct analysis of audio-files can be facilitated by appropriate software such as Sound Forge.

Although we have had only limited experience of such software, the direct analysis of auditory data does offer some real benefits in that the data can be directly experienced in acoustic modes and hence analyzed in their own right.

However, the problem with any auditory data-record is that sound disappears as it is uttered, being a temporally realized mode (unlike writing, a permanent and spatially realized mode). As a result, it is elusive and requires time-consuming repetition and rewinding in order for the analyst to take in the information (although, it must be said, a similar problem confronts the analyst of video, and is in any case considerably lessened by the ease of digital file navigation controls in editing software programs). Most researchers, however, are likely to find most useful a combination of reading transcriptions and listening to audio recordings. The written "version" always excludes the acoustic modes of the original recording, which in turn represents a reduction of the original live acoustic soundscape affected by the microphone's position, direction, and sensitivity. The many modes of vocal expression (tone, volume, pauses, accent, rhythm, stress, and so on)—not to mention the "background" noises of the setting itself—all get left behind during transcription unless painstaking notation procedures are used to represent these, as conversation analysts require (see Ashmore & Reed, 2000). It is undoubtedly the case that more experimentation with direct audio analysis will take place in social research in the near future.

Multimedia Integration and Multimodality

Literature on visual methods now abounds and sound-data, too, is receiving increasing attention in the methodological literature, but little work has been done on the integration of different media within one project. We would emphasize, following theorists of multimodality (e.g., Kress & Van Leeuwen, 2001), that the ways in which different media communicate are to be understood as particular orchestrations of multiple semiotic *modes*. Different media share some modes (e.g., photographs and video both capture the physical modes of objects, such as size, position, color, shape) but not others (a photograph obviously lacks the ability to capture movement). Multimodality emphasizes that bringing together data recorded in different media (as in a typical multimedia Web page) produces a meaning-making environment that is not simply a sum of the various media present (Kress, 1998). Different media deploy modes of meaning differently. Our use of various media in our data-records (video footage, audio recordings, photographs, scanned images, written fieldnotes) shows how different kinds of ethnographic insight are afforded by each medium (see Dicks et al., 2006).

It follows from this that there is no such thing as multimedia analysis per se. Our experiments suggest that diverse media cannot be lumped together and subjected to generic analysis. Instead, analysis has to proceed initially by examining each media-specific dataset in turn, that is, photographs have to be analyzed separately from video footage and written fieldnotes. Different procedures of analysis are applicable to different media and contain different kinds of information—for example, an image of a space presents it as a map, while a textual account provides a narrative or itinerary of it (see Hastrup, 1992). Analysis needs to take account of these differences. However, this is not something we go into here, as the analysis of sound, video, photography, and written data are each topics with a vast literature in their own right. What we do acknowledge is that more work is needed on how multimedia data-records dialogue with each other. What network of meanings is produced by linking together on-screen a photograph, a fieldnote, and a piece of video? How do the insights of video analysis relate to those obtained from analysis of fieldnotes? We have tried to start thinking about the issues at stake in the analytic integration of multimedia (see Dicks et al., 2006), but much more work is needed on this.

From Analysis to Authoring: Hypermedia Data-Transparency

The question of how video-records dialogue with written records is not only an issue for analysis, it is also germane to the task of hypermedia authoring and the representation of findings. In hypermedia authoring, all data-records can potentially be made available to the reader through hyperlinking. This is one—perhaps the most—significant affordance of hypermedia for social research. In conventional "writing-up activities," the data-records usually remain hidden in the computer's memory or in the filing cabinet and are not presented to the reader. This is because print-derived writing conventions do not allow the author to provide much in the way of access to data-records—which make a limited appearance in academic articles as quotes, selections, and extracts rather than be reproduced extensively. In the case of Web-authoring, by contrast, there is potential to exploit the powers of hyperlinking to present the data-records in their entirety to the reader and allow them to be inspected quite freely. In addition, all the analysis that has been conducted can also become part of the material available to the reader. Rather than the researcher's analysis remaining hidden from readers as in conventional models, its physical manifestations—the network of linkages or the coded records themselves—can be presented in such a way that readers are empowered to navigate their way around them and come to understand how the analysis has been conducted and organized. This has profound implications for enhancing the transparency of the analytic process.

Accordingly, the dataset itself—overlaid with the researcher's analytic annotations and codes, or (if hyperlinking has been used for analysis) reorganized into dynamic networks of hyperlinked elements—can become part of the dissemination. Further, this annotated, coded, and/or hyperlinked dataset can then be creatively linked into the *narrative* that the author produces. By this we mean the product created through what is classically known as the "writing up" of research, in which the author presents a coherent set of statements, findings, claims, arguments, explanations, and other kinds of exegesis to demonstrate to the reader what key points have been distilled from the analysis conducted and how these contribute to the academic field that is being addressed. This narrative embodies the conclusions of the research conducted (and it has certain key functions—to persuade, to show validity, and to address other aspects of the "scholarly apparatus"). It is to be expected that this narrative will need to be organized sequentially in order to be clearly understood (more on this below). Yet this is not to say that it, too, cannot be presented through clickable multimedia on-screen, as there is no need to sacrifice sequentiality. Instead, it can be presented through sequential Web pages containing links into the analyzed dataset.

To sum up, there are three aspects of analysis and authoring that can all potentially be incorporated into a hypermedia Web-based dissemination:

1. The dataset itself
2. The dataset plus analysis
3. The findings and conclusions—linked in to either or both of the above

This third potential is highly significant, because it means that any aspect of the author's narrative can potentially be linked into appropriate parts of the data/analysis so that the reader can reflect on the evidential basis upon which the author's conclusions have been reached. The potential benefits of being able to inspect the dataset and the analysis, and to thereby see how conclusions are underpinned, represents a considerable enhancement of the transparency of social research.

Potential Problems

There is, however, a question over the extent to which this level of transparency is entirely desirable. It may be that it sets up unrealistic expectations on the part of readers—that they can quickly come to terms with large amounts of second-hand, unfamiliar data, understand how analysis has been conducted, and thereby be in a position to appraise and assess authors' conclusions. This is unlikely to be realistic unless readers are prepared to invest considerable effort and time in familiarizing themselves with the dataset. Otherwise, there could be a danger of unpracticed readers launching attacks on authors' findings based on partial, uninformed, and undigested readings of the data. What is actually required in order to do justice to someone else's data is a kind of reading more akin to secondary analysis. Therefore, we suggest that these kinds of highly data-transparent hypermedia readings that are very demanding on the reader's time, ability, and commitment should not be viewed in the same light as routine readings of research that need to be done relatively swiftly and economically.

There is another sense in which hypermedia data-transparency presents both opportunities and costs. This refers to the way in which hypermedia blurs the stages of analysis into that of authoring and representation, since hyperlinking produced in analysis can also be accessed by readers. On the one hand, this blurring allows the writer to keep incorporating insights and arguments right up until the moment in which he or she decides to end the authoring process. On the other hand, there are two related dangers. One is that the analysis strategy becomes impossibly unwieldy and complex; as more and more links are produced, more and more relationships are discovered. Hypertext/media representations such as those that can be created using *StorySpace* allows different ways of showing the linkages made, which helps in organizing them, but still—just as in coding strategies, which can also become impossibly unwieldy—there comes a "cut-off point" where a decision has to be made to bring the linking phase to a halt.

The other danger is that the later stages of analysis become overshadowed by (re)presentational considerations, so that the demands of screen-based audience-presentation (such as readability, screen-design, navigation, and so forth) come to govern the direction that analysis takes. For instance, in the following steps in the hypermedia analysis process, the last two clearly impinge on decision making about representation:

1. In initial analysis, "rough" coding is followed by intensive data-to-data and data-to-memo hyperlinking (as above).

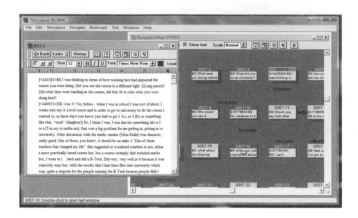

Figure 6.2 Screen shot from *StorySpace* showing the node 00575–5, an excerpt from interview data that has been linked to other excerpts and to analytic memos.

2.   In the later stages of analysis, the researcher begins to formulate an interpretation of the data, and so to write analytic texts (or create mini-films, perhaps) that will elucidate key aspects of the emerging analysis. These can be seen as *interpretative nodes* that, as analysis proceeds, will soon go beyond simple analytic memos and begin to incorporate the findings themselves.
3.   These interpretative nodes will in the process be hyperlinked to selected data nodes—that is, to the relevant data-records including, where appropriate, video, sound, and photographs.

Consequently, at the end of the analysis stage, the researcher is likely to have produced a number of interpretative nodes hyperlinked to data nodes. In addition, through the process of analytic hyperlinking, these data nodes will in turn be hyperlinked to other data nodes (see Figure 6.2). In the latter stages of analysis, the author knows he or she is creating nodes that will be read by readers, and therefore simultaneously begins to consider how to order and structure them for representational purposes. Because hypermedia analysis and representation both take place in the same medium (the computer screen), there is bound to be a danger that analysis will be influenced by screen-design and presentational concerns: this is an issue that needs further acknowledgement and discussion in the literature.

The Process of Hypermedia Authoring

Let us imagine that by the end of analysis phase, you have assembled—perhaps using *StorySpace* as in Figure 6.2—a complex network of hyperlinks among multiple parts of your dataset and analytic memos. Interview transcripts have been divided into nodes, and nodes linked together, so that the interview set presents a complex network of named associations. See Figure 6.2, which shows a view from our *StorySpace* "map" view.

The power of hypermedia as an authoring activity lies in authors' ability to create sophisticated linking between researcher-defined elements of information, or *nodes*. In a hypermedia work, a node can contain any type of media element: for example, a photograph, a scanned image, a piece of video footage, or a sound-recording. Links between nodes may be "basic" in that they merely close one node and open another at its beginning: hence, one might have a Web page in which a piece of video is played and then disappears on a mouse-click to be replaced with a photograph, a piece of text, or another image. However, in the age of ubiquitous Web-authoring, we have become accustomed to Web pages laid out in magazine-page format, with different clickable nodes positioned simultaneously across the page in a mosaic—often with left- and right-hand columns for menus and indexes. These allow pop-up windows to be activated, so that video or sound can be played without leaving the page.

In fact, there has developed quite a standard set of expectations for Web page layout such that Web pages that depart radically from these seem inaccessible or frustrating. Artists are increasingly using the Web to disseminate their work and frequently wish to distinguish their work from commercially oriented or purely informational Web pages. They frequently use much less in the way of text and more in the way of music, sound, and images; artists often also eschew the signposting or indexing conventions of the mosaic-model, preferring the reader to have the feeling of a journey that is not merely about accessing information. It is possible that as researchers use the Web more frequently for authoring purposes, they too will develop conventions and expectations that will govern how a "typical" research-oriented Web page will look. Nevertheless, there are many difficult decisions to be made as to how to link data with analytic content and how to guide the reader around the infinitely elastic writing space of digital "pages"; becoming adept at screen design and navigational tools requires expending effort and time. Unlike print articles or film, both conventionally unilinear in their structure, hypermedia involves making decisions about organizing and ordering content—whether sequentially and/or multi-linearly. We have written extensively about the pitfalls and challenges of this kind of writing elsewhere (Dicks & Mason, 2003, 2008).

The EHE that we produced over the period 2003–2005 uses the "mosaic" model of Web page (see Figure 6.1). It is multi-linear and yet also sequential. It contains three major "trails" that take the reader on journeys through the analysis conducted. On each page, there are clickable links that take the reader into relevant parts of the dataset that evidence the analytic point in question, or which lead into pages containing further analytic or methodological reflections. If a reader follows a link and leaves the main trail, there is a variety of means provided to help them get back again and assist with orientation (e.g., there is the Back button; there is color-coding of each domain of the EHE; and there are tabs at the top of the page that allow the reader to return to the trail). There is also a "Next" button on each page. If the reader simply clicks on each of these, they will be conducted through a progressive, ordered sequence of pages with a step-by-step narrative. By following this sequential order, the reader keeps track of the authors' "default" reading-path, which contains the communicative steps we wish to convey. The decision to offer this default reading-path via the "Next" buttons reflects our view that authors will always want to present material in sequential order to allow academic argumentation to be represented in a logical and progressive manner.

Nevertheless, the real gains in reading research in hypermedia form are made when the reader leaves the default reading-path and departs on a journey of their own—into the dataset itself. Here, the reader will be able to read an interview transcript, listen to a section of an interview recording, watch a piece of video footage, or examine the fieldnotes relating to a particular fieldwork episode. You will recall from the above that, in our EHE, many of these records are hyperlinked with each other in a way that highlights their interconnections and relationships. Hence, when the reader leaves the trail in order to read an interview transcript, for example, they will find links made available to related interview transcripts and, indeed, to other media-records in the dataset as a whole. This allows readers to explore the dataset from a particular angle, hence becoming able to explore their own analytic pathways and begin to produce their own insights.

We have also experimented with a more controlled, less multi-linear kind of representational form, what we have called a "hypermedia essay" (Dicks Hurdley, 2009). This represents an attempt to engage more self-consciously and directly with the demands of the scholarly apparatus (Biella, 1993). Our aim was to produce a hypermedia output that would pass muster as a scholarly "essay," while at the same time take advantage of the unconventional affordances of hypermedia technology—for multi-linearity, and for granting the reader access to data-records. The result is a more carefully controlled kind of Web-presentation with a contents page "menu" of options at the top of each page, and highlighted links on each page to literature references, glossary, and bibliography. As in the EHE, the authoring process meant selecting from our complete dataset of media files and deciding how to link these electronically to each other and to authored written text. Working out this linking structure meant selecting what to link with what and how (e.g., a clickable link to a pop-up, a new page, or to a different section). In line with our aim of producing a more controlled text, we opted for a unilinear structure in which the reader clicks from "page" to "page" each with conventional headings (e.g., The Research Setting; Our Research Questions; Our findings), but where each page still offers clickable links, taking readers further into authored exposition, or into the data-records themselves. Many of these links activate short edited films designed to allow the reader to understand the research setting visually and aurally, rather than having to rely on detailed verbal description as in a print-article.[6] We hope to test out these experiments in the near future by submitting our hypermedia work for scholarly peer-review; this in spite of the fact that we remain highly conscious of the lack of available electronic journals using formats suitable for multimedia, hyperlinked work.

Future Directions

Up to this point, we have concentrated on technology that was available to us off the shelf and explored the potential for its use. Attempting to prognosticate the future is a process fraught with uncertainty but some possibilities can be seen in current new-media outside of the social sciences. One option is to explore "Web 2.0" programs.

The greatest obstacle to the use of hypermedia in qualitative research has been the software. Proprietary programs often will not "talk" to each other, rapidly go out of date and cost money to update, or else get overtaken by competitors. With each program bearing its own assumptions and having its own, sometimes steep, learning curve, it can be a daunting task to attempt to work effectively in all of them. One potential way forward, then, might be to embrace the potential of "Web 2.0" technologies that are deliberately designed to share, manipulate, and transform data.

For example, "tagging" can create emergent folksonomies of multiple datasets that can be shared and visualized through sites such as "Delicious" (a social bookmarking site—http://delicious.com/) and be used to create trails through Web pages using "Diigo" (a social annotation site—http://www.diigo.com/). Wiki sites, as made famous by Wikipedia, can be used to enable collaborative authoring and versioning not just between members of research teams but between researchers and research participants. Online image and video sharing sites such as Flickr.com and YouTube.com allow for annotation and linking. The use of social networking sites such as Facebook to create innovative digital art indicate that the potential is also there for equally innovative research methods. Similarly, the emergence of "micro-blogging" integrated with mobile phones through text messaging as in the Web site Twitter.com shows how even seemingly restrictive formats can be utilized creatively.

The use of Web 2.0 sites in qualitative research is still in its infancy (Mason & Thomas, 2007, 2008) but the influence of Wesch's digital ethnography project amply demonstrates its potential (2009). There are, however, considerable ethical issues to overcome, as most such sites requiring the hosting of what could be sensitive research data on distant servers may include undesirable terms and conditions of use. Given that these are programs run by private companies, the possibility of the company going out of business and making data unrecoverable is also a distinct risk.

Conclusions

We hope that this chapter has given some insight into the potential, but also the dilemmas, involved in doing hypermedia social research. We would point out that this kind of emergent technology is not an easy one to adopt. It is fraught with problems of meeting accepted standards of ethics, scholarly criteria, and accessibility. It is also incredibly resource-intensive and time-consuming to employ. To date, experience suggests that the conservatism of academia and the business models that go hand-in-hand with scholarly publishing has resulted in a distinct lack of enthusiasm for innovative media forms. Perhaps ironically, the most creatively linked networks of academic publishing can be found in the sciences and medical research where publications are routinely cross-linked, tagged, and commented on by readers. For example, the British Medical Journal online site has a very rich assemblage of linked material. On the other hand, qualitative research, and ethnography in particular, valorizes the rich, complex, messy "thickness" of its data yet the field seems reluctant to move beyond the printed page despite the fact that social researchers have been arguing for novel forms of representation for many decades.

Despite the barriers, we believe that paying attention to the issues involved in pursuing hypermedia research will be rewarded, since, as we move further into the digital age of Web-based representation, researchers will indeed increasingly turn to electronic forms of analysis, representation, and dissemination. We also believe that there are significant gains to be had in this transition to a digital age for both authors and readers. In granting readers more extensive and interactive access to datasets and analysis, they can trace and understand more fully the process of constructing research conclusions and understand the evidence that underpins them. In presenting these through hypermedia pathways that allow readers to explore and authors to represent analysis in more multi-linear and flexible kinds of ways, the affordances of both multimedia data and hypertext are clear.

The question remains of whether published social research will remain moored on the firm land of older, print-based formats or begin to venture further out into the digital world of Web 2.0 and hypermedia, with all the risks—and potential—that they entail. Answering that question is beyond us but it seems infeasible to expect the future generations of researchers, who will have grown up in a culture soaked in ubiquitous computing and permanent connections, who will have been used to creatively redeploying communications technology to suit their needs, who will have learned how to transliterate from Web to mobile device to face-to-face speech, to give all that up when it comes time to try to adequately represent the complexities of culture in scholarly publications. For all the risks and difficulties we have outlined that hypermedia publishing creates, a still greater risk is that the format for publishing social research becomes so divorced from the culture in which it exists that it starts to become irrelevant.

Notes

1. For this section, I am indebted to the input of Matt Williams, who has written extensively on these issues in an online guide we produced for an ESRC-funded project on qualitative data archiving. This guide is available online at: http://www.cardiff.ac.uk/socsi/hyper/QUADS/guide.html

2. In our own case, we have decided to restrict access to our EHE only to those academic researchers whom we know and can trust—only issuing passwords to these.

3. This is quite a complex assertion that could be further explored. Depending on the definition of hypertext being utilized, for example Aarseth's very general depiction of hypertext as a form of electronic text (1997), an electronically coded data set could be seen as a type of hypertext. Even if this stance is taken, however, a coding structure is only very minimally hypertextual. Some CAQDAS programs, such as Atlas-ti do now possess some hypertext functionality but it tends not to be integrated with the coding mechanisms.

4. There is an exception to this generalization in textual biblical studies. As Kelle notes (1997, 2000) cross-referencing is a form of textual analysis that has long been used in the study of religious texts and has been implemented in programs marketed specifically as "text analysis" (e.g., Code-A-Text) rather than "data analysis."

5. However, it has to be recognized that many of the links made in StorySpace risk being lost when exported to HTML; we found that we had to recreate many links from scratch. This indicates the problems presented by using two different kinds of programming language for analysis and authoring.

6. To ensure that all data-records can be accurately identified and contextualized, meta-data were attached to each hyperlinked data-extract (e.g., pseudonyms and roles of participants, date and time of recording, technology used, etc.). From the meta-data, readers can gain access to the relevant page of the EHE—where that data-record is to be found in its entirety—and thereby explore a whole network of associated hyperlinked records in the EHE, hence potentially becoming able to build their own analysis. In this way, the hypermedia essay does not have closed walls; it is an open structure that invites wider exploration—while still retaining an internal sequential logic with beginning, middle, and end.

References

Ashmore, M., & Reed, D. (2000). Innocence and nostalgia in conversation analysis: The dynamic relations of tape and transcript. *Forum Qualitative Sozialforschung/Forum: Qualitative Social Research*, *1*(3), http://www.qualitative-research.net/index.php/fqs/article/view/1020/2199.

Atkinson, P. (1990). *The ethnographic imagination: Textual constructions of reality*. London: Routledge.

Back, L. (2007). *The art of listening*. Oxford: Berg.

Banks, M. (1992). Which films are the ethnographic films? In Crawford, P. I., & Turton, D. (Eds.), *Film as ethnography*. Manchester: University of Manchester Press.

Banks, M. (2001). *Visual methods in social research*. London: Sage.

Barbash, I., & Taylor, L. (1997). *Cross cultural filmmaking*. Los Angeles: University of California Press.

Barbules, N. C. (1998). Rhetorics of the Web: Hyperreading and critical literacy. In Snyder, V (Ed.), *Page to screen: Taking literacy into the electronic era*. London: Routledge.

Biella, P. (1993). Beyond ethnographic film: Hypermedia and scholarship, in Rollwagen, J, R. (Ed.), *Anthropological film and video in the 1990s*. Brockport, NY: The Institute Inc.

Bolter, J. D. (2001) *Writing space: Computers, hypertext, and the remediation of print*. Hillsdale, NJ: Lawrence Erlbaum.

Bush, V. (1945). As we may think. *Atlantic Monthly*, *176*, 101–108. Reprinted in Steve, L., & Suzanne, R. (Eds.). (1986). *CD ROM: The new papyrus* (pp. 3–20). Seattle: Microsoft Press.

Clifford, J. & Marcus, G. E. (1986). *Writing culture: The poetics and politics of ethnography*. Berkeley, CA: University of California Press.

Coffey, A., Atkinson, P., & Holbrook, B. (1996). Qualitative data analysis: Technologies and representations. *Sociological Research Online*, *1*(1), Retrieved on August 9, from http://www.socresonline.org.uk/1/1/4.html

Collier, J., & Collier, M. (1986). *Visual anthropology: Photography as a research method*. Albuquerque: University of Mexico Press.

Corti, L., & Backhouse, G. (2005). Acquiring qualitative data for secondary analysis. *Forum Qualitative Sozialforschung/Forum: Qualitative Social Research*, *6*, Retrieved on August 9, from http://www.qualitative-research.net/index.php/fqs/article/view/459

Dicks, B., & Hurdley, R. (2009). Using unconventional media to disseminate qualitative research. *Qualitative Researcher*.

Dicks, B., & Mason, B. (1998). Hypermedia and ethnography: Reflections on the construction of a research approach. *Sociological Research Online*, *3*(3). Retrieved on August 9, from http://www.socresonline.org.uk/3/3/3.html

Dicks, B., & Mason, B (1999). Cyber ethnography and the digital researcher. In Armitage, J. & Roberts, J (Eds.), *Exploring cybersociety: Social, political, economic and cultural issues*. (Vol. 1), Newcastle, UK: University of Northumbria Press.

Dicks B., & Mason B. (2003). Ethnography, academia and hyperauthoring. In Ovieda, O., Barber, J., & Walker, J. R. (Eds.), *Texts and technology*. New Jersey: Hampton Press.

Dicks, B., & Mason B. (2008). Hypermedia methods for qualitative research. In Hesse-Biber, S., & Leavy, P. (Eds.), *The handbook of emergent methods*. New York: Guilford Publications.

Dicks, B., Mason, B., Coffey, A., & Atkinson, P. (2005). *Qualitative research and hypermedia: Ethnography for the digital age*. London: Sage.

Dicks, B., Soyinka, B., & Coffey, A. (2006). Multimodal ethnography. *Qualitative Research*, *6*, 77–96.

Economic and Social Research Council. (2003). *A review of ethics and social science research for the strategic forum for the social sciences*. Department of Sociology, University of York.

Geertz, C. (1973). On thick description: Toward an interpretative theory of culture. In Geertz, C. *The interpretation of cultures*. New York: Basic Books.

Hall, T. A., Lashua, B. D., & Coffey, A. (2008). Sound and the everyday in qualitative research. *Qualitative Inquiry, 14*, 1019–1040.

Hastrup, K. (1992). Anthropological visions: Some notes on visual and textual authority. In Crawford, P. I. & Turton, D. (Eds.), *Films as ethnography*. Manchester: Manchester University Press.

Kelle, U. (1997). Theory building in qualitative research and computer programs for the management of textual data, *Sociological Research Online, 2*(2), Retrieved on August 9, from http://www.socresonline.org.uk/2/2/1.html.

Kelle, U. (2000). Computer-assisted analysis: Coding and indexing. In Bauer, M. W. & Gaskell, G. (Eds.), *Qualitative researching with text, image and sound*. London: Sage.

Kincheloe, J. L. (2005). On to the next level: Continuing the conceptualization of the bricolage. *Qualitative Inquiry, 11*, 323–350.

Kress, G. (1998). Visual and verbal modes of representation in electronically mediated communication: The potentials of new forms of text. In Snyder, I. (Ed.), *Page to screen: Taking literacy into the electronic era*. London: Routledge.

Kress, G., & Van Leeuwen, T. (2001). *Multi-modal discourse*. London: Arnold.

Landow, G. P. (2005). *Hypertext 3.0: Critical theory and new media in an era of globalization*. Baltimore: John Hopkins Press.

Lee, R. (2004). Recording technologies and the interview in sociology, 1920–2000. *Sociology, 38*, 869–889.

Lee, R. M., & Fielding, N. G. (Eds.). (1991). *Using computers in qualitative research*. London: Sage.

Lincoln, Y., & Denzin, N (Eds.). (2003). *The landscape of qualitative research: Theories and issues*. (2nd ed.). London: Sage.

Loizos, P. (1993). *Innovation in ethnographic film*. Manchester: Manchester University Press.

Maloney, R. S., & Paolisso, M. (2001). What can digital audio data do for you? *Field Methods, 13*, 88–96.

Marcus, G. (1994). The modernist sensibility in recent ethnographic writing and the cinematic metaphor of montage. In Taylor, L. (Ed.), *Visualising theory: Essays from V. A. R. 1990–1994*. New York and London: Routledge.

Mason B., & Dicks B. (2002). Going beyond the code: The production of hypermedia ethnography. *Social Science Computer Review, 19*(4), 445–57.

Mason, B., & Thomas, S. (2007). Tags, networks, narrative: Exploring the use of social software for the study of narrative in digital contexts. In *Proceedings of the 18th conference on hypertext and hypermedia* (pp. 39–40) Association of Computing Machinery.

Mason, B., & Thomas, S. (2008). *A million penguins: Research report*. Leicester, UK: Institute of Creative Technologies, De Montfort University.

Nastasi, B. K. (1999). Audiovisual methods in ethnography. In Schensul, J., LeCompte, M. D., Nastasi, B. K., & Borgatti, S. P. (Eds.), *Enhanced ethnographic methods: Audiovisual techniques, focused group interviews and elicitation techniques*. Walnut Creek CA: AltaMira Press.

Nelson, T. (2009). *Project Xanadu*. Retrieved on March 9 from http://www.xanadu.com/.

Pink, S. (2001). *Doing visual ethnography*. London: Sage.

Richardson, L. (2000). Evaluating ethnography. *Qualitative Inquiry, 6*, 253–255.

Rose, G. (2001). *Visual methodologies*. London: Sage.

Thorne, B. (1980). You still takin' notes?: Fieldwork and problems of informed consent. *Social Problems, 27*, 284–297

Weaver, A., & Atkinson, P. (1994). *Microcomputing and qualitative data analysis*. Avebury: Aldershot.

Wesch, M. (2009). *Digital ethnography*. Retrieved on March 9 from http://mediatedcultures.net/ksudigg/.

Yardley, A. (2004). Creativity country: A study of the phenomenon of creativity in disrupted life. Unpublished thesis. Retrieved on August 9, from http://www.creativitycountry.net.au/creativity/creativity_country.htm.

Yardley, A. (2008). Piecing together—A methodological bricolage [25 paragraphs]. *Forum Qualitative Sozialforschung/Forum: Qualitative Social Research, 9,* Retrieved on August 9, from http://www.qualitative-research.net/index.php/fqs/article/view/416.

Chapter 7

Emergent Digital Ethnographic Methods for Social Research

Dhiraj Murthy

Digital ethnography, which applies new media technologies to ethnography, presents exciting possibilities for richly descriptive research, as well as potential pitfalls (especially in terms of ethics). The literature on the subject (e.g., Dicks, 2005; Dicks, Soyinka, & Coffey, 2006; Coffey, Renold, Dicks, Soyinka, & Mason, 2006; Hine, 2000; Howard, 1988; Masten & Plowman, 2003) has grown significantly over the years in response to the implementation and development of these new media technologies. Though much of this work discusses methodological implementation, it is largely limited to Web 1.0 and first generation digital technologies (most of which are over a decade old). Building on my previous work on the subject (Murthy, 2008), this chapter is designed to introduce cutting-edge research technologies—both that are used and could be used—in digital ethnography. Four emergent technologies—Blogs/Wikis (as fieldnotes and research Web sites), digital pens, CMS Groupware, and embedded technology (the "cyborg ethnographer")—will be discussed in-depth. The aim of this chapter is to equip social researchers in academia and industry with the knowledge to understand these technologies and their methodological applications to digital ethnographies. Ethical considerations relevant to digital ethnography such as informed consent, "lurking," privacy, and intellectual property will also be introduced by examining specific digital ethnographies and existing ethical frameworks/guidelines.

What Is "Digital Ethnography"?

> Every day, we witness mobile professionals at work—on the subway, at the park, in cafés. On mobile phones, they chat with business partners and write text messages. On their laptop computers, they surf the Web and post blog entries. Yet, despite the availability of these tools, many professionals rely on paper notebooks. Yeh et al. (2006, p. 571)

Norman Denzin (2004, p. 4) explains that online qualitative research is an: "interdisciplinary, transdisciplinary, and sometimes counterdisciplinary field...[which] is inherently political and shaped by multiple ethical and political positions." Like any other "field" method, successful online qualitative research is critically reflexive and socially rooted. Digital ethnography is a component of the online/digitally mediated qualitative research Denzin introduces above. However, it is different than virtual ethnography, which is completely "in, of and through the virtual" (Hine, 2000, p. 65); in other words, it does not involve face-to-face ethnographic work. Digital ethnography, unlike "virtual" or "cyber" ethnography, is not limited to ethnographic accounts of cyberspace and its concomitant communities and social networks (or what Latham and Sassen (2005) refer to as "digital formations"). Rather, digital ethnography is ethnography mediated by digital technologies. It encompasses virtual ethnography, but is broader in its remit. Digital ethnography includes, but is not limited to, the use of digitally mediated fieldnotes, online participant observation, blogs/wikis with contributions by respondents, and online focus groups. As this definition suggests, digital ethnographies can be ethnographic accounts of both offline and online groups. The "digital" in this mode of ethnography stems from the methods rather than merely the target ethnographic object. This distinction is important as this chapter is focused on digital ethnography. That being said, the two are not mutually exclusive and I will also examine some aspects of virtual/cyber ethnography.

The emergent literature on digital/cyber/virtual/Internet ethnography (e.g., Domínguez et al., 2007; Teli, Pisanu, & hakken, 2007; Dicks & Mason, 1999; Bryman, 2008; Davies, 2008, pp. 151–170) introduces this distinction for those interested in further understanding it. The questions and conclusions that have emerged from this work emphasize the ability of the methodology to document virtual communities and organizations, engage vulnerable or more inaccessible groups/respondents, and—in the case of digital ethnography rather than virtual ethnography—efficiently conduct face-to-face ethnographic work. This literature also highlights the shortcomings of some of these methods, especially virtual ethnography. For example, Gobo (2008, p. 110) claims that "the internet ethnographer merely observes and analyzes the texts which appear on the screen, without being able to meet their writers... [which makes it] difficult to associate this research technique with ethnography." This critique and others will be evaluated in the following section.

What Does Digital Ethnography Contribute to the Field of Ethnography and What Are Some of Its Weaknesses?

"Virtual reality" is not a reality separate from other aspects of human action and experience, but rather a part of it. Therefore, ethnographers should define the field or setting of their research on the basis of their research topic, rather than arbitrarily or prematurely excluding one arena or the other. Garcia, Standlee, Bechkoff, & Yan (2009, p. 55).

An ethnography, as discussed in the previous section, is a "digital ethnography" if its data-gathering methods are mediated by computer-mediated communication (CMC) or digital technologies. In digital ethnography itself, there is a spectrum. For example, face-to-face ethnographic fieldwork that is documented using wiki-based fieldnotes would be on one end of the spectrum, while a cyber ethnography conducted wholly online (both in terms of observation and fieldnotes) would be at the other end.

Digital ethnography not only presents the possibility of the written ethnography in a new multimedia form (i.e., the ethnography is presented online), but it also adds a new array of data-gathering methods, many of which draw respondents into your project or potentially make them "stakeholders." However, digital ethnographic methods also have their inherent weaknesses and your research design process should take these into account. The most powerful critique is not against digital ethnography per se, but rather virtual ethnography's elimination of face-to-face observation and interviewing. Gobo's claim, mentioned above, exemplifies this critique.

Gobo's charge is a valid and very powerful attack against cyber ethnography (though not digital ethnography per se), as one of the pillars of "traditional" face-to-face ethnographic work is being able to record and represent the studied individuals, groups, and communities through thick description. A key aspect of ethnographic work has been the attempt to represent the "authentic" speech acts of respondents. Gobo's argument is founded upon the argument that one cannot accurately represent "speech" from respondents without physical face-to-face interaction. That being said, all ethnographic accounts are abstractions and selective representations. As Clifford (1986, p. 118) notes, the mere "textualization" of ethnographic interviews has been considered by some logocentric theorists to be "corrupting," as there is "a loss of immediacy, of the face-to-face communication [...], of the presence and intimacy of speech." Following Clifford, Gobo's argument can apply to "traditional" physical ethnography as well in that the written account abstracts and potentially misrepresents the speech of respondents.

Furthermore, virtual worlds, for example, are social worlds dependent on cyberinfrastructure and "speech" within these spaces is always technologically mediated (whether communicating through text, digitally encoded voice, or image). Boellstorff (2008, p. 61) argues that a failure to realize this equals the rendering of virtual worlds ethnographically inaccessible:

> To demand that ethnographic research always incorporate meeting residents in the actual world for "context" presumes that virtual worlds are not themselves contexts; it renders ethnographically inaccessible the fact that most residents of virtual worlds do not meet their fellow residents off-line.

Boellstorff's argument is critical in that virtual worlds are built and maintained through the implicit notion that residents will not meet each other off-line. Therefore, off-line participant observation and interviewing would not truly capture the experiences, communities, and interactions of virtual worlds. Additionally, contemporary society is highly digitally mediated and our identities, communities, and relationships are increasingly enacted through virtual spaces. Garcia et al. (2009, p. 53) argue that ethnographers need to take stock of these marked changes and "must incorporate the Internet and CMC into their research to adequately understand social life in contemporary society."

In some cases, much of one's life can occur in a virtual world. For example, there are highly developed economic systems in three-dimensional virtual worlds such as Second Life, which, at the time of writing, has a population of over 20 million residents,[1] clearly illustrating that certain individuals dedicate a significant amount of their time actually engaging in virtual "living." Therefore, ignoring the powerful role of the virtual in our social lives ultimately creates extremely selective ethnographic accounts. In the case of Second Life, residents have even constructed virtual graveyards to remember people who have died off-line. As Hughes, Palen, Sutton, Liu, & Vieweg (2008) observe, a virtual graveyard and virtual memorial for victims of the Virginia Tech shooting in 2007 were put up in Second Life. These spaces of mourning resembled off-line memorial sites on the

Virginia Tech campus and included candles, poetry, flowers, and music. As these examples highlight, distinctions between a virtual life and "real life" ultimately collapse as the latter subsumes the former, blurring any difference between the two.

Another question surrounding cyber ethnography, which is evaluated by Wellman and Gulia (1999, p. 331), is whether "online relationships between people who never see, smell, or hear each other [can] be supportive and intimate." In his ethnography of Second Life, Boellstorff (2008) immersed himself in Second Life, "constructing" a house called "Ethnographia" and eventually conducting 30 formal ethnographic interviews, 30 informal ethnographic interviews, and a series of focus groups with Second Life residents (Boellstorff, 2008, pp. 76–78). He never meets any of his respondents off-line. Rather, all his ethnographic interviews, observation, and focus groups are done wholly in Second Life. Even his informed consent forms are presented by Boellstorff's avatar to the avatars of potential respondents (Boellstorff, 2008, p. 77). He concludes that his work is firmly ethnographic and that Second Life is firstly a social "world" (albeit a virtual one) in which a researcher can conduct participant observation, focus groups, questionnaires, and employ other ethnographic research methods.

That being said, Boellstorff (2008) is careful to highlight some of weaknesses of this type of ethnographic work. A key shortcoming, from his perspective, is that the ease in which researchers are able to obtain data from online sources (e.g., copy and pasting text-based conversations or recording webcam sessions) is also a double-edged sword. Specifically, he believes that handwriting is an important part of the ethnographic field experience in that researchers are "forced" to record a lot of observations, which they may not feel to be important at the time, but may end up being consequential (Boellstorff, 2008, p. 75). Boellstorff's observation is an important one and reminds us that some of the "productivity advantages" generated by digital ethnographic methods can have real consequences in limiting the qualitative data gathered.

Another weakness may be that virtual ethnography cannot be combined with face-to-face ethnographic work. Hine (2000, p. 49), for example, argues that face-to-face ethnographic interviews with online respondents can "threaten the experiential authenticity that comes from aiming to understand the world the way it is for informants." Hine's question is an important one in that the social worlds respondents inhabit online are, in some ways, best understood by participating, observing, and interviewing online. However, if Hine's argument holds, a weakness of accounts exclusively gathered online is that they present only one side of that respondent's life—their online one.

An additional shortcoming of some digital ethnographic methods is the inability of researchers to interpret the bodily gestures and other visual cues of respondents. Illingworth (2001) conducted an ethnography of patients undergoing assisted reproduction treatment. She found that respondents would have been reluctant to participate in her ethnography if the interviews were conducted face-to-face rather than online. However, a weakness of this research design, as Illingworth herself notes, is that the lack of physical interviews gave her no visual clues to decipher interview data in nuanced ways. Now (as Illingworth conducted her work in the late 1990s), video chatting and respondent-uploaded videos could help address this weakness but would not totally ameliorate it. Ultimately, the abstractions cyber ethnographers often make can be farther along a spectrum as they are not able to "read" visual cues such as body language. Therefore, we should be mindful of Gobo's argument and take care to triangulate data exclusively gathered from online sources. Despite some of the weaknesses surrounding cyber and digital ethnography, its collaborative aspects and its ability to transparently present ongoing research findings to respondents and the public are attractive features.

Here are some benefits to consider when evaluating digital ethnographic methods for your research project (specific applications will be detailed in the following section):

1. Respondents can be seamlessly given a greater stake in the ethnographic project through the use of research Web sites/blogs/wikis. This is not to say that digital ethnographies turn researcher/respondent power relations on their head. Rather, digital ethnographies have the potential to at least make the ethnographic process more transparent.
2. Digital ethnographic methods are an efficient means to simultaneously capture heterogeneous data sources such as text, audio, photographic images, and video.
3. Respondents are likely to be more intimate online, as Miller and Slater (2000) have found. Furthermore, Carter (2005) found that digital ethnographers can establish trust and comfort online through sustained dialogic interactions (in much the same way as researchers are able to do with their off-line subjects).
4. Digital ethnographic methods provide an efficient mechanism to triangulate qualitative data due to online databases and programs.
5. The collaborative aspects of digital ethnography represent a major contribution to the field of ethnography. For example, wiki technology, Web pages that permit users to easily edit online, are being used by researchers (e.g., Brown, Lundin, & Rost, 2004) to create fieldnotes, which enabled multiple researchers in their field research groups to share data findings.

What Digital/Cyber Ethnographies Have Been Conducted and What Can Be Learned From These?

I will briefly introduce some select digital and cyber ethnographies and then detail several specific applications. I will begin with early Web 1.0 digital ethnographies and then examine newer cases that utilize Web 2.0 technologies. I will also introduce some cases in which digital ethnography is combined with face-to-face ethnographic methods.

First-generation cyber ethnographies like that of Ward (1999), who examined the Web sites @Cybergrrl and Women Halting Online Abuse (WHOA), highlight the reflexive qualities of online ethnography as well as conceptualizing online fieldsites as a "hybrid" that is neither exclusively physical nor virtual. During this time, ethnographers were also evaluating the strengths and weaknesses of covert verses overt digital and cyber ethnography. Markham (1998), for example, covertly studied chat rooms and Multi-User Dungeons (MUD's), real-time virtual game worlds that are purely text-based, and conducted her ethnographic interviews online (with some chat-based interviews lasting hours). At the time of her study, both her cyber-ethnographic methods and her use of online covert observation were highly contentious. Early cyber ethnographies such as Ward and Markham represent the vanguard of this field.

Hine (2000) researched online reactions to the Louise Woodward "British nanny case," a trial highly covered by the media in which a 19-year-old British au pair was convicted of involuntarily killing the 8-month-old baby she was looking after. Hine conducted eth-nographic observation through newsgroups and Web sites and ethnographic interviews through e-mail/newsgroups. For example, she contacted authors of Web sites comment-ing on Louise Woodward (which she found through the search engine Infoseek) and sent them e-mails[2] asking them to participate in her research. Through these digital methods, she obtained a response rate of approximately 33% (Hine 2000, p. 73). Hine (2000, p. 76) also kept "fieldnotes" on "visits" to Web sites, an act that simultaneously legitimized the Web sites as fieldsites. In these fieldnotes, she kept printouts of pages on the Web site and notes regarding new messages or posts.

Smith (2004) conducted "electronic eavesdropping" in her study of British General Practitioners. She conducted "virtual participant observation" by covertly "lurking" (i.e., not making oneself known) on a listserv e-mail list of British doctors for 15 months. Smith clearly considered the listserv a research "setting" and actively analyzed the unsolic-ited data she gathered from it. Williams (2006), on the other hand, conducted overt online participant observation and synchronous focus groups in a three-dimensional virtual world (which he terms "Cyberworlds") over 6 months to explore the question of deviance within online communities. He became a member of Cyberworlds and conducted his focus group in a virtual "open field" (i.e., unpopulated virtual green countryside) to which respondents were privately invited. What was particularly attractive to Williams was that the venue of the focus group could be brought to respondents via their modems rather than having to endure the complexities of bringing respondents to an off-line physical venue.

Carter (2005) conducted an ethnography of "Cybercity," a virtual community. Carter researched the community over 3 ½ years. She used online and off-line methods: a ques-tionnaire and face-to-face interviews. She also had 21 respondents write short stories/monologues about their time in Cybercity. The actual digital ethnographic methods she employed were not cutting-edge, but the level of ethnographic richness in her e-mail/text-based interviews was high. Carter presents extracts from interviews with six of her respondents regarding friendship and intimacy online versus off-line. The responses she received from respondents are thoughtful and reflective. For example, one of her respon-dents observes that in Cybercity, one "might lose that sense of personal conversation, espe-cially when compared to talking face to face" (Carter, 2005, p. 157). After conducting these virtual interviews, she used her built-up rapport in Cybercity to encourage her respon-dents to meet with her off-line. She ultimately met with four respondents off-line (Carter, 2005, p. 150). Kanayama (2003) conducted an ethnography, using participant observation and face-to-face interviewing, of an online mailing list based in Japan, "senior-ml," in order to explore the engagements of elderly Japanese people with online communities. She conducted participant observation for 10 months on the list. Kanayama also served as a "technical volunteer" for the list and assisted senior citizens to gain the technical skills to participate in the e-mail list. She also conducted telephone interviews with some respondents. Both Carter's and Kanayama's ethnographic work is best characterized as multimodal, incorporating both virtual and digital ethnographic methods.

Chapman and Lahay (2008) conducted an ethnography of SNS sites and differential usage in the United States, France, China, and South Korea through 36 face-to-face inter-views. Their research uses conventional face-to-face ethnography to explore the digi-tally mediated subject. Their semi-structured interviews explored familiarity with social networking sites, usage patterns, and perceptions, among other things. At one level, the project can also be considered to be a digital ethnography as Chapman and Lahay used a live video feed during each interview so that members of their international research team, who are based in the countries mentioned above, could simultaneously "be there" during the interview process. Enabling distant researchers to observe the interview process real time though one-way video feeds is a valuable digital ethnographic method in that it keeps teams of researchers, regardless of proximity, involved in the ethnographic process. Chapman and Lahay's work highlights new ways in which traditional ethnographic methods such as face-to-face interviewing can be fused with emergent digital technologies.

Below, I will examine some specific digital ethnographic applications in detail. These are fieldnotes with blogs/wikis, embedded ethnographic technologies (the "cyborg ethnographer"), digital pens, and CMS groupware.

Fieldnotes With Blogs/Wikis

As many ethnographers have attested to over the years, a fundamental aspect of a successful ethnography is the "strength" of one's fieldnotes (Sanjek, 1990). I use "strength" here broadly, encompassing "accuracy," spontaneity, and diversity of data types. Digital ethnography, whether it uses wikis, blogs, or other technological innovations, presents potentialities for new types of fieldnotes that can be inputted online from the field and embedded with video streams, audio transcripts of interviews, digital pictures, and, of course, textual fieldnotes. The ability to construct fieldnotes that simultaneously gather multiple data points from a single device with a small form factor (rather than being lumbered with a digital camera, video camera, digital transcriber, and paper notebook) is alluring—especially in more remote fieldsites.

My current research explores a transnational diasporic Muslim music scene and my fieldsites include recording artists' studios, club/concert venues, and the residences of respondents. Given the diversity of my fieldsites and the involvement of a remote research assistant, I began exploring potential digital ethnographic methods. Taking into consideration the studies mentioned above, my project bears resemblance to those of Carter (2005) and Kanayama (2003) in that I decided to conduct a multimodal ethnography, which fused face-to-face and virtual ethnographic methods. I concluded that I would need a publicly accessible Web site as well as a means to create multimodal fieldnote entries for the project.

The configuration our research team is using consists of Apple iTouches[3] with Canon PowerShot digital cameras to create multimodal fieldnote entries from the field. In this pilot configuration, I am able to record the audio (and video clips) of ethnographic interviews and observations on the iTouch[4]/digital camera, upload digital pictures from the field automatically to a flickr.com album (with the location of where the picture was taken automatically saved), and key fieldnotes in real time (which are automatically time-stamped—Wi-Fi access is needed to do this[5]). For those with a larger budget, the use of an iPhone could potentially eliminate the need for a separate camera.[6]

To implement this genre of configuration:

1. Purchase an Internet-ready mobile device/tablet, digital camera with video recording capabilities, and an Eye-Fi Share Wireless SD Flash Memory Card[7] or another similarly equipped auto-uploading memory card.

2. Create a free image sharing account at Flickr[8] (or a similar photo sharing service) and, in the registration process, choose the appropriate privacy settings to make the album public, private, or semi-private.

3. Select a method by which you wish to maintain your online fieldnotes. You can choose to maintain them for free on public "blog sites" such as Blogger,[9] Vox,[10] or LiveJournal.[11] The most apparent downside to these "free" Web sites is that your data is stored on commercial Web servers and this may also present intellectual property/privacy issues depending on your research. Secondly, advertisements may be displayed on these blog sites. Some of these ads may not only qualitatively change the aesthetic of your research blog, but may also be considered offensive/annoying by yourself or your respondents (as you may not have control of the ads displayed). If your research project needs to avoid this situation for whatever reason, consider using a premium ad-free online blog service such as TypePad or having your IT department install blogging/CMS software on its own servers.

4. Configure your Eye-Fi memory card to automatically upload field photographs from your digital camera to your Flickr or some other photo sharing account. If you are using TypePad or Vox as your fieldnote software, Eye-Fi can be configured to upload your photographs from the field directly to your TypePad or Vox site.

Another key advantage of this setup is that I can code the fieldnotes by "tag"[12] labels as I create fieldnote entries. Upon finishing an entry, I check the relevant box for the "category" of data being submitted and then enter keyword tags before I submit the entry online (See Figure 7.1 for an example of this). Though the "intellectual labor involved in coding" remains, the "administrative labor of applying and altering a coding scheme" (Dohan and Sánchez-Jankowski, 1998, p. 488) is radically reduced if one is continuously coding in the field rather than ex post facto using CAQDAS software. CAQDAS software would allow you to change coding schemes on-the-fly and most packages are able to have a flexible coding scheme. However, what they currently do not have is seamless integration with mobile devices such as the iPhones and Internet tablets. Blog software such as WordPress[13] has a free iTouch/iPhone application, which can be downloaded directly from Apple's iTunes store at www.apple.com/itunes/. Once downloaded, researchers can enter field entries and code them real time. Importantly, photographs taken in the field on the iPhone can be embedded into the blog entry through the WordPress iPhone application (See Figure 7.1 for an example from my research). The instantaneous nature of this form of qualitative research is useful to individual researchers, but is most advantageous to group-based research projects.

In collaborative ethnographies, researchers can also agree on a list of "tags" and "categories" beforehand and program them into the software they are using for their fieldnotes. In my case, I am using the free open-source blog software WordPress, which allows research categories and tags to be coded prior to creating "posts" (i.e., fieldnote entries in my case). WordPress can be used through wordpress.com or can be installed on servers in one's institution or company. These fieldnotes can be password protected if the blog software is maintained on your institution's servers. I was previously using Movable Type, another freely available blog software. A key reason for my decision to switch to Word-Press was its iPhone support (mentioned above), which I feel is of tremendous value to

Figure 7.1 Entry from the author's research blog.

ethnographers. In-depth text and video tutorials on installing and configuring WordPress can be found online.[14]

The tagging process is of critical value to this ethnographic method as it is the coding system that blog software uses. After I tag each field entry, a "tag cloud" is created on the front page of my research Web site. A larger size "tag" (see Figure 7.2) reflects more entries or more recent entries (depending on what software you are using). The tag cloud, therefore, serves as a visual map of keywords of one's research and provides an extremely convenient clickable index to navigating one's field entries. It serves as a sort of table of contents on-the-fly that takes you to the selected section of your fieldnotes with a click. For example, a tag cloud representing research on the lived experiences of rheumatoid arthritis sufferers might include the following tags: arthritis, bursitis, chronic illness, humira, knee replacements, knees, medication, methotrexate, pain, physical therapy, prednisone, R. A., rheumatoid, rheumatoid arthritis, rheumatologist, surgery, and weight gain. If you were to click on "humira," for example, all of your entries concerning this rheumatoid arthritis medication would be displayed on a single page. Because the tag cloud also enlarges tags with more entries (see Figure 7.2), a researcher would be able to quickly visually compare the frequency of entries on the medications being studied: humira, methotrexate, and prednisone.

Respondents can also tag material or even tag people to help researchers map out communities. For example, Farrell, Lau, and Nusser (2008) examined tagging in business settings and found that respondents voluntarily tagged individuals in a company, which allowed the researchers to see the emergence of respondent-perceived communities in the workplace. If "football team" was tagged by respondents, a researcher would not only discover the presence of an office football team, but also know who exactly are members of the team.

In addition, if respondents are allowed to upload data (images, audio, or video) to your research wiki/blog/site, they can be asked to tag or mark a caption to it. Van House

10th althawra appreciated article aug better blog book chapter church cloud cnn com coming **comments** conduct congrats dakster9 dm **dmurthy** draft email entries facebook feedback feel finished flash flickr forgot gallery ge getting gig happy hope http idea index interested interview intrigued islamoyankee isna kaitfoley kominas korea life live looking love meet mention mulling muslim nataliejill oct online padycakes participated people photo positive **posted** punk read role saggsyndicate san scene scholars search sep sf shore site software start story subscribe sure **tags taqwacore** taqwatweet thanks think thoughts took tour trendcrusher **twitter** tyson venue visualization web world writing year yellowbuzz yes

Figure 7.2 Tag cloud (from author's research).

and Ames (2007), for example, collected over 400 photographic images from respondents who were provided with custom-designed auto-uploading camera phones. Thirty-nine percent of the images were descriptively captioned and, as such, could be analyzed individually and collectively with this in mind. Furthermore, if employing a methodology such as theirs, the ethnographic researcher could then analyze the data by keyword/caption. Searching for a particular campus social group, in the case of Van House's and Ames' research, an ethnographer could see the images that respondents associated with the group.

Ethno-Goggles: Cyborg Ethnographer?

Tennent, Crabtree, and Greenhalgh (2008) developed a multimodal qualitative field data collection system, which they call "Ethno-Goggles." Using unobtrusive glasses with an embedded camera, microphones disguised as in-ear "bud" style headphones, a digital pen, and a laptop computer with digital replay system (DRS) software hidden in a backpack, Ethno-Goggles is currently in development stages (Tennent et al., 2008, p. 8).

Fieldnotes are "tagged" using a digital pen, a device that looks just like a regular ink-based pen, but happens to be digitizing and storing all keystrokes written with it. The ethnographer uses a special piece of "paper" with microdots to handwrite fieldnote entries and to label the entries with keyword tags. An iPhone or PDA serves as a remote control to this data collection system. The strength of a heterogeneous qualitative data collection system such as Ethno-Goggles is that a researcher can simultaneously capture a mountain of qualitative data and easily tag it in real time. Furthermore, because this system is disguised (despite a cornucopia of technology), it is especially suitable for covert ethnography. Its uses in overt ethnography are well-suited to gathering vox-populi interview data "on the street" or in other urban ethnographic fieldsites. Similarly, this type of system is useful for ethnographies that rely on video from the eye of an observer rather than from that of a video camera. By this I mean that interactions with respondents (even when they are aware you are recording them) are more likely to be less staged than interactions recorded on handheld video cameras. Because the embedded video camera is invisible, respondents are less likely to play up to the camera (again, even if they are aware of the camera, they soon forget it as it is out of sight).

With this array of technology, the ethnographer becomes a sort of Haraway-esque cyborg ethnographer, collecting data as he or she walks around, observes, and interacts with respondents and fieldsites. As discussed, there are strengths to this, but the status as cyborg ethnographer is also its weakness. The researcher, being connected to a whole host of wires/devices, is restricted in movement and actions and, as such, is less likely to be comfortable and "natural" in interactions with respondents. There is no doubt that this affects the data gathered and presents a barrier to building rapport with respondents. Furthermore, the researcher has to monitor the many devices to make sure they have not malfunctioned or run out of batteries. Tennent et al. (2008, p. 8), themselves, note that the battery life of the system is a mere 2 hr and if the researcher fails to shut it down before batteries run out on the laptop, data corruption can occur.

Clearly, there are large ethical questions in some uses of this technology. Indeed, philosophically, covert implementations of Ethno-Goggles or similar technologies mirror debates surrounding covert ethnography in general. For example, recording audio covertly has always been a research method with complex ethical implications, especially among vulnerable groups. These are issues that individual IRBs would need to consider carefully and researchers should make clear what exactly is being captured by the technology and why a method like this was chosen over other data-gathering methods. If this type of technology is being implemented in covert research, there is a reasonable likelihood that an IRB would not approve it. In any event, I see the best use of this technology for overt research. Indeed, the developers of Ethno-Goggles see the technology as useful to ethnographers because they can focus on their respondents, rather than focusing on their cameras and keeping respondents in the viewfinder.[15] In overt implementations of video capture technology, researchers should make clear to respondents that the camera is out of sight and that they are most likely to forget that they are being filmed. This should be explicitly highlighted in informed consent agreements as an expected part of the research process and respondents should be made aware that they should refuse participation if they are not comfortable.

Digital Pens

Digital pens,[16] such as the one implemented in Tennent et al.'s work (2008) mentioned above, are a good first port of call when evaluating digital ethnographic methods. They serve as a "gateway" method, combining traditional paper fieldnotes with digital technologies. Becvar, for example, uses digital pens and blogs about her digital pen-based research.[17] Becvar and Hollan (1) observe that despite "recent digital alternatives for recording field data […], many investigators still prefer the flexibility and portability of paper-based media." They rightly highlight that a pen and a paper notebook is a "natural medium for recording data in the field" (Becvar & Hollan, 2005, p. 1) as it is easily porta-ble, ubiquitous, and cheap. Yeh et al. (2006, p. 571) also add that paper notebooks "turn on instantly" and have "infinite battery life." Furthermore, it is a medium that is highly con-ducive for contemporaneous fieldnotes and brainstorming in the field. That being said, as Becvar and Hollan note, it is challenging to archive and digitally code paper notebooks. Their solution to moving from pen and paper to laptops and iPhones is to use digital pens for fieldnotes, coding, and even data analysis. In their ethnographic research, they deploy the Anoto digital pen,[18] which works like a standard ballpoint pen, but simultaneously captures what you have written into a digital file (with time and date stamps) that can be uploaded wirelessly to your computer through Bluetooth,[19] a communication technology standard on many laptops and mobile phones. The collection of these digital fieldnotes on one's computer forms a digital field notebook, which can be shared with other research-ers, respondents, clients, or the general public. Furthermore, as Becvar and Hollan (2005, p. 2) note, segments of handwritten data can be easily tagged/categorized by circling or highlighting, enabling ethnographers to organize these digitally encoded and written fieldnotes by keywords and analyze them alongside other coded digital data types such as video and audio.

Brown et al. (2004, p. 8) use Anoto digital pens to capture fieldnotes and the handwrit-ten text is displayed side by side with the researchers' wiki page so that the handwritten notes can be directly consulted during the "typing up" of fieldnotes. Stifelman, Arons, & Schmandt (2001) also transparently integrate audio into a paper notebook (what they term "The Audio Notebook") by enabling researchers to tap on sections of the written page, an action that retrieves audio data recorded when those fieldnotes were taken.[20] There is also an advantage in terms of data backup to using digital pens like Anoto in qualitative fieldwork. For example, if the digitization mechanism of pen failed in the field, an ethnographer still has ink without switching pens. Similarly, if a digital file gets cor-rupted, a paper backup is there for the researcher to scan/photocopy/consult. If a paper copy is lost, the digital copy is there.

Yeh et al.'s ButterflyNet (2006), which is a system designed for field biologists, inte-grates Anoto digital pens. Though ButterflyNet was not designed for social scientists, it highlights the potential to integrate digital pens into complex field applications that com-bine GPS, written fieldnotes, and contemporaneous audio and video. However, there is a reasonable cost barrier to designing and implementing this type of system, most likely relegating it to grant-funded and commercial applications. That being said, ButterflyNet is open-source software that can be downloaded from the Stanford University HCI Web site.[21] Furthermore, its creators are exploring its potential use among social scientists (and may perhaps release versions that facilitate adoption in the social sciences).

CMS Groupware

Brown, Lundin, Rost, Lymer, & Holmquist (2007, p. 416) discuss one way in which they taught graduate students digitally mediated group-based ethnographic methods. Their student groups were charged with conducting ethnographies of, for example, a local sci-ence center and a repair workshop for trucks, planes, and buses. Their fieldnotes were maintained online as wikis, multiuser editable Web pages (the most well-known use of wiki technology is Wikipedia). Using the open-source software TikiWiki,[22] students created fieldnote entries that were easily shared and modified by the members of the group. One example entry, titled "Blue Chip," that Brown et al. (2007, p. 416) include, notes a meeting with a respondent in the aviation industry and includes a wiki entry describing an ethnographic interview with the respondent and an embedded digital photograph of an airplane (from the fieldsite). As Brown et al. (2007, p. 416) note, TikiWiki enabled their field groups to create forums, blogs, and workflow integration. Furthermore, the software has multilevel privacy features that enable groups to make notes confidential, publicly editable, or shared/edited with clients and academic advisors.

TikiWiki is a groupware/CMS (Content Management System) software package, which combines a Web front-end with a powerful database-driven backend. In lay terms, TikiWiki provides a one-stop solution for digital ethnographers who wish to maintain online fieldnotes, image databases, map data, and other field-generated data. TikiWiki can also seamlessly distribute ongoing ethnographic data (e.g., new fieldnotes or photographs) so that interested individuals and groups are fully up to date. Researchers and respondents interacting with TikiWiki only require basic computer skills. Those who have implemented TikiWiki in ethnographic research emphasize that end users do not need to be familiar with programming languages or HTML (e.g., Callén et al., 2007, p. 17).

Implementing TikiWiki from the ground up for the purposes of digital ethnographic work requires moderate to advanced computer skills. Those already comfortable with installing Web server software, can download it directly from http://www.tikiwiki.org. David Lankes, a TikiWiki expert, made a short video[23] detailing how to configure TikiWiki for those proceeding with self installation. For those without the requisite technical skill set, private companies have set up preconfigured and easy to use TikiWiki services. For example, SiteGround[24] provides fully comprehensive TikiWiki hosting services with unlimited technical support for $5.95/month, eliminating the need for TikiWiki servers at an academic institution or business. Once TikiWiki has been installed and configured, you can customize it quite easily to accommodate your individual project's needs. For example, Callén et al. (2007) used TikiWiki to create a Web site for their ethnography of the politics of Riereta.net, a "technoactivist" virtual community. In their TikiWiki space, they presented their research objectives, methodologies, etc. Additionally, these pages invited respondents to provide suggestions on the research project, reconstruct the history of the Riereta community, complete questionnaires, and even read the provisional text of each chapter of their book as it was being written (Callén et al., 2007).

Collaborative fieldnote entries and data sharing are one aspect of CMS groupware. This genre of software applications also offers other highly useful applications such as collaborative video analysis. One specific application of interest is Fraser, Biegel, Best, Hindmarsh, & Heath (2005), in which the researchers discuss how qualitative video data can be synchronously analyzed and coded by multiple geographically distant researchers. Their custom-designed software application is built upon their argument that general CAQDAS software systems view video and collaborative features as "add-ons" rather than as integral components. They view this as a serious shortcoming of existing CAQDAS software. In their EQUIP DATASPACE application, video is played in multiple locations and researchers use a text box to write up analysis and can conduct "freeform annotation" by "writing on" the video display box using a type of digital stylus. Though technologically sophisticated and extremely powerful for visual ethnographers, an implementation like theirs is expensive (with multiple data stores and custom-configured software and equipment), time-consuming, and requires specialized knowledge/training.[25] That being said, the idea of collaborating on video data analysis need not be expensive or a burden. Rather, one can use free Web sites and software to do this. For example, you could start a research group on Facebook (and it can be private if needed) and upload a video and engage in an online chat session (also using Facebook's chat feature) and, during this process, code video into CAQDAS such as ATLAS.ti or HyperRESEARCH using video time stamps and "tag" data. Granted, this does not allow you a seamless coding experience like Fraser's EQUIP, but it is easy to set up and uses existing technical skill sets. This type of solution allows collaborative visual ethnographers to hit the ground running.

Can Digital Ethnography Be Combined With Face-to-Face Ethnography?: The Case for Multiple Ethnographic Methods

Some researchers, such as Murthy (2008), say yes and argue that combining digital and face-to-face ethnography can increase data validity through triangulation. Many of the case studies mentioned above (such as Martínez Alemán & Wartman, 2009; Kanayama, 2003) use multiple methods that employ some combination of cyber, digital, and "traditional" ethnography. Even some studies of virtual worlds (e.g., Carter, 2005) have successfully employed multiple methods. And not using multiple methods can lead to narrow accounts of cyber communities and Web-based social spaces. For example, McLelland (2008) conducted a virtual ethnography of race and racism on the Japanese discussion-based Web site "2-channeru" in which he observed and analyzed postings on the site's public forums. In this specific case, conducting face-to-face or telephone interviews would have helped contextualize the discourses in that some of the posters may have been intentionally "flaming," that is, posting hate messages to get attention[26] (though this is not to say that the posts are not racist). Like off-line ethnographic work, triangulated data makes for a more rigorous qualitative account.

A good example of ethnography that successfully employs multiple methods is Bernal's work (2006, 2005) on Eritrean diasporic identity that combines her digital ethnography of the first and most prominent diasporic Eritrean Web site, Dehai,[27] with physical ethnography in Eritrea (and with diasporic Eritreans around the world). In Bernal's case, she contextualized postings on the site through ethnographic interviews with members and the Web site's founders. Another example of an effective use of online and off-line methods is Kendall's ethnography (2002) of a MUD (a type of multiuser gaming community described earlier) over 3 years, which included online participant observation and off-line ethnographic observation and interviews. She found her off-line interactions to be significant in her interpretation of her online ethnographic data.[28] These ethnographers managed to successfully integrate online and off-line data in their analyses and interpretation. This is hardly a seamless process. In Kendall's case, she spent a year on the BlueSky MUD as an active user, becoming familiar with the spaces of this virtual world and its inhabitants. Only after she developed a strong rapport with a collection of BlueSky users did she attend informal off-line gatherings and conduct face-to-face interviews. For her, the success of her off-line interviews both in terms of an understanding of her respondents, as well as the meanings of their "lives" in BlueSky was contingent on her intense online ethnographic work. Furthermore, Kendall was able to further develop her theorization of gender construction within MUDs based on her online ethnographic work when she met with respondents off-line. For example, one of her respondents constructed a male character named "Phillipe." When Kendall met Phillipe face-to-face, she discovered that the person behind the character was a woman named Toni. At the time of Kendall's interview with Toni, very few BlueSky users knew of this. In her face-to-face interview with Toni, Kendall (2002, p. 104) discovered that her respondent chose a male character because she "wasn't really sure of the environment" and "liked the notion of not being [herself]."

A particularly unique case is that of Johannes Fabian (2008), a veteran field anthropologist who transcribed and digitized an interview with a healer in Katunga, Zaire over 30 years ago and recently posted it on the Internet. Obviously, the "text" came from traditional face-to-face ethnography, but its transformation into Internet-mediated "text" allows anyone with Internet access to "read" and critique the recorded ethnographic interview. In this sense, the original physical ethnography has taken on a digital ethnographic component. If nothing else, the Internet—an often textually driven space—promotes perhaps a phonocentric reading of Fabian's interview than a logocentric one.

What Are the Costs/Benefits?

> But the bulk of information technology is complex and expensive. It requires massive capital investment in large teams of researchers. Only the most powerful interests in society— governments and large private corporations—have the resources to promote it. Kumar (1995, p. 34)

Since Kumar wrote this almost 15 years ago, much has changed in terms of the accessibility of technology. For example, custom-designed software applications and more feature-rich hardware are expensive and continue to stay well out of the reach of some ethnographers. Costs vary and the impacts of these costs differentially affect institutions, graduate students, and independent researchers. Though the digital divide remains very much alive, albeit in new forms, as Selwyn (2004) argues, a "base" toolkit is within reach of most researchers—basic laptop, consumer grade high resolution digital camera, broadband Internet access, and freely downloadable/accessible software. Extras like an Eye-Fi geotagging memory card (mentioned previously) are relatively inexpensive ($100). Furthermore, conducting straightforward qualitative surveys online start free at Web sites (e.g., surveymonkey.com, zoomerang.com, and surveygizmo.com) and tutorials on how to implement these surveys can be found in methods books (e.g., Thomas, 2004) or are freely available online.[29] That being said, custom-made qualitative data-gathering widgets for Facebook or iPhone applications can cost thousands, reaffirming the stratifications within ethnographic research online.

Nonetheless, the benefits of digital ethnography are compelling. As mentioned previously, these benefits include, but are not limited to, global datasets/respondents, the speed of data collection, high portability of data (and ease of sharing with coresearchers in digital collaborative ethnographic projects), and the ease by which visual ethnographers can collect video and photographic data. Furthermore, digital ethnography presents new modalities for involving respondents, as well as disseminating research with respondents in the wider public. Therefore, in proposals to implement digital ethnographic methods, the costs of these technologies should be explained alongside their potentially enormous benefits.

What Are the Ethical Implications of These New Technologies?

The ethical implications raised by the above-mentioned studies and methods vary enormously. One difficulty is that newer technological innovations are quickly exceeding the scope of ethics guidelines, which take time to develop. Such is the case with the Association of Internet Researchers' (AoIR) ethical guidelines of 2002,[30] which covers listserv/Web forums well, but predates social networking and other Web 2.0 applications. That being said, key sections of guidelines such as AoIR continued to be highly relevant. For example, when conducting online research with particularly vulnerable respondents, guidelines that are even a decade old (e.g., Schrum, 1995; Sharf, 1999) continue to be insightful as core issues of privacy and "lurking," for example, remain in Web 2.0 applications.

The increasing shift of people's lives into the public domain also means that ethnographers need to be diligent in their treatment of continually emerging ethics issues. For example, Moreno, Fost, and Christakis (2008) discuss the ethics of using social networking Web sites. Light, McGrath, and Griffiths (2008) call for an ethics policy in conducting research via Facebook and other social networking sites (SNS). Another critical ethical issue is that if one obtains informed consent to quote from a Web forum, Facebook group, etc., it is not always possible to provide complete and total anonymity through pseudonyms and the removal of identifying information. "Googling" identifying data can often make it very easy to reveal sources. One solution to this, which Boellstorff (2008, p. 83) uses, is to not only anonymize screen names, but to also paraphrase quotations in order to "make them difficult to identify using a search engine." Williams (2005, p. 412), in his research of the virtual world "Cyberworlds," received a request from one respondent who asked him to remove any reference to his distinctive emoticon as any publishing of it would make his responses instantly known by residents of Cyberworlds. As Joinson (2005, p. 26) observes, researchers using digital and cyber-ethnographic methods, in many cases, should recognize that "true anonymity is not strictly possible." Joinson advises on using detailed informed consent forms and, when necessary, storing identifying information and responses on separate computers (which are presumably not networked). Furthermore, in proposals to Institutional Review Boards (IRB), academic researchers should be explicitly clear on possible ethical issues so that the shortcomings in technical knowledge on the part of review boards do not lead to ethical oversights.

A key purpose of IRB review of research proposals is to protect participants in terms of privacy, potential harm, and keeping them informed on the scope and implications of the research. Digital ethnographic methods do have unique ethical implications. Some of these, as Rutter and Smith (2005, p. 85) argue, are due to the nature of online and digitally mediated spaces as "unconventional" research settings. By this they mean that technologically mediated fieldsites are not the norm for ethnographers. For them, negotiating informed consent and announcing/maintaining their research identities in continually shifting virtual environments was never a straightforward task. However, in Rutter and Smith's work on RumCom.local, they were able to gain the trust of their respondents online and off-line through the type of honest self-presentation that ethnographers use in face-to-face ethnography. I would urge researchers to carefully think through the ethical implications of the technologies mentioned in this chapter. For example, maintaining publicly accessible fieldnotes and allowing your respondents access to comment not only requires detailed informed consent agreements, but also high levels of attention to confidentiality and the privacy of participants in your research. Some of the devices mentioned in this chapter may not pass the approval of an IRB. As mentioned previously, covert uses of ubiquitous capturing technologies such as Ethno-Goggles would most likely raise eyebrows in IRB panels. That being said, every case is different and the responsibility of covert researchers using cutting-edge digital technologies to disclose fully ethical implications to IRBs is even greater. As Stern (2004, p. 284) sagely advises, "researchers [should...] remember that behind every online communication is a real, living, breathing person."

These ethical implications are not a negative aspect of digital ethnography. Rather, the method offers ethnographers an opportunity to reflexively evaluate the impacts of their work and to respectfully and responsibly inform potential and actual respondents of what the research will involve. Ultimately, digital ethnographic methods have an immense potential to enliven and enrich the qualitative ethnographic experience and ethical considerations should be carefully attended to but should be viewed as safeguards rather than as stumbling blocks to high-quality social research.

Do Digital Ethnographic Technologies Require a Different Set of Skills?

Digital ethnographic technologies do require a set of technology-based skills. However, basic PC skills and skills gained from using existing ethnographic software are transferable. For example, consider the case of hosting an ethnographic focus group on Facebook. The process of joining Facebook and using an online "wizard" to set up a focus group does not require much more of a skill set than using "normal" Web-based applications. Similarly, the skills gained in using CAQDAS (e.g., ATLAS.ti, NUD*IST, NVivo, and HyperRESEARCH) are transferable to digital ethnographic tools. For example, many digital ethnographic methods involve "tagging." ATLAS.ti and HyperRESEARCH, for example, both foster data "tagging" skills in their users (Brown et al., 2007). Their analytic structure is organized along data categories and sub-tags. For example, when you want to deposit text, images, or other ethnographic data in CAQDAS, you classify it in a very similar process to tagging. As Friedman (2005) highlights, anthropologists and professional archivists have been "tagging" off-line through conventional systems of classification and categorization. Tagging online employs the same organizational and analytic structures—just deployed through the medium of computer-mediated communication. The difference is that this tagging, when put online, becomes a networked taxonomy. This is termed a "folksonomy," a collaborative system of subject-indexing in which users—rather than professional archivists or researchers—classify information collectively through "tags."

Because these methods of categorization are different to conventional off-line research methods, there currently exists a gap in training between what is being taught in social research courses and what skills are needed to tag online. Therefore, until the teaching of ethnography in undergraduate and graduate curriculums encompasses online "tagging," a barrier to maintaining a networked research folksonomy will persist. That being said, social research handbooks and manuals across a broad array of social science disciplines discuss tagging and provide modes of training (e.g., Thomas, 2009; Salmons & Wilson, 2009; Fielding, Lee, & Blank, 2008; Jank & Shmueli, 2008). As these pedagogical texts become integrated in method courses, the training gap should disappear.

Conclusion

This chapter has not advocated the death of paper-based ethnographic methods. As Sellen and Harper (2002) highlight that there are major "myths" surrounding paperless professional work. Fieldwork is no exception. Yeh et al. (2006) argue that digital technologies should complement paper (and I would argue non-digital ethnographic methods in general). In this vein, I have introduced various digital ethnographic methods and technologies such as digital pens, wikis, blogs, and embedded "cyborg" technologies. Creating an antagonism between digital and non-digital ethnographic methods is not only counterproductive to the future of ethnography, but overlooks the fact that both modalities of qualitative data collection have inherent strengths and weaknesses. Furthermore, digital ethnographic methods are not necessarily replacements to traditional physical ethnographic methods. Digital pens, for example, are an accessible and relatively nonintrusive gateway into digital ethnography. (Though, they too can be a distraction if batteries fail and a field researcher becomes preoccupied.)

However, we should not fall victim to the zeitgeist of new technologies. We should remember that new media spaces, like their off-line counterparts, can be "colonizing, racializing, gendering, sexing, classifying, stratifying, fetishizing, deceiving, authenticating, mesmerizing, transgressing, clarifying, stunning, muting, distracting, subjecting, cherishing, preserving, cluttering, and so on" (Clarke, 2005, p. 218 cited in Bell, forthcoming). It is our job as ethnographers to critically evaluate digital and virtual ethnographic methods. This chapter has mapped out some cutting-edge technologies, how they can be implemented, and their ethical implications. However, technologies are always evolving and their reception by respondents does as well. Therefore, a careful consideration of one's fieldsite(s), respondents, and ethical questions, among other things, is critical to technology choices in one's research design.

Another purpose of this chapter has been to keep the literature on digital ethnographic methods up to date. However, the terrain of digitally mediated research is always changing and new technological developments for use in ethnographic research will continue to emerge. In the future, I envision social researchers regularly using custom-built applications in social networking sites (e.g., Facebook) to collect highly sophisticated sets of qualitative data; conducting interviews and observation in complex virtual worlds; and working in virtual research teams in which ethnographers are located in multiple physical locations, observing and interviewing respondents locally, while contributing to a large-scale comparative ethnography.

Additionally, as new media technologies become more and more pervasive in the everyday lives of our respondents, ethnographers will be presented with new ways in which to apply emergent digital ethnographic methods for social inquiry. I am particularly convinced that advances in ubiquitous computing (ubicomp), everyday computational objects such as cell phones, will present radical increases in the scope and reach of digital ethnographic methods. Ubicomp devices will continue to not only increase in their raw processing power, but also in their convergence of technologies (imaging, video conferencing, GPS, and even motion sensing). Furthermore, if ubicomp becomes more ubiquitous across class, gender, racial, and international lines, digital ethnographers will have unparalleled abilities to collect a whole array of rich qualitative data that is contemporaneous, socially diverse, and wide-ranging.

Notes

1. As of July 2010. See http://secondlife.com/statistics/economy-data.php for the most recent statistics.
2. For example, see Hine (2000: 73) for the actual text she used.
3. A Nokia N810 Internet tablet was evaluated as well. For a demonstration video of a Nokia 810, see http://www.youtube.com/watch?v=wDe1gd-pBRo
4. The iTouch does not include a built-in microphone like the iPhone. Therefore, if you wish to deploy this configuration, you will need to purchase a 2G iTouch with Apple's optional premium microphones/headphones.
5. Though Wi-Fi is not needed if an iPhone is deployed.
6. That being said, the quality of pictures taken with an iPhone is usually much lower in comparison to good quality point-and-shoot digital cameras.
7. http://www.eye.fi/
8. http://www.flickr.com
9. http://www.blogger.com
10. http://www.vox.com
11. http://www.livejournal.com
12. See the literature on tagging (Ardet & M., 2004; Friedman, 2005; Mason & Thomas, 2007; Riddle, 2005; Speller, 2007) for more information.
13. http://www.WordPress.com
14. http://codex.wordpress.org/Installing_WordPress and a video tutorial can be found at http://www.dailymotion.com/video/x5lpe4_install-wordpress-tutorial_school
15. http://redress.lancs.ac.uk/resources/launch.php?creator=Tennent_Paul&title=Ethno_Goggles
16. http://www.youtube.com/watch?v=ekjw1ewyAUU
17. http://amayabecvar.blogspot.com/
18. See http://www.anoto.com
19. For an overview of Bluetooth, see Ferro and Potorti (2005).
20. Livescribe, another manufacturer of digital pens, has a blog section on ethnographic uses of their digital pens. See http://www.livescribe.com/blog/tag/ethnography/
21. http://hci.stanford.edu/bio
22. http://tikiwiki.org
23. http://tikiwiki.org/tiki-index.php?page=TikiMovies
24. http://www.siteground.com/tikiwiki-hosting.htm
25. See a PowerPoint presentation of their set up at http://www.ncess.ac.uk/events/conference/2005/papers/presentations/ncess2005_fraser.pdf for pictures and diagrams of how EQUIP dataspace works.
26. See Donath (1999) for more on flame posting.
27. http://www.dehai.org
28. Some other examples include Aoyama (2007), who conducted a "cyber ethnography" of the "nikkei," the Japanese diasporic population in Peru using the social networking website hi5 and physical ethnography in Lima. Davis (2008) conducted an ethnography of Myspace in which she observed 97 of her "Friends" rather than physically unknown respondents.

29. See http://www.acsu.buffalo.edu/burgosm/Impatica/Survey-Monkey-Tutorial.html
and http://support.uiwtx.edu/MediaTraining/PDF&Powerpoints/SurveyMonkey/Survey%20
Monkeyfull.ppt
30. http://aoir.org/?page_id=54

References

Aoyama, S. (2007). Nikkei-ness, a cyber-ethnographic exploration of identity among the Japanese Peruvians of Peru. MA dissertation. Mount Holyoke College.

Becvar, L. A., & Hollan, J. D.(2005). Envisioning a paper augmented digital notebook: Exploiting digital pen technology for fieldwork. Distributed Cognition and Human-Computer Interaction Laboratory, Department of Cognitive Science. La Jolla, CA: UCSD.

Bell, S. (Forthcoming). Digital methods for collecting and analysing data. In Bourgeault, I. L., DeVries, R., & Dingwall, R. (Eds.), *Sage handbook on qualitative health research*, London: Sage.

Bernal, V. (2006). Diaspora, cyberspace and political imagination: The Eritrean Diaspora online. *Global Networks*, 6(2), 161–79.

Bernal, V. (2005). Eritrea on-line: Diaspora, cyberspace, and the public sphere. *American Ethnologist*, 32(4), 660–75.

Boellstorff, T. (2008). *Coming of age in second life: An anthropologist explores the virtually human.* Princeton, NJ: Princeton University Press.

Brown, B., Lundin, J., & Rost, M. (2004). Wikis in the field: Collaborative ethnography as a learning experience. *ACM.*

Brown, B., Lundin, J., Rost, M., Lymer, G., & Holmquist, L. (2007). Seeing ethnographically: Teaching ethnography as part of CSCW. *Ecscw, 2007,* 411–30.

Bryman, A. (2008). *Social research methods.* (3rd ed.). Oxford: Oxford University Press.

Callén, B., Balasch, M., Guarderas, P., Gutierrez, P., León, A., Montenegro, et al. (2007). Riereta. Net: Epistemic and political notes from a techno-activist ethnography. *Forum Qualitative Sozialforschung/Forum: Qualitative Social Research,* 8(3).

Carter, D. (2005). Living in virtual communities: An ethnography of human relationships in cyberspace. *Information, Communication and Society,* 8(2), 148–67.

Chapman, C. N., & Lahav, M. (2008). International ethnographic observation of social networking sites. In *CHI '08 extended abstracts on human factors in computing systems.* Florence, Italy: ACM.

Clifford, J. (1986). On ethnographic allegory. In Clifford, J, Marcus, G. E., & School of American Research (Santa Fe N.M.) (Eds.), *Writing culture: The poetics and politics of ethnography.* A School of American Research Advanced Seminar (pp. 98–121). Berkeley: University of California Press.

Coffey, A, Renold, E., Dicks, B., Soyinka, B., & Mason, B. (2006). Hypermedia ethnography in educational settings. *Ethnography and Education,* 1(1), 15–30.

Davies, C. A. (2008). *Reflexive ethnography: A guide to researching selves and others.* (2nd ed.). London: Routledge.

Davis, J. L. (2008). Presentation of self and the personal interactive homepage: An ethnography of Myspace. MS dissertation. Texas A&M.

Denzin, N. (2004). Prologue: Online environments and interpretive social research. In Johns, M. D., Chen, S.-L., & Jon Hall, G. (Eds.), *Online social research: Methods, issues, & ethics* (pp. 1–12). New York, Oxford: Peter Lang.

Dicks, B., & Mason, B. (1999). Cyber ethnography and the digital researcher. In Armitage, J., & Roberts, J. (Eds.), *Exploring cybersociety: Social, political, economic and cultural issues.* Newcastle, UK: University of Northumbria Press.

Dicks, B. (2005). *Qualitative research and hypermedia: Ethnography for the digital age, new technologies for social research.* London: Sage.

Dicks, B., Soyinka, B., & Coffey, A. (2006). Multimodal ethnography. *Qualitative Research*, 6(1), 77–96.

Dohan, D., & Sánchez-Jankowski, M. (1998). Using computers to analyze ethnographic field data: Theoretical and practical considerations. *Annual Review of Sociology*, 24(1), 477–98.

Domínguez, D., Beaulieu, A., Estalella, A., Gómez, E., Schnettler, B., & Read, R. (2007). Virtual ethnography. *Forum Qualitative Sozialforschung/Forum: Qualitative Social Research*, 8(3).

Donath, J. S. (1999). Identity and deception in the virtual community. In Smith, M. A., & Kollock, P. (Eds.), *Communities in cyberspace* (pp. 29–59). London; New York: Routledge.

Fabian, J. (2008). *Ethnography as commentary: Writing from the virtual archive*. Durham, NC; London: Duke University Press.

Farrell, S., Lau, T., & Nusser, S. (2008). Building communities with people-tags. In *Human-Computer Interaction—Interact 2007* (pp. 357–360).

Ferro, E., and Potorti, F. (2005). Bluetooth and Wi-Fi wireless protocols: A survey and a comparison. *IEEE Wireless Communications*, 12(1), 12–26.

Fielding, N., Lee, R. M., & Blank, G. (2008). *The sage handbook of online research methods*. Los Angeles: Sage.

Fraser, M, Biegel, G, Best, K., Hindmarsh, J., & Heath, C. (2005). Distributing data sessions: Supporting remote collaboration with video data. *Proc. ICeSS*.

Friedman, P. K. (2005). Folksonomy. *Anthropology News*, 46(6), 38.

Garcia, A. C., Standlee, A. I., Bechkoff, J., & Yan, C. (2009). Ethnographic approaches to the Internet and computer-mediated communication. *Journal of Contemporary Ethnography*, 38(1), 52–84.

Gobo, G. (2008). *Doing ethnography*. Los Angeles; London: Sage.

Hine, C. (2000). *Virtual ethnography*. London: Sage.

Howard, A. (1988). Hypermedia and the future of ethnography. *Cultural Anthropology*, 3(3), 304–15.

Hughes, A. L., Palen, L., Sutton, J., Liu, S. B., & Vieweg, S. (2008, May). "Site-seeing" in disaster: An examination of on-line social convergence. Paper presented at the Proceedings of the 5th International ISCRAM Conference, Washington DC.

Illingworth, N. (2001). The Internet matters: Exploring the use of the Internet as a research tool. *Sociological Research Online*, 6(2).

Jank, W., & Shmueli, G. (2008). *Statistical methods in e-commerce research*. Statistics in Practice. Hoboken, NJ: Wiley.

Joinson, A. N. (2005). Internet behaviour and the design of virtual methods. In Hine, C. (Ed.), *Virtual methods: Issues in social research on the Internet* (pp. 21–34). Oxford, New York: Berg.

Kanayama, T. (2003). Ethnographic research on the experience of Japanese elderly people online. *New Media Society*, 5(2), 267–88.

Kendall, L. (2002). *Hanging out in the virtual pub: Masculinities and relationships online*. Berkeley, CA; London: University of California Press.

Kumar, K. (1995). *From post-industrial to post-modern society: New theories of the contemporary world*. Cambridge, MA: Blackwell Publishers.

Latham, R., & Sassen, S. (2005). *Digital formations: It and new architectures in the global realm*. Princeton, NJ: Princeton University Press.

Light, B., McGrath, K., & Griffiths, M. (2008). Facebook's ethics. In *Facebook: a network, a research tool, a world?* Liverpool John Moores University.

Markham, A. N. (1998). *Life online: Researching real experience in virtual space*. Ethnographic Alternatives Book Series. Walnut Creek, CA; London: Altamira Press.

Martínez Alemán, A. M., & Wartman, K. L. (2009). *Online social networking on campus: Understanding what matters in student culture* (1st ed.). New York: Routledge.

Masten, D. L., & Plowman, T. M. P. (2003). Digital ethnography: The next wave in understanding the consumer experience. *Define Management Journal*, 14(2), 75–81.

McLelland, M. (2008). "Race" on the Japanese Internet: Discussing Korea and Koreans on "2-Channeru." *New Media Society*, 10(6), 811–29.

Miller, D., and Slater, D. (2000). *The Internet: An ethnographic approach*. Oxford; New York: Berg.

Moreno, M. A., Fost, N. C., & Christakis, D. A. (2008). Research ethics in the Myspace era. *Pediatrics, 121*(1), 157–61.

Murthy, D. (2008). Digital ethnography: An examination of the use of new technologies for social research. *Sociology, 42*(5), 837–55.

Rutter, J., & Smith, G. W. H. (2005). Ethnographic presence in a nebulous setting." In Hine, C. (Ed.), *Virtual methods: Issues in social research on the Internet* (pp. 81–92). Oxford; New York: Berg.

Salmons, J., & Wilson, L. (2009). *Handbook of research on electronic collaboration and organizational synergy* (2 vols). Hershey: Information Science Reference.

Sanjek, R. (1990). *Fieldnotes: The makings of anthropology*. Ithaca: Cornell University Press.

Schrum, L. (1995). Framing the debate: Ethical research in the information age. *Qualitative Inquiry, 1*(3), 311–26.

Sellen, A. J., & Harper, R. (2002). *The myth of the paperless office*. Cambridge, MA: MIT Press.

Selwyn, N. (2004). Reconsidering political and popular understandings of the digital divide. *New Media Society, 6*(3), 341–62.

Sharf, B. F. (1999). Beyond netiquette: The ethics of doing naturalistic discourse research on the Internet. In Jones, S. G. (Ed.), *Doing Internet research: Critical issues and methods for examining the net* (pp. 243–56). Thousand Oaks: Sage.

Smith, K. M. C. (2004). Electronic eavesdropping: The ethical issues involved in conducting a virtual ethnography. In Johns, M. D., Chen, S-L., & Jon Hall, G., (Eds.), *Online social research: Methods, issues, & ethics* (pp. 223–238). New York; Oxford: Peter Lang.

Stern, S. R. (2004). Studying adolescents online: A consideration of ethical issues. In Buchanan, E. A. (Ed.), *Readings in virtual research ethics: Issues and controversies* (pp. 274–287). Hershey, PA: Information Science Pub.

Stewart, K., & Williams, M. (2005). Researching online populations: The use of online focus groups for social research. *Qualitative Research, 5*(4), 395–416.

Stifelman, L., Arons, B. & Schmandt, C. (2001). The audio notebook: Paper and pen interaction with structured speech. In *Proceedings of the SIGCHI conference on human factors in computing systems*. Seattle, WA: ACM.

Teli, M., Pisanu, F., & Hakken, D. (2007). The Internet as a library-of-people: For a cyberethnography of online groups. *Forum Qualitative Sozialforschung/Forum: Qualitative Social Research, 8*(3).

Tennent, P., Crabtree, A., & Greenhalgh, C. (2008). Ethno-goggles: Supporting field capture of qualitative material. In *4th international e-social science conference*. University of Manchester: ESRC NCeSS.

Thomas, M. (2009). *Handbook of research on Web 2.0 and second language learning*. Hershey, PA: Information Science Reference.

Thomas, S. J. (2004). *Using Web and paper questionnaires for data-based decision-making*. Thousand Oaks, CA: Corwin Press.

Van House, N, & Ames, M. (2007). The social life of cameraphone images. Paper presented at the Computer/Human Interaction 2007, San Jose, CA.

Ward, K. J. (1999). The cyber-ethnographic (re)construction of two feminist online communities. *Sociological Research Online, 4*(1).

Wellman, B., & Gulia, M. (1999). Net surfers don't ride alone: Virtual communities as communities. In Wellman, B. (Ed.), *Networks in the global village: Life in contemporary communities* (pp. 331–366). Boulder, CO: Westview Press.

Williams, M. (2006). "Policing and cybersociety: The maturation of regulation within an online community. *Policing and Society, 16*(4), 1–24.

Yeh, R. B., Liao, C., Klemmer, S. R., Guimbretiere, F., Lee, B., Kakaradov, B., et al. (2006). Butterflynet: A mobile capture and access system for field biology research. Paper presented at the Association for Computing Machinery, Montréal, Québec, April 22–27.

Chapter 8

New Fieldsites, New Methods:
New Ethnographic Opportunities

Laura Robinson and Jeremy Schulz

Introduction

As the rapid rate of the adoption and normative use of information technologies acceler-
ates, sociologists must expand the sociological imagination to explore a host of questions
related to mediated communication. From Twitter to YouTube, the media convergence
anticipated at the close of the millennium is coming into being. Blogs, vlogs, Web browsing, e-mail, and old time television, radio, and phone are all increasingly accessible via
digital technologies. Furthermore, not only can we consume these digital media, but we
can now produce them easily and quickly. Yet, sociological methods have not kept pace
with the profound changes in communication ensuing from the Information Revolution.
Although the quotidian use of new media continues to grow by leaps and bounds, there is
little consensus on how we can best collect and analyze new media data.

This chapter begins to address these issues by examining how ethnographic methods have been adapted to explore new media and digital communication. We find that
three central tensions have shaped the adoption of ethnographic methods in new media
environments since the advent of cyberethnography in the mid 1990s. The three tensions
that we identify and discuss are the character of mediated interaction (e-mail, IM, blogging, texting, etc.) as a social process, text as interaction, and the relationship between the
observer and the observed. Our analysis draws upon both the current work in the field
and foundational works that established cyberethnography as a legitimate methodological undertaking. Each section presents a history of salient texts detailing methodological
growth and innovation. We bring these texts together to close each section with an eye to
methodological and ethical implications under the heading "Stories from the Field." This
section provides analysis of challenges in methodological adaptation and related ethical
concerns that will be of increasing importance vis-à-vis user-driven content.

We close our chapter with a review of how the strengths of traditional ethnography
are especially suited to examine future waves of digital phenomena. In evaluating the
commonalities between traditional and mediated ethnographic practice, we argue that
although new twists in the evolution of the Internet may require ethnographers to continually adapt their methodological tool kits, they will not reduce the salience of the method.

In reviewing different tensions in the evolution of cyberethnographic methods, we find that the seeming newness of much of the cyberethnographic endeavor is a reworking, rather than a replacing, of traditional ethnographic methods. Finally, just as cyberethnographers argued a decade ago that the novelty of the Web will likely fade as information technology increasingly becomes just another taken-for-granted part of everyday life (Webb, 1999), we argue that once cyberethnography has been incorporated into the corpus of sociological methods, its legitimacy will be beyond question.

Mediated Interaction as a Social Process

As we will explore in this section, since its inception, cyberethnography has largely valorized the constructionist aspects of social interaction. Cyberethnographers train their lenses on microsocial interaction and smaller-scale interactional patterns. Often, these micro-interactional patterns may be conceptualized along Goffmanian lines (Cavanagh, 1999; Robinson, 2007). More specifically, Goffman (1959) conceptualized the social world in terms of theatrical performance or "dramaturgy." Goffman's extended metaphor of dramaturgy describes the social world as a theater in which social actors play different roles for different performances. From a Goffmanian point of view, all of our actions and interactions are performances through which we enact different roles or personae for different audiences and different contexts. Like Goffman, cyberethnographers have been quick to focus on the *dramaturgical*, *ritualistic*, and *ludic* aspects of the interactions taking place in online environments. Also like Goffman, cyberethnographers have concerned themselves with the kinds of interpersonal "engagements" and "encounters" that make up the micro-interactional order (Goffman, 1959; Turner, 2002).

However, each wave of cyberethnographic invention and practice has approached the intersection between interaction and identity from a different angle. The research efforts of the first cyberethnographers were animated by a transformative vision of what Miller and Slater call online "sociality" (Miller & Slater, 2000, pp. 72–74). The first generation of cyberethnographers took advantage of rich new fieldsites offered by Multi-User Dungeons (MUDs) and other text-based sites and virtual worlds that encouraged mediated sociality via role or identity play. Celebrating the transformational potential of these cybervenues, these "pioneering" cyberethnographers touted the potential that virtual environments offered for the emergence of a new kind of self-identity and personhood qualitatively different from that which flourished in off-line social environments (Robinson and Schulz, 2009, 1). In these new spaces of interaction, identity was framed solely as a matter of "projection" (Baym, 1998; Reid, 1999; Zhao, 2005) because the old identity categories tied to the body no longer held sway. As Correll explained, people who are engaged in online chat exercise a degree of control over their "fronts and idealizations" that they would find impossible to replicate in off-line contexts (Correll, 1995, p. 287).

In the early utopian views of the liberating promise of the Internet, a number of these pioneering cyberethnographers drew attention to the anonymity and "pseudoanonymity" (Donath, 1999, p. 53) of online environments as the foundations for their claims of a new kind of social process of identity formation. For them, the state of near-total anonymity on MUDs and chatboards meant that participants could create and sustain whatever self-presentations their online interlocutors would accept as genuine within the confines of that particular online interactional space. One of Turkle's informants (1995) describes, "I'm not one thing, I'm many things. Each part gets to be more fully expressed in MUDs than in the real world" (185). In their view, such a situation necessarily gave rise to identity play and kinds of experimentation that would be simply unfeasible in off-line environments (Donath, 1999). Thus, they argued that MUD environments lead to uncommon states of "disinhibition" among users who feel free to adopt any persona they wish without risk to their off-line reputations or identities (Reid, 1999, p. 113).

This preoccupation with the transformative effects of anonymity led many pioneering cyberethnographers to proclaim the virtual realm a *sui generis* social arena operating in accordance with its own rules and logic (Boellstorff, 2008; Kendall, 2002). They envisioned the cyberrealm as a medium for interaction that posed fundamentally different dramaturgical and identity construction possibilities than the off-line realm, where individuals are physically co-present (Zhao, 2005). Pioneering cyberethnographers mirrored the users they studied in that they were invested in the discontinuity between the social life they observed in online environments and the social life they witnessed in off-line environments. Turkle, Stone, Rheingold, and others focused on the "intentional identities" and identity signaling games that enabled MUDers and other denizens of online environments to flout the normal rules of microsocial interaction tied to physical co-presence. For example, in "furry" MUDs, participants could adopt animal surrogates and frolic with other animals to indulge their animal appetites (Robinson, 2007). Their accounts of virtual interaction highlighted the liberating potential of the medium, as an environment where individuals' conduct and identities were no longer tethered to their physical bodies (Rheingold, 1993; Stone, 1995; Turkle, 1995).

It was not by chance that pioneering cyberethnographers paid inordinate amounts of attention to the online activities of gamers, MUDers, and other individuals who capitalized on the anonymity of their online worlds. The college students and young adults who populate Sherry Turkle's groundbreaking 1995 book *Life on the Screen* spent up to 80 eighty hours a week living what amounted to alternative lives as MUDers and gamers. Howard Rheingold, author of *The Virtual Community: Homesteading on the Electric Frontier*, foregrounded users' quests to be "somebody else" or even "several people at the same time" (1993, p. 151). In her work, Allucquére Rosanne Stone focused on the ease with which MUD users cultivated fictitious characters that bore little resemblance to their off-line selves, but which were all the same entirely real to both their creators and their audiences. Recounting the tale of Sanford Lewin, a middle-aged male New York psychotherapist who impersonated a disabled woman and deceived countless others in the process, Stone concluded that the advent of the virtual persona signals a fundamental shift in our notion of personhood. From now on, she declared, "it's personas all the way down" (Stone, 1995, p. 81).

However, by the late 1990s, the tide began turning when ethnographers sought to "legitimize" (Robinson and Schulz, 2009) cyberethnography as an extension of off-line traditional ethnographic practice. These legitimizing cyberethnographers made note of the complex interplay and interpenetration between online and off-line identity and sociality among participants in online environments (Kendall, 2002, pp. 44–45; Markham, 1998, pp. 87, 162–163). Increasingly, these cyberethnographers argued that many people who go online do so in order to provide themselves with "another context" in which to interact with others, not to create alternative or substitute lives for themselves. Unlike pioneering ethnographers, legitimizing cyberethnographers such as Kendall and Markham did not presume that every person who went online did so in order to concoct a new self-identity or self-presentation. While acknowledging the medium's potential as a facilitator of identity masquerade, legitimizing cyberethnographers underscored the variability in the extent to which online lives and off-line lives blur together. Increasingly, arguments for master identities housing both online and off-line representations displaced transformationist emphasis on identity play and deception (Wertheim, 1999). Today, the emergence of social networking sites such as MySpace and Facebook confirms how individuals blur their online and off-line lives.

However, to accomplish their goal, these cyberethnographers sought to validate virtual ethnography by taking issue with the idea that a deep involvement in online worlds necessarily transforms the participants' sense of self and weakens the hold of social identity categories related to embodied characteristics like ethnicity, gender, and age. Not all individuals' off-line self-identities are tightly coupled with the intentional "representations" that they fashion for their forays into the online world (Kendall, 2002, pp. 222–223). These scholars also parted company with pioneering cyberethnographers inasmuch as they granted the possibility that online relationships and identities could cross over into the off-line world or vice versa. In sum, these legitimizing cyberethnographers took up an "integrationist" rather than a "segmentalist" (Nippert-Eng, 1996) perspective on these two domains of interaction, seeing them as essentially coterminous and continuous realms of social interaction and identity performance (Markham, 1998, p. 197). This shift in the field reflected a larger transformation in the overall population of Internet users in the United States. Increasingly as Internet use became more normative in American society, scholars shared a vision of a master self encompassing both online and off-line identities as the normative assumption for studies of the Internet (Robinson, 2007).

Stories From the Field: Methodological and Ethical Implications of Mediated Interaction

Cyberethnographers have conducted participant observation in a wide range of fieldsites including but not limited to economic venues, digital support groups, and political communities. Across these different kinds of fieldsites, the move toward the conceptualization of online identities as synonymous with off-line identities has important implications regarding how cyberethnographers treat online identities. Regardless of the kind of fieldsite they enter, cyberethnographers take care to recognize how members of a fieldsite perceive the linkage between their online and off-line identities. At the same time, cyberethnographers must strategically make their own off-line identities as researchers transparent in their online presentation of self.

Regarding members' identities, cyberethnographers must ask themselves how respondents frame the relationship between their online and off-line identities. It is impossible to fully understand the social processes at play in a particular community without ascertaining this fundamental distinction. For example, in her own work, Robinson has found that respondents conceptualized cyberidentities as part of their master identity frames. In Robinson's work (2005; 2008) on 9/11 digital discourse fora in Brazil, France, and the United States, community members often referred to their online identities to underscore their authority to speak to a range of issues. Whether in reference to ideological debates, discussion of discriminatory reprisals, or debates over authority to speak for national collectives, forum participants made explicit reference to their own off-line identities to bolster their authority when speaking in online venues. At the same time, forum members also made reference to other participants' presentation of their off-line identities as a means to criticize those who did not share their views. For example, in posts about firsthand knowledge of the 9/11 terrorist attacks, those community members claiming physical proximity to New York or Washington told personal stories in which they described their experiences as eyes on the ground. To do so, they bolstered online authority via reference to off-line status, their places of residences or employment, titles at work that could be checked by other participants, and other identifiers that bolstered their right to claim such knowledge.

These identity claims were critical to the factionalized debates central to the forum communities. Therefore, understanding this identity work was critical to unlocking the frictions within communities' group dynamics. For example, on the Brazilian and French fora, expatriate Brazilians and French living in the United States referenced their personal experience on 9/11 and their expatriate status. Doing this double identity work allowed them to reference their lives in their countries of origin in order to maintain their own status as Brazilian or French nationals, while also claiming to speak for the American collectivity. By contrast, their critics attempted to drive them out of the online communities by using their off-line expatriate status as a tool to critique them as "outsiders" who, having "turned their backs" on their countries of origin, no longer had any "right" to speak for their respective national collectivities.

Given the centrality of certain off-line identity claims, the shift toward an integrationist view of online and off-line identities also gives rise to new ethical concerns of how cyberethnographers should respect privacy in cyberspace. In sum, if our identities in cyberspace are extensions of our off-line identities, they must be afforded the same ethical consideration as they would be given in the off-line world. In addition to using pseudonyms to protect members' identities or user handles just as one would with off-line identities or real names, cyberethnographers must also consider how to best present their off-line identities as researchers in online environments.

While similar to off-line fieldsites, in cyberspace there is another ethical twist to announcing a researcher's presence. When traditional ethnographers venture into off-line fieldsites, they listen to what people are saying and engage their informants in conversational exchanges. In observing how their informants are relating to each other, they are often physically co-present and observable to all interactants. In the case of online fieldwork, there is the issue of what it means to be a pure observer or a participant observer in an environment that is neither public nor fully private. This issue has a bearing on the controversies over the advisability of "lurking" (Miller & Slater, 2000; Bell, 2001) in online environments in order to collect data. Unlike the situation faced by off-line ethnographers, who are often embedded in interactional spaces that are either public or private, the cyberethnographer faces difficulties in making this determination in cyberspace.

This has clear ethical implications for cyberethnographic practice; the cyberethnographer who chooses to "lurk" and witness the online proceedings without drawing the notice of the respondents is assuming that the fieldsite is essentially a public space (Soukup, 2000). However, simply because a site is not password protected does not mean that participants in the site consider it a "public space." Just as locals at a park or coffee shop who have staked out their "turf" in the off-line world, online community members may not necessarily consider their site a public space open to anyone who wishes to enter, whether or not there are any rules in place to stop individuals from loitering or lurking.

The ethical dilemma in cyberspace is that the researcher may lurk without being seen in ways that are impossible in the off-line world. For this reason, the cyberethnographer who eschews lurking may do so because she feels that such unobtrusive observation is inappropriate in an environment where some participants might assume that they are taking part in private interactions. When in doubt, many cyberethnographers recommend dialogue with participants regarding the private versus public character of the fieldsite.

This being said, cyberethnographers must also remember their "invisibility" to others. While in the off-line world the ethnographer's physical presence may signal to others that they may be observed, this is not the case in cyberspace. As this indicates, cyberethnographers who engage in unobtrusive observation may not intentionally do so. On the Internet, although cyberethnographers may announce their status and intentions, participants may not receive their messages if they are not present when they are posted. Whether posted as a textual post or blog entry, cyberethnographers' announcements of arrival may not be read after they have been posted. This risk is heightened when cyberethnographers observe real-time interaction on a text-driven site where past messages are not accessible once they have been superseded by a new generation of messages.

This introduces an ethical tension that is not necessarily present in the off-line world. On the one hand, cyberethnographers who wish to announce their presence must do so continuously to ensure that users are aware of their presence. On the other hand, they must do so with caution to avoid disrupting naturally flowing interactions or becoming an irritant to members of an online community. In the off-line world, it would be unnatural for the ethnographer to continually disrupt ongoing interactions in the physical world by holding up a sign saying, "The ethnographer is present." Online, the cyberethnographer cannot be expected to continually post: "Remember everyone, you are under ethnographic observation." In reviewing these and related concerns, the Association of Internet Researchers uses the language, "guidelines not recipes," to indicate that all such ethical decisions are necessarily context dependent (Ess et al., 2002).

One solution is to embed a link to one's professional homepage into one's signature on posts or communications. By linking to a Web page detailing the researchers' activities and status as an ethnographer through a signature link, cyberethnographers may maintain their ethical commitments to announcing their presence as researchers while doing so in a manner that seems natural rather than obtrusive. In his work on open source in Brazil, Takhteyev (2009) went one step further. As part of his observation of the Lua community, he started a related open source project, with a Web site (now at http://spu.tnik.org/) that he inserted into his participation in the project and for his normal "professional" mail. This strategy validated his role of researcher in two ways. First, it provided a transparent account of his engagement in the field that was visible to all community members. Second, this strategy ensured that he would be viewed as a full-fledged member of the community by virtue of his skills.

In like manner, it can also be helpful to use one's professional e-mail address in personal communications as yet another implicit signal of one's professional identity as a researcher. Robinson's work (2006a) on the eBay Black Friday walkout offers an example of why these subtle reminders may be important to preserving the researcher's credibility. While observing the eBay community's walkout in response to new administrative policies, Robinson had asked several community members if they would like to answer questions about the community protest. Unbeknownst to her, her invitation was reposted by community members on other community chat rooms and forwarded to other community members by e-mail. In one instance, the researcher's academic affiliation was not included and she was contacted immediately by an eBay member who suspected Robinson of being an informant working for eBay! Fortunately, a quick e-mail from her university account with links to appropriate Web pages validated Robinson's identity as a researcher and allowed her to garner valuable data from a respondent confident of Robinson's true identity.

Text as Interaction

The discussion thus far has primarily dealt with how social processes occur in cyberspace through the medium of text, indicating the centrality of text-based interactions to much of cyberethnographic inquiry. This leads us to the second central tension in the shaping of cyberethnographic methods: the idea of text as interaction. The MUDs, bulletin boards, and other online fieldsites that have traditionally been subject to the gaze of early cyberethnographers were, of necessity, entirely built around text-based platforms designed to process only text-based inputs and outputs. Thus, to the present, most cyberethnographies have examined online interactions occurring exclusively in the form of written communications, whether linguistic or paralinguistic, and excluded the possibility of spontaneous nonlinguistic communication characteristic of face-to-face interaction (Turner, 2002). To make these mediated social processes meaningful, cyberethnographers have argued that it is possible to regard these written communications as closer to live interaction than recorded interaction, in Steve Jones' terms more "practice" than "product" (Jones 1999, p. 15). Recent studies have enlisted increasingly sophisticated analytical techniques to analyze a variety of text-based interactions. Sociological studies of email interactions (Menchik and Tian, 2008) and blogging (Tian and Menchik, 2009) have drawn on the work of sociolinguists such as Bakhtin and semioticians such as Peirce in order to shed light on the dynamics of identity work in online environments.

Since the advent of the field of ethnography, qualitative researchers have long debated whether the object of analysis is live interaction or merely the traces of interaction. The off-line ethnographer analyzes social interaction and talk as one coherent "flow" of social interaction unfolding in the phenomenological present. Much of this interaction consists of talk, but this talk itself constitutes an ongoing flow of action in which the observer can immerse herself. Thus, many ethnographers are taught to pay careful attention to the talk that forms an integral part of the ongoing social interaction in most societies and cultures (Agar 1980, pp. 105–108). It is only when the ethnographer records speech that concerns social interactions temporally or physically far removed from the here and now that she treats this talk as "second-order" account-giving rather than an aspect of the ongoing interaction. Thus, traditionally for ethnographers, the here and now is the experiential locus for the object of observation and the act of observation as well.

Given these understandings, cyberethnography's critics have argued that computer-mediated communications resemble documents and other memorializations of completed interactions that have already slipped into the past. Because of the asynchronous character of Internet-mediated communication, when the cyberethnographer analyzes the transcripts of archived chat or MUD interaction, he or she is doing archival research similar to the research undertaken by an historian. For an ethnographic purist, then, the cyberethnographer who studies archived chat is necessarily studying what the off-line ethnographers Pollner and Emerson have labeled "dead sociality" (Pollner and Emerson 1983, p. 251).

In response, cyberethnographers have contested this definition of interaction by arguing that these communications can be experienced not as memorializations of some originary act, but as live ongoing interactions. They believe that with text- or image-mediated interaction, the observer is witnessing something akin to the living sociality of ongoing off-line interaction. In taking this stance, cyberethnographers have advocated approaching computer-mediated communication as a double-sided object. It is in recognition of this double-sided character of online interaction that Hine conceptualizes the object of cyberethnographic observation as a couplet comprised of a cultural performance and the "artefact" corresponding to this performance (Hine 2000, p. 39). From this angle of vision, text takes on a dual existence housing both the past and present in one.

One way of understanding this is to imagine how individuals interpret past text in the present. For example, when individuals visit the online auction house eBay and read a member's profile, they witness text representing past interactions that this member has had with other members. This textual commentary turns the past into the present when the individual reads it as the necessary preliminary step in deciding whether or not to bid on an item. In this sense, text is not a dead archive of the past, but in a dramatic fashion, all past text becomes the basis for the present act or interaction with the site. In parallel manner, when an individual visits the online video site YouTube, the videos on display are the result of other users' choices, comments, and ratings. In all such cases, the present cyber-reality may be interpreted as a continual accumulation of all past input by members or participants. This might be likened to the way traditional ethnographers use textual evidence from off-line fieldsites such as information on bulletin boards, advertisements, handouts, manuals, or other print information they encounter in their off-line fieldsites.

In addition, legitimizing ethnographers have made other arguments for the use of text as data. From their angle of vision in off-line participant observation, the ethnographer witnesses a host of cues via what Goffman termed "face engagement," in which individuals produce a rich array of verbal and bodily cues signaling meanings, intentions, and social identities (Goffman, 1959). Cyberethnographers drew upon a Goffmanian framework to argue that participant observation of face engagement and shared social practices could occur via text (Robinson, 2007). To make this case, cyberethnographers referenced the Chicago School as setting an important precedent for using text written by members to understand their own meanings without the intervening lens of the researcher. Significantly, this approach allows the cyberethnographer to record and analyze the interactions of third parties interacting with each other in pure form. In this sense, cyberethnographic text is both the data and medium through which participant observation is conducted (Cavanagh, 1999), a process that has fascinating implications for the research process. Off-line, ethnographers must perform all interpretive tasks themselves by transcribing all of their observations into text in the form of fieldnotes. Online, informants translate their own experiences into textual form by creating their own textual translations of the off-line range of interactive cuing mechanisms. Given this contrast, cyberethnographers may tout one of the virtues of cyberethnography as its ability to produce one fewer lens of distortion because the text is the interaction that is recorded verbatim as data (Hine, 2000).

Stories From the Field: Methodological and Ethical Implications of Text as Interaction

The use of text also introduces new methodological implications regarding the collection and use of text as data. In Robinson's work on both 9/11 (2008) and eBay France and eBay USA (2006b), she recorded her data by archiving entire Web pages to capture all ongoing interactions as experienced by participants. While data analysis programs can be helpful, they should be used in tandem rather than in lieu of archiving. Archiving entire Web pages offers several advantages. First, when reviewing data at a later date, the cyberethnographer may wish to revisit conversations or comments as they occurred in cyberspace. Archiving ongoing Web pages allows cyberethnographers to preserve data in the format in which respondents experience it and to make each subsequent exploration of the data a fresh view of the original interactions. Second, this technique allows cyberethnographers to accurately trace the threads of interaction over minutes, hours, and days. Comments or posts that may not seem significant at first view may acquire salience in light of continued conversation or repetition. By archiving Web pages of chat or continuous interaction, cyberethnographers may keep an accurate ongoing record of all exchanges between community members and preserve the integrity of larger community dialogues and debates.

The archiving of such data brings us to ethical concerns of how cyberethnographers should protect anonymity of respondents when publishing or sharing their findings. When recording textual data that is posted under user names, clearly it is necessary to change user names to protect anonymity just as with data in the off-line world. However, as search engine technologies become more advanced, there is an increased risk that researchers' replication of data can inadvertently reveal off-line identities.

Today, there are new twists engendered by the rapid growth of social networking sites that rely on the convergence of media consumption and production known as Web 2.0 or user-generated Web site content. While this may potentially occur with data from any non-password protected site, this is especially problematic when studying sites such as MySpace that explicitly reveal individuals' real names and off-line identities. Reproducing textual data from a social networking site such as MySpace or Facebook can allow anyone with enough Internet savvy to track down respondents' real identities. For example, if an individual's MySpace account allows "public" access, a simple online search may allow anyone to pull up that person's profile. By typing in a single quotation from someone's MySpace page using quotation marks, it is theoretically possible for anyone to pull up those profiles and see photos and other identifying information.

To test this ethical concern, we replicated some quotes taken from studies of MySpace to see if we could find out respondents' identities. We used a simple Google search in which we typed in an exact phrase from someone's MySpace page that a researcher had quoted. We were able to find the exact user profile of the person quoted by using a phrase as simple as "Are we still gonna go play Frisbee?" Although the article's author had given this individual a pseudonym, this provided approximately two minutes of anonymity. A Google search based on "Are we still gonna go play Frisbee?" revealed two possible MySpace profiles in which this quotation was used. One of them was a perfect match to the other identifying information provided in the author's description of the respondent. As this indicates, quotes that may seem innocuous are often unique enough to reveal personal identities.

While quotes about playing Frisbee may not pose extraordinary potential ethical conflicts, it is easy to imagine how data revealing information about sensitive populations could pose an enormous risk for those under study. To push this concern further, we visited a non-password protected pro-anorexia online community. We again selected a quote that had no personal identifying information that may be paraphrased as, "How can I be alive with such a big belly?" Taking this quote out of context, we again ran a simple Google search putting the text in quotation marks. Not only were we given an exact match to the girl, but also her picture. If we found these individuals so easily, so can almost anyone else with an Internet connection. Please note that given our success in finding these individuals' personal information, we are not replicating the exact quotation in either of the examples given.

With employers and educational institutions increasingly "looking up" applicants' social networking site profiles, the ethical implications for researchers to protect anonymity is increasingly important. Cyberethnographers must face a unique set of ethical challenges. On one hand, we want to preserve the integrity of our informants' words. On the other hand, the ethical risks to do so may be too great. Should a cyberethnographer be studying a sensitive population, she must take precautions to project anonymity. These may include, but are not limited to, running searches on quotations to make sure that they do not reveal their authors' real identities. While simply correcting spelling errors is one option to thwart search engines, cyberethnographers may have to consider the necessity of altering the text through the use of ellipses or even paraphrasing some parts of respondents' words while preserving the meaning. While there is little discussion regarding what cyberethnographers can do, increased dialogue on this issue is both timely and needed.

Observer and Observed

Just as cyberethnographers have come to recognize that the object of their analysis can be constituted in a variety of different ways, they have also recognized the complex relationship between the observer and the observed that is, in many ways, unique to cyberethnography. More specifically, cyberethnographers have come to acknowledge that, whenever they undertake cyberethnographic research, they are coming face-to-face with interactional environments that pose special challenges for those seeking an in-depth understanding grounded in direct observation. When off-line ethnographers carry out conventional participant observation (Hammersley & Atkinson, 1989; Schatzman & Strauss, 1973), they can perform acts of straightforward firsthand observation and, at the same time, put themselves in the shoes of the participant in order to convey what it feels like to be a participant in the world under observation. This approach privileges what the anthropologist calls "direct observation" (Agar, 1980, p. 127).

However, the cyberethnographer must make a choice whether or not to privilege online data or use a combined approach to online and off-line data gathering. Since its inception, many of cyberethnography's practitioners have been divided between those who advocate studying online phenomenon uniquely in virtual venues and those who argue for a blending of online and off-line fieldwork. In this dilemma, we come full circle to our original discussion of mediated social processes in relation to the social construction of identity begun in the first part of this chapter. As we discussed, one of the central tensions between pioneering and legitimizing cyberethnographers was the negotiation of online and off-line identity projects. These opposing stances also play out in terms of methodological choices. Some choose to conduct all fieldwork virtually, while other researchers choose to conduct both on- and offline fieldwork; this latter approach allows the researcher to compare on- and offline identity performances. While both approaches rely on ethnographic methods of participant observation and ethnographic interviews, each of these approaches provides a different fit between research questions and data.

Regarding the former, cyberethnographies relying uniquely on online fieldwork analyze members' contributions to chat rooms, bulletin boards, and MUDs (Markham, 1998; Ward, 1999). This type of ethnography is uniquely marked by participant observation online and relates members' experiences as encompassed by the virtual medium. Markham gives a self-reflexive account of her participant observation in a MUD that illuminates members' accounts of "ways of being." Ward conducted her participant observation in two virtual communities, The Cybergrrl Web Station and Women Halting Online Abuse. This approach accepts presentation of the virtual self; the orienting goal is to understand members' actions and perceptions of a particular virtual community.

A number of arguments have been used to validate the use of data collected in purely online fieldsites. From a theoretical standpoint, Goffmanian analysis of public and private life may be used to illuminate the nature of online and off-line selves and interaction (Cavanagh, 1999). Goffman's work (1959) provides numerous, pre-Internet examples of the multiplicity of identity performance in which the identity performances that individuals produce vary substantially in the context of their reception and the character of their intended audiences. Cyberethnographers, following Symbolic Interactionist approaches, have argued that the online self, as constituted by its identity performances, is continuous with the off-line self, even though it enacts itself in a disembodied environment (Robinson, 2007). Taking such a Symbolic Interactionist approach privileges members' understandings of their online and off-line identities.

In addition, from a methodological standpoint, in determining whether online fieldwork alone is sufficient, it is crucial for the cyberethnographer to understand how members understand the relationship between their online and off-line selves. One question of central importance to cyberethnographers is whether or not members of virtual communities also interact in the off-line world. If there are no connections between online and off-line interactions on the part of members, it has been argued that validating online participation observation with off-line verification can create a bias:

> The point for the ethnographer is not to bring some external criterion for judging whether it is safe to believe what informants say, but rather to come to understand how it is that informants judge authenticity … we cannot assume a priori that authenticity is as problematic for online members as it is for the cyberethnographer. (Hine, 2000, p. 49)

For this reason, those espousing this stance believe that it is not necessary to initiate face-to-face interaction in the off-line world because of the potential to distort participant observation by placing "the ethnographer in an asymmetric position, using more varied and different means of communication to understand informants than are used by informants themselves" (Hine, 2000, p. 48). Walstrom (2004) argued that this epistemic positioning gives the cyberethnographer an advantage over the off-line ethnographer. For, while the purely off-line ethnographer cannot know what it is like, from a subjective standpoint, for participants to interact in online environments, the online ethnographer can easily put herself in the participants' virtual shoes. From this perspective, the cyberethnographer must consider whether or not online members perceive the virtual-physical distinction as critical to their experience in a particular virtual fieldsite. Such knowledge can only be determined by extended participant observation online. According to Hine (2000), "The decision to privilege certain modes of interaction is a situated one. If the aim is to study online settings as contexts in their own right, the question of off-line identities need not arise" (22). From this perspective, it is valid to conduct all participant observation and ethnographic interviewing via mediated interaction.

On the other hand, sometimes cyberethnographers need to conduct observation and ethnographic interviewing across both online and off-line realms. This is true when members of a community or fieldsite extend their online relationships into off-line spaces (Baym, 2000). If members of an online community also meet in the off-line world, conducting ethnography in both online and off-line settings may be necessary. Humphreys (2007), for example, examines a series of interactions some of which take place on the virtual site Dodgeball and some of which take place in off-line venues where people meet up in bodily co-presence. Miller and Slater combine online data gathering and analysis with an off-line house-to-house survey in their study of the online Trinidad community to see the impact of the Internet on households in the region. A two-pronged data-gathering strategy was the choice of researchers like Turkle (1995), Kendall (2002), and Correll (1995) who sought to combine online and off-line ethnographic observation and interviewing. Turkle met many of her respondents face-to-face, while Kendall and Carter attended off-line "meets" where community participants would get together in the flesh.

Kendall's research (2002) on BlueSky presents an excellent example of when online and off-line ethnographic methods are ideal complements to best study how participants interact both online and off-line. In Kendall's case, gaining a complete and nuanced understanding of BlueSky participants' identities and relationships necessitated leaving the online world because many of the ties between the participants had an off-line dimension, as well as an online dimension. Kendall's foray into the off-line world demonstrates the necessity of ethnographic sensitivity to respondents' experiential horizons. Because her respondents also interacted with each other in the off-line world, Kendall was following in their footsteps when she initiated off-line contact with them. Because she used the same means of communication as the participants and had access to the same amount and quality of information as they did, her observations conveyed what Hine calls "experiential authenticity" (Hine, 2000, pp. 48–49). For her, there was no conflict between using as many data-gathering channels as possible and staying faithful to the subjective experiences of her own respondents.

Stories From the Field: Methodological and Ethical Implications for the Observer Observed

This discussion brings us to our final section on the ethical implications of conducting fieldwork using new digital technologies. Earlier text-based cyberethnographers conducted much of their fieldwork via a computer screen first with dial-up modems and then with high-speed connections. By and large, their data collection neither captured the subject's image nor rendered the ethnographer into an observable object herself. Today, however, Web 2.0 is based on highly interactive visual content. Cyberethnographers and their respondents can use highly mobile handheld devices to record multimedia and create their own digital representations both cheaply and easily.

Lange's work on YouTube offers insight into some the ethical implications of Web 2.0 cyberethnographic fieldwork. Lange complemented her online fieldwork with off-line participation in YouTube meet ups in the off-line world. She filmed these events and then posted her ethnographic video-based data on YouTube and her own Web site comprised of video blogs or "vlogs." Lange obtained informed consent before recording participants' images and voices for her video-based and interview data collection. However, in certain instances such as reproducing screen shots of YouTube participants' online videos, Lange (2007a) might choose to "fuzz out" certain identifying information such as faces or logos if she had any concerns about reproducing the unredacted images. As Lange's work (2007b) indicates, cyberethnographers may need to add multimedia skills to their methodological toolkits to engage in multimedia fieldsites (See Figure 8.1).

Further, while most scholarly publications still rely on text-based evidence published in paper journals, Web-based publications that can easily hyperlink to images, music, and video are increasingly common. As we saw earlier, just as the publication of text from Web sites may allow us to find the "real" identity of respondents with an online search, the release of visual ethnographic evidence may also put informants at risk in ways that would have been unimaginable before Web 2.0. As media convergence continues, cyberethnographers must carefully think through how to protect anonymity while preserving the authenticity of visual data (See Figure 8.2).

Finally, Lange's work illustrates how user-generated Web 2.0 media can radically change the relationship between the observer and the observed. Should the cyberethnographer venture into the off-line world, she must consider how she will become the object of scrutiny by those under observation. The cyberethnographer must face new concerns about how her identity may become part of a feedback loop with those she is studying. Lange's work (2007c) indicates how multi-modal Web 2.0 produces fieldwork in which the researcher may become the object of study herself. Indeed, respondents may choose

Figure 8.1 Anthrovlog (http://www.anthrovlog.com/).

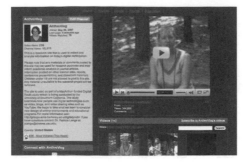

Figure 8.2 YouTube (http://www.youtube.com/user/AnthroVlog). Screen shot taken by Patricia G. Lange on October 8, 2007.

to publicize the fieldworker's personal identity. Lange describes her research with video bloggers from a "media-savvy group." She explains that, in the course of her fieldwork, her picture was taken without her knowledge and posted to Flickr, an online photo site, without her consent:

> …they have the power to capture events I attend and put the images on the Internet. They can identify me, disclose personal information, and manipulate my image without my even knowing it…"data" was collected on me, as my interactions were documented in photographs (and possibly also video) and distributed globally.…(2007c, p. 4).

Lange (2007c) was put in a position of comparative powerlessness in that respondents were able to record and reproduce her image and identity at will because of new media technologies. Lange cautions that some researchers and institutional sponsors are ill equipped to meet these challenges: "Although many human subjects protocols are set up with the assumption that the researcher alone records and analyzes materials, in fact in the video blogging community the power of recording and distribution may exceed that of any individual researcher" (p. 5). As she explains, "Ironically, the more I sought to control my image, the less control I actually had" (p. 4). As this indicates, ethical concerns must be reexamined in light of new technologies for both subjects and researchers alike.

Discussion: Where Are We Now?

As today's digital fieldsites are born, change, and die in an instant, cyberethnographers must continue to be flexible. Many of the challenges of data collection and analysis have no clear models or methodological exemplars from which to draw explicit guidance. Rather, ethnographers must plunge into a host of textual, pictorial, and aural data that may be here this morning, changed this afternoon, and gone tomorrow. While daunting, we believe that ethnography's traditional strengths are ideally suited to studying the elastic and ever-changing nature of mediated communication. More specifically, according to

The National Science Foundation's report, qualitative methods are especially appropriate for examining "naturally occurring processes" and "phenomena of social life," as well as "cultural practices" and "manifestations of globalization at the micro level" (Lamont and White, 2008, p. 17). In contrast to ethnography, much social science inquiry uses quantitative methods following what has been termed the logico-deductive or positivist model (Emerson, 2001). While valuable in its own right, this paradigm orients itself toward very different goals than ethnography. Unlike ethnography's emphasis on engagement with respondents, the logico-deductive mode of research often valorizes a distanced posture toward the objects of study (Burawoy, 1998). Rather, the researcher uses strategies related to the linkage between data and theory that aim to verify or disconfirm theoretical propositions framed in advance of empirical research. Analysts adopting this approach maintain distance from respondents to avoid introducing any bias into the research process; subjects are often decontextualized from natural settings in order to control for the effects of context (Burawoy, 1998). Finally, in achieving these ends, the formalized language of science is privileged over the language of everyday life used by those under study such that accounts of the social world rely on "experience-distant" terms (Emerson 2001, p. 35). From the ethnographic perspective, this process creates what may be termed a nonnaturalist social ontology because empirical engagement plays but an ancillary role in the research process (Emerson, 2001). We believe that these orientations are not ideal for examining naturally occurring processes on the Internet in order to reveal cyber cultural practices.

By contrast, online and off-line, ethnographic methods conceptualize engagement with subjects via fieldwork and participant observation as central to the research process to shed light on emergent social phenomena. Off-line and online, the ethnographer relies on contact and communication with "members," or those under study, and seeks to communicate with them about their understandings of the social world (Burawoy, 1998). For many ethnographers, a full description and analysis of social processes is not possible when employing the logico-deductive emphasis on detachment and the nonnaturalist social ontology. Rather, for ethnographers, uncovering members' meanings is crucial to the methodology's goal of understanding social processes and interactions from the point of view of those under study (Emerson & Pollner, 1988). Given the rapidly changing nature of mediated communication, which is but one part of the Information Revolution, we advocate the flexibility and innovative potential of cyberethnography to examine our society in flux.

Future Directions

Whether taking notes on a Blackberry in Brasília, typing them into a laptop computer in Ulan Bator, or jotting them down with a pen and paper in Silicon Valley, ethnographers conduct extended fieldwork to gather data through the observation of naturally occurring settings and interactions (Hammersley & Atkinson, 1989). For ethnographers and cyberethnographers alike, naturalistic forms of evidence include categories and orientations originating in common sense or folk idioms that capture the reality of "everyday life" rather than the formalized idiom of social science. Rather than offering objectified descriptions of the social fields in which social actors operate, the ethnographer relies on the categories cognitively accessible to social actors and concentrates on reporting members' emic categories by using members' own terms and words as windows into their social worlds (Emerson, 2001). Many ethnographers aspire to capture the "subject-centered" dimension of social reality by entering subjects' ongoing life worlds through participant observation. Ethnographers conduct ongoing fieldwork to appreciate the interactions and practices as they are seen through the eyes of the actors engaged in producing them (Emerson, 2001). For all of these reasons, we believe that traditional ethnography's orientations are an ideal fit with the rapidly changing nature of mediated communication as the field of Internet studies continues to be built.

However, to do so, we must continually adapt off-line ethnographic practice to the constraints and possibilities afforded by digital fieldsites. As increasing generations of individuals in developed nations grow up "wired," we believe that the novelty of cyberethnography will likely fade as information technologies become just another accepted part of everyday life. Simultaneously, once cyberethnography has been incorporated into the field of sociology, its legitimacy will be beyond question (Webb, 1999). As we have seen in this chapter, in the middle of the 1990s, ethnographers introduced the idea of the virtual world as a nonphysical space of flows that centered on connection, not location. Today, as the depth and complexity of interactive venues deepens, social phenomena originating in the online world are increasingly spilling over into the off-line world.

As these arguments indicate, physical face-to-face interactions and virtual interactions are increasingly but two possibilities among other forms of mediated communication including, but not limited to, the cell phone, iPod, and video conferencing. In sum, the dynamics of mediated interaction must be recognized as having the same level of complexity as face-to-face interaction. For this reason, we close this chapter by urging cyberethnographers to increasingly conceptualise mediated environments and interaction in terms of a range of possibilities. Already, the online auction house eBay provides a wealth of examples of how mediated and face-to-face forms of interaction coexist. The exchange of goods in the off-line world based on actions and interactions on the eBay site forms one point of online and off-line crossover for which members regularly engage in varied forms of mediated communication including phone and snail mail. Creating even greater possibilities of online and off-line interactions, eBay also holds events in the off-line world that promote the virtual site through face-to-face encounters.

Taking this further, the prevalence of cell phones and other handheld communication devices will make it necessary for cyberethnographers to consider an even greater range of communication possibilities. With media convergence, cell phones and other handheld devices are offering a new array of communication possibilities, thereby multiplying the potential platforms for digital communication. For this reason, we believe that cyberethnographers will increasingly extend their fieldsites beyond the computer to a sophisticated array of personal communication devices. This is already happening as the Internet becomes increasingly available via cell phones. At the same time, a new host of Web sites offer an increased range of communication media reliant on media convergence. Likening itself to the iPod, Dimdim claims to be the world's easiest Web conference Web site because it allows users to simultaneously give live video Web presentations using whiteboards, Web pages, and shared voice. Lifestrea.ms is yet another kind of convergence site that aggregates individuals' communications from Twitter, Facebook, MySpace Photos, etc. into a bundled communication package.

As these possibilities indicate, conceptualizing the fieldsite as accessible via a cell phone or Blackberry will prompt new challenges and questions about how to study interactions in real time versus asynchronous communication, how to analyze digital images, and how to best study other new forms of multimedia interaction. Even as we develop new research strategies suited to studying text-based mediated interaction, video-based and audio-based interaction is mushrooming on various digital media. Traditional methodological tools and constraints do not suffice when it comes to collecting data composed of a communicative mélange of images, sound, and text, which is increasingly the norm given media convergence. Today's webcams allow visual computer-mediated communication (CMC) to jump from text to image in what will perhaps soon be called its "primitive" form. Video clips and sound tracks are embedded in Web sites and linked to posts. Not only are the media mixed, but they no longer form or follow linear structures. Virtual ethnographies of video- and audio-based interaction will have to be even more attentive to issues of embedding and context. To be sure, written and spoken language will always be central to examining interaction, but cyberethnographers will also need to consider varied multimedia forms of communication.

Of further importance, both scholars and students must tackle these issues together. We must consider how future technologies may change the very way ethnography is taught and how the craft is disseminated. It is likely that in years to come we will collectively redefine normative classroom environments. Increasingly, the training of ethnographic methods will take place in wired settings. Simultaneously, training will increasingly incorporate technological tools. Now we might imagine the use of texting for jotting. However, the future promises even more dramatic shifts. These shifts will be equally salient in terms of publishing work in digital venues and sharing work through constantly evolving personal electronic devices. We can only begin to imagine the scope of the evolving ethical challenges that we must face together.

In closing, examining ethnographic practice in light of digital technologies, this article sheds light not only on issues connected to methodology but invites larger questions that will grow ever more pressing as the Information Revolution continues to unfold. We believe that increasingly cyberethnographers will creatively avail themselves of their sociological imagination in order to unearth the forms of social life that will exist and multiply in this new virtual world. Given the increasing salience and centrality of virtual environments to everyday experience, it has become imperative to conduct rigorous ethnographic research on the new forms of social life emerging in this domain. Such research requires a solid foundation. The fast pace of change, however, demands constant methodological innovation. We must consider cyberethnography as an ever-evolving form of research with wider implications for both sociology and the field of new media studies.

References

Agar, M. (1980). *The professional stranger: An informal introduction to ethnography*. New York: Academic Press.
Baym, N. (1998). The emergence of on-line community. In Jones, S. (Ed.), *Cybersociety 2.0: Revisiting computer-mediated communication and community*. Thousand Oaks: Sage.
Baym, N. K. (2000). *Tune In, Log On: Soaps, Fandom, and Online Community*. Thousand Oaks: Sage.
Bell, D. (2001). *An introduction to cyberculture*. New York: Routledge.
Boellstorff, T. (2008). *Coming of age in second life: An anthropologist explores the virtually human*. New Jersey: Princeton University Press.

Burawoy, M. (1998). The extended case method. *Sociological Theory, 16*, 1.

Cavanagh, A. (1999). Behaviour in public?: Ethics in online ethnography. *Cybersociology Magazine: Research Methodology Online*, 6.

Correll, S. (1995). The ethnography of an electronic bar: The lesbian café. *Journal of Contemporary Ethnography, 24*, 3.

Donath, J. (1999). Identity and deception in a virtual community. In Smith M. & Kollock P. (Eds.), *Communities in cyberspace*. London: Routledge.

Emerson, R. (2001). *Contemporary field research: Perspectives and formulations*. Prospect Heights: Waveland Press.

Emerson, R., & Pollner, M. (1988). On the uses of members' responses to researchers' accounts. *Human Organization, 47*.

Ess, C. and the AoIR ethics working committee. (2002). Ethical decision-making and Internet research: Recommendations from the aoir ethics working committee: www.aoir.org/reports/ethics.pdf.

Goffman, E. (1959). *The presentation of self in everyday life*. New York: Anchor Books.

Hammersley, M., & Atkinson, P. (1989). What is ethnography? In Atkinson, P. (Ed.), *Ethnography: Principles in practice*. New York: Routledge.

Hine, C. (2000). *Virtual ethnography*. Thousand Oaks: Sage.

Humphreys, L. (2007). Mobile social networks and social practice: A case study of dodgeball. *Journal of Computer-Mediated Communication, 13*, 1.

Jones, S. (1999). *Doing Internet research: Critical issues and methods for examining the net*. Thousand Oaks: Sage Publications.

Kendall, L. (2002). *Hanging out in the virtual pub: Masculinities and relationships online*. Berkeley: University of California Press.

Lamont, M., & Patricia W. (2008). *Workshop on interdisciplinary standards for systematic qualitative research*. Washington: National Science Foundation. http://www.nsf.gov/sbe/ses/soc/ISSQR_workshop_rpt.pdf.

Lange, P. (2007a). Fostering friendship through video production: How youth use YouTube to enrich local interaction. San Francisco: International Communication Association Conference.

Lange, P. (2007b). Publicly private and privately public: Social networking on Youtube. *Journal of Computer-Mediated Communication, 13*, 1.

Lange, P. (2007c). Collecting data and losing control: How studying video blogging challenges human subjects frameworks. Vancouver: Association for Internet Researchers Conference.

Markham, A. (1998). *Life online: Researching real experience in virtual space*. Walnut Creek: Altamira Press.

Menchik, D., and X. Tian. (2008). Putting Social Context into Text: The Semiotics of Email Interaction. *The American Journal of Sociology, 114*, 2.

Miller, D., & Slater, D. (2000). *The Internet: An ethnographic approach*. New York: Berg.

Nippert-Eng, C. (1996). *Home and work: Negotiating boundaries through everyday life*. Chicago: University of Chicago Press.

Reid, E. (1999). Hierarchy and power: Social control in cyberspace. In Smith & Kollock (Eds.), *Communities in cyberspace*. London: Routledge.

Rheingold, H. (1993). *The virtual community: Homesteading on the electric frontier*. Reading, MA: Addison-Wesley.

Robinson, L. (2005). Debating the events of September 11th: Discursive and interactional dynamics in three online fora. *The Journal of Computer-Mediated Communication, 10*, 4.

Robinson, L. (2006a). Black Friday and feedback bombing: An examination of trust and online community in eBay's early history. In Hillis K., Petit M., & Epley N. (Eds.), *Everyday eBay culture, collecting, and desire*. New York: Routledge.

Robinson, L. (2006b). Online Art Auctions à la française and à l'américaine: eBay France and eBay USA. *The Social Science Computer Review, 24*, 4.

Robinson, L. (2007). The cyberself: Symbolic interaction in the digital age. *New Media and Society*, *9*, 1.

Robinson, L. (2008). The moral accounting of terrorism: Competing interpretations of September 11, 2001. *Qualitative Sociology*, *31*, 3.

Robinson, L. & Schulz, J. (2009). "New Avenues for Sociological Inquiry: Evolving Forms of Ethnographic Practice" *Sociology*. Volume 43: 4.

Schatzman, L., & Strauss, A. (1973). *Field research: Strategies for a natural sociology*. Englewood Cliffs: Prentice-Hall Inc.

Soukup, C. (2000). The gendered interactional patterns of computer-mediated chatrooms: A critical ethnographic study. *The Information Society*, *15*, 3.

Stone, A. R. (1995). *The war of desire and technology*. Cambridge, MA: MIT Press.

Takhteyev, Y. (2009) *Coding places: Coding places uneven globalization of software work in Rio de Janeiro, Brazil*. Doctoral dissertation: UC Berkleley: School of Information Management and Systems.

Tian X, and Menchik D. (2009). Online Interaction with Unidentifiable Others. San Francisco: The Annual Meeting of the Society for Symbolic Interactionism.

Turkle, S. (1995). *Life on the screen: Identity in the age of the Internet*. London: Weidenfeld and Nicolson.

Turner, J. (2002). *Face to face*. Stanford: Stanford University Press.

Walstrom, M. K. (2004). Ethics and engagement in communication scholarship: Analyzing public, online support groups as researcher/participant-experiencer. In Buchanan E. A. (Ed.), *Virtual research ethics: Issues and controversies*. Hershey: Information Science Publishing.

Ward, K. (1999) Cyber-ethnography and the emergence of the virtually new community. *Journal of Information Technology*, *14*, 1.

Webb, S. (1999). Cyberspace as everyday life. *Cybersociology Magazine: Research Methodology Online*, 6.

Wertheim, M. (1999). *The pearly gates of cyberspace: A history of space from dante to the Internet*. New York: Norton.

Zhao, S. (2005). The digital self: Through the looking glass of telecopresent others. *Symbolic Interaction*, *28*, 3.

Chapter 9

Online Focus Groups

David L. Morgan and Bojana Lobe

As Bill Gates famously noted, "The Internet changes everything," so it is hardly surprising that online technologies are having a major impact on social science research. The revolutionary role of information communication technologies has been particularly important in creating new online options for collecting data. The power of this technology means that Web surveys, online qualitative interviews, and virtual ethnographies are now joining more traditional forms of research. Indeed, many of the Web-based applications that are already inherent to online computer use are appropriate for social science data collection (e.g., e-mail, instant messengers, blogs, social networking sites, Skype, etc.). As these examples demonstrate, online research is highly dependent on available technology, and the continuing evolution of this technology has created opportunities as well as challenges for collecting both qualitative and quantitative data.

For focus groups, online versions of this method have already been appearing for over a decade (e.g., Gaiser, 1997; Parks & Floyd, 1996). During that time, several different Internet technologies have been adapted as formats for online focus groups. This flexible approach to technology for conducting focus groups online is quite consistent with the overall evolution of traditional, face-to-face focus groups in the social sciences. In particular, that "traditional" approach largely evolved from marketing research, based on the earlier work of Merton and Lazarsfeld, which began over 70 years ago (Morgan, 1997). During the two decades that social scientists have rediscovered focus groups, this method has proven to be a highly flexible and adaptable tool, which can collect data across a wide range of research topics and cultural settings. One of the clearest messages from that experience is that there is no "one right way" to do focus groups, and we believe the same is true of online focus groups. Our emphasis here is thus on clarifying the advantages and disadvantages of different approaches for conducting online focus groups, both in terms of how they compare to each other and in terms of how each compares to face-to-face focus groups. In other words, we start with the assumption that each format for online focus groups has some advantages that would make it more suitable for some purposes, as well as some limitations that would make it less suitable for other purposes.

The layout for the chapter begins with a brief consideration of the more general issues about using online technologies for social science data collection, followed by a more specific presentation on technologies for online focus groups. The main section of the chapter then discusses the methodological and practical issues involved in conducting focus groups in online environments. The next section examines those issues in more details, within the context of a research project that used online focus groups. We conclude with a look at future directions in the emerging approaches to online focus groups.

Online Technologies and Social Science Data Collection

With the increasing expansion of the Internet (Hine, 2005a; Van Selm & Jankowski, 2006), a great many researchers in the social sciences can find some aspect of their interests on the Internet. As Mann and Stewart (2000, p. 5) note, social scientists are using the Internet for research that is concerned not only "with the study of online behavior" but also "with using computer-based tools and computer-accessible populations to study human behavior in general." Our goal is to examine online focus groups as a method for collecting data, rather than a way to study online behavior itself.

For the purposes of this chapter, "online technologies" will refer to information communication technologies that can be accessed through the use of Internet-connected computers. In this sense, online technologies are also known as "virtual environments" or "Web-based applications." Research methods that use online technologies all rely on what is known as "computer-mediated communication," where two or more people interact via a set of hardware- and software-based tools. Within this framework, the more traditional forms of interviewing are discussed as occurring in a "face-to-face" setting. The obvious question is: How well do online technologies for data collection compare to their traditional counterparts? Van Selm and Jankowski (2006, p. 435) distinguish a continuum of three positions on this issue, where the two end points make claims about either the ability to use traditional methods with only minimal changes or the need to invent new data collection methods with no direct equivalent in the "off-line" environment. In contrast, the intermediate stance is to adapt existing technologies in the online environment in ways that capture the essence of traditional methods, and a number of researchers are already developing online versions of qualitative interviews in general and focus groups in particular (O'Connor, Madge, Shaw, & Wellens, 2008).

Following that intermediate path, the main approach to creating online focus groups has been to adapt the method to existing software, with the assumption that participants will use the technology to interact in ways that produce useful data. This makes sense, from a practical perspective, because there are only a limited number of options for modifying online technologies. Even so, the conclusion that online technologies can be used to capture aspects of traditional, face-to-face methods says little about the desirability of doing so. On the one hand, we will discuss ways that online technologies make it easier to do some things that would be difficult in a traditional setting. On the other hand, we will also point out the aspects of traditional focus groups that are harder to accomplish via the Internet. Hence, the real issue is not so much what it takes to adapt an existing method for use online, as it is the ways that traditional and online uses of the "same" method are either similar or different.

Any attempt to compare face-to-face and online focus groups immediately raises more general questions about how to assess differences between alternative approaches to focus groups. Unfortunately, the current literature on face-to-face focus groups is not very useful for this purpose, because it concentrates almost exclusively on matching different research goals to different ways of conducting face-to-face focus groups (e.g., Krueger &

Casey, 2000; Morgan & Krueger, 1998). As a result, we lack explicit techniques for assessing differences in either the nature or the quality of the data produced by either traditional focus groups or their online counterparts. Our strategy for the rest of this chapter will thus be to assess the more obvious advantages and disadvantages of conducting focus groups one way rather than another. Ultimately, researchers who use focus groups will want to know how face-to-face and online groups differ in the *actual data* that generate, but that is an issue that goes well beyond the scope of this chapter.

Alternative Technologies for Online Focus Groups

By taking Van Selm and Jankowski's "intermediate" option (2006) and considering ways to create a match between face-to-face focus groups and online technologies, the first test is whether these technologies can indeed capture the most essential aspects of traditional focus groups. This is an easy question to answer, because science researchers uniformly agree that group interaction is the key distinguishing feature of focus groups (e.g., Morgan & Krueger, 1998; and O'Connor et al., 2008). For example, Morgan (1997) defined focus groups as a "research technique that collects data through group interaction on a topic determined by the researcher" (p. 6). Similarly, he stated, "*The hallmark of focus groups is their explicit use of group interaction to produce data and insights that would be less accessible without the interaction found in a group*" (Morgan, 1997, p. 2; emphasis in the original). Thus, an online technology meets the defining characteristics of a focus group when it allows a researcher to ask questions that generate meaningful interaction among the participants.

   Drawing on an earlier discussion by O'Connor & Madge (2001, 10.6), we offer the following list of shared advantages for online groups:

   For participants, holding the groups online increases comfort and convenience by:

1. eliminating issues related to arranging transportation (especially among groups with limited ability to travel);
2. minimizing the need to juggle schedules (especially for groups such as mothers, caregivers and those who work at home);
3. avoiding concerns about personal appearance.

For researchers, holding the groups online reduces costs and effort by:

1. reducing the need to locate or pay for a place to moderate the group;
2. reducing the complexity of recruiting by using a variety of "many-to-one" forms of contact;
3. eliminating the need for taping and transcribing by using written interaction.

Shifting to a comparison of the different technologies for online focus groups, the most important distinction is between "synchronous" and "asynchronous" formats (Jacobson, 1999; Mann & Stewart, 2000). Traditional face-to-face focus groups are inherently synchronous because the participants interact in real time. Similarly, there are several forms of synchronous online communication that allow real-time responses to other participants' comments; examples of online technologies for synchronous focus groups include instant messengers and chat rooms. In contrast, online technologies that use asynchronous interaction do not require the participants to be connected to the Internet at the same time, and thus allow people to respond at their convenience; examples of online technologies for asynchronous focus groups include discussion forums and e-mail lists. One way to summarize these distinctions is to say that traditional focus groups require the participants to meet at the same time and in the same place, while synchronous online focus groups allow the participants to be in widely separated locations, and asynchronous online groups do not require meeting at either the same place or the same time.

For our purposes, we will describe instant-messenger sessions as an example of synchronous online focus groups and discussion forums as an example of asynchronous focus groups. Both these formats for online focus groups begin with a metaphor that links each technology to interaction in traditional focus groups:

1.   An instant-messenger session is like a focus group because the participants react directly to each *other's* statements in the ongoing discussion.
2.   A discussion forum is like a focus group because participants can pick up and pursue various aspects of the overall topic.

Instant-Messenger Sessions as Synchronous Online Focus Groups

The most common use for instant messaging technology (or IM, as it is commonly known) makes it possible for several users who are on the Internet at the same time to exchange text messages. The classic format for an IM session is a separate window on each person's computer screen, which allows the users to interact by adding their own comments to the ongoing stream that makes up the session. Figure 9.1 shows a simplified version of an instant messenger with a hypothetical focus group discussion among women whose husbands all have early onset Alzheimer's Disease. The main part of the window contains the comments with the names for each participant. These comments move up the screen and out of sight as the conversation proceeds, but a scroll bar makes it easy to review earlier parts of the discussion. On the right side of the figure is a list of the participants, and the bottom of the window contains the field where the current participant can enter and send text. The field at the bottom is a "typing progress indication" that shows whether one of the other participants is about to add a comment to the discussion, in which case, the current participant may want to wait and see that entry before writing and sending his or her own comment.

To use an IM session for conducting a synchronous focus group, the moderator begins by contacting each of the participants who has agreed to participate in the discussion. Once all the participants have joined the focus group, each person in the conversation sees a window similar to Figure 9.1, with the same stream of text in each window. The next section of the group would follow the same schedule as a traditional group, with the moderator using the IM system to share some basic instructions before asking the first question.

To illustrate the nature of conversation in focus groups that use IM, Box 9.1 presents a longer extract from the hypothetical conversation in Figure 9.1 (see O'Connor & Madge, 2001 for an extract from a real discussion using similar software). As the conversation in Box 9.1 indicates, most of the comments in IM sessions are rather short. Indeed, examining a series of extracts from published articles indicates that comments as long as 50 words

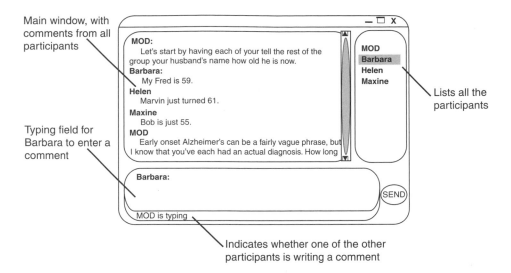

Main window, with comments from all participants

Typing field for Barbara to enter a comment

Lists all the participants

Indicates whether one of the other participants is writing a comment

Figure 9.1 Typical format for an Instant Messenger (IM) window.

are almost uncommon. Because these relatively brief comments are being entered in real time, they often show up on the screen in quick succession. This format is undoubtedly influenced by two elements of the technology. First, the input window for comments is almost always rather small. Second, because of the constant flow of messages from others, taking the time to compose a longer comment may well mean that the discussion has shifted somewhat, so that this contribution will essentially be out of order. Indeed, the problem of maintaining continuity is quite common in IM sessions, even without longer comments. This is simulated in Box 9.1 by the entry where Maxine needs to repeat her question to Barbara.

Overall, this stream of comments shows the typical format for the data from a synchronous online focus group using instant messaging technology. The discussion can continue for as long as the session is scheduled to last, and all of the text generated during the session is automatically saved. The data is thus ready for analysis as soon as the group is completed.

Discussion Forums as Asynchronous Online Focus Groups

The most common use for discussion forums on the Internet is to bring together people with a common interest, whether that shared interest deals with the same chronic illness, a mystery novel author, or the merits of the latest computer software. Discussion forums on these topics allow people to "post" various comments and queries, to which the other participants then reply. The asynchronous nature of these postings means that the discussion can continue for an indefinite amount of time. In academic circles, discussion forum are frequently found as a "bulletin boards" within online courses; other common versions of online discussion forums can be found in blogs and as part of "conferencing" software.

Box 9.1. *Hypothetical instant-messenger discussion about early onset Alzheimer's disease.*

MOD: Let's start by having each of you tell the rest of the group your husband's name and how old he is now.
Barbara: My Fred is 59.
Helen: Marvin just turned 61.
Maxine: Bob is just 55.
MOD: Early onset Alzheimer's can be a fairly vague phrase, but I know that you've each had an actual diagnosis. How long ago did you get that diagnosis and where did you go to get it?
Helen: We got the diagnosis 5 years ago. Our regular doctor suggested the clinic at [hospital] and they did a whole bunch of tests to confirm it.
Maxine: We went to the same hospital, but that was all Bob's idea. He knew he had a problem.
MOD: How long have you known?
Maxine: Two years.
Barbara: It was either two or three years ago for Fred.
Barbara: And I wish I had gone to [hospital] too, but I took him to [clinic] and they took forever.
Maxine: What was the problem?
Helen: It only took 2 weeks at [hospital].
Maxine: Barbara, why did it take so long?
Barbara: They couldn't make up their minds. The doctors just kept running test after test and debating and debating for six months. I got so frustrated I yelled at one of them.
Helen: Even the doctors don't know that much about early onset AD.

Participating in these discussions typically requires that the user officially joins the forum and establishes an online identity, which will be associated with each entry this person posts. Depending on the forum topic, membership may be granted automatically or, for more sensitive topics, it may require permission from a representative of the current membership. *Some* Internet forums have literally hundreds of members, but only a much smaller subset *is* likely to be posting during any given time period.

As Box 9.2 illustrates, the interaction in discussion forums comes from the running responses to previous postings. The most common format involves a "threaded discussion," where a specific original posting generates a sequence of replies, which make up the "thread" for the interaction around that particular topic. These threads can include a long series of postings, where all of the replies to an initial posting will carry the subject line. Another feature that supports the continuity of these discussions is to include "quoted text" from a previous posting when replying to that posting. This typically takes the form of a quotation at the start of the entry, to establish a context for the comments that follow, as illustrated in Box 9.2 by Charlotte's reply to Jeanette.

Box 9.2. *Hypothetical discussion forum about early onset Alzheimer's disease.*

MOD at 12:01 PM, March 1, 2009

Subject: Support

One topic that came up earlier is the whole question of support—who gives you support and who doesn't, plus who does what. What are your experiences with getting support?

Jeanette at 1:30 PM, March 1, 2009

Subject: No help from children

We were saying before how hard it is to get support, people just don't want to be around someone who has Alzheimer's, especially someone who has it so young. But my real problem is our two children. We have a son who lives a long way away but my daughter is just up the road about 20 miles, and I hardly see her either.
I know she has 4-year-old boy herself, but I used to see so much of her and my grandson before Sam started having problems. I think she's afraid to have little Tommy see him that way. I guess I could understand that, but she doesn't phone or anything.

Alicia at 5:19 PM, March 1, 2009

Subject: Reply to: No help from children

I think it is a real problem when you don't get help from children, especially if they live close.
But every time we talk about family I keep wondering if I'm the only one who doesn't have children. I think that is a very different situation.

Charlotte at 10:05 PM, March 1, 2009

Subject: Reply to: No help from children

> Jeanette wrote:
> We keep saying how hard it is to get support, people just don't want to be around someone who has Alzheimer's. But my real problem is our two children. We have a son who lives a

My problem is just the opposite. Is there such a thing as TOO MUCH support? Our son lives all the way in New York City, but he calls every two or three days to tell us about the latest thing he read in the paper or saw on TV. And it's almost always about the kind of AD you get at 85 instead of early onset.
We've got caller ID on our phone and last night I saw it was him and just let it ring.

Now I feel real guilty.

To use a discussion forum for an online focus group, the research team invites a set of participants to join a new forum, where the ability to post and reply is limited to those specific participants. The data collection typically begins with the moderator posting a question that serves as the starting point for the comments and replies that make up the discussion. Moderators also have the option of specifying a time limit for a discussion topic, such as noting that this question will be closed for further comments after a given number of days. The data from the discussion forum postings are automatically available as text at any time.

Choosing Between Synchronous and Asynchronous Formats for Online Focus Groups

The choice of a synchronous or an asynchronous format for an online focus group project depends on several factors. The most important issue is the same as any other choice of a research design: Which method is a better fit to the goals of the project? For example, the interaction in synchronous focus groups comes closest to the exchange of remarks in traditional focus groups, but will the relatively brief comments in these sessions be sufficient for a project's purposes? Similarly, the longer, more reflective passages in discussion forums may be desirable, but the discontinuous nature of these discussions may provide too little follow-up on key points.

There are also practical issues to consider, for both the research team and the participants, when choosing between synchronous and asynchronous focus groups. For the research team, each synchronous group has the advantage of taking only a short a short period of time; however, if too few participants show up, then that group has to be replaced with further recruitment efforts. By comparison, asynchronous groups have a disadvantage due to the longer time that it takes to gather data from each session; however, a concentrated recruitment effort can make it possible to conduct more than one group at the same time. For the participants, it is important to consider whether they will be able to meet the synchronous format's requirement that they all participate at the same time. Alternatively, there is question of whether enough of the participants are willing to continue contributing throughout the longer time that an asynchronous focus group requires.

Given these competing advantages and disadvantages between synchronous and asynchronous online focus groups, this chapter will concentrate on examining the differences between the two, rather than engaging in a contest to determine whether one is better than the other. We will pursue this strategy by comparing both synchronous and asynchronous groups to face-to-face focus groups, in order to show how each of these formats matches or differs from traditional practices. Our overall goal is thus to help researchers make well-informed choices about when to use either synchronous or asynchronous online focus groups.

Comparing Traditional and Online Focus Groups: Recruitment Processes

This section begins a three-part comparison of traditional, face-to-face focus groups with both synchronous and asynchronous focus groups. In this first section, we consider the

Table 9.1 Comparison of recruitment issues for different types of focus groups

	Face-to-face groups*	Synchronous groups	Asynchronous groups
Locating participants	Use existing lists, advertisements, and snowball sampling	Use existing lists, advertisements, and snowball sampling through Internet sites	Use existing lists, advertisements, and snowball sampling through Internet sites
Contacting participants	Contact participants by telephone, mail, or e-mail	Contact participants via e-mail or Web sites	Contact participants via e-mail or Web sites
Screening participants	Typically direct contact; limited assessment of accuracy at session	Can be done with online questionnaire, but no opportunity to assess accuracy	Can be done with online questionnaire, but no opportunity to assess accuracy
Sampling issues	Can use a variety of recruitment sources	Wider variety of recruitment sources, but digital divide issues	Wider variety of recruitment sources, but digital divide issues
Sufficient participants	Difficult to replace participants at the last minute	Participants do not all have to start at exactly the same time	Easier to contact alternate participants at the last minute

* For detailed coverage of recruitment options in traditional focus groups, see Morgan, 1998.

recruitment process, which is crucial for actually holding focus groups. Next, we examine a series of research design issues, including group composition, group size, and ethical considerations. We conclude by comparing the nature of moderating in these three formats for focus groups.

Successful recruitment is a crucial issue in focus groups, because it may be not be possible to conduct the group if there are too few participants. Recruitment thus requires serious attention, even though it may seem like a mundane or clerical issue. In this case, there are a number of noteworthy differences between the recruitment process for face-to-face versus online groups, but few differences between synchronous and asynchronous groups. Comparing synchronous and asynchronous groups, the biggest difference is the additional work that synchronous groups may need to find participants who are all available at the same time (which can, in this case, also include attention to time zones). Beyond that, the recruitment differences between synchronous and asynchronous groups are relatively minor, so the comments in this section will concentrate on the comparison between traditional focus groups and online groups in general. Table 9.1 compares traditional, synchronous, and asynchronous focus groups for each of the recruitment issues that follow.

Locating the Participants

The first step in recruitment is to locate potential participants. For face-to-face focus groups, the most likely ways are to use existing lists, advertisements, and snowball sampling. By comparison, online recruiting creates more options in each of these areas. On the Internet, the concept of using "an existing list" can be expanded to include e-mail lists, members of online forums and discussion boards, contacts through Facebook and MySpace friendship groups, and so on. For online "advertising," it may be possible to use sources such as blogs and Web sites for topics that are relevant to the topic. Using a snowball process to locate potential participants can also benefit from the online environment, because the range for online sources listed above multiplies the number of initial contacts that are available for starting a snowball search. Another important element of this difference between traditional and online recruitment is the basic requirement that participants in traditional focus groups must all be drawn from local sources, so that they can convene at the same place.

In addition, the advantages of using online resources to locate participants can be especially important in projects that involve categories of participants who are difficult to locate (Schensul, LeCompte, Trotter, Cromley, & Singer, 1999; Tates et al., 2009). Put simply, having the entire Internet to search makes it substantially easier to locate participants who match very specialized criteria for purposive sampling. Note, however, that sources with such carefully defined membership may be especially likely to limit contact with their members. Even so, it may still be possible to get authorization through the person who is in charge of that source—especially for academic research with university approval.

Contacting and Screening the Participants

At the next stage in the recruitment process, as Table 9.1 indicates, online resources also provide advantages for moving beyond, locating potential participants to contacting them, and inviting them to join the focus groups. For traditional focus group, these recruitment contacts typically rely on telephone calls, mailing, and, when possible, e-mail. In contrast, e-mail would be the entry level of contact for online recruiting. In essence, the resources available from the earlier use of online sources frequently translate into low-effort solutions for contacting potential participants. This reduction in effort is likely to be matched by a reduction in recruitment costs. For example, face-to-face focus groups require, at a minimum, that each participant receive instructions about how to reach the meeting site, and this often involves a mailing.

For many focus group projects, contacts with participants also involve a screening process to ensure they meet the purposive sampling criteria. In traditional focus groups, this kind of screening is often accomplished by brief telephone surveys. For online groups, this step can be modified to screen participants through an e-mail or Web-based questionnaire. More specifically, the earlier online contact with each potential participant can include a link to a Web survey that screens for the purposively specified inclusion criteria and also collects relevant background information.

One issue that is frequently raised with regard to online screening is that it can be hard to verify the actual identity of the participants—as symbolized by the well-known cartoon with a conversation between two dogs, where the one sitting in front of a computer says, "On the Internet, nobody knows you're a dog." This difficulty in confirming screening criteria on the Internet can be overstated, however, because face-to-face groups may have just as much difficulty confirming the crucial, topic-related aspects of screening. For example, it is unlikely that either traditional or online groups can conclusively determine that participants meet criteria related to health, marital status, past experience of life events, etc. Still, face-to-face groups do provide confirmation on some basic screening characteristics such as age, race, and gender.

Sampling Issues

One of the key elements in any purposive sampling process is to avoid bias in the final set of participants who are selected. While it is almost never possible to achieve meaningful representativeness in the small samples associated with qualitative research, it is just as important to make sure that the sample accurately meets the purposive criteria (Morgan, 2008). For example, imagine a study of men as single parents, where the researchers recruit from a school district that has an accurate list of such men. Further, suppose that researchers do not recognize that this is a relatively high-income school system; that could lead the researchers to discuss their results as if they applied to single fathers in general, without recognizing or stating the limitation that their results might not apply to all income groups. For both face-to-face and online focus groups, the screening process is one way to handle this problem, especially with the collection of relevant background information. When that kind of detailed screening is not possible, traditional focus groups have an advantage through meeting the participants, which makes it easier to detect more obvious discrepancies in the sample composition.

This type of bias can occur whenever the recruitment source is skewed in ways that the researcher either does not or cannot recognize. Unless the researcher is very familiar with the sample source, it can be very difficult to detect all the possible ways that it might be skewed in ways that would affect the research topic. Whenever the membership in source is skewed in some relevant way, simply following the purposive sampling criteria within this source can produce a set of research participants who meet the technical definition of those criteria, but not the broader intent behind those criteria. One recommended strategy for reducing potential bias is to recruit the sample from several different sources (Morgan, 1997). The idea is that using any one source for the sample may have produced a limited range of participants, but selecting the sample from several sources is likely to counteract this problem. Once again, this strategy applies to both face-to-face groups and online groups, but the online recruitment process has the advantage of providing more recruitment sources.

This issue may have special relevance recruiting online focus groups, due to what is known as the "digital divide" in access to and use of the Internet (Norris, 2001). Because Internet users are skewed toward younger people, males, and those in the middle and upper ends of the income distribution, online recruitment sources are almost inherently unrepresentative of the population as a whole. In response, advocates of online focus groups point out that this overall lack of representativeness may not be an issue, as long as the purposively selected participants meet the criteria for a particular research project. Although it might be possible to claim that this lack of representativeness is not an issue, so long as the participants in an online sample do indeed meet the purposive criteria for a particular research project, this argument still does not address the potential problems associated with selecting a sample from a biased source of participants. For example, the relatively rare set of older, low-income women who can be located online may differ in unknown ways from the much larger number of potential participants who meet these criteria but do not use the Internet. It is important to note, however, that in various versions of this same, general bias problem will arise any time a set of focus group partici-pants are recruited from some preexisting list, which is skewed in ways that are unknown to the researchers. Of course, these concerns do not apply to any study that directly targets Internet users as part of the research topic.

Ensuring Sufficient Participants

One final topic under the broad heading of recruitment is making sure that enough of the people who promise to participate in each focus group actually do so. In traditional focus groups, this problem is known as preventing "no-shows," and the same fundamental prob-lem can occur with online groups. Some of the classic means for minimizing this problem are emphasizing the importance of participating, recontacting and reminding participants shortly before the group, and maintaining a list of "alternates" who can be substituted when a participant gives notice that they cannot attend. Another classic strategy for motivating participants to attend focus groups is to offer "incentives" and especially monetary pay-ments, and this is an area where face-to-face groups have an advantage because these kinds of rewards are harder to guarantee over the Internet. In contrast, any strategy that involves recontacting those who have agreed to participate will favor online groups, due to the ease of using prior connections. In addition, the possibility of rapid communication online may well make it easier to bring in alternate participants on relatively short notice. Interestingly, this last aspect of recruitment is one area where there is a difference between synchronous and asynchronous groups, because instant messaging requires all of the participants to be connected at the same time but discussion forums do not. This provides at least some extra time to replace nonparticipants in asynchronous focus groups. In general, however, the strongest way to ensure that there are enough participants is to over-recruit beyond the minimal number of participants who are necessary, and there is no reason to believe that this would differ between face-to-face and online groups.

Overall, the recruitment process creates several clear differences between traditional face-to-face focus groups and either synchronous or asynchronous online groups, and the majority of these differences favor the options for online recruitment. Still, it is important for researchers to consider how their specific research project might be affected by using participants who are drawn solely exclusively as Internet users, as illustrated by the poten-tial issues associated with the digital divide.

Comparing Traditional and Online Focus Groups: Research Design Issues

As suggested earlier, the research design for any social science project needs to begin with an emphasis on meeting the goals for the project, but it must also take into account the more practical concerns of both the research team and the research participants. This sec-tion covers those issues with regard to a broad number of topics that the literature on tra-ditional, face-to-face groups has examined in some depth: using less structured or more structured approaches to the discussion, determining the group composition, choosing the number of participants for the group, and dealing with ethical issues. Table 9.2 com-pares traditional, synchronous, and asynchronous focus groups on each of the following design issues.

Table 9.2 Comparison of research design issues for different types of focus groups

	Face-to-face groups	Synchronous groups	Asynchronous groups
Less-structured groups	Straightforward	Best option for this type of focus group	Straightforward
More-structured groups	Straightforward	Difficult for this type of focus group	Require moderator to use careful control
Questioning strategies	Well-developed set of options	Little information	Little information
Group composition	Depends on local availability	Wider range of options through Internet	Wider range of options through Internet
Using segmentation	Straightforward, but can be limited to local availability	Straightforward, and easier to locate specific types of participants	Straightforward, and easier to locate specific types of participants
Choosing group size	4–6 preferred for high engagement and 8–12 for low engagement	Preferred size range of 3–5	Little information of preferred size range
Data confidentiality	Participants will hear each other's information	Participants will hear each other's information; data can be hacked	Participants will hear each other's information; data can be hacked
Identity confidentiality	Moderately strong	Data can be hacked	Data can be hacked

Matching Group Goals to Group Structure

One of the classic design choices in face-to-face focus groups is whether to use a less structured or a more structured approach. Less structured groups emphasize a wide-ranging conversation among the participants, where the moderator avoids an active role in directing the discussion; in addition, less structured groups typically use a smaller number of broad questions. In contrast, more structured groups emphasize a carefully controlled discussion, where the moderator actively directs the group to keep them on topic; in addition, more structured groups typically use a larger number of tightly focused questions. These two different formats for moderating and asking questions are associated with two different goals for focus groups where less structured groups use open, participant-oriented discussions to match the goals of exploratory research, while more structured groups use relatively controlled, researcher-oriented discussions to match the goal of pursuing depth and detail.

Traditional face-to-face groups use the preliminary instructions to establish the degree of structure by describing the expected roles that the moderator and the participants will play. In less structured groups, the instructions emphasize that the participants will pursue their own conversation for each question, rather than waiting for more directions from the moderators. In more structured groups, the instructions emphasize that the moderator will help the participants stay "on topic" and move the group through the questions in an orderly fashion. This initial statement is reinforced through the nature of the interview questions, where the first question is especially important. In less structured groups, the first question is designed to encourage an open-ended discussion of a relatively broad topic. In contrast, the first question in more structured groups is designed to produce an orderly discussion of a relatively specific topic.

Despite the centrality of design decisions about the degree of structure for face-to-face focus groups, this subject has received very little attention in the literature about online focus groups. Nevertheless, it is possible to speculate about issues surrounding the degree of structure in online groups, as well as how these issues might differ between synchronous and asynchronous formats. The first consideration is how the relevant instructions could be communicated in online groups. The obvious equivalent is for the moderator to paste the same content into the participants' screens. Unfortunately, 5 min of informal, oral instructions can easily amount to several hundred words, which could fill several screens with text. One tempting solution for dealing with this much text in an online setting is to e-mail the instructions, as part of the basic information to participants prior to the group. That way, a description of factors related to the degree of structure could be included within the longer set of instructions. Sending out this kind of "homework" is frowned on in traditional focus groups, because there is no way to tell which participants actually pay attention to it. Even so, some version of this approach might be adaptable for online groups.

For synchronous groups, handling the starting instructions is just one of several potential issues related to the degree of structure. In this case, the size of the comments window in IM sessions limits the ability to paste in a detailed set of instructions, because reading them requires participants to scroll through several pages. Overcoming this limitation may indeed call for sending out the full set of instructions prior to the group, and then starting the session with a shorter, bulleted set of instructions that would reinforce the key points. With regard to the broader question of using either less structured or more structured approaches in synchronous groups, the rapid give and take in this format definitely seems to favor research designs that call for less structure. In particular, that type of online interaction makes it harder to perform the tasks that the moderator's role requires in a more structured group, that is, leading the participants through a series of predetermined questions, while carefully allocating the amount of time devoted to each question. Note, however, that these suggestions for research design decisions about structure in synchronous groups should be evaluated within the context of any given project. For example, if the research involved participants who were quite familiar with a well-defined topic, then there is every reason to believe that the discussions in such groups could produce the kind of depth and detail that is usually associated with a more structured approach.

For asynchronous groups, the longer time period available can be well suited for both less structured and more structured designs. From the beginning, the use of more detailed instructions to establish the degree of structure are less problematic, because this material can be posted at the starting point for a discussion board (although there is no guarantee that all the participants will read that material). The primary things that the moderator needs to establish at this point are the number of questions and the amount of time devoted to each, along with an explanation for the reasons behind those decisions. For less structured groups, the introduction might establish that the discussion would last for eight days, with two days apiece for each of four questions, along with an explanation that the goal is to generate a wide-ranging discussion for each question. Alternatively, more structured asynchronous groups might involve one day apiece for each of eight questions, where the goal is to discuss each topic in as much depth and detail as possible.

We will cover one final subject under the heading of group structure, and this is the nature of the questions that make up the interview itself (for a book-length discussion about asking questions in face-to-face groups, see Krueger, 1998). Although this design issue would ordinarily receive its own separate section, there is very little literature about the how to write questions for either synchronous or asynchronous groups. This is a serious omission for two reasons. First, the nature of the questions as well as their precise content is just as essential for online groups as it is for face-to-face groups. For example, as noted earlier in this section, the nature of the first question is often important for establishing a less structured or more structured format for the rest of the discussion, and this concern should be just as relevant in online groups as it is in face-to-face groups. The second reason for concern is that online focus groups are likely to present a series of issues that are different from the existing literature on strategies for asking questions in face-to-face groups. For example, creating either a less structured or a more structured asynchronous online group would benefit from knowing the kinds of questions that encourage either longer, reflective postings or shorter, more targeted comments. Thus, whether it is a matter of what can be learned from questioning strategies in face-to-face groups or the adaptation of those strategies in online groups, there is clearly a need for more explicit attention to the nature of the questions in online focus groups.

Determining the Group Composition

In essence, decisions about the group composition for focus groups are another form of purposive sampling. Like any form of purposive sampling, the researchers need to devote considerable care in determining who will be an effective source of the data. Focus groups pose an additional challenge in decisions about group composition, because they require attention to both how well the participants match the research topic and also how likely they are to generate a good group dynamic during the discussion. These considerations make choices group composition a central element in the design process, because these choices frequently have impact on the quality of the data.

In face-to-face groups, there are a series of recommendations for thinking about how the group composition will affect the group dynamics:

1. At a minimum, the group dynamics require that the participants will feel comfortable talking to each other about this topic.
2. The group dynamics will be even better when all the participants are interested in sharing their own thoughts about the topic.
3. The best group dynamics occur when the participants are not only interested in sharing their own thoughts but also in hearing what others have to say about the topic.

Just as in face-to-face groups, choices about group composition are also likely to influence the group dynamics in online groups. In all three cases, design decisions about group composition are tied to a pair of goals that represent the needs of both the participants and the researchers (Morgan, 1996). For the participants, this should make it easier for them to understand and respond to each other's perspectives on the topic, which produces a more comfortable flow of interaction. For the researchers, the role that group composition plays in increasing the quality of the interaction is also likely to increase the quality of the data from those discussions.

When the participants represent a mix of potentially different perspectives on the topic, the research design for face-to-face groups often calls for "segmenting" the groups to produce homogeneous sets of participants, rather than mixing different kinds of participants within any one group (Morgan, 1997). Note, however, that segmentation of the group composition in face-to-face groups increases the demands associated with both locating specific categories of participants, as well as ensuring that enough members of each category can meet together at the same time for their specific group. Hence, separating focus group sessions into specialized types of participants gives online groups a distinct advantage, both searching for specialized categories of participants and in bringing them together.

The most common way to encourage this kind of interaction is to use research designs that create homogeneity within the groups—where the most important element of "homogeneity" revolves around the participants' relationship to the research topic, but where other criteria such as background characteristics may play a secondary role. When the participants represent a mix of potentially different perspectives on the topic, face-to-face groups have a strong tendency toward "segmenting" the groups so that each group has a homogeneous set of participants, rather than mixing different kinds of participants within the same group (Morgan, 1997). It is worth recalling, however, that searching for categories of participants for segmented group composition can lead to substantially more recruitment effort, where such a search for specialized types of participants would favor online focus groups.

Although the overall logic of creating homogeneous groups meets the need to create workable group dynamics for face-to-face groups, the nature of the interaction in online groups is different enough to call some of those assumptions into question. For example, in a synchronous group with a small number of participants (3–5), short and rapidly rotating exchanges in a format like an IM session could make it easier to conduct a mixed group—unless the topic is politically or emotionally charged. Alternatively, the interaction in an asynchronous focus group often involves not only a longer time period but also a larger number of participants, which could accommodate the development and comparison of different points of view on the topic. There certainly is no guarantee that either of these strategies would work, but they point to the larger opportunity for exploring options regarding group composition, rather than simply following the reliance on homogeneity in face-to-face focus groups. In addition, the lessons that online groups may teach us about group composition may show us ways to adapt similar strategies for face-to-face groups.

Choosing the Group Size

In face-to-face focus groups, the classic advice is to use smaller groups (4–6 people) when the participants are highly engaged in a topic, and larger groups (8–10 people) when the participants have less personal involvement with the topic. For example, when participants share an intense personal experience, a smaller group will allow each of them to say a fair amount about their experiences and feelings. For a topic with less personal meaning to the participants, a larger group creates the possibility for a sequential pattern of interaction, starting with comments by several individuals who have some awareness of the topic, which can stimulate a number of more wide-ranging responses from the rest of the group, which will thus produce the desired degree of interaction. This same advice about the size of groups and participants' level of engagement with the topic can also be expressed in a reverse, by emphasizing the potential *burden on participants* in groups that have an inappropriate size. Thus, a small group where the participants are less engaged with the topic will place a burden on each to keep the conversation going, while a large group where the participants are highly engaged will produce a burden to restrain their remarks so that everyone has a chance to contribute.

For online focus groups, this approach to determining group size is a poorer fit for synchronous than for asynchronous groups. In particular, the relative rapid and short exchanges in Internet messengers are likely to create problems for larger groups, regardless of the participants' level of engagement with the topic. We will cover this in much more detail in the later presentation of our empirical example, where group size (ranging from 3–5) was the primary independent variable for comparing synchronous groups. For now, suffice it to say that synchronous groups with smaller size are almost always more orderly groups. Once again, however, this generalization should be considered with the context of a specific research project. For example, one situation that might make larger sizes more workable for synchronous groups would be topics where the participants have levels of engagement that are high enough to increase the likelihood that they will follow instructions that emphasize letting everyone take turns in an orderly fashion.

For asynchronous groups, there is a better match with face-to-face groups, where a smaller number of participants who have a high level of engagement will generate a steady flow of postings and replies on a discussion board, while a larger group with a lower level of engagement is likely to generate enough initial postings to start an active discussion. Equivalently in terms of the burden on participants from inappropriate group sizes, a small number of participants with a low level of interest in the topic could well have difficulty maintaining a meaningful number of postings, while a large number of participants who were highly engaged with the topic could generate a wide range of comments and replies that would be hard to follow. In less extreme cases, however, discussion boards can have an additional advantage. The reason is this technology's ability to maintain a more precise monitoring of each participant's degree of participation, through reports on not just number and length of each participant's postings but also which postings each person has or has not read.

As a final design issue with regard to group size, all three focus group formats run into problems when the initial size choice turns out to be inappropriate. Unfortunately, resolving the problems of inappropriate group sizes are difficult to accomplish without redesigning this aspect of the project as a whole. When it is possible to make this kind of change, the most likely solution is simply to modify the size of the groups. In addition, note that it may be necessary to rewrite the questions in ways that would help generate the desired level of participation in these smaller or larger groups.

Ethical Issues

Concerns about ethics are the last area we will discuss with regard to research design. Placing ethical issues last does not, however, minimize their importance, because *there is no reason to even consider a research design that raises irresolvable ethical issues*. The first issue that arises for both Internet research in general and online focus groups in particular is whether new research environment requires a different set of ethical guidelines. Thomas

(2004) argues that there is no need to invent "new ethical rules for online research or try to reduce ethical behavior in Internet research—or any other—to an immutable set of prescriptions and proscriptions." What he suggests is "an increased awareness of and commitment to" already established ethical principles that apply across traditional research methods (p. 187).

Even though we agree that most of the central aspects of existing ethical guidelines apply to online focus groups, there are some differences between the online and off-line environment that need to be carefully considered. Three of these issues have been examined further by a special task force (Ess & A. E. W. Committee, 2002). First, online research poses a greater risk to individual privacy and confidentiality because of the enhanced accessibility of information on the Internet. In particular, skilled hackers could still penetrate even relatively high-level security procedures. Second, researchers may face a greater challenge in obtaining informed consent, because the use of pseudonyms and multiple online identities makes it harder to ascertain a participant's identity. Finally, it can be more difficult to decide which approaches are ethically appropriate, due to the greater diversity of online venues (e-mails, chat rooms, Web pages, instant messaging, discussion forums, etc.), as well as the unusually wide range of participants who can be reached through online media (e.g., people from different cultural or legal settings).

One additional ethical issue that is specific to focus groups involves the things that the participants learn about each other during the course of this discussion. Although the research team can create procedures to assure the confidentiality of the data they collect, there is essentially no way to keep participants from violating each other's privacy once the group is over. This concern can be even more serious for online groups, where it is often possible for the participants themselves to capture the text of their discussions. The most common way to deal with this issue is to address it explicitly during the initial instructions, *but this only addresses the issue*, rather than truly resolving it. A different approach is to gather consent forms with the participants' real names, and then assign pseudonyms for the participants to use during the group. White and Thomson (1995) refer to this as "anonymizing" the group. Interestingly, the same reliance on pseudonyms that can threaten meaningful, informed consent in online groups can also serve as an advantage for anonymizing participation, based on the familiarity of pseudonyms on the Internet.

Overall, there are good reasons to adopt Thomas's view (2004) that the fundamental ethical questions posed by new technologies are not new and, thus Internet research ethics cannot be separated from the "broader social milieu" (p. 198). This means that an inclusive approach to ethical issues, based on current standards, is the most appropriate starting point for online focus groups. There are also, however, situations where it may be necessary to consider the additional issues that arise from using this specific online technology for researching a specific topic with a specific set of participants.

Moderating

Moderators play a vital role in both face-to-face and online focus groups. In this section, we will consider two basic things that moderators do in focus groups: they probe participants' responses to the interview questions, and they guide the direction of the overall discussion (Table 9.3).

Table 9.3 Comparison of moderating issues for different types of focus groups

	Face-to face groups	**Synchronous groups**	**Asynchronous groups**
Probing responses	Direct requests	Can use well-timed text inserts	Careful monitoring for timely requests
Nonverbal interaction	Important resource	Not relevant?	Not relevant?
Following up responses	Relatively easy to apply at appropriate times	Possible, but more difficult with well-timed text inserts	Careful monitoring for timely requests
Restoring off-topic interaction	Relatively easy to both refocus on original or pursue emergent topics	Inserts work better for refocusing on earlier topics than pursuing new topics	Careful monitoring can handle both refocusing and pursuing new topics
Managing overly active exchanges	Can ask for pause, mention problem, restart discussion	Difficult because rapid exchanges are common	Timely interventions are crucial for diverting and restoring
Minimizing distractions	Rare, due to presence of moderator and participants in one setting	Distractions from both online and offline sources must be prevented	Longer time period can make it hard to reengage distracted participants
Avoiding departures	Rare, obvious, and unsolvable	Common, hard to detect or resolve	Common, but e-mail can resolve

Managing Responses to Interview Questions

As we pointed out in the section on group structure, it is important for a moderator's actions to match the choice of either a more structured or less structured approach to conducting the group. As we also noted in that section, the first question plays a particularly important role in moving the discussion toward the appropriate level of structure, and this applies not only to the content of that question but also to the moderator's handling of the responses to that initial question. In essence, this is the point where a moderator shifts from being the central object of attention into the role of managing the discussion among the participants. For a less structured approach, moderators should begin with a style that primarily facilitates a conversation among the participants themselves. Alternatively, for a more structured approach, moderators should establish a style where they can do more to direct the group's discussion.

The present section emphasizes the role that moderators play in managing the discussion of each question once it has been asked. These activities involve the ways moderators work with responses that are directly related to answering the current question; as such, they include many of the most basic ways that moderators interact with participants. As a result, much of the material we cover here will also be relevant for the following section on guiding the direction of the overall discussion. We have chosen to describe most of those activities in this section so we can maintain a coherent description of moderating. In addition, we will cross-reference this material at the relevant points in the other sections.

Probing Participants' Responses

One of the most common things that moderators do during the discussion is to probe the responses from individual participants. The most obvious goal of this probing is to hear more about the specific content associated with this participant's statement. We will cover several forms of probing that pursue this goal, but we will begin the simplest type of probes, which are sometimes called "free probes," in the sense that moderators are free to ask them at various points in the discussion, as a way to hear more about many different kinds of comment. Examples include statements like: "Can you give me an example of that?" "Help me understand what you mean by...." " "Tell me more about that," and so on. In addition to eliciting more material about a specific comment, the moderator can also use these kinds of probes to signal all the participants about the kinds of content that are especially appropriate for the discussion.

In face-to-face focus groups, an experienced moderator can easily inset these probes into the flow of the participants' conversation. Probes of this nature should, in principle, be just as useful for online focus groups, but are harder to implement in both synchronous and asynchronous focus groups. For synchronous groups, O'Connor and Madge (2001; see also O'Connor et al. 2008) have developed a system for inserting pretyped comments in the sequence of remarks in IM exchanges. This procedure begins before the first group, when members of the research group write up a series of probes, such as those illustrated above, so that a moderator can cut and paste these prewritten statements into the discussion. This reduces the problem of moderators trying to type up simple probes during the rapid interaction that can occur in synchronous focus groups. In particular, inserting prewritten probes increases the ability to request more information about a specific remark, before it gets lost in the larger flow of exchanges. In addition, the effectiveness of using inserted text is aided by the fact that the moderator's remarks appear in a distinctive color, so that the other participants will easily recognize that a moderator is making a brief, targeted request. Despite the utility of this strategy, it still requires that moderators have probes available that are clearly relevant for the current context; alternatively, they need to find some way to tailor a more generic prewritten probe. In addition, the pace of exchanges must be slow enough to ensure that the probe can be clearly associated with a particular remark. By comparison, the continuous, direct contact between moderators and the participants in face-to-face groups can make it much easier to deliver the right probe to the right person at the right time. Note, however, that these things do not occur automatically; instead, they depend on moderators who are well trained in working with face-to-face groups.

For asynchronous online groups, the slower pace makes it easier to place these probes at the appropriate location in the ongoing discussion. Further, the discussion board technology makes it possible to attach these probes via the "reply" feature in this technology. Where problems can occur is when the discussion gets dispersed over a number of different threads and subtopics, which is likely to happen during the longer period that is available in these focus groups. For moderators, this means that effective probing of specific remarks requires careful monitoring of the full set of remarks throughout the various segments of the discussion. This possibility for relatively dispersed interaction in asynchronous focus groups can also reduce the effectiveness of moderator's direct request for replies to a participant's posting, if that participant has moved on to a different section of the overall conversation. Although these limitations on probing response probably are not as great as the ones in asynchronous groups, they still demonstrate the advantages of the spontaneity in face-to-face groups.

A different aspect of probing, where face-to-face focus groups have an unquestionable advantage, is the use of *nonverbal communication*. More specifically, moderators in face-to-face groups can often find opportunities to use "nonverbals" as an alternative to explicitly stated probes. Examples (from Western culture) include the use of an outstretched hand to encourage a participant to say more, or the lift of an eyebrow to create a quizzical look that "asks" for clarification. Beyond pure nonverbal interaction, moderators can also accomplish some of the same purposes through *paraverbal interaction*, where communication consists of sounds that are not actually words, as well as deliberate silence. Not surprisingly, online researchers have noted the lack of these resources:

> Using other traditional interviewing devices such as probes is also problematic; periods of silence and pauses have different connotations online and there is no possibility of using an enquiring glance or verbal prompts such as "…mmhmm…" in order to encourage participants to expand on certain points…. Alternative mechanisms need to be employed by the researcher. (O'Connor & Madge, 2001, p. 10.2)

Unfortunately, the authors fail to suggest what those "alternative mechanisms" might be.

Following Up on Participants' Responses

Another frequent technique that moderators use to pursue a topic is to ask follow-up questions. The main difference between a probe and a follow-up question is that the latter consists of a substantive query that moves the conversation in a particular direction. Follow-up questions are often preplanned, based on topics that the research team has anticipated asking. In many cases, preplanned follow-up questions are often explicitly included with the original question, so that moderators are alerted to the desirability of discussing this aspect of the topic at this point in the interview. In face-to-face groups, moderators can use any mention of the desired topic as a basis for asking a follow-up question about that topic, such as "You've just mentioned something that we're interested in hearing more about. What else can people say about…." Alternatively, if the amount of discussion time for a question is nearing the end and the specified topic has not come up yet, a moderator can say, "I notice that no one has mentioned [topic] yet. What do you think about that?" The point behind questioning techniques such as this is that they temporarily draw attention to moderators in a face-to-face focus group, and then explicitly return responsibility for the conversation to the participants. Of course, as before, these tactics require moderators to have the necessary skills.

In general, it is relatively easy for online focus groups to adapt both the overall concept of preplanned follow-up questions and many of the tactics that moderators in face-to-face focus groups use to ask such questions. For synchronous focus groups, the previous process of inserting prewritten text could be used for follow-up questions, in much the same way that moderators in face-to-face focus groups will already be cued to follow up on specific topics. Similarly, moderators in asynchronous focus groups can either follow up on a given topic when it occurs or post a question about that topic if it does not come up by itself. It is also the case, however, that follow-up questions in both types of online groups can be subject to the same limitations that we already noted for probing. For example, in synchronous focus groups, the flow of interaction may be so rapid that it is difficult to insert the follow-up question effectively; alternatively, in asynchronous groups, a moderator may not be monitoring the appropriate location during the time when it would be most useful to ask the follow-up question.

Coping With Off-Topic Discussions

After moderators present a question, they also keep the participants within the overall topic for that question. All too often, however, it requires careful judgment to determine when the participants are so far off-topic that it is time to address that concern. In particular, it is almost impossible to tell whether the next comment will take the discussion in an exciting, new direction versus even further off-topic. The standard advice for this situation relies on the distinction between less structured or more structured focus groups. Moderators typically allow less structured groups to stray further, due to the exploratory orientation of these groups, which puts more value on the possibility of discovering "an exciting, new direction" for the research. In contrast, moderators in more structured groups typically intervene sooner, due to the goal of hearing about things in-depth and detail, which puts more value on hearing as much as possible about a specific set of topics.

When moderators decide that the discussion is offtrack, the classic response involves breaking into the discussion, noting the group has gotten too far away from the topic in the question, and then asking the group to "refocus" on the original question. Moderators in face-to-face groups can accomplish this by simply catching the group's attention and then repeating the core content of the original question. Online moderators can use variations on the resources we have already discussed to bring groups back on target, and these strategies are likely to be effective; at the same time, they are also trickier to implement than in face-to-face groups. Thus, synchronous groups would have ready-made inserts for dealing with the general issue of refocusing a discussion that was too far offtrack, but this inserted text could require time for editing to match the current context in the conversation. For asynchronous groups, moderators would post instructions that pointed the group back to the core topics in the discussion, but this would once again require careful monitoring of the full discussion, so that this request was posted in a timely manner at an appropriate location.

Although all three kinds of focus groups have relatively straightforward tactics for returning a group back to the desired topic, the situation is rather different when moderators decide to pursue a topic that emerges from a discussion that seemed to be headed off target. For any format, they may not require any action at all, if the participants naturally follow that strand of the conversation. If, instead, they merely mention it and then wander away, the moderator will want to refocus them on that emergent topic. For face-to-face groups, this involves saying something like, "Excuse me, but could we go back to [topic]; I'd really like to hear more about that." For a synchronous group, however, this could require a fair amount of work to insert a similar probe, because it would probably have to be inserted spontaneously. For an asynchronous group, the moderator can more easily post a remark that matched the basic content of the face-to-face comment, but this would require a very timely action, before the group posted a series of remarks leading in some other direction.

This last comment summarizes a theme that has appeared throughout our presentation in this section on managing responses to interview questions: many of the problems mentioned are more likely to present less serious challenges in asynchronous rather than synchronous focus groups. A related theme is the greater ability for managing these issues in face-to-face focus groups as opposed to online groups. There is, thus, a progression in the ability of moderators to manage the discussion of interview questions, where the available options make this easiest in face-to-face focus groups and most difficult in synchronous groups, with asynchronous groups occupying the middle position. The issues in the next section will show a similar progression.

Guiding the Direction of the Overall Session

Managing Overly Active Group Exchanges

So far, our consideration of moderating has centered on ways that moderators work with responses from individual participants, but moderators also need to deal with responses that involve two or more participants. The most basic version of this problem occurs when the intensity of the conversation leads to several participants talking at the same time. This is another case where it is easier for moderators in face-to-face focus groups to gain control over the situation. In particular, when moderators in face-to-face groups make even a moderately assertive request for people to pause and stop talking, that is usually enough to produce silence. After that, a moderator simply needs to explain the problem and ask the participants to be more orderly as they restart their discussion. This example is a reminder that even when moderators in face-to-face groups are playing a less active role in the discussion, their obvious presence serves as a reminder that they can make requests to the participants. It is also worth noting that these requests are least likely to disrupt the discussion when they reinforce elements of the instructions from the beginning of the session.

The problem of separating out the voices of multiple participants is more difficult in online focus groups. In particular, rapid exchanges in online groups can create a situation where participants "write over one another," so that it is not clear when an entry is either a new remark or a reply to a previous remark. The problem of overlapping comments is most serious when participants are generating very rapid responses in IM-based synchronous groups, where it has the nickname "blurring." Internet Messenger technology is susceptible to this blurring of responses because it allows participants to enter new remarks as fast as they can type them. As a result, when several participants generate a burst of comments it is difficult to determine who is replying to whom.

One useful resource in this situation is for moderators to emphasize the IM window's built-in typing progress indicator (as shown at the bottom of the illustration in Figure 9.1). To use this technique, moderators must recognize the first signs of blurring, so they can insert preventive instructions. This prewritten text asks the participants to be aware of the typing progress indicator, and not to type when that field indicates that someone else is already preparing a comment. A set of such inserted instructions might read:

MOD: Can we all please pause for a moment?
MOD: I notice we're "writing over" other's comments, so watch the progress bar.

MOD: If someone else is already typing, please wait before you start typing.

MOD: Then you can see what that person has to say before you respond.

Note that this approach also implicitly asks the participants to take more time reading and reflecting on the stream of messages, rather than jumping into an already blurred set of exchanges.

Asynchronous focus groups can also generate a similar kind of blurring when several people are posting on more or less the same topic at more or less the same time. Even if the participants are using subject lines for threading and connecting to quotes from previous messages, it may still be difficult to determine which postings introduce new ideas and which ones continue previous themes. For example, this can happen in a complex discussion if different people respond to different subject lines when they are actually commenting on very similar things. In that case, participants in a discussion board will experience "blurring" as they try to sift through the topics in a series of recent posting. For moderators in asynchronous focus groups, the best defense is continual monitoring of as much of the total discussion as possible, and posting an effective intervention before the problem leads to an annoying level of confusion. Although these problems with overlapping remarks may not be as serious in asynchronous focus groups as in synchronous groups, they still require careful attention.

Managing Distractions and Departures

Although there are many other aspects of moderating, the last one that we will cover here concerns the effort that it takes to manage distractions and departures during the course of the groups. More specifically, the most severe version of these problems happens when participants not only cease participating but actually leave the group all together. These departures should not be confused with a human subject's guarantee that all participation is voluntary and people are free to leave. Further, it is not simply a matter of participants who remain in the groups but simply cease their active participation. Instead, distractions involve things outside the group proper that interfere with participation while departure basically amount to "sneaking out" of the group.

Moderators in face-to-face focus groups seldom need to deal with either distractions or departures, because of the self-contained nature of the setting. The most frequent example of these problems consists of participants who leave for a bathroom break or some other personal need without coming back. It typically takes the moderator about 5 min to recognize that the participant is not returning, and by that point there is nothing that can be done. Yet, even if this is the most frequent form of distraction or departures in face-to-face groups, it happens so rarely that it barely deserves mentioning. In addition, the most common way of calling attention to and coping with this situation is with some form of mild humor, such as, "Well, [person] certainly seems to be taking a long time in the bathroom—either that or they are gone forever."

Compared to the bounded setting of face-to-face groups, distractions or departures are potentially much more troubling in the virtual environment for online groups. Once again, these problems have the most consequences in synchronous focus groups. Because of the short length and small size of these groups, anything that detracts from engagement in the discussion can have a noticeable effect. Starting with distractions, the major concern involves individual participants who are pursuing other activities when they are supposed to be interacting with the groups. This means that they are essentially "popping in and out" of the discussion in ways that make them poor partners for an active conversation. Further, they are likely to be less engaged and up-to-speed when they return after missing a segment of the discussion. Even though it is theoretically possible to catch up by scrolling back through the previous remarks, they must do that at the expense of keeping track of the current exchanges.

The kinds of distractions that can occur in synchronous focus groups can originate from both online and off-line sources. Some of the online activities that can reduce attention to the group include reading e-mails, playing computer games, or even taking part in other IM sessions with friends. Off-line distraction often depends on the participants' actual locations. For example, if they are at home, they might be talking on the phone or watching television. The best way to minimize any of these sources of distraction in synchronous groups is through prevention, starting at the earliest point of contact. In particular, this issue can be mentioned along with the flexibility of choosing a time for group: "It is very important that you spend the whole hour interacting with the rest of the group, so please choose a time when you will not have any other distractions that might interfere with your participation in the session." In addition, the instruction could be reinforced at the beginning of the session with a reminder of the importance of staying fully engaged throughout the discussion.

Distractions in asynchronous focus groups take many of the same forms as those in synchronous groups, except they occur over longer periods of time, where a participant may not be posting for two or more days simultaneously. Once again, the general idea is that something else becomes more interesting or more important than participating in the group. The possibility of longer time periods in asynchronous groups is also a factor, because the amount of effort that it would take to catch up with discussion may deter the participant from reengaging. Fortunately, the format of asynchronous groups does give the moderator an additional option that goes beyond prevention, through the possibility of sending the (non)participant a private e-mail that encourages rejoining the discussion.

Turning to the more severe problem of participants who completely depart from the group in either both synchronous or asynchronous focus groups, this is in many ways a continuation of the same problems that began with distractions. From a moderator's point of view, the online venue can make it very difficult to distinguish between participants who are too distracted to participate fully versus those who have disconnected—let alone telling the difference between either of those cases and participants who are still there but are simply being quiet during this part of the discussion. At present, there seem to be few consensual strategies for solving the problems of detecting and repairing departures in online focus groups, which may well reflect an inability to adapt procedures from face-to-face focus groups, where this concern is largely absent.

As this concludes our consideration of moderating, we would like to return to the theme that we raised at the end of the first half of this section: the idea that moderators experience a progression in their ability to manage focus group discussions, where synchronous groups pose the greatest difficulties, asynchronous groups offer better options, and face-to-face focus groups provide the most useful strategies. We would like to expand on that argument but noting both the likely sources of this ordering, as well a set of mitigating factors for each of the three types of focus groups.

For synchronous focus groups, the difficulties in managing the responses to questions are primarily due to the possibility of rapid exchanges between the participants, but one way to increase the moderator's ability to respond quickly is through inserting prewritten comments. For asynchronous focus groups, their advantages arise from both the more periodic posting of comments over a longer period and the ability to reply to specific comments, but these advantages have their limitations when the overall discussion becomes complex and widely dispersed. For face-to-face focus groups, the major source of their advantages comes from the more direct contact that moderators have with participants, but this can require a skilled moderator, one who knows when and how to make appropriate comments.

Once again, these conclusions follow our overall goal comparing the relative advantages and disadvantages of each format for conducting focus groups. Most importantly, we want to remove any impression that moderating is either inherently harder in synchronous groups or inherently easier in face-to-face groups. For some research projects, the fast-moving pace of synchronous groups may not pose any problems whatsoever, while the need for highly skilled moderators might eliminate face-to-face groups as a viable option. Hence, the bottom line, as always, is that these three approaches to focus groups each have a unique set of advantages and disadvantages, so deciding among them depends on the goals of your research.

An Empirical Study of 30 Experimental Online Focus Groups

As a part of a broader online mixed-methods experiment, an empirical study of 30 online focus groups was conducted to address several of the issues discussed above (Lobe, 2008). The research was conducted on a portal called Slo-Tech (http://www.slo-tech.com), which is Slovenia's main Web site for Internet users who are active in the field of information technology. The community associated with this portal included 20,000 registered members. The overall research goals were defined as studying the topic of Web site usability, in terms of quality attributes related to how easy and efficient it was to use the existing interface for the Web site. There were three specific research questions: What does the term "Web site usability" mean to these community members? What is their attitude to the current usability of the Slo-Tech site? What would they want to be changed on the portal in order to improve its usability?

Research Design

All of the focus groups were conducted in a synchronous format for two reasons. First, from a substantive point of view, this was primarily an applied research topic, which did not call for the level of reflection that would occur over a longer, asynchronous data collection. Second, from a methodological point of view, we specifically investigated the most appropriate number of participants in online synchronous focus groups that used instant-messenger (IM) technology.

In terms of the actual data collection, the focus groups were conducted in a way that allowed the participants to use a variety of IM clients, including MSN, AIM, Pidgin, and

Windows Live. These programs are easily compatible with each other, which means that the participants in the same discussion could use a variety of IM programs without any problems. It is also important to recognize that all of the participants were quite familiar with IM, due to their technological backgrounds. In addition, the participants needed little explanation of the three research questions because they were all quite familiar with the Web site in question.

Recruitment Process

Slo-Tech users were invited to participate in online focus groups in various steps, through a process that was highly influenced by the fact that we were working with a community who were attached to a Web site that already included a number of built-in features. First, the call for focus-group participation was published in the news section of the Slo-Tech portal, where it was available for comments and responses from the entire user community. Next, all of the users who commented on the initial news announcement about the research project received an invitation to participate, which was sent via a personal messaging feature within the portal's overall system. A list of the respondents who were willing to participate in the focus groups was created, including both their instant messaging contact information and the suggested time slots when they would be available for participation. Later, each of the participants was contacted via instant messaging to finalize the arrangements for the focus groups.

Online Moderating Issues

As we mentioned earlier, moderation is a vital process for a successful focus group. The moderator signed in at least 20 min prior the beginning, and when a participant joined the conversation window, the moderator greeted them and thanked them for participating. The moderator used informal language in a "chatty" way and encouraged them to use an informal language, not paying attention to the grammar. The moderator's comments also included emoticons, which were quite familiar to this group's participants. A special attention was given to the participants' typing skills.

Beside the usual issues (trying to keep the discussion focused and getting the participants to open up), the moderator was dealing with the additional challenge of preventing too much uncontrolled interaction. As we noted above, these issues of maintaining continuity can be a distinct problem in synchronous focus groups. To encourage greater continuity, the moderator asked participants to pay attention to the "typing in progress" indicator (see Figure 9.1) used in all groups as a way to encourage greater control over posting and replying, and to avoid typing when someone else was already writing a comment. In addition, the moderator asked the participants to read all the comments that were being posted before adding their own replies. Surprisingly, there were only in a few cases when two typing icons emerged, and these all occurred in the focus groups with the largest number of participants. The question of maintaining continuity in these IM sessions was thus closely connected to the number of participants, which is discussed below.

The Number of Participants

Of the 30 focus groups in the experiment, 10 were conducted with three participants, 10 with four, and 10 with five. The groups with five participants were indeed highly interactive, but to the extent of producing a confusing stream of comments. These comments were extremely short (normally only a few words), and it was hard to tell when these participants were either adding their own remarks or replying to earlier statements. There was also a considerable amount of overlap among the comments during any short period of time, leading to a "blurring" of the discussion. According to Puchta and Potter (2006), in face-to-face focus groups, overlapping is often due to incorrect predictions about where the previous participant's contribution was going to end, and that definitely seemed to be the case in these larger groups (p. 11). Finally, the pattern of rapid fire exchanges in the five-person groups also limited the moderator's ability to play an active role in the discussion.

The online focus groups with four participants were still highly interactive, but they maintained more continuity with less blurring, in comparison to the groups with five participants. The more orderly nature of these groups produced comments and replies that were well articulated. These groups were also easier to moderate than the larger ones. There was, however, one notable problem with regard to both the nature of the interaction and the challenges of moderating, based on a tendency for these groups to divide into pairs, with two people starting to chat with each other and ignoring the rest of the conversation. In the literature on traditional focus groups, these pairwise interactions are characterized as "side conversations," and moderators are instructed to act quickly to bring the two participants back into the general conversation (Morgan, 1996). In the present case, this was harder to accomplish, due to both the limits of online moderating and the fact that each pair of participants made up half of the four-person group.

The evidence shows that the focus groups with three participants were the most beneficial. All issues were easily covered. Increased self-involvement and self-disclosure was observed. The answers were more elaborated and better formulated. Participants were more attentive to the typing-indicator sign and did not "jump into the words" of the other participants. Thus, overall conclusion for the optimal number of participants in this particular set of online focus groups would be three, with four participants a workable possibility with a moderator who is skilled enough to keep side conversations to a minimum.

Of course, these results need to be considered within the specific context of this study. In this case, the contextual factors include both the high level of familiarity that the participants had with the topic and their equally high engagement in discussing the topic with other like themselves. Even so, it is hard to escape the conclusion that synchronous focus groups are likely to provide higher quality data with considerably fewer participants than are recommended for traditional face-to-face focus groups.

Conclusions

As we stated at the beginning of this chapter, there is no one right way to do focus groups, which means that face-to-face focus groups are not inherently superior to online focus groups; similarly, synchronous or asynchronous focus groups are simply different uses of online technology where the choice of one or the other depends upon the nature of the research project. Our approach throughout has thus been to compare these three formats for conducting group interviews. In particular, we have emphasized the advantages and disadvantages of each format across a wide variety of issues associated with focus groups. The purpose of these comparisons, has been to help researchers evaluate these three different ways to do focus groups. This ability to evaluate the available options for focus groups is essential in making decisions about which method to use and how to use that method. Just as important is the need to express specific goals, because choices about methods can only be judged by how well the strengths of a given method meet the needs of a research project.

Our comparisons of these three options have followed what Van Selm and Jankowski (2006) called an "intermediate stance" toward online technology. This intermediate stance rejects the extreme positions of either inventing totally new criteria for each method or simply using the existing standards from the equivalent off-line method; instead, this stance advocates adapting an online method to meet the core elements of the more traditional version of that method. This intermediate approach led us to use the large body of knowledge about traditional face-to-face focus groups as the frame of reference for describing the relative advantages and disadvantages of both synchronous and asynchronous focus groups. Now, however, we wish to reassess the usefulness of this intermediate stance as an approach for the *future directions* of online focus groups.

At this point in time, we believe there is no question that both synchronous and asynchronous focus groups have demonstrated their ability to apply online technologies in ways that match the most essential features of traditional focus groups, that is, producing informative qualitative data through interactions between participants who are guided by a moderator. Having achieved success with this intermediate stance, it is now time to take a more creative stance and pursue more ambitious goals. Our view of this creative stance for online focus groups is not to abandon the basic principles of face-to-face focus groups, but rather to move beyond using traditional focus groups as the main standard for assessing online groups.

In order to take a more creative stance, research about online focus groups should concentrate on developing new options and revising the existing ones, while maximizing the value of the interaction that is so central to focus groups. This stance points to goals that are quite different from answering the question, "I wonder how I could adapt this technology to produce something that looked as if it evolved from a face-to-face focus group?" Instead, researchers who work with online focus groups should begin experiencing what the master violin teacher Shunryu Suzuki called "beginner's mind"—a concept he borrowed from Zen Buddhism to capture the curiosity, enthusiasm, and willingness to experiment what new students often bring to their field. From that perspective, the future of online focus groups should be driven by the question "I wonder what would happen if...."

References

Bampton, R., & Cowton, C. J. (2002). The e-interview. *Forum Qualitative Sozialforschung/Forum: Qualitative Social Research, 3*(2).
Burns, E. (2005). The online battle of the sexes. *ClickZ*. Retrieved on June 11, 2006, http://www.clickz.com/stats/sectors/demographics/article.php/3574176.

Castells, M. (2000). *The rise of the network society* (2nd ed.). Oxford; Malden, MA: Blackwell Publishers.

Chen, P., & Hinton, S. M. (1999). Realtime interviewing using the World Wide Web. *Sociological Research Online, 4*(3), 21. Retrieved from *http://www.socresonline.org.uk/4/3/chen.html.*

Christians, C. G., & Chen, S. S.-L. (2004). Introduction: Technological environments and the evolution of social research methods. In Johns, M. D., Chen, S. S.-L., & Hall, G. J. (Eds.), *Online social research: Methods, issues, & ethics* (pp. 15–23). New York: Peter Lang.

Coomber, R. (1997). Using the Internet for survey research. *Sociological Research Online, 2*(2). Retrieved from http://www.socresonline.org.uk/.

Denzin, N. K. (2004). Prologue: Online environments and interpretive social research. In Johns, M. D., Chen, S.-L., & Hall, G. J. (Eds.), *Online social research: Methods, issues, & ethics* (pp. 1–12). New York: Peter Lang.

Ess, C. (2004). Epilogue: Are we there yet? Emerging ethical guidelines for online research. In Johns,M. D. Chen, S. S.-L., & Hall, G. J. (Eds.), *Online social research: Methods, issues, & ethics* (pp. 253–263). New York: Peter Lang.

Ess, C., & A. E. W. committee (2002). Ethical decision-making and Internet research. Retrieved from http://www.aoir.org/reports/ethics.pdf.

Frankel, M. S., & Siang, S. (1999). Ethical and legal aspects of human subjects research on the Internet. Retrieved on July 12, 2006, http://www.aaas.org/spp/sfrl/projects/intres/report.pdf.

Fricker, R. D. J., & Matthias, S. (2002). Advantages and disadvantages of Internet research surveys: Evidence from the literature. *Field Methods, 14*(4), 347–367.

Gaiser, T. J. (2005). Conducting on-line focus groups. *Social Science Compuer Review, 15*(2), 135–144.

Hewson, C., Yule, P., Laurent, D., & Vogel, C. (2003). Internet research methods: A practical guide for the social and behavioural sciences. London: Sage.

Hine, C. (2000). *Virtual ethnography*. London: Sage.

Hine, C. (2005a). Virtual methods and the sociology of cyber-social-scientific knowledge. In Hine, C. (Ed.), *Virtual Methods* (pp. 1–13). Oxford: Berg.

Hine, C. (Ed.). (2005b). *Virtual methods: Issues in social research on the Internet*. Oxford: Berg.

Illingworth, N. (2001). The Internet matters: Exploring the use of the Internet as a research tool. *Sociological Research Online, 6*(2). Retrieved from http://www.socresonline.org.uk/.

Jacobson, D. (1999). Doing research in cyberspace. *Field Methods, 11*(2), 127–145.

Joinson, A. N. (1998). Causes and implications of disinhibited behaviour on the Net. In Gackenbach,J. (Ed.), *Psychology and the Internet: Intrapersonal, interpersonal, and transpersonal implications* (pp. 43–60). New York: Academic Press.

Joinson, A. N. (1999). Anonymity, disinhibition and social desirability on the Internet. *Behavior Research Methods, Instruments and Computers, 31*(3), 433–438.

Joinson, A. N. (2001). Self-disclosure in computer-mediated communication: The role of self-awareness and visual anonymity. *European Journal of Social Psychology, 31*, 177–192.

Joinson, A. N. (2003). Understanding the psychology of Internet behaviour: Virtual worlds, real lives. Basingstoke: Palgrave Macmillan.

Joinson, A. N. (2005). Internet behaviour and the design of virtual methods. In Hine,C. (Ed.), *Virtual methods: Issues in social research on the Internet* (pp. 21–34). Oxford: Berg.

Jones, S. (2004). Introduction: Ethics and Internet studies. In Johns, M. D., Chen,S. S.-L., & Hall, G. J. (Eds.), *Online social research: Methods, issues, & ethics* (pp. 180–185). New York: Peter Lang.

Katz, J. E., & Rice, R. E. (2002). Social consequences of Internet use: Access, involvement, and interaction. Cambridge, MA: MIT Press.

Kiesler, S., Siegal, J., & McGuire, T. W. (1984). Social psychological aspects of computer mediated communication. *American Psychologist, 39*, 1123–1134.

Kiesler, S., & Sproull, L. S. (1986). Response effects in the electronic survey. *Public Opinion Quarterly, 50*(3), 402–413.

Kitchin, R. M. (1998). Towards geographies of cyberspace. *Progress in Human Geography*, *22*(3), 385–406.

Kivits, J. (2005). Online interviewing and the research relationship. In Hine,C. (Ed.), *Virtual methods: Issues in social research on the Internet* (pp. 35–49). Oxford: Berg.

Krueger, R. A. & Casey, M. A. (2000). *Focus groups: A practical guide for applied research* (3rd ed.). Thousand Oaks, CA.: Sage.

Krueger, R. A. (1998). Developing questions for focus groups. In Morgan,D., & Krueger, R. (Eds.), *The focus group kit* (Vol. 3). Thousand Oaks, CA: Sage.

Lobe, B. (2008). Integration of online research methods. Information technology/social informatics collection. Ljubljana: University of Ljubljana, Faculty of Social Sciences.

Lozar Manfreda, K. (2001). *Web survey errors*. Ljubljana: University of Ljubljana, Faculty of Social Sciences.

Mann, C., & Stewart, F. (2000). Internet communication and qualitative research: A handbook for researching online. London: Sage.

Markham, A. N. (1998). *Life online: Researching real experience in virtual space*. Walnut Creek, CA.: Altamira Press.

Martin, C. L., & Nagao, D. H. (1989). Some effects of computerized interviewing on job application responses. *Journal of Applied Psychology*, *74*, 72–80.

Mitchell, W. J. (1995). *City of bits: Space, place, and the infobahn*. Cambridge, MA.: MIT Press.

Morgan, D. L. (1988). *Focus groups as qualitative research*: Thousand Oaks, CA.: Sage.

Morgan, D. L. (1996). Focus groups. *Annual Review of Sociology*, *22*, 129–152.

Morgan, D. L. (1997). *Focus groups as qualitative research* (2nd ed.). Thousand Oaks, CA.: Sage.

Morgan, D., & Krueger, R. (1998). *The focus group kit*. Thousand Oaks, CA: Sage.

Morgan, D. L. (2008). Purposive sampling. In Give, L. M. (Ed.), *The sage encyclopedia of qualitative research methods*. Thousand Oaks, CA.: Sage.

Nguyen, D. T., & Alexander, J. (1996). The coming of cyberspacetime and the end of polity. In Shields, R. (Ed.), *Cultures of Internet: Virtual spaces, real histories, living bodies* (pp. 99–124). London: Sage.

Norris, P. (2001). Digital divide: Civic engagement, information poverty, and the Internet. Cambridge, MA: Cambridge University Press.

O'Connor, H., & Madge, C. (2001). Cyber-mothers: Online synchronous interviewing using conferencing software. *Sociological Research Online*, *5*(4). Retrieved from http://www.socresonline.org.uk/.

O'Connor, H., & Madge, C. (2003). Focus groups in cyberspace: Using the Internet for qualitative research. *Qualitative Market Research: An International Journal*, *6*(2), 133–143.

O'Connor, H., Madge, C., Shaw, R., & Wellens, J. (2008). Internet-based interviewing. In Fielding, N., Lee, R., & Blank, G. (Eds.), *The sage handbook of online research methods* (pp. 271–289). Thousand Oaks, CA.: Sage.

Oringderff, J. (2004). "My way": Piloting an online focus group. *International Journal of Qualitative Methods*, *3*(3), 69–75.

Parks, M. R., & Floyd, K. (1996). Making friends in cyberspace. *Journal of Communication*, *46*(1), 80–97.

Pastore, M. (2001). Online consumers now the average consumer. Retrieved on June 11, 2006, http://www.clickz.com/stats/sectors/demographics/article.php/5901_800201.

Puchta, C., & Potter, J. (2006). *Focus group practice*. London: Sage.

Reid, D. J., & Reid, F. M. (2005). On-line focus groups: An in-depth comparison of computer-mediated and conventional focus group discussions. *International Journal of Market Research*, *47*(2), 131–162.

Rheingold, H. (1993). *The virtual community: Homesteading on the electronic frontier*. Reading, MA.: Addison-Wesley Pub. Co.

Rice, R. E. (1984). Mediated group communication. In Rice, R. E. (Ed.), *The new media: Communication, research, and technology* (pp. 129–156). Beverly Hills: Sage.

Schensul, J., LeCompte, M., Trotter, R. T., Cromley, E. K., & Singer, M. (1999). Mapping social networks spatial data & hidden populations. In Schensul, J. & LeCompte, M. (Eds.) *Ethnographer's toolkit* (Vol. *4*). Walnut Creek, CA: Left Coast Press.

Shields, R. (2003). *The virtual*. London: Routledge.

Short, S. E. (2006). Focus group interviews. In Perecman, E. & Curran, S. R. (Eds.), *A handbook for social science field research: Essays & bibliographic sources on research design and methods* (pp. 103–115). London: Sage.

Slater, D. (2002). Social relationships and identity online and offline. In Lievrouw, L. A., & Livingstone, S. M. (Eds.), *Handbook of new media: Social shaping and consequences of ICTs* (pp. 533–546). London: Sage.

Sproull, L. S. (1986). Using electronic email for data collection in organisational research. *Academy of Management Review, 74*, 159–169.

Sproull, L. S., & Kiesler, S. (1986). Reducing social context clues: Electronic mail in organizational communications. *Management Science, 32*(11), 1492–1512.

Tates K., Zwaanswijk M., Otten R., van Dulmen S., Hoogerbrugge P. M., Kamps W. et al. (2009). Online focus groups as a tool to collect data in hard-to-include populations: Examples from paediatric oncology. *BMC Medical Research Methodology, 9*(15). Retrieved from www. biomedcentral.com/1471-2288/9/15.

Terrance, A. L., Johnson, G. M., & Walther, J. B. (1993). Understanding communication process in focus groups. In Morgan, D. L. (Ed.), *Successful focus groups: Advancing the state of art* (pp. 51–64): Thousand Oaks, CA.: Sage.

Thomas, J. (2004). Reexamining the ethics of Internet research: Facing the challenge of overzealous oversight. In Johns, M. D., Chen, S. S.-L., & Hall, G. J. (Eds.), *Online social research: Methods, issues, & ethics* (pp. 187–201). New York: Peter Lang.

Van Selm, M., & Jankowski, N. W. (2006). Conducting online surveys. *Quality & Quantity, 40*, 435–456.

Wallace, P. M. (1999). *The psychology of the Internet*. Cambridge, MA: Cambridge University Press.

Walther, J. B. (1995). Relational aspects of computer-mediated communication: Experimental observations over time. *Organisational Science, 6*(2), 402–413.

Walther, J. B. (1996). Computer-mediated communication: Impersonal, interpersonal, and hyperpersonal interaction. *Communication Research, 23*(1), 3–43.

Walther, J. B., & Parks, M. R. (2002). Cues filtered out, cues filtered in: Computer-mediated communication and relationships. In Knapp, M. L., & Daly, J. A. (Eds.), *Handbook of interpersonal communication* (pp. 529–563). Thousand Oaks, CA.: Sage.

White, G. E., & Thomson, A. N. (1995). Anonymized focus groups as a research tool for health professionals. *Qualitative Health Research, 5*(2), 256–61.

Chapter 10

Digital Repositories, Folksonomies, and Interdisciplinary Research: New Social Epistemology Tools

Karim Gherab-Martin

Introduction

The term "Web 2.0" has become a popular expression for new practices that are proving successful on the Internet. Tim O'Reilly (2005), who created this expression, has written an influential article in which he presents a comprehensive description of the Web 2.0 phenomenon. Among the issues discussed in the article, one of the more pressing issues is the *social Web*, as it is characterized by the fact that the users themselves produce the resources that they, in turn, utilize. In other words, the producer and the consumer are indistinguishable; the user of a typical Web 2.0 Web site acts both parts at once. Alvin Toffler (1980) coined the term "prosumers" almost three decades ago for this fusion of producers and consumers. In short, what distinguishes Web 2.0 projects from others is that they put the user "in the driver's seat," thereby creating implications for the behavior and social interaction of the participants.

This chapter describes digital repositories as *trading zones*, which are places in which interdisciplinary contact and exchange of ideas take place. Techniques known as *social tagging* or *folksonomies* are proposed as a way to optimize this interdisciplinary exchange of knowledge. First, the origin of the *trading zone* concept will be described and explained as it applies to science, as well as the two possible types of digital repository. The social-tagging technique will be presented, including the story of its origins and an analysis of its advantages and disadvantages. Social-tagging systems have come to fruition in a concept known as *folksonomies*. Using examples from cognitive psychology, we will see how *folksonomies* foster improved interdisciplinary relations. Finally, the concept of *long tail* will be introduced, which is a key element implemented in some hypotheses and speculations about the future.

Trading Zones

Some years ago, Peter Galison (1996, 1997) wrote about *trading zones* for the exchange of knowledge between different scientific cultures. According to Galison, trading zones are "an intermediate domain in which procedures could be coordinated locally even when broader meanings clashed" (1997, p. 46). That is, it is "an arena in which radically different activities could be locally, but not globally, coordinated" (1997, p. 690). He also borrowed theories from anthropology to show the way in which a technical sublanguage (a kind of *Pidgin*[1]) emerges that allows those cultures to understand each other and trade knowledge issues. Every culture has its own language and the understanding between cultures does not come about through the translation of one language into another. Instead, it comes through the emergence of a local language. This language develops through the creation of terms that have local meaning and that both cultures consider suitable agents of their mutual understanding. In science, there would be a type of interaction among cultures and subcultures similar to that described by anthropologists as occurring among different ethnic groups.

By referring to cultures, we do not necessarily mean different disciplines as various subcultures exist within any given discipline. For instance, theoreticians, experimenters, and instrument-designers constitute different subcultures within a scientific field since they may use different concepts, jargon, tools and methodologies, and social practices. Hence, after some time, new disciplines are born from more developed languages, as is the case of *Creole*[2], being a cultural by-product[3] of *Pidgin*. These subcultures will eventually evolve their own journals, scientific societies, awards, university courses, and Ph.D. programs.

Galison points out that the statistical Monte Carlo method, conceived and developed by mathematicians John Von Neumann and Stanislaw Ulam, was an emergent statistical technique based on the quick progress of programming technologies after World War II. It is also a unifying element among supposedly unrelated sciences. The so-called Monte Carlo method is a numerical computation that consists of introducing random values into an algorithm designed to solve a particular scientific problem. Therefore, it is not an elegant differential equation describing the ongoing, deterministic evolution of a physical system. Instead, it relies on computer power to carry out innumerable algorithmic computations on random numbers discretely introduced. This method was proving useful in various disciplines, and it allowed researchers to switch more easily from one discipline to another. Thus, Monte Carlo simulations were the trading zone that allowed scientists in such unrelated fields as meteorology, nuclear physics, thermonuclear weapons, poison gas, probability theory, computer science, and industrial chemistry to use the same techniques and understand each other in order to reach a specific goal after World War II, which was to build the Hydrogen Bomb.

Monte Carlo meant something different to each discipline (or subdiscipline), depending on the concrete problem to which specialists wanted to apply it. In some cases, it was a matter of a simple numerical computation while in other cases, it represented a tool for visualizing graphs or interpreted the stochastic movement of particles or a physical process of radiation transport. Thus, the meaning of concepts associated with the terms "experiment," "randomness," and "proof" were gradually changed. For example, "experiment" became a series of computer-simulated runs, whether it be a chemical reaction, physics problem, logic proposition, or mathematical proof. Galison (1997, p. 753) has further shown how the term "game" entered the vocabulary shared by different groups of specialists. Game Theory is a specialty within mathematics that has turned out to be very fruitful in various branches of knowledge such as, for example, sociology, economics, and military strategy. Though the word "game" has different local meanings in different disciplines, it came to have a global meaning among specialists, making it easier for them to communicate and exchange results and knowledge.

Digital Repositories

The concept of the trading zone is useful in understanding how digital repositories should be conceived. A digital or academic repository is an online open access archive for collecting, preserving, and disseminating intellectual outputs, usually scientific research articles and documents. By definition, archives contain primary sources, such as letters, scientific papers, and theses (as well as patents, technical reports, and even computer software), whereas libraries preserve secondary literature, such as books, and tertiary sources, such as encyclopedias. There are basically two kinds of digital repositories: Institutional Repositories (IR), and Subject Repositories (SR), also known as Disciplinary Repositories. In both cases, scholars self-archive their works as a final step in their research projects (Harnad, 2001).

Both IRs and SRs can be built either as *preprint* repositories, which are articles that have not been peer-reviewed yet, or as *postprint* repositories, which are articles that have already been peer-reviewed. Furthermore, both preprints and postprints arc called *e-prints*. It is important to understand that both IRs and SRs allow for open access (i.e., free) preprints.[4] IRs may contain both preprints and postprints while SRs usually contain more preprints. This owes to historical factors related to differences in culture and research practices within various disciplines (Till, 2001). For example, prior to the advent of the Internet,[5] distribution of preprints was part of the physics culture, but not a customary practice in other disciplines. Physicists had developed mechanisms whereby preprints were exchanged prior to submitting them to journals; this was successful cultural practice that has allowed the percentage of physics articles rejected by leading journals to be much lower than in other scientific fields. Hence, physicists view the SRs as a place to exchange, file, and deposit their preprints. The most well-known example of an SR was created by physicists and is known as the *arXiv*.[6] This online preprint repository contains more than 553,888 papers[7] and is an arena in which physicists, mathematicians, computer scientists, quantitative biologists, and statistics scientists self-archive and exchange articles. The tremendous success of *arXiv* has prompted scientists in other fields to join in the practice of exchanging preprints in this manner. Examples of other current SRs are *CogPrints*,[8] with more than 3,358 e-prints,[9] and the Nature Publishing Group's newly-created *Nature Precedings*,[10] with more than 1,885 e-prints.[11] *CogPrints* contains articles in psychology, neuroscience, linguistics, computer science, philosophy, and medicine. Though *Nature Precedings* specializes in biology, it accepts preprints from other disciplines, with the exception of physics. According to the criteria for posting on *Nature Precedings*, "We will *not* post submissions from fields in the physical sciences that are already well served by preprint servers as *arXiv.org*."[12]

SRs have two interdependent objectives that enable the researcher to present and discuss preliminary findings with peers[13] prior to submitting the finalized copy to a journal, and to establish that a researcher is the first to discover a scientific finding. Publication of the article in a journal constitutes officialization (or institutionalization) of peer-reviewed results, which is crucial for obtaining recognition and prestige within one's academic community.

SRs are gradually shaped by the participants' interventions and become trading zones when researchers of different subcultures exchange files. They are a daily meeting place for the exchange of knowledge, such as ideas, proposals, and empirical data, with different sections for different kinds of subjects. They are "markets" in which scholars, following specific self-archiving protocols, deposit the products they want to show their peers.

IRs are online archives[14] set up by academic institutions such as universities[15] and research councils in order to meet four main goals:

1. To make the research carried out by scholars of an institution visible through open access.
2. To group all research output in a single location.
3. To store and preserve other documents like theses, lectures, and technical reports.
4. To provide quantitative studies (scientometrics) for funding institutions.

The recent success of IRs can be attributed to initiatives within the open access (OA) movement in response to the huge increase in price of academic journals belonging to commercial entities—the so-called "serials pricing crisis."[16] OA initiatives have proposed that scholars voluntarily self-archive their postprints in IRs[17] or that the institutions that pay them make it mandatory to self-archive. Many commercial journals and scientific societies have claimed that this may be damaging to science (Royal Society, 2005) while defenders of OA have shown in a great number of case studies[18] that open access e-prints get more citations and have greater academic visibility and influence on other researchers in that discipline; this is argued to benefit science as well as the researchers themselves. In any event, not all scientific fields lend themselves well to OA, particularly the self-archiving initiative. Preprint repositories do not make much sense in sectors such as nanotechnology, as well as food and pharmaceutical industries where researchers do not publish their results until their innovations have been patented. For our purposes, we will focus on SRs and, more specifically, preprints.

From Social Bookmarking to Folksonomies

Citation indexing has become essential as a basic metrical element in the attempt to develop a science of science (called *scientometrics*), but this may be only one special case among the myriad descriptors scholars could use to trade. Although still not widely used by academic repositories, the practice known as *social tagging* could be an example (see Figure 10.1). A *tag* is a keyword attached to a piece of information that usually describes a digital object that could be a link, a Web site, a document, a blog, a photograph, a sound, or a piece of software, and allows it to be found again by browsing, filtering, or searching. *Tagging* means assigning some words to an item, which is a technique that has been popularized by many Web sites associated with Web 2.0. Launched in 2003, Del.icio.us[19] seems to have pioneered social tagging as we know it today and coined the term *social bookmarking*.

A brief historical overview will help clarify conceptual differences between some of the expressions used in this chapter, such as "social bookmarking," "social tagging," and "folksonomies." The reader should note, however, that using these expressions as though they

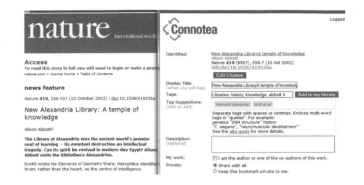

Figure 10.1 The window on the left side of the image is the Web page we want to bookmark. This Web page (belonging to the *Nature* publishing group's Web site) contains the article "New Alexandria Library: A temple of knowledge," published by *Nature* in 2002. In the window on the right, *Nature* gives us the chance to classify the article by assigning it either tags of our choice or tags suggested by the tool (called *Connotea*). At the bottom of this window, we see that *Connotea* offers us the options of keeping the bookmark private or sharing it with all other *Connotea* users.

were synonymous has become a widespread practice among authors. The origin of these three notions shows how natural it was for these techniques to be accepted by Internet users. In the mid-1990s, the amount of information on the Web and the number of users began to proliferate, making it necessary to organize the content. As one would expect, Web pages were organized by subject, in keeping with a taxonomic tradition going back at least as far as Aristotle and his *Categories* (Barnes, 1984, p. 4). At first, Web pages appeared that provided lists of links by subject. This approach was taken by *Yahoo!*, which enlisted an army of specialists who set about finding and evaluating the most relevant links on the Web. It later constructed a gigantic hierarchy tree to organize these links. As the Web increased in size, browsers began to offer the option of using bookmarks to make it easy for users to save links to Web sites of interest. In the case of Internet Explorer, for example, bookmarks were called *Favorites*; a unique tag could be associated with each bookmark, which was generally a keyword or brief description in the form of a title.

Over time, the number of bookmarks users collected also began to increase sharply, to the point that it became difficult to manage them. Specifically, it was becoming much more complicated to find and retrieve a desired link among so many saved links. The advent of the powerful search engine *Google* made it much easier to find a particular link; one could simply type a word into the search engine instead of looking for the desired bookmark in the list of links organized by subject. *Yahoo!* and *Google*, the two most powerful search engines at the time, became the best examples of two conflicting paradigms (Brin & Page, 1998). *Yahoo!*'s hierarchical structure organized Web sites by subject matter with experts working to filter out the bad Web sites from the good ones. On the other hand, *Google's PageRank* technique (Page, Brin, Motwani, & Winograd, 1998/1999) linked one page to another page and treated each link as if it were a vote, with more weight being given to the vote of Web sites that were themselves the target of many links and had received many votes. In other words, while *Yahoo!* hired experts and took a top-down (hierarchical) approach to organizing content, *Google* simply made use of the link structure already built anarchically (bottom-up) by hundreds of thousands of unknown users;

the links received by a Web site being an indicator of its reputation. The result is well-known: *Google*'s technique prevailed.

Now, in the twenty-first century, Web sites have appeared that make extensive use of social bookmarking, as shown in the previously mentioned *Delicious*. The success of *Google*, with its "social" approach using *PageRank*, *Amazon*,[20] with its system of recommendations based on the purchasing similarities of certain user profiles, and *Wikipedia*,[21] with more than 20,000 articles written in more than 18 languages by the year 2002, probably influenced the decision on the part of *Delicious* to create a Web site where any user could save bookmarks online and associate as many tags as necessary with any bookmark. Furthermore, the user could make all such tags visible to the public. *Delicious* was able to respect its users' privacy and, at the same time, openly show all tags that all users had assigned to each link saved in *Delicious*. This enabled any user to see the tags most often used by another user, which were the most popular tags associated with a particular Web site, or all links associated with a specific tag. To put it another way, in gambling on a collaborative tagging effort, *Delicious* did more than enable users to share links or bookmarks (social bookmarking); it enabled them to share tags associated with those bookmarks, known as social tagging, which was an ingenious addition that launched a sensible improvement. It did not take long for the idea of assigning tags to links to be extended[22] to other types of objects such as blogs (*Technorati*[23]), photographs (*Flickr*[24]), videos (*YouTube*[25]), and citations (*Diigo*[26]) published online, as well as books (*LibraryThing*[27]) and scientific articles (*CiteULike*,[28] *Connotea*,[29] *2Collab*,[30] *BibSonomy*[31]). It is these last two that will be our focus here. First, however, let us introduce and explain the term *folksonomy* along with the benefits it affords and the drawbacks it entails.[32]

In a folksonomy,[33] the item's creator is free to use whatever words he or she likes as tags. The item's viewers can also tag it using whatever words they choose. Thus, a *folksonomy* is a collection of tags[34] on a Web site in which many users informally tag many items. It is essentially a social-tagging system in which the user is free to write keywords or phrases that have a particular meaning for him or her. As a result, the expression "social tagging" has a broader and more flexible meaning than "folksonomy" because the first takes in both the free-tagging and controlled-tagging systems, in which there are more restrictions on the choice of keywords. Meanwhile, the second leaves the user free to choose his or her own keywords. A folksonomy, therefore, is a social-tagging system in which the user is free to choose the keywords he or she desires. We can then visualize a folksonomy as a social free-tagging system. Understandably, many librarians have been reluctant to accept the free-tagging of books and archives because the lack of control could result in erroneous, spiteful, or worse conflicting tags (Peterson, 2006). As we will see, however, librarians are also aware of the advantages of folksonomies (Spiteri, 2006), which is why some libraries are cautiously beginning to try them out in tagging their resources. As an example, the University of Pennsylvania library has already developed *PennTags*,[35] which are defined as "a social bookmarking tool for locating, organizing, and sharing your favorite online resources."[36] Likewise, the Ann Arbor District Library has several lists of tags grouped under various criteria in the *Catalog*[37] section of its Web site: "Top 10 Tags," "10 More Recent Tags," and "10 Random Tags." Peterson (2008) reviews other projects already underway.

It must be stressed that the primary purpose of social bookmarking, social tagging, and folksonomies is to enable the user to store links and create a personal catalog of bookmarks and their associated tags to facilitate their subsequent retrieval. For example, all bookmarks for Web sites with similar content could have one tag in common and be grouped together. Tagging an item consists primarily of committing it to memory for personal reasons using the available technology.[38]

Once tags are assigned to a specific bookmark (or other digital object), however, both the tags and the bookmark (or digital object) may be at the disposal of all other users who may, in turn, locate the tagged bookmarks (or objects) via the tags created and identify other users with similar interests. Because tagging is done in a public forum, the social dynamic forces users to choose relevant tags.

This way of categorization is based on the user's culture and knowledge background. Thus, folksonomies allow for new words and several languages because environments change in all countries, scientific disciplines evolve, knowledge expands, tools improve, new techniques and practices are continually set up, and sometimes groups of people or scientific communities modify the way they refer to scientific and popular objects. This aspect of folksonomies is the key to understanding what this chapter attempts to argue, which is that folksonomies may have a crucial bearing on the modes of communication in science.

Tag Clouds: Visualizing the Structure of Tags

Tags are usually sorted by their importance: the more often an item is tagged with a specific keyword, the greater the weight is given to that item. This can be displayed with a *tag cloud*, that is, a graphic illustration showing a set of related tags distinguished by font size, font color, and so on (see Figure 10.2). For instance, older tags can be represented by lighter colors whereas newer ones appear in darker colors. More frequently used tags can be larger than rarely used tags. In this way, we notice how the use of a particular keyword for an item evolves over time as long as viewers continue to tag day by day. In some Web sites, tags can be sorted by alphabetical order, by popularity, by latest additions, and by similarity so that tags with similar meanings or users can appear as neighbors in the tag cloud.

There are also tools for visualizing a folksonomy user's tag cloud that is a graphical representation of a particular user's most-used tags. For example, *Extispicious*[39] enables one to view the tag clouds of *Delicious* users (see Figure 10.3).

(29) Agriculture(43) anthropology(581) archaeology(48) biology (79) Civilization (169)cultural studies(19) Culture(128) culture diffuson(18) development (21) disease(35) ecology(55) economics(57) environment(62) epidemiology (19) ethnology(48) evolution(114) geography(149) germs(14) history (1,452)jared diamond(17) Natural History (22) nf(15) non-fiction(808) own(52) paperback (15) politics(38) popular science (24) prehistory (16) pulitzer prize(68) read(105) Science(454) social evolution (49)Social History(33) social science(42) societies (13) society(95) sociology (261) tbr(25) technology(70) unfinished (14) unread (102) war(29) WishList(23) World (36) World History (145)

Figure 10.2 LibraryThing's tag cloud for the book *Guns, Germ and Steel*, written by Jared Diamond. The book was tagged by 9,193 members up to February 12, 2009. The numbers in brackets indicate the number of tags per keyword. Screen shot borrowed from http://www.librarything.com/.

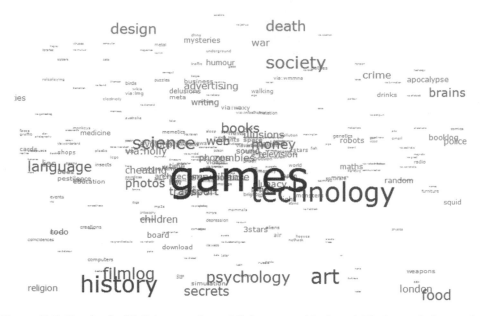

Figure 10.3 Tag cloud of *Delicious* user *kevan* (all the tags used by *kevan*). The larger the keyword, the more often *kevan* has used that keyword to tag bookmarks. Apparently, *kevan* is interested in games, technology, history, art, and psychology websites (+ brains). Screen shot borrowed from http://kevan.org/extispicious.

A study conducted by Sinclair and Cardew-Hall demonstrated that tag clouds are particularly useful for browsing or serendipitous discovery. Their experiment showed that users are inclined to use tag clouds rather than search boxes in the following two situations: "The first was where the information-seeking task was broad and non-specific [...]. The second was when the tag cloud contained a keyword relevant to the question" (Sinclair & Cardew-Hall, 2008, p. 23). In other words, when the search is for specific information, the search box is preferable, except when the tag cloud only contains the expression we want to find. However, when the search is for more general information, the tag cloud is suggested as the better option. Another important aspect of tag clouds is that they appear to be especially advantageous to users who are conducting a search in a language other than their own. Given that English has become the *lingua franca* of scientific, technological, and medical research, researchers for whom English is a second language may find tag clouds to be a very practical tool.

Advantages and Drawbacks of Folksonomies

Folksonomies[40] have advantages and drawbacks when it comes to taxonomic classification. Let us begin with the advantages. Classification by subject follows a hierarchy to ensure that every object has only one location. A few examples will show that objects organized by folksonomies can be in many places and accessed in many ways. In an article comparing taxonomic classification with social tagging, Clay Shirky (2005) shows that the procedure for tagging documents and other items is more flexible than filing them in folders. Even though a book may deal with several subjects, librarians have no choice but to catalog it univocally and shelve it under only one subject. For both cataloging and monetary reasons, it does not seem practical to have multiple copies of an actual book on different shelves. In the case of a digital book, while there are no financial barriers to making multiple copies, the number of different folders in which copies would have to be filed would make it unmanageable. Therefore, it would make more sense to increase the number of identical tags rather than the number of identical books.

Let us consider the following case in point. John Von Neumann, who was probably the finest mathematician of the twentieth century, made important contributions in various disciplines such as quantum physics, game theory, which is used in economics and military strategy, information theory, communication theory, and computer architecture. Traditional cataloging would force us to keep Von Neumann's books and documents in a single location, such as a shelf or folder, by discipline. Let us imagine that we have been appointed librarians of a digital library and we are faced with cataloging a digital copy of Von Neumann's 1932 book entitled *Mathematical Foundations of Quantum Mechanics*. We could place it in a Mathematics or Physics folder. If we place it in only one of those folders, then users who are looking for it in the other folder will not find it. If we decide to keep it in both folders at the same time, then we must have two copies of the book, which could generate confusion.[41] One way to solve this problem would be to forget about cataloging the book by subject and instead create a Von Neumann folder. However, this could become even more complicated. Now, suppose that we want to catalog another book by Von Neumann entitled *Theory of Games and Economic Behavior*, which was written in 1944 in collaboration with Oskar Morgenstern. We must then decide between placing the book in the Von Neumann folder or in a new Morgenstern folder and create subfolders for the subject matter. Or we could give priority to the subject matter folders[42] and create subfolders under each one for the authors' names. The process would become even more complicated if we wished to catalog the book entitled *From Mathematics to the Technologies of Life and Death* by Steve J. Heims, who draws comparisons between the life and works of Von Neumann and another mathematician named Norbert Wiener. We have no mention of either Von Neumann or Wiener in the title, nor of the comparison of them, nor of their connection with World War II. Obviously, choosing the ideal folder structure becomes infinitely more complicated as we add more and more books and intend to have copies in every folder. In addition, however, we must decide which type of folder should have priority because our library users may have different purposes and expectations; they could be mathematicians, physicists, or economists interested in searching by discipline, perhaps biographers searching by author, historians who want to search by dates or even casual readers who know nothing of Von Neumann and his book.

With the tagging system, we are able to assign tags to each book or document so that, in the first instance, the Von Neumann book could be tagged as "Mathematics," "Physics," "Von Neumann," and "1932." The second book could be tagged "Economics," "Game Theory," "Von Neumann," "Morgenstern," and "1944." Finally, we could assign tags such as "Biography," "Von Neumann," "Wiener," "Comparison," "World War II," and "History" to the Heims book. We would not have to make several copies of each book and simple Boolean filtering would enable us to retrieve what we are seeking. In a folksonomy, tags supplied by prosumers can be more subtle, less orthodox, less precise, or more personal, depending on the user's knowledge background. Moreover, with tags, it is possible to locate texts that may not include a particular word string. For example, while the Heims book is not likely to contain the string "ethics of science in the West," any reader could attach a tag with that very phrase, making it easy for other readers interested in this tag to find this book. This shows that the Internet is still far from being fully automated and remains a social network that is highly human-dependent in terms of searching for and retrieving digital objects.

Folksonomies also promote the dissemination of neologisms—that is, new terms, new meanings, or new turns of phrase. Every new scientific outcome, every new instrument, every new formula, and every new technology involves the emergence of a new lexicon that should be propagated. Folksonomies are optimal for this task because they allow freedom in tagging and are not subject to the inflexibility of a thesaurus or the ontologies of librarians and information scientists. Because users can browse through a variety of tags, which allows the linguistic freedom and flexibility to classify an object in multiple ways, folksonomies increase the chances of serendipitous discovery.

Without restrictions on words, language is much more fluid. Thus, social free-tagging encourages the use of natural and personal language with room for subtleties. The thesaurus attempts to force classification of a reality. Not all realities lend themselves to such a hierarchical structure, however, because while the experts consider properties to be *objective*, searches are made by users who have *subjective* desires and beliefs that, in turn, hinge on their contexts and circumstances. Meanings are tied to the origin, educational level, culture, values, and moods of both the person who is tagging and the person who is retrieving some particular information or object.

Another advantage of folksonomies, and social tagging in general, is that they allow for community activity because they encourage browsing and sharing activities. They create online communities of interest (Spiteri, 2006) because users can identify other users who share the same interests simply by checking the co-occurrences as they create tags.

Two final, positive considerations must be highlighted. Tagging is inexpensive in comparison to classification done by trained experts. The more information there is to categorize, the more expensive and time-consuming it will be if done by a group of experts. Furthermore, free-tagging "is easy, enjoyable and quick to complete: it is an activity with low cognitive cost, which provides immediate self and social feedback" (Tonkin, 2006).

Of course, there are also drawbacks. Folksonomies have been criticized because they rely on unstructured annotations (Tanasescu & Streibel, 2007). Tags are susceptible to fraud, corruption, spamming,[43] and collusion. Free tagging, Peterson (2006) criticizes, "is a scheme based on philosophical relativism" in which anyone tagging could put "white horse" on a photograph showing a black horse. Worse yet, with folksonomies, the most appalling sacrilege in logic can be committed; namely, an object could be declared to be A and not A simultaneously. Therefore, folksonomies have inherent *inconsistencies* and are not as reliable as taxonomies.

Also, social free-tagging leads to other problems (Noruzi, 2007) such as synonymy, polysemy, and "language gap." Because synonymy refers to different words with similar meanings, it may become an issue in searching because if the user filters on one single tag, he or she cannot be certain that all search possibilities have been exhausted (Golder & Huberman 2006, pp. 199–200). Polysemy refers to a single keyword that may have multiple meanings. For example, "jaguar" could refer to the animal or make of an automobile while "red" could indicate a color or a political orientation. These homonyms give rise to the problem of "tag ambiguity" and the resulting difficulties in searching.[44] The pro-sumer's language is also an important factor, in this regard, for "bird" could be tagged in English (bird), in Spanish (*pájaro*), in French (*oiseau*), and any other language. Moreover, there have been cases (Guy & Tonkin, 2006) of users mixing languages in the same tag.

Other types of issues are the *depth problem* and the *basic-level problem*. Both refer to the specificity of the tags. The depth problem is more general and results from the user's lack of precision in tagging an object by using general categories or specific names for keywords. The basic-level problem, which is a concept derived from cognitive psychol-ogy (Tanaka & Taylor, 1991), is related to the tagger's knowledge background (Golder & Huberman, 2006, p. 200). For example, suppose we are in a Web site that has photographs of animals. Most likely, a dog expert would use the tag "beagle" to describe a photograph of a dog of that breed, and a bird expert would tag a photograph of a robin as "robin." If the dog expert has no knowledge of birds and the bird expert knows nothing about dogs, then they would probably use the tags "bird" and "dog," respectively, to refer to their col-league's photographs. As a result, someone using the tag "dog" to search for dogs will not get those results that have only the tag "beagle."

Another problem is related to meta-noise, which are misspelled, inaccurate, and irrel-evant tags. Likewise, there are users who turn a folksonomy into a personal journal and archive ("to read," "my dog," etc.). The occurrence of plurals, which refers to one user tagging an item in singular and another tagging the same item in plural, also contributes to meta-noise.

Tag redundancy is another issue. For example, abbreviations exist such as "televi-sion" and "TV," or "laboratory" and "lab," "plane" and "airplane," and even "San Fran-cisco" and "Frisco." A related problem stems from users coding the same thing in two different ways: for example, "water" and "H2O," or "three" and "3," or "good to see" and "good 2 c." Furthermore, redundancy problems can come in several varieties: the *word order problem* ("2009 February 10," "10th February 2009," etc.), the *punctuation problem* ("open_source," "Tele.com"), and the use of symbols such as &, #, @, ñ, ü, ç, etc. ("Black & White," "Player #1," "@home," "Español," "Français").

It has been demonstrated (Sen et al., 2006; Golder & Huberman, 2006, p. 206) that, when tagging an item, a user may be influenced by other users' tags, especially when the computer system gives him or her the option to choose from among the most popular tags utilized for that item. The tendency to utilize the same tags to tag similar items may result from a process of imitation, in some cases. In other cases, however, it may be due to knowledge or jargon shared by experts on a specific subject.

To solve these problems, interdisciplinary projects have been initiated to develop systems that some have called *tag gardening* (Peters & Weller, 2008). For example, many informa-tion scientists have proposed to combine the folksonomy approach with some controlled vocabulary (Gruber, 2006; Guy & Tonkin, 2006; Noruzi, 2007; Peters & Weller, 2008) to cre-ate a kind of *collabulary* (collective vocabulary) approach, in the words of Anderson (2007). This is a rich, informal but systematic tagging classification system[45] so that viewers could, for example, choose from a set of formal keyword synonyms suggested automatically by the system in finding an item (MacLaurin, 2007). In fact, automatic recommendation systems already exist that offer users a list of the most popular tags for the resource when he or she is tagging a new item. A sentence that would be appropriate for the Web, then, is this: "Many of the people who sometimes use tag *A* have decided to use tag *B* for this item. Would you like to use *B* instead of *A*?" The most-used tags are usually the most relevant, just as the most-cited articles and most-linked Web sites are deemed to have greater authority in the academic realm and in some search engines (such as Google), respectively.

Folksonomies and Subject Repositories

One of the objectives of this chapter is to suggest that these open tags be used for SRs since tags are widely used by successful Web 2.0 projects. Instead of following a hierarchical structure like taxonomic classification (thesauri, ontologies), the Web is witnessing a sort of network-tagging that is not ranked but highly multi-contextual, multi-cultural, and interdisciplinary. In keeping with the folksonomies approach, I propose that not only the author chooses metadata to tag articles stored in SRs but that any number of researchers in the same or other disciplines be permitted to add tags as they see fit, perhaps using a *collabulary* approach. This should be done with some caution, however, since science is the realm in which truth has an incalculable value. This is not a proposal to abandon subject taxonomic classification systems, but to complement them with social-tagging systems. As Stock (2007, p. 101) has pointed out, both systems can coexist in "a proposal to mash-up the benefits of the 'old' science databases (professional indexing, citation indexing, full-text processing) and the benefits of folksonomies (authentic language use of the readers, multiple interpretations, and new ranking options)."

In this way, any given article could be tagged in the distinct "language" of various disciplines, some seemingly quite unrelated. Nowadays, a scientist who writes an article has to prepare an abstract and a set of keywords to go with it. When writing the abstract, the scientist knows very well whom he is addressing and takes care to use the appropriate language with its familiar rhetoric to capture the attention of the desired readers. Likewise, when choosing keywords, he or she will employ terms and expressions germane to the specific discipline; the jargon he or she knows is used and will be easily recognized by his or her peers. However, a researcher from another discipline or even one from a different subculture within the same discipline may find that jargon difficult to understand. In many cases, the jargon of an academic community can evolve very quickly, perhaps in connection with new ideas, new phenomena, or new instruments, depending on the degree and rate of progress in that discipline. There are also cases where two or more disciplines refer to the same or similar objects, processes, and methodologies that use different expressions for them.

For example, in 1993, an innovative type of theoretical physics experiment was proposed called *Interaction-Free Measurements* (Elitzur & Vaidman, 1993) by its authors to denote a surprising process of obtaining information from an object without the need of an interaction. This idea involved speculation about an experimental set-up that would prove the existence of a strange quantum phenomenon that was not foreseen by quantum physicists, apparently. Shortly afterward, experimental physicists proved the effect with a real device. The interesting thing about this is that there has been a dispute that is still not entirely settled about the name that should be given to the phenomenon and to this type of experiment. The focus of the dispute was on the term "free" in connection with the term "interaction" because the physicists all agreed that there was some type of interaction, even though they did not know about the "what" or the "how" of it. Various proposals have been made, but we will only mention a couple of them. Some experimental physicists have opted for the expression "Quantum Interrogation Measurements" (Hosten, Rakher, Barreiro, Peters, & Kwiat,

2006), which comes as no surprise since *interrogating* Nature is precisely what experimental physicists do. While the theoretical physicists had chosen a rather vague term ("interaction") and added to it a problematic term ("free"), some experimental physicists were reluctant to get too involved because this represents a position consistent with *positivist* philosophy in which all metaphysical speculation is rejected. Another expression, "Absorption-Free Measurements," has been proposed by a biologist interested in applying this quantum technology to X-ray radiation in biology (Mitchison & Massar, 2001). We may ask why this biologist used the term "absorption" instead of "interaction." An object absorbing a physical particle is a specific type of interaction within the group of possible interactions that could occur between them. Surely, the biologist thought the term "absorption" was less risky and more appropriate for what was observed in the experiment. We can add another reason, however, which is the one that interests us in this chapter. This biologist chose the term "absorption," consciously or not, to indicate a connection between this physics phenomenon and his own research field—biology. His objective was to develop an X-ray technique whereby information (e.g., the existence of a tumor) could be obtained about biological tissues without those tissues absorbing the radiation. Also, the term "absorption" is certainly more likely than the term "interaction" to attract the attention of biologists.

Even though these assertions clearly cross the threshold into the treacherous realm of speculation, it is worth mentioning a series of experiments conducted by cognitive psychology experts on the types of words different epistemic subjects chose to name objects. In identifying an object, we can access three levels of classifications named *superordinate*, *basic*, and *subordinate*. Various experiments, particularly Rosch, Mervis, Gray, Johnson, and Boyes-Braem (1976), have demonstrated that virtually everyone uses basic-level terms (e.g., "dog," "fish," "chair," "hammer," "car") when asked to spontaneously name an everyday object. Empirical evidence shows that for the overwhelming majority of people, the basic level is more accessible than the more general superordinate level (e.g., "animal," "furniture," "tool," "vehicle") and the more specific subordinate level (e.g., "beagle," "trout," "desk chair," "Porsche"). Moreover, Tanaka and Taylor (1991) conducted new experiments that revealed two additional characteristics, which Rosch et al., had already intuited in 1976. In these experiments, the individuals selected could freely choose the words they wanted to associate with the photographs they were shown. On the one hand, Tanaka and Taylor demonstrated that experts were inclined to use subordinate-level terms, such as "robin" or "beagle," to a significantly greater degree than nonexpert individuals, many of whom used basic-level terms such as "bird" or "dog." On average, 57% of expert responses corresponded to subordinate level and 43% to basic level. On the other hand, they pointed out that the extent to which experts from different fields used subordinate-level terms could vary considerably depending on practices in each field. Thus, bird experts used subordinate-level terms 76% of the time and basic-level 21% of the time when identifying photographs of birds, while dog experts used subordinate-level terms 40% of the time and basic-level terms the other 60% of the time when identifying dogs. This discrepancy, the authors argued, could be attributed to differences between conceptualizing birds and conceptualizing dogs in terms of culture and technique. Identifying birds by type and the physical differences between them, such as color, wing shape, and beak length, plays an important role in ornithologists' work. Meanwhile, dog experts focus on other factors, such as the rhythm of movement, fierceness, obedience, and uses in society, in addition to the breed and physical appearance.

The same can happen with scientific articles. Differences in scientific practices, theoretical suppositions, representation techniques, and research methodologies can lead reader-researchers to utilize different levels of classification to refer to the same objects, texts, images, or charts. Therefore, by adding folksonomies to informal, scientific communication, readers may play an active role, since they can tag documents with terms taken from their professional or personal environment.

Folksonomies and Scientometrics

Scientometrics is a discipline that *measures* the dynamics of science by conducting quantitative studies of science and technology. Its sphere of analysis includes scientific documents, the performance of researchers and scientific institutions, and scientific journals. Its origins go back to the mid-twentieth century when Eugene Garfield (1955) introduced his *citation index*,[46] which can be defined as "an ordered list of cited articles each of which is accompanied by a list of citing articles" (Garfield, 1964, p. 650). This is the inverse of scientists' usual procedure: at the end of a *paper*, scientists give the bibliography on which they base and support their arguments, theories, and experiments. However, Garfield's proposal called for a bibliography of sources that *cite* the paper rather than sources *cited by* the paper.

Development of citation indexing has progressed to the point that knowledge maps by discipline can be created, which enable a researcher interested in the subject to see the influence of interdisciplinary relationships and other features. This is accomplished through citation analysis techniques such as the so-called *bibliographic coupling*,[47] which relates those articles that cite the same article, and *co-citation*,[48] which relates those articles that have been cited by a third article.

These techniques have been extended to the analysis of authors themselves: the "author co-citation analysis," which relates those authors cited by a (same) third author, and so on. Thus, there are technologies for mapping the "intellectual space" of individual disciplines in which the proximity of the points representing the authors reflect their academic similarity (See Figure 10.4 for an example). These techniques for indexing citations between articles and authors create an interdisciplinary map that allows newly emerging disciplines to be recognized (See the example in Figure 10.5).

It is not difficult to imagine folksonomies as a realm in which scientometrics could advance considerably. When a user tags a link on the Web, he or she is showing interest in it and stores it in his or her catalog. The same occurs with researchers and scientific articles in *Connotea*, *CiteULike*, and *2Collab*.[49] Therefore, just as scientometrics has taken advantage of a behavior that already existed, such as the act of citing, folksonomies also make their contribution by capitalizing on a behavior, such as the act of tagging, in conducting its quantitative and qualitative studies.

We have seen how information scientists identify interdisciplinary influences by analyzing citations between articles and between authors. Indeed, creating a link to or a citation of some article stored in a repository becomes a form of purchasing. Scholar *B* metaphorically purchases an idea, theoretical piece, or empirical result from scholar *A* by linking to and citing his work. Scholar *B* is borrowing the idea from scholar *A* to support his or her own idea or perhaps to make a contribution in the scientific field to which he or she belongs.

The same approach may be applied to folksonomies, but it is a bit complicated in this instance. In citation analysis, we had two basic units: articles and authors. In folksonomies, we have three basic units: articles, authors, and tags. In fact, Hotho, Jäschke, Schmitz, & Stumme, (2006) have proposed defining a folksonomy F as the set of four

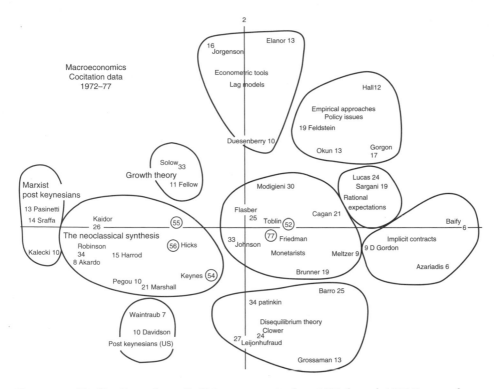

Figure 10.4 The "intellectual space" of Macroeconomics from 1972 through 1977. Borrowed from McCain, K. W. (1990). Mapping authors in intellectual space: A technical overview. *Journal of the American Society for Information Science*, 41(6), 439. Copyright (1990, John Wiley & Sons). Reprinted with permission of John Wiley & Sons, Inc.

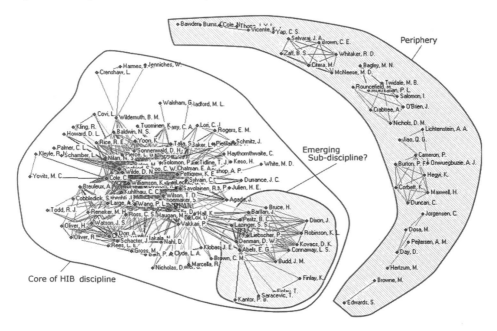

Figure 10.5 Intense interaction among articles (in the form of citations) generates a sort of independent bubble, which is interpreted as the emergence of a new subdiscipline. Image taken from McKechnie, Goodal, and Lajoie-Paquette (2005).

elements: F = (*U*, *T*, *R*, *Y*), where *U*, *T*, and *R* are finite sets, and denote *users*, *tags*, and *resources*, respectively. *Y* is a ternary relation between *U*, *T*, and *R* and represents the corresponding event of a user assigning tags to a resource.

In fact, new retrieval techniques and new generation search engines are trying to interpret tagging trends (Peters & Stock, 2007) by indexing information not only by counting links but also by counting tagging co-occurrences since librarians and information scientists use the concept of co-citation. Scholars do not simply categorize objects; they also optimize their future findability. Though it may seem surprising, *Google*'s creators (Brin & Page, 1998) had already written something similar in the final section of their article, entitled "Future Work."

As an example, I mention a recently created algorithm, its authors named *FolkRank*, the key idea of which "is that a resource which is tagged with important tags by important users becomes important itself" (Jäschke, Marinho, Hotho, Schmidt-Thieme, & Stumme, 2007). One would expect other algorithms to appear as *FolkRank* did and undergo debugging so that recommendation technologies for articles will be more sophisticated than technologies that merely recommend the most popular tags. Digital technology is highly malleable and will permit us to build any architecture we deem most suitable for the epistemological collaboration model information scientists are willing to design. We might, for instance, give more weight to a tag edited by a recognized specialist, or we could open an array of different weights depending on who is tagging, what discipline the tagger is from, and so on. This is similar to the way Google's *PageRank* gives more weight to the more reliable nodes or Web sites. Furthermore, the combinations are potentially infinite. Still, we must bear in mind that every choice of a key expression used to tag an article will certainly be not just an epistemic decision, but a decision explicitly or implicitly conditioned by a set of values, beliefs, and wishes. People from different cultural backgrounds and different scientific fields may use drastically different terms to tag the same concept. Some of the problems that plague print journals will reappear. However, they will reappear in different form because the amount of information is vastly greater and the technological tools available are considerably better.

The model proposed here for SRs is a kind of simulation of scientists' social activities, representing the interdisciplinary exchange of knowledge and perhaps a social epistemology dynamic of science. Up to a point, tags "transport" not only epistemic parameters, but also beliefs, desires, subjective value judgments, and other educational and cultural parameters from one scientific "tribe" to another. As a result, with the right technological tools, we will be able to make a great deal of implicit knowledge explicit. This knowledge, prior to the advent of the Internet, could be transmitted only in telephone conversations or professional conferences. Neither of those is preserved for scientometric studies, nor are e-mails, generally speaking.

I believe that dynamizing the exchange of preprints would require taking one step closer to incorporating folksonomies into SRs. I also stress that the concept of scientific trading zone in combination with the social-tagging approach is a good illustration of how SRs should work. It would be of value to conduct experiments on the exchange of terms among researchers, distinguishing them by discipline. As we have already seen, experts differ from one discipline to another in their ratio of cognitive use of subordinate-level terms.

As in Galison's anthropological analogy, neologisms arise and evolve in folksonomies too. In case studies to date, it has been observed that the terms a user first enters into the system are the general terms that correspond to what we have called "basic level." Predictably, the last to be assigned are the more specific terms, which correspond to the subordinate level. There are several studies that have analyzed the semiotic evolution of tags, showing that users generally tag in a consistent manner and coincide on tag names.[50] Thus, the extent to which certain keywords/tags are used stabilizes over time. As Golder and Huberman (2006) have stated, however, the use of certain tags expands rapidly, reflecting either new interests or a change in tagging practices. That is, new keywords assigned to a certain type of object reflect these new interests and changes. This has been the case with the computer term "ajax," which recently came into use to refer to a set of emerging computer technologies that had no name. The term "ajax" represented an innovation that, over time, has been changing the way many people think of and refer to the technologies they are using. Naturally, these same people began to utilize this keyword for the tags they used to bookmark Web sites and other objects related to *ajax*. In a sense, neologisms, which are a type of *Pidgin*, serve to bring different users into agreement on how to tag certain types of resources until, eventually, it becomes routine discourse, which is a type of *Creole*. As it was being incorporated into the discourse, the term "ajax" gradually shifted from basic level to subordinate level.

This has a direct bearing on science. New ideas, languages, metaphors, techniques, practices, rules, and beliefs can be traded in SRs through the preprints, citations, and tags that researchers have associated with them. Making all this a reality, however, requires that the tags be converted to a new scientific currency besides citations. For that to occur, scholars would somehow have to be encouraged by a "symbolic value" that would increase their visibility and reputation as good contributors. For example, one idea is that if a researcher in discipline *A* tags an article by a researcher in discipline *B* and many of discipline *A*'s colleagues discover and cite that same discipline *B* article, then that researcher in discipline *A* should be credited in the scientometric analyses.

In general, the graph of tags assigned to an object in a folksonomy follows a power law curve (see Figure 10.6).

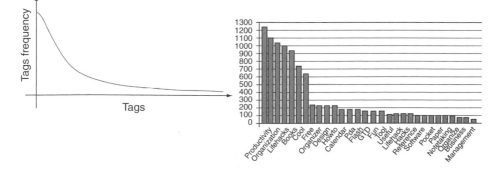

Figure 10.6 The type of curve characteristic of folksonomy is shown. In (a) the theoretical curve has been drawn, and (b) shows actual *Delicious* (empirical) data taken from Kipp, M. E. I., & Campbell, D. G. (2007). Patterns and inconsistencies in collaborative tagging systems: An examination of tagging practices. *Proceedings of the American Society for Information Science and Technology, 43*(1), 1–18. Copyright (2007, John Wiley & Sons). Reprinted with permission of John Wiley & Sons, Inc.

As the graphs show, there is a *long tail* of tags seldom used by prosumers where, for example, the majority of misspelled words are found. Let us imagine a set of tags used to characterize an online scientific article. My hypothesis is that many seldom-used tags residing in the *long tail* are interdisciplinary terms that academic search engines should be able to find. Current research projects on nonacademic folksonomies are focused primarily on determining the most popular terms so as to help search engines improve their services. We must not forget about the seldom-used tags, however, for I believe that many of them are crucial to the enhancement of interdisciplinary studies. In reality, for a digital repository of scientific preprints, it would be difficult to predict the distribution of basic-level and subordinate-level tags on the typical folksonomy curve. We could speculate, for example, that scientists in discipline X will utilize 30% basic-level tags and 70% subordinate-level tags, which are specialized discipline X terms, when identifying a text pertaining to discipline X. Likewise, scientists in discipline Y may utilize 80% basic-level tags and 20% subordinate-level tags, which are specialized discipline Y terms. Thus, the long tail would be composed of 30% basic-level tags pertaining to discipline X and 20% subordinate-level, specialized tags pertaining to discipline Y. It would be interesting, then, to conduct experiments of this type to determine the extent to which this hypothesis may be confirmed.

Future Directions

It is hard to anticipate what the map of scientific communication and knowledge exchange will look like in the future; it is obvious, however, that the long-standing academic journals model will be complemented by new computer tools. The current model has been around for more than 3½ centuries and has served its purpose reasonably well in the print era. A new era has dawned, however, thanks to the emergence of the Internet and the development of digital technology. Blogs, wikis, folksonomies, SRs, IRs, and OA are slowly but inexorably transforming the traditional ways of communicating and exchanging knowledge as well as the way sources are located and cited.

Commercial journals are not immune to the paradigm shift that is occurring; certain publishing groups such as Nature and Springer have already shown their position on folksonomies by operating *Connotea* and *CiteULike*, respectively. It would be a mistake, however, to reduce this paradigm shift to a mere technological adaptation. It is more subtle than that—it also involves a new way of understanding science.

As could be expected, the new technological systems, the digital universe, will give us a portrait of the research world much more like its contemporary reality than that suggested by the traditional system of great journals. The ideal image of that kind of representation is the interpretation of science offered by positivism, the Archimedean conception of science, tiered, hierarchical, and reductive. There is some sociological translation of this in a hierarchical academy, in which honors are given through equally objective and precise methods, such as impact indexes, awards, and honors of all kinds. It is a portrait that may have been a faithful representation of science in the beginning years of the last century, but certainly has nothing in common with our current world.

Conclusion

Scholarly social-tagging systems such as *Connotea*, *CiteULike*, and *2Collab* are not digital repositories. I believe that interdisciplinary bridges such as those I have described here would be much more effective in a digital repository where all the articles would be accessible and visible to researchers. Serendipity is important for scientific research. SRs that combine many disciplines and maintain an accelerated pace of preprint exchange, such as *arXiv*, are perfect candidates for the implementation of academic folksonomies. These are known as *trading zones*. In a sense, it could be said that preprints are part of the research process while postprints represent the institutionalization of the results. Clearly, folksonomies are of more interest for SRs, where preprints foster an ongoing interaction among researchers than for IRs in which e-prints, which are a mix of preprints and postprints, are static. IRs have been and are the ethical and political answer to the problem of OA to scientific research. Scientists themselves have not created these as tools or used them as *trading zones*.

To find and identify interdisciplinary tags in the long tail of folksonomies is to enhance interdisciplinary research. The fact that case studies of and experiments with folksonomies have been focused on the most popular tags is beneficial to research. However, they should not overlook the *long tail* and all its hidden potential.

Obviously, the current journal model will have to be adapted to fit the technological reality. The boundary lines between disciplines and between university departments will become less and less distinct. Digital technology and the Internet have made it possible to develop tools for social collaboration that never existed before, and utilities are gradually being consolidated. These tools will benefit interdisciplinary exchange, in particular, bringing to light areas of research that were once hidden in the shadows. Science has had no choice but to consign certain sectors of knowledge to the shadows because they did not conform to the geometry of its hierarchical scheme of organization. As a result, every new discovery was forced to reside on a particular bookshelf or in a particular, predetermined academic realm. The academic journals model mirrors the organization of knowledge by subject matter—a system that has remained intact because of power structures that favor local hierarchies, most likely, but also because of certain technological limitations that maintain the *status quo*.

Over time, the new technological utilities will probably disrupt the equilibrium of currently existing power structures within the scientific community. The measure of power in science today is the number and caliber of articles published; membership on an editorial board is another measure of power that has sometimes fostered intellectual elitism and thwarted new and fresh ideas that were in conflict with the system's accepted paradigm. The hope is that new technologies such as folksonomies will gradually weaken, to some extent, the local power structures that are established at journals and in university departments and evaluation groups. While the complete disappearance of power structures is inconceivable, and elimination of the reward system would be detrimental, Merton's promise of a more universal and communal science is no longer a Utopian vision—and power is likely to be more evenly distributed.[51]

Notes

1. Pidgin is "a language containing lexical and other features from two or more languages, characteristically with simplified grammar and a smaller vocabulary than the languages from

which it is derived, used for communication between people not having common language; a lingua franca." (Oxford English Dictionary Online)

2. A *creolized language* is "a language which has developed from that of a dominant group, first being used from a second language, then becoming the usual language of a subject group, its sounds, grammar, and vocabulary being modified in the process." (*Oxford English Dictionary Online*)

3. "A Pidgin is a first-generation *lingua franca*, spoken by everybody as a *second* language; when in subsequent generations it becomes the *first* language of a community, it is a Creole." (*Oxford English Dictionary Online*)

4. With the consent of journals, many IRs and SRs also contain postprints. The reasons for this consent would require a lengthy explanation, and it has no special relevance to our subsequent considerations. Complete, detailed, and updated information is available on Peter Suber's magnificent website dedicated to open access for scientific articles: http://www.earlham.edu/peters/.

5. In a way, the preprints exchange culture is a distant continuation of the exchange of letters that was so commonplace among scientists prior to the mid-seventeenth century when scientific societies and their associated journals came into being.

6. http://arxiv.org/

7. August 17, 2009.

8. http://cogprints.org.

9. August 17, 2009.

10. http://precedings.nature.com.

11. August 17, 2009.

12. http://precedings.nature.com/about#intro.

13. Digital repositories have certain advantages over e-mailing. The preprint is deposited once into the SR and remains visible and accessible online to the entire community. Any addition or modification is made on the same Web site. In contrast, keeping track of versions can be unduly complicated and make e-mailing chaotic. Also, with e-mailing, it is always possible that someone was inadvertently left off the mailing list whereas, with SRs, there is universal access.

14. For further information on IRs, see Ware, M. (2004). *Pathfinder research on Web-based repositories*. London: Publisher and Library/Learning Solutions.

15. The University of Southampton's institutional repository (http://eprints.soton.ac.uk/) is a paradigmatic example. A list of all the world's digital repositories may be viewed at http://www.opendoar.org/.

16. There is an historical reconstruction in Guédon, J. -C. (2001). In Oldenburg's long shadow: Librarians, research scientists, publishers, and the control of scientific publishing, (accessed on August 17, 2009) http://www.arl.org/resources/pubs/mmproceedings/138guedon.shtml.

17. This route to OA is known as the "green" road. Actually, there is another route to OA called the "golden" road, which argues that journals themselves should provide open (free) access to all articles (Guédon, 2004). This, of course, brings up the problem of finding a new business model to cover the journals' expenses—an issue that is beyond the scope of this chapter and will not be addressed here. For further information on the subject, see Cockerill, M. (2006). Business models in open access publishing. In Jacobs, N. (Ed) (pp. 111–120), and also Waltham, M. (2006). Learned society business models and open access. In Jacobs, N. (Ed.) (pp. 121–130). For an institutional approach, see House of Commons UK, Science and Technology Committee. (2004). *Scientific publications: Free for all?* Tenth Report of Session 2003–2004, (Vol. 1). http://www.publications.parliament.uk/pa/cm200304/cmselect/cmsctech/399/399.pdf (accessed on August 17, 2009).

18. See http://opcit.eprints.org/oacitation-biblio.html for a complete and updated bibliography of case studies on the relation between open access to scientific articles and the increase in citations received.

19. Now called Delicious.com.

20. http://www.amazon.com/

21. http://www.wikipedia.org/

22. Not all initiatives have followed the same model. There are Web sites that allow links or digital objects to be tagged and read by anyone, and there are other Web sites where tags may be read by the general public but only authors are permitted to tag their own objects.

23. http://technorati.com/

24. http://www.flickr.com/

25. http://www.youtube.com/

26. http://www.diigo.com/

27. http://www.librarything.com/

28. http://www.citeulike.org/

29. http://www.connotea.org/

30. http://www.2collab.com/

31. http://www.bibsonomy.org/

32. There also are Web sites that specialize in finding tags on several social tagging Web sites at once.

33. The term "folksonomy" was proposed by Thomas Vander Wal on July 24, 2004.

34. It should be pointed out that some researchers make the following distinction: they use the expression personomy when speaking of the set of tags utilized by a particular user and the expression folksonomy when speaking of the set of tags utilized by all users. It is a useful distinction; here, however, we are addressing folksonomies primarily, and in the sense indicated, so we will use this term in all cases, without making distinctions.

35. http://tags.library.upenn.edu/

36. http://tags.library.upenn.edu/help/

37. http://www.aadl.org/catalog

38. Social tagging capitalizes on this personal motivation by implementing an open system—that is, by allowing each user's tag to be visible to all other users. Other services may mandate privacy and, therefore, put a closed system in place. This is the case with Gmail.com, for example—an e-mail account in which e-mails received can be labeled instead of being filed in folders.

39. http://kevan.org/extispicious

40. There are several case studies on the structure of tags chosen by the users, a few of which are listed here: Lund, Hammond, Flack, and Hannay, (2005), Guy and Tonkin (2006), Spiteri (2007), Bruce (2008). For a case study on the semiotic dynamic, see Cattuto, Loreto, and Pietronero, (2007).

41. Shirky (2005) details the complications arising from this strategy.

42. With the passage of time, the names of some disciplines may undergo modification or even disappear, or they may be blended or combined—biochemistry or quantum computation, for example. Folksonomies can more readily put new concepts into practice.

43. Some people call this specific tagging-related spam spagging. Spagging contributes to erroneous classifications and "dilution of meanings."

44. It is important to mention an interesting project called extreme tagging by its authors (Tanasescu & Streibel, 2007), which proposes the tagging of tags to improve the semantics of social tagging systems and eliminate tag ambiguity.

45. There has been discussion as to the name that should be given to what we are calling "folksonomies" or "social tagging" here. Many names have been suggested (Hammond, Hannay, Lund, & Scott, 2005), such as "folk classification," "ethnoclassification," "distributed classification," "social classification," "open tagging," "free tagging," and "faceted hierarchy," but it appears "folksonomy" is the expression that is taking hold.

46. For information on the origins of citation indexing, as well as an exercise in philosophical abstraction—in the form of an attempt to make generalizations about citation indexing using Karl R. Popper's World III concept—see González-Quirós and Gherab-Martín (2008).

47. Bibliographic coupling is widely used in bibliometrics and citation studies. If articles X and Y both cite article Z, then we expect that X and Y may be related to each other, even though they do not reference each other.

48. Co-citation is also widely used in bibliometrics and citation studies. If article C cites both articles A and B, then we expect that A and B may be related to each other, even though they do not reference each other. If A and B are both cited by many others (C, D, E, F...), we expect that A and B have a stronger relationship.

49. It is important to remember that Connotea, CiteULike, and 2Collab are not article repositories per se but social bookmarking sites that redirect to each article's actual location. In other words, they are hyperlink (and tag) repositories.

50. This should not be surprising because they are general, basic-level terms.

51. This work has been undertaken thanks to funds coming from the Spanish Ministry of Science and Innovation as part of the research project FFI2008-03599 – Philosophy of Human and Social Technosciences.

References

Anderson, P. (2007). What is Web 2.0? Ideas, technologies and implications for education. *JISC Technology & Standards Watch* (February 2007).

Barnes, J. (Ed.). (1984). *The complete works of Aristotle*. Princeton: Princeton University Press.

Brin, S., & Page, L. (1998). The anatomy of a large-scale hypertextual Web search engine. *Computer Networks and ISDN Systems, 30*, 107–117.

Bruce, R. (2008). Descriptor and folksonomy concurrence in education related scholarly research. *Webology, 5*(3). (Accessed on August 17, 2009) http://www.webology.ir/2008/v5n3/a59.html.

Cattuto, C., Loreto, V. & Pietronero, L. (2007). Semiotic dynamics and collaborative tagging. *Proceedings of the National Academy of Sciences (PNAS), 104*(5), 1461–1464.

Elitzur, A. C. & Vaidman, L. (1993). Quantum mechanical interaction-free measurements. *Foundations of Physics, 23*(7), 987–97.

Galison, P. (1996). Computer simulations and the trading zone. In Galison, P., and Stump, D. (Eds.), *The disunity of science: Boundaries, contexts, and power*. California: Stanford University Press.

Galison, P. (1997). *Image and logic. A material culture of microphysics*. Chicago: The University of Chicago Press.

Garfield, E. (1955). Citation indexes for science: A new dimension in documentation through association of ideas. *Science, 122*(3159), 103–111.

Garfield, E. (1964). "Science Citation Index": A new dimension in indexing. *Science, 144*(3619), 649–654.

Golder, S. A. & Huberman, B. A. (2006). Usage patterns of collaborative tagging systems. *Journal of Information Science, 32*(2), 198–208.

González-Quirós, J. L., & Gherab-Martín, K. (2008). *The new temple of knowledge: Towards the universal digital library*. Australia: Common Ground Publishing.

Gruber, T. (2006). Where the social Web meets the semantic Web. *Lecture Notes in Computer Science, 4273*, 994.

Guédon, J.-C. (2004). The "Green" and "Gold" roads to open access—The case for mixing and matching. *Serials Review*, 30(4), 315–328. doi:10.1016/j.serrev.2004.09.005.

Guy, M. & Tonkin, E. (2006). Folksonomies: Tidying up tags? *D-Lib Magazine, 12*(1). (Accessed on August 17, 2009) http://www.dlib.org/dlib/january06/guy/01guy.html.

Hammond, T., Hannay, T., Lund, B., & Scott, J. (2005). Social bookmarking tools (I): A general review. *D-Lib Magazine, 11*(4). (Accessed on August 17, 2009) http://www.dlib.org/dlib/april05/hammond/04hammond.html.

Harnad, S. (2001). The self-archiving initiative. *Nature, 410,* 1024–1025.

Hosten, O., Rakher, M. T., Barreiro, J. T., Peters, N. A., & Kwiat, P. G. (2006). Counterfactual quantum computation through quantum interrogation. *Nature, 439*(23), 949–952. doi:10.1038/nature04523.

Hotho, A., Jäschke, R., Schmitz, C., & Stumme, G. (2006). Information retrieval in folksonomies: Search and ranking. *Lecture Notes in Computer Science, 4011,* 411–426.

Jäschke, R., Marinho, L., Hotho, A., Schmidt-Thieme, L., & Stumme, G. (2007). Tag recommendations in folksonomies. *Lecture Notes in Artificial Intelligence, 4702,* 506–514.

Lund, B., Hammond, T., Flack, M. & Hannay, T. (2005). Social bookmarking tools (II): A case study–Connotea. *D-Lib Magazine, 11*(4). (Accessed on August 17, 2009) http://www.dlib.org/dlib/april05/lund/04lund.html.

MacLaurin, M. B. (2007). Selection-based item tagging. *United States Patent 20070028171, Code A1, assignee: Microsoft Corporation.* Publication date February 1, 2007, filing date July 29, 2005. (Accessed on August 17, 2009) http://www.freepatentsonline.com/y2007/0028171.html.

McKechnie, L., Goodall, G. R., & Lajoie-Paquette, D. (2005). How human information behaviour researchers use each other's work: A basic citation analysis study. *Information Research, 10*(2).

Mitchison, G. & Massar, S. (2001). "Interaction-free" discrimination between semi-transparent objects. *Physical Review A, 63* (032105).

Noruzi, A. (2007). Folksonomies: Why do we need controlled vocabulary? *Webology, 4*(2). (Accessed on August 17, 2009) http://www.webology.ir/2007/v4n2/editorial12.html.

O'Reilly, T. (2005). What is Web 2.0? Design patterns and business models for the next generation of software. (Accessed on August 17, 2009) http://www.oreillynet.com/lpt/a/6228.

Page, L., Brin, S., Motwani, R., & Winograd, T. (1998/1999). *The PageRank citation ranking: Bringing order to the Web.* Technical Report. Stanford InfoLab. (Accessed on August 17, 2009) http://ilpubs.stanford.edu:8090/422/.

Peters, I., and Stock, W. G.(2007). Folksonomy and information retrieval. *Proceedings of the 70th Annual Meeting of the American Society for Information Science and Technology* 15, CD-ROM.

Peters, I. & Weller, K. (2008). Tag gardening for folksonomy enrichment and maintenance. *Webology, 5*(3). (Accessed on August 17, 2009) http://www.webology.ir/2008/v5n3/a58.html.

Peterson, E. (2006). Beneath the metadata: Some philosophical problems with folksonomy. *D-Lib Magazine, 12*(11). (Accessed August 17, 2009) http://www.dlib.org/dlib/november06/peterson/11peterson.html.

Peterson, E. (2008). Parallel systems: The coexistence of subject cataloging and folksonomy. *Library Philosophy and Practice,* (April).

Rosch, E., Mervis, C. B., Gray, W., Johnson, D., & Boyes-Braem, P. (1976). Basic objects in natural categories. *Cognitive Psychology, 8,* 382–439.

Royal Society. (2005). Royal society warns hasty "open access" moves may damage science. (Accessed on August 17, 2009) http://www.royalsoc.ac.uk/news.asp?id=3881.

Sen, S., Lam, S., Rashid, A., Cosley, D., Frankowski, D., & Osterhouse, J. (2006). Tagging, communities, vocabulary, evolution. *Proceedings of the 20th Anniversary Conference on Computer Supported Cooperative Work* (pp. 181–190). Banff, Alberta, Canada.

Shirky, C. (2005). Ontology is overrated: Categories, links, and tags. (Accessed on August 17, 2009) http://www.shirky.com/writings/ontology_overrated.html.

Sinclair, J. & Cardew-Hall, M. (2008). The folksonomy tag cloud: When is it useful? *Journal of Information Science, 34,* 15–29.

Spiteri, L. F. (2006). The use of folksonomies in public library catalogues. *Serials Librarian, 51*(2), 75–89.

Spiteri, L. F. (2007). Structure and form of folksonomy tags: The road to public library catalog. *Webology, 4*(2). (Accessed on August 17, 2009) http://www.webology.ir/2007/v4n2/a41.html.

Stock, W. G. (2007). Folksonomies and science communication: A mash-up of professional science databases and Web 2.0 services. *Information Services & Use, 27,* 97–103.

Tanaka, J. W., & Taylor, M. (1991). Object categories and expertise: Is the basic level in the eye of the beholder. *Cognitive Psychology*, *23*, 457–482.

Tanasescu, V., and Streibel, O. (2007). Extreme tagging: Emergent semantics through the tagging of tags. In *Proceedings of the International Workshop on Emergent Semantics and Ontology Evolution (ESOE2007) at ISWC/ASWC 2007*. Busan, South Korea.

Till, J. E. (2001). Predecessors of preprint servers. *Learned Publishing*, *14*, 7–13.

Toffler, A. (1980). *The third wave*. New York: Morrow.

Tonkin, E. (2006). Folksonomies: The fall and rise of plain-text tagging. *Ariadne*, *47*, (April). (Accessed on August 17, 2009) http://www.ariadne.ac.uk/issue47/tonkin/.

Part III

**Emergent Data Collection Methods:
New Forms of Data Production**

> Chapter 11

Studying Mailing Lists: Text, Temporality, Interaction, and Materiality at the Intersection of E-Mail and the Web

Anne Beaulieu and Mette Terp Høybye

Introduction

The present chapter considers what it means to talk about mailing lists as an emerging technology and to use them in research. There is nothing very spectacular about mailing lists, and to use them as sites and tools for empirical research may seem like a trivial choice. There is indeed a tendency to look to new or computationally significant technologies to find novelty or a large "impact" of technology on knowledge. Not so very long ago, mailing lists *were* a new thing, and studied as such in the late 1990s. There have been several newer, more complex technologies developed since then, and scholarly attention has tended to follow these developments and has addressed, for example, blogs, podcasts, and social networking. As well as novelty, the scale of technologies also tends to draw attention. New initiatives to provide tools for research, whether under the label of cyberinfrastructure or e-science, have a high profile and carry promises of large-scale and radical innovation. In comparison, mailing lists appear not to be so novel, small, mundane, and nearly invisible, both to users of these lists and to researchers. Yet, it is precisely this aspect of mailing lists that makes them interesting as a scholarly tool. Within a decade, mailing lists have become a known entity to scholars in the Western world, something scholars effectively put to use or deliberately ignore. As a pervasive technology, mailing lists are eminently unnoticeable. And this is precisely why we think they are worthy of further attention, not only in the early phases where they were seen as new, but also at the point where they are part of everyday practices. A technological practice that becomes mundane, that fades into the background, may be as equally important to consider as a cutting-edge technology, not only because the number of users is much greater, but precisely because such taken-for-grantedness signals that these applications have become essential parts of research and everyday practices in infrastructures.

What is there to say about something as ordinary as a mailing list? Following a critical approach to the study of technology, we consider in this chapter how the mailing list is configured, how it is set in contrast to (or associated with) other technologies or aspects of the web, and how this in turn shapes what we can learn using and studying mailing lists. Rather than emphasizing a definition of a mailing list, we demonstrate in this chapter that the boundaries and definition of the mailing list can fruitfully be taken as an empirical question. Such an approach enables the researcher to apprehend the entwinement of applications, such as mailing lists that have web interfaces and searchable archives, making them at once software and network. By avoiding compartmentalized or generalized conceptualization, we can also encompass in our analysis the way a mailing list can be alternately a mail event, a web-based hypertext or a searchable database. As a form, mailing lists distinguish themselves from other applications through a number of features: they involve e-mail communication, delivered via (semi-) automated software running on mail servers and addressing an audience of subscribers. As we move through the reflections and discussion of this chapter, we will note different ways of defining mailing lists and the consequences of different definitions. By showing the link between these, we seek to address the relation between research methods as forms of social practice, technologies, and mediated settings, paying attention to the characteristics of digital networks (internet, web) that may present particular challenges for social researchers.

Illustrative Cases

The reflections in this chapter about mailing lists as emerging technologies are related to two larger ethnographic projects on thematically different mailing lists. One is Beaulieu's ethnographic project to investigate women's studies and information and communication technology (ICT), where an analysis of WMST-L became a subproject in the ethnography. This project aimed to explore how ICT is used to enhance research practices, and how ICTs get adapted to suit the needs of this particular field of scholarship. As is detailed later in the chapter, mailing lists were first used as part of an inventory of the resources used in the field, and one of the lists became a "site" of research in its own right. This dual role represents the strength of mailing lists in serving as an informative tool that provides insight into what is going on in a given area or for a given group of subscribers (peripheral awareness) and also as a site to consider mediated social interactions. The mailing list that became especially important for the project is WMST-L, a women's studies mailing list established in 1991 and based at the University of Maryland College Park. At the time of the study, the list had more than 4,800 subscribers in 47 countries ranging from the United States and Canada to Israel, various countries in Europe, Saudi Arabia, Brazil, Singapore, and Australia. Participants are mainly scholars from the field of women's studies. All communication on the list is in English. Beaulieu subscribed to the list between January 2005 and June 2007, reading it daily and making fieldnotes about it. She further studied the content of e-mails to the list in detail for the month of November 2005.

The second illustrative case is Høybye's study on SCAN-BC-LIST (Scandinavian Breast Cancer Mailing List) (Høybye, Johansen, & Tjørnhøj-Thomsen, 2005) investigating the social interactions that occur in support groups mediated by the internet. The study investigated the social mechanisms and dynamics that made the group useful in the rehabilitation of cancer patients. By focusing on the stories told on a breast cancer internet mailing list, Høybye investigated how the overwhelming experience of breast cancer and the isolating and mentally debilitating effects of the illness may be counteracted. The list was founded by a Danish breast cancer survivor in 1999 as a closed group for people with breast cancer, speaking a Scandinavian language to discuss all aspects of life with breast cancer. Participants on the list were mainly women with breast cancer, though a few close relatives to women suffering from breast cancer also joined. Geographically, the majority of participants were living in Denmark, but Norwegian and Swedish women also used the list. Danish women living in other places of the world, like Greenland, Faeroe Islands, France, and Germany, also took part in the list and found it to be a place to communicate the experience of illness in their native language. The mailing list was hosted by the Association of Cancer Online Resources (ACOR), an American-based NGO hosting a large number of cancer related mailing lists. In 2004, the list was closed on ACOR and moved to Yahoo Groups under the new name Scan-bc-listen, due to an internal matter on the list (as will be further elaborated below). Høybye conducted an ethnographic fieldwork on the mailing list for 8 months in 2000, participating in daily list activities of reading and posting. She left the list after the fieldwork but rejoined the list in April 2002 to tell the list about her research findings. Following this, she was invited by the list owner to stay on as a member, but is not actively engaging in the list anymore. At the start of Høybye's ethnographic fieldwork, the mailing list had 39 members, but has since grown to more than 130 subscribers. As in the study of Beaulieu, the mailing list was at the same time both a site for, as well as a tool of research providing a particular insight to the experience of cancer and the social interactions formed in response of this experience.

Ways of Studying Mailing Lists

There is a large body of work on mailing lists, and rather than attempt to review all this literature, we focus here on conveying a sense of the various approaches to using mailing lists, both in terms of the intellectual framework of these approaches and in the methods used. A number of themes are prominent in accounts of both the promised and sought after outcomes of digitization of work in general, and the use of mailing lists in particular. Views that new technologies lead directly and unproblematically to new insights tend to persist in promissory documents about new technologies ("hype") (Beaulieu & Wouters, 2009). The early association of computerization and efficiency in research is a strong one. It endures (Barjak, 2006) and has been associated with group interactions via e-mail lists by improving the codification of knowledge (Steinmueller, 2000) or access to information (Brown, 2001). This assumption is linked to a view that the interaction between knowledge creation, and technology is a progressivist one, where technology will enable scholars to keep doing what they are already doing, but better and faster. This approach, which focuses on the impact of a technology, has been called the "standard mode" in which information is central, to the exclusion of social relations (Kling, McKim, & King, 2003). Yet, as we will see, the interaction is more complex. By embracing the importance of social relations in the study of technology, we can better understand how technologies come to be used, and remain open to two-way influences of practices and technology and to the possibility that new practices may be arising.

Many studies of mailing lists set out to test various claims about the possibilities offered by technologies, a strategy that is common in technology studies (VKS, 2007). Based on surveys or detailed analysis of contribution patterns, these studies have variously focused on the possibility of bridging gaps between center and periphery in scientific communities (Matzat, 2001; Barjak, 2006); on the idea that e-mail can facilitate collaboration over distances and across national boundaries (Sooryamoorthy & Shrum, 2007); or on the possibility of bridging gaps between lay people and scientists (Hine, 2002). Scholarship that sets out to examine such claims is not so unusual, as this is one of the dominant forms of writing about internet culture. In this work, technologies have been characterized as potentially flattening communication hierarchies enabling access to those previously excluded. Such expectations were not always confirmed: Hine found in a participant-observer study that rather than overcoming boundaries, discursive practices were used to recreate boundaries between specialists and outsiders (Hine, 2002).

Other scholars have studied in a detailed manner the contributions to lists in terms of features of participant identity, analyzing the gender of subscribers and of contributors, length and frequency of contributions (Sierpe, 2000), and patterns of use and subscription (Brown, 2001). This work especially emphasized the liberatory or nonhierarchical potential of lists presumably embedded in the technology. The potential for all subscribers to have equal access to public debate and interaction on the list signaled, for some, a new kind of discursive space where the absence of (gendered) bodies (Korenman & Wyatt, 1996; Sierpe, 2000) and the possibility of emerging voices (Korenman, 1999; Guy, 2000) were especially highlighted.

Other work has characterized the functions that mailing lists can play, from sustaining communities (Marshall, 2004) to serving information needs (Talja, Savolainen, & Maula, 2004), or in the way mailing lists might be shifting distinctions between formal and informal communication in science (Walsh, 1996; Barjak, 2006).

Also noteworthy in this work is that mailing lists have been labeled a tool, a technology, and an application. Mailing lists could justifiably be labeled as one or the other, or as all of these. While this may at first seem confusing, we think it is important to maintain openness to the richness and multiplicity of what the mailing list might be and what it might mean for scholarly practices. Mailing lists are part of larger technical systems, like internet protocols and telecom media, which themselves are embedded in social and institutional contexts, qualifying them as infrastructures. In what follows, we share our own conceptualizations of mailing lists. An important aspect of our work is that it does not present the web and computer-mediated communication as impoverished or purely textual media (Steinmueller, 2000). It rather seeks to highlight the innovative and productive aspects of e-mail and of the web as infrastructure for shaping research practices as social actions. As a consequence of this conceptualization of digital and networked technologies, the embedding of interactions is very important for the present analysis.

Time, Timing, Cycles, and Mailing Lists

Though the content of mailing lists is continuously shaped by the social life of the list, it is at the same time positioned in time and retained as archived material, searchable, and accessible even years past its production. For some projects, the archival time will be more appropriate while for others, the way time and timing are experienced and shaped in relation to the mailing list will be more important. It is nevertheless important to realize the diversity of temporalities at play around these technologies. With mailing lists and other technologies where "time stamps" offer a valuable source of information for researchers, this view of time can easily dominate, because of its automated form and seemingly objective quality. We are keen to see this temporal understanding of mailing lists denaturalized and enriched with attention to other aspects. The dominant understanding that sees time in mailing lists as chunks of chronologically ordered, individual pieces of writing is one approach, but as we have discussed, there are other very significant temporal aspects. These include continuous interactions between participants and technology, lived experience in social time, and the temporality that is shaped by the writing in which we engage as researchers.

Several aspects of mailing lists can be invaluable sources of insight. Beyond the obvious textuality of messages, other aspects of mailing lists are important in constituting their role and meaning. The intensity and rhythm of responses can be indicative of the importance of particular topics or of the prominence of specific posters. Such aspects are furthermore not always retrievable in archives of lists. In our work, we have found that there is a great deal of modulation in the rhythms of interactions on mailing lists. Silence as well as floods of messages can be observed.

The mediated environment of mailing lists is, as all social practice, embedded in time. Studying mailing lists therefore needs to include temporality as a key element shaping contents of mailing lists and the kinds of uses they are put to. The temporality of mailing lists operates at different levels in the social network it forms. Time of writing and time of posting, for example, are not necessarily the same. Distribution protocols for lists (i.e., digests) and for infrastructure (i.e., routing) also mean that readers do not all receive the list in the same way—let alone have the same reading practices. This means that the individual's experience of time intersects in different ways with the collective of the mailing list. These differences can reflect negotiations of boundaries of social space or the fact that individuals may draw back from the list. Attention to such time cycles can, therefore, reveal interesting aspects of participation in a mailing list.

Besides the chronology of the mailing list that can be traced in its archives or in one's mailbox, there are other aspects of temporality at play. Whether or not we pay attention to these has implications for how we conceptualize mailing lists. If we look at the mailing list as marked by the temporality of linear and singular actions of writing, we tend to embrace a view that we can stand aside and observe the passage of time without attention to context and embodiment, an epistemological approach that is founded on an illusion of disembodiment (Ingold, 2000, p. 196). As we will discuss later, embodiment is an important element in interacting with technologies (Høybye, n.d.), especially if we think about ways of being copresent with our object of study (Beaulieu, 2010).

Such awareness to the changes in time and movement provide useful insights in the social practices of a particular list. While other communication technologies structure social practice as synchronous (as the immediate interaction of posts and responses), the mailing list conversation is structured by the writing of files posted as e-mails that most commonly move on to be saved as files in a mailing list archive. This possibility of working on a post or on a reply to a thread on a mailing list off-line, over time, formulating cohesive argumentation and rewriting passages, forms a distinct social interaction, which sets mailing lists apart from other communication technologies. One woman in Høybye's study of the SCAN-BC-LIST (Høybye et al., 2005) was an immigrant to Denmark and conveyed in interviews how she found it difficult at times to communicate in Danish and would never send off a post or reply to the list before she had worked thoroughly with her writing and spelling, not to stand out as the one with the peculiar phrasing or misspelling on the list. Researchers studying mailing lists have to take into account the meaning of such modulation of social time on the list.

Likewise, a geographical spread across time zones may affect the way in which conversation is structured, causing discussions not only to flow asynchronously but also to be delayed. While this is not a unique feature of mailing lists, but applies to most social media, some related structural elements in mailing lists amplify the time gaps. An example of this is the commonly used option to have mailing list posts collected by the LIST SERV and sent off in one daily digest e-mail. Responses to posts received in this way may be substantially delayed with great implications for the discussion on a list.

Paying attention to the temporality of mailing lists, through our own presence in the list for example, opens up important knowledge on the movement of participants in the social network. Time passing is not something we conceive or see, as onlookers, but something we affect (Merleau-Ponty, 1964, p. 421). In becoming able to identify what is socially significant in mailing lists, we need to develop a "feel" for relevance mediated by our own bodily and sensory experience (Hastrup, 1994, p. 227) of the space. Taking part in a mailing list, we develop such a "feel" for the social life and practice in this space that will facilitate our understanding of the timing of responses and the meaning of "silence."

Members of the SCAN-BC-LIST would often be very active writers when they first joined the list, very engaged in learning from the stories of fellow breast cancer survivors and seeking information and advice supporting their own situation. This intersection of personal and collective temporality was not always parallel, since not everyone joined at the same time. As others have also observed (Sandaune, 2008), the individual constantly evaluates and to a certain extent adjusts the personal and social life of a mailing list. Hereby, members not only assess and adjust to the existing exchanges of a mailing list, but start to contribute as they enter the social life of writing and creatively appropriate the list. On the SCAN-BC-LIST, members would find the list useful for some time, some a few months, and others years and then draw back from the list, as other individual priorities surfaced. Some members would unsubscribe to the list, while others would just stop writing or "become quiet," as it was described by other group members. Reasons for drawing back but not taking the definite step of unsubscribing were most often phrased as a personal need for knowing that immediate access to the list was possible at a later stage, should one be in need of the contact. Mailing lists are not fixed structures, but projects that entail always-moving and emergent relations, constantly reflecting the lives, interests, and concerns of its members.

This empirical material serves to show that when studying mailing lists, we need to pay attention to time and temporality in different scales. Furthermore, this stresses that our research is always deeply embedded in the temporality of our object of study, which has all kinds of implications not only for our immediate practice but also for our ethical consideration and the presentation of our research. Issues of time can affect ethical issues in two ways, either alleviating concerns for doing harm or else increasing this possibility. For example, there are times when a list may be more vulnerable to what we write about it, because our findings may be taken up in social and political debates (e.g., "science wars"), or because hosts, moderators, and participants to the list may be under scrutiny (institutional reviews or evaluations). Also, given the often considerable amount of time that elapses between the production of data and publication, list membership may have changed significantly. This is not necessarily problematic, since much research will aim to identify structural elements in lists and it may even have the advantage of making it less sensitive to publish about lists, since individuals may have moved on, thereby alleviating some ethical concerns. But the level of dynamism of lists over time (expected turnover of members, level of stability in hosts) should be noted as an important element to contextualize results.

Furthermore, timing is not only a function of intensity of interaction but can also be deeply meaningful. Silence, apart from drawing back from active conversation, can also be a collective or personal experience of silence. At the SCAN-BC-LIST, silence would follow difficult news of progressive cancer or relapse in a member, or the news of a member's death. Silence on the list resembled holding your breath, before engaging vigorously in writing to support and relieve the member once again inflicted by illness. Silence at other times was experienced by individuals as a response to issues they raised or stories they told that did not conform to mailing list practice. This could be issues that went somewhat off topic, which other members would not assess as related to breast cancer or stories that were somehow perceived as discouraging and did not support the socially desirable story of "fighting breast cancer." Such posts could elicit limited comments, but never really spurred active interaction. This is significant because it shows that not posting is not necessarily a sign that nothing is happening on a mailing list.

In this way, temporality of a mailing list also enacts the authority of the mailing list, as structured by the list administrator or by more unregulated social practices for determining wanted or unwanted discussions. Studying mailing lists by engaging in the social practices of the list will open up an understanding of how the authority of a particular setting is endorsed by its members. While the content of mailing list discussions is most commonly guided by directives given by the list administrator, the daily interaction on mailing lists may negotiate these directives in diverse ways. Below, we shall look more closely at how such interactions function as a form of boundary-keeping in lists.

Public/Private and Front/Backstage of Lists

One of the perennial debates for researchers around mailing lists concerns the perception of communication as simultaneously private and public, in particular related to how ethical concerns are framed in Internet Studies (Sveningsson, 2009). We take up this discussion here to explore ways of understanding audiences and purposes of lists and how presence is established by contributors. We also focus on the "traffic" on lists (flow or over-flow of list e-mails and private e-mails) and on the visibility of both contributors and researchers. We also discuss how mailing list posters modulate their audience and create expectations about public and private discourse on the list.

As we noted in our introduction, it is important to consider the embedding of mailing lists within other modes of communication or other cultural forms. When studying mailing lists, a common approach has been to study list archives (Seale, Ziebland, & Charteris-Black, 2005; Gooden & Winefield, 2007) as providing a full account of the interactions on the list. Some have argued that such archives can be places for ideal or unobtrusive observation on the internet (Paolillo, 1999; Schaap, 2002). Even though the social space of the internet is strongly shaped by textual exchanges in a literal sense (Schaap, 2002), the assumption that the text is a fixed and final product to be collected for further study, and that there is "less to miss" in a text-based world (Thomsen, Straubhaar, & Bolyard, 1998), cuts off insights into other backstage exchanges that interact with and shape the full public "traffic" of mailing lists. This can be essential to an understanding of how social interaction is produced, negotiated, contested, and reproduced in mailing lists. Several scholars have documented that exchanges of e-mails on lists are often accompanied by bilateral or small group exchanges, either face-to-face, telephone, or e-mail messages addressed to specific users (Hine, 2002; Høybye et al., 2005). This phenomenon qualifies the idea that the archive is not a definitive account of interactions, since they provide only a partial perspective, insofar as the archive does not encompass interaction spurred by the list and involving participants, but using other channels. These "backstage," less public exchanges can contribute important insights into the social dynamics of the mailing list. Such a backstage message can undermine the authority of extremely prominent posters. In other cases, they can provide background to particular debates or explanations as to why certain positions are not forthcoming in a discussion, for example, because they provoked too much controversy in the eyes of participants, eliciting waves of aggressive responses (flaming), or otherwise threatening the functioning of the list.

SCAN-BC-LIST presents itself as a mailing list open to everyone with an interest in breast cancer with the aim of encouraging and supporting breast cancer survivors. Active participants on the list are mainly women with breast cancer, but there are also a few members who are close family members of a cancer survivor, such as husband, mother, or sister. The stories these family members tell are obviously different as they convey their experience of someone else's illness, but many of the issues they raise, for example, with regard to treatment options and late effects, are very similar. Though included on the list, their integration could not be sustained beyond the point where their family member died from breast cancer. Commonly, family members would inform the list about the death of their family member and, with no further interest in membership, politely leave the list. However, losing his wife to breast cancer, one man on the list decided to stick around. After some weeks, other members politely asked if he would be leaving them soon, to which he replied that he had experienced such support from the list and they were so important to him, that he would like to stay around a bit longer. Responses to this request on the list were mainly empathic but along with the open discussion, a private discussion between the list administrator and other core members evolved around the man's right to stay on the list. Their point was that the list was not a place for mourning and commemoration, but a place for the living, ongoing struggle with breast cancer. After having discussed the issue privately for some time, the administrator took the issue out in the open on the list, and disclosed that she had decided that he was no longer fit for membership of the list and would be excluded. Some members defied this position and found her to be overruling the social community, since the messages that had been on list were not so openly opposed to his membership. This caused some discussion but only a few women left the list to show their disagreement. In a personal communication to Høybye, the list owner later remarked that "a mailing list is basically not a democracy, despite all the social exchanges."

This empirical example shows how social interactions and negotiations of boundaries are not at all times fully displayed in text on the lists, but also have bilateral exchanges, as we discussed above. Such exchanges only become possible to include in research if one is invited into them. This may raise questions about the positioning of the researcher, such as whether material is shared with the researcher as "potential ally" or as "researcher." The ethics of using such material, which is by definition more private than interactions on list, should be carefully considered. The ethical issue is that informants might provide us with different kinds of materials at different times, and do so with different kinds of understandings of what we might do with it. The ethnographer needs to be very sensitive to such changes in expectations, for example, whether an e-mail is meant to be a personal communication and, therefore, outside the bounds of what can be used for research. Again, this makes the point that social research on mailing lists should go beyond studies of mailing list archives and engage the social action of particular lists. Such a participatory approach to research demands that the researcher continuously negotiate and reflect on her or his position on the list, such as being included in off-list discussions and negotiations.

The distinction between public and private is also a prominent element in many discussions about the ethics of studying mailing lists. In studies of the internet, that particular distinction has taken the shape of a major divide and has enforced binary thinking in much research. Identifying a setting as either public or private assigns the interactions to different ethical regimes, with implications for practices of researchers (Beaulieu, 2009). The ethical issues are framed in the following way: if a mailing list is identified as public, the researcher's accountability is often deemed minimal, while the study of a setting identified as private may mean that researchers must obtain informed consent from list members—a daunting task. From what we describe above, given that boundaries of mailing lists may not always be clear-cut, it may be difficult to assign them unilaterally to the private or public domain. In our work, we have used the mailing list as a way of performing research ethics, in the concrete sense of being accountable to members. For example, we have used lists to announce our activities and publications (including this chapter!). We see this as one of the ways of instantiating an ethical form of research, in which an ongoing relationship with participants is part of the researcher's accountability. But, being aware that participants often wish to see their own work acknowledged and feel a sense of ownership (Bakardjieva & Feenberg, 2001), we have also contacted individual members to inform them that we were using passages of their messages in our work and to open up an opportunity for discussing this.

Ethnographic presence, as a research strategy, is embedded in a relation of power and dialogue. Hastrup notes that the asymmetrical relationship between the researcher as author and the informant as contributor "is of a peculiarly creative nature, provided it is recognized. The ethnographer's presence, however violent, is in some way the only alternative to silence about the other worlds, because her sharing of this world is a source of authority about its objective reality; no reality can ever be exhaustively apprehended in its own categories" (Hastrup, 1992). Presence on a mailing list becomes, as we argue here, an essential point of knowledge-making and a moral involvement with the field that generates new creativity and anticipation.

Further, this approach has deep ethical implications as we, in this investigation of other social and cultural forms of the mailing list, also may position ourselves in specific "fractional" relations. The practice of research, on the other hand, cannot be without ethical bearing. Ethical considerations are always embedded, as we are at all times positioned in an ethical relation to the world and the Other, which goes beyond the standardized rules of informed consent, etc., that are often expected to alleviate ethical concerns. Rules do not govern personal and disciplinary knowledge interests, and can therefore not be evaluated independently of our individual interests. Further, we cannot rely on ethical rules to ensure that the people participating in research fully realize the implications of their participation. We should be aware that our interests might at times run counter to those of the participants, despite our good intentions and despite the fact that the participants have given informed consent.

Genres and Types of Lists

We have noted that the textuality of lists is one of their main constitutive elements. As such, they have been approached as structured pieces of text, for example, using threads as units of analysis. While threads can indicate a cluster of exchanges about a topic or question, researchers have also found that a single thread can contain very different kinds of messages (Bodourides, Mavrikakis, & Vasileiadou, 2002). It is also important to recall that a thread is partly sustained by the automated features of e-mail and mailing list archiving systems—a subject heading endures, by default, unless changed by the respondent. On the SCAN-BC-LIST, it was common practice to use headings as active "warning signals" if the post conveyed disturbing news of some kind (e.g., a recurrence of cancer or death of a list member). Headings can therefore be indicators, but not guarantors, of the relevance of a message to the thread or of coherence or interaction between posters.

Lists vary in terms of the models of authorship and audience they support. Many tend to have low levels of traffic and serve mainly for announcements. Often, such lists also have a centralized or designated few users who take on the role of posters to the list—even when this is not necessarily demanded by the set up of the list and any subscriber might post themselves (one-to-many). In such settings, membership of the list is a telling element, since the list is constituted as a medium directed at an audience. Other genres of lists have a much more diverse set of posters and can be characterized as discussion lists rather than announcement lists. Again, the distribution of posters can be skewed toward a small number of very vocal/active posters (few-to-many). In this type of list, it may be relevant to question the various views represented in the interactions, since debates can often make clear, dominant, and dissenting views within groups. It then becomes important to understand how the list fits into a particular setting (Hine, 2002) and who might be included and excluded from discussion.

An example of how mailing lists are situated in particular ways is the case of mailing lists in women's studies. WMST-L came into focus through initial participation in another mailing list, the NextGenderation, which originated at Utrecht University in the Netherlands. This context for the research is important in that it is through the use of connective research strategies (Hine, 2007) that WMST-L came into focus, and became a subproject in the ethnography. Beaulieu first became aware of NextGenderation (NG) because it had arisen from a summer school held at the department that was the focus of her project. However, wishing to focus on academics' uses of ICT in this project, NG did not seem like an appropriate object of study. Beaulieu was advised to look at WMST-L by some informants. Not only are the connections between the lists important, but the contrast between the two lists is also revealing. When Beaulieu began reading NG, it struck her as being very concerned with demonstrations and activism, and not much about women's studies. Carefully examining such value judgments is part of ethnographic enquiry, and she began to try and make explicit what it was about this list that made it unrecognizable as an "academic list." As part of the interrogation of her personal assumptions underlying this judgment, she sought out what would be a "proper academic list" and subscribed to WMST-L. While the two lists share the label of women's studies mailing lists and are both vibrant settings, they are also quite dissimilar, and show how a mailing list might be adapted and serve very different visions of women's studies.

Besides the differences in the topics emphasized, the two lists felt very different. NG is robust, noisy, and inclusive, while WMST-L is very focused. The lists are also supported by different styles of software, a difference that affects their functionality and the organization of postings on the list. Both lists are used for spreading information (announcements, calls for papers, conferences, and jobs), but support very different kinds of interactions. Interaction on the lists, in the form of responses by other subscribers, makes visible a form of intersubjectivity, and is an aspect of the list that is especially suitable for ethnographic investigation (see Beaulieu, 2004; Hine, 2002). The two lists display different patterns of interactions; whereas NG has dynamics of connection and crystallization that support coalition politics and can sustain a wide diversity of topics, WMST-L encourages dynamics of participation and consolidation. This has implications for the scope of issues that can be supported by the list, and for the persistence of the knowledge generated in the space of the list (also discussed in the next section). The free-roaming, messy, and inclusive mode of NG was part of the reason why it felt nonacademic. This messiness made Beaulieu worry about whether she had a proper object of study, given her brief to study research and ICT.

Beaulieu realized that a properly "disciplined" mailing list was what she had been seeking and had found in WMST-L. Through sustained attention to the practices on the list and an exploration of the various connections and uses made of the list, the entwinement of disciplinarity and efficiency in this women's studies mailing list drew her attention and became an important subproject to her main fieldwork. Modernist approaches to knowledge, characterized as seeking out appropriate expertise for advice, and faith in instrumentalization, reliability, and predictability (Marshall, 2004, among others, can be found in the WMST-L (Beaulieu, 2005). WMST-L was configured to support modernist values about knowledge and technology. The contrast between the lists showed how mailing lists can take on divergent forms with different effects and status.

Infrastructures and Mailing Lists

Mailing lists depend on infrastructures to function, and some features of infrastructures constrain what can best be done on the list. To give one example, large-scale infrastructures have a shaping effect on on-list interactions, beyond decisions of individual list moderator or participants. This is because the internet, as a network, is set up to send packets of information with maximum efficiency. This means that the software running on the internet as a network does not privilege maintenance of the strict order of postings. Rather it privileges a relatively smooth flow of data over the whole network. A clear consequence of this for mailing lists is that internet protocols are not well-suited for discussions in which sequential turn-taking is important.

Also of great significance is the way digital technologies can merge or be distinguished from each other on the internet. We noted in an earlier section that it is important to understand how mailing lists are used distinctly from other technologies, and why, for example, one might wish to circumvent the public stage of the list by sending a personal e-mail. It can be extremely relevant to explore lists beyond what results in the operations supported by listserv software. Such a broader view makes visible the creative and productive work done around the list.

There are also instances where lists are deeply embedded in, rather than distinguished from, other applications. In the case of WMST-L, analysis of the list shows how it sustains sharing, debating, and spreading of knowledge. However, through the use of web-based technologies, the list also serves a role in the consolidation of knowledge. While a number of elements in WMST-L seem continuous with fairly traditional debates (scholarship versus politics) or display the usual expectations of computerization movements (Hine, 2006), novel forms of interaction are also visible around WMST-L. One of these practices is the consolidation of postings to the list, in order to form a "file," and making this resource available on a web site related to the list. Such files draw together the material and discussions that have arisen on the list in relation to a particular topic or discussion. The various contributions are brought together so as to constitute a resource, but the contributions are not seamlessly merged, so that the file retains some of the multi-vocality of list interactions.

This is therefore a very potent intersection of web and mailing list applications, where two very different forms reinforce and complement each other. By posting such files on the web as discrete units on a theme, they also become more visible than the list archives and more likely to serve as a resource for research or teaching.

This particular form, files derived from a list and posted to the web, is also interesting in the way it brings together consolidation (an aspect of formal communication) with distributed expertise and individual voices (an aspect of informal communication), in order to create a novel kind of authoritative knowledge that is situated in a discussion (a type of knowledge valued in women's studies). Furthermore, the files are treated as authoritative without claiming to be definitive. When similar debates arise at different times and subscribers engage in the debate, (rather than respond with a "pointer," asking the poster to look at the file on the web site), the moderator will add these later threads to the existing file, indicating that they are another episode in the discussion. This practice constitutes a very rich source for analysis of developments in the field[1] and of the history of the list.

In turn, the files are often referred to in discussions on the list, as a resource to be drawn upon or renewed by reviving the discussion. In this respect, the list can be conceptualized as a persistent conversation that is laid on top of the archive, a spot of e-mail interactivity embedded in the web. As such, it is an interesting mix of the traditional modern investment in the archive and a late modern focus on the importance of conversation, communication, and remediation. Constant talk on the list and the related creation of resources supports modernist investments in canons and archives, while a great deal of the visibility and usefulness of these archives is contingent on a particular conversation, enabled by networks. It would be interesting to explore whether this element of contingency, and the subsequent tension with efforts of consolidation, exist in other fields where new practices around ICT are developing.

Such interactions between kinds of applications and their relation to infrastructure highlight the importance of the way mailing lists associate with and distance themselves from other kinds of digitals tools, and the work involved in doing so.

Social Dynamics in Mailing Lists

As has been reflected from several perspectives, social life on a mailing list is shaped by ongoing negotiations of positions and boundaries. Multiple elements shape group dynamics and participation in a list can have multiple meanings. It is not the case, for example, that all subscribers experience this access to a list as membership of a "community." Certain boundaries affecting social dynamics pertain to a set of "ground rules" outlined by the list owner, while others are more subtle, ongoing discussions of mailing list practice, relevant topics, specific behaviors, etc. When the SCAN-BC-LIST started out in 1999 on the ACOR server, it took the example of the large American breast cancer mailing list hosted with ACOR. The SCAN-BC-LIST owner had been a member of the American list during the initial stages of her own breast cancer treatment and wanted to take up the concept as a model for the Scandinavian list. The limited set of ground rules she set up copied the American example to a great extent and dealt with positioning the list as a space for open, nonreligious, nonpolitical discussion on breast cancer issues. These rules were meant to encourage a sincere discussion in a well-mannered tone of writing.

The founding members of SCAN-BC-LIST, beside the list owner, were women with breast cancer. They had come together through writing in the Guest book on the personal web site of the list owner, a site that she had made to tell her personal story of breast cancer with the hope that the experience could be useful to others in a similar situation. Other women had started commenting on her story in the Guest book at the site, and a small group of five women decided to start up a Scandinavian mailing list for discussing breast cancer. The woman who owned the web site and had experience with the American breast cancer mailing list became the list owner and was also the one doing the work to establish the list on the internet and the ACOR server. She thus gained a key position, but also a position that would not remain uncontested by the other women in the "founding" group who all felt a certain kind of ownership and had a stake in defining the founding history. With time, as the number of members on the list increased, negotiations of the right to define the list's socially desirable practices became increasingly common.

An example is the incident described above, where the list owner excluded the widowed husband of a former list member. Some members on the list openly disputed this decision, and in a series of posts, raised a discussion challenging of the right of the list owner to make such decisions "on behalf of the group." The list owner categorically countered such challenges by referring to her "founding" right, stressing that the list was not a community with democratic rights. With time though, the list owner became increasingly fed up with such disputes. Issues of governance can, therefore, be the object of negotiation and tension: who has the right to pose which actions can be contested, especially when such actions have consequences for the list, or when they are undertaken in the name of the list. The breast cancer lists exemplify one way in which such discussions can take place. Other lists differ; for example, NextGenderation uses a consensus model.

As an unrelated major life event occurred in the life of the list owner, she decided it was time for her to move on and invest her time and energy in other matters. She discussed this off the list by e-mail and telephone with several long-time group members before she openly wrote her decision as a post on the list. Her decision to quit the list became a major event in the life of the mailing list and several participants tried to persuade her not to leave. From the discussions on the list, there was a feeling that the list was in need of a new leader.

The other most active member on the mailing list at that point, besides the list owner, was a woman who was part of the "founding" group. She was the most obvious "heir" to the list ownership because of her strong commitment to the discussion on the list. However, for reasons that shall not be discussed here, the list owner did not want to leave the list to her and transfer the ownership of the list hosted with ACOR. It was therefore agreed between the two women that the list should instead migrate from ACOR to a new space. The new list owner chose Yahoo! Groups as the new host. The list owner explained this plan of migration to the members of the list in a post and described a transition period that allowed members to move their membership to the new list before the old list closed, allowing time for less active members to get the message as well.

The new list started out 5½ years after the start up of SCAN-BC-LIST. The new list carried the new but related name Scan-bc-listen, adding a Danish ending (-en) to the word "list," and hereby transforming it from an English to a Danish word. This clearly reframed the new list within a more Danish context, which emphasized a tendency building up over the last years on the old list that more Danish women and less women from other Scandinavian countries used the list.

What further occurred in the course of migration and transformation of the list was a repositioning of external boundaries. As explained above, the SCAN-BC-LIST was open to all persons with an interest in breast cancer. The presentation of the mailing list specifically mentioned that persons with a professional interest in breast cancer (physicians, nurses, patient advocates, etc.) were welcome on the list. Scan-bc-listen, however, drew new boundaries and the new list owner decided to present the list as a space open to women with an experience of breast cancer, hereby excluding further participation of professionals, researchers, and also of men with breast cancer. (Høybye was specifically invited though to join the new list, despite her lack of a personal breast cancer experience due to her long-term involvement with the list.) This is in line with Hine's observation that discursive practices can be used in boundary making between specialists (women with breast cancer, in this case) and outsiders (Hine, 2002). Yet, lists do not only create boundaries between inside and outside, subscriber and nonsubscriber. As illlustrated by this episode, the social landscape of the list itself is highly differentiated, on the basis of "ownership," commitment over time, and personal history. Mailing lists, therefore, cannot automatically be assumed to represent egalitarian communities. The basis for membership is also something that can shift fairly radically, and in a number of ways, as discussed in this example: through "technical" choices of a server, changes in regulations about list membership, and linguistic presentation of a list's title. Finally, as we have seen from the episode where events unrelated to the list (in the owner's life) had a big impact on the list itself, mailing lists have their own dynamics, without being isolated from the other social spheres of subscribers and owners.

Conclusion and Future Directions

We hope to have shown that mailing lists become configured in particular ways in different contexts. As such, this material demonstrates the variety of meanings that a mailing list can have and the number of different ways a mailing list can be used. This richness would be lost if technological determinism guided research, and it would be misguided to consider that mailing lists create automatically or even sustain particular modes of communication, such as pluralistic and participatory spheres. While mailing lists might provide new modes of participation and interaction, it is also the case that technologies do not spontaneously create social relations and do not necessarily carry values with them.

We have also shown, however, that some features of technology do orient users to certain actions (e.g., how the possibility of turn-taking on a mailing list is shaped by packet routing on the internet). Infrastructure and technology are certainly important elements of mailing lists, but they are not the main determinant for their use.

Working with mailing lists has a number of consequences for the researcher and can shift research practices in various ways. First, and perhaps most visibly, mailing lists constitute new sources for empirical investigations. As such, they can be usefully contextualized in a number of ways by the research—whether in terms of other modes of mediated communication, as alternatives to (or in combination with) face-to-face communication, or as a source of information and sociality that has particular or unique features. Mailing lists are also significant in their relation to other technologies and sources: hyperlinks, archives, face-to-face meetings, and related web pages can all intersect with mailing lists. This means that boundaries have to be drawn around the object of study, a necessary part of all social research. Yet, the study of digital tools and settings seems to be accompanied by much concern for this particular issue (Beaulieu, 2004; Hine, 2009). An important question is therefore why does it seem to be more difficult to draw boundaries around an object like a mailing list than around other complex, embedded notions like "a family" or "an election"? One answer might be that objects like mailing lists, because they are mediated, show more clearly that they are linked to other phenomena. Yet, this argument would also apply to other mediated intersections, such as a book, whose footnotes also potentially take the researcher toward other sites of investigation. Another answer would be the status of such objects as emerging research technologies, for which conventions may not yet be stable and in which boundaries may not yet be taken for granted. As a result, there is a lack of common sense or tacit agreement about these objects and about what counts as their proper boundaries. Ideally, though, the question would be posed in productive rather than anxious terms, and would direct researchers to be aware of the multiple ways they constitute their objects and of the consequences of this for their research. If too much worry about whether new technologies can be (part of) objects of study can be paralyzing, too much complacency about what constitutes a mailing list is another danger.

As we discussed in the introduction, for most scholars, mailing lists are probably already part of their practice. Mailing lists are often used as a tool for orientation, when seeking to become familiar with a new field. Researchers often spend time lurking on a list before formally embarking on a project that involves the list. Such lurking shapes our expectations of settings and should be reflected upon as a formative part of research. Furthermore, it is highly likely that researchers involved in projects that do not focus primarily on mailing lists will still encounter them in the course of their research. Mailing lists then serve as tools of peripheral awareness for researchers in the field and their role in orienting research should be noted, even when they are not the main objects of research.

The seeming mundaneness of mailing lists has further consequences. Not only do researchers tend to take them for granted, but they are also widely neglected and undervalued by ICT departments, by administration of universities, and by computer science researchers. It is often assumed that nothing more than a server is needed to run a list. Yet mailing lists can have thousands of subscribers, and while a number of functions such as registration and password support have been developed, there is still the need for human intervention to smooth out problems between users and systems. Many lists also rely on moderators who aim to enhance the functioning or quality of the list by maintaining their focus and/or limiting the noise on the list. Such labor is rarely recognized, let alone supported and rewarded. Furthermore, university policies about archiving of e-mail or limits to (kinds of) traffic often do not take into account what consequences they might have on uses and users of mailing list.

In the area of visualization research, however, innovative approaches to lists are much more visible. Work on mapping "very large scale conversations" by Warren Sack (2000) and more recent work of the Sociable Media group at MIT (http://smg.media.mit.edu/) on visualization of interaction is especially promising. By drawing on the contents and features of mediated interactions, new representations of lists become possible, offering new ways of exploring discussions or of finding patterns of interactions. Such developments have great potential to enhance mailing lists for both users and researchers, and offer interesting avenues for exploring mailing lists and developing new ways of using them. In spite of any innovations that might arise, what remains crucial in using mailing lists for research is to consider their context and specificity. As we have shown, mailing lists vary in the ways they are used, depending on the context in which the list is made to function—from the highly public to the highly restricted—and from the nearly unidirectional to the highly interactive. Furthermore, lists tend to function at the intersection of other technologies such as web sites and e-mail, a trend that is likely to grow as applications are built to allow contributions to flow from one platform to another (e-mail to twitter to blog, etc.). For this reason, the specific configuration of a list must always be taken as an important point of inquiry in any research project. By paying attention to both context and specificity, the mailing list as tool and object of research can be well matched to the problems to be investigated in a research project.

Note

1. For example, a debate about naming departments and degrees "women's studies" versus "gender studies" is archived in five instalments, dating from 1994, 1998, 2002, 2005, and 2008, http://research.umbc.edu/korenman/wmst/womvsgen.html.

References

Bakardjieva, M., & Feenberg, A. (2001). Involving the virtual subject. *Ethics and Information Technology, 2*, 233–240.

Barjak, F. (2006). The role of the Internet in informal scholarly communication. *Journal of the American Society for Information Science and Technology, 57*, 1350–1367.

Beaulieu, A. (2004). Meditating ethnography: Objectivity and the making of ethnographies of the Internet. *Social Epistemology, 18*, 139–164.

Beaulieu, A. (2005). Next generation e-science? Women's studies and the Internet. Paper presented at the Internet Research 6.0: Internet generations, October 5–9, Chicago, United States of America.

Beaulieu, A. (2009). Review of *Internet inquiry: Conversations about method*, Resource Center for Cyberculture Studies, (accessed on June 16) http://rccs.usfca.edu/booklist.asp.

Beaulieu, A., & Wouters, P. (2009). E-research as intervention. In Jankowski, N. (Ed.), *E-research: Transformations in scholarly practice*. New York: Routledge.

Beaulieu, A. (2010). From co-location to co-presence: Shifts in the use of ethnography for the study of knowledge. *Social Studies of Science, 40* (3), 453–470.

Bodourides, M. A., Mavrikakis, M. & Vasileiadou, E. (2002). Email thread, genres and networks in a project mailing list. Paper presented at Association of Internet Researchers International Conference, October 13–16, in Maastricht, The Netherlands. (Available at http://aoir. org/?page_id=106).

Brown, C. (2001). The role of computer-mediated communication in the research process of music scholars: An exploratory investigation. *Information Research, 6,* (online).

Cubbison, L. (1999). Configuring listserv, configuring discourse. *Computers and Composition, 16,* 371–381.

Fry, J. (2006). Coordination and control of research practices across scientific fields: Implications for a differentiated e-science. In Hine, C. (Ed.), *New infrastructure for knowledge production: Understanding e-science* (pp. 167–188). London: IDEA Group.

Gooden, R. J., & Winefield, H. R. (2007). Breast and prostate cancer online discussion boards: A thematic analysis of gender differences and similarities. *Journal of Health Psychology, 12,* 103–114.

Guy, E. (2000). Classification and participation: Issues in a study of an Internet mailing list. Paper presented at Workshop W4 on Classification Schemes in CooperativeWork, (CSCW 2000), December 2–6, in Philadelphia.

Hastrup, K. (1992). Out of anthropology: The anthropologist as an object of dramatic representation. *Cultural Anthropology, 7,* 327–345.

Hastrup, K. (1994). Anthropological knowledge incorporated. In Kirsten, H., & Hervik, P. (Eds.), *Social experience and anthropological knowledge* (pp. 224–240). London: Routledge.

Hine, C. (2002). Cyberscience and social boundaries: The implications of laboratory talk on the Internet. *Sociological Research Online, 7,* U79–U99.

Hine, C. (2006). Computerization movements and scientific disciplines: The reflexive potential of new technologies. In Hine, C. (Ed.), *New infrastructure for knowledge production: Understanding e-science* (pp. 26–47). London: Idea Group.

Hine, C. (2007). Connective ethnography for the exploration of e-science. *Journal of Computer Mediated Communication, 12*(2) (January 2007), (accessed on June 16, 2009) http://wwww. jcmc.indiana.edu/vol12/issue2/hine.html.

Hine, C. (2009). How can qualitative Internet researchers define the boundaries of their projects? In Markham, A., & Baym, N. (Eds.), *Internet inquiry: Conversations about methods* (pp. 1–20). Thousand Oaks, CA: Sage.

Høybye, M. T., Johansen, C., & Tjørnhøj-Thomsen, T. (2005). Online interaction: Effects of storytelling in an Internet breast cancer support group. *PsychoOncology, 14,* 211–220.

Høybye, M. T. (n.d.). Armchair anthropology revisited: Engaging in social experience on the Internet.

Ingold, T. (2000). The perception of the environment: Essays on livelihood, dwelling and skill. London: Routledge.

Kling, R., McKim, G., & King, A. (2003). A bit more to IT: Scholarly communication forums as socio-technical interaction networks. *Journal of the American Society for Information Science and Technology, 54,* 47–67.

Korenman, J. & Wyatt, N. (1996). Group dynamics in an e-mail forum. In Herring, S. (Ed.), *Computer-mediated communication: Linguistic, social and cross-cultural perspectives* (pp. 225–242). Amsterdam/Philadelphia: John Benjamins Publishing.

Korenman, J. (1999). Email forums and women's studies: The example of wmst-l. In Hawthorne, S. & Klein, R. (Eds.), *Cyberfeminism: Connectivity, critique, creativity* (pp. 80–97). North Melbourne: Spinifex.

Marshall, J. (2004). The online body breaks out: Asence, ghosts, cyborgs, gender, polarity and politics. *Fibreculture,* (3) (accessed on June 16, 2009) http://journal.fibreculture.org/issue3/issue3_marshall.html.

Matzat, U. (2001). *Social networks and cooperation in electronic communities. A theoretical-empirical analysis of academic communication and Internet discussion groups.* Amsterdam: Thela Publisher.

Merleau-Ponty, M. (1964). Eye and mind. In Merleau-Ponty, M. & Edie, J. M. (Eds.), *The primacy of perception, and other essays on phenomenological psychology, the philosophy of art, history and politics*. Evanston: Northwestern University Press[AB15].

Paolillo, J. (1999). The virtual speech community: Social network and language variation on IRC. *Journal of Computer-Mediated Communication*, 4(4) (June), (accessed on June 16, 2009) http://jcmc.indiana.edu/vol4/issue4/paolillo.html.

Sack, W. (2000). Conversation map: An interface for very-large-scale conversations. *Journal of Management Information Systems*, *17*, 73–92.

Sandaune, A-G. (2008). The challenge of fitting in: Non-participation and withdrawal from an online self-help group for breast cancer patients. *Sociology of Health and Illness*, *30*, 131–144.

Schaap, F. (2002). *The words that took us there: Ethnography in virtual ethnography*. Amsterdam: Aksant Academic Publishers.

Seale, C., Ziebland, S., & Charteris-Black, J. (2006). Gender, cancer experience Internet use: A comparative keyword analysis of interviews and online cancer support groups. *Social Science and Medicine*, *62*, 2577–2590.

Sierpe, E. (2000). Gender and technological practice in electronic discussion lists: An examination of JESSE, the library/information science education forum. *Library & Information Science Research*, *22*, 273–289.

Sierpe, E. (2005). Gender distinctiveness, communicative competence, and the problem of gender judgments in computer-mediated communication. *Computers in Human Behavior*, *21*, 127–145.

Sooryamoorthy, R., & Shrum, W. (2007). Does the Internet promote collaboration and productivity? Evidence from the scientific community in South Africa. *Journal of Computer Mediated Communication*, *12*(2) (July), (accessed on June 16, 2009) http://jcmc.indiana.edu/vol12/issue2/sooryamoorthy.html.

Steinmueller, E. (2000). Will information and communication technology improve the "codification of knowledge"? *Industrial and Corporate Change*, *9*, 361–376.

Sveningsson, E. M. (2009). How do various notions of privacy influence decisions in qualitative Internet research? Responses by Elizabeth Buchanan and Stern, Susannah. In Markham, A., & Baym, N. (Eds.), *Internet inquiry: Conversations about methods*. Thousand Oaks, CA: Sage.

Talja, S., Savolainen, R., & Maula, H. (2004). Field differences in the use and perceived usefulness of scholarly mailing lists. *Information Research*, *10*(1) (accessed in March 2009) http://informationr.net/ir/10–1/paper200.html.

Thomsen, S. R., Straubhaar, J. D., & Bolyard, D. M. (1998). Ethnomethodology and the study of online communities: Exploring the cyber streets. *Information Research*, *4*(1) (July), (accessed in June 2009) http://informationr.net/ir/4–1/paper50.html.

VKS. (2007). Messy shapes of knowledge-STS explores informatization, new media, and academic work. In Hackkett, E., Amsterdamska, O., Lynch, M., & Wajcman, J. (Eds.), *The handbook of science and technology studies* (3rd ed.) (pp. 319–351). Cambridge, MA: MIT Press.

Walsh, J. (1996). Computer networks and scientific work. *Social Studies of Science*, *26*, 661–703.

Chapter 12

Online Data Collection and Data Analysis Using Emergent Technologies

Michael Dal

Introduction

During the last decade or so, the collection and handling of quantitative research data has undergone considerable changes. Along with the development of better hardware and software, new techniques and methods have been introduced to aid research in different areas. In quantitative research schemes where the investigator aims to determine the relationship between independent and dependent variables in a population, new computer techniques have made it possible and easy to implement online data collection. This method is currently emerging and becoming more and more common for conducting surveys for both academic and commercial purposes.

What Is Online Data Collection?

Before we discuss the advantages and disadvantages of using online data collection in further detail, it is necessary to define what we exactly refer to when using this term. First of all, online data collection must be understood simply as a quantitative research method. A descriptive quantitative study is characterized as measuring things as they are. The measuring is typically done through surveys, and in the theoretical literature on research methods it is also often referred to as *survey research* (i.e., Creswell, 2003).

All theoretical literature on quantitative research methods agrees that quantitative research should be divided into two types of studies (1) *experimental* and (2) *nonexperimental research* (Gall, Gall, & Borg, 2007; McMillan, 2008). Experimental studies are sometimes also known as repeated-measure studies and often involve intervention, because the researchers do more than just observe subjects (Gay, Mills, & Airasian, 2006). Nonexperimental studies are also called observational because the researcher observes subjects without intervening. Online data collection belongs to the latter category of nonexperimental quantitative research often used to assay variables of interest in quantitative studies.

A definition of online data collection that will work for our purposes in this chapter is that it is a method to be used in quantitative nonexperimental research that can be conducted in a descriptive, predictive, and explanatory manner and carried through as cross-sectional, longitudinal, or retrospective research.

Different Types of Online Data Collection

Using the Internet for organized research purposes is a relatively recent phenomenon. The first studies made over the Internet used a list server to publicize a brief, open-ended questionnaire. The response rate for this study was very limited and only few individuals returned suitably detailed responses (N<20) (Greguras & Stanton, 1996). The next step in digitalizing surveys was to develop programs that could analyze data that had been fed to the computer. Typically, the sample population was asked to fill in a survey that was published as part of a computer program and distributed through e-mail. The respondents then filled out the survey on their computers and sent it back to the researcher by e-mail. The researcher then had to manually register the results in a database, a process that has since been simplified.

The rapid development of the Internet and its overriding importance for communication and distribution of information has affected the methods of data collecting. Today it is much easier to collect data over the Internet, and online data collection is becoming more visible in different academic research areas.

Today we can generally distinguish between two types of online data collection: (1) collecting data from a Web site and (2) collecting data by sending out e-mail messages.

The first method refers to collecting data randomly from a Web site. This can be done if you have a site about a specific subject; the readers of the site are asked to take part in a survey about the discussed topic after reading about it. This method of collecting data can, however, be rather inaccurate. Collecting randomly on a Web site does not secure that the survey reaches all members of the possible population and this can result in sampling error. Using data collected randomly from a Web site can also involve coverage error. Thus, some units of the population may have no chance of taking part in the survey, some units may have multiple chances, and some units may not even qualify for the survey. Also, this method of collecting data excludes calculating a reliable response rate. Even if one uses a site-counter in order to know how many page-views a Web site has received, the researcher does not have the possibility of knowing how many people in fact have read the Web site and therefore belong to the potential population. Therefore, it is almost impossible to find out a reliable response rate because the researcher only has exact information about the numbers of participants of the survey. The response rate in most educational and social surveys is of importance because it gives the researcher a hint on the reliability of the results. However, in some survey studies the response rate has no or only minor importance.

One can conclude that using data collected randomly from a Web site does involve some serious limitations, as seen from a methodological point of view and this kind of data has a reduced reliability. The second type of online data collection is considered to be more reliable because it is based on sending out e-mail messages to a known or unknown target group. This method is based on inviting a sample population to take part in an online survey by e-mail, where the researcher introduces the survey and includes a link to the survey. This may help overcome the aforementioned potential sources of errors. The researcher chooses and demarcates the survey population beforehand and also decides what units of the population should be contacted. For example, if the researcher is conducting educational research, he or she decides whether the sample population would be a group of teachers or a group of students. Furthermore, it can be decided what specific subpopulation the survey should reach (teachers of science, foreign-language learning, etc.). Knowing the exact number of the sample population also makes it possible to calculate the response rate.

Today, it is rather easy to construct online surveys in the Hypertext Mark-up Language (HTML) by using common Web site programs, such as FrontPage, Web Expression, and Dreamweaver (Hester, 2001; Laahs, McKenna, & Vanamo, 2005; Leeds, 2009). However, surveys made in that way may not be particularly reliable because it can be difficult to register whether a respondent answers the survey more than one time if the survey is supposed to be anonymous. A more safe and reliable method is to use one of the many data collecting programs offered on the Internet such as Surveymonkey and Tric-Trac (Survey-Monkey.com, 2008; TricTrac, 2008). The use of these programs is mostly free of charge, unless you are going to conduct a bigger survey that involves over 300–400 respondents. In such cases, the researcher is offered use of the programs for a reasonable fee. One of the advantages of collecting data over the Internet is that the answers are automatically collected in a database and the researcher can fetch them at any time.

Other Digital Surveys and Polls

Online data collection today is not reserved only for the academic world. It is also frequently used to conduct surveys for commercial purposes. When surfing the Internet, we have probably all received a pop-up window asking us to fill out a questionnaire about the design of a Web site, our views on a certain matter, etc. If you engage in e-commerce or purchase things on the Internet, you will often be presented with a questionnaire on the product you have bought or information about the product. These kinds of surveys can be categorized as descriptive and cross-sectional and they are supposedly done to measure costumers' evaluations of a certain service and/or product for commercial purposes.

Today we also find short online surveys that aim to measure the population's point of view on certain controversial matters. These surveys are also referred to as interactive polls. The participants are asked to choose from two or three possibilities concerning views on a specific topic and by submitting the answer they get to see the total results of the poll. In the examples shown below, participants are asked about their opinion on the influence of politics on the tradition and symbolism of the Olympic torch and their attitude about whether racism or sexism is a bigger problem in the United States (Figure 12.1).

The reliability of interactive polls like this has been widely discussed. One of the main questions is: What is the motivation for the participants to take part in a poll like this? Besides expressing our own view on the presented topic, one can also simply be curious to see what the trend is concerning the topic presented. In that case, one tends not to answer the question from one's own conviction but just from a wish to see the result. Polls like this are also accused of shaping the population's opinion on "hot" issues, such as those of a political nature.

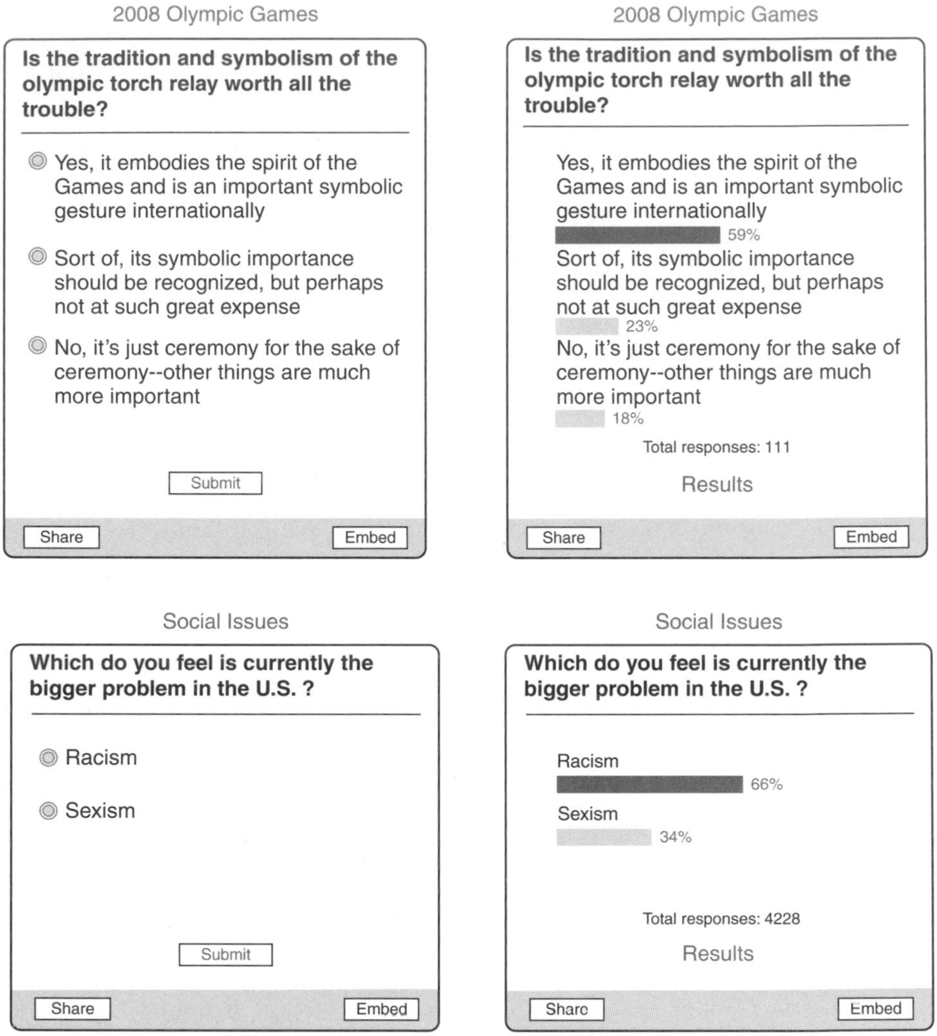

2008 Olympic Games

Is the tradition and symbolism of the olympic torch relay worth all the trouble?

◉ Yes, it embodies the spirit of the Games and is an important symbolic gesture internationally

◉ Sort of, its symbolic importance should be recognized, but perhaps not at such great expense

◉ No, it's just ceremony for the sake of ceremony--other things are much more important

Submit

Share   Embed

2008 Olympic Games

Is the tradition and symbolism of the olympic torch relay worth all the trouble?

Yes, it embodies the spirit of the Games and is an important symbolic gesture internationally
59%
Sort of, its symbolic importance should be recognized, but perhaps not at such great expense
23%
No, it's just ceremony for the sake of ceremony--other things are much more important
18%

Total responses: 111

Results

Share   Embed

Social Issues

Which do you feel is currently the bigger problem in the U.S. ?

◉ Racism

◉ Sexism

Submit

Share   Embed

Social Issues

Which do you feel is currently the bigger problem in the U.S. ?

Racism
66%
Sexism
34%

Total responses: 4228

Results

Share   Embed

Figure 12.1 Example of an interactive poll.

Interactive polls have also developed into more sophisticated polls where the participants can assess a product or an opinion and also provide their own comment on the matter in question. Such polls are becoming more and more popular to use with products found on the Internet. An example of this is found on the site for the cartoon Wulfmorgenthaler (Wulffmorgenthaler ApS, 2008). For every cartoon strip, the readers are urged to rate and comment on it (Figure 12.2).

The example shown below has been rated with 9 stars out of 10 and has been commented on 265 times. Some of the comments are shown underneath the cartoon strip.

Data can be collected online in different ways and for different purposes. But what are the advantages and disadvantages of using online data collection? This question will be discussed in the following paragraphs.

JUNE 9TH, 2008

CURRENT RATING: PURE AND BEAUTIFUL
★★★★★★★★★☆

COMMENTS (265)

anna from Sweden
August 29, 2008

This is the best strip ever.. it's priceless :D

Thank you, you'r great, keep up the good work!!

eddie from Canada
August 29, 2008

Man some people take political correctness just way to far. lighten up it's a comic and its funny.
i'm hooked on these comics they have a great twisted sense of humour .

fpk from China
August 24, 2008

To all those who think this is not a joke about women wearing a burka:
I dare to disagree. The joke is very much about the burka-lady, I think.

And to those who think this is discrimination or even racism:
Everybody should have the right to be mocked. It would be discrimination if some were excluded from this great cltural achievement.

Cheer up a little!

fpk from China
August 24, 2008

To all those who think this is not a joke about women wearing a burka:
I dare to disagree. The joke is very much about the burka-lady, I think.

And to those who think this is discrimination or even racism:

RATE HERE

WORLD CLASS

∧
- A MIRACLE
- PURE AND BEAUTIFUL
- UNFORGETTABLE JEWEL
- I ACCEPT IT
- TRULY OKAY
- JUST BELOW AVERAGE
- NOT GOOD ENOUGH, FOOL?!
- IT SUCKS SO MUCH!
- WORST CREATION EVER
- NOOOOOOOOOOOO!
∨

NO CLASS   RATE

Figure 12.2 Example of an interactive poll with comments.

Reasons for Using Online Data Collection

Data collection with paper-and-pencil methods has frequently been used in social and educational research. Targeting, for example, schools and their constituents with paper-and-pencil surveys has proven to be very efficient because the researcher is typically secured a rather high response rate, around 80–90%.

Over the years, it has become much more difficult to obtain data from workplaces and schools; some organizations simply have an official policy that prohibits its employees or its student and teacher population to take part in time-intensive paper-and-pencil surveys during work or school time unless it has a purpose that directly benefits the organization. A leader from one upper secondary school reported that during one term, the school was asked to take part in more than 30 paper-and-pencil surveys; each survey took an average of 15 min to fill out and time intended for teaching was used for survey purposes.

Using Web-based data collection partly would solve this problem, because then the response process would not take valuable time from teaching or work, because it typically would be done in the respondents' spare time.

In a nonexperimental, retrospective, and descriptive study of teachers' assessment literacy (Mertler, 2003), a population of 197 teachers in the United Kingdom were randomly split into two groups: one group received a paper-and-pencil version of a survey and the other group a Web-based version of the same survey. The object of the research was to find out how traditional and Web-based delivery modes compare. The paper-and-pencil group was asked to participate in the survey by mail, whereas the Web-based group received an e-mail message containing the same letter and a link to the survey. It is reported that the most common reason for nonresponse among teachers in the paper-and-pencil group was that they did not have the time to respond. Many teachers simply indicated that their schedules at school were too busy to permit them to do any "extra things."

The teachers belonging to the Web group did not make the same complaint, but instead some of the teachers belonging to this group complained that they simply not could open the survey. When encountered with a hyperlink that did not work, the respondents were apparently unaware that the URL could be copied and pasted into a browser window; they simply gave up and did not try further to access the survey. Today, we have a tendency to believe that everyone is technologically literate, knows about browsers, and can surf painlessly on the Internet. This example indicates that not all individuals are literate in this sense.

However, technology today is a very integrated part in all parts of society and our lifestyle and is getting to be a "natural" component in our daily life, and as such it is getting to be more usual to contact and communicate through the Web. In fact, young people today regard paper-and-pencil surveys as "old fashioned" and rather outdated (Lefever, Dal, & Matthiasdottir, 2007).

In the wake of developing the Internet into an important place for communication, one can argue that it has also become a more natural setting for presenting surveys, just as telephones were in the past.

Besides being a natural and modern media, the Web also ensures fast access to the survey. Another advantage is that the use of Web-based surveys protects against missing and miswriting data because the data are directly uploaded. The researcher also has direct access to the data through the Web. Also, there is the question of cost benefit. The avoidance of postage costs makes it much cheaper to carry out a Web-based survey than a paper-and-pencil survey.

Reliability and Response Rate of Online Web Surveys

The main question about the difference of using an online survey or a paper-and-pencil survey lies in whether the former is as reliable and effective as the latter. To date, only a few studies have discussed this question. Some researchers have devoted attention to developing and testing different aspects of Internet survey methodology. These studies focus on, among other things, the research process as it pertains to sampling and comparing response rate. Response rates as low as 30% have been considered reasonable in self-completed postal or mail surveys made for paper-and-pencil (Saunders, Lewis, & Thornhill, 2003).

On the other hand, it is reported that most virtual surveys in 1999 showed a response rate as low as 15–29% (Comley, 2003). Yet other research studies from the same year report that Web surveys often have a response rate from 25–60% (Matz, 1999). How high a response rate you get depends very much on the subject of the surveys and the sample population. In a comparative study of computer-assisted and paper-and-pencil self-administered questionnaires in a survey on smoking, alcohol, and drug use done by Debra Wright and her research team in 1998, the authors conclude that their findings support the notion that a Web-supported survey and a paper-and-pencil survey yield similar estimates of sensitive information in self-report data collection with adolescent and young adult respondents. The authors argue furthermore that computerized self-administered surveying may hold particular promise for surveying and interviewing children and adolescents about highly sensitive issues, because this group has a high level of comfort with computers (Wright, Aquilino, & Supple, 1998, p. 351).

The above mentioned research results are all of rather old date. Newer research reveals that using online surveys is becoming more common and more efficient. Today, different methods of collecting data online are being used. Schillewaert and Meulemeester (2005) did a study on comparing response distributions of off-line and online data collections methods. Respondents were recruited in four different ways, by traditional mail, e-mail, telephone, and Internet pop-ups. E-mail contact was the first method used to contact the sample population. Three hundred of the possible respondents were sent an e-mail with a general explanation of the survey topics and including a link to a Web site. This method generated 152 responses, which equals a response rate of almost 51%. Secondly, a pop-up was activated on a high traffic Web site over a period of 3 days. If a visitor was willing to participate, he or she could click through to an online questionnaire. This method generated a sample of 291 responses. Thirdly, mail surveys containing official letterhead and prepaid envelopes were sent to 707 participants. These letters generated 219 completed questionnaires, equaling a response rate of 31%. Finally, a sample of 400 people was contacted by telephone, which generated a response rate of 35% or 140 responses. The study as a whole ended up with a sample of 801 valid responses from a total population of about 1700 persons. The numbers in the study indicate that Web-supported survey methods today result in better response rates than more traditional survey methods.

Time Management and the Range of Surveys

To carry out a paper-and-pencil survey involves a number of resources. First of all, the researcher has to make copies of the survey and often it is costly to distribute the questionnaires because it is either done by mail requiring stamps—or by sending out personnel to supervise the data collection. When the data has been collected, the researcher must use time and often also money to let assistants convert the collected data into a digital form. These features do not apply to online data collection and therefore it is less costly because of the low cost distribution over e-mail, the Internet or Web panel, and the automatic collection of the results into a database. Besides being less costly, online surveys also tend to be more accurate, because there are only very limited risks for making typing errors in the process of recording the data. The recording is only done by the respondents themselves and no other persons are involved.

Provided that the technical expertise is present and that the computer is loaded with the right software and connected to a reliable Internet connection, Web surveys certainly are more expedient and less time consuming to use for both the researcher and the sample population. Also, the participation in a Web survey is not bound to time and location because participants can approach a Web survey when it is convenient for them as long as they have access to a computer connected to the Internet. A positive consequence of this is that it is rather easy to gather data from a larger geographic area. In the European research project *DIVIS-digital video streaming and multilingualism* (Dal, Hottmann, & Sassen, 2008), a Web survey was launched for participants in 15 European countries. The project was a cross-sectional and descriptive study of how much language teachers use video production in foreign-language classes. The survey was open over a 2-week period. During that period, 514 foreign-language teachers responded to the request for participation in the survey. The number of responses was satisfactory for the purpose of the survey and an assessment of the participation later revealed that it probably would have been difficult to get the same number of participation by using the paper-and-pencil method within the same timeframe. The DIVIS-survey is thus a good example of how online data collection makes it easier to gather a large amount of data over a larger geographical area within a rather short time frame.

In many cases, the target population is unknown to the researcher, but in those cases where the target group is well defined and known to the investigator it is extremely easy to implement Web surveys for different purposes. This is often done within bigger organizations and institutions to measure employees' attitudes toward different matters concerning the workplace. As such, surveys of this type have developed into some kind of a tool for democracy on workplaces. If there exist differences of opinion on certain matters concerning the workplace, management has the possibility of sending out a survey covering the issues in order to explore the ruling opinion among the staff. The results of such surveys can then be considered in decision making. The same would apply to a group of known customers or users of certain products.

Difficulties in Using Online Data Collection

Web surveys can be applied in different research areas with great benefit because of their effectiveness, and there can be little doubt that the number of surveys being conducted over the Web is increasing dramatically (Witt, 1998). But collecting data online also involves some limitations and difficulties. Ethical matters are one of the issues that the researcher should be aware of.

In a cross-sectional and explanatory study on the use of information and communication technology in teaching and learning in upper secondary schools in Iceland (Lefever et al., 2007), the researchers report that some ethical questions arose from the use of a Web-based survey. To reach the sample population, the research team decided to collect student and teacher e-mail addresses from school authorities. A request of participation was then sent out by e-mail to 8,000 students and over 400 teachers. Some respondents reacted with aggravation to the request because they thought of the e-mail as spam. Some participants wanted to know how the research team had got hold of their e-mail address and indicated that they felt that the e-mail address was their own personal property and should therefore not be used to put forward a request of this nature without being asked beforehand. The official position of the school authorities was, however, that the student and the teacher e-mail accounts were the property of the institutions, and as the research team had obtained permission from the relevant authorities, the request of participation was looked upon as a legal request. However, the question of privacy and ownership of e-mail accounts is under constant debate within several sectors of society and should, therefore, be carefully considered when collecting e-mail addresses to be used in Web surveys.

Other researchers (Carbonaro & Bainbridge, 2000) point out the ethical importance of the Web survey having a built-in security system to ensure credibility and anonymity. If not, there is a danger that the respondents will not feel secure and confident in taking part in the survey. When dealing with online data collection, ethical issues are of great importance and concern to both those who sponsor the research and those who collect the data. Of course, the usual considerations for ethical treatment of participants apply. By large, these issues are simple enough to resolve, but there are some special concerns that should be addressed when conducting online research.

Informed consent is readily obtained by staging the survey so that the first page is formed as an information page and consent form rather than a part of the survey. When filling out a survey in paper-and-pencil format, the respondent will be asked to agree to the consent by signing the consent. With online surveys, it is not possible to get an actual signature, so the respondent will instead be confronted with an on-screen button saying "I agree," and by clicking this link the participants accepts the terms of the consent form and proceeds to the actual survey.

This way of agreeing and accepting the terms of consent could at first be seen as problematic. However, this format is widely used in lieu of a signature, for example, when entering credit card information online, or when accepting the terms of a software license prior to installation, so there are ample precedents for its use.

When filling out a hard copy of a survey, data confidentiality is typically achieved through some restriction such as "the data will be kept locked up and only accessible to the researcher." For an online data file, confidentiality is achieved in that the data are stored on a computer in a personal account that is accessible only to someone who knows the account user ID and password, which of course is just the researcher.

Anonymous participation is as important as ever. Respondents need to be informed of this component and should not have to provide any more personal information than is absolutely required for the research program. In general, the Web page software will log as header lines the IP address of the computer the respondent accessed the survey page from. The IP address is a code made up of numbers separated by three dots that identifies a particular computer on the Internet. But otherwise, only the demographic information the respondent explicitly enters will be stored. However, some of the domains associated with an IP address are personalized, and may provide too much identifying information. Therefore, it is a good idea to edit the data file periodically and erase these headers.

In an online survey, it is best not to ask for an e-mail address that will be stored in the main data file. Participants may, however, wish to be informed of the general results later, so the best way to accommodate this request is to transfer them from the survey page to a "thank-you" page, and on the latter have a place for them to enter an e-mail address that will go into a separate data file. In this way, the information in the survey has no direct connection to the e-mail address.

Treating the information given by the respondent as strictly confidential and guarding their privacy is one of the primary responsibilities of the researcher.

Some Common Sources of Errors

Groves (1989) identifies several potential sources of error that surveys need to overcome including (1) coverage error, (2) sampling error, (3) measurement error, and (4) nonresponse error. *Coverage error* refers to a situation where some units of a population may have no chance of selection, while other units may have multiple chances and some units may not even qualify for the survey. *Sampling error* refers to the result of only surveying a portion of the survey population rather than all of its members. *Measurement error* refers to inaccurate answers to questions and stem from poor question wording, poor interviewing, survey mode effects, and/or the answering behavior of the respondent. Finally, the *nonresponse error* refers to not getting some people in the sample to respond to a survey request. If they had done so, it would have provided a different distribution of answers than those who did respond to the survey.

Designing a survey with the aim of generalizing sample results to a defined population, means that all four sources of error must be kept low. A special emphasis on the reduction of one type of error will not typically compensate for ignoring other error sources.

When using Web surveys, it can seem easy to collect hundreds, thousands, or even tens of thousands of responses at virtually no cost, except for constructing and e-mailing the survey. This can encourage the researcher to think that the singular emphasis of increasing the numbers of respondents results in reduction of survey error. A necessary means of reducing sampling error is to increase the number of respondents. However, obtaining large numbers of completed questionnaires under the condition of letting anyone respond who wants to fill out the questionnaire does not necessarily prevent coverage error, and one cannot even calculate sampling error, since the underlying assumption behind the calculation requires knowledge about the probabilities of selection.

The main goal of respondent-friendly Web surveys is to decrease the occurrence of measurement and nonresponse error in surveys. That is why it is important that a Web survey is constructed in a manner that increases the likelihood that sampled individuals will respond to the survey request and that the respondents will do so accurately by answering each question in the manner intended by the researcher. The respondents must also be able to comprehend what is expected of them, know what actions are required for responding, and be motivated to take those actions. Questionnaire design features that are difficult to understand take excessive time for the respondents to figure out or embarrass people and are uninteresting to complete and decrease people's likelihood of responding to a Web survey. Therefore, it is of great importance that the researcher constructs a design that aims to present a questionnaire to respondents in such a way that each person to whom it is sent has an equal chance of receiving and responding to it.

Today, admittance to the Internet generally should not represent a problem. However, some people have more or less admittance to computers, and some have better software and are generally better at operating a computer than others. The researcher must have this in mind when constructing a respondent-friendly questionnaire. It is tempting to use colors, innovative question displays, split screens, embedded programs and applets, animation, a sound track, and other design features that are available today. These features, however, can negatively influence the response rate and increase the likelihood of nonresponse error.

Recently, the Gallup Organization conducted an experiment by comparing completion rates for two types of questionnaires. A questionnaire, which was labeled as "plain," used no graphics, was only presented in black print and white background, and placed answer categories in the traditional left-hand position used for most paper questionnaires. The other type of questionnaire, which was labeled "fancy," used bright colors with constantly changing background, HTML-tables etc.

The "fancy" questionnaire required more computer memory, which meant that the respondents with browsers that had less power were likely to spend a longer time receiving a questionnaire. Also, slower browsers were more likely to bring in the questionnaire with disabled response features or even become overloaded and crash.

The result of the experiment showed that the recipients of the "plain" version completed significantly more pages, more write-in boxes, and were less likely to quit before reaching the last page. It also took this group of recipients less time to complete the survey. A total of 93.1% of those who logged into the plain version completed all of it, whereas only around 80% of those entering the fancy version finished (Christian, 2003).

Due to these results, a respondent-friendly Web survey faces an unusual challenge. Instead of implementing the newest technology and designing at the cutting edge of modern technology, there seems to be a need to hold back on incorporation of advanced features and create simpler questionnaires that require less computer power.

Another area of concern regarding Web surveys is that of reliability and fraudulent respondents. This concern addresses the question of how one can ensure that respondents only answer the survey once. Additionally, the respondents can easily forward the survey to somebody else that does not belong to the demarcated sample population.

When constructing a Web survey with help from Web design programs such as Front-Page or Dreamweaver, it can be very difficult to build in the kind of security to protect against this fraud. In most of the available survey design programs, however, this problem has been taken care of by equipping the programs with some kind of a cookie control, where the program places a cookie in the respondent's computer when he or she has completed the survey. A cookie is a small string of text stored on a user's computer by a Web browser. A cookie consists of one or more name-value pairs containing bits of information such as an identifier for a server-based session, or other data used by Web sites. The cookie then prevents the respondent from answering the questionnaire again on the same computer. Another popular method is IP address control. This means that the program automatically registers the respondents' IP addresses and excludes a respondent if his or her IP address already has been registered. In other cases, the program operates as password-protected, where the respondents have to give up a password to enter the survey. Yet another method is based on java-script. JavaScript is a scripting language used to enable programmatic access to objects within other applications. It is primarily used in the form of client-side JavaScript for the development of dynamic Web sites. Some online survey programs have a piece of JavaScript that register the respondents' IP addresses and the program will then automatically exclude already registered IP addresses.

All these methods have some advantages and disadvantages. Let us assume that we have sent out an e-mail request to a sample population in an institution. If the employees in the institution do not have access to their own laptop or stationary computer, using cookie or IP address controls would then not be a preferable option because the computers would be excluded from the survey after the first user of the computer has completed the survey. Using password-protected surveys can also be disputable because of the question of anonymity. If a survey is password-protected, the researcher has to connect passwords to each participant and the answers could therefore be more easily traceable and endanger the credibility and anonymity of the survey. In other words, using these kinds of participation controls can involve some practical problems. In most cases, though, respondents operate from their own personal computer, especially if the request for participation in a survey is mailed to their personal e-mail.

The difficulties of using Web survey can also be of a technical nature. Lefever et al. (2007) discuss, among other things, external technical problems arising from the Internet service provided. Sending out a big number of e-mails can result in piling up messages because the sending and receiving servers cannot handle the volume of messages sent through the system. It can result in uncertainty as to whether the message has been delivered to the recipients. When sending out one and the same message to 8,000 recipients, it can in some ways be compared to send out insignificant junk mail, and it also presents a problem that e-mail messages announcing surveys frequently are interpreted as such. In such cases, there is a danger of the message being deleted without hesitation and/or automatically diverted to other folders by screening programs so the recipient does not see the message and therefore is unable to answer the survey. This can lead to sampling errors and uncertainty of the actual numbers of participants in the survey.

Collecting and using e-mail addresses can involve certain difficulties. It is important that the e-mail address is the one normally used by the recipient. Today, it is rather common that one person has more than one e-mail address. Some of the e-mail addresses registered to a person may, therefore, be inactive or only frequently used. This was the case in research conducted in Iceland (Lefever et al., 2007), where the student population was contacted by the e-mail addresses provided by the school authorities. In Iceland, the upper secondary schools provide students with e-mail addresses and those were the addresses the research team used to contact the students. It was evident, however, that students had more than one e-mail address and did not necessarily use the one provided by their school. Therefore, the e-mail message with the request for participation in the survey did not reach all the student respondents. This resulted in a sampling error, because the survey only reached a portion of the survey population rather than all the intended members. From this perspective, one can conclude that it can be difficult to obtain lists of participants. If the researcher does not have specific knowledge on the participating population, gathering e-mail addresses can present a problem, and instead of having a demarcated sample population, research must sometimes be based on volunteer sampling rather than probability sampling.

Volunteer sampling as opposed to probability sampling was the case in the DIVIS-research (Dal et al., 2008). The group of respondents was defined to be language teachers in Europe. This is a rather broad definition of the sampling population and it was not possible to collect e-mail addresses from all the involved European countries. It would have been rather time consuming and costly and the research did not demand a stringent probability sampling. Instead, the request for participation in the questionnaire was sent to professional organizations representing language teachers all over Europe and they were asked to forward the request through their post list for members. The participation was thus based on volunteer sampling, which is also reflected in the frequency of respondents from the different countries. In some cases, only 10 participants responded from one country; 80–90 people responded from other countries. That is why it is not, in this particular study, possible to make a contrastive analysis between the represented countries, and that was not the purpose of the survey. The research was cross-sectional and descriptive, and the main purpose was to get an idea of the extent to which students' video production is used in language teaching in Europe and whether language teachers wanted to use video as an active tool in their foreign-language classes.

The study, however, shows some of the problems arising when voluntary participation is implemented. If the respondents do not wish to complete the survey, they are free to "surf elsewhere." The fact is that the respondents do not feel any pressure to finish the survey. Participants in a survey tend to continue due to face-to-face social pressures, but that is not applicable when using an online version. If the respondents want to withdraw, they can do it without any further consequences. To overcome the danger of losing the respondents during the survey, the researchers in the DIVIS project discussed the possibility of rewarding participants by offering presents through a form of lottery. This was never carried through, but as long as participation in a survey is anonymous, withdrawal will be a perceived option by the participants.

Designing and Analyzing a Web Survey

When designing a Web survey, the surveyor must consider different aspects, ranging from what information should appear on the screen to what programming tools are used to present it. It is important to consider aspects such as the length of the questionnaire, the style of the first page, how the response boxes are placed, respondents' interest in the surveyed subject, and so on and so forth.

One of the first things that the survey constructor must have in mind is the front page of the survey. A potential respondent may be directed to the first page of a survey from a Web site or an e-mail request. In either case, it is important that the respondent knows that he or she has arrived to the right Web site. Therefore, it is important that there is a short introductory message on the first screen; it should not be loaded with all kinds of instructions on how to fill in the questionnaire or if the questionnaire is easy or difficult to participate in. It seems preferable just to bring a short message welcoming the participants to the survey.

In addition, the initial question tends to imply and define whether the questionnaire is easy or difficult to complete. The first question should be attention grabbing and confirm to the respondent that it is worthwhile to continue.

Another basic principle is that all questions should be presented in as simple a style as possible. If the survey is too complicated and difficult to work through, there is a risk of the respondents giving up the task and not completing the survey. The questions can be of different types. Most surveys operate with closed questions that can often be answered with *yes* or *no*, multiple choices, or having respondents agree or disagree with a statement on a level from 1 to 5 for example. If the surveyor uses open-ended questions, they are normally answered through written text. In either case, it is important to provide specific instructions on how to take each necessary computer action for responding to the questionnaire. For example, note that radio buttons require clicking an alternative button in order to erase a previous answer, while check boxes require a single click in order to erase them. Respondents may not know how to operate a scroll bar in order to see the entire question or the next questions. Some respondents may not know exactly what a drop-down menu is, how to access hidden categories or how open-ended answers are to be entered. Each of the techniques described above may be obvious to experienced computer users, but need to be explained to less experienced respondents.

One of the clear advantages of Web surveys is that, similar to interview surveys, respondents can be directed to skip several questions without being aware that it is happening. Asking respondents to scroll past questions they are not being asked to complete will probably increase frustration as well as errors. That is why a screen-by-screen construction technique is preferable. A Web questionnaire should be constructed in such a way that the respondents have a feeling of scrolling from question to question. If there is a need to skip questions, this should be done in such a way that the respondents are lead through to the question through different screens.

It is also an advantage if each question or a group of questions can be displayed within the area of a screen. When the number of answer choices or answers belonging to one and the same group exceeds the number that can be displayed on one screen, you should consider double-banking, that is continuing the line of questions on a new page, with appropriate navigational instructions being added.

Web surveys are, in most cases, under control of the respondent and can thus be categorized as a self-administered questionnaire. A type of question with a known defect in self-administered questionnaires is the so-called "check-all-that-apply" questions (Keysurvey.com, 2008). In this kind of question, the respondents are asked to check items from a long list. Research shows that one of the problems of using this kind of question is that participants often try to satisfy the surveyor by checking all or many answer choices until they think they have satisfactorily answered the question. In addition, the order of reading answer choices tends to bias responses in favor of the first categories (Weisberg, Bowen, & Krosnick, 1996; Presser, 2004). If one decides to use these kinds of questions, it is a good idea to require the respondent to make a certain number of selections or divide your answer choices with subheaders. Open-ended questions also often produce poor answers on self-administered surveys. The intention of using open-ended questions is to let the respondents get a chance to go into details about a certain subject. However, the literature on the subject suggests that respondents give rather incomplete answers and the researcher cannot use follow-up-probes (Jenkins & Dillman, 1997).

Analyzing a Web Survey

The results from a Web survey will be automatically gathered in a database that the constructor of a survey can access. A database of this kind can be saved in a text-file format that can be accessed through Notepad, Word, or other word processing programs. As such, it can be almost impossible to read and understand, but from there the data can easily be exported to a spreadsheet application and analyzed with conventional analyzing software such as SPSS (SPSS Inc., 2007). As soon as the data has been entered in the analytic software, the surveyor can deal with the data as he or she pleases. Having digitized information makes it easy to calculate the frequency for each of the questions, the ratio, and the correlation between different questions, and it is easy to cross tab. It is not within the frame of this chapter to go thoroughly into the different analyzing methods of surveys. There already exists literature, both old and newer, that thoroughly deals with this subject (Gay et al., 2006; Gall et al., 2007; Johnson & Christensen, 2008).

If a researcher has chosen to use one of the many data collecting programs on the Internet, the service often offers online reports for free or at a very low cost. However, these reports are often rather simple reports measuring for frequency or another simple equation. If one wants to go deeper into the results, it is recommended to use professional analyzing software.

Dyslangue—A Case Study

The Dyslangue project was a cross-national European project supported by the European Counsel. The objective of the project was to develop a research-based method of teaching foreign languages to dyslexic students in a European context. In order to develop the project further, it was necessary in the beginning to make a quantitative and a qualitative study on how schools and language teachers deal with dyslexic students in the participating countries: Austria, Denmark, and Iceland. The quantitative part of the research was conducted through an online survey (Dal, Arnbak, & Brandstätter, 2005) and in the following the methodological issues related to this research and the Web-based survey will be discussed.

The main objective of this research was to collect information on school policy concerning dyslexic students, on teaching dyslexic students a foreign language, and which method the teachers think is the most beneficiary to the development of foreign-language skills in dyslexic students. The survey was performed in 124 lower secondary schools in Austria, Denmark, and Iceland during the spring of 2004. The study can therefore be characterized as a cross-sectional study, because the data are collected from the participants during a relatively brief time period (also called contemporaneous measurement).

The sample population was identified by where the schools were situated geographically. In order to be able to make comparative studies between the different schools in the different countries, it was decided that schools from rural areas would not be included. Thus the criteria were that the participating schools should be situated in an urban area and have a student population of more than 250.

Because of the nature and the objective of the study, the researchers decide to use probability sampling and not volunteer sampling. In each country, certain schools were picked out as target schools due to the criteria mentioned above. A total of 152 schools were selected, but only 124 schools accepted to take part. After obtaining permission from the school administrators to involve staff members in the study, one or two language teachers in each school were selected to take part in the survey, which ensured that each school did not weigh more than others in the final results. In order to avoid coverage error, the selected sample population was contacted first by telephone to get a confirmation that they were willing to participate in the study and then by e-mail with more information about the survey and a link to the questionnaire.

Each participant was given a special code. This was done to incorporate some means of personal identification, to gain more control over the e-mail survey, and ensure that participants only answered the questionnaire once. The method also made it possible for the researchers to encourage participation by sending out reminders to the participants who eventually had not yet answered the survey.

The Dyslangue questionnaire consisted of a total of 16 questions. The questionnaire was divided into three sections beginning with a section of general questions about the participant's age, school etc. The second section covered information about school policy concerning dyslexic students. The third section contained more specific questions concerning points of views on teaching dyslexic students a foreign language and on assessment. Most of the questions were closed questions. Only one question, which related to the participant's general comments on the topic of dyslexia and foreign-language acquisition, was open ended. The questionnaire was otherwise constructed by applying yes/no and agree/disagree options. One question was designed as a "check-all-that-apply" question and four questions were formed as allegations that the respondents had to agree or disagree with on a scale from 1 to 6 where 1 equaled "agree" and 6 equaled "totally disagree." All respondents answered all the questions of the survey and as such the survey was successful.

The design of the questionnaire was deliberately very simple and pictures, logos, or other extra materials were only applied to a small extent (Figure 12.3).

The findings of the quantitative study revealed that there is a general assumption in school systems across the participating countries that children with special needs should be included in the normal classroom and in a majority of the participating schools dyslexic students are integrated into normal foreign-language classes.

It is noteworthy that the majority of the respondents claimed that most schools do not offer support to students experiencing difficulties learning a foreign language and almost a fifth of the respondents claimed that their school does not at all acknowledge that dyslexic students have problems learning a foreign language. These results indicate that generally the schools' policy is to include dyslexic students in foreign-language classes and to a certain extent acknowledge that dyslexic students do have difficulties learning a foreign language, but at the same time most of the schools do not have any policy on how they can offer support for the same group of students. The schools thus are generally acknowledging the idea of inclusion, but at the same time the results from the survey indicate that many schools on the other hand really do not have the proper knowledge to do so.

The findings also revealed that a majority of the teachers claim to sometimes give special attention to dyslexic by doing things such as preparing special tasks for the dyslexic students. From the collected data, the researchers concluded that despite this awareness the teachers do not work methodically and continuously support the dyslexic students in foreign-language classes. The most common way to support dyslexic students seems to be letting them work with both books and tapes. Other tools are only used sporadically, but some of the respondents particularly mention picture dictionaries. More advanced tools such as a spelling checker with a prediction program and programs with speech feedback seems to be used only sometimes, but an advanced tool such as a "talking pen" is only used in very few cases.

The analysis of the findings resulted in a series of new questions that needed to be answered, such as what can schools do to improve their policy on dyslexic students and

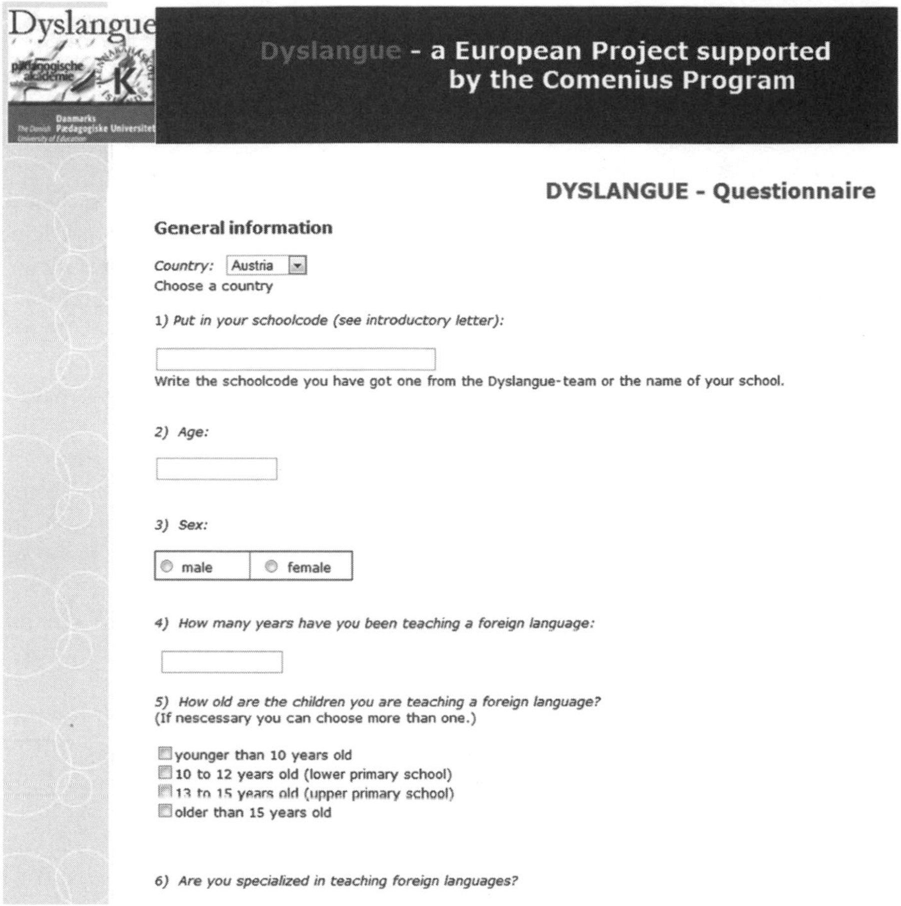
Dyslangue
pädagogische akademie
Danmarks Pædagogiske Universitet
Dyslangue - a European Project supported by the Comenius Program

DYSLANGUE - Questionnaire

General information

Country: Austria
Choose a country

1) Put in your schoolcode (see introductory letter):

Write the schoolcode you have got one from the Dyslangue-team or the name of your school.

2) Age:

3) Sex:

male | female

4) How many years have you been teaching a foreign language:

5) How old are the children you are teaching a foreign language?
(If nescessary you can choose more than one.)

- younger than 10 years old
- 10 to 12 years old (lower primary school)
- 13 to 15 years old (upper primary school)
- older than 15 years old

6) Are you specialized in teaching foreign languages?

Figure 12.3 Screen shot of part of the Dyslangue survey.

foreign-language learning, what possibilities does the school have to help dyslexic students to participate in language classes, and what tools are available for the teachers to help dyslexic students in language classes? These questions were later followed up in interviews with a selected group of the participants and the results from these interviews, combined with the description of different teaching methods, was used to produce more specific guidelines for foreign-language teachers (Dal, Arnbak, & Brandstätter, 2008).

Though the researchers made an effort to ensure that the participants would respond to the e-mail request, few participants responded immediately. Reminders were then sent out to the participants and in a further attempt to increase the response rate, the researchers even made direct telephone calls or made personal contacts with the participants in some cases. A great majority of the respondents expressed a positive reaction when they first got a letter or phone call from the research group, but even so, many participants did not immediately take the time to fill out the questionnaire. However, it was necessary for the study to get a suitably high response rate to secure reliability, and in some cases the research team contacted the respondents as often as four times to get them to act.

This group of respondents was later asked why they had delayed in filling out the questionnaire. The most common answer was that the teachers had rather busy workdays and doing extra things like filling out a survey was simply a low priority. In this aspect, their answers equal the findings of Mertler (2003), who found that many teachers simply regard their schedules at school as too busy to permit them to do anything extra. The same group of respondents was also asked if they found it unnecessary or pointless to participate in a study like the Dyslangue study. Everybody expressed satisfaction with their participation and said it had been "interesting," "noteworthy," and "exciting" to participate. All participants thought that the objective of the study out from a professional view was "necessary" and "relevant." Also, a majority of the respondents expressed deep concerns for how the school system in some cases neglects the needs of the dyslexic students in foreign-language learning.

The time and effort put into reaching the sample population evidently paid off, because from the selected 124 schools, 148 participants completed the questionnaire, a response rate of almost 100%. However, the experiences from the survey leave us with an intriguing question of why it took a longer time for some of the participants to finish the questionnaire. It was obviously not because they found the study uninteresting or unnecessary. Thus, other reasons must have caused the slowness and the lateness of the respondents, such as forgetfulness, absent-mindedness, or a designation of low priority. One of the respondents expressed that she received many requests to participate in different kinds of surveys and that this particular request more or less drowned in the crowd, though she acknowledged that the object of the study certainly had her attention.

The research team discussed whether it would have been more helpful if the survey had been conducted by using a paper-and-pencil survey. They concluded, though, that it would probably have been far more time consuming to collect data in the more traditional way. In fact, the research team agreed that the response rate was as high as it was because of the use of online data collection.

The Dyslangue study draws attention to the important question of how and what researchers must do to reach a sample population. In this particular case, the research team had carefully demarcated and selected the sample population, obtained the necessary permissions, and personally contacted the participants. In spite of this, a lot of energy was used in reminding and getting the group of respondents to participate in the study. This called attention to the need for more research on new and better methods to reach different kinds of sample populations.

It is important to remember that this particular nonexperimental quantitative study was only one section of the whole research project, which also included interviews and further qualitative research, which will not be commented on here. One of the principles behind the quantitative study was to delimit the amount of questions to ensure that the questionnaire would not consist of too many questions. Experiences from other surveys show that it is important to be as precise as possible when asking questions and to keep the questionnaire within a certain length in order to avoid nonresponse error. If one needs more information from the respondents, it is always possible to make and send out another questionnaire.

The online survey used in the Dyslangue project was in many ways successful. Though the survey was conducted in three different countries and therefore over a large geographical area, the response rate was unusually good. Using a Web survey made it possible to immediately collect the data in one database. Also, it was possible to closely follow the participation rate so reminders could be sent out by e-mail when needed. In this survey, the participants were selected on the basis of certain criteria. Each recipient was given an identification tag that ensured that it was possible to track whether a participant had filled out the questionnaire more than once. The selected group was small enough to keep close track of the whole group, which made this particular study different from surveys based on volunteer sampling. In the volunteer sampling method, it is not possible to keep close track of the participants in the same manner, simply because the surveyor does not always have the necessary information of who the participants are. If an online survey needs to be reliable and probable, as it was the case in the Dyslangue survey, researchers must be ready to use time and effort to demarcate and select potential participants and keep close track of the participation rate during the collection process. Otherwise, there is a danger that survey errors such as nonresponse error and sampling error will have an unfortunate influence on the results of the survey and thus make the data unreliable.

Emerging Possibilities of Presenting a Web Survey

As stated before, it may be a two-edged decision to implement the newest technology and use advanced features when designing surveys. Research calls attention to the advantage of creating rather simple questionnaires that require less computer power in order to secure easy access to the survey (Christian, 2003).

However, today it is rather common that users have access to high-speed Internet connections and more powerful computers. Just within the last couple of years, the standard in computing has increased dramatically. The next generation will automatically be an integrated part of the rapid development of new technology as it opens up emerging possibilities of presenting surveys and new methods that may better ensure that participants take an interest in the subject of a survey, which also ensures more reliability.

One of the biggest challenges in using surveys lies in defining, reaching, and activating the sample population. The development of new communication technology has changed our views on how we can communicate most effectively. Communicating through hard copies such as newspapers, books, brochures, posters, public notices, etc., is today considered to be a slow method of communication. The advantage of this way of communication is that it is evident and easy to confirm and verify. Communicating with help from live pictures, chat machines, blogs, e-mails, and other forms of new technology is more diffuse and floating.

One can argue that the floating form of communication today has a greater impact on daily life than the hard copies. One of the consequences of this development is that the illustrious media also have gone online and today newspapers are being published both as a hard copy and as soft copy online. More books today are also published as e-books. E-books are usually read on personal computers or smart phones, or on dedicated hardware devices known as e-book readers or e-book devices. Many cell phones can also be used to read e-books.

Using Web surveys makes it possible and easier to use new and different features when presenting a survey. Most Web surveys are today directly transferred from paper to a digital form and therefore often look very much like a paper-and-pencil survey on the screen. However, using Web surveys makes it possible to present a survey with different kind of picture materials such as short movie clips, still pictures, cartoons, clip art, different shapes to illustrate and stress certain points in a survey, and so on. Illustrating a survey with features like this may be one way of attracting the participants to take part in surveys in the future. The danger is, however, that the survey will be too decorated and therefore confusing and difficult to take in for the respondent.

Multimedia presentations can be used to explain certain matters concerning the survey or simply to present the aim of the survey. Let us say that a researcher wants to present the subject and the aim of the survey for a sample population. Instead of writing a long notice in the beginning of the survey, this can be done even more effectively by making a short video where images and music can present the main goal of the survey, as well as explain the participants why there is a need for making a survey in this particular area.

Using pictures, music, and different kinds of interactivity are all methods to make the participants more comfortable taking part in the survey and can thus be said to be effective methods to catch the attention of the participants. However, researchers also have to keep in mind that using this kind of material tends to make it more time consuming for the respondents to participate in a survey.

One of the key findings in research done by Mertler (2003) was that the respondents complained of limited time to take part in extra things such as surveys. This calls attention to the fact that material of this kind should be used with considerable circumspection. The constructor of a Web survey must be very much aware of the exact purpose of including interactive and multimedia features in a survey and aware of the pros and cons.

It may be a good idea to present the topic and the purpose of the survey in a video clip. It can have more than one purpose. Firstly, the respondents get to see the person(s) behind the research, and an oral presentation is always a good way of drawing interest. Secondly, a video presentation can make the participants familiar with the purposes and the topic of the survey. This can especially be effective when reaching a population of professionals such as teachers. They will beforehand most likely be interested in involving themselves in the subject of the survey. The aforementioned research Dyslangue (Dal et al., 2008) can serve as an example of this. While most of the participants thought of the topic of the survey as interesting and important, many did not answer the survey without receiving a reminder by e-mail. A short video presentation may have helped to focus on the necessity of answering the survey immediately.

Multimedia can also be used in an effective way for commercial purposes. An example of that is the entertainment packet at the airline Icelandair. All the planes at Icelandair are today equipped with a video screen for each seat. The screen is a touch screen that makes it easy for passengers to navigate on. Each video screen is equipped with a headset.

During the flight, each passenger then has the possibility to choose different kinds of entertainment, movies, music, games, shopping possibilities, documentaries on Iceland, and even an introductory language lesson in Icelandic. Also, the passengers have the option of participating in a survey. If you open the survey, you are welcomed by a video presentation that explains the object of the survey. It seems to be an effective way of reaching a specific sample population, but exactly how effective it is one can only make a guess of because the company does inform about the response rate.

One of the common characteristics of the new methods of communication is the possibility of interactivity. When presenting a survey, it may be a good idea to use an interactive presentation form where the participating population gets to know the results of the survey immediately after finishing. When the respondents have answered a question sheet, there is the possibility of showing the present results as graphics or in numbers, especially if the questions are of such nature that can be measured in numbers. The interactivity makes the participating population more curious and it can, therefore, result in a bigger response rate. An interactive survey could be built up from the same principle as the interactive polls, especially if it is a survey with multiple-choice questions. After finishing the questionnaire, the participating respondent could find out how many people have totally participated in the survey until now and how the answers are distributed in each question. To get a more analyzed result will demand involvement from the researchers themselves, but getting a rough picture can be a highly motivating factor for the sample population. This kind of interactivity indicates that you as a respondent do not only take part in the survey for the sake of the researcher or the team behind the survey but also partly for your own sake to satisfy your own inquisitiveness. In many ways interactivity thus makes it more satisfactory for the respondents to take part in a survey and it can have a positive effect on the response rate of the survey.

The aspect of interactivity could also be presented in other ways, for example, by giving the sample population the opportunity to comment on issues or the survey when taking it. Imagine if a big work place would like to find out how its employees feel about certain matters concerning the work place. The participants of the survey could get the opportunity to go more into details about certain issues by commenting on them further in public. Instead of just choosing between certain possibilities or answering a question with a simple yes or no, the participants could have a chance to write comments that were visible for other participants to read and others to reply to. In that way, a survey not only would serve as an instrument for measuring opinions but also be an instrument to let the participants express their opinion on the issues in question and even discuss them among each other online. In this way, the participants would have the opportunity to inform both the researcher and the other participants of what motives he or she has for choosing the answer they in fact chose. In some research, this could be of specific interest, especially if the research is about controversial issues.

In this type of interactive survey, one would presuppose that the issue of the survey would be the topic of the discussion among the participants and as such the comments would rather help the researcher to understand more about the survey than contradict it. Perhaps it can even give the researcher a hint of how interested the participants are in the survey and the topic that is surveyed. In educational research, this can be of some importance. Let us say we want to survey how a group of students feel about a topic concerning their school or school culture, for example, student harassment or sport activities during and after school time; an interactive discussion as suggested above could give a hint of the students' point of views and their reason for filling out the survey. If a majority of the students finds the topic of the survey or the survey unnecessary or even ridiculous, it gives the researcher a hint of the level of motivation among the students and this piece of information must be included as an aspect when analyzing the results.

Including the interactive opportunity for the participants to react to and discuss the issue of a survey sets a certain frame for the comments. The participants would typically comment on questions presented in the survey in the same way that comments to online newspaper articles reflect on and are limited to the issues mentioned by the journalist. In that way, the researcher presents a certain agenda through the survey.

Online research tools also provide an opportunity to observe a group without presenting the researcher's own agenda. It could be in the purpose of following the development of an issue, or reviewing a public exchange that took place in the past, or outside the influence of researchers and policymakers. This can be done by collecting data from online discussions. It may be synchronous, such as real-time chat, or instant messaging, or asynchronous, such as a list server or bulletin board. It may be text only or provide facilities for displaying images, animations, hyperlinks, and other multimedia. Tools for online conversation are becoming increasingly sophisticated, popular, and easy to access; these tools increase the appeal of using online discourse as a source of data. Examples of these are popular blogs and digital communities such as Facebook and LinkedIn. Such sites are potentially important, and whether you are looking for ways to improve interactions within a group, studying the interactions of a community that interests you, or assessing student learning, online discussions can be a valuable instrument for collecting data.

The nature of online discussions, though, is quite different from that of an online survey and should therefore be managed quite differently when handling and analyzing them. Management of online discussions demands qualitative techniques and not quantitative techniques, as is the case with surveys. As such, there is an essential difference between dealing with online surveys and online discussions. The study of online discourse is still emerging, and there still is much about the handling and analysis of this kind of data that has not yet been addressed and fully examined.

Another emerging possibility of presenting an online survey is through mobile phones, smart phones, and other forms of media that can connect to the Internet such as iPods and iPhones. These media are widely used as a vital instrument of communication among young as well as older generations. SMS (Short Message Service) and MMS (Multimedia Messaging Service) are a part of what could be called normal communication practice and some companies offer software that enable researchers to run their own SMS survey. It is done by creating a questionnaire online, which the researcher makes into hard copy of the survey and distributes it to the sample population. Respondents then enter their results in their cell phones using a single SMS. The results will then be posted to a server, where the researcher has access to the data. Some companies offer the technical facilities for this service (Page 2009; Software Realisations, 2009).

Finally, it should be mentioned that researchers today have rather easy access to a variety of commercial software and shareware survey solutions including easy facilities access to interactive and multimedia features. If you enter "survey" in Google you will get links to several surveys building software for creating and distributing surveys. The offered programs consist of an intuitive wizard interface for creating survey questions and distributing a survey via e-mail or your Web site, and tools for analyzing and viewing the results and the results will mostly be available in real time. The amount of results from searching for surveys on Google suggests that a huge amount of companies are developing new software in this field and it seems that tomorrow's researchers will have a vast numbers of choices for making online surveys even more interesting and tempting to participate in for the respondents.

Conclusion and Future Directions

Collecting empirical evidence is an important part of most academic research. The quantitative research techniques have developed methods designed to ensure objectivity and reliability. The theoretical literature on quantitative research agrees on classifying quantitative research into experimental and nonexperimental research. The use of the Internet to conduct surveys provides enormous opportunities as well as challenges. Online data collection is a research technique that belongs to the nonexperimental quantitative research.

The use of online data collection is not only reserved for academic purposes. New digital techniques are emerging and online surveys are widely used for commercial purposes as well as for letting a population state their point of view on controversial matter through interactive polls. We can therefore conclusively state that online data collection is an emerging technique used in nonexperimental quantitative research, and it is a technique that is increasing dramatically.

Even though there evidently are many advantages to using online data collection, there are also some difficulties. First of all, there are ethical issues. Collecting e-mail addresses must be done in such a way that it secures the privacy of the addressee. Also, there is the concern of the reliability and quality of responses. In this regard, it is important to secure that the respondent can only answer the questionnaire once to minimize the risk of distorted sampling. Another area of concern is related to technical problems and issues in implementation of the Web survey, and finally there is the issue of collecting lists of participants and the fact that online data collection is more often based on volunteer sampling than probability sampling.

When designing a Web survey, the designer needs to aim explicitly at reducing three or four survey errors that typically prevent accurate surveys from being done, that is, nonresponse, measurement, and coverage of the survey population. Also a Web survey must be respondent-friendly, which means that it interfaces effectively with the wide variety of computers and browsers possessed by respondents and the response task easy and interesting to complete. In this chapter, some basic principles important in the design of self-administered surveys have been presented.

Tomorrow's researchers, however, will without doubt have vast numbers of new choices for making online surveys even more interesting and tempting to participate in for the respondents. The challenge of tomorrow will thus be to incorporate these new possibilities in order to follow the development of communication technology and in order to keep up with tomorrow's user population.

References

Carbonaro, M., & Bainbridge, J. (2000). Design and development of a process for Web-based survey research. *The Alberta Journal of Educational Research, 46*(4), 39–394.
Christian, L. M. (2003). Influence of plan vs. fancy design on response rates for Web surveys. Washington, DC: Department of Sociology, Washington State University.
Comley, P. (2003). Pop-up surveys. What works, what doesn't work and what will work in the future. http://www.virtualsurveys.com/sites/com.vs-web/files/Pop-Up%20Surveys.%20 What%20works,%20what%20doesn't%20work%20and%20what%20will%20work%20 in%20the%20future%202000–03–01.doc.
Cresswell. (2003). *Research design* (2nd ed.). Thousand Oaks, CA: Sage Publications.
Dal, M., Arnbak, E., & Brandstätter, H. (2005). *Dyslexic students and foreign language learning— survey conducted among teachers in lower secondary schools*. Reykjavík: Iceland University of Education Research Centre.

Dal, M., Arnbak, E., & Brandstätter, H. (2008). *Dyslexia and foreign language learning—what to do?* Reykjavik Iceland University—School of Education.

Dal, M., Hottmann, A., & Sassen, D. (2008). *EU projects DIVIS and speech bubbles.* Kulturing in Berlin e.V 2008 (accessed on 20.20.2008).

Gall, M. D., Gall, J. P., & Borg, W. R. (2007). *Educational research an introduction* (8th ed.). Boston: Allyn and Bacon.

Gay, L. R., Mills, G. E., & Airasian, P. W. (2006). *Educational research competencies for analysis and applications* (9th ed.). Upper Saddle River, NJ: Pearson Merrill Prentice Hall.

Greguras, G. J., and Stanton, J. M. (1996). Three considerations for I/O graduate students seeking academic positions: Publish, publish, publish. *The Industrial-Organizational Psychologist, 33*(3), 92–98.

Groves, R. M. (1989). *Survey errors and survey costs.* New York: Wiley.

Hester, N. (2001). Macromedia dreamweaver ultradev 4: Training from the source. Berkeley, CA: Macromedia Press.

Jenkins, C. R., & Dillman, D. A. (1997). Chapter 7: The language of self-administered surveys. In Lyberg, L. (Ed.), *Survey measurement and process quality.* New York: Wiley-Interscience.

Johnson, B., & Christensen, L. B. (2008). *Educational research quantitative, qualitative, and mixed approaches* (3rd ed.). Los Angeles: Sage Publications.

Keysurvey.com. (2008). *Check all that apply.* Keysurvey.com 2005 (accessed on October 23, 2008). Available from http://www.keysurvey.com/WebHelp/CheckAll.htm.

Laahs, K., McKenna, E., & Vanamo, V.-M. (2005). *Microsoft SharePoint® technologies: Planning, design, and implementation.* Amsterdam: Elsevier/Digital Press.

Leeds, C. (2009). *Microsoft expression Web 2: Step by step.* Redmon, Washington, DC: Microsoft press.

Lefever, S., Dal, M., & Matthiasdottir, A. (2007). Online data collection in academic research: Advantages and limitations. *British Journal of Educational Technology, 38*(4), 574–582.

Matz, M. C. (1999). *Administration of Web versus paper surveys: Mode effects and response rates.* University of North Carolina 1999 (accessed on June 4, 2008). Available from ERIC Webportal http://www.eric.ed.gov/.

McMillan, J. H. (2008). *Educational research—Fundamentals for the consumer.*Brvikovs, A. E. (Ed.) *Education.* New York: Pearson.

Mertler, C. A. (2003). Patterns of response and nonresponse from teachers to traditional and Web surveys. *Practical Assessment, Research & Evaluation, 22,* http://pareonline.net/getvn.asp?v=8&n=22.

Page, A. (2009). *How to conduct a SMS survey using a cell phone connected SMS gateway and MS access.* Code Project 2007 (accessed on March 6, 2009). Available from http://www.codeproject.com/KB/winsdk/sms_gateway_survey.aspx.

Presser, S. (2004). *Methods for testing and evaluating survey questionnaires.* Wiley series in survey methodology. Hoboken, NJ: Wiley-Interscience.

Saunders, M., Lewis, P., & Thornhill, A. (2003). *Research methods for bussiness students.* London: Pitman Publishing.

Schillewaert, N., & Meulemeester, P. (2005). Comparing response distributions of offline and online data collection methods. *International Journal of Market Research, 47*(2), 163–178.

Software Realisations. (2009). *SMS survey—instant survey with SMS.* SMS Survey 2009 (accessed on May 12, 2009). Available from http://www.smssurvey.co.za/.

SPSS Inc. (2007). *SPSS base 16.0 user's guide.* Chicago: SPSS Inc.

SurveyMonkey.com. (2008). *SurveyMonkey.com* 2009 (accessed on May 24, 2008). Available from http://www.surveymonkey.com/.

TricTrac. (2008). *TricTrac.com.* TricTrac 2008 (accessed on August 25, 2008). Available from http://www.trictrac.com/.

Weisberg, H. F., Bowen, B. D., & Krosnick, J. A. (1996). *An introduction to survey research, polling, and data analysis* (3rd ed.). Thousand Oaks, CA: Sage Publications.

Witt, K. J. (1998). Best practices in interviewing via the Internet: Proceeding of Sawtoo Software Conference. Paper read at Sawtooth Software, Inc., Washington, DC.

Wright, D. L., Aquilino, W. S., & Supple, A. J. (1998). A comparison of computer-assisted and paper-and-pencil self-administered questionnaires in a survey on smoking, alcohol, and drug use. *Public Opinion Quarterly, 62*(3), 331–377.

Wulffmorgenthaler ApS. (2008). *Wulffmorgenthaler.* Wulffmorgenthaler ApS 2001–2007 (accessed on August 5, 2008). Available from http://www.wulffmorgenthaler.com/.

> Chapter 13

Collaborative Research Tools: Using Wikis and Team Learning Systems to Collectively Create New Knowledge

Robert Fitzgerald and John Findlay

Introduction`

In the first decade of the twenty-first century, technological and social change is accelerating faster than ever before. Seemingly isolated and "under control" local or regional issues are now being transmitted throughout global economic, technological, and management systems in minutes and days rather than months and years. The global financial crisis is one recent example of this. Major differences between the experts (scientists and other researchers) about issues such as global warming, the use of nanotechnology or nuclear power often polarize the key debates producing conflict and little action. Decision theory has taught us that expertise is highly domain specific and therefore differences in opinion and strategy are understandable and to be expected. However, the real problem arises when experts move from their *descriptive* expertise to the *normative* activity of making predictions as to what constitutes ideal or optimal social practice. Many years ago, Rittel and Webber (1973) made the important distinction between wicked and tame problems. Tame problems are those that can be solved by the technical applications of expertise and knowledge. Wicked problems as those that are contentious and controversial with no clear solution—they are social problems such as welfare or poverty, requiring a social dialogue between experts and nonexperts. Wicked problems are not solved by information alone. In his 1980s best-selling book about the paradigm shift from the Industrial Age to the Information Age, futurist John Naisbitt noted, "We are drowning in information but starved for knowledge" (1982, p. 17). Three decades later, it could be argued that we are now drowning in knowledge, but starved of its wise application to the wicked problems that face us.

Solving Wicked Problems Through Democratized Research

There is a pressing need for processes of social research and some aspects of the natural sciences to become more democratized, so that nonexperts can not only participate directly in the process of knowledge creation, but also in its immediate implementation. In fields such as knowledge management or business innovation, there is already a shift away from the traditional model of expert-neophyte to communities of knowers. Here, citizens play an active role as content creators, self-managing their community teams to participate more or less equally in the production and consumption of knowledge. The citizen journalism movement is one such example, where local citizens armed with mobile phones and other devices report on the news as it happens. The initial reaction of the traditional news media was to ignore or ridicule this movement as ill informed and amateurish, but now every major news service encourages their viewers to share and contribute their stories. The power of this form of journalism is unquestionable—who can forget the YouTube video of Neda Agha-Soltan's death during the protests in Iran in June 2009. Within a short space of time, this video became a symbol of the Iranian protests and the widespread condemnation of the Iranian government's handling of the protests. As this example shows, central to increasing community participation has been the role played by new information and communication technologies, in particular Web 2.0 applications designed around what has been termed an "architecture of participation" (O'Reilly, 2004). However, most Web 2.0 tools are designed to achieve a technical requirement of participation, rather than higher forms of contribution implicit in learning and knowledge creation. Mayfield (2006) describes the power law of participation according to how people use different online tools. At the high end of the scale, which he calls collaborative intelligence, tools support the joint production of knowledge in which the object of inquiry is transformed with the active interaction of the participants through a process of synthesis. At the other end of the participation spectrum, which Mayfield characterizes as collective intelligence, participants engage in reproducing, comprehending, and classifying existing knowledge (Figure 13.1).

Mayfield's model offers a tantalizing account of the potential of participation to engage users in higher forms of activity or collaborative intelligence. Within the debate about the impact of Web 2.0 developments, some commentators allude to the potential for the many to create knowledge (Surowiecki, 2004) and the increased opportunities

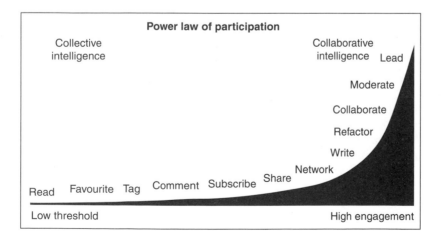

Figure 13.1

for social production of knowledge (Benkler, 2006), while others lament the loss of expertise and rigor (Keen, 2007) in this new environment. Researchers such as Hasan and Crawford (2006, p. 10) offer a more nuanced perspective and see people and technology as engaged in a complex socio-technological system of "self-directed knowledge work where people, engaged in a collective activity, are allowed and enabled to choose the technical components as needed to automate operations, leaving them with more time to deal with the knowledge components of their actions." In these socio-technical systems, there are shifts to new forms of joint production and new ways of knowing become possible. In the academic field, there is also a shift away from research conducted purely via the scientific method to a more inclusive connected approach to knowledge creation (Palmer, 1998).

Research as a Specialized Form of Learning

We begin this chapter with the proposition that good research is a specialized form of learning that engages participants in mutual inquiry and a dialectical or knowledge building discourse. In this chapter, we consider the potential of two emergent technologies, wikis and team learning systems, that both embody an architecture of participation that engages users in the coproduction of new knowledge via a process of research. In academe, research and learning are inextricably entwined in a form of ongoing research-education exchange, which is also dialectical, and is transformed as it is transferred or used (Shariq, 1999). As new theories are formulated and the new knowledge is applied, gaps develop in the theory that point to inconsistencies that evolve into new unanswered questions that become the subject of further research.

Although the scientific method has been extraordinarily successful, educational institutions have become the custodians of a curious form of inert knowledge (Palmer, 1998), presided over by "high priests" of both the knowledge and the methods for acquiring knowledge, access to which only a few are allowed. Academic institutions are designed to objectively discover new knowledge and acculturate chosen neophytes into their method of creating new knowledge. Further down the line in the school education system, the problem is critically apparent. Teachers, who often have little or no formal role in either the creation of new knowledge or the development of pedagogy, receive accreditation from the universities in both the practice of teaching and the field in which they specialize, such as mathematics, science, or the arts. The knowledge they pass on to their students is an inert, theoretical form that may bear little or no relationship to the practical kinds of knowledge or skills students will require to be successful in the workplace. The objective expert is often removed from the source of identified errors in a theory by several layers of obfuscation. The expert's role is to interpret what they know for "amateurs" who "are full of bias" (Palmer, 1998, p. 100) and to select some to be indoctrinated into the world of objective knowing. Experts are trained in methods designed to prevent their subjectivity from intruding on the interpretation of the object so it remains in its "pristine" form, but this ensures that most participants in the learning process remain disengaged from the learning process (Palmer, 1998) (Figure 13.2).

Palmer proposes a "connected knowing" model in which all participants in the research-learning process are in touch as both observers of and interactors with the

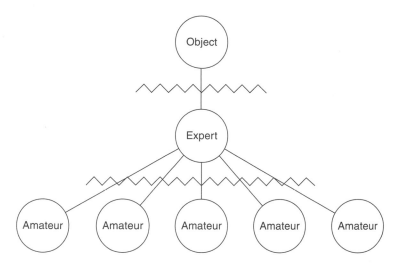

Figure 13.2

subject. He argues that this close relationship with the subject results in a more truth-ful and faithful type of learning that is more real and credible for the amateur than the remote, abstract scientific models that emerge from objective research. People arrive at truth via "an eternal conversation about things that matter, conducted with passion and discipline" (p. 104). Palmer's model affords the amateur a new status not as nonexpert but rather closer to the Latin meaning of the word "amateur" as a passionate and enthusiastic pursuer of an objective within a community of knowers (Figure 13.3).

This approach, which combines both research and teaching functions, allows the ama-teur to participate in the knowledge-creation process alongside experts. During the inter-action, the amateur learns through a process of immersion and imitation in the manner first identified by Vygotsky (1978) as collective play. Vygotsky showed that people learn in three main ways:

1. with support through the zone of proximal development, which has been described as the zone between what a learner can do independently and what they can do with guidance (as exemplified by the present "objective" education-research system);
2. through a process of inner speech or dialogue while engaging with an external tool, where a new skill is first practiced externally, then internalized;
3. through play with others with what begins as a process of imitation of the activity of others. Three mediating factors—tools, signs, and other people—are present in play so that people are able, via cooperation, to "raise the demand on themselves and with that bring themselves into the *zone of proximal development*" (Brostrom, 1999, pp. 250–251) and thereby master ideas they cannot achieve in nonplay settings.

In order to deal with growing size and complexity, many business organizations and some government agencies have found it necessary to decentralize their knowledge

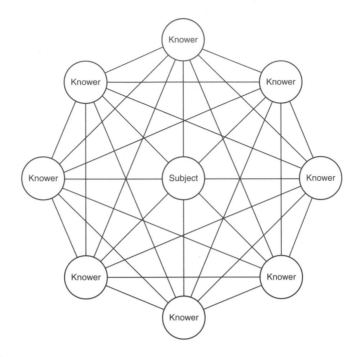

Figure 13.3

building and decision-making capabilities to the stakeholders. Accelerating change on many scales has made it difficult for centrally controlled organizations to function as successfully as they were able to in slower times. Sluggish behemoths of organizations tend to be displaced in a Darwinian competition by faster moving and more flexible organizations, capable of either rapidly implementing knowledge newly created by others or directly creating their own knowledge—to improve their products, processes, and decision-making methods. In a world in which accelerating change has become a critical factor, organizations can no longer plan rationally as their primary strategy. In order to deal with a multiplicity of scenarios, a playful approach to learning has emerged in the form of search conferences, brainstorming sessions to generate and link ideas that better fit the context, scenario planning, simulations, and case studies, in which groups work together in order to determine what might happen in the real-world. Leadbeater (2008) points to this new approach of playful joint-knowledge construction in his online book, "We think: Why mass creativity is the next best thing." He says:

> The power of mass creativity is about what the rise of the likes of Wikipedia and YouTube, Linux and Craigslist means for the way we organise ourselves, not just in digital businesses but also in schools and hospitals, cities and mainstream corporations. My argument is that these new forms of mass, creative collaboration announce the arrival of a society in which participation will be the key organising idea rather than consumption and work. People want to be players not just spectators, part of the action, not on the sidelines. (p. 1)

The emergent tools that most closely fit this new kind of world of playful co-creation, and which have applications in the world of research, are wikis and the Zing team learning system, both of which show potential to enable sharing, exchange, and joint production.

Emergent Research Tools: Wikis and the Zing Team Learning System

Wikis and the Zing team learning system (TLS) have separate origins and different applications. Wikis build on the metaphor of a *page*, while team learning systems draw on the metaphor of a *conversation*. The two notions are highly complementary, as will become clear in the following sections.

A wiki is a Web page that can be easily edited by a group of users. This somewhat simplistic description belies the collaborative power that can arise when groups of people need to work on a document together. In 1995, Ward Cunningham developed the first wiki as a system for Web publication. He wanted a system that was accessible, simple to use, and reliable and that would enable nontechnical users to publish material on the Internet. Core to his original specification was the principal that any author would automatically be an editor as well. In their early days, wiki systems used a specific editing language; however, with their widespread use has come the preference for more useable WYSIWYG (What You See Is What You Get) editors. Fitzgerald (2007) has argued that the combined author/editor role built-in to wikis supports a model of collaboration and knowledge building that is more consistent with constructivist approaches to learning (Vygotsky, 1978) and the development of communities of practice (Wenger, McDermott, & Snyder, 2002). Each wiki page comprises four different views of the document: Article, Discussion, Edit, and History.

The Article tab represents the current version of the document, while the Discussion tab is a place where comments and discussions are recorded about the development of the document. The Edit section allows the user to modify the page, while the History tab provides a complete revision history of the document and has the facility to compare versions and/or revert pages to a previous version. This rich descriptive environment documents both the process and the product.

Wikis have a role to play at different stages of the research process. At the start of research work, they are not only a richly connected way to access both the history of the development of knowledge in a field, along with the messy contradictions and competing ideas, but also a place that flags the latest ideas and provides links to connected ideas—akin to a giant Wittgensteinian language game. For the researcher, Wikipedia-style sites are becoming the first port of call to obtain a broad overview of the state of the art and locate immediate links to journal articles and other references, sometimes even the original source documents from the researchers who initiated the field. Although wikis may not necessarily be as exhaustive as a library, both physical in the forms of documents and artifacts, and virtual, as is now available online, a wiki helps to organize information and research articles around themes and related themes so that what people regard as the most vital or interesting is brought forward for the community's attention. Wikis also allow data and other artifacts to be shared with other researchers and they can be very useful at the stage when joint authors are sparking off each other's ideas. Wikis are generally readily accessible with several service providers such as www.wikispaces.com and pbwiki.com, allowing users to establish a public wiki at no charge, with private and customizable wikis available from $US5 to $US50 per month.

There is no question that over recent years, Wikipedia has become a popular and valued source of information that enables collaborative interaction among users (LeLoup & Ponerio, 2006; Lih, 2004). The potential of wikis to engage users has been documented in the area of e-government (Wagner, Cheung, & Ip, 2006) and in what has become known as participatory journalism (Lih, 2004). A key feature of wikis makes them well suited to the rapid development and sense-making required in research. Wikis promote a short edit-review cycle within a highly visible (and often public) environment where the complete history of the page edits is easily accessible.

The result is that knowledge can be quickly developed and authenticated by the community of users (Lih, 2004), supporting both member checking and more elaborate community authentication. Social media researchers Bruns and Bahnisch (2009) identify the features that make wikis exemplary forms of social media including:

1. their relatively low threshold of participation—the system is accessible to a wide range of users;
2. highly granular participation tasks—a variety of tasks can be undertaken from simple editing through to major conceptual organization;
3. an assumption of user equipotentiality—users are able to actively participate in the system irrespective of their skill or experience;
4. shared ownership of content—a collaborative model of knowledge creation is promoted where the community owns the content.

In addition to the research benefits that arise from the use of wiki systems, perhaps one of the most compelling comes from researchers' need to demonstrate that their research process is open for comment and critique. Too often, research constructs participants as *sources of data* who only have a role to play during that data collection phase. Research plans and processes are usually predetermined and often closed to comment and critique. According to writers such as Jenkins (2006) and Bruns (2008), we live in a highly participatory world of blogs and wikis where users want to share their opinion and cocreate. Researchers that set themselves as the experts and do not engage participants as cocreators may well find it increasingly difficult to recruit participants and are ultimately at risk of producing low-quality research findings.

Zing Team Learning System

The Zing team learning system is a tool that brings together into a single platform four aspects of human interaction: decision and learning processes, communicating and relating processes, facilitation and leadership methods, and mechanisms for recording and sharing ideas. Taken together, these four aspects allow the neophyte or amateur to perform many of the roles of an expert consultant or teacher and help people create new knowledge together. The tool guides participants—researchers, learners, or decision makers—through a series of open-ended discussable questions to arrive at a conclusion, decision, action plan, new model, or theory. Each session is led by a facilitator who employs a facilitation model or "etiquette" to organize or orchestrate the group activity so that all the participants engage in the same activity at the same time. The most frequently used "etiquette" is known as the Talk-Type-Read-Review cycle, which involves discussing the topic for several minutes, typing the ideas, reading the ideas aloud, and looking for patterns in the ideas, which is a sense-making step. Other etiquettes can also be used to organize the group process. Participants using a team learning system are presented with a series of rich questions that guide their discussion. The participants discuss a question and then type their ideas, which are presented on the screen. Participants are able to not only see their own ideas as they are generated, but also all other ideas as they form. The data is coded so that the concept is recorded together with the identity of the contributor (Figure 13.4).

In a team learning session, all the participants "talk" at the same time, which gives everyone at the meeting an opportunity to have an equal say, whereas in a conventional business meeting the order of discussion is determined by a chairperson or by taking turns, and in the classroom, the order is often determined by the teacher. Another advantage of the tool is the ease with which neophyte facilitators can quickly master the role of facilitator (Findlay & Newman, 2005).

The ability to view all the ideas as they are created ensures that participants recall or make connections to related ideas, which promotes assimilation, orchestration, and integration. As the narrative is revealed and shaped, the developing ideas become triggers or scaffolds for further and usually richer and more integrated ideas.

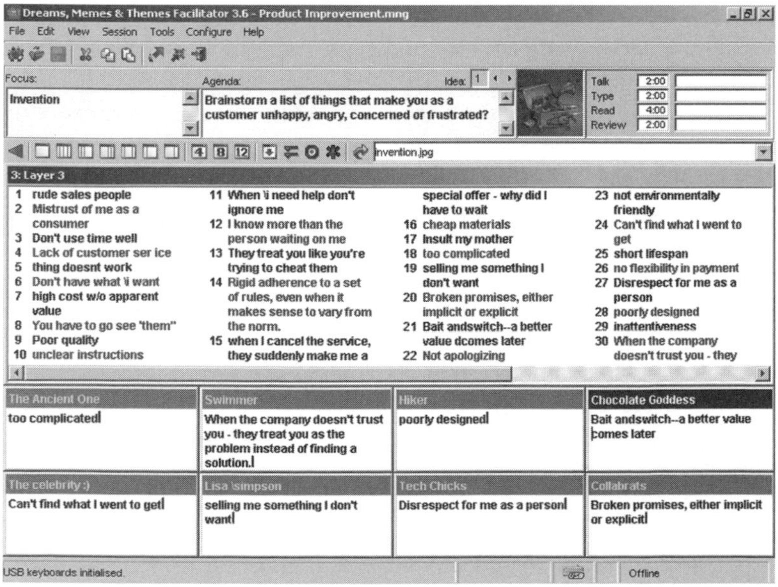

Figure 13.4

In the research field, team learning systems have been used for data collection (Waters & Callan, 2003; Findlay, 2009; Whymark, Callan, & Purnell, 2004), activity theory research (Findlay, 2009; Lee & Crawford, 2002), ethical dilemma analysis (Findlay & Newman, 2005), social research (Fitzgerald & Findlay, 2004; Caldwell, 2006), focus groups (Ward & Hawkins, 2003; Moyle & Fitzgerald, 2008), and Q methodology (Hasan & Crawford, 2006; Meloche & Hasan, 2008). The following five examples illustrate the range of possible research applications of the Zing team learning system.

Example 1: Focus Group Research

Whereas most focus group research seeks to perpetuate the expert knower-amateur relationships and to minimize the interactions between the participants, the team learning tool facilitates a dynamic type of conversation that evolves and allows the researcher to ask "abductive," "what if" type questions that project the discussion beyond the current paradigm.

Caldwell (Caldwell, 2006; Caldwell, Bhowon, Daby, & Harris, 2009), an education consultant and former Dean of Education at Melbourne University, has conducted numerous focus groups using the team learning system with head teachers and principals in Africa, Australasia, Asia, Europe, and South America. The workshops have had a dual purpose: to collect data about issues facing educators around the world as they seek to adapt to accelerating societal change, and to plan how to implement the changes. Participants share their knowledge and perspectives about the future directions of school education and arrive at new conclusions via a guided "vibrant and exhilarating" conversation. Typical of a guided discussion process is the following sequence of questions asked of teachers, principals, and administrators in Maritius in 2007, where Caldwell tags each question so it relates to an integrated theoretical model the participants are asked to consider and use:

1. What differences would a visitor observe if your school is offering a world-class quality education in 2012 (vision)?
2. What new knowledge and skills are needed by teachers at your school if this vision is to be realized (intellectual capital)?
3. In what ways can individuals, organizations, and institutions, not currently involved, assist your school in its efforts to offer a world-class quality education (social capital)?
4. What changes in values, beliefs, and attitudes are needed in your school and its community if the school is to succeed in its efforts to deliver a world-class quality education (spiritual capital)?
5. What changes in planning and budgeting processes in your school will help ensure that scarce resources are well-targeted (financial capital)?
6. What changes will be required in the roles of school leaders (leadership and governance)?

Findlay (2009), Dodd (private communication, 2007), and Phillips (2009) have separately used the tool to conduct "student voice" focus groups to collect data from students about their school or classroom experiences, as inputs to programs to help school principals and teachers understand how their students are responding to different pedagogical approaches. Students were asked what they like or do not like about both school and their lessons, and which pedagogical approaches they prefer or least like. Findlay, Fitzgerald, and Hobby (2004) reported on a series of focus groups conducted with teachers and students in the United Kingdom. They showed that senior students were more socialized into the school system and did not expect changes from schools, whereas junior secondary students still hoped for improvements that would improve their learning experiences. The Zing system enabled the researchers to work with the students to create a narrative about their experience of school. Asked about their patterns of computer use at school and home and what changes they would prefer to the way they learned and school was organized, the senior students said "there is little or no opportunity to use these tools" in school and spent very little time using computers at school "because they are shoddy" and there are "too many restrictions." They wanted schools to be more flexible, involve "more interaction" and greater use of technology, and allow students to "take more control over their learning" and "have their own opinions" and enjoy "better teacher techniques" for "different types of learners."

Example 2: Action Research

Newman and Findlay (2008) employed an action research approach to concurrently develop a new software program known as "Working Wisely" on the team learning system platform and undertake research into the use of professional discourse by early childhood professionals. The development task was to translate a complex paper-based generic process for resolving ethical dilemmas into a series of 10 guided discovery workshops. The research task was to use the feedback from the participants to inform the design process and to develop an understanding of how rich, dialectical, and dialogical discourse models married to ethical discourse can bring about personal change and a change in their relations with the children and families they served. A set of workshops was devised in which participants were presented with a series of ethical dilemmas. At each stage of the process, the participants were asked to consider how they would deal with each new complication, and at the end of the workshop to then develop their own theoretical models and rubrics. During the course of the research project, there was a shift from informal everyday language by the participants in the project, which is summarized by one person who reported she now "felt more like a professional than a child-minder."

Example 3: Nominal Group Technique

The nominal group technique (NGT) is a rapid decision-making method that obtains multiple inputs from group members on a particular problem or issue and then applies a structured group technique for prioritizing those inputs (Delbecq & van de Ven, 1971). Willcox and Zuber-Skerrit (2003) report on the use of the tool for action research using NGT. In this process, participants are asked to contribute their responses to a broad research question in several rounds of idea generation. Then, without criticism or comment so they are open to be influenced by all the ideas, participants choose a small number of ideas they regard as the most important, place them in rank order, and consolidate the votes. The technique is regarded as nominal because the groups act individually within a group context. Wilcox and Zuber-Skerrit compared the tool with a flip-chart process and showed the tool compressed the research cycle from 2 hr to 30 min, reduced research fatigue and provided a "fun" experience.

Example 4: Q Methodology

The Q methodology is a systematic research procedure used to study people's opinions or attitudes. Participants are presented with a set of statements about a topic and asked to rank order in a process referred to as Q sorting. The team learning system speeds up the collection of statements for the Q methodology research, whether from face-to-face or online participants. The tool then allows them to rank the statements in order of importance, which can be used as input for Q method analysis software. Hasan and Crawford (2006) reported on the use of the online version of the team learning system to remotely collect statements for a Q methodology research activity from geographically dispersed participants. Hasan, Meloche, Pfaff, and Willis (2007) employed a face-to-face version of the team learning system to survey subjective attitudes toward the use, adoption, and acceptance of a corporate wiki and explain the lack of use. In both examples, the factors that emerged reflected the priority views of the participants. Meloche and Hasan (2008, p. 3) said that the use of the team learning system "is particularly effective in the Concourse stage of Q Methodological research where the participants can freely engage in conversations and the material is freely typed and projected for all to see. The process engages the participants and promotes discussion. The researcher is also provided with a digital copy of the discussion and no additional or obvious effort is required of the participants."

Example 5: Voting and Surveys

The team learning system allows poll or survey data to be collected simultaneously from multiple users. The participants contribute their responses in real time. The contributions and the aggregated results are in full view of all the participants. Voting tools include Yes–No for a simple poll, an X–Y tool to chart two factors (e.g., risk analysis, where the probability of an event is assigned one number and the impact a second number), a rank-order tool, a weight tool, and a scale-voting tool. The team learning tool allows the facilitator to prepare a variety of surveys using response scales that vary from 3 to 7 items.

The voting system also allows researchers to conduct instant polls during the course of a research activity to collect self-report data about the state of individual members of the group or the group as a whole. Findlay (2009) used the tool to collect data about the level of engagement of work groups and classroom learners before, during, and after a workshop activity in order to determine the impact on the interaction by different kinds of teaching styles. Findlay applied the concept of Flow to study high-level engagement. The Flow experience, which has been widely studied by Csikszentmihalyi (1975), is a state of "optimal experience" in which people report feelings of concentration and enjoyment. Flow can be experienced in any kind of activity, but is most easily experienced when playing games, engaging in highly skilled work, and being creative. Flow seems to occur when the task is not so difficult that a participant becomes anxious, nor too easy for the participant to be bored.

Using an online survey adapted from Novak, Hoffman, & Duhachek (2003), Findlay developed a set of Flow items using a Likert scale (strongly disagree, disagree, uncertain, agree, and strongly agree). Eleven propositions were presented, each associated with the dimensions of Flow, which include a sense of clear goals, immediate feedback, the match of personal skills to the challenge, the merger of action and awareness, a focus on the task, a feeling of being in control, the loss of self-consciousness, the transformation of a personal sense of time so participants lose track, and a level and a sense of fun/enjoyment. The 11 propositions were:

1. I know what I am doing
2. This is fun and enjoyable
3. I feel connected to the task.
4. I feel connected to other people
5. I am focused on what I am doing
6. I feel comfortably unaware of myself
7. The time went very quickly
8. I am in control of my own destiny
9. I am unaware of my surroundings
10. This task is worth doing anyway
11. This task is challenging but I can do it

Studies of the student groups found that most groups experience the flow state during a team-meeting activity, except when the teachers continued to lecture and ask closed questions (Findlay, 2009).

Each of the previous five examples highlights the versatility of the team learning system to be employed across a wide range of research activities. In addition to generating rich data, the highly visual "shared" view of that data allows participants to quickly and easily engage in thematic analysis of the data. So in addition to member-checking opportunities, participants can also engage in collective sense-making. Moreover, the team learning system makes it possible to collect text conversations (written speech acts) identified by author and time sequence that can be subjected to social network analysis in order to see whether a change in the connectedness or relatedness of a group occurs. Findlay (2009) drew on a research model based on complexity theory principles developed by Losada (1999), who showed that peak team performance is highly correlated with group connectivity as measured by the number and strength of speech acts. Disconnected groups become highly connected teams via a phase transition (Findlay, 2009) similar to the phase transitions in physical or chemical systems (Kauffman, 1995). Two types of social network analysis are then possible:

1. two-model analysis, which can be used to examine the pattern of concept generation by participants in a discussion over the course of an entire learning or decision-making activity; and
2. directed graphs analysis, to identify if and when the concepts generated by a group spread rapidly throughout the group in such a contagious manner that a change occurs in both the relationships between participants and the shared knowledge of the group.

In the figure below, a two-mode analysis is shown with the blue ideas in the center representing the emergent knowledge of the group. The red dots represent participants in an extended text conversation and the blue squares represent the concepts generated by one or more participants (Figure 13.5).

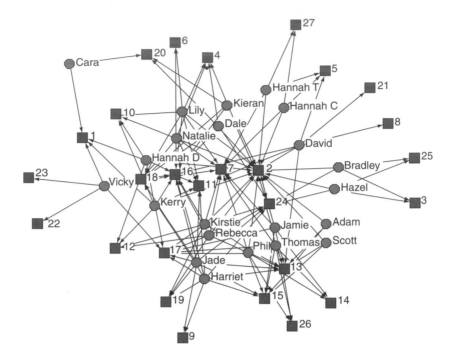

Figure 13.5

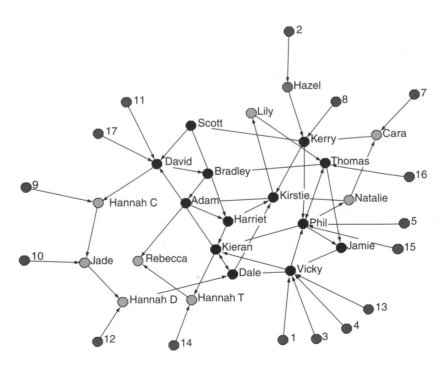

Figure 13.6

A directed graph analysis can be employed to map the flow of the conversations and where they intersect. Findlay (2009) shows that closed questions result in no or minimal change in the state of the group, whereas rich questions often stimulate richly connected clusters of concepts that coalesce out of a conceptual "soup" of possibilities, which becomes prototypical shared knowledge of the group. A transition occurs when concepts generated by some of the participants appear to autocatalyze other concepts. When the density of the interactions reaches a critical point, a large component forms (Erdos & Renyi, 1959), which may result in a runaway reaction. Figure 13.6 below shows a directed graph of classroom discussion where the concentration of interaction points suggests a transition or phase shift in the knowledge-creation process.

In summary, while the team learning system supports traditional data collection activities, it also allows researchers to engage in more participatory methods both in terms of data generation and analysis. When combined with social discourse analysis these, methods afford researchers new ways of collaboratively generating knowledge and understanding the knowledge construction process. The next section will examine the relative strengths and weaknesses of wikis and team learning systems.

Strengths and Weaknesses of Wikis and Team Learning Systems

In a sense, team learning systems and wikis are complementary tools for knowledge creation. Both allow information to be recorded and shared with others, who can then further evolve what is written, so that it moves asymptotically toward a more perfected form. Both make visible a large number of complex ideas.

Team learning systems support the process of crudely integrating complex streams of ideas into higher-level concepts, models, theories, and proposals for action, whereas wikis help multiple users perfect a description of a model of theory in all its explanatory richness.

Timing: Wikis allow ideas to evolve by keeping a record of what was previously said, allowing comparisons to be made between versions, but, unlike the TLS, which allows all the participants to engage in the same activity at the same time, wikis do not permit two users to work on the same page at the same time, although they can edit adjacent pages. Wiki also allows previous versions to be recalled if they are considered superior to the current version, or bring back into consciousness an element that is missing from the latest version. A wiki has the advantage of being able to display the collective wisdom of the group (for themselves or others) in all its informational or conceptual richness, as a resource for all members to draw upon or to further develop. The TLS allows previous work to be viewed and added to, but usually only to make visible previous stages of the discourse, which may be beneficial to later stages.

Making ideas visible: The process of knowledge creation depends to a large degree on making as much of the data/information visible as possible for the researcher (and coresearchers), in order to observe, detect, and extrapolate from patterns in the data.

Although wikis facilitate a kind of shared working, the participants do not have a common real-time thinking space, and so are unable to see and build on each other's ideas at the same time, which limits opportunities for purposeful collective knowledge creation.

On the other hand, the team learning system has a common real-time space in which multiple users contribute and see each other's ideas simultaneously, thereby allowing the immediate further development of the ideas, either within a current focus question or under the guidance of a sequence of questions to some purposeful conclusion. The TLS also helps to resolve conflicts between competing ideas by supporting the dialectical development of overarching ideas, which helps participants develop superior explanations of the phenomenon under investigation. Each person is able to contribute their own perfected version and show it to others at the same time so the best elements of ideas become apparent and can subsequently be incorporated into a new, more all-embracing version. In a sense, the TLS works in the same way that a human brain works, by bringing multiple streams together at the same time, so they can be compared and evolved or resolved. Ideas are presented in "newspaper columns" for readability and alternating colors, so that a large number of ideas can be packed into a small space and the data can be easily reviewed.

Concept integration: An advantage of the team learning system as a tool for purposeful knowledge creation is the ability to use rich question sequences to guide the collective thinking of participants. These kinds of tools are not present in wikis. Various versions of the team learning system, such as Researching Well (Findlay, 2007), offer processes to support concept integration, triangulation, sense-making, and theory formation. The team learning system also helps to resolve the muddle of competing types of thinking that occur in "free-for-all" discussion, which is the model adopted by wikis in general.

Data collection: The team learning system allows researchers to collect data about past or current activities. It can also be used concurrently with an experiment, both to deliver an experimental treatment and to obtain the participants' response to the treatment. The tool can also be used to enlist the participants as coresearchers by inviting them to contribute to theory formation about their own activities. The tool has the advantages of simultaneous concurrent input and the consolidation of all contributions into a single html or Word document that can be immediately processed in other ways, such as copying all the ideas to a mind-map or undertaking a concept analysis. Because all contributions are time stamped and identified by the author, the overall flow of a discussion can also be analyzed.

Although wikis can also be used to collect data, this is not a primary purpose, and generally can only be achieved with considerable effort, such as embedding questions or treatments within a page, or converting the page headings into questions.

Accessibility: Wikis are Web-based tools that are easily accessible to participants for very low cost, between $5 and $20 per month. On the other hand, team learning systems are generally inaccessible and require an initial investment of $US5–10,000 for a basic portable wired USB, wireless system, or a network of computers. The tool is mostly used in face-to-face settings and although Web-based versions are available, real-time sessions with multiple participants require high-level facilitation skills.

Usability: Wikis are generally very intuitive to use and require little or no training for participants. One person acts as the organizer, and invites others to join and participate at times of their own choosing. On the other hand, the team learning system is a synchronous tool and depends for its success on all participants being present for the entirety of the session and able to coordinate their activities with each other. Good leadership or facilitation skills are required. The team learning system makes it easy for neophyte facilitators to conduct complex meetings because they simply follow the question sequence. If they need to diverge and ask supplementary questions or introduce a previously planned question sequence that performs a specific function (e.g., action plan, stakeholder analysis, or feedback loop), the facilitator types in and selects a new question, or loads a new question sequence from a repository of question sets. This kind of feature is not present in wikis. However, researchers need to be able to give clear instructions so the group members learn how to perform the same thinking or discourse activities at the same time. Researchers also need to be able to craft suitable questions, which can be as difficult as crafting primary and secondary research questions.

Version control: Wikis provide a tool for comparing and perfecting drafts in a side-by-side comparison of the written word, whereas the team learning system supports the collection and evolution of ideas. Effectively, this allows for resolving conflict between concepts. Because every version of contributions and changes is archived, frequent minor changes can result, and even after a few iterations the amount of data that is collected can become overwhelming and be difficult to compare and analyze.

Exploration: In conventional data collection activities, where only one person talks at a time or data is collected via pre-prepared forms, emergent concepts are difficult to explore. An advantage of the team learning system is the facility for the researcher to observe where a conversation is going and be able to ask supplementary questions to delve deeper into the subject. Facilitators also need to know their subject area well enough to decide which other aspects of a conversation may be worth pursuing. This kind of feature is not available in wikis.

Adaptability: One of the main advantages of the team learning system is the ability of the designer/facilitator to create question sequences to perform a specific existing or new research function, such as deciding/crafting the research question and sub-questions. In some versions of the team learning system, neophyte researchers are able to learn the language of research through a series of guided discovery workshop activities, for example:

1. Variables: Your car has stopped. Make a list of possible reasons (the variables) why the car may have stopped.
2. Theory: A house brick has just landed on your front doorstep. What is your best guess for why this has happened?
3. Research questions: Thinking about life, the universe, and everything, craft a series of questions you would like to have answered.
4. Data: You have been given $50,000 to collect data about the differences between men and women. What data must you collect, for example, height, weight, etc.?
5. Data collection: Here is an image of planet earth from space. What can you see: location, size, shape, etc., for example, white swirls… (do not jump to conclusions)?
6. Data analysis: Here are three series of numbers (a) 1,1,2,3,5,8,13,21; (b) 1,4,9,16,25; (c) 99,92,85,78,71. What patterns can you see in these numbers?
7. Interpretation: Give your best explanation for the apparent difference between the size of the moon at the horizon and when it is overhead.
8. Ethics: Brainstorm moral and related issues around research, for example, not doing harm, privacy, etc.

Other research methods that have been captured in the tool include one that guides the neophyte researcher through a series of stages in the research process: focus group method, a triangulation method, a concept integration method, and a research project plan and grant application method. For example, this question sequence from Researching Well captures the kind of thinking that is employed when attempting to establish patterns in the data:

1. What evidence do we have, for example, fingerprint on the murder weapon, who is present?
2. In what ways is the evidence connected, for example, fingerprints on the knife are Mrs. Smith's, does Mrs. Smith have an alibi?
3. In what ways is the evidence about some factor/aspect connected in two or more ways, for example, how are the suspect, knife, and alibi all connected?

Developmental: As the team learning system becomes more widely adopted, new versions of the tool are being created that provide researchers with unique arrangements of question sequences that capture specific learning, decision making, or research methods (Findlay, 2009). In a sense, the tool is retroviral, having the unique ability to create new versions in a symbiotic relationship with researchers and academics. Wikis do not have a facility to create, save, and reuse tools that could guide a group through a thinking or learning process. However, they could be adapted to perform this function in a rudimentary way through the use of template pages, a feature found at PBworks.com.

Interoperability: Wikis and team learning systems, like many other tools used to collect, analyze, or represent social research data, are at an early stage of development. Each of the tools performs a discrete function, with minimal integration with other tools or ability to transfer data from one tool to another without some kind of intermediate processing. New versions of the team learning system are expanding its range of applications in the social sciences by simply creating new thinking, learning, decision making, or research questioning processes and publishing new versions of the software.

There is limited interconnection between team learning systems and wikis. Integration with data analysis tools such as social network and concept analysis software would help to further democratize and decentralize research activities. In this scenario, research would no longer be seen as separate from learning.

The team learning system and wikis rely on humans to make decisions about the narrative that is created, as the human brain continues to be superior to technology in making fine judgments, particularly in linguistic environments where meaning is rapidly evolving.

Knowledge-building activities are similar to retroviral activity, which rather than merely producing more of itself, evolves to a new form during the creation process. The meaning of concepts and their relationship to other concepts undergo a phase transition similar to the change in state from a solid to a liquid, liquid to a gas, or a gas to plasma. The characteristics of the components and the rules of interacting with other components also change.

It is our view that the role of the academic researcher is not diminished by the creation of user-centered theory/knowledge building tools, unless of course academics try to resist the broader societal changes that are already upon us. The role of the social research academic is to explore, discover, and invent new ways to conduct social research and to foster that in their research students—their apprentices. However, this role may soon be usurped by the citizen academic or citizen researcher, the knowledge industry equivalent of the citizen journalist.

Conclusions

Wikis and team learning systems are two emergent technologies that appear to offer much to improving the process and product of research. Over the course of the next few decades, we expect to see the learning-research process become more democratized, in the same way that information and knowledge has become more routinely available and accessible to all. Over time, we may see research head in the same direction as citizen journalism. Citizen academics and researchers of tomorrow will no doubt directly collect their own data and use smart tools for sense-making and theory building to create their own theories and begin applying what they learn. We can also expect to see the emergence of new kinds of tools that help humans track whether the knowledge we create is being applied wisely, to use the "wisdom of crowds" to know what is working and what is not. It is quite likely that a struggle will result between experts currently responsible for the creation and wise application of knowledge and citizen researchers in much the same way as the artisans at the start of the Industrial Age or the secretaries and clerks at the start of the Information Age resisted change. As new theoretical knowledge becomes more powerful and beneficial, it often has a dark side, if produced or used inappropriately. As a result, the fruits of research are now scrutinized more closely than at any time in the history of human civilization. It is no longer possible for new pharmaceuticals to be unleashed on an unsuspecting populace without first conducting extensive trials, to ensure that the new drugs are both therapeutic and safe. It has become increasingly difficult in many countries for both government and private enterprises to be established without first consulting the neighbors who will have to live with the consequences. In the same way that engineers and builders in Western countries found during the latter half of the twentieth century they could no longer build major projects such as infrastructure without first engaging the community affected by the project, it will become increasingly difficult to commercialize the fruits of management, psychological, medical, scientific, and biological research, without the participation of the broader community.

We anticipate that a new generation of social tools will become necessary to support the democratization of the knowledge-creation process. It is often only when a new technology is used that we understand how it could develop in the future and what improvements would make the technology more useful and powerful. Our analysis of the use of wikis and team learning systems for the research process suggests that tools are required to support the process of knowledge integration and formation rather than just data collection and analysis. The knowledge-creation process has reached the stage where the most powerful new learning can only take place when we emphasize synthesis between people rather than objective analysis and truth alone. Wikis and the team learning system are examples of social research tools that can help us achieve this goal.

References

Benkler, Y. (2006). *The wealth of networks: How social production transforms markets and freedom.* New Haven, CT: Yale University Press.

Brostrom, S. (1999). Drama games with 6-year-old children: Possibilities and limitations. In Engestrom, Y., Miettinen, R., & Punamaki, R-L. (Eds.), *Perspectives on activity theory* (pp. 250–263). Cambridge, MA: Cambridge University Press.

Bruns, A. (2008). *Blogs, wikipedia, second life and beyond: From production to produsage*. New York: Peter Lang.

Bruns, A., & Bahnisch, M. (2009). *Social media: Tools for user-generated content: social drivers behind growing consumer participation in user-led content generation [Volume 1: state of the art]*. http://eprints.qut.edu.au/21206/1/Social_Media_-_State_of_the_Art_-_March_2009.pdf

Caldwell, B. (2006). *Re-imagining educational leadership*. Camberwell: ACER Press; London: Sage.

Caldwell, B., Bhowon, R., Daby, S. C., & Harris, J. (2009). *Mauritius on the move: Re-imagining school leadership*, iNet (International Networking for Educational Transformation). http://www.ssat-inet.net/pdf_secure/Mauritius%20on%20the%20move.pdf

Csikszentmihalyi, M. (1975). *Beyond boredom and anxiety*. San Francisco: Jossey-Bass.

Delbecq A. L., & van de Ven, A. H. (1971). A group process model for problem identification and program planning. *Applied Behavioural Science, 7*, 466–491.

Ellyard, P. (1995). *Education 2001: A preferred future for Victorian state education*. Melbourne: Victorian State Secondary Principals Association.

Erdos, P., & Renyi, A. (1959). On random graphs. *Publicationes Mathematicae, 6*, 290–297.

Findlay, J., Fitzgerald, R., & Hobby, R. (2004). *Learners as customers*. Proceedings of the International Conference on Educational Technology (ICET), Singapore.

Findlay, J., & Newman, L. (2005). Exploring ethical issues via ethical dialectical discourse using a face-to-face team learning system, *Eighth Annual Ethics & Technology Conference at St. Louis University*, June 24–24.

Findlay, J., & Fitzgerald, R. (2006). *Rich design: Engaging students as capable designers and co-creators in auto-catalytic learning contexts*. Proceedings of World Conference on Educational Multimedia, Hypermedia and Telecommunications.

Findlay, J. (2007). *Researching well* (Version 3.6). [Computer software]. Sydney: Zing Technologies.

Findlay, J. (2009). *Learning as a game. Exploring cultural differences between teachers and learners using a team learning system*. Unpublished doctoral dissertation, University of Wollongong, Australia.

Fitzgerald, R., & Findlay, J. (2004). *A computer-based research tool for rapid knowledge-creation*. Proceeding of World Conference on Educational Multimedia, Hypermedia and Telecommunications.

Fitzgerald, R. (2007). Open source learning: Wikis as an exemplary model of collaboration and knowledge creation. In St. Amant, K., & Still, B. (Eds.), *Handbook of research on open source software: Technological, economic and social perspectives* (pp. 681–689). Texas Tech University. PA: IGI Global.

Hasan, H., & Crawford, K. (2006). *Innovative socio-technical systems for complex decision-making*. Paper presented at the international conference on creativity and innovation in decision making and decision support (CIDMDS), London.

Hasan, H., Meloche, J., Pfaff, C., & Willis, D. (2007). *Beyond ubiquity: Co-creating corporate knowledge with a wiki*. Paper presented at mobile ubiquitous computing, systems, services and technologies, Papeete, French Polynesia (Tahiti).

Jenkins, H. (2006). *Convergence culture: Where old and new media collide*. New York: NYU Press.

Kauffman, S. (1995). *At home in the universe: The search for laws of self-organisation and complexity*. London: Penguin.

Keen, A. (2007). *The cult of the amateur: How the democratization of the digital world is assaulting our economy, our culture, and our values*. New York: Doubleday.

Leadbeater, C. (2008). *We-think: Mass innovation, not mass production: The power of mass creativity*. http://www.wethinkthebook.net.

Lee, M., & Crawford, K. (2002). *Collective activity to change: A case of expansive learning*. Paper presented at the fifth congress of the International Society for Cultural Research and Activity Theory. Amsterdam.

LeLoup, J., & Ponerio, R. (2006). Wikipedia: A multilingual treasure trove. *Language Learning & Technology*, *10*(2), 12–16. http://llt.msu.edu/vol10num2/net/.

Lih, A. (2004). *Wikipedia as participatory journalism: Reliable sources? Metrics for evaluating collaborative media as a news resource.* Paper presented at the 5th international symposium on online journalism. http://jmsc.hku.hk/faculty/alih/publications/utaustin-2004-wikipedia-rc2.pdf

Losada, M. (1999). The complex dynamics of high performance teams. *Mathematical and Computer Modelling*, *30*, 179–192.

Mayfield, R. (2006). *Power law of participation.* http://ross.typepad.com/blog/2006/04/power_law_of_pa.html.

Meloche, J., & Hasan, H. (2008). *ICT devices as ubiquitous tools for information seeking activity.* Paper presented at The Second International Conference on Mobile Ubiquitous Computing, Systems, Services and Technologies. *UBICOMM 2008.* Spain: Valencia.

Moyle, K., & Fitzgerald, R. (2008). Electronic focus groups. In Hansson, T. (Ed.), *Handbook of digital information technologies: Innovations and ethical issues* (pp. 340–352). Pennysylvania: IGI Global.

Naisbitt, J. (1982). *Megatrends.* New York: Warner Books.

Newman, L., & Pollnitz, L. (2002). *Ethics in action. Introducing the ethical response cycle.* Canberra: Australian Early Childhood Association.

Newman, L., & Findlay, J. (2008). Communities of ethical practice: Using new technologies for ethical dialectical discourse. *Journal of Educational Technology & Society*, *11*(4), 16–28.

Novak, T. P., Hoffman, D. L., & Duhachek, A. (2003). The influence of goal-directed and experiential activities on online flow experiences. *Journal of Consumer Psychology*, *13*(1–2), 3–16.

O'Reilly, T. (2004). *The architecture of participation.* http://www.oreillynet.com/pub/a/oreilly/tim/articles/architecture_of_participation.htmPalmer.

Palmer, P. J. (1998). *The courage to teach: Exploring the inner landscape of a teacher's life.* San Francisco: Jossey-Bass.

Phillips, A. (2009). *Case studies: Wimbledon park primary school.* Wimbledon http://www.viewsandvoices.co.uk/.

Rittel, H., & Webber, M. (1973). Dilemmas in a general theory of planning. *Policy Sciences*, *4*, 155–169.

Shariq, S. (1999). How does knowledge transform as it is transferred? Speculations on the possibility of a cognitive theory of knowledgescapes. *Journal of Knowledge Management*, *3*(4), 243–251.

Surowiecki, J. (2004). *The wisdom of crowds: Why the many are smarter than the few and how collective wisdom shapes business, economies, societies and nations.* New York: Double Day.

Vygotsky, L. (1978). *Mind in society.* Cambridge, MA: Harvard University Press.

Wagner, C., Cheung, K., & Ip, R. (2006). Building semantic webs for e-government with wiki technology. *Electronic Government*, *3*, 36–55.

Ward, S., & Hawkins, L. (2003). Have portable GSS will travel: Focus groups at professional conferences. In Whymark, G. (Ed.), *Transformational tools for 21st century minds: TT21C2003* (pp. 60–65). Eveleigh: Knowledge Creation Press.

Waters, N., & Callan, J. (2003). A team approach sets the stage to enhance learning outcomes in classrooms. In Whymark, G. (Ed.), *Transformational tools for 21ˢᵗ century minds: TT21C2003* (pp. 60–65). Eveleigh: Knowledge Creation Press.

Wenger, E., McDermott, R., & Snyder, W. (2002). *Cultivating communities of practice: A guide to managing knowledge.* Cambridge, MA: Harvard Business School Press.

Whymark, G., Callan, J., & Purnell, K. (2004). Online learning predicates teamwork: Collaboration underscores student engagement. *Studies in learning, evaluation, innovation and development*, *1*(2), http://sleid.cqu.edu.au/viewarticle.php?id = 40.

Willcox, J., & Zuber-Skerritt, O. (2003). Using the Zing team learning system (TLS) as an electronic method for the nominal group technique (NGT). *ALAR Journal*, *8*(1), 61–75.

> Chapter 14

Using Emerging Technologies in Focus Group Interviews

Kathryn Moyle

Introduction

Emergent technologies are defined here as those new technologies that are being adopted by an increasing number of researchers with a view to add value to or improve their research methods. This is not to suggest that emergent technologies are beneficial to research per se, but that emergent technologies are used with that intention. Emergent technologies by definition, however, are those about which there is a limited literature, but are increasingly being used in the field. In Australia, one emergent technology, the *Zing* system, has been adapted to assist in the collection of data in face-to-face focus group interviews in education research.

"Education research" is the conduct of planned, systematic, and creative acts to investigate and understand questions and problems concerning the processes of teaching and learning of individuals within communities and societies (Creswell, 2008; Kervin, Vialle, Herrington, & Okely, 2006). The processes of education and knowledge creation are socially constructed (Giroux, 2001), and so education research is often social, political, and cultural in nature and can be complex and multidisciplinary (cf. Johnson & Christensen, 2004). Qualitative research paradigms (Guba & Lincoln, 1998) often suit such fields of education inquiry because the complexities and interrelationships afforded by qualitative research theories and methods match the demands of complex, robust education research. Interactions between innovations in both research methods and emerging technologies are paving the way for refining traditional methods of data collection and analysis in qualitative education research.

The choice of a particular research method is dependent upon the problem or issue to be investigated. Qualitative data is used by researchers interested in the reasons for certain human behaviors, structures, and/or activities, and involves asking questions about "how" and "why" things are or are not a certain way (Creswell, 2007). Qualitative data is often textual and is collected through methods such as observation, individual interviews, and focus groups (Denzin & Lincoln, 2005). To take into account the diversity and complexity of many research problems, emerging technologies are increasingly being used to gather both quantitative and qualitative data (cf. Jonassen, 2004).

The electronic *Zing* system was used to assist in the data collection of two recent national research projects in Australia: *Leadership and learning with information and communication technologies* (ICT) (Moyle, 2006) and *Student voices—learning with technologies* (cf. Moyle & Owen, 2008). Typically, Australian Government-funded research is undertaken within strict timelines. *Zing* supports the rapid and efficient collection of electronic data through focus group interviews. *Zing* was originally developed in Australia as a group facilitation and knowledge creation tool. It is marketed as a tool for team-building, strategic planning, and for business process reengineering (Zing Technologies, n.d.). The interface of the *Zing* system is designed to foster group processes, described as "talk-type-read-review" (Zing Technologies). Over the past 5 years, the *Zing* system has been adapted for use in education research in Australia to assist the processes and outcomes of data collection used in face-to-face (or synchronous) focus group interviews.

The *Leadership and learning with ICT* national research project was conducted in 2005 on behalf of the Australian Government-funded institute *Teaching Australia, Institute for Teaching and School Leadership*. This research set out to investigate the relationships between school leadership and teaching and learning with technologies. The data was collected with *Zing* through 40 face-to-face focus group interviews with over 400 educational leaders.

The *Student voices—learning with technologies* research was a national research project funded by the Australian Government. This research investigated students' views of learning with technologies. The participants in this research were primary and secondary school students, vocational education and training (VET) students, international higher education students, preservice teacher education students, and early career teachers. Both online surveys and face-to-face focus group interviews using *Zing* were used to collect the data from all student cohort groups.

Zing was used to collect data in the *Student voices—learning with technologies* research to add depth and richness to the data from the online surveys by further investigating issues of interest that emerged from that data. A total of 40 focus group interviews were conducted involving almost 300 participants. Each focus group interview consisted of a homogenous group of participants. That is, only one cohort of students participated in any given focus group interview: primary students participated in focus group interviews with other primary students; preservice teachers with other preservice teachers; and so on.

Both these Australian research projects successfully incorporated the *Zing* technology into the data collection methods employed. This chapter reflects on the issues and benefits of this innovation to data collection in education research and on its applicability in other research settings. It does so by drawing on the experiences gained from conducting face-to-face focus group interviews using *Zing*, to enable the collection of robust data in a timely manner that met external funding requirements.

Collecting Data From Focus Group Interviews

Focus groups can be considered to be a form of "group interview" (Puchta & Potter, 2004), although this view is contested. Bloor, Frankland, Thomas, and Robson (2001) suggest that there are distinctions that can be drawn between group interviews and focus groups. They suggest the distinctions rest in the outcomes achieved from the respective discussions held in these different groups. Bloor et al. argue that researchers use the discussions in focus groups to observe the group interactions, whereas in group interviews the researcher is interested in the answers the group is able to provide. However, both the processes and the outcomes from the discussions in group interviews are of interest. As such, in this paper, group interviews and focus groups are considered as synonymous, and are referred to as "focus group interviews."

Focus group interviews in education research consist of small groups of informed people, participating in social processes and facilitated conversations, to respond to research questions relevant to specified research outcomes (Morgan, 2004; Puchta & Potter, 2004). The discussions are recorded and analyzed to identify participants' views about the particular research topics. The records of the conversations, once transcribed, become textual data (Kvale & Brinkmann, 2009). Views recorded can be both individual as well as group-agreed opinions. Focus group questions are used to stimulate discussion so that the researcher can record the conversations held in response to the research questions. That is, focus group interviews involve situated interactions between informed participants, based upon specific investigative questions.

Meaningful education research contributes to understandings of social constructions of reality, which, Berger and Luckmann (1966) argue, occur through the use of language, where language is understood to refer to the rules for generating speech and texts. Indeed Robin Usher (1996) proposes that language has a central place in education research since most education research practice is textually based. That is, where education research involves human beings engaged in conversations, this leads to the generation of texts, and such "textual practices" can be interpreted broadly to include written notes and recorded verbal conversations collected and then transcribed into written texts. Understanding the social construction of education and the role of textual practices in those social constructions, then, is fundamental for undertaking education research (Herda, 1999). Focus group interviews using *Zing* generate textual data.

Focus group interviews can also be conceptualized as "research conversations" (Merton, Fiske, & Kendall, 1990). Conversation is a basic form of human interaction (Kvale & Brinkmann, 2009); conversations are speech acts that occur in social contexts (Herda, 1999). Interviews are primarily linguistic occurrences, and the main characteristic of an interview is discourse: "meaningful speech between interviewer and interviewee as speakers of a shared language" (Mishler, 1993, pp. 10–11). The transactions of focus group interviews are carried out in conversations premised upon mutual assumptions about how the communication should be undertaken (Puchta & Potter, 2004). That is, the research questions are presented by the researcher to the group, and the responses from the participants provide data that can inform the findings of the identified research questions and create new knowledge.

"Research conversations" form the location or the "construction sites" (Kvale, 1996) for qualitative research data. At these "construction sites," there is an interdependence between human interaction, data production, and knowledge creation, with those taking part in the "research conversations" being the constructors of the research data (Burgess, 1988; Herda, 1999). The meanings of the questions and answers held within these conversations are contextually grounded (Mishler, 1993), and the conversations are used to establish meanings that are jointly understood. Indeed, according to Ricoeur (1988), it is through the process of discussion and debate that some interpretations of meaning are maintained and others discarded.

Conversations in focus group interviews are facilitated so that the discourse is oriented to the interpretative context established within the group. Underpinning this approach to research, the data collection and analysis methods are based on hermeneutic research theory, where the "knower" and "known" are interrelated:

> the interpreter's perspective and understanding initially shapes his [sic] interpretation of a given phenomenon, but the interpretation is open to revision and elaboration as it interacts with the phenomenon in question. (Tappan, 2001, p. 50)

Interpretative research is based on the view that there is not one single "truth," and that all truths are partial (Lincoln & Guba, 2000). Discussions and debates in focus group interviews allow for multiple and partial viewpoints to be presented and recorded. Focus group interviews, then, enable different collective and individual views of the world, and multiple interpretations of what is considered "real" or "legitimate" to be presented. Research that involves many focus group interviews and hence many participants also offers the potential to the researcher of hearing over time the same or similar themes emerging in response to the research questions. That is, the collection of data from informed participants can reach a point of "data saturation" (Denzin & Lincoln, 2005; Flick, 1998). In focus group interviews, data saturation occurs when new views or information are no longer being heard by the researcher.

To determine whether data saturation has been achieved requires the researcher to have access to sufficient participants to get to a point of saturation, and requires the researcher to undertake initial analyses of the data throughout the study. Both the *Leadership and learning with ICT* and *Student voices—learning with technologies* research projects involved the conduct of many focus group interviews with many participants. Several different themes emerged during the course of the data collection, and often similar or the same views on the research questions were presented. There was a convergence of views among several of the informed participants around the respective themes that emerged.

Traditional Methods of Collecting Data From Focus Group Interviews

The collection of data in focus group interviews traditionally has occurred through the use of recording devices: often with a tape recorder and written notes taken by an observer (Krueger & Casey, 2000). The tape-recorded conversations are then transcribed and coded, turning the conversations into texts. The written notes taken together with the transcripts of the group interview conversations become the data ready for analysis. Thus, conversations in educational research become the data collected through focus group interviews.

There are strengths and weaknesses to conducting focus group interviews, however. Benefits include the flexibility of the format, which allows the researcher to explore unanticipated issues and encourage interaction among the participants. Discussions in the focus group interviews can enable the clarification of issues and allow views to be both challenged as well as accepted. Through the analysis of focus group interviews, researchers can create new knowledge and are able to identify what should be done in the future and why.

Traditional recording of data through note-takers and audio recordings, though, can be a limitation to focus group interviews. The intervention of others observing and noting the discussions while not necessarily taking part in them can work against the notion of establishing research conversations in which the participants and the researcher develop joint understandings and constructions of meaning.

Collecting data using note-takers and tape recorders can also be disconcerting to the participants, while transcriptions are laborious and time-consuming for the researcher to produce. Audio recordings can be problematic for the taping of group conversations as the types of microphones necessary to suitably record group conversations tend to also pick up extraneous background noises such as feet tapping, planes flying overhead, and the like. The use of such audio recording devices can also inhibit some participants' conversations. Without the use of video recordings of the focus group interviews, however, (which are sometimes difficult to justify with university ethics committees), it can be difficult for transcription purposes to determine from audio alone as to who was speaking at any given time. A further challenge of recording the data from focus group interviews can be how to ensure that the range of themes generated in the conversations are adequately and accurately recorded.

The traditional methods of data collection in focus group interviews can also mean that individual and group views are at risk of being dissipated through the processes of collection and transcription. That is, where note-takers and audio recordings only are used, participants' views pass through the "filter" of these third parties in the transcription processes. Indeed, as Silverman (1993, p. 124) has observed:

> There cannot be a perfect transcription of a tape-recording. Everything depends upon what you are trying to do in the analysis, as well as upon practical considerations involving time and resources.

Zing is a new tool for conducting research that removes the "third party filter." It is usually used to facilitate group processes, and little use of it has been made as a data collection tool as outlined in this chapter. It is against this backdrop then, that the benefits and limitations of incorporating *Zing* into focus group interviews for qualitative education research are discussed. To understand how *Zing* can be applied to qualitative data collection methods, a brief description of what the *Zing* system is and how it can be applied to education research now follows.

What Is Zing?

The *Zing* system comprises keyboards and the *Zing* software, which allows multiple keyboards to be linked to a single "host" computer. The keyboards are wireless and the cursors all work on the same screen simultaneously. Each keyboard has its own self-contained space on the screen of the "host" computer. With the use of a datashow and large screen, all participants and the researcher are able to see this screen. The screen-view enables 8, 12, or 16 self-contained spaces to be displayed concurrently, thereby accommodating up to 16 keyboards and 17 cursors to operate at once. In both, the *Leadership and learning with ICT* and the *Student voices—learning with technologies* research, eight keyboards and the associated screen-view of eight working spaces were used.

The *Zing* technology, originally developed to assist in strategic team-building activities, has been adapted to be a data collection tool in face-to-face focus group settings for research purposes. *Zing* is of assistance in recording the discussions held in focus group interviews facilitated by the researcher. The group interview questions can be shown visually on the *Zing* software interface as well as read aloud by the researcher. The participants are encouraged to discuss the interview questions with each other in order to clarify their ideas and then to record their views using the keyboards. In this way, each participant can have a conversation with others in the focus group interview, and also directly enter his or her own views into the computer with the use of one of the keyboards, without mediation from a third party. Participants can concurrently see what other people have written, but the participants are not aware of who has what keyboard space on the screen.

Once the participants have discussed and completed their responses to the question, with the aid of the *Zing* software the responses can be read through by the whole group, and participants invited to make observations, identify themes, and add further comments. *Zing* allows both the researcher and the participants to reflect upon and revise their statements before finally submitting them into the research process. At the conclusion of each group interview, the *Zing* system can generate text reports of the responses from all the participants.

Since *Zing* works from a portable laptop computer and the keyboards are wireless, it can be moved and set up in different locations. This portability is beneficial for national research where many focus groups arc conducted in a variety of settings, and the participants involved are drawn from a diverse set of locations.

Using Zing to Collect Data Through Focus Group Interviews

The inclusion of *Zing* in focus group interview research methods has to be constructed as an integral part of the overall group interview processes, and as such, planned at the outset. The researcher must reflect on his or her skills to facilitate group conversations and take into account the practical requirements of including technologies as an integral part of the research method, within the context of the underpinning research theory being applied. These are all fundamental requirements for achieving the desired research outcomes from focus group conversations.

Role and Capabilities of the Researcher

Consistent with traditional approaches to focus group interviews, the use of the *Zing* system is based on the facilitation of group processes to foster research conversations and generate knowledge construction. Group interview processes require an expert researcher/facilitator to ensure the group processes meet the research objectives and the participants stay focused on the research task (Krueger & Casey, 2000; Puchta & Potter, 2004).

To foster research conversations in focus group interviews requires the researcher to have an understanding not only of the issues identified for discussion, but to also have an understanding of the "self" in the research (Herda, 1999). The recognition of the place of the "self" in qualitative research processes implies recognition by the researcher of the reflexive nature of knowledge construction (Harris, 2001). Drawing on his ethnographic work, Stephen Ball (1993) has argued that understanding the place of the "self-as-researcher" requires an understanding of one's preconceptions. Ball further argues that education researchers have to engage in self-reflexivity and to place their preconceptions on hold if they are to gain meaningful data through qualitative research methods. Furthermore, Michael Apple (1995) has argued that understanding the self as a researcher is required in order to be an authentic and honorable researcher.

One of the roles of the researcher using *Zing* in focus group interviews is to facilitate the group's conversations so that the best possible data can be collected, by jointly using discussion and the keyboards for participants to record their views. To facilitate group processes, the researcher has to demonstrate professionalism, self-confidence, and authenticity, and maintain personal integrity (Krueger & Casey, 2000). Facilitating focus group interviews requires the researcher to foster processes to generate answers to the questions; manage the technologies, time, and space available for the research conversations; encourage participation in the conversations by the participants; and respect individuals' and the group's wisdom. In doing so, the researcher encourages the group processes for knowledge creation, while at the same time "reading" the dynamics of the group.

The skills of the researcher as a facilitator, then, are an important factor in this research method, if focus group interviews are to be constructed as "research conversations." To assist the researcher, the *Zing* system incorporates tools that scaffold the processes required to lead the group through guided conversations. The *Zing* system is handled by one person who uses the software and hardware to foster the group processes. As the facilitator of a group interview, the researcher selects the research questions entered into the computer. The researcher facilitates the conversations around those questions so that the views and ideas raised by the participants during a session are recorded. That is, the participants are encouraged to discuss the questions and to contribute their views and ideas using the *Zing* keyboards. Once the views of the participants are recorded, the researcher can facilitate a process whereby the participants can review and reflect on all the responses made and offer further responses if they so choose.

Following each group interview in both the *Student voices—learning with technologies* and the *Leadership and learning with ICT* research projects, all participants of each group were made the offer by the researcher to have the transcript from the group interview session in which they participated e-mailed to them. This strategy meant that the participants received something back for their participation in the group interview, rather than it simply being a one-way activity where they "give" and the researcher "takes." Both the conversations and the data collected were thereby transacted. To achieve such transactions, however, is dependent upon the role the researcher plays in such contexts, and on his or her capabilities of facilitating such approaches to data collection for research purposes.

Zing and Power Relationships

Focus group interviews use people's voices as part of a research methodology that can be affected by the power relationships between the researcher and the participants. A weakness of traditional focus group interviews is that the discussions can be sidetracked or dominated by one or a few vocal individuals (cf. Bloor et al., 2001).

Focus group interviews conceptualized and structured as "research conversations," however, place an emphasis on the talking by the participants, and on the researcher listening to how the participants interpret, understand, and explain their world and their experiences. Research methods that use "research conversations" place an emphasis not only on participants talking but also on listening as a research tool (Forester, 1980; Herda, 1999). The role of the researcher in such contexts is to foster the conversations held in small group situations, and this requires the researcher to listen to the voices of the participants: what they say about their choices and the constraints in their daily lives, and how they explain their own social reality. As Reinharz observes,

> …before you can expect to hear anything worth hearing, you have to examine the power dynamics of the space and the social actors. Second, you have to be the person someone else can talk to, and you have to be able to create a context where the person can speak and you can listen. That means we have to study *who we are and who we are in relation to those we study*. Third, you have to be willing to hear what someone is saying, even when it violates your expectations or threatens your interests. In other words, *if you want someone to tell it like it is, you have to hear it like it is.* (Reinharz in Fine 1994, p. 20; Fine's emphasis)

The role of the researcher is to listen to the participants, which in turn empowers them (Casey, 1995). Listening requires the researcher not to dominate and control the airspace but to share it, and to attend to the messages being told. Such an approach requires constructing the relationships between the researcher and the participants so that the researcher moves away from a position of a "neutral observer" to that of being engaged in the relationship (albeit temporarily) (cf. Casey; Herda, 1999). To achieve this sort of relationship between the researcher and the participants requires consideration of where the power lies within the research method and how that is reflected in the structure of the research conversations (Casey). It requires the researcher to recognize that he or she is not accorded an elite or privileged external position from which to conduct the discussions, but requires the researcher to be conversant with the issues in order to hold meaningful and meaning-making conversations with the participants in the research.

People like being listened to because it legitimates their experiences (Bruner, 1986; Casey, 1995). Placing an emphasis on listening and the joint construction of meaning though (Mishler, 1993) requires that the researcher move away from being an interviewer or participant observer to a co-conversant, able to intelligently listen to and, where necessary, discuss the topics under discussion in the group interview.

In both, the *Leadership and learning with ICT* and the *Student voices—learning with technologies* research projects, the use of the *Zing* system and the datashow to project the responses of each participant onto a large screen provided the participants in each focus group interview with a sense of distance from the responses. Each participant logged onto the *Zing* system using a number or pseudonym with which to identify himself or herself rather than using a real name. This meant that all the responses, although projected onto a screen, stored participants' identities anonymously. This approach allowed all the members of the focus group interview to see the responses of other participants but did not enable the identification of given comments to specific people. In this way, while the discussions in the focus group interviews could enable both assent and dissent, each individual could present his or her views without fear of intimidation or ridicule from others.

An advantage of using the *Zing* system to collect the conversations from the focus group interviews was that it gave each voice equal weight, as each participant was able to record his or her own views through the keyboard, irrespective of other discussions going on within the group. Several participants reflected on this aspect of the research method by recording sentiments similar to the following two responses to the question: "Is there anything else you would like to add?"

> *I liked this system—gives each person a chance to voice their opinion.*
> *Not just the loudest that get to have their say. You can have your say anonymously without worrying about what others think or are going to say.*

Planning Research to Include *Zing*

The conduct of focus group interview sessions requires planning in advance (Bloor et al., 2001). Including the *Zing* system as a seamless component of a qualitative research method for data collection requires that the planning is both robust and detailed, determining approaches to the following issues:

1. What questions should be asked?
2. How many questions can be asked in the timeframes available?
3. What should be the logical flow of questions to ensure conversations are maintained?
4. What "types" of participants will provide the views and information the researcher is seeking?
5. How can confidentiality of the views of the participants be assured?
6. What venues would be appropriate in which to hold the focus group interviews? and
7. What layout of the furniture will enable effective discussion and data collection?

Cutting across these questions is: How will *Zing* be set up and used to assist in the data collection in the focus group interviews?

Zing Processes and Creating the Research Questions

Zing has proved useful for collecting data where the questions are designed to investigate participants' views and opinions about particular issues. Questions are determined prior to the focus group interviews and entered into the host computer before starting the sessions. Like all research, the quality of the research questions is important to the quality of the research data subsequently collected (cf. Puchta & Potter, 2004). The quality of the data collected in focus group interviews using *Zing*, similarly, is in part dependent upon the quality of the group interview questions developed.

The quality of the questions, however, is not only important for the collection of data. Focus group interviews are usually conducted with participants informed about the issues or questions being investigated. As such, in the focus group interviews the participants implicitly or explicitly will put under scrutiny the credibility and legitimacy of the researcher. The group interview questions then, should flow logically one from the other and be seen as meaningful and relevant by the participants, and therefore worthy of discussion.

In the *Leadership and learning with ICT* research project, the group interview questions grew out of a background paper prepared to investigate the policy context and existing research within Australia and overseas concerning the relationships between school leaders and the integration of technologies into teaching and learning. The purpose of the background paper was to assist in the development and clarification of what was to be researched. It was considered important that the focus group interview questions commenced from what was already known about the relationships between school leadership and the integration of technologies into teaching and learning in school education, and that the questions intersected with the lived experiences of the participants. That is, the research was positioned to build on existing knowledge, not to replicate past studies.

The research design of the *Student voices—learning with technologies* research was informed by a literature review of blind peer-refereed studies published since 2002 that investigated the views and perspectives of students in relation to their own learning with technologies. The purpose of the literature review (Moyle & Owen, 2008) was to examine published literature since 2002 to

1.   ascertain what recent research had already been undertaken in the field in Australia and overseas;
2.   identify the various research methods already used in the existing studies;
3.   determine the gaps in these existing studies; and
4.   determine what "next steps" in new research could be undertaken.

This literature review showed that apart from evaluation studies, little recent Australian research had been deliberately and exclusively undertaken to listen to students' views and perspectives about their learning with technologies (Moyle & Owen, 2008). The literature review also provided insights into the topics and types of questions that could be asked of students, in order to build the field of knowledge.

In both the *Leadership and learning with ICT* and the *Student voices—learning with technologies* research projects, the focus group interview questions were developed and then "roadtested" with people who shared the characteristics of the likely participants for the research. In the *Leadership and learning with ICT* research project, the first draft of the focus group interview questions was tried with two school principals. The second draft of the questions and the focus group interview processes using *Zing* were tried with a cross-section of education technology leaders drawn from the Catholic, State, and Commonwealth government education sectors, and from universities. The final version of the group interview questions was endorsed by a small reference committee established to provide input into the *Leadership and learning with ICT* research project.

In the *Student voices—learning with technologies* research project, both the online survey questions and the *Zing* focus group interview questions were tried with the respective cohorts of students before the questions were administered for data collection purposes. The trials involved ascertaining, particularly with the students who were under the age of 18, whether the questions were easily understood and had meaning for them. The researcher was also interested in ensuring that the focus group questions provided richer or deeper data in addition to those collected through the online surveys. Based on the feedback received from the people trying the questions, and on the observations of the researcher of how the questions were treated by the respective cohorts, the final questions were determined.

Length of Focus Group Interviews

Consistent with the processes required to prepare for any focus group interview session, detailed planning is required of the following individual components in the research, and of their interrelationships:

1. the group interview questions;
2. the processes to be used within groups; and
3. the roles the respective participants are to play in the research.

An optimum time for focus group interviews with adults using *Zing* is between 60 and 90 min. The number of questions covered in the allocated time for any given *Zing* group interview in part depends on the degree to which participants are informed about the issues under discussion. Irrespective of the length of time allocated to the interviews though, the questions have to be carefully worded and be suitably penetrating to maintain the interest of the participants and to elicit the depth of responses sought.

In the planning stages of the *Leadership and learning with ICT* research project, it was ascertained through the processes of developing the background research paper and trying out both the research questions and the data collection method that the maximum amount of time for maintaining the group's commitment and concentration to the tasks in the group interview using *Zing* was a period of no longer than 90 min. As such, the final selection of questions was developed so that adult participants could reasonably address them within a 1½-hr session.

In the *Student voices—learning with technologies* research project, however, the length of the focus group interviews conducted with both the adult and child participants tended to be no longer than an hour. Generally, within an hour, no more than five questions were discussed.

In addition to the times scheduled for the group interviews, in both the *Leadership and learning with ICT* and the *Student voices—learning with technologies* research projects, about 1 hr was left between each session in order for the researcher to save the data from the previous group interview and to become refreshed before facilitating the next session.

Types of Questions Suitable to Use With Zing

It has become apparent through using *Zing* to collect data in two national research projects that the benefits afforded by collecting data in this way are influenced by the types of questions used. Questions appropriate to use with *Zing* are open-ended questions, where no options or predefined responses are proposed. That is, the participants provide their own answers to the questions without being provided a fixed set of possible responses. Although *Zing* can be used to collect responses to closed, single-response questions, such questions do not maximize the functionality of the *Zing* system. *Zing* works well when the questions are designed to encourage participants to provide answers that draw on their knowledge, experiences, and understandings. As such, using *Zing* with open-ended questions combined with facilitated processes that encourage the participants to discuss their answers with others, and to use the keyboard to enter their own views, including explanations for their answers, enables a breadth and depth of data to be collected.

The general approach used with fostering focus group interviews using *Zing* is to

1. introduce the participants to the *Zing* keyboards and the *Zing* interface screen;
2. facilitate discussion using a consistent suite of group interview questions; and
3. conclude each session with the question: "Is there anything else you would like to add?"

Introducing Zing—Focusing Participants

At the beginning of each focus group interview session using *Zing*, the researcher has to teach the participants how to use *Zing* to record their views. The use of "focusing questions" in the "*Zing* orientation" encourages participants to bring their thinking to the task at hand. Focusing questions when using *Zing*, then, have the dual purposes of both teaching the participants how to use *Zing* and also addressing questions related to the study.

In the *Leadership and learning with ICT* research project, the researcher asked participants to address the following two focusing questions:

1. briefly describe the type of work you do; and
2. identify what factors have helped you to include technologies in your work.

In the *Student voices—learning with technologies* research project, one focusing question was used with all cohorts of students. All participants in every focus group were asked to describe the types of technologies they use for learning purposes at home or outside of their education or training institution.

To answer the focusing questions, the participants learned how to use the keyboards and to become accustomed to using the working space on the *Zing* interface screen. At the same time, the responses to these questions provided background information for the researcher about the participants in the focus group interview and enabled her to "pitch" the presentation of the research questions in the group sessions, to connect with the participants' experiences.

Focus Group Interview Questions

Following the "*Zing* orientation," the researcher moves into the research questions identified for the study. Examples of the types of open, education research questions that work well with *Zing* are questions such as the following:

1. Could you describe the ways in which you prefer to learn?
2. How do you use technologies for your learning at school?
3. How would you like to include technologies into your learning?
4. Could you describe the ways in which you like your teachers to assist you to learn with or without technologies?
5. In what ways has teaching and learning with technologies been encouraged or discouraged during your teaching practicum?

Open-ended questions were used in both the *Student voices—learning with technologies* and the *Leadership and learning with ICT* research projects to encourage discussion among the group interview participants. In these studies, the research questions were designed with the specific purpose of generating responses both for practical and policy purposes.

All *Zing* sessions conclude with the question "is there anything else you would like to add?" This question allows participants to provide input on any issue he or she feels has not been covered, or not covered sufficiently, during the course of the group interview session. Several participants in both the *Student voices—learning with technologies* and the *Leadership and learning with ICT* research projects took the opportunity to add further comments at this stage of the focus group session. As indicated earlier, some participants in both research projects made unsolicited, positive comments about using *Zing* to record their views in the focus group interviews.

Using Zing Flexibly

Beyond this generalized approach to using *Zing*, the *Zing* system also provides flexibility in the way questions can be presented to the group. Each question used in a focus group interview using *Zing* is selected by the researcher from those questions entered into the host computer. The questions selected are then discussed by the group. As with traditional focus groups, the researcher has control over the order of questions discussed and the amount of time allocated to the discussion of each question. Even though the research questions have been entered onto a computer, the *Zing* technology is sufficiently flexible to not force a "lock-step" approach to the questions, but rather, the interface maintains the researcher's flexibility to delve into topics of specific interest to any given cohort of focus group participants, for a period of time that is at the discretion of the researcher.

A researcher highly competent at facilitating group conversations while "driving" the *Zing* system can also seamlessly include variations to the generalized approach, when appropriate. In this way, one of the benefits of focus group interviews, that of the flexibility of the focus group format that allows the researcher to explore unanticipated issues and encourage interaction among participants, is maintained when using *Zing*. Furthermore, *Zing* in the hands of a competent facilitator allows the group to pursue a new issue of interest not covered in the existing questions, because the researcher can easily move to a place in the system that enables the participants to record their views to unexpected topics.

Environments for Focus Group Interviews

Central to fostering group interviews that address the research questions in dynamic ways is the construction of an environment that is conducive to the conversations being relaxed and free-flowing (Krueger & Casey, 2000). To construct group interview conversations that allow for the open exchange of ideas requires that participants feel able to freely contribute to the conservations (Puchta & Potter, 2004), and this requires planning. Interactions between the practical issues such as the selection and comfort of venues, the ease with which the sessions occur, and the likely impact of the environment and the constitution of the focus groups, on whether the focus group interviews themselves live up to the methodological ambitions underpinning them (cf. Stewart, Shamdasani, & Rook, 2006), have to be considered prior to the conduct of the focus group interviews.

The physical place or location of the researcher in the group interviews has to be considered, because the role of the researcher is to facilitate not to dominate the conversations, and to encourage participants to both discuss and record their views. Creating a welcoming environment that includes *Zing* requires the researcher to carefully plan the approaches to be used in the focus group interviews and to recognize the iterative relationships between the data collection method being employed and the number and type of participants; the ease of access to the room by the participants; the degree of comfort of the room and the furniture; the setup of the room so that it is conducive to fostering conversations; the size of the text of the data-projected images on the screen; and the appropriate lighting for the participants to see each other, their keyboards, and the screen. Furthermore, the researcher must set up the room and the equipment in ways that do not create hazards with the electrical cords.

In both, the *Leadership and learning with ICT* and the *Student voices—learning with technologies* research projects, the room was set up so that the data screen was placed at the front of the room, and "U" shape of tables and chairs for the participants spanned out in front of the screen. The researcher sat at the bottom of the "U" toward the back of the room, to drive the technology and facilitate discussions. The setup of the room using *Zing* provided multiple foci for the participants: the researcher read aloud the question to which she was asking the participants to respond; and the participants were encouraged to discuss their responses with other participants, record their responses using the keyboards, and review the responses of others that were projected on the large screen. These processes enabled the researcher to position herself as a facilitator of group conversations rather than only as a collector of responses to interview questions. The use of the data screen and the keyboards tended to prevent participants from addressing their verbal responses to questions only to the researcher.

The focus group interviews in the *Leadership and learning with ICT* project were conducted in comfortable surroundings suitable for a group interview: usually in a conference room hired and set up specifically for that purpose. The venues for the *Listening to students' and educators' views'* research (Moyle & Owen, 2009) varied depending on the cohort of students involved.

At all group interview sessions for the *Leadership and learning with ICT* project, refreshments such as coffee, tea or soft drinks, and biscuits were available to the participants throughout the session. Care in the selection of the venue was exercised so that, as appropriate, any sectoral or "political" interests were avoided, with comfortable, well-ventilated, "sector neutral" venues used. Consideration was also given to the accessibility of the venue to the participants likely to attend. Wherever possible, cheap or free car parking was easily available at the venue.

The planning required to undertake data collection processes that include technologies such as *Zing* also requires additional thought and time management by the researcher. The setting up and packing up of the equipment, and ensuring before the focus group interview session that the layout of the room is appropriate, requires time to be allocated to this task. Technologies have to work, otherwise the research method can be compromised.

When collecting the data for both the *Leadership and learning with ICT* and the *Student voices—learning with technologies* research projects, the researcher arranged to arrive at each venue for the focus group interviews an hour prior to the first group interview. The purpose of the early arrival was to set up the equipment and check that the technologies were all working as they should, without putting the researcher under any undue pressure as a result of lack of preparation time. It also allowed time for the researcher to undertake any troubleshooting with the technologies, should it be required. This preparatory work enabled the technologies, then, to slip into the background during the group interviews, and allowed the researcher and the participants to discuss the issues at hand.

Participants

Undertaking "research conversations" in focus group interviews means that as researchers, we enter into relationships with participants. The identification and recruitment of participants is a critical step for establishing focus group interviews and gaining the data sought to address the research questions. Usually, participants in focus group interviews are invited to participate because they are able to proffer informed views about the issues under discussion. The researcher, however, has to determine the constitution of the focus groups in light of the demographics of the participants. This requires the researcher to hold in the front of his or her mind the goals of the research and bear in mind that a "one size fits all" method is not necessarily a helpful approach to interviewing (Reinharz & Chase, 2001).

When determining who should be invited to attend which focus group interview, the researcher has to determine whether homogeneous groups of participants are required or not, and if so, the degree to which the "homogeneity" of the focus groups is interpreted. These are professional considerations for the researcher, but have to be considered to ensure the participants are able, as far as is possible, to freely and openly discuss the research questions.

Consideration of the constitution of the focus groups requires acknowledgement that participants from different cohorts may be more powerful than others, and this in turn may affect the social dynamics in the group. It is possible to predict where there are likely to be differential power dynamics, and strategies can be put in place to offset these predicted power differentials between participants, unless, of course, the intention of the research is to observe these differentials in action. To illustrate, school students who are minors are generally a less powerful group than their adult teachers and parents. As such, a researcher is more likely to elicit honest responses from students if the group is a homogoneous student group (Eder & Fingerson, 2001) than if their parents or teachers also participate in the same focus groups as the students. Similar considerations about the relationship between the researcher and the participant and how power intersects with research methods have been highlighted by researchers interested in research involving disempowered groups, although no broad cohort such as "women," for example, will be homogenous: privileged women are more likely to be accustomed to speaking and being heard, for example, than are less powerful women (cf. Reinharz & Chase, 2001).

If homogenous groups of participants are required, then the common characteristics sought have to be determined at the outset. Alternatively, the researcher may not be concerned with the degree of homogeneity that exists in the groups of participants: if so, a justification for the constitution of the groups is nonetheless required. That is, the relationship of the characteristics of participants to the purposes of the research have to be determined prior to inviting participants to be involved in the focus group interviews. The literature review prepared to inform the *Student voices—learning with technologies* research project and the background paper prepared as part of the *Leadership and learning with ICT* research informed the types of participants identified for these respective research projects.

One of the research purposes for the *Student voices—learning with technologies* project was to investigate students' views across different levels of education and training. A cross-section of students drawn from years 5 and 6 in primary schools; years 9 and 10 in secondary schools; training students drawn from a cross-section of trades; international students studying education at university; and preservice teacher education students, were identified as participants. The funding agency for this research also requested that teachers in their first 5 years of teaching be asked to reflect on their experiences of learning with technologies while at university. These characteristics guided the selection of students as participants in the research. It was also determined at this stage that all focus group interviews would be homogenous, that is, students from the same age cohort only would participate in any given focus group interview. This was decided for two reasons: firstly, to avoid unequal power relationships within the focus groups, given the participants ranged in age from primary-aged school students to middle-aged preservice teacher education students; and secondly, the structure of the focus groups allowed an analysis within and across each cohort of students of their common and differing views, without having to extract this data artificially from the transcript of each focus group interview.

The background paper that informed the *Leadership and learning with ICT* research was used to determine that the research participants would be educational leaders in the schools' sector, and would be drawn from both the government and nongovernment school jurisdictions from across Australia. It was assumed that since the participants in the research were identified leaders in the field of technologies in school education, entering an environment that included technologies would not be alienating to the participants. It was anticipated that the background experiences of the participants would contribute to making them feel comfortable in the research setting. In fact, it was found that while most participants in this research were familiar with technologies generally, they had not used *Zing* previously, and so the participants found the sessions edifying in themselves.

Informed Consent and Maintaining Anonymity Using Zing

All participants in both studies were recruited through written invitations, which included an information sheet and an informed consent form. All adult participants who attended a focus group interview in either the *Student voices—learning with technologies* or the *Leadership and learning with ICT* research project, were also provided with an informed consent form and the information sheet as they arrived at the venue. Each group interview session began with an explanation about the research project and the purpose of the informed consent form.

To assist with maintaining participants' anonymity, the processes of acquiring and managing the acquisition of informed consent, and the log-on to the *Zing* system were linked. Each adult informed consent form had a unique number on it and the participant was asked to use that number rather than his or her name when logging onto the *Zing* system. This process ensured each participant's anonymity when recording his or her responses to the group interview questions and when his or her responses were projected onto the *Zing* interface screen, but at the same time allowed the researcher to identify the data of each participant that completed an informed consent form. In this way, should it be required, the researcher was able to withdraw a specific person's data if at some later stage he or she withdrew consent.

A feature of the *Zing* system is that it enables the data recorded through all the keyboards to be converted into a word-processed document with a few computer commands. The software also records comments according to each keyboard. As each consenting participant used the number allocated on his or her respective informed consent form, the transcripts kept all participants' names anonymous to other participants, but could be cross-checked to each individual by the researcher if required.

Adult participants were asked not to submit the signed informed consent form until the end of the group interview session so they were in a position to reflect upon the processes and their submitted comments (albeit their comments were recorded anonymously), so they could assess whether they were indeed willing to give informed consent.

Similar processes of gaining informed consent were used with the adult participants in the *Student voices—learning with technologies* research project. Informed consent for participation in the group interviews by students under the age of 18, however, was required from the parents or guardians of these students. An information sheet and informed consent form were sent home to the parents of potential student participants and those students who returned to the researcher with signed informed consent forms were able to participate in a focus group interview session. To protect these students' identities, they were asked to create a "make believe" name when logging onto *Zing*. By using a pseudonym, the identity of each student was protected within the group and in the processes of data analysis.

Participants and parents of children under the age of 18 were invited to include an e-mail address on the informed consent form if they wanted to receive a copy of the transcript of their group interview session. To make such an offer required that all child participants in the focus group sessions used pseudonyms when responding to the research questions. The process of linking the log-on to the *Zing* system with the processes of acquiring and managing informed consent, however, made these tasks seamless within the overall processes of each group interview.

Preparing the Data for Analysis

This chapter thus far has focused specifically on the processes of data collection through focus group interviews using *Zing*. One of the benefits of *Zing*, however, is that the data can rapidly be made ready for analysis. As such, a brief outline of how the data was collected and prepared for analysis, in both the *Leadership and learning with ICT* and the *Student voices—learning with technologies* research projects, is provided here.

There was an emphasis in the *Leadership and learning with ICT* research on conversations that provided opportunities for the participants to develop their own interpretations, understandings, and explanations to each of the group interview questions. As the researcher was also the facilitator of the focus group interviews, she attended all 40 sessions and listened to the conversations the participants held. Facilitating the groups with the adapted processes of "talk-type-read-review-respond" enabled the researcher to become familiar with the common themes emerging through the focus group interviews. At the completion of each session, the participants' recordings into the *Zing* system were electronically turned into text. This provided the researcher with the opportunity to review the texts after each session. This process enabled reflexivity between the process of data collection and the initial processes of analysis. Indeed, Ball (1993) has argued that reflexivity in data collection and analysis provides rigor in education research.

Once the focus group interviews were completed, all the transcripts generated through the *Zing* system were coded by the researcher and analyzed to identify the major themes that emerged for each question (cf. Denzin & Lincoln, 2005; Ezzy, 2002). The transcripts generated through the *Leadership and learning with ICT* research project provided a range of views about the relationships between leadership, teaching, and learning with technologies. The transcripts provided the basis for the development of the findings and creation of new knowledge from the research. The themes raised by the different individuals and groups were reflected upon and discussed in the research findings, and these provided insights for future policy directions.

Similarly, in the *Student voices—learning with technologies* research project, once the 40 focus group interview sessions were complete, the responses to each question, within and across each cohort of participants, were coded and analyzed for recurring themes. The data from the focus group interviews were then placed alongside the findings from the online surveys, and these were used to provide deeper insights into the findings from the online surveys. Again, adapting the *Zing* group processes to "talk-type-read-review-respond" enabled the researcher to engage in research conversations and become familiar with the common themes emerging.

The use of *Zing* for the data collection phase in both these national research projects enabled the data for these projects to be collected in a timely manner. Through the *Zing* software functions, the generation of textual data collected directly from the responses provided by the participants enabled the data to immediately be prepared electronically, ready for analysis.

Conclusion

Zing is an emergent technology that has been used in two national, Australian education research projects to assist the processes of data collection from focus group interviews, where textual data is collected and interpreted. *Zing* was originally developed to assist groups of people to work collaboratively to create, sort, rank, and/or evaluate concepts using interactive processes supported through the *Zing* technology (Findlay, 2000). Publications to date about *Zing* have tended to focus upon *Zing*'s role as a "knowledge-building" tool or to support nominal group techniques (Whymark, Callan, & Purnell, 2004; Willcox & Zuber-Skerritt, 2003), rather than to address how it has been used specifically and purposefully as a research tool to support data collection. As such, to include the *Zing* system into the data collection approaches for the focus group interviews in the national, Australian education research projects outlined here represented new work and required the researcher to be reflexive, and to reflect upon and adapt existing approaches to focus group data collection techniques. As a result of this work though, it has been found that *Zing* offers improvements to traditional methods of data collection used in focus group interviews. Indeed, the beneficial characteristics of using face-to-face, synchronous focus group interviews for data collection are maintained, while *Zing* also provides the researcher with the added ability to ensure that all the voices in the group are "heard" equally, by putting the keyboard for recording their respective views, directly into the hands of the participants. This functionality of *Zing* provides the capacity for participants to simultaneously record their views directly, rather than indirectly through transcription processes.

Applying emergent technologies such as *Zing* to assist in collecting qualitative data also has applicability to other forms of social science research. One of the strengths of the *Zing* system for social science research is that it is sympathetic to interpretative research methods. The discussion, exchange, and recording of views and ideas that the *Zing* system supports, facilitates joint constructions of knowledge (Elliott, 2002), irrespective of the field of inquiry. While *Zing* is beneficial for collecting data in group interviews or focus groups, it could also be usefully applied to other research methods such as case studies, narrative research, action research, and actor network theory: indeed, any qualitative research method where the views on a particular issue are to be sought from a range of individuals, either as a snapshot in time or periodically over time.

The capacity for *Zing* to be applied to different social science data collection methods, however, requires the application of *Zing* to occur based upon the functionality for which it was designed, that is, to enable individuals and groups of people to undertake knowledge-building activities (Elliott, 2002). Not all emerging technologies add value to existing research methods, and so regular reexamination of the interrelationships between technologies and different research methods is necessary if theories and methods are to be honored, and high quality data is to be collected.

To include *Zing* in social science research methods requires the researcher to bring together an understanding of theories of research, data collection methods appropriate to the theory informing the specific research, and an understanding of the practical requirements of carrying out the data collection using technologies. That is, the research method and the functionality of the technology must iteratively support each other. In addition, with *Zing*, the researcher has to reflect on his or her skills to facilitate group conversations, and to simultaneously manage the practical requirements of including technologies as an integral part of the research method, within the context of the underpinning theory for the research. Thoughtfully applied, however, the *Zing* system can add value to existing data collection methods, and enable the data collection to be meaningfully undertaken, consistent with interpretative research methods.

Characteristics of the *Zing* functionality that support data collection for social science research include the use of open-ended questions, where participants are encouraged to tell their stories or outline their views in their own words, using the *Zing* keyboards and screen interface. The respective self-contained working spaces in *Zing* provide anonymity for the participants. The computer image projected onto a large screen provides a sense of distance between what the participants are writing and the words on screen, and as such offer participants the capacity to be frank in their responses to the questions, while taking part in processes where they contribute their views to larger group discussions. To collect data through research conversations using *Zing* though, also requires the researcher to ensure the room layout is comfortable to enable meaningful talk within the group to occur, while ensuring participants' keyboards are set up and work properly. Furthermore, the participants have to be able to easily see the screen, and the words on the screen have to be large enough that the researcher and all the participants can effortlessly read the research questions and the respective responses of the other participants. Once a data collection session is completed, the *Zing* system with a few keystrokes can generate text reports of the responses from participants, again maintaining each individual's anonymity. Both the researcher and the participants can rapidly receive a text transcript of their *Zing* session, but with identities remaining confidential. Once the data becomes textual, different analyses can be undertaken such as a thematic analysis or a critical discourse analysis, depending on the aim of the researcher. It is the interplays between these respective functions of the *Zing* system, and the processes of qualitative data collection, that enable *Zing* to be beneficial to social science research.

In conclusion then, this chapter has discussed how face-to-face focus group interviews, assisted by the *Zing* system, have been used as a method of robust data collection ready for analysis. This method of data collection places technologies in the hands of the participants in face-to-face settings. Reflecting upon how *Zing* has been used to collect data in two Australian, national research projects, it is possible to predict that such an approach is applicable to other contexts. It would appear that wherever a researcher is interested in collecting textual data, traditionally by transcribing audio or video recordings, then in those circumstances, *Zing* offers functionality that when linked with the research processes, offers improvements to social science data collection methods, irrespective of the field of inquiry. Not all emergent technologies offer improvements to, or offer different strategies by which to collect data for research purposes. However, the functionality of *Zing*, when used in conjunction with research methods that value the joint constructions of meaning, enables benefits to these data collection methods to be afforded.

References

Apple, M. (1995). *Review of research in education 21 1995–1996*. Washington, DC: American Educational Research Association.
Ball, S. (1993). Self-doubt and soft data. In Hammersley, M. (Ed.), *Educational research: Current issues* (pp. 32–48). London: Open University, SAGE Publications.
Berger, P., & Luckmann, T. (1966). *The social construction of reality: A treatise in the sociology of knowledge*. New York: Anchor Press.
Bloor, M., Frankland, J., Thomas, M., & Robson, K. (2001). *Focus groups in social research*. London: SAGE Publications.
Bruner, J. (1986). *Actual minds, possible worlds*. Cambridge, MA: Harvard University Press.
Burgess, R. (1988). Conversations with a purpose: The ethnographic interview in educational research. In Burgess, R. (Ed.), *Studies in qualitative methodology*. (Vol. 1, pp. 137–155). Greenwich: JAI Press.

Casey, K. (1995). The new narrative research in education. In Darling-Hammond, L. (Ed.), *Review of research in education* (Vol. 21, pp. 211–253). Washington, DC: American Educational Research Association.

Creswell, J. (2007). *Qualitative inquiry & research design: Choosing among five approaches* (2nd ed.). Thousand Oaks, CA: SAGE Publications.

Creswell, J. (2008). *Educational research. Planning, conducting and evaluating quantitative and qualitative research* (3rd ed.). Upper Saddle Creek: Pearson Education International.

Denzin, N., & Lincoln, Y. (Eds.). (2005). *The SAGE handbook of qualitative research*. Thousand Oaks, CA: SAGE Publications.

Eder, D., & Fingerson, L. (2001). Interviewing children and adolescents. In Gubrium, J., & Holstein, J. (Eds.), *Handbook of interview research: Context and method* (pp. 181–159). Thousand Oaks, CA: SAGE Publications.

Elliott, A. (2002). Scaffolding knowledge building strategies in teacher education settings. In Crawford, C., Willis,D. A., Carlsen, R., Gibson, I., McFerrin, K., Price, J., et al. (Eds.), *Proceedings of society for information technology and teacher education international conference 2002* (pp. 827–829). Virginia: Association for the Advancement of Computing in Education.

Ezzy, D. (2002). *Qualitative analysis. Practice and innovation*. Crows Nest: Allen and Unwin.

Findlay, J. (2000). *Zing technologies and grouputer (Version 5.1.203)*. Eveleigh: AnyZing Technologies Ltd.

Fine, M. (1994). Dis-tance and other stances: Negotiations of power inside feminist research. In Gitlin, A. (Ed.), *Power and method. Political activism and educational research* (pp. 13–35). New York: Routledge.

Flick, U. (1998). *An introduction to qualitative research: Theory, method and applications*. London: SAGE Publications.

Forester, J. (1980). Listening: The social policy of everyday life—critical theory and hermeneutics in practice. *Social praxis, 7*, 219–232.

Giroux, H. (2001). *Theory and resistance in education: Towards a pedagogy for the opposition* (2nd ed.). Westport: Bergin and Garvey.

Guba, E., & Lincoln, Y. (1998). Competing paradigms in qualitative research. In Denzin, N., & Lincoln, Y. (Eds.), *The landscape of qualitative research: Theories and issues* (pp. 195–220). Thousand Oaks, CA: SAGE Publications.

Harris, M. (2001). The place of self and reflexivity in third sector scholarship: An exploration. *Nonprofit and voluntary sector quarterly, SAGE Journals*, 747–760.

Herda, E. (1999). *Research conversations and narrative. A critical hermeneutic orientation in participatory inquiry*. Westport, Connecticut; London: Praeger.

Johnson, B., & Christensen, L. (2004). *Educational research: quantitative, qualitative, and mixed approaches* (2nd ed.). Boston: Allyn and Bacon.

Jonassen, D. (Ed.). (2004). *Handbook of research on educational communications and technology* (2nd ed.). New Jersey; London: Lawrence Erlbaum Associates.

Kervin, L., Vialle, W., Herrington, J., & Okely, T. (2006). *Research for educators*. Melbourne: Thomson Social Science Press.

Krueger, R., & Casey, M. A. (2000). *Focus groups. A practical guide for applied research*. Thousand Oaks, CA: SAGE Publications.

Kvale, S. (1996). *InterViews. An introduction to qualitative research interviewing*. Thousand Oaks; London; New Delhi: SAGE Publications.

Kvale, S., & Brinkmann, S. (2009). *InterViews: learning the craft of qualitative research interviewing*. Los Angeles: SAGE Publications.

Lincoln, Y., & Guba, E. (2000). Paradigmatic controversies, contradictions, and emerging confluence. In Denzin, N., & Lincoln, Y. (Eds.), *Handbook of qualitative research* (2nd ed.). Thousand Oaks, CA: SAGE Publications.

Merton, R., Fiske, M., & Kendall, P. (1990). *The focused interview. A manual of problems and procedures* (2nd ed.). New York: The Free Press.

Mishler, E. (1993). *Research interviewing. Context and narrative.* Cambridge, MA: Harvard University Press.

Morgan, D. (2004). Focus groups. In Hesse-Biber, S., & Leavy, P. (Eds.), *Approaches to qualitative research: A reader on theory and practice* (pp. 263–285). New York: Oxford University Press.

Moyle, K. (2006). *Voices from the profession.* Canberra: Teaching Australia, Australian Institute for Teaching and School Leadership.

Moyle, K., & Owen, S. (2008). *Students' expectations about learning with technologies: A literature review.* Canberra: University of Canberra. http://www.aictec.edu.au/aictec/webdav/site/standardssite/shared/Learner_Research_Literature_Review.pdf.

Moyle, K. and Owen, S. (2009). *Listening to students and educators views of learning with technologies. The views of learners and early career educators about learning with technologies in Australian education and training, Research findings,* Department of Education, Employment and Workplace Relations (DEEWR) Canberra, http://www.deewr.gov.au/Schooling/DigitalEducationRevolution/Resources/Pages/Resources.aspx#stuvoice

Puchta, C., & Potter, J. (2004). *Focus group practice.* London: SAGE Publications.

Reinharz, S., & Chase, S. (2001). Interviewing women. In Gubrium, J., & Holstein, J. (Eds.), *Handbook of interview research: Context and method* (pp. 181–159). Thousand Oaks, CA: SAGE Publications.

Ricoeur, P. (1988). *Time and narrative* (Vol. 3). Chicago: University of Chicago Press.

Silverman, D. (1993). *Interpreting qualitative data. Methods of analysing, talk, text and interaction.* London: SAGE Publications.

Stewart, D., Shamdasani, P., & Rook, D. (2006). *Focus Groups. Theory and practice* (2nd ed.). Thousand Oaks; London; New Delhi: SAGE Publications.

Tappan, M. (2001). Interpretive psychology: Stories, circles, and understanding lived experience. In Tolman, D., & Brydon-Miller, M. (Eds.), *From subjects to subjectivities: A handbook of interpretive and participatory methods* (pp. 45–56). New York: New York University Press.

Usher, R. (1996). A critique of the neglected epistemological assumptions of educational research. In Scott, D., & Usher, R. (Eds.), *Understanding educational research* (pp. 9–32). London: Routledge.

Whymark, G., Callan, J., & Purnell, K. (2004). Online learning predicates teamwork: Collaboration underscores student engagement. *Studies in Learning, Evaluation, Innovation and Development.* 61–71. Australia: Central Queensland University.

Willcox, J. & Zuber-Skerritt, O. (2003). Using the Zing TLS as an electronic method for the NGT. *Action Learning and Action Research Journal.* 59–72. Australia: Action Learning, Action Research and Process Management (ALARPM) Association Inc., Interchange and Prosperity Press.

Zing Technologies. (n.d.) *Zing.* Sydney: Zing Technologies http://www.anyzing.com/whyzing.html.

> Chapter 15

Toward Experimental Methods in Collaborative Computing Research

Gregorio Convertino and John M. Carroll

Introduction

Disciplines such as Human-Computer Interaction (HCI), Computer-Supported Cooperative Work, and Information Systems are relatively new research areas that emerged after the invention of computers in 1946. These disciplines are still in the process of defining their theories and corpora of research methods. A unique trait that these technology-related disciplines share is that the research aims at advancing both science and technology development. The researchers and their interdisciplinary teams pursue the goal of producing new knowledge but also aim at engineering new tools for practical uses.

This chapter focuses on research in Computer-Supported Cooperative Work (CSCW) and Groupware, which is software typically aimed at groups of knowledge workers in organizations. Hereon, we will refer to these research areas as "*Collaborative Computing*" (CC) research. The thesis proposed on research methods within CC research is that for a well-informed exploration and development of emergent collaborative technologies, we need to utilize and to integrate the full arsenal of empirical methods and, specifically, we need to integrate lab-based and field-based studies. In addition, to integrate field and lab methods, we also need to contextualize them to better serve the specific needs of CC research. We will show that *this field is lacking the proposed field-to-lab integration and is still missing native experimental lab methods*. As a "case study" that concretely articulates our thesis about how we should investigate emergent collaborative technologies, we present a research program on awareness and knowledge sharing in computer-supported teams, where field studies are integrated with laboratory studies.

In the following sections, the emergence of CC research and its novelty will be discussed, as well as the methodologies, implications, and some basic deficiencies in current research methods.

Collaborative Computing Research: Brief History

Collaborative Computing research became its own field in the early 1980s (Grudin, 1994). The emergence of this new field was prepared by the combination of a few key events that had occurred throughout the 1970s. These included the advent of the personal computer for nonprofessional users, the technological advancements in telecommunication systems that enabled computer networks (LAN), and the diffusion of software applications for automating office work such as word processors and spreadsheets.

During the 1980s, personal computers were introduced to support nonexpert users and nonprogrammers. Researchers of human-computer interaction (HCI), which mostly consisted of psychologists and computer scientists, started developing specific research methods to study the interaction between users of the personal computer, as individuals, and specific software applications (e.g., the thinking-aloud method, the GOMS method). The studies of editing applications became so common that text editors were defined as the "white rats" of HCI researchers (Carroll, 1997).

The research on groups and groupware followed the research on single-user applications. As personal computers became powerful enough to support groups of office workers through file-sharing, word processors, spreadsheets, e-mail, and shared output devices (e.g. printers), small groups became an important new market for vendor companies. Thus, office systems, office automation systems, or office information systems became widespread (see Grudin, 1994, 2008). An illustrative example of an early office system is the spreadsheet. The intuitive conceptual model of the spreadsheet program (i.e., VisiCalc) combined with a simple interactive tabular interface led to the first popular spreadsheet program, Lotus 1-2-3 (1983), running on an IBM personal computer. The spreadsheet was one of the first office applications allowing knowledge workers to partially automate their work and collaborate with their colleagues (Nardi, 1993). Soon after, a series of more advanced collaborative technologies for file-sharing and group communication entered the workplace, such as electronic mail, desktop conferencing and videoconferencing systems, collaborative document editors, and electronic meeting rooms or systems for group decision making.

In the meantime, the research on Office Automation became its own area and remained influential for nearly a decade, during the early 1980s. Two conferences, the annual Office Automation and the Biannual Office Information System, and two journals, *Office: Technology and People* and *ACM Transactions on Office Information Systems*, were born in this period. The research on applications for minicomputers in office settings was added to prior research on applications for mainframes or management Information Systems (IS).

In this context, researchers and practitioners, mostly from computer science, social sciences, and management sciences in academic or industrial labs in the United States and Europe, saw the opportunity to study and engineer computer systems that could support collaboration in groups or organizations, rather than just individual workers. While several technical challenges had been addressed, it soon became clear that the harder challenges pertained to understanding how groups and organizations operate and, then, translating such understanding better collaborative systems that address the newly specified requirements or needs.

During the second half of the 1980s and the 1990s, this interdisciplinary group of researchers and practitioners constituted a community that focused on CC applications and began sharing prototypes and empirical results at workshops and conferences such as the biannual ACM CSCW and ACM Group conferences, which replaced the prior Office Information Systems conference in North America, and the biannual European CSCW (ECSCW) conference. Previously, several of these researchers had studied individual users or developed prototypes for single-user applications (HCI), while others had studied or prototyped management information systems for organizations, such as Management and Information Sciences (see Grudin, 1994, 2008).

Since the 1990s, CC research has expanded considerably, becoming a visible field. The community remains interdisciplinary in its composition. It includes ethnographers, psychologists, computer scientists, engineers, and other professionals. Additionally, the collaborative tools have dramatically changed the collaborative practices of workers in organizations. Several of these changes have been documented and investigated by the CC community. The research findings appeared in several international conferences, an area-specific journal (i.e., CSCW or Computer Supported Cooperative Work journal, published by Springer), and other journals in the areas of Human-Computer Interaction and Information Systems.

Collaborative Computing: Innovative Technology

The set of tools investigated in CC research is very diverse, although they all support some aspect of collaboration. CC research has evolved along with the appearance and innovation of new tools. During the 1980s, the Graphical User Interfaces represented a key innovation that changed the interaction with computers. Since then, with the diffusion of computer networks, several other innovations have emerged. Tools such as e-mail, videoconferencing, and the Internet (WWW) have changed how people communicate, get information, and collaborate.

Early collaborative applications focused mainly on supporting communication and collaborative editing, for example, e-mail, chat or Instant Messaging, bulletin boards, or shared text editors. Other applications supported groups in performing a common task and provided a shared workspace (Ellis et al., 1991). Examples of these applications include electronic meeting rooms used for colocated meetings (Nunamaker et al., 1991), group decision-making systems (gBIS, Concklin & Begeman, 1988), and commercial systems for the enterprise such as Lotus Notes, which supported electronic mail, teleconferencing, and a shared database (Lotus, 1989). Similar applications have followed including Microsoft NetMeeting and Ray Ozzie's Groove Networks.

During the late 1990s, the variety of the collaborative systems available increased significantly due to the rapid diffusion of e-mail clients for asynchronous communication, video conferencing systems for meetings, content-sharing via the Internet (or Web pages), and multiuser domains and collaborative virtual environments for social gaming.

Since 2000, the variety of tools has increased even further with the emergence of a new generation of Web-based collaborative tools (Web 2.0 tools such as wikis, blogs, photo-/video-/bookmarks-sharing tools, social networking tools) and the increasing availability of networked mobile devices making it possible for people to share, coordinate, and collaborate through computers outside the traditional walls of offices and work hours. Moreover, the collaborative tools within traditional work settings are also increasingly Web-based. Presently, medium and large enterprises are more and more often adopting Web services such as commercial platforms that include tools or features for collaboration, coordination, and information sharing. These platforms include IBM Lotus Bluehouse (called LotusLive, from 2009), SAP NetWeaver, and Windows SharePoint Services.

Collaborative Computing: Innovative Research

The two key consequences of research on collaborative systems for knowledge workers have been that the new and more efficient forms of collaboration enabled. For example, electronic mail and teleconferencing systems enable distributed (or remote) collaboration, either synchronous or asynchronous, *in ways that were not possible before*. Additionally, several collaborative tools, such as those for task management or for decision-support, help groups *reduce their process costs or improve their productivity*. For example, electronic brainstorming tools can enable more cost-effective idea generation in groups.

The rapid evolution of the technology suggests that the spectrum of possible forms of collaboration and the very definition of collaborative technology have changed over time. On the other hand, the fundamental functions that these various tools support remain moderately stable. Such functions include: communication and information sharing via e-mail, instant messaging, shared databases; coordination and mutual awareness via shared calendars, buddy lists, versioning systems; and cooperative production via workspaces for collaborative writing, drawing, or decision making.

More recently, some collaborative Web-based tools also support *new* functions for large sets of people. For example, social networking tools (e.g., LinkdIn, Beehive, Facebook, or Twitter), applications for sharing bookmarks (e.g., Del.icio.us), wiki (e.g., MediaWiki), and thematic blogs support new social functions such as staying connected or informed or building social capital. These tools are typically targeted at social units larger than small groups of knowledge workers, such as communities of interest or professional communities of practice or learning (e.g., containing up to hundreds of members).

In summary, what is emergent about CC technologies are the new endeavors in which communication, coordination, collaboration, and socialization are made possible. The goal of CC researchers is to develop and test solutions (i.e., user interfaces or features in the back-end) that improve the quality and efficiency of these work endeavors.

To this end, understanding the human behavior around innovative technology is necessary but not sufficient. Differently from social and behavioral researchers, for the CC researcher the technology is also a primary object of interest, by itself and in relation to the humans. In other terms, CC research is an applied research area, where the ultimate goal is not to just to understand collaboration but also to apply the findings in order to improve the technology.

While a new class of human-computer-human interactions has been enabled and is now available for investigation, CC researchers are still in the process developing midrange theories and research methods native to their field. After three decades of work, a key challenge for the scientific research in the CC community is to properly balance their efforts between two basic, competing goals: (1) understanding the new phenomena induced by the latest collaborative technology, which is constantly changing, and (2) establishing general scientific foundations for the new field of study, such as a stable corpus of theories and methods.

Research Methods in CC Research State of Research Methods

Since the 1980s, there have been two main themes in the debate on methods in HCI (Carroll, 2003) and Human Factors (Meister, 2004). The first theme pertains to the maturity of the methods. They were primarily imported from the fields of Psychology (lab experiments and survey-based studies), Computer Science (simulation studies with conceptual models), and Social Sciences (ethnography and case studies). That is, HCI theories and models were not as mature or standardized as the theories and models in the more established sciences such as Physics. This consequently led to prolonged research and an unmanageable body of empirical data; this also spawned the second theme for debate, which pertains to the costs and efficiency of methods to evaluate technology.

Two classes of methods can be distinguished in the context of this debate: on one hand, the *systematic research methods* used by scientists to acquire new understanding (i.e., identify general principles) and design innovative prototypes (i.e., test general principles); on the other hand, the *usability evaluation methods* implemented by the practitioners to provide focused feedback during the development of new technologies (e.g., industrial products).

Traditionally, the efforts of CC research have primarily focused on the development of new technologies such as commercial products or research prototypes, and in part on characterizing new and old collaborative practices in the workplace. Much less attention has been given on to how to develop more rigorous research methods for systematically studying collaboration and assess the effects of specific properties of the technology on specific attributes of the users' behaviors. A few researchers have started arguing for the need to fill in such a gap in methodology, as suggested by the next section.

Analyses of Research Methods

Very few scholars have analyzed the state of research methods adopted in CC research. Some have found that the methods are often *ad hoc*, or *nonstandard*, and *informal*. Pinelle and Gutwin (2000) performed a meta-analysis of 45 papers from eight venues of the ACM CSCW conference between 1990 and 1998. They analyzed the research papers that presented new groupware applications or those that evaluated existing applications. They found that almost one third of the groupware applications presented were not evaluated in a formal way. Many applications received only an informal evaluation. Across all the papers, the methods used included very heterogeneous collection and analysis techniques, which suggest that CC research lacks a uniform corpus of native methods or a set of agreed principles for choosing the methods.

Plowman, Rogers, and Ramage (1995) analyzed a complementary segment of research literature: a sample of research papers about workplace studies from the European CSCW conference or the Journal of CSCW. This meta-analysis also revealed that there were very few studies that focused on systematic evaluation of technology in the workplace. Moreover, very few contributed design guidelines that were specific enough to offer useful guidance. Instead, numerous research papers contributed a case study and then concluded with general or semi-intuitive recommendations for design (Ramage, 1999).

Other researchers have observed that the methods are often selected based on their cost and the phase of development of the technology (Herskovic, Pino, Ochoa, & Antunes, 2007). In contrast, it has been argued that in the interest of sound scientific research different types of methods should be integrated for a more comprehensive assessment of the same phenomena in different conditions (Twidale, Randall, & Bentley, 1994; McGrath, 1995). Specifically, lab-based methods could be integrated with field methods, or the lab or field methods could be integrated with computational simulations. Herskovic et al. (2007) came to similar conclusions after examining the very diverse set of methods used to assess groupware systems.

These studies pointed to the value of integrating multiple methods *within a study*. But it can also be argued, more generally, that it is beneficial to integrate multiple methods at the level of research programs, or *within series of related studies*. We argue that running series of studies as part of coherent, applied research programs better suits the needs of CC research than running isolated studies. The object of study is complex and the CC research community is young and needs conditions that favor the accumulation of theory and methods native to this field (this argument finds inspiration in the *research programmes* approach proposed by Lakatos, 1978).

Other researchers have pointed to the lack of explicit mapping between the methods selected and the conceptual model and the goals driving the research (e.g., Neale, Carroll, & Rosson, 2004; Steves & Scholtz, 2005). In fact, the selection of specific measures and, later, the interpretation of the data collected via these measures are guided (either explicitly or implicitly) by the conceptual model (or theory) and the goal of the researchers. Thus, it is more beneficial if the researchers map explicitly their methods onto the conceptual model that they assume. In contrast with atheoretical or opportunistic approaches, such a model-based approach enables better comparisons and accumulation of findings across studies on a related phenomenon. Shapiro (1994) also pointed to the disadvantages of using theory-agnostic methods in this applied field.

More recently, Convertino, George, and Councill (2006) conducted an extensive analysis of the papers published at the ACM CSCW conference: 466 research papers from 1986 to 2006. They found that the most common *level of analysis* chosen for the research (individual, group, or organizational) was the group level, comprising 70–80% of the total analysis, while 20–25% of papers focused on organizations or communities. More recently, the studies of these broader socio-technical systems are gradually increasing, as Web applications enter the consumer domain and then the workplace. These papers also categorized the type of the *predominant contribution* made by each paper (theory development, technology design, or an empirical study) and found a decline in the contributions on theory, while the papers containing empirical studies of work practices or system evaluations increased from about 40% to 70%; the contributions about technology design remained relatively high over the years. Finally, they categorized the papers based on the *basic functions of cooperative work* being studied (communication, coordination, or cooperative work) and found that the studies focused predominantly on the functions of coordination (or awareness) and communication (or information sharing).

For this chapter, we extended the above-mentioned analysis and conducted a more in-depth meta-analysis on the papers published in the first two ACM CSCW conference venues in 1986 and 1988, and in the recent venue in 2006. The meta-analysis revealed that there has been a strong increase in the proportion of research papers reporting about empirical studies. In 2006, compared to the papers from the late 1980s, the informants were more often from academia or IT industry (research) settings, most likely because they are more accessible to researchers. Over 2/3 of the empirical studies involved study participants either from academia (1/3) or the IT industry (1/3) compared to 25–45% during the first two venues (1986 and 1988). For the data analysis, qualitative methods have remained the dominant technique (about 53% of the papers in 2006, compared to 43–50% during the first two venues), while the percentage of studies using quantitative analysis has increased (from about 13–29% during the first two venues to 38% in 2006) together with the studies that use formal manipulation of research variables (from 13–17% in the first two venues to 34% in 2006).

This recent meta-analysis provided evidence consistent with the prior meta-analyses. No systematic effort to integrate different types of methods in the same research projects was found. The studies tended to be unilaterally oriented either toward naturalistic field methods or controlled lab studies. Moreover, the overall ratio between field and lab studies constantly remained in favor of field studies (about six field studies for each lab study). The lab studies focused on short tasks while field studies focused on longer tasks, but there were no systematic attempts to integrate findings between the methods of these two. Finally, just one third (36%) of the empirical studies had an explicit definition of research questions or hypotheses, and even fewer (13%) had a clear mapping to the explicit models or concepts being investigated.

Deficiencies in Current Research Methods

The meta-analyses presented in the previous section suggest that the field of CC research is the result of a successful collaboration between groups of researchers from different schools of thought (i.e., field researchers versus experimentalists, corporate versus academic researchers). However, these groups continue to differ significantly in their biases, agendas, access to technology, types of research settings, and informants. In the interest of promoting a more homogeneous discussion about the problems, the solutions, and the criteria, we point below to a few basic deficiencies in current research methods and then propose our solution.

The debate on research methods has often lacked a rigorous distinction between research and non-research methods. On one hand, the researchers' methods are primarily used to experiment with proof-of-concept prototypes and the aim is to gain a *general* understanding of regularities in the interaction between the users and the technology prototypes. On the other hand, practitioners' techniques, such as usability evaluation methods, are primarily used to assess prototypes and are aimed at informing the development of *specific* commercial products developed in the software industry. The discussion about these two classes of research methods should be distinct because the goals are different. This chapter focuses on the former, the *research methods* used by scientists.

A first general deficiency pertains to the lack of integration between field and lab methods. The overall offset of methods in research projects tends to be *unilaterally oriented* toward either field methods, such as ethnography and ethnomethodology imported from Sociology (e.g., studies of work practices), experimental methods, such as laboratory methods from Psychology (e.g., experiments with videoconferencing prototypes), or simulation methods, such as analysis and computational modeling of social networks from Computer Science (e.g., information flows via e-mail).

A second deficiency is that research methods (i.e., techniques for manipulation, control, and measurement) have been *imported* without adaptation from other disciplines, although the object of the study and the end goal of researchers have changed. The selection of research methods is driven by "surprisingly orthodox strategies" (Randall, Twidale, & Bentley, 1996, p. 16). The methods currently used are mostly those imported from disciplines such as Psychology, Social Sciences, and Computer Science. Instead, we believe that traditional methods such as Psychology's lab experiments or ethnomethodology need to be contextualized to adequately capture the complexity of collaborative technologies being used in realistic conditions.

A third deficiency pertains to the relationship between methods and theory. Once imported, the research methods tend to remain *ad hoc* (nonstandard, e.g., Inkpen,

Mandryk, DiMicco, & Scott, 2004) and are often not explicitly related to the theoretical models of the phenomena being studied. The measures selected are often heterogeneous, spanning from quantitative indicators of performance of individual users to qualitative accounts of complex practices of organizations. Rarely do researchers map their measures onto the theoretical concepts to clearly motivate their selection.

CC researchers have recognized that the evaluation of CC technology is difficult (Grudin, 1988) and needs to occur in a realistic context (Twidale et al., 1994). However, prior meta-analyses of the methods have suggested that either the procedures adopted in field studies are *unsystematic* and mostly based on informal observations *or*, when procedures are systematic and occur in the lab, the study conditions observed are often too *simplistic* (e.g., Twidale et al.; Pinelle & Gutwin, 2000; Randall et al., 1996).

A general consequence of the above-mentioned deficiencies is that it is difficult for researchers to compare, validate, and accumulate results across studies. In the long term, this leads to inefficient reuse of knowledge and unsuccessful systems because designers may fail to consider the relevant known factors that affect the success of their system.

Proposed Approach to Research Methods

Several researchers have pointed to some of the deficiencies listed in the prior section (e.g., Carroll, Singley, & Rosson, 1992; McNeese, 1996; Neale et al., 2004; Steves & Scholtz, 2005; Damianos et al., 1999). However, there has not been any systematic empirical effort aimed at reducing these deficiencies within a research program. We propose a methodological approach that has three basic properties:

1. *Comprehensive in methods.* The research program integrates multiple measurement strategies. At the level of the program, the results from field studies are integrated with results from laboratory studies. At the level of each study, different types of data are collected about the same central concept (e.g., awareness or common ground in CSCW).
2. *Centered on group process.* The unit of analysis of the research is the work group and the focus of investigation is on global variables that characterize group process, such as the processes of awareness and knowledge sharing in teams. Measures of the quality of the collaboration process are collected over time and related to group performance.
3. *Model-based* (or theory-driven). The investigation is explicitly directed by theory: a conceptual model guides the selection of measures and the interpretation of results.

Implementing the Approach

The rest of this chapter describes a research program as a concrete illustration (i.e., a case study) of how this integrated approach can be employed (Convertino, 2008, PhD thesis). The research program consisted of field studies integrated with laboratory studies.

Two pairs of laboratory experiments, each grounded on a prior field study, investigated, respectively, the processes of awareness and common ground (or knowledge sharing) in computer-supported teams. Each field study informed the design of the laboratory experiments that followed. This setup helped us to implement lab methods that allowed us to collect novel findings about awareness and common ground, which we could later take back to the field. The two subsections below describe, specifically, the two pairs of laboratory experiments following the field studies.

Studies of Activity Awareness

The first half of the research program focused on studying the process of activity awareness in computer-supported distributed teams (2002–2005). Several researchers have documented that when *collaborators work in the same place for an extended period of time (e.g., air traffic controllers in a control room), they tend to align and integrate their activities seamlessly, without interrupting each other, as they work together* (Harper, Hughes, & Shapiro, 1989). Activity awareness (AA) is the process of developing and maintaining this ability of monitoring and coordinating within long-term collaboration. While the opportunities to collaborate remotely via collaborative technology are increasing, the AA process is very often impaired and explicit coordination efforts are needed in these distributed work settings. Thus, CC researchers are developing novel software tools that can better support AA in these settings.

Traditionally, the studies of awareness in collaboration have used, unilaterally, either qualitative methods in naturalistic settings (ethnographic studies), or, experiments in the laboratory with prototypes and simplified short-term experimental tasks. Instead, in our research program we combined a field study with two laboratory experiments on AA.

Following the approach described above, the goal of this first half of the program was to measure and understand the AA process, compare two collaborative software systems, and provide directions for better awareness tools. Explicit conceptual models of AA were used to orient the study. The measures selected were focused on AA as a critical aspect of group process in long-term group work. The research team studied the work of distributed groups or pairs performing a long-term collaborative editing project. A comprehensive set of methods was used: from the findings of the field study to the design of two laboratory studies that followed. Moreover, within each study, multiple measures for the awareness construct were considered.

The field study was conducted over two years, in a school setting, with distributed groups of students and teachers (Neale et al., 2004). Small groups of students distributed across two classrooms collaborated remotely on a science project over a 26-week period (Carroll, Neale, Isenhour, Rosson, & McCrickard, 2003). The BRIDGE software supported the remote collaboration (Ganoe, Convertino, & Carroll, 2004, Ganoe et al., 2003).

The researchers analyzed videos, field notes, digital artifacts, and system logs. Using this data, they identified common factors that disrupted the collaborators' AA process (Carroll et al., 2003; Neale et al., 2004). Four classes of breakdown situations and typical events that induced these four situations were found: that is, disruptive events related to the group, the task, the tool, and the situation or external context. The behaviors exhibited by collaborators in the breakdown situations indicate lack of activity awareness: in fact, explicit coordination efforts are required to reestablish the collaborators' awareness after these events occur. For example, if a collaborator changes the task schedule in the shared calendar without communicating it to the remote partners, then as the incongruence arises the partners will become confused and ask for clarifications in order to gain awareness and move forward with the collaboration.

The two laboratory studies that followed the field study had the goals of, first, validating the experimental method and, then, extending the descriptive findings from the field study with the systematic investigation of possible causal relations that could be inferred between changes in the variables manipulated and the resulting changes in the measures of the AA process. The experiments were conducted in scaled but representative settings.

The first laboratory study was conducted with six remote pairs of collaborators who performed a four-session collaborative school project (Convertino, Neale, Hobby, Carroll, & Rosson, 2004). Although shorter in duration, the collaboration task was analogous to the one observed in the field.

For this study, drawing on the findings of the field study, the researchers had defined a set of scripted scenarios. Each scenario contained one of the typical disruptive events that had caused collaborative breakdowns in the field. In the laboratory study, these scenarios were run as experimental manipulations with the support of a trained confederate, who played the role of the partner. Thus, a study participant and the confederate composed each of the six pairs. The confederate followed a script for each scenario. Because the scenarios were designed to simulate awareness-related situations that had been observed repeatedly in the field, they lent ecologic validity to the laboratory methods. At the same time, the experimental method enabled us to systematically measure the effects of these typical collaborative situations on AA (Figure 15.1).

The results of this laboratory study supported the validity of the lab method. The pairs of collaborators were clearly engaged in the work, performed the project with autonomous initiative, conducted lively discussions, solved problems collaboratively and creatively, and, more importantly, exhibited AA deficits that were representative of those observed in the field.

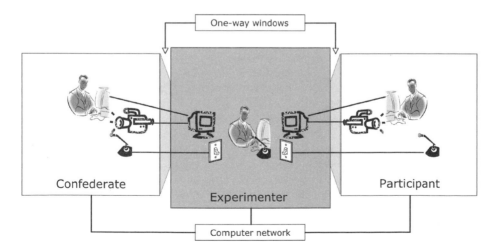

Figure 15.1 Activity Awareness study: collaboration in a distributed setting, via a software prototype.

The results showed that in more than half the cases where experimental manipulations (i.e., scenarios) were introduced, the participants did not become aware of critical disruptive events, such as the collaborator misplacing useful content in the wrong tool within the shared workspace. Participants lacked awareness of these events even after receiving a systematic prompt that drew their attention toward the event. Additionally, similarly to the participants of the field study, the participants of this lab study tended to lack awareness of the overall shared plan, the actual work time available, and the current status of the activity. In summary, the first lab study supported the validity of the approach and provided a method for systematically measuring awareness in a laboratory.

The second laboratory study implemented an extended version of this experimental method. It measured multiple aspects of the AA process over time and compared the effects of two CSCW systems, BRIDGE and Groove (see the conceptual model in Figure 15.2).

Each pair completed a four-session collaborative project over a period of about 3 weeks. The participants performed not only collaborative work but also individual work for each session. They produced new content during the individual sessions and shared this content during the subsequent session, which was collaborative. This doubled the overall time spent in each work session compared to the first study, where the participants performed only collaborative work and were given simulated "results" of individual work before each session. Additionally, this second lab study included multi-session scenarios to introduce manipulations in the collaborative setting over a period of two to three sessions.

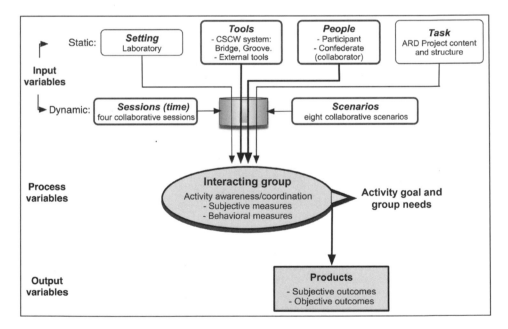

Figure 15.2 Activity Awareness Group Process Model. Classes of variables manipulated, controlled, or measured in the experiment. Bold boxes and arrows indicate the effects focused upon. Blue labels indicate the research questions. This conceptual model adapts the model proposed by McGrath (1984).

Table 15.1 First lab study of Activity Awareness: scripted scenarios used.

Scenario	Breakdown factor	What the confederate (C) does in the scenario
Tool use	*Tool factors: the planning tool is used*	The confederate (C) encourages the use of a planning tool
Additional work	*Task factors: the task is extended*	C completes additional work because of new teachers' instructions: three additional vocabulary terms were added
Schedule change	*Situational factors: the class schedule changes*	C changes the dates in the planning tool: two dates were changed in the planning tool because the class schedule changes
Completion failure	*Situational factors: unavailability of the Internet connection*	C fails to complete a task because of local contingencies: additional information was not gathered from the Web
Role change	*Group dynamics: a task is executed ahead of schedule*	C executes a task ahead of schedule because of his habit to work alone and uncertainty with the partner's abilities
Task data change	*Task factors: the content of the task changes*	C executes a task because of new teachers' instructions: the levels of pollutant considered were different from what is listed in the activity guide
Tool change	*Tool factors: the task is completed in a different tool*	C completes a task in a tool that is different from the one they had previously agreed on

This permitted the systematic examination of the effects of breakdown factors that occur over multiple sessions, thereby modeling more closely the properties of actual long-term collaboration than in the prior lab study.

The findings of this second lab study confirmed that many critical events tend to remain unnoticed while using current collaborative software systems. This leads to extra coordination costs for the collaborators. The subjective measures of AA suggested that AA develops as a process over time (i.e., over the four sessions). These measures were also good predictors of the perceived quality of the final outcomes (e.g., the final report); i.e., the greater the perceived awareness the better the perceived quality of the outcomes.

The behavioral measures of AA, specifically, suggested that the two software workspaces led to different levels of AA, collaboration efficiency, and coordination costs in their users: overall, the BRIDGE research system provided better support than Groove.

Across the two systems, the participants were less aware if the disruptive events occurred over multiple sessions rather than within one session only. Also, the individuals with high metacognitive skills exhibited a higher level of awareness overall, which suggests that metacognition is a relevant cognitive ability to be considered in the future when modeling the process of AA and when designing the tools that can support it (Figure 15.3) (Table 15.1).

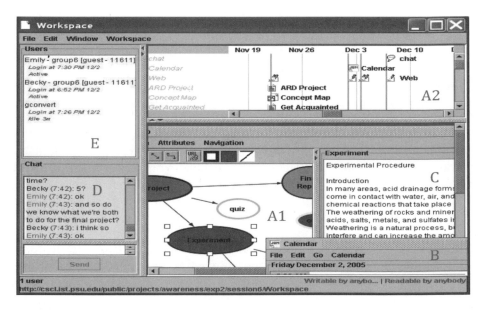

Figure 15.3 a (top) Groove workspace. Includes a large tabbed panel (A) for navigation among the shared documents (C) and planning tool (B), chat tool (D), and list of active users (E). b (bottom) BRIDGE workspace. Includes integrated timeline (A2) and concept map (A2) for navigation among the shared documents (C), and planning tool (calendar) (B), chat tool (D), and a list of active users (E). Versions of documents are accessible from the timeline (A2).

Studies of Common Ground

The second half of the research program focused on studying common ground building (2005–2008). From a theoretical standpoint, the *process of building Common Ground* (CG) in teamwork is defined here as an *underlying subprocess of the general process of building AA*, which was the focus of the first half of the program (Carroll, Rosson, Convertino, & Ganoe, 2006). Collaborators working together for extended periods of time gradually accumulate mutual knowledge, beliefs, assumptions, and shared coordination protocols (i.e., Common Ground; Clark, 1996). Being able to easily share and validate knowledge and protocols is essential for collaborating effectively and efficiently. Not surprisingly, CG has been the focus of many studies of Computer-Mediated Communication (Monk, 2003) and research prototypes (e.g., McCarthy et al., 1991; Kraut, Gergle, & Fussell, 2002).

Prior research has traditionally investigated CG building in the context of communication, whether in face-to-face or computer-mediated settings. Instead, our research program studied CG building in the context of cooperative work. The work processes include but are not limited to communication. In this context, the communication is not a stand-alone process but is instrumental to higher-order group functions, such as group production (e.g., McGrath, 1984).

The research program investigated the development of CG in teams performing an emergency-management planning task. Drawing on the results of a prior field study of emergency-

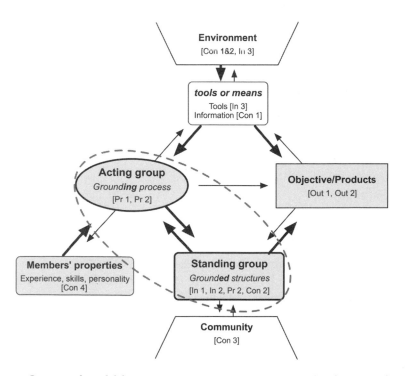

Figure 15.4 Conceptual model for Common Ground: Variables manipulated, measured, and controlled in the study of common ground in teamwork.

Table 15.2 Examples of manipulations and measures by model component

Variable class	Measurement or manipulation	Specific examples
Input	[In 1 & 2] Previously shared knowledge	• Three repeated runs of the task (within group) • Pre-briefing for half of the teams (between groups)
	[In 3] Medium/setting condition	• Paper/face-to-face versus software/distributed condition (between groups)
Process (acting, standing group)	[Pr. 1] Subjective measures (questionnaire)	• Common ground: perceived gain of shared knowledge; quality of communication; ease of understanding, and expression • Awareness: perceived interpersonal awareness, awareness over time
	[Pr. 2] Objective measures (recall, video and artifact analysis, communication logs)	• Common ground built: post-task recall • Communication efficiency. Content: queries, breakdowns, ellipsis, references. Structure: turn counts/duration, simultaneous speech turns • Coordination efficiency: facilitation and decision
Output (product)	[Out. 1] Subjective measures (questionnaire) [Out. 2] Objective measures (logs of judgments, final plan)	• Performance and satisfaction: perceived quality of the product • Breadth of analysis: coverage of relevant information • Decision quality: final plan optimality
Control (task, environ. member)	[Con. 1, 2, 3] Constant factors (study method)	• Task, setting, and member properties: for example, information distribution, laboratory, team gender
	[Con. 4] Control measures (questionnaire)	• Members' properties: background experience, relevant skills, personality factors

management teams, the researchers conducted two laboratory studies with, respectively, collocated teams using a paper prototype (Convertino et al., 2008) and distributed teams using a software prototype (Convertino, Mentis, Slavkovic, Rosson, & Carroll, 2009).

As for the earlier studies of AA, the studies in this second half program were also led by an explicit conceptual model of CG (Figure 15.4), centered on group process (i.e., CG building while the teams perform repeated runs of the same type of collaborative task), and comprehensive in methods. In fact, two laboratory studies drew on the findings of the prior field study and included multiple measures of CG (see Process measures in Table 15.2). The two laboratory studies used the same task, experimental design, and measures: three-member teams performed three repeated runs of a collaborative planning task on shared maps. This consistency enabled the researchers to measure the effect of specific Medium/Setting conditions on CG building (see Table 3, Input).

The field study with local emergency-management teams in Central Pennsylvania had pointed to the need for better technologies for knowledge sharing and collaboration. The researchers found that the teams were periodically engaged in various planning activities on maps every year. A central activity was the "tabletop exercise" where team members walk through an emergency scenario and revisit agreed response procedures using a shared map at a meeting table. For example, a scenario could be responding to an emergency at the local airport. Typically, the teams trained to rehearse the interdependencies and build a shared planning experience, thus facilitating improvisation during actual crises (Schafer, Ganoe, & Carroll, 2007, Schafer et al., 2008). The team members needed to rapidly analyze large amounts of information and balance the contributions from different professionals.

These findings suggested that a software system for collaborative planning could be built to make the knowledge-sharing process more efficient and unbiased. Therefore, the goal of the second half of this (applied research) program was to inform the design of such a collaborative software prototype via the systematic investigation of how teams shared knowledge while working in conditions that are representative of those observed in the field.

The first lab study investigated collocated (or face-to-face) teams using a paper prototype (Figure 15.5). Like the teams observed in the field, the three-member teams collaborated on an emergency-planning task, in a laboratory. Paper maps, post-it notes, and other physical materials were used as the tools for collaborative planning. The experimental setup for studying face-to-face teams and the use of a paper prototype allowed this first study to validate the experimental task and measure, develop, and learn specific design requirements for the software prototype being built. Furthermore, the experimental setup systematically measured the CG process as the teams kept working on a complex planning task. The outcomes of this study were the reference task, some initial measurements of CG, and the software prototype (Convertino, Zhao, Ganoe, & Carroll, 2007b; Convertino et al., 2009).

Figure 15.5 Common Ground study: collaboration in a face-to-face setting, using paper maps on a tabletop.

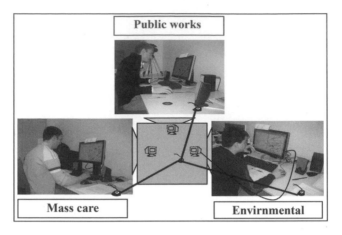

Figure 15.6 Common Ground study: collaboration in a distributed setting, via a software prototype.

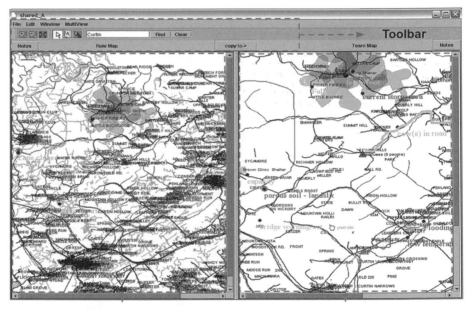

Figure 15.7 Common Ground study: software prototype user interface.

The second lab study investigated distributed (or remote) three-member teams that collaborated via the software prototype, in a laboratory (Figures 15.6, 15.7). Since the experimental task, method, and measures were the same, the results of this second study were compared to those of the prior lab study.

Two factors were manipulated within each study: the amount of shared experience of the task (i.e., three repeated runs) and prior knowledge of the team roles (half of the team were pre-briefed on the roles). A third factor was manipulated between the two lab studies: the Medium/Setting condition (paper/face-to-face versus software/distributed).

The results of both studies show that that the amount of CG within the teams increased over the three repeated runs, as the shared experience increased. Also, the perceived and objective measures of performance increased as the amount of shared experience and CG increased. The two Medium/Setting conditions (paper/face-to-face teams versus software/distributed teams) affected the team performance: as expected, paper/face-to-face teams encountered lower costs for building CG than the software/distributed teams. The ratings of ease of communication and satisfaction were higher for the paper/face-to-face teams than for the software/distributed teams. However, despite these extra costs imposed by the distributed setting, the software prototype enabled the teams to perform better than those using paper (i.e., they performed the task in less time). Moreover, the ratings of shared knowledge gained increased in both of the Medium/Setting conditions (Convertino, Mentis, Ting, Rosson, & Carroll, 2007a; Convertino, Mentis, Rosson, Carroll, & Slavkovic, 2008; Convertino et al., 2009).

After establishing that CG increased, a more in-depth analysis of verbal interactions in both studies revealed in what ways such increment of CG occurred. In both studies, the team became more efficient in transferring information over time. For example, they used less query–reply dialogue acts (i.e., pull acts) and more direct information add dialog acts (i.e., push acts); the latter require an implicit understanding of when content is needed. They also decreased the number of explicit moves devoted to managing the group process, which suggests an increasing number of shared assumptions about *how to* conduct the task together over time. The increment in the amount of CG led to more efficient work, as shown by the improved performance measures.

Compared to the paper medium, the software tool made the process of sharing information more explicit, keeping users focused on the content. The dialog patterns were also affected by medium and setting. The software-based teams exhibited an enhanced effect in increasing their push dialog acts (i.e., efficient strategy for information transfer). On the other hand, these teams, who had to collaborate in a distributed setting via the software medium, tended to increase rather than decrease the proportion of explicit agreement and judgment acts. This is probably due to the lack of visual cues in the distributed condition (i.e., Medium/Setting effect): participants were consistently more vocal in confirming and discussing judgments in the distributed condition than in the collocated or face-to-face condition.

Overall, the results from the studies on common ground suggest that as the team keeps working together, the members develop not only common knowledge about the content or facts but also about the process and the team strategies built to better complete the task. As enough shared knowledge about the process, or *process common ground*, is established, the teammates need fewer explicit acts to regulate their work process because shared assumptions can be made. As a result, the efforts are gradually turned toward establishing *content common ground*, which leads to greater efficiency, as observed in both the lab studies.

The comparison between the two studies suggests that collaborative technology—when well designed—gives us the unprecedented opportunity to catalyze a faster development of process common ground by leveraging specific functions that allow teams to share knowledge, manage actions, and make decisions more efficiently despite the extra cost imposed by the distributed setting. This consideration also applies to the software systems that support activity awareness (AA) in long-term and distributed collaboration.

The lessons learned about the CG building in the research program have motivated more focused experiments and the development of new software prototypes with enhanced functions. An example is a new software prototype implemented for the first time on a Web platform. It supports distributed collaboration on maps but also provides new collaborative visualizations. These are designed to improve the sharing of the content but also the sharing of process information among domain experts in a team (Convertino, Wu, Zhang, Ganoe, Hoffman, & Carroll, 2008; Wu, Zhang, Convertino, & Carroll, 2009).

Implications for Social Sciences

This chapter pointed to the problem that lab-based and field-based methods are currently not well integrated and that experimental methods native to the field of Collaborative Computing are missing. We pointed to the deficiencies of current methods, proposed a new integrated approach, and presented an empirical research program as an illustration of how the approach can be employed. In the research program, two pairs of laboratory experiments, each grounded on a prior field study, investigated, respectively, the general construct of activity awareness in distributed cooperative work and then the narrower construct of common ground in distributed cooperative work on maps. The program showed that each field study informed the design of the laboratory experiments that followed. This helped us to implement lab methods that allowed us to collect interesting findings that we could later take back to the field. This section draws a few implications of this empirical research work for social science.

In his seminal paper on methods for social psychology, "Methodology Matters," McGrath (1995) distinguishes three parallel domains that social researchers need to consider while doing scientific research: substantive, conceptual, and methodological. We describe below what each domain comprises, in general, and within our research program, specifically:

1. The *substantive domain* includes all the "real" social phenomena of interest for the researchers: that is, the object of investigation. In our research program, it comprises the phenomena being studied, that is, the actual behaviors and the prototype features related to awareness (AA) and common ground (CG) building in computer-supported collaboration.
2. The *conceptual domain* includes the properties and relations that are "abstracted" and defined in order to make sense of the phenomena investigated: that is, theoretical models. In our research program, it comprises the explicit conceptual models of AA and CG that were defined on the basis of prior group theory and activity theory (Figures 15.2, 15.4).
3. The *methodological domain* includes the techniques for investigating the phenomena of interest in the substantive domain according. McGrath (1995) distinguishes three types of techniques: manipulation, measurement, and control. Our research program introduced a number of experimental techniques for investigating AA and CG. In each study, a few relevant factors were manipulated. In order to test possible causal relations with the construct investigated (AA or CG), multiple measures of the construct were collected,

while several other related factors were controlled or kept constant. The manipulations, the task, and the tools used mirrored phenomena observed in prior fieldwork.

The research program presented contributes directly to the methodological domain of CC research (i.e., a new field-to-lab integrated approach and new experimental lab methods). Our contribution has also a few more general implications for research methods in social sciences, the development of social theories, and the design of social technologies.

Implications for Research Methods

Following McGrath's schema (1995) for behavioral and social sciences, we can view the methodological domain of CC research as comprised of three classes of techniques, respectively, for measurement, manipulation, and control. These are well described in the literature of Psychology and Social Sciences. But there has been no analysis of how these should be adapted to address the specific needs of CC research. Similarly to psychologists and social scientists, CC researchers are interested in maximizing the following: the generalizability of the findings with respect to specific user populations, the realism with respect to the work condition, and the precision in the measurement of the user behaviors of interest. But, the different object of study (i.e., computer-supported collaboration) and research goals (e.g., guiding technology design) require that the techniques for conducting CC research and the criteria for evaluating it need to be adapted in order to reflect these differences. Below, we present a few adapted versions of the three classes of techniques that we used for studying AA and CG in the research program.

Measurement Techniques

Toward More Valid and Informative Measures

In the real world, collaborative systems are often used for long-term projects. To date, experimental research in CC has focused predominantly on short-term tasks and lacks valid experimental methods for systematically studying collaboration during extended cooperative work projects. Compared to the studies of social and behavioral researchers, CC research is more strongly applied. For example, it is both a common and a desired practice for CC researchers to include "implications for design" as part of the discussion of the main findings in their research papers. Thus, in such an applied research context, the requirement of strong *validity* for the methods used with respect to real users and work conditions is particularly critical.

On the other hand, *statistical power* is also important. Running a larger sample of groups is preferable in order to draw reliable findings from the data (e.g., highly reliable variables). But, the high costs involved in studying work groups performing nontrivial tasks over a long period imposes the need to trade off some statistical power to increase the validity of the methods used and, thus, of the findings obtained.

For example, in the second experiment on activity awareness, we could have studied 56 pairs working on a 2-hr task, rather than 14 pairs working on an 8-hr task (4 hr of individual and 4 hr of collaborative work) with less overall costs. But the object of study for the research program was to study activity awareness in the realistic context of long-term collaboration. In addition, we studied awareness in an experimental context so that relevant variables could be manipulated, measured, or kept constant, which is generally unfeasible in a field study.

The current criteria for assessing the soundness of CC studies, such as sample size and statistical significance results, are often imported without adaptation from the parent disciplines (see reviewers' criteria for conferences or journals). We argue, instead, that the assessment of the findings from experiments on long-term collaboration needs to assign greater value to those techniques that increase validity, while some degree of experimental control is preserved.

Another strategy to compensate for the high costs of rigorous research in CC is to increase the benefits of the research by collecting more informative data sets. To this end, in our research program, multiple data types were collected: subjective (questionnaires), behavioral (observation and audio-video recordings), and work-performance measures (keystroke-level system logs, artifact analysis). This allowed a comprehensive assessment of the investigated construct (AA or CG) in relation to the factors manipulated.

The use of *multiple measures* for the same construct in the research program was important for two reasons. First, it increased the reliability of the findings: convergent measures of increasing awareness in the first AA lab study and convergent measures of increasing CG in the paper prototype study. Second, some discrepancies between the different measures enabled additional understanding of the investigated phenomenon. For example, in the first AA lab study an informative difference was found between the overt and the covert responses of participants to a specific scenario (i.e., the partner had changed to the task schedule): the participants avoided overtly expressing frustration about the unnoticed change made by the partner, but on the other hand the event had affected their covert responses during the collaboration. Furthermore, we also found differences between the perceived and objective performance measures in the work groups. For example, in the results of the CG lab studies, the subjective ratings of performance correlated with both objective and subjective measures of common ground but they were not a good indicator of some objective measures of team performance (e.g., quality of final plan). These divergences suggest new questions that can be addressed by future focused studies.

Process Plus Outcome Measures

An important decision is choosing the appropriate *measurement approach* to properly assess collaborative systems. For example, does the better systems lead to an improved group outcome (or performance) while requiring the same process costs, or does it reduce the process costs (or increase group efficiency) while leading to the same group outcomes (or performance)?

We argue that a comprehensive approach for measuring the support of AA or CG should consider both process and outcome or summative performance measures. Prior experimental research on computer-mediated communication has suggested that the participants in constrained work conditions might get the work done efficiently by adding extra effort of their own or at the expense of a secondary task (Monk et al., 1996). This would be unlikely to happen with users in a naturalistic setting. If this happens in an experiment that only uses performance measures, such as the number of errors and total task completion time, then the effects on process would not be captured and thus the results would be misleading. In our studies, the measures of process, which were our focus, were related to the measures of outcome (or performance). For example, in the second AA lab study, it was observed that while the final reports from the two systems were similar in the overall quality of the reports (i.e., a measure of performance), both behavioral responses and system logs indicated lower levels of awareness and greater coordination efforts, such as more switches between tasks done by the pairs working in the Groove workspace than for those working in the BRIDGE workspace. The potential lack of sensitivity of performance measures was successfully addressed by also collecting measures of process.

An Embedded Measure of Efficiency

In the second AA lab study, keystroke-level logs were aggregated and used to measure the duration and intensity of work in the workspace. From this data we extracted a *metric of collaboration efficiency* considering only the interaction logs from a 5-min task, a quiz task, repeated by the pair over the second, third, and fourth sessions. The metric was then related to the measured level of AA. This measurement technique, experimented here for the first time, appears promising for a number of reasons. It is a cost-effective technique to measure changes in the performance level during multi-session projects. It avoids unnecessary control on the overall collaborative project (i.e., all the tasks) and preserves more ecologic validity. Finally, it appears more sensitive to changes in efficiency than summative performance measures for the entire group project (i.e., in our study, a project of four 2-hr sessions over multiple weeks), which is affected by a broader range of unknown or uncontrollable noise factors.

CC researchers could use similar task-level metrics, nested in larger experimental group project, for measuring collaborators' efficiency or effectiveness. These can provide cost-effective benchmark indicators for comparing collaborative systems and can be easily related to other measures of process. For example, in the second lab study the efficiency metric correlated with the perceived level of AA. Lastly, this type of metrics can complement the current summative performance measures, such as time and errors, by allowing CC researchers to measure the changes of group efficiency or performance over time.

Manipulation Techniques

Specific manipulation techniques were developed for studying AA and CG. Below is a summary of these techniques from the two pairs of lab studies presented above (see section 3):

1. Within-group: Repeated measurements after each *session* or *task run* enable assessing changes of the dependent variable, such as AA or CG, over time. This occurs as the amount of shared experience increases (i.e., Session and Run as independent variables).

2. Within-group: The *experimental confederate* plays the role of the remote partner and uses *scripted scenarios* to introduce events in the collaborative setting, following a schedule. The participant's awareness of the changes is measured through recordings of his or her behavior, such as Breakdowns Factors or Scenario as independent variable.

3. Between-groups: Comparison of functionally equivalent *collaborative systems*, such as Groove and BRIDGE, or versions of a collaborative medium, paper

and SW prototypes used in a collocated or distributed setting, respectively (i.e., Medium/Setting condition as independent variable).

4. Between-groups: In half of the groups, known as the treatment condition, as they started to collaborate, the members are *pre-briefed* about the partners' roles in addition to their own role. In the other half, known as the control condition, the members are only briefed about their own role. This manipulates the amount of shared knowledge that the group has at the outset of collaboration (i.e., pre-briefing on roles as independent variables).

All these techniques are novel for CC research. They were developed for the first time to study either activity awareness in a collaborative editing task or common ground in a geo-collaborative task. The experimental confederate, who followed scripted scenarios, was used in the two AA lab studies and the pre-briefing on roles was used in the two CG lab studies. Both of these techniques have been refined since their first use.

Control Techniques

When experimenters use a realistic task, repeated measures, and/or a between-groups factor, the expected sample size of an experiment in CC research is generally small. A lesson learned is that, in these conditions, the researchers are likely to encounter sampling problems. Across the compared between-subject conditions, the samples of teams may unexpectedly differ on variables that the researchers did not intend to manipulate. It is, therefore, important to verify if relevant variables, especially those that are likely to have an effect on the dependent variable, happen to be different between experimental conditions. If this is the case, then their effect needs to be taken into account. For example, in the second AA lab study, we found that some individual differences, such as differences in the participants' metacognitive skills, had an effect on their level of activity awareness but were not equally distributed between the two samples, BRIDGE and Groove participants. These were included as covariates when running the statistical analyses, which avoided a misattribution of part of the measured differences between the BRIDGE and the Groove participants.

In summary, the techniques for measurement, manipulation, and control presented above (section 15.4) in our studies represent early attempts to develop native experimental methods for CC research. In fact, earlier in the chapter (section 15.2) we have argued that this field has a clear need for more studies that develop and validate measures, procedures, and reference tasks (see the call for reference tasks by Whittaker, Terveen, & Nardi, 2000).

Why a Research Program?

Conducting a research program rather than single-isolated studies is a more productive strategy for research on constructs such as AA and CG. This is motivated by the difficulty of evaluating the impact of collaborative systems on collaboration (Grudin, 1988) and the difficulty of measuring experimentally such multi-determined collaborative phenomena.

We presented a research program where these phenomena were studied incrementally. For example, among the studies on AA, the first lab study validated the laboratory method, which modeled events and conditions observed in the prior field study. The second lab study, built on the results from the first study, introduced an extended version of the laboratory method. In this second study, more variables were manipulated or controlled, the participants also performed individual work sessions, multi-session scenarios were added to model disruptive events across sessions, and a more comprehensive questionnaire was used to measure AA based on a more articulated definition of AA proposed in Carroll et al. (2006).

Rather than using single-isolated studies, we propose that series of studies that form coherent research programs suit better the needs of CC research than single-isolated studies. We consider research programs a more effective strategy to incrementally investigate complex collaborative phenomena such as activity awareness and enable the accumulation of results across studies, while the theory and methods used are more clearly related. Our vision for CC research draws on the methodology of research programs described proposed by Lakatos (1978). His view of science integrates Popper's and Kuhn's prior propositions on science and suggests that empirical science is generally led not only by the negative epistemology of falsification of specific scientific hypotheses, but also by the positive epistemology of constructing scientific knowledge stage by stage using a research program.

Future Trends in Research Methods

The rapid diffusion of Web-based (or Internet-based) technologies for collaboration and knowledge sharing is causing relevant changes in the research methods for studying collaboration and, more generally, online social behaviors.

Researchers have long moved beyond the study of behaviors of individual users sitting in front of a single desktop computer. Nevertheless, many of the research methods currently used continue to be derived and limited from this legacy (e.g., Chi, 2009). Phenomena such as wiki-based communities (e.g., Wikipedia) and Web-based software platforms that are now used in large organizations or on the public web are forcing researchers to update their methods of investigation.

A new development is the "Living Laboratory" approach. Similarly to Information Retrieval and Library researchers, CC researchers are using this approach to test the effects of specific features of experimental prototypes with real online users (i.e., in vivo). Examples of new Web-based technologies include tools such as wikis, blogs, tools for sharing bookmarks, annotations, photo and video, and tools for managing personal or professional contacts (e.g., online social networks). These tools can be studied openly on the Web or internally in large organizations (e.g., business enterprises) (e.g., Convertino et al. 2010).

In the future, CC research may engage with real users through "Living Laboratories" in which they evaluate system prototypes available on the Internet or intranets of large organizations. This suggests that the field may need experimental platforms and procedures through which researchers can run studies with access to large number numbers of users, different locations worldwide, and various social behaviors. Therefore, systematic studies could be done in ways and at scales that were not possible before. These new conditions might increasingly blur the boundaries and increase the interchange between Collaborative Computing and Social Science (e.g., see Kraut et al., 2004 on Psychological Research Online).

Acknowledgments

Gregorio Convertino thanks John M. Carroll, his coauthor and PhD advisor, and Mary Beth Rosson, PhD co-advisor, who supported this research for 6 years. Funding was provided by the National Science Foundation: grant award IIS 0113264 (2002–2004) and by the U.S. Office of Naval Research: grant award N000140510549 (2005–2008). See Convertino's Ph.D. thesis (2008).

References

Arrow, H., McGrath, J. E., & Berdahl, J. L. (2000). Small groups as complex systems. Sage awareness: Synchronizing task-oriented collaborative activity. *Int. J. Hum.-Comput. Studies*, *58*(5), 605–632.

Carroll, J. M., Singley, M. K., & Rosson, M. (1992). Integrating theory development with design evaluation. *Behavior & Information Technology*, *11*, 247–255.

Carroll, J. M. (2000). Making use: Scenario-based design of human-computer interactions. Cambridge, MA: The MIT Press.

Carroll, J.M., Neale, D.C., Isenhour, P.L., Rosson, M.B. & McCrickard, D.S. (2003). Notification and awareness: Synchronizing task-oriented collaborative activity. International Journal of Human-Computer Systems 58, 605–632.

Carroll, J. M., Rosson, M. B., Convertino, G., & Ganoe, C. H. (2006). Awareness and teamwork in computer-supported collaborations. *Interacting with Computers*, *18*(1), 21–46.

Chi, H. E. (2009). A position paper on "Living Laboratories": Rethinking ecological designs and experimentation in human-computer interaction. Proceedings of HCII, 597–605.

Clark, H. H. (1996). *Using Language*. Cambridge, MA: Cambridge University Press.

Convertino, G., Neale, D. C., Hobby, L., Carroll, J. M., & Rosson, M. B. (2004). A laboratory method for studying activity awareness. Proceedings of the third Nordic conference on Human-computer interaction (NordiCHI), ACM Press, 131–222.

Convertino, G., George, T., & Councill, I. (2006). Mapping the intellectual landscape of CSCW research, interactive posters, CSCW 2006 Conference, Alberta, Canada, 2006. Paper also presented at the 2009 HCI-C Winter Workshop, Fraser, CO.

Convertino, G., Mentis, H., Ting, A., Rosson, M. B., & Carroll, J. M. (2007a). *How does common ground increase?* Proceedings of Group 2007. ACM Press, 225–228.

Convertino, G., Zhao, D., Ganoe, C., & Carroll, J. M. (2007b). A role-based multi-view approach to support GeoCollaboration. Proceedings of HCI International 2007 Conference, Springer.

Convertino, G., Zhang, Y., Asti, B., Rosson, M. B., & Mohammed, S. (2007c). Board-based collaboration in cross-cultural pairs. First International Workshop on Intercultural Collaboration (IWIC), Kyoto University, Japan Lecture Notes in Computer Science, Vol. 4568. Ishida T., Fussell S. R., Vossen P. T. J. M. (Eds.), XIII.

Convertino, G., Farooq, U., Rosson, M. B., Carroll, J. M., Meyer, B. J. F. (2007d). Supporting intergenerational groups in computer-supported cooperative work (CSCW). *Special issue on Designing Computer Systems for and with Older Users, Behaviour and Information Technology*, *26*, 275–285.

Convertino, G. (2008). Awareness and knowledge sharing in collaborative computing experimental methods, Ph.D. Thesis, College of Information Sciences and Technology, Pennsylvania State University, August.

Convertino, G., Mentis, H., Rosson, M. B., Carroll, J. M., & Slavkovic, A. (2008a). Articulating common ground in cooperative work: Content and process. Proceedings of CHI. ACM Press. Florence.

Convertino, G., Wu, A., Zhang, X. L., Ganoe, C. H., Hoffman, B., & Carroll, J. M. (2008b). Designing group annotations and process visualizations for role-based collaboration. In Liu, H. (Ed.), *Social computing, behavior modeling, and prediction*. Springer.

Convertino, G., Mentis, H., Rosson, M. B., Slavkovic, A., & Carroll, J. M. (2009). Supporting content and process common ground in computer-supported teamwork. Proceedings of CHI (pp. 4–9). Boston: ACM Press NY.

Convertino, G. Grasso, A. De Michelis, G. Millen, D.R. Chi, E. H. (2010). (Collective Intelligence In Organizations (CIorg): Tools and Studies. Workshop at ACM Group 2010 conference, Sanibel Island, FL (USA). www.parc.com/ciorg

Damianos, L., Hirschman, L., Kozierok, R., Kurtz, J., Greenberg, A., Walls, K., et al. (1999). Evaluation for collaborative systems. *ACM Computing Surveys, 31*, 3e.

Ganoe, C. H., Somervell, J. P., Neale, D. C., Isenhour, P. L., Carroll, J. M., Rosson, M. B. & McCrickard, D. S. (2003). Classroom BRIDGE: using collaborative public and desktop timelines to support activity awareness. ACM UIST 2003: Conference On User Interface Software and Tools. New York: ACM, 21–30.

Ganoe, C. H., Convertino, G., & Carroll, J. M. (2004). The BRIDGE workspace: Tools supporting activity awareness for collaborative project work, NordiCHI. Finland: Tampere.

Grudin, J. (1988). Why groupware applications fail: Problems in design and evaluation. *Office: Technology and People, 4*(3), 245–264.

Grudin, J. (1994). Groupware and social dynamics: Eight challenges for developers. *Communications of the ACM, 37*(1), 92–105.

Harper, H. R., Hughes, J. A., & Shapiro, D. Z. (1989, September13–15). Working in harmony: An examination of computer technology in air traffic control. Proceedings of the ECSCW '89 conference (pp. 73–86), Gatwick.

Herskovic, V, Pino, J., Ochoa, S., & Antunes, P. (2007). Evaluation methods for groupware systems. Proceedings of CRIWG 2007. Lecture Notes in Computer Science (Vol. 4715, pp. 328–336), Springer.

Inkpen, K., Mandryk, R., DiMicco, J., & Scott, S. (2004). *Methodology for evaluating collaboration in co-located environments. Interactions 11(6). Extended abstracts of CSCW*. New York: ACM Press.

Kraut, R. E., Gergle, D., & Fussell, S. R. (2002). The use of visual information in shared visual spaces: Informing the development of virtual co-presence. Proceedings ACM CSCW.

Kraut, R. M., Olson, J., Banaji, M., Bruckman, A., Cohen, J., & Couper, M. P. (2004). Psychological research online: Report of board of scientific affairs' advisory group on the conduct of research on the Internet. *American Psychologist, 59*(2), 106–117.

Lakatos, I. (1978). The methodology of scientific research programs, philosophical papers, 1. In Worrall, J., & Currie, G. (Eds.). Cambridge, MA: Cambridge University Press.

Leonard, V. K., Jacko, J. A., Yi, J. S., & Sainfort, F. (2006). Human factors & ergonomic methods. In Salvendy, G. (Ed.), *The handbook of human factors & ergonomics* (3rd ed.). New York: John Wiley and Sons.

McCarthy, J. C., Miles, V. C., Monk, A. F., Harrison, M. D., Dix, A. J., & Wright, P. C. (1991). Four generic communication tasks which must be supported in electronic conferencing. *ACM/SIGCHI Bul., 23*, 41–43.

McGrath, J. E. (1984). *Groups: Interaction and performance.* Englewood Cliffs, NJ: Prentice Hall.

McNeese, M. D. (1996). Collaborative systems research: Establishing ecological approaches through the Living Laboratory. Proceedings of the 40th Annual Meeting of the Human Factors Society, *2*, 767–771). Santa Monica, CA: Human Factors Society.

Meister, D. (1999). The history of human factors and ergonomics. New Jersey: Lawrence Erlbaum Associates, Mahwah.

Meister, D. (2004). *Conceptual foundations of human factors.* Mahwah, NJ: Lawrence Erlb. Ass.

Monk, A. (2003). Common ground in electronically mediated communication: Clark's theory of language use. In Carroll, J. M. (Ed.), *Toward a multidisciplinary science of HCI*. MIT Press.

Neale, D. C., Carroll, J. M., & Rosson, M. B. (2004). Evaluating computer-supported cooperative work: Models and frameworks. Proceedings of CSCW'04, New York: ACM Press.

Pinelle, D., & Gutwin, C. (2000). A review of groupware evaluations. In WETICE'00: 9th International Workshop on Enabling Technologies (pp. 86–91). IEEE Computer Society.

Plowman, L., Rogers, Y., & Ramage, M. (1995). What are workplace studies for? Proceedings of ECSCW 95 conference (pp. 309–324).

Prinz, W., Mark, G., Pankoke-Babatz, U. (1998). Designing groupware for congruency in use. Proceedings of the CSCW 1998 conference (pp. 373–382).

Ramage, M. (1999). The learning way: Evaluating co-operatives systems. PhD thesis, Lancaster University.

Randall, D., Twidale, M., & Bentley, B. (1996). Dealing with uncertainty: Perspectives on the evaluation process. In Thomas, P. (Ed.), *CSCW Requirements and Evaluation*. London: Springer Verlag.

Schafer, W. A., Ganoe, C. H. & Carroll, J. M. (2007). Supporting Community Emergency Management through a Geocollaboration Software Infrastructure. *Computer-Supported Cooperative Work: The Journal of Collaborative Computing*, 16, 501–537. DOI 10.1007/s10606-007-9050-7.

Schafer, W., Carroll, J. M., Haynes, S. & Abrams, S. (2008). Emergency management planning as collaborative community work. *Journal of Homeland Security and Emergency Management*, 5(1), Article 10, 1–17.

Schmidt, K., & Bannon, L. (1992). Taking CSCW seriously: Supporting articulation work. *Computer Supported Cooperative Work*, 1(1–2), 7–40.

Shapiro (1994). The limits of ethnography: Combining social sciences for CSCW. Proceedings of the 1994 ACM CSCW conference, (pp. 417–428) New York: ACM Press.

Steves, M. P., & Scholtz, J. (2005). A framework for evaluating collaborative systems in the real world. Proceedings of HICSS.

Straus, S. G., & McGrath, J. E. (1994). Does the medium matter? The interaction of task type and technology on group performance and member reactions. *Journal of Applied Psychology*, 79(1), 87–97.

Straus, S. G. (1999). Testing a typology of tasks. *Small Group Research*, 30(2), 166–187. SAGE Publications.

Twidale, M., Randall D., & Bentley, R. (1994). Situated evaluation for cooperative systems. Proceedings of the CSCW 1994 conference (pp. 441–452). New York: ACM Press.

Whittaker, S., Terveen, L., & Nardi, B. A. (2000). Let's stop pushing the envelope and start addressing it: A reference task agenda for HCI. *Human-Computer Interaction*, 15, 75–106, Lawrence Erlbaum Associates, Inc.

Winograd, T., & Flores, F. (1986). *Understanding computers and cognition: A new foundation for design*. Norwood, NJ: Ablex.

Wu, A., Zhang, X., Convertino, G., & Carroll, J. M. (2009). CIVIL: Support geo-collaboration with information visualization. Proceedings of ACM Group. ACM Press.

Chapter 16

Emergent Technologies for Assessing Social Feelings and Experiences

Albertine Visser and Ingrid Mulder

Introduction

Emerging technologies such as mobile Internet, ambient environments, and IPTV (Internet Protocol TeleVision) are increasingly social networked systems and consequently ease sharing of experiences. We refer to "sharing experiences" in the remainder of this chapter when one person uses emerging technology for sharing his or her feelings or thoughts with someone else. However, even though facilitation of sharing experiences by technology is readily available, assessing sharing experiences is not necessarily straightforward. Difficulties arise in assessing sharing experiences because thoughts and emotions involved in social interactions are mainly internal processes. Furthermore, many factors influence a person's feelings, including the appraisal of (social) events, one's psychophysical state, and subjective experiences (Roesch, Fontaine, & Scherer, 2006), which can affect a sharing experience. In addition, an experience is moment dependent, which implies that assessment should be done during the moment of the experience instead of the more common subsequent assessment (Sanders, 2001). Moreover, because sharing experiences happens in a social environment, which is hard to establish in an artificial context, people's natural context should be assessed as well. The above-stated issues stress the need for finding new ways of assessing sharing experiences, which is of particular interest for interactive media user evaluations. Various tools tackling difficulties in assessing sharing experiences have been developed in the past. These tools use psychophysiological and contextual measurements for gaining understanding of social interactions by assessing emotions, feelings, locations, and activities. The assessment tool WiShare was developed to particularly assess sharing experiences in interactive media. Researchers and designers developing interactive media can use the tool to gain more insight in personal and interpersonal feelings *during* moments that people are using interactive technology. This chapter informs you about (technical) tools for measuring social interaction, in particular the WiShare tool. Also, we show you how the WiShare tool can be used in practice.

Understanding (Sharing) Experiences

To assess feelings in sharing experiences, we first need to understand the concept of experience. Sanders (2001) made a clear conceptual model that shows that it is important to measure experiences in the moment. Asking people about an experience afterward means that they have to recall memories. An experience is a result of our memories and imagination lasting only for the moment. A vital moment-to-moment changing aspect of experience is emotion. However, neither for experience nor for emotion is there a universally agreed-upon definition. Roughly speaking, emotion can be distinguished from feeling and mood, although there is an overlap between these concepts. Nevertheless, emotion is generally presumed to have several components: physiological arousal, motor expression, action tendencies, and subjective feeling (Roesch et al., 2006). Additionally, an emotion has usually a short duration, in contrast to a mood, which can last for days or weeks. A feeling is more specific than emotion as it refers to a private, mental experience of an emotion, rather than the physical expressions of emotion. Roesch et al even stated that feeling is the component of subjective experience of emotional arousal that is often conscious and can be verbalized by using emotional words or expressions. In this way, feelings can be seen as a very important component of emotion in assessing them, since through feelings people can speak about having an emotion. The feeling component can be viewed as a reflection of the changes occurring in all other components; it situates the experience in the total context of our self with its history, preferences, and present state being affected by a particular event. This view on feelings is in accordance with Appraisal Theory, which assumes that emotions are produced by evaluating events on certain criteria that are person dependent (Hewstone & Stroebe, 2002, p. 151). In essence, a certain event can be perceived as being positive or negative (valence), producing a whole range of different emotions depending on the person's arousal level (Scherer, 2005, p. 695). This two-dimensional representation of emotion is a well-known model used in studying subjective feelings of people.

Social interaction has a key influence on sharing experiences and therefore both personal and interpersonal feelings play a large role in experiencing. Research indicates that social contact in general is associated with high positive emotions (Kahneman & Krueger, 2006, p. 3; Brandstatter, 1991, pp. 173–192). Happiness in life is strongly correlated with having close personal relationships; its absence is linked to unhappiness and depression. Social contact can provide people with positive social feelings as a sense of presence and connectedness. The social feelings most referred to in the relevant literature are social presence (Short, Williams, & Christie, 1976, p. 65), social connectedness (Lee & Robbins, 1998, p. 338), and social awareness (Dourish & Bly, 1992, p. 541). To assess these social feelings, different measurements methods are used, which are discussed in the next section.

Methods of Assessing Experiences

Various methods can be used for assessing experiences; these methods and their advantages and disadvantages are outlined below and are used for gathering requirements for an assessment tool for sharing experiences.

Questionnaires

A questionnaire is a common method for measuring user experiences. Questionnaires are the most used methods for measuring social feelings, as well as in the fields of psychology and HCI. To measure social presence, different questionnaires were developed as semantic differential scales: the Networked Mind Questionnaire and the IPO Social Presence Questionnaire (van Baren & IJsselsteijn, 2004; Harms & Biocca, 2004, p. 246; Short et al., 1976, p. 74). The Social Connectedness Scale was developed to measure social connectedness as an attribute of the self (Lee & Robbins, 1998, p. 338). Questionnaires very much related to social connectedness (more as a feeling of staying in touch) also exist, like the Personal Acquaintance Scale (Starzyk, Holden, Fabrigar, & MacDonald, 2006, p. 833). The Affective Benefits and Costs in Communication Questionnaire (ABC-Q) focuses on the affective benefits of awareness systems, rather than focusing on connectedness following the face-to-face model (van Baren, IJsselsteijn, Romero, Markopoulos, & de Ruyter, 2003). Questionnaires are usually used for measurement before and after the experience, which means that it is highly reliant on self-reported recollection, which can allow cognitive biases. In this line, using interviews and focus groups to gather data about social experiences also rely on recall self-reports, although there is more room for explanation.

Observation

Another way of gathering (social) user experience data is observation. Although, in comparison to questionnaires, observation is not relying on self-reports from people, it can still be highly obtrusive for the observed person, who might not to behave as he or she naturally would. Also, without any form of self-report from the participant, conclusions are purely based on external expressions of internal experiences that may not be enough to obtain a reliable representation of the real experience. Asking people to keep a diary is a form of indirect observation and can also include pictures, drawings, and pieces of audio and video. Logging can be seen as another form of indirect observation. In computer-mediated communication, interaction can be logged easily. Software is available that unobtrusively logs participants' activities. An example of interaction logging software is Noldus uLog (van Drunen, van den Broek, & Heffelaar, 2008).

Lab and Field Studies

Gathering experience data can be done not only in the field but also in a lab environment (Sharp, Rogers, & Preece, 2006, p. 585). A lab experiment is much more controlled, which makes it easier to gather data in a shorter amount of time. However, a major drawback of a lab is that participants do not behave as they would assumingly behave outside a lab. Measuring experiences in the field has the challenges of technical constraints (e.g., logging interaction and providing working prototypes) and less control of participants' actions.

For measuring user experience in the field, the Experience Sampling Method (ESM) is often used to collect in situ subjective feedback from people (Consolvo & Walker, 2003, pp. 24–31; Froehlich, Chen, Consolvo, Harrison, & Landay, 2007). Using this method, participants fill out several brief questionnaires every day by responding to alerts. Because ESM does not rely on recalling memory but on current feelings and activities, this reduces cognitive biases. Tactile or audible alerts call for responses given in various ways, such as typing, writing, picture-making, or speaking. ESM does have some disadvantages (Scollon, Kim-Prieto, & Diener, 2003, p. 5); it can be quite intrusive and interruptive for people. There are situations in which people are less likely or not able to respond, for instance in a swimming pool or in a meeting. Furthermore, the influence of reactivity (the effect of the participant's awareness of his or her responses) may have an influence on future feelings and activities. In addition, ESM is based on self-report that might be affected by social desirability and provides little information about uncommon or brief events, which are rarely sampled.

In response to these issues with ESM, the Day Reconstruction Method (DRM) has been developed to lessen burden and gain information about rarely sampled events (Kahneman, Krueger, Schkade, Schwarz, & Stone, 2004, p. 1776). DRM allows participants to reconstruct the previous day to gain continuous feedback about experiences. In this way, DRM asks for less effort from participants and is less interruptive than ESM. However, the feedback of the participants is more reliant on recalled memory because of the greater period between experiencing and reporting. A combination of the ESM and DRM methods was developed by Khan, Markopoulos, & IJsselsteijn (2007) to limit the disadvantages of both methods.

Psychophysiological Measurement

A method that is not reliant on self-report is psychophysiological measurement. It is possible to gain information about peoples' experiences by measuring pupil size, heart rate, skin temperature, skin conductance, and blood pressure as well as by measuring facial expressions, speech prosody, eye movements, body postures, respiration, and brain activity (Partala, 2005). A problem with these measurements is that it is quite hard or even impossible to measure in the field. Moreover, even in a lab environment, participants are usually restricted in their movements or even completely "wired up," although much research is underway to make psychophysiological measurements unobtrusive (Ouwerkerk, Pasveer, & Langereis, 2008, pp. 163–193) The intrusive character of these measurements influences both the freedom of movement and the experience itself. Furthermore, self-report is still needed in addition to psychophysiological measurement, since physiological data is not able to accurately recognize emotions of individuals (Picard & Daily, 2005; Ward & Marsden, 2003, p. 199).

Methods Especially Assessing Emotions

Since feelings and emotions are very important in experiencing, several methods to measure these internal processes exist. The circumplex model of affect, which provides a semantic structure of emotions on the dimensions of valence and arousal, is frequently used as the basis of emotion studies (Russell, 1980, p. 1161). Images representing emotions are often used in emotion research, for example, the Self-Assessment Manikin (Bradley & Lang, 1994, p. 49) and the Product Emotion Measurement (Csikszentmihalyi & Larson, 1987, p. 526). Hole and Williams (2008) are developing a new approach to measuring emotions based on Appraisal Theory, the Emotion Sampling Device, which uses a simple and short questionnaire that can be answered at any time and in any context.

New Methods for Assessing Experiences

New methods and tools that deal with problems of intrusiveness, self-report, and measuring in the field are in development. An example of such a tool is the Electronically Activated Recorder (EAR) (Mehl & Pennebaker, 2003, p. 857). Participants have to keep this device with them continuously to record pieces of audio. User data about where, how, and with whom time is spent can be gathered without asking participants to self-report. Another tool is the SenseCam, which combines a camera with a number of sensors (that automatically take pictures at "good" times) in a pendant around the neck (Gemmell, Williams, Wood, Lueder, & Bell 2004). Ethical issues arise with tools such as the EAR and the SenseCam. Confidentiality and anonymity of users have to be taken into account when developing assessment tools, especially when assessing in real contexts. Users should always be informed about when and what is captured and what will be done with the captured data and should give their consent before assessment.

Context-aware systems are usually not developed as a measurement tool for user experiences but can be used for it. According to Dey (2001), "a system is context-aware if it uses the context to provide relevant information and/or services to the users, where relevancy depends on the user's task." Features of context-aware systems can be used to gather data about where the user is, what the user is doing, and whom the user is with. Currently three context-aware measurement tools have been developed or are in development for measuring the user experience. The Context-Aware Experience Sample tool is designed to ask the user questions only in moments and during activities of interest (Intille, Rondoni, Kukla, Ancona, & Bao, 2003). In this way, the interruption of the ESM technique is minimized. The tool uses GPS, a heart rate monitor, and algorithms that recognize activities of the user. Another measurement system using context-aware data is MyExperience (Froehlich et al 2007). MyExperience captures both objective and subjective in situ data on mobile devices. User data can be gathered through logging of device usage, user context (e.g., calendar appointments), environmental sensing (e.g., Bluetooth sensors), and user experience samples (e.g., self-report survey and SMS). A third measurement tool is the SocioXensor, which supports in situ data collection methods as logging and experience sampling on a person's mobile phone (ter Hofte, Otte, Peddemors, & Mulder, 2006; Mulder & Kort, 2008, pp. 601–612). The SocioXensor collects context data (e.g., by use of GPS and Bluetooth), usage data, and experience data by using ESM.

To Challenge Existing Methods

Although context-aware systems designed for assessing experiences aim to minimize problems with recalling memory, self-report, and obtrusiveness, these problems to a lesser extent still exist. Ideally, researchers would like to measure subjective data during an experience without disturbing the experience. Experiences in a social context, when shared, make these measurement issues even more complex because of the influence of social feelings. Until now, context-aware systems have not focused on assessing social feelings. The challenge is in designing a mobile tool for in situ assessment of social feelings during moments of sharing experiences in a nonintrusive manner.

Requirements for an Assessment Tool

The explorative probing diary as described in Visser and Mulder (2008) has been used to get more insight into (assessing) sharing experiences. Based on the results of this probing diary study and the shortcomings of existing methods discussed in the above section, there are certain requirements for the design of an assessment tool. Results of the probing diary study identified 12 main requirements for an assessment tool of sharing experiences. These are described below in Table 16.1.

Table 16.1 Requirements for an assessment tool.

#	Requirement	Explanation
1	The tool should (continuously) measure during a sharing experience at moments of interest (depending on assessment goals).	By automatic logging of user behavior as location, activity, and social interaction, interesting moments can be detected.
2	The tool should take little effort and time to use.	As participants indicated and literature showed, people do not want to spend much time on effortful research tasks during their daily activities. Giving participants small, effortless tasks will increase the chances of completed data.
3	The tool should be motivating to use.	The participant should be motivated to use the measurement tool, to minimize negative feelings of irritation or dislike. One could think of a nice-looking or fun tool. Also tasks that take much time and effort will not be motivating.
4	The tool should measure information about the users' (social) context automatically and unobtrusively.	Behavior as well as feelings should be measured automatically and unobtrusively. Measuring behavior should be possible using sensor technology. However, feelings can only to a certain extent be measured automatically. Moreover, social feelings have not been measured automatically in previous studies.
5	The tool should be wearable or mobile.	Since the tool should measure in situ, the user should and should easily be able to take the tool with him or her constantly.

6	The tool should be able to reflect the data given by the user.	Resulting from the probing diary study, the user finds it important to know what data is collected by the tool and would probably like to reflect on it.
7	The tool should give enough opportunity to express oneself (about thoughts and feelings considering sharing experiences).	Participants in the probing diary study indicated that they liked to express themselves freely, without being restricted to certain predetermined options.
8	The social relationship between the user and the person the user is sharing experiences with should be clear.	Social relationship has a large influence on a sharing experience: social feelings tend to be stronger in close relationships. The social relationship should, therefore, be clear before using the assessment tool.
9	The tool should discover social needs/wishes in sharing experiences.	As found in the results of the probing diary study, the participants had not so much difficulties in expressing wishes in sharing experiences as expressing their feelings. Therefore, the tool should focus on wishes as a means to inform how to enhance sharing experiences.
10	The social feeling to be measured should not be a stable, relatively hard to influence feeling over time, but should show variance over moments of experiencing.	Social connectedness, presence, and awareness are in some definitions defined as moment independent feelings. It is important to take into account these different definitions referred to in the literature.
11	The social feeling to be measured should be well defined.	Social feelings have multiple, even overlapping definitions. When measuring a social feeling, a clear definition should be selected.
12	The social feeling to be measured should be able to be measured with a validated questionnaire.	In order to evaluate the assessment tool, its results will be compared to results of conventional methods, like validated questionnaires for measuring social feelings.

As described before, many methods exist to measure experiences. To fulfill the above requirements, we chose a mixture of the methods Experience Sampling (ESM) (Csikszentmihalyi & Larson, 1987, p. 526) and Day Reconstruction (DRM) (Kahneman et al., 2004, p. 1776), as previously done by Khan et al, (2007). When using ESM, it is possible to measure in situ during the moment; using DRM, the tool will take less time to use during this moment. Furthermore, data that can be unobtrusively and automatically logged (such as location and activity) should be collected by context-aware systems and not through self-report. As for psychophysiological measurements, these could give very useful, objective data without burdening users. However, since these measures still need additional self-report, for the first version of the assessment tool these measures will not be taken into account, but should be kept in mind when further developing the tool. In the next section, the development of the WiShare tool is explained.

Development of the WiShare Tool

The WiShare tool for assessing social feelings is designed to assess social connectedness and social presence. Social presence is defined as "the sense of being with another in a mediated environment" (Biocca, Harms, & Burgoon, 2003, p. 456) and social connectedness as "an emotional experience, evoked by, but independent of, the other's presence; psychological involvement" (Rettie, 2003) and as "a feeling of staying in touch" (IJsselsteijn, van Baren, & van Lanen, 2003, pp. 924–928). These (definitions of) social feelings are both moment dependent and addressed by validated questionnaires. The sharing experiences model described by Visser and Mulder (2008) shows that people can indicate two important elements of a sharing experience: what is shared and what is wished to be shared, for example, information about context, thoughts, or feelings. An attempt will be made to let people indicate their feeling of social presence and connectedness through answering questions about sharing of context, thoughts, feelings, and wishes. It is assumed that this should be easier and take less effort than directly asking about social feelings, since participants indicated in the probing diary study (Visser & Mulder2008) that they have trouble describing their feelings. Also, social feelings usually are fairly unfamiliar concepts to users (IJsselsteijn & de Ridder 1998) and "understanding of presence should not be assumed by directly asking participants how present they feel" (van Baren & IJsselsteijn, 2004).

Through different iterations with user evaluations, an interactive prototype of an adequate assessment tool has been developed in line with the interaction lifecycle model (Sharp et al., 2006, p. 413), which allows multiple iterations of development phases. The tool will be referred to as the WiShare tool: named after the wishes we have when we are or are not sharing experiences. The technical implementation of the WiShare tool will be discussed first, followed by user evaluations that gave input to the development of the WiShare tool, which exists of a Web application on a pocket PC or ordinary PC, and a vibrating bracelet. The Web application is accessible through a pocket PC that should be able to monitor user behavior as location (e.g., using GPS, Bluetooth) and activity (usage logging). This data is used for analysis and to request the user to report about sharing experiences in certain situations. The user can be requested to quickly report about a certain experience on the pocket PC by a vibration of the bracelet. The Web application is also accessible on an ordinary PC for filling in questionnaires about reported sharing experiences. In addition to triggered requests, random requests can also be sent or the user can take the initiative to report at moments he or she wants. In this way, the WiShare tool could also be used in cases when no user behavior can be monitored. The Web application is implemented using Flash (action script), XML, PHP, and mySQL. After logging in on the Web application, a flash application is shown in which the user can indicate his or her sharing experience. The flash application sends the data of the avatar positions, date, time (if monitored), location, and activity to a database. Each moment (can be found on the "moments" Web page) has a specific link to a questionnaire, which displays a reported moment visualization in flash and information about date, time, and other monitored data retrieved from the database. When the user sends the filled in questions, this data plus date and time of sending is also sent to the database.

User behavior can be monitored in several ways in addition to within the WiShare tool, depending on the system that is evaluated. For instance, if the evaluated system is on a pocket PC, user location could be monitored using the GPS and Bluetooth available on this pocket PC. Activity within the system could be monitored using code especially written for the desired purpose. Per system evaluation, decisions should be made about what needs to be monitored and the best ways to monitor user behavior considering the system's goals and possibilities. In the section "User lab evaluation," techniques used for monitoring user behavior are explained.

Explanation of the WiShare Tool

The visualization of the WiShare tool exists of two dimensions: the sharing of context (blue avatar icons) and the sharing of thoughts and feelings (cloud icons) (Figure 16.1). In the bottom left corner is an avatar that represents the user. The Real avatar is the person with whom the user is reporting sharing experiences. The Wish avatar is how the user would like to have the sharing experience. The avatars can be dragged with a mouse pointer (or pocket PC pen) onto the square field. In future versions of the WiShare tool, it should be possible to let users pick a favorite avatar from a list. In this version of the tool, it is not possible to report sharing experiences with multiple people, because evaluating the tool in a social network would make user testing in this first phase of development more complex and bring practical issues.

In short, the closer the Real avatar is dragged to the Me avatar, the more that is shared at a certain moment. When the user feels the avatars are well positioned, the user clicks OK to send the data (Figure 16.1). If the user is not sharing at a certain moment when he or she wants to send a sharing experience, he or she can indicate this by checking the (not default) "I don't share" radio button. The user is thus able to indicate a wish.

Once the user sends data of sharing experiences, they answer a questionnaire for each sharing experience. The questionnaire contains the following open questions:

1. What did you share (in addition to the activity)?
2. What did you think and feel at this (sharing) moment?
3. What did the other person think and feel at this (sharing) moment?
4. If you had a wish for this (sharing) moment, what was it?
5. If you had a wish for this (sharing) moment, what did you miss in this (sharing) moment?
6. What other remarks would you like to share about this (sharing) moment?

Evaluation of the WiShare Tool

We had the WiShare tool evaluated at different stages in the development of the tool. The conceptual design of the tool is evaluated by means of an expert brainstorm and a Web survey. The main aim of the Web survey is to validate the conceptual design (the visualization) as measuring social presence and social connectedness; also, the usability of some first visualizations of the tool has been tested. We used the results of the expert review and the Web survey to develop a first version of the WiShare tool. Since the tool should facilitate describing sharing experiences, a diary study was conducted in which participants were asked to reflect on their sharing experiences using the WiShare tool. The results of this diary gave input for developing an improved second version of the tool. In a final evaluation with pairs of users in a lab setting, participants evaluated the second

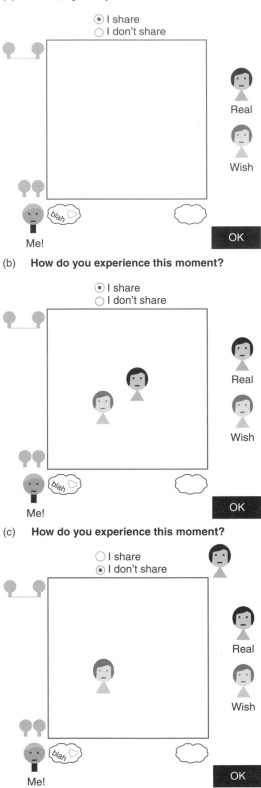

Figure 16.1 Three examples of screens of indicating a sharing experience.

version of the WiShare tool. In the following sections, we discuss only the diary study and the final user evaluation in the lab. These evaluations inform how the tool should be used in practice.

Diary Study

In the diary study, participants evaluated a first version of the interactive prototype of the WiShare tool. The main aim was to check if the requirements for the WiShare tool were met and if the tool was understandable and usable.

Method

Participants

Ten participants participated in this study (five male and five female). The participants were between 21 and 63 years old; the average age was 31. Four of the participants (two male and two female, no students) also participated in the probing diary study, which informed the conceptual design. The participants were required to use the Internet on a daily basis. All participants were rewarded with a credit note of 15 €.

Procedure

During one week, participants had to describe their sharing experiences with a certain person that was close to them and with whom they had contact on a daily basis. After a week of describing sharing experiences, we interviewed each participant about how he or she experienced the act of describing their sharing experiences and valued the usability of the Internet version of the WiShare tool.

Tasks

We asked participants to describe their sharing experiences with one specific person close to them by means of the WiShare tool. The participants had to answer the question "how much feelings, thoughts and context do I share with the other person?" at moments when they shared or wished (not) to share experiences. We asked them to report about the sharing experience the moment it occurred, using the Internet version of the tool when available or otherwise the paper version. On the paper version of the tool, the participant had to draw the Real and Wish avatars at the correct place and write down the date and time of the moment, plus answer questions about the moments. In the Internet version, the participants could drag the avatars to the right place and send this data to the database. They could fill in the belonging questions about the moments at a later time, on paper or the Internet. After 1 week, or at the time of the interview, the participants needed a minimum of five described sharing experiences on paper and a minimum of five described sharing experiences on the Internet.

Material

The participants received a letter containing forms with a visualization of the WiShare tool and the belonging questions together with an explanation of the tasks. The interview questions were based on the requirements explained in the above section "Requirements for an Assesment Tool."

Analysis

We analyzed interview results to explore if the WiShare tool met the requirements we previously outlined. Also, four people qualitatively analyzed understandability of the WiShare tool in an expert rating session.

Results

In total, participants reported 98 moments, of which 62 were reported on the paper version. We will first discuss the interview results, followed by the results of the expert rating brainstorm.

Interview

Most participants preferred the paper version because they could take this version with them and could better express themselves writing instead of typing. Two participants did not even use the Internet version at all. The participants had no major problems with using the tool; however, most of them indicated it took some time to be able to use it easily. The participants generally interpreted the thoughts and feelings scale as the amount of communication at a certain moment; they indicated no difficulties with interpreting the visualizations.

Expert Rating Brainstorm

To analyze the collected 98 moments, an expert rating brainstorm was organized. Four User-System Interaction students from the Eindhoven University of Technology were asked to each rate 49 moments so two times an inter-rater reliability could be calculated. The experts rated the moments on a three-point scale: 1 = the WiShare tool is applied well in this situation; 2 = the WiShare tool is almost applied well in this situation; 3 = the WiShare tool is not applied well in this situation. Before rating, the experts received the same instructions about the WiShare tool as the users received and were asked not to talk to each other during rating. For both pairs of raters/experts, a weighted Cohen's kappa (for ordinal data) was calculated (Cohen, 1976, p. 213; Landis & Koch, 1977, p. 159). The raters had an inter-rater reliability of 0.57 (moderate agreement) and 0.67 (substantial agreement).

After rating, the experts discussed in pairs the moments they rated. This discussion provided information about in which situations the WiShare tool was difficult to apply and why. Several useful remarks were made during this discussion.

The experts noticed that it was easier for the participants to fill in the thoughts and feelings dimension than the context dimension, because there seems to be a lot of variation between moments in the context dimension in similar situations. Also, the experts themselves had different interpretations of sharing context; it could refer to the mental or physical distance people experience. Furthermore, it seemed that participants sometimes just wanted a different context or sharing at a different moment instead of wanting to share more or less. In these situations, the wish avatar was difficult to position. The experts mentioned that the tool does not provide an option to show how large a wish is. Sometimes a big wish was visualized as separating the avatars as much as possible, although this would in theory mean a wish for sharing much more. Moreover, it was not possible in the current visualization to convey not sharing and wishing to share, although some participants tried to visualize these moments. One expert remarked that it was not clear as to what was meant with "sharing thoughts and feelings": is it about thinking and feeling the same or about what you tell about each other's thoughts and feelings? Although none of the participants made this remark, we determined that "sharing thoughts and feelings" may need more explanation. The experts had trouble judging visualizations in which the avatars were placed half over each other. It could mean that the participant did not have a wish or had a wish for sharing a bit more or less. One expert suggested to make the tool more intuitive by changing the dimensions so the "Me" avatar will be in the right upper corner instead of in the left lower corner.

Discussing difficulties in applying the WiShare tool led to the discussion of improving the tool. To make it possible to visualize no sharing, there should be a "no sharing" option on the visualization. Also, to make it possible to have no wish, the avatars should be transparent to keep them visible when putting them on top of each other. Since the term context defined as "your environment, activity, and situation" seemed to be confusing, one expert suggested changing the definition into "your environment and activity," because "situation" can also refer to your inner thoughts and feelings.

Discussion

Most results (if possible to implement concerning material and time) of the diary study were used to design an improved second version of the WiShare tool. First of all, the participants chose the moments they wanted to report themselves, as well as the moment of reporting. This is not how the tool should be used; the user should get an alert and immediately fill in the visualization. Second, the moments the participants reported were everyday moments. This implies that the tool is used in situations that will not necessarily be involved when using the tool to evaluate a new interactive media application. However, for the purpose of this diary study, these issues were less important because our main aim was to evaluate understandability and usability of the tool and testing requirements. Regardless of the above-stated validity issues, the results were used for realizing an improved second version of the tool to use in the user lab evaluation.

User Lab Evaluation

After developing the second version of the WiShare tool, the tool was evaluated in a user lab context similar to contexts of real use of the tool. Unfortunately, due to technical constraints, it was not possible to evaluate the tool in a field test. First, user behavior logging and alerting the user based on his or her behavior seemed impossible for a short term. Second, the two available vibrating bracelets soon appeared not to be stable enough for user testing. Third, the WiShare tool worked on a pocket PC, but imperfectly. Sending data from the visualization responded very slowly or not at all, which would cause frustration for the user. Thus, we used a lab test to optimally prepare the WiShare tool for a field test.

The user lab evaluation had two main goals. The first goal of the experiment was to observe the influence of different activities, different communication media, and different personal views on sharing experiences between friends. We chose the application MSN Live messenger to be evaluated by the WiShare tool due to its many possibilities in sharing experiences. Two different activities (watching TV and playing games) in three different communication conditions (text chat, audio and video chat, and being together in one room) were performed by the users in pairs of friends. Since the content of the games and TV programs differed over the tasks, we expected each person to also evaluate this content, and therefore the sharing experience, differently due to personal taste. User activities and behavior were logged and triggered alerts for the WiShare tool.

The second goal was to research the utility and usability of the WiShare tool for assessing sharing experiences, by attaining useful results from the WiShare tool for informing new development of social interactive media and good understandability and usability of the tool by means of user interviews.

Method

Participants

In total, 18 people, 8 female and 10 male, participated in this study. Their average age was 31 (SD = 7); the youngest participant was 14, the oldest 41. Fourteen participants had a higher education level of which six were scientists. Two participants were scholars. We recruited four participants via acquaintances, adverts on Internet forums, and adverts spread at public places such as a library and schools. Fourteen participants were employees of the Telematica Instituut where the study was conducted. The participants were required to have experience using computer and Internet, and to know the other person participating at the same time (preferably being friends or close colleagues). Participants recruited outside the company received a credit note of 10 €; participants working in the company received a small gift. Two participants used an instant messaging (IM) program less than once a month; other participants use IM a number of times a week or a month. The most used IM program was MSN, used for talking to friends, colleagues, acquaintances, and family. Most participants used IM only for text chatting and to share documents.

Procedure

Two participants participated together at the same time in the test. First, participants received a short explanation of the tasks and the WiShare tool Web application. A Bluetooth dongle on a necklace, which could give a beep, was put around their neck. Then, the participants were separated and brought to different rooms where they each sat behind a

Table 16.2 Participants' tasks

User 1—tasks	User 2—tasks
Invite your friend for a MSN game Het Duel you and your friend would like to play. Turn off your webcams.	Invite your friend for a MSN game. You and your friend would like to play Bejeweled. Turn on your webcams.
Invite your friend to watch a film trailer you both would like via Messenger TV. Turn on your webcams.	Invite your friend to watch a movie trailer you both would like via Messenger TV. Turn off your webcams.
Invite your friend to play the game Text Express 2 together in your room.	Invite your friend in your room to watch a film trailer via MSN TV.

computer for doing the tasks. They first had some time to practice a bit with the WiShare tool. After 5 min, the participants were free to start their tasks. During each task, participants received an alert on their Bluetooth dongle, which meant the WiShare tool had to be used. When the participants were done with their tasks after about 45 min, they had to fill in the online questionnaires belonging to the reported moments. In addition, we gave a questionnaire about usability and a form with general questions about personal and social Internet networks behavior. Each participant was personally asked how they experienced the tasks and the WiShare tool.

Tasks

In total, six joint tasks had to be done, and each participant was responsible for three of these tasks (Table 16.2). In all six tasks, participation of both participants was needed. Tasks involved playing a game via MSN messenger with or without a video chat, watching a film trailer via MSN messenger with or without a video chat, and playing a game or watching a film trailer while together in one room. We made a randomization scheme to change the order of the tasks for each pair of participants.

The participants were told that they had about 3–8 min for one task and that they could (but were not obliged to) stop the task once they received an alert. When they received an alert, they had to fill in the visualization of the WiShare tool. After finishing the tasks, the participants filled in the WiShare questionnaires about the reported moments. We also asked the participants to tell which film trailer they watched (if they watched a film trailer) and to give a mark from 1 (not nice) to 5 (very nice) to indicate how much they liked the game or film trailer. The form with general questions about social Internet networks behavior contained questions about the relationship between the participants and overall use of instant messaging.

Material

Two rooms next to each other were furnished as living rooms. Both contained a desk and a laptop plus a webcam for the participants to do their tasks. A second laptop was installed as a replacement for the pocket PC to fill in the WiShare tool. Another computer with a webcam was installed to make it possible for the test leader to hear and see what happened in the two rooms. We mainly used these observations to intervene when the participants needed help or when technical errors appeared.

We used MSN Live Messenger with the extension application Messenger Plus! to be able to view both rooms simultaneously. Also, Internet activity of both laptops of the participants was logged by the use of a specially programmed central logging machine using MySQL tools. The output of the central logging machine was also visible on the observation laptop. The MSN conversations were saved but unavailable during observation. The activity (watching a film trailer or playing Text Express, Bejeweled, or Het Duel) was sent to the WiShare tool. An alert was automatically sent to the Bluetooth dongle 2 min after starting an activity, which was established by a specially programmed notification system. When the participants filled in the WiShare visualization, the activity and time were sent to the WiShare database and displayed in the WiShare questionnaire as a mnemonic. Unfortunately, it was technically impossible to automatically send information about the "sharing condition" (text chat, video chat, being together) or the film trailer to the questionnaires, which would have supported a stronger remembrance of the moment.

Analysis

We explored the influence of the content conditions (playing a game or watching a film trailer) and communication medium (being together, video chat, or text chat) on a sharing experience for individuals. It is assumed that more interactivity in a sharing experience is appreciated as more sharing of context, thoughts, and feelings. Playing a game was expected to be more interactive than watching a film trailer; being together was assumed to be more interactive than a video chat, which in turn is more interactive than a text chat. The positions of avatars on the WiShare visualizations were divided into categories to make analysis easier (grid). Using this categorization, a wish is recognized when the Wish and Real avatar differ on position at least half of the size of the avatar (to be fairly sure about the wish being different than the real situation, because sometimes users tend to partly overlap the avatars). Within a pair of participants, we analyzed the relationship between personal views and experiencing. It is assumed that when a pair of participants has a different opinion about a sharing experience, the participants feel as if they share less. Next, we analyzed the WiShare questionnaires to get insight into the understandability and usability of the tool, opinions about sharing experiences, and wishes in sharing experiences. Also, the short interviews gave an indication of usability of the tool.

Results

Before discussing the results, we should note that the test had to deal with a lot of technical issues. This was partly caused by network problems and faults in the script of logging the data and sending alerts. Furthermore, MSN Live Messenger caused errors when starting a game or a film trailer. Because of these technical issues, quite a lot of data is missing, since some participants could not do all their tasks, thus in the analysis N is lower than the number of participants.

Influence of Content and Communication Medium

The data of each participant are difficult to compare with other participants' data since experiencing is very personal. Quite large deviations exist between people in filling in the WiShare visualization. To answer the question of whether content has an influence on the evaluation of a sharing experience, we performed a Wilcoxon Signed Ranks Test on the positions of the Real avatar. There was a significant effect of content on evaluating a sharing experience for the context dimension ($Z = -2.213$; $p = 0.027$ at $\alpha < 0.05$), indicating that overall watching a film trailer was evaluated as sharing more context than playing a game. This is a striking result, because we assumed that playing a game would be more interactive and therefore would cause a feeling of sharing more instead of less. We performed Friedman Tests on the Real avatar positions to research predicted influences of communication medium. The results of the tests suggest that the sharing of context, thoughts, and feelings significantly increases when using richer communication media (context: $p = .002$ at $\alpha < 0.05$; thoughts and feelings: $p = .009$ at $\alpha < 0.05$).

Influence of Personal View

Unfortunately, due to many missing values, we can do no statistical tests to reliably explore the relationship between different opinions about content and evaluation of sharing experiences within participant pairs. However, it is possible to explore if a negative or positive personal view has an influence on the evaluation. We asked participants to give a value from 1 (nice) to 5 (very nice) to indicate if they liked the game or film trailer. Kruskal-Wallis tests were used to test if there is a difference in sharing context, thoughts, and feelings for different values. Results from the tests give no significant results for influence of different personal views on content for context sharing (TV: $\chi^2 = 0.417$, $p = 0.812$; game: $\chi^2 = 1.538$, $p = 0.463$) and thoughts and feelings sharing (TV: $\chi^2 = 0.774$, $p = 0.679$; game: $\chi^2 = 2.333$, $p = 0.311$). These results indicate that the user's evaluation of a sharing experience is not effected by his or her evaluation of the content.

Wishes

The wishes in the sharing experiences are visualized in Figures 16.2 (be together and play a game), 16.3 (video chat and play a game), 16.4 (text chat and play a game), 16.5 (be together and watch a film trailer), 16.6 (video chat and watch a film trailer), and 16.7 (text chat and watch a film trailer). The arrows indicate the position from the Real avatar to the Wish avatar. A dot indicates that the position of the Real and Wish avatars are equal. A green arrow or a dot represents a good interpretation of the visualization in the sense that when a participant fills in a wish on the visualization, he or she explains this wish in the questionnaire. A purple arrow or a dot represents the participant filling in the WiShare tool wrongly. Each arrow and dot is labeled with the wishes that were stated in the WiShare questionnaires.

The position, direction, length, and color of the arrows and dots provide information about how a sharing moment is experienced. Comparing playing a game in the conditions being together, video chat, and text chat (Figure 16.2, 16.3, and 16.4), participants had most wishes for more sharing in the text chat condition. As can be seen especially in the text chat condition, the direction from Real to Wish is mainly from the right upper corner (little sharing) to the left down corner (much sharing). Note that relatively more errors have been made in the being together condition (despite much missing data). Although in the visualizations it has been shown that more interactivity in a condition is indicated by sharing more (as was also statistically discussed above), the arrows and dots also show personal differences in appreciation. The wishes give an explanation, referring to missing interaction, missing sharing, missing a feeling of competition, and social interaction between two participants, for example, "more input from the other during the game." Wishes also (more concretely) refer to wanting to talk or play longer and wanting to have the same playing field. However, participants also had wishes that do not seem to directly

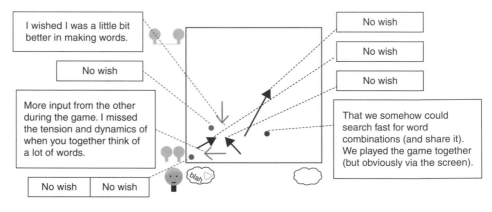

Figure 16.2 Playing a game while being together.

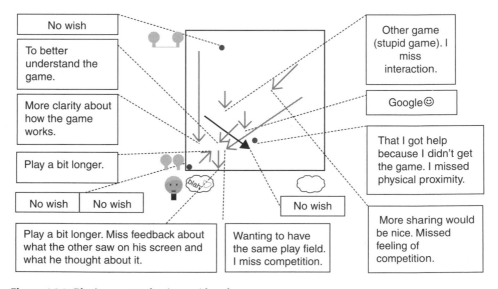

Figure 16.3 Playing a game having a video chat.

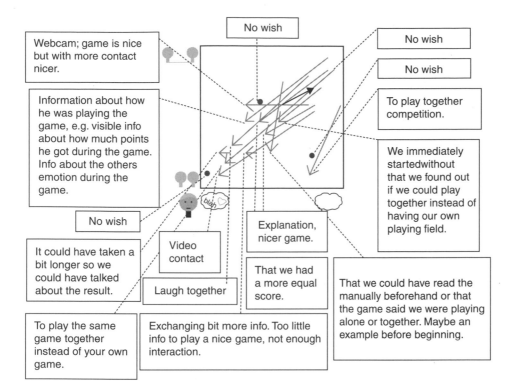

Figure 16.4 Playing a game having a text chat.

refer to the sharing experience, such as the wish to have a better comprehension of the game and the wish to be better at playing the game.

The conditions of being together, video chat, and text chat (Figures 16.5, 16.6, and 16.7) show quite similar outcomes when watching a film trailer as when playing a game. Again, less interactivity is interpreted as less sharing and causes more wishes (more arrows) and wishes for more sharing (longer arrows). Participants have wishes about sharing more and having more interaction, but also have wishes about technical aspects and content, such as to have better quality or a longer film trailer.

Some participants wrongly filled in visualizations and/or questionnaires while watching a film trailer, which indicates several issues with the WiShare tool. It could be that participants forgot their wish once they had to fill in the questionnaires. Also, not all wishes were specifically about social interaction between the two participants (e.g., "I wanted to share it with more people that I saw this movie is coming" and "home theater"). Furthermore, the visualization could have been unclear to fill in. We will next explore the usability of the tool.

Usability

Interviews conducted after the test provided several remarks that could help improve usability. The WiShare tool appeared to be hard to use at first. Placing the Wish avatar

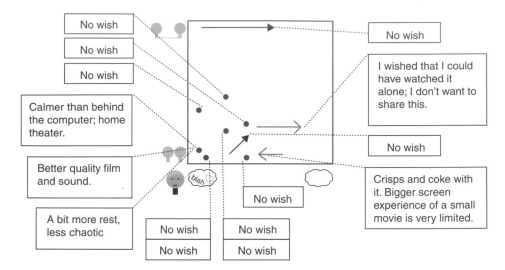

Figure 16.5 Watching a film trailer being together.

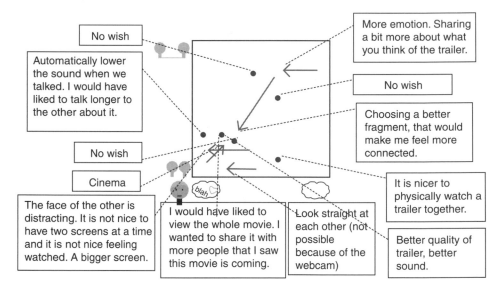

Figure 16.6 Watching a film trailer having a video chat.

was the most difficult task. Some participants mentioned that the tool was counterintuitive because participants expected that moving the avatars to the right upper corner means more sharing instead of less sharing. Opinions about the scales differed between suggestions for textual or numbered scales to very much liking the used scales. For most participants, it took much effort to remember what activity (if not automatically logged

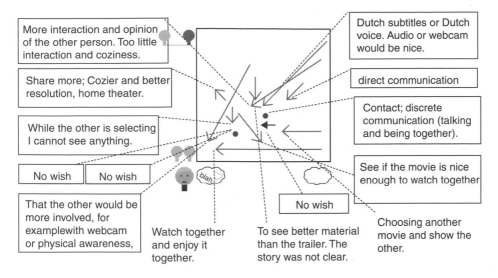

Figure 16.7 Watching a film trailer having a text chat.

due to technical issues) and condition (being together, video chat, text chat) belonged to which moment when filling in the questionnaires. This stresses the findings of the diary study, since users needed means to remember the moment; the positions of the avatars were not enough.

Discussion

The aim of the final user lab evaluation was an overall evaluation of the WiShare tool concerning predicted assessment and usability of the tool. Assuming that interactivity has a great influence on appreciation of sharing experiences, we explored different conditions in content and communication media. As for the influence of content, watching a film trailer was considered as sharing more context than when playing a game (regardless of the communication medium), which was an unpredicted outcome. Participants felt that they were sharing more context, thoughts, and feelings when they had a video chat, compared to a text chat, and even more so when they were together. The wishes stated in the final user evaluation not only referred to social interaction, but also to concrete wishes for a better user experience. Probably more factors, such as quality of media, influence the appreciation of the sharing experience. Participants indicated that filling in the visualization of the tool was not easy, especially filling in the wishes. This could be explained by the variety of wishes that exist in a sharing experience, beyond the wish for more or less sharing of context, thoughts, and feelings. Automatic logging of activity and other situation elements was very important in making users better remember sharing moments and thus making the tool more user friendly.

Concluding Thoughts

The goal of this research was (to get insight in how) to design a tool for in situ measurement of social feelings during moments of sharing experiences between related users in a nonintrusive manner. The assessment tool is meant to inform product designers to optimally design social systems and give researchers insight into sharing experiences in interactive media.

The first steps to achieve this goal were to reach an overview of methods assessing social interactions and gain insight into how literature and people perceive social feelings in sharing experiences. We identified main requirements of the tool based on literature and end users' feedback, which were implemented in the WiShare tool. The WiShare tool aims at gathering richer data compared to existing technologies as ESM and MyExperience by combining short questions about feelings and (automatic) contextual logging. Also, the WiShare tool focused on nonintrusive assessment by using emergent technology in contrast with psychophysiological measurements currently available. User evaluations revealed which requirements were met and which aspects of the tool still needed, and therefore need attention.

The evaluation showed that the WiShare tool assesses social feelings in sharing experiences as we intended. Information about design improvements for a better quality of a sharing experience can be found in participants' wishes for sharing experiences, which provide information about what users miss in a certain sharing experience. The tool provides social researchers information about in what situations people feel they share less or more context, thoughts, and feelings and helps them understand how these feelings of sharing are influenced.

General Findings

1. The WiShare tool measures sharing of context, thoughts, and feelings during a sharing experience at moments of interest.
2. The tool takes little effort and time to use, but can be improved to require even less effort.
3. The tool measures information about the users' (social) context automatically and unobtrusively. The WiShare tool is a prototype focusing on user self-report, however, it can easily be extended with automatic logging functionality in the emerging technology. As indicated in the user lab evaluation, sensing of user behavior is possible as well.
4. The tool discovers social wishes in sharing experiences.
5. The tool is not unpleasant to use; however, different ways of motivating users to use the tool should be explored.

Future Directions

This chapter elaborated upon the Wishare tool to stimulate the current debate on methodological innovation and to inspire social researchers. The design and evaluation of the Wishare tool illustrates how social researchers could benefit from emergent technologies in getting more grips on social phenomena such a sharing of thoughts and feelings in mediated communication. Current methods for social research are not appropriate for assessing such social feelings in the moment of experiencing. Although the current version of the Wishare tool did not meet all identified needs, our exploration was helpful in getting a better understanding in the assessment of social feelings and experiences. Lessons learned from the current study yielded in several recommendations to improve the tool for future use. First, we originally developed the tool for designers of interactive media to gain insight in the quality of sharing experiences to inform their redesign of interactive media. Although designers were involved in the current study, we did not explicitly ask them whether the data gathered with the WiShare tool was helpful for redesigning. In the next phase of research, these designers should play a role in the development of the tool. Second, one aim in the beginning of this research was to search for a social concept that could be assessed by the tool. There is a discrepancy between how users understand their feelings during sharing experiences and how literature assesses these social feelings. It is still a challenge to translate users' views on sharing experiences into social concepts as stated and assessed in literature. The refined WiShare tool might therefore be helpful for social researchers as well, as it gains a clear insight in what users are truly feeling during a moment of sharing experience. Interestingly the automatically measured activity and situation appeared to be very important for users in remembering the moment, a factor that should get a main focus in the future. We originally developed the tool to assess social feelings in sharing experiences in a social network. Users should be able to visualize in the WiShare tool sharing experiences with more than one friend. Although not taken into account in this research, using the tool for sharing experiences with multiple people could have an effect on, for instance, the usability of the tool. Future work should consider these possible effects. Last, the WiShare tool should be extended with technologies available for assessing (social) feelings. At this moment psychophysiological measurements as heart rate, skin temperature, body postures etcetera are not yet suitable enough for in situ contextual research. However, these measurements can give much insight in people's feelings at a certain moment. Using these measurements as an addition to the WiShare tool would make the tool more valid and reliable.

Acknowledgments

Many thanks to the University of Technology Eindhoven (especially Panos Markopoulos) and the Telematica Instituut Enschede for giving us the possibility to do research on the WiShare tool.

References

van Baren, J., IJsselsteijn, W. A., Romero, N., Markopoulos, P., & de Ruyter, B. (2003, October). Affective benefits in communication: The development and field-testing of a new questionnaire measure. Presence 2003. Aalborg, Denmark.

van Baren J., & IJsselsteijn, W. (2004). Compendium of presence measures. Deliverable 5: Measuring presence: A guide to current measurement approaches. Available at http://www.presence-research.org and www.presence-research.org.

Biocca, F., Harms, C., & Burgoon, J. K. (2003). Toward a more robust theory and measure of social presence: Review and suggested criteria. *Presence, 12*(5), 456–480.

Bradley, M. M., & Lang, P. J. (1994). Measuring emotion: The self-assessment manikin and the semantic differential. *Journal of Behavior Therapy and Experimental Psychiatry, 25*, 49–59.

Brandstatter, H. (1991). Emotions in everyday situations. Time sampling of subjective experience. In Strack, F., Argyle, M., & Schwarz, N. (Eds.), *Subjective well-being: An interdisciplinary perspective* (pp. 173–192). Oxford: Pergamon Press.

Cohen, J. (1976). Weighted kappa: Nominal scale agreement with provision for scaled disagreement or partial credit. *Psychol Bull, 70*, 213–220.

Consolvo, S., & Walker, M. (2003). Using the experience sampling method to evaluate Ubicomp applications. *IEEE Pervasive Computing Mobile and Ubiquitous Systems: The Human Experience, 2*, 24–31.

Csikszentmihalyi, M., & Larson, R. (1987). Validity and reliability of the experience-sampling method. *Journal of Nervous and Mental Disease, 175*, 526–536.

Dey, A. K. (2001). Understanding and using context. *Personal and Ubiquitous Computing, 5*, 20–20.

Dourish, P., & Bly, S. (1992). Portholes: Supporting awareness in a distributed work group. Proceedings of ACM CHI, 541–547.

van Drunen, A., van den Broek, E. L., Heffelaar, T. (2008, August). uLog: Towards attention aware user-system interactions measurement. Proceedings of Measuring Behavior, Maastricht, The Netherlands, 26–29.

Froehlich, J., Chen, M., Consolvo, S., Harrison, B., & Landay, J. (2007). MyExperience: A system for in situ tracing and capturing of user feedback on mobile phones. Proceedings of MobiSys, San Juan, Puerto Rico.

Gemmell, J., Williams, L., Wood, K., Lueder, R., & Bell, G. (2004, October 15). Passive capture and ensuing issues for a personal lifetime store. Proceedings of the 1st ACM Workshop on Continuous Archival and Retrieval of Personal Experiences. New York, USA.

Harms, C., & Biocca, F. (2004). Internal consistency and reliability of the networked minds measure of social presence. Proceedings of the Seventh Annual International Presence Workshop. Valencia, Spain: Universidad, 246–251.

Hewstone, M., & Stroebe, W. (Eds.). (2002). Introduction to social psychology (3rd ed.). Oxford: Blackwell Publishers Ltd.

ter Hofte, H., Otte, R., Peddemors, A., & Mulder, I. (2006, November 4–8). What's your lab doing in my pocket? Supporting mobile field studies with SocioXensor. (Demonstration) CSCW Conference Supplement. Banff, Alberta, Canada.

Hole, L., & Williams, O. (2008, June 24–25). Capturing the user experience. Paper for CREATE, London.

IJsselsteijn, W. A., & de Ridder, H. (1998, June 10–11). Measuring temporal variations in presence. Paper presented at the Presence in Shared Virtual Environments Workshop, University College London.

IJsselsteijn, W. A., van Baren, J., van Lanen, F. (2003). Staying in touch: Social presence and connectedness through synchronous and asynchronous communication media. In Stephanidis, C., & Jacko, J. (Eds.), Human-computer interaction: Theory and practice (Part II, pp. 924–928).

Intille, S. S., Rondoni, J., Kukla, C., Ancona, I., & Bao, L. (2003). A context-aware experience sampling tool. In CHI '03 Extended Abstracts. ACM Press, New York, 972–973.

Kahneman, D., Krueger, A. B., Schkade, D. A., Schwarz, N., & Stone, A. A. (2004). A survey method for characterizing daily life experience: The day reconstruction method. *Science, 306*, 1776.

Kahneman, D., & Krueger, A. B. (2006). Developments in the measurement of subjective well-being. *Journal of Economic Perspectives, 20*(1), 3–24.

Khan, V. J., Markopoulos, P., & IJsselsteijn, W. (2007, June 21). Combining the experience sampling method with the day reconstruction method. Proceedings of CHI Nederland Conferentie, Eindhoven.

Landis, J. R., & Koch, G. G. (1977). The measurement of observer agreement for categorical data. *Biometrics, 33*, 159–174.

Lee, R. M., & Robbins, S. B. (1998). The relationship between social connectedness and anxiety, self-esteem, and social identity. *Journal of Counseling Psychology*, *45*(3), 338–345.

Mehl, M. R., & Pennebaker, J. W. (2003). The sounds of social life: A psychometric analysis of students' daily social environments and natural conversations. *Journal of Personality and Social Psychology*, *84*(4), 857–870.

Mulder, I., & Kort, J. (2008). Mixed emotions, mixed methods: The role of emergent technologies to study user experience in context. In Hesse-Biber, S., & Leavy, P. (Eds.), *Handbook of emergent methods in social research* (pp. 601–612). New York: Guilford Publications.

Ouwerkerk, M., Pasveer, F., & Langereis, G. (2008). Unobtrusive sensing of psychophysiological parameters. In Westerink, J. H. D. M., Ouwerkerk, M., Overbeek, T. J. M., Pasveer, W. F., & de Ruyter, B. (Eds.), *Probing experience. From assessment of user emotions and behaviour to development of products* (pp. 163–193). Netherlands: Springer.

Partala, T. (2005). Affective information in human-computer interaction. Dissertations in Interactive Technology, Department of Computer Science, University of Tampere, Finland.

Picard, R., & Daily, S. B. (2005). Evaluating affective interactions: Alternatives to asking what users feel. Presented at the 2005 CHI Workshop "Evaluating Affective Interfaces," New York: ACM.

Rettie, R. M. (2003). Connectedness, awareness and social presence. Presence 2003, 6th Annual Workshop on Presence.

Roesch, E. B., Fontaine, J. R., & Scherer, K. R. (2006, September 21–28). The world of emotions is two-dimensional... or is it? Presentation at the 3rd HUMAINE Summer School, Genova. Available at http://emotion-research.net/ws/summerschool3/ and http://emotion-research.net/ws/summerschool3/.

Russell, J. A. (1980). A circumplex model of affect. *Journal of Personality and Social Psychology*, *39*, 1161–1178.

Sanders, E. B. N. (2001). Virtuosos in the experience. In Proceedings of the 2001 IDSA Education Conference.

Scherer, K. R. (2005). What are emotions? And how can they be measured? *Social Science Information*, *44*(4), 695–729.

Scollon, C. N., Kim-Prieto, C., & Diener, E. (2003). Experience sampling: Promises and pitfalls, strengths and weaknesses. *Journal of Happiness Studies*, *4*, 5–34. Kluwer Academic Publishers.

Sharp, S., Rogers, Y., & Preece, J. (2006). *Interaction design: Beyond human-computer interaction*. West Sussex: John Wiley & Sons Ltd.

Short, J., Williams, E., & Christie, B. (1976). *The social psychology of telecommunications*. London: John Wiley & Sons.

Starzyk, K. B., Holden, R. R., Fabrigar, L. R., & MacDonald, T. K. (2006). The personal acquaintance measure: A tool for appraising one's acquaintance with any person. *Journal of Personality and Social Psychology*, *90*, 833–847.

Visser, A., & Mulder, I. (2008, June 24–25). Gaining insight in (assessing) sharing experiences by means of a probing diary study. Proceedings of CREATE 2008, London, (CD-Rom), the BCS HCI Group and the Ergonomics Society.

Ward, R., & Marsden, P. (2003). Physiological responses to different Web-page designs. *International Journal of Human-Computer Studies*, *59*, 199–212.

Chapter 17

Data Mining and Research: Applied Mathematics Reborn

Bert Little

> Facts are stubborn, but statistics are more pliable.
>
> Mark Twain

Introduction

A term popularized in 2009, "data mining" is used to refer to a wide array of actions thought to be analytical. Techniques falling under this rubric range from using MS Excel© to sort rows of data to sophisticated mathematical algorithms that include matrix algebra and its derivative multivariate techniques. At NASA's most recent Knowledge Discovery in Databases—Association for Computing Machinery meeting in 2009, its data mining group was renamed *Advanced Analytics,* which is more acceptable formal terminology and probably will overtake data mining as the descriptor for this approach to data analysis (Little & Schucking, 2008).

Data are an implicit component of data mining. Traditionally, data mining is paired with a data warehouse, which is usually a very large database (VLDB). However, the definition of a database suited for data mining varies considerably. Data mining techniques are usually designed for samples of tens or hundreds of thousands of rows of data, and often the data may encompass the universe of information on a given topic.

An important difference between traditional statistical analysis, involving samples of a few hundred observations, and data mining of VLDBs is the test of statistical significance. Tests of significance are based on probability distributions and assume a certain amount of sampling error, but huge VLDBs violate traditional statistics' assumption that all data are relatively small samples of some distribution from a population.

In this chapter, data mining is defined, how to structure data for data mining (i.e., data warehouse) is explained, and the leading specific techniques are discussed. Finally, a vignette of a data mining project is presented end-to-end as an example of how someone might develop a data mining project.

Data Mining Techniques and Applications

Data mining's short history draws together sophisticated techniques from several different fields. Traditional statistics provides a quantitative basis for data mining. Machine learning and artificial intelligence contribute the rule-based analytical techniques and emulation of human brain functions (e.g., neural networks). In addition, relational database management systems (RDBMS) from computer science provide data mining with the quantitative underpinnings driving data mining.

Data Mining—Mathematical, Statistical, and Algorithmic Foundations

Data mining is erroneously advertised as a "new" technology. It could as accurately be termed advanced analytics or applied mathematics-statistics-VLDB computing, because data mining is a combination of techniques from all these areas.

It is important for the reader to appreciate that well-established mathematical, statistical, and computer science techniques are at work behind the scenes in data mining. This chapter concludes with an example of data mining with a sociological slant applied to a specific real-world problem in which large amounts of data are merged (or joined) in a data warehouse and are analyzed to quantitatively deduce (mating) behavior (Little, 2004).

The mathematical bases for many data mining analytical techniques are matrix algebra and linear programming, including such techniques such as regression, multiple regression, principal component analysis (PCA), factor analysis, discriminant analysis, canonical correlation analysis, and other matrix decomposition techniques (e.g., type III sums of squares) used in analysis of variance (ANOVA), analysis of covariance (ANCOVA), multivariate analysis of variance (MANOVA), and multivariate analysis of covariance (MANCOVA). Simple statistical tests such as t-tests or chi-squares fail (yield false positives) with huge samples because the denominator drives meaninglessly small differences to statistical significance. In medicine, the question is often whether the statistically significant difference is clinically significant. In the social sciences, a similar question may be posed—is this a meaningful difference?

Another difference between standard textbook statistical analysis and data mining is the use of algorithms. An algorithm is technically a sequence of steps that lays out a series of instructions with the end point, or output, being a solution to a problem. Algorithms can be tandem applications of formulae to data in a sequence of steps to produce a "deterministic" solution, but researchers are often interested in the statistical analysis, which is probabilistic. In addition, probabilistic algorithms are used in simulation studies where transition from one step to another is not a deterministic outcome of pushing data through a formula but instead randomness is introduced through a probabilistic process like sampling and resampling a data set, sampling a probability from a table, or computing it using a stochastic term (Han & Kamber, 2006).

A major strength of data mining when sufficient data are available is the use of sampling and resampling. For example, a technique called SEMMA ("sample, explore, modify, model, and assess") can optimize building, testing, and assessing statistical models to avoid over-fitting a model to a localized solution. The goal of data mining analysis is usually to derive a model that can be generalized to other data of similar nature. In SEMMA, creating three data sets through random sampling without replacement provides a dataset for exploration (model one), a dataset for modifying the initial model, and model fine-tuning and assessment (Olson & Delen, 2008).

Data Mining Applications

Data mining in retail business is used to optimize where certain items are placed in a grocery store. For example, lecturers explaining "market basket" analysis frequently cite the urban legend that data mining is responsible for Wal-Mart placing baby diapers near beer in the grocery stores. However, the online myth buster Snopes.com asserts this data mining heuristic is in fact a myth, and indeed, with a little fieldwork, one can discover that baby diapers are not colocated with beer (at least not in a local Wal-Mart in Texas). Although this amusing anecdote is not true, market basket analysis really is used for the purpose claimed: to determine patterns of association of products purchased during the same shopping trip. The information is used, for example, to print a point of sale coupon when the computer system recognizes that Items A, B, C, and D are usually purchased together, but the customer did not purchase item D on this shopping trip. The discount coupon for item D is intended to encourage purchase of item D through a reminder with an economic incentive.

Other practical data mining applications include medicine, science, technology development, and government. In 2004, the U.S. Government and Accountability Office (GAO) issued a report (GAO, 2004) identifying 199 data mining projects in the U.S. federal government. Applications ranged from astrophysics in NASA to financial accounting in the General Services Administration (GSA) to one of the author's data mining projects, entering its 10th year in 2010. This USDA Risk Management Agency project also was the subject of the GAO 2005 case-study report (GAO, 2005), which also included case studies of the Department of State, GSA, FBI, and the IRS. In this report, data mining was defined as the use of statistics and algorithms applied to large databases to discover patterns that may be used to predict future behavior (GAO, 2005).

In 2009, almost any data analysis might be labeled data mining because the phrase has become so popular. Popularity is driven by the immense amount of data currently available, and data mining techniques are increasingly made accessible to a wider user-base. In this chapter, data mining is considered to be the analysis of VLDBs (tens of thousands of rows with numerous variables) using advanced and multivariate techniques and algorithms.

Databases, Data Warehouses, and Additional Mythos

The phrase "data warehouse" brings to mind data analysis (data mining) because the two have been paired since the phrases were introduced. Data warehouses—VLDBs for some investigators—are methods of storage. General consensus distinguishes between data warehouses, which have data about the data they contain (i.e., metadata), while many VLDBs may be simple flat files (e.g., in Microsoft SQL Server™). In 2009, "data fusion" was used to describe the process of building a data warehouse. Importantly, the lion's share (> 80%) of time and effort in a data mining project lies in preparing the data (warehouse) for analysis (Little & Schucking, 2008).

Classification Analysis

The classification of individuals into groups is a general problem that is attacked from different angles. The approach depends upon the type(s) of data available and the objective

Table 17.1

Characteristic	Database	Data warehouse
Structure	Table Format	Table plus metadata
Complexity	Low	High
Data quantity	Sample, relatively small	Huge, possibly universe of data
	(*N>100*)	*N*>>100,000
Amount of data	Limited	Terabytes to petabytes or beyond
Optimization	Transactions, limited history	Large Scale with long history
Scope of data	Single source system	Data merged from many sources
Longitudinal	Rarely	Very frequently

Beginning with a flat ASACII file, sometimes referred to as flat text the data are numerically encoded and can be read digitally. Generally, flat text files have no information about the data represented in the variable at hand, except in some instances the first row is actually a header that includes only the variable name.

of the analysis. Classification can be approached from the perspective of discovery as in cluster analysis, testing an existing classification as with discriminant analysis, or exploring the decision rules that drive the classification (decision trees, rules, classification, and regression trees-CART).

Cluster Analysis

Cluster analysis is a method of unsupervised learning. It is a common technique for statistical data analysis used in many fields, including machine learning, data mining, pattern recognition, image analysis, and bioinformatics. Clustering or cluster analysis is the placement of a set of observations into subsets called *clusters*. Observations in the same cluster are more similar in some sense than observations in another cluster. Cluster analysis differentiates mainly between types of relationships between clusters. Some cluster analyses simply separate groups in two dimensions. Other clusters attempt to show the relationship among groups, such as in a phylogeny, or hierarchical clusters. Importantly, cluster analysis can help generate grouping hypotheses that can be further tested using discriminant analysis (Abonyi & Feil, 2007).

Discriminant Analysis

A regression-based technique, discriminant analysis allows the analyst to use predefined groups to experimentally discover independent variables that best define the groups through predicting the group membership of each member (row) of the dataset. Discriminant analysis is often used to test groupings discovered through cluster analysis (Fernandez, 2003; McCue, 2007).

In discriminant analysis, it is important that the data be well behaved (i.e., close to normally distributed) and that groups be similar in size (i.e., number of members). When only two groups are analyzed, regression of a binary independent on the dependents is exactly equal to a discriminant analysis. For example, analysis of binary groupings such as upper income versus lower income can be accomplished using either regression or discriminant analysis. However, for the spectrum of incomes (low, low middle, middle, high middle, lower high, middle high, upper high), discriminant analysis must be used.

The territorial map is a visual tool for assessing the discriminant functions derived. On the map, functions (synthetic variables) are plotted on an x–y axis for each observation in the database.

Regression

Simple linear regression is a powerful analytical technique. It is often used as the single analytical technique. Linear regression relies on the two parameters A (intercept) and B (slope), in addition to dependent variables (Y) and independent variables (X).

Multiple Regression

Multiple regression is the expansion of simple regression analysis to include many independent (x-axis) variables, thus extending the standard regression formula [$y = a + bx$] to one that includes many x's (variables). The major advantage is that it allows the influence of many independent variables (x) on the dependent variable (y). Often the bivariate relationship among the variables in a multiple regression can be revealing (Figure 17.1). However, relationships among more than two variables can be challenging. For example, the left panel in Figure 17.2 reveals a linear relationship between $Y1$, $X2$, and $X3$. However, the relationship is much weaker, less linear between $Y1$, $X1$, and $X2$ (Figure 17.2). Such findings should guide the investigator in modeling data in multiple regression analyses (Larose, 2006).

Principal Components Analysis (PCA)

Principal components analysis (PCA) is a regression-derived data reduction technique that decomposes the correlation matrix using orthogonalization, and creates synthetic variables that are linear combinations of the raw data. The synthetic variables summarize the information in the raw data and are often used as variables in further analyses (Han & Kamber, 2006).

Factor Analysis

Factor analysis uses the synthetic variables derived from PCA and optimizes their ability to capture information by refining the computation of principal components. The optimized synthetic variables are called factors. Factors differ from the original PCA in that they have

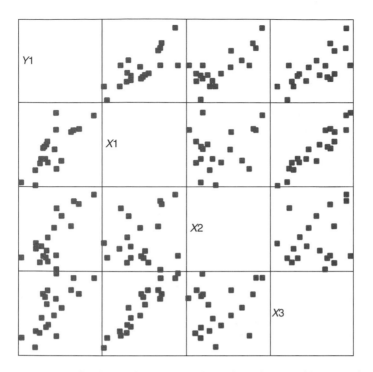

Figure 17.1 Scattergrams for three independent and one dependent variable in a multiple regression.

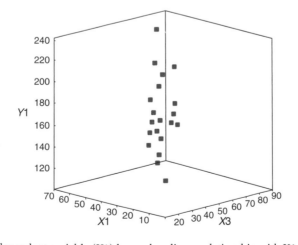

Figure 17.2 The dependent variable (Y1) has a clear linear relationship with X1 and X3, but not with X1 and X2.

been "rotated" to maximize the correlation of the factor with the raw data. Different kinds of rotations are available, but the two most commonly used are varimax and quatrimax. Varimax is used to maximize relationships among variables, and quatrimax is used to optimize variance at the row (individual observation) level (Han & Kamber, 2006).

Canonical Correlation

Canonical correlation is a derivative of PCA where two sets of variables are analyzed using PCA. The result is two sets of synthetic variables that are in turn correlated to discover patterns in the data. This technique, like PCA and factor analysis, is most often used when there are very large numbers of variables. Usually some intuitive grouping is used to choose which raw variables are included in the two sets of variables that will be reduced (Han & Kamber, 2006).

Decision Trees

Decision trees are also known as *b-trees* because decisions are usually modeled as binary (0, 1 or no, yes). They may be used alone as an analytical technique in a graphic representation of sets (groups) and subsets (subgroup) of data. The sub-setting of data and techniques of determining what/who will belong to the subsets allow decision trees to crosscut many analytical methods.

A decision tree in data mining is frequently part of a predictive model (i.e., predicting an outcome from observations on several-to-many variables). Outcomes are often group membership. Because frequently there will be only two groups, the progenitor of decision trees was named the *b-tree*.

In addition to the simple graphic tree structure, decision trees used in more advanced analysis include classification analysis trees and regression trees, whose "leaves" represent the classifications of entities (rows) into a "leaf" or terminal node (DeVille, 2006).

Decision trees in data mining are types of predictive models because information about an item is mapped to conclusions about resulting target values. Types of decision trees include classification trees for discrete data and regression trees for metric or continuous data. In this tree structure, leaves represent classification and "branches" represent the intersection of features that resulted in the classifications.

Decision Rules

Decision rules are the verbal description of a graphical decision tree that indicates class or group membership based on a hierarchical sequence of decisions. Individual decision rules in a set of rules indicate class membership, and are indicated by the intersection (i.e., use of AND) of all rules for contingent observations. For example:

IF *condition$_1$* **AND** ... *condition$_n$* ARE **<u>TRUE</u>** **THEN** CLASS=*class$_1$*.

Thus, if all conditions (condition$_1$ through condition$_j$) are satisfied (TRUE), then the entity under consideration is a member of class$_i$. In the alternative, failure to satisfy these conditions indicates that the entity is NOT a member of class$_i$.

Decision rules can be verbalized from the corresponding graphical decision tree or can be induced directly from observations. In practical use, rules are derived from actual data (observations), a decision tree is constructed, and then rules are derived from the tree. Some software packages (e.g., SAS Enterprise Miner) can assist in deriving decision rules with its "English rules" and decision tree construction routine (Fernandez, 2003; Huang & Webb, 2006).

Classification Analysis and Regression Trees (CART)

Classification analysis and regression trees (CART) analytical techniques can produce either classification or regression trees. If the dependent variable is categorical, then classification is the result. If the dependent is a metric/continuous numeric, the result is a regression tree (Berk, 2006).

Classification trees are derived from the iterative application of a collection of rules based on values of certain variables in the modeling data set:

1. Rules are optimized by testing splits (classifications) based on the ability of the variables' values to differentiate between observations in different groups based on the dependent variable.
2. When a rule is chosen and the node splits into two "groups," the same logic is used to split each "child" node.
3. Usually a criterion for iterative improvement is specified. Node splitting stops when the CART procedure is not able to improve on the previous classification.

Branches of each tree end in a terminal node:

1. Each observation falls into one and exactly one terminal node.
2. Each terminal node is uniquely defined by a set of rules.

An example of Breiman's Random Forests provides an informative illustration of CART for Fisher's Iris data, based on observations of the flower's measurements made in the 1930s. Classification into each of three groups is graphically shown for the Iris data in Figure 17.3.

Deviation Analysis

In statistics, deviation or outlier analysis refers to measuring the distance, especially the absolute distance, between one number in a set and the mean of the set. Outliers are usually marked as those occurring outside the 95% confidence interval, although higher limits may be applied for greater reliability. Deviation analysis has been used in data mining to observe anomalous behavior from large data sets. Extending the analysis to the multivariate case

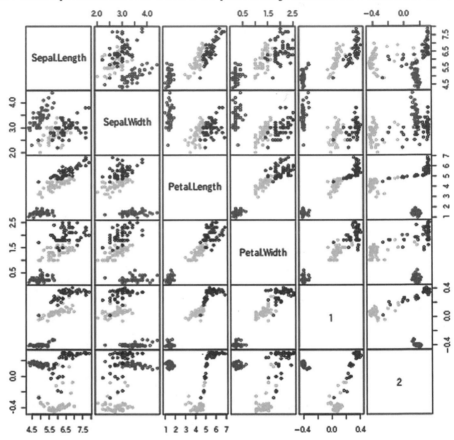

Figure 17.3 Classification and regression using Fisher's famous Iris data. Note that in the regression the multiple scatter plots that three separate groups emerge.

makes it possible to identify independent variables that can predict the observations that will be outliers. This approach can be especially informative when searching for anomalies that may indicate fraud or some other "deviant" behavior (Moss & Atre, 2003).

Rough Sets

Rough sets are a formal approximation of a conventional set in terms of a pair of sets that give the *lower* and the *upper* approximation of the original set. In the standard version of rough set theory, the lower- and upper-approximation sets are crisp sets, but in other variations, the approximating sets may be fuzzy sets. Hence, group membership may not be as clearly defined as under cluster or discriminant analysis, but the "statistical" nature of the set allows for observations that may not necessarily belong exclusively to one set or the other (Bouchon-Meunier, Lesot, Detyniecki, Marsala, & Rifqi, 2007).

Taxonomic Induction

Induction of a taxonomy—classification—for the analysis of groupings is an automated method for identifying groups. Two methods are used for taxonomic induction: pattern-based and cluster-based. Pattern-based taxonomies are constructed based upon the similarities of items within a set. Sometimes investigators will use a correlation between observations to produce this kind of classification.

Cluster-based taxonomies usually hierarchically cluster items based on similarity determined by a vector of quantifiable features. Cluster approaches have the main advantage of being able to discover relationships between items that are not explicitly indicated in the data being analyzed (Yang & Callan, 2009). It is generally held that classifications produced by cluster-based taxonomies are not as reliable as those derived from pattern-based taxonomies.

However, no systematic analysis has compared cluster- versus pattern-based analyses for automated taxonomy under various analytical conditions. For individual analyses, an iterative approach is probably warranted, and the investigator must choose between the taxonomies, testing the accuracy of each methodology using a resampling technique.

Artificial Intelligence

Artificial intelligence (AI) is a branch of computer science whose goal is to create machines that are intelligent in the sense that they can perceive their environment and take premeditated action to improve the chances that their actions are successful. AI is mentioned here because one of the mainstays of its approach is modeling how the human brain uses decisions based on rules to function (Han & Kamber, 2006).

"Artificial" Neural Network

An artificial neural network is modeled after how it is perceived that brains work. Human brains contain approximately 10^{11} neuron cells that communicate with one another through exchange of electrical signals. Neurons have one or two axons that function as outputs and many dendrites that input electrical signals. Neurons have a certain threshold of signal input that accumulates from all the potentiated dendrites. Neurons will fire once they reach their point of potentiation (activation), sending electrical signals down axons to other neurons.

The neural networks metaphor is applied to AI neural networks on a smaller scale. Contemporary computers lack the power of 20 billion neurons. However, a few neurons can be implemented virtually, and elicit an intelligent response from a neural network.

Neurons are organized in layers: (1) input layer, (2) hidden layer, and (3) output layer. The input layer will have entries, and, depending on the strength of connection to each neuron in the next layer, the input signal will be sent to the next layer. Strength of the connection or influence is called a weight. The value of each neuron in each layer will depend on the weight of the connection and the values of the neurons of the previous layer.

An "artificial" neural network is an interconnected group of nodes, similar to the immense network of neurons in the human brain. The analogy of the brain to the artificial neural network is INPUT (graph as left side), the HIDDEN (middle), and the OUTPUT (right side) layers. The OUTPUT layer is the computational target or dependent(s). INPUT is the information available. The HIDDEN layer, or the perceptron, is the locus of the most intense computation (Ripley, 2007).

Forecasting

> *"Predicting the future is hard, especially if it hasn't happened yet."*
>
> —Yogi Berra

The process of predicting an outcome in the future based on unknown situations is known as forecasting. Prediction is similar to forecasting because both terms can refer to time series, cross-sectional, or longitudinal data. Risk and uncertainty are central to forecasting and prediction. Forecasting is commonly used in the analysis of time-series data. Like many other techniques, it is regression-based: linear regression, nonlinear regression, autoregressive moving average (ARMA), and autoregressive integrated moving average (ARIMA) (Hetland, 2004). On the other hand, simple prediction does not necessarily include time.

Association Rules

In data mining, association rule learning is a popular and well-researched method for discovering interesting relations between variables in large databases (Han & Kamber, 2006). Association rules have been used to discover regularities between product sales in supermarkets, as discussed earlier with the beer and baby diapers urban legend.

In Table 17.2, the set of items is milk, bread, butter, and beer, where 1 = purchase, and 0 = no purchase. An example of an association rule could be milk, bread → butter. Customers who buy milk and bread ought to also buy butter. This rule is supported by 40% of the transactions (i.e., two of five transactions where value = 1 follow this rule). Confidence in the rule and its lift (improvement in classification) can also be computed.

Bayesian Classification

A naive Bayes classifier is a simple probabilistic classifier based on applying Bayes' theorem with strong (naive) independence assumptions. A more descriptive term for the underlying probability model would be "independent feature model."

Naive Bayes classifiers make the assumption that the presence or absence of a given characteristic of a certain class is unrelated to the existence of any other characteristics. A baseball might be considered round and white and about 3 in. in diameter. These features depend on the existence of the other features, but a naive Bayes classifier considers that

Table 17.2 Examples database with four items and five transactions.

Examples database with four and five transactions

Transaction ID	Milk	Bread	Butter	Beer
1	1	1	0	0
2	0	1	1	0
3	0	0	0	1
4	1	1	1	0
5	0	1	0	0

all these properties independently influence the probability that this sphere is a baseball. Dropping the size and color factors as one must under Bayesian assumptions, the ball could be a soccer ball, basketball, or ping pong ball, hence the uncertainty of Bayesian classifiers.

In a human supervised learning environment, naive Bayes classifiers can be trained (i.e., supervised by a human or an iterative process) to be effective. A major advantage naive of Bayes classifiers is that a small amount of training data is needed to estimate the means and variances necessary for classification (Han & Kamber, 2006).

Visualization

Visual Data Mining or Graphical Data Mining

Visual data mining is an educated inspection of data plotted in various ways. Perhaps the most interesting example of "visual data mining" is the Minard graphic of the French Army's march to Russia in the winter of 1812–1813. It has troop size and temperature over time embedded in a single drawing (Figure 17.4).

Thus, "visual data mining" is really an educated understanding of the graphic and the data. Sometimes patterns are recognized that were not amenable to numeric analysis, or visual patterns may inspire a numerical analysis (Simoff, Bohlenand, & Mazeika, 2008).

Text Mining

Text mining—analysis of unstructured textual or narrative data—is a growing field of interest. Medical records, conversations, newspapers, and e-mails are amenable to analysis. Most text mining tools can ingest a variety of data and search for patterns.

Although text mining is beyond the scope of this chapter, it is included because, as data mining evolves, use of free form text will become a part of the ensemble of techniques routinely used and referred to as data mining (Feldman & Sanger, 2007; Zanasi, 2007).

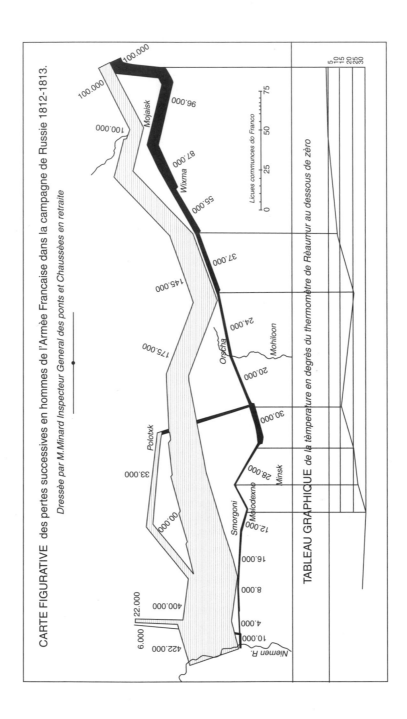

Figure 17.4 Early "visual data mining": Minard's Graph of Napoleon's March to Russia.

The Future of Data Mining, Advanced Analytics, and Data Warehouses

The future of data mining and data warehouses depends largely on the laws enacted to protect privacy. Currently, mining of prescription data for use in research is a critical controversy because it uses private information—Personally Identifiable Information (PII). Although any information that can potentially be linked back to an individual is protected to avoid violating personal privacy, in certain cases, access to personally identifiable information is necessary to carry out important research such as medical outcomes analysis. Mining prescription data is being blocked because it is known that the results will be used to enhance the profit margin of companies who wish to market specific medications. When the smoke clears from this debate, other debates will arise centered on PII. Researchers who wish to avoid such difficulties will focus on the use of "de-identified" data.

Case Study: Data Mining Marriage, Demographic, and Birth Defects Data

In this vignette (case study), data mining techniques are used to extract patterns of marriage and population demographic structure that are related to the occurrence of birth defects being tracked in an actual, ongoing research project. The case study demonstrates the essentials of defining a problem, formulating a data solution, and structuring an analysis to disclose associations that may point to possible causation.

The objective of the case study is to assess the risk of birth defects in Texas associated with parental consanguinity. The data warehouse challenge is to acquire data from different sources and combine (join, merge, fuse) it into a single data warehouse at the greatest possible level of detail (high granularity).

Approximately 6 million Texas marriage records, including the bride's maiden name and groom's surname, were available for the period of 1961 to 2001. The Texas Department of Health Vital Statistics maintains a separate database with the number of live births that occur by county per year. Texas began a birth defects' registry in 1996 to monitor the occurrence of congenital anomalies at the county level. The database contains approximately 70,000 cases of birth defects. The U.S. Census from the year 2000 was available at the county level for 20 million Texas residents.

Surname isonomy (when the bride's surname is the same as the groom's) is an established method to estimate population level of inbreeding. Birth defect surveillance data available for Texas at the county level were joined into a VLDB that contained marriages at the county level. Age, gender, and ethnicity data from the 2000 U.S. census were joined at the county level into a single database (data warehouse) and normalized by county population. Three types of birth defects were chosen for preliminary analysis: (1) one known to be associated with an autosomal recessive inheritance pattern (Ventricular Septal Defect—VSD); (2) one of unknown etiology, speculated to be associated with a possibly autosomal recessive (Ebstein's Anomaly); and (3) one known to not be related to parental consanguinity (Fetal Alcohol Syndrome—FAS), which is environmentally caused (i.e., teratogenic).

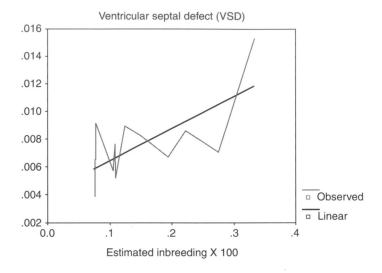

Figure 17.5 Incidence of ventricular septal defect regressed on estimated inbreeding ($R^2 = 0.43$, $\beta = 0.232$, $P < 0.03$).

Several different regressions were used to assess the ability of estimated local inbreeding to predict the local incidence of three birth defects analyzed. It was hypothesized *a priori* that estimated inbreeding was strongly related to the incidence of VSD. Therefore, the slope of the regression line was expected to be positive (Figure 17.5). For the second birth defect analyzed, it was unknown whether or not incidence of Ebstein's

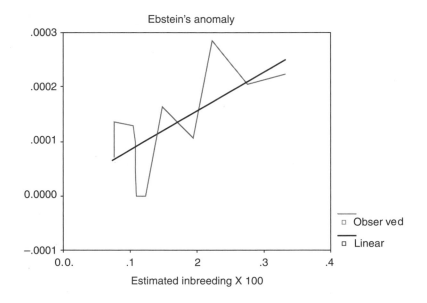

Figure 17.6 Incidence of Ebstein's anomaly regressed on estimated inbreeding ($R^2 = 0.46$, $\beta = 0.007$, $P < 0.02$)

Anomaly was strongly influenced by estimated inbreeding. No *a priori* hypothesis existed, and the analysis was truly exploratory data mining (Figure 17.6). For the third birth defect analyzed, the *a priori* hypothesis was that the relationship between fetal alcohol syndrome and estimated inbreeding would not be different from a regression slope of zero.

VSD was strongly related to estimated inbreeding in the regression analysis, and VSD is well known to be associated with an autosomal recessive pattern of inheritance. Results of this analysis suggest that VSD is inherited in an autosomal recessive (i.e., aa, Aa, AA) manner (Figure 17.5). Ebstein's Anomaly is a rare congenital heart defect, with no clear etiology. Some investigators have proposed that the defect is related to environmental exposures during the first 6–8 weeks post conception (e.g., lithium). Other investigators have suggested that Ebstein's Anomaly is due to a rare recessive gene. Findings in the present analysis suggest that Ebstein's Anomaly is due, at least in part, to recessive genetic inheritance because increased estimated inbreeding is positively related to the incidence of the birth defects. However, the greatest emphasis has been placed upon possible teratogenic causes of Ebstein's Anomaly. The present study's findings are important to the etiology of Ebstein's Anomaly because they provide strong evidence that inbreeding significantly increases the risk for this rare birth defect, indicating a major recessive gene effect.

Fetal Alcohol Syndrome (FAS) is caused by maternal alcohol abuse during gestation. It is not related to level of inbreeding, nor is it primarily caused by any known genetic mechanism. FAS was included in the present analysis as a "negative control." The negative finding for FAS incidence regressed on estimated inbreeding was confirmatory because it was known *a priori* that no relationship should exist between the dependent and independent variables (Figure 17.7).

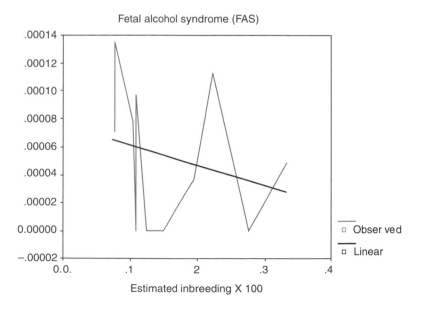

Figure 17.7 Incidence of fetal alcohol syndrome regressed on estimated inbreeding ($R^2 = 0.06$, $\beta = -0.0001$, P = NS).

Conclusion

Data mining techniques combined with the data warehouses or VLDBs contemporarily available are very powerful ways to investigate disease topics in population genetics important to human health. Substantive discoveries that can help direct genomic and clinical research await the construction of joined VLDBs and data mining analysis. Similarly, sociologists have an enormous opportunity because so many available data sources are relevant to human behavior. Relevance to human behavior is enhanced further when several sources are combined at a common level of data structure to address a specific behavioral hypothesis. In the case study, mating behavior and its relevance to birth defects were derived from publicly available data. Many research discoveries await the curious sociologist who creatively merges (joins, fuses) data from several sources and uses advanced analytics.

References

Abonyi, J., & Feil, B. (2007). *Cluster analysis for data mining and system identification.* Birkhauser Verlag, AG: Basel.

Berk, R. A. (2006). An introduction to ensemble methods for data analysis. *Sociological Methods Research, 34,* 263–295.

Bouchon-Meunier B., Lesot, M-J., Detyniecki, C., Marsala, C., & Rifqi M. (2007). Real-world fuzzy logic applications in data mining and information retrieval. In Wang, P. P., Ruan, D. & Kerre, E. E. (Eds.), *Fuzzy logic: A spectrum of theoretical and practical issues* (pp. 219–243). Berlin: Springer-Verlag.

Chatfield, C. (1999). *The analysis of time series: An introduction* (pp. 66–91) Boca Raton, FL: Chapman and Hall/CRC.

DeVille, B. (2006). *Decision trees for business intelligence and data mining: Using SAS enterprise miner.*™ Cary. North Carolina: SAS Press.

Feldman, R. & Sanger, J. (2007). *The text mining handbook advanced approaches in analyzing unstructured data.* Cambridge, MA: Cambridge University Press.

Fernandez, G. (2003). *Data mining using SAS applications.* Boca Raton, FL: Chapman & Hall/CRC.

GAO. (2004, August). *DATA MINING: Federal efforts cover a wide range of uses.* Washington, DC: Government Printing Office.

GAO. (2005, August). *DATA MINING: Agencies have taken key steps to protect privacy in selected efforts, but significant compliance issues remain.* Washington, DC: Government Printing Office.

Han J, & Kamber M. (2006). *Data mining: Concepts and techniques* (pp. 227–271) San Francisco: Morgan Kaufmann Publishers.

Hetland, M. L. (2004). A survey of recent methods for efficient retrieval of timer sequences. In Last, M., Kandel, A. & Bunke, H. (Eds.), *Data mining in time series databases* (pp. 22–42) River Edge, NJ: World Scientific Publishing.

Huang S., & Webb G. I. (2006). Efficiently identifying exploratory rules' significance. In Williams G. J., & Simoff, S. J. (Eds.), *Data mining: Theory, methodology, techniques, and applications.* Berlin: Springer-Verlag.

Larose, D. T. (2006). *Data mining methods and models* (pp. 93–146). Hoboken, NJ: John Wiley and Sons.

Little, B. B. (2004). Data mining and population genetics of birth defects: Preliminary investigation. In *Data Mining V* (pp. 415–422). Southampton: Wessex Institute of Technology Press.

Little, B. B., & Schucking M. L. (2008). Data mining, statistical data analysis, or advanced analytics: Methodology, implementation, and applied techniques. In Fielding, N., Lee, R.M., & Blank, G. *The sage handbook of online research methods* (pp. 419–452). London: SAGE Publications LTD.

McCue, C. (2007). *Data mining and predictive analysis: Intelligence gathering and crime analysis* (pp. 121–122) Oxford: Butterworth-Heinemann.

Milic-Frayling, M. (2007). Text processing and information retrieval. In Zanasi, A. *Text mining and its applications to intelligence, CRM and knowledge management*, (pp. 1–39) Southampton: Wessex Institute of Technology Press.

Moss, L. T., & Atre S. (2003). Data Mining. In *Business intelligence roadmap: The complete project lifecycle for decision-support systems* (pp. 301–316) Boston: Pearson Education Inc.

Olson, D. L., & Delen D. (2008). *Advanced data mining techniques* (pp. 19–27) Berlin: Springer-Verlag.

Ripley, B. D. (2007). *Pattern recognition and neural networks*. Cambridge, MA: Cambridge University Press.

Simoff, S. J., Bohlenand, M.H. & Mazeika, A. (2008). Visual data mining: An introduction and overview. In Simoff, S. J. *Visual data mining: Theory, technique, and tools for visual analytics*, (pp. 1–12) Berlin: Springer-Verlag.

Yang, H., & Callan J. (2009). A metric-based framework for automatic taxonomy induction. Paper presented at the Proceedings of the Joint Conference of the 47th Annual Meeting of the Association for Computational Linguistics and the 4th International Joint Conference on Natural Language Processing. Singapore. http://www.cs.cmu.edu/ huiyang/publication/acl2009.pdf (accessed on August 12).

❯ Chapter 18

Knowledge Mining and Managing: Emergent Tools and Technologies in Web-Based Intelligent Learning Environments

Nittaya Kerdprasop

Introduction

The World Wide Web (WWW) is becoming an ordinary tool that enables common people to acquire, create, and distribute information electronically. The ease of use and availability everywhere at any time are key factors leading to a great success of Web technology. In recent years, numerous Web-based environments have been developed to support various kinds of applications such as electronic commerce, recommendation systems, automated customer support, and online shopping. Web-based learning environments are the recent developments of Web technology in the areas of electronic learning (e-learning) and distance education.

A Web-based learning environment (WLE) is a software system designed and developed to support teaching and learning using both the Web and the Internet as the major media in an educational setting. Therefore, a WLE is a suite of computer programs that facilitates e-learning. These facilities include course creation and delivery, learning tracking and assessment, enrollment, and administration. This kind of system has many other names such as Learning Management System (LMS), Course Management System (CMS), Learning Content Management System (LCMS), and Virtual Learning Environment (VLE). The well-known systems such as Moodle (http://moodle.org), ATutor (http://www.atutor.ca), and WebCT and Blackboard (http://www.blackboard.com) have been adopted by many institutions and organizations worldwide to deliver online courses.

Despite the success and popularity of Web-based online courses, people soon realized that these online materials are nothing more than a group of static hypertext pages (Tzouveli, Mylonas, & Kollias, 2007; Li, Lau, Shih, & Li, 2008) designed once and used by any learner regardless of their diversities in capabilities, needs, and perceptions. Since then, the issues of content adaptability and intelligent curriculum sequencing have become the major research goals for the development of advanced Web-based educational systems (Pahl, 2003; Xu & Wang, 2006; Kritikou et al., 2007). The term Web-based intelligent learning environment (WILE) has been introduced (Kazi, 2004) to refer to the integrative approach of intelligent technology and Web-based educational systems.

Automatic knowledge acquisition and discovery from learners' data repositories and knowledge bases are major sources of intelligence facilitating the creation of adaptive functionality of the most current WILEs (Amershi & Conati, 2007; Lazcorreta, Botella, & Fernandez-Caballero, 2007; Romero & Ventura, 2007; Chen & Liu, 2008). It is thus the main objective of this chapter to discuss advances and trends in WILEs with the emphasis on the many roles of knowledge-mining technology to the development of intelligent infrastructures.

Knowledge-Mining Technology: Basic Concepts and Its Applications

Knowledge mining (Michalski, 2003; Markellou, Rigou, & Sirmakessis, 2005; Kerdprasop & Kerdprasop, 2008) is the discovery of hidden knowledge stored in various forms and placed in large data repositories. Hidden knowledge refers to models and patterns that implicitly exist in the data set and are unknown a priori. For instance, consider the set of data instances $\{(0, 3), (1, 6), (2, 15), (3, 30)\}$. The explicit knowledge is that this data set contains four data, represented as a (x, y)-pair. The implicit knowledge that are hidden in the data set is a pattern $y = 3x^2+3$, and a model $y = ax^2+b$. A pattern is an expression describing a subset of the data, whereas a model is a representation of the source generating the data. In the knowledge-mining context, we refer to both patterns and models as new knowledge automatically discovered from data sources. This emerging technology was originally coined (Fayyad, Piatetsky-Shapiro, Smyth, & Uthurusamy, 1996) as knowledge discovery in databases or KDD, also known as data mining in the field of statistics. In this chapter, we use the term "knowledge mining" to state the fact that the process discovers hidden knowledge from not only raw data, but also from previously discovered patterns and meta-data. Knowledge mining, thus, can be characterized by the following scheme:

(stored data and meta-data) + previously discovered knowlegde → new knowlegde

This section presents basic concepts of the knowledge-mining process and discusses many kinds of knowledge to be discovered from educational data. The knowledge discovery technology often reveals interesting patterns and dependency relationships hidden in large data. It is thus beneficial to educators to understand how this emerging technology is applicable to the development of Web-based intelligent learning environments, as well as the insight that such knowledge-mining tasks provide. Researchers and educational software developers should also gain benefits from the awareness of the emergence of this intelligent-related technology, as it will soon be a major part of computer-assisted learning tools.

The Process of Knowledge Mining

The whole process of knowledge mining works around data, meta-data, and previously discovered patterns. It can be conceptually shown as in Figure 18.1.

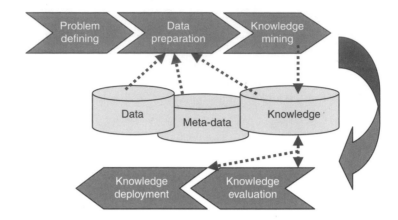

Figure 18.1 The process of knowledge mining.

The initial step (problem defining) of knowledge mining focuses on setting the goal or specifying the problem, which can be achieved through understanding the task objectives and organization requirements. Defining the problem is important because it will guide activities in subsequent steps to collect only relevant data, perform mining with the appropriate algorithm, and keep only pertinent and actionable knowledge. A clear problem statement should define what is to be accomplished and what the desired outcome is likely to be. For instance, if the objective of mining is to reduce the number of dropouts at junior college level, the specific problem statements might be, "Is there an association between financial support and students' decision to leave school?" or, "Are there interdependencies among different groups of dropouts?"

The second step (data preparation) covers all activities necessary for preparing high quality data suitable for mining via algorithms. This data preparation step includes collecting data from multiple sources, transforming the data format, and selecting data representatives with minimum but sufficient attributes. Data preparation is typically time consuming and likely to be performed iteratively. Meta-data and background knowledge are kinds of supportive information that can be applied in this step. Supporting tools that are useful for this step can be as simple as a notepad program, or more sophisticated tools such as those provided by SPSS or SAS data exploration packages.

The third step is knowledge mining, which is the search for and extraction of interesting patterns (local generalized structures) or models (global generalized structures) from data. Such patterns and models are called knowledge. This step is the backbone of the knowledge-mining process. Several techniques are available, but their application needs some adjustment to obtain optimal results.

The fourth step (knowledge evaluation) is to assess the accuracy and interestingness of the discovered knowledge over some threshold values. Accuracy is correctness of the induced model and it can be evaluated by using another set of data called test data. The required level of model accuracy has to be set by users or miners. Interestingness of the induced model is somehow a more subtle issue than the accuracy metric. Evaluating interestingness depends considerably on the judgment of miners or domain experts. Accurate and interesting knowledge is finally fed to the deployment step to become actionable information for an organization or to act as background knowledge for other knowledge-mining tasks.

Different Knowledge-Mining Tasks on Educational Dataset

The knowledge-mining step, as shown in Figure 18.1, can be conducted with different kinds of algorithms. Despite hundreds of available algorithms, they may be grouped roughly according to the task that specific algorithm performs into three categories: *classification*, *association*, and *cluster analysis*.

For the purpose of demonstration, each knowledge-mining task will be performed on the dropout data at the secondary level (7th grade through 12th grade) in the school year 2003–2004 (Sable & Gaviola, 2007). This dropout data was reported annually by the state education agencies throughout the United States including the District of Columbia, Puerto Rico, American Samoa, Guam, the Commonwealth of the Northern Mariana Islands, and the U.S. Virgin Islands. The data files have been collected and made publicly available by the National Center for Education Statistics (NCES, http://nces.ed.gov), U.S. Department of Education. Data file for school year 2003–2004 includes only dropout data for school districts enrolling 1,000 or more students. A dropout is an individual who enrolled in school at some time during the previous school year but does not enroll at the beginning of the current school year. The school year is the 12-month period starting at October 1.

NCES does provide a caution that the data file should not be used to compute state-level estimation of public school dropouts because the reported data are restricted to state education agencies with membership of 1,000 or more. However, we can investigate the dropout patterns and dependencies among different dropout groups with the knowledge-mining technology. For simplicity, we will use only dropout data reported by school districts from the California and Florida states. (The formatted data, ready-made for mining with the Weka system, are available upon request; please e-mail to nittaya@sut.ac.th).

Each data record (also called data instance in the data-mining community) is a report from each school district and the record contains 15 variables (or attributes). The first three attributes are Locale (i.e., location of the school divided into eight categories: 1 = large city, 2 = midsize city, 3 = urban fringe of a large city, 4 = urban fringe of a midsize city, 5 = large town, 6 = small town, 7 = rural, outside metropolitan, and 8 = rural, within a metropolitan), LO-offered (i.e., the lowest grade of the school), and HI-offered (i.e., the highest grade offered by the school). Attributes 4–9 are the total number of student enrollments in grade 7 through 12. The nonzero number was grouped into four intervals: 1–999, 1,000–4,999, 5,000–9,999, 10,000–infinity and encoded in the dataset as [1–1K), [1K–5K), [5K–10K), [10K–UP), respectively. Attributes 10–15 are the total number of dropouts at grade 7 through 12. The nonzero number was grouped into five intervals: 1–50, 51–99, 100–500, 501–999, 1,000–Infinity and accordingly encoded in the dataset as [1–50], [51–99], [100–500], [501–999], and [1,000–UP]. The number "−2" may appear in the dataset and it represents the "non-applicable" case, number "−1" means "data was not reported by the agency" and "0" encodes "no occurrence of the data element." The first three data instances of California school districts are shown as follows:

8, KG, 12, [1 − 1K], [1 − 1K], [1 − 1K], [1 − 1K], [1 − 1K], [1 − 1K], 0, 0, 0, 0, 0, 0
3, KG, 8, [1 − 1K], [1 − 1K], − 2, − 2, − 2, − 2, 0, 0, − 2, − 2, − 2, − 2
7, KG, 12, [1 − 1K], [1 − 1K], [1 − 1K], [1 − 1K], [1 − 1K], [1 − 1K], [1 − 50], 0, 0, 0,
[1 − 50], [1 − 50]

In this knowledge-mining demonstration, we adopt the Weka (Waikato environment for knowledge analysis) system (http//www.cs.waikato.ac.nz/ml/weka/), which is open source software (i.e., free software that provides source code for anyone to modify it) used for knowledge mining and data analysis.

Classification

The *classification* task is to find major characteristics that can classify correctly the specified target attribute. The algorithm normally applied for this task is J48 (Witten & Frank, 2005), which is known as a decision-tree induction algorithm because it can find (or induce) a pattern from the given data and display the pattern graphically as tree. The leaf nodes at the bottom of the tree are the predicted decision, whereas the nodes at the upper levels are conditions to be fulfilled prior to making the decision.

Our objective is to draw some patterns from the dropout data of 565 public school districts in the California state compared with the patterns induced from the dropout data of 70 public school districts in the Florida state. The results of mining the 12th grade dropout patterns in the California state as compare to the Florida state are shown in Figure 18.2. The two patterns are slightly different. In the California pattern, the total number of

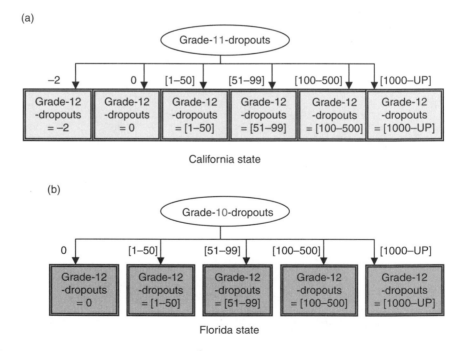

Figure 18.2 Decision trees for classifying and predicting the attribute *Grade-12-drop-outs*.

12th grade dropouts can be predicted from the total number of 11th grade dropouts. This pattern is 77.2% accurate measured with the 10-fold cross-validation method. But in the Florida pattern, the total number of 12th grade dropouts can be predicted from the total number of 10th grade dropouts (accuracy = 82.8% with the same measurement method as in the California mining). These results reveal the nature of knowledge-mining technology that it is data dependent. If the data change, the mined knowledge may change.

Besides decision-tree induction, the classification task can be performed using various kinds of machine-learning techniques such as artificial neural network, genetic algorithm, fuzzy rule induction, rough set theory, support vector machines, case-based reasoning, and many others. To derive cause-and-effect relationships or causal knowledge with some level of uncertainty, *Bayesian belief network* or *Bayesian network* is utilized because it can convey both qualitative and quantitative information.

Bayesian network (Han & Kamber, 2006; Larose, 2006) is a directed acyclic graph with nodes to represent variables or attributes, arcs to represent probabilistic correlations or dependencies between attributes, and conditional probability tables associated with each node. The table associated with the root node, which is an independent variable, contains unconditional probabilities. If there is a directed arc from node X to node Y, then X is a parent of Y, and Y is called a descendant of node X. Given parent node(s), a variable is said to be conditionally independent of its non-descendants in the network.

Decision tree (as shown in Figure 18.2) can be used to predict the future outcome given the learned pattern from the past data. But if we are interested in finding explanation about dependency relationships among data attributes or to learn cause-and-effect relationships, Bayesian network should be employed. The Bayesian network-learning result of California 12th grade dropouts versus the result obtained from the Florida state data is shown in Figure 18.3 (conditional probability tables are omitted due to space limitation). To learn the cause-and-effect relationships using the Weka system, we have to set the search algorithm to ICS search; otherwise, with different search algorithms the learned network simply represents conditional dependencies among data attributes.

The Bayesian network in Figure 18.3(a) tells us that the total number of 12th grade enrollment and the total number of 8th grade dropouts are two direct causes of the number of 12th grade dropouts. Figure 18.3(b) depicts the Bayesian network learned from the Florida school districts. It can be noticed that in addition to the total number of 12th grade enrollment and the total number of 8th grade dropouts, the other three attributes (i.e., the total numbers of 7th, 9th, and 10th grade dropouts) also affect the number of 12th grade dropouts.

Association

With the same set of data, we can perform *association analysis* to discover correlations or relationships that hold among data attributes. The results of association analysis are reported as the "IF-THEN" rule. The "IF" part states the antecedent or condition of the proposition that must be true. The "THEN" part is the conclusion. In Weka, the "IF-THEN" rule is displayed as *Antecedent ==> Conclusion*. Association rules do not convey the cause-and-effect relationships; they simply state that if the event(s) in antecedent part does occur, the event(s) in the conclusion part must also occur. Therefore, they represent the co-occurrence relationships. The following rules show the best five results (in terms of confidence value or accuracy of the rule) of association analysis conducted with the Apriori algorithm (Agrawal, Imielinski, & Swami, 1993) on California and Florida school districts data, respectively.

(a)

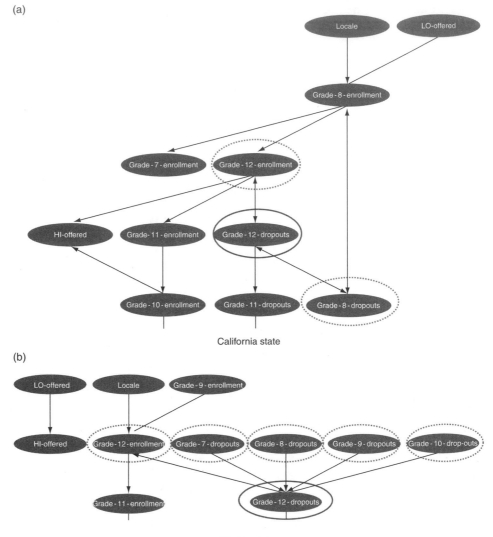

California state

(b)

Florida state

Figure 18.3   Bayesian networks showing that (a) in California state, the numbers of *Grade-12-enrollment* and *Grade-8-drop-outs* are two direct causes of the occurrence of value in the attribute *Grade-12-drop-outs*, and (b) in Florida state, numbers of *Grade-12-enrollment*, *Grade-7-drop-outs*, *Grade-8-drop-outs*, *Grade-9-drop-outs*, and *Grade-10-drop-outs* are all direct causes of the occurrence of value in the attribute *Grade-12-drop-outs*.

California school districts

1.   *Grade-7-enrollment = [1–1K] ==> LO-offered = KG conf:(0.99)*
2.   *Grade-7-enrollment = [1–1K] & Grade-8-enrollment = [1–1K] ==> LO-offered = KG conf:(0.99)*
3.   *Grade-8-enrollment = [1–1K] ==> LO-offered = KG conf:(0.99)*

4. *Grade-7-enrollment = [1–1K) ==> Grade-8-enrollment = [1–1K) conf:(0.99)*
5. LO-offered = KG & Grade-8-enrollment = [1–1K) ==> Grade-7-enrollment = [1–1K) conf:(0.99)

Florida school districts

1. *HI-offered = 12 ==> LO-offered = PK conf:(1)*
2. *LO-offered = PK ==> HI-offered = 12 conf:(1)*
3. *Grade-8-dropouts = [1–50] ==> LO-offered = PK conf:(1)*
4. *Grade-8-dropouts = [1–50] ==> HI-offered = 12 conf:(1)*
5. *HI-offered = 12 & Grade-8-dropouts=[1–50] ==> LO-offered = PK conf:(1)*

Each association rule is annotated with confidence value (conf) to give information regarding how accurate the rule is. Given the association rule $X ==> Y$, the confidence value of this rule is the proportion of number of data instances that contain both X and Y events to the number of data instances that contain X (the occurrence or absence of Y does not affect the count of event X). The value 1 is the most accurate association, whereas a value less than 1 implies that the rule might contain some error. Taking the last association rule in Florida school district as an example, the rule states the relationship that "if the highest grade offered by the school is 12 and the number of 8th grade dropouts is in the range [1–50], then the lowest grade offered by this school is pre-kindergarten."

Cluster Analysis

Another commonly performed mining task is *cluster analysis*. Several algorithms exist that perform cluster analysis. However, the most fundamental and widely used algorithm is the k-means algorithm (MacQueen, 1967). The parameter k is the number of clusters that users have to specify. The result of running k-means is the *cluster centroids* (or center points) that report the characteristics of representatives in each cluster. If we set k to be 5 and run k-means on our data, we will obtain 5 centroids reporting characteristics of each data subgroup. For instance, the first cluster of Florida school districts might be: a group of public schools located in rural area not within a metropolitan; the lowest grade mostly offered by these schools are pre-kindergarten; the highest grade mostly offered are grade 12; numbers of students enrolled in 7th, 8th, 9th, 10th, 11th, 12th grades are in the same range, that is 1–999; numbers of 7th through 12th grade student dropouts are also in the same range of 1–50. Other groups of students in different school districts can be interpreted in the same manner. If we change the number of clusters (i.e., vary k to different values), characteristics of each data cluster should also change.

Current Tools and Technology That Support Mining in Web-Based Learning Systems

Most intelligent learning systems are composed of five main components (Karampiperis & Sampson, 2006; Pahl, 2003): student modeling, content and domain expert modeling, structure and communication module, pedagogical strategy module, and supporting module. These components cover activities and people involved in WILE. Currently, knowledge-mining technology has been adopted to introduce intelligent behavior associated with various parts of such environments. In this section, we discuss the available technology supports and recently proposed approaches to mine knowledge; the discussion is based on these five components.

Student Modeling

Web-based education is a form of computer-supported learning in which course contents are delivered via the Internet. In such an educational setting, learning activities can take place pervasively through the support of Web servers. The server mediates courseware transmission and records Web access in log files. The Web logs normally contain learners' navigation on Web sites including accessing time, Web traversal paths, and responses. These Web logs are major data sources widely used to perform mining in order to gain some knowledge about learners' behavior. Zaiane (2001) is among the first data-mining researchers interested in acquiring knowledge from Web logs. The early work of Zaiane focuses on the data preparation step of Web usage mining. Web mining is a powerful technology to obtain knowledge about how students learn the course materials, in which order the students study subtopics, which topics have been skipped, how much time the students spend on each topic, and how a pedagogical strategy affects students with different learning paces and styles.

Chen, Hsieh, and Hsu (2007) were also interested in gaining knowledge about students' understanding of course contents. This research team adopted association analysis to mine the learners' profiles for capturing deviation from common learning patterns. The deviations that reflected misconceptions of students during the learning process could be inferred from incorrect testing items. Chen et al. also proposed a remedy approach for the students to correct their comprehension on the subject matters by delivering course materials with easier difficulty level but covey the similar learning concept. Ceddia, Sheard, and Tibbey (2007) developed a tool named WAT (Web log analysis tool) to analyze sequences of Web site interactions of students to determine whether they understand the core concept of a specific topic.

Lee, Chen, Chrysostomou, and Liu (2009) mined students' behavior by means of decision-tree induction with the main goal of discovering cognitive style of learners in order to manage flow of course contents suitable for each student. Decision tree is a data structure used to classify the cognitive style (field dependent/independent) of students during their learning sessions. Web navigational behavior of the students was observed and transformed into training data to induce a decision tree. Romero, Gonzalez, Ventura, del Jesus, and Herrera (2009) proposed a genetic algorithm approach to mine usage data of the Moodle course management system. Moodle is a free and open source licensed software designed to help educators create online courses and assessments. The Moodle system normally accumulates a great amount of information that is valuable for the mining and analyzing of students' behavior. The analysis results were in the form of descriptive rules such as "*IF course = CS101 & number_assignments = High & number_posts = High THEN mark = Good.*" Such a rule is a student model describing relationships between student activities on modules provided by the e-course and the final mark obtained in that course.

Content and Domain Expert Modeling

An educational system that is meant to be intelligent has to provide at least two function-alities: content adaptiveness and personalization. AHA! (De Bra et al., 2003) is an adaptive educational system working with hypermedia data in the form of XML files. This system has a log file designed to record, in addition to normal timestamps and user's identifica-tion, a flag field marking access to the concept fragment of each user. Concepts repre-senting domain knowledge fragments are defined as knowledge attributes whose value is updated when users read related Web pages. By analyzing the knowledge attribute values, the user's level of knowledge on the studied topics may be assessed. Kristofic and Bielikova (2005) proposed to improve the adaptation technique by means of knowledge discovery. The techniques proposed are association analysis, sequential patterns, and traversal pat-tern discovery. Association rule mining was employed to learn relations between concepts. The results were used in the process of recommending relevant concepts. The authors also extended the association algorithm to discover the sequential patterns that students navi-gated the concepts. Their final outcome was a recommendation system to suggest learning concepts relevant to each user.

Wang, Tseng, and Liao (2008) proposed an adaptive system designed particularly for teaching English as a second language course. Given students' profiles, the system adopts a decision-tree induction algorithm to discover the most adaptive learning sequences suit-able for each group of students for particular teaching content. The students' profiles have been created from the pretesting, posttesting, and student models that contain five attri-butes: gender, personality (e.g., introverted, neutral, extroverted), cognitive style (i.e., field dependent, field independent), learning style (i.e., sensing thinking/feeling, intuition feel-ing/thinking), and students' grades from the previous semester (i.e., low, medium, high). The final output of the system is a recommendation such as, "*For a female student with neutral personality, mildly introverted and has an intuition-feeling learning style, Suggestion is she should be assigned a learning sequence as <Main idea, Details, Vocabulary, Inference, Critical reading>.*"

Biletskiy, Baghi, Keleberda, and Fleming (2009) proposed an adjustable personaliza-tion approach to deliver learning objects to learners. The authors argued that current learning objects have been created by various suppliers targeting several groups of learn-ers such as students, employees, and professionals. To serve the specific needs of each learner, some kind of personalization has to be adopted. The authors propose to compare the learner profile and the learning object descriptions and deliver objects most relevant to each learner. A comparison metric such as similarity measurement can be used in this approach. Feedback about content usefulness and suitability from the learner is also obtained to adjust the learner's profile on the issue of preference.

Structure and Communication Module

Current Web-based educational systems provide services that are transmitted synchro-nously (such as video conferencing) and asynchronously (such as discussion Web boards and e-mail). Online students can register in many courses and seek course materials from several lecturers that may be located at different sites. Such a physically distributed environment needs advanced technology in order to handle the dynamic aspects of sites and information resources. Handi (2007) proposed a MASACAD system designed with a multi-agent approach to customize information presented to students. An advantage to adopting the multi-agent paradigm is that the changing environment of a course, for example, may be accommodated, as in students leaving a course or registering for a new course. The students' profiles may be updated accordingly without intervention from human administrator.

Chen (2008) proposed an intelligent learning system with personalized learning path guidance. The system collects the incorrect testing responses of each learner in a pre-testing session, and then applies the genetic algorithm to generate appropriate learning paths. Personalized curriculum sequencing has been conducted through consideration of courseware difficulty level and the continuity of learning concept. The system is meant to replace the freely browsing learning mode in order to increase learning performance by reducing disorientation during the learning process.

Pedagogical Strategy Module

In a Web-based educational setting, the Web provides not only information and content accessible through browsing, but also interactive pedagogical models through Web boards, blogs, and other communication methods. Recently, Martin, Alvarez, Fernandez-Castro, and Urretavizcaya (2008) presented the SIgMa (suggestions for improving educational aspects in Magadi) system to be an adaptable feedback generation tool for teachers. This tool analyzes students' performances using statistical calculations and data-mining techniques to discover anomalous behavioral patterns that reveal situations difficult for the students. The system provides feedback by means of a rule-based system to make suggestions for learning improvement. The suggestions are also adapted to teaching strategies and preferences. Shih, Chiang, Lai, and Hu (2008) also applied data-mining techniques, mainly decision-tree induction, in their Web-based self-assessment system. The system has been used to study disturbances of high-risk freshmen students, first-year students who have trouble following class contents and thus highly probable to fail in their study, providing counselors with the proper information to better bolster their counseling services.

Supporting Module

The supporting module provides technology in terms of hardware and software to be an infrastructure for the learning environment. Marshall, Chen, Shen, and Fox (2006) developed the GetSmart system in integrating course management, digital library, and concept mapping components to support the information search process. The authors view concept mapping as a knowledge visualization tool that can provide both a course map view of learning topics and a methodology to support personal knowledge acquisition. The authors report that from their field study, they observed improvement in the scores of the students' online quizzes after including concept mapping in the curriculum. Chen, Kinshuk, and Chen (2008) also based their study on concept maps. They proposed a construction of domain concept maps from academic articles by applying text-mining techniques. The domain concept map is a graphical representation of knowledge structure in which nodes represent concepts and links represent relationships between concepts. They concluded, in their study, that the concept maps could show the whole picture and core knowledge about a subject domain. This approach can support the domain experts upon constructing concept maps of the subjects.

Romero, Ventura, and Garcia (2008) studied Moodle as an infrastructure of the intelligent educational system. They proposed a case study to apply data mining to education that would investigate the following aspects: assessing students' learning performance, providing adaptive courses and recommendations based on learning behavior, evaluating learning objects, providing feedback to both teachers and students, and detecting atypical students. Chen and Chen (2009) presented a mobile formative assessment tool using hybrid data-mining techniques, that is, correlation analysis, fuzzy clustering analysis, k-means clustering, fuzzy association rule mining, and fuzzy inference. The objective of this tool was to identify key formative assessment rules according to the learners' portfolios.

New Proposal: Knowledge Mining as an Embedded Component in WILE

During this decade, we have witnessed the development of tools customizing knowledge discovery techniques to support intelligent educational systems. Some tools are embedded in the course management system while some operate stand-alone as knowledge acquisition and representation applications.

In this section, the new design of the integrated Web-based intelligent learning environment (WILE) has been proposed to achieve a full-scale integration of knowledge intensive tasks. The core of WILE is the data and knowledge repository in which the knowledge objects are moved around the four main stages: knowledge object generation, knowledge acquisition and extraction, knowledge object indexing and mapping, and knowledge application. The process of knowledge mining has been applied to acquire knowledge objects that will be subsequently processed in the indexing and mapping stage. This stage supports the search for suitable contents to present to learners. Performance and learners' preference are then captured and stored to be used later in the knowledge-mining stage.

A Framework for Implementing Knowledge Mining and Managing Features in WILE

In a framework (Kerdprasop & Kerdprasop, 2008) of the Web-based intelligent learning environment (Figure 18.4), a repository is defined as a collection of three distinct levels of resources: data, information, and knowledge. Data is the most primitive resource storing raw representations of facts, concepts, learning objects, and other instructional materials. These basic resources are stored in the formats suitable for communication and processing by related modules in the environment. Information is a supplement to raw data, such as meta-data, to describe the meaning, relevance, and purpose of stored data. Information is also intended to be used in knowledge generation, sharing, and discovery guidance. In other words, information refers to any heuristics applied to the process of knowledge

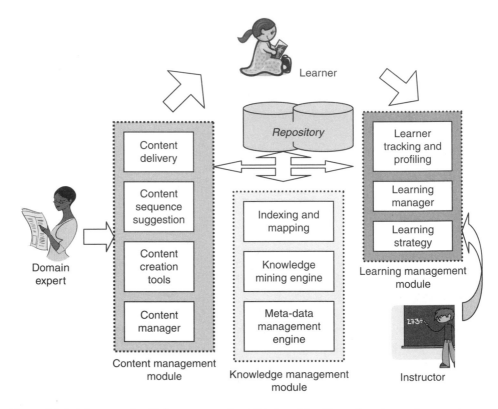

Figure 18.4 A framework of infrastructures in a Web-based intelligent learning environment.

mining and management. Knowledge is the most sophisticated entity stored in a repository as knowledge objects, which represent the relationships among data, correlation, and high level of data abstraction. Relationships can take many forms such as rules, vectors, or even mathematical formulas. Knowledge is thus data with semantics.

Data, information, and knowledge stored in a repository are key components of the designed framework. The three major modules of the proposed system communicate through the repository. Some components such as the knowledge-mining engine (or a mining software) are even data-driven; the knowledge-mining engine is data dependent and the mining results may be different if the data contents have been changed.

The three main modules in the proposed framework are learning management, content management, and knowledge management. This framework is proposed to support Web-based learning with several learning schemes including adaptive, autonomous, and collaborative learning.

The *learning management module* provides the following capabilities:

1. Enables instructors to post syllabi, class schedules, assignments, lecture notes, slides, and other supplemental materials for learners to access via Web browsing tool.

2. Enables instructors to conduct assessments in various forms such as online tests, surveys, quizzes using a variety of standard question formats, for example, multiple choice, true/false, essay, short-answer, matching, etc.
3. Enables learners to submit assignments remotely either as file upload or interactive through Web interface.
4. Provides profiling tools to collect the personal data of learners and a tracking tool to observe learners' actions, including like and dislike information.
5. Provides tools to compare the created profile with the available contents in order to create and deliver customized learning materials suitable for a learner's preference and ability.
6. Facilitates instructors and learners to engage in collaborative discussion on assignments and course content.

The *content management module* provides the following capabilities:

1. Allows content developers to import and export content through the authoring tools.
2. Allows the content manager to individualize the presented content.
3. Enables the content manager to archive old but useful contents and assign numbers on different versions of contents of the same topic.
4. Creates an interface for learning management modules in getting desired form for delivered content.
5. Creates an interface with a data repository that contains learners' personal information and other meta-data such as knowledge assets that are created by knowledge management modules. It applies this data to create a personalized sequence of content material suitable for each learner.

The *knowledge management module* provides the following capabilities:

1. Provides tools to collect different kinds of data such as learners' personal data, tracked data of learners' performance and behavior, and data related to content sequences that were presented in the past with the evaluation results according to that content sequence. These valuable data are stored in the data repository in different files that may take different formats.
2. Provides tools to discover valuable knowledge assets from the collected data.
3. Supports the indexing and mapping of knowledge objects that are discovered by the knowledge-mining engine.

The major actor of the learning management module is a learning manager component, which acts as a conductor controlling and synchronizing every component within the module. The manager component is also responsible for interfacing with the repository. This is also the case for the content manager component in the content management module. The content-creation tools in a content management module support the creation of all types of digital content materials such as word documents, spreadsheet data, pictures in standard formats, video content, animation, and multimedia data.

For the knowledge management module, the knowledge-mining engine is responsible for the synchronizing process. Indexing and mapping is a component for storing and searching knowledge objects to be used in the learning process. The meta-data management engine is a tool to incorporate background knowledge that may be useful for the mining component.

Architecture of the Knowledge Management Module: An Agent-Based Model

The design of a knowledge-mining engine in the knowledge management module (Figure 18.4) should base on the agent technology. An agent has been defined (Wooldridge & Jennings, 1995) as a computer system designed to work in some environments. It has the capability to act autonomously in order to meet its designed goals. In complex and dynamic environments, multi-agents are often utilized as a collaborative group of performers. Agents may coexist on a single processor or they may be physically separated to perform activities on their own and build a community through communication. Intelligent agents (Wooldridge, 2002) employ additional capabilities such as goal-directed task accomplishments, response due to changes in their environments, ability to interact with other agents, and learning through inductive and deductive reasoning to improve performances as they perform their assigned tasks.

A practical agent-based model should comprise of three layers: data source layer, agent layer, and external layer. A community of agents is in the agent layer, which is situated to help users to access and obtain only promising knowledge for their discovery tasks. Locating and accessing, filtering, and mining are three major activities of these agents.

Locating and accessing. At the lowest level of the framework, multiple heterogeneous data sources are located in an enterprise environment. These data sources may be distributed across a network such as the Internet or an Intranet. The resource agent is thus responsible for making the underlying data available to the data transformation agent in the upper filtering sub-layer. The resource agent also monitors changes in data contents to report any corresponding modification to the data-update agent.

Filtering. The agents in this class are the most autonomous and sophisticated ones due to the self-adjusting and specific functioning aspects. The agents in this class are composed of data-update agent, data transformation agent, cleansing agent, feature selection agent, and data sampling agent.

Mining. The agents in this class are mainly responsible for performing the data-mining techniques. Data obtained from the filtering sub-layer will be turned into valuable and actionable knowledge by these agents.

Running example: Knowledge mining for the personalization purpose

Personalization functionalities such as personalized learning plans, learning materials, and tests as well as appropriate advice (dependent on individual characteristics) are obviously a key success of Web-based intelligent learning environments. We illustrate the process of knowledge mining based on the learning technique of rough set theory to support the purpose of personalization.

The notion of rough sets was introduced by Zdzislaw Pawlak in the early 1980s (Pawlak, 1982, 1991) as a new concept of sets with uncertain membership. Unlike fuzzy set, uncertainty in rough set theory does not need probability or the value of possibility to deal with vagueness. This is rather formalized through the simple concepts of lower and

(a)

	score1	score2	level
s1	0–20	0–20	basic
s2	0–20	21–40	basic
s3	0–20	41–60	basic
s4	0–20	41–60	basic
s5	0–20	81–100	advanced
s6	41–60	41–60	advanced
s7	21–40	61–80	advanced
s8	21–40	21–40	advanced

A decision table for student's performance classification

(b)

	score1	score2	level
s1	0–20	0–20	basic
s2	0–20	21–40	basic
s3	0–20	41–60	basic
s4	0–20	41–60	basic
s5	0–20	81–100	advanced
s6	41–60	41–60	advanced
s7	21–40	61–80	advanced
s8	**21–40**	**21–40**	**advanced**
s9	**21–40**	**21–40**	**basic**

A decision table with different classification results regarding students S8 and S9

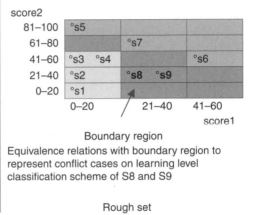

Equivalence relations for the above decision table represented as rectangular regions

Crisp or conventional set

Boundary region

Equivalence relations with boundary region to represent conflict cases on learning level classification scheme of S8 and S9

Rough set

Figure 18.5 An example showing the concept of a conventional set versus a rough set.

upper approximation that are, in turn, defined on the basis of set. Given the input data, the rough set-based system generates a list of certain and possible rules.

The input data is a decision table comprised of conditional attributes, or conditions for short, and a decision attribute. Figure 18.5a gives an example of a decision table containing information of eight students. There are two conditions: *score1* (the first pretest score of each student), and *score2* (the second pretest score). These scores are intervals of numeric values. The level attribute (either basic or advanced) is a decision that is based on the students' performances. Conditions together with decision attribute form an information system.

A decision table is a representation of real-world data. Each row represents one object. Rough set theory is based on the formation of *equivalence relations* within the given data. Equivalence relations, also called *indiscernibility relations*, partition data in a decision table into groups of similar objects based on the values of some attributes.

Suppose we are given additional information on the ninth student with exactly the same attribute values as the eighth student except that their performance levels are different. It is such conflicting cases that inspire the rough set concept. Given the two decision sets of advanced/basic level, the uncertain cases such as s8 and s9 (as shown in Figure 18.5b) can be approximated in their membership by means of lower and upper approximation. The *lower approximation* of X is the set of all objects that certainly belong to X.

The *upper approximation* of X is the set of all objects that definitely do not belong to X. The area between these two sets is called the *boundary region* of X, the set of all objects that cannot be classified as not belonging to X. If the boundary region is empty, it is a *crisp* (precise) set; otherwise, the set is *rough*. The set of advanced-level students in Figure 18.5a is a crisp set, whereas it is a rough set in Figure 18.5b.

Figure 18.5a represents the concept of crisp set (or conventional set) as each student, s1 through s8, can be assigned exclusively either in a basic-level set, or an advanced-level set. The assignment is based on the *score1* and *score2* values. Such concept, however, cannot be applied to the situation shown in Figure 18.5b because the new student, s9, whose performance is exactly the same as s8 but assigned to a different learning level. Therefore, s8 and s9 raise uncertain cases. We put the two cases in the boundary region because we are uncertain about its correct set assignment.

The knowledge-mining engine in the proposed framework exploits rough set theory as a theoretical foundation to deal with precise and uncertain information systems. The induced knowledge is represented as decision rules stored in the knowledge base. These rules are intended to be used as a guide for composing course content customized to meet the specific requirements of each learner.

A database containing learners' profiles and tracking records is a starting point of the knowledge induction process. A data extractor component creates a decision table in a format appropriate for the knowledge induction engine. A set of equivalence relations is analyzed and two classes of rules, that is, certain and possible rules, are derived and stored in the knowledge base. The steps in inducing decision-supported knowledge are explained via a running example.

The student data in Figure 18.5b will be used as an example to explain the steps in inducing decision-supported knowledge. The hierarchical information or ontology on interval order such that 81–100 > 61–80 > 41–60 > 21–40 > 0–20 is used as background knowledge for decision-rule generalization. Suppose there is a request from the learning manager consulting the knowledge-mining engine to create a set of decision rules to help decide the learning level of the new student based on the first pretest score. This student obtained 52 points in the first pretest. The steps on inducing decision rules are as follows.

(1) The request asks about students' level with *score1* as a condition. Since *score1* is not a core attribute, this attribute alone cannot be used to derive a set of equivalence relations. Hence, a decision table containing *score1* and *score2* attributes as in Figure 18.5b is constructed.

(2) Then, the following decision rules are generated.

Certain Rules
IF (score1 = 0–20 ∧ score2 = 81–100) THEN level = advanced
IF (score1 = 21–40 ∧ score2 = 61–80) THEN level = advanced
IF (score1 = 41–60 ∧ score2 = 41–60) THEN level = advanced
IF (score1 = 0–20 ∧ score2 = 0–20) THEN level = basic
IF (score1 = 0–20 ∧ score2 = 21–40) THEN level = basic
IF (score1 = 0–20 ∧ score2 = 41–60) THEN level = basic
Possible Rules
IF (score1 =21–40 ∧ score2 =21–40) THEN level = advanced

(3) The induced decision rules are generalized according to the background knowledge. The final decision rules are as follows.

R1: IF (score1 > 20 ∧ score2 > 60) THEN level = advanced

R2: IF (score1 > 40 ∧ score2 > 40) THEN level = advanced

R3: IF (score1 > 20 ∧ score2 > 20) THEN level = possibly advanced

Advice From the Knowledge Induction Engine

The learning level depends on the score obtained from the second pretest.

IF score2 > 40 THEN level = advanced.

IF score2 > 20 THEN level = possibly advanced.

Research Challenges and Future Directions

Despite the promising results of knowledge mining applicable to a limited domain of Web-based learning presented in the literature, the practical aspect of such applications is still in its infancy. This is due to the fact that knowledge mining is not a systematic task; it requires intuition and experiences in adjusting the techniques at every step to obtain the most relevant and actionable knowledge. Knowledge mining is still a task of experts, not at all for a novice or occasional user.

One solution that would abet the improvement of knowledge-mining techniques for typical educators that are not the experts in this field is to customize the process and make the technique more user-friendly. To achieve such a goal, constraint mining (De Raedt, Guns, & Nijssen, 2008), in which the mining engine can be made more specific through constraint specifications, and higher-order mining (Roddick, Spiliopoulou, Lister, & Ceglar, 2008), in which the mining results can be mined again to deliver only interesting and useful knowledge, may be used. More specifically, mining algorithms should be made more powerful to provide users with the answers they are looking for. In order to serve the specific needs of users from various and totally different fields, such as social science researchers and medical practitioners, the mining system should be made domain-specific with the intelligent user interface. Existing general mining systems such as Weka can, nevertheless, convey some useful knowledge to users at the expense of quite significant learning time.

The issue of knowledge object representation and managing for the mobile devices working on stream data is also a research challenge for the next decade. These devices are, by nature, limited in memory capacity. Knowledge caching and storing schemes need specific design for such mobile-learning environment.

Current Web-based learning environments provide tools and mechanisms to support knowledge creation and delivery, electronic document access and management, e-learning, and knowledge sharing through collaborative workspaces. Standards such as SCORM for learning objects, modeling languages, and content structures enable the rapid generation of instructional materials and other learning-related elements. These materials in electronic form are widely dispersed and stored in various servers globally. The trends for the next generation of learning environments are the ability to efficiently exchange the available instructional materials, the functionality to create on-the-fly courseware contents that serve the specific needs of the learner, and the support for advanced technologies that allow the learning system to search Web documents semantically and organize knowledge assets intelligently.

Learning environments in the new decade require an efficient fusion mechanism to integrate new technologies such as semantic Web, smart agents, and declarative knowledge-mining engines. Semantic Web is a concept evolved from Web technology in which the semantics (or meaning) of Web documents are defined to facilitate the search on Web content (Antoniou & van Harmelen, 2008). A new form of Web content with attached meaning may introduce some standards for the knowledge asset format and make the knowledge exchange and sharing more feasible.

Agents comprise an important computing paradigm used in hundreds of applications. Current software agents work autonomously and pervasively to some extent. Software developers attempt to design and develop smart agents that can be personalized to reflect the user's preferences and constraints. Such preferences may be inferred from users' behavior. The attempts to create smart agents are now reaching the demonstration level. The real usable applications can be anticipated within the next decade.

It can be noticed that semantic Web and smart agents are two different concepts that can support each other; semantic Web should be efficiently implemented with an agent technology, and vice versa agents may become smarter with the support from semantic Web and knowledge-mining technologies. These three main concepts are, nevertheless, in the evolving stage. The new advancement in these areas will certainly benefit the development of intelligent learning environments.

Conclusions

Recent developments in information and communication technology certainly influence the design and implementation of educational systems. The emergence of the World Wide Web in the early 1990s has resulted in substantial change in both the content representation and the delivery mechanism. XML (eXtensible Markup Language) is an acclaimed technology as the main content representation format. The main advantage of XML over other hypertext languages, such as HTML, is its property of being in an interoperable data interchange format. This language technology helps improve the courseware design concept toward interoperability, which is one of the major design criteria for most software products these days.

Improvements in hardware and communication technology, such as mobile microprocessors and wireless communication, have evolved learning environments into mobile and distributed platforms. Such information infrastructures provide learners with remote access to experts and distributed resources. *Web Browser* is a software device that offers learners open and flexible accessibility to distant course contents. The organization of learning resources has also been changed from creating and delivering large inflexible course content to producing database-driven learning objects that can be reused, searched, and modified independently of the delivery media.

Interoperability, accessibility, and reusability are therefore the main design concepts of current instructional systems. These concepts have shifted the learning paradigm from static learning to collaborative, adaptive, and autonomous learning. Collaborative learning allows for direct contact between instructors and groups of learners through the communication technologies ranging from e-mail and shared workspaces to video conference systems. Adaptive and autonomous learning allow learners to take control over their own organization of learning pace and scheme.

In parallel to advancement of the Web technology, knowledge discovery in databases or data mining has also emerged as a new field. Knowledge discovery in databases is the process of searching and extracting hidden patterns from data that are too large to be efficiently analyzed by humans with simple tools such as a spreadsheet program or database software. Instead, analysis of such huge datasets has to be done automatically via a suite of complicated software. The knowledge discovery process should be done in an intelligent manner and provides useful knowledge in a reasonable time. Knowledge typically appears in a form of patterns that reflect any kind of relationships existing among data attributes. Such relationships include classification rules, association rules, and characteristics of data subgroups in summarized form. However, the discovered patterns represent local relationships, instead of the global ones, because the discovery process is performed on data samples or only some portions of the whole database. The patterns may change if the data samples are modified. Therefore, evaluation on the discovered patterns is an essential post-mining step that has to be done under the supervision of domain experts prior to the delivery of discovered patterns to the stage of knowledge deployment.

The new proposal that embeds knowledge management modules to induce knowledge and manage stored knowledge objects can efficiently supplement the content management and the learning management modules currently existing in most Web-based learning systems. In this chapter, we argue that with the matured technology of knowledge discovery in databases, the integration of knowledge-mining capability to the creation, delivery, and management of learning and knowledge objects should be the next step in e-learning. The proposed architecture of learning environments will enable the convergence of e-learning with knowledge management. A repository containing learner-related materials is a valuable source of knowledge to support personalization information for independent learners.

The contribution of this chapter is the design and prototype implementation of a knowledge-mining system to provide an integrated, flexible, and efficient platform supported by a community of agents. The agents in the system refer to the computer programs capable of controlling their own decision-making and acting. Their decisions are based on the perception of changes in the environment and the predefined goals of each agent. The proposed agent-based platform provides mechanisms of data browsing, extracting, data arrangement, data-quality evaluation, knowledge mining, knowledge processing, and knowledge customization for the whole process of knowledge discovery. The agent model is designed with three-layer architecture. The data source layer is at the back-end and is responsible for locating and accessing data from the remote sites. The external layer is the user interface part. These agents work autonomously and cooperatively to deliver knowledge assets that meet specific interests of each user. This intuitive idea is illustrated through a running example in which the induction process is based on the rough set theory.

Acknowledgments

The research results presented in Section 18.4 has been conducted at Data Engineering and Knowledge Discovery (DEKD) Research Unit, fully funded by Suranaree University of Technology. The author has also been supported by grants from the National Research Council of Thailand (NRCT).

References

Agrawal, R., Imielinski, T., & Swami, A. (1993). Mining association rules between sets of items in large databases. Proceedings of ACM SIGMOD International Conference on Management of Data, 207–216.

Amershi, S., & Conati, C. (2007). Unsupervised and supervised machine learning in user modeling for intelligent learning environments. Proceedings of 12th International Conference on Intelligent User Interface, 72–81.

Antoniou, G., & van Harmelen, F. (2008). *A semantic Web primer* (2nd ed.). Cambridge, MA: MIT Press.

Biletskiy, Y., Baghi, H., Keleberda, I., & Fleming, M. (2009). An adjustable personalization of search and delivery of learning objects to learners. *Expert Systems with Applications*, doi:10.1016/j. eswa.2008.12.038.

Ceddia, J., Sheard, J., & Tibbey, G. (2007). WAT-A tool for classifying learning activities from a log file. Proceedings of 9th Australasian Computing Education Conference (ACE2009), 11–17.

Chen, C., Hsieh, Y., & Hsu, S. (2007). Mining learner profile utilizing association rule for Web-based learning diagnosis. *Expert Systems with Applications*, *33*, 6–22.

Chen, C. (2008). Intelligent Web-based learning system with personalized learning path guidance. *Computers & Education*, *51*, 787–814.

Chen, N., Kinshuk, W., C., & Chen, H. (2008). Mining e-learning domain concept map from academic articles. *Computers & Education*, *50*, 1009–1021.

Chen, S., & Liu, X. (2008). An integrated approach for modeling learning patterns of students in Web-based instruction: A cognitive style perspective. *ACM Transactions on Computer-Human Interaction*, *15*(1), 1:1–1:28. doi:10.1145/1352782.1352783.

Chen, C., & Chen, M. (2009). Mobile formative assessment tool based on data mining techniques for supporting Web-based learning. *Computers & Education*, *52*, 256–273.

De Bra, P., Aerts, A., Berden, B., De Lange, B., Rousseau, B., Santic, T., et al. (2003). AHA! The adaptive hypermedia architecture. Proceedings of 14th ACM Conference on Hypertext and Hypermedia, 81–84.

De Raedt L., Guns T., Nijssen S. (2008). Constraint programming for itemset mining. Proceedings of International Conference on Knowledge Discovery and Data Mining (KDD), 204–212.

Fayyad, U. M., Piatetsky-Shapiro, G., Smyth, P., & Uthurusamy, R., (Eds.). (1996). *Advances in knowledge discovery and data mining*. Cambridge, MA: AAAI/MIT Press.

Han, J., & Kamber, M. (2006). *Data mining: Concepts and techniques* (2nd ed.). San Francisco: Morgan Kaufmann.

Handi, M.S. (2007). MASACAD: A multi-agent approach to information customization for the purpose of academic advising of students. *Applied Soft Computing*, *7*, 746–771.

Karampiperis, P., & Sampson, D. (2006). Automatic learning object selection and sequencing in Web-based intelligent learning systems. In Ma, Z. (Ed.), *Web-based intelligent e-learning systems: Technologies and applications*. Hershey, PA: Information Science Publishing.

Kazi, S. A. (2004). A conceptual framework for Web-based intelligent learning environments using SCORM-2004. Proceedings of the IEEE International Conference on Advanced Learning Technologies (ICALT'04), 12–15. doi:10.1109/ICALT.2004.1357365.

Kerdprasop, N., & Kerdprasop, K. (2008). Knowledge mining in Web-based learning environments. *International Journal of Social Sciences*, *3*(2), 80–83.

Kristofic, A., & Bielikova, M. (2005). Improving adaptation in Web-based educational hypermedia by means of knowledge discovery. Proceedings of 16th ACM Conference on Hypertext and Hypermedia, 184–192.

Kritikou, Y., Demestichas, P., Adamopoulou, E., Demestichas, K., Theologou, M., & Paradia, M. (2007). User profile modeling in the context of Web-based learning management systems. *Journal of Network and Computer Applications*. doi:10.1016/j.jnca.2007.11.006.

Larose, D. (2006). *Data Mining: Methods and Model*. New Jersey: John Wiley & Sons.

Lazcorreta, E., Botella, F., & Fernandez-Caballero, A. (2007). Towards personalized recommendation by two-step modified Apriori data mining algorithm. *Expert System with Applications*. doi:10.1016/j.eswa.2007.08.048.

Lee, M. W., Chen, S. Y., Chrysostomou, K., & Liu, X. (2009). Mining students' behavior in Web-based learning programs. *Expert System with Applications, 36*, 3459–3464.

Li, Q., Lau, R., Shih, T., & Li, F. (2008). Technology supports for distributed and collaborative learning over the Internet. *ACM Transactions on Internet Technology, 8*(2), 10:1–10:24. doi:10.1145/1323651.1323656.

MacQueen, J. (1967). Some methods for classification and analysis of multivariate observations. Proceedings of 5th Berkeley Symposium on Mathematical Statistics and Probability, (1), 281–297.

Markellou, P., Rigou, M., & Sirmakessis, S. (2005). Knowledge mining: A quantitative synthesis of research results and findings. In Sirmakessis, S. (Ed.), *Knowledge mining*. The Netherlands: Springer-Verlag.

Marshall, B., Chen, H., Shen, R., & Fox, E. (2006). Moving digital libraries into the student learning space: The GetSmart experience. *ACM Journal on Educational resources in Computing, 6*(1), 1–20.

Martin, M., Alvarez, A., Fernandez-Castro, I., & Urretavizcaya, M. (2008). Generating teacher adapted suggestions for improving distance educational systems with SIgMa. Proceedings of 8th IEEE International Conference on Advanced Learning Technologies, 449–453.

Michalski, R. S. (2003, March). *Knowledge mining: A proposed new direction*. Invited Talk at the Sanken Symposium on Data Mining and Semantic Web (pp. 10–11) Japan: Osaka University. Retrieved from http://www.mli.gmu.edu/papers/2003–2004/03–5.pdf.

Pahl, C. (2003). Managing evolution and change in Web-based teaching and learning environments. *Computers & Education, 40*, 99–114.

Pawlak, Z. (1982). Rough sets. *International Journal of Information and Computer Science, 11*(5), 341–356.

Pawlak, Z. (1991). *Rough sets, theoretical aspects of reasoning about data*. Dordrecht, The Netherlands: Kluwer Academic Publishers.

Roddick, J. F., Spiliopoulou, M., Lister, D., & Ceglar, A. (2008). Higher order mining. *ACM SIGKDD Explorations Newsletter, 10*(1), 5–17.

Romero, C., & Ventura, S. (2007). Educational data mining: A survey from 1995 to 2005. *Expert Systems with Applications, 33*, 135–146.

Romero, C., Ventura, S., & Garcia, E. (2008). Data mining in course management systems: Moodle case study and tutorial. *Computers & Education, 51*, 368–384.

Romero, C., Gonzalez, P., Ventura, S., del Jesus, M. J., & Herrera, F. (2009). Evolutionary algorithms for subgroup discovery in e-learning: A practical application using Moodle data. *Expert Systems with Applications, 36*, 1632–1644.

Sable, J., & Gaviola, N. (2007). *NCES common core of data local education agency—Level public-use data file on public school dropouts: School year 2003–04 (NCES 2007–372)*. National Center for Education Statistics, Institute of Education Sciences, U.S. Department of Education, Washington, DC. (http://nces.ed.gov/pubsearch/)

Shih, C., Chiang, D., Lai, S., & Hu, Y. (2008). Applying hybrid data mining techniques to Web-based self-assessment system of study and learning strategies inventory. *Expert Systems with Applications*. doi:10.1016/j.eswa.2008.06.089.

Tzouveli, P., Mylonas, P., & Kollias, S. (2007). An intelligent e-learning system based on learner profiling and learning resources adaptation. *Computers & Education*. doi:10.1016/j.compedu.2007.05.005.

Wang, Y., Tseng, M., & Liao, H. (2008). Data mining for adaptive learning sequence in English language instruction. *Expert Systems with Applications*. doi:10.1016/j.eswa.2008.09.008.

Witten, I. H., & Frank, E. (2005). *Data mining: Practical machine learning tools and techniques* (2nd ed.) San Francisco: Elsevier/Morgan Kaufmann.

Wooldridge, M., & Jennings, N. (1995). Intelligent agents: Theory and practice. *The Knowledge Engineering Review, 10*(2), 115–152.

Wooldridge, M. (2002). *An introduction to multiagent systems.* London: John Wiley & Sons.

Xu, D., & Wang, H. (2006). Intelligent agent supported personalization for virtual learning environments. *Decision Support Systems, 42,* 825–843.

Zaiane, O. (2001). Web usage mining for a better Web-based learning environment. Proceedings of the Advanced Technology for Educational Conference, 60–64.

Part IV

Audiovisual, Mobile, and Geospatial Technologies' Impact on the Social Research Process

Chapter 19

The Use of Audiovisuals in Surveys

Tom W. Smith and John Sokolowski

Introduction

Surveys are increasingly using computers and other new technologies in more innovative ways (Couper, 2005). The advances are especially notable in the utilization of audiovisuals for both the presentation of questions and the collection of responses. These innovations have the potential to fundamentally change the nature of survey research and expand on the data that can be captured.

In some ways, there is little new in the use of audiovisuals in social-science research. For example, psychologists for 60 years or more in pretest/posttest designs have shown subjects film clips as the treatment between the tests (Lorge & Ordan, 1945). Likewise, surveys for decades have regularly used visuals in the form of show cards with response options such as depictions of the feeling-thermometer scale, and less frequently have presented still photographs of people or places for evaluation (Davis, 1955).

But in other ways, the change has been profound. Over the last 20 years, the rise of both Web-based surveys and computer-assisted personal interviews (CAPI) has enormously increased the capacity of surveys to use audiovisuals. First, audiovisuals have moved out of the psychologists' laboratory and into people's living rooms. This greatly increases the external validity of the audiovisual studies both by reaching larger and more representative samples and by collecting the data in more natural settings. Second, the technological advances mean that audiovisuals in the field can show and capture a full range of sounds and images. Computer-generated visuals and high-quality, moving audiovisuals can be displayed and recordings during the interviews can capture time-stamped, digitized audiovisuals as well.

Typology of Audiovisual Surveys

The use of audiovisual recordings in surveys can be broken down in several ways. First, the medium of recording can be audio, visual, or audiovisual. These media can either be real (i.e., recording of actual sights and/or sounds), virtual (i.e., machine-generated graphics and sounds), or a combination of the two (e.g., real images and/or speech that have been altered by computers). If real, the images could be staged with actors following a script or natural involving people actually engaged in the activity of interest. Additionally, the visual medium can be static with still images or dynamic with moving images. Second, the audiovisual recordings can be used as stimuli as part of the question-asking process or for recording responses as part of the data capture and preservation stage. These two dimensions form a framework for illustrating the use of audiovisuals in surveys.

Stimulus/Audio

On the 2002 General Social Survey (Davis, Smith, & Marsden, 2007) recordings representing doctors discussing medical matters with patients were played for respondents who were then asked several questions about the staged doctor/patient interchange that they had just heard (Levinson et al., 2005). Another example is audio computer-assisted self-interviewing (audio-CASI) in which the computer "reads" questions to respondents and respondents directly enter their answers into the laptop without having to verbally or directly disclose their answers to an interviewer. The development of audio-CASI won the 2002 Innovators Award of the American Association for Public Opinion Research. It has been shown to increase truthful responses to sensitive questions (Couper, 2005; Couper, Singer, & Tourangeau, 2003; Renker & Tonkin, 2007; Tourangeau & Smith, 1996, 1998) and is also an alternative to written self-completion when the target population is illiterate or poorly educated (Hewett, Erulkar, & Mensch, 2004).

Stimulus/Visual

Harris (2002) studied how respondents classified people racially using computer-altered images of actual people to mix physical characteristics. A National Opinion Research Center (NORC) housing study used actual pictures of garages, walls, and other structural features of buildings to guide people in their ratings of the condition of their own property. Loftus (1999) showed people videos of staged accidents and other scenes and tested their ability to accurately recall details under various conditions.

Stimulus/Audiovisual

Rasinski et al. (1999) recorded eight staged interviews of a person being asked about sensitive topics such as abortion and driving under the influence. The interviews experimentally varied elements such as whether a third party was present during the interview and the age of the interviewer. Respondents shown the recordings were asked how truthful they thought the person being interviewed would be and other questions about the recorded interview. McKinlay et al. (2006, 2007) recorded staged consultations between patients and doctors. Their physician respondents were asked to diagnose and prescribe treatment for the presented conditions (see also Kales et al., 2005). Furthermore, they used a factorial design with 16 combinations of patient age, gender, race, and socioeconomic status to ascertain the impact of these patient characteristics on their assessments. Southwell (2005) had a national sample of teens evaluate health campaign advertisements and Valentino, Hutchings, and White (2003) in the Detroit Area Study showed political-campaign ads on laptops. Studies in Chicago and Detroit have shown videos of neighborhoods with actors of different races (Krysan et al., 2005; Krysan and Couper, 2003).

Data Capture/Audio: This procedure is known as Computer Audio Recorded Interviewing (CARI) and is discussed in detail in the following section.

Data Collection/Visual

A number of studies have asked interviewers to rate the physical attractiveness of respondents. Such ratings are subject to great interviewer variability (Cable & Judge, 1997; Macintyre & West, 2008). A digital camera or a laptop with a webcam could be used to record respondents' images and these could then be rated in a consistent manner by a team of evaluators. In a NORC study of Human Development in Chicago Neighborhoods, videos were shot of 27,000 block faces covering the 80 sampled areas. These were used not only to allow researchers to get a qualitative "feel" for where people lived, but also so that objective facts about the area could be observed and coded (i.e., percentage of windows broken, amount of trash on the streets). The recordings also allowed researchers to have raw data that could be analyzed in various different and unanticipated ways rather than just extracted information that had been observed and counted such as the number of broken windows, but that had not been visually recorded.

Data Collection/Audiovisual

The NORC Nonshared Environment in Adolescent Development Study (1988–1992) made recording of interactions between family members in addition to conducting interviews and using self-administered questionnaires. Suchman and Jordon (1990) recorded several GSS interviews (not with actual GSS respondents) and analyzed them to assess cognitive problems with the questions and/or interviewer behavior.

CARI

To more fully illustrate the nature and utility of the new audiovisual approaches, the example of CARI will be considered. The focus here is on (1) what CARI is and how it works, (2) the development of CARI, (3) what technological challenges have been resolved and what challenges remain in its usage in field surveys, (4) how CARI is currently used, and (5) future developments, including suggestions on how CARI can be most effective.

CARI is an exciting technological advance that has the potential to both improve data quality (Edwards et al., 2008; Herget, Biemer, Morton, & Sand, 2005; Arceneaux, 2007; McGee, 2007) and expand substantive analysis (Grogger, 2008). CARI gives survey researchers insights into the in-person interview respondent/interviewer exchange never before possible. CARI allows for the digital recording of in-person interviews capturing the verbal exchange between the interviewer and respondent. CARI allows field-survey researchers the advantage telephone-survey researchers have long enjoyed, where data-quality monitors have had the ability to listen-in on the interviewer/respondent exchange. While telephone-survey researchers can typically monitor interviewer sessions in real time, field-survey researchers using CARI can monitor snippets of an in-person interview, or the entire in-person interview, after the interview has been completed and the audio files have been received by data-quality monitors. In terms of data quality, CARI can be used in addition to standard procedures such as recontacting respondents to ensure the validity of the interview, provide interviewing protocol feedback to interviewers, provide survey-questionnaire designers with insights into how well interviewers administer questions and how well respondents comprehend the questions asked, and offer the ability to digitally record the respondent's responses to open-ended verbatim questions (Biemer, Herget, Morton, & Willis, 2000).

CARI also opens up new avenues of research using paradata that were previously unavailable. Paradata are auxiliary information that measure various components of the survey data-collection process including information on contact attempts, question probing, etc. During the analysis stage, these data can be obtained from the coding of the verbal exchange between the interviewer and respondent. For example, researchers can determine the number of times a question needed to be repeated by an interviewer or the number of times the respondent needed a question clarified.

Finally, CARI can be used for substantive research. For example, Grogger (2008) examined 520 validation interviews from the 1997 National Longitudinal Survey of Youth. He found that Black respondents with distinctly Black voice patterns earned less than Whites with comparable job skills and also less than other Blacks with less distinctive Black speech. Other research areas that depend on audio records, which can be delivered by CARI include discourse analysis and response-latency studies (Bassili & Scott, 1996; Mulligan et al., 2003; Yan & Tourangeau, 2007). Discourse analysis involves the detailed analysis of speech and syntax patterns. Response-latency studies center on the precise measurement of the timing of responses to questions.

How CARI Works

CARI works through the audio-recording mechanisms on an interviewer's laptop, namely, the laptop microphone and soundcard. Each laptop is equipped with either an internal or external microphone and a command file indicates which portions of the interview are recorded, that is, the command file contains programming code instructing the laptop to record a certain set of questions or the entire interview. The command information can be programmed directly into the CAPI instrument software such as Blaise (Thissen & Rodriguez, 2004) or it can exist independently of the CAPI instrument software. For the 2008 GSS, NORC computer scientists successfully implemented the CARI command file to work independently from the main questionnaire that was programmed in SPSS' MR interview software. The command file can be written to a survey's specifications. The recording time can be specified to stop the recording after the interviewer administers a specific question that was set for recording by proceeding past the CAPI screen, which contained the original question to the next question screen. Additionally, the recording can be set to stop after a predetermined length of time regardless of whether the interviewer completed the administration of the question and had proceeded to the next screen. The command file can also be written with instructions to record random portions of the interview, if so desired. It also has the flexibility of being updated throughout a data-collection field period. If, for example, researchers wanted to record a variable that was not specified for recording when data collection began, an updated command file including instructions to record the new variable(s) could be sent to an interviewer's laptop through a remote update via a secure encrypted Internet connection. One advantage of having the command file work independently from the questionnaire is that should researchers decide on updating the command file, they do not have to update the questionnaire software to do so. Theoretically, researchers could be recording different questions for different interviewers, if that was the research goal, by placing different command files with different instructions on each interviewer's laptop.

At the beginning of a CARI interview, respondents are made to read a statement contained in the informed consent statement typically required by an organization's Institutional Review Board (IRB), which indicates that portions of the interview will be recorded for quality-control purposes; this will not affect the strict confidentiality of the respondent's responses. If the respondent consents to the interview and recording, the recording mechanism is turned on. If the respondent consents to the interview, but does not consent to recording, the recording mechanism is turned off. The interviewer also can have the recording mechanism turned off partway through an interview, if after initially consenting to recording, the respondent changes his or her mind.

The recording files are then transmitted over the Internet through a secure encrypted connection along with the questionnaire and other survey data to the organization's central office computer. If the survey organization does not have this capability, or if the audio files are too large to transmit remotely, as might be the case if an entire in-depth interview was recorded, interviewers could transfer the audio files from their laptop to a zip disk and ship the recordings to a centralized location where the audio files can be uploaded and reviewed. Initial deployments of CARI utilized this technique (Herget, Biemer, Morton, & Sand, 2005). With dial-up connections being the norm for interviewers during initial deployments of CARI, the sending of large audio files over the Internet was not entirely feasible. Improvements in file-transfer technology and compression, and more widespread use of broadband Internet connections in the homes of field interviewers have made the remote transfer of audio files to a centralized computer via the Internet much more feasible today.

CARI Development

The first deployment of CARI took place in 1999 on the National Survey of Child and Adolescent Well-being (NSCAW). The NSCAW was conducted by Research Triangle Institute (RTI). NSCAW was a national study of children in the child welfare system, plus a supplement of children in the foster care system. Survey respondents included children, their caregivers, the child welfare caseworker, and teachers. This initial deployment of CARI on a major national field project acted as the first significant CARI field test to determine the feasibility of the application. In the years that followed, RTI and NSCAW's sponsor, the U.S. Department of Health and Human Services (DHHS) collaborated on a number of CARI feasibility studies (Biemer, Herget, Morton, & Willis, 2000; Herget, Biemer, Morton, & Sand, 2005). The U.S. Census Bureau also conducted CARI laboratory tests to evaluate the potential implementation of CARI into all of the Census Bureau's CAPI surveys (Arceneaux, 2007). From these feasibility studies, lab tests, and evaluations, the following key issues were addressed:

1. *System Performance*: No degradation of CAPI performance was found. This was the consensus across the research organizations. Initial concerns that the implementation of CARI would lead to laptop hardware or software performance degradation were invalidated. There were no signs that interviewers could determine when CARI recording was occurring. The CARI system appeared to unobtrusively operate on the interviewer's laptop computers.

2. *Data Security*: It was found that when CARI files were transmitted remotely over the Internet, the files could be subject to the same type of encryption to which other survey and questionnaire data are subjected.

3. *Audio Quality*: The only notable discrepancy between the RTI feasibility studies and the Census Bureau's lab tests is the reported audio quality of the recordings. The Census Bureau did note positive findings in their CARI evaluation in regards to audio quality, but did indicate that more research is needed before CARI can be implemented for use in current Census Bureau surveys. While RTI reported that 90% of the audio files collected in NSCAW were of the highest audio quality, it suggested that CARI technology does produce high-quality recorded interviews. Although the Census Bureau observed a high-quality audio file rate of 85.6%, it deemed this audio quality rate unacceptable. Additional research on the quality of CARI recordings collected on the National Centre for Social Research's (NatCen) English Longitudinal Study of Ageing (ELSA) in Britain complicates the matter further. NatCen found that for more than a third of the completed cases, random, individual sound files were inaudible. While for most cases, the interviewers themselves were clearly audible, most likely because they were sitting close to the laptop and thereby the microphone, the recording of respondents were generally much quieter because they were further away from the recording device, making it difficult to understand what respondents said (McGee, 2007).

    What is not clear is the configuration setting of the laptops used to record the audio files of the organizations using CARI (Nelson et al., 2007). RTI has noted that its standard configuration is 16-bit bandwidth, 11.25 KHz sampling rate, and a single channel. Recording two channels (stereo) requires twice the storage space and provides no extra quality since a single laptop microphone is generally used. Audio quality is also affected by sampling rate, compression, and audio file format (Thissen, Sattaluri, McFarlane, & Biemer, 2007).

    The location of the microphone, whether it is external or internal, and if it is an internal microphone, where it is located within the laptop, along with the quality of the microphone and soundcard can also affect the quality of the recordings. Despite all of the CARI audio files collected by survey-research organizations to date, more research into the quality of the audio files and the system requirements and specifications required to produce high-quality CARI audio files are needed since clear and audible audio files are critical to the success of CARI applications.

4. *Respondents' Reactions*: Respondent reactions to CARI have been positive. In terms of respondent CARI consent rate, a variety of organizations have found that over 80% of respondents agree to CARI recording. RTI found 85% of caseworkers, 83% of caregivers, and 82% of child interviews consented to CARI recording in the NSCAW. These results were seen as rather positive given the sensitive nature of the survey. On a much less sensitive survey, RTI found that 93% of respondents agreed to CARI recording (Wrenn-Yorker & Thissen, 2005).

NatCen's ELSA survey yielded an 89% CARI cooperation rate. And on the 2008 GSS, 86% of respondents agreed to CARI recording.

Overall it has been found that more than 70% of respondents reported that they had no reaction one way or the other when initially requested for permission to record portions of the NSCAW interview. In the same survey, nearly 69% of respondents reported that their answers were not influenced by the audio recording, 16.4% reported that their answers were influenced "a little," and about 15% reported that their answers were influenced "somewhat" or "a lot." Those respondents who answered "a lot," "somewhat," or "a Little" were asked a follow-up item on how they thought their answers were influenced. Over 47% of the respondents reported that their awareness of the recording probably influenced them to provide more accurate responses, 36.8% reported that the recording had no effect, and 15.8% reported that it influenced them to provide less accurate responses. This research showing that CARI has little influences on respondent answers is supported by similar research regarding the recording of telephone interviews (Basson, 2005), which show no social-desirability effects. The extent to which CARI does influence respondent answers is more likely to improve data accuracy.

5. *Interviewer Reactions:* On the positive end, approximately 82% of NSCAW interviewers felt positive or neutral about the use of CARI overall. About 87% of interviewers were positive or neutral about using CARI to detect case falsification and 89% of interviewers were positive or neutral about using CARI as a tool to evaluate and provide feedback to interviewers. The more negative feelings toward CARI tended to come from more experienced interviewers. More experienced interviewers were more likely to exhibit negative feelings toward CARI. Experienced interviewers exhibited negative feelings toward a change in the status quo and saw CARI as a sign that "management" does not trust the interviewers.

6. *CARI Validation System:* Reviewing three 30-sec audio files was found to be sufficient for monitors to reach a consensus on the validity rating of the interview. Additional analysis showed that the CARI-based verification approach was less expensive than traditional approaches by 20–30%.

7. *CARI Performance Monitoring:* It was also found, through a review of an interviewer's audio files, that CARI would be a useful tool when combined with performance monitoring procedures such as supervisor's evaluations and the examination of an interviewer's response rates and cost/production ratio to successfully evaluate performance and provide feedback to field interviewers. To date, CARI has primarily been used to detect inappropriate interviewer behavior including data falsification, and to evaluate interviewing protocols and provide feedback to interviewers.

Current Use as a Validation Tool

Of its many usages, CARI has been used primarily to detect falsified interviews. To detect falsification, data-quality monitors listen for no voices on the audio file while room noises are audible, instances when the interviewer can be heard, but appears to be speaking to himself or herself, instances when the respondent answers too quickly or laughs in inappropriate places, and instances when the respondent makes comments suggesting the interview is being falsified, or the same respondent's voice is heard in recordings of multiple interviews (Thissen & Rodriguez, 2004).

In addition to acting as a detection tool to identify falsified cases, CARI also acts as a deterrent. Interviewers on CARI surveys certainly know CARI is being used to monitor their work and to ensure interviews are not falsified. To the extent that CARI acts as a deterrent to case falsification is difficult to quantify and this issue has not yet been thoroughly explored to date.

Exclusively using CARI for validation on field projects can lower validation costs by 20–30%, although there are a number of issues that currently prevent it from being used as the primary tool to identify interviewers who are falsifying interviews. While CARI can be used to detect falsification and acts as a deterrent to falsification, it has not shown that it can fully replace traditional validation methods such as callbacks. The type of survey utilizing CARI is an important factor in determining how well CARI can be utilized by survey researchers for interviewer validation. Area Probability (AP) samples are the perfect example of a type of survey that still requires traditional callback validation. While AP samples can certainly use CARI as a validation supplement, it is difficult to see how AP samples can solely use CARI as the primary tool to detect case falsification. Through callback validation for AP surveys, survey researchers are able to confirm that the interviewer contacted the correct sampled address and correctly selected the appropriate respondent. To verify that these two key-study protocols for AP surveys were correctly followed by an interviewer, these items would need to be confirmed with the respondent through either a telephone callback or the receipt of a paper validation questionnaire. With CARI, these two items would have to be confirmed with the respondent and recorded using CARI in the main questionnaire. This would be difficult to achieve as it would be very apparent to the interviewer what researchers would be trying to accomplish with these questions.

For panel and other reinterview type field projects, capturing CARI audio files of respondents during the first wave of the survey would prove invaluable for validation of interviews on future waves of the survey. Implementing strict validation and callback procedures during the first wave of data collection would ensure the CARI audio files collected do, in fact, contain the respondent's voice. Implementing CARI on subsequent waves of the survey would allow for decreased validation costs and more efficient validation as survey-research organizations would have the respondent's voice on record from the first wave of the survey for quick and accurate comparison during subsequent waves. In order for survey-research organizations to save CARI audio files from round to round for ongoing surveys, it would require clearance from the organization's IRB. If one were reasonably taking the view that the audio files are just another piece of survey data, such as respondent address or gender, it is hard to imagine an IRB having an issue with this procedure, especially if an organization's CARI audio files are subjected to the same stringent, data-protection protocols as more traditional response data.

One other limitation of CARI as a validation tool is that the best data available have shown that researchers can reasonably expect that 10% of respondents will refuse audio recording. This is coupled with the fact that an undetermined percentage of the CARI audio files will be of low and unusable quality. It is unlikely that much can be done to improve the cooperation rate for CARI, but several steps can be taken to improve the technical quality of the audio recordings. First, interviewers can be trained to facilitate better recordings by making sure that ambient noise is within acceptable limits, that the recording device is not obstructed, and that the respondent is close enough to the laptop to be adequately picked up. Second, audio recording and compression standards can be chosen to enhance the quality of recordings. Finally, laptops can be used that have better placement of their recording device and quieter keyboards to reduce extraneous noise. Even if a panel or reinterview survey has a repository of respondent audio files from a prior round of the survey for comparison in future survey waves, there will be a significant percentage of the cases where there are inaudible audio files or no audio files for comparison. In these cases, some other kind of validation method will need to be utilized.

Current Use as a Performance Monitoring Tool

Combining CARI and interviewer-behavior coding provides a very useful tool for highlighting interviewer training needs (McGee, 2007). Indeed, a major benefit of CARI is its extremely high potential to improve interviewing methods under a quality-improvement initiative. The mere presence of CARI is likely to exhibit a positive effect on an interviewer's behavior knowing they will be receiving feedback on the audio files captured. Interviewers who know they are being recorded are more likely to stick to study protocols and not to exhibit behavior they know is inappropriate. Through a review of CARI audio files, trained data-quality monitors can listen to the interviewer/respondent exchange and assign a predetermined code based on what was heard. Based on the codes assigned to an interviewer's audio files, either positive or negative feedback will be received. Feedback to the interviewer would generally be provided by his or her manager. On the 2008 GSS, NORC field supervisors had access to all of the CARI recordings for all interviewers he or she supervised through the NORC Case Management System (CMS), CM Field. Field supervisors found these recordings to be an extremely effective management tool to verify the authenticity of completed interviewers and to monitor interviewer performance. CARI can identify areas where interviewers need retraining and can highlight areas where interviewers excel for future project assignments. CARI can work to correct the inappropriate behavior of experienced interviewers and works as an extension of training for new interviewers.

In order for timely and accurate feedback to be provided to interviewers, some kind of CARI coding application is required. The coding application would provide a link to the audio file and code frames with the ability of the coder to assign a code that indicates the quality of the audio file and an interviewer-performance code (Sokolowski, Daquilanea, & Fennell, 2008). Examples of interviewer-performance codes would include: question not read, question misread, improper prompt, and insufficient probe. The type of questionnaire and the kinds of quality initiatives desired by the researchers can inform the type of feedback given to interviewers and the contents of the code frames. Quality-improvement methods such as these may supplement other validation activities, evaluate interviewing techniques, and assess data quality.

The costs of implementing a full-blown, CARI-monitoring system can be significant. On the 2008 GSS, it was estimated that if the project were to monitor and code an average of 5 min of audio per case for all completed cases, the task would comprise 4% of the project's total budget. Cost is an issue for survey researchers, as CARI is a new technology that many existing surveys have not fully incorporated into their budgets. Survey researchers need to find ways to balance the benefits of CARI coding and find ways to incorporate this work into their surveys.

Survey-research organizations have taken great strides to incorporate CARI into their validation protocols and have worked to initiate CARI-monitoring systems to enhance interviewer performance. While these areas have seen the utilization of CARI's potential, there are relatively large holes in the literature regarding the two other areas where CARI has the potential for a significant impact: (1) using CARI to identify questionnaire and data problems, and (2) using CARI to capture responses to open-ended questions.

Future Use of CARI

Although the recording of the interviewer/respondent exchange has the potential to aid questionnaire designers and cognitive psychologists in the development of sound survey questions, so far there has been little literature that has documented how CARI can aid in the identification of questionnaire problems and how it can help with questionnaire design. However, the recording of questionnaire administration has shown itself to be a great tool for question pretesting (Basson, 2005).

CARI can also be used to collect verbatim responses, although no literature that documents how effective CARI can be in this area exists. The 2008 GSS used CARI to record respondent responses to the standard Census Industry/Occupation (I/O) battery of questions (Sokolowski, Daquilanea, & Fennell, 2008). The results of this initiative are forthcoming. NORC researchers will be examining the audio file coding of I/O responses versus the interviewer coding of the same responses to determine what, if any, the differences are and which is the better vehicle for collecting this type of information.

Advances of Audiovisuals

The main benefits of using audiovisuals in surveys are that both the questioning and the data collection can become more extensive and complete. In many cases, simple spoken survey questions are poor substitutes for what the researcher really wants to measure. For example, asking about a campaign theme or slogan may be useful, but showing actual political ads greatly increases what can be evaluated. Similarly, asking directly about race or gender may not be nearly as powerful nor valid as having respondents view visuals in which the race and/or gender of people have been randomized. In many cases, the audiovisual presentation can be closer to the real-world phenomenon of interest than a traditional, ask-and-answer question. At the data-collection end, audiovisual recording can capture much more detail (e.g., full verbatims of open-end responses) and valuable ancillary information (e.g., body language in addition to verbal responses) than traditional modes. In many cases, such as in discourse analysis or response-latency studies (Bassili & Scott, 1996; Mulligan et al., 2003; Yan & Tourangeau, 2007), the data of value can only be analyzed from recorded data.

Another benefit of the current, advanced forms of audiovisuals comes from them being computerized and digital. The development of computer-assisted interviewing, in general, and its integration with audiovisual programs, in particular, have, of course, been the conduit for their expanded use in surveys. This means that the audiovisual components can interface with other elements of the survey. For example, on the presentation side it is becoming increasingly possible to artificially generate audio from text in what is known as text-to-speech systems (TTS) (Couper, 2005; Couper, Singer, & Tourangeau, 2004). At the data-collection end, responses are more directly and easily amenable to computerized and quantitative analysis. For example, discourse analysis is done more easily and reliably with CARI and computerized analysis routines than with analog recordings, hand transcriptions, and manual data coding (Kendall & French, 2006). Also, time stamps can be used to measure response latency (Couper, 2005).

One more benefit of audiovisuals is their versatility. Traditional question modes have to narrowly predefine what information is to be collected and in what form it is to be coded and analyzed. Of course, audiovisuals still have to be used to address relevant issues in meaningful ways, but because more information is captured and preserved in its unedited form, it has more utility and can more readily be used for multipurposes and in ways beyond those initially intended. For example, the recordings of collected data can be used for both methodological and substantive purposes. Methodically, CARI can be used as a quality-control device to assess how well interviewers are administering and recording responses to questions and as a cognitive tool to assess questions with the object of improving their design (Bassili & Scott, 1996). Substantively, CARI can be used to capture fuller responses to open-ended questions, including preserving natural language, and to record precise verbal responses for detailed discourse analysis (Bauer & Gaskell, 2000; Schober & Bloom, 2004).

Cautions Involving Audiovisuals

While the gains of using audiovisuals in surveys are clear and compelling, their use does raise a number of cautions. First, there will be mode effects (Hecht, Corman, & Miller-Rassulo, 1993; Muller & Scott, 1984; Tourangeau & Smith, 1996, 1998; Trapl, 2007). Questions using audiovisual stimuli will certainly produce different results than analogous measures not using audiovisuals or using only more limited forms such as real, still photographs. These differences are not necessarily a problem, especially if the enhanced, audiovisual measures are more reliable and valid. However, their improved measurement capacity has to be proven, not merely assumed. In addition, for trends analysis, the mode differences are especially problematic. Since the use of advanced audiovisuals in surveys has been limited to date, the mode effect of various different versions is largely unknown. For example, do people respond to computer graphics differently than real images? What is the difference between color and black-and-white presentations? What difference does accents and gender make in audio recordings?

Second, at the data-collection end privacy is a major concern. Recording respondent's faces and voices not only means that more identifying information beyond such traditional identifiers as name, telephone number, and/or birth date are being stored, but that detailed, verbatim responses to specific and possibly sensitive questions are being preserved. These increased privacy issues mean respondents must be fully informed of the risks involved and give explicit consent to the audiovisual recordings and that the survey researchers must have strict security protocols to prevent the disclosure of the identifying recordings.

Third, surveys are already complicated endeavors involving such experts as sampling statisticians, survey methodologists, substantive specialists, data-collection managers, and quantitative analysts. Major use of audiovisuals necessitates the adding of experts in these technologies (Couper, 2005) and, if staged presentations were being used, of working with directors and thespians (Rasinski et al., 1999; McKinlay et al., 2006).

Fourth, with more detailed audio and/or visual information being collected, both the coding and analysis of data become more difficult. While more information is clearly a positive, simpler approaches may be better, quicker, and less costly in some cases.

Finally, while the basic technological issues such as programming, sound and visual quality, and backing up recorded data have been adequately worked out at both the presentation and data-collection ends, such technical matters still need careful consideration and testing. The more complicated a survey application is, the more development effort is needed to "debug" it and field test it under real-world conditions. Moreover, even when technologically sound, extra challenges are inherent in using these approaches. For example, CAPI interview files are usually transmitted by interviewers back to the central office over the Internet. Since CARI can enormously increase the size of interview files, this can create a problem especially when interviewers have only slow Web-connectivity and/or when whole interviews are recorded.

In addition, one must also be cautious about the different varieties of audiovisuals and what differences they may make. For example, the use of either computer-morphed, actual images or entirely computer-generated images has both advantages and disadvantages over using real images. One potential advantage of using computer-generated graphics is the minimization of unintentional variance. For example, much social-science research wants to compare how respondents evaluate different types of people that vary among other things in terms of race, gender, and age. Thus, job discrimination studies want to determine to what extent race is a factor in hiring decisions. This is often examined by having applicants who are "identical" on all relevant attributes except race and then finding out whether one race is treated more or less favorably than others. With real-world recordings, it is very difficult to match the applicants on all their nonracial attributes such as height, body mass, voice, eagerness, and well-spokenness. With computer-imaging, all factors beside racial features can be more easily held constant. Similarly, computerized voice-generation and modification techniques can be used to change accents, volume, timbre, pitch, and other vocal traits while visuals, if any were used, are held constant. Another advantage is that machine-generated images may be less expensive to prepare than actual visuals involving actors, sets, etc.

Probably the largest potential disadvantage is that computerized images are still recognizable as virtual rather than real. While there is some evidence that people may process and respond to computer-generated and real images in a similar manner, this is far from established (Couper, 2002, 2005). Thus, there is less face validity for survey questions using the virtual rather than the actual.

Future

Several factors are encouraging audiovisual expansion in the near future. First, the computing power and versatility of laptops will continue to advance as will Internet-based applications. While so far the use of audiovisuals in Internet-based surveys has primarily been on the stimulus side, the expansion of voice over Internet protocol (VOIP), webcams, and related devices will increasingly make their use at the data-collection side practical.

Second, their use will migrate from the cutting edge to the standard-product center; a transition that is already well along for CARI and audio-CASI. For example, most CAPI programs can readily handle CARI additions and in the future CAPI programs are likely to have CARI as an integrated option. Other audiovisual uses will diffuse in a similar manner. In general, the pattern is to have the new technologies developed by industry leaders like NORC and RTI and then to spread into more general use by other data collectors.

Third, while stimulus and data-collection usages have essentially been separate to date, there is nothing that necessitates this. It is already possible to have survey questions that both contain audiovisual presentations and capture verbal and visual responses.

Finally, since the audiovisuals are digitized and computer driven, they can be easily used in versatile and powerful ways. McKinlay et al. (2006, 2007) of course, already have used a factorial-vignette design. In the standard factorial-vignette approach, key elements of the question such as the gender, race, and educational level of the referent person are randomly varied across subsamples. With the new audiovisual applications, the randomization can be extended to varying the sounds and images. For example, the vignettes can portray people of different genders and races and/or with different accents. Not yet adopted, but already entirely practical with existing equipment and programs is the use of interactive, audiovisual presentations (Couper, 2005). For example, item-response-theory (IRT) techniques could be utilized to decide which follow-up audiovisual items would be administered based on responses to the earlier IRT items. Similarly, in an audio-video display a respondent could be presented with an argument for a particular position. Then the respondent would evaluate the argument by agreeing or disagreeing with the advocated position and/or assessing the strength of the presented case. In response to those evaluations, the respondent could then be given selected follow-up audio-video arguments. These might be counter-arguments to try and dissuade the respondent from supporting the original proposition or new arguments in favor of the proposal to win over the unpersuaded.

In addition, the audiovisual information can also be used to weight or qualify analysis of the simple-coded responses. For example, response-latency measures can be used to distinguish between fast and slow responders. Similarly, analysis of body language and voice patterns can be used to detect signs of confusion, hesitancy, mendacity, and other response patterns. For example, based on audio and visual cues, responses to sensitive topics could be analyzed by evidence of truthfulness.

In the longer term, developing technologies offer even more possibilities such as the voice-recognition processing of audio survey responses and face recognition and other visual techniques for analyzing the images involving survey responses.

In sum, audiovisual technologies have become a valuable tool in survey research and will increasingly make contributions as innovative technologies are developed and use diffuses to surveys in general. While using audiovisuals at both the stimulus and response-capture phases greatly increases the power and versatility of surveys, it does not make them easier to design or analyze. Developing more complex instruments needs considerable conceptual and technical skills and analyzing the enormous volume and complexity of audio and visual information necessitates extensive data processing and new statistical procedures. Using audiovisuals makes survey research better, but not easier.

References

Arceneaux, T. (2007). Evaluating the computer audio-recorded interviewing (CARI) household wellness study (HWS) field test.

Bassili, J. N., & Scott, B. S. (1996). Response latency as a signal to question problems in survey research. *Public Opinion Quarterly, 60,* 390–399.

Basson, D. (2005). *The effects of digital recording telephone interviews on data quality.* ASA Proceedings of the Joint Statistical Meetings, 3778–3785, Alexandria, VA: American Statistical Association.

Bauer, M. W., & Gaskell, G. (2000). *Qualitative researching with text, image, and sound: A practical handbook.* Thousand Oaks, CA: Sage.

Biemer, P., Herget D., Morton, J., & Willis, G. (2000). The feasibility of monitoring field interview performance using Computer Audio Recorded Interviewing (CARI). Presented at the Survey Research Methods Section, American Statistical Association, Indianapolis.

Cable, D. M., & Judge, T. A. (1997). Interviewers' perceptions of person-organization fit and organizational selection decisions. *Journal of Applied Psychology, 82,* 546–561.

Couper, M. P. (2002). New technologies and survey data collection: Challenges and opportunities. Paper presented to the International Conference on Improving Surveys, August, Copenhagen.

Couper, M. P., Singer, E., & Tourangeau, R. (2003). Understanding the effects of audio-CASI on self-reports of sensitive behavior. *Public Opinion Quarterly, 67,* 385–395.

Couper, M. P., Singer, E., & Tourangeau, R. (2004). Does voice matter? An interactive voice response (IVR) experiment. *Journal of Official Statistics, 20,* 551–570.

Couper, M. P. (2005). Technology trends in survey data collection. *Social Science Computer Review, 23,* 486–501.

Davis, J. A. (1955). Living rooms as symbols of status: A study in social judgment. Unpublished Ph.D. dissertation, Harvard University.

Davis, J. A., Smith, T. W., & Marsden, P. V. (2007). General social survey cumulative codebook: 1972–2006. Chicago: NORC, see www.gss.norc.org.

Edwards, B. et al. (2008, September). *Computer Audio-Recorded Interviewing (CARI): A toll for data quality assessment on comparative surveys.* Paper presented to the International Conference on Social Science Methodology, Naples.

Grogger, J. (2008). Speech patterns and racial wage inequality. Harris School Working Paper 08.13. University of Chicago.

Harris, D. R. (2002). In the eye of the beholder: Observed race and observer characteristics. Research Report 02–522, Population Studies Center, University of Michigan.

Hecht, M. L., Corman, S. R., & Miller-Rassulo, M. (1993). An evaluation of the drug resistance project: A comparison of film versus live performance media. *Health Communications, 5,* 75–88.

Herget, D., Biemer, P., Morton, J., & Sand, K. (2005). *Computer Audio Recorded Interviewing (CARI): Additional feasibility efforts of monitoring field interview performance.* Paper presented at the Federal Conference on Statistical Methods.

Hewett, P. C., Erulkar, A. S., & Mensch, B. S. (2004). The feasibility of computer-assisted survey interviewing in Africa: Experience from two rural districts in Kenya. *Social Science Computing Review, 22,* 319–334.

Hicks, W. et al. (2008, May). *CARI: A tool for improving data quality now and next time.* Paper presented to the American Association for Public Opinion Research, New Orleans.

Kales, H. C. et al. (2005). Effect of race and sex on primary care physicians' diagnosis and treatment of late-life depression. *Journal of the American Geriatrics Society, 53,* 777–784.

Kendall, T., & French, A. (2006). Digital audio archives, computer-enhanced transcripts, and new methods in sociolinguistic analysis. *Digital Humanities,* 110–112.

Krysan, M., & Couper, M. P. (2003). Race in the live and virtual interview: Racial deference, social desirability, and activation effects in attitude surveys. *Social Psychology Quarterly, 66*, 364–383.

Krysan, M. et al. (2005, May). *Disentangling the effects of race and class on residential preferences: Results from a video experiment.* Paper presented to the American Association for Public Opinion Research, Miami Beach.

Levinson, W. et al. (2005). Not all patients want to participate in decision making: A national study of public preferences. *Journal of General Internal Medicine, 20*, 531–535.

Loftus, E. F. (1996). *Eyewitness testimony.* Cambridge, MA: Harvard University Press.

Lorge, I., & Ordan, H. (1945). Trends, survey, and evaluation studies. *Review of Educational Research, 25*, 360–376.

Macintyre, S., & West, P. (2008). Social, developmental, and health correlates of "attractiveness" in adolescence. *Sociology of Health and Illness, 13*, 149–167.

McGee, A. (2007). CARI on NatCen: Using a combination of Computer Assisted Recorded Interviewing (CARI) and behavior coding to measure data quality in the English longitudinal study of ageing (ELSA). *Survey Methods Newsletter, 25*, 9–17.

McKinlay, J. et al. (2006). How do doctors in different countries manage the same patient? Results from a factorial experiment. *Health Services Research, 41*, 2182–2200.

McKinlay, J. et al. (2007). Sources of variation in physician adherence with clinical guidelines: Results from a factorial experiment. *Journal of General Internal Medicine, 22*, 289–296.

Muller, E. J., & Scott, T. B. (1984). A comparison of film and written presentations used for pregroup training experiences. *Journal for Specialists in Group Work, 9*, 122–126.

Mulligan, K. et al. (2003). Response latency methodology for survey research: Measurement and modeling strategies. *Political Analysis, 11*, 289–301.

Nelson, S. C. et al., (2007). Computer Audio Recorded Interviewing (CARI): Maximizing audio quality. Unpublished NORC report.

Rasinski, K. A. et al., (1999). Methods of data collection, perceptions of risks and losses, and motivation to give truthful answers to sensitive survey questions. *Applied Cognitive Psychology, 13*, 465–484.

Renker, P. R., & Tonkin, P. (2007). Postpartum women's evaluations of an audio/video computer-assisted prenatal violence screen. *CIN, 25*, 139–147.

Schober, M. F., & Bloom, J. E. (2004). Discourse cues that respondents have misunderstood survey questions. *Discourse Processes, 38*, 287–308.

Sokolowski, J., Daquilanea, J., & Fennell, K. (2008, March). *Computer-Assisted Recorded Interviewing (CARI) developments at NORC: Recordings as a source of paradata for management.* Paper presented at the Federal Computer-Assisted Survey Information Collection (FedCASIC) Conference, Washington, DC.

Southwell, B. G. (2005). Between messages and people. *Communication Research, 32*, 112–140.

Suchman, L., & Jordon, B. (1990). Interactional trouble in face-to-face interviews. *Journal of the American Statistical Society, 85*, 232–241.

Thissen, M. R., & Rodriguez, G. (2004). *Recording interview sound bites through Blaise instruments.* Paper presented at the International Blaise Users' Conference, Ottawa, CA.

Thissen, R., Sattaluri, S., McFarlane, E. S., & Biemer, P. (2007, May). *Evolution of audio recording in field surveys.* Paper presented at the American Association for Public Opinion Research Conference, Anaheim, CA.

Tourangeau, R., & Smith, T. W. (1996). Asking sensitive questions: The impact of data collection mode, question format, and question content. *Public Opinion Quarterly, 60*, 275–304.

Tourangeau, R., & Smith, T. W. (1998). Collecting sensitive information with different modes of data collection. In Couper, M. P., Baker, R. P., Bethlehelm, J., Clark, C. Z., Martin, J., Nicholls II, W. L., and O'Reilly, J. M. (Eds.), *Computer assisted survey information collection.* New York: John Wiley & Sons.

Trapl, E. S. (2007). Understanding adolescent survey responses: Impact of mode and other characteristics of data outcomes and quality. Unpublished Ph.D. dissertation, Case Western Reserve University.

Valentino, N. A., Hutchings, V. L., & White, I. K. (2002). Cues that matter: How political ads prime racial attitudes during campaigns. *American Political Science Review*, *96*, 75–90.

Wrenn-Yorker, C., & Thissen, M. R. (2005, March). *Computer Audio Recorded Interviewing (CARI) technology*. Paper presented at the Federal Computer-Assisted Survey Information Collection (FedCASIC) Conference, Washington, DC.

Yan, T., & Tourangeau, R. (2007). Fast times and easy questions: The effects of age, experience, and question complexity on Web survey response times. *Applied Cognitive Psychology*, *22*, 51–68.

Chapter 20

The Use of Mixed Methods Thinking in Documentary Development

John W. Creswell and Bernard Rogers McCoy

The Use of Mixed Methods Thinking in Documentary Development

As interest expands in mixed methods research, new applications are appearing for its use. Interest has developed in applying it in different disciplines, including studies in social psychology, social work, psychology, nursing, family medicine, health services research, and organizational studies (Creswell, 2010). Furthermore, mixed methods research has attracted world-wide attention with published reports from Sri Lanka (Nastasi et al., 2007), Germany (Bernardi, Keim, & von der Lippe, 2007), Japan (Fetters, Yoshioka, Greenberg, Gorenfo, & Yeo, 2007), the United Kingdom (O'Cathain, Murphy, & Nicholl, 2007), and other countries around the world. By adding mixed methods procedures to existing designs, researchers are able to conduct case studies (Luck, Jackson, & Usher, 2006), experiments (Sandelowski, 1996), and narrative studies (Elliot, 2005).

A new application for mixed methods research is in the area of visual methods, specifically in the development of documentaries. For example, in Nobel Laureate Al Gore's award-winning documentary, *An Inconvenient Truth*, the inclusion of individual stories about global warming as well as trends and statistical data about the changing climate are used, thereby illustrating the increasing use of mixed methods in more visual modes of research (http://www.climatecrisis.net/aboutthefilm/). Another example is Michael Moore's documentary, *Bowling for Columbine*. Moore's examination of gun violence in the United States takes its audience from a look at the security camera tapes in the Columbine High School massacre to the home of Oscar-winning NRA President Charlton Heston, from a young man who makes homemade napalm to the murder of a 6-year-old girl by another 6-year-old. Moore also injects gun violence, gun ownership, and gun purchase statistics from the United States, Canada, and other foreign countries into his documentary. (http://www.bowlingforcolumbine.com/about/synopsis.php)

Less obvious, however, is how both qualitative and quantitative forms of data are combined to provide a story line for documentaries. The basic idea behind mixed methods research is that the inquirer thoughtfully combines both qualitative and quantitative data, and uses design principles to inform this combination. Indeed, a recent development in the mixed methods literature is to consider mixed methods more than simply a combination of "methods." It is also combining multiple perspectives that, in combination, provide a better understanding than a single method (i.e., qualitative or quantitative alone) (Greene, 2007). Indeed, mixed methods becomes more than "methods" but also a way of thinking about (and visualizing) the social world.

This chapter explores the use of mixed methods thinking in documentaries. We begin with an overview of mixed methods research, the elements of qualitative and quantitative research in this approach, and the design possibilities being discussed within mixed methods literature. To illustrate how documentary developers might incorporate both mixed methods design and data elements, we then turn to an award-winning documentary, *Breaking Down Barriers* (College of Journalism and Mass Communications, University of Nebraska-Lincoln, Lincoln, Nebraska) to illustrate the implicit mixed methods design used in its development and the inclusion of elements of qualitative and quantitative data. Based on this analysis, we end with recommendations for incorporating mixed methods thinking into documentary development.

Data Elements and Designs in Mixed Methods Research

The core idea of mixed methods research is to collect, analyze, and combine qualitative and quantitative data in a single study (or sustained program of inquiry) to best understand a research problem (Creswell, 2009a). The central assumption is that the use of both forms of data provides a better understanding of the problem than either qualitative or quantitative data alone. This better understanding comes from the collection of more evidence, the strengths each form of evidence provide (detailed, contextually situated qualitative data and trends, generalizable quantitative data), and the evidence of stories of individuals (qualitative) as well as the frequency and magnitude of numbers (quantitative). During its 20-year history, mixed methods has increasingly become a stand-alone research methodology and has experienced increased legitimacy as a methodology alongside more traditional approaches such as surveys, experiments, and ethnographies. Central to mixed methods is that the researcher collects and analyzes both qualitative and quantitative data and integrates the two databases (Creswell & Plano Clark, 2011).

At a general level, these two forms of data might be differentiated as qualitative text data (i.e., word) or image data (i.e., pictures) versus quantitative numeric data (Creswell & Plano Clark, 2011). Another distinction views the differences in scoring data. Qualitative data, such as interview data, are considered to be open-ended in that the researcher, when collecting such data, does not have predetermined response categories into which the responses are assigned. Alternatively, quantitative data, such as information collected on surveys or questionnaires, is scored using closed-ended items with predetermined response categories. Qualitative data types are continually evolving, but they might be characterized as open-ended interviews, open-ended observations, documents (e.g., diaries, minutes of meetings), and visual methods (e.g., pictures, videos, relics). Quantitative data, on the other hand, are collected on instruments (e.g., surveys), behavioral checklists (e.g., observing behavior and then checking response categories), and found in documents such as census reports and attendance records. However, the distinctions between the forms may not be apparent. For example, interview data may be collected using both open-ended questions and responses as well as closed-ended questions in which the researcher checks responses off on a predetermined scale. But for purposes of our

Table 20.1 A comparison of qualitative, quantitative data elements in research*

Criteria of differences	Qualitative	Quantitative
Focus	Particularity	Generality
Understanding sought	Meaning	Causality
Type of participants	Unusual	Representative
Relationship of researcher to participants	Closeness	Distance
Type of evidence gathered	Social construction	Observations and measurement
Analysis of the data	Diversity within the range integrated synthesis	Central tendency of the mean Componential analysis
Whose viewpoint counts	Insider viewpoint—dialogue	Outsider viewpoint
Who holds expertise	Practical wisdom of participant	Expert knowledge of researcher
Picture of interest	Micro	Macro

*Adapted from Greene & Caracelli (1997).

discussion, it is helpful to see the two forms of data as distinct, yet supportive, when they appear in documentaries.

Another helpful distinction is to consider that there are elements of qualitative research typically distinct from elements of quantitative research. Greene and Caracelli (1997) have made the claim that an alternative set of characteristics is associated with knowledge claims associated with postpositivism and interpretivism (see Table 20.1). These, in turn, are often associated with quantitative and qualitative methods, respectively. These will be used in this way in our discussion of Table 20.1. It should also be noted that we view these differences not as opposites or dichotomies, but rather as different ends on continua. Moreover, also shown in Table 20.1, we have added the column of criteria of differences to the original table advanced by Greene and Caracelli (1997) so that the elements could be related to the process of research that spans from the broader introduction to a study (i.e., focus, understanding) and onto data collection (i.e., participants), analysis, and the larger picture developed (i.e., macro and micro). Characteristics of the tendency toward knowledge claims associated with qualitative and quantitative are detailed in many texts (e.g., Creswell, 2008; Fowler, 2002; Marshall & Rossman, 2006).

The focus of qualitative research is typically on the particular, a specific place, group of people, or setting, whereas in quantitative research, the focus is on the general, such as a population, common places where people gather (e.g., markets), or issues experienced by many people (e.g., immigrants). By studying these places or people, the researcher seeks to understand a research problem. In qualitative research, the inquirer looks for the meaning ascribed to the problem or issue by the participants being studied. In quantitative research, the investigator looks for causality, which identifies the factors that influence an outcome. The participants providing information also differ. In qualitative research, the inquirer asks questions of individuals who can provide insight into the problem. For example, this may mean interviewing unusual individuals that may not be representative of those thought to provide the best information. In quantitative research, the investigator chooses to study individuals who are representative of the overall population, since the intent is to generalize the findings from a sample to a population. The relationship between the researcher and the participants may differ: in qualitative research, the inquirer goes into the setting to study individuals. Often, a close relationship is forged between the inquirer and those being studied. In quantitative research, a distance is built by the researcher into the relationship. The idea is for the researcher to be impartial and objective. Thus, by sending out an impersonal survey by mail, the researcher has created distance with the participants; in the same sense, the experimental researcher creates standardized procedures so that researcher bias does not enter into the experiment.

Differences also appear in the data gathering and analysis procedures. In qualitative research, the evidence gathered explores the meaning individuals ascribe to a phenomenon. This information is often socially constructed, in that meaning is derived by individuals interacting with each other and sharing their meaning. In quantitative research, the investigator seeks to measure specific variables and constructs and isolates the concepts that can be measured successfully (i.e., valid and reliable measures). Analysis of the data for the qualitative researcher takes the form of looking for diverse perspectives. The more perspectives there are from different individuals and different sources, the more successful the qualitative project. Also, reporting these diverse perspectives need to be brought together into a complex whole—an integrated synthesis of view. Thus, one finds that qualitative reports provide an expansive view of a problem by mapping the diverse factors that influence the central issue being explored. Rather than developing such a broad picture of the issue, the quantitative researcher proceeds in the opposite direction, to reduce the information down to its essence. A focus on the central tendency of the mean provides such a perspective, as well as analyzing each variable one by one or by comparing groups. This fulfills a componential analysis of analyzing the parts. Also, during this analysis, the question develops as to whose viewpoint counts and who holds expertise to provide information. For the qualitative researcher, the participants' views count the most, and thus it is important to share specific quotes from individuals in the results. By using open-ended questions, the researcher defers to the participant to construct the story, a participant with good practical wisdom. Alternatively, in quantitative research, the investigator holds immense power and influence through the identification of theories, the selection of variables, and the choice of measurement instruments. The researcher serves as the expert and, in many ways, directs the study. Finally, the picture assembled by the researcher differs between qualitative and quantitative research. The qualitative researcher, having studied a specific setting and reporting individual voices as well as detail, constructs a micro analysis of the research problem. The reader of such a study learns through the detail presented in the report. Alternatively, the quantitative researcher develops an explanation of broad trends, thereby assembling a macro picture for the reader. Whereas the qualitative researcher goes down deep, the quantitative researcher constructs a broad, panoramic view.

In tandem, both qualitative and quantitative pictures provide a more complex understanding than either picture alone. This understanding is driven by the synergistic pairing of objective information (quantitative research) with more subjective and powerful elements of human emotion and experience (qualitative research). The challenge in this method, however, is determining how to assemble the qualitative and quantitative elements in a study. Those involved in mixed methods designs have addressed this issue in recent years, making progress in the development of different forms of mixed methods designs. A number of authors from different social and human science disciplines have offered classifications or typologies of mixed methods designs (see Creswell & Plano Clark, 2011). For purposes of our discussion of mixed methods designs and documentaries, it is helpful to discuss five basic types.

Concurrent mixed methods designs. The basic idea of a concurrent (also called a triangulation or parallel) design is to collect both qualitative and quantitative data separately, to analyze each data individually, and then to merge or bring together the two databases. The intent of this design is that each form of data brings a different picture to the study, with the results that a more complete understanding emerges from collecting, analyzing, and integrating the two forms of data. In this design, the two forms of data are collected concurrently or at nearly the same time. Thus, it is often an efficient design in which the researcher visits the field once and collects data. Also, the amount of information can vary with more qualitative data collected than quantitative, or vice versa. In documentary development, the two forms of data can be brought together in a unified story line in which, for example, qualitative interview data are combined with quantitative official studies reporting numbers.

Exploratory sequential mixed methods designs. These designs differ from the concurrent design in that the data are collected sequentially. In order to explore the problem of interest, the researcher first collects qualitative data and analyses it (in phase one). The qualitative findings then help to inform phase two of quantitative data collection. In short, one phase builds upon another. Furthermore, the researcher cannot begin a study by collecting quantitative data with specific theories, variables, and measures because these are not known in advance of the study. With certain populations and groups of people, these theories and measures are simply not known. Thus, a need exists to begin the study by exploring qualitative data collection in an open-ended manner. Though the amount of qualitative and quantitative information can vary in this type of design, the initial qualitative phase typically contains the most information and is given emphasis by the researcher in the study. Applied to documentary development, an exploratory sequential design would involve initial exploration of the topic through individual interviews in order to explore the issues and then build into a follow-up phase in which quantitative data such as official reports are incorporated to indicate general trends that support the interview data.

Explanatory sequential mixed methods design. This design is the same type as the exploratory design except that instead of beginning the study with qualitative data collection followed by quantitative data collection, the investigator reverses the sequence and begins with quantitative data collection. The intent of this type of data collection is to use follow-up qualitative data (in second phase) to help explain the initial quantitative results (in the first phase). The initial quantitative phase yields important results, though they are only general and not explanatory. As with the exploratory design, the amount of information collected at each phase can differ. Typically, however, the priority is given to the initial quantitative phase with a minor follow-up qualitative phase. Applied to documentary development, the documentary would start with quantitative pie charts, trend graphs, and official statistics, and then move on to individual interviews in which individuals give testimony to the accuracy of the quantitative data. In this way, the viewer sees both the broad trends and the specific evidence that give the trends authenticity.

An embedded mixed methods design. This type of design might be seen as a meta-design incorporating the above types of concurrent and sequential designs. The intent of this design is to use the procedures of collecting, analyzing, and integrating both qualitative and quantitative data and to embed these mixed methods procedures within traditional designs. Thus, mixed methods procedures are being used within existing experimental designs, within narrative studies, within ethnographies, within case studies, and other types of design. To illustrate this example, assume that the documentary illustrates a multiple case study of four immigrant groups to the United States. A story line is developed by the documentary writer in which both qualitative personal interviews and quantitative comparisons are made of different types of immigrant groups. The writer includes these two data sources as merged by merging them within the case analysis of each immigrant group or by having one type of data build on the other to present case analyses of each group. This form of a documentary may be seen as a traditional case study involving both qualitative and quantitative data.

Transformative mixed methods design. This type of design can include all of the above possibilities of design. The intent is to provide an overarching transformative lens onto the process of mixed methods research (see Mertens, 2009). Transformative means that the overall intent of the study is to encourage a transformation or improvement in the lives of underrepresented groups in our society, such as women, ethnic and racial groups, the disabled, gays, or lesbians. The researcher uses the transformative lens in all phases of the research project. It becomes an orienting device to specify the type of issue being explored (e.g., the marginalization of women), frame the research questions in a directional manner (e.g., are women treated unequally (as compared to men) in the workplace?), shape ethical considerations in data collection (e.g., will the data collection procedure serve to further marginalize the women?), and suggest an agenda for action as a distinct outcome of the study (e.g., improved salaries for women) (Mertens, 2003, 2009). In a documentary, this design would involve using a transformative lens throughout the project, including beginning with an issue of an underrepresented group and posing advocacy-type questions that implore change at the end of the documentary. Further, qualitative and quantitative data would be inserted into the story line either in a concurrent fashion where both forms of data provide evidence for the story or in a sequential fashion in which one form of data builds upon the other.

The Documentary, *Breaking Down Barriers*

How specifically would the elements of qualitative and quantitative data and a mixed methods design be used in a documentary? We choose the documentary *Breaking Down Barriers* as an example because it contains both qualitative and quantitative elements, illustrates one of the mixed methods designs, and has won awards for excellence.

This documentary was developed in 2007 by four students (Rachel Anderson, Megan Carrick, Justin Peterson, and Chris Welch) in the field of journalism at the University of Nebraska-Lincoln. In 2006, these students had chosen to focus on issues of immigration between Germany and the United States by examining educational opportunities afforded to immigrants in both countries. The four students traveled to Germany to interview Turkish immigrants about their experiences in German society. The students also interviewed sociologists, politicians, community leaders, educators, and citizens about Turkish immigrants in Germany. In the United States, they interviewed Latino immigrants as well as sociologists, politicians, community leaders, educators, and citizens about these immigrants. As the students worked to gain the trust of the immigrants whose lives and families they chronicled, they found that people from different cultures mutually benefited by working and communicating with each other. The students also discovered that people can find better ways to break down barriers of ethnic perception that often divide them. In 2008, *Breaking Down Barriers* won a number of prominent college journalism competitions, including the Robert F. Kennedy Journalism Award. This award honors the outstanding reporting of the lives and strife of disadvantaged people throughout the world.

Developing the documentary. A documentary is a form of visual methods which has been used in social science research (Banks, 2001; Mertens, 2009; Pink, 2007; Rose, 2007; Stanczak, 2007). For example, the visual and participatory methodologies (e.g., photovoice and video documentaries) are currently being used to explore the issue of HIV/AIDS in rural South Africa (see http://cvm.za.org/ hosted by the University of KwaZulu-Natal in South Africa). Representations such as these often tell a story of individual struggle or an issue in society. Documentaries often follow the classic story construction of three acts: the situation, the conflict, and the resolution (Personal communication with Joel Geyer, December, 2008). Rabiger (2004) uses the analogy that a documentary presents information for an audience to consider in much the same way that evidence is presented to a jury. One approach to documentary development is the "diamond" style:

> A package not only should start strong, it needs to end strong. . . . This might be called the diamond approach with a beginning or top tip that introduces a problem by finding a person who has it and serves as the story's "main character." The middle or center of the diamond explores and explains the problem and offers expert comments and information on it. Then the bottom tip of the diamond or end refers back to the main character, the person and the problem at the heart of this story, and concludes with some information and picture you want the audience to carry away from the piece. (Kolodzy, 2006, p. 152)

Others have endorsed this "diamond approach" as well (Tuggle, Carr, & Huffman, 2007), and it bears a strong resemblance to a qualitative-quantitative-qualitative mixed methods approach referred to as a "sandwich" model of design (Sandelowski, 2003). Still, documentarians argue about what a documentary is. Certainly, images have no fixed or single meaning and do not capture an objective reality (Pink, 2007). Co-construction of reality is an important goal for a documentarian, such as in *Breaking Down Barriers*, in which the students sought out interpreters and established rapport with participants in both Germany and the United States.

This 51-min documentary, *Breaking Down Barriers*, was developed through a series of decisions and steps (Personal communication with Bernard McCoy, October, 2008). The students needed to consider how the documentary would be portrayed. This included attention to approach, form, and style. In addition, they also had to develop a shooting schedule which consisted of a timeline for setting up interviews, gathering and recording archival video clips, and taking photographs. The students had one year to complete the project and deliver an edited documentary. They also worked with faculty advisors to solicit funds from German and United States groups and to assemble a working documentary budget. Finally, they had to identify the audience for the documentary, as well as the market for its distribution.

An initial proposal for the documentary was followed by a 3-month script development process. This process included conducting research on the topic, writing a documentary script, and having it reviewed, accepted, and modified by faculty project supervisors. Preproduction included continuing script development, making contacts, setting up interviews, preparing interview questions, and coordinating travel logistics. Next, the documentarians went into the field and over a 5-month period videotaped interviews and the settings that would be used in the documentary. Students collected roughly 40 hour of videotaped interviews and location shots, along with dozens of archival photographs, for the 51-min documentary. This was followed by logging and editing selected interviews and supporting video into a rough-cut version of the documentary, which helped determine how well the script translated visually to the screen. During the roughly 300 hour editing process, the script and visual content continued to be reviewed and revised as natural sound, interviews, music, and narration were layered in from an approved script. Postproduction consisted of digital "tweaking" of the video and audio, as well as adding titles and credits. The writers then created a close-captioned script for television broadcast. Finally, DVD copies were made for public distribution and screenings.

The story line. The documentary opens in Act One with the Sanchez family, consisting of Antonio and Georgina Sanchez and their three children in Lincoln, Nebraska. A school bus arrives at their home. The Sanchez family had come to the United States from Mexico more than a decade ago and recently migrated from California to Nebraska. The Sanchez's found this move to be beneficial to their empowerment in American society because of better educational and employment opportunities.

From *Breaking Down Barriers*

> Narrator: *"It's move-in day, and the Sanchez's are carrying their lives to a home rich with possibilities. They call it their fulfillment of the American Dream. To get here though, Antonio works two jobs. In addition to his supervising job at a local brick company, he also has a job in the kitchen of a Lincoln country club."*
>
> Antonio Sanchez says: *"The biggest change is the opportunity, if you work hard, you can have whatever you want. Myself, I have to work two jobs to try to support my family. I am thinking that my kids can have a better education. They can have better jobs, and probably live a better quality of life."*

After this opening, and nearly 5,000 miles away, we meet the Erberger family in Berlin, Germany. Like the Sanchez family, the Erberger's are also a family of five and both parents are immigrants. Nuri and his wife, Nur, and children came to Germany from Turkey. We learn that Nuri has adapted to life in Germany by understanding the culture and speaking German at home. But his wife, Nur, has a different story, as she talks about coming to Berlin from Turkey when they married. Much like Georgina Sanchez in the United States, Nur feels like an outsider. As the family's primary care provider, she has less time to learn the German language and to socialize outside her family.

From *Breaking Down Barriers*

Nur Erberger: *"I am a teacher and I left all my friends in Turkey. I want to have German friends, because they are a different culture. But I couldn't do it because of the language. Most of the Turkish people, who are working here, are not really interested in communicating with the German people, or trying to integrate themselves into the society which they are living in. For this reason, I could not communicate with Turkish people here well either."*

Act Two delves more deeply into the dynamics of the immigrant experience. We learn how several native Germans view their immigrant population. We also learn about Germany's three-tiered school system in which most German students' educational futures are decided for them by the age of 10. Top students move into the Gymnasium tier, a path to the universities, while the middle students go to the Realschule tier, leading to universities or good vocational schools. The bottom level students go to the Hauptschule tier, where there are few opportunities for educational advancement. In the German educational system, the immigrant students are often grouped together into the Hauptschule tier.

From *Breaking Down Barriers*

Narrator: *"Being an immigrant student in a Hauptschule is not an enviable position. Many Turkish students go to school already knowing their futures will be less promising than their native German counterparts. Maybe this sense of inferiority is at the root of the unruly behavior in the classrooms."*

Evidence is then brought forward in the documentary from a 2007 United Nations' report that compared the educational performance of immigrant and native students in 17 countries in a graphic. The documentary students chose to present quantitative data at this point because they believed the information came from an independent source that the documentary's audience would consider to be objective and credible. The visual sequence here begins with a graphic of the United Nations' report cover page and transitions into an animated bar chart. As these graphics appear the narrator says the following:

From *Breaking Down Barriers*

Narrator: *"A study by the Program for International Student Assessment, looked at 15-year-olds in 17 developed countries with significant immigrant populations. It found that Germany had one of the widest proficiency gaps between native and immigrant students. The average immigrant student in Germany is two years behind their native counterpart. Compare that to the United States where the proficiency gap between native and immigrant students is just under one year. This report found that Germany had one of the widest proficiency gaps between native and immigrant students. Second generation Turkish immigrants were even further behind that of their first generation parents."*

Act Three looks at educational solutions for immigrants in both Germany and the United States. In Lincoln, Nebraska, and in Berlin, Germany, we are taken into settings in which parent groups have formed to help immigrant families support their children in the schools. We learn about ways in which the German and U.S. governments are helping to improve educational opportunities for immigrant students, especially problems posed by language barriers. We are taken into classrooms at Berlin's Heinrich-Zille elementary school in which German is the only language spoken by native Germans and immigrants alike.

From *Breaking Down Barriers*

Narrator: *"Unlike many mainstream German schools, these students are allowed to embrace their own cultural identity. Heinrich-Zille students come from a wide range of backgrounds and work together to understand each other."*

Heinrich-Zille Principal Inga Hirschmann: *"You have to look at children and what they can do.... It might be something completely different one day. Still, by social needs, there should be a big mixture. Diversity, that's what we believe in."*

We go into another German school, Aziz-Nessin, a so-called "European-style" school in which Turkish students speak both German and Turkish in their classes as they learn alongside their fellow German students. Transitioning back to Nebraska, we visit a public school program known as English Language Learners Program in which immigrants and native students learn together in one classroom, with immigrants receiving additional lessons to help sharpen their English language skills.

The documentary ends by raising one last question, "Can the tolerance and cultural diversity we observed in some of the schools we visited, spread to the rest of society?" From the narrator, we learn that there may be no perfect answer to questions like these, but that solutions are more likely when people communicate and work together with underrepresented and marginalized groups. The narrator continues:

"Could Nebraska schools attempt some of the solutions we saw in Germany for some of our own immigrants? Solutions are being tried here too. Lincoln teachers say they see improvements when they urge immigrant students to embrace their own cultures as they learn more about the language and culture of America. We found that neither country has it all figured out. If we look around us, there are better ways of doing things. But by learning, educating, and communicating, people are capable of working together and breaking down the barriers."

Mixed Methods Thinking in *Breaking Down Barriers*

An analysis of *Breaking Down Barriers* from a mixed methods perspective shows the type of mixed methods design it employs as well as the elements of qualitative and quantitative data. Of the five types of mixed methods designs mentioned earlier, this documentary illustrates the use of a transformative mixed methods design (Mertens, 2009). It began by studying underrepresented and marginalized groups—the Turkish in Germany and the Mexicans in the United States. We learn from the narrator that there were themes of "resistance," that "societies were not open to immigration," and that we need a "wall of acceptance." The interviews of the two families did not further marginalize them because they were conducted in neutral settings to the families, such as their homes, their evening meals in a restaurant, and in local immigrant-oriented school tutoring sessions, markets, and nightclubs. In the end, the documentary advocated for collaborative solutions to help acclimate the immigrants to their new cultural settings through initiatives in parent-student groups, in classrooms, and in policy assessments.

This documentary, however, was more than simply transformative, calling for change. It involved a central story line as found in documentaries (Personal communication with Joel Geyer) supported by both qualitative and quantitative data. A mixed methods interpretation of this documentary showed that the qualitative and quantitative data elements (as presented earlier in Table 20.1) flowed concurrently back and forth throughout the story line. The introduction of both forms of evidence would suggest a "concurrent design" to mixed methods, but with a stronger emphasis on the qualitative data (the interviews, the individual stories, the local settings) than the quantitative data (the statistical charts). Rather than this weaving of qualitative and quantitative together in a "concurrent design," the documentary might have started with the qualitative stories situated in specific settings, and the meaning of being immigrants in another culture. This would then have been followed by an ending with quantitative trends presenting national reports of immigrant issues (an exploratory sequential design). Indeed, there was some semblance of this design—it was 26 min (over half) into the documentary before quantitative numeric data were introduced in the form of the United Nations policy report. Alternatively, the project might have begun with national trend data about immigrants followed by individual stories of families to illustrate some of the trends (an explanatory sequential design). The "diamond" model could also have been used (fitting the "sandwich" mixed methods design model mentioned earlier) in a three-phase project. In this design, the opening of the documentary might have provided a family story to give meaning to being an immigrant (qualitative), followed by tracing the factors influencing stigmatism as an immigrant (quantitative), and ended with stories exploring (qualitatively) the meaning of one or two of these factors. These design options could certainly have been used and with different outcomes and different emphases in the project. Our discussion, however, will trace the most predominant design used in this documentary—a transformative concurrent design—and the elements that provided evidence for this type of mixed methods design.

A closer inspection of the qualitative and quantitative elements as presented in Table 20.1 can illuminate how both forms of data in combination (or concurrently) play important roles in the documentary. As shown in Table 20.2, the elements are stated again, but this time they are applied to specific scenes in the documentary. In terms of focus, there was much detail to suggest a specific qualitative focus. It began with the bus coming down the street and continued on in the documentary by the discussions around kitchen and dining room tables and the Christmas tree, and the use of music indigenous to the Mexican and Turkish cultural groups. A general quantitative focus appeared in the form of the more typical settings in which people of all cultures might gather, such as the general market, the school rooms, or the life of the city at night. In one scene in the Turkish market in Berlin, the person interviewed was not a Turk but a German man who commented on the novelty of the market.

Table 20.2 Elements found in *Breaking Down Barriers*

Criteria of differences	Qualitative	Qualitative elements in documentary	Quantitative	Quantitative elements in documentary
Focus	Particularity	Focus on details of bus, street, home table, Christmas tree, local music	Generality	Focus on general markets, schools, city life
Understanding sought	Meaning	Stories of individuals (their lives, history)	Causality	Identifying factors that influence acculturation
Type of Participants	Unusual	Turks in Germany Mexicans in the United States	Representative	Immigrants
Relationship of Researcher to Participants	Closeness	Video camera Personal interviews in homes	Distance	Language interpreters
Type of Evidence gathered	Social construction	Families interacting Symbols of flags	Observations and measurement	Bar chart
Analysis of the data	Diversity within the range	Multiple individuals tell	Central tendency of the mean	Trends over time
	Integrated synthesis	their stories Different contexts being explored (home, school)	Componential analysis	Comparison of Mexicans in the United States with Turks in Germany Comparison of religions
Whose viewpoint counts	Insider viewpoint	Dialogue of interviews	Outsider viewpoint	Narrator narrating a story
Who holds expertise	Practical wisdom of participant	Individual stories (children, teachers, officials)	Expert knowledge of researcher	Narrator framed the final questions
Picture of interest	Micro	Individual lives of two families	Macro	Immigrant experiences

The documentary developers sought out qualitative meaning by including many stories told by individuals of the Sanchez family and the Erberger family. Meaning was constructed through individual perspectives involving both words and emotion. However, the viewer learns as well about causality, such as the factors that influence bringing immigrants into the dominant culture via parent groups, classroom approaches, and policy recommendations.

The participants were both unusual and representative. In Germany, one does not immediately consider the unusual presence of a Turkish population, although through the documentary we learn why they came to Germany as laborers. In the United States, the Mexicans would be considered an underrepresented group. In both countries, the immigrants are studied as representative minority populations within other cultures. As immigrants, both the Turkish and Mexicans were looking for better opportunities that they believed existed in their adopted countries.

The relationship between the interviewers and the interviewees may have been characterized as close to a degree, since on the one hand, it was as close as the cameras of the researchers who entered the homes of the individuals who panned up close to faces and recorded personal stories. Also, there may have been distance built into the documentary between the interpreters and the student researchers because of multiple languages (Spanish Turkish and German) used by the participants. Throughout, one is conscious of a narrator telling a story, perhaps even imposing a view of the scenes and creating somewhat of a distant narrative for the listener.

The evidence provided had both qualitative and quantitative elements. People were talking around the table and sharing their stories in a manner of the social construction of meaning. The flags of Germany and the United States were shown as symbols of different meanings. On the other hand, when the documentary referred to the United Nation's policy statement, an animated bar chart was constructed to measure the differences in learning performance between immigrants and natives in Germany and the United States. As we consider the manner in which the evidence was analyzed and presented, we see many diverse qualitative perspectives presented from children, parents, group leaders, policy-makers, school officials, and interpreters. From a qualitative synthesis standpoint, we have a larger picture assembled by the time the documentary ends: a synthesis of many perspectives all focused on what it means to be an immigrant in another culture. On the other hand, we were also conscious of the quantitative presentation of trends over time (e.g., as the historical portrait of Turks in Germany unfolded), the continual quantitative comparison of different groups both religious as well as demographic, such as the Mexicans versus Turkish, and the comparison of two different regions of the world (Germany and the United States). In the documentary, the United States is portrayed as an ethnic melting pot for immigrants who feel they may be integrated into the culture without sacrificing their identity. In contrast, Germany is portrayed as more stagnant in which most Turks feel that they have to "assimilate" or sacrifice their identity in order to be accepted into the majority culture.

In this documentary, we also saw that individual stories were important while the story line was being told by a narrator. Who, in the end, held the expertise? It seemed to be a blend of the many individuals interviewed and the narrator, but, in the end, it was the narrator who raised the final questions. Still, we see the micro picture of individual lives—people and their families—in two different cultural settings allowing us to gain a profound perspective of the macro situation of immigrants.

Discussion

We learned that the documentary *Breaking Down Barriers* had both a transformative element of mixed methods research in advocating for the transformation of the lives of immigrants. This advocacy assumed the form of studying underrepresented groups, posing questions of resistance and acceptance, gathering data in a respectful way, and calling for change. The documentary also had strong elements of a concurrent mixed methods design in which both the qualitative and the quantitative elements were interwoven and flowed back and forth. Unquestionably, in this flow, the qualitative data in the form of stories and context weighed more heavily in the design than the quantitative data. But this type of design is only one possibility, and others, including a "diamond" approach going from qualitative to quantitative and back to qualitative, might have been used.

Regardless of the design, this documentary showed evidence of both qualitative and quantitative elements in the focus of the study, how understanding was obtained, the data collection and analysis of information from participants in the study, and in the overall picture assembled. Our analysis is undoubtedly limited to this one documentary, the data elements of qualitative and quantitative approaches derived from Greene and Caracelli (1997), and to our interpretive stance toward the documentary as a faculty advisor to the project and as one familiar with the various design possibilities in mixed methods research. It should also be noted that the documentary developers did not intend to incorporate a mixed methods design within the project. Only after-the-fact did we as researchers distill the type of design that "fit" the documentary.

Regardless of these limitations, we have specific recommendations that surfaced from this study for incorporating mixed methods thinking into documentary development:

1. Include in the plans and proposals for a documentary two lists—the qualitative data sources to be included as well as the quantitative data sources so that the alternative data sources can be made explicit. Consider that the quantitative numbers can give credence to the qualitative stories—a synergy. Hall and Howard (2008) advance a synergistic approach in which two or more options interact so that their combined effect is greater than the sum of the individual parts.

2. Consider the full array of mixed methods design possibilities early in the development of the documentary process. Weigh the advantages of each based on their intent as indicated in this discussion. The design possibilities should not be limited to two phases (as in the exploratory sequential design with a qualitative first phase and a quantitative secondary phase), but it might include more than two phases that would resemble the "diamond" sandwich model.

3. Draw out a visual (a story board) of the procedures of flow of qualitative and quantitative data in the documentary. The use of visual procedures has become well-accepted within the mixed methods literature (Creswell & Plano Clark, 2011). This visual approach can help others critique and review the flow of activities and the types of data in a documentary proposal. Story boards also offer unique visual context. They help documentary producers recognize and generate visual ideas and perspective that textual outlines may miss.

4. Documentarians need to be open to changing the presentation of qualitative and quantitative data based on the strength of the information gathered. A strong interview or story character can create a powerful emotional impact or statement which appeals to the viewer's heart and mind in ways quantitative research cannot.

5. Consider in the mixed methods field other uses for mixed methods thinking in the use of visual methods. How would this thinking apply to the use of photograph elicitation techniques (Banks, 2001), innovative visual methods such

as the idea of human imagination and dreams as sites for ethnographic fieldwork (Pink, 2007), or where the research site is a "virtual" site on the Internet (Hine, 2000)? In this study, the visual medium consisted of a documentary. How would mixed methods approaches be similar or different if the thinking were applied to television news reporting, to advertisements, to newspaper story development, or to short story plot construction? The applications of mixed methods to visual and print media seem endless.

With this beginning of a link between visual methods and documentaries, new sites for applying mixed methods will undoubtedly emerge. Mixed methods may be viewed not as only a method or methodology, but also as a "way of thinking" or perceiving everyday life. This "thinking" would go beyond simply viewing mixed methods as data—stories (qualitative) or trends (quantitative)—but it would expand into how understandings are derived (such as by meaning or causality) or how understandings are shaped by proximity of closeness or distance. A Native American healer might be seen as having both practical wisdom (qualitative) and expert knowledge (quantitative). Two commentators at a sporting event—a "color" commentator and a "play-by-play" commentator—would be an instance in everyday sporting life of qualitative and quantitative mixed methods thinking. The connection made between visual materials and mixed methods made in this chapter is but a point of departure for such thinking. Hopefully, this discussion will encourage mixed methods writers to consider new applications in visual methods and support documentary developers as they systematically include both qualitative and quantitative data in their project designs.

References

Banks, M. (2001). *Visual methods in social research*. London: Sage.

Bernardi, L., Keim, S., & von der Lippe, H. (2007). Social influences on fertility: A comparative mixed methods study in Eastern and Western Germany. *Journal of Mixed Methods Research, 1,* 23–47.

College of Journalism and Mass Communications. Lincoln, Nebraska: University of Nebraska-Lincoln, *Breaking Down Barriers*, September 5, 2007.

Creswell, J. W. (2008). *Educational research: Planning, conducting, and evaluating quantitative and qualitative research* (3rd ed.). Upper Saddle River, NJ: Pearson.

Creswell, J. W. (2009a). *Research design: Qualitative, quantitative, and mixed methods approaches*. (3rd ed.). Thousand Oaks, CA: Sage.

Creswell, J. W. (2009b). Mapping the field of mixed methods research. Editorial. *Journal of Mixed Methods Research, 3,* 95–108.

Creswell, J. W. (2010). Mapping the developing landscape of mixed methods research. In Tashakkori, A., & Teddlie, C. (Eds.). *SAGE handbook of mixed methods in social & behavioral research, (pp. 45-68)*. Thousand Oaks, CA: Sage.

Creswell, J. W., & Plano Clark, V. L. (2011). *Designing and conducting mixed methods research* (2nd ed.). Thousand Oaks, CA: Sage.

Elliot, J. (2005). *Using narrative in social research: Qualitative and quantitative approaches*. London: Sage.

Fetters, M., Yoshioka, T., Greenberg, G. M., Gorenfo, D. W., & Yeo, S. (2007). Advance consent in Japanese during prenatal care for epidural anesthesia during childbirth. *Journal of Mixed Methods Research, 1,* 333–365.

Fowler, F. J. (2002). *Survey research methods* (3rd ed.). Thousand Oaks, CA: Sage.

Greene, J. C. (2007). *Mixed methods in social inquiry*. San Francisco: Jossey-Bass.

Greene, J. C., & Caracelli, V. J. (1997). Defining and describing the paradigm issue in mixed-method evaluation. In Greene, J. C., & Caracelli, V. J. (Eds.), *Advances in mixed-method evaluation: The challenges and benefits of integrating diverse paradigm* (pp. 5–17. San Francisco: Jossey-Bass.

Hall, B., & Howard, K. (2008). A synergistic approach: Conducting mixed methods research with typological and systemic design considerations. *Journal of Mixed Methods Research*, 2, 248–269.

Hine, C. M. (2000). *Virtual ethnography*. London: Sage.

Kolodzy, J. (2006). *Convergence journalism: Writing and reporting across the news media*. Lanham, MD: Rowman & Littlefield.

Luck, L., Jackson, D., & Usher, K. (2006). Case study: A bridge across the paradigms. *Nursing Inquiry*, 13, 103–109.

Marshall, C., & Rossman, G. (2006). *Designing qualitative research* (4th ed.). Thousand Oaks, CA: Sage.

Mertens, D. M. (2003). Mixed models and the politics of human research: The transformative-emancipatory perspective. In Tashakkori, A., & Teddlie, C. (Eds.), *Handbook of mixed methods in social and behavioral research* (pp. 135–166). Thousand Oaks, CA: Sage.

Mertens, D. M. (2009). *Transformative research and evaluation*. New York: The Guilford Press.

Nastasi, B. K., Hitchcock, J., Sarkar, S., Burkholder, G., Varjas, K., & Jayasena, A. (2007). Mixed methods in intervention research: Theory to adaptation. *Journal of Mixed Methods Research*, 1, 164–182.

O'Cathain, A., Murphy, E., & Nicholl, J. (2007). Integration and publications as indicators of "yield" from mixed methods studies. *Journal of Mixed Methods Research*, 1, 147–163.

Personal communication with Bernard McCoy. Broadcasting, College of Journalism and Mass Communications, University of Nebraska-Lincoln, October 15, 2008.

Personal communication with Joel Geyer. Senior Documentary Producer, Nebraska Educational Telecommunications, Lincoln, Nebraska, December 15, 2008.

Pink, S. (2007). *Doing visual ethnography* (2nd ed.). London: Sage.

Rabiger, M. (2004). *Directing the documentary*. (4th ed.). Amsterdam: Elsevier.

Rose, G. (2007). *Visual methodologies* (2nd ed.). Thousand Oaks, CA: Sage.

Sandelowski, M. (1996). Using qualitative methods in intervention studies. *Research in Nursing & Health*, 19, 359–364.

Sandelowski, M. (2003). Tables or tableaux? The challenges of writing and reading mixed methods studies. In Tashakkori, A., & Teddlie, C. (Eds.), *Handbook of mixed methods in social and behavioral research* (pp. 321–350). Thousand Oaks, CA: Sage.

Stanczak, G. C. (Ed.). (2007). *Visual research methods*. Thousand Oaks, CA: Sage.

Tuggle, C. A., Carr, F., Huffman, S. (2007). *Broadcast news handbook*. New York: McGraw-Hill.

Chapter 21

Digital Storytelling as an Emergent Method for Social Research and Practice

Aline Gubrium and K. C. Nat Turner

Introduction

Media production contains expanded possibilities for multimodal representation, shared authorship, and interactivity, and with that new methods for doing research on a range of subjects in a variety of disciplines from education to public health. Kress (2003) argues the shift from word to image presents new possibilities for communication and representation that may have far-reaching cognitive, social, technological, and economic consequences that deserve more theorizing and study. The concept of multimodal media production (MMP) explains the myriad of modalities people use to understand the world they live in, express themselves, be entertained, and defend themselves, including documentaries, digital stories, hip hop music, digital video poetry, music videos, computer games, public service announcements, youth radio, web sites, blogs, wikis, and others (Turner, 2008). Outside the school setting, people use MMP as a way to engage with their everyday life experiences. These technologies are no longer separate from us; they are ubiquitous to the ways we now live our lives. For any social research project, it is necessary to understand how people are learning and making meaning of their lives. Increasingly, the public is using MMP to publicly document, comment upon, and create their own meaning of events around them.

This was trenchantly demonstrated through user-generated content covering the case of Oscar Grant. Oscar Grant was a young man living in Oakland, California who was assassinated by a police officer while coming home on the Bay Area Rapid Transit (BART), early in the morning on New Year's Day 2009. What was particularly remarkable about this incident was that so many people photographed and video recorded the event, thereby publicly documenting this to record police malfeasance. Within hours of the event, raw footage of the murder, as well as commentary on the raw footage, was posted on YouTube. What is so striking about this example is that media production was not just constructed online. As a form of popular social research and activism, people also worked "off-line," pulling a variety of clips, both user-generated and from the mass media, produced about this event as elicitation materials for conducting interviews with "experts," such as community activists. These clips were also used to draw upon these resources to create various

MMPs about the shooting. As one example, Jasari X (n.d.) produced a hip hop song/ music video/documentary/digital story about the shooting. What was especially compelling in this case was that MMPs such as this were eliciting a visceral response from the people to get out on the streets and demand that this police officer be brought to justice. Using these technologies, which are all pervasive, the public essentially served as a cop watch that monitored police brutality. Increasingly, this phenomenon is one example of much larger phenomena around the world to document injustices and organize protest movements (Rheingold, 2002; Yang, 2007). Essentially, the people themselves served as ethnographers, specifically as participant observers, interviewers, and documentarians, producing counter narratives of the incident.

Narrative inquiry is especially useful in helping researchers to more richly capture how people make sense of their experiences. In particular, the "thinking through" of events and experiences may be seen, in part, through the recording of these phenomena. Therese Riley and Penelope Hawe (2005) write of "internalized soliloquies" that serve as data in narrative research: "These are the conversations one has with oneself or imagined others" (p. 230). Internalized soliloquies signal the narrative sense that people make of their experiences in their social worlds and the ways that people represent their experiences to themselves and to others. However, narratives may be just as useful for interrogating the social and cultural as they are for investigating individual or group phenomena (Riessman, 2008).

As an emergent technological method in social research, digital storytelling adds to the picture of narrative inquiry. As a community-based participatory research (CBPR) method, digital storytelling may be used to investigate individual, group or sociocultural understandings of health, while also increasing community members' participation and input on studies of health issues and other community concerns (Gubrium, 2009). Digital stories are 3–5 min visual narratives that synthesize images, video, audio recordings of voice and music, and text to create compelling stories (Lambert, 2006). As a project outcome, a digital story may serve as an artifact of "internalized soliloquies," in which the storyteller is having "conversations" with imagined others, as well as sociocultural understandings and identity performances constructed by participants in the digital storytelling process.

In this chapter, we begin by describing the digital storytelling process. We then present the emergence of digital storytelling as a research method and discuss how digital storytelling serves as an innovative method in social research, proposing ways that the process may be analyzed. Indeed, the process of digital storytelling serves as much as a site for analysis as does the product of digital storytelling. As a component of analysis, we review how the stories produced may be intertextually transcribed for analytical purposes. Finally, to provide clarity for the reader in terms of how digital storytelling may be useful in social research and practice, we provide a case-study example of digital storytelling in a classroom setting. Here, we examine the case as a forum for discussing the prospects and problems associated with using this method in social research and practice.

Digital Storytelling Process

As a CBPR method, digital storytelling may bolster community building and community members' abilities to address local issues of concern. The method is based on a Freirian model of using images to generate dialogue and to tap into the "funds of knowledge" that people already have (Moll, 1992). These generative images are used to reflect on and tell stories about their lives as a way of coming to understand and challenge oppression (Freire, 1970).

> To Freire (1970), the purpose of education is human liberation, which means that people are the subjects of their own learning, not empty vessels filled by the knowledge of experts. To promote the learner as subject, Freire proposes a listening-dialogue-action approach.... The first step is listening to the generative themes or issues of community members in order to create a structural dialogue in which everyone participates as co-learners to jointly construct a shared reality of themselves as individuals in their social context. Individuals must not only be involved in efforts to identify their problems but also to engage in conscientization to analyze the societal context for these problems. (Wallerstein & Duran, 2002, p. 42)

As with other Freirian approaches and many narrative research methods, the goal is to listen to the themes or collective issues of participants. The creative aspect of digital storytelling transforms these themes and shared understandings into physical form, such as a digital story. One affordance of a digital story is that people can publicly represent their experiences through multiple modes that elicit greater illocutionary force.

The process codified as digital storytelling originated in the San Francisco Bay Area at the Center for Digital Storytelling (CDS) (www.storycenter.org). The center has played an integral part in the production of digital stories in conjunction with oral and local history projects (Meadows, 2003; Tucker, 2006), K-12 and higher education programs (DUSTY, n.d.), public health and youth services (Dupain & Maguire, 2005, 2007), domestic healthcare and international health and development programs (Silence Speaks, n.d.), and Spanish language projects in the United States (Contando Nuestras Historias, n.d.), and in countries such as Norway, India, and Brazil (Hull, Zacher, & Hibbert, 2009; Lundby, 2008; Sahni, 2003; U.C. Links, 2002). In each of these cases, the ways that digital stories have been produced were adjusted and adapted to fit the needs and interests of participating communities.

Gubrium (2009) reviewed the digital storytelling process, especially as it relates to health promotion research and practice, in a prior publication. CDS follows a train-the-trainer model in which those who have experience with digital storytelling, known as the trainers, train others, known as the participants, to construct their own digital stories. To be a digital storytelling trainer, you do not have to be a technology or storytelling "expert"; you just have to have completed your own digital story and be willing to share the process with others. Thus, the train-the-trainer model moves away from the idea of "experts" running the show. During a workshop, participants "learn by doing" and produce their own digital story over the course of three 8-hr days. By the end of the workshop, all participants have constructed a digital story. The aim is to have participants construct their *own* digital story and to avoid having the trainer construct a story for them.

Training workshops may include as many participants as can be accommodated by available computers. However, we recommend that the number of participants not overwhelm the number of trainers available, as trainers are expected to work closely with participants in a mentoring relationship. While 3-day workshops are the norm, a concentrated period of time better allows for undisturbed participation in the digital storytelling process. Time allocation for completing a workshop should be flexible according to the daily schedules of participants. All told, participants should expect to devote approximately 24 hr to complete a story.

Participants are usually asked to come to the first workshop session with a page to a page and a half draft of their story, or at the very least an idea for their story in mind, and to bring along digital photos, print photos to be scanned, or video clips they may want to incorporate into their stories. In terms of subject matter for the story, the digital storytelling process is notably fluid. For example, if the aim of a project is to better understand high school student perspectives on sexual health education, the workshop trainers may ask the participants to focus on constructing a story that takes their experiences with sexual health education into consideration. The research and practice process, thus, is initially driven by the research or advocacy topic, but the content comes from the experiences of participants. Other workshops, however, may contain a more open agenda and ask only that participants focus on constructing a story that is meaningful to them.

Workshops and the digital storytelling process are commonly organized into phases, but there is also flexibility in this. The first phase of the workshop is usually devoted to an overview of digital storytelling in which participants become better acquainted with the process. As participants often arrive at a workshop not quite sure how to identify a digital story, the moderator may present digital story samples to the group in order to exemplify the final product. Trainers may then present a brief lecture on the seven elements of digital storytelling as conceptualized through the CDS: point of view, dramatic question, emotional content, voice, soundtrack/music, economy, and pacing (Lambert, 2006). These elements represent the basic ingredients of a multimedia story and are kept in mind throughout the production process. Participants are asked to consider these elements when revising their own stories and when listening to and commenting on other participants' stories during collaborative discussion sessions. Participants also may be asked to take part in several talking or writing activities, which can be used as warm-up activities to encourage a less formal writing style.

The digital storytelling process is a highly collaborative and interactive one. Indeed, participant observation of the production process may serve as a site for the analysis of the social construction of narrative and identity. The second phase of the workshop deals with participants crafting the script of their stories, beginning with the story circle process. The purpose of a story circle is to create a safe and comfortable space for participants to present the first draft or initial idea for their stories and to allow group cohesion in discussing and mutually mentoring each other in story construction. In this regard, storytelling can serve as a kind of medicine for healing (Ladson-Billings & Tate, 1995). Story circles can be used by participants for discussing difficult experiences and may provide the first outlet for participants to acknowledge and create something positive from these circumstances. All participants are given the same amount of time to present and discuss their stories, with listening participants encouraged to consider the seven elements of storytelling when discussing the storyteller's narrative. This provides a shared format for both story construction and supportive commentary. Out of the discussion of participants' stories, a unity of mission develops that forms a sense of collaborative accomplishment. In our experience, social research incorporating MMP methods, in particular those projects that incorporate social networking sites or other virtual methods, is shifting toward looking at how people are collaborating using these new media (boyd, 2007; Jenkins, 2006). This collaborative nature disrupts traditional notions of authorship that see thinking and learning as individual in nature, instead of rooted in a sociocultural context where people collaborate in knowledge production. Using their "collective intelligence," digital storytelling groups bring their knowledge to bear on particular issues in the community (Levy, 1956/1998).

After the story circle is completed, workshop trainers may present a tutorial on working with a digital image editing application, such as *Picasa*, which is available for free download from the Internet, or *Photoshop Express*. Participants are taught to scan printed photos into their computers and to visually modify scanned and digital photos for use in the digital story. Trainers can add a separate lecture on photography and/or run a photo activity with participants so that they may think more critically about the visual representations they use to develop their digital stories.

Participants revise their story scripts with the assistance of the workshop trainers, and are asked to consider comments made about their idea/draft during the story circle. They then record a voiceover of their scripts, which is used as the audio portion of the digital story. Voiceovers are usually recorded in a room separate from the main training area. This provides the participants privacy in audio recording their stories and allows for better acoustics in recording. Trainers work with participants to teach them how to use the voice recording software, advise them how to properly position themselves in front of the microphone, and encourage them to speak as much as possible with their natural speaking voice.

While some participants record their voiceovers, other participants create storyboards for their digital stories. A storyboard serves as a visual layout or menu for digital story construction. A storyboard consists of a large sheet of paper, on which participants align oral/aural elements of their stories, such as story scripts and soundtrack/musical elements, with visual elements, such as photos, video clips, or scanned visual objects. Participants are taught to consider the timing and placement of elements of their stories, such as the order of parts of their story, as well as the interaction between elements (Lambert, 2007).

The final phase of the digital storytelling workshop centers on incorporating components of the digital story (visual, oral, and aural elements) into a nonlinear video editing application such as *iMovie* (available for free on a Mac) and *Final Cut Express* for Macs or *MovieMaker* (available for free on a PC) and *Adobe Premiere* for PCs. Through a trainer-provided tutorial, participants learn how to import and work with their source materials within the application, beginning a rough edit of their digital stories. A range of collaborative practices takes place among participants and trainers in making choices in the production process.

By the end of the workshop, each participant should expect to have a digital story ready to present to the group. As part of a collaborative effort, workshop closure is important in the digital storytelling process. Screening each digital story at the end of the workshop is a way of celebrating the groups' collective accomplishments (Lambert, 2007). The first showing of a digital story is usually restricted to participants and trainers within the workshop, helping to sustain the safe space and group cohesion built over the course of the workshop.

Digital Storytelling as a Method for Social Research

More than 20 years ago, feminist and postmodern social researchers led a discussion of the ways that we produce and represent the individual, society, and culture through social research and representation by challenging the norm of the detached social scientist and inviting the "objects of investigation" to "talk back" in scholarly texts (Clifford & Marcus, 1986). Few of these critics, however, challenged the notion of written text as the central medium for empirical data. Shifts in the everyday use of technology from written texts to multimodal texts have implications for social research (Kress, 2003). While written texts remain a central practice and expectation in social research, some researchers are interested in turning to new media for scholarly production.

More recently, varied disciplines in social research, including anthropology, sociology, and cultural geography, have reinvigorated the discussion of the relevance of ethnographic knowledge. In public health, nursing, education, and other applied fields, community-based participatory research (CBPR) has gained prominence as an approach to ethnographic scholarship and understandings applied in practice. In response to the critique of ethnographic representation, visual social researchers have begun to embrace CBPR approaches. Digital and visual approaches to participatory research offer opportunities to open up the social research process and to share research with a diverse array of audiences. In this regard, digital storytelling serves as an exemplar. The digital storytelling process and product offers up an array of visual, oral, textual, and aural ethnographic empirical material for analysis, while both are largely directed and produced by the digital storyteller.

Digital Storytelling Innovation

Digital storytelling is rooted in community arts and oral history traditions. It first emerged as a method of community activism, most notably linked with radical community theater in the San Francisco Bay area. Thus, the roots of digital storytelling do not lie in social research so much as in community building and pedagogical or alternative literacy efforts (Meadows, 2003). The method is said to have originated with Joe Lambert's and the late performance artist Dana Atchley's collaborative work on "storying" lives through community theater production. While staging their theater productions, the two community artist activists realized that the people in the audience watching the performances were also interested in producing their own stories. CDS workshops emerged in the early 1990s as a response, with Lambert and partner Nina Mullen, committed to helping other people tell their own stories, using emerging digital technologies as media for producing their own stories (Beeson & Miskelly, 2005).

As a method of social research, the aims of digital storytelling may be linked to an iteration of participant observation popular in Great Britain in the late 1930s through the mid-1960s, that later reemerged in the early 1980s (Fyfe, 2007). The Mass Observation Movement claimed that any person could serve as observer and that only through "mass observation," which is the everyday observations of millions of people involved in public events, could we have a mass science of everyday life. According to this perspective, each individual observing an event, whether through diaries, interviews, conversations, or the direct observations and recordings of field notes, serves as a point of observation (Hubble, 2006). Known as an "anthropology of ourselves," the Mass Observation Movement was not "issue based, but holistic, seeking to observe the [previously] unobserved, and resisting objectification of those observed by not only being about the people, but also for them and created by them" (Fyfe, 2007, p. 5). The digital storytelling process can be used to create similar individual or group observation points on everyday life, as the aim of this process is also to understand the everyday life experiences of ordinary people (Fyfe, 2007). Thus, the epistemological roots of digital storytelling are quite similar to that of the Mass Observation Movement, which foregrounds local understandings as empirical data.

As a method of social research and activism, however, digital storytelling moves beyond the observational qualities of Mass Observation. Analysis of the process begins from the interlocution of participant and trainer/researcher with the researcher present and helping to work with the population she is trying to learn from in projects aimed at improving the material conditions of participants' lives (Freire, 1970). This active involvement on the part of the researcher reflects the philosophical or epistemological perspective of phenomenology that is aimed at facilitating reflection in order to represent the life-world of participants (Barab & Roth, 2006; Favret-Saada, 1980; Merleau-Ponty, 1973; Ranciere, 1991). Seeking to respect the uniqueness of every individual and experience, phenomenology challenges the idea that there is no one singular universal truth. Instead, it seeks to understand how local knowledge relates to the historical and social context from which it arises. Thus, multiple purposes may be realized from the digital storytelling process, as it serves up both empirical data for analysis and may be implemented as a vehicle to challenge social injustices in local and international arenas.

While digital storytelling has been used in primary, secondary, and adult education as a way to increase student access to alternative forms of literacy (DUSTY, n.d.; Educause Learning Initiative, 2007; Kajder, 2006; Ohler, 2007), it is an incipient method for use in social research and research in health programming and practice. Research efforts incorporating digital storytelling tend to center on identity as a locus of concern (de Leeuw & Rydin, 2007), research-based practice, or research that contributes to knowledge production and intervention (Beeson & Miskelly, 2005; Burgess, 2006; Chavez et al., 2004; Marcuss, 2004; Meadows, 2003), and research on pedagogical processes, such as literacy projects and conceptual learning projects (Hull & Nelson, 2005; Mahiri, 2004; Morrell, 2004). As an emergent method in social research, digital storytelling may be used to address social inequities and to shed light on individual and community understandings of experience. Organizations such as Stories for Change (n.d.) mobilize workshop trainers and facilitators specifically to use digital storytelling to incite action within and between local groups.

Daniel Meadows (2003), director of *BBC Wales—Capture Wales*, describes the shift of power in representation played out through digital storytelling:

> No longer must the public tolerate being "done" by media—that is, no longer must we tolerate media being done to us. No longer must we put up with professional documentarists recording us for hours and then throwing away most of what we tell them, keeping only those bits that tell our stories their own way and, more than likely, at our expense. If we will only learn the skills of Digital Storytelling then we can, quite literally, "take the power back." (Meadows, 2003, p. 192)

Invoking a sort of grassroots empowerment that may be felt by participants of the digital storytelling process, Meadows seemingly responds to a 1980s crisis in social research and representation in which "the native" was invited to "talk back" (Clifford & Marcus, 1986).

Digital storytelling plays with the notion of empirical reality in terms of who is in control of producing and interpreting reality. As process and artifact, digital stories may be linked to the social construction of memory. For example, de Leeuw and Rydin (2007) use digital storytelling as media to study children's lives. They note the accessibility and user-friendly qualities of digital storytelling and other participatory media methods in studying children's lives. Their central research question is to analyze the ways that children represent and express their experiences of migration. De Leeuw and Rydin use digital stories as sites for analysis to investigate the ways that children socially construct their experiences of cultural identity. Echoing Meadows' claim (2003), they regard children as media producers, with their media productions serving as sites for analyzing the social construction of identity.

In their Media Clubs project, children participated in any number of media clubs, one of which included a variant of a digital storytelling workshop. De Leeuw and Rydin (2007) focus on a small set of participating children's media productions from these clubs that serve as exemplars for analyzing self-representational processes and identity construction. Here, digital storytelling may be used as a "process of active construction of personal history through the use of what Hoskins (2001) calls 'memory devices,' pointing to photo albums, home videos [and I add here, digital stories]. The medium at least partly becomes memory" (de Leeuw & Rydin, 2007, p. 460). The process allows participants to use expressive means to construct individual and collective identities and to represent their memories from the past, present, and future (de Leeuw & Rydin, 2007).

Indeed, the digital storytelling process may serve as a trigger for the social construction of memory. The Charlestown Digital Stories project (Digital Stories @ UMBC, n.d.), focused on remembering and relating forgotten memories, is a collaborative project between students at the University of Maryland, Baltimore County's New Media Studio (NMS), and residents of the Charlestown Retirement Community. Digital stories produced during the project are broadcast on Retirement Living Television, a cable network syndicated in the Mid-Atlantic and New England, dedicated to serving the needs of adults over the age of 50. The Charlestown project serves as an example of an intergenerational initiative, with younger students and older retirement community resident participants working together in the digital storytelling process (Shewbridge, 2007). Students participating in the Charlestown project noted in their evaluations of the digital storytelling workshop that they found commonalities and relevance between their own experiences and those of the retirement community residents. Importantly, both young and older participant groups noted that several components of the digital storytelling workshop, but especially the story circle activity, encouraged them to remember and relate forgotten memories.

Analyzing the Digital Storytelling Process and Outcome

While the process of producing a digital story has been codified to some extent, the ways to analyze a digital story are in a nascent stage of development. Social researchers using digital storytelling as a method of narrative inquiry should take note of other methods of narrative and visual analysis. The analyst might think of the various modes of representation demonstrated through the digital storytelling process, as well as within the product of digital storytelling. During the digital storytelling process, participants involved are constructing their stories or voiceover scripts to be read aloud as narration for the digital story. The script itself, then, could be analyzed as a textual artifact, with "what," "how," "why," "when," and "for whom" questions asked of the script and the storyteller. "What" questions would be the focus of a thematic analysis. Focusing on these questions, the analyst would explore the generative themes of the story. In addition, the analyst could look at visual images used by the storyteller to tell his or her story in relation to key themes of the story.

"How" questions are the focus of a more structural analysis of the digital story. In this sort of analysis, the aim would be to look at the types of speech and images used to produce the story to better understand the meaning of the story through a microanalysis of the language used (Riessman, 2008). Through a structural analysis, the researcher strives to understand how the digital storyteller uses language to produce meaning.

Focusing on "why," "when," and "for whom" questions of the text, the researcher may delve into dialogic/performance analysis terrain. This perspective sees stories more as social artifacts, in which the storyteller produces identities through storytelling with an audience or audiences in mind. In a dialogic/performance analysis, the notion of identity is problematized; identities produced through storytelling are not static. Rather, they are seen as polyvocal, with meaning produced through storytelling up for interpretation through a dialogic interpretation of the story between the storyteller, the researcher analyzing the story, and the audience viewing/listening to the story (Bakhtin, 1981). Dialogic/performance analysts "treat identities as dynamically constituted in relationships and performed with/for audiences" (Riessman, 2008, p. 137). Identity performances are the locus of concern and the amalgamation of text, visuals, and soundtrack of the digital story are analyzed as sites for identity production. Therefore, digital stories are not seen as individual productions, as might be the perspective taken in thematic or structural analyses. Rather, digital stories may be viewed as sites for the production and transformation of identities of the small groups or social networks that produce them. In turn, the work of these social networks may hold implications for addressing issues of social justice. For instance, the digital stories produced by a group of community member participants may be seen as representative of group/community concerns and shared through the Internet. As a group performance, digital stories may enable participants to talk about issues of importance and to build a group culture capable of mobilizing larger numbers of people to address these issues at local and state government levels (Yang, 2007).

Visual analysis may employ multiple modes of inquiry. Noted cultural geographer and visual analyst Gillian Rose (2001) writes of three sites of inquiry in conducting a visual analysis of data including representation, production, and performance. The first site of inquiry is the representation itself. With a digital story in mind, the researcher looks at the image or digital story and responds to the "what" questions produced in the story. The focus here is on key themes generated in the story. The seven elements of storytelling (Lambert, 2006) are relevant terms for analysis in this mode of inquiry. Guiding questions for analysis might ask about the point of the story (the point of view and dramatic question), what is included and what is left out of the story (known as economy), and how the component parts of the story, such as the voiceover, images, and soundtrack, are stylistically produced via voice and soundtrack/music and arranged through pacing to create a particular mood (known as emotional content) for the story.

Another site of inquiry is the production process of the digital story. Here, the researcher focuses on the "how" questions, with guiding questions for analysis focusing on *how* and when the digital story was made (known as the socio-historical context behind the digital story), the social identities produced through the collaboration of the participants during the digital storytelling process, and the intended social identities of the recipients or audience of the digital story. An ethnographic analysis of the digital storytelling process is equal to, if not more important than, the artifact produced through the process (de Leeuw & Rydin, 2007). Field notes on participant observation taken by the researcher or facilitators during the digital storytelling process, such as those focusing on observations taken from introductory writing and oral storytelling activities, story circles, the script revision process, and the event of putting the story together on the computer, as well as interviews of participants and facilitators before, during, and after the workshop might be material for analysis in considering the production of the digital story. In addition, feedback from audiences viewing the digital stories could also serve as data in analyzing the story of production.

A third site for inquiry is the performative qualities of the digital story. When interrogating the "audiencing" process of digital storytelling (Riessman, 2008), the researcher might look at the individual and group responses to the digital story, the other types of stories that the viewers may associate with the particular digital story being viewed, any written text or curricular material that is designed to guide the viewer in watching and discussing the digital story, as well as the ways that the digital storyteller situates his/her identity within the confines of the digital story artifact, as well as in discussions and explanations of his/her digital story during semi-public workshops and public community exhibitions.

Our take on digital storytelling is inspired, in large part, by Riessman's perspective (2008) that personal narratives, read here as digital stories, are largely about the telling of social worlds:

> Whether personal narratives are spoken, written, or visual, they do not generate unmediated and unclassed portraits of an "essential" self....An investigator cannot elicit an autobiographical story that is separable from wider conditions in which it is situated and constructed...[visual narratives] are performances of "selves," crafted with an audience in mind—a "staging of subjectivity." (Riessman, 2008, p. 177)

Indeed, an analysis of the production and artifact of digital storytelling allows for an analysis of power relations. The researcher may gain a deeper understanding of narrative constraints placed on meaning-making in relation to structures of power, such as race, class, and gender, by looking at the language used in a digital story, the ways that the narrator chooses to situate herself within her story, and reflecting upon what is possibly left *unsaid* in a digital story. In doing so, we might ask ourselves as the audience why and when we are made privy to some stories and not others, how digital stories are completed according to the context in which they are produced, and how the process and production of meaning-making interact with institutional and/or sociocultural norms (Riley & Hawe, 2005, pp. 231–232).

Transcribing Digital Stories: An Intertextual Method

We have used an intertextual transcription method to visually represent and begin to understand how people make meaning across the different modalities of visual, chronological, aural and oral, emotional, gestural, and textual elements found in a digital story. The transcript features multiple tracks, representing linguistic and nonlinguistic elements of the story. Below is an example of one digital story transcript we have completed. We chose this particular digital story because it is exemplary of an issue of interest to social researchers—gun violence—and due to its brevity.

During a year-long social research study on multimodal media production in the development of multiliteracies, Nat worked with middle-school students in an extended-day program called Digital Underground Storytelling for You(th) (DUSTY). The transcript example provided here represents a digital story produced by a 6th grade student, Edward, who participated in the DUSTY program. Edward is a student with an Individualized Education Plan (IEP), typically provided for students with special needs. A visual artist who writes and illustrates his own science fiction chapter books, Edward proclaimed a love for video games and animated cartoons and distaste toward rapping, unlike many of the other boys in the course. Whereas his media practices and talents were usually kept private, the DUSTY program provided him with an opportunity to share these interests and practices in a public forum at school.

After Edward completed his digital story, Nat interviewed him about the story in order to better understand his choice in topic for the digital story, his choice of visual materials to represent the topic, and the sociocultural context of his story production. It is important to note that while Nat interviewed Edward, he used the digital story as an elicitation device. Therefore, the "interview transcript" part of the intertextual transcript reflects the particular scene of the digital story they are discussing (Figure 21.1).

Interview Transcript

E: It was on about stop guns in Newton and it was all the death in Newton caused by guns all the mayham, death, violence and other things.

Image:	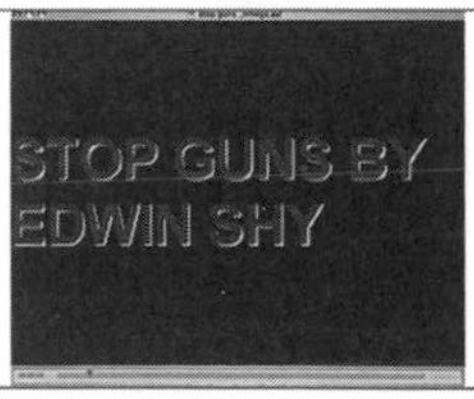		
Time (sec.):	0–3	3–8	8–11
Soundtrack:	[None]	[None]	[None]
Script:	My PSA is titled Stop Guns.	I am tired of all the deaths in Newton. Everyday a	Police car is going to Hillside. It is very sad.
Location represented:	Virtual space	Police gun heist	Random community
Emotion:	Powerful suggestion	Shock	Sadness
Features of visual objects:	Blue letters on black	Big guns	Police car
Special effects:	Still title page	Long pause	Still image
Text on screen:	Stop guns by Edwin Shy	[Illegible tags on guns]	London Police Community Service

Figure 21.1 Multimodal media transcript sample 1.

Image:			
Time (sec.):	11–16	16–18	8–11
Soundtrack:	[None]	[None]	[None]
Script:	It is very sad that adults, children, and teens all have a gun.	They always think that guns will help, but they are wrong.	It will only get worse. Do you think that God
Location represented:	Representation of Newton	Police station	Police station
Emotion:	Community	Arrest	Arrest
Features of visual objects:	Strip mall business	Hand gun	Hand gun
Special effects:	Long image	Quick image	Quick image
Text on screen:	[Unintelligible store name/logo]	[None]	[None]

Figure 21.2 Multimodal media transcript sample 2.

Image:		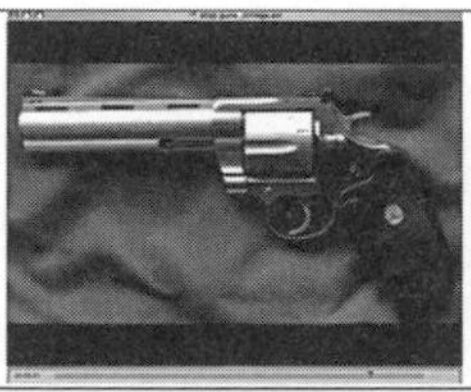	
Time (sec.):	22–27	27–32	33–37
Soundtrack:	[None]	[None]	[None]
Script:	has made us to make guns war and death? So stop with all the	guns, death, and war and bring peace to all for God.	[None]
Location represented:	Police gun heist	Anywhere in U.S.	Virtual space
Emotion:	Threatening	Fear	Inspiration
Features of visual objects:	Many types of big guns	Magnum	Green letters on black background
Special effects:	Long image	Long image	Still title page
Text on screen:	[None]	[None]	THE END!

Figure 21.3 Multimodal media transcript sample 3.

KCNT: What images did you include in your PSA to address that?
E: Death, Newton, Hillside and police car...oh yeah death (Figure 21.2).

Interview Transcript

E: Well, it's kinda like I suppose its kinda like [unintelligible] some kids may have guns secretly its for teens and adults because you never know if they have a gun or not. Until they get drastic measures and figuring out things that's what they say (Figure 21.3).

Interview Transcript

E: Well around me I always see a lot of guns and death and even saw one gun when I was five years old when I was in Houston so that is why I picked "stop guns" because guns are way to viol...sometimes guns are useful but now they are used for just to many things now.

> KCNT: Have you ever seen that before?
> E: No but once this mysterious character put a big gun behind my house when I was living on Hillside. I think probably like a M-10 or something.
> KCNT: Put it behind your house?
> E: Yeah but we didn't get blamed they understand someone just put it behind there because someone saw this one teen with a machine gun in his hand

Edward combines multiple modalities to, in effect, multiply meaning. For example, the multiple images of so many guns and the large size of the guns reinforce the point of Edward's digital story, which is about the urgency of gun control. The moment in the digital story where he says "I am tired of all the deaths in Newton," he presents a picture of a variety of nearly 30 large guns to link the deaths with gun violence. Again at the point where he says "Everyday a police car is going to Hillside. It is very sad," his inclusion of a photo of a police car opens the analysis up to several possibilities. As an explicit image, the police could represent an ideal version of police coming to the rescue. However, alternatively as an implicit image, it could also serve as a critique of the criminalization of Edward's community. Unprompted, Edward suggests the possibility of being blamed for gun violence, which indicates a potential irony to include an image of a police car with the words "community service" on the side.

We found the process of analyzing Edward's digital story akin to analyzing other discursive genres such as song lyrics or poetry. While he does not write or present his story in a traditional essay format, his digital story is equally sophisticated in the different ways that he produces meaning. Additionally, as with other genres, social researchers looking into analyzing how individuals are making meaning would ideally interview the producer and then work in teams to co-construct interpretations of the story. Essentially, this produces a more active analysis, which accounts for the collaborative nature of digital storytelling.

While we are aware of the move to recognize multimodal texts, we feel compelled to use print text to transcribe multimodal media because it continues to be the currency of academia. In addition, a reader who does not have access to multimedia can still get a sense of the whole MMP. This multimodal form of transcription takes its influences from theories of communication, literacy, and multimodality (Finnegan, 2002; Hull & Nelson, 2005; New London Group, 1996); we hope it can be a kind of bridge to MMP. This system could allow a researcher to chart the meaning participants make in their media and to show changes in how they choose to represent themselves. Intertexuality is especially important in MMP as participants "remix" by selectively cutting, pasting, and combining resources, to represent, produce, and perform identities and the knowledge they are constructing (Erstad, Gilje, & de Lang, 2007). By decoupling modalities, we highlight the meaning and effect of each mode individually, as well as the choices participants make to combine certain modalities together to multiply meaning (Lemke, 1998). Additionally, the researcher could use participants' meta-level analysis of their multimodal media by including their interview notes as part of the transcription (Bauman & Briggs, 1990).

Challenges and Benefits of Digital Storytelling

A Case Study of Digital Storytelling in the Classroom

In Spring 2008, Aline, a feminist and medical anthropologist who uses narrative methods to better understand women's health issues and to construct health interventions rooted in a social justice framework, taught a public health and social justice course that introduced students to digital storytelling within the context of community-based participatory health research. Student reflections on this course and lessons learned about digital storytelling are also reviewed in another publication (Gubrium, 2009). After the course ended, Aline consulted with Nat, a literacy researcher studying multiliteracy development using multimodal media production. Nat holds a special interest in the language and literacy practices of culturally and linguistically diverse urban adolescents in school and nonschool settings. Aline sought Nat's contribution to this chapter because of his expertise with transcribing and analyzing digital stories as sources of social research data. In this section, we present an analytical case of using digital storytelling in a classroom setting, especially examining the representation, process, and performance of participants involved in a public health and social justice course.

Digital storytelling was situated in the course as a method for community organizing and civil engagement in health promotion activities. For the first half of the semester (7 weeks), 14 graduate students, most of whom were taking a Master's of public health program or a Master's in public policy program, were trained in the digital storytelling process. Students met for a 2½-hr period every week. By the middle of the semester, each student had produced a digital story related to his or her own experiences. The students were not asked to construct digital stories based on a particular topic, such as health or social justice. Rather, the only guideline they were given was that they construct a story that was meaningful to them, written in their own voice, and about themselves. For the second half of the semester, students partnered with a range of other youth, both on and off campus, to train them in the digital storytelling process. The graduate students registered for the course were asked to meet weekly with partnering students to provide cohesive and consistent training sessions in digital storytelling.

At the end of the semester, digital storytelling participants, those registered for the course and partnering students, participated in a gallery exhibition of their work. The exhibition, which was held at a historical museum located across the street from a school for pregnant and parenting young women that was also the site of digital storytelling training, provided a public location to screen the digital stories. Community members, healthcare providers, students and their family and friends, school and university faculty and students, and key community stakeholders were invited to view and discuss the digital stories. The digital story public exhibition, itself, serves as a site for social researchers interested in conducting a dialogic/performance analysis of the digital story product and the spectacle of this production (Best & Kellner, 1999).

Aline chose to emphasize a train-the-trainer approach in the course, in which students learned how to produce a digital story themselves as a way to learn how to train others how to produce a digital story. The goal of this training was that, as public health professionals, the students might incorporate the method into their own community health research, programming, and advocacy work. Students were asked to contribute at least one weekly post to a course-based blog, which served as a virtual forum for student reaction and dialogue on the digital storytelling process. All students were asked to create their own blog name, known as a pseudonym, in posting their responses, which are reflected in this chapter. Here, we analyze and summarize some of the students' blog posts to indicate various research and practice challenges and benefits associated with digital storytelling.

Digital Storytelling Challenges

While digital storytelling can serve as a method for participants to produce something concrete and tangible out of their experiences, thus serving as a forum for advocacy on issues of concern, a number of challenges may be faced in running a digital storytelling workshop. One initial challenge faced may be how to approach an Institutional Review Board (IRB) about incorporating digital storytelling as part of the research process. As a nascent method for social research, the procedure for applying to the IRB for approval to use digital storytelling as a research method is not well established. Issues that may arise in seeking approval include addressing informed consent. In particular, obtaining participant consent to air digital stories in a public forum for advocacy, such as a web site or a public exhibition, and, in relation to consent, maintaining the confidentiality of participants if digital stories are to be used in media and advocacy campaigns, especially if stories contain recognizable images of the participant or others depicted in the story. Within the context of the digital storytelling training sessions, all participants were asked to sign consent forms to air their digital stories and/or to use their stories for educational or research aims. However, they were asked to sign consent forms only *after* they had produced their digital stories, as we wanted to make sure that participants had the chance to experience the digital storytelling process, as well as to know the final outcome of this process—the sort of story they had produced. Asking participants to sign a consent form before participating in the workshop or having a final product in hand did not provide them with adequate information to give true consent.

Other challenges arose during the second half of the semester, when graduate students trained other students to produce digital stories. In terms of using digital storytelling as a social research method, one main challenge of using this method, as opposed to other qualitative methods such as interviews or focus groups, is that the method is heavily dependent upon the mutual ability of participants and trainers to devote a significant amount of time to completing a workshop. Two graduate students in the social justice course met this challenge and, unfortunately, were not able to overcome it. The students attempted to run a digital storytelling workshop through an after-school program for middle-school youth, developed through a public school-based initiative. Due to the fact that attendance at the after-school program was optional for students and that virtually no mandates were placed on students to consistently participate in the program week after week, the graduate students found it extremely difficult to run the workshop. They also found that communication among the people directing the program (administrators), people on the ground organizing and running the program (teachers, volunteers, and the two graduate students running the training sessions), and students participating in the after-school program were poor. This limited the graduate students' ability to properly organize for each session. Not only were the graduate students never sure of which middle-school students would show up for the program each week, they were also unsure of what technological equipment (computers, scanners, microphones, external hard drives) would be available or working during the session, or what classroom space they would be allotted during each session. Quality of the equipment, especially in under-resourced urban schools, is an important consideration when attempting to engage participants in the technology-dependent practice of multimodal media production.

One of the graduate students spelled out her frustrations working in this setting. While she found digital storytelling compelling as a method for youth to represent their own experiences and produce something concrete out of these experiences, she realized that one major obstacle in accomplishing her goal of running a complete digital storytelling workshop was the very collaborative nature of the digital storytelling endeavor. Ironically, while this collaborative quality may serve as a boon in other contexts, here it served as a barrier to accomplishing the task at hand: "An organization's culture can interrupt the flow of the digital storytelling process. Going into this setting, an educational institution, allowed me to see that while the application of the digital storytelling process was extremely pertinent…collaboration among different levels of personnel…was difficult. Everyone had a different vision of digital story engagement" (Guevara David). In this case, running the workshop within a more rigidly defined institutional setting, such as in school as part of the regular school day, might have provided easier and more consistent access to students, as well as access to the equipment required for use during the workshop.

In addition to the context of participation, graduate students working with middle-school students felt especially challenged by the age of the workshop participants. Both noted that the maturity level of participants should be considered when planning workshop sessions. One graduate student commented on the need to consider the participant's potential attention span and ways to keep participants actively engaged in workshop activities. Workshop organizers should keep in mind that with pedagogical components regularly incorporated into the digital storytelling workshop, such as the lecture on the seven elements of storytelling, younger participants may quickly grow bored with a presentation model quite similar to the one they face in school, day in and day out. The graduate student working with middle-school students noted: "having to work on the story narrative before working with the 'cool' technology may have…been seen as a drawback (or boring) by some of the youth involved. Working on a story seemed like something you did *in* school, not after school" (Guevara David). Not only do facilitators need to take into the need to be flexible with project activities and related materials, they should also be willing to shift the schedule of workshop activities to accommodate the needs of different participant groups.

When working with a diverse array of participants, especially in an out-of-school setting, the facilitator/researcher must allow for flexibility in the process and realize that their own agenda or plan for the session may not mesh with that of the participants in the session. This signals a possible tension in the digital storytelling process. How does one run a workshop based on a CBPR approach which, from a grass roots approach, has participants producing and directing stories in their own flavor, while *at the same time* run a workshop focused on a particular research topic and provide training in a method that, due to technological and time constraints, does not allow for so much flexibility? Several students in the social justice course seemingly responded to this conundrum with frustration, as they realized that while some amount of flexibility was needed in planning the workshop so that it was sensitive to the needs and abilities of the participants involved, allowing participants too much leeway in the workshop was negatively associated with the ability of participants to complete a digital story.

Digital Storytelling Benefits

While accommodating the needs of individual participants in a workshop may provide a challenge to the researcher/facilitator, in our overall experience of conducting workshops, participants comment that the digital storytelling process is quite therapeutic. Graduate students participating in the social justice course spoke of a cathartic experience in producing a digital story about difficult experiences. For example, one graduate student showed her adoptive mother her digital story about their mother–daughter relationship on Mother's Day. Another graduate student, an African-American woman who is currently attending a predominantly white university, produced a digital story about body image. She related that the digital storytelling process was therapeutic for her because she was finally able to produce something concrete out of experiences that she had held onto for so long and was able to share her experiences in an MMP format to which she felt many viewers would be able to relate.

Not only do participants experience catharsis from a tangible digital storytelling product, they also note a therapeutic aspect to participating in activities associated with the storytelling process. In particular, activities associated with script construction, such as story circling and interaction with others centered on revising the draft, allow participants to shape and represent experiences the way they see fit. One graduate student reflected this sentiment when commenting upon her training work with participants in a school for pregnant and parenting young women: "Being able to put their story into words, which I guessed many of them had not done before, was wonderful to observe and I have a better understanding of the importance of this aspect of the digital storytelling process" (Shannon). Instead of dreaming about what they could achieve and simply dismissing it, the workshop participants were learning a method for systematically representing their hopes and aspirations. Research shows that focus on future/possible selves is a key ingredient for bolstering resilience and perseverance (Carey & Martin, 2007). For oppressed communities, digital storytelling offers a site for unpacking and articulating their oppression, as well as resisting and challenging oppression; digital storytelling can also act as a vehicle for healing wounds caused by oppression through the development of critical consciousness (Freire, 1970).

In contrast to top-down approaches in which policy makers, academics, public health practitioners, and others seen as "experts" may generalize an experience for a targeted community, digital storytelling allows participants to construct and represent their own experiences. In the context of research, the story circle process may serve much the same role as a focus group, in that it allows participants to discuss issues of concern in a group setting. In contrast to the traditional focus-group method, however, story circles allow participants to guide the topic of discussion.

The final day's airing of digital stories produced in the workshop often proves to be quite moving for participants, as they unveil their finished product to other participants in the group. For some participants, this may be the first time they have opened up about an important experience. Moreover, for many participants, this is the first time they have created a tangible media production to represent their experiences, which lead to new possibilities to see and be seen. Indeed, in our experience conducting digital storytelling workshops, we have seen how the digital storytelling process allows both researcher/facilitators *and* workshop participants to position themselves as participant observers in the research process, thereby allowing both parties new and varied perspectives on the social construction of meaning in everyday life.

Practicing *conscientization* (Freire, 1970), and as participant observers in this regard, workshop participants become more conscious of the ways they choose to represent their experiences. Over the course of the semester, Aline saw workshop participants become active agents in the construction of stories about their experiences. They made decisions about ways to position themselves and their experiences within the context of their written scripts, the ways they talked about and explained their experiences during the story circle, the ways they narrated their stories during the voiceover recording, the types of images they used to represent their experiences, and the soundtrack and sound effects they used to create a particular type of mood within their production. Participants' digital stories clearly stood as an active portrayal of the ways that they chose to position themselves as certain kinds of people with particular kinds of experiences, depending on the story they wished to produce.

Within the context of the social justice course workshop, the discussions Aline held with graduate students and other workshop participants while encouraging them to craft their script narratives or while training them to use various applications to assemble their digital stories were illuminating for her as a researcher and teacher, and she gained a more nuanced perspective of their lived experiences. To be sure, she gained a much finer understanding of her students over the course of the digital storytelling process than she might have in a more traditional classroom setting. She also saw how workshop participants were emboldened by being given the reins to drive the meaning-making of their own experiences as they produced their digital stories. The digital story became a representation and a performance of how they preferred their experiences to be seen by others. As an emergent method for social research, especially research aimed at addressing social problems, digital stories serve to humanize people whose behaviors, attitudes, and experiences may otherwise be represented through a set of facts and figures. As one graduate student pointed out, "[digital stories] really ha[ve] the potential to reach people in their hearts, and [help them to] understand that those they are serving are not just bodiless statistics or potential voters, but real people...." (Clarkie).

Conclusion

We enumerate some of the challenges of digital storytelling in this chapter. From addressing IRB concerns in seeking approval to conduct research based on participant-produced movies, to the difficulties that may be encountered in running a digital storytelling workshop, to the "between a rock and a hard place" position the researcher may find himself or herself when attempting to negotiate the needs of participants with the fiduciary and professional demands of funding agencies and the academy, using digital storytelling as a method for social research is not without its difficulties.

One site for future research will be to reflect upon ethical issues related to digital storytelling and other visual methods used in social research project. Topics of discussion in this regard include the following: issues of presentation and self-representation and ways that digital stories may contribute to or challenge visual/multimedia stereotypes; the ethics of digital storytelling production in relation to the story circle process in ethnographic research and maintaining the original intent of reflective conversation, catharsis, and empowerment, as well as consent to participate in the process; the ethics of access to the digital storytelling product, especially related to the release and target audience for the distribution of the digital story as well as how the chosen display for the stories affects the story presentation and interfaces with issues of consent and release of materials; repercussions of using digital storytelling as a research method, including IRB concerns, publication of materials, ethical issues encountered during data analysis, and the potential for conflicting agendas based on digital storytelling as a research method versus method of intervention; various meanings of participation in the digital storytelling process, focusing on the CDS philosophy in which digital story production is driven by the participant to the way the process is actually practiced as guided by a predetermined research agenda; and how relationships of trust and rapport may or may not be established when incorporating digital storytelling into the social research process. Indeed, the very act of considering digital storytelling as a method for *research* may be antithetical to the philosophy of digital storytelling and establish a relationship of exploitation between researcher and participant.

However, despite challenges in carrying out the digital storytelling process, analyzing the digital storytelling product and maintaining fidelity to its original Freirian intent, we believe that the benefits of digital storytelling outweigh its drawbacks. Digital storytelling serves as a potentially fruitful method for social research and advocacy. The method's innovative quality stems from its ability to serve, in true Freirian fashion, as a method for research, intervention, and community action. The nature of the digital storytelling process offers participants and researcher/facilitators the possibility to open up the social research process as an "active" and collaborative method in which both parties serve as virtual researchers in the meaning-making process.

In this respect, we see a future direction for digital stories to be incorporated as visual elicitation devices for interview and focus-group-based social research, similar to that of participant-produced photos in the Photovoice focused group discussion method (Wang & Burris, 1997). "Much of the creativity of the Freirian approach has been in the development of codes [also known as triggers]…that codify the generative themes [of discussion] into a physical form…so that participants can 'see' their reality with new eyes and consequently develop alternative ways of thinking and acting" (Wallerstein & Duran, 2002 p. 42). Digital stories mesh well with a Freirian-structured questioning approach in which group dialogue is facilitated through the use of visual elicitation triggers for discussion. However, not only do participant and researcher/facilitator create meaning in this process, audiences viewing the digital story are also afforded a modicum of interpretive leverage. In this regard, digital storytelling goes one step further than what was deemed innovative for social research in the 1980s and 1990s by acknowledging the agency of participants in the research process and by casting novel agency upon digital storytelling audiences, thereby opening up the production of media as a *popular* form, to be consumed *and produced* by the masses.

Applying an ethnographic lens to the digital storytelling process allows for a sophisticated analysis of meaning-making endeavors, heralding the potential for digital storytelling as an innovative method for social research projects interrogating identity as a locus of concern. The digital storytelling process and product may be analyzed from multiple narrative vantage points. "What," "how," "why," "when," and "for whom" questions signal the narrative intent of the digital storyteller. Responses to these questions center on the collaborative and situated nature of the social construction of identity.

Analytical responses to "what" questions focus on the generative themes of the story and may be used by participant, researcher/facilitator, and audiences alike to assess community concerns and may serve as a launching point for a formative social research project. Analysis of "how" questions foreground the artistry of the storyteller, displaying a much more dynamic role for digital storytelling participant in the social research process than might be revealed in thematic/content analyses. "Why," "when," and "for whom" questions beckon a dialogic/performance analysis of digital stories as socially produced artifacts. From this analytical perspective, meaning is produced through a dense configuration of narrative intention and interpretation. Practiced and symbolic social interactions among storytellers, researcher/facilitators, and audience serve as sites for the transformation of identities of the social networks producing and viewing the digital story. Finally, the digital storytelling process is useful for a narrative inquiry of power relations and may be especially useful for social researchers seeking to understand phenomena from a particular sociocultural or historical juncture. From a Foucauldian perspective, digital stories may be seen as deriving from particular "discursive regimes." Rhetorical and discursive practices within mirror a larger sociopolitical or economic calculus of the topic at hand (Foucault, 1995).

In terms of the practicalities of conducting a digital storytelling analysis, in this chapter we have spelled out one way for conceptualizing a transcript to capture the vicissitudes of the digital story product. The intertextual transcription method presented herein, that represents visual, chronological, aural and oral, emotional, gestural, and textual elements, points to the multiple modalities used to produce meaning in a digital story. This transcription method literally allows the researcher to chart the meanings participants attach to different elements of their media production and to illustrate, albeit rather statically, the dynamics of identity representation. Future research is needed to develop qualitative data analysis software that moves beyond a textual analysis approach to more faithfully represent conceptualizations of multimodal media production. Digital storytelling is one new way for researchers to engage and contribute to community, group, and individual efforts to use MMP to publicly document, comment upon, and shape the events around them. As these multimodal literacy practices expand, so will the need for social research methods that can account for the real economic and social changes that take place as a result.

References

Bakhtin, M. M. (1981). *The dialogic imagination: Four essays by M.M. Bakhtin* (Emerson, C., & Holquist, M., Trans.). Austin: University of Texas Press.

Barab, S. A., & Roth, W.-M. (2006). Curriculum-based ecosystems: Supporting knowing from an ecological perspective. *Educational Researcher, 35*(5), 3–13.

Bauman, R., & Briggs, C. (1990). Poetics and performance as critical perspectives on language and social life. *Annual Review Anthropology, 19,* 59–88.

Beeson, I., & Miskelly, C. (2005). *Digital stories of community: Mobilization, coherence and continuity: Fourth media in transition conference.* Paper presented at the MiT4: The Work of Stories.

Best, S., & Kellner, D. (1999). Debord and the postmodern turn: New stages of the spectacle [Electronic Version]. *Illuminations.* Retrieved on March 2, 2009 http://www.uta.edu/huma/illuminations/kell17.htm

boyd, d. (2007). Why youth (heart) social network sites: The role of networked publics in teenage social life. In Buckingham, D. (Ed.), *MacArthur foundation series on digital learning—Youth, identity, and digital media volume.* Cambridge, MA: MIT Press.

Burgess, J. (2006). Hearing ordinary voices: Cultural studies, vernacular creativity and digital storytelling. *Continuum: Journal of Media & Cultural Studies, 20*(2), 201–214.

Carey, J. C., & Martin, I. (2007). *What are the implications of possible selves research for school counseling practice?* School Counseling Research Brief 5.2. Amherst, MA: Center for School Counseling Outcome Research.

Chavez, V., Israel, B., Alex, J., Allen, I., DeCarlo, M. F., Lichtenstein, R., Schulz, A., et al. (2004). A bridge between communities: Video-making using principles of community-based participatory research. *Health Promotion Practice, 5*(4), 395-403.

Clifford, J., & Marcus, G. E. (Eds.). (1986). *Writing culture: The poetics and politics of ethnography.* Berkeley: University of California Press.

Contando Nuestras Historias. (n.d.). Spanish Language Projects. Retrieved on November 14, 2008 http://www.storycenter.org/casestudies.html

de Leeuw, S., & Rydin, I. (2007). Migrant children's digital stories: Identity formation and self-representation through media production. *European Journal of Cultural Studies, 10*(4), 447–464.

Digital Stories @ UMBC. (n.d.). Digital stories from Charlestown. Retrieved on March 11, 2009 http://www.umbc.edu/oit/newmedia/studio/digitalstories/ctds.php

Dupain, M., & Maguire, L. (2005). *Digital story book projects 101: How to create and implement digital storytelling into your curriculum.* Paper presented at the 21st Annual Conference on Distance Teaching and Learning.

Dupain, M., & Maguire, L. (2007). Health digital storytelling projects. *American Journal of Health Education,* 33–35.

DUSTY. (n.d.). *D.U.S.T.Y.* Mission. Retrieved on October 5, 2005 http://oaklanddusty.org/mission.php

Educause Learning Initiative. (2007). 7 things you should know about . . . digital storytelling. Retrieved on July 6, 2010, *www.educause.edu/eli.*

Erstad, O., Gilje, O., & de Lang, T. (2007). Remixing multimodal resources: Multiliteracies and digital production in Norwegian media education. *Learning, Media and Technology, 32*(2), 183–198.

Favret-Saada, J. (1980). *Deadly words: Witchcraft in the Bocage.* Cambridge, MA: Cambridge University Press.

Finnegan, R. (2002). *Communicating: The multiple modes of human interconnection.* London: Routledge.

Foucault, M. (1995). *Discipline and punish: The birth of the prison.* New York: Vintage Press.

Freire, P. (1970). *Pedagogy of the oppressed.* New York: Seabury Press.

Fyfe, H. (2007). *"Habits of the heart" storytelling and everyday life.* Paper presented at the George Ewart Evans Centre for Storytelling Research Seminars 2007.

Gubrium, A. (2009). Digital storytelling: An emergent method for health promotion research and practice. *Health Promotion Practice, 10*(2), 186–191.

Gubrium, A. (2009). Digital storytelling as a method for engaged scholarship in anthropology. *Practicing Anthropology, 31*(4), 5–9.

Hoskins, A. (2001). New memory: Mediating history. *Historical Journal of Film, Radio and Television, 21*(4), 333–346.

Hubble, N. (2006). *Mass-observation and everyday life*. Houndmills-Basinstoke: Palgrave Macmillan.

Hull, G., & Nelson, M. (2005). Locating the semiotic power of multimodality. *Written Communication, 22*(2).

Hull, G., Zacher, J., & Hibbert, L. (2009). Youth, risk and equity in a global world. *Review of Research in Education, 33*.

Jasari X. (n.d.). OG3-Oscar grant-this week with Jasiri X episode 16. Retrieved on March 11, 2009 http://www.youtube.com/watch?v=zSFs1CQYDgY

Jenkins, H. (2006). *Convergence culture: Where old and new media collide*. New York: New York University.

Kajder, S. B. (2006). *Bringing the outside in: Visual ways to engage reluctant readers*. Portland, ME: Stenhouse Publishers.

Kress, G. (2003). *Literacy in the new media age*. London: Routledge.

Ladson-Billings, G., & Tate, W. A. (1995). Toward a critical race theory of education. *Teachers College Record, 97*(1), 47–68.

Lambert, J. (2006). *Digital storytelling: Capturing lives, creating community*. Berkeley: Digital Diner Press.

Lambert, J. (2007). *Digital storytelling cookbook*. Berkeley: Digital Diner Press.

Lemke, J. L. (1998). Metamedia literacy: Transforming meanings and media. In Reinking, D., Labbo, L., McKenna, M., & Kiefer, R. (Eds.), *Handbook of literacy and technology: Transformations in a post-typographic world* (pp. 283–301). Hillsdale, NJ: Erlbaum.

Levy, P. (1956/1998). *Becoming virtual: Reality in the digital age* (Bononno, R. Trans.). New York: Plenum Press.

Lundby, K. (Ed.). (2008). *Digital storytelling, mediatized stories: Self-representations in new media*. New York: Peter Lang.

Mahiri, J. (2004). Street scripts: African American youth writing about crime and violence. In Mahiri, J. (Ed.), *What they don't learn in school*. New York: Peter Lang Publishing Inc.

Marcuss, M. (2004). *The new community anthology: Digital storytelling as a community development strategy*. Boston, MA: Federal Reserve Bank of Boston.

Meadows, D. (2003). Digital storytelling: Research-based practice in new media. *Visual Communication, 2*(2), 189–193.

Merleau-Ponty, M. (1973). *The prose of the world* (O'Neil, J. Trans.). Evanston: Northwestern University Press.

Moll, L. C. (1992). Funds of knowledge for teaching: Using a qualitative approach to connect homes and classrooms. *Theory into Practice, 31*(1), 132–141.

Morrell, E. (2004). *Linking literacy and popular culture*. Norwood: Christopher-Gordon Publishers, Inc.

New London Group. (1996). A pedagogy of multiliteracies: Designing social futures. *Harvard Educational Review, 66*(1), 60–92.

Ohler, J. B. (2007). *Digital storytelling in the classroom: New media pathways to literacy, learning, and creativity*. Thousand Oaks, CA: Corwin Press.

Ranciere, J. (1991). *The ignorant school master*. Stanford: Stanford University Press.

Rheingold, H. (2002). *Smart mobs: The next social revolution*. Cambridge, MA: Basic.

Riessman, C. K. (2008). *Narrative methods for the human sciences*. Los Angeles: Sage Publications.

Riley, T., & Hawe, P. (2005). Researching practice: The methodological case for narrative inquiry. *Health Education Research, 20*(2), 226–236.

Rose, G. (2001). *Visual methodologies: An introduction to the interpretation of visual materials*. Thousand Oaks, CA: Sage.

Sahni, U. (2003). Personal communication.

Shewbridge, W. (2007). *All the good stories: Intergenerational digital storytelling as process and product*. Paper presented at the MiT5: Creativity, Ownership and Collaboration in the Digital Age International Conference.

Silence Speaks. (n.d.). Digital storytelling in support of healing and violence prevention. Retrieved on November 14, 2008 http://www.silencespeaks.org/

Stories for Change. (n.d.). About stories for change. Retrieved on November 15, 2008 http://storiesforchange.net/about_stories_for_change

Tucker, G. (2006). First person singular: The power of digital storytelling. *Screen Education*, (42), 54–59.

Turner, K. C. N. (2008). *Multimodal media production in the development of multiliteracies.* Berkeley: University of California.

U.C. Links. (2002). From Berkeley to Brazil through the fifth dimension. Retrieved on October 5, 2005 http://www.uclinks.org/what/newsletter/nl1/nl1.1.pg9.html

Wallerstein, N., & Duran, B. (2002). The conceptual, historical, and practice roots of community based participatory research and related participatory traditions. In Minkler, M., & Wallerstein, N. (Eds.), *Community-based participatory research for health* (pp. 27–52). San Francisco: Jossey-Bass.

Wang, C., & Burris, M. A. (1997). Photovoice: Concept, methodology, and use for participatory needs assessment. *Health Education & Behavior, 24*(3), 369–387.

Yang, K. W. (2007). *Organizing MySpace: Youth walkouts, pleasure, politics and new media.* Unpublished manuscript, San Diego, CA.

> Chapter 22

Mobile Phones as Sensors for Social Research

Nathan Eagle

Introduction

Mobile phones have the potential to generate unprecedented data for social research. By installing custom logging applications on higher-end phones, it is possible to quantify behavioral information including tone of voice, the people typically proximate on Saturday nights, and even an individual's media consumption habits. However, mobile phones are playing an increasingly important role in social research due not only to these growing technical functionalities, but also to their ubiquity around the world. Every one of the approximately 4 billion mobile phones in use today have continuous access to information about an individual's social behavior, including communication and movement data.

In the last decade we have witnessed the fastest technology adoption in human history. More than 1 billion mobile phones were sold during 2008, 10 times as many as the number of personal computers sold that year, at a rate of one new phone for every six people on Earth. In many developed countries, the mobile phone penetration rate has exceeded 100% of the population. However, mobile phones are now available to the majority of people who earn more than $5 a day, resulting in the fact that the majority of mobile phone subscribers today live in the developing world, dramatically changing the prospects of conducting social research in these underserved regions. And the potential functionality of this ubiquitous infrastructure of mobile devices is dramatically increasing. Many of these phones currently have a processor equivalent in power to the ones in our desktop computers just a decade ago. No longer constrained to simply placing and receiving voice calls, or even simple calendar and address book applications, the possibilities are staggering now that billions of people are essentially carrying pocket-sized, networked computers throughout their daily lives.

Mobile phones are ideally suited to provide insight into social behaviors. They are inconspicuous, typically carried by the majority of a population, and have passive sensing capabilities that make them such an important tool to study human populations. Mobile phone service providers have access to behavioral and social network data for over 4 billion people; indeed, there are many nations whose entire population is accounted for in these databases. Additionally, the ability to program today's mobile phones has enabled them to be transformed into data gathering sensors by researchers working independently of mobile phone operators. This chapter will outline two techniques for collecting data from mobile phones, each with its own set of privacy implications. The first comes from an analysis of data from the mobile phone service provider, whereas the second comes from installing a logging application directly on a phone.

Background on Phones as Sensors

The very nature of mobile phones makes them an ideal vehicle to study both individuals and societies: people habitually carry a mobile phone with them and use it as a medium through which to do much of their communication. This recent ubiquity of mobile phones means that the majority of humans today already have the habit of keeping a charged behavioral sensor with them at all times. Now that handset manufacturers are opening their platforms to developers, standard mobile phones can be harnessed as networked wearable sensors. The information available by installing custom logging software on today's phones includes the user's location (cell tower ID), people nearby (repeated Bluetooth scans), communication (call and SMS logs), as well as application usage and phone status (idle, charging, etc). However, as discussed below, every mobile phone today also creates logs of communication and movement patterns that are stored within mobile phone service provider databases around the world.

Data Collection: Service Providers. While obtaining access to these operator databases is not a trivial process for researchers, today's mobile phone service providers occasionally allow academic researchers limited access (see González, Hidalgo, & Barabási, 2008; Onnela, et al., 2007). This data, typically referred to as call data records (CDR), consists of all communication events (phone calls and text messages) as well as the cellular tower that enabled the communication to occur. Beyond documentation of voice and text-message communication and location estimates based on cellular towers, occasionally mobile operators have additional data about their subscribers, including demographic information, socioeconomic status, prepaid scratch card denominations, air-time sharing and transfers, and additional product adoption data.

It is important to emphasize the typical constraint on CDR: location of a phone is only logged if it is actively being used to communicate. While a mobile phone continuously monitors signals from proximate cellular towers, due to power constraints it typically does not continuously send back similar signals alerting the nearby towers of its particular location.[1] Therefore, the only method of obtaining continuous cellular tower data is by installing a logging application on the mobile phone itself, as described in the next section.

Data Collection: Handsets. To capture more detailed information about the movements of a mobile phone, along with a variety of additional rich behavioral data, it is necessary to install a custom application onto a mobile phone. There have been a variety of projects that have involved such applications that log communication events as well as visible cellular towers and Bluetooth devices on a set of subjects' phones including HIIT's Context project (Raento, Oulasvirta, Petit, & Toivonen, 2005), MIT's Reality Mining project (Eagle & Pentland, 2006), and the PlaceLab (LaMarca et al., 2005; Chen et al., 2006) research at Intel Research. Additionally, other research projects have demonstrated the utility of cellular tower data for a broad spectrum of applications ranging from contextual image tagging (Davis, Good, & Sarvas, 2004) to inferring the mobility of an individual (Sohn et al., 2006). Generally, this logging software records between one and four of the cellular towers with the highest signal strength, however, recent research suggests it is possible to localize a handset down to 2.5-m accuracies if the number of detected towers is dramatically increased (Otsason, Varshavsky, LaMarca, & Lara, 2005). Similar accuracies are obtained if the phones are equipped with GPS, which is becoming increasingly prevalent on today's high-end phones. However, continuous location tracking is not yet realistic due to the significant power requirements required by the GPS chipset.

While location is obviously an important feature in this data, the proximity of other Bluetooth devices has proved to be equally important behavioral information. Bluetooth, a short-range wireless standard initially designed as a cable replacement, has been installed on over 1 billion devices worldwide. A byproduct of this technology is that today's Bluetooth-enabled phones can detect other Bluetooth devices carried by people nearby. When a Bluetooth device is visible, any other device conducting a scan within 3–5 m will be able to detect its unique MAC address. By combining this proximity information with location, time, and date, it becomes possible to infer the nature of relationships between individuals. For example, regular proximity detected by a coffee machine in the afternoons represents a very different relationship than proximity detected downtown late on Saturday night (Eagle, Pentland, & Lazer, 2009).

Collecting data using these custom logging applications on mobile phones does not require the consent of the mobile service providers. Despite having the phones programmed to automatically send back the behavioral data over the operator's data connection, the majority of the research projects mentioned above occurred unbeknownst to the operators. Streaming data to the research team also aids their ability to follow and control the study; should the experiment not be running according to expectations, it can be modified as soon as this is noticed. And by not requiring a data-sharing agreement with a service provider, this type of handset-based data collection is much more accessible to researchers. However, as discussed in the section on implementation details, writing a custom logging application requires the skill of an experienced mobile phone programmer. Luckily, mobile phone logging software like HIIT's ContextLogger and Nokia's Simple-Context application is open-source and can run on many high-end Nokia handsets, which

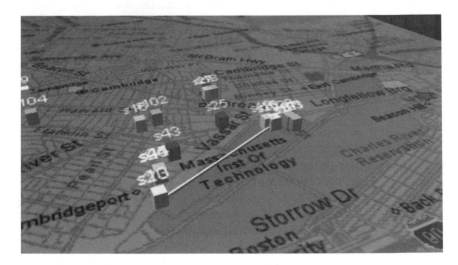

Figure 22.1 Movement and communication visualization of the Reality Mining subjects.

has made it extremely popular for this type of research. Figure 22.1 is a visual representation of the type of data logged by ContextLogger.

Location of individual subjects is based on approximate location of cell towers, while the links between subjects are indicative of phone communication.

Existing Data Collection Methods for Social Research

While the current social research relies on data that is generally adequate for the analysis required, much of today's social research data suffers from common problems: the reliance on self-report data, the absence of extensive longitudinal data, and the necessity to limit the size of the study due to the time-consuming and burdensome nature of the data collection. However, as technological social network data becomes increasingly prevalent, it has suddenly become possible to ask an entirely unprecedented set of new research questions.

Trade-offs in Traditional Social Data Collection. For over a century, social scientists have studied relatively small, cohesive social groups (Tonnies, 1887). Interaction and relationship data collection began in earnest in the 1930s (A Davis, 1941), typically through surveys as well as by placing an observer in a particular social setting who continuously took notes on the behavior of the group. Figure 22.2a depicts data collected from a human observer placed in the Western Electric Company who was studying the interaction patterns between 12 employees (F Roethlisberger, 1939). This traditional method of conducting ethnographic research is still quite prevalent and captures rich sociological data, yet is constrained to a limited number of subjects simply due to its time-consuming nature. However, a new method of collecting data on social systems has emerged with the prevalence of the Internet. Today, researchers can automatically collect large-scale social network datasets from digital information such as e-mail, represented in Figure 22.2b (Huberman, Adar, & Fine, 2005). These networks represent a larger number of people and have a variety of interesting properties, yet the rich interpersonal relationship information that was traditionally collected by the human observer has been lost.

(a)   (b)

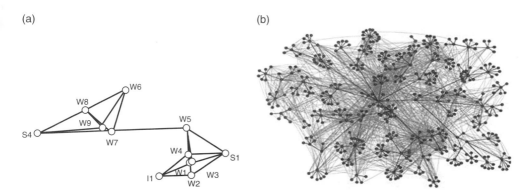

Figure 22.2a was generated from the rich, low-level relationship data collected by an observer watching the interactions among 12 employees in the Western Electric Company in 1935 (Rich Interaction Data (1935)). Figure 22.2b is a representation of the social network of hundreds of Hewlett Packard employees collected from sparse e-mail data in 2003 (Sparse e-mail data (2004)).

The evolution of social network analysis. Figure 22.2a was generated from the rich, low-level relationship data collected by an observer watching the interactions among 12 employees in the Western Electric Company in 1935. Figure 22.2b is a representation of the social network of hundreds of Hewlett Packard employees collected from sparse e-mail data in 2003.

Dealing with the inherent trade-offs between traditional ethnographic and today's automated, digital social network data has spawned attempts to generate both rich and large-scale data. Agent-based models have been proposed as a solution to this problem of dearth of data and detail by simulating people's behavior in groups using simple rules. However, this has been seen not only as an oversimplification of human behavior, but also, in many instances, as completely wrong. Some models of gossip dissemination across an organization of agents make the assumption that individuals move randomly, an assumption that almost all people could recognize as spurious (Moreno, Nekovee, & Pacheco, 2004).

The limitations of these methods can be seen as the rationale behind why social scientists, unlike almost any other type of scientist, are still conducting analysis and publishing papers on datasets collected well over 50 years ago (Freeman, 2003). The massive technical breakthroughs over the past few decades that have revolutionized virtually every other science have yet to dramatically impact social science. The data from Figure 22.2a, collected by the human observer on the behavior of those 12 workers back in 1935, are still some of the best data a social network analyst can get today. However, we are beginning to enter another era of technical breakthrough—a breakthrough that will manifest itself by outfitting each employee in tomorrow's electric company with his own personal observer that tirelessly logs everything he does. Sociologists are now becoming aware of the possibility that the data collected by the human observer of 1935 could now be collected by today's pervasive mobile phone.

Reliance on Self-Report Measures. A series of early studies comparing self-report and observational data found surprisingly large divergences between the two (H Bernard, P. Killworth, & L. Sailer, 1979; Bernard, Killworth, & Kronenfeld, 1984; Marsden, 1990). Since these early studies, researchers have relied almost exclusively on self-reports of network ties. Some researchers have argued that observational data capture only snapshots of interaction, while self-report data provide a truer picture of the long-term social structure (Freeman, Romney, & Freeman, 1987). It is certainly true that self-reported interactions are behaviors mediated by beliefs about what constitutes a relationship, ability to recall interactions, how memorable certain people are, etc. These beliefs and recollections about one's relationships may have a considerable impact on certain outcomes. In fact, in the extreme, there are some relationships that exist only as a belief (e.g., unrequited love). Surveys will thus always remain an essential measurement instrument in social network analysis. However, it is indisputable that, in many circumstances, actual behavior has an effect independent of people's beliefs and recollections about that behavior, despite the fact that much of social network research is written as if self-report data are equivalent to behavioral data.

Study of Macro-networks. The reliance on self-reports also presents a practical problem: thorough network data are time-consuming and burdensome for respondents to report. This limits the size of social systems that can be studied with self-report data, as well as the number of observations over time that can be collected. (For a system of size N, where one collects P observations of interactions, the number of sociometric questions each respondent needs to reply to is $(N - 1) * P$.) Given the need to maintain exceptionally high response rates for social network research, most social network research is thus limited to a single observation of relatively small systems. This is beginning to change with the development of electronic devices to measure interaction automatically. However, social network analysis has largely been limited to sharply bounded groups. In contrast, mobile phone data is already being collected on 4 billion people, in virtually every country on Earth.

Absence of Longitudinal Data. Most data used for social research (including those generated by mobile phones) tend to analyze static, behavioral snapshots. However, longitudinal data are essential to discriminating between cause and effect in behavioral data. For example, in some ongoing research on the effect cities have on their inhabitants' social networks, we can find that individuals who live in cities tend to have different types of social networks than those who live in rural areas, as hypothesized in previous studies (Fischer, 1982). However, a legitimate critique of this result is that the original question has gone unanswered. With the current "snap-shot" data, we are unable to determine whether the city attracts individuals who already have a signature social network, or whether indeed the city itself influences the network of its inhabitants. To obtain a better answer to this question, it is necessary to have longitudinal data. Now that we have over 3 years of data on every mobile phone subscriber in a country, we can identify individuals who live in rural areas during year 1, and then move to urban areas in year 2. By comparing the before and after social networks, we can get a better idea of a city's effect. Indeed with several years of data, we can also learn if these individuals maintain these new relationships created by the urban area if they move back to their rural home.

A New Set of Social Research Questions

The rapid technology adoption of mobile phones, enabling researchers to unobtrusively collect continuous human behavioral data, opens new avenues of understanding across a variety of domains. Through the analysis of the aggregate social networks that make up a society, we can gain deeper insights into the behavior of individuals, organizations, and cities. However, because the phones themselves are networked, their functionality transcends merely a logging device, but rather they can be used for social network intervention—supplying introductions between two proximate people who do not know each other (Eagle & Pentland, 2005). The mobile devices of tomorrow will see what the user sees, hear what the user hears, and learn patterns in the user's behavior. This will enable them to make inferences regarding whom the user knows, whom the user likes, and even what the user may do next. Although a significant amount of sensors and machine perception are required, it will only be a matter of a few years before this functionality will be realized on standard mobile phones. The following section details some of the first steps toward answering some of these questions.

Experience Sampling. Subjects in experience sampling method (ESM) studies typically carry a device that prompts them with questions about their current activities, context, and state of mind (Csikszentmihalyi & Larson, 1987). Recent advances in information technology, such as Web-based surveys or even experience sampling methods on handheld computers (Barrett & Barrett, 2001) have helped facilitate gathering survey data, yet these techniques are unable to eradicate its fundamental flaws: bias and sparsity. The method described by Hulkko et al. (2004) can be contrasted with computerized experience sampling (ESMc). Traditionally, in most computerized ESM the questions are posed by and answered on handheld computers (such as Palm Pilots or the HP IPAQ).

Computerized ESM has of course, in general, advantages over standard paper-questionnaires: the subject does not have to accurately note answering times (and so the times, provided by the technology, tend to be more accurate), the ability to generate dynamic questionnaires, and the digital nature of the resulting material. These are inherited by smartphone-based ESM, with stricter limitations on screen size and input modalities. The main advantage of smartphones is then not the technical capabilities as such, but the ability to bring these capabilities to new settings, where people are unwilling or unable to carry additional devices or where such devices would affect the phenomena under study even more, for example, taking out a mobile phone can be quite invisible and acceptable in social settings, whereas a handheld computer will likely bring extra attention to the subject.

Intille, Rondoni, Kukla, Ancona, and Bao (2003) describe a system where the researcher can specify rules on when questions are asked, and which questions, based on contextual variables such as location. This limits the sampling to the times when a subject is performing a particular activity, rather than burdening the subject with a very high question rate. Answering experience sampling questionnaires while mobile may task the available cognitive and attentional resources.

Technologically, the main advantage of the camera-equipped smartphone is the always-available networking, enabling flexible posing of questions and monitoring of the answers, as well as the ability to use images to both document the surroundings and to trigger memories in later analysis sessions. Additionally, the programmability of the smartphone opens up avenues of optimized questionnaires (Kurhila et al., 2001), which show that modeling the reasons underlying answers allows the questionnaire to be adapted, so that a minimum number of questions will be answered while maintaining the level of information gained. However, care should be taken in the experiment design that the results are not fully determined by the hypothesized model of activities or reasons. While typically ESM questions are triggered at random intervals, incorporating mobile phones as the data gathering instrument enables the surveys to be driven by a particular detected behavior or event.

There have been several systems designed to enable the researcher to specify rules defining when questions are asked, and which questions, based on contextual variables such as location (Intille et al., 2003; Holmquist, Falk, & Wigström, 1999; Verkasalo & Ámm⊢ Áinen, 2007). In our recent Helsinki study, phones were programmed to launch a survey question about the type of relationship the user had with the individual he or she just called. This limits the sampling to the times when a subject is performing a particular activity rather than burdening the subject with a very high question rate. The programmability of today's mobile phones (smartphones) opens up avenues of optimized questionnaires: Kurhila et al. (2001) show that modeling the reasons underlying answers to questions allows the questionnaire to be adapted, so that a minimum number of questions will be answered while maintaining the level of information gained.

Mobility Patterns. The recent analysis of data from mobile phone service providers has led researchers to increased insight into human movement patterns. While some researchers take issue with labeling these insights as "universal laws of human movement," it is clear that through the analysis of cellular tower location data from hundreds of thousands of people, it is possible to finally quantify some of the more fundamental rules of human mobility. In a highly cited *Nature* paper from 2008, González, Hidalgo, and Barabási (2008) used data from mobile phone operators to show that human movement trajectories can be parameterized using gravity models. The recent analyses of data from mobile phone service providers have given us new insights into the aspects of human movement patterns that are shared in all societies. As researchers replicate these findings in increasing numbers of countries and cultures, we are beginning to observe general rules governing the "physics of society." The volume of data that is now available from across the globe will allow us to determine to what extent these rules are universal.

Urban Studies. The analysis of cellular tower data not only provides insight into human movement patterns, but also sheds some light on how individuals use the urban infrastructure within a city. Ratti, Pulselli, Williams, & Frenchman (2006) have demonstrated the possibility of using mobile phones for urban analysis: to quantify the dynamics of complex urban activities. As alluded to in the previous section, we are also hoping to use our mobile phone data to learn more about the effect cities have on their inhabitants and social networks.

Using information from communication logs and top-up denominations to characterize attributes such as socioeconomic status and region, we have shown that rural and urban communities differ dramatically not only in terms of personal network topologies, but also in terms of inferred behavioral characteristics such as travel (Eagle, Montjoye, & Bettencourt, 2009). To our knowledge, this is the first comprehensive comparison between regional groups of this size.

In Eagle et al. (2009), we proposed the use of cell phone usage data to test, elaborate, and quantify classical hypotheses in sociology, social psychology, and economics about behavioral changes and human and social adaptations as a result of life in large cities versus smaller urban areas and rural settings. We have argued that this type of data can now supply statistical coverage of the majority of the population, albeit through technologies that allow us to measure specific quantities that are correlates of cost, rhythms of life, and the dynamics and structure of social networks.

We have found support for, and quantified here for the first time on a large scale, arguments for the diversification and growth of personal networks as individuals live or move to large urban areas. We have also found evidence that this growth results in an optimization process whereby the burden of maintaining a large number of social contacts is partially mitigated by the fact that most of these contacts are weak, taking up less of the individual's time. At the same time, we could characterize several other personal attributes of cell phone users and their geographic disparity.

Finally, we were able to test statistically two alternative hypothesis for the origin of these effects, namely, whether individuals change behavior to conform with their social environment (behavioral adaptation) or instead migrate to realize their preferences for larger and more intense social environments of the large city or a smaller number of stronger links characteristic of rural areas (differential selection). We found strong support for differential selection over behavior adaptation, though future work is under way to further test the viability of these two alternative scenarios (Figure 22.3).

The Stability of Society. With adequate longitudinal data, it becomes possible to quantify the dynamics within social networks to gain insight into the evolution of groups. Using an analysis of phone communication logs and a coauthorship network involving 4 million and 30,000 people, respectively, Palla, Barabási, and Vicsek (2007) showed that smaller groups persist longer if their members do not change, whereas the opposite holds

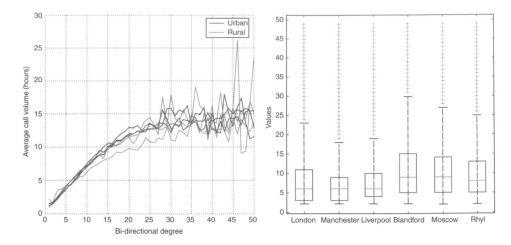

Figure 22.3 Urban versus rural social networks. The figure on the left shows how both urban and rural call volumes plateau at the same rate despite the increase in the number of contacts. The figure on the right shows the distribution of contacts within three urban and three rural areas of the United Kingdom. Contrary to previous opinion, individuals living in rural areas within the United Kingdom tend to have more contacts, as evidenced by their calling patterns.

true for larger community, which are more likely to persist only if the group actively alters membership.

One of the major open questions is whether the characteristics previously correlated with temporal stability and evolution in the study above can be generalized. Using several different community detection algorithms over a sliding window of communication logs representing every phone call made in a country over 4 years, we are attempting to rigorously validate these results and uncover other characteristics of both stable and unstable communities.

Social Network Diversity across Demographics. In our analysis of communication logs from the United Kingdom, individuals who communicate with a variety of different people have a greater socioeconomic status. While it is not possible to establish causality between this behavior and socioeconomic status, there is a significant ($R = .75$; $p < .001$) correlation between a region's communication diversity and its index of deprivation, a metric used to quantify a region's socioeconomic status within the United Kingdom (Eagle, Macy, & Claxton, 2010). It certainly seems plausible that some cultures encourage interactions with others while other groups prefer to remain insular. In the United States, this type of culture was shown above to be associated with business school students, and in the United Kingdom the culture appears to be associated with individuals of higher socioeconomic status. The question whether this result is universal across countries is actively being pursued (Figure 22.4).

Behavioral Structure across Demographics. Human life is inherently imbued with routine across all temporal scales, from minute-to-minute actions to monthly or yearly patterns. Many of these patterns in behavior are easy to recognize; however, some are subtler. Using a dataset generated from a logging application installed on the phones of 215 randomly sampled subjects from a major U.S. city, we attempted to quantify the amount

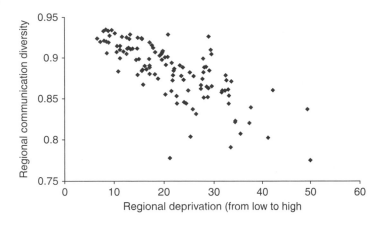

Figure 22.4 A preliminary plot of regional communication diversity and the corresponding index of deprivation (a socioeconomic status measurement that is a combination of metrics such as average income levels, access to healthcare, and education). This data came from the UK call graph consisting of 250 million hashed phone numbers and 12 billion phone calls. It can be seen that the regions with a culture of creating diverse social ties tend to be the least deprived. Diversity of communication behavior has a significant correlation of $r = -.75$ with the regional index of deprivation.

of predictable structure in an individual's life using the standard Shannon information entropy metric,

$$H = -\Sigma p \times \log_2(p)$$

After providing informed consent, these subjects were given phones that logged the ID of the four cellular towers with the strongest signal strength every 30 sec. Additionally, the phones conducted Bluetooth scans every minute. Bluetooth beacons, static devices that simply report their identity when a proximate phone conducts a Bluetooth scan, were installed in the homes of each subject; as the beacons are detected only if the phone is within 10 m of it, detection implies the subject is at home. Additional data about the ambient audio environment was also collected, but not used for this analysis. The data was compressed on the mobile phone and uploaded to a central server after each day. By offering a smartphone and free service, over 80% of the randomly selected individuals agreed to participate in the study. The demographic information we have about the subjects is evenly distributed among ethnic groups and income levels, accurately reflecting the distribution of the city's inhabitants. No longer constrained to the study of academics or researchers, our data represents one of the first comprehensive behavioral depictions of the inhabitants within a major urban city.

The means and variances of the entropy metric are segmented across demographics in Table 22.1. Of particular note is the high variance of the entropy metric, indicating that there are individuals across all demographics whose behavioral patterns are seemingly unstructured (Eagle, Quinn, & Clauset, 2009).

Complex Social Systems. Attempting to understand and model the complex collective behavior of organizations and societies made up of idiosyncratic individuals is certainly a daunting task. Physicists have recently been quick to jump on the problem with their own set of tools, applying techniques such as statistical mechanics to ignore the micro-behavior of a system (i.e., the speed of each individual particle in a balloon or actions of an individual in society), and rather provide guidelines for the behavior of the aggregate (i.e, the air pressure in the balloon or the current cultural fad). Even in the early 1970s, physicists began successfully mapping human movement in groups to the theory of particle movement in gases (Henderson, 1971). Today's physicists are now taking on much larger social phenomena: decision making, contagion dissemination, the formation of alliances and organizations, as well as a wide range of other collective behavior (Newman, 2001; Huberman et al., 2005; Domingos & Richardson, 2001; Albert & Barabasi, 2002; Watts & Strogatz, 1998; Eubank, Guclu, & Anil Kumar, 2004).

Diffusion & Influence. A different type of social data collected by mobile phone service providers is the adoption of service (tariff) plans and other telecommunication products, which may be thought of as the spread of a social contagion. Individuals who have a particularly good experience with a particular product will tell their friends about it, increasing the probability that their friends also adopt the product (Hill, Provost, & Volinsky, 2006). Other research has shown that this probability of adoption does not increase linearly with the number of adopter friends. While the probability of adoption more than doubles when an individual goes from one adopter friend to two, each additional adopter friend after the second has a decreasing impact on the individual's behavior (Backstrom, Huttenlocher, & Kleinberg, 2006).

In our larger datasets (consisting of more than 500,000 people), there are particular individuals who hold influence over others in their peer group; when they adopt a particular product or service, the individuals whom they call subsequently adopt the product as well. Through the analysis of the diffusion of these social contagions over a call graph, it may become possible to learn more about the social dynamics inherent within a population. Other researchers have used the adoption of products such as mobile instant-messaging chat applications as a method of quantifying the influence of individual subscribers (Szabo & Barabasi, 2006) (Figure 22.5).

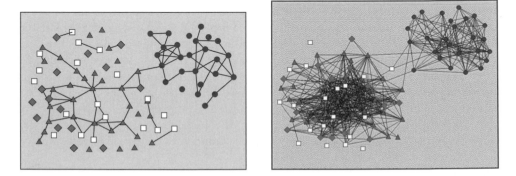

Figure 22.5 Friendship (left) and daily proximity (right) networks share similar structure. Blue circles represent incoming Sloan business school students. Red triangles, orange diamonds, and white squares represent the senior students, incoming students, and faculty/staff/freshmen at the Media Lab.

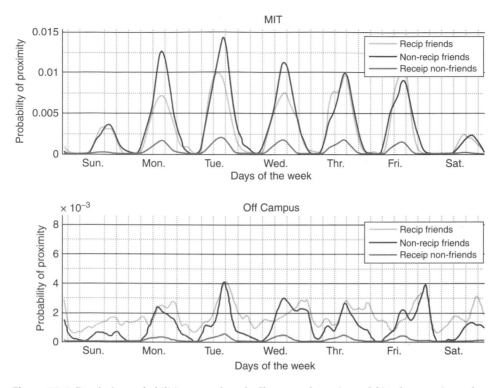

Figure 22.6 Proximity probabilities at work and off campus for reciprocal friend, nonreciprocal friend, and non-friend dyads. Probability of proximity is calculated for each hour in the week and is generally much higher for friends than non-friends. However, it is also apparent that nonreciprocal and reciprocal friend dyads have different temporal and spatial patterns in proximity, with reciprocal friends spending more time together off campus in the evenings.

Relationship Inference. In the first part of this chapter, we discussed how information about location and proximity can be gathered using logging applications installed on mobile phones. The knowledge of a shared context between two users can provide insight into the nature of their association. For example, being near someone at 3:00 p.m. by the coffee machines confers different meaning than being near him or her at 11:00 p.m. at a local bar. However, even simple proximity patterns provide an indication of the structure of the underlying friendship network, as shown in Figure 22.6. The clique on the top right of each network are business students, while the group of senior students are at the center of the clique on the bottom left. The first-year students can be found on the periphery of both graphs.

A key finding of this study is that using just the proximity data from mobile phones, it is possible to accurately predict 95% of the self-reported friendships between the subjects (Eagle et al., 2009). Thus, we can accurately predict self-reported friendships based only on objective measurements of behavior. These findings imply that the strong cultural norms associated with social constructs such as friendship produce differentiated and recognizable patterns of behavior. Leveraging these behavioral signatures to accurately characterize relationships in the absence of survey data has the potential to enable the

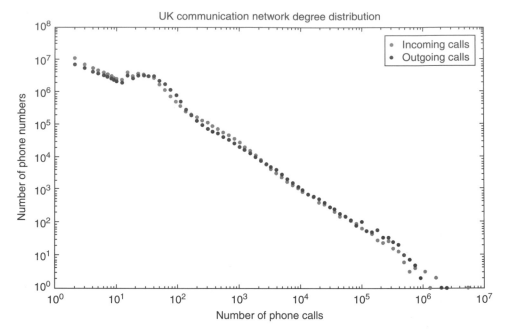

Figure 22.7 Degree distribution for Communication Network of the United Kingdom.

quantification and prediction of social network structures on a much larger scale than is currently possible.

Unsurprisingly, nonreciprocal friendships fall systematically between these two categories. This probably reflects the fact that friendships are not categorical in nature, and that nonreciprocal friendships may be indicative of moderately valued friendship ties. Thus, inferred friendships may actually contain more information than is captured by surveys that are categorical in nature. A pairwise analysis of variance (a standard technique to compare two distributions typically referred to as an ANOVA) shows that data from friendships, nonreciprocal friendships, and reciprocated non-friend relationships do indeed come from three distinct distributions ($F > 9$; $p < .005$). Some of the information that permits inference of friendship is illustrated in Figure 22.7. This figure shows that our sensing technique is picking up the commonsense phenomenon that office acquaintances are frequently seen in the workplace, but rarely outside the workplace. Conversely, friends are often seen outside of the workplace, even if they are coworkers.

Measuring Social Distance. In 1967, Stanley Milgram conducted the "small world experiment" in an attempt to count the number of ties between any two randomly sampled people. His famous results showed that the average path length (the number of edges that separate two nodes in a network) for the social network of people living in the United States is approximately 5.5. However, because Milgram only allowed his subjects to select a single contact as the individual that has the most likely shortest path between two nodes, the path he mapped was not necessarily the shortest path between two people. More recent attempts at this experiment using e-mail imposed the same sampling constraint (Watts, Muhamad, & Sheridan Dodds, 2003). However, with a complete set of social network data, a much more complete view of the aggregate social network becomes possible. Using 1 month of data from almost 250 million Microsoft's instant messenger accounts, researchers within Microsoft discovered a shortest path distance of 6.6 (Leskovec & Horvitz, 2008). Defining distance as the path length while studying subgraphs of mobile phone networks, Onnela et al. (2007) found that ties that span a longer range tend to be weaker. Analyzing a corporate e-mail network, Adamic and Adar found that as the distance within the organizational hierarchy increased between two individuals, the typical tie strength, as measured by e-mail volume, unsurprisingly also decreased (Adamic & Adar, 2005). Liben-Nowell, Novak, and Kumar, (2005) demonstrated how geography is related to small world social networks. By studying the accounts with public location and a list of friends on the public blogging site LiveJournal, they were able to show that the probability of *A* forming a tie with *B* is inversely proportional to the number of people geographically closer to *A*.

Mobile Social Software. Several wireless service providers now offer location-based services to mobile phone subscribers using cell tower IDs. Users of services such as Dodgeball.com can expose their location to other friends by explicitly naming their location using SMS. Social Net is a project using RF-based devices (the Cybiko) to learn proximity patterns between people. When coupled with explicit information about a social network, the device is able to inform a mutual friend of two proximate people that an introduction may be appropriate (Terry, Mynatt, Ryall, & Leigh, 2002). Jabberwocky is a mobile phone application that performs repeated Bluetooth scans to develop a sense of an urban landscape. It was designed not as an introduction system, but rather to promote a sense of urban community (Paulos & Goodman, 2004). More recently, companies like Loopt and Boostmobile have had marginal commercial success with these friend tracking services, however, with the launch of Google Latitude, these location-based friend finder services have suddenly crossed the chasm into the mainstream market.

Data Analysis Techniques. Dynamic Bayesian Networks (DBNs) have been widely used for quantifying and predicting human behavior. Hidden Markov Models are popular types of DBNs that typically model time-series data as a series of observations useful to infer a phenomenon that is not observed (hidden). A useful property of these models is their generative nature. The transition probabilities associated with an individual's previous behavior and conditioned on the current observed data permit researchers to estimate future behavior. For analysis of human movement, typically these models involve location coordinates that are much more precise than cellular tower data, such as GPS data. These models are trained on general human movement (Ashbrook & Starner, 2003) or more specific data such as transportation routes (Liao, Patterson, Fox, & Kautz, 2007).

Media Consumption. Much of the state-of-the-art research on using mobile phones as behavioral sensors comes from industry rather than the academic research community. Beyond logging communication, location, and proximity, companies like IMMI are beginning to take advantage of an additional sensor: the microphone. By programming the phones to also record and transmit 10 sec of ambient audio every minute, IMMI has been able to determine exactly the media content to which their panelists are being exposed. This includes information down to which television show is being watched, or radio ads or song being played. The software has gotten so good that it is being used to test the efficacy of advertisements. Because they are tracking not only advertising consumption, but also purchasing decisions such as going to a film (which is determined in a similar way using the films' ambient acoustics), IMMI can determine how well an advertisement can influence behavior. Clearly, while the analysis of ambient audio presents a variety of privacy concerns, it certainly presents an additional dimension to behavioral data for social research.

Economic Indicators. By tracking enough people periodically with GPS, it becomes possible to use that sampling to infer buying patterns beyond consuming media. Companies such as Mao Networks are using anonymized GPS traces of thousands of individuals to predict economic outcomes. For example, they can track how many people are going into a specific retail chain store located across the country. This information can subsequently be sold to investment firms such as hedge funds, who use this data to make better predictions about whether this company will make their numbers during the next quarter.

Disease Monitoring. Beyond academics and start-ups, the other entity with an obvious interest in mobile phone data is the government. One of the additional application areas for these temporal proximity networks is to model the dissemination of a contagion, whether it is an airborne pathogen or a Bluetooth virus. The majority of epidemiological models are based on a compartmental SIR framework (which stands for the three types of people in the model: susceptible, infected, and recovered); the host population is partitioned into those that are susceptible, infected, or immune to a particular pathogen (Anderson & May, 1991). These deterministic models assume that the rate at which new infections are acquired is proportional to the number of encounters between susceptible and infected individuals, and leads to an effective reproductive ratio that is dependent on a threshold density of susceptible people (Kermack & McKendrick, 1991). Thus, the reproductive ratio is dependent not only on parameters intrinsic to the disease such as latent and infectious periods, but also on contacts between infectious and susceptible hosts. However, compartmental models of this kind implicitly assume that the host population is well mixed, such that the probability of infection is equal for all. Social network structures are clearly not always well mixed, however, and the complexities of host interactions may have profound implications for the interpretation of epidemiological models and clinical data. Standard mean-field models do not account for heterogeneities of risk between individuals due to the finite number, variability, and clustering of social contacts. Studies have shown that network structure can significantly affect the processes occurring on social networks, including the dynamics and evolution of infectious diseases. Some have investigated the effect of network structure on the evolution of disease traits such as infectious period and transmission rates, as well as invasion thresholds for epidemics, (e.g., Read & Keeling, 2003). Others have explored the role of spatial contact structure in the evolution of virulence (van Baalen, 2002; O'Keefe & Antonovics, 2002).

The accurate quantification of the host contacts, and therefore the associated variability in the probability of infection, is clearly of great importance. Hypothetical models are valuable for understanding the kind of effect different social network structures would have on disease spread; however, we suggest that the proximity information that can be captured with today's mobile phones gives a much more realistic interpretation of human social network dynamics. With detailed data on mixing parameters within a social network, epidemiologists will be armed with more information to make predictions about our vulnerability to the next SARS, as well as greater insight into preventing future epidemics. We note that our high resolution dynamic proximity network data have a great potential to contribute to the growing body of research on epidemiology from the network perspective, that is, proximity is a major contributing factor in infection. In particular, traditional network epidemiology concerns itself with the question of percolation; however, we have shown that the mean degree does not rise above the threshold for a connected graph until it is roughly a few hours in length. However, information (and pathogens such as mobile phone or biological viruses, or even rumors) can obviously still spread by virtue of the sequential nature of the adjacency matrices.

A project that used mobile phones as behavior sensors aimed to detect, localize, and estimate the time of a bioterror attack. BACTrack was designed to be installed on a sample of inhabitants of an urban area. By coupling self-report health status with high resolution location histories, it becomes possible to identify if the subjects reporting illness were in the same location at some point in the past. This not only enables the government to locate the site and time of an attack, but also to identify other individuals who were exposed, even before they report any symptoms.

Implementation Challenges

Handset Data Collection Difficulties. Unfortunately, most people do not use mobile phones that can run the logging applications mentioned earlier. Therefore, collecting data generated by mobile phones almost always requires giving out high-end phones to a set of subjects over an extended period of time, which obviously presents a variety of challenges. One major issue with using the logging software that runs on Nokia S60 GSM phones is that while they are suitable for almost all of the global mobile phone networks, they will work only on two major U.S. networks (T-Mobile and AT&T). Additionally, the least expensive S60 phones cost upward of $250, so outfitting a large study is an expensive undertaking, even if the mobile phone service is not being covered. Additionally, while it is possible to have the data stored directly on the memory cards of the subjects' phones, the researchers may find it beneficial to have the phones upload the latest behavioral data automatically every evening. This makes it possible to immediately detect if there is an error with the software and intervene upon the detection of a particular behavior. However, service providers generally charge for the data usage when uploading data from a mobile phone. Because the subjects typically are not getting any value out of this daily data usage, they typically need to be reimbursed for the associated expenses. Generally, 1 month of data typically takes up 10MB, which costs anywhere between $5 and $15 to upload.

Client-Side Data Collection: Data Errors. While logging applications that are installed on phones are now fairly robust and can be assumed to be running anytime the phone is on, the dataset generated is certainly not without noise. The following section describes errors introduced into the data through device failures and human factors, such as forgetting the phone at home or turning it off.

Bluetooth Errors. The 10-m range of Bluetooth, along with the fact that it can penetrate some types of walls, means that people not physically proximate may incorrectly be logged as such. By scanning only periodically, shorter proximity events may also be missed. Additionally, from the 5-million logged Bluetooth scans in our dataset, we have found that there is a small probability (between 1–3% depending on the phone) that a proximate, visible device will not be discovered during a scan. However, to detect other subjects, we can leverage the redundancy implicit in the system. Assuming both of the subjects' phones are actually scanning, the probability of a simultaneous crash or device discovery error is less than 1 in 1,000 scans. In our tests at MIT, we have empirically found that these errors have little effect on the extremely strong correlations between interaction (survey data) and the 5-m Bluetooth proximity scans. These problems, therefore, produce a small amount of background noise against which the true proximity relationships can be reasonably measured. However, social interactions within an academic institution are not necessarily typical of a broader cross-section of society and the errors may be more severe or more patterned. If testing in a more general population shows that the level of background noise is unacceptable, there are various technical remedies available. For instance, if someone is not involved in a specific group conversation but just walking by, then she will often enter and leave the log at a different time than the members of the group. Similar geometric and temporal constraints can be used to identify other anomalous logs.

Human-Induced Errors. The two primary types of human-induced errors in this dataset result either from the phone being off or separated from the user. The first error comes from the phone being either explicitly turned off by the user or exhausting the batteries. According to our collected survey data, users report exhausting the batteries approximately 2.5 times each month. One fifth of our subjects manually turned the phone off on a regular basis during specific contexts such as classes, movies, and (most frequently) when sleeping. Immediately before the phone powers down, the event is time-stamped and the most recent log is closed. A new log is created when the phone is restarted and again a timestamp is associated with the event. Additionally, 6 of the 100 phones in the study were either lost or irreparably destroyed (most notably, one phone was repeatedly run over by a large bus). The subjects who had these phones were given spare phones if available, or otherwise were forced to drop out of the experiment.

A more critical error occurs when the phone is left on but not carried by the user. From surveys, we have found that 30% of our subjects claim never to forget their phones, while 40% report forgetting them about once each month, and the remaining 30% state that they forget the phone approximately once each week. Identifying the times when the phone is on, but left at home or in the office, presents a significant challenge when working with the dataset. To grapple with the problem, we developed a forgotten phone classifier. Features include staying in the same location for an extended period of time, charging, and remaining idle through missed phone calls, text messages, and alarms. When applied to a subsection of the dataset that had corresponding diary text labels, the classifier was able to identify the day the phone was forgotten, but also mislabeled a day when the user stayed home sick. By ignoring both days, we risk throwing out data on outlying days, but have greater certainty that the phone is actually with the user. A significantly harder problem is to determine whether the user has temporarily moved beyond 10 m of his or her home or office without taking the phone. Casual observation indicates that this appears to happen with many subjects on a regular basis and there does not seem to be enough unique features of the event to classify it accurately. However, as described in the survey comparison section, this phenomenon does not diminish the extremely strong correlation between detected proximity and self-report interactions. Lastly, as discussed in the relationship inference section, while frequency of proximity within the workplace can be useful, the most salient data comes from detecting a proximity event outside MIT, where temporarily forgetting the phone is less likely to repeatedly occur.

Missing Data. Because we know when each subject began the study, as well as the dates that have been logged, we can know exactly when we are missing data. This missing data is due to the two main errors discussed above: data corruption and powered-off devices. On average for the Reality Mining study, we had logs accounting for approximately 85.3% of the time since the phones were deployed. Less than 5% of this is due to data corruption, while the majority of the missing 14.7% is due to almost one fifth of the subjects turning off their phones at night.

Other Measures: Surveys & Diaries. In return for the use of the phones, students have been asked to fill out Web-based surveys regarding their social activities and the people they interact with throughout the day. Comparison of the logs with survey data has given us insight into our dataset's ability to accurately map social network dynamics. Through surveys of approximately 40 senior students, we have validated that the reported frequency of (self-report) interaction is strongly correlated with the number of logged Bluetooth IDs (BTIDs) (R = .78; p = .003), and that the dyadic self-report data has a similar correlation with the dyadic proximity data (R = .74; p < .0001). Interestingly, the surveys were not significantly correlated with the proximity logs of the incoming students. Additionally, a subset of subjects kept detailed activity diaries over several months. Comparisons revealed no systematic errors with respect to proximity and location, except for omissions due to the phone being turned off.

Service-Provider Side Data Collection. Mobile phone service providers already have a wealth of information about movement and communication in their call data records (CDR). While there are obvious benefits to using existing CDR for social research, many times the benefits are outweighed by the issues and limitations associated with these types of data. The first obstacle is simply obtaining access to CDR data. Even upon agreement from a service provider, we have found that it takes months for legal documents to be written and signed before such data-sharing agreements can be finalized.

Additionally, one of the major limitations with data from mobile phone service providers is the fact that the researcher is constrained to only communication events and cellular tower location data when the phone is being used to make or receive a call or text message. This means that for the vast majority of time, the phone's location is unknown. Besides the limitations associated with the behavioral data automatically generated, collecting survey data of the subscribers is typically prohibited by the service providers. And many service providers, particularly in the developing world, have no demographic information about any of their subscribers. However, some providers do collect fairly detailed information about demographics including gender, pay scale, and address. While mobile phone service providers have a financial incentive to maintain the quality of their data for billing purposes, the sheer magnitude of this type data can be incredibly daunting to any researcher. For our analysis of data from the United Kingdom involving over 100 million phone numbers, we needed to obtain a computer with 8 terabytes of extremely fast access drives (RAID 10), 64 gigabytes of memory, and 8 processors. Even with a machine such as this, we were unable to hold the full social network in memory, which makes calculating particular network metrics, such as distance, all the more challenging. Custom software needed to be written for the CDR analysis that is always in a continual state of development.

Location Estimation. Getting continuous access to the locations of a particular phone is typically not an easy task. Location inference has traditionally been done using a landline phone's area code or information about the cellular towers near a mobile phone.

GPS chip-sets have become increasingly common in high-end phones, however, enabling services that can query the location of a particular phone with an accuracy of up to 10 m. Through the analysis of tower transitions, or simply the latitude/longitude coordinates from the GPS, it is possible to infer the amount and speed of travel for an individual phone user.

While many phones currently have GPS that provides exact latitude and longitude coordinates, repeated use of the GPS dramatically affects the phone's battery life. An alternate method of localizing a phone that requires no additional power is by using cellular tower data, data that every phone already has access to. There has been a significant amount of research that correlates cell tower ID with a user's location (Bar-Noy, Kessler, & Sidi, 1995; Kim & Lee, 1996). For example, Laasonen, Raento, and Toivonen (2004) describe a method of inferring significant locations from cell tower information through analysis of the adjacency matrix formed by proximate towers. They showed reasonable route recognition rates, and most importantly, succeeded in running their algorithms directly on the mobile phone.

Obtaining accurate location information from cell towers is complicated by the fact that phones can detect cell towers that are several miles away. Furthermore, in urban areas it is not uncommon to be within range of more than a dozen different towers. The inclusion of information about all the current visible towers as well as their respective signal strengths would help solve the location classification problem, although multipath distortion may still confound estimates. There are several techniques that have been developed to equate the cellular tower information with location.

It is possible to calculate the posterior probability that a subject is home, $P(L_{HOME})$, conditioned on the four towers currently detected by the phone, T_{ABCD}, using the likelihood, the marginal, and the prior probability of being at home (inferred either by the time of day or static Bluetooth beacon data):

$$P(L_{HOME}|T_{ABCD}) = \frac{P(T_{ABCD}|L_{HOME})P(L_{HOME})}{P(T_{ABCD})}$$

While the Bayesian model above works well in many cases, simply using the ratio of tower counts copresent with the Bluetooth beacon tends to fail if the phone regularly moves beyond 10 m of the beacon while still staying inside the home. Instead of normalizing by total number of times each tower is detected, it is possible to obtain additional accuracy by incorporating the signal strengths from the detected towers. There are many models for signal strength of a single cellular tower; $P_t(S_t|L)$, one such model, uses training data to estimate Gaussian distributions over functions modeling signal propagation from cellular towers (Schwaighofer, Grigoras, & Tresp, 2004). In our case, the training data comes from the signals of towers detected at the same time as the Bluetooth beacon in the subject's home, and the inference is binary (home or not home); however, these models are easily extendable for more broad localization.

The two models above generate a probability of being at home associated with a single sample of detected towers (i.e., the four tower IDs and their respective signal strengths). However, during the times when a subject is stationary, the phone continuously collects samples of the detected towers' signal strengths. These samples can form "fingerprint" distributions of the expected signal strengths associated with that particular location. It is possible to detect deviations within these distributions of signal strengths using a pairwise analysis of variance (ANOVA). Training the home distributions on the times when the beacon is visible (or if there are no beacons, on times when the subject is likely home such as from 2:00 a.m. to 4:00 a.m.), an ANOVA comparing this home distribution with a distribution of recent tower signal strengths makes it possible to identify if the subject is truly at home, or is at a next-door neighbor's house. In previous work, such tower probability density functions have successfully localized a phone down to the office-level (Eagle & Pentland, 2006).

Location inference has traditionally been done using a landline phone area code or information about the cellular towers near a mobile phone. GPS chip-sets have become increasingly common in high-end phones, however, enabling services that can ping the location of a particular phone with an accuracy of up to 10 m. Through the analysis of tower transitions, or simply the latitude/longitude coordinates from the GPS, it is possible to infer the amount and speed of travel for an individual phone user. Aggregate data about travel patterns is a key variable for quantifying the pace of life within different cultures, epidemiological models, and next-generation applications such as anticipatory computing.

Ethical Issues and Implications

IRB/Human Subjects Approval. As will be discussed in subsequent sections, the projects that involved logging continuous behavioral data on mobile phones raise many privacy concerns for both the participants and the IRB. To receive Human Subjects Approval, the researchers needed to explicitly describe each type of data collected from both participants and nonparticipants. We made it clear that participants have the option to delete any data they are not comfortable submitting to the study, as well as the ability to disable the logging application at their discretion. Particular emphasis was placed on the data captured from people who were not participants in the study. This data includes the Bluetooth hardware addresses, as well as phone numbers logged by the subjects. In the past, we have made the case that the Bluetooth hardware address is an anonymous identification number that does not provide any information about the identity of an individual.

However, this argument does not hold for the communication logs, which include the phone numbers and (if available) the individuals' names from the phone's address book. To be able to capture this data, we used the precedent of ongoing e-mail studies within academia. Similar to call logs, e-mail headers provide the identity and contact information of individuals not in the study. As with the e-mail studies, we made the point that these phone logs were the property of the participants in the study, and were submitted with their approval. To ensure additional security, we performed a one-way (MD5) hash on all of the phone numbers that turned each number into a unique ID and made it impossible to get back to the original number. By removing any identifiable information within the dataset, we were allowed to share the dataset with other researchers outside the immediate scope of this project.

For server-side data, IRB approval becomes significantly easier, pending the following agreements. Because the data already exists, the IRB's largest concern was that the data must be completely de-identified such that it is impossible for the researchers to obtain the identity of a particular subscriber. We ensured that the service provider de-identified the CDR by having them assign a unique, randomly generated series of characters (a hash-id) to each phone number. The service providers then simply replaced every phone number in the data with the associated hash-id. While anonymized temporal communication data can be exploited (Backstrom et al., 2006), this hashing technique proved sufficient for most university IRBs.

Privacy

The privacy implications associated with using mobile phones as sensors for social research scare some people, and perhaps with reason. However, this type of research remains within the confines of academia. While for experiments like the Reality Mining project, each of the subjects read and signed a detailed consent form approved by MIT's Committee on the Use of Humans as Experimental Subjects (COUHES), describing all the types of information we were gathering, this is simply not the case with data collection from mobile phone service providers. The hundreds of service providers around the world are already continuously logging every mobile phone user's communication behavior as well as location from nearby cell towers—and most of the 4 billion individuals being tracked are not even aware of it.

To some, the privacy implications of this chapter are more salient than any of the other results. There are inherent connotations with a machine's logging of human behavior and George Orwell's concept of Big Brother. Regardless of whether this is a fair comparison, researchers interested in becoming involved with this field should become well-versed in the privacy literature. Mining the reality of our 100 users raises justifiable concerns over privacy. However, the work done in experiments like the MIT Reality Mining study was conducted with human subject approval and consent of the users. Outside the lab, we envision a future where phones will have greater computation power and will be able to make relevant inferences using only data available to the user's phone. In this future scenario, the inferences are done in real time on the local device or on a user's personal computer, making it unnecessary for private information to be shared with a central system.

In a democratic and open society, the argument that privacy concerns can be balanced by various benefits of convenience can be plausibly made. However, benevolent governments are not guaranteed indefinitely, and putting in place a vast system for information gathering has some rather disturbing consequences in a less than benevolent society. It is interesting to note that there are over 500 million people in China who daily carry what is essentially an always-on surveillance device. It still is unclear what governments will do with this type of data, and what kind of backlash it will have on the user population.

A pervasive information gathering system could be put to nefarious uses, especially in the hands of an unscrupulous government. But while we could (and perhaps should) raise attention to those obvious dangers, at the end of the day, having a centralized cellular infrastructure implicitly creates such an information gathering system; and if the system exists, why not use it for public service applications? Currently, society's use for this new type of data from mobile phones is to place an individual at the scene of a crime. If we, as a society, agree that it is acceptable to use this data against an individual, then using it to better support the individual does not appear as controversial.

There does not appear to be a conclusive answer to the question about whether or not the privacy concerns surrounding mobile phones outweigh their potential benefits. The case that this chapter has tried to make is that assuming we do live in a society (benevolent or not) that has a ubiquitous cellular infrastructure, it makes sense to start thinking about beneficial ways we (as engineers/designers/politicians/scientists and so on) can start using the resultant data.

Informed Consent. An important consideration for any study of this kind is that the telecommunication industry does not generally seek consent from their subscribers to participate in research. While privacy laws throughout the world differ regarding call log record regulations, it is the researcher's responsibility to ensure that the data is appropriately hashed such that it is impossible to gain access to any individual's actual phone logs or personal information: an increasingly challenging, yet critical requirement.

For data collection on handsets, prior to starting the study, each subject typically must read and sign a detailed consent form listing the type of data to be gathered, providing sample data, detailing how the data would be treated, and describing what it would be used for. A sample of this consent form is available on the Reality Mining Web page (http://reality.media.mit.edu/pdfs/consent.pdf). Upon reading the consent form, subjects are given a phone and instructions on its operation. Every subject was shown how to disable the logging application; while very few subjects ever used this feature, just having the functionality provided piece of mind to many subjects when being introduced to the study. However, even with these privacy protection measures, the ability to automatically collect continuous behavioral data from 100 users raises justifiable concerns. When the study was described to others outside of MIT, reactions were typically apprehensive. While this experiment may be possible at a technical university where people are comfortable with the technology and its limitations, there may need to be significant differences in research design should this scale to a more typical demographic.

The Price of Privacy. In general, companies have found that people are usually willing to relinquish a portion of their privacy in exchange for something of (typically surprisingly small) value (Huberman et al., 2005). Consumers, for example, have been willing to divulge personal information, such as the names of their friends and relatives, to receive free gifts or reduced rates for a service. For the majority of people, the benefits of paying with a credit card outweigh the perceived intrusion of providing a company access to information on the location and content of each purchase. To track the buying behavior of specific demographics, many retail stores issue personalized coupons. Loyalty-reward cards are another example of consumers trading information about their shopping behavior for discounts on purchases.

In the e-commerce space, many Web retailers ask customers to log on to receive personalized recommendations. For most consumers, the personalization that results from logging on to a Web site such as Amazon.com is worth having the enormous amount of data that is generated from their visit linked to their identity; this information ranges from the products they browsed, links they clicked, to the duration (down to the millisecond) that they spent on each page. Simply a look-up of an IP address gives the store information about a Web browser's location. In the mid-1990s, when this information gathering was just becoming broadly deployed, companies began testing the limits of what they could do with this information. It turned out that while customers did not complain about the actual data collection (although it seems reasonable to assume that many were unaware it was even taking place), there was a large reaction against sharing this data. In one example, Amazon's early Web site gave users information such as, "Other people from Stanford University also purchased these products." While this information was useful to many, the perceived privacy violation led to a vocal group insisting that this type of functionality be permanently removed.

How Privacy Scales. This chapter has introduced several applications for this new mobile data on a variety of scales ranging from individual, to dyad, to group. These different focuses each have their own unique privacy implications. While not all of the applications will appeal to the most privacy sensitive among us, the trade-offs of sharing private information and the potential benefit of an application may yield a successful compromise for most people.

Privacy and the Individual. For individual applications, such as the automatically generated diary, very little private information needs to go beyond an individual's phone and personal computer. The inferences about a user's context and situation can be completed as a client application rather than by using the existing server-based model. Instead of uploading the phone logs to our central server, we can send them to a user's trusted personal computer. This modified application will be able to display named locations and the people associated with the phones numbers already in the phone's address book. However, because there is no central repository mapping Bluetooth IDs (BTIDs) to individual names, establishing the identity of the proximate people becomes a more difficult task. Inferring these mappings will be addressed in the next section.

Dyadic Privacy Implications. Using the friendship correlations described in Figure 22.7, it is possible for a phone to infer a relationship between its user and another person's mobile phone. The next time that particular BTID is logged, the phone could open a dialogue box alerting the user that a friend with a Bluetooth phone might be nearby. If the user agrees that there is a friend nearby with a mobile phone, a list of names from the phones address book could present itself and the user could select a particular contact to associate with the discovered BTID.

Data Aggregation of the Organization. Inherent to the nature of group behavior analysis is the fact that behavioral data is disclosed. While applications such as the six-person research group's proximity network would require complete disclosure of proximity data, it may be feasible to collect statistics about a larger aggregate while keeping the individual researchers' identities anonymous. Given an adequately large sample size, an individual may be able to compare his behavior with organizational averages. Initially, assuming that this aggregate data can be submitted anonymously, the dynamics of organizational rhythms can still be analyzed without violating the privacy of the individual.

Privacy Guardrails: Context versus Content. While compromises can be made regarding particular privacy trade-offs, there are some specific societal norms regarding privacy that should always be adhered to. These privacy guardrails are related to the general public's expectation of privacy. Data should remain private if there is a reasonable expectation that the data is private, which often relates to content versus context. The content of interactions, whether they are face-to-face, over the phone, or e-mail, typically has the expectation of being private. Just as it is against societal norms to eavesdrop on a conversation between two people, so is it not appropriate (nor legal in many states) to record a conversation unless both parties are formally notified.

However, context is different from content. If two people are talking in an office with the door open, while it is unacceptable to stand at the entrance listening to the conversation, it is not socially inappropriate to wait outside the office, out of earshot, but still in view of the two people engaged in conversation. In this case, by leaving the door open, the two people have acknowledged that their context is public information. The public can see that both people are inside the office and, therefore, that contextual information is not private. Similarly, information about approximate location and proximity is contextual and carries less of an expectation of privacy. However, while content is inherently much more sensitive than context, users should always have the option of keeping their contexts private as well. Just as individuals have the right to close their office door to establish that their current context is private, they should always have the right to disable the logging software on their phone.

While some may argue that this type of pervasive behavioral data should not be collected, it is a fact of life in the twenty-first century the data discussed here will continue to be aggregated by the hundreds of mobile phone service providers throughout the world, whether or not it is shared with researchers. Therefore, while academics must remain cognizant of the privacy issues surrounding the analysis of personal information, society has much to gain from these studies and their potential for use in solving social problems ranging from disease outbreaks to urban planning. To achieve these goals, new tools will be needed to grapple with data sets that are many orders of magnitude larger than have previously existed.

A New Set of Tools

Increasingly, answers to the important questions of structure, function, and dynamics require biologists and social scientists to sift through ever growing amounts of data. Many conventional techniques, however, effectively fail at the giga-, terra-, and petascales, sometimes because their assumptions fail for data sets with thousands of dimensions, but also because they cannot handle data of this magnitude. Thus, there is a clear and pressing need for new techniques that can compress this data to a more manageable size and automatically extract understanding.

Massive datasets on the order of petabytes can defy analysis via conventional techniques because of problems with dimensionality reduction, including normalizing different dimensions, lack of well-behaved distance metrics or local analysis methods, and huge computations.

Networks offer a way to accomplish both tasks by representing data in a fundamentally different way. Today, networks are a powerful and increasingly popular tool for studying complex systems of all kinds: they provide an abstraction of a system's interacting parts that is both general enough to encompass important features of real systems, effectively compressing the original data below the petascale, while preserving structurally important features, yet simple enough to provide clear insight and support efficient computations. By capturing only the important topological or functional interactions in a system, networks compress high-dimensional data while preserving structurally important features.

To be practical, these methods must scale efficiently, taking $O(n \log n)$ time to run, where n is the number of nodes in the network. To be useful scientifically, these methods must be based on rigorous mathematical and statistical principles. Our approach to achieving these goals includes techniques from computer science and machine learning such as local computation, compression, sampling, divide and conquer, parallelization, and approximations, as well as clustering, statistical inference, generative models, model selection, and techniques for controlling model complexity. This approach will boost relatively simple techniques to the peta- or terrascales, boost more sophisticated techniques to the gigascale, and more generally bring a powerful new set of tools to the analysis of petascale behavioral data.

Future Directions

For almost a century, social scientists have studied particular demographics through surveys or placing human observers in social environments such as the workplace or the school. Subsequently, the tools to analyze survey and observation data have become increasingly sophisticated. However, within the last decade, new methods of quantifying interaction and behavior between people have emerged that no longer require surveys or human observation. The new resultant data sets are several orders of magnitude larger than anything before possible. Initially, this data was limited to representing peoples' online interactions and behavior, typically through analysis of e-mail or instant-messaging networks.

However, social science is now at a critical point in its evolution as a discipline. The field is about to become inundated with massive amounts of data that is not just limited to human behavior in the online world; soon, datasets on almost every aspect of human life will become available. And while social scientists have become quite good at working with sparse datasets involving discrete observations and surveys of several dozen subjects over a few months, the field is not prepared to deal with continuous behavioral data from thousands—and soon millions—of people. The old tools simply will not scale. Skills associated with large-scale data analysis will be critical to the generation of social scientists who are no longer studying small groups but rather the petabytes of data about an entire society's movements, transactions, and communication patterns—continuously being inadvertently generated by technology from mobile phones to credit cards.

The analysis of this new type of data is inherently multidisciplinary. To deal with the massive amounts of continuous human behavioral data that will be available in the twenty-first century, it is going to be necessary to draw on a range of fields from traditional social network analysis to particle physics and statistical mechanics. We will be borrowing algorithms developed in the field of computer vision to predict an individual's affiliations and future actions. Tools from the burgeoning discipline of complex network analysis will help us gain a better understanding of aggregate behavior. And it is my hope as an engineer that these new insights into our own behaviors will enable us to develop applications that better support both the individual and the group. Indeed, by increasing our understanding of complex social systems, we can better inform the design of social structures such as organizations, cities, office buildings, and schools to conform to how we, as an aggregate, actually behave, rather than how some CEO, architect, or city planner thinks we do (Ball, 2006).

Beyond the Traditional Social Sciences. This latest technical breakthrough will have not only a dramatic impact on everyday people's lives, but also on the academic communities that study them. These academics range from physicists interested in modeling large groups of people using statistical mechanics, to sociologists looking to quantify the evolution of social networks, to computer scientists attempting to teach computer commonsense facts about human life, to social psychologists studying organizational and team behavior, and to epidemiologists modeling how a contagion disseminates across a proximity network.

Beyond Phones. Within the last decade, the amount of behavioral data about human societies has grown by many orders of magnitude. While new methods of quantifying continuous e-mail and other online interactions have resulted in part of this wealth of information, much of the data is not limited to human behavior occurring online. With the ubiquity of telecommunication systems, credit cards, RFIDs, and a growing suite of additional tracking technologies, it is rapidly becoming possible to quantify detailed dynamics of real-world complex social systems. The digital traces, not of our movement or communication patterns, but rather of our purchasing of items such as orange juice and paper tissue has been shown to be useful when attempting to detect the onset of flu outbreak within a community (Farzad Mostashari & Jessica Hartman, 2003). Tracking the dissemination of American currency has also been used as a proxy for inferring human movement patterns, which then enables large-scale epidemiological models to be better grounded in actual behavioral data (Brockman, Hugnagel, & Geisel, 2006). An increasing number of vehicles are becoming equipped with networked GPS, that not only provides (and contributes to) real-time traffic data, but also generates a wealth of much more detailed human movement data (Eriksson, Balakrishnan, & Madden, 2008).

Union of Academic and Industry Interests. While collecting behavioral data using mobile phones originated within academia, it did not take long before companies formed to embark on similar pursuits. Whether for the purposes of quantifying vehicular traffic, economic outcomes, or media consumption, mobile phones have been proven commercially viable as a behavioral sensor. As such, the union between academia and these companies can certainly be mutually beneficial. While academics can lend their expertise in data collection and theory, these companies have many times more budget for data collection than any singular academic project. In previous relationships, academics helped consult on these types of projects in exchange for the chance to publish on the data collected. However, typically the contract also empowers the companies to have the option to review any paper prior to publication, and censor the findings as needed. While this is a common clause in many of such contracts, it is rarely, if ever, actualized. Looking forward, we will continue this trend of analyzing digital traces—there will be an increasing number of studies involving data collected not necessarily with a particular academic hypothesis in mind, but rather leveraging the fact that corporations are beginning to take an increased interest in collecting such data for commercial purposes. The nature of this relationship between academia and industry will inherently change the structure of the research questions, determining who and what is studied in reflection of the partnership based on the stakeholder interests. While this is not an ideal situation for academics, it should be familiar, as for over a decade we have been analyzing the digital traces of behavior—data not generated from any particular experiment, but rather simply from the fact of living in the twenty-first century. Regardless of these details, the motivation to make this collaboration work should be huge. Ultimately, this union between academics and industry has the potential to enable insights that will actively improve the lives of the billions of people who generate this data and the societies in which they live.

Conclusion

Whether it is used to study the differences between groups of local students, quantify the behavioral effects of urbanization, or infer the relationships between ethnic tribes across a continent, the data left in the wake of mobile phones can provide invaluable information about the dynamics of our species. While some may argue that this type of pervasive behavioral data should not be collected, it is a fact of life in the twenty-first century that the data discussed here will continue to be aggregated by the hundreds of mobile phone service providers throughout the world, whether or not it is shared with researchers. Therefore, while academics must remain cognizant of the privacy issues surrounding the analysis of personal information, society has much to gain from these studies and their potential for use in solving social problems ranging from disease outbreaks to urban planning.

However, this rush to quantify large-scale human behavior should not be thought of as a quest to end a universal equation for human behavior; we are not trying to create something whereby it is possible to feed data in, and to have emerge an elegant deterministic description of human behavior. Rather, as Ball (2004) notes, increased understanding of complex social systems will be actualized by an accumulation of examples of how patterns of behavior emerge from the idiosyncratic actions of many individuals. This understanding may not only lead us to building applications that better support the individual and group, but also better inform the design of organizations, schools, and office buildings so as to conform to how we actually behave and enhance and encourage beneficial social interactions.

Social science is rapidly becoming inundated with massive amounts of data on individual, dyadic, team, organizational, and global behavior. This deluge of data is beginning to have dramatic repercussions on a field that has had the same state-of-the-art data gathering instruments for nearly a century. However, new tools will be needed to grapple with data sets that are many orders of magnitude larger than have previously existed. And while these new datasets will certainly not replace the surveys and other traditional data gathering techniques, I hope this chapter has shown how these data compliment each other to enable researchers to ask questions never before possible.

Acknowledgments

The author would like to thank Prof. Alex ("Sandy") Pentland for the instrumental role he played in this research. This work has been partially supported by the Santa Fe Institute.

Note

1. Operators can also "ping" a phone to have it report back to a nearby tower; however, this requires additional power from the phone and therefore typically is impractical for continuous location tracking.

References

A. Adamic and E. Adar, "How to search a social network", *Social Networks*, 27(3):187–203, July 2005.

B. Albert, R., & Barabasi, A. (2002). Statistical mechanics of complex networks. *Reviews of Modern Physics*, *74*, 47–97.

Anderson, R., & May, R. (1991). Infectious diseases of humans: Dynamics and control. Oxford University Press

Ashbrook, D., & Starner, T. (2003). Using GPS to learn significant locations and predict movement across multiple users. *Personal and Ubiquitous Computing*, *7*, 275–286.

Ball, P. (2004). *Critical Mass*, Farrar, Straus and Giroux, New York.

Backstrom, L., Huttenlocher, D, & Kleinberg, J. (2006). Group formation in large social networks: Membership, growth, and evolution. *Proc. 12th ACM SIGKDD Intl. Conf. on Knowledge Discovery and Data Mining*, 44–54.

Ball, P. (2006). Critical mass: How one thing leads to another. *Farrar, Straus and Giroux*, 528.

Bar-Noy, A., Kessler, I., & Sidi, M. (1995). Tracking strategies in wireless networks. *Electrical and Electronics Engineers in Israel*.

Barrett, L., & Barrett, D. (2001). An introduction to computerized experience sampling in psychology. *Social Science Computer Review*, *19*(2), 175–185.

W. H. Bernard, P. Killworth, and L. Sailer. 1979. "Informant accuracy in social networks. Part IV: A comparison of clique-level structure in behavioral and cognitive network data." *Social Networks 2*: 191–218.

Bernard, H. R., Killworth, P. D., & Kronenfeld, D. (1984). The problem of informant accuracy: The validity of retrospective data. *Annual Review of Anthropology*, *13*, 495–517.

Brockmann, D., Hufnagel, L., & Geisel, T. (2006). "The scaling laws of human travel," *Nature*, 439, 462–465.

Chen, M., Sohn, T., Chmelev, D., Haehnel, D., Hightower, J., Hughes, J., LaMarca, A., Potter, F., Smith, I., & Varshavsky, A. (2006). Practical metropolitan-scale positioning for gsm phones. *UbiComp 2006 Ubiquitous Computing—8th International Conference*, 225–242.

Csikszentmihalyi, M., & Larson, R. (1987). Validity and reliability of the experience-sampling method. *The Journal of Nervous and Mental Disease*, *175*(9), 526–536.

Davis, A., Gardner, B. B., & Gardner, M. R. (1941). *Deep South*. Chicago: The University of Chicago Press.

Davis, M., Good, N., & Sarvas, R. (2004). From context to content: Leveraging context for mobile media metadata. *Proceedings of the 12th annual ACM international conference on Multimedia*, 188–195.

Domingos, P., & Richardson, M. (2001). Mining the network value of customers. *Proceedings of the seventh ACM SIGKDD international conference on Knowledge discovery and data mining*, 57–66.

Eagle, N., & Pentland, A. (2005). Social Serendipity: Mobilizing Social Software. *IEEE Pervasive Computing*, 4 (2): 28–34, 2005.

Eagle, N., & Sandy, A. (2006). Pentland. "Reality mining: Sensing complex social systems." *Personal and Ubiquitous Computing*, *10*(4), 255–268.

Eagle, N., Pentland, A., & Lazer, D. (2009). Inferring social network structure using mobile phone data. *Proceedings of the National Academy of Sciences*.

Eagle, N., de Montjoye, Y., & Bettencourt, L. (2009). Community Computing: Comparisons between Rural and Urban Societies using Mobile Phone Data. *IEEE Social Computing*, 144–150

Eagle, N., Quinn, J., & Clauset, A., "Methodologies for Continuous Cellular Tower Data Analysis." Proc. 7th International Conference on Pervasive Computing (Pervasive '09), 342–353.

Eagle, N., Macy, M., & Claxton, R. (2010). Network Diversity and Economic Development. *Science* 328(5981), 1029–1031.

Eriksson, J., Balakrishnan, H., & Madden, S. (2008). *Cabernet: vehicular content delivery using WiFi.* ACM MOBICOM, 199–210.

Eubank, S., Guclu, H., & Anil Kumar, V. (2004). Modelling disease outbreaks in realistic urban social networks. *Nature*, *429*(6988), 180–184.

Freeman, L. Romney, A., & Freeman, S. (1987). Cognitive structure and informant accuracy. *American Anthropologist, 89*, 310–325.

Freeman, L. (2003). Finding social groups: A meta-analysis of the southern women data. In Ronald Breiger, Kathleen Carley and Philippa Pattison (eds.) *Dynamic Social Network Modeling and Analysis*. Washington, D.C.: The National Academies Press.

González, M. C., Hidalgo, C. A., & Barabási, A. L. (2008). Understanding individual human mobility patterns. *Nature, 453*(7196), 779–782.

Henderson, L. (1971). The statistics of crowd fluids. *Nature, 229*(5284), 381–383.

Hill, S., Provost, F., & Volinsky, C. (2006). Network-based marketing: Identifying likely adopters via consumer networks. *Statistical Science, 21*(2), 256–276.

Hulkko, S., Mattelmäki, T., Virtanen, K. & Keinonen, T. (2004). Mobile probes. In *Proceedings of the Third Nordic Conference on Human-Computer interaction* (Tampere, Finland, October 23–27, 2004). NordiCHI '04 (pp. 43–51). New York, NY: ACM Press.

Holmquist, L., Falk, J., & Wigström, J. (1999). Supporting group collaboration with interpersonal awareness devices. *Personal and Ubiquitous Computing, 3*(1–2), 13–21.

Huberman, B., Adar, E., & Fine, L. (2005). Valuating privacy. *IEEE Security & Privacy, 3*(5), 22–25.

Intille, S., Rondoni, J., Kukla, C., Ancona, I., & Bao, L. (2003). A context-aware experience sampling tool. *Conference on Human Factors in Computing Systems*, 972–972.

Kermack, W., & McKendrick, A. (1991). Contributions to the mathematical theory of epidemics—I. 1927. *Proceedings of the Royal Society of London. Series A, 115*(772), 700–721.

Killworth, P. D., & Bernard, H. R. (1977). Informant accuracy in social network data II. *Human Communication Research, 4*(1), 3–18.

Kim, S., & Lee, C. (1996). Modeling and analysis of the dynamic location registration and paging in microcellular systems. *IEEE Transactions on Vehicular Technology, 45*(1), 82–90.

Kurhila, J., Miettinen, M., Niemivirta, M., Nokelainen, P., Sil, T., & Tirri, H. (2001). Bayesian modeling in an adaptive on-line questionnaire for education and educational research. *PEG 2001: Intelligent Computer and Communications Technology*, 194–201.

Laasonen, K., Raento, M., & Toivonen, H. (2004). Adaptive on-device location recognition. *Lecture Notes in Computer Science, 3001*, 287–304.

LaMarca, A., Chawathe, Y., Consolvo, S., Hightower, J., Smith, I., Scott, J., Sohn, T., Howard, J., Hughes, J., Potter, F., Tabert, J., Powledge, P., Borriello, G., & Schilit, B. (2005). Place lab: Device positioning using radio beacons in the wild. *Proceedings of the Third International Conference on Pervasive Computing*, 116–133.

Leskovec, J., & Horvitz, E. (2008). Worldwide buzz: Planetary-scale views on an instant-messaging network. *Proc. 17th International World Wide Web Conference*, 915–924.

Liao, L., Patterson, D., Fox, D., & Kautz, H. (2007). Learning and inferring transportation routines. *Artificial Intelligence, 171*(5–6), 311–331.

Liben-Nowell, D., Novak, J., & Kumar, R. (2005). Geographic routing in social networks. *Proceedings of the National Academy of Sciences, 102*(33), 11623–11628.

Marsden, P. (1990). Network data and measurement. *Annual Review of Sociology, 16*, 435–463.

Moreno, Y., Nekovee, M., & Pacheco, A. (2004). Dynamics of rumor spreading in complex networks. *Physical Review E, 69*(6), 066130.

Mostashari, F. & Hartman, J. (2003). Syndromic surveillance: A local perspective. *Journal of Urban Health, 80*(2).

Newman, M. (2001). The structure of scientific collaboration networks. *Proceedings of the National Academy of Sciences, 98*(2), 404–409.

O'Keefe, K., & Antonovics, J. (2002). Playing by different rules: The evolution of virulence in sterilizing pathogens. *The American Naturalist, 159*(66), 597–605.

Onnela, J.-P., Saramäki, J., Hyvönen, J., Szabó, G., Lazer, D., Kaski, K., Kertész, J., & Barabási, A.-L. (2007). Structure and tie strengths in mobile communication networks. *Proceedings of the National Academy of Sciences, 104*(18), 7332–7336.

Otsason, V., Varshavsky, A., LaMarca, A., & Lara, E. (2005). Accurate GSM indoor localization. *Proceedings of UBICOMP*, 141–158.

Palla, G., Barabási, A., & Vicsek, T. (2007). Quantifying social group evolution. *Nature, 446*(7136), 664–667.

Paulos, E., & Goodman, E. (2004). The familiar stranger: Anxiety, comfort, and play in public places. *Conference on Human Factors in Computing Systems*, 223–230.

Raento, M., Oulasvirta, A., Petit, R., & Toivonen, H. (2005). ContextPhone: A prototyping platform for context-aware mobile applications. *IEEE Pervasive Computing, 4*(2), 51–59.

Raento, M., Oulasvirta, A., & Eagle, N. (2009). Smartphones: An emerging tool for social scientists. *Sociological Methods & Research, 37*(2), 426–454.

Ratti, C., Pulselli, R., Williams, S., & Frenchman, D. (2006). Mobile landscapes: Using location data from cell phones for urban analysis. *Environment and Planning B: Planning and Design, 33*(5), 727–748.

Read, J., & Keeling, M. (2003). Disease evolution on networks: The role of contact structure. *Proceedings: Biological Sciences, 270*(1533), 2565–2571.

Roethlisberger, F.J., & Dickson, W.J. (1939), *Management and the Worker*, Cambridge, MA: Harvard University Press.

Schwaighofer, A., Grigoras, M., & Tresp, V. (2004). GPPS: A Gaussian process positioning system for cellular networks. *Advances in Neural Information Processing Systems, 16*, 579–586.

Sohn, T., Varshavsky, A., LaMarca, A., Chen, M., Choudhury, T., Smith, I., Consolvo, S., Hightower, J., Griswold, W. G., & de Lara, E. (2006). Mobility detection using everyday GSM traces. *Lecture Notes in Computer Science, 4206*, 212–224.

Szabo, G., & Barabasi, A. (2006). Network effects in service usage. *Arxiv preprint physics*.

Terry, M., Mynatt, E., Ryall, K., & Leigh, D. (2002). Social net: Using patterns of physical proximity over time to infer shared interests. *Conference on Human Factors in Computing Systems*, 816–817.

Tönnies, F. (1955 [1887]). *Community and Organization* [Gemeinschaft und Gesellschaft]. London: Routledge and Kegan Paul.

van Baalen, M. (2002). Dilemmas in virulence management. In *Adaptive dynamics of infectious diseases: In pursuit of virulence management* (pp. 60–69).

Verkasalo, H., & Áinen, H. (2007). A handset-based platform for measuring mobile service usage. *Info—The journal of policy, regulation and strategy for telecommunications, 9*(1), 80–96.

Watts, D., & Strogatz, S. (1998). Collective dynamics of "small-world" networks. *Nature, 393*(6684), 409–410.

Watts, D., Muhamad, R., & Sheridan Dodds, P. (2003). An experimental study of search in global social networks. *Science, 301*(5634), 827–829.

Chapter 23

Bringing the Research Lab into Everyday Life: Exploiting Sensitive Environments to Acquire Data for Social Research

Geert de Haan, Sunil Choenni, Ingrid Mulder,
Sandra Kalidien, and Peter van Waart

Introduction

This chapter discusses the concept of sensitive environments. Sensitive environments are essentially spatial and public areas like streets or school that are provided with an intelligent infrastructure that collects sensory information of users while they move and interact. Such sensitive environments offer researchers an environment which enables them to automatically collect lots of data. However, when data collection takes place through a sensitive environment instead of by interviews, questionnaires, and structured observations, it consequently changes the nature of social research and imposes new types of questions: How to design the environment to fit the research questions. How do we deal with huge datasets in a sensible way? How can we interpret data that might be incomplete or uncertain in a meaningful and useful way? In the remainder of this work, we discuss the use of sensitive environments as a tool for social research embedded within everyday life.

To describe where the concept of a sensitive environment comes from and why it is necessary, we first focus on the wider context of human centered design. Research and development in the field of human centered design evolve in different directions and levels, which are not necessarily divergent. There is a practical need to develop and implement systems according to the concept of human centered design, since many information and communication technology (ICT) systems appear to fail in real life (Dobson, 2007). Dobson describes the classical and much sited case of the London Ambulance Service in which the ICT system turned out to be unusable in real life. A core element of the ICT system, the ambulance dispatch system, was designed to ensure that an ambulance would be available at the scene of an accident within a certain amount of time. On paper, the ICT system worked well and met all stated requirements. In real life, however, it turned out that among others, certain human requirements had been overlooked in the transition of command from the human operator to the ICT dispatching system, such as, allowing ambulance personnel time to recover after some gruesome accidents or anticipating changes in the demand for ambulance services.

It has been pointed out that an important factor for this failure is that these systems do not meet the expectations and values of the users. In finding answers, several backgrounds and disciplines have joined the research field; however, understanding real-life behavior appears to be complex.

A promising direction to understand human behavior and values is to exploit sensitive environments. In a sensitive environment, data is sensed, which makes it possible to derive information such as "who is where, and possibly, doing what," more or less like an anthropologist or a sociologist might do in an observation study of a particular group to establish a social network map of the inhabitants of a street, the power structure in a governing board, etc. A sensitive infrastructure need not be sophisticated; all that is necessary is that it has some sensing devices like a surveillance camera, an automatic light switch, or an entrance gate to the metro that registers the number of passers-by. Sensors may be placed in an environment accidentally or for different purposes than research. For example, the automatic light switch is only put there to have the lights off when no one is there.

When the sensors are intentionally placed in an environment for research or development purposes, the term "Living Lab" may be used (eJOV, 2008) to indicate that the research laboratory has moved into the everyday life. The automatic light switch with some added wiring may also be used to get a rough estimate of how many people are in a particular room at a certain time. Likewise, to create a social network map of the inhabitants of a street, a surveillance camera might be used with some software to analyze movement patterns between households to get a first idea about interactions between households. In a sensitive environment, computing and sensing capabilities are embedded in the environment by means of devices and creative tools. These tools and devices are focused on the (continuous) gathering of data about people; examples include RFID (Radio Frequency Identification) applications, Bluetooth, or mobile phones. For example, RFID and Bluetooth may be used to refine the example of creating a social network map since these wireless techniques can be used to provide people and devices with unique identity codes. With the proper placement of sensors, the interaction patterns in a street may be refined from household interactions to interactions between individuals. As such, insights in these data can be used to obtain a better understanding of user behavior. It should be clear, however, that the amount of sensor data may be huge and difficult to handle and, besides, there is not always a clear understanding of how to interpret sensor data, consider, for example, how to deal with the interaction pattern of the postman. Furthermore, we expect that in the future even more data will be able to be gathered since emerging technologies are becoming increasingly available and affordable for people in more contexts for more purposes. Technologies for wireless networks, image capture, storage, and display get cheaper and more functional. According to Juniper Research (Juniper Research, 2009), sales of smart phones, mobile phones with multimedia and Internet abilities may help to cushion the downturn in the mobile handset market due to the recession. Juniper forecasts that in 2013 about 23% of all handsets sold will be smart phones, creating a 300 million annual market. Also GSA, the Global mobile Suppliers Association with members like Nokia and Sony Ericsson, shows figures in their market update statistics on GSM and mobile broadband subscriptions, indicating that GSM growth is slowing down in western countries but wireless Internet is rapidly growing almost everywhere (GSA, 2009). Another dynamic characteristic of these emerging technologies is that they become personalized, they stay and go with one person, and they are consequently used in various contexts. In other words, sensing capabilities in these devices people carry with them can be part of the sensing infrastructure as well.

Different types of devices and creative research tools may give rise to different types of data ranging from structured to unstructured data and from numerical to categorical data. The analysis of the gathered data can be done from different assumptions. In the so-called closed world assumption (Genesereth & Nilsson, 1987), it is assumed that collected data is true and complete, while in the case where this assumption does not hold, it is assumed that the collected data is incomplete and uncertain. This definition of the closed world assumption sounds fairly theoretical, however, in the context of ICT it generally comes down to the question whether or not the data used by computer applications is predefined. Within a database of a payroll application, for example, data fields named *address* or *balance* have well-defined meanings. This is because their specific meanings have been defined within the "closed world" of the database and the payroll application by software engineers when the database and application were created. In a different database, such as an office telephone register, an *address* field may have a very different meaning, interpretation, and format. Most importantly, in general, there is a notable difference between the terms used within the closed worlds of ICT systems and the open world of everyday life. Consider, for example, that in plain English there are many different ways to use terms like *balance* or *address* and it is not always clear what is exactly meant when they are used.

Related to the closed world assumption is the structuredness of data. Within a closed world, the meaning of terms or data fields is well structured: not only are the terms defined in advance but also the relations between them are. Within an art database, there is a structured relation between a *painter* and a *painting* but this relation does not have to be true for painters in everyday life. Consider, for example, that in text documents the co-occurrence of *painter* and *painting* may be completely accidental, when "the painter removed the painting to paint the wall" and, nevertheless, a search engine like Google will report a hit.

To analyze a huge collection of structured data under the closed world assumption, both data mining and statistical tools can be used. A major difference between data mining and statistics is that data mining tools help to generate useful hypotheses, while statistics is focused on the rejection or acceptance of a predefined hypothesis (Choenni, Bakker, Blok, & de Laat, 2005a). An example of data mining is comparing data in different databases related to welfare or unemployment benefits in order to find frauds, or to analyze airline passenger data to determine who might be a terrorist. To analyze semi-structured and/or unstructured data, we propose to use text mining and information retrieval tools. The best-known example of an information retrieval tool is probably Google, which looks for the occurrence of a particular search text in a collection of documents. More advanced information retrieval tools are also able to distinguish between the different meanings of terms, like the bank of the balance and the one in the park. Text mining tools go one step further and analyze the relations among text terms, as such text mining tools are able to consider the context in which terms are used and sometimes to "understand" what a document is about.

Multisensor data-fusion techniques will be tailored for personalized applications (Waltz & Llinas, 1990). In such applications, measurement by different sensors will be combined in order to serve the information needs of a single user. A good example of multisensor data fusion is the digital camera that "knows" where its pictures are taken, and the GPS positioning information is fused with the digital image. We note that contemporary analyzing tools are equipped with visualization modules for different types of users (Laudon & Laudon, 1999).

Analyzing data in the case that the closed world assumption does not hold is in its childhood. The processing of data in this case leads to scenario studies or how to exploit this data in such a way that it adds value to the data analysis processed under the closed world assumption.

In this chapter, we discuss the potentials and concerns that are entailed by sensitive environments. We expect that the exploitation of these environments may be beneficial for, among others, social scientists. Suppose a group of people is provided with wireless identity tags and camcorders in a sensitive environment within an office, a library, or an urban area. When the sensitive environment is setup, it is possible to track who is where, with whom, and preferably doing what, the setting would enable researchers to collect data to study, for example, interaction patterns among people in more and less formal settings, without the need to interfere with the ongoing activities. Data collected in these environments may be complementary to data gathered by questionnaires or interviews. Observation data may be used to validate or support answers to questions or the questions may be used to give meaning to or resolve ambiguities in the observations. These data may give rise to a wide variety of innovative applications. However, if the collection and processing of these data are not submitted to rules and regulations, it may violate the privacy law (Kalidien, Choenni, & Meijer, 2009). We give an overview of analyzing methods and tools that may be applied to different data types. We also distinguish the role of the time dimension in analyzing data. Furthermore, we discuss how data that are uncertain and for which the closed world assumption does not hold can be collected and exploited for a better understanding of human behavior.

Sensitive Environments

While most methods and tools for data collection are explicit, that is, users are involved in an explicit way, emergent technologies also provide opportunities for getting insight into human behavior in an implicit and less obtrusive manner. By embedding a sensor network in an environment, it is possible to track users' patterns of interaction with and usage of appliances and movements from one location to the other. When such a sensitive environment is used for research purposes, and the research laboratory is moved into the real-life world, the sensitive environment is referred to as a "Living Lab" (eJOV, 2008).

The first applications benefiting emergent technology were mainly motivated by the desire to monitor elderly and disabled people, that is, observing people that are hard to reach for "data collection," for example, using movement sensors to determine if these people are well. The next generation in emergent technology includes the adoption of biosensors, which measure phenomena such as skin temperature or heart beat frequency; in this way, it is possible to infer stress and excitement levels, for instance while the user is playing with an interactive game. However, most examples of environments collecting context data concentrate on logging of usages or track changes in location. One of the first examples of a sensitive environment as well as an example of a Living Lab is the Active Badge System, developed around 1991 at Olivetti Research Lab (Want, Hopper, Falcão, & Gibbons, 1992). In this system, researchers wore badges with a small transmitter whose location could be monitored by a number of receivers dispersed over the laboratory building. This system allowed people to determine the whereabouts of their colleagues and whether or not they could be approached. Even though the system was used on a voluntary basis and could be switched off, it did evoke a lot of discussion about privacy issues. A more recent and much more advanced example of a "logging" environment is the intelligent coffee corner (Mulder, Lenzini, Bargh, & Hulsebosch, 2009), where people taking coffee can use a variety of services offered in the intelligent environment at the coffee corner's site. In the intelligent coffee corner, real-life data is collected by employees carrying detectable devices (e.g., Bluetooth-enabled mobile phones or PDAs and WLAN-enabled laptops) with them and a RFID-enabled badge, which is needed to open doors in order to access the different floors in the office building.

It might be clear that sensitive environments open a wealth of possibilities for real-life data as they enable researchers to come close to people. It moves research out of laboratories into real-life contexts and provides opportunities to nonintrusively study social phenomena in users' social and dynamic context of daily life.

Mulder et al. (2009) stress the need for methodological guidelines and tools that effectively combine the intelligent features of such environments with the strengths of methods and tools traditionally used in social science research, like interviews and focus groups. In the example to create a social map of the interaction patterns among inhabitants of a residential area, it is possible to use data from surveillance cameras or RFID tags to identify and measure the frequency of the interaction patterns. This would be fine when research questions can be answered using purely numeric data. However, it is more likely that researchers will also want qualitative data to investigate why particular interactions take place, and it takes an interview or questionnaire to find out if people are relatives of each other or perhaps postmen. Notwithstanding, it is necessary to have reliable data collection systems as well as (automatic) solutions for capturing and analyzing user behavior, taking into account people's sensitivity to privacy.

When the aim of trying to create a sensitive environment is not how to build a failsafe system but rather to utilize as much information from real life as possible to serve its inhabitants, it may not be a good idea to create yet another closed system using certain and well-defined data but rather to strive for systems that provide "surplus value" for the users. To create a reliable electronic banking system requires the design of systems that provide absolute certainty about the identity of the bearer of a bankcard and the amount of money on his or her balance. Furthermore, any cash withdrawal system should only allow for interactions guarded by valid and reliable means of identification, such as a PIN code to guarantee the relation between identity and balance. Although having to use a PIN code for identification is a system requirement following from the choice, or perhaps, the need to use certain ICT systems, it therefore is not something that users might need or even appreciate. In the context of banking systems, users might appreciate sound advice or transactions without hassle as surplus values of a banking system, for example, in comparison to other systems.

In order to design a sensitive environment in which any kind of information available is used to serve any kind of "user" or "inhabitant," it is rather unnecessary to strive for a closed information system. In order to design a sensitive environment, a system should utilize as many sources of information as possible, much like the way in which we, human beings, function best in environments that provide information from all our different senses. In general, human beings do not function very well in environments that feature information that is restricted to visual or visual-spatial information only, as most ICT systems force us to do.

Information systems aiming to support sensitive environments should include any kind of information that is available, both in terms of whether it is available at all, as well as in terms of whether information is available in a structured, well-formed, reliable, deterministic, and explicit form. In the context of designing information systems, it is important to realize that human beings, in contrast to information systems, do not require structured information; it may be helpful but is not a prerequisite for functional behavior. Human beings do not fall silent when information is unknown; rather, they tend to predict or fill-in what is unknown or unreliable in the environment. In addition, most human knowledge remains tacit and thus implicit (Polanyi, 1958).

In short, a sensitive environment can be seen as an intelligent infrastructure that collects sensory information of users while they move and interact. Although such an environment eases data collection processes as lots of data can be captured automatically, benefits for data analysis are not often that obvious. How do we deal with huge datasets in a sensible way? How can we interpret data that might be incomplete or uncertain in a meaningful and useful way? In the remainder of this work, we focus on making sense of real-life datasets.

Data Analyzing Tools

Equipping our environment with different types of measurement tools, such as sensors, interactive white-boards, cameras, etc., results in the collection of a vast amount of data. Depending on the nature of a measurement tool, different kinds of data will be collected. At a high abstraction level, we distinguish three types of data: structured, unstructured, and semi-structured (Bocij, Greasley, & Hickie, 2009).

Structured data can be regarded as numbers or facts that can be conveniently stored and retrieved in an orderly manner. This is due to the fact that the semantics of the data are well defined. Database and data warehouse systems are developed to facilitate the storage of structured data. The database of a bank-account system, for example, describes the amounts of currency in bank-accounts, identified by account numbers, connected to (legal) persons, who reside at postal addresses, which in turn consist of a street name, an address number, a city name, a postal code, and possibly a state or country code. Such an account system allows one to select the postal addresses of all the people whose name is "Smith" or "Jones" and who own more than a certain amount of money. The bank-account system allows for operations like selection by name or address because the elements of the database—account numbers, names, and address elements—relate to each other by means of predefined relations. Therefore, these systems contain, in general, structured data. The opposite of structured data is unstructured data.

Unstructured data refers to data that lacks predefined relations. Unstructured data will most often refer to textual documents; data in these documents are ambiguous and therefore not well defined. Information retrieval systems such as Google are developed to facilitate, store, and retrieve unstructured data. Since the data used by Google has no predefined relations between bank-account numbers, owner names, and addresses, Googling for "Smith" or "Jones" will result in a long list of banks, bank-account owners, addresses, museums, horses, and whatever, each with "Smith" or "Jones" in its name. The fundamental differences between these systems are summarized in Table 23.1.

Table 23.1 Difference in handling structured versus unstructured data

Aspect	Structured data	Unstructured data
Matching	Exact	Partial and best
Model	Deterministic	Probabilistic
Query language	Formal	Natural
Answers to questions	Exact	Relevant
Output sensitivity to errors	No	Yes

As Table 23.1 shows, for the handling of structured data, a question needs to be formulated in a formal query language, which in turn is used to search for data that exactly match to the question. Therefore, a data retrieval system is capable to return exact answers without errors to the user. Let us assume that a patent office has automated the applications of patents, and information with regard to patents can be obtained via a Web site. A question like "give me the patents that have been submitted by Dr. Knuth" will be typically handled by systems that facilitate the retrieval of structured data. Whereas a question like "give me the patents that significantly contributed to the development of information retrieval systems" will be typically handled by systems that facilitate the retrieval of unstructured data, for the following reasons: the phrase "significantly contributed" is subjective to a certain extent and therefore not well-defined; and to answer the question, a large set of patents, which are textual documents, have to be examined.

The third type of data we distinguish is semi-structured data, which is in between structured and unstructured data and has some regular structure. For example, in a book we recognize, besides unstructured data, some regular structure in the make-up. A book is divided into chapters, a chapter into sections, and a section into paragraphs. Today XML (eXtended Markup Language) is becoming the standard to model semi-structured data (Elmasri & Navathe, 1994). If a book is understood to be a long string of characters, like the file of a word-processor, then XML may be used to indicate which parts of the string contain book elements like the names of the authors, the title, the chapters, the textual data, etc. by means of MARKUP tags like < TITLE> ... < \ TITLE>, <AUTHOR> ... <\AUTHOR>, or < TEXT> ... < \TEXT>. XML is used for a particular document type, to describe which markup tags there are and how they relate. In HTML, the language to markup documents for the World Wide Web, XML is used to describe the tags that determine how documents are presented in Web browsers. Note that HTML is concerned with the presentation rather than the structure of documents. Although XML enables the structured application of data, it will only in very simple and trivial cases allow for a complete structural definition of the available data. Generally, the greater part of the data, like the text in sections of a book, will remain unstructured.

Although the need for analyzing tools for semi-structured and unstructured data is widely recognized, the majority of data analyzing tools pertain to structured data. In the following, we discuss the concepts behind analyzing tools that pertain to structured and unstructured data. The concepts behind semi-structured analyzing tools can be considered a mix of the concepts applied to analyze structured and unstructured data.

Analyzing Structured Data

A wide variety of analyzing tools is reported in the literature (Fayyad, Piatetsky-Shapiro, Smyth, & Uthurusamy, 1996). The suitability of each tool depends on the analysis that should be performed on the data that is collected. Consider, for example, a shop that attaches an RFID sensor to its shopping baskets that is equipped with several sensor readings. Suppose that customers are requested to take a basket before entering the shop. In such a setting, we may collect RFID sensor data that pertain to the position of a customer at a certain time t, which can be modeled as a triple (*basket_id, position, time*) (Farina & Studer, 1985). Furthermore, we may collect data with regard to items in the basket, which may be modeled as a sequence of [$item_1$, $item_2$,..., $item_n$]. Note that time plays a crucial role in the data collected by the sensors, while this is not the case with regard to the data in the basket. The former collection of data will be referred to as time dependent data, while the latter will be referred to as time independent.

As said before, two approaches can be used to analyze time independent data: a statistical or a data mining approach (Choenni et al., 2005a). The starting point of the statistical approach is to collect data and analyze data that might be relevant in rejecting or accepting a hypothesis. The starting point of data mining is collecting data that might not be related to a specific problem at hand and searching for interesting hypotheses. Note that a hypothesis can be regarded as a model of the real world. Although both approaches have a different starting point, the goal is to come up with a useful and adequate model of the real world for a problem given at hand. We illustrate the differences and similarities between data mining and statistics by means of an example. Let us assume that we have collected and stored several items in the baskets of each customer. A typical data mining question on the collected data is: "Search for an interesting hypothesis for me that might be relevant to my shop fitting." Such a question might result in an association between diapers and beer such as, the selling of diapers leads to the selling of beer. On the basis of this result, a shop owner may decide to store beer and diapers next to each other for the sake of convenience for customers. A typical statistical question on the collected data might be, "Is there an association, for example, correlation, between beer and diapers?" In both questions, the interest in an association between beer and diapers is expressed. However, in the data mining question the interest is expressed in an implicit manner, while in the statistical question it is done in an explicit way.

This difference in the formulation of questions has major consequences for the development of technology used for data mining and statistics. To answer the data mining question, all associations need to be inspected in order to find the interesting ones, while in the case of statistics the association between diapers and beer needs to be computed. We note that an exponential complexity is involved in answering the data mining question, that is, if we have n variables then 2^n possible associations need to be inspected. Therefore, an important issue in data mining is how to control complexity. Furthermore, we observe that traditional statistical techniques are tailored toward the handling of data mining questions. For example, classification and clustering concepts are extended to determine the profiles of entities, such as customer, researchers, etc.

The main goal for tools that focus on time dependent data is to track or predict the location of a moving object, such as an airplane or a car, at a certain time or within a time frame. For tools and concepts in the field of multisensor data fusion, the goal is to determine the location of an object on the basis of data that is obtained from different sources, for example, sensors. In our shopping-basket example, we may be interested in what departments of a shop, for example, the food or fashion department, a customer is interested in. Suppose that the shop is equipped with a sensor network such that whenever a customer enters or leaves a certain department of the shop, this data is read by the sensor readings and stored in a database. To compute the time that a customer has spent in a department, data of the sensors that noted that a customer has entered and has left the department can be processed. Moreover, data from the sensor reading may also be used to determine the popular routes in the shop.

Today, we observe also an emerging trend to exploit comprehensive sensor networks to serve for answering "navigational" queries such as "what is the closest best restaurant?" Mobile location-based services employ information from wireless networks such as GPS and Wi-Fi to establish one's location relative to some beacons such as route-maps as in car-navigation systems, places of interest like touristic sites, buildings or works of art as in e-guide systems. Navigational queries are not limited to establishing locations relative to stationary beacons; the beacons may also be other people carrying GPS or Wi-Fi devices, such as in mobile mixed-reality games (Benford et al., 2006) or the GRINDR iPhone application to "meet guys near you" (Grindr, 2009).

Analyzing Unstructured Data

The explosive growth of the Web has entailed a boost in the development systems that are capable of handling unstructured and semi-structured data. Today, the Web has become a huge knowledge resource, containing information about many subjects. The challenge the user faces is finding the information he or she needs and generating useful knowledge from a vast amount of semi- or unstructured data. Information retrieval systems facilitate users in finding documents that might be relevant for them (Croft, 1993; Baeza-Yates & Ribeiro-Neto, 1999), while text mining systems search for useful knowledge, such as associations and regularities within the data (Tan, 1999; Berry, 2004). We briefly discuss the issues and potentials behind these systems.

In the field of information retrieval, effort is put into building systems that are capable of handling the information needs of a user. Information needs formulated by a user are not necessarily exact, as they are in traditional (database) applications, but rather vague and incomplete (Choenni et al., 2005a). Often an information need is expressed by a set of keywords. Suppose that we have a system containing a digital library and a user needs to gain some information about information systems. Therefore, he or she consults this system by typing the keywords "information systems" in order to find all relevant documents that deal with this subject. It should be clear that there are many documents about this subject, and therefore it is not trivial to select the proper documents for this user. Furthermore, a document dealing with information systems can be of interest for one user but not for another, even though both express their information need by the same keywords.

Another issue that should be taken care of by information retrieval systems is to recognize that keywords not explicitly mentioned by users may still be of interest to them. For example, since a database is a major component of an information system, documents about databases also may be of interest for a user who used "information systems" as a keyword and did not explicitly mention databases. By means of an interactive session with the user, an information retrieval system attempts to discover what precisely the information need of a user is and to meet this need. The data generated in the interactive session may be stored and analyzed to better understand users. This understanding can be exploited to serve users better whenever they use the system again (Choenni, Harkema, & Bakker, 2005b). Text mining may be applied as a tool to analyze the data such that it contributes to a better understanding of users.

In the field of text mining, we may distinguish roughly two directions. The first takes as its starting point a database that contains structured data; the goal is to extend this database with unstructured data from other sources. The general approach is to transform the unstructured data into structured data, and then to apply the data mining process. Suppose that we distribute a questionnaire to the customers in our shop example. The goal of the questionnaire is to find out to what extent customers are satisfied by the services in the shop. Customers are asked to answer a set of open and closed questions. In general, the answers of each customer to the open questions can be added to an existing database, as long as the database makes a distinction between different customers. To add the unstructured data for mining purposes in the database requires significantly more effort. The answers to each open question should be classified into a limited number of subjects with which the database is extended. Techniques for information retrieval and extraction are used to facilitate this step. We note that information extraction has as its goal to extract facts from a vast amount of texts. For each subject, the answers of the customers should be clustered into a limited number of clusters. Then, each customer's answer should be mapped on one of these clusters, which will be stored in the databases. Suppose that a questionnaire is sent out to customers and one of the questions pertains to complaints about the items in a shop. Let us assume that the items in the shop are supplied by a limited number of suppliers S1 to S7 and we want to know from the answers on the questionnaire to which suppliers the complaints pertain mostly. Then, for each supplier, we have to make a list of items that are delivered by this supplier. From the questionnaires, we have to extract the items and have to map each item to a supplier.

A generalized approach is to model documents in databases (Blok, Choenni, Blanken, & Apers, 2004). To keep them manageable, not all the terms of a document can be stored in databases. Therefore, a selection of words should be made that will be recorded in a database. In literature, it is proposed to make this selection on the basis of the so-called document and term frequencies. Term frequency is defined as the occurrence of a term in a document related to the term with the highest occurrence in the document. The document frequency of a term is defined as the number of documents in which this term occurs related to the total number of documents. The higher these frequencies for a term, the more important this term is and should be therefore recorded in the databases. Such a database can then be mined with data mining tools.

To conclude, one direction of text mining focuses on extending databases with the unstructured data by processing the data in such a way as to create neatly categorized and structured data.

The second direction of text mining is focused on the analysis of documents. The goal is to determine to what extent two sets of documents are associated with each other or to what extent these sets differ from each other. For example, association may be measured in the amount of overlapping terms between documents. Results from this approach might be useful in the examination of patents, books that will be purchased for a library, etc.

Processing Uncertain and Incomplete Data

Earlier, a number of distinctions were made between different types of data, for example, between structured and unstructured data and between knowledge or information that may be derived from data mining operations versus knowledge or information that required information processing or text mining. In reality, as opposed to data modeling, no such strict distinctions do exist, and for this reason we propose a combined approach both to think about data modeling in sensitive environments as well as to make optimal use of existing data sources.

In traditional ICT, data is generally explicitly defined and used for the purpose of the systems being designed. For example, in order to design a public transport billing system, one might use a personal balance card as a means to keep track of the distance traveled and the amount charged. As such, the notions of the personal identity of the traveler and the balance, be it in miles, clicks, or euros, are to be represented by means of the balance card. Such a card is, of course, not a natural thing but rather a burden to its keeper. Assuming, furthermore, that the card is dedicated to the local or national public transport system or even to the transport company, it follows that the public transport billing system and the balance card constitute a closed system. In general, closed information systems only have a few well-defined possible relations to the real world in which they operate.

It may be noted that in order to function properly, information systems, in contrast to human beings, require exactly the type of information that is well-structured, well-formed, reliable, deterministic, and explicit. When the aim is to design ICT systems to support human beings, rather than to design ICT systems for administration or business purposes, in these circumstances, the question then is how to utilize unstructured, ill-formed, unreliable, etc., information in systems that require the opposite.

Earlier in this chapter, we argued that it is sometimes possible to turn implicit and uncertain data into explicit information, as in the case of the relation between diaper and beer sales. In that example, statistics or data mining established the relation. In advance, the data about beer sales and diaper sales were structured explicitly. The relation between the two categories was not explicitly known but could be established by using the drag-net of data mining: calculating statistical correlations between (sales) categories and filtering out those that surpass a certain level of significance. After this, further analysis may reveal the nature of the relation, for example, that there is a certain category of buyer that links diaper and beer sales.

The interesting point here is that uncertain data should not be avoided but rather used to make deterministic data more interesting or useful. Consider, for example, that when buying books, people might be interested in other books that are in some respect similar to the ones they already know, as is exemplified by Amazon's "people who bought the book also bought...." To answer a question like this, it is not necessary to know exactly, reliably, and in well-defined ways what people's interests are. The only thing that needs be known is the purchasing outcome of others. Of course, if customer's interests were known, in addition to the data about other people's purchasing behavior, the recommendation system would be even better able to advise a customer.

Some Illustrating Examples

As an example, consider the recommendation system behind the Amazon online bookstore. What is required for a good recommendation system is some sort of basic data set

· consisting of other people's opinions and choices that is large enough to analyze the data and organize it into interesting or otherwise significant patterns in behavior. These patterns, in turn, may be interpreted by a process of sense making to yield directly applicable results. In Davenport and Glaser (2002), an advanced knowledge management system is described in a medical context. On the basis of knowledge in the medical field and the experiences of medical colleagues, the system advised what drugs might be prescribed for a certain disease.

Outside the well-defined ICT environment, we might essentially do the same, except that the data or information may not be derived from the well-defined deterministic environment of the information system but from the outside world. In this case, the information is not the result of an analysis process that is fed into a sense making process, but rather the opposite: a process of sense making is applied to the outside world such that phenomena that may not be observed directly may be predicted from observable phenomena such as data available about past behavior. An example of such a "sensible relation" is that—other things being equal—a person's interest in an object, for example, a painting in a museum, a dress in a shop window, or a stereo in a car, may be established by measuring the time spent inspecting the object by art lovers, shopping addicts, or car burglars, respectively.

A major disadvantage of the type of data that is laid down in predefined ICT systems is its limited utility: this type of data is defined, collected, and put into databases with specified purposes. Even if such data is brought together from multiple sources, it is generally very difficult to use such data for any other purpose than the one underlying the raison d'être of the ICT systems.

Looking at the interesting types of data in the real-life world, a major disadvantage of data outside ICT systems is that it is, unfortunately, less reliable. It is one thing that common sense may yield a number of interesting or sensible relations between items in the outside world, but it is quite another thing to ask for the validity and reliability of these relations.

Given the limited utility of the one type of data and the limited reliability of the other, it may be interesting to ask what may be gained from bringing the two types of data together. In this case, the idea is to start with the most reliable data and add observed data from the outside world to create additional information.

As an example, consider a museum that provides electronic touring guides to its visitors. The example is loosely based on two European Community IST (Information Society Technology) projects: COMRIS and i-MASS. Both of these projects concern research on "ubiquitous computing," a term coined by Mark Weiser (Weiser, 1991), to expand the utilization of computers outside the working context and support people in a natural way in everyday life. The i-Mass project concerned, among other things, the technical information infrastructure to adapt the presentation and content of information in museums to the characteristics of its visitors (de Haan, 2002). The COMRIS project concerned the design of a ubiquitous device to present information from a range of heterogeneous sources to support attending a large conference or exhibition (de Haan, 1999).

When the visitor arrives at an interesting piece of art, he or she types in some number connected to the specific item and the touring guide provides the visitor with information about the item, such as biographic information about the artist, the materials used, and so on. A slightly more advanced electronic touring guide might provide visitors with the opportunity to select a level of explanation that is most suitable to his or her level of expertise. In both these cases, it is the visitor who has to interact with the e-guide device.

This may not always be possible or desirable. In addition, one might ask why it is the visitor who has to make decisions.

As an alternative, it may be possible to build some intelligence into the device or into the environment to sense the location of the visitor and to help decide which level of expertise is appropriate for the particular visitor. Suppose that the identity of a museum visitor is known in advance from the ID data on his or her museum card. The ownership of the museum card may be taken to support the idea that this person is more knowledgeable about art than the average museum visitor, which may then be used to instruct the electronic guide to present information at a more advanced level. In addition, the card might be used to store a visitor's personal settings and preferences.

In a similar vein, when an e-guide might wirelessly sense that it is near a certain location, a beacon or a piece of art, the vicinity information may be utilized in different ways. In such a case, the visitor is relieved from the task of instructing the e-guide about his or her whereabouts or the required level of complexity in the guidance information. In addition, when a visitor spends considerable time in the vicinity of a particular item, the e-guide might provide additional or more comprehensive information about the item than the standard message. In this case, the e-guide system might infer from the visitor's hanging-around behavior that additional explanation is appropriate. In both these examples, information is used from a single source: the amount of time that the e-guide receiver senses that it is in the vicinity of the transmitter associated with a certain location or piece of art.

In a slightly more complex design, it may be possible to use data from different sources to create additional information. Visitors who spend a considerable amount of time near impressionist paintings and who spend, in a consistent manner, relatively little time near naive or abstract paintings may reveal a particular interest in impressionism as an indication that some sort of expert explanation might be appropriate for this visitor. It may be noted that a relation between time near something and amount of interest may not always exist. Even if it seems that people are interested in impressionist art, it may be that in reality people are merely interested in the availability of seats in the room where the paintings are on display. However, at least in the context of visiting museums, there is presumably little harm done in presenting the "wrong" information, especially compared to the benefits of those visitors who are served better.

The utilization of information from multiple sources may become even more advanced when information is used from outside the particular context of use. As an extension of the museum example, consider that through the visitor's museum card or some other publicly accessible identity token, it may be possible to establish a link to information about the visitor on the Internet, such as his or her homepage, information from social-networking sites such as Orkut or Facebook, or professional information from sources such as LinkedIn or company Web sites.

Internet information from sources like these is often and negatively associated with marketing, fraud, and security purposes, often notably different from the personal intentions and wishes of those whom it concerns. Public information, however, may also be used to empower people by using the information in such a way as to adapt the environment according to their own purposes. In the context of the running example, suppose that, upon entering a museum, visitors allow the e-guide system to utilize the information that is available about them on the Internet. This time, however, the purpose is not to perform some security check or try and sell something to the visitor but rather to enhance the person's visiting experience by providing guiding information that is optimally adapted to his or her personal interests and experience.

The e-guide system might utilize the Internet for information about the visitor in various ways, using more or less advanced techniques, ranging from simple keyword matching, to personal profiling and agent-based metadata analysis using semantic Web techniques. When a visitor has a homepage, for example, finding a keyword expression such as "impressionist painting" under a heading "interests" may be taken as a direct reference to a specific interest or a specific level of expertise. More often, keyword analysis will yield indirect references to interests and expertise when sets of words like "Pisarro," "beer," or "knitting" may either strengthen, weaken, or be neutral in their relation to certain interests or levels of expertise.

Some problems are true for individual keyword-interest relations, which may not be very strong or valid or may not even be reliable. Keyword matching, profiles, and semantic analysis, however, are hardly ever concerned with single keyword matches. On the contrary, since concern is with large numbers of such relations and value networks, an analysis will yield useful relations, if only by sheer number. This is especially true when concern is not with a single data source but when there are many homepages, profiles, or function descriptions at stake. Indeed, whereas ICT systems under the closed world assumption tend to be restricted to single database systems featuring a certain level of reliability and validity, the idea to create useful information from a multitude of different data and different data sources inherently supports the notion to rely on sound data patterns.

To summarize this section, first, it is necessary to open up the closed systems in order to make the trapped data inside available for different purposes. In principle, the data inside closed systems is only meaningful to the purposes for which those systems were built in the first place, and this may be done in different ways. Having the data readily available, they can be related to different sets of less structured and less reliable data, such as unstructured text on the Internet or semi-structured XML data. Finally, by relating the different types of data using a sufficiently large number of sources, where each source provides a different perspective on environment, it will not only be possible to increase the reliability and certainty of the information, but it will also be possible to create more utility and meaningfulness than was available in the resources.

Benefits and Potentials in Data Collection

In the previous sections, we briefly mentioned some of the benefits of sensitive environments. In this section, we discuss the impact of data collected in sensitive environments in social research and some innovative applications that might be entailed by the data. To gain insight in social phenomena, a standard tool that is used by researchers is surveys. Valuable data can be collected form surveys and interesting hypotheses can be answered from these data (as illustrated earlier in the shop fitting example).

However, using surveys for collecting data to answer explicit as well as implicit questions also has restrictions which lead to certain challenges. One restriction is that the reliability of surveys is dependent on the number of participants in a survey. Often, the participation in a survey is voluntary. One challenge is that there are not enough participants in a sample to make reliable statistical statements. Secondly, composing a questionnaire can be quite time-consuming. Specific items on the research subject must be chosen carefully at hand and often a pretest is needed to see how effective a certain item is. The processing and analyzing of the data is often also quite time-consuming (athough nowadays many surveys are made by the Internet). Nevertheless, analyzing questionnaires may cost a lot of time, especially in the case of "open" questions, for example, "What do you think of this product?" instead of "closed" questions, answered with, for example, yes, no, do not know. In the case of open questions, there is a wide range of interpretation, while in the case of closed questions the interpretation is fixed. Another challenge may be that different interviewers interview in a different way; this means that the interreliability among interviewers may not be optimal. By training interviewers, one may increase the interreliability among interviewers; however this also costs time and money.

Yet another challenge of surveys is that there are different ways of sampling. For instance, participants may be recruited by taking a sample of the central population register in one survey. In another survey, the sampling may be done by means of postal codes or telephone registers. Some interviews may be held at the participants home, while others are made by telephone or e-mail. Comparing the results of different surveys about the same object may not be evident in this way. Also, comparing the results of surveys over different periods may not be evident when different sampling methods have been used.

In addition, the restricted memory of a respondent may influence the results, especially in the case of questions about the past, for example, "Did you drink more beer compared to 5 years ago?" From psychological research, it is known that human memory is not a simple recorder of events but an active process, influenced by irrelevant external factors like emotions, suggestions, intentions, how questions are formulated, etc. As a result, it is very difficult to have people act as eyewitnesses, particularly about their own lives (Loftus, 1996).

By exploiting (implicit) data by means of technology, one may profit in a more efficient way from the data. For example, in the case of sampling, a sensor in the shop basket automatically registers all clients visiting a shop. In this way, no interviewers are needed and also a broad variety of possible hypotheses may be captured. In the case of a survey, specific items must be thought of at hand. Another example is that in some large shops, customers can scan all products themselves and pay with their credit card instead of waiting in the line at the cash register. In this way, implicit data about consumer behavior is registered without the need for composing questionnaires and sampling. Using the same technique in different regions may lead to the comparison of different regions. Also, by exploiting technology the challenge of restricted memory is overcome, since data is registered each time a customer enters the shop. As illustrated above, in many cases one may benefit from replacing survey data with register data, in the case that the environment is adjusted adequately with existing measurement technology.

The data collected in sensitive environments may also open directions for new applications in the near future. This might be completely new directions that are based on tracking data or existing applications that are enriched with a tracking dimension. An example of the latter has already been given in the context of navigational queries. Database systems are now able to handle additional queries such as "give me the closest best restaurant from the position where a user is." An example of new directions that are completely based on tracking data is to manage crowds in cities and traffic jams. Big events always attract many people, which often lead to congestions and traffic jams. By keeping track of the mobile phones of people, one may follow the developments of the traffic and movement of people. Authorities may use this knowledge to control the movement of people and/or traffic whenever congestions arise.

Data from sensitive environments may also have an impact in the field of direct marketing, also referred to as pervasive advertizing (e.g., van Waart & Mulder, in press). Since the movement of people can be tracked at individual level, it becomes easy to find out their travelling behavior. Therefore, more effective offers by marketing departments may be made to them, especially when this data can be combined or integrated with other data, such as the reading interest, preferences for food and so on. Market researchers still use a small palette of traditional techniques to get insights in what their customers want. These methods, such as interviews, focus groups, or surveys, usually focus on what people say they do. Differently put, insights gained will be those that can be expressed by people themselves, and the data consequently do not reveal customer insights. Creative research tools promise to be different and yield, therefore, different insights as well. In the current chapter, we elaborated on how to deal with uncertain data in a meaningful way.

It should be clear that the collection of data in sensitive environments has potential in several domains. However, the counterpart of this potential is the possible violation of people's privacy. How to deal with privacy issues in innovative applications that may expose the identity of individuals is considered as a major challenge (see a.o. Broder, 2000; Choenni & van Dijk, 2009).

Conclusions

This chapter started with the observation that an important factor in the failure of information systems in real life is that these systems do not meet the expectations and values of the users. The concepts of sensitive environments and Living Labs, in which information systems continuously collect and process data about their users, may provide a better understanding of the needs and limitations of them. Consequently, this understanding may be incorporated in the design of contemporary information systems, which increases the acceptance of information systems by its users, and, therefore, reduces the chances of failure of an information system. Since the understanding of the behavior, needs, and limitations of people is also a cornerstone in social research, the collection and processing of data in the context of sensitive environments may become an effective and efficient vehicle to answer questions raised by social researchers.

A widely accepted method to study a real-world phenomenon is to capture the phenomenon in a model, which is the subject of further analysis and reasoning. Data collected in real life are used to derive models of a phenomenon or to underpin a model that is built on the basis of theories. However, for a single phenomenon, one may devise many models. We recall that in general a model for a phenomenon can be regarded as a simplified map of the real-world phenomenon. Depending on the research questions, one model may be marked as better than another model. To study the behavior, needs, and limitations of people, interactions with and among people have been proved to be indispensable to collect the proper set of data for building suitable models. Therefore, we propose to create sensitive environments that also focus on the support of interactions.

In order to create sensitive environments that support people's interactions with each other, the general goal of Human Centered ICT approaches, it will be necessary to make the data in closed ICT systems available for other purposes than those for which the specific systems were built in the first place. As illustrated in the foregoing, the data from ICT systems for surveillance purposes might also be used for, for instance, keeping in touch with one's neighbors. Mere access to data does not ensure that it can be used meaningfully. Meaning might be added by means of some analytical process. In this chapter, we propose to seek external data to facilitate changing streams of low-level data into meaningful information. Using external information, from the Internet, for example, in combination with well-structured data also helps to create information that is sufficiently reliable for further processing in ICT systems, in order to shape a meaningful context containing meaningful information. An example of these new opportunities is illustrated, in the foregoing, by means of an electronic guiding system for museums that uses a combination of well-defined and less well-defined data sources to allow for automatic adaptation of the subject and of the level of explanation to the interests, wishes, and experience of museum visitors, thus enhancing the experience of visiting a museum. The electronic guidance systems have become more and more sophisticated in the past recent years due to the success of PDAs, GPRS-enabled phones, and Smart Phones, in combination with technologies like Java, RFID, and Wi-Fi (Santoro, Paternò, Ricci, & Leporini, 2007). Most e-guides in actual use still require the user to indicate the item of interest and other settings, but location-aware e-guides are commercially available. E-guides featuring automatic adaptation to the type of user or usage have—to our knowledge—not yet left the research phase of development (Baus, Cheverst, & Kray, 2005).

Only when we succeed in crossing the border between structured and unstructured data will we be able to create true ubiquitous computing system, supporting everyday life using ICT. We have argued that to design such systems requires the utilization of a range of different types of data, such as structured, semi-structured, and unstructured data, each requesting specific methods for analysis, including data mining, statistics, multisensor data fusion, and techniques as advanced as reasoning with uncertainty and incomplete information. Applying some general principles behind human behavior in the natural world, it follows that the most interesting and useful types of information are those that are presently not used or underutilized in ICT systems that tend to depend on well-defined, reliable, and valid information, thus creating closed world systems: systems with few and well-defined interfaces to the outside world, such that they are only usable for the specific purpose that they are designed for. Although data mining technologies have as goal to exploit collected data also for other purposes than data is initially collected for, these technologies are primarily focused on structured data. In order to provide sensitive environments to support people in everyday life, including personal wishes and intentions, it is necessary to look beyond the technologies of the closed world assumption and utilize less well-structured data and information. The sheer abundance of less well-structured and less reliable data sources will not only create new opportunities to design more useful systems answering the needs and demands of everyday life, but also increase the reliability and utility of the data that is already available and used in information systems.

In general, extracting models from these wide variety types of data will lead to better and more reliable models that may be used to understand people behavior and social phenomena in society. In many cases, social researchers will be relieved from issues that are involved in data collection, such as the design and processing of questionnaires and model building. Therefore, it is possible that social researchers will shift their efforts toward the interpretation of models in the future.

Research and development related to sensitive environments evolves in several directions, which are not necessarily divergent. Two main streams may be distinguished, the so-called technical- and application-oriented streams. The technical-oriented stream, mainly consisting of computer scientists, mathematicians, and electrical engineers, primarily focuses on proper ways to represent different types of data in computer systems and to reason/combine these data in an efficient and robust way. The application-oriented stream primarily focuses on the set up of sensitive environments and devising and implementing innovative applications with the rich set of different type of data that is nowadays available. We note that new technology is also deployed for efficiency purposes, for example, in the case of product development rather than research purposes. During this process, they often have to face technical challenges and shortcomings. These challenges and shortcomings are communicated to the technical stream, which may use them as a source of inspiration for their research agenda. It should be clear that in such a setting, both streams are complementary to each other.

References

Baeza-Yates, R., & Ribeiro-Neto, B. (1999). *Modern information retrieval.* New York: Addison Wesley/ACM Press.

Baus, J., Cheverst, K., & Kray, C. (2005). A survey of map-based mobile guides. In Meng, L., Zipf, A., & Reichenbacher, T. (Eds.), *Map-based mobile services: Theories, methods and implementations* (pp. 197–216). Berlin: Springer.

Benford, S., Crabtree, A., Flintham, M., Drozd, A., Anastasi, R., Paxton, M., et al. (2006). Can you see me now? *ACM Transactions on Computer-Human Interaction, 13*(1), 100–133.

Berry, M. W. (Ed.). (2004). *Survey of text mining, clustering, classification and retrieval.* New York: Springer.

Blok, H. E., Choenni, R., Blanken, H., & Apers, P. (2004). A selectivity model for fragmented relations: Applied in information retrieval. *IEEE Trans. Knowl. Data Eng., 16*(5), 635–639.

Bocij, P., Greasley, A., & Hickie, S. (Ed.). (2009). *Business information systems: Technology, development and management* (4th ed.) Pearson Education Limited.

Broder, A. J. (Ed.). (2000). Data mining, the Internet, and privacy. In *Proceedings of International WEBKDD'99 Workshop* (pp. 56–73) August 15, 1999, in San Diego, CA. Springer LNCS 1836. Berlin/Heidelberg: Springer Verlag.

Choenni, R., Bakker, R., Blok, H. E., & de Laat, R. (2005a). Supporting technologies for knowledge management. In Baets, W. (Ed.), *Knowledge management and management learning: Extending the horizon of knowledge-based management.* New York: Springer Verlag.

Choenni, R., Harkema, S., & Bakker, R. (2005b). Learning and interaction via ICT tools for the benefit of knowledge management. In Baets, W. (Ed.), *Knowledge management and management learning extending the horizons of knowledge-based management.* New York: Springer Verlag.

Choenni, R., & van Dijk, J. (2009). Towards privacy preserving data reconciliation for criminal justice chains. In *Proceedings of the 10th Annual International Conference on Digital*

Government Research: Social Networks: Making Connections between Citizens, Data and Government, (pp. 223–229) DG.O 2009. ACM.

Croft, W. B. (1993). Knowledge-based and statistical approaches to text retrieval. *IEEE Expert,* 8(2), 8–12.

Davenport, T. H., & Glaser, L. (2002). Just in time delivery comes to knowledge management. Harvard Business Review, July.

Dobson, J. (2007). Understanding failure: The London ambulance service disaster. In Dewsbury, G., & Dobson, J. (Eds.), *Responsibility and dependable systems* (pp. 130–161). London: Springer Verlag.

eJOV. (2008). *eJOV—The Electronic Journal for Virtual Organizations and Networks 10, Special Issue on Living Labs,* (November). Retrieved from http://www.ejov.org/apps/pub. asp?Q=2993&T=eJOV%20Issues&B=1 (accessed July, 2009).

Elmasri, R., & Navathe, S. (1994). *Fundamentals of database systems* (2nd ed.). Menlo Park: Addison-Wesley.

Farina, A., & Studer, F. A. (1985). *Radar data processing: Introduction and tracking, research studies* (Vol. 1). New York: Wiley Press.

Fayyad, U., Piatetsky-Shapiro, G., Smyth, P., & Uthurusamy, R. (Ed.). (1996). *Advances in knowledge discovery and data mining.* AAAI/The MIT Press.

Genesereth, M. R., & Nilsson, N. (1987). *Logical foundations of artificial intelligence.* San Mateo, CA: Morgan Kaufmann Publishers.

Grindr. (2009). Grindr—Meet_Guys_Near_You_on_your_iPhone. (Accessed on June 28) http:// www.grindrguy.com/Grindr_iPhone_App/.

GSA. (2009). GSM/3G Stats & Market Update. (Accessed on July 17) http://www.gsacom. com/.

de Haan, G. (1999). The usability of interacting with the virtual and the real in COMRIS. In Nijholt, A., Donk, O., & Van Dijk, D. (Eds.), *Proceedings of interactions in virtual worlds, TWLT 15,* (pp. 19–21). May, Enschede, the Netherlands.

de Haan, G. (2002). The design and evaluation of intelligent access to mankind's collective memory. In Bagnara, S., Pozzi, S., Rizzo, A., & Wrigth, P. (Eds.), *Proceedings of the 11th European conference on cognitive ergonomics, ECCE-11—Cognition, culture and design* (pp. 47–53). September 8–11, Catania, Italy.

Juniper Research. (2009). Next generation smart phones: Players, opportunities & forecasts 2008–2013. (Accessed on July 20, 2009) http://www.juniperresearch.com/shop/viewreport. php?id=171.

Kalidien, S., Choenni, R., & Meijer, R. (2009). Towards a tool for monitoring crime and law enforcement, In *Proceedings ECIME 2009, 3rd European Conference on Information Management and Evaluation.* Gothenburg, Sweden: Academic Publishing Limited.

Laudon, K. C., & Laudon, J. P. (1999). *Essentials of management information systems* (3rd ed.). New Jersey: Prentice Hall.

Loftus, E. F. (1996). *Eyewitness testimony* (2nd ed.). Cambridge, MA: Harvard University Press.

Mulder, I., Lenzini, G., Bargh, M. S., & Hulsebosch, B. (2009). Reading the tea leaves in an intelligent coffee corner: Challenges for understanding behavior. *Behavior Research Methods,* 41(3), 820–826.

Polanyi, M. (1958). *Personal knowledge. Towards a post critical philosophy.* London: Routledge.

Santoro C., Paternò, F., Ricci, G., & Leporini, B. (2007). A multimodal mobile museum guide for all. In *Proceedings of the 9th International Conference on Human Computer Interaction with Mobile Devices and Services. Mobile HCI,* (pp. 21–25). September 9–12, Singapore.

Tan, A. H. (1999). Text mining: The state of the art and the challenges. In *Proceedings of the PAKDD 1999 Workshop on Knowledge Discovery from Advanced Databases.* April 26. Beijing, China.

van Waart, P., & Mulder, I. (2009). Meaningful Advertising: Pervasive Advertising in the experience economy. In: J. Müller, P. Holleis, A. Schmidt, M. May (Eds.). Proceedings of the 2nd Workshop on Pervasive Advertising (workshop in conjunction with Informatik 2009. Lubeck. 2 October 2009), pp. 22–27.

Waltz, E., & Llinas, J. (1990). *Multi sensor data fusion*. Boston: Artech House Radar Library.

Want, R., Hopper, A., Falcão, V., & Gibbons, J. (1992). The active badge location system. *ACM Transactions on Information Systems*, *10*(1), 91–102.

Weiser, M. D. (1991). The computer for the twenty-first century. *Scientific American*, September, 94–104.

> Chapter 24

Using Technology and the Experience Sampling Method to Understand Real Life

Anne Kellock, Rebecca Lawthom, Judith Sixsmith, Karen Duggan, Ilana Mountian, John T. Haworth, Carolyn Kagan, David P. Brown, John E. Griffiths, Jenny Hawkins, Claire Worley, Christina Purcell, and Asiya Siddiquee

Introduction

Social scientists are still puzzling over how best to access human experience. Historically, the strength of the natural sciences paradigm resulted in a belief that more stringent measurement could deliver more accurate experiences. This quantitative stronghold has lessened due to the "turn to language." Approaches that embraced this qualitative stance have addressed key issues of power, reflexivity, and transparency within the research process. There are however, still many tensions when addressing experience in this way. Researchers have sought to unpack human experience using a variety of methodological approaches ranging from ethnography, discourse analysis to observational methods, and interviews. However, the ways in which these methods and analytical tools are utilized are continually critiqued and reflected upon. Qualitative researchers have been mindful of the use of self in research and the contextual nature of the data. A key issue in collection and interpretation of the work is more than a consideration of the researcher role, rather the usage of the technology that seems hugely relevant to the method. In the same way that social science researchers emphasized that language was not a transparent medium, technology is itself in need of interrogation. In this chapter, we present an original approach to accessing experience, which is both visual and word based. In outlining how the method was utilized, we also reflect critically upon the approach and the ways in which technology interfaces with the capture of human experience.

The Experience Sampling Method (ESM) was first used by Csikszentmihalyi, Larson, and Prescot (1977) for the random collection *in situ* of self reports about a respondent's subjective states and daily experience. Respondents answer questions in a diary several times a day in response to signals from a preprogrammed devise such as a watch or radio pager. Brandstatter (1991) considered that time-sampling methods can be designed to overcome some of the flaws and restrictions inherent in traditional retrospective questionnaire methods used to measure subjective experience. An extensive guide to the method, used to undertake research into the experience and quality of people's everyday experience, has been written by Hektner, Schimidt, and Csikszentmihalyi (2008). The investigation of the relationship between the activity undertaken, skills, challenges, enjoyment, and subjective well-being in daily life has been of particular concern (Haworth, 1997). Delle Fave (2007) notes that the ESM can be used to capture emotions, motivations, and cognitive processes as they occur, and that it reduces the problem of distortion of memories occurring in retrospective methods. This has been the case in the current research; however, like many methods, the ESM is seen as complementing and not replacing other research methods.

In the research presented here, the ESM has been used as a method to investigate subjective appreciation of participants' everyday experiences, with a special emphasis on the visual, first undertaken by Haworth (2009a) and developed from his research into both creativity and well-being. Within this chapter, there will be an explanation of the method and its research potential. These discussions are based on the group analysis of a research project conducted with staff and students at a higher education institution using the ESM with photography. The research project aimed at investigating participants' assessments of their everyday life experiences in keeping with the previous research of Haworth (1997, 2009a).

The chapter will comment on the way this technological innovation can be practiced and its applicability across disciplines and the type of questions the application of this technology could help answer. Some of the issues stemming from this research project regarding visual methods, ethics, power in research relationships, and research in institutional settings have been previously discussed in Mountian et al. (forthcoming, 2009). In this paper, issues of power are at the centre of research processes, the filtering of pictures to be taken, and are implicated in shaping the performances of participants. Taking these issues into account, this chapter will further consider the potential applications of ESM in research.

The chapter will present the strengths and weaknesses of the method, along with the technical aspects of ESM used in the research project, including sampling, tasks undertaken, questions answered, design of response card, and color coding of questions around subjective understandings of well-being (Haworth, 2009b). Further, implications of using scales to measure subjective understandings of well-being will also be considered, including a critique of the methods. This analysis will be illustrated by visual and textual/verbal interpretations of the data; the focus will be on well-being and on creativity. The chapter will also comment on the potential applications across disciplines, the usage of ESM as photo-elicitation and photo-documentation, and the combined visual and textual approach allowing a rich collection of data.

Methodology and Method

This higher education research project involved ESM using mobile-phone technology including a camera first utilized by Haworth (2009a). In essence, participants were provided with a mobile phone with integrated camera as a research tool that allowed them to capture pictures of their daily activity and experiences over the period of 1 week. Twelve members of a department at the Manchester Metropolitan University participated in this project including administrative staff, researchers, research students, professors, supervisors, lecturers, and line managers. The project was designed as part of a team-building activity, aiming to provide a focus for both collective purposeful activity across the group as well as to promote shared understanding of well-being.

Here, details of the ESM will be presented in the following text including sampling details, tasks undertaken, specific questions answered during the ESM data collection, and design of response card. Details will also be presented of the color coding of the questions on subjective well-being, which have been used to visually present the images of daily life (Haworth, 2009a, 2009b). Implications of using 3-point scales to measure subjective well-being will also be considered further on.

The participants in the study took two photographs each morning initially to capture the day and date as well as a further image to portray a wider context of the day, such as a view of their garden or a part of a newspaper. An example of this is given in Figure 24.1. For the rest of the day, the phone was preset to beep an alarm eight times through the day. To facilitate this, the day was divided into eight sections of 1½ hr each. The alarms were preset, over the 1½-hr intervals by a person independent of the project in order to "surprise" the participant. This was done in an attempt to prevent anticipation of the alarm to predetermine activity. Once the beep sounded, the participant took a photograph of the main activity they were doing. Framing of the photograph was entirely under the participants' control in the sense that they could decide who or what was depicted in the photograph. In addition, they answered a series of questions by voice recording into the mobile phone. The questions were set in order to provide some qualitative description of the activities involved in and to enable participants to record their comments in explanation of answers given to preset questions. Eight preset questions, five of which were based on the theory of "optimal experience" (Csikszentmihalyi & Csikszentmihalyi, 1988), determined the degree of enjoyment, interest, challenge, skill level, happiness, and visual interest felt at the time of the activity:

1. What was the main thing you were doing?
2. How much were you enjoying the activity? (1–3)
3. How interesting did you find the activity? (1–3)
4. How challenging did you find the activity? (1–3)
5. Were your skills: (1) less than required by the challenge; (2) equal to the challenge; or (3) more than required by the challenge?
6. How visually interesting did you find the scene? (1–3)
7. How happy were you feeling at the time? (1–3)
8. Any other brief comments.

These were graded 1–3 representing low to high ratings of experience such that a rating of 1 represented low enjoyment, interest, etc. and a rating of 3 represented high enjoyment, interest, etc.

Traditionally, the ESM method uses questionnaire diaries and electronic pagers that are preprogrammed to bleep at randomly selected times during the day. However, here, the mobile phone/camera was used to take a picture at each signal, a method first developed by Haworth (2009a) as a part of his research into creativity and well-being. The addition of this visual method enabled multiple possibilities of data interpretation involving "an artistic object for contemplation" in several ways:

Figure 24.1 A week in the life, Participant 11.

1. as individual visual profiles for comparative research;
2. or as analysis of themes across a group of individuals;
3. and between groups." (p.)

This form of visual data collection within the ESM also stimulated a great deal of personal and social reflection after data collection had been completed. Critical review of the photographs in parallel with the qualitative and quantitative data encouraged retrospective analysis of the activities and the ways in which they supported, maintained, or promoted well-being. In some cases, this opened up new opportunities and possibilities of ways of seeing activity and experience, and introduced new trains of imagination.

In discussing the visual in ethnographic research, Pink (2004) recognizes the interweaving of objects, texts, images, and technologies in people's everyday lives and identities. She advocates a reflexive approach to research, focusing on subjectivity, creativity, and self-consciousness, abandoning the possibility of a purely objective social science. Rose (2007) notes that photographic images, whether moving or still, are currently the most popular sort of image being created by social scientists because they can carry or evoke three phenomenon—information, affect, and reflection—particularly well. She documents that researchers have pointed to several reasons for using photos, including the way they convey "real, flesh and blood life"; make their audiences bear witness to that life; and give research participants a means to reflect on aspects of their lives that they may usually give little thought to. Rose also notes that research ethics are particularly important in this type of research; the social relations of a research project are ethical. The present research is a collaborative group project, where participative research within a group is understood as collaborative research. This involves the process being open to the understandings of all participants, who must be allowed to withdraw from a project at any stage and specify in which way their data can be used.

The photographic data for each individual across the week was constructed into a series of posters, for example, Figure 24.1. In this figure, the 7 days are shown horizontally, whereby the first two images for each are the date and context photographs and the eight below are those taken when the alarm sounded. Finally, the data was compiled into a data-collection book that included a copy of the posters that were made, reflections, and comments made when the voice recordings were transcribed. The posters were exhibited at the RIHSC Conference at Manchester Metropolitan University in 2007 in an exhibition entitled "Tapping into visual worlds" and have been presented in several seminars and conferences since.

The ESM method with its innovative visual component was subject to research evaluation. Each participant completed individual reflections immediately after the project ended and reflections of the experience of taking part in the project. In addition, the sensitivities of opening up personal data to collective analysis were revealed in a focus group conducted 6 months later. This provided enhanced personal and methodological reflexivity, which framed diverse understandings of the research process.

Critique of the ESM as Used in This Project

This section will examine the perceived strengths and weaknesses of this innovative method, primarily drawing on learning achieved when using and reflecting on the ESM in the project described above. The following themes concerning methodological process emerged from the data analysis and from individual and socially shared reflections that were carried out at both data collection and project end. Firstly, initial reflections were carried out immediately after the week of photographic research had taken place. Secondly, reflections were carried out 6 months later when reviewing the photographic images and posters revealed the very different responses reported by participants on their experiences of documenting a week in their lives in ways that created not only verbal descriptions but also visual records. These have been organized into two sections below: the first concerns the strengths of the method and the second relates to weaknesses.

The Strengths and Opportunities of Using the Experience Sampling Method

Raising Awareness of the Taken-for-Grantedness of Everyday Life

The photographs within the research highlighted the taken-for-grantedness of everyday life within the context of ordinary, everyday activities. The focus on mundane activities or even interesting activities allowed participants to focus on details of their daily lives. By reviewing the images, an opportunity was created to see daily patterns of activity that might not otherwise have been obvious. The reflective stands taken within the project enabled us to examine those daily patterns made visible within the photographic context and to consider why such patterns exist. Indeed, reviewing our week through the eyes of the photographs enlightened us to the behavioral structures of our lives as evidenced in that particular week and prompted much consideration of why our lives were shaped in those particular ways. The social context of our lives became highly visible not only to ourselves but to others, very much underlining the connection between people, places, and organizational hubs. In this way, the taken-for-granted patterns of activity that we rarely think about seemed to make sense only within such contexts. This was not always a positive experience. For some participants, the visible patterning of life was difficult to accept personally and to share in open public scrutiny, for others the permanent record of the week made it a detailed and memorable record enhanced by our developing knowledge of the complexity of its very ordinariness.

Recognizing Your Place in Space and Time

In viewing the photographs, it was possible to make direct and immediate connections with our own environments, contexts, situations, events, and people that we spend our time with. Such connections were seen to be forged through micro actions, the small and seemingly inconsequential spaces that are the context of our lives, momentarily consuming, instantly forgotten, yet constitutional of our identity. This paradox arising between that which is seen as inconsequential but is later recognized as hugely important in making us who we are can be realized in the choices we made not only about framing photographs but also describing our actions. This was exemplified in the case of the series of photographs taken by one participant whose activities throughout 1 day encompassed work-related meetings, socializing, dog walking, and engaging in sport. She reflected that those very activities were symbolic of her internal representation of self at this time in her life, as well as building a social picture of who she felt she currently was for others to see. Taken together, the ESM with critical analysis, personal and social reflection resulted in raising awareness of everyday activities and what is important in imbuing our daily lives with a range of meanings that situated us in space and time.

There is also an element of choice in our depiction of space and time that is made evident through the images. Do we elect to be outside or watching television? The following is a quotation from an original personal reflection:

> There's little evidence of cross-over between work and home in terms of socialising, but a strong sense of enjoyment of each other's company in our working life. We're not all about work. For me, there's a strong outdoors element which contrasts with the indoor working environments I frequent.

The method also allowed reflection upon the contrast between the parts of our lives that people feel are typical or frequent and those that are seen as more infrequent or spontaneous. As an example, the same participant was surprised to find few photographs of driving to work when she felt that she spent "at least half my life doing this." On the other hand, drinking coffee in cafes was featured frequently, which led this participant to think differently about her balance between work and social life. Another participant was pregnant during the data-collection week and experienced morning sickness—her photos remind her of the physical state she was in at the time and the subsequent outcome of the week (a new family member).

The week stood out to participants as one that was particularly remembered due to the photographic reminders, as well as the intense scrutiny of the week developed through the reflections and commentary that accompanied the photographs. Indeed, the photographs acted as such a strong reminder that some participants feel they remember this week much more vividly than any other at that time. The isolation of that week is also worthy of consideration within the longer-term temporal context. Many changes have occurred for several participants since the data was collected, the periods of reflection and the final outcome of the project. Births, deaths, gaining or changing jobs, and moving continents all illustrate the complex tapestry of everyday life-cycle experiences. For these participants, the visual seemed to act as a more pertinent documentation of a week, evoking a recreation of "who I was and what I was doing" at that time in contrast to "who I am now and what I am doing." Emotional consequences have been experienced, which again link to issues of identity. In some senses, the posters can be read as a different "me," perhaps one that was happier or more stressed, more chilled out or more lonely. Certainly, emotions experienced during the reflections differed considerably to those experienced at the time of data collection when the participant was busily engaged in the here and now. In this way, the ESM method together with a depth of reflection holds the potential to impose new or different emotions on the same events and to recreate the historical "me" with relevance to the current "me."

Banks (2001, p. 12) describes "*good*" visual research as research that sees both the internal and external narratives, naming this the *multivocality* of an image, that is, being able to communicate the multiple narratives arising from the image (Banks 2001, p. 15). In revisiting the photographs, participants are able to reflect upon their images and recognize the external context of a life lived while recalling internal narratives of selfhood.

In reflecting on the project at a later date, participants noted significant change from when the photographs were taken, at a specific time, to "now," when the reflections were made. These included the change in weather, social environment, and, for example, growth in the garden. Memory is stronger on more personal events than on work-orientated tasks. The following two quotations demonstrate later reflections and how work has become forgotten:

> It is winter now, cold, dark windy outside. The pictures show a different time…nice and bright, sometimes sunny weather.
>
> I can't remember the work that I was engaged in at the time, so all the work related pictures simply tell me I was working on the computer, sitting in meetings, etc, but little beyond that.

In addition to the self recognition aspect—the noting and denoting of life over a week—the method can generate data that can be available for public perusal or attest to a particular way of life. The process is akin to bearing witness.

Bearing Witness to Our Own Lives

This section notes how photographs illustrate our lives, making them available for reflection. The photographs were viewed in a way that showed our lives as we chose to photograph them at a specific time, which may be different from how we consider our lives upon reflection. We are faced with the "objective facts" of space and place. There is an anchoring to place but the psychological significance of being and doing in place are not made available in the photographs. Hagerstrand's notion () says that only being physically able to be in one place at one time has implications for us, telling us about the choices we make and also what we have chosen not to do, places we have chosen not to be in. This is rather an important point to consider when using visual methodologies. The immediacy of what is represented can easily be mistaken for what is significant for people in place, in time, and thereby the "not thereness" of our existence in other places is hidden from analysis or reflection. Our positive choices come to define us in ways that can only ever partially touch upon the holism of our experiential worlds. While this issue is rarely the focus of research, it became a critical point of discussion among the group. The hidden or "not thereness" aspects of lives were theorized and speculated upon (as if representativeness of experience or self were intrinsic to the work). Certainly, the making of choices on photographic perspectives did influence participants as they engaged with the technology in the study.

In bearing witness, participants made decisions as to what would be shown in the photographs. Some participants tried to vary the focal points for a range of reasons such as the aesthetics of their images or to show variation in their activity. Further, it could be said that some photographs thus misrepresented the action at the time or at least showed a particular perspective. Due to ethical concerns involved in visual research, certain encounters (e.g., student supervision) did not involve students (or those who refused permission for the photographs to be taken) and so a photograph of an empty chair is taken. While this signals that event to the participant concerned, it may have a range of meanings to others, for example, the empty chair in gestalt therapy or a symbol of loneliness. This is why the verbal and textual accompaniment of thick description is crucial to the interpretation of the photographs. That is not to say that the person's description of their activity should be taken as factual "truth." Rather, the social construction of explanations (which becomes available through analysis and reflection) of both photographic and verbal evidence together lies at the heart of understanding as articulated in this particular project. This is what is made available to an audience in this project and it is this that they can themselves interpret.

Through bearing witness in retrospect, that is, viewing the photographs at a later date, participants see themselves from a different perspective. For example, their state of well-being from the collection of images is holistically explored. One participant said:

> So what do I see (re. self)…someone who is pretty active both at work and at home. A comfortable if not sparkling life.

Further, the audience seems to become part of the process in the later reflections where participants wanted to justify some of their photographs, especially photographs that were missing or seen to be out of character:

> This is totally out of character for me and it was in fact a game from my childhood. Equally it was a game which requires great amounts of patience and is more of a "thinking" game.

And:

> This was an abnormal week for me…first time in about 30 years I was alone in the house…looks as if I am house proud.

What is interesting here is the way in which presentation of the home self is almost manipulated to fit an image of the working self. Aspects of the person that are acceptable at home (the playfulness, the tidy person) seem not to fit so well to the image of a busy academic whose concern is less with the pragmatics of everyday life. It is almost as if the choice of photograph taken happens within the context of the place inhabited. What this might say about identity in a different context may or may not feel acceptable. In this way, the notion of well-being at home set against the notion of well-being at work come to be very different issues. The manipulation of presentation of self and hence of "identity-made-visible" was very much part of the data-collection experience:

> I chose to take a picture of the date in my diary also as I thought it would look quite good but also consistent and orderly, which I like to be. (See Figure 24.1)

This also shows that the participant wanted the audience to witness this part of their identity. Interestingly, this manipulation was required at the point at which the photograph was taken. Usually within verbal research, such manipulation of past events can happen at the time of the interview, that is, I can say I was working at home last Friday during an interview, while in fact I was enjoying a shopping trip. However, use of the photographic method reduces the freedom with which manipulations of self-identity are possible, and forward thinking about how the photographic image can be interpreted is required.

In exhibiting the posters and sharing the photographs in the group analysis sessions, bearing witness to who we were also became a legitimate activity of others. The participants and those viewing the exhibition were provided with their own opportunity to reflect on their own photographs and those of the other participants.

The concept of exploring and sharing data underlined the profoundly social nature of human existence. Photos and verbal reflections attested to the interdependencies present in everyday life. This relatedness was termed understanding reliance.

Understanding Reliance

Being forced to bear witness to our own lives brought into focus our inevitable personal and social reliances. As Aronson (2003) pointed out, we are not islands. However, we are also not just social animals. We are immersed in a physical world that bears witness to as well as structures our lives (Bell, Greene, Fisher, & Baum, 2005). Our reliance on technology is integral to our working lives, at once enabling and confirming the importance of our work and hence our useful contributions to society. The use of technology within the academic sphere has transformed the way in which people work. In the first instance, working from home has become very much part of the working week and this is shown in many of the photographs and across most all of the participants. The embedding of work at home has at one and the same time offered not only freedom in space and time to do work where and when that person is most disposed but also constrictions in social and family life when that work predominates in the home environment. In this study, photographs of work at home (mostly characterized by computer screens) were often explained in terms of tight deadlines and heavy workloads. There were few descriptions of well-being linked to work at home, although verbal reflections supported the notion of well-being as a product of work at home. Our reliance on technology to facilitate our work at home was very much a storied part of our efforts to maintain our home–work life balance or integration.

Other forms of reliance included computer-mediated communication, relationships (romantic and childcare) and particular lifestyles such as playing tennis, pets, and other social patterns. Notions of interdependence are displayed in many of the visual accounts where colleagues, family members, and friends create a sense of connectedness. For example, in one participant's visual diary there are many different pictures of children across the bank-holiday weekend (nine children in all) and associated parents. The account enumerates not only the sheer number of house guests and childcare undertaken over the weekend but also the fondness of the relationships and enmeshed social lives. The quotidian tasks of childcare (all children being below 7 years of age) are dispersed with images of parties (for the children involving bouncy castles) and glimpses of adults socializing—drinks and dinners in evenings and cups of tea the morning after. The stand-out nature of this week in capturing the sheer connectedness of lives tells us much about the power of this methodology to illustrate the everyday interdependency of lives.

The various participants' photographs and stories enabled their different roles to become visible, such as a mother, researcher, worker, partner, friend, etc. This is also demonstrated by the way the photographs portray us as individuals, family members, and a team of colleagues. Photographs show colleagues working together (e.g., in meetings) but also as partners in shared social experiences and as individuals, at work and at home. Through examining the accompanying voice recordings, well-being associated with the home–work balance.

Legacy: Shared Learning

Part of the original intention of the project was to develop further the team relationships within the research institute. All were members of this setting, although occupying rather different roles (with respect to tenure and status). While many members had worked collaboratively on external research projects, the experience of all working together gave personal and methodological insight. For funded research, bidding, co-supervision working relationships often assume a shared and implicit understanding. However, working with such an intimate technology and showing photos for analysis and interpretation garnered a rather different set of assumptions to be unearthed. The shared learning that has come about from the project is considered to be a legacy. There are several areas here that are thought worthy of mention and these are listed below:

1. Taking more photographs of everyday personal life as opposed to "special occasions"—participant's memory of this week and their engagement within it is enhanced by the visual record and quotidian nature of the data.
2. The documentation of the crossover from personal to work life being key to understanding work and personal life integration (or lack thereof)—for some this prompted personal reflection and career shifts, for others it documents the shifting territories of work and family and self.
3. The change in the way visual methods are used in current research work—in using these methods with other participants who may be less aware of the implications, for example, young people, community residents, etc.—the utilization of the visual alongside other forms and associated ethical awareness has been reflected and acted upon.
4. Looking for the missing bits of life (those absent from the visual data) and seeking them elsewhere—for some, the representation of self provoked "therapeutic" mindfulness about over-reliance on technology and over-investment with work, which required action.
5. Utilizing the methods inspired new projects with visual methodologies or added visual elements to current projects—using self as participant and data has yielded a rich curiosity around visual literacy and what it offers.
6. The curiosity of others in what participants were doing allowed a window into their lives for friends and family that may not normally be aware of their usual work activity—the visual exhibition has been shown at research conferences and commented upon positively.
7. Inspiring others to take more photos of own everyday life—the visual diary and exhibition posters presented a snapshot of real life rarely documented in "normal people" (non-celebrity).
8. Generated critique conceptually, ethically, practically—it is possible that in utilizing our own data there was added investment in the critique.

The project generated joint working sessions, analytical training developments, paper writing, decision making, and sharing of world views. Much of this process was at times difficult and demanding, as in demonstrating arguments or analysis; we needed to point to evidence from each others' data, which of necessity enmeshes personal, social, and working lives. The reality and luxury of this project is both a personal legacy (a physical record and individual subjectivity on this), and a group legacy (shared activities, developing understandings, and shifting relationships and roles). The transitions and shifts of life are articulated in the next section.

A Disappearing Life

A poignant observation that has taken place is that the photographs document a disappearing life. Through undertaking the ESM project, participants took photographs of everyday life that would not normally be captured. Personal and work lives are reflected here but often of very ordinary activities that normally become forgotten over time. Within a usual week, it would be unlikely for participants to take a photograph of, for example, making a cup of tea or writing reports, yet here, they remain as means of documenting our time. Some participants felt that aspects of their roles during which they spend a lot of time, such as research activity, report writing, or marking, are rarely recorded. Visual methods and in particular the ESM offers social researchers a way of mapping experience over a time period and portraying phenomena not easily or readily shown (either through lack of interest or visibility). Ethnographic methods can use visual but are more likely to be textual data (word based). Documenting life for marginalized people (e.g., older adults, homeless) offers a window into everyday narratives that are rarely voiced in other methods.

Methods are usually evaluated in relation to the adequacy of other data, settings, or participants. Unusually here, we had individual and joint reflections about our own positionality in relation to the data and experience of using the method. We document some of the challenges during the processes of collection and interpretation.

The Perceived Weaknesses of Using the ESM

Intrusiveness

One of the main concerns regarding this method of research has been the intrusive nature of the ESM. There were three main areas where this affected some of the participants. Firstly, the random beeps broke the flow of activity and interrupted participants' activities, at times with irritating results. Secondly, as the ESM ran over a bank-holiday weekend and thus into the private lives of participants, it was felt that there was an intrusion into personal time and leisure space. Thirdly, the final area of intrusion was that of the photographs revealing a private life, one that some participants did not feel comfortable revealing within the group. For example, certain participants may have felt the impress of power in terms of demonstrating work commitment in nonwork time. Additionally, the normative nature of family life was featured in some visual accounts and this may have made other ways of living less viable for shared consumption. Participants expressed unease at whether all activities were represented in the accounts and felt some aspects of life (e.g., working outside working hours, family engagement) were more acceptable than others (e.g., socializing, using the toilet).

The "Not Me-ness"

Some participants commented that the photographs did not portray their life and that the timing of the beeps missed parts of their lives that they felt were important in showing a rounded person. On the one hand, this was a product of the way in which the study had been set up as in the case of one participant who commented that she gets up early and so the beeps missed several hours of her usual day. For her, the photographs offered only a superficial reading of her life, and one that missed important aspects of the way she organized herself in space and time. To some extent, the life of the person she viewed in the photographs was seen at a distance from her own experience of that same life. In cases where the participants felt the photographs were not representative of their usual lives, a clear rationale was often provided in explanation. There is a desire to provide more information to explain that there is more to their identity than is evident in the photographs. The narrative filled in the missing elements and built a truer picture of self in analysis and reflection. For some, the research reflects a stage of life that was temporary and now can be viewed with some distance. For example, one participant was pregnant and photos of mornings and clothes reminded her of a particular embodiment from which she has moved on.

On the other hand, the partiality of the photographic rendering of a life was located in the hands of the participants who could choose or not choose to take a photograph as each alarm sounded. This resulted in some people's weeks containing many photographic blanks (see Figure 24.2) while others were rather fuller (see Figure 24.1). In these cases, the evidence of the absent "me" reflected the empowerment of participants as they negotiate the photographic method.

In considering objectivity versus subjectivity, the photographs tell a very compelling story, objectively present. We know, through our subjectivity, that we are not wholly there and so we tell the story of the missing me, for the benefits of self, but also for the audience. The potential fixed nature of the photographs provided some dissonance as participants felt a need to distance themselves from the permanence of the visual record.

Nontypicality

As indicated above, the project did not take place over the course of a usual working week and included a long weekend as well as four ordinary work days. It was felt that this was not a true representation of a usual week for many of the participants. Further, the week coincided with a school holiday and so some participants were also spending more time at home than usual or juggling their busy work schedule and childcare. Timing of the week may well need careful consideration in relation to the research question considered.

Other Weaknesses

The following weaknesses are drawn from group analysis and discussions. They form a mixture of personal reflections, as well as themes that have emerged from group discussions. These weaknesses range from the social engineering of activities, feelings about the

Figure 24.2 A week in the life, Participant 7.

experience as a whole, and some group negativity, as well as issues around privacy and negative reflections on life.

An important methodological concern in the current research using the ESM is that of social desirability responses, self-presentation, and demand characteristics. Socially desirable responding may occur in investigations due to respondents attempting to present themselves in the best light and give answers that they think are required. For example, one participant elected not to play a game on her computer for the entire week so that the camera would not "catch" her doing this when she felt she should have been working or doing a more meaningful activity. This is a concern in social science research in general (Haworth, 1996), where performance in a research task is often a source of pressure. However, it may be even more of an issue in research involving images of personal daily life. For example, Rose (2007) found that in family pictures displayed there were enduring pictures of occasions presenting happy family portrayals rather than depicting more ordinary events such as daily chores or the "truth" such as children falling out at a party.

Within the current project, there is some choice in what photograph is taken at an ESM signal. But here, taking a picture of watching a soap series on TV at two consecutive bleeper signals was not thought to give the best impression. While the timing of the ESM signals is not known to the participant, it is possible to plan behavior in advance, to some extent, depending on the circumstances of the person and technological competence. However, compared to other methods of social research, the potential for changing behavior is much less because the ESM signal comes somewhat as a surprise. Behavior and feelings are also recorded at the time of the signal or at the latest within 15 min of the signal, so the potential for adjusting the recall of behavior and feelings is much less. These issues of what counts as data and how individuals see themselves are the demand characteristics of research. Normally, as researchers we are mindful of these in relation to participants' expectations. In this research project, participants are simultaneously both aware of demand characteristics and potentially playing them out.

There were a considerable range of feelings about the experience as a whole. Some participants missed the beeps following the completion of the week's activity and enjoyed being able to capture parts of their lives in this way. Others felt nervous during the week about missing the beep and not being able to fulfill data requirements.

The relationships between participants that existed prior to the study and beyond were felt to be under scrutiny by some participants. The power imbalances that are a feature of everyday life and work environments were experienced by some participants who withdrew before the end of the project. This impact on group dynamics is interesting as implicit underpinning assumptions, on issues such as participation and informed consent, were more visible and, hence, more explicitly reflected upon. The personal nature of the research and the visual permanency of the record foregrounded group collaboration. While all did not share these concerns, working within a participatory framework we have documented them and have written about them elsewhere (Mountian et al., 2009).

The visual and, therefore, immediate nature of the self-presented was commented upon by participants. For one participant, the rendering of the lack of leisure in a week together with the relentless portrayal of computers made her consider her work role and enjoyment in it. Subsequently, she has gained a different position. For another participant, the absence of other people in the pictures afforded them an unrecognizable portrait of their life, while evaluative judgments on one's own life (the house improvements, messiness of houses, or social weekends) were addressed to the group collective. Certain participants felt that privacy was compromised and that accurate reflections were not obtained (toilet encounters, bathing, sexual activity, and other socially unacceptable behavior that they may have been engaged in). It is interesting to comment on the prior qualitative experiences of group members where text-based data was commonly used. The inclusion of the visual as the shared nature of the project meant that representations were possibly seen as shortcut windows into individuals' lives. Hence, the typicality or representation issue that was utilized as a defense.

Participants engaged in the project predominantly worked within a qualitative social science paradigm so issues of meaning, interpretation, and reflexivity became issues of contestation. However, aside from the richness of the visual, the project also allowed numerical analysis—interpreting ratings given by individuals at the time of the image capture. In the next section, we turn to this.

Quantitative Analysis

Research involving the ESM is typically analyzed numerically to investigate the relationship between activity undertaken and subjective experience. A particular concern has been the investigation of "flow" or optimal experience, which has been characterized by the perception of high environmental challenges matched by personal skills. Flow can to be accompanied by high levels of concentration, involvement, enjoyment, control, and intrinsic motivation. Flow is considered to be important for quality of life and personal growth (Csikszentmihalyi, 1990; Delle Fave, 2006). While we have reflected upon the method above, it seems pertinent to present a flavor of the numerical data. First of all, it is necessary to consider the measurement scales used in the study.

The measurement scales for subjective well-being and challenge use three points: 1= low, 2 = moderate, 3 = high. This very simple scale has the advantage of being visually simple if on a card and easy to visualize if given as an instruction on a mobile phone. It can be used with category analysis. It is also easy to code into dimensions of a color—such as pale red = low enjoyment, bright red = moderate enjoyment, deep red = high enjoyment—which is useful for visually illustrating subjective well-being. However, the scale obviously has only limited discrimination. It may result in more 2s being recorded than the end points of 1 and 3. In Clarke and Haworth (1994) 7-point scales were used to measure subjective well-being and challenge, and used with correlation analysis. It is easier to decide to record 6 on a 7-point scale than an end point if some element of doubt about intensity of feeling is felt. In analysis of challenge, however, in line with other studies, points 6 and 7 are combined to give a score of high, 3, 4, and 5 are combined as moderate and 1and 2 are combined as low. Using a 7-point scale in this way is likely to produce a greater incidence of "flow" than using a 3-point scale. Color coding could still be used with a 7-point scale by collapsing into a 3-point scale.

In the current project, just over 9% of signals were recorded as flow, where high challenge (score 3 on a 3-point scale) is met with equal skill. Half of these were enjoyable flow, that is, flow in which enjoyment is recorded as 3 (high). In just over half the instances of enjoyable flow, interest and happiness were also recorded as 3 (high). Enjoyable flow experiences are considered important for psychological growth and well-being (Csikszentmihalyi, 1988; Clarke & Haworth, 1994). The mode for flow experiences in the group was three per week, and the mode for enjoyable flow experiences was two per week. Two thirds of flow experiences occurred at work and one third at leisure (nonwork, though this was not a five-day working week). It may be that the proportion of signals experienced as flow would be higher if the study had used 7-point measurement scales, particularly if points 6 and 7 are combined for the measurement of high challenge, as in Clarke and Haworth (1994).

The enjoyable flow experiences at work include Web training course, marking, reading, training, and research meetings. Enjoyable flow experiences at leisure included computer games, social meetings, gym activities, and playing with a pet (dog). It must be emphasized that as in other studies (e.g., Clarke & Haworth, 1994), high enjoyment came from both moderate- and low-challenge activities, and could be associated with high interest and happiness. In many cases, this cluster of positive subjective experiences came from social activities in leisure:

- Participant 10, day 2, signal 7. Drinks for a group of friends (Figure 24.3).
- Example of an enjoyable flow experience associated with high interest and high happiness at work is participant 5, day 6, signal 2. Training course, group discussion (Figure 24.4).
- Example of an enjoyable flow experience associated with high interest and high happiness at leisure is participant 9, day 5, signal 8. Playing with a dog (Figure 24.5).

This analysis of group data could be developed from and drawn on research and concepts presented in Haworth and Veal (2004) and Haworth and Hart (2007). This could include an analysis of themes across the group, such as the incidence of "flow" (as shown above), the pursuits involved, and the relationship between work, leisure, and well-being.

Figure 24.3 Day 7, Signal 7, Participant 10.

The Visual ESM and Research Into Creativity and Well-Being

A photo-ethnographic project "The Way We are Now" originated from both practice-led research into creativity (www.creativity-embodiedmind.com, Haworth, 2009a) and research into well-being (www.wellbeing-esrc.com, Haworth & Hart, 2007). A presentation was made on "The Way We are Now" at the IMPACT 5 international printmaking

![Figure 24.4 image]

Figure 24.4 Day 6, Signal 2, Participant 5.

Figure 24.5 Day 4, Signal 8, Participant 9.

conference concerned with the study of slices of time and the production of visual political-poetic statements (www.creativity-embodiedmind.com).

In this study, a photograph was taken each day of a heading to an article in three newspapers: The Guardian, the Sun, and the Lancashire Telegraph. Each day a photograph was also taken of a topical image in the newspapers. The two images from the newspapers for each day (one of the headings to the news paper articles, the other of a topical image) constitute a media view of the world. They provided a comparative view to the images of daily life taken at the ESM signals for the 7 days. The print for autumn can be seen in detail in the gallery at www.creativity-embodiedmind.com. The large format canvas print was shown, along with other digital prints resulting from the practice-led research into creativity, in an exhibition at Blackburn Museum and Art Gallery in the spring of 2008. Rose (2007) indicates that the results from research can be presented in different ways, including visual documentation to be read in its own terms. This is in line with the more general turn in the social sciences toward placing a greater weight on the importance of the senses in knowing (Howes, 2005). The implication of showing the work needs some independent audience research.

The process of undertaking the project can stimulate visual awareness. The readily ignored mundane can be brought into focus. The creative process in fine art can be stimulated with new trains of imagination arising. For example, a three-dimensional cylindrical print is being constructed, which will constitute a new form of portrait. The ideas for the cylinder print occurred during the process of making the first large format print, and related to the structure of that print. On the upper part of the cylinder will be the band of modified images taken from the newspapers. The seven vertical strips of images, one for each day, will have further graphic work associated with them related to the questions in the ESM study. Each day will form a tube in the overall cylinder. The outside of the cylinder will also have graphic work on it based on the life history of the person doing the ESM (based on a graphic technique used in sociological research). The sound recordings made in association with each image could be selectively activated electronically. The idea for the cylinder is also based on modern theories of the brain and consciousness relating to quantum computing occurring in tubules in nerve dendrites (Woolf & Hammeroff, 2001; www.consciousness.arizona.edu).

Prints have also been made where each image taken at an ESM signal has color codings alongside it of the answers to the questions asked at the ESM signal. For example, the question on enjoyment is coded, low enjoyment: pale red, moderate enjoyment: bright red, high enjoyment: deep red. The question on interest in activity is coded, low interest: pale blue, moderate interest: bright blue, high interest: deep blue. Challenge is coded using orange; Skills is coded using green; Visual Interest is coded using purple; and Happiness is coded using yellow. The key to the color codings is presented with the print. An example of part of day 1 for the winter ESM, and the key to the color codings, can be seen in the paper "The Way We are Now" on the Web sites www.creativity-embodiedmind.com and www.wellbeing-esrc.com. A large format print on "A day in the life of ———" was shown in an exhibition of digital art at an international conference on Towards a Science of Consciousness in Hong Kong in June 2009. The print was shown with the color codings of well-being and a brief outline of the method with reference to the paper "The Way We are Now," which would enable the viewer to undertake the project. The print can be seen in the gallery at www.creativity-embodiedmind.com. A paper on the research and its relevance to research into consciousness was also presented at the conference, which had the theme of "Investigating Inner Experience: Brain, Mind and Technology." An important topic of research discussed at the conference was the importance of social mirrors for the formation and development of consciousness (www.socialmirrors.org). Undertaking the project on "The Way We are Now" can constitute a mirror for the self, and others if it is shared. A project such as "A day in the life of ———" if undertaken by many people and particularly from different regions of the world, could be a valuable global mirror, which could possibly help with well-being and sustainable lifestyles. Prints could be shown on a dedicated Web site and other electronic networks and in a large exhibition space such as the Turbine Hall at the Tate Modern in the UK, and elsewhere. A DVD could be included on a probe into deep space.

Conclusions

The role of technology in accessing social experience presents social scientists with problems and challenges. In an increasingly multimodal world, where individuals (at least in Global North contexts) routinely access various forms of technology on a daily basis, how best to maximize technology to access this experience? While the visual approach can assist hugely in unpacking real life, there are also challenges. The work outlined in this chapter attests to the importance of joint meaning making and interpretation of image-based data. The ESM can provide a diarized mapping of quotidian lives, promising a richer glimpse of everyday "normative" living. In engaging with technology, education, participation, and collaboration are the key to the process. We feel that the spirit of this approach is much in line with calls for decolonizing methodologies (Tuhiwai Smith, 1999), which aim to decouple knowledge and knowledge generation from researchers in order to collaborate with the researched. Everyday technology such as mobile telephones and cameras offers possibilities in this arena.

As noted earlier, the ESM method with photos does stimulate reflection and change in perceptions. The addition of the visual presents some rather surprising challenges in consent, interpretation, and ethics. The method can break the mould of looking/perceiving and interpretation of data. It can open up new opportunities and possibilities for new ways of seeing things, and introduce a new train of imagination (Haworth, 2009a). If used collaboratively, it can potentially empower people by giving them a feedback loop, a different representation, or a public affirmation of identity. It has therapeutic uses, development purposes, and much potential as a research practice. In this chapter, we have aimed to give a flavor of the research process, the visual data, methodological reflections, and quantitative data. Underpinning this approach is an assumptive framework which contextualizes the visual in a larger narrative.

In further research, the project could be undertaken by different individuals and groups in society. The method could also be used to investigate a day in the life of individuals in different countries across the world. A Web site such as www.wellbeing-esrc.com could, if funded perhaps by a mobile-phone company, be used as a clearing house to which individuals could post the data. Worldwide visual representations could also be presented in an exhibition. They may have an impact on visions of sustainability. In privileging the visual, the methods can be used with diverse groups to explore various interpretations of cultural/ethnic lives.

The method could also be used to investigate a day in the life of individuals in different countries across the world. Worldwide visual representations may have an impact on visions of sustainability.

References

Aronson E. (2003). *The social animal.* New York: Worth Publishers.

Banks M. (2001). *Visual methods in social research.* London: Sage Publications Ltd.

Bell P. A., Greene, T. C., Fisher, J. D., & Baum, A. S. (2005). *Environmental psychology.* London: Routledge.

Brandstatter H. (1991). Emotions in everyday life situations. Time sampling of subjective experience. In Strack, F., Argyle, M., & Schwartz, N. (Eds.), *Subjective well-being: An interdisciplinary perspective.* Oxford: OUP.

Clarke S. E., & Haworth J. T. (1994). "Flow" experiences in the daily life of sixth form college students. *British Journal of Psychology, 85,* 511–523.

Csikszentmihalyi M., Larson R., & Prescot S. (1977). The ecology of adolescent activity and experience. *The Journal of Youth and Adolescence, 6,* 281–294.

Csikszentmihalyi M. (1988). Society, culture and person: A systems view of creativity. In Sternberg, R. J. (Ed.), *The nature of creativity: Contemporary psychological perspectives.* Cambridge, MA: Cambridge University Press.

Csikszentmihalyi M., & Csikszentmihalyi I. S. (Eds.). (1988). *Optimal experience: Psychological studies of flow in consciousness.* Cambridge, MA: OUP.

Csikszentmihalyi M. (1990) Flow: the psychology of Optimal experience. Ny: Harper and Row.

Delle Fave A. (2006). The impact of subjective experience on the quality of life: A central issue for health professionals. In Csikszentmihalyi, M., & Csikszentmihalyi, I. S. (Eds.), *A life worth living: Contributions to positive psychology.* Oxford: OUP.

Delle Fave A. (2007). Theoretical foundations of ESM. In Hektner, J., Schimdt, J. A., & Csikszentmihalyi, M. (Eds.), *Experience sampling method: Measuring the quality of everyday life.* London: Sage Publications Ltd.

Hagerstrand T. (1975). "Space, time and human conditions", in A Karlquist, Lundquist, F Snickars (Eds.), Dynamic Allocation of Urban Space, Farnborough, Hants.

Haworth J. T. (1996). *Psychological research: Innovative methods and strategies.* London: Routledge.

Haworth J. T. (1997). *Work, leisure and well-being.* London: Routledge.

Haworth J. T., & Hart G. (Eds.). (2007). *Well-being: Individual, community and social perspectives.* Basingstoke, UK: Palgrave Macmillan.

Haworth J. T. (2009a). Explorations in creativity, technology and embodied mind. In Freire, T. (Ed.). *Understanding positive life: Research and practice on positive psychology.* Lisboa: Climepsie Editores.

Haworth J. T. (2009b). *The way we are now* Leisure Studies.

Haworth J. T and Veal, A. J. (2004). Work and Leisure. London: Routledge.

Hektner J., Schimidt J. A., & Csikszentmihalyi M. (2008). *Experience sampling method: measuring the quality of everyday life.* London: Sage Publications Ltd.

Howes D. (Ed.). (2005). *Empire of the senses.* Oxford: Berg.

Mountian I., Lawthom R., & Kellock, A., et al. (2009). On utilising a visual methodology: share reflections and tensions. In Reavey, P. (Ed.), *Visual psychologies: Using and interpreting images in qualitative research.* Chapter accepted.

Pink S. (2004). *Doing visual ethnography: Images, media and representation in research.* London: Sage Publications Ltd.

Rose G. (2007). *Visual methodologies: An introduction to the interpretation of visual materials* (2nd ed.). London: Sage Publications Ltd.

Tuhiwai Smith L. (1999). *Decolonizing methodologies: Research and indigenous peoples* New York: Zen Books Ltd.

Woolf N., & Hameroff S. R. (2001). A quantum approach to visual consciousness. *Trends in Cognitive Sciences, 5*(11), 427–478.

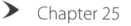

Chapter 25

Geospatial Analysis Technology and Social Science Research

Steven J. Steinberg and Sheila Lakshmi Steinberg

Introduction

While the consideration of space and place are not new to the social sciences, our ability to analyze and understand these relationships has been greatly enhanced by a variety of new and emerging technologies. Since the turn of the millennium, several technologies developing separately and in parallel have come together to greatly enhance our ability to collect, obtain, and assess spatial information. Geospatial technologies such as Geographic Information Systems (GIS) have existed for more than 40 years, but did not become readily available to the nonspecialist until the mid 1990s. By the early part of the millennium, the Global Positioning System (GPS) was publicly accessible and locations were no longer being intentionally scrambled by the United States Department of Defense. At around the same time, the Internet was just becoming a popular mainstream communication tool that would in just a few years provide unprecedented access to a wide array of geospatial data, including global images popularized by companies like Google and more recently GPS-enabled cell phones, cars, and a variety of Internet-based mapping tools and other location-based technologies aimed at the consumer market.

With the explosion of consumer mapping and location-based services, GIS, GPS, and global image sets obtained from satellites and aircraft-based remote-sensing systems became commonplace. New applications of these tools and data seem to appear on almost a daily basis, and with them emerge new opportunities to enhance the social science research highlighted in this chapter.

Although mapping environments and the human interactions within them is not a new concept to social science researchers, a number of emerging technologies provide tremendous access for the application of a computer-based sociospatial approach to research and analysis (Steinberg & Steinberg, 2009). Historically, these maps were drawn and analyzed by hand, greatly limiting their utility. More recently, with the emergence of inexpensive computers and a wide array of free or inexpensive geospatial technology and data, encountering some form of geospatial information is nearly unavoidable. Mapping technology is pervasive on the Internet and in cell phones and cars. Questions such as "Where am I?" or "How do I get to my destination?" are no longer difficult to answer for even the moderately capable user of these tools. Location-based services aimed at the consumer have found a niche in social networking, allowing individuals to make their specific location visible to friends and marketing and advertising applications that can point you to the nearest latte, or even suggest a nearby restaurant that meets your dining preferences. For service providers, these same technologies are used to efficiently route emergency response vehicles or ensure package deliveries are optimized to use a minimum of fuel.

Why Use a Sociospatial Perspective?

With the emergence of geospatial technology across a continually growing variety of applications, basic access to geospatial information and tools is not difficult. For the social science researcher, the utility and value of these technologies may remain elusive. Perhaps more important than being impressed by fancy technological feats and bird's-eye images of your neighborhood are the fundamental questions of how space matters to your research question. What value does location bring to my work? How will location help me to understand interactions and effects? How does it help to understand people within a larger environmental context? And perhaps most importantly, how do I use all of this information without getting overwhelmed by the data and technology?

In this chapter we focus on three specific geospatial technologies, Geographic Information Systems (GIS), Global Positioning Systems (GPS), and Remote Sensing. As a group, these are often referred to as geospatial technologies. Each of these technologies in some manner accounts for location of data in space and time, and all of them are relatively new. Because these technologies emerged from disciplines far removed from the social sciences (engineering, physics, and computer science), we will first briefly discuss each one before moving to a discussion of their application to sociospatial research.

Remote Sensing

Remote sensing is the oldest of the three core technologies discussed here, having begun in earnest in the 1920s and 1930s. However, compared to social science methods that have been developed over centuries, remote sensing is barely a toddler. Generally, remote sensing refers to the collection and recording of data from a distant location, without direct physical contact. In practical terms, data sources include aerial photographs and satellite images. Numerous other remote-sensing data sources are available and are detailed extensively in the literature. One important primary value of remotely sensed data for the social scientist is that it provides a synoptic view of a region at a particular time. This is eminently valuable to social scientists seeking to obtain an unbiased view of past conditions or to explore how an area has changed or developed over time. Remotely sensed images provide a time machine that allows the researcher to understand historic physical conditions of a city, rural or natural environment in ways that are not necessarily obtainable through other sources.

In contrast to maps and written or interview-based data sources, remotely sensed data provides an uninterpreted perspective, unbiased by the recollections, motives, or capabilities of understanding of a particular individual. This is not to imply that remotely sensed data is a panacea—images have limits. For example, important information may be obscured by clouds, trees, or shadows. The imaging technology used may lack the required detail or may have been collected at a time that does not meet the objectives of your research. Perhaps most important to understand about remotely sensed data is that because it is a raw, unbiased view of the world, it requires interpretation by the researcher to be useful. If you are exploring the development of neighborhoods in and around a city over the last century, but cannot determine the difference between a high rise apartment building and an office building in an aerial photograph, there may be little value to the remotely sensed data. Ultimately, use of imagery is only as good as the ability of the researcher to understand and interpret it. In many cases, ancillary data provides the needed support, for example, demographic data from a national census.

One important final note about data acquired via remote-sensing techniques is that these technologies can allow the researcher to see information beyond the range of normal human vision. Sensors capable of imaging infrared and thermal information provide the ability to assess conditions such as the health of crops and other vegetation, identify urban heat islands or cooking fires, or assess water quality. Other sensors are capable of seeing through clouds, fog, forest canopy, or darkness. Such technologies allowed for some of the first anthropological studies of difficult-to-reach locations and populations in the Amazon in the 1960s. These same technologies are used today for a variety of studies on wide-reaching topics such as food security, human rights and development around the world, and the effects of natural disasters such as hurricanes, tsunamis, and forest fires. With the emergence of more frequent and more accessible image data around the world, social scientists have an increasing ability to explore a variety of questions with a multi-disciplinary sociospatial perspective.

Global Positioning Systems

The GPS first developed and maintained by the United States Department of Defense was largely developed during the 1960s and 1970s. Public access to this satellite-based navigation was not available until 1995. For the first several years, the GPS signal was scrambled by the Department of Defense as a security measure, making it difficult to use in nonspecialist applications. Since the spring of 2000, scrambling of the GPS signal has been discontinued, making the system available to a wider range of users. The availability of inexpensive GPS receivers quickly followed, as did the development of onboard navigation in vehicles. By 2004, cell phones incorporating GPS were developed and are now relatively commonplace.

As an emerging geospatial technology, GPS is the youngest and least developed. One issue for social science researchers is that of confidentiality. In some situations, tagging data obtained in the field to a specific location is not appropriate, or additional precautions may be required to ensure protection of human subjects. Unlike remote sensing, which is a secondary data source, GPS data is most often collected by the researcher as primary data while in the field. Therefore, GPS data requires the researcher to consider the implications of such data in context of their research question and analysis.

At its root, GPS is a location technology that tells the researcher exactly where on the surface of the earth they are located. In urban or densely populated settings, the unit of analysis may be the census block or neighborhood, easily identified with a street address or similar label. However, for research conducted in rural settings or where other means of georeferencing data is lacking, GPS can be especially useful. This is especially significant when one orients more off of topography and general settlement patterns within the context of the larger, less-populated environment, such as occurs in rural areas.

GPS provides other benefits to studies that look at the movement of subjects over time. Because people are mobile, obtaining data at regular intervals can be important to understanding social interactions, access to resources or services, or patterns of movement. With the growth in popularity of GPS-enabled phones and other GPS-enabled devices, it becomes relatively simple to track movements in space and time, either by recording the information for download or in real time. In fact, some Internet-based social networking and mapping services provide the capability for individuals to broadcast their location to approved contacts in real time. This real-time accessing of data is something that has value to the public when using their GPS-enabled car or cell phone to locate their friends or family members or the nearest gas station as they are driving cross country. Photographs can be "geo-tagged" to note the location where they were taken, and even linked to Web-based maps so friends and family can follow along with their loved one's vacation. While any of these tasks could be accomplished via maps, phone calls, or simply asking a local for directions, as new location-based tools emerge, such tasks become more available and accessible to almost anyone. Perhaps more importantly, these tools can be used in business and emergency response systems to provide the current location and estimated time of arrival for a package in shipment, or the location of an accident to first responders.

In the academic realm, these tools are valuable as a mechanism for field data collection, especially as inexpensive computers and geospatial software have become more commonplace on University campuses. Geospatial analysis methods have emerged as both useful and ever increasingly important technology in both academic and nonacademic realms. While the potential benefits of GPS as an emerging technology are continually evolving, immediately apparent benefits come from the links between GPS and other traditional data collection methods. Many commonly available GPS-enabled cell phones now include the ability to take photos and record video, sound, and written notes. Such devices are relatively inexpensive and provide social scientists with new opportunities for data acquisition. The computer or GPS data recorder provide an electronic field notebook capable of integrating many, if not all of the techniques used by social scientists into one integrated environment. Many professional-grade GPS units are beginning to incorporate digital cameras and full featured data loggers that can be programmed for direct input of field notes, survey responses, or other information into georeferenced digital data formats compatible with popular software packages including statistical packages, databases, and GIS software. In all cases, data collected with GPS becomes an excellent means for input to a geographic information system.

Geographic Information Systems

In their simplest form, GIS are spatially aware computer databases. A less precise, but more accessible description of GIS would be to call it a computerized map. However, GIS is much more than maps, it is an analysis system from which maps are one of the common end-products. GIS systems have four primary components or functions: (1) data storage; (2) data access and retrieval; (3) data analysis; and (4) data output and visualization. What differentiates GIS systems from other database and analysis software programs are the tools incorporated in them that permit complex spatial analysis and visualization of geospatial information. The most compelling of these to both researchers and the general public is most often the display of data in a map-based format. Because maps are a visual medium, in many cases they can more easily display and interpret information and patterns than is possible via statistical output or lengthy narratives. In addition to its analytical capabilities, GIS is also an integrative technology, allowing a diverse array of data to be brought together in an effort to understand questions of interest to the social scientist. In practice, this means that any data collected or obtained by a researcher that contains location information can be stored and potentially analyzed within a GIS environment.

As was the case for remote sensing and GPS, GIS were originally developed for very different sorts of data and analysis. Early GIS developed in Canada in the 1960s was targeted at management of natural resources, for example, mapping of vast forest stands or geologic resources (location, size, type, and value). Military needs also sparked development of other common components of modern GIS such as three-dimensional terrain mapping. While mapping natural features such as trees, rivers, and mountains were the first applications, it was not long after that demographers at the U.S. Census Bureau began to develop GIS mapping techniques that could be applied to mapping of human populations and their characteristics. By 1970, GIS was an important component of the work of the census bureau, although these uses were largely sequestered to the back rooms of government-computing centers, and not in the realm of the average social science researcher.

Since the value and strength of GIS is in answering spatial questions, it is important to consider how space relates to questions of interest. These may be questions exploring issues of spatial correspondence, relative location, distance, direction, pattern, and clustering. For example, are particular demographic groups more or less associated with certain other social or environmental variables of interest? Are crimes clustered in particular areas? Is there differential access to services?

Nonetheless, it is important to keep in mind two issues in relation to GIS. First, it is not a panacea. GIS have their place in the toolbox of the social scientist, but are not a replacement for existing methods of qualitative and quantitative analysis. By contrast, GIS is a supplement that can be used by social scientists to enhance and extend their exploration and understanding of the questions of importance to them. Second, GIS is complex. While some basic GIS concepts and skills can be learned via tutorials, workshops, or courses, it is important to stay within your capabilities. As an analogy, consider how prepared you were to conduct research following a first course in research methods or statistics. Many professionals continue to find it useful to consult with a statistician when developing a sampling design or analysis. By the same token, it may be important to consult or collaborate with experts in geospatial analysis when using GIS and the other geospatial tools discussed here.

As a developing profession, there are not yet accrediting bodies for University curricula in geospatial sciences, but some guidance for what a geospatial professional should know, including professional certifications, are emerging via organizations such as the University Consortium for Geographic Information Science (UCGIS), the GIS Certification Institute (GISCI), and the American Society for Photogrammetry and Remote Sensing (ASPRS).

Does My research Have a Spatial Component?

When considering the sorts of research that are best addressed with a sociospatial perspective, a key consideration should be, "Is space important to my question?" Spatial questions are those in which the hypothesis has some relationship to position in the landscape or environment in which the study subjects operate. While location may not be a driving variable in all social science research situations, it certainly is worth considering as a potential factor, especially given our improved ability to collect and analyze data in space and time. Consider that people and societies do not occur randomly on the landscape, but rather in proximity to essential resources such as water, food, and transportation. Differences in power or influence between various populations or subgroups may alter this distribution. Geospatial analysis of one's data can assist in identifying and analyzing such patterns in space and time.

For example, groups of people may have strong ties to a location for one of several reasons, including access to a natural resource and social ties to family, friends, or community. Questions examining differences between populations are often spatial, for example looking at differential access to resources or exposures to negative social and environmental geographies. A variety of geospatial tools and techniques are also available to explore networks, which may have a physical influence on populations, such as road and river networks, or may be conceptual as in the case of social relationships, which may have little to do with true geography. An example of this may be the patterns of social interaction that occur in a neighborhood. There may be some neighbors with whom one interacts, and others who may live physically next door, but due to social distance one may have little to no interaction with these neighbors. The same is true for groups of people who live in a community. People tend to interact with others who share similar values, perceptions, and attitudes, so it is not uncommon to see physical patterns of interaction mirror specific social structures and statuses.

While the visuals generated via sociospatial analysis are compelling, and certainly a significant reason to consider use of these technologies, it is important to note the nonvisual benefits to using these approaches. For example, most individuals new to GIS are surprised to learn that early GIS systems had no graphical capabilities; in fact, the primary outputs were statistics in tabular format. In most analytical and spatial modeling situations, this is still the case. The value of GIS in these situations is often the ability to generate and extract spatial statistics related to correspondence, distance, direction, pattern, and other such parameters. These statistics are often exported to traditional statistical analysis software for inclusion with other parameters collected through traditional means, including observation, survey, and content analysis. Inclusion of spatial parameters in analysis and development of correlation and regression models or other statistical analyses can often provide additional insights that might be otherwise overlooked. And conversely, sometimes assumptions about relationships between contextual features (social, physical, or otherwise) do not always prove to be statistically significant when examined more rigorously in a sociospatial context. However, now that the spatial outputs have become available to the general public, it makes the technology increasingly more appealing and understandable. We often notice with discussion of spatial data that people understand spatial concepts much better when a visual portrayal or output is provided. That is the beauty of geospatial technologies taken together as a whole.

Sociospatial Grounded Theory

One particularly useful approach to exploring the importance of space in a social science research setting is sociospatial grounded theory (Steinberg & Steinberg, 2006). Grounded theory, introduced by social scientists Glaser and Strauss (1967), emphasizes the generation of theory from the data. It is an inductive process of theory generation where one seeks to first identify patterns and themes in data and then generate conceptual models based on these themes.

Once identified, themes are used to develop a coding scheme (Strauss & Corbin, 1998). As Charmaz (2006) notes, "with grounded theory methods, you shape and reshape your data collection and, therefore, refine your collected data" (Charmaz, 2006, p. 14). In a spatial context, this may include coding and examining the social and environmental context in which the study subjects operate. The spatial data may come from a variety of secondary and primary sources, including data generated by members of the subject community via participatory mapping approaches, referred to in the literature as Participatory GIS (PGIS) or Public Participation GIS (PPGIS). Sociospatial grounded theory draws from the local knowledge of the individuals most familiar with the area under study and may surface questions or theories that would be missed by a researcher who is not a member of the population or community of interest. Sociospatial grounded theory begins with the notion that the answer and understanding of an issue lies with the people who inhabit or interact with a particular place. Sociospatial refers to an examination of space and social indicators in a holistic fashion (Steinberg & Steinberg, 2009). As alluded to previously, people and societies do not operate in a vacuum. The context in which they interact and function includes the natural and built environments as well as a variety of social and political factors.

When we wrote *GIS for the Social Sciences: Investigating Space and Place*, we developed the concept of sociospatial grounded theory (Steinberg & Steinberg, 2006). This is rooted in the notion that the truth lies in the field, and that local people possess important knowledge about a particular topic of study. Sociospatial grounded theory is a research process that guides the researcher through field-based data collection, spatial analysis, and theoretical development. It is an iterative process that begins with the people in the context of their place.

Steps for sociospatial grounded theory are (Steinberg & Steinberg, 2006, p. 80)

1. Determine a topic of interest;
2. Determine a geographic location of interest;
3. Collect the data (qualitative and spatially linked social data);
4. Geocode the data (link data to location on a map);
5. Ground truth the data (validate data in person or via another source);
6. Analyze the data and look for spatial and social patterns;
7. Generate theory (spatial and social).

Geospatial Analysisw

Data visualization is, of course, an important component of geospatial analysis at several stages in the process. Sometimes exploring individual data sets on a map or combining multiple data sets in different combinations can highlight patterns that are not visible using traditional analytical tools. The human brain is particularly adept at seeing patterns in data and more importantly at picking out anomalies in those patterns. Noticing patterns including clustering, directionality, or dispersion of data across a study region raises questions about the underlying causes. For example: Are crimes clustered around ATMs or convenience stores? Are people suffering from particular health issues associated with particular industrial sites? Even if the potential correlations are not apparent to the researcher, placing such data before local community members in PPGIS sessions may raise possibilities that would otherwise go unnoticed.

Not only does the grounded sociospatial approach provide a means to generate theory to guide research and analysis, but it also engages participants in the research process in ways that go beyond traditional data collection methodology. Furthermore, it actively empowers community members as knowing valuable, place-based knowledge that can actively inform the research process.

There are multiple benefits of using these emerging technologies in sociospatial research. While space has been considered in social science research for decades, if not centuries, use of actual maps and spatial analysis had been ignored or minimally used. At a base level, this is because mapping research data was a time-consuming and tedious process done by hand on paper. Furthermore, robust statistical methods for analyzing spatial data were lacking. Not until the advent of computers did digital mapping techniques become widespread. And more recently, vast amounts of high quality and accessible spatial information have become available to support these approaches. By the 1980 U.S. Census, data was mapped in GIS using consistent and relatively accessible standardized methods. Thus, a social scientist seeking to examine the rich demographic datasets collected via the census, in theory, had access to the requisite information. Nonetheless it was not until some years later that the supporting software, Internet access, and data organization matured to a level that has begun to be truly accessible to researchers. As these rapidly emerging technologies have continued to develop, additional supporting datasets have followed quickly.

With each passing year, digital map data becomes more easily accessible. In many countries, national census and a wide array of other social and environmental data are collected and stored in geospatial formats readily accessible with GIS software and analysis tools. With this rapid proliferation in both public and private sector data sources, there are two important caveats. First, regardless of the source, there is a risk of coming across data that is poorly documented as to its origin, method of collection, quality assurance and quality control (QA/QC) information, and other important documentation about the data itself, referred to as metadata. While data is easy to obtain and transmit electronically, this does not mean all data is of equal quality or utility in analysis of a particular research question. Similarly, with the ever-improving software tools for the development of high quality and attractive cartography, it is easy to be fooled by maps and remotely sensed images that, while visually stunning, may not be rigorously documented and assessed, or worse, are designed to intentionally mislead or provide a particular perspective. It becomes ever more essential that the researcher has a critical eye when considering data sources and outputs.

With these issues in mind, the value of considering a sociospatial perspective is in the potential for important explanatory parameters necessary to understanding social processes and subsequent research findings. Such understanding can also be valuable when research is used as a basis for policy making or other outcomes based upon such research. Everything that happens in social research occurs in some sort of space: built environments, natural settings, or conceptual spaces. Space is not an accidental occurrence, but rather an intentional or unintentional choice or construct of individuals and the societies in which they operate. Therefore, neglecting to consider a spatial perspective in social science research potentially leaves out this important component of the research setting.

Geospatial Technology as an Enabler

Geospatial technologies are in many ways enabling technologies that became possible through a series of factors ranging from geopolitical events, which allowed for the declassification of military technologies, to marvels of engineering that have enabled humans to fly and place satellites into orbit with GPS and sensor technology, to the development of the computer hardware and software necessary to manage and manipulate all of the information. While these and many other technological developments allowed for innovations in mapping, imaging, geolocation, communication, and data analysis, it was not any single event or planned research and development program that led to the development of these technologies. Rather, they emerged organically as creative individuals saw possibilities for using and combining them in new ways. This process continues on an almost daily basis, as new geospatial applications and data, particularly those contributed by the general public, become available. As the aforementioned technologies become available, people find ways to use them to realize their ideas and to develop new applications. For this reason, we refer to geospatial technologies as enabling technologies. They simply allow researchers to more easily, or perhaps for the first time, explore questions and analyze data in valuable ways.

Examples of mapping span thousands of years of human culture, providing compelling evidence that individuals and societies have a desire to understand their place in the world and spatial relationships in the environments in which they operate. However, at various points throughout history, mapping lay in the domain of the educated, elite, and religious institutions or governments. Mapping did not begin to become democratized until well after the turn of the millennium, and as these emerging technologies continue to reach the across cultural, educational, and language barriers in the coming years, we will continue to gain a more holistic and representative view of the world.

Data Surrounds Us

Recently a new term, Volunteered Geographic Information (VGI), has come into use to capture the concept of geographically referenced data shared via one of a growing number of Web-based services, media outlets, and Web sites (Goodchild, 2007). In this model, largely driven by growing access to geospatial technology in cell phones, vehicles, and consumer GPS units, any individual becomes simultaneously a participant, mobile remote sensor and reporter providing information about almost any topic at any time. While these enabling technologies are prevalent, they do raise questions about data quality and privacy. However, these same technologies and the data resulting from them may prove valuable sources of information for social science researchers.

What once may have taken years or even decades to map and understand using manual tools can now be mapped almost instantaneously using technologies ranging from aircraft and satellite-based imaging systems, largely maintained by governments and for-profit corporations, to VGI synthesized by citizens with access to GPS and high-speed Internet connections. Furthermore, the increasing presence and availability of secondary spatial data leads many researchers to rely solely on such existing data. Of course, these technologies could not have come into existence without the development of an array of technologies that were impossible to consider even a few decades ago. Geospatial technology relies on a long list of technological achievements including photographic and digital-imaging technologies, aerospace platforms, computers, high-speed communication networks, coordinated data collection by governments, and the creative individuals and research communities in both academia and industry that brought them all together. Since many of these technologies were initially developed for military purposes, their availability to the research community and the public has also relied on geopolitical factors such as an end to the Cold War, which allowed for the eventual declassification and public access to these tools. As recently as a decade ago, many of the geospatial capabilities we have today were not available to the average researcher.

Evolving Knowledge and Theory

Coupled with the technological innovations that allowed sociospatial analysis to develop as a research method, there was and continues to be a need for expanded theoretical views about how and why space is important in social settings. Because many of the early developments in geospatial analysis developed in fields outside of the social sciences, little attention was paid to social issues. Data analysis instead focused on issues such as mapping terrain and analysis of natural systems such as plant and animal habitats. The theoretical basis for analysis of social systems has lagged behind and there is ample room to develop theories and test them further. Until recently, students in the social sciences received little or no formal exposure to geospatial analysis techniques and even now it is rarely a component of formal curricula outside of geography departments.

As an emerging area of inquiry, there may be developing epistemological concepts that will help to further the application of geospatial technology in social research. Additional developments in our understanding of the relevance of space are likely to evolve in conjunction with a set of technologies such as those discussed here; nonetheless, there is already a strong epistemological basis for integrating a spatial perspective drawn from a variety of social science disciplines.

One of the greatest strengths geospatial technologies bring to social research is that of placing information in context of the natural, constructed, or conceptual spaces that are so essential to individuals, societies, and cultures. There is an extensive literature relating to the importance of place in its many forms. This becomes especially salient for understanding people within the context of their space and place. Geospatial technologies provide the researcher a basis for the examination and quantitative assessment of space;

however, there are limits to the utility of this approach as well. Previously mentioned are issues of assigning data to a specific location, given concerns of confidentiality. While there are a variety of mechanisms to mask or degrade this information to larger units of analysis, it becomes incumbent on the researcher to do so.

Additionally, because mapping technology was designed by engineers and programmers with an eye to the most spatially accurate information feasible, mapped locations have a tendency to be overly precise for some types of social data. For example, a spiritually or religiously important area or landscape may have fuzzy boundaries. It would be an oversimplification to assume you could interview members of an indigenous community to define a precise boundary for a traditional hunting ground so that you could then cross a centimeter to the opposite side of that line drawn to build a new shopping mall. While mapping information can be valuable, maps are, by necessity, abstractions and simplifications of reality and must therefore be analyzed and used with this in mind.

In a variety of cultural or social contexts, there are vague or fuzzy boundaries that should not always be mapped and analyzed as explicitly as they are represented by computers and their geoprocessing algorithms. Some progress has been made in representing fuzzy boundaries in GIS, but even so, these algorithms cannot always address the realities of the social systems we are studying. Another example might be that of perceived situations related to mapping emotional or psychological states. Some people may find alleys or paths through a park surrounded by trees and shrubs, a scary setting all of the time, others only during darkness, and still others not at all. As with other conceptual spaces, it would be silly to believe that simply crossing a line on the map will transition from a scary setting to a safe one, although we use phrases such as "the wrong side of the tracks" in our everyday language. Does crossing a street or railroad track really change the context so drastically? More often, such situations are better analyzed as gradients transitioning from one state to another. Ultimately, a GIS can be used to analyze and explore such questions; it is simply a matter of selecting the right software methods. Thus, as is true of any research, analysis should be driven by the researcher's question as opposed to the software tools used to analyze the data.

All Geospatial Analysis Is Not Created Equal

When considering a sociospatial perspective, there are a number of considerations to evaluate. First and foremost is the relevance of space and place as a component of the research question. Second, it is important to consider what spatial data will be required, and how it will be obtained. Existing geospatial datasets, including a variety of demographic variables, may provide a good beginning; however, there may be additional data to be georeferenced to the map. For example, content analysis of newspaper articles can be georeferenced by a location name in the byline or other location descriptions provided in the article. Data collected via written or mail survey may be referenced to street address, zip code, or town. Data may also come from government agencies, local organizations, and private firms, including some who provide geospatial data for a fee.

Evaluation and consideration of the most appropriate and useful data can make a prospective study go smoothly, whereas poor up-front planning can lead to significant problems when it comes time for analysis, not to mention lead delays and additional expenses. If one's personal experience and training are not sufficient, it is valuable to get the assistance of an experienced geospatial professional early in the process, before costly mistakes are made.

For primary data, there is obviously greater control in how the spatial information is collected and recorded. For in-person field work, GPS coordinates may be an option to map precise locations that may be generalized or aggregated for purposes of confidentiality. The advantage of using GPS in the field is that more precise measurements of location, distance, and direction can be obtained for purposes of analysis. Use of technology in the field does present some added considerations. Field staff must be properly trained in the use of the field equipment so that recorded information is accurate and consistent. Practical matters such as planning for ample batteries, storage media, and backups of data are also important to ensure the technology does not impede data collection.

When it comes time for the analysis of data, of course the potential is great and typical research protocols apply. The special case of geospatial data may necessitate training or assistance from individuals with the appropriate skill sets. If GPS data is being incorporated from the field, understanding accuracy and any post-processing done with the data is important. If remotely sensed images are a component of the study, they can provide valuable insight and a longitudinal view of the environment across years or even decades. In these cases, calling in an experienced remote-sensing image analyst can be useful. Similarly, when it comes to analysis of sociospatial data in a GIS system, it is helpful to draw on an experienced analyst who understands the numerous geoprocessing and geostatistical options available in GIS software. While an introductory course in GIS can provide a basic level of competence in conducting GIS operations and generating simple maps and summary statistics, it is easy to become quickly overwhelmed by the software and thousands of analytical commands and options available.

Much like statistics, geospatial analysis and the special case of sociospatial analysis are both tools and disciplinary areas of scientific expertise. Specialists in any field can gain experience in using statistical tools and software, and even become competent in statistical analysis. However, for significant research, it is still a good idea to call on a statistician early in the process of experimental design and sampling as well as at the point of conducting data analysis. By the same token, a social scientist can develop a good competency with geospatial data collection, sampling, and analysis, but may find it useful to call upon a geospatial scientist when the complexity of the research goes beyond that experience.

As with any specialist, sometimes their personal understanding of the data is lacking. Like statisticians, geospatial analysts are often called in to assist on a broad array of research topics, often outside their own area of expertise. Given GIS and remote sensing were largely applied to natural resource and environmental disciplines early on, many geospatial professionals were trained in these application areas and may have little or no understanding of social science research and analysis. For the social scientist working alongside such individuals, it is important to learn how to communicate project data and analysis requirements to the geospatial analysts who conduct the analysis, checking in frequently throughout the process and ultimately validating results against ground truth, either with verification visits to a subset of field locations, or by taking the data back to the community in participatory GIS sessions to validate results with personal knowledge and experience.

While geospatial analysis techniques have been available for several decades, for many years research using these techniques was largely limited to those working in natural resource management fields and later in urban and community planning. While there are numerous reasons for this, the primary one is that remote sensing and later GIS were largely developed by and for practitioners in these fields. Simultaneously, geography, the primary social science field that would have logically participated in the development of geospatial analysis techniques, had been eliminated as a field of study at many of the major universities in the United States. A case in point, Harvard University, a key player in the development of computer-based mapping in the 1960s, had eliminated its geography program more than a decade prior. Of programs that persisted, many were in disarray in the latter half of the twentieth century, struggling with their own identities as GIS was developing as a technology and discipline (Dear, 1988). Because geographers were exploring postmodern and feminist perspectives, including consideration of imagined or conceptual spaces, GIS was not a focus for geographers until decades later.

Many geographers in the academic realm largely ignored the development of geospatial analysis, leaving it to computer scientists and natural resource management disciplines. With the social scientists out of the picture, it is easy to understand why GIS and its supporting technologies took on a much more natural science and engineering focus for the first three decades of its development. More recently, geography and other social sciences have rediscovered the value of a spatial perspective and are returning to the table, or in many cases joining in for the first time.

The majority of data is spatial, including most of the data used in social science research. It is generally accepted that at least 80% of all data has a spatial component of some sort, meaning it occurs in, or is collect at, a particular location on the surface of the earth (Foresman, 1998). Consider the following exercise: Make a list of data types you frequently use and then for each, determine if it is collected or occurs in a particular location. Odds are all or most of the data on your list will occur in a particular location. For example, surveys are collected from households, or purposively at particular locations (e.g., outside a grocery store, in the park, stratified by neighborhood, comparisons of red and blue states). Given the prevalence of the spatial component to data and data collection, it may be surprising that a sociospatial perspective and geospatial analysis techniques have not been the standard operating procedure for social science researchers.

Of course, some social scientists have always used these techniques in some manner, but as discussed previously, it was not until well after the turn of the millennium that a combination of emerging technologies came together to make these approaches accessible to the mainstream. Nonetheless, there is a significant computer and technology component to geospatial analysis as well as an entire set of new concepts and terminology that are unfamiliar to practitioners of these disciplines. This has resulted in slow adoption of geospatial technology in these disciplines that, from an adoption-diffusion perspective (Rogers, 2003), fall into the late majority and laggard categories. Adoption-diffusion, as described by Rogers, arranges adoption of new technologies or approaches into several categories ranging from early adopters (those who want to be the first to use the latest technologies) to early majority (who tend to adopt technologies once they are relatively sure the bugs are out and cost has dropped somewhat) to late majority (those who need to see everyone else is doing it too) to the laggards who insist that the old ways are fine and adopt the newer approaches either when forced (the old technology is no longer available) or simply it becomes obvious that the new technology really is a better option.

With some exceptions, most researchers in the social sciences, as well as the business community, mass media, and general public, did not become aware of geospatial technologies in a significant way until well after the beginning of the millennium, particularly in the past several years. It was difficult to locate University courses relating geospatial analysis in the social sciences before 2005 and it is still a developing area. For this reason, while the potential for geospatial analysis in social science research is vast, because social scientists were not intimately involved in the first 40 years of geospatial analysis development, many of the existing tools and techniques tend to focus on questions with very specific natural resource and business analysis applications in mind. As more social scientists incorporate these tools and techniques into their work, techniques will continue to be adapted from those established in geospatial analysis approaches and new ones will be developed.

However, some extremely positive results come from these delays in bringing emerging geospatial technologies to bear in social science research. First, the technology itself has matured to a level that is relatively less complex and expensive than in the past. In fact, with the rapidly emerging and innovative tools available on the Internet, many aspects of sociospatial data acquisition and analysis can be accomplished for free or inexpensively. Simultaneously, personal computers and commercial geospatial software prices have dropped, making even high-end commercial software affordable and available to researchers across all disciplines. Second, because geospatial technology and more specifically a sociospatial approach to analysis with geospatial tools are emerging, there is great potential for social science researchers to participate in moving these techniques forward and extending them into additional areas of social research.

The relevance and value of a sociospatial perspective is not new, but the possibilities for the application and analysis of social data are vast. When colleagues or students ask us what sorts of questions can be examined with geospatial technology, our honest answer is, anything you are interested in! Because so much of the data we work with has a spatial component, and because we have long understood that social systems are not isolated from the environments in which they operate, it just makes sense to consider the role space plays when we conduct social science research. We operate in a world where research questions cross disciplinary boundaries and data are drawn from a variety of sources. As integrating technologies, the array of geospatial tools discussed here are a natural fit for the collection, organization, analysis, and display of research questions, data, and results.

Why Now?

While sociospatial research has been carried forward in various forms for centuries, the adoption of the emerging technologies has taken longer to migrate into social research. Perhaps, the most important innovations in recent years have come with the rapid adoption of digital mapping technologies used by media outlets to report details of presidential elections as well as in reporting on major events such as military conflicts, natural disasters, disease outbreaks, and genocide. As the media continue to place social and environmental information before the public in a geospatial context, including combinations of remotely sensed images, demographic and other supporting data, the level of awareness of these technologies has rapidly taken hold. In just a few years, the average person who would never had considered or thought about geospatial technology now has access to vast amounts of geospatial information via applications such as Google Earth, a variety of Internet-based mapping sites that assist in map-based trip planning, and a wide array of social networking sites that link people and locations together via cell phones and wireless computing connections.

This is a situation where commercial development, media saturation, and public awareness have significantly outpaced the inclusion of geospatial technologies by social researchers as a core component of their training and in how they conceptualize and conduct research. Of course, another aspect of this transition to emerging technology may simply be generational. With the substantial demographic turnover in faculty and government agency staff, many who began their careers in the 1970s, a new generation of technology-savvy individuals has been entering the ranks of researchers and is finding new and innovative ways to take advantage of these emerging technologies.

Combining Skills and Experience in Sociospatial Research

By their very nature, sociospatial research efforts will generally require a multidisciplinary mixed-methods approach. All of the accepted and well-tested social science techniques still apply, but now coupled with the new capabilities and methods of the geospatial realm. Since sociospatial research also considers the environmental context, additional disciplinary expertise may be required to address issues relating to both the built and natural environmental domains.

Sociospatial projects develop through an integration of environmental and social skills. The sociologist brings the interviewing, survey, and social science skills, while the environmental scientist brings the environmental/spatial analysis skills needed to examine patterns in the physical data. Specialists in any number of supporting disciplines— economics, health, criminology or psychology, anthropology, and many others—may have perspectives that can further benefit decisions relating to data collection and analysis. Because essentially any topic can be viewed from a multidisciplinary perspective, we both strongly believe that any issue or problem behind one's research question can benefit from a sociospatial approach. Why? Such an approach facilitates examination of different types of data simultaneously and allows for easy pattern identification. Furthermore, spatial portrayal of data crosses the language and literacy barrier and, therefore, allows for greater communication about data, process, and policy with a much larger audience. It also enables quick communication with policy makers to highlight patterns and trends in a short time frame.

So why would a social researcher want to attempt to integrate a complex set of computer-technologies into their research? Perhaps, most compelling is the fact that many researchers already are using geospatial or sociospatial techniques. While the concept of sociospatial analysis was being applied more than 100 years ago, the terminology and the modern geospatial tools and techniques were unavailable to assist these researchers in their endeavors. It was all done by hand; the geographic information relied on paper and pencil. One classic example was the work of Charles Booth, *Life and Labour of the People in London* (1903). Beginning in 1886, Booth initiated an extremely in-depth study of poverty in London. Booth and his team visited every single street in London to document the social, economic, and environmental conditions of residents (Fearon, 2007).

Among other issues, Booth was interested in examining the relationship between space, social class, and a number of other demographic and environmental characteristics. Booth's grounded-theory approach eventually disproved original statistics that had underestimated the poverty rate in London at 25%. When his detailed examination was completed more than a decade later, he found poverty was actually closer to 35% (Fearon, 2007). While Booth's research took more than a decade from beginning to end, the same analysis could be completed and analyzed using geospatial techniques in much quicker fashion than Booth's manual approach. Booth employed both quantitative and qualitative methods (he took detailed field notes on the survey gathering process of poverty data). He was definitely ahead of his time as a researcher, using a mixed-methods approach incorporating interviews and survey data with field observations and map analysis; a simultaneously broad yet narrow view of poverty could be accomplished using this process. Had Booth had access to a GIS in 1903, he could have really provided some interesting analysis to policy makers, and it would not have taken more than a decade to complete.

Examples of Sociospatial Analysis in Social Research

The following sections provide examples of modern sociospatial research that utilizes geospatial analysis tools and techniques. In each of these cases, we utilized one or more of the emerging technologies described earlier in this chapter. The examples are provided primarily as a means to provide readers with an understanding of the process and practice of sociospatial research. We hope that one or more of these examples will give you insight into how you might begin to incorporate a sociospatial perspective and geospatial technologies in your own research. Of course, the best way to accomplish that is to seek out opportunities to learn more about approaches to collecting and analyzing geospatial information relevant to your own work. Then seek out those around you who are experienced with geospatial tools and techniques and involve them in your research process, or better yet, if you have the time and motivation, seek out opportunities to learn more about them yourself. As more social science research incorporates these tools, additional examples will appear regularly in the literature and the community of social science researchers incorporating geospatial techniques will continue to grow.

Sociospatial Analysis of Farmworker Health

As a first example, we present a study that employed a mixed-method sociospatial approach to study agricultural worker health issues related to pesticide use in Monterey and Tulare counties in California. This project used GIS to effectively integrate and overlap environmental and social data related to farmworker health and pesticide use. Because farmworkers live and work in places where they and their families are potentially exposed, there were clear benefits to incorporating a spatial perspective. We examined the affect of these environmental and social factors on farmworkers and their families. One important benefit of the map-based approach was that the visual portrayal of data was effective across language and literacy barriers. Accessing farmworker organizations was accomplished in partnership with Poder Popular, a community-based group to empower farmworker communities throughout the state of California. For the data collection and analysis, we combined sociospatial data consisting of both mapped and interview data integrated to tell the story of farmworkers, their communities, and pesticide drift using a sociospatial analysis approach (Steinberg & Steinberg, 2009).

An important aspect of any sociospatial study is the acquisition and manipulation of existing geospatial data that is believed to have relevance. Our decisions about which data to consider were based on a variety of factors as described earlier in this chapter. In particular, we sought to obtain all of the potentially important contextual data including information about built and natural environments as well as a variety of social, demographic, and political data. Some data were obtained based on the suggestions and outcomes of participatory GIS sessions.

Pesticide application data was obtained from the California Department of Pesticide Regulation's 2005 statewide pesticide database. This database provides detailed information regarding all commercial pesticide applications by pounds of individual active ingredient for each public land survey section in the state. We georeferenced key pesticides applied in each county and linked resulting information to a geospatial database for each study county. Additional physical and environmental data included county parcels and zoning information and locations of schools in each of the six cities analyzed for the study. We also drew together available social science data for political and demographic characteristics including California State Senate and Assembly districts to identify elected representatives whose regions showed the highest levels of agricultural chemical use.

Environmental data included topography derived from the 10m resolution National Elevation Dataset (NED) and wind forecast data from the National Oceanographic and Atmospheric Administration (NOAA). Wind data was used to develop maps showing a weekly average wind speed and direction at 4-hr intervals during a representative week of the growing season when pesticides are typically applied.

Sociospatial methods include key-informant interviews, ethnographic methods, public participation GIS, participant observation at community meetings, and environmental mapping. Prior to field visits, we interviewed key informants (targeted individuals from government agencies, community groups, and nonprofit organizations working on pesticide issues) to determine the issues and active chemical ingredients of greatest concern. Field visits to both counties were made in the summer of 2006 to carry out a community-based participatory research (CBPR) approach as a means to understand community members' interest in and knowledge about pesticides. Particular emphasis was placed on the amount and types of specific pesticides and fumigants used near schools, neighborhoods, and community gathering places. Specific locations or names of locations were obtained whenever possible to ensure information could be later linked to the geospatial data obtained from other sources described earlier (Figure 25.1).

Public participation GIS (PPGIS) is a technique for obtaining georeferenced data derived from local knowledge. We overlaid National Aerial Photography Program (NAPP) color images of the six study communities with GIS data showing roads and parcels as a base for community members to provide input on locations where they had observed or experienced pesticide drift. The PPGIS process was also used to identify sensitive sites such

Figure 25.1 Community members participating in a public participation GIS session. Directions provided to participants specify data and other information to be noted and colors to use for each data category. For this activity, GIS data was layered over aerial photography and printed at large scale allowing groups of six to eight people to interact and mark up each of the maps.

as schools, hospitals, and nursing homes, places where community members participate in outdoor activities including parks and open spaces, and locations where farmworkers live. The PPGIS approach provided an additional and extremely rich dataset based on local knowledge. Where existing geospatial data sources (e.g., U.S. Census Data and the respective county assessor's office) were available, the results of the PPGIS were cross-referenced with geospatial sources or spot-checked on the ground as a means of accuracy assessment (Figure 25.2).

These interviews provided insight into primary issues of relevance related to pesticide use, pesticide drift, agricultural worker health, and community issues for these regions. Analysis of interviews helped us to understand issues related to pesticide drift, how farm-workers are affected by drift, where and how they go to seek treatment in instances of possible exposure to pesticides, and other specific areas of concern in these communities. Furthermore, by conducting interviews with various parties related to this issue—including nonprofit organizations working to reduce pesticide use and exposure, agricultural and county officials, farmworkers, and community members—issues of importance for policy emerge. The interviews provide the basis of the farmworker/pesticide drift interaction and perspective presented in the final research report (Steinberg & Steinberg, 2008).

Pesticide data was examined for the region surrounding the three Poder Popular communities in each of the study counties. We examined both the total amount of pesticide applied in 2005, as well as the amount of individual pesticides of concern. The Department of Pesticide Regulation summarizes application rates by public land survey sections of approximately 1 square mile (640 acres). As an approximation of the total pesticide impact associated with a particular community, we examined a region approximately three times the diameter of the developed area of the community. For the five smaller communities of Gonzales, Greenfield, Cutler & Orosi, Woodlake, and Lindsay, the developed area of the community was approximately 1 mile in diameter with populations of between 7,250 and

Figure 25.2 In this figure is a close-up of a small portion of one map marked up by community members in a participatory GIS session. Data captured in such sessions is later converted into digital information for analysis in GIS.

15,000 people. For these towns, we totaled all pesticide applications for 2005 within a 3-mile radius of the center of the community (approximately 28.3 square miles).

The city of Salinas, in Monterey County, is substantially larger in size, with a population of nearly 150,000. The developed area of Salinas measures approximately 3 miles in diameter, so for Salinas, pesticide applications for 2005 were totaled within a 9-mile radius of the center of the city (approximately 254.5 square miles). Salinas has a unique layout representing a doughnut with a sizable area of agricultural production remaining in what is now the middle of the city, and located literally across the street from a major hospital.

A topic that arose among community members interviewed in this study was the possibility of establishing buffer zones around schools. A buffer zone is a region of some specified (legislated) distance around school grounds with limitations on if, how, and when particular pesticides may be applied. In California, the establishment of buffer zones is handled on an individual county basis. To assist in illustrating the impacts of a proposed buffer zone of a ¼ mile (1,320 feet), the maximum proposed at the time of this study, we identified schools for the entire county as well as for each of the study communities. Parcels associated with school structures were overlaid on the NAIP photography and inspected to ensure that all playgrounds and athletic fields associated with the school were included in the analysis. In many cases, a school owned multiple parcels, and buffers had to be generated for the total extent of the grounds rather than just the location of the school building.

For each study community, we aggregated the total acres of agriculturally zoned land falling into the ¼-mile buffer zones as well as the percentage of the total amount of agricultural lands surrounding the community. For areas surrounding towns, this naturally overestimates the percent of agricultural lands affected relative to the outlying areas of the county. For example, in Tulare county, of the over 5.6 million acres of agricultural land, 35,420 acres are located within ¼ mile of a school or school grounds, representing 0.63% of the total. In Tulare County, within the 3-mile radius (28.3 square miles) surrounding each of the Poder Popular communities, buffer zones would have the largest impact upon agricultural lands in the community of Woodlake with just over 2.3% (208 acres) of agriculturally zoned lands falling within ¼ mile of a school. In Lindsay, just over 2.2% of these lands are within ¼ mile of a school and for Cutler & Orosi just over 1.8%.

Exploring these data further, it became apparent that many schools are located at the periphery of these and other communities, perhaps due to the availability and price of these parcels as urban and suburban development grow outward from the city center. We observed very similar patterns and results in Monterey County as well.

The PPGIS methodology offered insight into perceived conditions affecting a community where gaps exist in the scale of publicly available data. While no pesticide data was available at a finer scale than 1 square mile, participants were often able to identify streets or fields related to specific incidents of pesticide drift. Cross-referenced demographic data confirmed the validity of differences perceived by participants; however, participants were often able to identify demographic regions at a much finer scale than the U.S. Census block group level. Sensitive sites within the community are often not included in land use or parcel data, as some community locations, like churches or residential homes, have

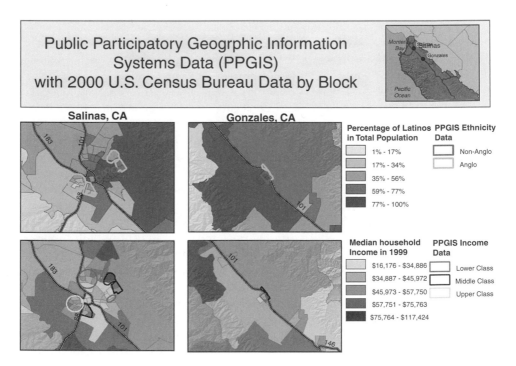

Figure 25.3 After data is converted into digital form, it is easily integrated with other supporting geospatial datasets for analysis. In the above example, regions of the PPGIS maps that were marked for locations of Latino neighborhoods and income level are compared with 2,000 U.S. Census data.

secondary purposes unique to the community served and would otherwise go unnoticed as sensitive (Figure 25.3).

Broadband Internet Access and Demand

A second example is a study that again combined data from a wide array of sources using a mixed-methods approach and geospatial technology in the organization, collection, analysis, and modeling of results. This study utilized a variety of social science methods, including mail, telephone and Web-based surveys, community-based participatory research (CBPR), graphic facilitation, statistical analysis, spatial analysis, economic modeling, and spatial modeling, all in an effort to characterize and understand the availability and demand for broadband Internet connectivity in four rural northwestern California Counties (Redwood Coast Connect, 2009).

As broadband Internet connectivity has spread over the last decade, its availability has provided a wide array of new capabilities to governments, businesses, and individuals. However, in many areas, particularly rural regions, access to high-speed affordable Internet connections is lacking. What was less certain and a major component of this research was the level of demand and the economic feasibility for providing such service in rural areas. A number of factors contribute to limited access to broadband. Costs to install and maintain broadband infrastructure are relatively high so, for many providers, it does not make sense to install over long distances to reach a limited number of customers. An important aspect of the project was the recognition that successful broadband deployment requires more than just assuring that requisite infrastructure is available. In order to ensure a comprehensive and successful deployment, five issues must be considered: access, applications, affordability, accessibility, and assistance.

The long-term goal of the project is to identify approaches to make available ubiquitous broadband to all rural communities in the region through the aggregation of users, engagement of providers, simplification of county and municipal policies, and tapping the ingenuity of entrepreneurs in the region. The initial planning process involved a multipronged approach including a series of community meetings with businesses and community members throughout the region. Written, phone, and online surveys of current and potential business and residential customers were conducted to develop an understanding of the demand for broadband. Survey data was geocoded to the address of the current or desired broadband access and combined with a variety of physical, infrastructural, and environmental data to develop a better understanding of both current broadband availability and the potential for extending access to areas with unmet demand (Figure 25.4).

The study provided a benchmark of current regional readiness to participate in the changes that high-speed communications entail. Such readiness assessment is critical to addressing a viable plan for broadband deployment. This project has already led to positive impacts for the entire region by demonstrating a business case for broadband infrastructure investment. Increased broadband accessibility will increase opportunities for business development, job creation, and access to quality health care and educational opportunities.

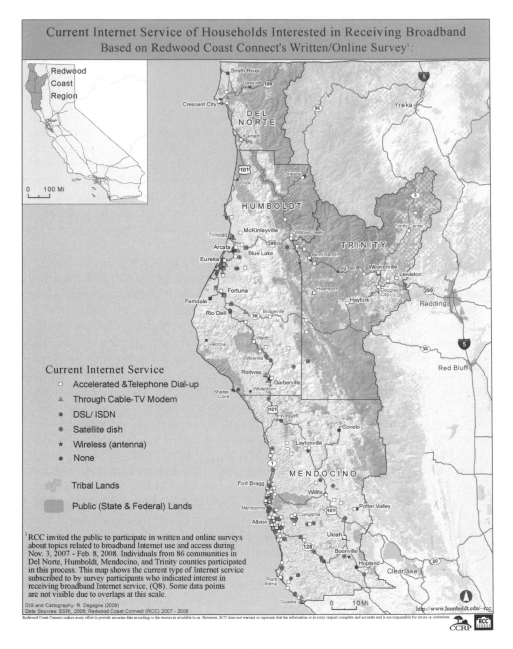

Figure 25.4 An example of a GIS map derived from a combination of social science and geospatial data sources. This map shows the density and distribution of Internet connectivity through four rural counties in Northern California.

Analysis of the geospatial data was completed by the Institute for Spatial Analysis at Humboldt State University using ArcGIS 9.2 (ESRI). Scenario modeling was developed with CommunityViz Professional 3.1 (Placeways). Publicly available interactive maps were served using ArcGIS Server 9.2 implemented on an ArcGIS Server platform (Inline Corporation).

Geospatial data was acquired from a variety of sources including commercially available telecommunications data (TeleAtlas), as well as a wide array of publicly available data from Federal, State, County, and local sources. Where additional detailed data was required, we worked directly with broadband providers to develop maps of their coverage areas. Survey data included street address information, and responses were geocoded to allow for accurate mapping of demand.

A first step in the GIS analysis was to acquire and evaluate available data. We acquired over 500 geospatial data sets covering some or all of the four counties studied at state, county, and municipality levels. After review, layers for portions of the study area that contained acceptably similar information were merged into a single data layer. For example, broadband footprints by individual providers were combined into a single broadband access footprint layer. Additional data sets were compiled for a variety of information types including telecommunications and transportation infrastructure, county parcels and zoning, government buildings, schools, businesses, demographics, and others. Data layers were individually evaluated and when appropriate, aggregated. Additional data layers were developed from geocoded questionnaires collected at public meetings as well as mail and phone surveys. Other information was georeferenced from a variety of print and digital sources not initially provided in georeferenced formats. We ultimately had nearly 200 geospatial data layers associated with the study, with over 100 compiled into a comprehensive geodatabase made publicly available via an ArcGIS Server online mapping system.

One of the more challenging aspects of obtaining accurate broadband coverage footprints was the variety of forms in which data was or was not available. Some providers were unwilling to share detailed coverage information under the premise of competition. In these cases, we were limited to coarse resolution (3 km raster data) provided by the California Emerging Technology Fund. In other cases, we were provided standard road maps with coverage areas marked in yellow highlighter, which we hand-digitized and georeferenced. For some of the fixed wireless providers, we were provided information on tower locations and transmitter specifications allowing spatial modeling of coverage footprints using viewshed analysis tools in ArcGIS in conjunction with elevation data from the national elevation data (NED) at 10 m resolution. In a few cases, providers were willing and able to provide coverage footprints in GIS compatible formats.

Because there are relatively low population densities in rural regions and large tracts of public land, it is not appropriate to assume that housing or demand is equally distributed in census blocks as is common in more urbanized regions. Because county parcel information was not available in digital form for the entire study region, we could not reliably determine which parcels were zoned residential. We modeled housing as a surrogate for actual parcel data. To ensure populations were allocated only to areas that were appropriate, housing units were allocated only on private lands (excluding the substantial areas of State and Federal public lands in the study region) and within a reasonable distance of roads based on average distances observed.

Our objectives to develop available coverage maps and to generate demand areas from geocoded survey data were met. This data is now being used by telecommunications consultants, community interest groups and policy makers throughout the region to move forward in seeking additional broadband access for their respective communities and constituents. Two specific products developed by the Institute for Spatial Analysis to support the development of demand scenarios are notable. First, a Web-based mapping tool that provides the telecommunications consultants for the project with access to over 100 geospatial data layers via ArcGIS Server. This interactive mapping tool provides detailed information about demand location, willingness to pay, and a variety of other important factors derived from the georeferenced survey data and other geospatial data sources acquired and developed through this project. It was essential that project data be available via a Web-based interface, since project consultants were located in multiple states as far as 750 miles away. The ArcGIS Server permitted project consultants to explore and interact with the geospatial data while working together from multiple locations.

To facilitate exploration of various scenarios for extending broadband coverage, we developed an interactive modeling tool using the CommunityViz 3.1 software extension for ArcGIS. This tool permitted us to provide tools allowing a user to set parameters based on distance to extend coverage, number of new customers desired (including capture rates for anticipated subscriptions), as well as costs per mile to extend the infrastructure. These tools allow interactive mapping based on the data and parameter settings. As the user alters values in the system, the ArcGIS map display is updated to show the households that would be captured under a given scenario. Such tools can be useful to individual providers and entrepreneurs considering investments in broadband capacity, as well as to communities and policy makers who may need to rely on government assistance to facilitate access to broadband in areas that would not make financial sense to private sector investors.

It is clear that rural communities desire and could benefit from greater access to broadband services such as are available in the more urbanized and suburban areas of California. The most significant hurdles to achieving the goal of ubiquitous broadband include limited numbers of businesses and households that are sometimes perceived as insufficient to justify the cost of extending broadband services to these regions. Our preliminary work indicates that demand may be substantially higher than previously believed, and access, even in the larger communities, is often substantially lower than expected.

By incorporating sociospatial techniques to understand demand and willingness to pay on the part of community members and business owners in combination with a clear view of the physical and spatial environment in which they operate, it becomes possible to better understand the realities faced by broadband providers. Substantial distances between clusters of prospective customers, coupled with environmental and policy obstacles, can be better understood when viewed spatially.

Proper Use of Geospatial Technology

There are several potential ethical issues that may arise when working with geospatial tools in social science research. Most obvious is the risk of disclosure of the identity of human subjects participating in a study by too precisely providing information about their location. For example, it would be rare for a researcher to provide specific addresses or GPS locations of study subjects and in the research realm, protocols for the protection of human subjects would not permit such information to be disclosed. There are several means available to mask such information when reporting the results of a study. One common method is to aggregate study populations into groups covering large enough geographic area, for example, by neighborhood, town, or census block. Data aggregation is a common method for masking individual identities when there are sufficient numbers and variation among study subjects, especially when the information collected is not outwardly visible. However, aggregation may not be sufficient if there are extremely small numbers of participants from a particular group; for example, if a study involves a small town with a single black family, mentioning race in combination with other information may result in an unintentional disclosure of confidential information.

In such cases, the geographic unit of aggregation may need to be expanded to include a larger number of subjects, or other methods of masking data may be necessary. Another means of masking information is to remove geographic identifiers from the study, for example, rather than using the name of the town, simply describing it as "a small rural town in the upper Midwest." It may also be important to mask data by avoiding associated place names such as rivers, lakes, or highways. For example, a mitten-shaped outline for an unnamed state is a likely giveaway even to the casual reader if a map is shown. Even more so if this is tied to dots on the map showing where in the state the study was conducted. While it is clear that maps are a valuable means for communicating the results of a spatial study, they may also present risks of disclosure of confidential information when they provide too much detail. In such cases, a map may not be an appropriate means for reporting results and researchers may opt to use charts, tables, and statistical output from the geospatial analysis.

It is not only important to consider these risks for studies involving human subjects, but also those that may disclose other sensitive information. For example, a researcher studying topics related to particular activities or behaviors considered socially unacceptable or illegal may need to mask information about where those activities are taking place. Examples may include locations where illegal drugs are being dealt or used, where homeless spend their nights camped out, or where underage high-school students are able to purchase alcohol or have their parties.

When relative locations (distances, directions, or concentrations of data points) are important to communicate visually, doing so without the supporting information of roads, rivers, and political boundaries may go a long way to masking the specific location of the data collection (Figure 25.5). As an additional protection, if data will be made available in digital formats, geographic coordinates can be shifted so that points do not map their actual location on the surface of the earth. For example, geographic coordinates collected with GPS units are often recorded using Universal Transverse Mercator (UTM) system coordinates, which measures locations in meters and can be adjusted by adding or subtracting a specific value to all of the resulting coordinates. Thus, coordinates recorded in the field for New York City (587187, 4515215) and Montreal, Quebec (610940, 5039477) can be shifted by any amount in either the positive or negative direction without altering the relative locations of these points.

For example, shifting all values by (−500000, −4000000) would result in new values of (87187, 515215) for New York and (110940, 1039477) for Montreal. On a Cartesian coordinate system, these will plot in correct relative locations as the original, true locations, but if placed onto a map, they will lie quite distant from the actual location, thus masking it, so long as the magnitude and direction of the shifts are not disclosed. This can

(a)

(b)

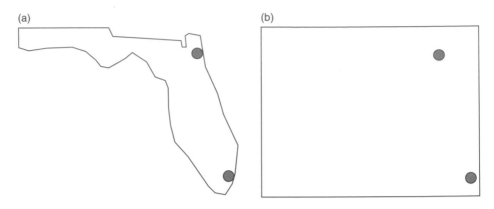

Figure 25.5 In this simple example, two data points shown with a state outline (A) provide a reader enough information to identify the two large southeastern cities examined. The same two data points shown without a state outline (B) effectively mask this information. Relative geospatial information such as the distance and direction between these points is retained for purposes of analysis. A similar approach could be used for other units of analysis, for example, neighborhoods within a city or even houses on a block. Leaving identifiable geographic features such as political boundaries, roads, or water bodies off of maps included in a report can help to mask confidential information.

be validated via simple Cartesian geometry by computing the distance as the hypotenuse of a right triangle using the Pythagorean Theorem. In both computations, the result is the same: 523,800 m, or 523.8 km. This same logic works at local scales of neighborhoods or towns, and in general the accuracy is better for distances at a local scale than a regional or global scale.

In addition to confidentiality in studies involving human subjects, other situations may necessitate similar precautions, for example, anthropologists and archeologists may wish to mask locations of important cultural and historical sites. Ethical considerations may also relate to the effects of reporting geographic details of organizations or businesses in studies where providing such details could lead to unanticipated economic or political ramifications for those entities. While these issues are not unique to studies incorporating geospatial analysis, there may be additional considerations because such studies have the potential to specifically locate these features or individuals.

One aspect of the geospatial data and confidentiality that is sometimes surprising to people is the level of detailed information that can be gleaned from aerial photographs and satellite images. While on the surface this may appear to be a breach of confidentiality, it is not. From a legal perspective, information obtained passively via imaging systems is not considered an invasion of privacy in the United States and many other countries, in fact, international open skies treaties explicitly allow for aerial imaging. At the national level, many countries have regular programs of aerial image acquisition for mapping, tax assessment, and law enforcement purposes. These data are very commonly available to both researchers and the general public for free or a fee. Private imaging firms also collect and market a variety of aerial and satellite-acquired images. While a wide array of images are available, it is also important to remember that the vast majority of these are months or even years old and rarely show conditions at the current moment. From the perspective of the social science researcher, the ethics of imagery of this sort is not so much what is shown, but how these images are interpreted and presented in the context of the research. Older images are excellent sources of information regarding past conditions but can also be misleading if this is not clearly stated. While less likely, it is also possible for images to be digitally altered to change or hide information presented. Therefore, it is important to know the source and details of data used in a study, and when possible to use primary data.

Future Directions

As a new and continually evolving field, the application of geospatial techniques in social science research is at the early stages of development. Computer-based geospatial analysis tools are just a few decades old. During most of the development of geospatial analysis, these techniques were largely developed by natural scientists, and at best minimally considered by social scientists. As this has begun to change, particularly in the last 5 years, a variety of new possibilities are emerging. Even in the months during which we have worked on this chapter, new tools and applications have emerged. One thing that is certain is that geospatial tools and research methods will continue to evolve. Some of the more likely innovations will relate to better three-dimensional visualizations for built and natural environments and more available and accurate geolocation via common tools such as cell phones, vehicle navigation systems, and digital cameras. No doubt innovative researchers, individuals, and companies will continue to develop additional tools not yet imagined. This is perhaps the most promising aspect for these technologies for social science researchers: the immense opportunity to incorporate these and other new technologies in collection and analysis of data to assess relationships and interactions between and among social parameters and their environments.

Perhaps the greatest opportunity for the future development is simply putting these tools and techniques into the hands of researchers and future researchers via formal workshops and continued integration of geospatial coursework into social science curricula. In our own experience, we find that when introduced to these tools, social science students and practitioners come up with new and different applications for their own research and subsequent careers. In some cases, these ideas are implemented immediately using existing tools and techniques, while in others we must work to develop a means to accomplish them, and in yet others, they may have to wait until additional tools become available. We have presented a variety of examples for the application of geospatial and sociospatial analysis techniques here, and no doubt as you have considered them, other innovative ideas have come to mind.

Conclusion

Given that a vast majority of data has a connection to a particular location, it seems appropriate that we consider these spatial components when conducting social research. As geospatial technologies have emerged into the mainstream in the past decade, they continue to become increasingly more accessible, inexpensive, and easy to use. A vast array of possibilities for the social scientist has emerged and some researchers have begun to incorporate geospatial technologies into their work. For many social researchers, the consideration of space and place is not a new concept; in fact, it predates the existence of all of the emerging technologies discussed in this chapter. What is new is our ability to completely and fully interrogate our data to better understand how and perhaps why space plays such an important role in social systems.

As is the case with any area of disciplinary expertise, the geospatial realm is complex and potentially overwhelming to the newcomer. We encourage you to try a few of the approaches to sociospatial research that have been presented here. If you need assistance, find your local expert. Geospatial specialists are commonly found on University campuses and in government agencies and consulting firms. Courses in geospatial analysis are also becoming more common, and most institutions of higher education offer at least one, though it may be hosted by a department you may not consider. While geospatial courses are often housed in geography departments, they are also common in natural resource disciplines such as forestry or agriculture, or on some campuses, engineering. As with most computer and telecommunications technologies, what is emerging today will quite likely be commonplace tomorrow. We encourage you to embrace these emerging technologies and use them to further your research and understanding of whatever topics you choose.

In the situations where we have incorporated geospatial techniques over the last several years, without exception we find that the research is enhanced by the inclusion of the spatial component, and perhaps more importantly the research has been exceptionally well received by both colleagues in the research community as well as decision makers and the public. The visual component of geospatial tools is a powerful means of communication and at a very practical level, location matters.

References

Booth, C. (1903). *Life and labour of the people in London.* London: MacMillan and Company Limited.

Charmaz, K. (2006). *Constructing grounded theory: A practical guide through qualitative analysis.* Thousand Oaks, CA: Sage Publications.

Dear, M. (1988). The postmodern challenge: Reconstructing human geography. *Transactions of the Institute of British Geographers,* New Series, *13*(3), 262–274. Oxford, England: Blackwell Publishing.

Fearon, D . (2001). *Charles Booth: Mapping London's poverty, 1885–1903.* In Center for Spatially Integrated Social Science. (2007). CSISS classics. Santa Barbara. Regents of University of California (accessed on February 2007) http://www.csiss.org/classics/content/45

Foresman, T. W . (Ed.), (1997). *The history of geographic information systems: Perspectives from the pioneers.* Prentice-Hall.

Glaser, B. G., & Strauss, A. L. (1967). *The discovery of grounded theory: Strategies for qualitative research.* Chicago: Aldine Publishing Company.

Goodchild, M. F. (2007). Citizens as sensors: The world of volunteered geography, (accessed on April 22, 2009) http://www.ncgia.ucsb.edu/projects/vgi/docs/position/Goodchild_VGI2007.pdf.

Redwood Coast Connect, Final Report. (2009). (Accessed on April 29) http://redwoodcoastconnect. humboldt.edu/docs/RCC_Report_Final_04282009.pdf.

Rogers, E. M. (2003). *Diffusion of innovations* (5th ed.). New York: The Free Press.

Steinberg, S. J., & Steinberg, S. L. (2006). *GIS for the social sciences: Investigating space and place*. Thousand Oaks, CA: Sage Publications.

Steinberg, S. J., & Steinberg S. L. (2008). *People, place and health: A sociospatial perspective of agricultural workers and their environment*. Institute for Spatial Analysis & California Center for Rural Policy, Humboldt State University, (accessed on June 1) http://hdl.handle. net/2148/428.

Steinberg, S. L., & Steinberg, S. J. (2009). A sociospatial approach to globalization: Mapping ecologies of inequality, In Dasgupta, S. (Ed.), *Understanding the global environment* (pp. 99–117). Delhi: Pearson Longman.

Strauss, A., & Corbin, J. (1998). *Basics of qualitative research* (2nd ed.). Thousand Oaks, CA: Sage Publications.

> Chapter 26

Methods, Examples, and Pitfalls in the Exploitation of the Geospatial Web

Ross S. Purves

Introduction

The Web has become a ubiquitous part of the lives of many in the developed world. Although it is important to realize that major inequities continue to exist in terms of both access and ability to use the Web and associated tools, its pervasiveness can no longer be ignored. If we wish to book an airplane ticket, find out when the next bus arrives, locate a local pizza parlor, or apply for a visa-waiver[1] for entry into the United States, the Web is, in many cases, the first and sometimes the only means of completing the transaction.

Much of the information on the Web has a geographic component; it is somehow related to a location and the relevance of individual pages to a user's need may vary according to their current location. In the recent past, the rise of enabling technologies, such as Google Maps, has transformed the use of geographic data on the Web, with so-called *mash-ups*[2] (Butler, 2006) of a wide variety of information becoming easy to produce using relatively simple technologies. Furthermore, the ease of publicizing and exploiting a wide variety of information about our day-to-day lives and experiences through the Web has resulted in an increase in the diversity of Web content, ranging from government records to so-called *blogs* recording individual experiences. Through services such as Twitter and TwitPic, it is now possible for individuals to post information and images in real time, with such a service becoming a source for breaking news stories.[3] Within academic research, the term *Geospatial Web* has become a catchphrase, applied across research from highly technical domains seeking to develop complex standards for mapping technologies to research exploring the use of *vernacular* place names (e.g., Scharl & Tochtermann, 2007). This chapter will set out to elucidate the nature of the Geospatial Web by exploring some examples relevant to researchers in the social sciences, and discussing the data, methods, and importantly pitfalls that we must be aware of in exploiting it for research.

Like many zeitgeists, the definition of the Geospatial Web is vague and has morphed through time. However, for the purposes of this chapter, we will set out to define it by simply considering the Geospatial Web as the collection of data and services that allow us to collect, portray, manipulate, and analyze data with some form of geographic content from the broader Web. In other words, the Geospatial Web is simply treated as any part of the Web that is somehow related to geography. In the following case studies, the nature and the potential of exploiting the Geospatial Web, particularly with respect to social sciences, is illustrated.

Case Study 1: Where's Downtown?

Almost all of the time, human beings qualitatively communicate about places among one another without resorting to formal referencing systems. Thus, we are likely to describe a bar where we wish to meet as being "across the road from the supermarket, near the railway station" rather than give a set of coordinates. We almost always deal successfully with ambiguity in place names and use natural language to describe locations and routes to one another. We discuss going Downtown, and know that we mean travelling to a particular region of a city or talk about the Alps and expect the listener to picture the ice and snow-covered place that is the European Alps. But, where exactly is Downtown and is the city of Zurich in the Alps?

These questions matter because, on the one hand, they help us understand how humans communicate about space and place, and on the other, there is a need to deal with such referents in computers. Thus, for example, if we can say something about *where* Downtown is located, then perhaps we can carry out empirical research about *what* it is that is represented by Downtown. Equally, if we wish to carry out empirical research among Alpine dwellers, where should we go?

Downtown and the Alps are both examples of place names that can be described as *vague regions*, which may be referred to using *vernacular language* (e.g., Montello, Goodchild, Gottsegen, & Fohl, 2003; Jones, Purves, Clough, & Joho, 2008). Vague regions have no formally defined borders, thus differing from administrative regions, such as the United States or the Kanton of Zurich, that have formally defined, crisp borders. They are often referred to by using colloquial language not familiar to those from outside an area, for example, the appellation of "The Loop" for the Downtown area of Chicago.

Traditionally, such regions have been explored by linguists and geographers in their research, using methods such as textual analysis and empirical studies based on questionnaires (e.g., Aitken & Prosser, 1990; Montello et al., 2003). However, the advent of the Geospatial Web has seen an enormous increase in interest in research in this area. Though this research is driven by a need to allow Web search engines and advertisers to allocate services and respond to queries based on vague regions or vernacular names, it also has many academic applications.

Much recent work has focused on establishing the extent of such vague regions. Typical methods use either *georeferenced* information objects such as images, which are *tagged* as belonging to such regions (e.g., Ahern, Naaman, Nair, & Yang, 2007; Grothe & Schaab, 2008; Rattenbury & Naaman, 2009) or identify administrative place names with known locations that co-occur in text with vernacular place names (e.g., Jones, Purves, et al., 2008). Such place names must be identified as such through *geoparsing*, and assigned geographic coordinates by *geocoding* (Densham & Reid, 2003). Both sets

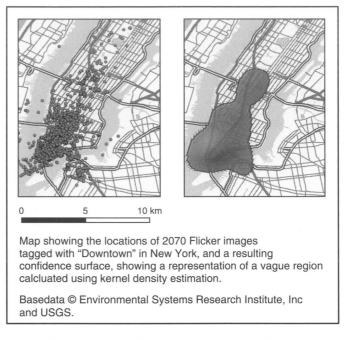

0   5   10 km

Map showing the locations of 2070 Flicker images
tagged with "Downtown" in New York, and a resulting
confidence surface, showing a representation of a vague region
calcluated using kernel density estimation.

Basedata © Environmental Systems Research Institute, Inc
and USGS.

Figure 26.1 Images in Flickr tagged with Downtown in the area of New York City, and a resulting confidence surface representing the vague region of Downtown, New York.

of methods thus result in sets of *points* or *areas*, to which researchers aim to ascribe boundaries, often through defining *confidence surfaces*. Figure 26.1 shows an example of this process for the Downtown area of New York City. Such a representation might then be used within a search engine to define the region desired by users querying for "Downtown pizza parlors" in New York, or as the region for carrying out empirical research on the views of residents and workers within the Downtown area of New York city.

Case Study 2: Analyzing Query Logs

Users' interactions with Web services, such as typical commercial search engines, are an extraordinarily rich data source, recording information about what, when, and how people search for information. Unsurprisingly, search engine query logs are a jealously guarded resource, primarily for reasons of commercial advantage, but also because of important privacy concerns. Query logs allow search engines to fine-tune the performance of their system to maintain an edge against competition, and can be compared to, for example, the data collected by supermarkets through loyalty cards on individual shopping habits. However, some data sources of this nature are in the public domain or are made available through licensing agreements between academic conferences and workshops and individual search engine companies.

A commercial search engine company has illustrated how its query logs can be used to provide early warnings of potential influenza epidemics more rapidly than official methods by counting queries related to influenza and its remedies, as well as mapping the locations from which these queries were made (Ginsberg et al., 2009). The work demonstrated that through such relatively simple methods, it was possible to accurately estimate influenza activity within the United States with a lag of about 1 day, in comparison to the 1–2-week lag in data produced through traditional data sources, which is usually based on reported visits to clinicians. This research suggests an important link between search engine queries and, in this case, health, which one might expect would be mirrored in other areas. For example, the level of public interest in individual political themes may be linked to other search queries.

Other researchers have investigated how users search for information by exploring how queries are spatially specified or refined when search results are initially unsatisfactory. Thus, a user may add a place name to search for pizza parlors, and refine this place name when the original search results contain either too few or too many relevant documents (Jones, Zhang, Rey, Jhala, & Stipp, 2008). Such research provides insights into how people think about space and place, as well as cognitive models of concepts such as nearness, which are key to our understanding of how we interact with the world around us.

It is clear that query logs provide an unrivalled insight into how people search for information, and what sorts of information enthrall large sections of the population on a daily basis. However, query logs can also provide detailed information about individuals and their behavior and, for this reason, ethical issues concerning the exploitation of query logs are a central question that must be considered in any research exploring such data.

Representing Location

Fundamental to the notion of a Geospatial Web is the idea that information can somehow be related to locations. For example, Longley, Goodchild, Maguire, and Rhind (2005) suggest that a fundamental atomic element of geographic information is a triplet consisting of an *attribute*, a *location*, and, potentially, a *time*. Thus, for example, a mountaineer may report that he or she is at the summit of Everest, a courier company may wish to deliver a package to a particular address, and a researcher may seek to describe infant mortality in the United States. It follows, therefore, that these locations may be represented by what humans might conceptualize as *points* (the summit of Everest), *lines* (the route of a delivery truck), and *areas* (a country). Points, lines, and areas are, in fact, the fundamental ways that geography goes about representing *discrete entities* in two dimensions, and closely match with one of the ways in which we typically describe and think about space in everyday life as being made up of hierarchically organized individual objects with relatively distinct borders (Mark, Freksa, Hirtle, Lloyd, & Tversky, 1999). However, properties such as temperature or elevation do not fit this model of discrete entities, since it is clear that they have values that are *continuous* and have no borders. In this model of space, known as a *field*, every location may be represented by a value for a given attribute (Longley et al.). In other words, wherever we are on the Earth's surface, we can report on, for example, temperature, elevation, or population density. Figure 26.1 shows examples of both such discrete entities, the locations of individual photographs represented as points, and a field representing a confidence surface for the vague region named New York. Note that the regions not colored can be considered to be associated with a very low confidence of being in Downtown.

Georeferencing

There are many ways in which we can report on our location, and it is important to understand these, and their implications, in considering how we can extract and explore geospatial information from the Web (Longley et al., 2005). Fundamentally, humans are typically happier describing their locations *qualitatively* through the use of *place names*, while computer representations of location tend to focus on *quantitative* models where discrete entities or fields are located through the use of *coordinate systems*. These coordinate systems are a form of metric georeference, which simplify mapping and calculations, but typically remove the *imprecision*[4] or *vagueness*, which may be inherent in a place name, be it a discrete point, line, or area. *Addresses* are a third method of describing location, which are typically used by humans when they wish to formally communicate a location unambiguously. However, formal addresses are still rarely used in everyday oral language. Typically, computers convert an address to a set of coordinates, which are considered to be very precise, signifying the location of an individual building when metric calculations are required, as in calculating distances in route planning applications.

Closely related to the idea of georeferences is the *granularity* with which a piece of information should be represented. For example, how should the picture in Figure 26.2 be described? Does it represent a typical Swiss scene (and thus Switzerland), a particular valley, or an individual village if we wish to use a place name? If we wish to represent it in a metric system, is the point where the photographer stood, the centre of the village that forms the focus of the scene or the centre of the area visible in the picture appropriate to use as a reference point? Should we consider the place name as an area and, if so, bounded by what? Though these questions are fundamental to our analysis of all geographic information, we will see them become particularly pressing because of some of the assumptions and uses to which we can put the Geospatial Web.

Fundamental resources in converting place names to coordinates and addresses are gazetteers, which are essentially dictionaries of place names that contain the types of features associated with a place name, such as a town, forest or river, and coordinates associated with those place names, typically in the form of points (Hill, 2006). Converting between place names, addresses, and coordinates is a basic task when working with data from the Geospatial Web. This will be discussed in more detail in the section entitled Geoparsing and Geocoding of Unstructured Data.

Geographic Scope

Typically, Web resources can be considered to have some *geographic scope*. Geographic scope was defined by Ding, Gravano, and Shivakumar (2000, p. 3) as "*the geographic area that the creator of a Web resource intends to reach*." Of course, such a concept is subjective and may vary with time and according to particular events. In an attempt to more completely describe the components that contribute to geographic scope, Wang, Xie, Wang, Lu, and Ma (2005) defined a triplet of *provider location*, *content location*, and

Figure 26.2 Does this picture represent Switzerland, the Engadine (a valley in Switzerland) or the village of Sent?

serving location. Provider location is the actual location of the owner of a Web resource. For example, in the case of a holiday company, the provider location may be the address of the holiday company. Content location is the area described by the resource. For example, a holiday company Web resource may advertise holidays in Paris, France, which is the area described in the advertisement. Finally, serving location describes the location of the audience of the Web resource. For instance, a holiday company advertising holidays in Paris, France may target prospective customers from the United States in order to garner sales abroad. The United States, in this case, is the serving location. Ding et al. and Wang et al. were primarily interested in these ideas in order to optimize the provision of Web resources through technologies such as location-based services and local advertising relevant to users. However, these concepts also have immediate relevance for research, which we can explore through the image shown in Figure 26.2. Here, the provider location is Zurich, since the "owner" of the image, that is to say the person who took the picture, lives there. The content location is the village of Sent in the Engadine Valley in Switzerland, and the serving location(s) are the British relatives of the owner who view the image. If the image is also described by text or a set of *tags*, we might be interested in investigating whether other resources describing Switzerland (e.g., with content locations in Switzerland) are more similar if the serving locations are also similar. In other words, do people characterize a place according to where it is, or to whom they wish to describe it?

Geospatial Data on the Web

In order to undertake any research based on the Geospatial Web, it is important to understand the nature of geographic information available on the Web. The nature of such information can be described in a number of ways, through discriminating between different representations of location and geographic scope, as well as structured and unstructured, authoritative and volunteered, and static and dynamic data. In the following section, we use these headings to introduce a tentative taxonomy of geospatial data on the Web and to illustrate both the nature of, and differences between, different sources of data before discussing how such data can be exploited.

Structured and Unstructured Data

Humans are readily able to identify information related to particular concepts in unstructured text. For example, if presented with a page of text, we can easily identify all the place names contained therein if the page is in a language with which we are familiar. By contrast, computationally identifying place names from such unstructured text is a nontrivial problem that will be discussed later. Until recently, Web pages contained very limited structural information, usually a few metadata fields used in indexing data and stylistic information related to the rendering of text on screen, such as title or section headings. However, as the recognition of the importance of semantics related to Web information has increased through the notion of the *Semantic Web* (Berners-Lee, Hendler, & Lassila, 2001), increasingly structured metadata tags have also been associated with data on the Web. One of the most common types of structured information relates to location. For example, Wikipedia introduced tags representing information related to location in the form of place name hierarchies and coordinate geometries. The distinction between these types of content is, in practice, often blurred since many Web pages contain both unstructured data, including references to place names and some form of metadata referring to location. However, the difference is important, since structured metadata information about location is often explicit and implicitly trusted, whereas in unstructured text, locational information must be inferred.

Authoritative and Volunteered Data Sources

Until relatively recently, the collection, production, delivery, and analysis of spatial data were predominantly the preserve of professionals, mostly national mapping agencies and academics with qualifications from the geosciences. Data produced by such groups have been considered, especially by the producers, to be authoritative, in what was seen by social scientists as a major weakness of the emerging field of Geographic Information Science (GIS) in the 1990s (e.g., Pickles, 1995). Thus, for example, national mapping agencies produced gazetteers in which regions were assigned crisp borders and place names did not necessarily equate with local usage. The most extreme examples of such practices are perhaps those of colonial empires, which are arbitrarily reassigned borders and ignored local appellations. However, it is important to realize that place names are often contested and dynamic, and that typical spatial datasets are ill-suited to deal with such issues. Associated with such "authoritative" spatial data were typically metadata, which described the quality and thus the *fitness for use* of data for a particular purpose. Standard[5] metadata fields included *positional accuracy* (e.g., how exactly are a property's borders recorded?), *attribute accuracy* (e.g., how often is a house misclassified as a factory?), *logical consistency* (e.g., can houses be found in lakes?), *completeness* (is every house recorded?), and *lineage* (who produced these data, for what purpose, and when?) (Veregin, 1999, p. 184). Equipped with such metadata, a user can decide if a particular task can sensibly be carried out with a particular dataset and how suitable datasets are for combination, when they have differing lineage and accuracy. In practice, the use and production of spatial metadata has remained the preserve of the specialist. Many examples of mash-ups have occurred in which data was inappropriately combined because mapping data was not supported by the underlying data accuracy. For instance, a right-wing British political party's membership list was leaked on the Internet in 2008. A mash-up was developed using the postcodes (equivalent to zip codes used in the United States) to map members of the party to point locations within the United Kingdom. However, postcodes actually refer to a number of dwellings, and a point representation thus implies more precision than is actually possible with the given data.[6]

The advent of Web 2.0 has led to a flood of so-called volunteered data (Goodchild, 2007) appearing on the Web. Perhaps the most obvious example is Wikipedia, whose entries are collaboratively created and edited by anyone with the time and inclination to do so. In the world of explicitly spatial data, GeoNames, a place names gazetteer, and OpenStreetMap are two examples of products that directly compete with existing authoritative spatial data and are generated by collaborative efforts. Such data may have major advantages over traditional data sources, since licensing conditions typically allow them to be used for a multitude of purposes on a share and share alike basis. Thus, after a hurricane in Haiti in 2008, OpenStreetMap data was quickly digitized and used to develop a routing service to efficiently channel aid to the region's devastated road network (Zipf, personal communication).

However, volunteered spatial data also encompass a wide range of resources and information objects that differ from traditional spatial data. People write blogs recording what, where, and when they performed an activity, which are rich in qualitative references to location. A multitude of services such as Twitter allow users to rapidly *tweet* about their activities, while mash-ups facilitate the delivery of information from individuals related to their current location. Flickr and other image-sharing Web sites allow users to post not only images and related tags, but also to georeference these images using a variety of means. In almost all of these examples, metadata describing the quality of geospatial information is either implicit or missing, and many mash-ups appear to ignore considerations of data quality.

A third category of geospatial data is volunteered but nominally authoritative information. Thus, for example, many police departments now broadcast quasi real-time dispatch information related to crimes in their local area, displaying these on mapping backdrops to any interested users. The data themselves are typically also available through so-called *feeds*, allowing third parties to mash-up Web services combining these and other datasets in new and unexpected ways.

Static and Dynamic Data Sources

The Web is, by its very nature dynamic, making it seem contradictory to refer to static data sources when discussing geospatial data on the Web. However, the Web takes the form of a continuum, ranging from materials which are intended to form a permanent record of the text of books and newspaper articles to dynamically updated reports of an individual's activities on a minute by minute basis such as those provided by Twitter, which may equally rapidly disappear from the Web. Such dynamic information mechanisms appear to respond very rapidly to ongoing events and have become a source of information mined by newswires for information on developing stories. In turn, such dynamism, and implicit levels of trust, poses difficult questions about accountability and information provision. For example, during an attack on Mumbai in 2008, many people "tweeted" updates to the ongoing events.[7] These Twitter feeds were picked up by news wires and reported, though the identity and actual location of those tweeting is often unknown. Equally, news organizations now typically use the Internet in the form of social networking sites, for instance, as a source for background information about events and people related to those events.

Implications of New Data Sources for Research With the Geospatial Web

The move from structured to unstructured, authoritative to volunteered, and collaborative and static to dynamic geospatial information on the Web brings with it a paradigm shift in the potential for research based on such materials. As we will see shortly, it is now possible to explore how large groups of people *appear* to think about and describe popular events through the traces they leave behind them on the Geospatial Web. People post images, text, and implement a wide variety of other media via the Internet to report on their experiences, which can in many cases, be considered to be *primary sources*, equivalent to written diaries kept in the past. However, unlike written diaries, material on the Web is typically viewable by anyone who finds the information. The extent to which this influences others producing similar materials, and the motivation for producing such materials are important questions that require further investigation if we are to exploit such data. For example, do people describe information so that others can find it or to accurately record their emotions and impressions? In the section entitled Example Analyses, we present examples of the analysis of volunteered data to explore presidential elections in the United States and how people describe landscapes in the United Kingdom.

Basic Methods and Resources for Exploring the Geospatial Web

Exploitation of the Geospatial Web has primarily taken place in three ways to date. Firstly, academics have sought to develop methodologies both to enhance and exploit the Geospatial Web. Research has explored, among other areas, the dynamic provision of basic mapping on the Web, as well as the effective integration of multiple data sources to provide information while minimizing cognitive load, methods implemented to retrieve geographically relevant information from the Web, methods that mine and analyze geographic information from the Web, and the effective visualization of the Geospatial Web.

Secondly, industry in the form of search engine companies, news wires, and a host of other sectors have realized the importance of relevant location information. Thus, companies such as Google, Microsoft, and Yahoo compete to deliver location-aware services that may be used with a minimum of knowledge, while hardware manufacturers such as Apple have implemented location awareness as a basic property of hardware devices such as the iPhone. In turn, such devices and the developments in associated software have led to a flood of new data types associated with locations.

Thirdly, a new community of *neogeographers* has come into being. Neogeography is defined by its adherents as a "new geography" where people "create and use their own maps" (Turner, 2006). Central to the notion of neogeography is that work is carried outside of the traditional domains of cartography and Geographic Information Science (GIS). Interestingly, neogeography itself has become a subject of study within these traditional research domains (e.g., Haklay, Singelton, & Parker, 2008). The notion of neogeography is, above all, important for this chapter in so far as neogeographers are responsible for many of the unusual and unexpected developments on the Geospatial Web.

Together, these three communities have developed methods to generate, collect, portray, manipulate, and analyze data from the Geospatial Web in a wide variety of ways. In this section, we will explore a basic set of methods for research with the Geospatial Web. It is important to realize that contrary to census records or disease statistics, the Geospatial Web is not a single entity under the control of a single community, but rather an amorphous and constantly evolving resource driven by a wide variety of motivations.

Basic Methods

Exploiting the Geospatial Web for research requires, as do other forms of research, a set of basic skills that are developed and applied. Equally important, it requires a critical application of these methods and careful consideration of the potential pitfalls associated with such data, which are further discussed in the section entitled Problems and Promise. Fundamental to any analysis of spatial data is a basic understanding of issues such as spatial autocorrelation, map projections, uncertainty and precision, geometric primitives, and methods for interpolation. These issues form the basis of typical introductory courses in GIS, and are also discussed in a wide range of GIS textbooks. It is strongly recommended that some time should be spent familiarizing oneself with such issues before embarking on research (Burrough & McDonnell, 1998; Longley et al., 2005; O'Sullivan & Unwin, 2003). Here, a selection of standard methods required in working with the Geospatial Web are described before two detailed case studies and are used to illustrate how these methods can be applied.

Collecting Data from the Geospatial Web

One of the strengths of the Geospatial Web is its size and breadth. However, dealing with very large volumes of disparate data is also a significant impediment to research, especially for those from outwith computing science. An important first step in such research is identification of appropriate resources. There are essentially two ways of obtaining data from the Geospatial Web; we can either build a data collection for a specific purpose or access publicly available research or commercial collections, normally after signing some form of license agreement with respect to the use and publication of results related to the collection.

Building data collections is nontrivial, but in specific cases, it can be accomplished in a straightforward manner with some programming experience through APIs (application programming interfaces) provided by service and data providers. These APIs are typically associated with licensing conditions. It is important to ensure that these allow research with and publication of data obtained through them. Examples of services with APIs include *image collections*, such as Flickr (www.flickr.com) and Geograph (www.geograph.org.uk), *social networking sites*, such as Twitter(www.twitter.com) and Facebook(www.facebook.com), *news wires*, such as Reuters (http://spotlight.reuters.com/), *mapping applications*, such as Google Maps (maps.google.com) and OpenStreetMap (www.openstreetmap.org/), and *geographic data*, such as GeoNames (www.geonames.org) and USGS (http://gisdata.usgs.gov/XMLWebServices/). Such APIs can provide opportunities to mine collections and relationships (e.g., Flickr images with particular tags or within a particular geographic area), allow the portrayal of information (e.g., displaying the locations of images from Flickr, after some processing, on OpenStreetMap), or provide other intermediate services (e.g., geocoding of tags in Flickr images using GeoNames).

If the aim is simply to build a snapshot of the Web independent of individual services (e.g., all Web pages mentioning Edinburgh), then the problem is much more complex and involves the development of *Web crawlers*, which may be thematically or geographically constrained (e.g., Davison, 2000; Thelwall, 2002). However, large search engine companies such as Google and Yahoo provide access for research purposes to their indexes thus allowing researchers to access their collections for research, with the obvious limitation that the methods used to crawl and retrieve documents are not transparent (e.g., http://research.google.com/university/search/). Such methods have been used to map Web coverage for a range of different services, and thus explore how complete the Web's reach might be considered to be in the United Kingdom (Pasley, Clough, Purves, & Twaroch, 2008).

Obtaining existing collections of data from the Geospatial Web is obviously a much simpler solution and therefore has much to commend it. However, few collections are freely available to download and, more typically, users are required to sign some form of a license related to data exploitation. Typical examples of existing collections include query logs and thematic collections of documents used in evaluation experiments. Query logs record information about the queries entered by users, sometimes including IP addresses (which can be used to locate users), the query itself, other queries made by the user, the results of the query, and information about clicks, which are the hyperlinks that users entered. Unsurprisingly, such information is closely guarded by search engine companies because of the commercial and ethical concerns involved. Commercially, query logs give information about how users reacted to search engine results, which therefore confer a commercial advantage to companies trying to garner more hits on their Web site. Ethically, query logs contain information about our everyday behavior that we are unlikely to want to share.

In 2006, researchers at the search engine company AOL released a query log containing supposedly anonymous data collected over 3 months, with around 10 million individual queries from some 600,000 individuals. By using a simple process of triangulation to build up a picture of a user from clues in queries, New York Times' journalists quickly identified one of the "anonymous" users.[8] Within days, AOL had apologized and removed the data from the Web. However, these data were quickly mirrored and remain accessible on the Web. Other search engine companies have released query logs, but usually after first stripping out information that may allow triangulation, and under strict conditions relating to the use and publication of data.

The use of query logs in general poses difficult legal and ethical questions. Is it acceptable to use data for research that a company no longer desires to be available, as is the case for the AOL query logs? How can we obtain informed consent for the use of data if the data is, by the very nature of its release to us, anonymous?

A wide variety of collections of other Web resources are available, either publicly or after signing some form of agreement. An example of a collection of Web resources is the Enron Email Dataset (http://www.cs.cmu.edu/~enron/), which consists of an archive of some 500,000 e-mails made public after Enron's collapse. Furthermore, numerous collections have been held for evaluation purposes, available for instance through the TREC (Text Retrieval Conference (e.g., Voorhees & Harman, 2008)) or CLEF (Cross-Language Evaluation Forum (e.g., Peters et al., 2008)) and other collections are available on a commercial basis, such as the archives of individual newspapers.

Geoparsing and Geocoding of Unstructured Data

Perhaps the most fundamental task in dealing with unstructured data is the process of unambiguously identifying place names in text, commonly known as *geoparsing*, and assigning a *geographic footprint* to a place name, which is known as *geocoding*. Furthermore, it may also be appropriate to assign a geographic scope (see the section entitled Geographic Scope) to a resource or a particular part of a text, which somehow combines multiple footprints found in a document. At first glance, this appears to be a trivial task, since humans can very effectively deal with vagueness and ambiguity. Thus, despite there being multiple cities with the name Sydney, more than one of which has an airport, it is still considered a newsworthy event when travelers accidentally end up in Sydney, Canada as opposed to Sydney, Australia (http://news.bbc.co.uk/1/hi/uk/2172858.stm). However, computational methods to resolve this problem are complex, and geoparsing attempts to resolve such dilemmas, typically use a variety of methods before falling back on a default scenario. In fact, geoparsers need not only deal with *geographic ambiguity*, but also the fact that many place names are also used in non-geographic senses. Think, for example, of the author *Jack London*. The challenge in providing an effective geoparser is to identify candidate place names, filter out instances that are not geographic, resolve geographic ambiguity and, finally, assign a set of coordinates to a place name, which is known as geocoding (e.g., McCurley, 2001; Densham & Reid, 2003). Typical approaches rely on methods from the more general class of methods in Named Entity Recognition to identify candidate place names (Mikheev, Moens, & Grover, 1999; Cunningham, 2002). Contextual clues may then be used to identify non-geographic senses of place names. For example, a lexical form, such as <firstName><placeName>, suggests that this instance of a place name is more likely to be a surname (Li, Srihari, Niu, & Li, 2003). Simple hierarchical relationships can help to resolve geographic ambiguity. For instance, an occurrence of Nova Scotia in a text referring to Sydney suggests that the Sydney in question is not in Australia, but rather Canada. Other clues, such as word co-occurrence or distances to place names can also be used in order to reduce ambiguity (Rauch, Bukatin, & Baker, 2003). For example, one might expect the word kangaroo to co-occur more with Sydney, Australia than Sydney, Canada (Overell & Rüger, 2008). In cases where ambiguity cannot be resolved, a default place name is often selected, which is often the place name with the greatest population or the highest position in an administrative hierarchy (e.g., a capital city rather than a small town) (Rauch et al). Having unambiguously identified a place name, a set of coordinates is assigned through looking it up in a gazetteer (Hill, 2006; Purves et al., 2007). Figure 26.3

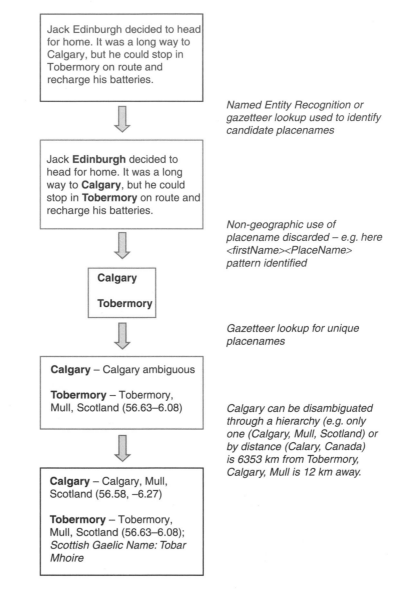

Jack Edinburgh decided to head for home. It was a long way to Calgary, but he could stop in Tobermory on route and recharge his batteries.

Named Entity Recognition or gazetteer lookup used to identify candidate placenames

Jack **Edinburgh** decided to head for home. It was a long way to **Calgary**, but he could stop in **Tobermory** on route and recharge his batteries.

Non-geographic use of placename discarded – e.g. here <firstName><PlaceName> pattern identified

Calgary

Tobermory

Gazetteer lookup for unique placenames

Calgary – Calgary ambiguous

Tobermory – Tobermory, Mull, Scotland (56.63–6.08)

Calgary can be disambiguated through a hierarchy (e.g. only one (Calgary, Mull, Scotland) or by distance (Calary, Canada) is 6353 km from Tobermory, Calgary, Mull is 12 km away.

Calgary – Calgary, Mull, Scotland (56.58, –6.27)

Tobermory – Tobermory, Mull, Scotland (56.63–6.08); *Scottish Gaelic Name: Tobar Mhoire*

Figure 26.3 Schematic representation of the geoparsing and geocoding process for a hypothetical text snippet (note that in reality, the process is more complex and that Tobermory is also ambiguous).

shows a schematic representation of the geoparsing and geocoding process for a hypothetical text snippet.

Many gazetteers primarily represent place names through point geometries. However, there are obvious advantages to representing place names more appropriately. For instance, cities could be better represented as areas and rivers as lines (Fu, Jones, & Abdelmoty, 2005). If all geographic features are represented as points, then it is impossible to identify locations that are contained by others. Thus, if both London and the United

Kingdom are represented as points, we cannot derive the relationship that the United Kingdom contains the city of London.

The final step in assigning a geographic scope to an individual Web resource is processing the individual footprints identified to assign one or more geographic footprints related to all or part of a resource. Thus, for example, a document describing Canadian national parks might be assigned an overall geographic scope of Canada, while individual snippets of the documents could be assigned scopes related to the geographic footprint of the national parks. The document scope of the snippet shown in Figure 26.3 might be given either as the bounding box of the island of Mull, or perhaps a bounding box containing Tobermory and Calgary, which would represent only the northern part of the island.

An important research area that has, until recently, only been addressed in a relatively simplistic manner is *reverse geocoding*. In reverse geocoding, for a given geographic footprint, an appropriate name should be assigned. To date, most methods simply assign the place name with the finest granularity contained by or intersecting the footprint. However, in practice the question of describing a location, given its footprint, is clearly related to not only the footprint itself, but to both the context within which the footprint is being applied and the context of an individual user. In turn, assigning place names to a footprint requires considering the context of the user related to the location. One may ask, "How well do they know the area? How often have they visited it? Why do they wish to add a geographic name?" In a promising approach, Naaman, Song, Paepcke, and Garcia-Molina (2006) explored how to add appropriate place names to groups of points representing photographs, and considered issues such as the *popularity* of place names in choosing which was more appropriate.

Basic Text Analysis

When working with unstructured information, the use of Named Entity Recognition techniques, as described in the section entitled Geoparsing and Geocoding of Unstructured Data, provides a means of identifying place names. Named Entity Recognition techniques themselves belong to a more general set of methods for text analysis, which, for example, aim to derive semantics related to unstructured text and vary widely in complexity. Here, we discuss only relatively simple methods of analyzing unstructured text through statistical analysis or *data mining*, which can be surprisingly powerful in analyzing textual content. Such data mining can be carried out using a wide variety of freely available tools, ranging from standard statistical analysis tools such as SPSS, SAS, and R, through the application of information retrieval toolkits to bespoke programmed solutions. The most simple text analysis method is the production of a simple ranked list of the terms[9] found in an individual resource, or collection of resources. By comparing the occurrence of terms between individual resources and the collection, it is possible to draw conclusions about the significance of occurrences of particular terms in particular documents. Typically, unstructured text is first *stemmed* to identify word roots (e.g., climbing; climbs →climb) and, later on, *stop words* (e.g., the, at, then, etc.) are removed before ranking is carried out (Porter, 1980; Croft, Metzler, & Strohman, 2009). If *controlled vocabularies* relevant to a particular domain exist, (i.e., the *Art & Architecture Thesaurus®* (AAT)), it is possible to rank terms from these vocabularies and their occurrence in particular Web resources in order to explore, for instance, the distribution of architectural styles in Web resources with differing geographic scopes. Since such vocabularies often contain information related to relationships between terms, we might also carry out more complex analyses where related terms were used to classify documents according to individual architectural styles.

If we wish to explore the similarities between individual resources, it is necessary to explore how often terms occur in both resources and a collection as a whole. These are a baseline method used in information retrieval, where *term frequency–inverse document frequency* (*tf-idf*) is used to weight the importance of individual terms' contribution in relation to relevance in search. *Term frequency* (*tf*) is simply the number of occurrences of a term in a document that is typically normalized to take account of document length. *Inverse document frequency* (*idf*) is the logarithm of the total number of documents in a collection divided by the number of documents containing a term. The *tf-idf* is then defined as the product of *tf* and *idf*. Thus, a term that commonly occurs in a single document but rarely occurs over the collection as a whole has a high value for *tf-idf*, while a term common in both the collection and a document is less discriminating and thus has a lower weight. If individual resources have been first assigned geographic scopes, it is possible to explore the similarity of descriptions of documents describing different locations through the use of measures, such as cosine similarity, which effectively compare vectors of *tf-idf* term weights (Croft et al., 2009).

A second set of methods used for exploring unstructured text takes advantage of the notion of co-occurrence. Thus, we might expect to find terms such as *unemployment*, *poverty*, and *depression* co-occurring within text more commonly than *unemployment* and *holiday*. The simplest forms of co-occurrence simply search for a pair of adjacent terms, with or without specification of order. It is possible to extend such methods in a logical way by using ordered or unordered windows and *n*-grams, which are sequences of *n*-terms. For example, White House is a bigram because it has two terms.

Finally, in textual analysis of the Geospatial Web, it is important to recall that we are interested in the geographic nature of the relationships we are exploring. This, in turn, requires us to explore not only the statistical significance of aspatial relationships that relate to the whole collection, but also spatial relationships. For example, the Chi-statistic relates observations to some expected level of occurrence. By mapping Chi-statistics for georeferenced information objects, it is possible to explore how occurrence varies with expectation in space and across different levels of spatial aggregation (Wood, Dykes, Slingsby, & Clarke, 2007).

Geographic Analysis of Geocoded Resources

Where unstructured resources have had geographic footprints assigned to them through geoparsing and geocoding or where resources that contain explicit geocoding are available, geographic analysis can be carried out in which either the geometry or attributes or geometry and attributes of Web resources are explored. The attributes of a Web resource may consist of both unstructured data and any structured data related to the resource. Typically, unstructured and structured data take the form of text, and are processed using methods, such as those described above to assign attributes of some measurement scale[10] to an individual footprint. In the case of structured data, they may also include data of known measurement scales with associated semantic information aiding processing.

Typical geographic analysis of Geospatial Web data could commence with geometries related to the data themselves and other data for analysis purposes. As discussed in the

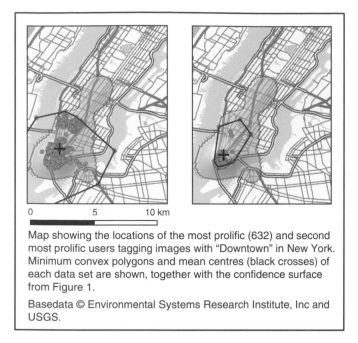

Map showing the locations of the most prolific (632) and second most prolific users tagging images with "Downtown" in New York. Minimum convex polygons and mean centres (black crosses) of each data set are shown, together with the confidence surface from Figure 1.

Basedata © Environmental Systems Research Institute, Inc and USGS.

Figure 26.4 Georeferenced images from the two most prolific users to tag images with Downtown in the New York area, and their mean centers and associated convex hulls—note that the convex hull described by the most prolific user extends along the route of the Staten Island ferry from Manhattan Island.

section entitled Representing Location, geographic footprints are typically represented as discrete entities, such as points, lines, or areas. Operations carried out on these entities can, for example, analyze entities with respect to their attributes. For instance, identifying all images taken by the same user, their geometry (such as finding the *mean centre* of all the images taken by a user), and spatial relationships between groups of geometries (such as finding the *intersection* of the areas containing all images taken by the two most prolific photographers in a data set). Figure 26.4 shows examples of these operations for the data discussed in the case study illustrated in Figure 26.1 describing Downtown New York. Such operations are the bread and butter of typical Geographic Information Systems, and the challenge for researchers is not in carrying out the operations, but in ensuring that the operations relate to meaningful research questions and are appropriate to the nature of the Geospatial Web data on which they are performed.

Example Analyses

In the following section, two example analyses are introduced and discussed. In both examples, methods such as those introduced above are applied and all of the data used were harvested from the Geospatial Web. The first example explores how traces of the

2008 presidential election were left on the Geospatial Web, while the second attempts to develop methods suitable for exploring *basic levels* in language using the Geospatial Web.

Images Tagged With Terms Related to Barack Obama and Voting Patterns in the 2008 Presidential Elections

Motivation

People leave *digital traces* on the Geospatial Web (Girardin, Dal Fiore, Ratti, & Blat, 2008), which may reflect individuals' feelings at particular moments and places in time. We might expect that these can be explored to gain an insight into popular culture at these points in time. Furthermore, events of national significance have different impacts in different regions, and it may also be possible to investigate such variation using the Geospatial Web. In this analysis, georeferenced images tagged with terms such as Barack Obama and Obama[11] in Flickr are analyzed and compared with voting patterns at the state level in the continental United States. The underlying hypothesis is that one might expect a positive relationship between visual images related to Barack Obama and votes cast for President Obama in the 2008 presidential elections.

Data and Methods

Georeferenced images were first harvested from Flickr if they included the tag "Obama" or "Barack Obama" irrespective of when they had been posted to the system using Flickr's API.[12] The dataset included all tags used by the photographer for that image and a unique user identifier that allowed images to be clustered by user. A dataset representing the continental United States was also obtained and images found within this area were retained, before the two datasets were plotted together in ESRI's ArcGIS®. A dataset containing data on the absolute number of votes cast for Senators Obama and McCain (the Democratic and Republican election contenders, respectively) by state was downloaded from a Federal Report[13] and the proportion of Democratic votes per state calculated.

Images were then assigned to states by testing for the area within which each point was found, and the number of images per state counted (Figure 26.5), before image counts were normalized as a function of population (Figure 26.6). Correlation coefficients for these normalized counts were calculated against the Democratic proportion of the vote, and finally a *tag cloud* was produced to visualize all terms, except for the terms "Barack" and "Obama," and their proportions associated with georeferenced images tagged with "Obama" and associated terms.

Results

A total of 45,299 georeferenced images with related tags were found in Flickr, 42,033 that lay within the continental United States. Figure 26.6 shows chlropleth maps and cartograms[14] (Gastner & Newman, 2004) of the Democratic share of the vote, raw image counts, and image counts normalized against population. Counts for Washington DC were removed from the cartogram representations, since the large counts associated with this very small area tended to remove much of the remaining variation from the representation.

Raw image counts give a misleading picture of the distribution of images, since large counts are often associated with states with large populations, as is the case for both

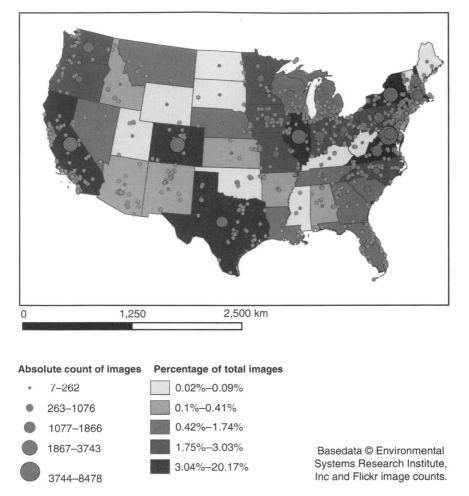

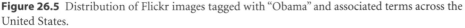

0   1,250   2,500 km

Absolute count of images	Percentage of total images
• 7–262	0.02%–0.09%
• 263–1076	0.1%–0.41%
● 1077–1866	0.42%–1.74%
● 1867–3743	1.75%–3.03%
● 3744–8478	3.04%–20.17%

Basedata © Environmental
Systems Research Institute,
Inc and Flickr image counts.

Figure 26.5 Distribution of Flickr images tagged with "Obama" and associated terms across the United States.

California and Texas. Normalizing for population gives a more representative picture of the distribution of image counts. In the cartograms, area is distorted to represent the variable under investigation. Thus, in the cartogram showing absolute votes for Obama, we can see the relatively larger area of California in proportion to its true area, this is shown in the chloropleth map representing share of the vote, and thus the increased proportion of votes for Obama in this state. Some interesting effects are visible. Populous states such as California and Texas account for many of the images associated with Obama, but when we normalize for the population, we observe the prominence of New Hampshire, which has a potential effect on its importance as the location of the first primary.

Though some correlations appear to be present in the data, it is not possible to state whether Flickr images relating to Obama are related to his share of the vote without carrying out some form of statistical analysis. The Pearson product moment correlation coefficient was calculated, with a null hypothesis being that no relationship exists between votes

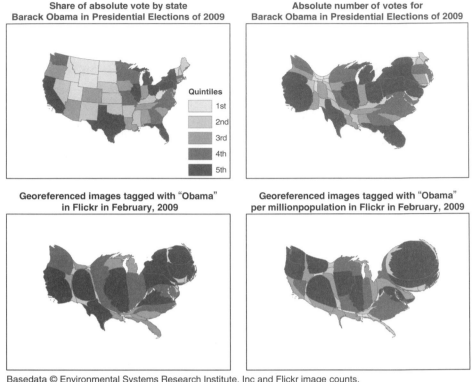

Basedata © Environmental Systems Research Institute, Inc and Flickr image counts.

Figure 26.6 Proportion of Democratic votes and georeferenced images found tagged with "Obama" and related terms, normalized against population, in the lower 48 U.S. states.

and normalized Flickr counts. The value of r was found to be 0.57, which indicates a statistically significant correlation at the $p < 0.01$ level, with a moderate degree of correlation.

On initial inspection of these results, it therefore appears that a weak relationship exists between georeferenced images taken and tagged with terms associated with "Obama" and votes cast. This might simply reflect that more images were taken by those celebrating a successful vote, and suggests that such data somehow relates to national trends. This, in turn, implies that the tag cloud shown in Figure 26.7 reflects terms used by voters for Obama during the 2008 presidential election, and suggests that such analysis may provide a potentially rich source of data for further research.

Exploring Descriptions of Place Through the Geospatial Web[15]

Motivation

The advent of the Geospatial Web and, more particularly, the development of volunteered, unstructured data sources provide a new opportunity to explore how geographically related or located concepts are described. In particular, it has the potential to provide access to very large volumes of data, which might be suitable for use to explore the results of

Figure 26.7 Tag cloud produced from from images shown in Figure 26.5—relative size reflects popularity of tag. Image created using http://www.wordle.net/ and licensed under a Creative Commons Attribution 3.0 United States License (http://creativecommons.org/licenses/by/3.0/us/).

empirical experiments. For example, research in environmental psychology and geography has sought to explore how places are *described* using natural language. One strand of this research has involved eliciting terms from participants in empirical experiments that are used to describe and categorize natural landscapes. Craik (1971) attempted to describe and differentiate between landscapes by recording adjectival qualities used in conjunction with photographic stimuli. Tversky and Hemenway (1983) looked at how environmental scenes were categorized using *basic levels*, which are terms that are informative but not overly specific. For example, *beach* is much more likely to fall into a basic level rather than *coastline* or *sublittoral zone*. Basic levels are typically characterized as being related to more associated concepts than more general super ordinate categories while subordinate categories add a limited number of additional concepts to a characterization (Mark, Smith, & Tversky, 1999). Smith and Mark (1999) used empirical experiments to explore *category norms*, similar to basic levels, for commonly used norms related to geographical concepts. In a number of works, mostly based on American subjects, one of the most striking results was that the most commonly identified geographical category norm was *mountain* (Battig & Montague, 1969; Smith & Mark, 1999, 2001; Van Overschelde, Rawson, & Dunlosky, 2004).

In information science, the Panofsky-Shatford facet matrix (Figure 26.8) was developed to categorize how subjects initially described art works and other objects (Shatford, 1986). This has been laterally applied to analysis of tasks such as requests for images from library collections (Armitage & Enser, 1997). Notably, the matrix considers three levels ("Specific Of," "Generic Of," and "About") and four facets ("Who?," "What?," "Where?," and "When?"), of which the "Where?" facet is of particular relevance to geographical concepts. "Where?/Generic Of" is categorized as a "*Kind of place geographic or architectural*," and commonly occurring terms describing this matrix element might be seen as representing basic levels or category norms. Thus, *mountain* can be seen as a *kind of geographic place*, while *Mount Etna* is an *individually named geographic location*.

Facets	Specific of	Generic of	About
Who?	Individually named persons, animals, things	Kinds of persons, animals, things	Mythical deings, abstraction mainfested or symbolized by objects or' beings
What?	Individually named events	Actions, conditions	Emotions, abstractions mainfested by actions
Where?	Individually named geographic locations	Kind of place geographic or architectural	Places symbolized, abstractions manifest by locale
When?	Linear time; dates or periods	Cyclical time; seasons,time of day	Emotions or aabstraction symbolized by or manifest by time

Figure 26.8 The Pansofsky-Shatford facet matrix.

If the Geospatial Web is a useful source of empirical data, then it ought to be possible to carry out experiments similar to some of those carried out by the researchers above and, for example, identify terms commonly used in describing images of natural landscapes and, furthermore, to explore the concepts associated with such common terms. The Pansofsky-Shatford facet matrix and associated research suggests that information objects and, particularly, images are likely to be described using concepts analogous to *basic levels* or *category norms*. Thus, it may be possible to analyze text associated with information objects from the Geospatial Web to explore such relationships in space.

Data and Methods

In the experiments described, a collection of images and textual descriptions obtained from Geograph (www.geograph.org.uk) was used to explore how geographic concepts were described in Great Britain. Geograph aims to collect "geographically representative" images and associated data for every $1\,km^2$ grid in the United Kingdom and Republic of Ireland. Geograph is a volunteered, *moderated*[16] collection and consists of structured and unstructured data. The structured data include the position of the image, keywords related to the image type, the author of both the image and caption, and the data on which the image was taken. The unstructured data include a title and caption describing the image. An example image and caption are shown in Figure 26.9.

The results reported here are based on an analysis of a snapshot of the Geograph dataset obtained under a Creative Commons license[17] on February 24, 2007, consisting of 346,270 images taken by 3,659 individuals.

Figure 26.9 Typical Geograph image—the associated caption reads: "Gatliff Trust Hostel on Berneray: Picture taken from the beach on Berneray of the historic Gatliff Trust Hostel. Visited in the 1990s, shortly before the causeway linking Berneray to North Uist was built."

To analyze image captions, a locally installed search engine was used to firstly index all image captions and, secondly, rank term occurrence and co-occurrence of terms identified as related to *elements*, *qualities*, and *activities* with basic levels. Since the methods applied here were based on simple term counts, structured vocabularies were required to identify terms that were candidate basic levels or attributes of those basic levels. Candidate basic levels were selected from lists of terms resulting from previous empirical experiments by Battig and Montague (1969) and Van Overschelde et al. (2004) that named "natural earth formations." Lists of terms were also selected from the results of Smith and Mark (1999, 2001) in which participants were asked to suggest terms belonging to categories such as "a kind of geographical feature," "something geographic," etc.

Candidate elements co-occurring with basic levels were identified by extraction of terms likely to relate to the components of a scene (Tversky & Hemenway, 1983) from WordNet (Miller, Beckwith, Fellbaum, Gross, & Miller, 1990). Candidate qualities were based on the adjectival qualities listed in Craik's work (1971) on landscape quality.

Results

Figure 26.10 shows a ranked list of terms obtained from the Geograph data for comparison with three sets of previous empirical work.

In a further comparison, the ranks of the first 10 terms of the Battig and Montague (1969) experiments were compared with the ranks of the same terms in the Geograph data, and a statistically significant ($p < 0.05$) correlation was found. This result, in turn, suggests that the Geograph collection has similar characteristics to previous empirical work, and that further research on co-occurrence is appropriate.

B&M	VanO	S&M	Geograph
Mountain	Mountain	Mountain	Road
Hill	River	River	Hill
Valley	Ocean	Lake	River
River	Volcano	Ocean	Village
Rock	Lake	Hill	Building
Lake	Valley	Country	Park
Canyon	Hill	Sea	Street
Cliff	Rock	City	Valley
Ocean	Canyon	Continent	Field
Cave	Plateau	Valley	Loch
	Tree	Plain	Land
	Plain	Plateau	Town
	Cave	Map	Forest
	Glacier	Road	Map
	Grand Canyon	Island	Sea
	Island	Desert	Woodland
	Stream	Peninsula	Tree
	Cliff	State	Beach
	Desert	Volcano	Country
	Beach	Forest	Glen

Figure 26.10 Ranked list of terms retrieved from experiments on Geograph and previous experimental work (top 10 terms from Battig and Montague (B&M), top 20 from Smith and Mark (S&M), Van Overschelde et al., (vanO)).

Term	Frequency	N
Beach		N = 2824
Sandy	0.26	553
Deserted	0.10	233
Eroded	0.09	288
Soft	0.08	181
Rocky	0.06	756
Warm	0.06	241
Glacial	0.06	290
Low	0.05	2866
Beautiful	0.05	1177
Lovely	0.02	919

Figure 26.11 Top 10 qualities co-occurring with beach.

Figure 26.11 shows the top 10 qualities selected from Craik's list (1971) of adjectives, which co-occur with beach. It appears that beaches are described in a variety of ways through terms related to geological processes (eroded, glacial), geological materials (rocky, sandy), and feeling (soft, beautiful, warm, and lovely).

This case study illustrates the potential for the use of Geospatial Web for complex analysis of unstructured text. It is possible to derive relationships between the attributes of what appear to be basic levels and to further identify candidate basic levels. Furthermore, since the information used is georeferenced, we can explore how the description of such basic levels and their use varies in space. One area where such methods have considerable promise is in the development of ontologies of geographic concepts that can then be used in more general text analysis.

Problems and Promise

In this chapter, the nature of the Geospatial Web has been introduced, along with a variety of potential methods for its analysis. However, these methods are from the perspective of a Geographic Information Scientist familiar with methods used in information retrieval and only scratch at the surface of the possibilities offered by this new data source. In completing the chapter, it is appropriate to explore not only the potential promise of the Geospatial Web, but to illustrate some of the problems afforded by the medium, both to caution researchers against uncritical application of methods and also to suggest potential directions for future research. The inclusion of more qualitative and critical analysis from social scientists familiar with the dangers of over-interpreting data can serve to strengthen research in a rapidly growing area.

When unstructured text is written from a single perspective such as a governmental advisory body, nongovernmental organization (NGO), or an individual publishing house, researchers are typically aware of the potential for bias in the materials produced. As one moves to more structured data such as unemployment statistics, crime figures, or hospital waiting times, critical media reporting typically makes us aware that such data may have been, at best, reinterpreted over time and, at worst, manipulated to present a better picture. However, by the time we reach typical spatial data, such as the borders of countries, the names of cities, or the surface areas of rain forests, most users uncritically apply these data in analysis. However, as was elaborated by Pickles (1995), such data are collected with a perspective in mind, which reflects one consensus at a particular time. In the case of what were termed here as *authoritative sources*, it may be possible through metadata to at least comment on the purpose behind the collection of the data through exploring the data's lineage. Thus, we might know that data on rain forest areas were collected by a local government, which receives subsidies for protecting rain forest, or an NGO concerned about rain forest decline.

However, in the case of *volunteered data* that has been argued to be a powerful data source when exploring qualitative ideas such as place, it quickly becomes apparent that formal metadata do not exist. For example, in the case of consensus materials such as Wikipedia, Geonames, or OpenStreetMap, many of the contributors use pseudonyms to author material. Although we may know when materials were edited, there is typically no way of knowing by whom or for what purpose. Discussion boards related to entries may provide a possible route to exploring the history of individual entries, and thus potentially exploring the motivations and interests of individual contributors. Still, they do not provide structured metadata that are associated with more traditional, authoritative data sources (Goodchild, 2007).

In the case of volunteered data consisting of individual information objects, the problem becomes even more acute. Typically, researchers have assumed that the very large numbers of objects mean that the dangers of bias are small. However, even in such large collections, small numbers of users may contribute to very large amounts of data. Figure 26.12 shows this relationship for the Flickr images used to explore images of Obama in the United States in the Example Analyses above. Here, we can observe in a cumulative histogram that only around 3% of images were contributed by people who tagged a single image, while 50% of images were tagged by users contributing more than 64 images.

Furthermore, individual users can cause the results of textual analysis of such collections to be significantly biased. Very high volume users often have specific interests

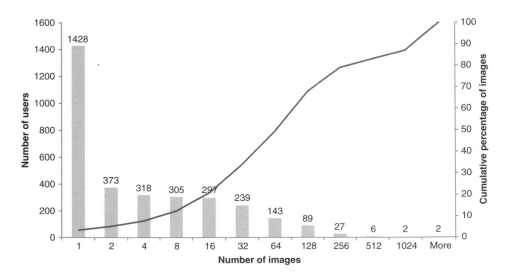

Figure 26.12 User contributions and cumulative histogram of georefenced images tagged with "Obama" and associated tags.

in diverse subjects, such as heritage railroads. They therefore use language that deviates markedly from the norm and, because of their large volume of contributions, associated terms are falsely identified as significant descriptors. It is therefore important to control for both very large contributors in the analysis of volunteered collections and terms frequently used by very small numbers of contributors.

A further problem with volunteered data, and potentially authoritative materials in the future, lies in the danger of circularities in descriptions and the influence of underlying data sources. For example, georeferenced objects uploaded by contributors typically receive coordinates in one of three ways. The coordinates may be directly read from a GPS sensor, in which the coordinates represent the place at which the data was captured. In the case of images, this may lead to bias, since the image captured may represent a place other than its location. This effect is clearly visible in Figure 26.1, where the area of the Downtown New York extends into the water because of the large number of images of the Downtown taken from ferries. Secondly, coordinates may be assigned through automated geoparsing of image tags for place names, which is then subject to the ambiguity as discussed above. Finally, users may assign coordinates through the use of a map interface. Here, if users have not zoomed in to sufficient detail, are unfamiliar with an area, wish to assign large numbers of coordinates quickly, or if the mapping for a region is not sufficiently detailed, then the resulting positions of objects may be both imprecise and inaccurate.

Recently, some organizations have started to use volunteered data to derive neighborhood boundaries for vernacular and other regions. Indeed, this approach was suggested in this chapter. However, if definitions of these regions are derived from volunteered data, then these definitions will most likely bias future volunteered data by incorporating this knowledge into georeferencing systems and thus defining the borders of vernacular regions. This problem of circularity is an important one when dealing with volunteered data which has, to date, received little attention. At what point do contributors cease to describe information based on their local knowledge or perception of an area and start to rely on a consensus derived from the Geospatial Web itself?

A third problem related to the Geospatial Web relates to ethical issues and privacy. As was reported here, New York Times journalists took a very short time to identify a search engine user through triangulation. As we all increasingly leave digital traces through the world, it becomes increasingly straightforward to identify individuals who have knowingly or unknowingly broadcast their locations. Thus, for example, it is possible to observe individuals taking images at particular locations with location-enabled devices such as iPhones, search the Geospatial Web for images taken at the corresponding time and place, and finally identify an individuals' dwelling or workplace by looking for clusters of images taken in one evening or over long periods of time.[18] Research on *obfuscation* focuses on "the means of deliberately degrading the quality of information about an individual's location in order to protect that individual's location privacy" (Duckham & Kulik, 2005). Examples of methods that obfuscate locations include adding imprecise coordinates or timestamps, or storing place names rather than coordinates. However, there is a pressing need for more research to explore whether users understand the permanence of the geospatial traces they leave on the Geospatial Web and to encourage more informed choices about these traces (e.g., Ahern, Eckles, et al., 2007).

A final problem in research related to the Geospatial Web lies in its theoretical underpinnings. In recent years, many articles coming from Information and GIScience have stressed the importance of *place*. However, many of these articles go on to treat places as named locations with shared common definitions. In many ways, this contradicts the qualitative roots of research on notions of place from social science. Though the Geospatial Web is an extraordinarily rich source for data mining, many researchers active in this area, including this author, have a limited background in qualitative methods from the social sciences. There is a pressing need for interdisciplinary research to strengthen the theoretical foundations of research in this area through a shared and constructive dialogue.

This chapter closes with a consideration of the promise of the Geospatial Web. It is clear that enormous volumes of data are being generated and made accessible, and that these data offer social scientists and other researchers with opportunities that previously did not exist. Furthermore, a revolution in the accessibility, affordability, and usability of tools for collecting, portraying, manipulating, and analyzing the Geospatial Web suggests that such data need no longer be the sole preserve of the technically skilled elite. Rather, through interdisciplinary collaboration and well-defined research questions, coupled with a good understanding of the underlying structure of the Geospatial Web, and the potential for problems of bias, exciting new research avenues are starting to emerge. To date, research exploiting the Geospatial Web has mostly been driven by computing scientists, excited by the potential of large volumes of new data to which existing methods can be applied, and to some extent by geographers and particularly Geographic Information Scientists, who see the opportunity to exploit a new source of spatial data. There are, however, few examples of research undertaken with such data from the perspective of social science. Clearly, the opportunity to explore materials such as those described in this chapter presents an unparalleled chance to gain access to a wide variety of materials, and to carry out geographically grounded analyses of such materials. Equally importantly, however, there is an opportunity to study the nature and motivation of contributors to the Geospatial Web itself. Do the Example Analyses presented in this chapter reflect more general patterns and views of the presidential elections in 2008 or how people perceive landscapes in the United Kingdom? Given that the data themselves were not published with research in mind, how can we deal with ethical considerations? If people have voluntarily relinquished anonymity by publishing materials on the Internet, what responsibilities do researchers have to maintain anonymity? Furthermore, comparative studies might consider differences in the use of the Internet between differing cultures, countries, and political systems. To what extent do political controls vary in the world view of those using the Internet and, in turn, influence what is contributed?

Acknowledgments

Although I am responsible for all errors in this chapter, much of the work has relied on the help of others. Livia Hollenstein prepared data for the Flickr analyses and Alistair Edwardes worked on the Geograph analysis. Together with Alistair Edwardes, Jo Wood, and Jason Dykes, I have had numerous fruitful discussions on the nature of the Geospatial Web. Ralph Straumann provided inputs to some early drafts and Sara Fabrikant provided some cartographic feedback. Some of the research reported in this chapter is part of the project TRIPOD supported by the European Commission under contract 045335. I would also like to gratefully acknowledge contributors to Geograph British Isles, see http://www. geograph.org.uk/credits/2007–02–24, whose work is made available under the following Creative Commons Attribution-ShareAlike 2.5 License (http://creativecommons.org/ licenses/by-sa/2.5/).

Notes

1. Visa-waivers are used by travellers from many countries to enter the United States without need for a Visa. Since early 2009, the only way to apply for a visa-waiver is through the Web.

2. Mash-ups chain together data and services from different sources to provide new ways of exploring and visualizing data on the internet.

3. http://www.bbc.co.uk/blogs/technology/2009/01/twitter_and_a_classic_picture.html

4. Imprecision implies that a location is reported to a level that may not allow us to locate it (e.g., locating a car as being in Switzerland) while vagueness suggests that the location itself has no definite borders (e.g., the south of France).

5. These metadata fields are based on the so-called famous five, introduced by the Spatial Data Transfer Standard in the United States.

6. http://www.guardian.co.uk/media/pda/2008/nov/19/politics-hacking

7. http://www.bbc.co.uk/blogs/theeditors/2008/12/theres_been_discussion_see_eg.html

8. http://www.nytimes.com/2006/08/09/technology/09aol.html?ex=1312776000&en=996f61c9 46da4d34&ei=5088&partner=rssnyt&emc=rss

9. A *term* is typically a word, but may also be a set of closely related words, for example, "United Kingdom."

10. Nominal (e.g., weather: rainy, sunny, cloudy, etc.); ordinal (e.g., income: low, medium, high); interval (e.g., temperature: 0°C); ratio (e.g., distance from city centroid: 13 km)

11. Barack Obama was the winning Democratic candidate in the 2008 U.S. presidential elections

12. An API is an application programming interface, which, subject to agreement with terms and conditions, allows third parties to access Web data through bespoke computer programmes.

13. http://www.fec.gov/pubrec/fe2008/2008presgeresults.pdf

14. In continuous cartograms as used here, area is distorted to represent the value of a variable associated with a polygon.

15. This case study is based on work reported in Edwardes and Purves(2007).

16. A moderator checks that content is relevant to the collection and approves it for use—in the case of Geograph, this means that images should be geographically representative (thus a picture of a railway station is likely to be approved, while a family snapshot rejected).

17. A variety of types of Creative Commons licenses are available—in this case the license was share-alike (meaning that the results of the work should be available under the same licensing) and attributive (meaning that all those who produced images should be acknowledged).

18. http://www.wired.com/gadgets/wireless/magazine/17–02/lp_guineapig

References

Ahern, S., Eckles, D., Good, N. S., King, S., Naaman, M., & Nair, R. (2007). Over-exposed?: Privacy patterns and considerations in online and mobile photo sharing. In *Proceedings of the SIGCHI conference on Human factors in computing systems* (pp. 357–366). San Jose, CA: ACM New York, doi: 10.1145/1240624.1240683.

Ahern, S., Naaman, M., Nair, R., & Yang, J. H. I. (2007). World explorer: Visualizing aggregate data from unstructured text in geo-referenced collections. In *Proceedings of the 7th ACM/IEEE-CS Joint Conference on Digital Libraries* (pp. 1–10). ACM New York.

Aitken, S. C., & Prosser, R. (1990). Residents'spatial knowledge of neighborhood continuity and form. *Geographical Analysis, 22*(4), 301–325.

Armitage, L. H., & Enser, P. G. B. (1997). Analysis of user need in image archives. *Journal of Information Science, 23*(4), 287.

Battig, W. F., & Montague, W. E. (1969). Category norms for verbal items in 56 categories: A replication and extension of the Connecticut category norms.

Berners-Lee, T. B., Hendler, J., & Lassila, O. (2001). The semantic Web. *Scientific American, 284*(5), 34–43.

Burrough, P. A., & McDonnell, R. (1998). *Principles of geographical information systems* (2nd ed.). Oxford: Oxford University Press.

Butler, D. (2006). Mashups mix data into global service. *Nature, 439*(7072), 6–7.

Craik, K. H. (1971). Appraising the objectivity of landscape dimensions. In Krutila, J. V. (Ed.), *Natural environments: Studies in theoretical and applied analysis* (pp. 292–346).Baltimore: John-Hopkins University Press.

Croft, W. B., Metzler, D., & Strohman, T. (2009). *Pearson—search engines: Information retrieval in practice.* Boston: Addison-Wesley. Retrieved on March 20, from http://www.pearsonhighered.com/educator/academic/product/0,3110,0136077846,00.html.

Cunningham, H. (2002). GATE, a general architecture for text engineering. *Computers and the Humanities, 36*(2), 223–254.

Davison, B. D. (2000). Topical locality in the Web. In *Proceedings of the 23rd Annual International ACM SIGIR Conference on Research and Development in Information Retrieval* (pp. 272–279). Athens, Greece: ACM New York, doi: 10.1145/345508.345597.

Densham, I., & Reid, J. (2003). A geo-coding service encompassing a geo-parsing tool and integrated digital gazetteer service. In *Proceedings of the Workshop on the Analysis of Geographic References held at HLT/NAACL.* Edmonton, Alberta.

Ding, J., Gravano, L., & Shivakumar, N. (2000). Computing geographical scopes of Web resources. In *Proceedings of the 26th International Conference on Very Large Data Bases* (pp. 545–556). San Francisco: Morgan Kaufmann Publishers Inc.

Duckham, M., & Kulik, L. (2005). A formal model of obfuscation and negotiation for location privacy. In *Proceedings of PERVASIVE 2005* (pp. 152–170). Springer.

Dykes, J., Purves, R., Edwardes, A., & Wood, J. (2008). Exploring volunteered geographic information to describe place: Visualization of the "Geograph British Isles" collection. In *Proceedings of GIS Research UK* (pp. 256–267). Manchester.

Edwardes, A. J., & Purves, R. S. (2007). A theoretical grounding for semantic descriptions of place. In *Lecture Notes in Computer Science* (Vol. 4857, p. 106). Springer.

Fu, G., Jones, C. B., & Abdelmoty, A. I. (2005). Building a geographical ontology for intelligent spatial search on the Web. In *Proceedings of IASTED International Conference on Databases and Applications (DBA-2005)* (pp. 167–172). Innsbruck, Austria.

Gastner, M. T., & Newman, M. E. J. (2004). Diffusion-based method for producing density-equalizing maps. *Proceedings of the National Academy of Sciences of the United States of America, 101*(20), 7499–7504, doi: 10.1073/pnas.0400280101.

Ginsberg, J., Mohebbi, M. H., Patel, R. S., Brammer, L., Smolinski, M. S., & Brilliant, L. (2009). Detecting influenza epidemics using search engine query data. *Nature, 457*(7232), 1012–1014, doi: 10.1038/nature07634.

Girardin, F., Dal Fiore, F., Ratti, C., & Blat, J. (2008). Leveraging explicitly disclosed location information to understand tourist dynamics: A case study. *Journal of Location Based Services, 2*(1), 41–56.

Goodchild, M. F. (2007). Citizens as sensors: The world of volunteered geography. *GeoJournal*, *69*(4), 211–221.

Grothe, C., & Schaab, J. (2008). An evaluation of kernel density estimation and support vector machines for automated generation of footprints for imprecise regions from geotags. In *International Workshop on Computational Models of Place (PLACE'08)* (pp. 15–28). Department of Geomatics, The University of Melbourne, Australia. Retrieved from http://repository.unimelb.edu.au/10187/2466.

Haklay, M., Singleton, A., & Parker, C. (2008). Web mapping 2.0: The neogeography of the geoweb. *Geography Compass*, *2*(6), 2011–2039.

Hill, L. L. (2006). Georeferencing: The geographic associations of information. Cambridge, MA: MIT Press.

Jones, C. B., Purves, R. S., Clough, P. D., & Joho, H. (2008). Modelling vague places with knowledge from the Web. *International Journal of Geographical Information Science*, *22*(10), 1045–1065.

Jones, R., Zhang, W., Rey, B., Jhala, P., & Stipp, E. (2008). Geographic intention and modification in Web search. *International Journal of Geographical Information Science*, *22*(3), 229–246.

Li, H., Srihari, R. K., Niu, C., & Li, W. (2003). InfoXtract location normalization: A hybrid approach to geographic references in information extraction. In *Proceedings of the HLT-NAACL 2003 Workshop on Analysis of Geographic References* (Vol. 1, pp. 39–44). Edmonton, Alberta: Association for Computational Linguistics. Retrieved on March 20, 2009, from http://portal.acm.org/citation.cfm?id=1119400.

Longley, P., Goodchild, M. F., Maguire, D. J., & Rhind, D. W. (2005). *Geographic information systems and science* (2nd ed.). Chichester: Wiley.

Mark, D. M., Freksa, C., Hirtle, S. C., Lloyd, R., & Tversky, B. (1999). Cognitive models of geographical space. *International Journal of Geographical Information Science*, *13*(8), 747–774.

Mark, D. M., Smith, B., & Tversky, B. (1999). Ontology and geographic objects: An empirical study of cognitive categorization. In *Spatial Information Theory: Cognitive and Computational Foundations of Geographic Information Science: International Conference COSIT'99, Stade, Germany, August 25–29, 1999: Proceedings* (p. 283). Springer.

McCurley, K. S. (2001). Geospatial mapping and navigation of the Web. In *Proceedings of the 10th International Conference on World Wide Web* (pp. 221–229). Hong Kong: ACM New York, doi: 10.1145/371920.372056.

Mikheev, A., Moens, M., & Grover, C. (1999). Named Entity Recognition without gazetteers. In *Proceedings of the Ninth Conference on European Chapter of the Association for Computational Linguistics* (pp. 1–8). Bergen, Norway: Association for Computational Linguistics. Retrieved on March 19, 2009, from http://portal.acm.org/citation.cfm?id=977037&dl=.

Miller, G. A., Beckwith, R., Fellbaum, C., Gross, D., & Miller, K. J. (1990). Introduction to wordnet: An on-line lexical database. *International Journal of Lexicography*, *3*(4), 235–244.

Montello, D. R., Goodchild, M. F., Gottsegen, J., & Fohl, P. (2003). Where's Downtown?: Behavioral methods for determining referents of vague spatial queries. *Spatial Cognition and Computation*, *3*(2&3), 185–204.

Naaman, M., Song, Y. J., Paepcke, A., & Garcia-Molina, H. (2006). Assigning textual names to sets of geographic coordinates. *Computers, Environment and Urban Systems*, *30*(4), 418–435.

O'Sullivan, D., & Unwin, D. J. (2003). *Geographic information analysis*. Hoboken, NJ: Wiley.

Overell, S., & Rüger, S. (2008). Using co-occurrence models for placename disambiguation. *International Journal of Geographical Information Science*, *22*(3), 265–287.

Pasley, R., Clough, P., Purves, R. S., & Twaroch, F. A. (2008). Mapping geographic coverage of the Web. In *Proceedings of the 16th ACM SIGSPATIAL International Conference on Advances in Geographic Information Systems* (pp. 1–9). Irvine, CA: ACM New York, doi: 10.1145/1463434.1463459.

Peters, C., Jijkoun, V., Mandl, T., Müller, H., Oard, D., Peñas, A., et al. (Eds.). (2008). *Advances in Multilingual and Multimodal Information Retrieval*. Lecture Notes in Computer Science (Vol. 5152). Berlin: Springer. Retrieved on March 19, 2009, from http://dx.doi.org/10.1007/978–3–540–85760–0.

Pickles, J. (Ed.). (1995). *Ground truth: The social implications of geographic information systems*. New York: The Guilford Press.

Porter, M. F. (1980). An algorithm for suffix stripping. *Program, 14*(3), 130–137.

Purves, R. S., Clough, P., Jones, C. B., Arampatzis, A., Bucher, B., Finch, D., et al. (2007). The design and implementation of SPIRIT: A spatially aware search engine for information retrieval on the Internet. *International Journal of Geographical Information Science, 21*, 717–745.

Rattenbury, T., & Naaman, M. (2009). Methods for extracting place semantics from Flickr tags. *ACM Transactions on the Web, 3*(1).

Rauch, E., Bukatin, M., & Baker, K. (2003). A confidence-based framework for disambiguating geographic terms. In *Proceedings of the HLT-NAACL 2003 Workshop on Analysis of Geographic References* (pp. 50–54). Association for Computational Linguistics. Retrieved on March 20, 2009, from http://portal.acm.org/citation.cfm?doid=1119394.1119402.

Scharl, A., & Tochtermann, K. (Eds.). (2007). The geospatial Web: How geobrowsers, social software and the Web 2.0 are shaping the network society. Secaucus, NJ: Springer-Verlag.

Shatford, S. (1986). Analyzing the subject of a picture: A theoretical approach. *Cataloging & Classification Quarterly, 6*(3), 39–62.

Smith, B., & Mark, D. (1999). Ontology with human subjects testing: An empirical investigation of geographic categories. *American Journal of Economics and Sociology, 58*(2), 245–272.

Smith, B., & Mark, D. M. (2001). Geographical categories: An ontological investigation. *International Journal of Geographical Information Science, 15*(7), 591–612.

Thelwall, M. (2002). Methodologies for crawler based Web surveys. *Internet Research: Electronic Networking Applications and Policy, 12*(2), 124–138.

Turner, A. (2006). *Introduction to neogeography*. Sebastapol, CA: O'Reilly.

Tversky, B., & Hemenway, K. (1983). Categories of environmental scenes. *Cognitive Psychology, 15*(1), 121–149.

Van Overschelde, J. P., Rawson, K. A., & Dunlosky, J. (2004). Category Norms: An updated and expanded version of the Battig and Montague (1969) norms. *Journal of Memory and Language, 50*(3), 47.

Veregin, H. (1999). Data quality parameters. In Longley, P. A., Maguire, D. J., Goodchild, M. F., & Rhind, D. W. (Eds.), *Geographical information systems* (Vols. 1–2, Vol. 1, pp. 177–189).

Voorhees, E., & Harman, D. (2008). TREC experiment and evaluation in information retrieval. *Information Retrieval, 11*(5), 473–475.

Wang, C., Xie, X., Wang, L., Lu, Y., & Ma, W. Y. (2005). Detecting geographic locations from Web resources. In *Proceedings of the 2005 Workshop on Geographic Information Retrieval* (pp. 17–24). Bremen, Germany: ACM New York.

Wood, J., Dykes, J., Slingsby, A., & Clarke, K. (2007). Interactive visual exploration of a large spatio-temporal dataset: Reflections on a geovisualization mashup. *IEEE Transactions on Visualization and Computer Graphics, 13*(6), 1176–1183.

❯ Chapter 27

Living Laboratories: Social Research Applications and Evaluation

Chris Fowler, Lindsay O'Neill, and Joy van Helvert

Introduction

Living Labs in all their different shapes and sizes are becoming more commonplace across the world. Successful trials of such facilities demand a range of differing skills and competences. They need teams that understand both human behavior and cutting-edge technology. Further, many of the products and services assessed in Living Labs are commercial products being assessed for their user acceptance before being launched into the market place. As we will see later, Living Labs therefore are the crucible within which academic and commercial worlds blend and react. This chapter particularly focuses on evaluation methods and issues. An evaluator is defined as an individual who collects and analyzes data about the usability or usefulness of different products or services being used in the Living Lab. The focus of the chapter is, therefore, on the user, what they do, and what they value in their interaction with technology. The testing of the technology per se is not in the remit of "social" evaluation.

The chapter begins (section 2) by offering a number of definitions of Living Labs and settles on one. It then explores issues concerning the choice of data collection methods, particularly how that choice can be influenced by different investigative approaches and theoretical perspectives (section 3). Section 4 drills down further and explores the formulation of the evaluation question. Section 5 sets out to help the reader appreciate a range of different data collection methods and provides descriptions of the different types. To help exemplify the use of the methods and techniques, and the reasoning behind their selection, section 6 provides some case studies that involved the use of the University of Essex's Living Lab or the i-space. Finally, section 7 looks at the more general challenges and issues of carrying out research and evaluation in Living Labs, and suggests some future directions for Living Labs.

Definitions

William Mitchell of MIT's Media Lab is generally acknowledged as the originator of the term "Living Labs." He defined them "...as a research methodology for sensing, prototyping, validating and refining complex solutions in multiple and evolving real-life contexts" (see Niitamo, 2005). In a similar vein, Feurstein and Schumacher (2006) define a core service of any Living Lab as one that facilitates "the co-creation of a product, service or application"; this definition is important for stressing the methodological detail of co-creation or participatory design, as well as noting the importance of innovation and not just research (see also Lasher, Ives, & Jarvenpas, 1991). CoreLabs (2008) extend the concept of Living Labs as "functional regions" where stakeholders have formed a Public-Private-Partnership (PPP) of firms, public agencies, universities, institutes, and people all collaborating for creation, prototyping, validating, and testing new services, products, and systems in real-life contexts. Inherent in the CoreLabs definition is what Ballon, Pierson, and Delaera (2005) call a "test and experimentation platforms" (TEP) approach to testing multiple services and technologies owned by different stakeholders in realistic settings. The approach identifies six TEP types (Prototyping Platform, Test Bed, Field Trial, Living Lab, Market Pilot, and Societal Pilot) and positions each type in a Focus (from testing to design) by Maturity (low to high) space. The Living Lab type is defined as "an experimentation environment in which technology is given shape in real-life contexts and in which (end) users are considered 'co-producers'." It is centrally positioned in the Focus by Maturity space as an Open Innovation Platform (see Eriksson, Niitamo, & Kulkki, 2005) and allows users to be both "co-producers" (a more design-based focus) and, we would argue, co-evaluators (a more test-based focus).

All of the above definitions stress three essential concerns for Living Labs—the *why*, *what*, and *how*. Folstad (2008) asked similar questions when surveying the Living Lab Literature. With respect to the why or purpose of the studies, he reported that two thirds of the 32 papers reviewed shared common purposes related to the Living Labs' contribution to the innovation and development process (context research, discovery, co-creation, evaluation, and technical testing), the Living Lab context (familiar and real world), and the characteristics of Living Lab studies (medium- or long-term and large scale, i.e. number of users). All of Folstad's studies addressed the area of Information and Communication Technologies (ICT) use, and he used a broad definition of ICT to include end-user solutions and network solutions. The context of use was the key to understanding what was studied. For most, it was important that the user was operating in a familiar context: these could be either real or simulated. This could be the difference, for example, between the participants using technology in their actual homes versus temporarily living in a purpose-built flat or "smart" house in a Living Lab study.

The importance of the context should not be underestimated. In particular, care must be taken to note the differences between the domestic (e.g., a Smart Home) and work contexts (e.g., a Smart Office). Organizational or work contexts are usually characterized by more controlling rules and procedures, duties and responsibilities, work flows, and less autonomy and discretion. Policy and practice in this context is normally well documented. In contrast, a domestic environment is much more diverse and flexible. For example, there is considerably more variation in the users' skills and competencies, and there is also limited support and no "quality control." The social rules are more tacit and complex, and often need to be negotiated. However, some researchers, ethnographers in particular, would argue that in the end, the investigator in both cases must observe what actually happens and not rely on descriptions of what should happen (see, e.g., chapters in Denzin & Lincoln, 1998).

On the question of "how" (methods and processes), a common theme in most of the prior definitions is the co-creation process and the way in which it supports innovation. This in part explains the emphasis, in some definitions, on a wider stakeholder representation. However, the term "laboratory" has its roots in a research tradition, and research and innovation processes do not necessarily share the same goals. Innovation processes are more about the creation of new concepts, products, and services, with an emphasis on design and evaluation. In contrast, research processes are concerned with explaining or understanding phenomena, with an emphasis on evidence collection and experimentation. Hence, Folstad came to the bleak conclusion that "future research on Living Labs methods is clearly needed" in order to ameliorate the profound lack of innovative methods that support co-creation.

There are, therefore, a number of different definitions of a "Living Lab." Before methods can be discussed, an operational definition is required. Thus, in the context of this chapter, a "Living Lab" is defined as:

> *An environment that is designed to support innovation through co-creation and evaluation of products and services being used in realistic but familiar contexts.*

This narrow definition is limiting, but provides focus by stressing the innovation process, co-creation, and context.

Choosing Data Collection Methods: Investigative Approaches and Theoretical Perspectives

People collect data to satisfy many different needs or for different purposes. In this respect it is important to understand the difference between research and innovation as an approach to data collection. The chosen approach defines the adoption of a particular data-gathering strategy, which in itself then influences the choice of methods. Innovators, for example, generally ask questions about people's interactions with their products and services. These questions refer to various attributes of the product, such as its usability. A second related factor refers to the theoretical disposition of the researcher or innovator. Many methods were developed to gather data to support a particular theoretical perspective. This does not prevent them from being used for other purposes, but does provide insights into their strengths and weaknesses.

Investigative Approaches

In the definitions section, we made a distinction between innovation and research. Innovation, we argued, emphasized the creation, evaluation, and exploitation of new products and services. It is essentially part of a commercial activity, where assessing the value of products and services (i.e., evaluation) is a key process. In contrast, research forms part of a scholarly activity that collects data or descriptions that helps build and test theories, explanations, or understandings of the world we live in. Research and evaluation, therefore, have different goals, though they share common methods.

Innovators will generate questions based on how people are expected to interact with their products and services. From the users' perspective, products and services have certain defining attributes that are valued and may be evaluated. Sommerville and Dewsbury (2007) adapted Laprie's Dependency model (1995) for domestic systems. The model is based on Batavia and Hammer's seventeen factors (1990) that affect the users' selection of assistive technologies in the home and include Sandhu's acceptability attributes (2002). The four top attributes they identified are "Fitness of purpose," "Trustworthiness," "Acceptability," and "Adaptability."

> "Fitness of purpose" refers to building the right system for the users. What is "right" is normally determined through a user-needs analysis. There is a strong emphasis on identifying the right set of functional requirements.
>
> "Trustworthiness" reflects the users' confidence that the system will deliver without any unforeseen side effects. These side effects could include issues about safety, data privacy and integrity, maintainability, and reliability.
>
> "Acceptability" addresses many of the nonfunctional requirements. For example, is the system usable? Is it well-integrated with other services in the home? Is it aesthetically pleasing? Is it affordable?
>
> "Adaptability" concerns the system adapting to the changing needs of the user over time or context. Inherent in adaptability is the notion of control. Systems should be adaptable but whether they are self-adapting or user adapted may impact acceptability.

Sandstrom and Keijer (2007) adopt a usability engineering approach to product attributes. The central concepts are "Usefulness," "Usability," and "Accessibility." Each of these can be further subdivided. For example, usability can be subdivided into "Physical/Technical Usability" and "Cognitive Usability" and the latter can be further divided into "Ease of use," "easy to understand," and so on. The problem with both the Dependability and Usability approaches is that they do not assign values, so the relative weights of each component cannot be compared. In one context, a user might "trade-off" lack of usability for enhanced functionality (usefulness). Some form of internal cost/benefit analysis usually takes place. More research is required to explore how to assign weights or values to the various product attributes and the impact of such weights on users' behavior (cf. value attribution process—van Helvert & Fowler, 2004).

Furthermore, in most evaluations, more than one product or service is used in the Living Lab. In other words, the emphasis is on the whole system and not necessarily on any subcomponent. This does not prevent evaluation of any particular product or service, but such evaluation takes place in the context of a wider socio-technical system: a situation that makes judgments and evaluations more complex, as they will depend on variations in the context. For example, the acceptability of a photo-display may vary according to what is being displayed (some pictures being more personal or private), where it is displayed (public and private spaces), and on what device it is displayed (e.g., a large TV versus a small picture frame). So, for example, it may be more acceptable to display private or personal images on a small display located in a bedroom rather than on a large display in the living room.

Although the end goal of research is to better understand and explain phenomena while innovation is more concerned with the process of creating new and valued products and services, some important similarities also exist between research and innovation. Both are trying to describe, explore, or explain behaviors, but for quite different reasons. With respect to both research and innovation, it is useful to differentiate between three different types of research strategies: descriptive, explorative, and explanatory (Wright & Fowler, 1980).

Investigators, whether researchers or innovators, adopt a descriptive strategy that is concerned with describing behaviors or contexts while their outputs are often the prerequisite for viable explanations. If we are interested in how technology is changing our everyday lives, then it would be useful to have a description of our everyday behaviors as a baseline for measuring subsequent change. Theories often arise from descriptions, but adopting a descriptive strategy will not help you prove or test a theory. A good description is, therefore, essential for both the research and innovation approaches.

Research from an empirical or positivistic tradition adopts an explanatory strategy that is epitomized by the experiment, where the researcher is concerned with the building and testing of conceptual theories and models (not products and services) through the generation of research hypotheses. Innovation is not directly concerned with theory testing, although it may provide insights into why people behave in certain ways and thus indirectly inform theory development. In natural settings, both the researcher and the innovators mainly rely on naturally occurring interventions. These might be predictable (habitual or routine behaviors) or unpredictable events (unscheduled or emergency induced behaviors). In both cases, behavioral changes would be expected. Such approaches require time to allow for a full and useful set of interventions to occur. This "quasi-experimental" approach (see also section 7) contrasts with the more traditional experimental approach in which the researcher holds some variables constant and manipulates others and measures the impact on a further dependent variable.

The explorative strategy is the most flexible and often contains elements of being both descriptive and explanatory. Investigators adopting an exploratory strategy often are looking for insights rather than explanations. These insights can then lead to a formal experiment being undertaken or more descriptive data being collected. For the innovator, new insights can suggest new products or service opportunities, whereas for the researcher it may suggest new hypotheses to be tested (hypothesis generation rather than hypothesis testing). Innovators choosing an explanatory strategy do so believing that they are confirming predictable outcomes based on some understanding of consumer behavior. In contrast, when choosing explorative strategies, the innovators are unsure of the outcomes, and are thus open to a range of unexpected possibilities.

Choice of strategy is not mutually exclusive. Living Lab investigations could and perhaps should adopt all three strategies. In an ideal world, you would expect investigations in a Living Lab to begin with a baseline description of "normal" behaviors (i.e., how and why people use existing technologies). New technologies could then be evaluated one at a time in the Living Lab, and these should have predictable outcomes (explanatory strategy). In most cases, the complexity of introducing multiple technologies to the same environment with many users cannot be predicted without considerable uncertainty arising (explorative strategy). The emerging behaviors also need to be described, thus forming a new baseline for future investigations (descriptive strategy).

Theoretical Perspectives

A method nearly always has a theoretical heritage. It is designed for a particular purpose but is often later used for other purposes. Although theory has its greatest influence on the interpretation of findings, clearly what and how data is gathered is also critical to the interpretation. Below, some key theories and associated methodologies are discussed, which may give an evaluator greater insight into selecting appropriate methods.

Symbolic interactionism is a perspective that allows for "understanding and explaining human social conduct and group life" (Hewitt, 1984). This perspective has its roots in the philosophy of pragmatism. Symbolic interactionists look at what people say about their motives and the real contexts of interaction in which they form their conduct instead of explaining what people do on the basis of assumptions about their motives. This has the advantage of not assuming that behavior is driven by a single set of meanings and, instead, studies the meanings people construct as they go. It is based on observation of people as they construct their conduct rather than making assumptions about their motivations.

Phenomenological research on the home describes the experience of "being-at-home" as a state of being and not a physical location. Researchers taking this approach look at how people "do" and "feel" at home, not how they "think about" the home. According to Mallett (2004), "As such many explore the 'dynamic processes and transactions' that transform a 'dwelling unit . . . into a home in the context of everyday life'" (Despres, 1991, p. 121). Critiques of this approach, or account of the "home," are that it fails to adequately consider the "social and discursive fields that impinge upon or from experience" (Mallett, 2004). Other criticisms are about the adequacy and accuracy of representations of people's experiences. Feminist critiques often implement this approach, claiming gendered experiences are overlooked or misrepresented. Mallett (2004) also notes that there has been little sustained analysis of methodologies used by phenomenologically inspired researchers in spite of many methods such as in-depth interviewing, ethnography, and episodic ethnography claiming to be legitimate.

Drawing on the social phenomenology of Alfred Schutz, ethnomethodology is a sociological perspective concerned with interaction. Harold Garfinkel introduced the approach in the 1960s, taking the view that objective social order is illusory. Instead, individual social actors "accomplish, manage and produce" (Holstein & Gubrium, 1998, p. 141) a personal sense of order out of a potentially chaotic social milieu (Holstein & Gubrium). The ethnomethodologist aims to expose tacit, everyday processes, and procedures that humans use to create order out of what they encounter. Though it is primarily concerned with the subjective experiences of social actors, there is an emphasis on the analysis of observed behavior; it is not concerned with the process of adjustment taking place within the individual. As Cohen (2000) claims, citing examples from Garfinkel(1967, pp. 268, 267), "he intentionally sets aside . . . the existential experience of thoughts and emotions, thereby leaving actors' private feelings and existential meanings out of the account." One data collection technique used by ethnomethodologists is to temporarily disrupt the "normal" social order in an everyday situation. Observations of the resulting human reactions help reveal what has been taken for granted in the unfolding interaction. Outcomes of such practice aim to describe how people account for and explain the order they experience in their lives.

Interpretative phenomenological analysis (IPA) is a relatively recent qualitative approach specifically developed within psychology. IPA is about understanding lived experience and how participants make sense of their experiences (see Smith & Osborn, 2003). It is concerned with meanings of experiences as interpreted by the individual experiencing it. It is an exploration of the individual's personal perception or account of an event or state and not an attempt to produce an objective record of it. The usefulness of the IPA approach celebrates this subjectivity; while examining the individual's constructed and experienced world, it accepts that this cannot be done directly or completely observed. IPA uses the researcher's own conceptions to make sense of the other world and the participants through interpreting activity. IPA employs qualitative methods and examines these interviews verbatim, pulling out key themes.

The action research approach, with its emphasis on subjects being co-researchers (see Heron, 1996), at first sight looks promising for the Living Lab. In the form of cooperative or collaborative inquiry, participants essentially take part in a reflective process that helps draw out new knowledge or understanding. It is particularly powerful in understanding how communities of practice or organizations operate by drawing up and analyzing different members' experiences or actions. It draws upon the participants' thoughts, images, and stories. The process not only creates knowledge but it also contributes "…directly to the flourishing of human persons, their communities, and the ecosystems of which they are part" (Reason & Bradbury, 2001). The true value of action research may come from research that combines participants with similar experiences from different laboratories rather than focusing on participants from a single Living Lab study.

One final approach that may be of value in the Living Lab context is Dervin's Sense-Making; a phenomenologically grounded methodology originally developed in the field of communications research. It provides a framework for investigation based on 'gaps'; moments when the actors normal process of making sense is interrupted. It suggests the actor moves through time-space, possessing an innate need to "bridge" any gaps that are encountered. Bridging is the act of constructing the best possible sense of a particular phenomenon by drawing on a range of sources, such as past experience, cultural/historical context, personal beliefs, values so on. In the context of the Living Lab, a Sense-Making approach might, for example, allow multiple research participants to experience the environment and the technologies within it. They would then be asked to reflect on their 'gap moments' and any 'bridges' they were able to construct. While each participants experience would be individual, collectively patterns and resonances emerge in 'gap' and 'bridge' descriptions that might usefully inform the innovation and design process (see Dervin, Foreman-Wernet, & Launterbach, 2003).

What the above approaches have in common is that they all rely on qualitative research methods in contrast to quantitative methods that are more associated with the positivistic tradition. Qualitative methods tend to fall into one of four types. First, participant observation, in which the researcher gains insights from being part of the group, society, or observed culture (i.e., observing prisoners' behaviors by pretending to be a prisoner), has a strong anthropological tradition that normally takes place over long time scales. However, its value for Living Labs research is doubtful because the time scales are too short, the groups may be too small, and intimate and unobtrusive observation involves an element of deceit that may not be acceptable. In contrast, the second and third data collection methods, which are direct observation and in-depth interviews, do not involve participation. As we will discuss later, they lend themselves well to Living Lab research. Finally, qualitative research uses sources or materials that have already been created by the participants. These could be diary entries, event logs, etc., which are also important methods for the Living Lab researcher.

One reason to understand the theoretical heritage of many data collection methods is not necessarily to recommend any particular methodology for the Living Lab evaluators. The reason is to highlight that whatever choice is made, it will come with considerable methodological "baggage" that needs to be appreciated if an informed choice is to be made.

Evaluation Claims and Criteria

The overall evaluation approach as determined by theoretical or investigative perspective is important for defining a broad class of methods that could be used. However, the asking of a specific evaluation question is also critical to choosing the right method. In evaluation parlance, such questions are often referred to as "evaluation claims" or "evaluation criteria," and there is a need to understand how such questions are generated.

Evaluation claims can come from many sources. One source is the stakeholders, normally the developers or marketing people, who will make claims about the capabilities and functionalities of their technology, products or services. These can be elicited by structured or semi-structured interviews (see section 5) with the stakeholders. A claim might be "Product X will automatically retrieve, record and make available to the user, in a timely manner, all relevant travel information." The evaluator is not interested in how the product, technically, achieves this end, only that it does, and it does it in a way that is acceptable to the user. The claim will need to be "unpacked." Terms like "automatic" or "timely" need to be operationally defined. It is also necessary to consider specific tasks that the user needs to carry out to fully "test" the claim. In the above example, the user may need to:

Task 1: Enter his daily travel plans (destinations, routes, and timings)
Task 2: Receive planned route at least 15 min before departure time
Task 3: Receive plan route regardless of location (e.g., any room in the house or car)
Task 4: Amend or cancel routes, timings, etc. regardless of location.

In a very structured or formal evaluation (e.g., taking place in a Usability Lab), these tasks effectively become the "experimental instructions." In less formal settings like Living Labs, the tasks are expectations that can themselves be tested. In other words, the result of the evaluation may be that the users never found an occasion to use product X; or if they did use it, a result may be that "most users wanted to receive traffic information whilst in the bathroom, but this location was not available" or even more precisely "the traffic information was spoken, and was often too complex to remember after one hearing."

Another way claims can be generated is through the use of scenarios. van Helvert and Fowler (2004) developed a method for creating and analyzing scenarios for development purposes (Scenario-based User Needs Analysis or SUNA). The scenario describes how the user or users will interact with the proposed product or service, and from these descriptions user needs can be extracted and Use Cases written. A Use Case is defined simply as an actor acting on an object (e.g., user switches on light). Where necessary, contextual information can be added (e.g., "when he or she wants to read"). Use Cases are also an important input for a particular design methodology called Universal Modeling Language (UML—see Fowler, 2000).

The scenarios, therefore, can be analyzed and any claims noted. However, Living labs often involve more than one user and often multiple services and products, and in these cases the scenario or scenarios may not provide enough detailed information. In these circumstances, an "Evaluation Use Cases" approach or template can be used. The template should contain at least three sections: The Goal and definition, the Use Case Description (UCD), and Dependencies. Below is an example of a completed template for a large European-funded project (Box 27.1) (Atraco—http://www.uni-ulm.de/in/atraco).

These rich descriptions are normally provided by the technologist but are essential for the evaluator to understand how the designers envisage their products and services being

---

Box 27.1. *WP7: Evaluation Use Case template*

WP ID: WP7   Author: John Smith   Date: June 1, 2009

1   Goal and Definition

Artifact adaptation: Adapt to specific instances of conceptually identical devices in order to provide a consistent response. For example, adapt to different types of lights (e.g., in different rooms) in order to provide the same light level even if one light might be more powerful than another.

Adapt to different user's perception of a specific artifact (e.g., A/C "cold" might be 17 degrees Celsius for one person, but 20 degrees Celsius for another).

2   Use Case Descriptions (UCD)

1   Inhabitant changes location; that is, goes to a different room with heterogeneous but conceptually identical devices (e.g., different lights). The artifact adaptation adapts the previously constructed "model" for the lighting by creating a new instance of it for the new room and adjusting it to reflect the individual characteristics of the lights present (maybe there are more, or they are less/more powerful…).

2   Device failure; that is, after a device/artifact "fails," a replacement is offered by the Sphere manager (e.g., a new light source or different speaker…). The artifact adaptation adapts the "model" in order to reflect the replacement device, which might be different in terms of its power output, efficiency.…

3   Contextual artifact adaptation; that is, an artifact is adapted because its context has changed. For example, a portable screen's brightness is increased when it is moved from the dimly lit bedroom to the brightly lit living room.

4   A change in occupancy. The "model" of an artifact may be tuned for a specific occupant. The following occupant will start his occupancy with the previous model (is this a privacy issue?), which will then be further adapted toward his personal preferences.

3   Dependencies on other WPs

4.1. Privacy policy issues (WP3)
4.2. Privacy components (WP6)
4.3. Personal preferences/user profiles (WP4)

used. The UCDs can then be used to extract "value claims" or "usability criteria" that need to be met by the product or service. A claim is a positive or negative effect on a given user of some feature of the product or service. For example, in the above UCD example a claim can be elicited that "portable screen's brightness is increased when it is moved from the dimly lit bedroom to the brightly lit living room," and this can be tested in the evaluation trial.

Evaluation criteria are stronger and more precise than claims, and are often used in usability testing. They normally contain a measure of some threshold that must be met or range that must be achieved if the product and service is going to be deemed as usable. For example, a usability criterion may be "that the lights must dim within 1 sec of activation." Criteria usually need further elaboration by providing more information about the context of use—for example, "activation will occur only when user X is detected in the lounge and only after nightfall."

As well as describing the overall evaluation methodology, the evaluator needs to specify the overall purpose of the study, who are the participants, how they will be selected (see section 6), what is to be evaluated, and an appropriate time schedule for the different evaluation activities. These are best presented in an "Evaluation Plan."

Data Collection Methods

There is a vast array of different data collection methods available. Some are strongly associated with particular methodological approaches (e.g., ethnomethodology, grounded theory), while others are classified according to whether they are directly collecting the data (e.g., observation) or indirectly relying on pre or post-event reporting (e.g., an interview or a secondary source). Finally, some data collection methods rely on the user to collect the data (e.g., diaries, blogs, cultural probes) while others depend on automated capture systems (e.g., computer logging) to collect the data.

In terms of data collection within a Living Lab, we need to return to the overall purpose of the investigation (approach and strategy) and the nature of the research question being asked (product or service attribute). With this in mind, most methods can be broadly divided into those where the data collection is in control of the investigator and those where it is collected by the users, such as those in self-reports. Within each class, a number of techniques can be identified:

1. Reflective Techniques. These are data collection techniques that require the users to remember and reflect on past events or behaviors.
    a. Verbal Reports (questionnaires and interviews). Verbal reports are generally "unobtrusive," as they usually take place either before or after the trial.[1] However, they rely on people being able to both remember and verbalize experiences; not all users are able, willing, or good at doing this. Pre- and post-trial questionnaires or interviews are useful for setting up baselines and noting any changes that may result from exposure to the trial. Quite often, they are used to measure change across "softer" variables, such as attitudes, perceptions, or experiences, and are descriptive. In more explorative and explanatory strategies, the pretests can be used to classify users into meaningful

subgroups (e.g., expert versus novice users). Ideally, such "strata" should determine the sampling frame. However, with Living Labs, particularly "Smart Homes," it is often impractical to use a large number of subjects (so the frame is impoverished), as subject recruitment can be problematic (see section 5 for a fuller discussion of these issues). Follow-up or posttrial interviews are commonly used. For Living Lab trials, they are usually "group" sessions[2] and normally take one of two forms. Firstly, there is the "walk-thru" in which the evaluators go through some data (e.g., their diary or an event log), asking the users to elaborate on a particular entry or event. An alternative is to ask the user to reconstruct the experience by providing a narrative of how they perceived their experiences. The evaluator needs to create a set of questions and probes that allow the narrative to unfold in a meaningful way.

b. Diaries are often used to allow participants to record their experiences in their own words. They tend to be reflective and are usually completed once a day or at least once a week. In this respect, they are not dissimilar to participant observation methods. They can be online (blogs) or off-line and written or recorded via audio or visual equipment. The data collected are usually both subjective and qualitative and are good at providing insights into people's feelings about events. Though experiences recorded can become distorted over time (i.e., memory lapses, reinterpretations, etc.), they can complement more direct sources and thus provide multiple views of the same event.

c. Event logs are a way of recording events at the time they happen or at the end of the day that the event occurred. A simple log records the day and time, and the event to be reported. They are particularly useful for recording acceptability, usability, and compatibility and also reliability and safety (trustworthiness) problems.

2. Observational Techniques. These are techniques that directly capture and record the behavior as it happens.

a. Video and audio recordings can be obtrusive, especially in Smart Home environments in which there are privacy issues (e.g., do you put a camera in the bedroom?). Most people adapt to being recorded, with their behaviors returning to their natural way of living in a relatively short period of time (days rather than weeks). Real time, uninterrupted recordings generate a huge amount of data, which takes time and effort to analyze. They provide a permanent and reusable record, allowing the investigator to revisit an event and corroborate evidence collected from other sources. A variation on video is to create a professional or semiprofessional documentary or filmed commentary on the users' reactions and behaviors. Although this can be a rich source of insight, it is still an "interpretation" that is edited and controlled by a film director. Another variation is to only record when a significant event is taking place (context aware experience sampling). For example, it may be possible to combine location-sensing devices with the recording. Therefore, if the investigator is interested in how a particular device is used, then the recording is only made when the user is near the device or switching the device on or off also controls the recording.

b. Data Logs. This includes information gathered by third parties (e.g., telephone usage from a telephone companies records), computers, and other physical devices (e.g., sensing devices). It does not include logs or records created by the participants themselves (see below). Data logging is an excellent method for capturing basic quantitative data about the use of a system such as how often it is used, by whom, for what, and what problems might have occurred (e.g., failed login). Usage logs are particularly powerful for tracking the use of Web sites (server logs). The log files created by the service can be analyzed (log file analysis) and the wealth of usage data extracted.

However, the following data is not normally captured by log files:

- Individuals' identities. A user is an IP address. Unless passwords are used, no data is collected that could reveal the user's identity.
- Number of users. Given that users cannot be identified, an IP address may actually be a computer agent, spider, or an ISP.
- Qualitative data. Log files cannot capture motivations or feelings or other qualitative aspects of use.
- Files not viewed. Log files reflect activity and not inactivity, so there is no information about unused pages, for example.
- Where the user went next. This transaction would be recorded only in the log of the subsequent site visited.

Also, always be careful about the inferences you make. For example, do not infer that the number of "hits" equals "use." Because hits represent exchanges between the client and the server, not all of those hits are initiated by the user.

Logs collected by third parties raise many trust and privacy issues, which must be legally protected. The investigator has no control over how the information was collected. Often, some form of summarization has occurred and key data may be lost. Logs captured by physical devices should also be used with care. For example, a log of where a participant has been and what they have used does not provide a great deal of insights into their motives. Though emotional or health sensors are becoming more popular, they suffer from both validity and reliability problems, as well as being currently rather obtrusive (wearing sensors, etc.).

3. Ethnographic Techniques
    a. Cultural probes (see Gaver, Dunne, & Pacenti, 1999) come from an ethnographic tradition and are very much concerned with capturing "actual" behaviors and people's feelings that happen in real time (rather than verbal reports after the event). Critically, they are user-created (i.e., self-reporting) rather than investigator-generated (e.g., through observation), and are thus less obtrusive and more ideal in domestic or personal situations.

Typical examples are:

- Self-directed photography
- Labeling
- Diaries/note book
- Tape recorders

The above form a typical cultural probe pack where users can "capture" key events using different media to record when they happen.

The use of probes provides designers with insights and clues about the users' behavior, that can then inspire innovative design ideas. This contrasts with the attempt to systemize and structure the process to answer specific questions from which these needs or requirements are derived.

This tension between the ideation and needs generation processes should be considered when making your final choice about how probes should be used.

It should be clear that all the methods and techniques described above can be used to collect data on all the product and service attributes. Depending on only one or even two data collection techniques is not advisable, nor usual, if you wish to build a rich picture of the users' behavior within the Living Lab. The actual choices and the decision behind making the choices should be noted in the Evaluation Plan.

Some Case Studies From the University of Essex's i-Space

This following section provides some case studies to help ground or contextualize the more abstract discussions in the previous section. It begins with a short description of the University of Essex's Living Lab, or i-space, and then describes three different case studies that used the facility.

The Essex's Living Lab is encapsulated by its i-space facility: a facility where new products and services can be explored and evaluated in a highly participative and user-centered way. The i-space is a two-bedroom domestic apartment built from the ground up to support easy experimentation with autonomous and pervasive computing, including hollow walls and a ceiling. Nearly every artifact is networked, including nonelectric artifacts such as chairs. The i-space is equipped with numerous networked appliances and sensors glued together with UPnP and Bonjour middleware. For example, there are location/tracking systems that can trace items to within 1 cm. Other devices include occupancy (at a room and furniture level), appliances (e.g., DVD players that report state), media streaming devices, communications systems, cameras, plasma displays, etc. The result is a setup that will provide a tangible manifestation of autonomous systems in a digital home to focus inter-disciplinary working, as well as provide a longer-term focus for actual experimentation. The i-space can, therefore, be classified as a "Smart Home" or flat.

Most of the techniques mentioned above in section 4 have been used in a number of studies that used the i-space or are related to the i-space. The first trial was an evaluation of a suite of telecommunication products and services. The main aim was to investigate how users perceive and use multiple telephony products in a single home. The product was essentially a Voice Over IP (VOIP) package that could be accessed either from a PC via a "softphone" or via a Digital European Cordless Telecommunications (DECT) or fixed phone. For comparison, there was also a fixed line (via the Public Service Telephony Network or PSTN). The DECT and fixed phones could be configured by the users to use VOIP or PSTN. The two services (VOIP or PSTN) had their own separate telephone numbers and bills.

The sponsoring company had highlighted some particular concerns, and combined with the short stay it was decided to use a scenario combined with a set of tasks and key questions for the participants to consider when undertaking the tasks. The scenario was based around "moving home." The products were already set up, but could be reconfigured to meet the participant's own particular needs. The Task List included retrieving messages from a message service on arrival, making at least two outgoing calls per day using the different handsets provided and receiving incoming calls on both the PSTN and VOIP services. They were asked to pay particular attention to certain service attributes, including audio quality, usability, and reliability. The participants did not have to pay for any calls.

The target participants were families of two or three people visiting students at the University. Six sets of participants were eventually selected and represented a fairly diverse sample (a researcher, a local government officer, a company director, two translators, and an engineer). Each set was briefed with respect to the scenarios, data collection methods, and support.

When participants arrived in the i-space, they were given a Task Sheet describing a fictional context for the evaluation. It asked them to imagine that they had just moved into their new i-space home and to adjust and evaluate the telephony with respect to their everyday living needs. The Task Sheet also contained a list of questions intended to direct participants' attention to some specific aspects of the setup into which the sponsoring telephony company wanted insights.

Alongside the Task Sheet, participants were given blank event log sheets and asked to document each incoming and outgoing call for the duration of their stay. Finally, participants were shown and talked through the Sense-Making technique. The closing interview utilized this technique by enquiring about gap moments, allowing the researcher/interviewer to step back from directing the interview along premeditated paths and encourage the emergence of topics, avenues, and areas of interest generated from the direct experience of the interviewee. This has the potential to reveal previously unexplored angles on the subject matter.

At the end of each session, a semi-structured qualitative group interview was conducted that lasted, on average, 50 min. The interview for Session 1 could not be conducted face-to-face due to inclement weather conditions preventing the evaluator from reaching the i-space. Instead, it was conducted over the telephone and written up from notes. The other three interviews were conducted face-to-face, digitally recorded, and subsequently transcribed into Word documents. All appropriate permissions were gathered. Additionally, completed event log sheets were gathered after each session. Logs from the company's online billing site were also compiled as a supplementary data source. It is important to note that although a potentially rich set of data was gathered, because of the contractual agreement, the time, available for detailed analysis was very limited.

The second trial explored the use of networked picture frames in supporting emotional closeness. The participant was a Chinese visiting fellow who was linked to her husband and child in China through a pair of networked picture frames located in the United Kingdom and China. Other possible scenarios could include linking grandparents to their grandchildren, parents separated from their children because of divorce or gap years abroad, and so on. The frame was used over a period of two weeks.

For the purposes of the study, two "off-the-shelf" networked picture frames were bought to connect two families separated by a large geographic distance. These were the PhotoVu PV1750 Wireless Digital Picture Frame (see http://www.photovu.com/pv1750.html for a full technical specification). These devices are fully compatible with a number of image-storing Web sites such as Flickr, iPhoto, and Google that use RSS feeds to upload and share photos. The devices have a screen size of 17 in. and resemble flat-screen televisions.

Both adult members of the family gave permission for their identities and family situation to be revealed in the report. One member of the family, LS, was undertaking a research project at the University of Essex, and lived in the i-space two-bedroom flat for several months while her husband (XS) and two-year-old son remained in China. In order to achieve a naturalistic context, LS and XS were asked to use their picture frames as and when they wanted to. Due to practical issues involving a delay at Shanghai customs, the second networked picture frame did not arrive until two weeks before the final interview was conducted. LS and XS's opinions and use of the picture frames may therefore be influenced by novelty effects.

LS was asked to keep a Weblog of her use of the picture frame. This included times and dates of when LS looked at or altered it, how she set it up, and how she shared photos with her husband or friends or relatives. It also recorded how she used it with other elements of the digital home, such as straight from a digital camera or from stored photos on the Internet. She was also asked to note any problems with usage, or anything she would like to do with the frame that is not currently possible. The Weblog was then deconstructed to examine patterns of behavior and recurrent themes.

One of the project's aims was to establish, using emotional sensing technologies, whether looking at or using the networked picture frame elicited any kind of emotional response. This seeks to understand the value of the frame from an emotional perspective in the context of everyday life. The emotional sensor is a device worn on the first finger and measures changes in skin resistance. Emotion or arousal increases sweating, which in turn changes the electrical properties of the skin by making it more conductive. After calculating baseline data, it can record a change in emotional response and arousal level of the individual. In this study, there were three possible emotional responses: (1) negative, (2) neutral, and (3) positive. LS used the emotion-sensing device on five separate sessions in which she exclusively used the picture frame (as opposed to looking at it while doing other activities) for 20 min. The device measures electrical impulses every 2 s; there were therefore 600 emotional responses per 20-min sessions.

It was initially intended to keep a system log of the picture frame, to record actual use as opposed to reported use, and examine any discrepancies. However, because one of LS's early choices was to set the picture frame's timer to be on from 8:00 a.m. to 11:00 p.m. (i.e., all the hours she was awake), there was no opportunity to record when the picture frame was switched on or off outside of those hours, and so no records of this event were kept.

Drawing on the Weblog and emotion sensing, LS was given an in-depth semi-structured interview about her use of the networked photo frame and how she incorporated it into her everyday life. This included questions that aligned with project aims and desired insights. Part of the interview was carried out in the presence of LS's husband, XS, about their shared use and experiences of the picture frames. This was achieved via Instant Messenger, with LS translating from Chinese to English.

The emotional sensing tool proved to be disappointing. It was difficult to correlate emotional changes with actual events (e.g., changing of a picture). However, it did confirm an overall positive emotional response. The Weblog was particularly useful because it was completed at the end of a session rather than at the end of the day, allowing the feelings and facts to be fresh in the participant's mind.

The third i-space trial explored how people used different prototype systems for capturing, organizing, displaying, and printing digital pictures. The trial was mainly addressing fitness-for-purpose and acceptability issues. Two types of cameras were used. One was a high-specification digital camera with network capabilities, that allowed images to be directly uploaded to a commercial Internet site, and the other was a mobile phone camera. On entering the i-space, any images on the mobile phone camera were automatically downloaded to a local computer via Bluetooth. These can then be organized and, in due course, be uploaded to the commercial site. The images could be displayed on four devices: a dedicated picture frame, a display on the fridge, the large LCD TV, and a tablet computer (acting as another picture frame). A color printer for local copies was available for use or hard copies could be ordered from the commercial Internet site. The PC Tablet had a prototyped system for organizing the images, sending them to different displays, printing images, and so on.

The sponsors had very clear ideas of the research questions they wanted to be answered. In general, these were concerned with fitness-for-purpose and acceptability, but they were broken down into quite precise questions (e.g., are different types of images captured by the camera and phone? Is auto-image transfer desirable?). In addition, previous work had suggested that there were distinct types of photograph users that fell into one of four personas. These personas were not used to select participants, but a pretrial questionnaire was developed that allowed us to classify the participants into one of the four persona types.[3]

Only three groups of participants were used in the study. The first group was of two sociologists from the University and the second group consisted of four Norwegian researchers attending a project meeting at the University. The third group was a pilot participant who tested the technology and methods in situ before the main participants arrived.

Four methods of data collection were used. One was the aforementioned persona identifier questionnaire. Participants were also asked to complete an event log where they noted major activities (e.g., printing) and any issues or problems they had in achieving the activity. A diary was also used to reflect on their experience more holistically and was usually completed at the end of the day. Data logs from the computers were also used to look particularly at the frequency of different types of interactions with the commercial site (uploading, etc). Finally, after the trial, there was an interview about the overall experience; the events and diaries were used as reminders and as prompts for questions.

The final case study used cultural probes to explore issues and tensions of multiple technology users in the home (e.g., a family accessing the Internet on a single PC, or the use of multiple mobile phones in the home). The researcher was interested in understanding the nature of any conflicts that might arise and the strategies and solutions adopted to resolve any conflicts. This was not undertaken in the i-space but explored the use of technology in the home; however, the techniques adopted could be easily used in a Living Lab. The study used multi-method qualitative data collection to gather information to form a number of case studies that could then be used to inform designers of future housing.

Cultural probes were used to promote thinking about the issues, trying to make the implicit more explicit. The issues could then be fully explored in subsequent interviews. The cultural probes used were:

- **Conflict and control diary**. Participants were asked to keep a record of their activities and the issues raised in their house that they felt were important to include in this diary. Also, they could record time and date, activities, location, other members of the household involved or present, and any notes on the set of prompts. Participants were asked to write their diary entries on the same days, two between Monday and Friday and the third day on Saturday or Sunday. Participants were instructed that, ideally, entries would be added at least every hour although they were told that making diary entries should not interfere with normal activities in the household. The importance of recording the information at the time it occurs, while the memory of the events was clear in their mind, was emphasized.

- **Self-directed photography**. Using Polaroid cameras that would allow instant descriptions and justifications of photos taken, participants were asked to take photographs of activities, locations, objects, people, ideas, events, or technologies that raised issues of particular importance to them in their house. On each photograph, the participants were asked to write their initials, time and date, location, and why they took the photograph and the participants were encouraged to take as many photographs as they felt they would like in order to illustrate the issues. Again, participants were reminded that there were no right or wrong photographs. Participants were also asked to keep photographs taken until the researcher returned, even if they decided not to submit them to the study. This was to get a measure of "discarded" or "inappropriate" photographs. In practice, no photographs were reported as being withheld from the study.

- **Paint-me-a-picture.** Participants were asked to create a picture through words, images, diagrams, or charts that represented their house using any or all of the materials provided. The materials provided included art paper, chalk, pens, writing paper, and Dictaphones. Participants were reminded in the instructions that there were no right or wrong ways to do this and that no two "pictures" would be alike. This was to reduce any uncertainty or participation anxiety concerning "accuracy." Examples were given in the instructions such as pencil sketches of the layout of the house and worded descriptions of the rooms. Also suggested was a collage that represents how they felt about the house with textures representing different aspects, technologies, objects, rooms, or spaces. Another suggestion was to use the provided tape recorder and tour the house describing how they feel, act, influence, and control the layout and activities that go on in the rooms. Participants were asked to use any or all of these methods to "paint me a picture" in words or art that represented their house.

- **Labeling conflicts**. Participants were given labels on string to attach to items/articles/objects/technologies or spaces in rooms that raised issues of particular importance to them in their house. They could also be used to indicate areas or items over which compromises were made. These labels could be tied or looped to objects and so were only temporary alterations to the house. On each label, participants were instructed to write their initials, the time and date, exact location of label—room and space or object—and why they used the label. As with the photographs, participants were instructed to use as many labels as they liked and were reminded that there were no right or wrong answers. Participants were also asked to take a photograph of the area the label was placed if it was to mark a space or activity in order to allow the investigator to understand the situation and context, and to label the photo with the same information.

These cultural probe activities were carried out over the space of a week and then collected. Interviews were then carried out with individuals from the shared households taking part. These interviews were in two parts. The first part was a Sense-Making Interview. This took a specific conflict event and explored how the individual made sense of a given situation and what resources were drawn upon to resolve any conflict. The second part was a more open, semi-structured interview to explore more general issues, as well as some of the issues raised in the cultural probe study.

Concerns, Challenges, and Future Directions

A significant number of Living Labs are only able to evaluate a few subjects at a time and, naturally, concerns are raised about how representative their samples are of the population as a whole. There are at least three ways of ensuring that a sample is a good representation of the population. The first way is size; the closer the sample size is to the population size, the more representative the findings are likely to be. There are techniques that allow you to determine an appropriate sample size according to the population being studied (e.g., Morgan, 2003). The second aspect concerns how the sample was created. It is possible to have a large but biased sample. Most investigators overcome this problem by random sampling from the population so any errors or bias should also be randomly distributed. Alternatively, a stratified sample could be used.[4] Here, certain strata are predefined (e.g., age, sex, socioeconomic class, etc.) and their proportions are determined for a given population. This creates the sampling frame. The strata and proportions are reflected in the sampling frame (e.g., 40% males; 60% females) and once determined, simple random sampling can be used. Of course, stratified sampling assumes that the strata and corresponding population proportions are known if bias is not to be introduced.

The third way is concerned with how the subjects or participants are assigned to conditions. An experiment, for example, will have at least two conditions, a control group, and an experimental group. Usually, the subjects will be randomly assigned to one or other conditions, ensuring that there is no deliberate bias and that the two groups are equivalent. Quasi-experimental designs were created to overcome the problem of not being able to randomly assign subjects in more "natural" experiments. One solution to this problem is to assess both groups before the intervention to ensure that they are equivalent.

For Living Labs, time series is perhaps the most important quasi-experimental design. In its simplest form, the participants act both as a control and experimental group. This is achieved by taking regular measures at fixed time intervals before, during, and after the intervention. The interventions could be naturally occurring and are not necessarily under the control of the investigator. They may also be investigator-induced interventions (e.g., introducing a new piece of technology into the home). In between these extremes, the investigator may try to focus the participants on certain technologies and behaviors, through, for example, the use of active scenarios, specific questions, or given tasks. If the intervention, in whatever form, is responsible for any effect, then there will be a corresponding change in the baseline behaviors. Over time, the behaviors should then return to their baseline level. For example, if we were interested in determining whether using smart energy monitoring devices reduces energy consumption, then we could adopt a time series design. Participants would use the appliances in the Smart Home without a monitoring device. Later on, the monitoring device is introduced and the impact on their behaviors is observed. Any change in energy consumption after the intervention could be attributed to the participants being more energy aware. Its strength lies in the fact that the same subject is measured before and after, so any effects cannot be attributed to inherent differences in the subjects themselves. Gradual change can be attributed to people maturing over time while sudden and short-lived changes in behavior are rarely due to maturity effects.

One potential quasi-experimental approach could result from exploiting the distributed nature of Living Labs. Most of the Labs, falling within our definition, are small and distributed throughout the world, with a particular density in Europe. The essence of the approach would be to view each Living lab as contributing a single set of data (as if they were a "subject" in an experimental design). Referring to the energy monitoring example previously mentioned, what if the same "experiment" was repeated in different labs across Europe and the different sets of data were combined to make a single set? In these circumstances, the results may be more valid and general. In a grander model, each lab could be a distinct "cell" in a design. For example, the UK Lab participants could be selected to represent a particular socioeconomic status and associated lifestyle (e.g., dual income, no children), whereas a lab in France may have participants with a different set of attributes (single income, two children) and so on. While the effect of culture may be a confounding variable, it may be possible to reduce its impact through tight control over the sampling procedures, or even statistically remove the effect from the results (assuming it can be reliably measured). Great care would need to be taken with such designs and they demand a degree of inter-Lab collaboration that may not currently exist.[5]

A further concern associated with sampling has to do with making decisions about the significance of any results. In "real" experiments, researchers can draw upon a whole range of inferential statistics to help them assess the probability that their findings are significant. The most powerful of these are called parametric tests. Unfortunately, these tests come with certain assumptions, one of which has to do with random sampling that most Living Labs have difficulty in meeting. The alternative, nonparametric statistics (see Corder & Foreman, 2009) make fewer assumptions, but can only be applied to data measured on nominal or ordinal (ranked) scales. Both kinds of tests can be used to compare groups or to measure the degree of correlation between variables. However, parametric statistics allow many more sophisticated comparisons (e.g., comparing multiple groups' means) and types of analysis (e.g., multiple regression) and can be applied to more than one dependent variable (multivariate analysis). Even in the case of time series analysis, reasonable inferences demand a lot of data points, though these can be achieved by a few subjects generating a lot of data.

Living Labs also have many challenges in recruiting participants and ensuring that the studies are ethical. Asking participants to give days, weeks, or even months of their time to live in a purpose-built flat has its caveats. The University of Essex-owned i-space attempted to overcome the problem by targeting parents of students who might wish to visit the campus, visiting research fellows in need of accommodation, and friends and families of University staff. For example, in the telecommunication trial described earlier, recruitment was pursued through administration contacts and e-mail circulars using both departmental and "All Students" mailing lists. Prospective participants had to be over 18 years of age in order to avoid the researchers undergoing police checks, have good English skills, and be willing to take part in approximately 6 hr of research work. It was stressed that no technical experience was required. There was little opportunity to create any kind of representative sample, given the small number of applications. There is no easy solution to the difficulties in recruiting suitable participants. Even the use of a subject panel proved difficult when a significant number of the potential participants were families of students, thus making the panel prone to significant "churn" over time.

The question of ethics is also important. Most universities have ethics approval procedures, particularly where human participants are involved. In the case of the University of Essex, the design, recruitment, documentation, and methods were all subject to ethical approval, and took time. Many professional societies (e.g., The British Psychology Society—BPS[6]) and research-funding bodies (e.g., Medical Research Council) have their own ethical guidelines for their members.

Particular attention should be paid to ensuring that informed consent is provided, assuring confidentiality, not deceiving the participant, properly briefing and debriefing them, making it clear that the participants have the right to withdraw at any time, and generally making sure that they are protected and not exposed to any unnecessary and harmful risks.

The future of Living Labs is not certain. There is a tendency for the greatest emphasis to be on the development of the technology and less on its social evaluation. The Living Lab teams need to have both social scientists and technologists working together. The inclusion of social scientists in the Living Lab team is necessary but not sufficient. Technologists and social scientists have different agendas, terminologies, and levels of influence. Too often, the social scientist is only involved in the evaluation, often late in the process, rather than being involved throughout the whole Living Lab process. The use of techniques like SUNA are very helpful in bringing together different members face-to-face (e.g., by the use of workshops), and in using natural language to describe a common set of user needs, expectations, and experiences. User needs not only lead to user requirements for development purposes but also play a key role in defining the evaluation criteria.

Living Labs could potentially have very significant impact on the world of social science research. They need to be correctly positioned in terms of what they can achieve and their limitations must be understood. They are essentially a "quasi-experimental" platforms sitting somewhere between the traditional customer behavior laboratory and the field trial. They have an element of co-creation not usually in terms of users being part of the design team, but in the sense that the users, not just the designers, are a major source of innovation. Users can and often do the most unexpected things. Future methods are likely to move from traditional behavioral science methods to complex, automated data capturing techniques in which the devices themselves retain a history of their use and abuse. Finally, setting up and maintaining international networks and other communities is essential so that practices and lessons may be more efficiently shared and that newly discovered methods and techniques can be more fully explored and tested.

Notes

1. The experience sampling method (ESM) and the ecological momentary assessment (ESA) are techniques that are designed to reduce memory distortion and lapses. These techniques use a timing device to trigger a self report or a survey usually on a portable computing device. However,

sampling rates must be controlled if the users are not to become irritated or the natural patterns of behaviour disturbed.

2. They do not have to be. Indeed undertaking individual interviews is one way of identifying different perceptions of the same event. However, a well-designed and executed group interview should also be able to uncover and elaborate on such individual differences.

3. Clearly, it would have been better to use the personas to select participants, however, as we argue later, this is not always possible or desirable due to the small numbers involved and the difficulties in recruiting participants.

4. There are other sampling alternatives including cluster, spatial, and quota sampling, but these will not be discussed in this chapter.

5. There are various European initiatives that could provide the framework for this short collaborative activity, for example, the European Network of Living Labs and Co-Labs.

6. See the BPS Code of Ethics and conduct (2006) at http://www.bps.org.uk/document-download-area/document-download$.cfm?file_uuid=5084A882–1143-DFD0–7E6C-F1938A65C242&ext=pdf.

References

Ballon, P., Pierson, J., & Delaere, S. (2005). *Test and experimentation platforms for broadband innovation: Examining European practice.* A paper presented at the 16th European regional conference of the International Telecommunications Society in Porto, Portugal.

Batavia, A. I., & Hammer G.S. (1990). Towards the development of consumer-based criteria for the evaluation of assistive devices. *Journal of Rehabilitation Research and Development, 27,* 425–436.

Cohen. I. J. (2000). Theories of action and praxis. InTurner, B. S. (Ed.), *The Blackwell companion to social theory.* Oxford: Blackwell.

Corder, G.W. & Foreman, D. I. (2009). *Nonparametric statistics for the non-statistician: A step-by-step approach.* New York: Wiley & Sons.

CoreLabs. (2008). CoreLabs from AMI@Work communities wiki. http://www.ami-communities.net/wiki/CORELABS.

Denzin, N. K. & Lincoln, Y.S. (Eds.). (1998). *The landscape of qualitative research: Theories and issues.* London: Sage Publications.

Dervin, B., Foreman-Wernet, L., & Launterbach, E. (Eds.). (2003). *Sense-making methodology reader: Selected writings of Brenda Dervin.* Cresskill: Hampton Press, Inc.

Despres, C. (1991). The meaning of home: Literature review and directions for future research and theoretical development. *Journal of Architectural and Planning Research, 8,* 96–115.

Eriksson, M., Niitamo, V. P., & Kulkki, S. (2005). *State-of-the-art in utilizing Living Labs approach to user-centric ICT innovation—A European approach.* A report from the Centre of Distance spanning Technology, Lulea University of Sweden.

Feurstein, K., & Schumacher, J. (2006). *CoreLabs—Best practice report.* http://www.ami-communities.eu/pub/bscw.cgi/d308423/D2.1a%20Best%20Practices.pdf.

Folstad, A. (2008). Living Labs for innovation and development of information and communication technology: A literature review. *The Electronic Journal of Virtual Organisations and Networks, 10,* 100–131.

Fowler, M. (2000). *UML distilled* (2nd ed.). Boston: Addison.

Garfinkel, H. (1967). *Studies in ethnomethodology.* Englewoods Cliffs, NJ: Prentice Hall.

Gaver, W., Dunne, A., & Pacenti, E. (1999). Design: Cultural probes. *Interactions, 6,* 21–29.

Heron, J. (1996). *Cooperative inquiry: Research into the human condition.* London: Sage Publications.

Hewitt, J. P. (1984). Self and society—A symbolic interactionist social psychology (3rd ed.). Boston: Allyn and Bacon.

Holstein, J. A., & Gubrium, J. F. (1998). Phenomenology, ethnomethodology and interpretive practice. In Denzin, K., & Lincoln, S. (Eds.), *The landscape of qualitative research: Theories and issues*. Thousand Oaks, CA; London: Sage Publications.

Laprie, J-C. (1995). *Dependable computing: Concepts, limits, challenges*. Paper presented at FTCS-25: 25th IEEE Symposium on Fault-tolerant computing, Pasadena, CA.

Lasher, D. R., Ives, B., & Jarvenpas, S. L. (1991). USAA-IBM partnerships in information technology: Managing the image project. *MIS Quarterly, 15*, 551–565.

Mallett, S. (2004). Understanding home: A critical review of the literature, *The sociological review, 52,* 62–69.

Morgan, R. H. (2003). Sample size estimation: How many individuals should be studied? *Radiology, 227*, 309–313.

Niitamo, V-P. (2005). The centre for knowledge and innovation research presentation. www.sric-bi.com/LoD/meetings/2005–06–08/VPNiitamo.ppt.

Reason, P. & Bradbury, H. (2001). *Handbook of action research*. London: Sage.

Sandhu, J. (2002). *Multi-dimensional evaluation as a tool in teaching universal design. Universial design: 17 ways of teaching and thinking*. Norway: Norway. Christopherson, J. Husbaken

Sandstrom, G., & Keijer, U. (2007). User values of smart home functions in residential living. In Sandstrom, G. & Keijer, U. (Eds.), *Smart homes and user values*. Gateshead: Urban International Press.

Smith, J. A., & Osborn, M. (2003). Interpretative phenomenological analysis. In Smith, J. A. (Ed.), *Qualitative psychology: A practical guide to methods*. London: Sage.

Sommerville, I., & Dewsbury, G. (2007). Dependable domestic systems design: A socio-technical approach. *Interacting with Computers, 19*, 438–456.

van Helvert, J, & Fowler, C. J. H. (2004). Scenarios for innovation (SUNA). In Alexander, I. & Maiden, N. (Eds.), *Scenarios & Use Cases stories through the system life-cycle*. London: Wiley.

Wright G., & Fowler, C. J. H. (1980). *Investigative design and statistics*. London: Penguin.

➤ Chapter 28

The Digital Home: A New Locus of Social Science Research

Anne Holohan, Jeannette Chin,
Vic Callaghan, and Peter Mühlau

In this chapter, we explore the hypothesis that emerging technology, in the form of the digital home, could provide a new way of exploring the implications of a digital lifestyle for consumption, policy, and social research purposes. We will illustrate how these methods are implemented by describing a working prototype of future digital homes called the iSpace and a methodology that empowers laypeople to customize the functionality of their digital homes called PiP. The ability of lay-users to customize products provides a powerful tool for market and social researchers to gain an insight to the needs and behavior of ordinary people. Moreover, a central innovation made possible by the technologies in digital homes is the opportunity for researching how the disaggregation of control over resources and institutional decision making evident in other parts of the information economy and networked world work in a model that is scalable from household to neighborhood, state, and beyond. We also discuss how and when the data from a digital home might add value to existing social survey and marketing approaches.

Introduction

Digital Lifestyles and Homes: A Multidisciplinary Vision

The vision for a digital lifestyle refers to the extensive integration of computing and communication technologies into our everyday lives, to such an extent that people and technology form symbiotic relationships, supporting an ever richer, more engaging, and deeply connected set of experiences. The notion of lifestyle implies the idea of change; that our "digital lifestyles" (our behavior, expectations, etc.) change incrementally with technological innovations and acceptance. Also, the consumption of digital technologies, and to some extent, lifestyle, is about choice (either unconscious or conscious). Thus, the vision for a digital lifestyle is highly multidisciplinary in nature embracing social and physical sciences in equal measure. Lifestyles are rooted in real-life environments such as homes, offices, transport, and cities where people live. It is possible to use real environments that ordinary people inhabit as test beds for new technology, a concept that has been dubbed a "Living Laboratory" by the EU who have established a network of facilities labeled the European Network of Living Laboratories (http://www.openlivinglabs.eu/). The iSpace used in this paper is an example of a Living Lab and is part of this European network.

An example of a digital lifestyle environment is the digital home in which most electronic appliances and systems feature a network connection. The arrival of Internet has enabled all manner of home appliances and devices to be connected to networks making it possible to adjust heating, open shutters, check that lights are off, start the washing machine, set the alarm, show who is at the door, check that a baby is asleep, and feed the pets even when away from home. Moreover, by connecting information and media sources to networks, it becomes possible to create new forms of entertainment, work or play by, for example, delivering films on demand or teleconferencing among friends.

Delivering this vision is not easy, and is the subject of ongoing research with many technical issues being considered such as end-user programming, security, reliability, and maintenance (Callaghan et al., 2007). Thus, there are also many pitfalls that can lead to poor acceptability and, consequently, living digitally poses a number of challenges to designers and users on a variety of technological, social, political, and cultural levels that we will discuss as part of this chapter (Johnson, Callaghan, & Gardner, 2008).

In order to investigate the possibilities for such digital homes, a handful of test beds have been built around the world to explore future visions where there is the progressive "instrumentation" of social environments through, for example, mobile and ubiquitous computing devices. In this paper, we draw on work from one such digital home test bed: the iSpace based at the University of Essex. The iSpace is a two-bedroom apartment built from the ground up to allow experimentation with new network-based home appliances and systems.

In this chapter, we propose that such digital homes offer an opportunity to provide useful social research data in a number of ways. Most basically, we can gather behavioral data that is produced as a by-product of a digital home. However, as the technology allows for innovative use of this data by households themselves, a rich seam of data on collective behavior and decision making for social research can be made available. For example, a family might govern the operation of their home appliance (manage) to conserve energy that would benefit them (lower energy bills) and the community (less greenhouse emissions). The smart technology (novel forms of sensors, agents, human-computer interaction (HCI), and networks within the home), under the management of the home occupant, collects usage data that is transmissible by Internet. From a single household level, and with the agreement of the occupants, the data can be transmitted to a variety of agencies (including for social research purposes), and Internet forums can be used to engage with other households to produce a collective for managing resources that is a blend of community and organization.

For social science, the greatest potential interest lies in the theoretical significance of this innovative use of technologies, but the greatest challenges are methodological as we will discuss later in the paper. The implications for social research go well beyond examining usage and behavior patterns of particular appliances. The digital home potentially offers one insight into a revolutionary way of organizing society as already argued by some in social science. In the 1960s and early 1970s, sociologists suggested that industrial society would give way to the "information society" with consequences in all fields of human endeavor (Bell, 1973). Later, Manuel Castells (1996) argued that the world is entering an "information age" in which digital information technology "provides the material basis" for the "pervasive expansion" of what he calls "the networking form of organization" in every realm of social structure (p. 468). He predicts new forms of identity and inequality, submerging power in decentered flows, and establishing new forms of social organization. More recently, Hardt and Negri in *Empire* (2000) have considered the consequences of the computer revolution and the widespread adoption and development of ubiquitous, pervasive, and ambient computing, which they argue will lead to a totally new postindustrial, informatization mode of production. For example, they argue that wealth creation will move from the manipulation of physical resources (e.g., mining coal from the ground) to information resources (e.g., mining knowledge from large collections of computer-based information servers). The effects of this, in terms of population behavior, were also considered by Clarke, who considered various scenarios and the consequences for the population as a whole (Clarke et al., 2007).

This chapter will first outline the emerging technologies that are refining existing research methods and enabling new forms of researching social behavior. Given the reach of these new technologies, there are clearly ethical issues relating to privacy, confidentiality, and access that should be addressed and that we will discuss below. We conclude by discussing the implications and limitations of the digital home for social and market research.

The Smart Home and the Digital Population Observatory Model (as a Concept)

There have been several research projects concerned with designing systems for realizing digital homes. By way of a few examples, Georgia Tech's "Aware Home" (Abowd & Mynatt, 2005) and Microsoft's EasyLiving project (Brumitt, Meyers, Krumm, Kern, & Shafer, 2000) that have investigated context aware systems (systems that present users with functions and options that change according to the users context). The Adaptive House project in Colorado (Mozer, 2005), The University of Texas Mav Home project, (Cook, Huber, Gopalratnam, & Youngblood, 2003), and the University of Essex iSpace (Hagras, Doctor, Lopez, & Callaghan, 2007; Doctor, Hagras, & Callaghan, 2005) have investigated a variety of artificial intelligence techniques to model user behavior and preemptively controlled the environment to meet the users' needs creating the so-called smart home.

A key feature of a smart home is that networked devices can be made to coordinate their actions to produce meta-services formed from communities of coordinating services, functions, and appliances. Thus, the home of the future will be a deceptively complex place containing tens or even hundreds of pervasive network-based services, some provided by physical appliances within the home, others by external service providers. Services could range from simple video entertainment streams to complex home care or energy conservation packages.

There are many visions for digital homes that speculate on how network services might change the nature of consumer products and peoples' lifestyles. The general expectation is that domestic services would be designed, packaged, and marketed by commercial companies. However, networked technology opens up the possibility to develop alternative models. For example, from a customer's perspective, it may be possible for end users (homeowners) to compose the functionality of digital homes based on aggregating coordinating sets of networked services. Such descriptions of composite services and their behaviors would form "virtual appliances" that could move with people as they migrate across differing environments (e.g., via the network, or contained in mobile phones), instantiating these functions wherever possible. For example, a homeowner could create a *"DVD Ambience"* virtual appliance that sets the ambient light level to a comfortable level whenever someone watches a DVD (by controlling the window blinds and the room's artificial lighting) or a *"Home Guard"* virtual appliance that checks and secures the home locks at bedtime. Naturally, there is a basic set of common needs that people have such as telephones, TVs, heating, etc., and these would form default "virtual appliances" in all homes. However, other, more novel, virtual appliances (composite service descriptions) created by lay people could even be traded between people as "innovations."

Further, this notion addresses the need in some people to be creative. For example, many people like to choose their own home furniture and wall coverings, personalizing their environments. The technology described in this paper enables these concepts to be applied to people "decorating" their own electronic spaces. In addition, this paradigm increases the control people have over the technology in their life, a requirement that numerous social research projects have reported as being essential to the acceptance of technologies in the home (Kook, 2003; Mäyrä, 2006).

The iSpace

The iSpace is a test bed for future digital or smart homes based at the Essex University campus. It takes the form of a two-bedroom apartment (see Figure 28.1), containing the usual rooms for activities such as sleeping, working, eating, washing, and entertaining. It comprises numerous regular but networked appliances such as telephones, media players, plasma screens, washing machines, refrigerators, lights, heating systems, etc., together with newer technologies such as speech and vision interaction (for commanding or configuring the environment), which interact with the user and sensors (e.g., detecting status of locks, food stocks, etc.) and tags (for tracking objects).

The iSpace (the home) is situated inside a larger community framework (the iCampus), which includes a wider instrumented environment (bars, shops) and wearables. The iSpace or home is an example of the wider concept that embraces other environments such as offices, shops, etc., showing that methods can be extrapolated to the wider networked environment domain.

In the next section, we provide a brief overview of iSpace technology that enables people to create micro services and government within the home, which we argue, can be extrapolated to inform macro government models and policies.

The Technical Methodology

A core tenet of the hypothesis we are arguing is that there are useful parallels between people forming policies to manage, for example, energy usage in their home, and policies

Figure 28.1 The iSpace.

being administered by local or central government. For this strategy to be effective, the technology needs to maximize home owners' choice and control.

A number of significant studies have investigated digital home requirements. For instance, the Samsung Corporation, in cooperation with the American Institutes for Research (AIR), conducted a study aimed at identifying smart-home requirements by interviewing and monitoring people in South Korea and the United States (Chung et al., 2003) One particularly important requirement discovered by the Samsung and AIR study was the need for people to be able to customize their home, a finding supported by many other studies (Mäyrä et al., 2006). There are many visions for digital homes that speculate on how users might be empowered to customize the electronic functionalities of their own home. An example of such a concept is that of MAps (meta-appliances and applications). MAps are "soft objects" that provide a means to aggregate elemental network services together to create virtualized forms of regular (e.g., TVs, air-conditioning, etc.) and novel (user created) appliances (Chin, Callaghan, & Clarke, 2009).

In terms of social science, MAps are uniquely useful as they form documents that described a person's real preferences with respect to some application or topic. For example, for energy policies, they would describe how a person set their heating in the home, office, or transport for a variety of differing contexts such as lone use, family use, or business. Thus, they are a rich and accurate source of data, albeit at a somewhat low and detailed level. However, they are amenable to higher-level aggregation over hundreds or thousands of people, potentially providing more meaningful higher-level statistics.

A key consideration to the design of the technology is how MAps are created (Callaghan et al., 2005). Chin has researched this issue and makes a strong case for nontechnical end-user methods that she sees as a key requirement to empowering the principle stakeholder of the digital home to engage with the technology (Chin et al., 2009). She points at two solutions, one based on highly automated autonomous agents that monitor people's behavior, using this historical information to build models that aim to configure the technology to meet the person's future needs. She argues that such approaches have drawbacks such as a reluctance of many people to allow their personal home spaces (and them) to be monitored by network-connected technology in this way and, second, that trying to second guess needs based on past experience will inevitably have annoying failures (as not all future needs will be described by past actions) and it does not allow creative thoughts for novel MAps that might exist in people's mind to be efficiently extracted. For those reasons, she has argued for and produced a prototype system referred to as PiP (Pervasive interactive Programming) that users can use to create MAps by demonstrating, in explicit teaching sessions, the behavior they require (for full technical details and needs see Chin et al., 2009). Being able to gather data on people's needs, by directly monitoring what they create (as against what people say they may like based on more abstract judgments), has the potential to provide more reliable, detailed, and timely information (Rowley & Wilson, 1975). In particular, our approach builds on "gaming" and the "priority-evaluator approach" to social research, which uses analogues of the real world (frequently in the form of games) in which people are given the freedom to configure resources as a means to obtain more reliable social research data (Rowley & Wilson, 1975). In the approach being advocated in this paper, we retain the idea of monitoring how people configure resources as a means to elicit peoples' choices and desires but dispense with the use of analogies in favor of using new generations of configurable technology, in particular digital homes and PiP, which directly involves the stakeholders being studied. Incidentally, Rowley's work is also relevant to this paper as he is also credited with the earliest use of bespoke portable microcomputer technology to augment social and market research, concepts that further motivate this research (Rowley, Barker, & Callaghan, 1986).

Concerning the data yielded by such end-user customization systems, because people are able to create and design the functionality of their own virtual appliances or environments, their decisions and design actions represent valuable information in terms of understanding peoples' needs. This is especially so because the networked nature of the system makes collection of this data relatively straightforward for both individuals and aggregations of large numbers of people. However, rather than the data being conventional questionnaire-style answers, it is more complex as it contains details of assemblies (MAps) of functions, together with their usage. Inferring what the MAps do and why the user created them require meta-data tagging by the user at the time of creation. Usage statistics (when certain functions are used and for how long) can be automatically collected by the system. MAps and end-user programming are just one approach, albeit an important approach, to governing digital homes.

In summary, with respect to social science research the two methodologies described above (end-user programming and autonomous agents) provide a source of data on peoples' behavior and preferences. The agent-based approach represents more passive data gathered from monitoring peoples' behavior with little active input from the person being monitored. In contrast, end-user programming (and its PiP implementation) involves active participation of the home occupant in making decisions and forming policies. As such, we argue that the data gained from end-user programming is more linked to conscious decisions and policy making and thus more useful for extrapolating higher-level policy information. Decision making and its relationship to our hypothesis is discussed further in the following section.

The Model of Governance and Its Implications for Social Research

Emerging technologies such as the digital home have the power to disrupt and transform existing social structures and social practices. The "digital home," through networking appliances inside the home to each other and beyond the household via the Internet, offers the opportunity to generate usage data and allow people to manage and share that data via the Internet in a way that will have a transformative impact on consumption and decision-making patterns. The most innovative aspect of digital homes is arguably their ability to empower households to manage their own usage data and to deliberate with other households over whether and how to share this data with outside stakeholders, such as energy companies or government agencies. This disaggregates, and has the power to allow innovative reconstitution of, existing decision-making practices and relationships between providers of resources and consumers, and governments and citizens. Existing resource management and e-deliberation solutions can provide a means through which users can form and federate groups that can then electronically manage, reflect, and debate the best use of ambient intelligence resources in servicing their own needs and that of the wider community. By rendering such activities explicit, but by also providing user friendly Web tools to browse and manipulate the related models, communities can be enabled to decide clearly how to collect, monitor, process, and distribute sensor data.

Managing a home is in many ways analogous to the process of government. There are finite resources with much competition for them. Opinions and information need to be gathered, deliberated on, rules decided on within households (effective formation of policies), and actions taken (cf. a micro-government) (Callaghan, Clarke, & Chin, 2008). The household can engage in deliberation on how best to manage the household resources and then go online, if they wish, to engage in deliberation at three levels to exchange information and views on how to manage their data, and how that data is used: within the household between individuals; with other households in a selected group, specifically the street/neighborhood, municipal level; and between citizens and interested parties and government. This approach enables householders/citizens to manage their own bounded domain—their own data—and if they wish to respond as a household or as a collective to specific policy and engage in deliberation on this policy with the government and other citizens. The government in turn could modify its policies in response to the findings and views of the households. These "micro-government" choices provide an opportunity for households to negotiate with commercial companies or state providers of resources, making the relationship much less passive and hierarchical than it is now. Taking the example of management of energy, existing technology can provide the means to monitor the power consumption of key appliances such as heating/cooling, lighting, hot water, washing machines, or TVs. Monitoring the individual power appliances is the minimal level of granularity needed to gain knowledge of personal behavior. This data from a digital home can feed policy formation as the data recorded can be transmitted to relevant parties/actors, for example, local municipal authority or central government. One can imagine a scenario where households, through negotiation, not only reduce their energy bills through the appliance specific data they are collecting but also could collectively share data on energy use with energy providers in exchange for lower fuel/energy charges. This would have implications for energy policy, including strategies to reduce the consumption of energy.

The emerging technologies used in "digital homes" offer opportunities to interrogate classical and contemporary social theories about the nature of social order. Contrary to some arguments in the Marxist tradition (Braverman, 1974; Schiller, 1976), rather than the information age leading to the increased control of capital through surveillance and deskilling and the further disempowering of labor, our model is part of a potential scenario where traditional power holders (capital, state) have some of their power decentralized or redistributed (Negri, 1988)—in this case, drawn down to households. IF (our emphasis) the lay user/worker/citizen is part of the process from the moment of inception, including easily customizable sensors, and IF there is use of the Internet forums for coordinating with other households, there is a significant new role for households and collectivities of households in the economy and polity. Households will have the information or data that the companies or state will require for efficiencies and this will provide bargaining power to previously passive consumers. The low level of cost for overcoming the hitherto material barriers for production of information (affordable sensors, access to Internet) means we have a scenario where anyone who is computer literate at a basic level will be able to own and manage their own information. Our model is aware of and tries to address this issue of access by including the means for customizing the sensors that does not require any technical knowledge.

With the ownership of data shifting to the individual, particularly the household level, and the necessity of negotiation for companies and bureaucracies who wish to gain access to the level of detail gathered, the structure and practice of institutions is impacted.

Institutions, from household to companies to government, have, since the industrial revolution, been predominantly characterized by hierarchical structure and top–down authority relationships. The information revolution and postmodern society have provided the tools and consequences to challenge this in the family (Stacey, 1996), organizations, (Powell, 1990) and government (Keck & Sikkink, 1998; Slaughter, 2004). The rise of the "network society" (Castells, 1996, 2000) has changed the rules so that information flows now determine structure, boundaries are much less important (or indeed even possible), and status is determined much more by expertise than formal position (Holohan, 2005). Knowledge has never been more democratically distributed or available regardless of formal status. Politically, this offers a potential citizen–polity relationship that goes well beyond the franchise, and allows for deliberation and input into policy decisions that is unprecedented (Habermas, 1991; Calhoun, 1993).

The "networked information economy" (Benkler, 2006) is challenging the old "industrial information economy." This is producing a society where decentralized individual action, specifically new cooperative action carried out through radically distributed, non-market mechanisms that do not depend on proprietary strategies, is becoming increasingly important in the fields of communication, information, and culture (Lessig, 1999). For instance, the music industry has moved from dominance by huge music companies to a much more diffuse and democratized model of music publishing and performing. The material barriers are largely gone (due to technologies, principally the Internet) and non-market, nonproprietary motivations, and organizational forms are increasingly common, resulting in effective, large-scale cooperative efforts such as the Open Source software movement. Eric von Hippel's idea (1988, 2005) of "user-driven innovation" has begun to expand that focus to thinking about how individual need and creativity can drive innovation at the individual level and its diffusion through networks of like-minded individuals. It is this feasibility of producing information through social (cooperative and coordinated individual action) rather than market or proprietary relations that is at the heart of our proposed model of scalable governance of households using data that is produced by sensors and shareable with others through the Internet. So for instance, householders can choose to share information on energy consumption not on demand from companies or government nor in a market place but through collective deliberation and deployment of data for specific purposes, such as assisting energy efficiencies to address challenges from global warming. The collective deliberation could be at a street level or neighborhood level or municipality or city ward level. While there are threats to privacy (discussed below), there are also benefits. For example, by participating in energy usage monitoring programs, ordinary citizens can both help the environment and save money by using less energy. In addition, as such information might help make the energy providers more efficient, these savings could be shared with the consumer in the form of a discount providing additional incentives for the citizen to participate.

Privacy and Ethical Implications

The social sciences, and indeed society, need to grapple with the danger of technological developments proceeding at a pace that would realize the fears around privacy and "Big Brother" scenarios. The more attention social science gives to emerging technologies such as the "digital home," the more such dangers can be highlighted and addressed.

Re-interrogating Marx and Weber, we can explore whether the new technology is increasing elite control of both politics and production through enhanced surveillance (Davis, Hirschl, & Stack, 1997).

Numerous reports have revealed that user acceptance of technology in digital homes has been shown to be linked to perceptions of privacy, which in turn is linked to the degree of control the user has over the technology (Chung et al., 2003; Mäyrä et al., 2006). In terms of digital homes, these issues have been linked to the balance of autonomous agents versus manual management of the environment (Callaghan et al., 2008). A search of the Internet will quickly reveal that much has been written over the years about such dangers. This fear is increased as our control, and system transparency, is reduced. Thus, if we are to live in digital homes, then questions such as "who has control?," "what is the extent of their control?," and "who has access to sensory data from our home and what use are they making of it?" are paramount. In terms of smart or digital homes, control comes down to the balance of technological autonomy versus user influence.

These concerns are graphically illustrated in the two-dimensional graph shown in Figure 28.2: the "3C framework" (Callaghan et al., 2008). To capture the balance of automation, there is an autonomy-axis that depicts the possibilities for configuration from manual (end user) to automatic (agent based). In terms of sociology, reactions to technology vary from love to fear, which are illustrated in an "attitude" axis that shows user reaction (philia versus phobia) to the different possibilities. The quadrants show differing combinations of technology and attitude, identifying potentially significant positions within this space. A general assumption underpinning this model is the view that the less understanding of and control over their technological environment people have, the more resistant or fearful they will be of it (and vice versa). The model is not normative but depicts a conceptual space of possibilities drawn from experiences of our research. Thus, for example, people that are technophobic may react to automated environments (where they have little say in how they operate) by trying to sabotage the technology. For example, people may cover or disconnect sensors to fool the system or prevent it monitoring them. In a system where technophobic people have control over the system, they may simply program the system to disable it, or make it work in an unconventional way, as a means of expressing their dissatisfaction. This is in contrast to the way people with technophilia tendencies may react. For example, for systems in which autonomous agents exercise total control over the environment they may marvel at the sophisticated technology and bask in the comfort it affords, whereas in a system that they can exercise control they may delight is creating novel functionalities. Of course these are extreme attitudes and behaviors and the diagram allows for more continuous variations.

Thus, in a digital or smart home the principal tool in the armory of privacy protections is control, which in practical terms resides in the balance of agent versus user management. By control or management, we mean maximizing the user's ability to make choices on what information is gathered and when and how it is used (including choices to "autonomise" the collected data). At a community level, this would require and enable groups at various levels of granularity (from families to neighborhood, town, and even to nations) to e-debate/deliberate what data should be made available to whom and for what purposes. Cheap storage, distributed systems querying, and perhaps peer-to-peer (P2P)-based backups could mean that sensor data could be stored relatively locally (minimizing exposure to massive theft and allowing the levels of security and robustness to be tailored to the group concerned).

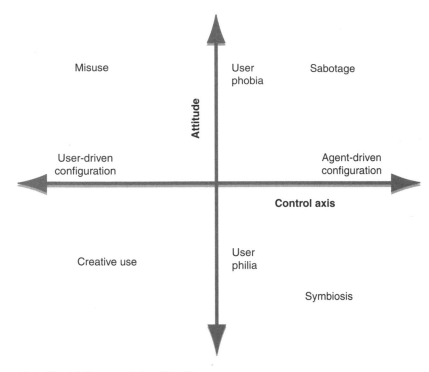

Figure 28.2 The 3C framework for digital homes.

In addition to people's desire for privacy, another barrier to people allowing detailed sensing of their domestic lives is rooted in a lack of trust in the officials or corporations who collect, store, have access to, and use such sensitive information. The 25 million personal data records lost in the United Kingdom in 2007 demonstrates the importance of addressing this issue. Local groups need to be able to negotiate about access of their data by "outside" bodies, for example, governments and corporation, from a position of power. These bodies would need to be forced to argue for access to data on the basis of earned trust, transparent procedures, and well-reasoned appeals to the common good or appropriate incentives. Agreement for access could be provisional (these are ongoing feeds of data so long-term relationships are key) and linked to systems for auditing security and usage and also for dealing with potential conflicts that may arise, for example, if one accessing body wishes to forward data to another one (a big concern with a lot of data privacy—you may trust the local police but not want them passing details to the CIA).

While in this paper we are focusing on the benefits of digital home technology, and how it might improve social research, which in turn could connect people and government in a more mutually effective relationship, it is equally clear that without careful planning and regulation of digital home technology it would be possible to create a modern equivalent of Bentham's Panopticon (Bozovic, 1995) or "Big Brother" (Orwell, 1949), turning homes into "gold-fish bowls" where our every move is monitored by third parties.

Blurring of Public and Private Spaces

As indicated above, it is already documented that the use of information technologies can itself pose a threat to confidentiality. The data collected and any accompanying communication that is typed rather than spoken leaves a physical trace referred to as a "data trace" that can be archived or preserved (Duffy, 2002, p. 85). Data traces can result in breaches of confidentiality if unauthorized people have access to research data stored on a computer that is connected to the Internet. In addition, in our example, protocols and standards for confidentiality need to be in place not just in the "smart home" but also in all relevant agencies: energy companies, government departments, market research companies, and social science departments in universities or research institutes. Such coordination represents a major challenge and can only really be addressed at the legislative level.

The difficulty in terms of the discussions via forums on the Internet, as to who and where and how to share the data, is the blurring of the boundary between public and private. Obviously, when people are in a public setting they can expect to be observed. Conversely, when they are in a private setting they do not. However, online this distinction is not clear (Barnes, 2004). Traditionally, there has been a clear divide between the public and private data with explicit consent required for inclusion of private data and measures taken to ensure that private data does not enter the public realm. But online flows of personal information are channeled through a public forum that poses no restrictions on audience access; anyone can view the discussion. Password-protected forums could be used, but this would restrict recruitment and participation in our proposed models; how else to entice neighbors over a relatively large geographical space, for instance to work together on sharing data, but to see the discussions and outcomes for oneself on the Internet? Traditionally, it is the discretion of the subject that determines the boundary between public and private. But messages exchanged online often create an illusion of privacy because contributors forget that other individuals can read those messages. Once individuals develop close Internet relationships, they can easily forget they are communicating in a public space (Barnes, 2004).

One practical solution is to ensure that while the public can access the deliberation forums, participation in the discussion requires membership. However, this does not deal with the problem of confidentiality for social science researchers, as participants using pseudonyms merely make the ethical problem one of dealing with multiple identities, as unless similar pseudonyms are substituted, online identities are not hidden if actual pseudonyms are written up in the research, as participants can be recognized by those familiar with their online pseudonyms (Beddows, 2008). This situation presents an as yet unsolved dilemma for Institutional Review Boards (IRBs), which exist to ensure the subjects of social research and participants in social research's rights are protected.

Situating "Digital Home" Research in Current Social Research

It is useful in the discussion of the potential of "digital/smart-house technology" to distinguish on the one side between *technology-specific* and *general research* and on the other between *market research* in a broad sense (including audience measurement and market research feeding into research and development) and *social research*. By technology-specific research, we refer to research that is generally concerned with the adoption, use, and adaptation of "digital home technology" or with the consequences of "digital home technology" for attitudes and behavior of the users and the social structure they are embedded in. With respect to the technology-specific research, the issues may overlap between market and social researchers although market researchers will be more interested in the adoption and use aspects while social researchers will be more tempted to examine the consequences of the technology. We have already addressed this, focusing on the implications for social research, in our discussion of the proposed model of disaggregated decision making and scalable governance.

General research is research that is interested in topics that are independent of the "digital home technology" and in a target population that is not the universe of actual or potential users of "digital home." Here, the perspectives of market researchers and social researchers diverge more strongly: Market researchers will be interested in the use of products and the market chances for new products, while social researchers will be primarily interested in the social organization of the domestic sphere. In the following, we focus on the potential and limitations for general research.

Most simply, the data collected in "digital homes" improves continuous measurement. The idea of continuous assessment is not new—for example diary surveys and audience measurement have been around for quite a while. However, the initiative to call in or complete the diary usually rests with the respondent. Technology has already been identified by researchers as improving continuous assessment and is giving much greater access into people's lives. For example, transaction data is already in use (credit or debit card use, video rental, etc.) and continuous measurement has been linked to the growth of portable Internet devices and mobile computing—mobile phones, Blackberries, etc. (Couper, 2003, p. 493). Traditional interviewer-administered surveys have very high costs for sampling, contacting, persuading, and interviewing, so interviewers have tended to maximize the interview and ask up to several hours of questions. Panel interviews, for the same high cost reasons, have tended to be months or years apart. However, there is existing evidence of the value of continuous measurement (Mundt, Bohn, King, & Hartley, 2002; Aaron, Mancl, Turner, Sawchuk, & Klein, 2004) and "digital home" technologies offer an opportunity to increase this value.

Collecting data in a "digital home" has potential for improving accuracy, as instead of surveying people's usage patterns in retrospect, where people report from memory, the hard data is much more accurate and complete. The pitfall of recall from memory is erased when you are working with real-time data; some obvious examples would come from research on diet, exercise, activities in the home, and mood. It also helps overcome observer fatigue: collecting data manually negatively influences the reliability of the data, apart from being very tedious, as the events of interest are rare and are interspersed with long periods of uninteresting activity (Philips Homelab http://www.research.philips.com/technologies/projects/homelab/index.html).

Thus, the core of the primary data to be expected from "digital homes" appears to be process-generated usage data from linked and integrated equipment. It is useful to compare the potential of usage data with the very established industry of audience measurement (e.g., Napoli, 2003). The data generated by "digital home technology" is similar to what is known as "passive" audience measurement data. Traditionally, meters were attached to working television sets to record set-tuning data for the household. The use of these data was limited and was complemented by diaries of the individual household members and by survey-based information about the sociodemography and other characteristics of the household and its members. Diaries have been largely replaced by "active people meters" that share with diaries the dependence on the active cooperation of the household members resulting in data of doubtful reliability. More recently, the emphasis is on "passive people meters" allowing also the recording of media consumption outside the home and reflecting the use of multiple platforms, in particular of the Internet. The infrastructure for audience measurement is a "single-purpose technology" set up because the data generated are of utmost economic importance, in particular in the planning of advertisement campaigns and the price-setting for television commercials. To secure that the audience data permit reliable and precise population estimates, audience measurement requires panels that are representative for the population of television viewers. This is typically done by some form of probability sampling. Panels need to be regularly updated to continue to represent the population and validated by "external coincidental surveys."

What are the implications of this tale for the potential of digital homes in social research? Of course "digital homes" may be useful for the "passive" generation of multiple platform media consumption data at the household level, and individual meters should not be a problem. But are there other areas for which "digital homes" can produce valuable data? Energy consumption may be another area and an intelligent energy monitoring system may help the end user to use energy more efficiently. But the energy producer has far less interest than television companies in details about who consumes their product—the revenue of the utility company is independent of whether a male in the age group between 25 and 34 consumes their product or a woman in her 70s. However, unlike audience measurement systems, "digital homes" are not set up because of the need to collect data. To the degree that data about usage patterns are the by-product of their operation, setup costs are low and so are the marginal cost of generating (but not of processing) the data. Data generated by "digital home technology" may hence find interest from groups who would not be willing to invest massively in a data-generating infrastructure but see enough value in the data to cover the marginal costs and finance the processing of the data, for example, appliance manufacturers or home care providers. The integrated nature of the system, in addition, appears to permit one to examine interdependencies in the usage of different components in the house. This may guide the analysis of substitution and complementary effects between different components and identify more general patterns of consumption ("lifestyles"). Moreover, new developments such as PiP are intended to allow users to translate mental concepts into designs of lifestyles or home functionalities they would like, but currently do not exist, with important implications for product research and development.

Limitations in this line of research are, first, that the natural unit of observation is the household and individuals have to be identified to permit data with individual household members as the unit of observation. Second, the research is confined to "home consumption," while there are obvious and important interdependencies between "consumption at home" and "outside the home," as the trend in audience measurement toward "portable" meters recording mobile and public media consumption shows. Potentially, the core ideas of digital homes can be extrapolated to the wider networked environment domain easing this limitation. Third, for the foreseeable future, the weak point of "digital home"-generated data from the point of view of social research is the quality of the sample. High-quality samples are representative for the target population, and that is typically achieved by (1) a sampling frame that has high and unbiased coverage of the target population, (2) a sampling strategy that permits the generation of unbiased samples from this frame, for example, probability sampling, and (3) efforts to avoid low and biased cooperation and response rate.

Usually surveys are linked to individuals and thus there is the problem of how to differentiate individual from household in usage patterns. This has important implications for sample design and coverage. There is also not a stable sample of Internet users; unlike the real world, people, even if technically on an e-mail list, can choose to go "off-line." Participants can also mislead others about their physical location, identity, gender, or age, which means the researcher cannot effectively characterize his or her sample audience. Participation in Internet surveys and online deliberation, if sharing data from digital homes, will be affected by people working from different technological platforms; in particular, access to appropriate equipment and Internet technology and variation in bandwidth all impact who participates.

At the time being, inhabitants of digital homes are a small fraction of the overall population in terms of socioeconomic characteristics and age distribution but also in terms of attitudes and traits not representative for the general population. Because innovators typically differ from late adopters of technologies, current people living in a digital home are also different from the universe of smart-house digital home inhabitants (including future ones) and the former cannot be considered as a representative sample of the latter. "Digital home" owners are hence a sampling frame with low and highly selective coverage of the general population. There appears to be no incentive for data users to equip a representative sample of houses with digital homes technology in order to avail of representative data—that is, a crucial difference to audience measurement. Additional problems may be posed in securing the cooperation and willingness to share the data by people living in digital homes, as was discussed above. This may crucially depend on how "intruding" respondents perceive the "smart-house" technology if used for research and how sensitive respondents regard the data transferred. Such noncooperation is unlikely to be random. With ubiquitous deployment not yet established, as of now "digital home technology" might be valuable in providing reliable data of highly selective samples for narrowly circumscribed fields in marketing research.

Less clear is how large the potential of usage data is for social research in the broader sense. First, scope of the recorded usage appears to be excessively narrow to command much social-scientific interest. For example, in a research field like the domestic division of work, even individually attributed usage data cover only a narrow range of household activities. Activities that are not technologically mediated or supported are not covered; domestic work outside of the house is disregarded; and for many in-home activities of technologically mediated or supported activities, recorded usage is at best proxy measurement of the household task being completed. Second, in the case that a variable of interest is generated by the "smart-house technology," there are severe limitations of "what you can do with the data" *if it stands alone*. The scope for experimental manipulation is limited and quasi-experimental designs of a "natural experiments" type are the best one can hope for. Moreover, lacking random assignment as a mechanism to allocate people to treatment and control conditions, additional covariates have to be established to control for heterogeneity or allow matching of the groups. For observational studies, the problem of covariates is even more severe as (limited) causal inference requires measurement of the conditions expected to be the causal *agents* as well as antecedents and side-effect of this condition to eliminate spurious relationships.

All this would require that "rich" data are collected in addition to the process-generated data, using most likely "traditional" survey methods. For example, audience measurement data are not frequently used outside of their commercial applications and if so, then in highly aggregated form that permits one to link the data with other data sources (e.g., Hyland, Wakefield, Higbee, Szczypka, & Cummings, 2006; Frechette, Roth, & Ünver, 2007). Most studies on media consumption or media impact rely on self-collected data on media usage using either diaries (e.g., Couldry, Livingstone, & Markham, 2007) or self-reported usage (e.g., Chiricos et al., 1997), that is, data that are clearly less reliable than "passively" measured media consumption. A main reason is that social-scientific research is not particularly interested in purely descriptive studies of media consumption but either aims to untangle the processes generating different patterns of media consumption or to examine the effect of these patterns on behavior or attitudes. For both research interests, data generated by audience measurement are far too "thin" to permit meaningful social research and it is likely that the same holds for data generated by digital homes. Finally, most social research aims to be generalized to target populations and the quality standards are typically much higher in social research when compared with market research. Even if a highly salient dependent variable is recorded (or can be derived from data recorded by the "digital home technology") and relevant covariates are additionally measured, the fact that as of yet the inhabitants of "digital homes" are a highly selective group diminishes the value of the data for most social research.

The value added to qualitative research by "digital homes" is less obvious but nonetheless significant. As the researcher goes in with tremendous amounts of information already, it is much easier to orient the researcher theoretically and to focus follow-up questions and observation or just observation and in-depth interviews. Having accurate usage patterns is useful, but interpretative data is also needed to fully understand the context of the use of sensors. In addition, the online forums—and potential accompanying off-line interaction—would be subject to ethnographic analysis. Online ethnography refers to a number of related online research methods that adapt ethnography to the study of the communities and cultures created through computer-mediated social interaction, in particular observation, participant-observation, and interviews. Some have contested that ethnographic fieldwork can be meaningfully applied to computer-mediated interactions (e.g., Clifford, 1997) but it is increasingly becoming accepted as possible (Garcia, Standlee, Bechkoff, & Cui, 2009). In fact, the term netnography has gained currency within the field of consumer research to refer to ethnographic research conducted on the Internet (Kozinets, 2002, 2006a, 2006b). The limitations of ethnographies of online cultures draw from its more narrow focus on online communities, its inability to offer the full and rich detail of lived human experience, the need for researcher interpretive skill, and difficulty generalizing beyond the community under study. These and the challenge of scale and confidentiality face the researcher of householders participating in forums to collectively manage household data.

Most promising from a social research point of view, as indicated in the discussion of a new form of scalable household governance, is the potential of the technology to enable and record household decisions and their outcomes, such as rules, in a variety of ways. Research interested in understanding how decisions in households are formed and how contextual factors (e.g., income differences between the partners) affect the process and the outcomes would be keen to have access to data that would test models of household decision making (or joint decision making of a group of households). Model-testing research is also less dependent on sample representation, if the goal is to test theories about general mechanisms and is more concerned about the internal validity of the findings rather than the external validity (similar to laboratory experiments).

Conclusion and Future Directions

This paper has explored the hypothesis that emerging technology, in the form of the digital home, can provide a new way of exploring the implications of a digital lifestyle for consumption, policy, and social research purposes. We illustrated how these methods are implemented by describing a working prototype of future digital homes called the iSpace and a methodology that empowers laypeople to customize the functionality of their digital homes called PiP. The ability of lay-users to customize products provides a powerful tool for market and social researchers to gain an insight to the needs and behavior of ordinary people. We also discussed how and when the data from a digital home might add value to existing social survey and marketing approaches. For social science, the greatest potential interest lies in its theoretical significance but the greatest challenges are methodological.

Most significantly for social theory, emerging technologies such as the digital home have the power to disrupt and transform existing social structures and social practices. The "digital home," through networking appliances inside the home to each other and beyond the household via the Internet, offers the opportunity to generate usage data and allows people to manage and share that data via the Internet in a way that will have a transformative impact on consumption and decision-making patterns. The most innovative aspect of digital homes is arguably their ability to empower households to manage their own usage data and to deliberate with other households over whether and how to share this data with outside stakeholders, such as energy companies or government agencies. This disaggregates, and has the power to allow innovative reconstitution of, existing decision-making practices and relationships between providers of resources and consumers, and governments and citizens. In effect, this innovation can transform institutions and impact the existing power structure in society.

Methodologically, for current social and market research, the value of the digital home lies in its ability to enhance existing methods or elements of methods such as continuous measurement and the generation of passive user data. Limitations in this line of research include the difficulties with the unit of observation currently being the household rather than the individual; it does not investigate the important interdependencies between consumption "at home" and "outside the home" and finally, the quality of the sample is currently irredeemably weak. Although the use of such data for social research is thus circumscribed by the hitherto experimental nature of digital homes and their as of yet limited availability to the general population, there is clear movement in industry and academia to address these issues, with exciting possibilities opening up for both social and market research as a result. In particular, from the research at iSpace discussed here, the possibility of accessing representative data of people's customization of appliances and the patterns of usage combination is one that would be of great interest to market researchers if sampling was not as problematic as it is currently.

Both, the theoretical and methodological potential and challenge of the digital home need to grapple with the danger of technological developments proceeding at a pace that would realize the fears around privacy and "Big Brother" scenarios. The more attention social science gives to emerging technologies such as the "digital home," the more such dangers can be highlighted and addressed.

Acknowledgment

We are pleased to acknowledge the valuable contribution of Michael Gardner to this paper.

References

Aaron, L. A., Mancl, L., Turner, J. A., Sawchuk, C. N., & Klein, K. M. (2004). Reasons for missing interviews in the daily electronic assessment of pain, mood and stress. *Pain, 109,* 389–398.

Abowd, G., & Mynatt, E. (2005). Designing for the human experience in smart environments. In Cook, D., & Das, S. (Eds.), *Smart environments: Technology, protocols, and applications* (pp. 153–174). London: Wiley.

Barnes, S. B. (2004). Issues of attribution and identification in online social research In Johns, M. D., Chen, S. S., & Hall, G. J. (Eds.), *Online social research: Methods, issues and ethics.* New York: Peter Lang Publishing Inc.

Beddows, E. (2008). The methodological issues associated with Internet-based research. *International Journal of Emerging Technologies and Society,* 6(2), 124–139.

Benkler, Y. (2006). *The wealth of networks.* New Haven: Yale University Press.

Bozovic, M. (Ed.). (1995). *Jeremy Bentham: The Panopticon writings.* London: Verso.

Braverman, H. (1974). *Labour and monopoly capital: The degradation of work in the twentieth century.* New York: Monthly Review.

Brumitt, B., Meyers, B., Krumm, J., Kern, A., & Shafer, S. (2000). EasyLiving: Technologies for intelligent environments. Proceedings of the Second International Symposium on Handheld and Ubiquitous Computing (pp. 12–29).

Calhoun, C. (1993). *Habermas and the public sphere* (Studies in contemporary German social thought) Cambridge, MA: The MIT Press.

Callaghan, V., Hagras, H. (2010). *Smart Homes,* Thematic Issue of Journal of Ambient Intelligence and Smart Environments, The Netherlands: IOS Press, 2(3), ISSN 1876-1364

Callaghan, V., Colley, M., Hagras, H., Chin J., Doctor, F., & Clarke, G. (2005). Programming iSpaces: A tale of two paradigms. In Steventon, A., Wright, S. (Eds.), *Intelligent spaces, the application of pervasive ICT part of the series computer communications and networks.* New York: Springer-Verlag. October, ISBN-13: 9781846280023.

Callaghan, V., Clarke, G., & Chin, J. (2008). Some socio-technical aspects of intelligent buildings and pervasive computing research. *Intelligent Buildings International Journal,* 1(1).

Castells, M. (1996). *The rise of the network Society, the information age: Economy, society and culture* (Vol. 1). Cambridge, MA; Oxford: Blackwell.

Castells, M. (2000, Second Edition). *The rise of the network Society, the information age: Economy, society and culture* (Vol. 1). Cambridge, MA; Oxford: Blackwell.

Chin, J., Callaghan, V., & Clarke, G. (2009a). End-user customisation of intelligent environments. In Nakashima, H., Aghajan, H., & Augusto, J. C. (Eds.), *Handbook of ambient intelligence and smart environments.* Springer-Verlag, December, ISBN: 978-0-387-93807-3.

Chin, J., Callaghan, V., & Clarke, G. (2009b). Soft-appliances: A vision for user created networked appliances in digital homes. *Journal of Ambient Intelligence and Smart Environments*, *1*(1), 69–75.

Chung, K. H., Oh, K. S., Lee, C. H., Park, J. H., Kim, S., Kim, S. H., et al. (2003). A user-centric approach to designing home network devices. In CHI '03 extended abstracts on Human factors in computing systems, 648–649.

Clarke G, Callaghan V, "Ubiquitous Computing, Informatization, Urban Structures and Density", Built Environment Journal, Vol. 33, No 2 2007.

Clifford, J. (1997). Spatial practices: Fieldwork, travel, and the discipline of anthropology. In Gupta, A., & Ferguson, J. (Eds.), *Anthropological locations: Boundaries and grounds of a field science* (pp. 185–222). Berkeley, CA: University of California Press.

Cook, D. J., Huber, M., Gopalratnam, K., & Youngblood, M. (2003). Learning to control a smart home environment. In *Innovative Applications of Artificial Intelligence*. Volume 4008, Springer Berlin/Heidelberg, ISBN 978–3–540–35994–4, 165–182.

Couldry, N., Livingstone, S., & Markham, T. (2007). *Media consumption and public engagement: Beyond the presumption of attention. Consumption and public life.* Basingstoke: Palgrave Macmillan.

Couper, M. P. (2003). Technology trends in survey data collection. *Social Science Computer Review*, *23*, 486.

Davis, J., Hirschl T., & Stack M., (Eds.). (1997). Cutting edge: Technology, information capitalism, and social revolution. New York: Verso.

Doctor, F., Hagras, H., & Callaghan, V. (2005). An intelligent fuzzy agent approach for realising ambient intelligence in intelligent inhabited environments. *IEEE Transactions on System, Man & Cybernetics-Part A*, *35*(1), 55–65.

Frechette, G. R., Roth, A. E., & Ünver, M. U. (2007). Unraveling yields inefficient matching: Evidence from post-season college football bowls. *Rand Journal of Economics*, *38*, 967–982.

Garcia, A. C., Standlee, A. I., Bechkoff, J., & Cui, Y. (2009). Ethnographic approaches to the Internet and computer-mediated communication. *Journal of Contemporary Ethnography*, *38*(1), 52–84.

Habermas, J. (1991). *The structural transformation of the public sphere: An inquiry into a category of bourgeois society.* (Studies in contemporary German social thought). Massachusetts: MIT Press.

Hagras, F., Doctor, F., Lopez, A., & Callaghan, V. (2007). An incremental adaptive lifelong learning approach for type-2 fuzzy embedded agents in ambient intelligent environments. *IEEE Transactions on Fuzzy Systems*, *15*(1), 41–55.

Hardt, M., & Negri, A. (2000). *Empire.* Cambridge, MA: Harvard University Press.

Holohan, A. (2005). *Networks of democracy: Lessons from Kosovo for Afghanistan, Iraq and beyond.* California: Stanford University Press.

Hyland, A., Wakefield, M., Higbee, C., Szczypka, G., & Cummings, K. M. (2006). Anti-tobacco television advertising and indicators of smoking cessation in adults: A cohort study. *Health Education Research*, *21*, 348–354.

Johnson,B., Callaghan, V., Gardner, G. (2008, July 21–22). Bespoke appliances for the digital home. IET International Conference on Intelligent Environments, Seattle, 61–69.

Keck, M. E., & Sikkink, K. (1998). *Activists beyond borders: Advocacy networks in international politics.* Ithaca, NY: Cornell University Press.

Kook Hyun Chung, Kyoung Soon Oh, Cheong Hyun Lee, Jae Hyun Park, Sunae Kim, Soon Hee Kim, Beth Loring, Chris Hass, "A User-Centric Approach to Designing Home Network Devices", CHI '03 extended abstracts on Human factors in computing systems, 2003, 648–649.

Kozinets, R. V. (2002). The field behind the screen: Using netnography for marketing research in online communities. *Journal of Marketing Research*, *39*(February), 61–72.

Kozinets, R. V. (2006a). Netnography 2.0. In Belk, R. W. (Ed.), *Handbook of qualitative research methods in marketing* (pp. 129–142). Cheltenham; Northampton, MA: Edward Elgar Publishing.

Kozinets, R. V. (2006b). Netnography. In Jupp, V. (Ed.), *The sage dictionary of social research* (pp. 193–195). London: Sage.

Lessig, L. (1999). *Code and other laws of cyberspace*. New York: Basic Books.

Mäyrä F., Soronen A., Vanhala J., Mikkonen J., Zakrzewski M., Koskinen I., et al. (2006). Probing a proactive home: Challenges in researching and designing everyday smart environments. *Human Technology Journal*, *2*(2), 158–186.

Mozer, M. (2005). Lessons from an adaptive home. In Cook, D., & Das, S. (Ed.), *Smart environments: Technology, protocols, and applications* (pp. 273–298). London: Wiley.

Mundt, J. C., Bohn, M. J., King, M., & Hartley, M. T. (2002). Automating standard alcohol use assessment instruments via interactive voice response technology. *Alcoholism: Clinical and Experimental Research*, *26*(2), 207–211.

Napoli, P. M. (2003). *Audience economics: Media institutions and the audience marketplace*. Chicago: University of Chicago Press.

Negri, A. (1988). *Revolution retrieved. Selected writings on Marx, Keynes, capitalist crisis and new social subjects*. London: Red Notes.

Orwell, G. (1949). *Nineteen eighty-four*. London: Penguin Books.

Powell, W. W. (1990). Neither market nor hierarchy: Network forms of organization. *Research in Organizational Behavior*, *12*, 295–336.

Rowley, G., & Wilson, S. (1975). The analysis of housing and travel preferences: A gaming approach. *Environment and Planning A*, *7*(2), 171–177.

Rowley, G., Barker, K., & Callaghan, V. (1986). The market research terminal and developments in survey research. *European Journal of Marketing*, *20*(2), 35–39, ISSN: 0309–0566, Publisher: MCB UP Ltd.

Scanlon, L. (2004). Rethinking the computer—Project oxygen is turning out prototype computer systems, *Technology Review*, July/August, 30–40.

Schiller, H. J. (1976). *Communication and cultural domination*. New York: International Arts and Sciences Press.

Slaughter, A. (2004). *A new world order*. Princeton, NJ: Princeton University Press.

Stacey, J. (1996). *In the name of the family: Rethinking family values in a postmodern age*. Boston: Beacon Press.

Sveningsson, M. (2004). Research ethics in Internet ethnography. In Buchanan, E. A. (Ed.), *Readings in virtual research ethics: Issues and controversies*. USA: Information Science Publishing.

von Hippel, E. (1988). *The sources of innovation*. New York: Oxford University Press.

von Hippel, E. (2005). *Democratizing innovation*. Cambridge, MA: MIT Press.

INDEX

Note: Page numbers followed by "*f*" and "*t*" denote figures and tables, respectively.